Cinema Sheet Music

to Richard L. Eshelman,
whose help, patience, encouragement,
and driving skills for the past twenty years
helped me accumulate this great collection
of sheet music which developed into this book

CINEMA SHEET MUSIC
A Comprehensive Listing of Published Film Music from *Squaw Man* (1914) to *Batman* (1989)

Donald J. Stubblebine, 1925-

McFarland & Company, Inc., Publishers
Jefferson, North Carolina, and London

British Library Cataloguing-in-Publication data are available

Library of Congress Cataloguing-in-Publication Data

Stubblebine, Donald J., 1925–
    Cinema sheet music : a comprehensive listing of published film
music from "Squaw Man" (1914) to "Batman" (1989) / by Donald J.
Stubblebine.
      p.   cm.
    Includes bibliographical references and index. ∞
    ISBN 0-89950-569-4 (lib. bdg. : 50# alk. paper)
    1. Motion picture music—Bibliography.   I. Title.
ML128.M7S88   1991
016.7821′4′0263—dc20   91-52514
                                                CIP
                                                MN

Manufactured in the United States of America

McFarland & Company, Inc., Publishers
  Box 611, Jefferson, North Carolina 28640

Acknowledgments

Over the years, many people have encouraged me and supplied me with very interesting sheet music. I can mention them only briefly but I am sure that each one of them, while reading this book, will know what part they played in its creation.

Collectors: Ralph Brauner, Joe Cantlin, Mike Emmyrs, Bill Engstrom, Joe Friedman, Vi Foerster, Bob Grimes, Phil Haggard, Alex Hassan, Jack Hefferman, Fred Hill, Jill Hobbgood, Harold Jacobs, Dave Jasen, Bob Johnson, Miles Kreuger, Sandy Marrone, David Morton, Henry Oakes, William Ott, Jack Reum, Abe Samuels, Chuck Saunders, Bill Simon, Steve Suskin, Larry Taylor, Stan White, Howard Wolverton, Saul Zalesch, Dave Zimmerman, Larry Zimmerman.

Music Publishers: Charlotte Day State, of Edwin H. Morris, who was my first friend in the music publishing business, who supplied me with endless amounts of music, and who gave me the first big boost of encouragement to pursue this hobby. Thanks to a later friend, Frank Military of Unichappell, for his generosity.

Music Dealers: John Aaron, Wayland Bunnell, Shirley Beavers, Carol Bireley, the Carpenters, Norman Levy of Colony Music, Reba Gartman, Beverly Hamer, Herb Huriwitz, Manny and Frances Kean, Lincoln Music, Joel and Helen Markowitz, Lillian and Dulcina McNeill, Tom Maturo, Tom Norcross, Dean Pappas, Trudy and Howard Clapper of the Pumpkin Patch, Allen Radwill, Paul Riseman, Julius Rutin, and John Van Doren.

Friends: Friends who have endured my eccentricities in collecting and writing over the last 20 years: Richard Eshelman, Regis Hauber, Dee Halstead, John Leed, Diane Jeral, and John Francis Marion. Friends who have boarded and fed me: Allan Behm, Jim and Phoebe Moyer, Dave Reffkin, Rose and Buster Snow, Charlotte Day State, and Saul Zalesch. Also, Walter Chapman for translations.

Libraries: Gillian B. Anderson, the staff, and fine music collection of the Library of Congress. Victor T. Cardell and the Archive of Popular American Music At U.C.L.A. The Theatre Collection of the Free Library of Philadelphia and its staff. Also, the private collections of Bill Engstrom, Vi Foerster, Joe Friedman, Bob Grimes, Phil Haggard, Alex Hassan, Dave Jasen, Bob Johnson, Henry Oakes, and Bill Simon.

Special Thanks to Chilton Company for forty years of income and benefits, to Bob Johnson for his cooperation and keen sense of competition, and to Dave Jasen for his firm insistence that this book be done.

Contents

Introduction

Music is a big part of our lives, surrounding us almost continuously. During this century, a majority of our best popular music has come from Broadway and Hollywood. It would be a fine thing if all this music could be preserved forever in its original form of presentation. Sad to say, when a Broadway show closes, most of the music as originally presented is gone forever. Some parts of it live on in recordings, sheet music and film versions. On the other hand, the music written for and presented in movies can live on indefinitely.

Early movies made the rounds of the largest downtown movie palaces and then on to the smaller neighborhood houses. Later most of them were brought back for double features and revival houses and from there to storage, where many films were lost through disintegration. Television arrived and created a new commercial use, and a cause for preservation. Possibly the biggest boost for movies was the videocassette, which created an endless market for an unlimited number of films, and better preservation.

Along with this great exposure of movies has come a renewed interest in the movie musicals and the music created for backgrounds and theme songs. What could be more logical than a book on exactly what music was available? This music could be used for private enjoyment and public performance. It could be used by historians to catalog how many songs and scores were written by known and unknown composers. It is essential to sheet music collectors and music lovers to know which music was published, and therefore still possibly available, somewhere.

My own moviegoing started at a very early age. My mother needed a companion on Tuesday night, which was "dish night." She also wanted me out of the house all day on Saturday for some peace and quiet—this meant serials, cartoons, newsreels, westerns, and movies for hours and hours. After my first exposure, I became addicted and saw at least four movies every week. At first, I favored the movie musicals where the music was obvious. In 1944, I saw the movie *Laura* and from then on became hooked on background music. Around this time, movie studios became aware of the commercial value of background music and theme songs—and pushed the recordings and sheet music.

Having collected recordings and other memorabilia for years, it was only inevitable that I start collecting sheet music. So, about twenty years ago, I started; my interest was in the colorful covers. I collect Broadway and Hollywood sheet music and they almost all have interesting covers. The movies proved to be a little bit more fascinating because of the endless number of movies represented, both feature films and short subjects. There is almost no way of knowing how many exist. These covers portray a history of motion pictures—showing the stars, movie scenes, and movie logos. To assemble a collection of this music is to preserve a history of motion pictures.

There have been several books on Broadway music but virtually no books on music from Hollywood. Using my collection as a start, I started a book on movie sheet music. My own collection amounted to 92 percent of the music. The balance of the music came from research at libraries and private collections. There are approximately 6,200 films and 15,000 songs.

There are probably another hundred or so pieces of movie sheet music of which I am unaware. Hopefully, some kind readers will pass on this information to me—to make this an even better and more complete book if it should go to a revised edition.

Purpose of This Book

This book provides a complete history of published film music for the last 75 years. There have been many books on film musicals—some of them even listing the songs in the films. Quite a bit of this music ended with the film and was never made available for the general public to play or record, and appreciate, however.

The main purpose of this book is to show sheet music collectors, musicians, historians, and the general public which film songs were actually published, and therefore available for their own enjoyment. For the sheet music collector, it will provide the information of what songs were published with collectible covers. For the musician, what songs were published in any format—be it colored cover, plain cover, professional copy, or part of an anthology book. For the historian, a history of movie music, composers, lyricists, publishers, etc. For the general public, a greater knowledge of an important part of their film enjoyment.

How to Use This Book

This book is a listing of all movie songs, movies, and songwriters. The following is a sample listing and an explanation of each item which is included:

1838[1]   Go West[2]
     MGM[3]   1940[4]   Marx Brothers, John Carroll[5]
          As If I Didn't Know[6]   Gus Kahn (w) Bronislau Kaper (m)[7]
               Feist[8]   Cover: Marx Brothers[9]

(1) *Number:* Number assigned to each movie—each of which is in alphabetical order. This number is used in all indexes to refer to this movie.

(2) *Movie Title:* Title exactly as listed on sheet music cover. Any pre-release title or subsequent title appears after this title.

(3) *Studio:* The studio which controlled the release and showing, and not necessarily the production company which made the film.

(4) *Date:* Date of release of film, which differs slightly in various reference books.

(5) *Stars:* Two leading stars of the film—in order to identify the film where there are several films with the same title.

(6) *Song Title:* Song title and spelling exactly as shown on cover. If there are no initials after this title, it is a single sheet with a full movie cover. Any initials after the title indicate the following:
   (PC)   Professional copy—black and white—with no cover.
   (BW)   Black and white cover, no pictures, with titles only.
   (VS)   Song was issued only in a selections book. Movies which had their own individual selections books are not listed in the index. Songs which came from miscellaneous selections books are identified in the index.
   (B)   British edition issued in England. These songs are included because they are related to important American movies which had no

American sheet music. Also included are important foreign films which had a wide distribution here by large Hollywood studios—some of which had sheet music published here and some in England.

(Q)   Questionable—advertised but may not have been published.

(7) *Composer and Lyricist:* Lyricist is listed as (w) and composer as (m). If two or more individuals worked on both, it is listed as (w,m) after all names. Music only is (m). Spelling and names appear exactly as shown on music and vary from time to time.

(8) *Publisher:* Original publisher of music as shown on cover. Many of these songs have been reissued by other publishers.

(9) *Cover:* This item is included for collectors and denotes cover variations with the stars, movie scenes, and movie logos which appear on covers.

Alphabetical Listing
of the Music

1 Aaron Slick from Punkin Crick (Paramount, 1952, Alan Young, Dinah Shore).

Chores/I'd Like to Baby You/ Life Is a Beautiful Thing/Marshmallow Moon/My Beloved/ Purt' Nigh, but Not Plumb/Saturday Night in Punkin Crick/Still Water/Why Should I Believe in Love?—Jay Livingston, Ray Evans (w,m), Famous. COVER: Alan Young, Dinah Shore, Robert Merrill, and Movie Scene.

2 Abdullah the Great (Abdullah's Harem) (The Royal Bed) (20th Century-Fox, 1956, Gregory Ratoff, Kay Kendall).

If Hearts Could Talk—Kay Twomey (w), Fred Wise (w), Georges Auric (m), Hill-Range. COVER: Percy Faith.

3 Abie's Irish Rose (Paramount, 1928, Nancy Carroll, Charles Rogers).

Little Irish Rose/Rosemary—Anne Nichols (w), J. S. Zamecnik (m), Sam Fox. COVER: Nancy Carroll.

4 Abie's Irish Rose (United Artists, 1946, Joanne Dru, Michael Chekhov).

Abie's Irish Rose—Mel Torme, Robert Wells (w,m), Burke-Van Heusen. COVER: Joanne Dru.

5 Abilene Town (United Artists, 1946, Randolph Scott, Ann Dvorak).

Every Time I Give My Heart/I Love It Out in the West/Snap Your Fingers—Kermit Goell (w), Fred Spielman (m), Hudson. COVER: Randolph Scott, Ann Dvorak, and Movie Scene.

6 Abou Ben Boogie (Universal, 1944, Cartoon).

Abou Ben Boogie—Tot Seymour (w), Vee Lawnhurst (m), Leeds. COVER: Cartoon.

7 About Face (Warner Bros., 1952, Gordon MacRae, Eddie Bracken).

If Someone Had Told Me/No Other Girl for Me/Piano, Bass and Drums/Spring Has Sprung/Wooden Indian—Charles Tobias (w), Peter DeRose (m), Witmark. COVER: Gordon MacRae, Eddie Bracken, and Girls.

8 About Last Night (Tri-Star, 1986, Rob Lowe, James Belushi).

If Anybody Had a Heart—J. D. Souther, Danny Kortchmar (w,m), Famous; So Far, So Good—Tom Snow, Cynthia Weil (w,m), Triple Star; If We Can Get Through the Night (VS)—Brock Walsh (w,m), Columbia; Living Inside My Heart (VS) —Bob Seiger (w,m), Columbia; Natural Love (VS)—Tom Snow, Cynthia Weil (w,m), Columbia; Shape of Things to Come (VS)—John Oates (w,m), Columbia; Step By Step (VS) —J. D. Souther, Karla Bonoff (w,m), Columbia; 'Til You Love Somebody (VS)—Bob Marlette, Sue Shifrin (w, m), Columbia; Trials of the Heart (VS)—Thom Bishop, Michael Day, Rocky Maffit (w,m), Columbia; True Love (VS)—Scott Kempner (w,m), Columbia; Words Into Action (VS)— Mike Lesson, Peter Vale (w,m), Columbia. COVER: Rob Lowe, Demi Moore, James Belushi, Elizabeth Perkins.

9 About Mrs. Leslie (Paramount,

1954, Shirley Booth, Robert Ryan).

I Love You So—Peggy Lee (w), Victor Young (m), Paramount. COVER: Shirley Booth, Robert Ryan.

10 Absence of Malice (Columbia, 1981, Paul Newman, Sally Field).

Absence of Malice—Dave Grusin (m), Gold Horizon; Who Comes This Night—Sally Stephens (w), Dave Grusin (m), Gold Horizon. COVER: Paul Newman, Sally Field.

11 Absent-Minded Professor, The (Buena Vista, 1960, Fred MacMurray, Nancy Olson).

Absent Minded Professor March/ Flubber Song/Serendipity—Richard Sherman, Robert Sherman (w,m), Wonderland. COVER: Fred MacMurray, Nancy Olson.

12 Accent on Youth (Paramount, 1935, Sylvia Sidney, Herbert Marshall).

Accent on Youth—Tot Seymour (w), Vee Lawnhurst (m), Famous. COVER: Sylvia Sidney, Herbert Marshall.

13 Accidental Tourist, The (Warner Bros., 1988, William Hurt, Kathleen Turner).

Accidental Tourist Theme—John Williams (m), Warner. COVER: William Hurt, Kathleen Turner, Geena Davis.

14 Accused, The (Paramount, 1988, Kelly McGillis, Jodie Foster).

Accused Theme—Brad Fiedel (m), Famous. COVER: Kelly McGillis, Jodie Foster, and Movie Scene.

15 Accused of Murder (Republic, 1955, Vera Ralston, David Brian).

You're in Love—Herb Newman (w), Buddy Bregman (m), Thunderbird. COVER: Gogi Grant.

16 Ace Drummond (Universal, 1936, John King, Jean Rogers).

Give Me a Ship and a Song—Kay Kellogg (w,m), Sam Fox. COVER: John King.

17 Across 110th Street (United Artists, 1972, Anthony Quinn, Yaphet Kotto).

Across 110th Street—Bobby Womack, J. J. Johnson (w,m), Unart. COVER: Anthony Quinn, and Movie Scene.

18 Across the Wide Missouri (MGM, 1951, Clark Gable, Ricardo Montalban).

Across the Wide Missouri—Ervin Drake, Jimmy Shirl (w,m), Revere. COVER: Clark Gable, and Movie Scene.

19 Actress, The (MGM, 1953, Spencer Tracy, Jean Simmons).

My Beautiful Lady (B)—C. M. S. McLellan (w), Ivan Caryll (m), Chappell. COVER: Jean Simmons.

20 Ada (MGM, 1961, Susan Hayward, Dean Martin).

Ada—Mack David (w), Bronislau Kaper (m), Miller; May the Lord Bless You Real Good—Warren Roberts, Wally Fowler (w,m), Gospeltone. COVER: Dean Martin, Susan Hayward.

21 Adam's Apple (Vitaphone, 1934, Musical Short).

Lookin' 'em Over/Rhythm in the Bow—Cliff Hess (w,m), Witmark. COVER: Black and white cover with title only.

22 Adam's Rib (MGM, 1949, Spencer Tracy, Katharine Hepburn).

Farewell Amanda—Cole Porter (w, m), Harms. COVER: Spencer Tracy, Katharine Hepburn, Judy Holliday.

23 Adios Amigo (Atlas, 1975, Richard Pryor, Fred Williamson).

Adios Amigo—William Stevenson (w), Luchi DeJesus (m), Brut. COVER: Richard Pryor, Fred Williamson.

24 Admiral Was a Lady, The (United Artists, 1950, Wanda Hendrix, Edmond O'Brien).

Everything That's Wonderful (PC) —Al Stewart (w), Earl Rose (m), Dreyer. COVER: None.

25 Adorable (Fox, 1933, Janet Gaynor, Henry Garat).

Adorable/My First Love to Last/ My Heart's Desire—George Marion (w), Richard Whiting (m), Movietone. COVER: Janet Gaynor, Henry Garat.

26 Adoration (Warner Bros.,

1928, Billie Dove, Antonio Moreno).

Adoration—J. Keirn Brennan (w), Karl Hajos (m), Famous. COVER: Black and white cover with title only.

27 Advance to the Rear (MGM, 1964, Glenn Ford, Stella Stevens).

Today—Randy Sparks (w,m), Miller. COVER: Glenn Ford, Stella Stevens, and Movie Scene.

28 Adventure (MGM, 1945, Clark Gable, Greer Garson).

El Yerbatero—Nicanor Molinare (w,m), Peer; Norah Girl—Fred Brennan (w), Herbert Shothart (m), Robbins. COVER: Clark Gable, Greer Garson, Joan Blondell .

29 Adventurers, The (Paramount, 1970, Bekim Fehmiu, Candice Bergen).

Adventure—Norman Gimbel (w), Antonio C. Jobim (m), Ensign; Corte Guay—Eumir Deodato (m), Famous; Love Theme of The Adventurers—Antonio C. Jobim (m), Ensign; Rome Montage—Eumir Deodato (m), Famous. COVER: Bekim Fehmiu, Candice Bergen.

30 Adventures of Bullwhip Griffin, The (Buena Vista, 1967, Roddy McDowell, Suzanne Pleshette).

Bullwhip Griffin—Mel Leven, George Bruns (w,m), Disney; Californee Gold/Girls of San Francisco—Richard Sherman, Robert Sherman (w,m), Wonderland. COVER: Blue cover with title only.

31 Adventures of Hajji Baba, The (20th Century-Fox, 1954, John Derek, Elaine Stewart).

Hajji Baba—Ned Washington (w), Dmitri Tiomkin (m), Remick. COVER: John Derek, Elaine Stewart, and Movie Scene.

32 Adventures of Ichabod and Mr. Toad, The (RKO Disney, 1949, Cartoon).

Headless Horseman/Ichabod/Katrina—Don Raye, Gene DePaul (w, m), Morris. COVER: Cartoon.

33 Adventures of Kathlyn, The (Selig, 1914, Kathlyn Williams, Charles Clary).

Kathlyn Waltz—Lee Orean Smith (m), Feist. COVER: Kathlyn Williams.

34 Adventures of Pinocchio, The (Sloman, 1939, Cartoon).

I'm Pinocchio—Morey Amsterdam (w), Tony Romano (m), Davis Schwegler. COVER: Cartoon.

35 Adventures of Robin Hood, The (Warner Bros., 1938, Errol Flynn, Olivia de Havilland).

Adventures of Robin Hood Piano Suite—Erich W. Korngold (m), Warner. COVER: Green cover with title only.

36 Adventures of Ruth, The (Pathe, 1919, Herbert Heyes, Ruth Roland).

Romantic Ruth—Annelu Burns (w), Madelyn Sheppard (m), Piantadosi. COVER: Ruth Roland.

37 Adventures of the Flying Cadets, The (Universal, 1943, Johnny Downs, Bobby Jordan).

Here Come the Air Cadets—Everett Carter (w), Milton Rosen (m), Robbins. COVER: Johnny Downs, and Cadets.

38 Adventures of Tom Sawyer, The (United Artists, 1938, Tommy Kelly, Ann Gillis).

Ain't You Comin' Out Tonight? (VS)/Dreamin' By a Stream (VS)/First Time I Smoked a Pipe (VS)/Hones' I Love You, Becky (VS)/I Did It, Teacher (VS)/Injun Joe (VS)/My Aunt Polly (VS)/Pleasant Dreams, Little Pirate (VS)/Prince in Patches (VS)/Sunday Clo's (VS)/Vacation Day (VS)/When You Run Away from Home (VS)/Whitewashin' Day (VS)/Wildwood Trail (VS)—Jules Loman (w), Louis Herscher (m), Sam Fox. COVER: Tommy Kelly, Ann Gillis.

39 Advise and Consent (Columbia, 1962, Henry Fonda, Charles Laughton).

Advise and Consent Main Theme—Jerry Fielding (m), Chappell; Advise and Consent Song—Ned Washington (w), Jerry Fielding (m), Chappell. COVER: Capital Dome.

40   Aesop's Fables (RKO, 1930, Cartoon).

Aesop and His Funny Fables— Gene Waite (w,m), Sonnett. COVER: Cartoon.

41   Affair in Trinidad (Columbia, 1952, Rita Hayworth, Glenn Ford).

I've Been Kissed Before—Bob Russell, Lester Lee (w,m), Shapiro Bernstein; Trinidad Lady—Bob Russell, Lester Lee, Fred Karger (w,m), Mills. COVER: Rita Hayworth, Glenn Ford.

42   Affair of Susan, The (Universal, 1935, Zasu Pitts, Hugh O'Connell).

Something in My Heart—E. Y. Harburg (w), Franz Waxman (m), Berlin. COVER: Zasu Pitts.

43   Affairs of Dobie Gillis, The (MGM, 1953, Debbie Reynolds, Bobby Van).

All I Do Is Dream of You—Arthur Freed (w), Nacio Herb Brown (m), Robbins. COVER: Debbie Reynolds, Bobby Van.

44   Affair to Remember, An (20th Century-Fox, 1957, Cary Grant, Deborah Kerr).

Affair to Remember—Harold Adamson, Leo McCarey (w), Harry Warren (m), Feist; Affair to Remember Theme—Harry Warren (m), Feist; Tiny Scout/Tomorrowland/You Make It Easy to Be True—Harold Adamson, Leo McCarey (w), Harry Warren (m), Feist. COVER: Cary Grant, Deborah Kerr.

45   Affair with a Stranger (RKO, 1950, Jean Simmons, Victor Mature).

Affair with a Stranger—Sam Coslow (w,m), Jefferson. COVER: Jean Simmons, Victor Mature.

46   Africa Addio (United Artists, 1967, Documentary on Africa).

Africa Addio Theme—Riz Ortolani (m), Unart. COVER: Black and white cover with title only.

47   African Queen (United Artists, 1952, Humphrey Bogart, Katharine Hepburn).

You're Mine (B)—Nicholas Bennett (w), Allan Gray (m), Maurice. COVER: Humphrey Bogart, Katharine Hepburn.

48   Africa Speaks (Columbia, 1930, Documentary on Africa).

African Serenade—Harry DeCosta (w), Nathaniel Shilkret (m), Feist. COVER: African Natives.

49   Africa—Texas Style (Paramount, 1968, Hugh O'Brian, John Mills).

Swahili Serenade—Mack David (w), Malcolm Arnold (m), Famous. COVER: Hugh O'Brian, and Animals.

50   After Midnight (Captain Carey, USA) (Paramount, 1950, Alan Ladd, Wanda Hendrix).

Mona Lisa—Jay Livingston, Ray Evans (w,m), Famous. COVER: Black and white cover with title only.

51   After the Ball (Anderson, 1924, Edna Murphy, Gaston Glass).

After the Ball—Charles Harris (w, m), Harris. COVER: Edna Murphy.

52   After the Fox (United Artists, 1966, Peter Sellers, Victor Mature).

After the Fox—Hal David (w), Burt Bacharach (m), United Artists. COVER: Sketch of Movie Scene.

53   After the Rain (The Painted Woman) (Fox, 1932, Spencer Tracy, William Boyd).

Beside the Coral Sea—L. Wolfe Gilbert (w), James Hanley (m), Movietone; Say You'll Be Good to Me— James Hanley (w,m), Movietone. COVER: Black and white cover with title only.

54   After the Thin Man (MGM, 1936, William Powell, Myrna Loy).

Blow That Horn—Bob Wright, Chet Forrest (w), Walter Donaldson (m), Robbins; Smoke Dreams— Arthur Freed (w), Nacio Herb Brown (m), Robbins. COVER: William Powell, Myrna Loy.

55   After the Verdict (International, 1930, Olga Tschechowa, Warwick Bond).

Two Smiling Eyes—Allan Stuart

(w), Alex Magnes (m), Sam Fox. COVER: Black and white cover with title only.

56 After Tomorrow (Fox, 1932, Charles Farrell, Marion Nixon).

After Tomorrow—James Hanley (w,m), Sam Fox. COVER: Charles Farrell, Marion Nixon.

57 After Tonight (Woman-Spy) (RKO, 1933, Constance Bennett, Gilbert Roland).

Buy a Kiss—Val Burton, Will Jason (w), Max Steiner (m), Berlin. COVER: Constance Bennett.

58 Against All Odds (Columbia, 1984, Jeff Bridges, Rachel Ward).

Against All Odds—Phil Collins (w, m), Columbia; Balcony (VS)—Stuart Adamson (w,m), Columbia; Making a Big Mistake (VS)—Mike Rutherford (w,m), Columbia; My Male Curiosity (VS)—August Darrell (w,m), Columbia; Violet and Blue (VS)—Stephanie Nicks, Stevie Nicks (w,m), Columbia; Walk Through the Fire (VS)—Peter Gabriel (w,m), Columbia. COVER: Jeff Bridges, Rachel Ward.

59 Age for Love, The (United Artists, 1931, Billie Dove, Charles Starrett).

I'm Chuck Full of Kisses—Dave Silverstein (w), Alfred Newman (m), Conrad; Just Another Night—Dave Silverstein (w), Con Conrad, Alfred Newman (m), Conrad. COVER: Billie Dove, Charles Starrett.

60 Agony and the Ecstasy, The (20th Century-Fox, 1965, Rex Harrison, Charlton Heston).

Agony and the Ecstasy Theme—Alex North (m), Miller. COVER: Rex Harrison, Charlton Heston, and Movie Scene.

61 Ain't Misbehavin' (Universal, 1955, Rory Calhoun, Piper Laurie).

Dixie Mambo—Charles Henderson (w), Sonny Burke (m), Northern; I Love That Rickey Tickey Tickey—Sammy Cahn (w), Johnnie Scott (m), Leeds; Little Love Can Go a Long, Long Way—Paul F. Webster (w), Sammy Fain (m), Northern; Ain't

Misbehavin'—Andy Razaf (w), Thomas Waller, Harry Brooks (m), Mills. COVER: Rory Calhoun, Piper Laurie, Jack Carson, Mamie Van Doren.

62 Airport (Universal, 1970, Burt Lancaster, Dean Martin).

Airport Love Theme—Alfred Newman (m), Shamley; Winds of Chance—Paul Francis Webster (w), Alfred Newman (m), Shamley. COVER: Airport.

63 Airport 1975 (Universal, 1975, Charlton Heston, Karen Black).

Airport 1975 Theme—John Cacavas (m), Leeds. COVER: Charlton Heston, Karen Black, Gloria Swanson, and Others.

64 Airport '77 (Universal, 1977, Jack Lemmon, Lee Grant).

Airport '77 Theme—John Cacavas (m), Leeds. COVER: Jack Lemmon, Lee Grant, and Others.

65 Alakazam the Great (AIP, 1961, Cartoon).

Magic Man (PC)—Les Baxter (w, m), Harlene. COVER: None.

66 Alamo, The (United Artists, 1960, John Wayne, Richard Widmark).

Ballad of The Alamo/Green Leaves of Summer/Tennessee Babe/Here's to the Ladies—Paul Francis Webster (w), Dimitri Tiomkin (m), Feist. COVER: John Wayne, Frankie Avalon, and Movie Scenes.

67 Alexander (Cinema Five, 1968, Phillippe Noiret, Marlene Jobert).

Where Is the Summertime?—Walter Marks (w), Vladimir Cosma (m), Croma. COVER: Phillippe Noiret.

68 Alexander's Ragtime Band (20th Century-Fox, 1938, Alice Faye, Tyrone Power).

Alexander's Ragtime Band/All Alone/Blue Skies/Cheek to Cheek/Easter Parade/Everybody's Doin' It Now/Everybody Step/For Your Country and My Country/Heat Wave/In My Haren/Lazy/Marching Along with Time/Marie/My Walking Stick/

Now It Can Be Told/Oh! How I Hate to Get Up in the Morning/Pack Up Your Sins and Go to the Devil/Pretty Girl Is Like a Melody/Ragtime Violin/Remember/Say It with Music/Some Sunny Day/That International Rag/This Is the Life/We're on Our Way to France/What'll I Do/When I Lost You/When the Midnight Choo-Choo Leaves for Alabam'/Y.M.C.A.—Irving Berlin (w,m), Berlin. COVER: Alice Faye, Tyrone Power, Don Ameche, Jack Haley, Ethel Merman.

69 Alfie (Paramount, 1966, Michael Caine, Shelley Winters).

Alfie—Hal David (w), Burt Bacharach (m), Famous; Alfie's Theme—Sonny Rollins (m), Ensign. COVER: Michael Caine, Shelley Winters.

70 Alfredo, Alfredo (Paramount, 1973, Dustin Hoffman, Stefania Sandrelli).

Alfredo Theme—Hank Hunter (w), C. Rustichelli (m), Chappell. COVER: Dustin Hoffman, Stefania Sandrelli.

71 Algiers (United Artists, 1938, Hedy Lamarr, Charles Boyer).

Algiers/C'est La Vie—Ann Ronell (w), Vincent Scotto (m), Robbins. COVER: Hedy Lamarr, Charles Boyer.

72 Alias Jesse James (United Artists, 1959, Bob Hope, Rhonda Fleming).

Ain't A-Hankerin'—Budd Burtson, Arthur Altman (w,m), United Artists. COVER: Bob Hope, Rhonda Fleming.

73 Alias Jimmy Valentine (Metro, 1929, Bert Lytell, Vola Vale).

Jimmy Valentine—Edward Madden (w), Gus Edwards (m), Remick. COVER: Bert Lytell, Vola Vale.

74 Alias Jimmy Valentine (MGM, 1929, William Haines, Lionel Barrymore).

Love Dreams—Mort Harris, Raymond Klages (w), William Axt, Dave Mendoza (m), Robbins. COVER: William Haines, Leila Hyams.

75 Ali Baba Goes to Town (20th Century-Fox, 1937, Eddie Cantor, Tony Martin).

I've Got My Heart Set on You/Laugh Your Way Through Life/Swing Is Here to Sway—Mack Gordon, Harry Revel (w,m), Robbins. COVER: Eddie Cantor, Louise Hovick, and Girls.

76 Alibi (United Artists, 1929, Eleanor Griffith, Regis Toomey).

I've Never Seen a Smile Like Yours—Justin Johnson, Eddie Frazer (w,m), Witmark; Then I'll Know Why—Paul Titsworth, Lynn Cowan (w,m), Sherman Clay; Your Love Is All—Harry Kerr (w), J. S. Zamecnik (m), Sam Fox. COVER: Regis Toomey, Irma Harrison, and Movie Scenes.

77 Alice Adams (RKO, 1935, Katharine Hepburn, Fred MacMurray).

I Can't Waltz Alone—Dorothy Fields (w), Max Steiner (m), Berlin. COVER: Katharine Hepburn.

78 Alice in Wonderland (Paramount, 1933, Charlotte Henry, Gary Cooper).

Alice in Wonderland—Leo Robin (w), Dimitri Tiomkin, Nathaniel Finston (m), Famous; Walk a Little Faster—Lewis Carroll (w), Dave Franklin (m), Famous; At the Banquet (VS)/Beautiful Soup (VS)/Drinking Song (VS)/Duchess Lullaby (VS)/Father William (VS)/Jabberwocky (VS)/Lobster Quadrille (VS)—Lewis Carroll (w), Dimitri Tiomkin, Nathaniel Finston (m), Famous; Morris Dance (VS)—Dimitri Tiomkin, Nathaniel Finston (m), Famous; Red Queen (VS)—Lewis Carroll (w) (Trad. Melody), Famous; Tweedle Dum, Tweedle Dee (VS)/Twinkle Twinkle Little Bat (VS)/Walrus and the Carpenter (VS)—L. Carroll (w), Dimitri Tiomkin, Nathaniel Finston (m), Famous. COVER: Movie Scenes.

79 Alice in Wonderland (RKO Disney, 1951, Cartoon).

Alice in Wonderland/All in the

Golden Afternoon—Bob Hilliard (w), Sammy Fain (m), Disney; How D'ye Do and Shake Hands—Cy Coben, Oliver Wallace (w,m), Disney; I'm Late/In a World of My Own—Bob Hilliard (w), Sammy Fain (m), Disney; March of the Cards—Sammy Fain (m), Disney; Twas Brillig—Don Raye, Gene DePaul (w,m), Disney; Unbirthday Song—Mack David, Al Hoffman, Jerry Livingston (w,m), Disney; Very Good Advice—Bob Hilliard (w), Sammy Fain (m), Disney; A E I O U, Caterpillar Song (VS)— Oliver Wallace (w,m), Disney; Caucas Race (VS)/Walrus and the Carpenter (VS)—Bob Hilliard (w), Sammy Fain (m), Disney. COVER: Cartoon.

80 Alice's Adventures in Wonderland (20th Century-Fox, 1972, Hywel Bennett, Michael Crawford).

Curiouser and Curiouser/I've Never Been This Far Before/Me I Never Knew—Don Black (w), John Barry (m), Morris. COVER: Cartoon.

81 Alice's Restaurant (United Artists, 1969, Arlo Guthrie, Pat Quinn).

Alice's Restaurant—Arlo Guthrie (w,m), Appleseed. COVER: Arlo Guthrie.

82 All Aboard (First National, 1927, Johnny Hines, Edna Murphy).

All Aboard—Herbert Crooker (w), John M. Hagen (m), Alfred. COVER: Johnny Hines.

83 All American (Universal, 1932, Richard Arlen, Gloria Stuart).

All American Girl—Al Lewis (w, m), Feist. COVER: Richard Arlen, Gloria Stuart.

84 All-American Coed (United Artists, 1941, Frances Langford, Johnny Downs).

Out of the Silence—Lloyd Morlin (w,m), Mills. COVER: Frances Langford, Johnny Downs.

85 All Ashore (Columbia, 1953, Mickey Rooney, Dick Haymes).

All Ashore/Boy Meets Girl/Buddy Boy/Catalina/Heave Ho, My Hearties/If You Were an Eskimo/I'm So Unlucky/Sir Francis the Dragon/Who Are We to Say—Robert Wells (w), Fred Karger (m), Mills. COVER: Mickey Rooney, Dick Haymes, and Movie Scenes.

86 All by Myself (Universal, 1943, Rosemary Lane, Patrick Knowles).

All to Myself—Buddy Pepper, Inez James (w,m), Robbins; I Don't Believe in Rumors—Harry Glick (w), Jimmy Lambert (m), BMI. COVER: Rosemary Lane, and Movie Scene.

87 All Fall Down (MGM, 1962, Eva Marie Saint, Warren Beatty).

All Fall Down Theme/All Fall Down Waltz—Alex North (m), Miller. COVER: Warren Beatty, Eva Marie Saint.

88 All Hands on Deck (20th Century-Fox, 1961, Pat Boone, Buddy Hackett).

All Hands on Deck—Jay Livingston, Ray Evans (w,m), Miller. COVER: Pat Boone, Buddy Hackett.

89 All I Desire (Universal, 1953, Barbara Stanwyck, Richard Carlson).

All I Desire—David Lieber (w,m), BMI. COVER: Barbara Stanwyck, Lyle Bettger.

90 All in a Night's Work (Paramount, 1961, Shirley MacLaine, Dean Martin).

All in a Night's Work—Ruth Roberts, William Katz (w,m), Famous. COVER: Dean Martin, Shirley MacLaine.

91 All in the Wink (Grant, 1963, Margaret Phillips, Vassili Lambrinos).

All in the Wink/For All/Get Yourself a Sweetheart/Lookin' at You/Pig Meat/Spain Away—Henry Nemo (w, m), Indano. COVER: Movie Scene.

92 All Men Are Enemies (Fox, 1934, Hugh Williams, Helen Twelvetrees).

Heart, My Heart—William Kernell (w), Louis DeFrancesco (m), Movietone. COVER: Helen Twelvetrees.

93 All Mine to Give (The Day They Gave Babies Away) (RKO, 1957, Cameron Mitchell, Glynis Johns).

My Very, Very Own—Norman Bennett (w), Max Steiner (m), Lamas. COVER: Cameron Mitchell, Glynis Johns, and Others.

94 All Quiet on the Western Front (Universal, 1930, Lew Ayres, Louis Wolheim).

All Quiet on the Western Front—Bernie Grossman (w), Lou Handman (m), Handman. COVER: Movie Scenes.

95 All Teed Up (MGM, 1930, Thelma Todd, Charley Chase).

Golfers Blues—Alice Howlett, Will Livernash (w,m), Quincke. COVER: Charley Chase.

96 All the King's Horses (Paramount, 1935, Carl Brisson, Mary Ellis).

Be Careful, Young Lady/Dancing the Viennese/King Can Do No Wrong, A/Little White Gardenia, A/When My Prince Charming Comes Along—Sam Coslow (w,m), Famous. COVER: Carl Brisson, Mary Ellis.

97 All the President's Men (Warner Bros., 1976, Robert Redford, Dustin Hoffman).

All the President's Men Theme—David Shire (m), Warner. COVER: Robert Redford, Dustin Hoffman.

98 All the Right Moves (20th Century-Fox, 1983, Tom Cruise, Craig Nelson).

All the Right Moves—Barry Alfonso (w), Tom Snow (m), Warner. COVER: Tom Cruise.

99 All the Way Home (Paramount, 1963, Jean Simmons, Robert Preston).

All the Way Home—Stanley Styne (w), Jule Styne (m), Famous. COVER: Jean Simmons, Robert Preston.

100 All the Young Men (Columbia, 1960, Alan Ladd, Sidney Poitier).

All the Young Men—Stanley Styne (w), George Duning (m), Columbia. COVER: Alan Ladd, Sidney Poitier, and Others.

101 All Through the Night (Warner Bros., 1942, Humphrey Bogart, Conrad Veidt).

All Through the Night—Johnny Mercer (w), Arthur Schwartz (m), Witmark. COVER: Humphrey Bogart, Kaaren Verne.

102 All Women Have Secrets (Paramount, 1939, Jeanne Cagney, Joseph Allen).

I Live Again—Ned Washington (w), Victor Young (m), Famous. COVER: Jeanne Cagney.

103 Alma, Where Do You Live? (Monopol, 1916, George Larkin, Ruth MacTammany).

Alma—George Hobart (w), Jean Briquet (m), Remick; Alma, Where Do You Live?—George Hobart (w), Adolf Phillipp (m), Remick. COVER: George Larkin, Ruth MacTammany.

104 Almost Summer (Universal, 1978, Bruno Kirby, Lee Purcell).

Almost Summer—Brian Wilson, Mike Love, Al Jardine (w), Brian Wilson (m), Stone. COVER: Students.

105 Aloma of the South Seas (Paramount, 1926, Gilda Gray, Percy Marmont).

Aloma—Frances DeWitt (w), Robert H. Bowers (m), Robbins Engel. COVER: Gilda Gray.

106 Aloma of the South Seas (Paramount, 1941, Dorothy Lamour, Jon Hall).

White Blossoms of Tah-ni—Frank Loesser (w), Frederick Hollander (m), Paramount. COVER: Dorothy Lamour, Jon Hall.

107 Along Came Jones (RKO, 1945, Gary Cooper, Loretta Young).

Round and Around—Al Stewart, Arthur Lange (w,m), Southern. COVER: Gary Cooper.

108 Along Came Sally (Aunt Sally) (Gainsborough, 1933, Cicely Courtneidge, Sam Hardy).

Winds in the West/We'll All Go Riding/You Ought to See Sally on

Sunday—Harry Woods (w,m), Mills. COVER: Cicely Courtneidge.

109 Along the Navajo Trail (Republic, 1945, Roy Rogers, Dale Evans).

Along the Navajo Trail—Larry Markes, Dick Charles, Eddie DeLange (w,m), Leeds. COVER: Roy Rogers.

110 Along the Santa Fe Trail (Warner Bros., 1940, Errol Flynn, Olivia de Havilland).

Along the Santa Fe Trail—Al Dubin, Edwina Coolidge (w), Will Grosz (m), Harms. COVER: Errol Flynn, Olivia de Havilland.

111 Alphabet Murders, The (MGM, 1965, Tony Randall, Anita Ekberg).

Amanda—Norman Newell (w), Brian Fahey (m), Miller. COVER: Tony Randall, Anita Ekberg.

112 Alvarez Kelly (Columbia, 1966, William Holden, Richard Widmark).

Ballad of Alvarez Kelly—Johnny Mercer (w), Johnny Green (m), Colgems. COVER: William Holden, Richard Widmark.

113 Always a Bride (Universal, 1953, Peggy Cummins, Terence Morgan).

I Love You Toujours (B)—Harold Purcell (w), Ben Bernard (m), Cinephonic. COVER: Peggy Cummins, Terence Morgan.

114 Always a Bridesmaid (Universal, 1943, Andrews Sisters, Patrick Knowles).

That's My Affair—Hy Zaret (w), Irving Weiser (m), Leeds; Yoo Hoo—Roy Jordan (w), John Wilfahrt (m), Leeds. COVER: Andrews Sisters, Frank Sinatra.

115 Always in My Heart (Warner Bros., 1942, Kay Francis, Walter Huston).

Always in My Heart—Kim Gannon (w), Ernesto Lecuona (m), Remick. COVER: Kay Francis, Walter Huston.

116 Always Leave Them Laughing (Warner Bros., 1949, Milton Berle, Virginia Mayo).

Always Leave Them Laughing—Milton Berle, Sammy Cahn (w,m), Remick. COVER: Milton Berle, Virginia Mayo.

117 Amadeus (Orion, 1985, F. Murray Abraham, Tom Hulce).

Amadeus Themes and Selections (VS)—Wolfgang A. Mozart (m), Leonard. COVER: A Hooded Figure.

118 Amateur Daddy (Fox, 1932, Warner Baxter, Marion Nixon).

Now I Lay Me Down to Sleep—James Hanley (w,m), Movietone. COVER: Black and white cover with title only.

119 Amateur Gentleman, The (United Artists, 1936, Douglas Fairbanks, Elissa Landi).

Did We Meet Or Was It a Dream? (B)—Clemence Dane (w), Richard Addinsell (m), Chappell. COVER: Silhouette of a Gentleman.

120 Amazing Mrs. Holiday, The (Universal, 1943, Deanna Durbin, Edmond O'Brien).

In Old Vienna (B)—King Palmer (w,m), Paxton. COVER: Deanna Durbin.

121 Amazing Quest of Ernest Bliss, The (Riches and Romance) (United Artists, 1937, Cary Grant, Mary Brian).

When Fortune Smiles (B)—Alister Fearn (w), Werner Bochmann (m), Wright. COVER: Cary Grant, Mary Brian.

122 Ambushers, The (Columbia, 1968, Dean Martin, Senta Berger).

Ambushers—Herbert Baker, Hugo Montenegro (w,m), Colgems. COVER: Tommy Boyce and Bobby Hart.

123 America (Griffith, 1924, Neil Hamilton, Erville Alderson).

America Themes-1976 Revival —Lee Irwin (m), Piedmont. COVER: D. W. Griffith.

124 America, America (Warner Bros., 1964, Stathis Giallelis, Frank Wolff).

America America/Family Farewell —Nikos Gatsos (w), Manos Hadjidakis (m), Harms. COVER: Stathis Giallelis.

125   American Anthem (Lorimar, 1986, Mitch Gaylord, Janet Jones).

Two Hearts—John Parr (w,m), Columbia. COVER: Mitch Gaylord.

126   American Beauty (Pallas, 1916, Myrtle Stedman, Elliott Dexter).

American Beauty—Alfred Bryan, Edgar Leslie (w), M. K. Jerome (m), Berlin; Perfect Love Song—G. Allen (w), E. G. Nomis (m), Turney. COVER: Myrtle Stedman.

127   American Dream (Warner Bros., 1966, Stuart Whitman, Janet Leigh).

Time for Love—Paul F. Webster (w), Johnny Mandel (m), Witmark. COVER: Stuart Whitman, Janet Leigh.

128   American Empire (United Artists, 1942, Richard Dix, Leo Carrillo).

Little Pal—Lew Pollack, Herman Ruby (w,m), Mills. COVER: Richard Dix, and Movie Scene.

129   American Gigolo (Paramount, 1980, Richard Gere, Lauren Hutton).

Call Me—Deborah Harry (w), Giorgio Moroder (m), Ensign; Love and Passion—Paul Schrader (w), Giorgio Moroder (m), Ensign; Night Drive/Seduction Love Theme—Giorgio Moroder (m), Ensign; Something in Return—Michael Lloyd (w), Giorgio Moroder (m), Ensign. COVER: Richard Gere.

130   American Hot Wax (Paramount, 1978, Tim McIntire, Jay Leno).

A B C's of Love (VS)—Richard Barrett, George Goldner (w,m), Regent; Goodnight It's Time to Go (VS) —Calvin Carter, James Hudson (w,m), Regent; Great Balls of Fire (VS)— Jack Hammer, Otis Blackwell (w,m), Regent; Hey Little Girl (VS)—Bobby Stevenson, Otis Blackwell (w,m), Regent; Hot Wax Theme (VS)—Kenny Vance, Ira Newborn, Paul Griffin (w, m), Regent; Hushabye (VS)—Doc Pomus, Mort Shuman (w,m), Regent; I Put a Spell on You (VS)—Jay Hawkins (w,m), Regent; I Want You to Be My Girl (VS)—Morris Levy (w,m), Regent; I'm Not a Juvenile Delinquent (VS)—George Goldner (w,m), Regent; Little Star (VS)—Morris Levy, Bobby Callender, John Peabody (w,m), Regent; Maybe (VS)— Richard Barrett (w,m), Regent; Mister Blue (VS)—DeWayne Blackwell, Regent; Mister Lee (VS)—Heather Dixon, Helen Gathers, Emma Pought (w,m), Regent; Reelin' and Rockin' (VS)—Chuck Berry (w,m), Regent; Rock and Roll Is Here to Stay (VS)— David White (w,m), Regent; Roll Over Beethoven (VS)—Chuck Berry (w,m), Regent; Sea Cruise (VS)— Huey Smith (w,m), Regent; Sincerely (VS)—Harvey Fuqua, Allan Freed (w, m), Regent; Speedo (VS)—Esther Navarro (w,m), Regent; Splish Splash (VS)—Bobby Darin, Jean Murray (w, m), Regent; Sweet Little Sixteen (VS)—Chuck Berry (w,m), Regent; That's Why (VS)—Berry Gordy, Tyran Carlo (w,m), Regent; There Goes My Baby (VS)—Lover Patterson, George Treadwell, Ben Nelson (w,m), Regent; Thousand Miles Away (VS) —James Shepherd, William Miller (w, m), Regent; Tutti Frutti (VS)—R. Penniman, D. LaBostrie (w,m), Regent; When You Dance (VS)—Andrew Jones (w,m), Regent; Why Do Fools Fall in Love (VS)—Frankie Lymon, Morris Levy (w,m), Regent; ZOOM (VS)—Esther Navarro (w,m), Regent. COVER: Phonograph Record.

131   American in Paris, An (MGM, 1951, Gene Kelly, Leslie Caron).

By Strauss—Ira Gershwin (w), George Gershwin (m), Chappell; Embraceable You/I Got Rhythm—Ira Gershwin (w), George Gershwin (m), Harms; I'll Build a Stairway to Paradise—I. Gershwin (w), G. Gershwin (m), B. G. Desylva (w), Harms; Love Is Here to Stay/Nice Work If You Can Get It/'S Wonderful—Ira Gershwin (w), George Gershwin (m), Chappell; Tra La La—Ira Gershwin (w), George Gershwin (m), Harms? American in Paris Miniature (VS)—George Gershwin (m), Warner; But Not For Me (VS)—Ira Gershwin (w), George Gershwin (m), Warner; Liza (VS)—Ira Gershwin, Gus Kahn (w), George Gershwin (m), Warner; Oh Lady Be Good (VS)/Someone to Watch Over Me (VS)/Strike Up the Band (VS)—Ira Gershwin (w), George Gershwin (m), Warner. COVER: Gene Kelly, Leslie Caron.

132 Americanization of Emily, The (MGM, 1964, James Garner, Julie Andrews).

Emily—Johnny Mercer (w), Johnny Mandel (m), Miller. COVER: James Garner, Julie Andrews.

133 Americano, The (RKO, 1942, Glenn Ford, Frank Lovejoy).

Americano—Tom Smith (w), Xavier Cugat, George Rosner (m), Marks. COVER: Glenn Ford, Ursula Thiess.

134 American Tail, An (Universal, 1986, Cartoon).

Somewhere Out There—James Horner, Barry Mann, Cynthia Weil (w,m), MCA. COVER: Cartoon.

134a Americathon (United Artists, 1979, Peter Reigert, Harvey Korman).

Get a Move On—Eddie Money, Paul Collins, Lloyd Chiate (w,m), Grajonca. COVER: Eddie Money.

135 Amorous Adventures of Moll Flanders, The (Paramount, 1965, Kim Novak, Richard Johnson).

Amorous Adventures of Moll Flanders Theme—John Addison (m), Famous; Lovely Is She—Norman Newell (w), John Addison (m), Famous. COVER: Kim Novak, Richard Johnson, Angela Lansbury.

136 Amours of Fanny Hill, The (Guild, 1963, Stars Unknown).

Don't Be in Such a Hurry/My Love Is Like a Red Red Rose—Robert Burns (w), Alexander Lazlo (m), Guild. COVER: Black and white cover with title only.

137 Amukiriki (Paramount,1955, Travelogue).

Amukiriki—Bob Russell (w), Jerry Livingston (m), Famous. COVER: Les Paul, Mary Ford.

138 Anastasia (20th Century-Fox, 1956, Ingrid Bergman, Yul Brynner).

Anastasia—Paul F. Webster (w), Alfred Newman (m), Feist; Anastasia Theme—Alfred Newman (m), Feist. COVER: Ingrid Bergman, Yul Brynner, Helen Hayes.

139 Anatomy of a Murder (Columbia, 1959, James Stewart, Lee Remick).

I'm Gonna Go Fishin'—Peggy Lee (w), Duke Ellington (m), Chappell. COVER: A Body.

140 Anchors Aweigh (MGM, 1945, Frank Sinatra, Gene Kelly).

All of a Sudden My Heart Sings—Harold Rome, Jamblan Herpin (w, m), Leeds; Charm of You, The—Sammy Cahn (w), Jule Styne (m), Feist; Chiapanecas—Albert Gamse (w), M. V. DeCamp (m), Marks; I Begged Her/I Fall in Love Too Easily—Sammy Cahn (w), Jule Styne (m), Feist; Waltz Serenade—Earl Brent (w), P. Tschaikowsky (m), Feist; We Hate to Leave/What Makes the Sunset?—Sammy Cahn (w), Jule Styne (m), Feist; Worry Song, The—Ralph Freed (w), Sammy Fain (m), Feist. COVER: Frank Sinatra, Gene Kelly, Kathryn Grayson.

141 Anderson Tapes, The (Columbia, 1971, Sean Connery, Dyan Cannon).

Anderson Tapes Theme—Quincy Jones (m), Screen Gems. COVER: Red cover with title only.

142 And Justice for All (Columbia, 1979, Al Pacino, Jack Warden).

There's Something Funny Going On—Alan Bergman, Marilyn Bergman (w), Dave Grusin (m), Gold Horizon. COVER: Gavel and Letters.

143 And Now Tomorrow (Paramount, 1944, Alan Ladd, Loretta Young).

And Now Tomorrow—Edward Heyman (w), Victor Young (m), Famous. COVER: Loretta Young, Alan Ladd, Barry Sullivan, Susan Hayward.

144 And the Angels Sing (Paramount, 1944, Dorothy Lamour, Fred MacMurray).

And the Angels Sing—Johnny Mercer (w), Ziggie Elman (m), BVC; Bluebirds in the Belfry—Johnny Burke (w), Jimmy Van Heusen (m), Paramount; For the First Hundred Years—Johnny Burke (w), Jimmy Van Heusen (m), Famous; His Rocking Horse Ran Away—Johnny Burke (w), Jimmy Van Heusen (m), Paramount; How Does Your Garden Grow/It Could Happen to You—Johnny Burke (w), Jimmy Van Heusen (m), Famous; Knockin' on Your Own Front Door/My Heart's Wrapped Up in Gingham—Johnny Burke (w), Jimmy Van Heusen (m), Famous; When Stanislaus Got Married—Johnny Burke (w), Jimmy Van Heusen (m), Famous. COVER: Betty Hutton, Dorothy Lamour, Fred MacMurray.

145 Andy Hardy Comes Home (MGM, 1958, Mickey Rooney, Sara Haden).

Lazy Summer Night—Harold Spina (w,m), Rooney. COVER: Mickey Rooney and Hardy Family.

146 Andy Hardy Meets Debutante (MGM, 1940, Mickey Rooney, Judy Garland).

Alone—Arthur Freed (w), Nacio Herb Brown (m), Robbins; Buds Won't Bud (BW)—E. Y. Harburg (w), Harold Arlen (m), Feist; I'm Nobody's Baby—Benny Davis, Milton Ager, Lester Santly (w,m), Feist. COVER: Mickey Rooney, Judy Garland.

147 Andy Hardy's Private Secretary (MGM, 1941, Mickey Rooney, Kathryn Grayson).

I've Got My Eyes on You—Cole Porter (w,m), Crawford. COVER: Mickey Rooney.

148 Andy Panda (Universal, 1939, Cartoon).

Andy Panda—Ann Ronell (w,m), Quincke; Andy Panda Polka—Irving Bibo (m), Eugene Poddany (m), Bibo. COVER: Cartoon.

149 Angel (Paramount, 1937, Marlene Dietrich, Herbert Marshall).

Angel—Leo Robin, Frederick Hollander (w,m), Popular. COVER: Marlene Dietrich, Herbert Marshall, Melvyn Douglas.

150 Angela (20th Century-Fox, 1955, Dennis O'Keefe, Mara Lane).

Angel Eyes (B)—Bill Lovelock, Wylie Grace (w), Mario Nascimbene (m), Southern. COVER: Dennis O'Keefe, Mara Lane.

151 Angels with Broken Wings (Republic, 1941, Binnie Barnes, Gilbert Roland).

Has to Be/In Buenos Aires/Three Little Wishes—Eddie Cherkose, Jule Styne (w,m), Mills. COVER: Binnie Barnes, Gilbert Roland, and Movie Scenes.

152 Angels with Dirty Faces (Warner Bros., 1938, James Cagney, Pat O'Brien).

Angels with Dirty Faces—Fred Fisher (w), Maurice Spitalny (m), Fisher. COVER: James Cagney, Pat O'Brien.

153 Animal Crackers (Paramount, 1930, Lillian Roth, Marx Brothers).

Why Am I So Romantic?—Bert Kalmar, Harry Ruby (w,m), Famous. COVER: Marx Brothers.

154 Anna (Lux, 1952, Silvana Mangano, Vittorio Gassman).

Anna—William Engvick (w), R. Vatro (m), Hollis; Baion (B)—Bob Godfrey (w), V. Roman (m), Latin American; If You Said Goodbye—Willie Stein (w), P. G. Redi (m), Hollis; Non Dimenticar, Don't Forget—Shelly Dobbins (w), P. G. Redi (m), Hollis. COVER: Silvana Mangano, Percy Faith, King Cole.

155 Anna Lucasta (United Artists, 1958, Eartha Kitt, Sammy Davis).

That's Anna—Sammy Cahn (w),

Elmer Bernstein (m), United Artists. COVER: Black and white cover with title only.

156   Annapolis (Pathe, 1927, John Mack Brown, Jeanette Loff).

My Annapolis and You—Charles Weinberg, Irving Bibo (w,m), Bibo Lang. COVER: John Mack Brown, Jeanette Loff.

157   Annapolis Story, An (Allied Artists, 1955, John Derek, Diana Lynn).

Engagement Waltz, The—Marlin Skiles (w,m), Sam Fox; Navy Blue and Gold (March)—J. W. Crosley (m), Melrose. COVER: John Derek, Diana Lynn, and Cadets.

158   Anne of Green Gables (Paramount, 1919, Mary Miles Minter, Paul Kelly).

Anne of Green Gables—Will Heelan (w), Will Haskings (m), Broadway. COVER: Mary Miles Minter.

159   Anne of the Indies (20th Century-Fox, 1951, Jean Peters, Louis Jourdan).

Anne of the Indies—George Jessel, Sam Lerner, Joe Cooper (w,m), Feist. COVER: Jean Peters, Louis Jourdan.

160   Anne of the Thousand Days (Universal, 1963, Richard Burton, Genevieve Bujold).

Farewell, Farewell—John Hale (w), Georges Delerue (m), Shamley. COVER: Richard Burton, Genevieve Bujold.

161   Annie (Columbia, 1982, Albert Finney, Carol Burnett).

Easy Street/I Don't Need Anything But You/I Think I'm Gonna Like It Here/It's the Hard Knock Life/Let's Go to the Movies/Little Girls/Maybe/Sandy/Dumb Dog/Sign! /Tomorrow/We Got Annie!/ You're Never Fully Dressed Without a Smile—Martin Charnin (w), Charles Strouse (m), Strouse. COVER: Aileen Quinn, Sandy.

162   Annie Get Your Gun (MGM, 1950, Betty Hutton, Howard Keel).

Anything You Can Do/Doin' What Comes Natur'lly/Girl That I Marry, The/I'm an Indian Too/Let's Go West Again (PC)/My Defenses Are Down/There's No Business Like Show Business/They Say It's Wonderful/You Can't Get a Man with a Gun—Irving Berlin (w,m), Berlin. COVER: Betty Hutton.

163   Annie Hall (United Artists, 1977, Woody Allen, Diane Keaton).

Seems Like Old Times—Carmen Lombardo, John Loeb (w,m), Almo. COVER: Diane Keaton.

164   Anonymous Venetian, The (Allied Artists, 1971, Tony Musante, Florinda Bolkan).

Valerie's Theme—N. Marcello (m), Marks; To Be the One You Love—Norman Newell (w), Stelvio Cipriani (m), Marks. COVER: Tony Musante, Florinda Bolkan.

165   Another Man's Poison (United Artists, 1952, Bette Davis, Gary Merrill).

Fatal Mood—Paul Sawtell (w,m), Young. COVER: Red cover with title only.

166   Another   Time,   Another Place (Paramount, 1958, Lana Turner, Barry Sullivan).

Another Time, Another Place— Jay Livingston, Ray Evans (w,m), Famous; Another Time, Another Place Theme—Jay Livingston, Ray Evans (m), Famous. COVER: Lana Turner, Barry Sullivan.

167   Any   Number   Can   Win (MGM, 1963, Alain Delon, Jean Gabin).

Any Number Can Win Theme— Michel Magne (m), Wood. COVER: Alain Delon.

168   Anyone   Can   Play (Paramount, 1968, Ursula Andress, Virna Lisi).

Anyone Can Play—Audrey Nohra (w), Armando Trovajoli (m), Famous. COVER: Ursula Andress, Virna Lisi, Marisa Mell, Claudine Auger.

169   Anything Can Happen (Paramount, 1961, Jose Ferrer, Kim Hunter).

Love Laughs at Kings—Jay Livingston, Ray Evans (w), Victor Young (m), Famous. COVER: Jose Ferrer, Kim Hunter.

170 Anything Goes (Paramount, 1936, Bing Crosby, Ethel Merman).

Anything Goes/I Get a Kick out of You—Cole Porter (w,m), Harms; Moonburn—Edward Heyman (w), Hoagy Carmichael (m), Harms; My Heart and I—Leo Robin (w), Frederick Hollander (m), Harms; Sailor Beware—Leo Robin (w), Richard Whiting (m), Harms; Shanghai Dee Ho—Leo Robin (w), Frederick Hollander (m), Harms; There'll Always Be a Lady Fair/You're the Top—Cole Porter (w,m), Harms. COVER: Bing Crosby, Ethel Merman, and Movie Scenes.

171 Anything Goes (Paramount, 1956, Bing Crosby, Donald O'Connor).

All Through the Night (B)/Anything Goes (B)/I Get a Kick out of You (B)/It's Delovely (B)—Cole Porter (w,m), Chappell; Second Hand Turban and a Crystal Ball (PC)/Ya Gotta Give the People Hok (PC)/You Can Bounce Right Back (PC)—Sammy Cahn (w), James Van Heusen (m), Harms; You're the Top (B)—Cole Porter (w,m), Chappell. COVER: Bing Crosby, Donald O'Connor, Mitzi Gaynor, Jeanmaire.

172 Any Wednesday (Warner Bros., 1966, Jane Fonda, Jason Robards).

Any Wednesday—Alan Bergman, Marilyn Bergman (w), George Duning (m), Remick. COVER: Jane Fonda, Jason Robards, Dean Jones.

173 Any Which Way You Can (Warner Bros., 1980, Clint Eastwood, Sondra Locke).

Acapulco—Larry Collins, Mary Leath (w,m), Senor; Any Which Way You Can—Milton Brown, Stephen Dorff, Snuff Garrett (w,m), Peso; Whiskey Heaven—Cliff Crofford, John Durrill, Snuff Garrett (w,m), Peso; You're the Reason God Made Oklahoma—Larry Collins, Sandy

Pinkard (w,m), Peso. COVER: Country and Western Singers.

174 Anzio (Columbia, 1968, Robert Mitchum, Earl Holliman).

This World Is Yours—Doc Pomus (w), Riz Ortolani (m), Columbia. COVER: Jack Jones.

175 Apache (United Artists, 1954, Burt Lancaster, Jean Peters).

Apache Love Song—Johnny Mercer (w), David Rakson (m), Unart. COVER: Burt Lancaster and Jean Peters.

176 Apache Woman (Golden Gate, 1955, Lloyd Bridges, Joan Taylor).

Apache Woman—Ronald Stein (w, m), BVC; Carrom's Theme—Ronald Stein (m), BVC; COVER: Black and white cover with title only.

177 Apartment, The (United Artists, 1960, Jack Lemmon, Shirley MacLaine).

Apartment Theme—Charles Williams (m), Mills; Key to Love, The—John Moran (w), Charles Williams (m), Mills; Lonely Room—Adolph Deutsch (m), United Artists. COVER: Jack Lemmon, Shirley MacLaine.

178 Apocalypse Now (United Artists, 1979, Marlon Brando, Robert Duvall).

Come Back to Love—I. Pennino (w), Carmine Coppola, Francis Coppola (m), Zoetrope; Satisfaction (PC)—Mick Jagger, Keith Richards (w,m), Abkco. COVER: The Moon and Helicopters.

179 Applause (Paramount, 1929, Helen Morgan, Joan Peters).

Give Your Baby Lots of Lovin'—Dolly Morse (w), Joe Burke (m), Remick; What Wouldn't I Do for That Man—E. Y. Harburg (w), Jay Gorney (m), Remick. COVER: Helen Morgan.

180 Appointment in Honduras (RKO, 1953, Glenn Ford, Ann Sheridan).

Appointment in Honduras—Lou Forbes (w,m), Disney. COVER: Green cover with title only.

181 April Fools (National General, 1969, Jack Lemmon, Catherine Deneuve).

April Fools—Hal David (w), Burt Bacharach (m), Blue Seas; Castle, The (PC)/I Remember the Rain (PC)/La La La (PC)/Peter's Pad (PC)/Safari Club (PC)—Marvin Hamlisch (m), April; Sugar Kite (PC)/Wake Up (PC) —Joel Hirschhorn (w), Marvin Hamlisch (m), April. COVER: Dionne Warwick.

182 April in Paris (Warner Bros., 1952, Doris Day, Ray Bolger).

April in Paris—E. Y. Harburg (w), Vernon Duke (m), Harms; Give Me Your Lips/I Know a Place/I'm Gonna Ring the Bell/It Must Be Good/That's What Makes Paris, Paree—Sammy Cahn (w), Vernon Duke (m), Harms. COVER: Doris Day, Ray Bolger.

183 April Love (20th Century-Fox, 1957, Pat Boone, Shirley Jones).

April Love/Clever in the Meadow/Do It Yourself/Give Me a Gentle Girl —Paul F. Webster (w), Sammy Fain (m), Feist. COVER: Pat Boone, Shirley Jones.

184 April Showers (Preferred, 1923, Colleen Moore, Kenneth Harlan).

April Showers—B. G. DeSylva (w), Louis Silvers (m), Harms. COVER: Colleen Moore, Kenneth Harlan.

185 April Showers (Warner Bros., 1948, Jack Carson, Ann Sothern).

April Showers—B. G. DeSylva (w), Louis Silvers (m), Harms. COVER: Jack Carson, Ann Sothern.

186 Apryl and Her Baby Lamb (Atlantis, 1957, Educational Film).

Apryl and Her Baby Lamb—J. Michael Hagopian (w,m), Atlantis. COVER: A Baby and a Lamb.

187 Arab, The (Metro, 1924, Alice Terry, Ramon Novarro).

Arab, The—Ted Barron (w,m), Barron. COVER: Ramon Novarro, Alice Terry.

188 Arabesque (Universal, 1966, Gregory Peck, Sophia Loren).

Arabesque Theme—Henry Mancini (m), Southdale; We've Loved Before —Jay Livingston, Ray Evans (w), Henry Mancini (m), Southdale. COVER: Gregory Peck, Sophia Loren.

189 Arch of Triumph (United Artists, 1947, Ingrid Bergman, Charles Boyer).

Arch of Triumph Song—Dave Oppenheim, Art Kahn, Ted Raden (w,m), Mills; Long After Tonight— Ervin Drake, Jimmy Shirl (w), Rudy Polk (m), BMI. COVER: Ingrid Bergman, Charles Boyer.

190 Are You There (Fox, 1930, Beatrice Lillie, John Garrick).

Bagdad Daddies—Grace Henry (w), Morris Hamilton (m), Red Star; Believe in Me—Joseph McCarthy (w), James Hanley (m), Red Star; It Must Be the Iron in the Spinach/Queen of the Hunt Am I, The—Grace Henry (w), Morris Hamilton (m), Red Star. COVER: A Window Facing the Sunrise.

191 Are You With It? (Universal, 1948, Donald O'Connor, Olga San Juan).

Daddy, Surprise Me/I'm Looking for a Prince of a Fella/Little Imagination, A/What Do I Have to Do?—Inez James, Sidney Miller (w,m), BVC. COVER: Donald O'Connor, Olga San Juan.

192 Argentine Nights (Universal, 1940, Andrews Sisters, Ritz Brothers).

Brooklynonga—Sid Kuller, Ray Golden (w), Hal Borne (m), Robbins; Hit the Road—Don Raye, Hughie Prince, Vic Schoen (w,m), Leeds; Rhumboogie—Don Raye, Hughie Prince (w,m), Leeds. COVER: Andrews Sisters, Ritz Brothers.

193 Arise My Love (Paramount, 1940, Claudette Colbert, Ray Milland).

Arise My Love—Ned Washington (w), Frederick Hollander (m), Famous. COVER: Claudette Colbert, Ray Milland.

194 Aristocats, The (Buena Vista, 1970, Cartoon).

Aristocats, The/She Never Felt Alone—Richard Sherman, Robert Sherman (w,m), Disney; Blues (VS)/Cat's Love Theme (VS)—George Bruns (w,m), Disney; Ev'rybody Wants to Be a Cat (VS)—Floyd Huddleston, Al Rinker (w,m), Disney; Goose Steps High, The (VS)/My Paree (VS)/Nice Melody (VS)/Pretty Melody (VS)—George Bruns (w,m), Disney; Scales and Arpeggios (VS)—Richard Sherman, Robert Sherman (w,m), Disney; Thomas O'Malley Cat (VS)—Terry Gilkyson (w,m), Disney. COVER: Cartoon.

195 Arizona Cowboy (Republic, 1949, Rex Allen, Teala Loring).

Arizona Waltz/Too-Lee Roll-Um—Rex Allen (w,m), AVA. COVER: Rex Allen.

196 Arizona Days (Grand National, 1937, Tex Ritter, Eleanor Stewart).

Arizona Days/High Wide and Handsome—Tex Ritter, Ted Choate (w,m), Sam Fox; Tombstone, Arizona (PC)—Tex Ritter, Jack Smith (w,m), Cole. COVER: Tex Ritter.

197 Arizona Sketches (Paramount, 1941, Western Short).

Prairieland Lullaby—Frank Loesser (w), Victor Young (m), Famous. COVER: Desert Scene.

198 Arizonian, The (RKO, 1934, Richard Dix, Margot Graham).

Roll Along Covered Wagon—Jimmy Kennedy (w,m), Berlin. COVER: Covered Wagon.

199 Arkansas Swing (Columbia, 1948, Gloria Henry, Hoosier Hot Shots).

That Lucky Feeling—Frances Clark (w), Robert Bilder (m), Dallas. COVER: Texas Rangers Singers.

200 Around the World (RKO, 1943, Kay Kyser, Joan Davis).

Candlelight and Wine/Don't Believe Everything You Dream/Great News Is in the Making/He's Got a Secret Weapon/Seasick Sailor, A/They Just Chopped Down the Old Apple Tree—Harold Adamson (w), Jimmy McHugh (m), Miller. COVER: Kay Kyser, Joan Davis, Marcy McGuire, and Others.

201 Around the World in 80 Days (United Artists, 1956, David Niven, Cantinflas).

Around the World/Away Out West—Harold Adamson (w), Victor Young (m), Young; India Countryside (B)/Passe Partout (B)/Around the World-Eight Themes—Victor Young (m), Young. COVER: Large Balloon.

202 Around the World Under the Sea (MGM, 1965, Lloyd Bridges, Shirley Eaton).

Around the World Under the Sea-Love Theme—Harry Sukman (m), Miller. COVER: Lloyd Bridges, Shirley Eaton, and Movie Scene.

203 Arrivederci Baby (Paramount, 1966, Tony Curtis, Rosanna Schiaffino).

Love Me Longer—Earl Shuman (w), Dennis Farnon (m), Famous. COVER: Tony Curtis, Rosanna Schiaffino, Movie Scenes.

204 Arthur (Warner Bros., 1981, Dudley Moore, Liza Minnelli).

Arthur's Theme, Best That You Can Do—Burt Bacharach, Carole B. Sager, Chris Cross, Peter Allen (w,m), Warner; Fool Me Again (VS)—Carole B. Sager (w), Burt Bacharach (m), Warner; It's Only Love (VS)—Carole B. Sager, Stephen Bishop (w), Burt Bacharach (m), Warner; Money (VS)—Burt Bacharach (m), Warner; Moving Pictures (VS)—Burt Bacharach, John Phillips (m), Warner; Poor Rich Boy (VS)—David Pack, Joe Puerta (w), Burt Bacharach (m), Warner; Touch (VS)—Burt Bacharach (m), Warner. COVER: Dudley Moore.

205 Arthur Two on the Rocks (Warner Bros., 1988, Dudley Moore, Liza Minnelli).

Love Is My Decision—Chris De-Burgh, Carole B. Sager, Burt Bacharach (w,m), Almo. COVER: Dudley Moore, Liza Minnelli.

206 Artists and Models (Paramount, 1937, Jack Benny, Ida Lupino).

Pop Goes the Bubble—Ted Koehler (w), Burton Lane (m), Famous; Public Melody Number One—Ted Koehler (w), Harold Arlen (m), Famous; Stop! You're Breakin' My Heart—Ted Koehler (w), Burton Lane (m), Famous; Whispers in the Dark—Leo Robin, Frederick Hollander (w,m), Famous. COVER: Jack Benny.

207 Artists and Models (Paramount, 1955, Dean Martin, Jerry Lewis).

Artists and Models/Bat Lady, The/Innamorata/Lucky Song, The/When You Pretend/You Look So Familiar —Jack Brooks (w), Harry Warren (m), Paramount. COVER: Dean Martin, Jerry Lewis.

208 Artists and Models Abroad (Paramount, 1938, Jack Benny, Joan Bennett).

Do the Buckaroo/What Have You Got That Gets Me/You're Lovely Madame—Leo Robin, Ralph Rainger (w,m), Famous. COVER: Jack Benny.

209 Art of Love, The (Universal, 1965, James Garner, Dick Van Dyke).

Art of Love, The—Don Raye (w), Cy Coleman (m), Northern; I Wish I Knew Her Name/Kick Off Your Shoes—Murray Grand (w), Cy Coleman (m), Northern; Nikki—James Lipton (w), Cy Coleman (m), Northern; So Long Baby—Murray Grand, Cy Coleman (w), Cy Coleman (m), Northern. COVER: James Garner, Dick Van Dyke, Elke Sommer, Angie Dickinson, Ethel Merman.

210 Ashes of Vengeance (First National, 1923, Norma Talmadge, Wallace Beery).

Ashes of Vengeance—Mabel Livingstone (w), Muriel Pollack (m), Photoplay. COVER: Norma Talmadge.

211 Ash Wednesday (Paramount, 1973, Elizabeth Taylor, Henry Fonda).

Summer Green-Autumn Gold—Paul F. Webster (w), Maurice Jarre (m), Famous. COVER: Elizabeth Taylor.

212 Ask Any Girl (MGM, 1959, Shirley MacLaine, David Niven).

Ballad for Beatniks/Blues About Manhattan, The—Larry Orenstein (w), Jeff Alexander (m), Robbins; I'm in the Mood for Love—Jimmy McHugh, Dorothy Fields (w,m), Robbins. COVER: Shirley MacLaine, David Niven, Gig Young.

213 Assassination Bureau, The (Paramount, 1968, Oliver Reed, Diana Rigg).

Life Is a Precious Thing—Hal Shaper (w), Ron Grainer (m), Famous; Assassination Bureau Movie Score—Ron Grainer (m), Famous. COVER: Diana Rigg, and Movie Scenes.

214 Astonished Heart, The (Universal, 1950, Noel Coward, Celia Johnson).

Astonished Heart Suite—Noel Coward (m), Chappell. COVER: Noel Coward, and Girl.

215 As Young As We Are (Paramount, 1958, Robert Harland, Pippa Scott).

As Young As We Are—Harold Barlow (w,m), Famous. COVER: Robert Harland, Pippa Scott.

216 At Close Range (Orion, 1986, Sean Penn, Chris Walken).

Live to Tell—Madonna Ciccone, Pat Leonard (w,m), Warner. COVER: Madonna.

217 Athena (MGM, 1954, Jane Powell, Edmund Purdom).

Athena—Bert Pollock (w), Hugh Martin, Ralph Blane (m), Feist; Girl Next Door, The/Imagine/Love Can Change the Stars/Venezia—Hugh Martin, Ralph Blane (w,m), Feist. COVER: Jane Powell, Edmund Purdom, Debbie Reynolds, Vic Damone.

218 Atlantic City (Republic, 1944, Constance Moore, Brad Taylor).

After You've Gone—Henry Creamer, Turner Layton (w,m), Mayfair; Blues My Naughty Sweetie Gives to Me—Art Swanstone, Charles McCarron, Carey Morgan (w,m), Marks; By the Beautiful Sea—Harold Atteridge (w), Harry Carroll (m), Shapiro Bernstein; On a Sunday Afternoon—Andrew Sterling (w), Harry Vol Tilzer (m), Von Tilzer. COVER: Constance Moore, Brad Taylor, Jerry Colonna, Paul Whiteman.

219 Atlantic Flight (Monogram, 1937, Dick Merrill, Jack Lambie).

Marking Time—Lyle Morine (w, m), Mills; Me Myself and I—Irving Gordon, Allan Roberts, Alvin Kaufman (w,m), Words Music. COVER: Dick Merrill, Paula Stone.

220 Atlantis (Siren of Atlantis) (United Artists, 1948, Maria Montez, Jean Pierre Aumont).

Oriental Song—Robert Lax (w), Michel Michelet (m), Ditson. COVER: Maria Montez.

221 At Long Last Love (20th Century-Fox, 1975, Burt Reynolds, Cybill Shepherd).

At Long Last Love (VS)/But in the Morning No (VS)/Find Me a Primitive Man (VS)/Friendship (VS)/From Alpha to Omega (VS)/I Get a Kick out of You (VS)/I Loved Him (VS)/It's Delovely (VS)/Just One of Those Things (VS)/Let's Misbehave (VS)/Most Gentlemen Don't Like Love (VS)/Picture of Me Without You (VS)/Poor Young Millionaire (VS)/Well, Did You Evah? (VS)/Which? (VS)/You're the Top (VS)—Cole Porter (w,m), Chappell. COVER: Burt Reynolds, Cybill Shepherd.

222 At the Circus (MGM, 1939, Marx Brothers, Kenny Baker).

Blue Moon (PC)—Lorenz Hart (w), Richard Rodgers (m), Robbins; Lydia, The Tattooed Lady/Two Blind Loves—E. Y. Harburg (w), Harold Arlen (m), Feist. COVER: Marx Brothers, Kenny Baker.

223 At the Stroke of Nine (Grand National, 1957, Patricia Dainton, Stephen Murray).

Vorslav Concerto, The (B)—Edwin Astley (m), Metro. COVER: Stephen Murray.

224 At War with the Army (Paramount, 1951, Dean Martin, Jerry Lewis).

Navy Gets the Gravy, The/Tonda Wanda Hoy/You and Your Beautiful Eyes—Mack David (w), Jerry Livingston (m), Paramount. COVER: Dean Martin, Jerry Lewis, Polly Bergen.

225 Auction of Souls (Selig, 1919, Aurora Mardiganian, Irving Cummings).

Armenian Maid—Wilbur Weeks (w), M. Alexander (m), Paull. COVER: Aurora Mardiganian.

226 Auntie Mame (Warner Bros., 1958, Rosalind Russell, Forrest Tucker).

Drifting—Kim Gannon (w), Bronislau Kaper (m), Witmark. COVER: Rosalind Russell.

227 Aunt Sally (Along Came Sally) (Gainsborough, 1933, Cicely Courtneidge, Sam Hardy).

Ain't She the Dainty/If I Had Napoleon's Hat/I Want a Fair and a Square Man/My Wild Oat/We'll All Be Riding on a Rainbow/Wind's in the West, The/You Ought to See Sally on a Sunday—Harry Woods (w, m), Mills. COVER: Cicely Courtneidge.

228 Author! Author! (20th Century-Fox, 1982, Al Pacino, Dyan Cannon).

Coming Home to You—Alan Bergman, Marilyn Bergman (w), David Grusin (m), Warner. COVER: Al Pacino.

229 Awakening, The (United Artists, 1927, Vilma Banky, Walter Byron).

Marie—Irving Berlin (w,m), Berlin. COVER: Vilma Banky.

230 Away All Boats (Universal, 1956, Jeff Chandler, George Nader).

Away All Boats—Lenny Adelson (w), Frank Skinner, Albert Skinner (m), Keys. COVER: George Nader, Julie Adams.

231 Awful Truth, The (Pathe, 1929, Ina Claire, Henry Daniel).

When I Gave My Heart to You— Walter O'Keefe, Bobby Dolan (w,m), DBH. COVER: Black and white cover with title only.

232 Babe (MGM, 1975, Susan Clark, Alex Karras).

When You've Gone Away—Carol Goldsmith (w), Jerry Goldsmith (m), MGM. COVER: Susan Clark.

233 Babe Ruth Story, The (Allied Artists, 1948, William Bendix, Claire Trevor).

After the Ball—Charles Harris (w, m), Harris. COVER: William Bendix, Claire Trevor.

234 Babes in Arms (MGM, 1939, Mickey Rooney, Judy Garland).

Babes in Arms—Lorenz Hart (w), Richard Rodgers (m), Chappell; Good Morning—Arthur Freed (w), Nacio Herb Brown (m), Chappell; God's Country—E.Y. Harburg (w), Harold Arlen (m), Chappell; I Cried for You—Arthur Freed, Gus Arnheim, Abe Lyman (w,m), Miller; I'm Just Wild About Harry (VS)— Noble Sissle (w), Eubie Blake (m), Witmark; Lady Is a Tramp, The (B)/ Where or When (B)—Lorenz Hart (w), Richard Rodgers (m), Chappell. COVER: Mickey Rooney, Judy Garland.

235 Babes in Toyland (MGM, 1934, Stan Laurel, Oliver Hardy).

I Can't Do the Sum/March of the Toys/Toyland—Glen MacDonough (w), Victor Herbert (m), Witmark. COVER: Movie Scene.

236 Babes in Toyland (Buena Vista, 1961, Ray Bolger, Tommy Sands).

Castle in Spain (VS)/Fioretta (VS) /Forest of No Return (VS)/Go to Sleep (VS)/I Can't Do the Sum (VS)/ Just a Toy (VS)/Just a Whisper Away (VS)/Lemonade (VS)/March of the Toys (VS)/Mother Goose Village (VS)/Never Mind Bo-Peep (VS)/ Slowly He Sank to the Bottom (VS)/ Tom and Mary (VS)/Toyland (VS)/ We Won't Be Happy Till We Get It (VS)/Work Shop Song (VS)—Mel Leven (w), George Bruns, Victor Herbert (m), Disney. COVER: Ray Bolger, Tommy Sands, Annette.

237 Babes on Broadway (MGM, 1941, Mickey Rooney, Judy Garland).

Chin Up! Cheerio! Carry On!— E.Y. Harburg (w), Burton Lane (m), Feist; Hoe Down—Ralph Freed (w), Roger Edens (m), Feist; How About You?—Ralph Freed (w), Burton Lane (m), Feist; Waiting for the Robert E. Lee—L. Wolfe Gilbert, Lewis Muir (w,m), Alfred. COVER: Mickey Rooney, Judy Garland.

238 Baby Doll (Warner Bros., 1956, Karl Malden, Carroll Baker).

Baby Doll—Bernie Hanighen (w), Kenyon Hopkins (m), Remick; Baby Doll Theme—Kenyon Hopkins (m), Remick; Shame, Shame, Shame— Ruby Fisher (w), Kenyon Hopkins (m), Remick. COVER: Carroll Baker.

239 Baby Face Nelson (United Artists, 1957, Mickey Rooney, Carolyn Jones).

I'm So in Love with You—Mickey Rooney, Harold Spina (w,m), Rooney. COVER: Mickey Rooney, Carolyn Jones.

240 Baby Peggy (Universal, 1923, Baby Peggy).

That's My Baby—Sidney Clare, Cliff Friend, Owen Murphy (w,m), Abrahams. COVER: Baby Peggy.

241 Baby Take a Bow (Fox, 1934, Shirley Temple, James Dunn).

On Account-a I Love You—Bud Green (w), Sam Stept (m), Movietone. COVER: Shirley Temple, James Dunn, Claire Trevor.

242 Baby the Rain Must Fall (Columbia, 1964, Steve McQueen, Lee Remick).

Baby the Rain Must Fall— Elmer Bernstein, Ernie Sheldon (w,m), Colgems. COVER: Glen Yarborough.

243 Bachelor and the Bobby Soxer, The (RKO, 1947, Cary Grant, Shirley Temple).

Bachelor and the Bobby Soxer,

The—Don Meyer, Howard Phillips (w), Joseph Meyer (m), Paul-Pioneer. COVER: Cary Grant, Shirley Temple.

244 Bachelor in Paradise (MGM, 1961, Bob Hope, Lana Turner).

Bachelor in Paradise—Mack David (w), Henry Mancini (m), Robbins. COVER: Bob Hope, Lana Turner.

245 Bachelor of Arts (Fox, 1934, Tom Brown, Anita Louise).

Phi Phi Phi—Sidney Clare (w), Richard Whiting (m), Movietone. COVER: Black and white cover with title only.

246 Bachelor Party (United Artists, 1957, Don Murray, E. G. Marshall).

Bachelor Party Theme—Alex North (m), Hecht Lancaster. COVER: Don Murray and Other Men.

247 Bachelor's Daughters, The (United Artists, 1946, Gail Russell, Claire Trevor).

Twilight Song—Jack Lawrence, Irving Drutman (w,m), Mutual; Where's My Heart—Kermit Goell (w), Fred Spielman (m), Hudson. COVER: Gail Russell, Claire Trevor, and Others.

248 Backbone (Distinctive, 1923, Edith Roberts, Alfred Lunt).

Yvone—Irving Caesar (w), Lewis Gensler (m), Harms. COVER: Edith Roberts, Alfred Lunt.

249 Back Door to Heaven (Paramount, 1939, William Ford, Patricia Ellis).

Home Town—Jimmie Kennedy, Michael Carr (w,m), Crawford; I Need a Friend—Nick Kenny, Charles Kenny, Pierre Norman (w,m), ABC. COVER: Patricia Ellis.

250 Back from Eternity (RKO, 1956, Robert Ryan, Anita Ekberg).

Back from Eternity—Franz Waxman (m), Lamas. COVER: Robert Ryan, Anita Ekberg, Rod Steiger.

251 Back Home and Broke (Paramount, 1922, Thomas Meighan, Lila Lee).

Back Home and Broke—Charles Harris (w,m), Harris. COVER: Thom-Meighan.

252 Back in the Saddle (Republic, 1941, Gene Autry, Smiley Burnette).

Where the River Meets the Range —Jule Styne, Sol Meyer (w,m), Mills; You Are My Sunshine (VS)—Jimmie Davis, Charles Mitchel (w,m), Western. COVER: Gene Autry.

253 Back Roads (Warner Bros., 1981, Sally Field, Tommy Lee Jones).

Ask Me No Questions—Alan Bergman, Marilyn Bergman (w), Henry Mancini (m), April. COVER: Sally Field, Tommy Lee Jones.

254 Backstage (Limelight) (Wilcox, 1935, Anna Neagle, Arthur Tracy).

Whistling Waltz, The—Harry Woods (w,m), Crawford. COVER: Anna Neagle, Arthur Tracy.

255 Back Street (Universal, 1932, Irene Dunne, John Boles).

Only a Back Street Girl—Irving Bibo, Joe Weil (w,m), Bibo Lang. COVER: Irene Dunne.

256 Back Street (Universal, 1961, Susan Hayward, John Gavin).

Back Street—Ken Darby (w), Frank Skinner (m), Keys Hansen. COVER: Susan Hayward, John Gavin.

257 Back to God's Country (First National, 1919, Nell Shipman, Wheeler Oakman).

Back to God's Country—Paul Sarazan, Jack Weil (w), Paul Sarazan (m), Berlin. COVER: Nell Shipman.

258 Back to School (Orion, 1986, Sally Kellerman, Rodney Dangerfield).

Respect (VS)—Otis Redding (w, m), East Memphis; Twist and Shout—Bert Russell, Phil Medley (w,m), Warner. COVER: Blue cover with title only.

259 Back to the Future (Universal, 1986, Michael Fox, Christopher Lloyd).

Back to the Future—Alan Silvestri (m), MCA; Power of Love, The—Johnny Colla, Chris Hayes, Huey Lewis (w,m), Cherry Lane, Back in

Time (VS)—Johnny Colla, Chris Hayes, Sean Hopper, Huey Lewis (w, m), MCA; Dance with Me Henry (VS)—Etta James, Johnny Otis, Hank Ballard (w,m), MCA; Earth Angel (VS)—Dootsie Williams (w,m), MCA; Heaven Is One Step Away (VS)—Eric Clapton (w,m), MCA; Johnny B. Goode (VS)—Chuck Berry (w,m), MCA; Night Train (VS)—Oscar Washington, Lewis Simpkins (w), Jimmy Forrest (m), MCA; Time Bomb Town (VS)—Lindsay Buckingham (w,m), MCA. COVER: Michael Fox.

260 Bad and the Beautiful, The (MGM, 1953, Lana Turner, Kirk Douglas).

Bad and the Beautiful—Dory Langdon (w), David Raksin (m), Robbins; Bad and the Beautiful Theme—David Raksin (m), Robbins. COVER: Lana Turner, Kirk Douglas.

261 Bad Boy (Fox, 1935, James Dunn, Dorothy Wilson).

As I Live and Breathe—Paul F. Webster (w), Lew Pollack (m), Movietone. COVER: Black and white cover with title only.

262 Bad Boy (Allied Artists, 1949, Audie Murphy, Lloyd Nolan).

Dream on Little Plowboy—Gene Austin (w,m), Feist. COVER: Audie Murphy, Lloyd Nolan.

263 Bad Company (Paramount, 1972, Jeff Bridges, Barry Brown).

Wandering Child—Harvey Schmidt (m), Famous; Bad Company—Ten Themes—Harvey Schmidt (m), Portfolio. COVER: Jeff Bridges, Barry Brown.

264 Bad Girl (Fox, 1931, James Dunn, Sally Eilers).

Come on Baby and Beg for It/Red Head—James Hanley (w,m), Movietone. COVER: Black and white cover with title only.

265 Bad Man from Red Butte (Universal, 1940, Johnny Mack Brown, Bob Baker).

Gabby the Lawyer/Where the Prairie Meets the Sky—Everett Carter (w), Milton Rosen (m), Robbins.

COVER: Bob Baker, Johnny Mack Brown, Fuzzy Knight.

265a Bad One, The (United Artists, 1930, Dolores Del Rio, Edmund Lowe).

To a Tango Melody—Irving Berlin (w,m), Berlin. COVER: Black and white with title only.

266 Bad Seed, The (Warner Bros., 1957, Nancy Kelly, Patty McCormack).

Bad Seed Themes—Alex North (m), Witmark. COVER: Blue cover with title only.

267 Bagdad Cafe (Island, 1988, Marianne Sagebrecht, Jack Palance).

Calling You—Bob Telson (w,m), Boodle. COVER: Marianne Sagebrecht, Jack Palance, and Others.

268 Bail Out at 43,000 (United Artists, 1957, John Payne, Karen Steele).

Who Knows—Alan Bergman, Marilyn Keith (w), Al Glasser (m), John Paul. COVER: Green cover with title only.

269 Balalaika (MGM, 1939, Nelson Eddy, Ilona Massey).

At the Balalaika—Bob Wright, Chet Forrest (w), George Posford (m), Feist; Dark Eyes—Howard Johnson (w), A. Salami (m), Feist; Magic of Your Love, The—Gus Kahn, Clifford Grey (w), Franz Lehar (m), Chappell; Ride, Cossack, Ride!/Shadows on the sand—Bob Wright, Chet Forrest (w), Herbert Stothart (m), Feist. COVER: Nelson Eddy, Ilona Massey.

270 Ballad of Josie, The (Universal, 1967, Doris Day, Peter Graves).

Ballad of Josie, The—Floyd Huddleston (w), Don Costa (m), Hawaii; Wait Till Tomorrow—Jack Lloyd (w), Gene DePaul (m), Shamley. COVER: Doris Day, Peter Graves.

271 Ball of Fire (RKO, 1941, Gary Cooper, Barbara Stanwyck).

Drumboogie (Q)—Gene Krupa, Roy Eldridge (w,m), Robbins. COVER: Unknown.

272 Bal Tabarin (Republic, 1952, William Ching, Muriel Lawrence).

You've Never Been in Love—Jack Elliott (w,m), Bourne. COVER: Vicki Benet.

273 Bal Week (World Wide, 1967, Religious Film).

Collegian's Prayer (PC)/There Is More to Life (PC)—Ralph Carmichael (w,m), Lexicon. COVER: None.

274 Bambi (RKO Disney, 1942, Cartoon).

I Bring You a Song (VS)/Little April Shower/Let's Sing a Gay Little Spring Song/Love Is a Song—Larry Morey (w), Frank Churchill (m), BMI; Thumper Song/Twitterpated—Helen Bliss, Robert Sour, Henry Manners (w,m), BMI. COVER: Cartoon.

275 Bamboo Blonde, The (RKO, 1946, Frances Langford, Ralph Edwards).

Along About Evenin'—Mort Greene (w), Lew Pollack (m), Mayfair. COVER: Frances Langford.

276 Bananas (United Artists, 1971, Woody Allen, Louise Lasser).

Bananas—Marvin Hamlisch (w,m), Unart. COVER: Woody Allen.

277 Bandido (United Artists, 1956, Robert Mitchum, Ursula Thiess).

Bandido—Jack Barnett (w), Max Steiner (m), Chappell. COVER: Robert Mitchum.

278 Band of Angels (Warner Bros., 1957, Clark Gable, Yvonne DeCarlo).

Band of Angels—Carl Sigman (w), Max Steiner (m), Witmark. COVER: Clark Gable, Yvonne DeCarlo.

279 Bandolero (20th Century-Fox, 1968, James Stewart, Dean Martin).

There's Got to Be a Better Way—Sammy Cahn (w), Jerry Goldsmith (m), Fox. COVER: James Stewart, Dean Martin, Raquel Welch.

280 Bandwagon, The (MGM, 1953, Fred Astaire, Cyd Charisse).

By Myself—Howard Dietz (w), Arthur Schwartz (m), Chappell; Dancing in the Dark/I Guess I'll Have to Change My Plan/I Love Louisa/ Louisiana Hayride/New Sun in the Sky—Howard Dietz (w), Arthur Schwartz (m), Harms; That's Entertainment—Howard Dietz (w), Arthur Schwartz (m), Chappell; Triplets—DBH. COVER: Fred Astaire, Cyd Charisse.

281 Bang the Drum Slowly (Paramount, 1973, Robert DeNiro, Michael Moriarty).

Bang the Drum Slowly Theme—Bruce Hart (w), Stephen Lawrence (m), Famous. COVER: Robert DeNiro, Michael Moriarty.

282 Banjo on My Knee (20th Century-Fox, 1936, Barbara Stanwyck, Joel McCrea).

There's Something in the Air—Harold Adamson (w), Jimmy McHugh (m), Robbins; Saint Louis Blues—W. C. Handy (w,m), Handy; Where the Lazy River Goes By/With a Banjo on My Knee—Harold Adamson (w), Jimmy McHugh (m), Robbins. COVER: Barbara Stanwyck, Tony Martin, Joel McCrea, Buddy Ebsen.

283 Banning (Universal, 1967, Robert Wagner, Jill St. John).

Eyes of Love, The—Bob Russell (w), Quincy Jones (m), Shamley. COVER: Robert Wagner, Jill St. John.

284 Barabbas (Columbia, 1961, Anthony Quinn, Silvana Mangano).

Barabbas—Earl Shuman (w), Mario Nascimbene (m), Columbia. COVER: Anthony Quinn, Silvana Mangano, and Others.

285 Barbarella (Paramount, 1968, Jane Fonda, John Phillip Law).

Angel Is Love, An/Barbarella/I Love All the Love in You/Love Drags Me Down—Bob Crewe, Charles Fox (w,m), Ensign. COVER: Jane Fonda.

286 Barbarian, The (MGM, 1933, Ramon Novarro, Myrna Loy).

Love Song of the Nile—Arthur Freed (w), Nacio Herb Brown (m), Robbins. COVER: Ramon Novarro, Myrna Loy.

287 Barbary Coast (United Artists, 1935, Miriam Hopkins, Joel McCrea).

Barbary Coast—Abner Silver, Al Sherman, Al Lewis (w,m), Engel. COVER: Miriam Hopkins, Joel Mc-Crea, Edward G. Robinson.

288 Barefoot Contessa, The (United Artists, 1954, Ava Gardner, Humphrey Bogart).

Beware Now (B)—Johnny May (w), M. Nascimbene (m), Chappell; Song of the Barefoot Contessa—Mario Nascimbene (m), Chappell. COVER: Ava Gardner, Humphrey Bogart.

289 Barefoot in the Park (Paramount, 1967, Robert Redford, Jane Fonda).

Barefoot in the Park—Johnny Mercer (w), Neal Hefti (m), Famous. COVER: Robert Redford, Jane Fonda.

290 Bargain with Bullets (Gangsters on the Loose) (Million Dollar, 1937, Les Hite, Eddie Barefield).

What Is Life Without You?—Tony Sacco, Charlie Crafts (w), Marty Arden (m), Inter. COVER: Birds and Clouds.

291 Barkleys of Broadway, The (MGM, 1949, Fred Astaire, Ginger Rogers).

Bouncin' the Blues (BW)—Harry Warren (m), Warren; Manhattan Downbeat (BW)/My One and Only Highland Fling/Shoes with Wings On/Swing Trot (B)—Ira Gershwin (w), Harry Warren (m), Warren; They Can't Take That Away from Me—Ira Gershwin (w), George Gershwin (m), Chappell, Weekend in the Country (BW)/You'd Be Hard to Replace—Ira Gershwin (w), Harry Warren (m), Warren. COVER: Fred Astaire, Ginger Rogers.

292 Barnacle Bill (All at Sea) (MGM, 1958, Alec Guinness, Irene Browne).

Barnacle Bill's Hornpipe (B)—John Addison (m), Robbins. COVER: Alec Guinness.

293 Barnyard Follies (Republic, 1940, Mary Lee, Rufe Davis).

Barnyard Holiday/Big Boy Blues/ Lollipop Lane/Poppin' the Corn—Johnny Marvin, Fred Rose (w,m), Mills. COVER: Mary Lee.

294 Barretts of Wimpole Street, The (MGM, 1934, Norma Shearer, Fredric March).

Wilt Thou Have My Hand—Elizabeth Barrett (w), Herbert Stothart (m), Robbins. COVER: Norma Shearer.

295 Barretts of Wimpole Street, The (MGM, 1957, Jennifer Jones, John Gielgud).

Wilt Thou Have My Hand—Elizabeth Barrett (w), Herbert Stothart (m), Robbins. COVER: Jennifer Jones.

296 Barricade (The Girl From Brooklyn) (20th Century-Fox, 1938, Alice Faye, Warner Baxter).

There'll Be Other Nights—Lew Brown (w), Lew Pollack (m), Movietone. COVER: Alice Faye, Warner Baxter.

297 Barrier, The (Beach, 1917, Mitchell Lewis, Edward Roseman).

Song of the North—Louis Weslyn (w), Frederick O. Hanks (m), Beach. COVER: Movie Scene.

298 Barrier, The (Paramount, 1937, Jean Parker, Leo Carrillo).

Moonlit Paradise—Harry Tobias, Jack Stern (w,m), Paramount. COVER: Jean Parker, James Ellison.

299 Barry Lyndon (Warner Bros., 1976, Ryan O'Neal, Marisa Berenson).

Sarabande—George Handel (m), Schirmer. COVER: Ryan O'Neal, Marisa Berenson.

300 Bar 20 Rides Again (Paramount, 1935, William Boyd, Jimmy Ellison).

Moon Hangs High, The—Dave Franklin (w), Sam Stept (m), Sam Fox. COVER: Jean Rouverol, Jimmy Ellison.

301 Bat, The (Allied Artists, 1959, Vincent Price, Agnes Moorehead).

Bat Theme, The—Lou Forbes (m), Miller. COVER: A Girl and a Bat.

302 Bathing Beauty (MGM, 1944, Esther Williams, Red Skelton).

Alma Llanera—Pedro Elias Gutierrez (w,m), Peer; Hora Staccato—Jascha Heifetz, Grigoras Dinicu (m), Fischer; I'll Take the High Note—Harold Adamson (w), Johnny Green (m), Chappell; Magic Is the Moonlight—Charles Pasquale (w), Maria Grever (m), Melody Lane; Tico Tico—Ervin Drake (w), Zequinha Abreu (m), Harris. COVER: Esther Williams, Red Skelton, Harry James.

303 Batman (Warner, 1989, Jack Nicholson, Michael Keaton).

Arms of Orion, The—Prince, Sheena Easton (w,m), Warner; Batdance—Prince (w,m), Warner; Batman Theme, The—Danny Elfman (m), Warner; Partyman/Electric Chair (VS)/Future, The (VS)/Lemon Crush (VS)—Prince (w,m), Warner; Scandalous (VS)—Prince, John Nelson (w, m), Warner; Trust (VS)/Vicki Waiting (VS)—Prince (w,m), Warner; Batman Themes #2–10 Themes—Danny Elfman (m), Warner. COVER: Batman Sign.

304 Battle Cry (Warner Bros., 1954, Van Heflin, Aldo Ray).

Honey Babe, The Marching Song—Paul F. Webster (w), Max Steiner (m), Witmark. COVER: Aldo Ray, Nancy Olson, Mona Freeman.

305 Battle Cry of Peace (Vitagraph, 1915, Charles Richman, Norma Talmadge).

Battle Cry of Peace March—J. Tim Bryan (m), Cadillac. COVER: Thais Lawton.

306 Battle of Britain (United Artists, 1969, Laurence Olivier, Michael Caine).

Battle of Britain Theme—Ron Goodwin (m), Unart. COVER: Airplanes.

307 Battle of Broadway (20th Century-Fox, 1938, Victor McLaglen, Brian Donlevy).

Daughter of Mademoiselle—Sidney Clare (w), Harry Akst (m), Mills. COVER: Victor McLaglen, Brian Donlevy, Louise Hovick.

308 Battle of Paris, The (Paramount, 1929, Gertrude Lawrence, Charles Ruggles).

Here Comes the Bandwagon/They All Fall in Love—Cole Porter (w,m), Harms; What Makes My Baby Blue?/ When I Am Housekeeping for You—Dick Howard (w), Jay Gorney (m), Spier Coslow. COVER: Gertrude Lawrence.

309 Battle of the Sexes, The (United Artists, 1928, Belle Bennett, Jean Hersholt).

Just a Sweetheart—Josef Pasternack, Nat Shilkret, Dave Dreyer (w, m), Berlin; Rose in the Bud—Percy Barrow (w), Dorothy Forster (m), Chappell. COVER: Belle Bennett, Jean Hersholt, Phyllis Haver.

310 Battle of the Villa Fiorita, The (Warner Bros., 1965, Maureen O'Hara, Rossano Brazzi).

Our Crazy Affair—Ervin Drake (w), Mischa Spoliansky (m), Witnark. COVER: Maureen O'Hara, Rossano Brazzi.

311 Battlestar Galactica (Universal, 1978, Richard Hatch, Dirk Benedict).

Battlestar Galactica Theme—Stu Phillips, Glen Larson (w,m), Duchess. COVER: Battle Scene.

312 Baxter! (National General, 1973, Patricia Neal, Britt Ekland).

Baxter Theme—Michael Lewis (m), Ambrit. COVER: Patricia Neal, Scott Jacoby.

313 Bayou (United Artists, 1957, Peter Graves, Lita Milan).

Bayou/Hold Me Close—Edward Fessler (w,m), Miller. COVER: Lita Milan.

314 Beach Blanket Bingo (AIP, 1965, Frankie Avalon, Annette Funicello).

Surfer's Life Is Fun, A (PC)—Guy Hemric, Jerry Styner (w,m), Dijon. COVER: None.

315 Beachcomber, The (Paramount, 1934, Charles Laughton, Elsa Lancaster).

Whistle a Happy Refrain—Dailey Paskman (w), Richard Addinsell, Bert Reisfeld (m), Marks. COVER: Charles Laughton.

316 Beaches (Touchstone, 1989, Bette Midler, Barbara Hershey).

Wind Beneath My Wings, The— Larry Henley, Jeff Silbar (w,m), Warner; Friendship Theme—Georges Delerue (m), Disney. COVER: Bette Midler.

317 Beach Party (AIP, 1963, Frankie Avalon, Annette Funicello).

Beach Party (PC)—Gary Usher, Roger Christian (w,m), Dijon. COVER: None.

318 Bears and I, The (Buena Vista, 1974, Patrick Wayne, Andrew Duggan).

Sweet Surrender—John Denver (w,m), Disney. COVER: Patrick Wayne, and Bear.

319 Beat Generation, The (MGM, 1959, Steve Cochran, Mamie Van Doren).

Beat Generation, The—Tom Walton (w), Walter Kent (m), Robbins. COVER: Mamie Van Doren, Louis Armstrong, and Others.

320 Beat Street (Orion, 1984, Rae Dawn Chong, Guy Davis).

Beat Street Breakdown—Reggie Griffin, Melvin Glover (w,m), Buttermilk; Strangers in a Strange World—Jake Holmes (w,m), Buttermilk. COVER: Dancers.

321 Beau Brummel (Warner Bros., 1924, John Barrymore, Mary Astor).

Beau Brummel Minuet—Francis Young (m), Fischer. COVER: John Barrymore, Mary Astor.

322 Beau Geste (Paramount, 1927, Ronald Colman, Neil Hamilton).

Beau Geste Themes—Hugo Riesenfeld (m), Robbins Engel; Song of the Legion March (B)—Ed Lockton, Frank Tours, Jim Bradford, Hans Spialek (w,m), Sam Fox. COVER: Ronald Colman.

323 Beau James (Paramount, 1957, Bob Hope, Vera Miles).

Beau James—Herbert Baker (w,m), Famous; Manhattan—Lorenz Hart (w), Richard Rodgers (m), Marks; Sidewalks of New York, The—Charles Lawlor, James Blake (w,m), Lewis. COVER: Bob Hope, Vera Miles.

324 Beau Sabreur (Paramount, 1928, Gary Cooper, Noah Beery).

Desert Stars (B)—Edward Lockton (w), Frank Tours (m), Keith Prowse; Thinking of You (Promo Song)—Joseph Grey (w), Allie Moore (m), Oxford. COVER: Gary Cooper.

325 Beautiful Blonde from Bashful Bend, The (20th Century-Fox, 1949, Betty Grable, Cesar Romero).

Beautiful Blonde from Bashful Bend—Don George (w), Lionel Newman (m), Feist; Every Time I Meet You—Mack Gordon (w), Josef Myrow (m), Feist. COVER: Betty Grable, Cesar Romero, Rudy Vallee.

326 Beautiful but Broke (Columbia, 1944, Joan Davis, Jane Frazee).

Just Another Blues (VS)—Dick Charles, Larry Markes, Jimmy Paul (w,m), Leeds; Keeping It Private— Morte Greene (w), Walter Donaldson (m), Leeds; Mister Jive Has Gone to Wat—L. Wolfe Gilbert (w), Ben Oakland (m), Lasalle; Shoo Shoo Baby— Phil Moore (w,m), Leeds. COVER: Joan Davis, Jane Frazee, Judy Clark.

327 Beauty and the Beast (Vitaphone, 1934, Cartoon).

Beauty and the Beast—Bert Kalmar, Harry Ruby (w,m), Remick. COVER: Cartoon.

328 Beaver Valley (RKO Disney, 1950, True Life Adventure).

Jing-a-ling Jing-a-ling—Paul Smith (w), Don Raye (m), Disney. COVER: Winter Scene.

329 Bebo's Girl (Continental, 1964, George Chakiris, Claudia Cardinale).

That's What I Live For—Alan Brandt (w), Carlo Rustichelli (m), Marks. COVER: George Chakiris, Claudia Cardinale.

330 Because of Him (Universal, 1945, Deanna Durbin, Charles Laughton).

Danny Boy—Fred Weatherly (w, m), Boosey Hawkes; Lover—Lorenz Hart (w), Richard Rodgers (m), Famous. COVER: Deanna Durbin.

331 Because of You (Universal, 1952, Loretta Young, Jeff Chandler).

Because of You—Arthur Hammerstein, Dudley Wilkinson (w,m), BMI. COVER: Loretta Young, Jeff Chandler.

332 Because They're Young (Columbia, 1960, Tuesday Weld, Michael Callan).

Because They're Young—Aaron Schroeder, Wally Gold (w), Don Costa (m), Columbia; Swingin' School—Kal Mann (w), Bernie Lowe, Dave Appell (m), Columbia. COVER: Michael Callan, Tuesday Weld, and Others.

333 Because You're Mine (MGM, 1942, Mario Lanza, Doretta Morrow).

Because You're Mine—Sammy Cahn (w), Nicholas Brodszky (m), Feist; Granada—Dorothy Dodd (w), Agustin Lara (m), Southern; Lee Ah Loo—John Lehmann (w), Raymond Sinatra (m), Feist; Song Angels Sing, The—Paul F. Webster (w), Irving Aaronson (m), Feist. COVER: Mario Lanza, Doretta Morrow.

334 Bedazzled (20th Century-Fox, 1967, Peter Cook, Dudley Moore).

Bedazzled—Peter Cook, Dudley Moore (w,m), 20th Century; Love Me—Dudley Moore (w,m), 20th Century; Sweet Mouth—Sammy Cahn (w), Dudley Moore (m), 20th Century. COVER: Cartoon sketch.

335 Bedevilled (MGM, 1952, Anne Baxter, Steve Forrest).

Embrasse, Hold Me Close—Richard Driscoll (w), Paul Durand (m), Disney. COVER: Anne Baxter, Steve Forrest.

336 Bedknobs and Broomsticks (Buena Vista, 1971, Angela Lansbury, David Tomlinson).

Age of Not Believing, The/Beautiful Briny/Old Home Guard, The/Portobello Road/Substitutiary Locomotion/Don't Let Me Down (VS)/Eglantine (VS)/Overture to Bedknobs and Broomsticks (VS)/Portobello Road Street Dance (VS)/Step in the Right Direction (VS)/With a Flair (VS)—Richard Sherman, Robert Sherman (w,m), Disney. COVER: Angela Lansbury, David Tomlinson.

337 Bedtime for Bonzo (Universal, 1951, Ronald Reagan, Diana Lynn).

Bedtime for Bonzo—Ted Berkman, Raphael Blau (w), Ted Berkman (m), Chappell. COVER: Ronald Reagan, Diana Lynn, Bonzo.

338 Bedtime Story, A (Paramount, 1933, Maurice Chevalier, Helen Twelvetrees).

Bedtime Story, A—Leo Towers, Harry Leon, Horatio Nicholls (w,m), Famous; Home Made Heaven/In the Park in Paree/Look What I've Got/Monsieur Baby—Leo Robin (w), Ralph Rainger (m), Famous. COVER: Maurice Chevalier, and Babies.

339 Beetlejuice (Warner Bros., 1988, Michael Keaton, Alec Baldwin).

Day-O—Irving Burgie (w,m), Cherry Lane. COVER: Michael Keaton, Alec Baldwin, Geena Davis.

340 Before Winter Comes (Columbia, 1969, David Niven, Topol).

Before Winter Comes—Carole Bayer Sager (w), Ron Grainer (m), Colgems. COVER: Topol, Anna Karina.

341 Beggars of Life (Paramount, 1928, Wallace Beery, Richard Arlen).

Beggars of Life—J. Keirn Brennan (w), Karl Hajos (m), Berlin. COVER: Wallace Beery.

342 Behave Yourself (RKO, 1951, Farley Granger, Shelley Winters).

Behave Yourself—Buddy Ebsen, Lew Spence (w,m), Disney. COVER: Farley Granger, Shelly Winters.

343 Behind the Eight Ball (Off the Beaten Track) (Universal, 1942, Ritz Brothers, Carol Bruce).

Mister Five by Five—Don Raye, Gene DePaul (w,m), Leeds. COVER: Fat Man.

344 Behind the Make-Up (Paramount, 1929, William Powell, Fay Wray).
Never Say Die—Leo Robin (w), Newell Chase (m), Famous. COVER: William Powell, Fay Wray, Hal Skelly.
345 Believe in Me (MGM, 1971, Michael Sarrazin, Jacqueline Bisset).
Believe in Me—Tylwyth Kymry (w), Fred Karlin (m), Hastings. COVER: Michael Sarrazin, Jacqueline Bisset.
346 Bella Donna (Paramount, 1923, Pola Negri, Adolphe Menjou).
Bella Donna—Harry B. Smith, Arthur Brilant (w), Ted Snyder (m), Berlin. COVER: Pola Negri.
347 Bell, Book and Candle (Columbia, 1959, James Stewart, Kim Novak).
Bell, Book and Candle Theme—Steve Allen (w), George Duning (m), Columbia. COVER: James Stewart, Kim Novak, and Others.
348 Bell Bottom George (Columbia, 1943, George Formby, Annie Firth).
If I Had a Girl Like You (B)—Phil Park (w), Harry P. Davies (m), Victoria. COVER: George Formby.
349 Belle of New York, The (Select, 1919, Marion Davies, Etienne Giradot).
Salvation Rose—Robert Levenson (w), Jack Mendelsohn (m), Stern. COVER: Marion Davies.
350 Belle of New York, The (MGM, 1952, Fred Astaire, Vera-Ellen).
Baby Doll/Bachelor Dinner Song (BW)/Bride's Wedding Day Song (BW)/I Love to Beat the Big Bass Drum (BW)/I Wanna Be a Dancin' Man/Naughty But Nice/Oops!/Seeing's Believing/When I'm Out with the Belle of New York—Johnny Mercer (w), Harry Warren (m), Feist. COVER: Fred Astaire, Vera-Ellen.
351 Belle of the Nineties (It Ain't No Sin) (Paramount, 1934, Mae West, Roger Pryor).

Memphis Blues—W. C. Handy (w, m), Morriss; My American Beauty/My Old Flame/Troubled Waters—Arthur Johnston, Sam Coslow (w, m), Famous; When a Saint Louis Woman Comes Down to New Orleans—Arthur Johnston, Sam Coslow, Gene Austin (w,m), Famous. COVER: Mae West.
352 Belle of the Yukon (RKO, 1945, Dinah Shore, Randolph Scott).
Ballad of Millicent Devere, The/Belle of the Yukon/Ev'ry Girl Is Diff'rent—Johnny Burke, Jimmy Van Heusen (w,m), Burke; I Can't Tell Why I Love You But I Do—Will Cobb (w), Gus Edwards (m), Mills; Like Someone in Love/Sleighride in July—Johnny Burke, Jimmy Van Heusen (w,m), Burke. COVER: Dinah Shore, Randolph Scott, Gypsy Rose Lee.
353 Belles on Their Toes (20th Century-Fox, 1952, Jeanne Crain, Myrna Loy).
Linger Awhile (B)—Harry Owens (w), Vincent Rose (m), Day. COVER: Green cover with title only.
354 Bells Are Ringing (MGM, 1960, Judy Holliday, Dean Martin).
Bells Are Ringing/Better Than A Dream/Do It Yourself/Drop That Name/Hello Hello There/I Met a Girl/Independent/Just in Time/Long Before I Knew You/Mu Cha Cha/Party's Over, The—Betty Comden, Adolph Green (w), Jule Styne (m), Stratford. COVER: Dean Martin, Judy Holliday.
355 Bells of Coronado (Republic, 1950, Roy Rogers, Dale Evans).
Save a Smile—Sid Robin, Foy Willing (w,m), Leeds. COVER: Green cover with title only.
356 Bells of St. Mary's, The (RKO, 1945, Bing Crosby, Ingrid Bergman).
Aren't You Glad You're You—Johnny Burke (w), Jimmy Van Heusen (m), Burke; Bells of St. Mary's, The—Douglas Furber (w), A. Emmett Adams (m), Chappell; In the Land of

Beginning Again—Grant Clarke (w), George Meyer (m), Feist; O, Come All Ye Faithful (B)—Traditional, Southern; Spring Is Here Again (B)—Eddie Lisbona, Bob Musel (w,m), Southern. COVER: Bing Crosby, Ingrid Bergman.

357 Beloved (Universal, 1934, John Boles, Gloria Stuart).

Beloved—Victor Schertzinger (w, m), Berlin. COVER: John Boles, Gloria Stuart.

358 Beloved Cheater (Robertson, 1919, Lew Cody, Doris Pawn).

That Beloved Cheater of Mine—L. Wolfe Gilbert, Edna Williams (w,m), Gilbert. COVER: Lew Cody.

359 Beloved Infidel (20th Century-Fox, 1959, Gregory Peck, Deborah Kerr).

Beloved Infidel—Paul F. Webster (w), Franz Waxman (m), Robbins. COVER: Gregory Peck, Deborah Kerr.

360 Be Mine Tonight (Universal, 1933, Jan Kiepura, Sonnie Hale).

Tell Me Tonight—Frank Eyton (w), Misha Spoliansky (m), Harms. COVER: Movie Scenes.

361 Ben (Cinerama, 1972, Lee Montgomery, Joseph Campanella).

Ben—Don Black (w), Walter Scharf (m), Jobette. COVER: Michael Jackson.

362 Bengazi (RKO, 1955, Richard Conte, Victor McLaglen).

Bengazi—Murray Arnold (w,m), Ranger. COVER: Richard Conte, Victor McLaglen, Richard Carlson, Mala Powers.

363 Ben Hur (MGM, 1959, Charlton Heston, Jack Hawkins).

Adoration of the Maji—Harry Wilson (w), Miklos Rozsa (m), Robbins; Ben Hur Love Theme/Christ Theme—Miklos Rozsa (m), Robbins; Mother's Love—Mary Ann Eager (w), Miklos Rozsa (m), Robbins; Star of Bethlehem/Ben Hur—Thirteen Themes —Miklos Rozsa (m), Robbins. COVER: Chariots.

364 Benji (Mulberry, 1974,

Peter Breck, Deborah Walley).

Benji's Theme—Evel Box (m), Mulberry; I Feel Love—Betty Box (w), Evel Box (m), Mulberry. COVER: A Dog.

365 Benny Goodman Story, The (Universal, 1956, Steve Allen, Donna Reed).

And the Angels Sing—Johnny Mercer (w), Ziggie Elman (m), BVC; Bugle Call Rag—Jack Pettis, Billy Meyers, Elmer Schoebel (w,m), Mills; Down South Camp Meetin'—Irving Mills, Fletcher Henderson (w,m), American Academy; Good-Bye—Gordon Jenkins (w,m), Southern; Goody Goody—Johnny Mercer, Matt Malneck (w,m), DBH; Jersey Bounce —Bob Wright (w), Bob Plater, Tiny Bradshaw, Ed Johnson (m), Lewis; Let's Dance—Fanny Baldridge, Gregory Stone, Joseph Bonime (w,m), Marks; Memories of You—Andy Razaf, Eubie Blake (w,m), Shapiro Bernstein; Moonglow—Will Hudson, Eddie DeLange, Irving Mills (w,m), Mills; Original Dixieland One Step —J. Russell Robinson, George Crandall (w), Nick LaRocca (m), Marks; Sing, Sing, Sing—Louis Prima (w,m), Robbins; China Boy (VS)—Dick Winfree, Phil Boutelje (w,m), Robbins; Don't Be That Way (VS)—Benny Goodman, Edgar Sampson, Mitchell Parish (w,m), Robbins; I Got It Bad (VS)—Paul F. Webster (w), Duke Ellington (m), Robbins; I'm Coming Virginia (VS)—Will Cook (w), Donald Heywood (m), Robbins; It's Been So Long (VS)—Harold Adamson (w), Walter Donaldson (m), Robbins; Lullaby in Rhythm (VS)—Walter Hirsch (w), Benny Goodman, Edgar Sampson, Clarence Profit (m), Robbins; One O'Clock Jump (VS)—Count Basie (m), Robbins; Sensation (VS)—Dixieland Jazz (m), Robbins; Stompin' at the Savoy (VS)—Andy Razaf (w), Benny Goodman, Chick Webb, Edgar Sampson (m), Robbins; Taking a Chance on Love (VS)—John Latouche, Ted Fetter (w), Vernon Duke (m), Robbins; Waitin' for Katy (VS)—Gus Kahn (w), Ted Shapiro (m), Robbins. COVER: Steve Allen, Donna Reed.

366 Bernadine (20th Century-Fox, 1957, Pat Boone, Terry Moore).

Bernadine/Technique—Johnny Mercer (w,m), Palm Springs. COVER: Pat Boone, Terry Moore.

367 Best Defense (Paramount, 1984, Eddie Murphy, Dudley Moore).

Best Defense Theme—Patrick Williams (m), Ensign. COVER: Dudley Moore, Eddie Murphy.

368 Best Foot Forward (MGM, 1943, Lucille Ball, Harry James).

Buckle Down Winsocki/You're Lucky—Hugh Martin, Ralph Blane (w,m), Chappell. COVER: Lucille Ball, Harry James, and Others.

369 Best Friends (Warner Bros., 1982, Goldie Hawn, Burt Reynolds).

How Do You Keep the Music Playing?—Alan Bergman, Marilyn Bergman, Michel Legrand (m), Warner. COVER: Burt Reynolds, Goldie Hawn.

370 Best Little Whorehouse in Texas, The (Universal, 1982, Burt Reynolds, Dolly Parton).

I Will Always Love You—Dolly Parton (w,m), Columbia; Aggie Song, The (VS)/Courtyard Shag (VS)/Hard Candy Christmas (VS)/Lil' Ole Bitty Pissant Country Place, A (VS)/Side Step, The (VS)—Carol Hall (w,m), Columbia; Sneakin' Around (VS)— Dolly Parton (w,m), Columbia; Texas Has a Whorehouse in It (VS)/Twenty Fans (VS)/Watch Dog, The (VS)— Carol Hall (w,m), Columbia. COVER: Dolly Parton, Burt Reynolds.

371 Best Man, The (United Artists, 1964, Henry Fonda, Cliff Robertson).

Best Man Theme—Mort Lindsay (m), Unart. COVER: Black and white cover with title only.

372 Best of Enemies (Fox, 1933, Buddy Rogers, Marion Nixon).

All American Girls/Hans and Gretchen/ We Belong to Alma—Val Burton, Will Jason (w,m), Movietone. COVER: Black and white cover with title only.

373 Best of Everything, The (20th Century-Fox, 1959, Hope Lange, Stephen Boyd).

Best of Everything, The—Sammy Cahn (w), Alfred Newman (m), Miller. COVER: Hope Lange, Stephen Boyd.

374 Best Things in Life Are Free, The (20th Century-Fox, 1956, Gordon MacRae, Dan Dailey).

Best Things in Life Are Free/ Birth of the Blues (B)/Button Up Your Overcoat/If I Had a Talking Picture of You/It All Depends on You/One More Time/Sonny Boy/ Sunny Side Up/Together/Without Love—B. G. DeSylva, Lew Brown, Ray Henderson (w,m), DBH. COVER: Gordon MacRae, Dan Dailey.

375 Best Years of Our Lives, The (RKO, 1946, Fredric March, Myrna Loy).

Among My Souvenirs—Edgar Leslie (w), Horatio Nicholls (m), Crawford; Best Years of Our Lives (B)— Jack Fishman (w), Peter Hart (m), Sterling; Lazy River (VS)—Hoagy Carmichael, Sidney Arodin (w,m), Peer. COVER: Fredric March, Myrna Loy, and Others.

376 Betrayal (Fraulein Doktor) (Paramount, 1969, Kenneth More, Suzy Kendall).

Betrayal Theme—Ennio Morricone (m), Famous. COVER: Suzy Kendall, Capucine.

377 Betrayed (MGM, 1954, Clark Gable, Lana Turner).

Johnny Come Home—Ronald Millar (w), Walter Goehr (m), Feist. COVER: Clark Gable, Lana Turner, Victor Mature.

378 Betsy Ross (World, 1917, Alice Brady, George MacQuarrie).

That's Why We Love You Betsy Ross—Ivan Reid, Peter DeRose (w, m), Haviland. COVER: Alice Brady.

379 Betty Boop (Paramount, 1930, Cartoon).

Betty Boop—Edward Heyman (w), John Green (m), Famous. COVER: Cartoon.

380 Betty Co-ed (Columbia, 1946, Jean Porter, William Mason).

Betty Co-ed—Paul Fogarty, Rudy Vallee (w,m), Fischer. COVER: Cheerleader.

381 Between Friends (Vitagraph, 1924, Alice Calhoun, Lou Tellegen).

Cecile (B)—Herbert Parsons (w, m), Miller. COVER: Alice Calhoun, Lou Tellegen.

382 Beverly Hills Cop (Paramount, 1984, Eddie Murphy, Judge Reinhold).

Axel F—Harold Faltermeyer (w, m), Famous; Don't Get Stopped in Beverly Hills—Hank Wolinski, Howard Hewett, Micki Free (w,m), Hip; Heat Is On, The—Keith Forsey (w), Harold Faltermeyer (m), Famous; Stir It Up—Danny Sembello, Allee Willis (w,m), Unicity; Neutron Dance (VS)—Danny Sembello, Allee Willis (w,m), Columbia; New Attitude (VS)—Bunny Hull, Jon Gilutin, Sharon Robinson (w,m), Columbia. COVER: Eddie Murphy.

383 Beverly Hills Cop II (Paramount, 1987, Eddie Murphy, Judge Reinhold).

Be There—Franne Golde, Allee Willis (w,m), Ensign; Better Way—Andre Cymone (w,m), Famous; Cross My Broken Heart—Stephen Bray, Tony Pierce (w,m), Famous; In Deep (PC)—Charlie Sexton, Scott Wilk (w,m), Famous; Shakedown—Harold Faltermeyer, Keith Forsey, Bob Seger (w,m), Famous. COVER: Eddie Murphy.

384 Beware (Astor, 1946, Louis Jordan, William Davis).

Beware Brother Beware—Morry Lasco, Dick Adams, Fleecie Moore (w,m), Preview; Long Legg'd Lizzie—Deek Watson, Herman Fairbanks (w, m), Rytvoc; Salt Pork West Virginia—William Tennyson (w,m), Pic. COVER: Louis Jordan.

385 Beyond a Reasonable Doubt (RKO, 1956, Dana Andrews, Joan Fontain).

Beyond a Reasonable Doubt—Alfred Perry (w), Herschel Gilbert (m), Lamas. COVER: Dana Andrews, Joan Fontaine.

386 Beyond Glory (Paramount, 1948, Alan Ladd, Donna Reed).

Beyond Glory—Jay Livingston, Ray Evans (w,m), Paramount. COVER: Alan Ladd, Donna Reed.

387 Beyond Mombasa (Columbia, 1956, Cornel Wilde, Donna Reed).

Beyond Mombasa (B)—Cindy Ryder (w,m), Campbell. COVER: Donna Reed, Eddie Calvert.

388 Beyond the Blue Horizon (Paramount, 1942, Dorothy Lamour, Walter Abel).

Full Moon and an Empty Heart—Mort Greene (w), Harry Revel (m), Famous. COVER: Dorothy Lamour.

389 Beyond the Valley of the Dolls (20th Century-Fox, 1970, Dolly Reed, Cynthia Myers).

Beyond the Valley of the Dolls—Stu Phillips, Bob Stone (w,m), Fox; Ampersand (VS)—Stu Phillips (w,m), Fox; Come with the Gentle People (VS)—Stu Phillips, Bob Stone (w,m), Fox; Find It (VS)—Stu Phillips, Lynn Carey (w,m), Fox; Girl from the City (VS)/I'm Coming Home (VS)—Paul Marshall (w,m), Fox;Incense and Peppermint (VS)—John Gilbert, Tim Gilbert (w,m), Fox; Long Run (VS)/ Look on Up at the Bottom (VS)—Stu Phillips, Bob Stone (w,m), Fox; Once I Had Love (VS)—Stu Phillips, Lynn Carey (w,m), Fox; Sweet Talkin' Candy Man (VS)—Stu Phillips, Bob Stone (w,m), Fox. COVER: Girls.

390 Beyond Tomorrow (RKO, 1940, Harry Carey, Charles Winninger).

It's Raining Dreams—Charles Newman, Harold Spina (w,m), Select. COVER: Black and white cover with title only.

391 Be Yourself (United Artists,

1930, Fannie Brice, Harry Green).

Cooking Breakfast for the One I Love—William Rose, Harry Tobias (w,m), Robbins; Kickin' a Hole in the Sky/Sasha, The Passion of the Pasha—William Rose, Ballard Mac-Donald (w), Jesse Greer (m), Robbins; When a Woman Loves a Man—William Rose (w), Ralph Rainger (m), Robbins. COVER: Fannie Brice.

392 Bible, The (20th Century-Fox, 1966, Michael Parks, Richard Harris).

Bible Song—Paul F. Webster (w), Toshiro Mayuzumi (m), Robbins; Bible Theme/Bible Musical Highlights—Toshiro Mayuzumi (m), Robbins. COVER: Noah's Ark.

393 Big (Touchstone, 1988, Tom Hanks, Elizabeth Perkins).

Heart and Soul (VS)—Frank Loesser (w), Hoagy Carmichael (m), Famous. COVER: Black and white cover with title only.

394 Big Bad Wolf, The (Disney, 1934, Cartoon).

Big Bad Wolf Is Back Again, The (VS)—Larry Morey (w), Frank Churchill (m), Bourne. COVER: Cartoon.

395 Big Beat, The (Universal, 1958, William Reynolds, Andra Martin).

Big Beat, The—Fats Domino, Dave Bartholomew (w,m), Travis; Call Me—Bernard Gasso (w), Irving Fields (m), Hansen; Can't Wait (B)—Grace Saxon, Barry Mirkin (w,m), Hansen; I Waited So Long—Jay Livingston, Ray Evans (w,m), Hansen; Lazy Love—Bernard Gasso (w), Irving Fields (m), Hansen; Take My Heart—Al Alberts, Dave Mahoney (w,m), Hansen; Where Mary Go (B)—Diane Lampert, John Gluck (w,m), Maurice; You're Being Followed (B)—Charles Tobias (w), Arthur Altman (m), Maurice. COVER: Singers and Musicians.

396 Big Boy (Warner Bros., 1930, Al Jolson, Claudia Dell).

Hooray for Baby and Me/Little Sunshine—Sidney Mitchell, Archie Gottler, George Meyer (w,m), Witmark; Liza Lee/Tomorrow Is Another Day—Bud Green, Sam Stept (w,m), Witmark. COVER: Al Jolson.

397 Big Broadcast (Paramount, 1932, Bing Crosby, Stuart Erwin).

Here Lies Love/Please—Leo Robin (w), Ralph Rainger (m), Famous. COVER: Bing Crosby, Kate Smith, and Other Stars.

398 Big Broadcast of 1935-1936 (Paramount, 1935, Jack Oakie, Lyda Roberti).

Cheating Muchachita—Marjorie Harper, Alfredo Lepera, Carlos Gardel (w,m), Famous; Double Trouble—Leo Robin, Richard Whiting, Ralph Rainger (w,m), Famous; I Wished on the Moon—Dorothy Parker (w), Ralph Granger (m), Famous; It's the Animal in Me—Mack Gordon, Harry Revel, (w,m), Famous; Miss Brown to You—Leo Robin, Richard Whiting, Ralph Rainger (w,m), Famous; Through the Doorway of Dreams—Leo Robin, Richard Whiting (w,m), Famous; Why Dream—Leo Robin, Richard Whiting, Ralph Rainger (w, m), Famous; Why Stars Come Out at Night—Ray Noble (w,m), Famous. COVER: Ethel Merman, Bing Crosby, Jack Oakie, and Others.

399 Big Broadcast of 1937 (Paramount, 1936, Jack Benny, Martha Raye).

Here's Love In Your Eye/La Bomba/Night in Manhattan/Talking Through My Heart/Vote for Mister Rhythm/You Came to My Rescue—Leo Robin, Ralph Rainger (w,m), Famous. COVER: Jack Benny, Martha Raye, Benny Goodman, and Others.

400 Big Broadcast of 1938 (Paramount, 1938, W. C. Fields, Martha Raye).

Don't Tell a Secret to a Rose/Mama, That Moon Is Here Again/Thanks for the Memory/This Little Ripple Had Rhythm—Leo Robin, Ralph Rainger (w,m), Paramount;

Sawing a Woman in Half—Jack Rock (w,m), Paramount; Waltz Lives On, The/You Took the Words Right Out of My Heart—Leo Robin, Ralph Rainger (w,m), Paramount; Zuni Zuni—Tito Guizar (w,m), Paramount. COVER: Dorothy Lamour, Bob Hope, W. C. Fields, Shirley Ross.

401 Big Brother (Paramount, 1923, Tom Moore, Edith Roberts).

Big Brother—Fred Rath, Joe Garren, Mel Shauer (w,m), Berlin. COVER: Tom Moore.

402 Big Bus, The (Paramount, 1976, Joseph Bologna, Stockard Channing).

Big Bus Theme, The—David Shire (m), Ensign. COVER: Joseph Bologna, Stockard Channing, and Others.

403 Big Caper, The (Unit. Artists, 1957, James Gregory, Mary Costa).

If You're Askin' Me—Alan Bergman, Marilyn Keith (w), Al Glasser (m), John Paul. COVER: Green cover with title only.

404 Big Chill, The (Columbia, 1983, Tom Berenger, Glenn Close).

Ain't Too Proud to Beg (VS)—Eddie Holland, Norman Whitfield (w, m), Columbia; Bad Moon Rising (VS)—J. C. Fogerty (w,m), Columbia; Dancing in the Street (VS)—William Stevenson, Marvin Gaye, Ivy Hunter (w,m), Columbia; Gimmie Some Lovin' (VS)—Steve Winwood, Muff Winwood, Spencer Davis (w,m), Columbia; Good Lovin' (VS)—Rudy Clark, Art Resnick (w,m), Columbia; I Heart It Through the Grapevine (VS)—Norman Whitfield, Barrett Strong (w,m), Columbia; I Second That Emotion (VS)—Smokey Robinson, Alfred Cleveland (w,m), Columbia;In the Midnight Hour (VS)—Wilson Pickett (w), Steve Cropper (m), Columbia; It's the Same Old Song (VS)—Eddie Holland, Lamont Dozier, Brian Holland (w,m), Columbia; Joy to the World (VS)—Hoyt Axton (w,m), Columbia; My Girl (VS)—Smokey Robinson, Ronald White (w,m), Columbia; Natural Woman (VS)—Gerry Goffin, Carole King, Jerry Wexler (w,m), Columbia; Quicksilver Girl (VS)—Steve Miller (w,m), Columbia; Tell Him (VS)—Bert Russell (w,m), Columbia; Tracks of My Tears (VS)—Smokey Robinson, Marv Tarplin, Warren Moore (w,m), Columbia; Too Many Fish in the Sea (VS)—Eddie Holland, Norman Whitfield (w,m), Columbia; Weight (VS)—James Robertson (w,m), Columbia; What's Going On (VS)—Marvin Gaye, Al Cleveland, Renaldo Benson (w,m), Columbia; When a Man Loves a Woman (VS)—Calvin Lewis, Andrew Wright (w,m), Columbia; Whiter Shade of Pale (VS)—Keith Reid, Gary Brooker (w,m), Columbia; Wouldn't It Be Nice (VS)—Brian Wilson, Tony Asher (w), Brian Wilson (m), Columbia; You Can't Always Get What You Want (VS)—Mick Jagger, Keith Richards (w,m), Columbia. COVER: Tom Berenger, Glenn Close, William Hurt, and Others.

405 Big Circus, The (Allied Artists, 1959, Victor Mature, Rhonda Fleming).

Big Circus, The—Paul F. Webster (w), Sammy Fain (m), Miller; Nearer to Heaven—Paul F. Webster, Sammy Fain, Paul Sawtell, Bert Shefter (w, m), Miller. COVER: Clown.

406 Big City (MGM, 1948, Margaret O'Brien, Robert Preston).

Don't Blame Me—Dorothy Fields (w), Jimmy McHugh (m), Robbins; I'm Gonna See a Lot of You—Janice Torre (w), Fred Spielman (m), Robbins; Ok'l Baby Dok'l—Sidney Miller (w), Inez James (m), Warren; What'll I Do—Irving Berlin (w,m), Berlin. COVER: Margaret O'Brien, Robert Preston, Betty Garrett.

407 Big Country, The (United Artists, 1958, Gregory Peck, Jean Simmons).

Big Country, The—Morty Neff, Jack Lewis (w), Jerome Moross (m), Unart. COVER: Diahann Carroll.

408 Biggest Bundle of Them All, The (MGM, 1968, Robert Wagner, Raquel Welch).

Along About Now—Carl Sigman (w), Riz Ortolani (m), Robbins; Biggest Bundle of Them All, The—Ritchie Cordell, Sal Trimachi (w,m), Hastings; Most of All There's You—Norman Newell (w), Riz Ortolani (m), Robbins. COVER: Raquel Welch.

409 Big Gun-Down, The (Columbia, 1968, Lee Van Cleef, Tomas Milian).

Big Gun-Down, The—Audrey Nohra (w), Ennio Morricone (m), Unart. COVER: Lee Van Cleef.

410 Big Hand for a Little Lady, A (Warner Bros., 1966, Henry Fonda, Joanne Woodward).

Mirror, Mirror, Mirror—Johnny Mercer (w), David Raksin (m), Witmark. COVER: Henry Fonda, Joanne Woodward, Jason Robards.

411 Big Jim McClain (Warner Bros., 1952, John Wayne, Nancy Olson).

Isle of Kuualoha—Roc Hillman (w), Robert Miller (m), Merit. COVER: Hawaiian Girl.

412 Big Land, The (Warner Bros., 1957, Alan Ladd, Virginia Mayo).

I Leaned on a Man—Wayne Shanklin (w), Leonard Rosenman (m), Witmark. COVER: Alan Ladd, Virginia Mayo.

413 Big Night, The (Paramount, 1960, Randy Sparks, Venetia Stevenson).

Big Night, The—Randy Sparks (w, m), Famous. COVER: Randy Sparks, Venetia Stevenson.

414 Big Parade, The (MGM, 1927, John Gilbert, Renee Adoree).

Agitato #5—William Axt (m), Robbins; Douce Fièvre—Louis Weslyn (w), Y. Ener (m), Manus; Sweet Little Woman o' Mine (B)—Frank Stanton (w), Floy Bartlett (m), Keith Prowse. COVER: Silhouette of Soldier.

415 Big Party, The (Fox, 1930, Sue Carol, Dixie Lee).

Bluer Than Blue Over You—Harlan Thompson, William Kernell (w), William Kernell (m), Red Star; Good for Nothin' But Love—William Kernell (w,m), Red Star; I'm Climbing Up a Rainbow—Harry Pease (w), Ed Nelson (m), Red Star; Nobody Knows But Rosie—Joseph McCarthy (w), James Hanley (m), Red Star. COVER: Sue Carol, Dixie Lee.

416 Big Pond, The (Paramount, 1930, Maurice Chevalier, Claudette Colbert).

Livin' in the Sunlight, Lovin' in the Moonlight—Al Lewis (w), Al Sherman (m), Famous; Mia Cara/You Brought a New Kind of Love to Me— Irving Kahal, Sammy Fain, Pierre Norman (w,m), Famous. COVER: Maurice Chevalier, Claudette Colbert.

417 Big Red (Buena Vista, 1961, Walter Pidgeon, Gilles Payant).

Emile's Reel/Mon Amour Perdu—Richard Sherman, Robert Sherman (w,m), Wonderland. COVER: Gilles Payant, and Dog.

418 Big Show, The (Republic, 1937, Gene Autry, Smiley Burnette).

Lady Known as Lulu, The—Ned Washington (w), Sam Stept (m), Remick; Mad About You—Ted Koehler (w), Sam Stept (m), Remick. COVER: Gene Autry.

419 Big Show-Off, The (Republic, 1945, Arthur Lake, Dale Evans).

Cleo from Rio—Dave Oppenheim, Roy Ingraham (w,m), Leeds. COVER: Freddy Martin.

420 Big Sky, The (RKO, 1952, Kirk Douglas, Dewey Martin).

Big Sky, The—Stan Jones (w), Dimitri Tiomkin (m), Mills; When I Dream (B)—Gordon Clark, Paul Logan (w), Dimitri Tiomkin (m), Morris. COVER: Kirk Douglas.

421 Big Store, The (MGM, 1941, Tony Martin, Marx Brothers).

If It's You—Ben Oakland, Artie Shaw, Milton Drake (w,m), Feist;

Tenement Symphony—Sid Kuller, Ray Golden (w), Hal Borne (m), Feist. COVER: Tony Martin, Marx Brothers.

422 Big Time (Fox, 1929, Lee Tracy, Mae Clarke).

Nobody Knows You Like I Do—Sidney Lanfield (w,m), DBH. COVER: Lee Tracy and Girls.

423 Big Town Girl (20th Century-Fox, 1937, Claire Trevor, Donald Woods).

Argentine Swing/Don't Throw Kisses/I'll Settle for Love—Sidney Clare (w), Harry Akst (m), Movietone. COVER: Claire Trevor, Donald Woods.

424 Big Trail, The (Fox, 1930, John Wayne, Marguerite Churchill).

Song of the Big Trail—Joseph McCarthy (w), James Hanley (m), Red Star; When It's Harvest Time in Peaceful Valley—Robert Martin, Ray McKee (w,m), Consolidated. COVER: John Wayne, Marguerite Churchill, the Pioneer Trio.

425 Bill and Coo (Republic, 1947, Ken Murray, George Burton).

Hum a Little Tune/Off to the Circus—Royal Foster, David Buttolph, Lionel Newman (w,m), BVC; Tweet Tweet—B. G. DeSylva, Lew Brown (w), Ray Henderson (m), Harms. COVER: Ken Murray, and Birds.

426 Billie (United Artists, 1965, Patty Duke, Jim Backus).

Billie—Diane Lampert (w), Dominic Frontiere (m), Unart; Funny Little Butterflies—Lor Crane, Jack Gold, Bernice Ross (w,m), Unart. COVER: Patty Duke.

427 Bill of Divorcement, A (RKO, 1933, John Barrymore, Katharine Hepburn).

Unfinished Sonata—Max Steiner (m), Sam Fox. COVER: RKO Tower.

428 Billy Budd (Allied Artists, 1962, Robert Ryan, Peter Ustinov).

Ballad of Billy Budd—Joseph Hooven, Jerry Winn (w,m), Miller; Billy Budd Theme—Anthony Hopkins (m), Miller. COVER: Robert Ryan, Peter Ustinov, Terence Stamp.

429 Billy Dooley Comedies (Paramount, 1929, Billy Dooley).

Dooley-Dooley-Do—Sterling Sherwin (w,m), Sherman Clay. COVER: Billy Dooley, and Girl.

430 Billy Jack (Warner Bros., 1969, Tom Laughlin, Delores Taylor).

One Tin Soldier—Dennis Lambert, Brian Potter (w,m), Trousdale. COVER: Tom Laughlin, Delores Taylor.

431 Billy the Kid Returns (Republic, 1938, Roy Rogers, Smiley Burnette).

Born to the Saddle (VS)/Trail Blazin' (VS)—Eddie Cherkose (w,m), Cole. COVER: Red Foley.

432 Bingo Long Traveling All Stars and Motor Kings, The (Universal, 1976, Billy Dee Williams, James Earl Jones).

Bingo Long Song, The—Berry Gordy, Ron Miller (w,m), Jobete; Razzle Dazzle—Ron Miller (w), William Goldstein (m), Stone. COVER: Cartoon Sketch.

433 Bird Man of Alcatraz (United Artists, 1962, Burt Lancaster, Karl Malden).

Bird Man—Mack David (w), Elmer Bernstein (m), Unart. COVER: Burt Lancaster.

434 Bird of Paradise (RKO, 1932, Dolores Del Rio, Joel McCrea).

Out of the Blue—Edward Eliscu (w), Max Steiner (m), Southern. COVER: Dolores Del Rio.

435 Bird of Paradise (20th Century-Fox, 1951, Louis Jourdan, Debra Paget).

Bird of Paradise—Malia Rosa (w), Peter DeRose (m), Robbins. COVER: Movie Scene.

436 Birds and the Bees, The (Paramount, 1956, Mitzi Gaynor, George Gobel).

Birds and the Bees, The—Mack David (w), Harry Warren (m), Famous; Each Time I Dream—Don Hartman (w), Walter Scharf (m), Famous; La Parisienne—Mack David (w), Harry Warren (m), Famous.

COVER: Mitzi Gaynor, George Gobel.

437 Birds Do It (Columbia, 1966, Soupy Sales, Tab Hunter).

Birds Do It—Howard Greenfield, Jack Keller (w,m), Columbia. COVER: Soupy Sales.

438 Birds, the Bees, and the Italians, The (Warner Bros., 1967, Virna Lisi, Gastone Moschin).

Birds, the Bees, and the Italians, The/There Will Always Be Tomorrow—Ray Collins (w), Carlo Rustichelli (m), Marks. COVER: Cartoon Sketch.

439 Birth of a Nation, The (Griffith, 1915, Mae Marsh, Lillian Gish).

Birth of a Nation (#1)—Billy James (w,m), Swisher; Birth of a Nation (#2)—Thomas Allen (w), Joseph Daly (m), Chappell; Birth of a Nation Music Score—Joseph Breil (m), Griffith; Perfect Song, The—Clarence Lucas (w), Joseph Breil (m), Chappell. COVER: Sketch of Couple.

440 Birth of a Nation (Griffith, 1915 [1930 Revival], Mae Marsh, Lillian Gish).

Close in Your Arms/I've Got You to Thank for That/Steamboat Song—Irving Bibo, Albert Von Tilzer (w,m), Sherman Clay. COVER: Red and black cover with titles only.

441 Birth of a Nation (Griffith, 1915 [1976 Revival], Mae Marsh, Lillian Gish).

Birth of a Nation Themes—Lee Irwin (m), Marks. COVER: D. W. Griffith.

442 Birth of the Blues (Paramount, 1941, Bing Crosby, Mary Martin).

Birth of the Blues, The—B. G. DeSylva, Lew Brown, Ray Henderson (w,m), Harms; By the Light of the Silvery Moon—Ed Madden (w), Gus Edwards (m), Remick; Cuddle Up a Little Closer—Otto Harbach (w), Karl Hoschna (m), Witmark; Memphis Blues—George Norton (w), W. C. Handy (m), Handy; My Melancholy Baby—George Norton, Maybelle Watson (w), Ernie Burnett (m), Shapiro Bernstein; Saint Louis Blues—W. C. Handy (w,m), Handy; Waiter and the Porter and the Upstairs Maid—Johnny Mercer (w,m), Famous; Waiting at the Church—Fred Leigh (w), Henry Pether (m), Harms; Wait 'Till the Sun Shines Nellie—Andrew Sterling (w), Harry Von Tilzer (m), Von Tilzer. COVER: Bing Crosby, Mary Martin, Brian Donlevy, Jack Teagarden.

443 Bishop's Wife, The (RKO, 1947, Cary Grant, Loretta Young).

Lost April—Emil Newman, Edgar DeLange, Herbert Spencer (w,m), Simon. COVER: Cary Grant.

444 Bittersweet (United Artists, 1933, Anna Neagle, Ferdinand Gravey).

I'll See You Again—Noel Coward (w,m), Harms. COVER: Sketch of Couple.

445 Bittersweet (MGM, 1940, Nelson Eddy, Jeanette MacDonald).

Call of Life, The/Dear Little Cafe/Green Carnations/If Love Were All/I'll See You Again/Kiss Me/Ladies of the Town/What Is Love/Zigeuner—Noel Coward (w,m), Harms. COVER: Nelson Eddy, Jeanette MacDonald.

446 Bitter Victory (Paid in Full) (Paramount, 1950, Lizabeth Scott, Robert Cummings).

You're Wonderful—Jay Livingston, Ray Evans (w), Victor Young (m), Famous. COVER: Black and white cover with title only.

447 Blackbeard the Pirate (RKO, 1952, Robert Newton, Linda Darnell).

Come to Me—Edward Heyman (w), Victor Young (m), Young. COVER: Green cover with title only.

448 Blackboard Jungle (MGM, 1955, Glenn Ford, Anne Francis).

Blackboard Jungle Love Theme—Charles Wolcott (m), Feist; Rock Around the Clock (B)—Max Freedman, Jimmy DeKnight (w,m), Kassner. COVER: Glenn Ford, Anne Francis.

449 Black Caesar (American International, 1973, Fred Williamson, Art Lund).

Down and Out in New York City —Bodie Chandler, Barry DeVorzon (w,m), Dijon. COVER: James Brown.

450 Black Hole, The (Buena Vista, 1979, Maximilian Schell, Tony Perkins).

Black Hole Score—10 Themes— John Barry (m), Wonderland. COVER: Space Ship.

451 Black Knight, The (Columbia, 1961, Alan Ladd, Patricia Medina).

Bold Black Knight, The/Whistling Gypsy, The—Leo Maguire (w,m), Box and Cox. COVER: Alan Ladd, Patricia Medina.

452 Black Lassie (Columbia, 1974, Johnny Stash).

Black Lassie—Thomas Chong, Richard Marin, Gene Page, Billy Page (w,m), Colgems. COVER: Cartoon Sketches.

453 Black Orchid (Paramount, 1959, Anthony Quinn, Sophia Loren).

Hurdy-Gurdy Song, The—Mack David (w), Allesandro Cicognini (m), Famous. COVER: Anthony Quinn, Sophia Loren.

454 Black Orpheus (Lopert, 1959, Breno Mello, Marpessa Dawn).

Batuque De Orfeu—Rossini Pacheco (w,m), Jungnickel; Felicidade —Vinicius DeMoraes (w), Antonio C. Jobim (m), Jungnickel; Macumba De Orfeu—Rossini Pacheco (w,m), Jungnickel; Manha De Carnaval—Antonio Maria (w), Luiz Bonfa (m), Jungnickel; O Nosso Amor—Antonio C. Jobim (w,m), Jungnickel; Samba De Orfeu —Antonio Maria (w), Luiz Bonfa (m), Jungnickel; Day in the Life of a Fool (VS)—Carl Sigman (w), Luiz Bonfa (m), Hill Range; Goodbye Tristesse (VS)—Hal Shaper (w), Antonio C. Jobim (m), Hill Range; Sweet Happy Life (VS)—Norman Gimbel (w), Luis Bonfa (m), Hill Range. COVER: Dancers.

455 Black Oxen (First National, 1923, Corinne Griffith, Conway Tearle).

When Romance Wakes—J. L. Johnston (w), Ned Freeman, Sam Messenheimer (m), Berlin. COVER: Corinne Griffith.

456 Black Rose, The (20th Century-Fox, 1950, Tyrone Power, Orson Welles).

Black Rose, The—Tom Pryor (w), Al Urbano (m), Cromwell; Black Rose Theme (B)—Richard Addinsell (m), Chappell. COVER: Tyrone Power, Orson Welles.

457 Black Sheep (Fox, 1935, Claire Trevor, Edmund Lowe).

In Other Words, I'm in Love— Sidney Clare (w), Oscar Levant (m), Movietone. COVER: Claire Trevor, Edmund Lowe.

458 Black Spurs (Paramount, 1965, Rory Calhoun, Linda Darnell).

Black Spurs—By Dunham (w), Jim Haskell (m), Ensign. COVER: Rory Calhoun, Linda Darnell.

459 Black Stallion (United Artists, 1979, Kelly Reno, Mickey Rooney).

Take Me in Your Heart—Italia Pennino, Roxanne Seeman (w), Carmine Coppola (m), Unart. COVER: A Stallion.

460 Black Sunday (Paramount, 1977, Robert Shaw, Bruce Dern).

Black Sunday Theme—John Williams (m), Ensign. COVER: Dirigible.

461 Black Watch (Fox, 1929, Victor McLaglen, Myrna Loy).

Flower of Delight—Harlan Thompson (w), William Kernell (m), DBH; COVER: Victor McLaglen, Myrna Loy.

462 Blame It on Love (Hotpoint, 1940, Alan Ladd, Joan Marsh).

Blame It on Love—Portia Lanning (w), Marvin Hatley (m), Hatley. COVER: Joan Marsh.

463 Blame It on Rio (20th Century-Fox, 1984, Michael Caine, Joseph Bologna).

Blame It on Rio/I Must Be Doing

Something Right—Sheldon Harnick (w), Cy Coleman (m), Notable. COVER: Girl in Bikini.

464 Blaze of Noon (Paramount, 1947, Anne Baxter, William Holden).

Blaze of Noon—Charles Henderson (w), Adolph Deutsch (m), Famous. COVER: Anne Baxter, William Holden.

465 Blaze O' Glory (Sono Art, 1930, Eddie Dowling, Betty Compson).

Dough-boy's Lullaby/Put a Little Salt on the Bluebird's Tail—Eddie Dowling, James Brockman, James Hanley (w,m), Shapiro Bernstein; Welcome Home—Ballard MacDonald (w), James Hanley (m), Shapiro Bernstein; Wrapped in a Red, Red Rose—Eddie Dowling, Joe McCarthy, James Hanley (w,m), Shapiro Bernstein. COVER: Eddie Dowling.

466 Blazing Across the Pecos (Columbia, 1948, Charles Starrett, Smiley Burnette).

Goin' Back to Texas—Joseph Brockman (w), John Cornell (m), Gordon. COVER: Charles Starrett.

467 Blazing Barriers (Monogram, 1937, Frank Coghlan, Florine McKinney).

C.C.C. Follow On—Bernie Grossman(w), Charles Duval (m), Sam Fox. COVER: Frank Coghlan, Florine McKinney.

468 Blazing Saddles (Warner Bros., 1974, Cleavon Little, Gene Wilder).

Blazing Saddles Theme—John Morris (m), Warner. COVER: Cowboy and Indian.

469 Blessed Event (Warner Bros., 1932, Dick Powell, Lee Tracy).

How Can You Say No—Al Dubin, Irving Kahal (w), Joe Burke (m), Witmark; I'm Makin' Hay in the Moonlight—Tot Seymour (w), Jesse Greer (m), Witmark. COVER: Dick Powell, Lee Tracy.

470 Bless the Beasts and Children (Columbia, 1972, Bill Mumy, Barry Robins).

Bless the Beasts and Children—Barry DeVorzon, Perry Botkin (w,m), Columbia; Bless the Beasts Solo Theme—Barry DeVorzon (m), Columbia. COVER: A Flower and a Gun.

471 Blind Date (Tri-Star, 1987, Kim Basinger, Bruce Willis).

Simply Meant to Be—Henry Mancini, George Merrill, Shannon Rubicam (w,m), Tri-Star. COVER: Kim Basinger, Bruce Willis.

472 Blindness of Virtue, The (Essaney, 1915, Bryant Washburn, Edna Mayo).

Blindness of Virtue, The—Harry Bewley (w,m), Bewley. COVER: Blindfolded Girl.

473 Bliss of Mrs. Blossom, The (Paramount, 1968, Shirley MacLaine, Richard Attenborough).

I Think I'm Beginning to Fall in Love—Geoffrey Stephens (w,m), Famous; Way That I Live, The—Norman Newell (w), Riz Ortolani (m), Famous. COVER: Shirley MacLaine, Richard Attenborough, James Booth.

474 Blithe Spirit (United Artists, 1945, Rex Harrison, Constance Cummings).

Blithe Spirit Waltz—Richard Addinsell (m), Sam Fox. COVER: Sketch of Girl.

475 Blob, The (Paramount, 1958, Steve McQueen, Aneta Corseaut).

Blob, The—Mack David (w), Burt Bacharach (m), Famous. COVER: Movie Scene.

476 Blockade (Unit. Artists, 1938, Henry Fonda, Madeleine Carroll).

Beloved, You're Lovely—Anne Ronell (w), Werner Janssen (m), Miller. COVER: Henry Fonda, Madeleine Carroll, Leo Carrillo.

477 Blonde from Brooklyn, The (Columbia, 1945, Robert Stanton, Lynn Merrick).

Just a Prayer Away—Charles Tobias (w), David Kapp (m), Shapiro Bernstein; My Baby Said Yes—Teddy Walters, Sid Robin (w,m), Leeds. COVER: Bob Stanton.

478 Blonde Venus (Paramount, 1932, Marlene Dietrich, Cary Grant).

Hot Voodoo—Leo Robin (w), Sam Coslow (m), Famous; I Couldn't Be More Annoyed (B)—Leo Robin (w), Richard Whiting (m), Famous; You Little So-and-so—Leo Robin (w), Sam Coslow (m), Famous. COVER: Marlene Dietrich.

479 Blondie Goes Latin (Columbia, 1941, Penny Singleton, Arthur Lake).

Querida—Chet Forrest, Bob Wright (w,m), Berlin. COVER: Penny Singleton, Arthur Lake.

480 Blondie Meets the Boss (Columbia, 1939, Penny Singleton, Arthur Lake).

Y' Had It Comin' to You—Sam Lerner (w), Ben Oakland (m), ABC. COVER: Cartoon Sketch.

481 Blondie of the Follies (MGM, 1932, Marion Davies, Robert Montgomery).

Why Don't You Take Me—Edmund Golding (w,m), Feist. COVER: Marion Davies.

482 Blood and Sand (Paramount, 1925, Rudolph Valentino, Lila Lee).

You Gave Me Your Heart—Francis Wheeler, Harry B. Smith (w), Ted Snyder (m), Berlin. COVER: Rudolph Valentino.

483 Blood and Sand (20th Century-Fox, 1941, Tyrone Power, Linda Darnell).

Chi Qui Chi/Green Moon/Torero/ Romance De Amer—Abe Tuvim (w), Vicente Gomez (m), Pampa. COVER: Tyrone Power, Linda Darnell, Rita Hayworth.

484 Bloodhounds on Broadway (20th Century-Fox, 1952, Mitzi Gaynor, Scott Brady).

Eighty Miles Outside of Atlanta—Harold Adamson (w), Jimmy McHugh (m), Chappell; I Wish I Knew—Mack Gordon (w), Harry Warren (m), Triangle; Jack of Diamonds—Paul F. Webster (w), Ben Oakland (m), Hub. COVER: Mitzi Gaynor.

485 Bloodline (Paramount, 1979, Audrey Hepburn, Ben Gazzara).

If Not for You—Larry Kusik (w), Ennio Morricone (m), Famous. COVER: A Girl's Neck.

486 Blossoms (Publix, 1928, Stars Unknown).

Blossoms That Bloom in the Moonlight—Ben Black, James Dietrich (w,m), Famous. COVER: Blossoms.

487 Blossoms on Broadway (Paramount, 1937, Edward Arnold, Shirley Ross).

Blossoms on Broadway—Leo Robin, Ralph Rainger (w,m), Famous; No Ring on Her Finger/You Can't Tell a Man by His Hat—Frank Loesser (w), Manning Sherwin (m), Famous. COVER: Broadway.

488 Blowing Wild (Warner Bros., 1953, Gary Cooper, Barbara Stanwyck).

Blowing Wild—Paul F. Webster (w), Dimitri Tiomkin (m), Witmark. COVER: Gary Cooper, Barbara Stanwyck, Anthony Quinn.

489 Blue (Paramount, 1968, Terence Stamp, Karl Malden).

Domingo De Ronda—Manos Hadjidakis (m), Famous. COVER: Terence Stamp and Movie Scene.

490 Blue Angel, The (Paramount, 1930, Marlene Dietrich, Emil Jannings).

Falling in Love Again—Frederick Hollander (w,m), Famous. COVER: Marlene Dietrich.

491 Blue Angel, The (20th Century-Fox, 1959, Curt Jurgens, May Britt).

Lola, Lola—Jay Livingston, Ray Evans (w,m), Robbins. COVER: May Britt, Curt Jurgens.

492 Bluebeard's Eighth Wife (Paramount, 1926, Gloria Swanson, Huntley Gordon).

Answering Eyes (B)—Jack Gartman (w), Louis Chapman (m), Ricordi. COVER: Gloria Swanson, Huntley Gordon.

493 Bluebird (Paramount, 1918, Robin MacDougall, Tula Belle).

Bluebird, Bring Back My Happiness—George Graff (w), Bert Grant (m), Berlin. COVER: Bluebirds.

494 Bluebird, The (20th Century-Fox, 1940, Shirley Temple, Spring Byington).

Someday You'll Find Your Bluebird—Mack Gordon (w), Alfred Newman (m), Robbins. COVER: Shirley Temple.

495 Blue Bonnet (National, 1919, Billie Rhodes, Ben Wilson).

Little Blue Bonnet—Fred Fisher (w,m), McCarthy Fisher. COVER: Billie Rhodes.

496 Blue Danube, The (Pathe, 1927, Leatrice Joy, Nils Asther).

Moonlight on the Danube—Byron Gay (w,m), Villa Moret. COVER: Leatrice Joy, Nils Asther.

497 Blue Gardenia (Warner Bros., 1953, Anne Baxter, Richard Conte).

Blue Gardenia—Bob Russell, Lester Lee (w,m), Harms. COVER: Anne Baxter, King Cole.

498 Blue Hawaii (Paramount, 1962, Elvis Presley, Angela Lansbury).

Almost Always True—Fred Wise, Ben Weisman (w,m), Gladys; Blue Hawaii—Leo Robin, Ralph Rainger (w,m), Famous; Can't Help Falling in Love with You—Hugo Peretti, Luigi Creatore, George Weiss (w,m), Gladys; Hawaiian Sunset/Island of Love—Sid Tepper, Roy Bennett (w, m), Gladys; Ku-u-i-po—Hugo Peretti, Luigi Creatore, George Weiss (w,m), Gladys; Moonlight Swim—Sylvia Dee (w), Ben Weisman (m), Daniels; No More—Don Robertson, Hal Blair (w, m), Gladys; Rock-A-Hula Baby—Fred Wise, Ben Weisman, Dolores Fuller (w,m), Gladys; Slicin' Sand—Sid Tepper, Roy Bennett (w,m), Gladys. COVER: Elvis Presley.

499 Blue Lagoon (Columbia, 1980, Brooke Shields, Chris Atkins).

Blue Lagoon Love Theme—Basil Poledouris (m), Golden Torch. COVER: Brooke Shields, Chris Atkins.

500 Blue Max (20th Century-Fox, 1966, James Mason, George Peppard).

Blue Max Love Theme—Jerry Goldsmith (m), Hastings; May Wine—Ernie Sheldon (w), Jerry Goldsmith (m), Hastings. COVER: James Mason, George Peppard, Ursula Andress.

501 Blue Montana Skies (Republic, 1939, Gene Autry, Smiley Burnette).

I Just Want You (VS)/Neath the Blue Montana Sky (VS)/Rockin' in the Saddle (VS)—Gene Autry, Fred Rose, Johnny Marvin (w,m), Western. COVER: Gene Autry.

502 Blues Brothers (Universal, 1980, John Belushi, Dan Aykroyd).

Rubber Biscuit—Charles Johnson (w,m), Levy; Soul Man—David Porter, Isaac Hayes (w,m), Birdees. COVER: John Belushi, Dan Aykroyd.

503 Blues in the Night (Warner Bros., 1941, Priscilla Lane, Betty Field).

Blues in the Night/Hang Onto Your Lids/Says Who? Says You, Says I!/This Time the Dream's on Me—Johnny Mercer (w), Harold Arlen (m), Remick. COVER: Priscilla Lane, Betty Field.

504 Blue Skies (Paramount, 1946, Bing Crosby, Fred Astaire).

All by Myself (plain cover)/Blue Skies (plain cover)/Couple of Song and Dance Men, A (PC)/Getting Nowhere/ Heat Wave (plain cover)/ I'll See You in Cuba (plain cover)/ I've Got My Captain Working for Me Now (plain cover)/Pretty Girl Is Like a Melody (plain cover)/Puttin' on the Ritz (plain cover)/Russian Lullaby (plain cover)/Say It Isn't So (plain cover)/Serenade to an Old-Fashioned Girl/We Saw the Sea (plain cover)/ You'd Be Surprised (plain cover)/ You Keep Coming Back Like a Song —Irving Berlin (w,m), Berlin. COVER: Bing Crosby, Fred Astaire, Joan Caulfield.

505 Blue Thunder (Columbia, 1983, Roy Scheider, Warren Oates).
Murphy's Law—Arthur Rubenstein (m), Gold Horizon. COVER: Space Helicopter.
506 Blue Veil, The (RKO, 1951, Jane Wyman, Charles Laughton).
Daddy—Bobby Troup (w,m), Republic; Devotion—Jack Brooks (w), Franz Waxman (m), Disney; There'll Be Some Changes Made—Billy Higgins, Benton Overstreet (w,m), Marks. COVER: Jane Wyman, Richard Carlson, Joan Blondell.
507 Bobbikins (20th Century-Fox, 1960, Shirley Jones, Max Bygraves).
Last Night I Dreamed—May Bygraves (w,m), Lakeview. COVER: Shirley Jones, Max Bygraves.
508 Bobby Deerfield (Columbia, 1977, Al Pacino, Marthe Keller).
Bobby Deerfield Theme—David Grusin (m), Warner. COVER: Red cover with title only.
509 Bobo (Warner Bros., 1967, Peter Sellers, Britt Ekland).
Imagine—Sammy Cahn (w), Francis Lai (m), Harms. COVER: Peter Sellers, Britt Ekland.
510 Body and Soul (United Artists, 1945, John Garfield, Lilli Palmer).
Body and Soul—Edward Heyman, Robert Sour, Frank Eyton (w), John Green (m), Harms. COVER: John Garfield, Lilli Palmer, Hazel Brooks.
511 Body Double (Columbia, 1984, Craig Wasson, Gregg Henry).
Relax—Holly Johnson, Mark O'-Toole, Peter Gill (w,m), Island. COVER: Girl in Window.
512 Body Heat (Warner Bros., 1981, William Hurt, Kathleen Turner).
Feel Like a Number—Bob Seger (w,m), Gear. COVER: Bob Seger.
513 Body Rock (New World, 1984, Lorenzo Lamas, Vicki Frederick).
Body Rock—John Bettis (w), Sylvester Levay (m), Warner. COVER: Lorenzo Lamas, Vicki Frederick.
514 Bofors Gun, The (Universal, 1968, Nicol Williamson, Ian Holm).
Bofors Gun Theme (B)—Carl Davis (m), Leeds. COVER: Black and white cover with title only.
515 Bold and the Brave, The (RKO, 1955, Mickey Rooney, Wendell Corey).
Bold and the Brave, The—Mickey Rooney, Ross Bagdasarian (w,m), Rooney. COVER: Mickey Rooney.
516 Bolero (Paramount, 1934, George Raft, Carole Lombard).
Raftero—Ralph Rainger (m), Famous. COVER: George Raft, Carole Lombard.
517 Bombardier (RKO, 1943, Pat O'Brien, Randolph Scott).
Song of the Bombardiers—Jack Scholl (w), M. K. Jerome (m), Remick. COVER: Pat O'Brien, Randolph Scott, Anne Shirley.
518 Bondage (Fox, 1933, Dorothy Jordan, Alexander Kirkland).
Command to Love/Penthouse Lament—Val Burton, Will Jason (w,m), Movietone. COVER: Black and white cover with title only.
519 Bonjour Tristesse (Columbia, 1958, David Niven, Deborah Kerr).
Bonjour Tristesse—Arthur Laurents (w), Georges Auric (m), Carlot; Bonjour Tristesse Dance—George Auric (m), Carlot. COVER: Sad Face.
520 Bonnie and Clyde (Warner Bros., 1967, Warren Beatty, Faye Dunaway).
Bonnie and Clyde—Charles Strouse (w,m), Witmark; Foggy Mountain Breakdown—Earl Scruggs (m), Peer; We Will Find a Way—Lee Adams (w), Charles Strouse (m), Witmark; Can't We Be Friends (VS)—Paul James (w), Kay Swift (m), Warner; Deep Night (VS)—Rudy Vallee (w), Charles Henderson (m), Warner; Golddiggers Song (VS)—Al Dubin (w), Harry Warren (m), Warner; Horsey Keep Your Tail Up (VS)—Walter Hirsch, Bert Kaplan (w,m), Warner; Lucky Day

(VS)—B. G. DeSylva, Lew Brown, Ray Henderson (w,m), Warner; Shadow Waltz (VS)—Al Dubin (w), Harry Warren (m), Warner; Sometimes I'm Happy (VS)—Irving Caesar (w), Vincent Youmans (m), Warner. COVER: Gene Hackman, Estelle Parsons, Warren Beatty, Faye Dunaway, Mike Pollard.

521 Bon Voyage (Buena Vista, 1962, Fred MacMurray, Jane Wyman).

Bon Voyage—Richard Sherman, Robert Sherman (w,m), Wonderland. COVER: Fred MacMurray.

522 Book of Numbers (Embassy, 1972, Freda Payne, Raymond St. Jacques).

Blue Boy Holler/I'm So Glad/ I Walk with the Lord—Al Schackman (w,m), Fab. COVER: Freda Payne, Raymond St. Jacques.

523 Boo Loo (Paramount, 1938, Colin Tapley, Jayne Regan).

Beside a Moonlit Stream—Sam Coslow, Frederick Hollander (w,m), Famous. COVER: Natives.

524 Boom (Universal, 1968, Richard Burton, Elizabeth Taylor).

Hideaway—Don Black (w), John Dankworth (m), Duchess. COVER: Richard Burton, Elizabeth Taylor.

525 Boots (Paramount, 1919, Dorothy Gish, Richard Barthelmess).

What Is the Harm in a Bit of a Walk—Elmer Clifton (w), Norman McNeil (m), Remick. COVER: Dorothy Gish.

526 Boots and Saddles (Republic, 1937, Gene Autry, Smiley Burnette).

Ridin' the Range—Fleming Allan, Gene Autry, Nelson Shawn (w,m), Sam Fox. COVER: Gene Autry.

527 Border Romance (Tiffany, 1930, Armida, Don Terry).

Yo Te Adoro, I Adore You—Will Jason, Val Burton (w,m), Bibo-Lang. COVER: Armida, Don Terry.

528 Bordertown Trails (Republic, 1944, Smiley Burnette, Sunset Carson).

It's My Lazy Day—Smiley Burnette (w,m), Stevens. COVER: Smiley Burnette.

529 Borneo (20th Century-Fox, 1937, Documentary of Borneo).

My Sweet Tahi—Lew Lehr (w), John Rocchetti (m), Movietone. COVER: Tropical Scene.

530 Born Free (Columbia, 1966, Virginia McKenna, Bill Travers).

Born Free—Don Black (w), John Barry (m), Columbia; Born Free Rhapsody—John Barry (m), Columbia. COVER: Virginia McKenna, Bill Travers, and Lion.

530a Born on the Fourth of July (Universal, 1989, Tom Cruise, Raymond Barry).

A Hard Rain's A-Gonna Fall— Bob Dylan (w,m), Warner. COVER: Blue and orange cover with title only.

531 Born to Be Kissed (The Girl from Missouri) (MGM, 1934, Jean Harlow, Franchot Tone).

Born to Be Kissed—Howard Dietz (w), Arthur Schwartz (m), Harms. COVER: Jean Harlow, Franchot Tone.

532 Born to Be Loved (Universal, 1959, Carol Morris, Vera Vague).

Born to Be Loved—Walter Bullock (w), Franz Steininger (m), Robbins. COVER: Carol Morris, and Others.

533 Born to Be Wild (Republic, 1938, Ralph Byrd, Doris Weston).

Story as Old as the Hills, A—Jack Lawrence, Peter Tinturin (w,m), Leeds. COVER: Black and white cover with title only.

534 Born to Dance (MGM, 1936, Eleanor Powell, James Stewart).

Easy to Love/Hey, Babe, Hey/ I've Got You Under My Skin/Love Me, Love My Pekinese/Rap, Tap on Wood/Rolling Home/Swinging the Jinx Away—Cole Porter (w,m), Chappell. COVER: Eleanor Powell.

535 Born Yesterday (Columbia, 1951, Judy Holliday, William Holden).

I Can't Give You Anything But Love—Dorothy Fields (w), Jimmy

McHugh (m), Mills. COVER: Judy Holliday, William Holden, Broderick Crawford.

536 Borsalino (Paramount, 1970, Jean Paul Belmondo, Alain Delon).

Borsalino Theme—Claude Bolling (m), Famous; Generique—Pierre De-Lange (w), Claude Bolling (m), Famous. COVER: Jean Paul Belmondo, Alain Delon.

537 Both Ends of the Candle (The Helen Morgan Story) (Warner Bros., 1957, Ann Blyth, Paul Newman).

Bill (B)—P. G. Wodehouse, Oscar Hammerstein (w), Jerome Kern (m), Harms; Can't Help Lovin' Dat Man (B)—Oscar Hammerstein (w), Jerome Kern (m), Harms; Man I Love, The (B)—Ira Gershwin (w), George Gershwin (m), Harms; Why Was I Born (B)—Oscar Hammerstein (w), Jerome Kern (m), Harms. COVER: Ann Blyth.

538 Bottoms Up (Fox, 1934, Spencer Tracy, John Boles).

I'm Throwin' My Love Away (PC)/Little Did I Dream—Harold Adamson (w), Burton Lane (m), Berlin; Waitin' at the Gate for Katy—Gus Kahn (w), Richard Whiting (m), Movietone. COVER: Spencer Tracy, John Boles, Pat Paterson, and Others.

539 Bought (Warner Bros., 1931, Ben Lyon, Constance Bennett).

Now You're in My Arms—Allie Wrubel, Morton Downey (w,m), Remick. COVER: Constance Bennett.

540 Bound for Glory (United Artists, 1976, David Carradine, Ronny Cox).

Bound for Glory—29 Guthrie Songs (VS)—Woody Guthrie (w,m), TRO. COVER: David Carradine.

541 Bowery Princess (Dimple) (20th Century-Fox, 1936, Shirley Temple, Frank Morgan).

Hey! What Did the Blue Jay Say? —Ted Koheler (w), Jimmy McHugh (m), Feist. COVER: Black and white cover with title only.

542 Bowery to Broadway (Universal, 1944, Maria Montez, Susanna Foster).

Just Because She Made Dem Goo-Goo Eyes—John Queen (w), Hughie Cannon (m), Paull Pioneer; My Song of Romance—Dave Franklin (w), Don George (m), Forster. COVER: Maria Montez, Evelyn Ankers, and Girls.

543 Boy Friend (20th Century-Fox, 1939, Jane Withers, Arleen Whelan).

Doin' the Socialite—Sidney Clare, Harry Akst (w,m), Mills. COVER: Jane Withers, Arleen Whelan, and Others.

544 Boy Friend, The (MGM, 1971, Twiggy, Christopher Gable).

Boy Friend, The (VS)/Fancy Forgetting (VS)/I Could Be Happy with You (VS)/It's Never Too Late to Fall in Love (VS)/It's Nicer in Nice (VS)/Poor (VS)/Room in Bloomsbury, A (VS)/Safety in Numbers (VS)/Sur le Plage (VS)/Won't You Charleston with Me? (VS)—Sandy Wilson (w,m), Chappell. COVER: Twiggy, and Girls.

545 Boy in the Plastic Bubble, The (Spelling, 1976, John Travolta, Robert Reed).

What Would They Say?—Paul Williams (w,m), Almo. COVER: John Travolta.

546 Boy o' Mine (First National, 1923, Ben Alexander, Irene Rich).

Dear Little Boy of Mine—J. Keirn Brennan (w), Ernest Ball (m), Witmark. COVER: Ben Alexander.

547 Boy on a Dolphin (20th Century-Fox, 1956, Alan Ladd, Clifton Webb).

Boy on a Dolphin—Paul F. Webster (w), Hugo Friedhofer (m), Robbins. COVER: Alan Ladd, Clifton Webb, Sophia Loren.

548 Boys from Syracuse, The (Universal, 1940, Allan Jones, Martha Raye).

Falling in Love with Love/Sing for Your Supper/This Can't Be Love/Who Are You?—Lorenz Hart (w),

Richard Rodgers (m), Chappell. COVER: Allan Jones, Martha Raye, Joe Penner, Rosemary Lane.

549 Boys in the Band, The (National General, 1970, Kenneth Nelson, Leonard Frey).

Boys in the Band—Sandy Linzer (w,m), Colgems. COVER: Nancy Sinatra.

550 Boys' Night Out (MGM, 1962, Kim Novak, James Garner).

Boys' Night Out, The—Sammy Cahn (w), James Van Heusen (m), Miller. COVER: Kim Novak, James Garner, Tony Randall.

551 Boys Town (MGM, 1938, Spencer Tracy, Mickey Rooney).

Boys Town on Parade—Bob Wright, Chet Forrest (w), Edward Ward (m), Feist. COVER: Spencer Tracy, Mickey Rooney.

552 Boy Ten Feet Tall, A (Paramount, 1964, Edward G. Robinson, Constance Cummings).

Boy Ten Feet Tall, A—Ned Washington (w), Les Baxter (m), Arch. COVER: Edward G. Robinson, and Boy.

553 Boy, What a Girl (Lippert, 1946, Ann Cornell, Roger Lampirez).

I Just Refuse to Sing the Blues—Roger Ramirez, Walter Bishop (w, m), Bishop. COVER: Ann Cornell.

554 Brass Target (United Artists, 1978, Sophia Loren, John Cassavetes).

Maria's Theme—Lawrence Rosenthal (m), Variety. COVER: Sophia Loren and Men.

555 Brat, The (MGM, 1919, Nazimova, Charles Bryant).

Brat, The—Harry B. Smith (w), Ted Snyder (m), Berlin. COVER: Nazimova.

556 Brazil (Republic, 1944, Tito Guizar, Virginia Bruce).

A Batucada Comecou/Blim Blem Blao—Ary Barroso (w,m), Southern; Brazil—Bob Russell (w), Ary Barroso (m), Southern; Quando Eu Penso Na Bahia—Ary Barroso (w,m), Southern; Rio De Janeiro/Tonight You're Mine —Ned Washington (w), Ary Barroso (m), Southern; Upa Upa—Ary Barroso (w,m). COVER: Virginia Bruce, Tito Guizar.

557 Breakfast at Tiffany's (Paramount, 1961, Audrey Hepburn, George Peppard).

Breakfast at Tiffany's—Henry Mancini (m), Famous; Lovers in the Park—Jay Livingston, Ray Evans (w), Henry Mancini (m), Famous; Moon River—Johnny Mercer (w), Henry Mancini (m), Famous; Moon River Theme/Something for Cat/Breakfast at Tiffany's Piano Score—Henry Mancini (m), Famous. COVER: Audrey Hepburn.

558 Breakfast Club, The (Universal, 1985, Emilio Estevez, Molly Ringwald).

Don't You-Forget About Me—Keith Forsey, Steve Schiff (w,m), MCA. COVER: Blue cover with title only.

559 Breakfast in Hollywood (United Artists, 1946, Tom Brennan, Bonita Granville).

If I Had a Wishing Ring—Marla Shelton (w), Louis Alter (m), Melrose; It's Better to Be By Yourself—Bob Levinson, Howard Leeds, King Cole (w,m), Capitol. COVER: Bonita Granville, Andy Russell, King Cole.

560 Breakin' (MGM, 1984, Lucinda Dickey, Adolpho Quinones).

Ain't Nobody (VS)—David Wolinski (w,m), Leonard; Body Work (VS) —Curtis Hudson (w,m), Leonard; Breakin' (VS)—Jerry Knight, Ollie Brown (w,m), Leonard; Cut It (VS)—Paul Fishman (w,m), Leonard; Freakshow on the Dance Floor (VS)—James Alexander, Michael Beard (w, m), Leonard; Heart of the Beat (VS) —Don Hart, Charlie Midnight (w,m), Leonard; Ninety-Nine and One Half (VS)—John Footman, Maxi Anderson (w,m), Leonard; Reckless (VS)—Chris Taylor, David Storrs (w,m), Leonard; Show Down (VS)—Joe Curiale, Ollie Brown (w,m), Leonard;

Street People (VS)—Jerry Knight, Ollie Brown (w,m), Leonard. COVER: Break Dancers.

561 Breaking the Ice (RKO, 1938, Bobby Breen, Charlie Ruggles).

Goodbye, My Dreams, Goodbye—Paul F. Webster (w), Victor Young (m), Miller; Happy as a Lark/Put Your Heart in a Song/Sunny Side of Things, The—Paul F. Webster (w), Frank Churchill (m), Miller; Tellin' My Troubles to a Mule—Paul F. Webster (w), Victor Young (m), Miller. COVER: Bobby Breen, Irene Dare.

562 Break the News (GFD, 1937, Jack Buchanan, Maurice Chevalier).

It All Belongs to You (B)—Cole Porter (w,m), Chappell. COVER: Jack Buchanan, Maurice Chevalier.

563 Breath of Scandal, A (Paramount, 1948, Sophia Loren, Maurice Chevalier).

Breath of Scandal, A—Al Stillman (w), Robert Stolz (m), Famous; Smile in Vienna—Patrick Michael (w), Sepp Fellner (m), Famous. COVER: Sophia Loren, Maurice Chevalier, John Gavin.

564 Breezing Home (Universal, 1937, William Gargan, Binnie Barnes).

I'm Hitting the Hot Spots/You're in My Heart Again—Harold Adamson (w), Jimmy McHugh (m), Feist. COVER: William Gargan, Binnie Barnes, Wendy Barrie.

565 Breezy (Universal, 1973, William Holden, Kay Lenz).

Breezy's Song—Marilyn Bergman, Alan Bergman (w), Michel Legrand (m), Leeds. COVER: William Holden, Kay Lenz.

566 Brewster's Millions (United Artists, 1935, Jack Buchanan, Lili Damita).

I Think I Can/One Good Tune Deserves Another/Pull Down the Blind—Douglas Furber (w), Ray Noble (m), Chappell. COVER: Jack Buchanan, Lili Damita.

567 Brian's Song (Columbia, 1972, James Caan, Billy Dee Williams).

Hands of Time, The—Marilyn Bergman, Alan Bergman (w), Michel Legrand (m), Colgems. COVER: Football Players.

568 Bribe, The (MGM, 1949, Robert Taylor, Ava Gardner).

Situation Wanted—William Katz (w), Nacio Herb Brown (m), Robbins. COVER: Robert Taylor, Ava Gardner, Charles Laughton, and Others.

569 Bridal Suite (MGM, 1939, Annabella, Robert Young).

When I Gave My Smile to You—Gus Kahn (w), Bill Buddie (m), Feist. COVER: Black and white cover with title only.

570 Bride Comes Home, The (Paramount, 1935, Claudette Colbert, Fred MacMurray).

Bride Comes Home, The—Tot Seymour (w), Vee Lawnhurst (m), Popular. COVER: Claudette Colbert.

571 Bride of the Regiment (First National, 1930, Vivienne Segal, Walter Pidgeon).

Broken Hearted Lover/Dream Away/One Life One Love—Al Bryan (w), Eddie Ward (m), Harms; When Hearts Are Young—Cyrus Wood (w), Sigmund Romberg, Alfred Goodman (m), Harms. COVER: Vivienne Segal, Walter Pidgeon.

572 Bride Wore Red, The (MGM, 1937, Joan Crawford, Franchot Tone).

Who Wants Love?—Gus Kahn (w), Franz Waxman (m), Robbins. COVER: Joan Crawford.

573 Bridge Ahoy (Paramount, 1936, Cartoon).

Let's Build a Bridge Today (VS)—Bob Rothberg (w), Sammy Timberg (m), Popular. COVER: Popeye.

574 Bridge at Remagen, The (United Artists, 1969, George Segal, Robert Vaughn).

Bridge at Remagen, The—Elmer Bernstein (m), Unart. COVER: Black and white cover with title only.

575 Bridge on the River Kwai, The (Columbia, 1957, William Holden, Alec Guinness).

Colonel Bogey March—Kenneth Alford (m), Boosey Hawkes; River Kwai March—Malcolm Arnold (m), Columbia; Bridge on the River Kwai-Themes—Malcolm Arnold (m), Shapiro Bernstein. COVER: Alec Guinness, William Holden, Jack Hawkins.

576 Bridges at Toko-Ri, The (Paramount, 1954, William Holden, Grace Kelly).

Bridges at Toko-Ri, The—Lyn Murray (m), Famous. COVER: William Holden, Grace Kelly.

577 Bridge Too Far, A (United Artists, 1977, Dirk Bogarde, James Caan).

Bridge Too Far, A/Dutch Rhapsody—John Addison (m), Unart. COVER: Dirk Bogarde, James Caan, and Other Stars.

578 Brief Moment (Columbia, 1933, Carole Lombard, Gene Raymond).

Say What You Mean—Joe Young (w), Gerald Marks (m), Berlin. COVER: Black and white cover with title only.

579 Brigadoon (MGM, 1954, Gene Kelly, Van Johnson).

Almost Like Being in Love/Brigadoon/Come to Me, Bend to Me/Down on MacConnachy Square/From This Day On/Heather on the Hill, The/I'll Go Home with Bonnie Jean/There But for You Go I/Waitin' for My Dearie—Alan Jay Lerner (w), Frederick Loewe (m), Sam Fox. COVER: Gene Kelly, Van Johnson, Cyd Charisse.

580 Bright Eyes (Fox, 1934, Shirley Temple, James Dunn).

On the Good Ship Lollipop—Sidney Clare, Richard Whiting (w,m), Movietone. COVER: Shirley Temple.

581 Bright Lights (First National, 1931, Frank Fay, Dorothy Mackaill).

Every Little Girl He Sees/Nobody Cares If I'm Blue—Grant Clarke (w), Harry Akst (m), Witmark; Song of the Congo—Herb Magidson, Ned Washington (w), Ray Perkins (m), Witmark. COVER: Frank Fay, Dorothy Mackaill, Noah Beery.

582 Bright Lights (Broadway Joe) (First National, 1935, Joe E. Brown, Ann Dvorak).

She Was an Acrobat's Daughter—Bert Kalmar (w), Harry Ruby (m), Harms; Toddlin' Along with You/You're an Eyeful of Heaven—Mort Dixon (w), Allie Wrubel (m), Harms. COVER: Joe E. Brown, Ann Dvorak.

583 Bright Road (MGM, 1953, Harry Belafonte, Dorothy Dandridge).

Suzanne—Harry Belafonte, Millard Thomas (w,m), Feist. COVER: Harry Belafonte.

584 Bright Shawl (First National, 1923, Richard Barthelmess, Dorothy Gish).

La Clavel—Katherine Lively (w,m), Flammer. COVER: Dorothy Gish.

585 Bring on the Girls (Paramount, 1945, Veronica Lake, Sonny Tufts).

Bring on the Girls/How Would You Like to Take My Picture/I'm Gonna Hate Myself in the Morning/Uncle Sammy Hit Miami/You Moved Right In—Harold Adamson (w), Jimmy McHugh (m), Famous. COVER: Veronica Lake, Sonny Tufts, Eddie Bracken, Spike Jones.

586 Bring Your Smile Along (Columbia, 1955, Frankie Laine, Keefe Brasselle).

Bring Your Smile Along (B)—Benny Davis, Carl Fischer (w,m), Dash; Mama Mia—Ned Washington (w), Lester Lee (m), Columbia. COVER: Frankie Laine, Keefe Brasselle, Constance Towers.

587 Broadcast News (20th Century-Fox, 1987, William Hurt, Albert Brooks).

Broadcast News Theme—Bill Conti (m), Warner. COVER: William Hurt, Albert Brooks, Holly Hunter.

588 Broadway (Universal, 1929, Glenn Tryon, Merna Kennedy).

Broadway/Chicken or the Egg/

Hittin' the Ceiling/Hot Footin' It/ Sing a Little Love Song—Con Conrad, Sidney Mitchell, Archie Gottler (w,m), DBH. COVER: Dancing Girls.

589 Broadway Babies (First National, 1929, Alice White, Sally Eilers).

Broadway Baby Dolls/Jig Jig Jigaloo—Al Bryan (w), George Meyer (m), Witmark; Wishing and Waiting for Love—Grant Clarke (w), Harry Akst (m). COVER: Alice White, and Girls.

590 Broadway Bad (Fox, 1933, Joan Blondell, Ginger Rogers).

Forget the Past—Sidney Mitchell (w), Harry Akst (m), Movietone. COVER: Joan Blondell, Ginger Rogers, Ricardo Cortez.

591 Broadway Bill (Columbia, 1935, Warner Baxter, Myrna Loy).

Old Man with the Whiskers, The— Haven Gillespie, Mitchell Parish, J. Fred Coots (w,m), Mills. COVER: Warner Baxter, Myrna Loy.

592 Broadway Butterfly (Warner Bros., 1925, Dorothy Devore, Louise Fazenda).

Butterfly—Gene Rodemich, Reeves Espy, Larry Conley (w,m), Mills. COVER: Night Club Scene.

593 Broadway Danny Rose (Orion, 1984, Woody Allen, Mia Farrow).

Agita/My Bambina—Nick Apollo Forte (w,m), Branch. COVER: Nick Apollo Forte.

594 Broadway Gondolier (Warner Bros., 1935, Dick Powell, Joan Blondell).

Flagenheim's Odorless Cheese/ Lonely Gondolier/Lulu's Back in Town/Outside of You/Pig and the Cow, The/Rose in Her Hair, The/ You Can Be Kissed—Al Dubin (w), Harry Warren (m), Witmark. COVER: Dick Powell.

595 Broadway Hoofer (Columbia, 1929, Marie Saxon, Jack Egan).

Hawaiian Love Song—Ballard MacDonald (w), Dave Franklin (m), Berlin. COVER: Black and white cover with title only.

596 Broadway Hostess (First National, 1935, Wini Shaw, Phil Regan).

He Was Her Man/Let It Be Me/ Playboy of Paree/Weary/Who But You—Mort Dixon (w), Allie Wrubel (m), Remick; Help Yourself to My Love (BW)—Herman Ruby (w), M. K. Jerome (m), Remick. COVER: Wini Shaw, Phil Regan.

597 Broadway Joe (Bright Lights) (First National, 1935, Joe E. Brown, Ann Dvorak).

She Was an Acrobat's Daughter— Bert Kalmar (w), Harry Ruby (m), Harms; Toddlin' Along with You/ You're an Eyeful of Heaven—Mort Dixon (w), Allie Wrubel (m), Harms. COVER: Joe E. Brown, Ann Dvorak.

598 Broadway Melody (MGM, 1929, Charles King, Anita Page).

Boy Friend/Broadway Melody/ Love Boat/Wedding of the Painted Doll/You Were Meant for Me—Arthur Freed (w), Nacio Herb Brown (m), Robbins. COVER: Charles King, Bessie Love, Anita Page.

599 Broadway Melody of 1936 (MGM, 1935, Jack Benny, Robert Taylor).

Broadway Rhythm/I've Got a Feelin' You're Foolin'/On a Sunday Afternoon/Sing Before Breakfast/ You Are My Lucky Star—Arthur Freed (w), Nacio Herb Brown (m), Robbins. COVER: Jack Benny, Robert Taylor, Eleanor Powell.

600 Broadway Melody of 1938 (MGM, 1937, Robert Taylor, Eleanor Powell).

Everybody Sing/Follow in My Footsteps/Got a Pair of New Shoes/ I'm Feelin' Like a Million/Sun Showers—Arthur Freed (w), Nacio Herb Brown (m), Robbins; You Made Me Love You—Joe McCarthy (w), James Monaco (m), Broadway; Your Broadway and My Broadway/Yours and Mine—Arthur Freed (w), Nacio Herb Brown (m), Robbins. COVER: Robert Taylor, Eleanor Powell, Judy Garland.

601 Broadway Melody of 1940 (MGM, 1939, Fred Astaire, Eleanor Powell).

Begin the Beguine—Cole Porter (w,m), Harms; Between You and Me/I Concentrate on You/I Happen to Be in Love/I've Got My Eyes on You/Please Don't Monkey with Broadway—Cole Porter (w,m), Chappell. COVER: Eleanor Powell, Fred Astaire.

602 Broadway Rhythm (MGM, 1944, Ginny Simms, George Murphy).

All the Things You Are—Oscar Hammerstein (w), Jerome Kern (m), Chappell; Amor—Sunny Skylar (w), Gabriel Ruiz (m), Melody Lane; Brazilian Boogie—Hugh Martin, Ralph Blane (w,m), Feist; I Love Corny Music/Irresistible You/Milkman Keep Those Bottles Quiet—Don Raye (w), Gene DePaul (m), Feist; My Moonlight Madonna—Paul F. Webster (w), Zdenko Fibich, William Scotti (m), Fischer; Pretty Baby (B)—Gus Kahn (w), Tony Jackson, Egbert Van Alstyne (m), Day; Solid Potato Salad—Don Raye, Gene DePaul, Hughie Prince (w,m), Feist. COVER: Ginny Simms, George Murphy, Tommy Dorsey.

603 Broadway Rose (Metro, 1922, Mae Murray, Monte Blue).

Broadway Rose—Eugene West (w), Otis Spencer, Martin Fried (m), Fisher. COVER: Mae Murray.

604 Broadway Scandals (Columbia, 1929, Sally O'Neill, Jack Eagen).

Can You Read in My Eyes—Sam Coslow (w,m), Spier Coslow; Does an Elephant Love Peanuts—James Hanley (w,m), Shapiro Bernstein; Kicking the Blues Away—James Hanley, Dave Franklin (w,m), Shapiro Bernstein; Rhythm of the Tambourine—Dave Franklin (w,m), Remick; What Is Life Without Love—Jack Stone, Fred Thompson, Dave Franklin (w,m), Berlin; Would I Love to

Love You—Dave Dreyer, Sidney Clare (w,m), Berlin. COVER: Sally O'Neill, and Movie Scenes.

605 Broadway Serenade (MGM, 1939, Jeanette MacDonald, Lew Ayres).

For Ev'ry Lonely Heart—Gus Kahn (w), Herbert Stothart, Edward Ward (m), Feist; High Flyin'/One Look at You—Bob Wright, Chet Forrest (w), Herbert Stothart, Edward Ward (m), Feist. COVER: Jeanette MacDonald, and Chorus.

606 Broadway Show (Independent, 1924, Short Subject).

When My Sugar Walks Down the Street—Gene Austin, Jimmy McHugh, Irving Mills (w,m), Mills. COVER: The Hotsy Totsy Boys.

607 Broadway Thru a Keyhole (United Artists, 1933, Constance Cummings, Russ Colombo).

Doin' the Uptown Lowdown/I Love You Pizzicato/When You Were the Girl on the Scooter/You're My Past Present and Future—Mack Gordon (w), Harry Revel (m), DBH. COVER: Constance Cummings, Russ Colombo.

608 Broken Blossoms (United Artists, 1919, Lillian Gish, Richard Barthelmess).

Broken Blossoms—Robert Long (w), Louis Gottschalk (m), Harms; White Blossom—Charles Towne (w), D. W. Griffith (m), Schirmer. COVER: Lillian Gish.

609 Broken Dreams (Monogram, 1933, Randolph Scott, Martha Sleeper).

Broken Dreams—Harry Kerr (w), Maurice Spitalny (m), Sam Fox. COVER: Randolph Scott, Martha Sleeper.

610 Broncho Billy (Essanay, 1914, Gilbert Anderson).

Broncho Billy—Don Meaney, H. Tipton Steck (w), Arthur Penn (m), Rossiter. COVER: Gilbert Anderson.

611 Bronco Billy (Warner Bros., 1980, Clint Eastwood, Sondra Locke).

Bar Room Buddies—Milton Brown,

Cliff Crofford, Steve Dorff, Snuff Garrett (w,m), Peso; Cowboys and Clowns—Steve Dorff, Snuff Garrett, Larry Herbstrit, Gary Harju (w,m), Peso; Misery and Gin—John Durrill, Snuff Garrett (w,m), Peso; Misery Loves Company—Jerry Reed (w,m), Lowery. COVER: Clint Eastwood, and Movie Scenes.

612   Brotherhood (Paramount, 1968, Kirk Douglas, Alex Cord).

Brotherhood Dance—Norman Gimbel (w,m), Ensign; Taste of Love —Norman Gimbel (w), Lalo Schifrin (m), Ensign. COVER: Kirk Douglas, Alex Cord.

613   Brotherly Love (Paramount, 1936, Cartoon).

Brotherly Love (VS)—Bob Rothberg (w), Sammy Timberg (m), Famous. COVER: Popeye.

614   Brothers (Columbia, 1930, Bert Lytell, Dorothy Sebastian).

I'm Dreaming—Dan Dougherty (w,m), Shapiro-Bernstein. COVER: Bert Lytell, Dorothy Sebastian.

615   Brothers Karamazov, The (MGM, 1958, Yul Brynner, Maria Schell).

Brothers Karamazov Love Theme —Bronislau Kaper (m), Robbins. COVER: Yul Brynner, Maria Schell, Claire Bloom.

616   Brother Sun, Sister Moon (Paramount, 1973, Graham Faulkner, Judi Bowker).

Brother Sun, Sister Moon/Crusader's Song/Little Church/Lovely Day/ There's a Shape in the Sky—Donovan (w,m), Famous. COVER: Graham Faulkner, Judi Bowker.

617   Buccaneer, The (Paramount, 1958, Yul Brynner, Claire Bloom).

Buccaneer Love Song, Lovers' Gold—Mack David (w), Elmer Bernstein (m), Famous; Buccaneer Love Song Solo—Elmer Bernstein (m), Famous. COVER: Yul Brynner, Claire Bloom.

618   Buck Benny Rides Again (Paramount, 1940, Jack Benny, Ellen Drew).

Drums in the Night/My Kind of Country/My My/Say It—Frank Loesser (w), Jimmy McHugh (m), Famous. COVER: Jack Benny, Ellen Drew, Phil Harris.

619   Buck Privates (Universal, 1941, Andrews Sisters, Abbott and Costello).

Apple Blossom Time—Neville Fleeson (w), Albert Von Tilzer (m), Broadway; Boogie Woogie Bugle Boy/Bounce Me Brother with a Solid Four/When Private Brown Becomes a Captain—Don Raye, Hughie Prince (w,m), Leeds; Wish You Were Here— Don Raye, Vic Schoen, Hughie Prince (w,m), Leeds; You're a Lucky Fellow Mr. Smith—Don Raye, Sonny Burke, Hughie Prince (w,m), Leeds. COVER: Andrews Sisters, Bud Abbott, Lou Costello.

620   Buck Rogers in the 25th Century (Universal, 1979, Gil Gerard, Pamela Hensley).

Buck Rogers Song—Suspension— Glen Larson (w,m), Duchess. COVER: Gil Gerard, and Movie Scenes.

621   Bud Abbott and Lou Costello in Hollywood (MGM, 1945, Bud Abbott, Lou Costello).

As I Remember You/I Hope the Band Keeps Playing—Ralph Blane, Hugh Martin (w,m), Feist. COVER: Bud Abbott, Lou Costello.

622   Buddy Holly Story, The (Columbia, 1978, Gary Busey, Don Stroud).

Everyday (VS)—Norman Petty, Charles Hardin (w,m), Columbia; Great Pretender, The (VS)—Buck Ram (w,m), Columbia; I'm Gonna Love You Too (VS)—Joe Mauldin, Niki Sullivan, Norman Petty (w,m), Columbia; It's So Easy (VS)—Buddy Holly, Norman Petty (w,m), Columbia; Listen to Me (VS)/Maybe Baby #1 & #2 (VS)/Not Fade Away (VS) —Norman Petty, Charles Hardin (w,m), Columbia; Oh Boy (VS)— Sunny West, Bill Tilghman, Norman Petty (w,m), Columbia; Peggy Sue (VS)—Jerry Allison, Norman Petty,

Buddy Holly (w,m), Columbia; Rave On (VS)—Sunny West, Bill Tilghman, Norman Petty (w,m), Columbia; Rock Around with Ollie Vee (VS)—S. Curtis (w,m), Columbia; That'll Be the Day #1 & #2 (VS)—Norman Petty, Buddy Holly, Joe Allison, Columbia; True Love Ways (VS)—Norman Petty, Buddy Holly (w,m), Columbia; Well All Right (VS)—Norman Petty, Buddy Holly, Jerry Allison, Joe Mauldin (w,m), Columbia; Whole Lotta Shakin' Goin' On (VS)—Sunny David, David Williams (w, m), Columbia. COVER: Gary Busey.

623 Buddy System, The (20th Century-Fox, 1984, Richard Dreyfuss, Susan Sarandon).

Here's That Sunny Day—Will Jennings (w), Patrick Williams (m), Warner. COVER: Richard Dreyfuss, Susan Sarandon, Jean Stapleton.

624 Bugs Bunny (Warner Bros., 1955, Cartoon).

Mister Easter Rabbit/Easter Song—Jack Segal (w), Maddy Russell (m), Witmark; Railroad Engineer—Tedd Pierce, Warren Foster (w,m), Witmark. COVER: Cartoon.

625 Bugsy Malone (Paramount, 1975, Scott Baio, Jodie Foster).

Bugsy Malone—Paul Williams (w, m), Twentieth Century Music. COVER: Scott Baio, Jodie Foster.

626 Building a Building (Disney, 1933, Cartoon).

Who'll Buy a Box Lunch (VS)—Frank Churchill (w,m), Berlin. COVER: Cartoon.

627 Bulldog Drummond (United Artists, 1929, Ronald Colman, Joan Bennett).

There's the One for Me—Jack Yellen (w), Harry Akst (m), Ager Yellen. COVER: Ronald Colman.

628 Bullet Is Waiting, A (Columbia, 1954, Jean Simmons, Rory Calhoun).

Jamie—Mann Curtis (w), Dimitri Tiomkin (m), Remick. COVER: Jean Simmons, Rory Calhoun.

629 Bullfighter and the Lady, The (Republic, 1951, Robert Stack, Joy Page).

How Strange—Peggy Lee (w), Victor Young (m), Young. COVER: Peggy Lee.

630 Bullitt (Warner Bros., 1968, Steve McQueen, Robert Vaughn).

Bullitt Theme—Lalo Schifrin (m), Warner; Great Divide—Norman Gimbel (w), Lalo Schifrin (m), Warner. COVER: Steve McQueen.

631 Bundle of Joy (RKO, 1956, Eddie Fisher, Debbie Reynolds).

All About Love/Bundle of Joy/I Never Felt This Way Before/Lullaby in Blue/Some Day Soon/Worry About Tomorrow, Tomorrow—Mack Gordon (w), Josef Myrow (m), Ramrod. COVER: Eddie Fisher, Debbie Reynolds.

632 Bunny Lake Is Missing (Columbia, 1965, Laurence Olivier, Keir Dullea).

Bunny Lake Is Missing Theme—Paul Glass (m), Chappell. COVER: Doll.

633 Buona Sera Mrs. Campbell (United Artists, 1968, Shelley Winters, Peter Lawford).

Buona Sera Mrs. Campbell—Mel Frank (w), Riz Ortolani (m), Unart. COVER: Gina Lollobrigida, Shelley Winters, Phil Silvers.

634 Burglars, The (Columbia, 1971, Omar Sharif, Jean Paul Belmondo).

Burglars Theme—Ennio Morricone (m), Colgems. COVER: Omar Sharif, Jean Paul Belmondo, Dyan Cannon.

635 Burning Rage (Cates, 1983, Barbara Mandrell, Tom Wopat).

To Me (PC)—Mack David (w), Mike Reid (m), Columbia. COVER: None.

636 Burning Sands (Paramount, 1941, Wanda Hawley, Milton Sills).

Burning Sands—D. Onivas (w,m), Robbins. COVER: Wanda Hawley, Milton Sills.

637 Bury Me Not on the Lone Prairie (Universal, 1941, Johnny Mack Brown, Fuzzy Knight).

Bears Give Me the Bird—Everett Carter (w), Milton Rosen (m), Robbins. COVER: Johnny Mack Brown, Fuzzy Knight, Nell O'Day.

638   Bush Pilot (Lippert, 1947, Rochelle Hudson, Jack LaRue).

True Love—Gordon Fleming, Harold Moon, Sam Hersenhoren (w, m), North American. COVER: Rochelle Hudson, Jack LaRue.

639   Business and Pleasure (Fox, 1932, Will Rogers, Joel McCrea).

Ole Aunt Mariar—James Hanley (w,m), Movietone. COVER: Black and white cover with title only.

640   Business Girl (First National, 1931, Loretta Young, Frank Albertson).

Constantly—Bud Green, Sam Stept (w,m), DBH. COVER: Black and white cover with title only.

641   Bus Stop (20th Century-Fox, 1956, Marilyn Monroe, Don Murray).

Bus Stop Song—A Paper of Pins —Ken Darby (w,m), Miller. COVER: Marilyn Monroe, Don Murray.

642   Buster (Warner Bros., 1988, Phil Collins, Julie Walters).

Groovy Kind of Love—Toni Wine, Carole Bayer Sager (w,m), Warner; Two Hearts/Big Noise (VS)—Phil Collins (w), Lamont Dozier (m), Warner; I Got You Babe (VS)—Sonny Bono (w,m), Warner; I Just Don't Know What to Do with Myself (VS) —Hal David (w), Burt Bacharach (m), Warner; Keep on Running (VS)—Jackie Edwards (w,m), Warner; Loco in Acapulco (VS)—Phil Collins (w), Lamont Dozier (m), Warner; Sweets for My Sweet (VS)—Doc Pomus (w), Mort Shuman (m), Warner. COVER: Phil Collins.

643   Buster Keaton Story, The (Paramount, 1957, Donald O'Connor, Ann Blyth).

Buster—Wilson Stone (w), Victor Young (m), Famous. COVER: Donald O'Connor, Ann Blyth.

644   Butch and Sundance, The Early Years (20th Century-Fox,

1979, William Katt, Tom Berenger).

Mary's Theme—Patrick Williams (m), Fox Fanfare. COVER: William Katt, Tom Berenger.

645   Butch Cassidy and the Sundance Kid (20th Century-Fox, 1969, Robert Redford, Paul Newman).

Butch Cassidy and Sundance Kid Medley—Hal David (w), Burt Bacharach (m), Blue Seas; Come Touch the Sun—Burt Bacharach (m), Blue Seas; Raindrops Keep Falling on My Head—Hal David (w), Burt Bacharach (m), Blue Seas; Sundance Kid (VS)/On a Bicycle Built for Joy (VS) /Old Fun City (VS)/Not Goin' Home Anymore (VS)/South American Getaway (VS)—Burt Bacharach (m), Hansen. COVER: Paul Newman, Robert Redford, Katharine Ross.

646   But Not for Me (Paramount, 1959, Clark Gable, Carroll Baker).

You Make Me Feel So Young— Mack Gordon (w), Josef Myrow (m), BVC. COVER: Clark Gable, Carroll Baker, Lilli Palmer.

647   Butterfield Eight (MGM, 1960, Elizabeth Taylor, Laurence Harvey).

Gloria—Mack David (w), Bronislau Kaper (m), Robbins. COVER: Elizabeth Taylor, Laurence Harvey, Eddie Fisher.

648   Butterflies Are Free (Columbia, 1969, Goldie Hawn, Eileen Heckart).

Butterflies Are Free—Steven Schwartz (w,m), Sunbury; Carry Me—Randy McNeill (w), Bob Alcivar (m), Colgems. COVER: Goldie Hawn, Edward Albert.

649   Bye Bye Barbara (Paramount, 1969, Eva Swann, Phillippe Auron).

Bye Bye Barbara—Mag Bodard (w), Nina Companeez (m), Famous. COVER: Black and white cover with title only.

650   Bye Bye Birdie (Columbia, 1963, Janet Leigh, Dick Van Dyke).

Bye Bye Birdie/How Lovely to Be

a Woman/How Lovely to Love a Woman/Kids/Lot of Livin' to Do, A/ One Boy/One Last Kiss/Put on a Happy Face/Rosie/Telephone Hour, The (VS)/Honestly Sincere (VS)/ Hymn for a Sunday Evening (VS)— Lee Adams (w), Charles Strouse (m), Morris. COVER: Teenagers.

651 Bye Bye Braverman (Warner Bros., 1968, George Segal, Jack Warden).

Braverman's Waltz—Herbert Sargent (w), Peter Matz (m), Columbine. COVER: Hand and a Grave.

652 By Love Possessed (United Artists, 1961, Lana Turner, Efrem Zimbalist).

By Love Possessed Theme—Sammy Cahn (w), Elmer Bernstein (m), Unart. COVER: Black and white cover with title only.

653 By the Light of the Silvery Moon (Warner Bros., 1953, Doris Day, Gordon MacRae).

Ain't We Got Fun (B)—Gus Kahn, Raymond Egan (w), Richard Whiting (m), Feldman; By the Light of the Silvery Moon—Ed Madden (w), Gus Edwards (m), Remick. COVER: Doris Day, Gordon MacRae.

654 Cabaret (Paramount, 1927, Gilda Gray, Tom More).

Cabarabia—Sidney Mitchell, Leon Flatow, Albert Gumble (w,m), Remick. COVER: Gilda Gray.

655 Cabaret (Allied Artists, 1972, Liza Minnelli, Joel Grey).

Cabaret/I Don't Care Much/Maybe This Time/Tomorrow Belongs to Me/Wilkomen/If You Could See Her (VS)/Married (VS)/Mein Herr (VS)/ Money Money (VS)/Two Ladies (VS) —Fred Ebb (w), John Kander (m), Time Square. COVER: Liza Minnelli.

656 Cabinet of Caligari (20th Century-Fox, 1965, Glynis Johns, Dan O'Herlihy).

Sounds of the Night, The—Johnny Mercer (w), Gerald Fried (m), Arch. COVER: Black and white cover with title only.

657 Cabin in the Sky (MGM,

1943, Ethel Waters, Lena Horne).

Ain't It De Truth—E. Y. Harburg (w), Harold Arlen (m), Feist; Cabin in the Sky—John Latouche (w), Vernon Duke (m), Feist; Happiness Is a Thing Called Joe—E. Y. Harburg (w), Harold Arlen (m), Feist; Honey in the Honeycomb—John Latouche (w), Vernon Duke (m), Feist; Life's Full of Consequence—E. Y. Harburg (w), Harold Arlen (m), Feist; Taking a Chance on Love—John Latouche, Ted Fetter (w), Vernon Duke (m), Feist; Things Ain't What They Used to Be—Ted Parsons (w), Mercer Ellington (m), Tempo. COVER: Cabin in the Sky.

658 Cabin Kids (Educational, 1936, Musical Short).

Little Bit of Rhythm—Saul Chaplin, Herman Pincus, Sammy Cahn (w,m), Williams. COVER: Brown and grey cover with title only.

659 Cabriola (Every Day Is a Holiday) (Columbia, 1966, Marisol, Angel Penalta).

Cabriola/I Can Live Without Love— Howard Greenfield (w), Augusto Alguero (m), Colgems. COVER: Marisol.

660 Cactus Flower (Columbia, 1969, Ingrid Bergman, Walter Matthau).

Time for Love Is Anytime, The— Cynthia Weil (w), Quincy Jones (m), Colgems. COVER: Ingrid Bergman, Walter Matthau, Goldie Hawn.

661 Caddy, The (Paramount, 1953, Dean Martin, Jerry Lewis).

Gay Continental, The/It's a Whistle-in Kinda Mornin'/It Takes a Lot of Little Likes—Jack Brooks (w), Harry Warren (m), Paramount; Mine to Love—Bebe Blake (w), Victor Young (m), Paramount; One Big Love/That's Amore/What Wouldcha Do Without Me/You're the Right One—Jack Brooks (w), Harry Warren (m), Paramount. COVER: Dean Martin, Jerry Lewis, Donna Reed.

662 Caddyshack (Orion, 1980, Chevy Chase, Rodney Dangerfield).

I'm Alright—Kenny Loggins (w, m), Milk Honey. COVER: Golfers.

663 Caddyshack Two (Warner Bros., 1988, Dyan Cannon, Robert Stack).

Nobody's Fool—Kenny Loggins, Michael Towers (w,m), Warner. COVER: Kenny Loggins.

664 Cadet Girl (20th Century-Fox, 1941, Carole Landis, George Montgomery).

It Happened, It's Over, Let's Forget It/She's a Good Neighbor/Uncle Sam Gets Around—Leo Robin (w), Ralph Rainger (m), Robbins. COVER: Carole Landis, George Montgomery, John Sheppard.

665 Cafe Rendezvous (Nu Art, 1938, The Kidoolers).

Little Wooden Whistle Wouldn't Whistle, The—Bobby Gregory (w,m), Von Tilzer. COVER: Black and white cover with title only.

666 Cafe Society (Paramount, 1939, Madeleine Carroll, Fred MacMurray).

Kiss Me with Your Eyes—Frank Loesser (w), Burton Lane (m), Paramount. COVER: Madeleine Carroll, Fred MacMurray.

667 Cain and Mabel (Warner Bros., 1936, Marion Davies, Clark Gable).

Coney Island/I'll Sing You a Thousand Love Songs—Al Dubin (w), Harry Warren (m), Remick. COVER: Marion Davies, Clark Gable.

668 Caine Mutiny, The (Columbia, 1954, Humphrey Bogart, Jose Ferrer).

Full Speed Ahead—Alfred Perry (w), Max Steiner (m), Chappell; I Can't Believe That You're in Love with Me—Jimmy McHugh, Clarence Gaskill (w,m), Mills. COVER: Humphrey Bogart, Jose Ferrer, Van Johnson, Fred MacMurray.

669 Cairo (MGM, 1942, Jeanette MacDonald, Robert Young).

Keep the Light Burning Bright (PC)—E. Y. Harburg, Howard Dietz, Arthur Schwartz (w,m), Feist; Wait-ing for the Robert E. Lee—L. Wolfe Gilbert, Lewis Muir (w,m), Alfred. COVER: Robert Young, Jeanette MacDonald.

670 Calamity Jane (Warner Bros., 1953, Doris Day, Howard Keel).

Black Hills of Dakota/Deadwood Stage/Higher Than a Hawk/I Can Do Without You/Just Blew in from the Windy City/Secret Love/Tis Harry I'm Plannin' to Marry/Woman's Touch, A—Paul F. Webster (w), Sammy Fain (m), Remick. COVER: Doris Day, Howard Keel.

671 Calcutta (Paramount, 1947, Alan Ladd, Gail Russell).

This Is Madness—Ben Raleigh (w), Bernie Wayne (m), Famous. COVER: Alan Ladd, Gail Russell.

672 Caldonia (Buzz Me) (Astor, 1946, Louis Jordan, Razz Mitchell).

Buzz Me—Danny Baxter (w,m), Preview. COVER: Louis Jordan.

673 Calendar Girl (Republic, 1947, Jane Frazee, William Marshall).

Calendar Girl/I'm Telling You Now/Lovely Night to Go Dancing—Harold Adamson (w), Jimmy McHugh (m), Mayfair. COVER: Jane Frazee, William Marshall, Kenny Baker.

674 California (Paramount, 1946, Ray Milland, Barbara Stanwyck).

California/California or Bust/Said I to My Heart—E. Y. Harburg (w), Earl Robinson (m), Paramount. COVER: Ray Milland, Barbara Stanwyck, Barry Fitzgerald.

675 California Dreaming (American International, 1979, Seymour Cassell, Glynnis O'Connor).

California Dreamin'—John Phillips, Michelle Phillips (w,m), ABC. COVER: A Man Heading West.

676 California Suite (Columbia, 1978, Alan Alda, Michael Caine).

California Suite Selections—Claude Bolling (m), Golden Torch. COVER: Alan Alda, Michael Caine, Jane Fonda, and Others.

677 Callaway Went Thataway

(MGM, 1951, Howard Keel, Dorothy McGuire).

Where the Tumbleweed Is Blue—Charles Wolcott (w,m), Miller. COVER: Howard Keel, Dorothy McGuire, Fred MacMurray.

678 Calling All Stars (Columbia, 1942, Musical Short).

My Heart Isn't in It—Jack Lawrence (w,m), Leeds. COVER: Black and white cover with title only.

679 Call It Luck (Fox, 1934, Pat Paterson, Charles Starrett).

I'll Bet on You—Sidney Clare (w), Richard Whiting (m), Movietone. COVER: Pat Paterson.

680 Call Me Bwana (United Artists, 1963, Bob Hope, Anita Ekberg).

Call Me Bwana (B)—Monty Norman (w,m), Unart. COVER: Bob Hope, Anita Ekberg.

681 Call Me Madam (20th Century-Fox, 1953, Ethel Merman, Donald O'Connor).

Best Thing for You, The/Can You Use Any Money/Hostess with the Mostes' on the Ball/It's a Lovely Day Today/Marrying for Love/Ocarina, The/Something to Dance About/That International Rag/Washington Square Dance/What Chance Have I with Love/You're Just in Love—Irving Berlin (w,m), Berlin. COVER: Ethel Merman, Donald O'Connor, George Sanders, Vera-Ellen.

682 Call Me Mister (20th Century-Fox, 1951, Betty Grable, Dan Dailey).

I Just Can't Do Enough for You Baby/Japanese Girl Like 'Merican Boy/Love Is Back in Business—Mack Gordon (w), Sammy Fain (m), Miller. COVER: Betty Grable, Dan Dailey.

683 Call of the Flesh (The Singer of Seville) (MGM, 1930, Ramon Novarro, Dorothy Jordan).

Lonely—Clifford Grey (w), Ramon Novarro, Herbert Stothart (m), Robbins. COVER: Ramon Novarro.

684 Call of the Prairie (Paramount, 1936, Jimmy Ellison, William

Boyd).

Call of the Prairie—Tot Seymour (w), Vee Lawnhurst (m), Famous. COVER: Jimmy Ellison, Muriel Evans.

685 Call of the Range (The Gentleman from Arizona) (Monogram, 1939, John King, Joan Barclay).

Call of the Range—Ted Cisco (w, m), Golden West. COVER: Desert Scene.

686 Call of the Rockies (Columbia, 1938, Charles Starrett, Iris Meredith).

Cowboy Has to Sing, A (VS)/Following the Sun All Day (VS)/Hangin' Blues (VS)—Bob Nolan (w, m), American. COVER: Bob Nolan.

687 Call of the Sea (Warner Bros., 1931, Henry Edwards, Crissie White).

Paquita (B)—Billy Milton, Basil Bartlett (w,m), Dix. COVER: Henry Edwards, Crissie White.

688 Call of the South Seas (Republic, 1944, Janet Martin, Allan Lane).

Blue Island—Ned Washington (w), Evan Newman (m), Forster. COVER: Janet Martin.

689 Call of the West (Columbia, 1930, Dorothy Revier, Matt Moore).

Sittin' on a Rainbow—Jack Yellen, Dan Dougherty (w,m), Ager Yellen. COVER: Dorothy Revier.

690 Call Out the Marines (RKO, 1942, Victor McLaglen, Edmund Lowe).

Beware!/Call out the Marines/Hands Across the Border/Light of My Life, The/Zana Zoranda—Mort Greene (w), Harry Revel (m), Greene Revel. COVER: Edmund Lowe, and Girl.

691 Calypso Heat Wave (Columbia, 1957, Johnny Desmond, Merry Anders).

Day Old Bread and Canned Beans—Claude Trenier, Damita Joe, Don Hill (w,m), Mobile; Jody—Scott Johnson, Rayon Darrell (w,m), Granson; My Sugar Is So Refined—Sylvia

Dee (w), Sidney Lippman (m), Goldsen; Run Joe—Walt Merrick, Joe Willoughby, Louis Jordan (w,m), Cheerio; Treat Me Like a Lady—George Thorne, Don Reed (w,m), Granson. COVER: Johnny Desmond, Merry Anders, and Other Stars.

692 Camelot (Warner Bros., 1967, Richard Harris, Vanessa Redgrave).

Camelot/Follow Me/How to Handle a Woman/If Ever I Would Leave You/I Loved You Once in Silence/Lusty Month of May, The/Simple Joys of Maidenhood, The/What Do the Simple Folk Do?—Alan Jay Lerner (w), Frederick Loewe (m), Chappell. COVER: Richard Harris, Vanessa Redgrave.

693 Cameo Kirby (Fox, 1930, J. Harold Murray, Norma Terris).

After a Million Dreams/Home Is Heaven—Heaven Is Home/Romance—Edgar Leslie, Walter Donaldson (w,m), Donaldson. COVER: J. Harold Murray, Norma Terris.

694 Camille (First National, 1927, Norma Talmadge, Maurice Costello).

Camille (B)—Hubert David, Guy Austin (w,m), Worton. COVER: Norma Talmadge.

695 Camille (MGM, 1936, Robert Taylor, Greta Garbo).

I'll Love Like Robert Taylor, Be My Greta Garbo—Fox Trot—Milton Benjamin (w,m), Benjamin. COVER: Robert Taylor, Greta Garbo.

696 Camping Out (Disney, 1934, Cartoon).

Ain't Nature Grand (VS)—Frank Churchill (w,m), Berlin. COVER: Cartoon.

697 Campus Rhythm (Monogram, 1943, Johnny Downs, Gale Storm).

Walkin' the Chalk Line—Jules Loman (w), Louis Herscher (m), Mills. COVER: Johnny Downs, Gale Storm.

698 Canadians, The (20th Century-Fox, 1961, Robert Ryan, John Dehner).

This Is Canada—Ken Darby (w,m), Longridge. COVER: Canadian Flag.

699 Can-Can (20th Century-Fox, 1960, Frank Sinatra, Shirley MacLaine).

Allez-vous-en, Go Away/Can-Can/C'est Magnifique/Come Along with Me/I Am in Love/If You Loved Me Truly/I Love Paris/It's All Right with Me/Let's Do It (B)/Live and Let Live/Montmart'/Never Give Anything Away—Cole Porter (w,m), Buxton Hill. COVER: Frank Sinatra, Maurice Chevalier, Shirley MacLaine, Louis Jourdan.

700 Candlelight in Algeria (20th Century-Fox, 1943, James Mason, Carla Lehman).

It's Love (B)—Muriel Watson, Jack Denby (w,m), Schaeur. COVER: Christine De Meurin.

701 Candy (Cinerama, 1968, Marlon Brando, Richard Burton).

Child of the Universe—Roger McGuinn (w), Dave Grusin (m), Pamco; Rock Me—John Kay (w,m), Trousdale. COVER: Young Girl.

702 Cangaceiro (Columbia, 1954, Alberto Ruschel, Marisa Prado).

Bandit, The—John Turner, Michael Carr (w), Alfredo de Nascimento (m), Leeds. COVER: A Hat and a Guitar.

703 Can Heironymus Merkin Ever Forget Mercy Humppe and Find True Happiness? (Universal, 1968, Anthony Newley, Joan Collins).

I'm All I Need/Lullaby/When You Gotta Go—Herbert Kretzmer (w), Anthony Newley (m), Duchess. COVER: Cartoon Sketch.

704 Cannonball Run-Two (Warner Bros., 1984, Burt Reynolds, Dom DeLuise).

Like a Cannonball—Steve Dorff, Snuff Garrett, Milton Brown (w,m), Peso. COVER: Burt Reynolds, Dom DeLuise, Frank Sinatra, and Others.

705 Can't Help Singing (Universal, 1944, Deanna Durbin, Robert Paige).

Any Moment Now/Californ-i-ay/

Can't Help Singing/More and More/Once in a Million Moons/Swing Your Sweetheart—E. Y. Harburg (w), Jerome Kern (m), Harms. COVER: Deanna Durbin.

706 Can This Be Dixie? (20th Century-Fox, 1936, Jane Withers, Slim Summerville).

It's Julep Time in Dixieland (BW)/Pick, Pick, Pickaninny/Uncle Tom's Cabin Is a Cabaret—Sidney Clare (w), Harry Akst (m), Movietone. COVER: Jane Withers.

707 Cantor's Son, The (Ero, 1938, Moishe Oysher, Judith Abarbanel).

Ask the Stars—Dailey Paskman (w), Alexander Olshanetsky (m), Marks. COVER: Jan Peerce.

708 Can't Stop the Music (Associated, 1980, Valerie Perrine, The Village People).

Go West/Manhattan Woman—Jacques Morali, Henry Belolo, Victor Willis (w,m), Columbia; Can't Stop the Music (VS)—P. Hurtt, B. Whitehead (w), Jacques Morali (m), Cant Stop; Give Me a Break (VS)—Jacques Morali, Henry Belolo, Ritchie Family (w,m), Cant Stop; I Love You to Death (VS)/Liberation (VS)—P. Hurtt, B. Whitehead (w), Jacques Morali (m), Cant Stop; Magic Night (VS)/Milkshake (VS)—Victor Willis (w), Jacques Morali (m), Cant Stop. Samantha (VS)—Jacques Morali, Henry Belolo, P. Hurtt (w,m), Cant Stop; Sophistication (VS)—Jacques Morali, Henry Belolo, P. Hurtt, Ritchie Family (w,m), Cant Stop; Sound of the City (VS)—Jacques Morali, Henry Belolo, P. Hurtt (w,m), Cant Stop; Y.M.C.A. (VS)—Jacques Morali, Henry Belolo, Victor Willis (w,m), Cant Stop. COVER: The Village People, Valerie Perrine.

709 Canyon Passage (Universal, 1946, Dana Andrews, Susan Hayward).

Ole Buttermilk Sky—Jack Brooks, Hoagy Carmichael (w,m), BVH; Rogue River Valley—Hoagy Carmichael (w,m), BVH. COVER: Dana Andrews, Susan Hayward, Hoagy Carmichael.

710 Caprice (20th Century-Fox, 1966, Doris Day, Richard Harris).

Caprice—Larry Marks (w,m), COVER: Doris Day, Richard Harris.

711 Captain Blood (Warner Bros., 1935, Errol Flynn, Olivia de Havilland).

Captain Blood Piano Suite—Erich W. Korngold (m), Warner. COVER: Brown cover with title only.

712 Captain Calamity (Grand National, 1936, George Houston, Marion Nixon).

Tell Me Why—Jack Stern, Harry Tobias (w,m), Sam Fox. COVER: George Houston, Marion Nixon.

713 Captain Carey, USA (After Midnight) (Paramount, 1950, Alan Ladd, Wanda Hendrix).

Mona Lisa—Jay Livingston, Ray Evans (w,m), Famous. COVER: Alan Ladd, Wanda Hendrix.

714 Captain Caution (United Artists, 1940, Victor Mature, Louise Platt).

Apple Song/Hilda/On a Little Island by a Sunlit Sea/Only One/Que Voulez Vous?—Foster Carling (w), Phil Ohman (m), BVC. COVER: Victor Mature, Louise Platt.

715 Captain China (Paramount, 1949, John Payne, Gail Russell).

Oh, Brandy, Leave Me Alone—Josef Marais (w,m), Frank. COVER: John Payne.

716 Captain from Castile (20th Century-Fox, 1947, Tyrone Power, Jean Peters).

Catana—Eddie DeLange (w), Alfred Newman (m), Robbins; La Venta/La Zarabanda—Vincent Gomez (m), Mills. COVER: Tyrone Power, Jean Peters.

717 Captain Horatio Hornblower (Warner Bros., 1951, Gregory Peck, Virginia Mayo).

Captain Hornblower Theme (B)/Lady Barbara Theme (B)/Sailing Theme (B)—Robert Farnon (m), Feldman. COVER: Gregory Peck, Virginia Mayo.

718 Captain January (20th Century-Fox, 1936, Shirley Temple, Guy Kibbee).

At the Codfish Ball/Early Bird—Sidney Mitchell (w), Lew Pollack (m), Movietone; Right Somebody to love—Jack Yellen (w), Lew Pollack (m), Movietone. COVER: Shirley Temple.

719 Captain Kidd (United Artists, 1944, Charles Laughton, Randolph Scott).

Captain Kidd—Roy Alfred (w), Marvin Fisher (m), Block. COVER: Charles Laughton, Randolph Scott, Barbara Britton.

720 Captain Newman, MD (Universal, 1963, Gregory Peck, Bobby Darin).

Captain Newman Theme, Blue Grotto—Frank Skinner (m), Northern. COVER: Black and white cover with title only.

721 Captain of the Guard (Universal, 1930, John Boles, Laura La Plante).

Can It Be/For You/Maids on Parade/You, You Alone—William Dugan (w), Heinz Roemheld (m), Handman. COVER: John Boles, Laura La Plante.

722 Captain's Kid, The (First National, 1936, May Robson, Sybil Jason).

Drifting Along/I'm the Captain's Kid—Jack Scholl, M. K. Jerome (w, m), Witmark. COVER: Guy Kibbee, Sybil Jason.

723 Captains of the Clouds (Warner Bros., 1942, James Cagney, Dennis Morgan).

Captains of the Clouds—Johnny Mercer (w), Harold Arlen (m), Remick; Bless Em All—Jimmy Hughes, Frank Lake, Al Stillman (w,m), Sam Fox. COVER: James Cagney, Dennis Morgan, Brenda Marshall.

724 Captain's Table, The (20th Century-Fox, 1959, John Gregson, Peggy Cummins).

Captain's Table, The (B)—Frank Cordell (m), Filmusic; No One—Paddy Roberts (w), Frank Cordell (m), Peer. COVER: John Gregson, Peggy Cummins, and Others.

725 Captain Swagger (Pathe, 1927, Rod LaRoque, Sue Carol).

Captain Swagger—Charles Weinberg, Irving Bibo (w,m), Bibo. COVER: Rod LaRoque, Sue Carol.

726 Caravan (Fox, 1934, Charles Boyer, Loretta Young).

Happy/Ha Cha Cha/Wine Song—Gus Kahn (w), Werner Heymann (m), Movietone. COVER: Charles Boyer, Loretta Young.

727 Cardinal, The (Columbia, 1963, Tom Tryon, Romy Schneider).

Cardinal Main Theme—Jerome Moross (m), Chappell; Cardinal Tango—Carolyn Leigh (w), Jerome Moross (m), Chappell; Cardinal Waltz—Jerome Moross (m), Chappell; Stay with Me—Carolyn Leigh (w), Jerome Moross (m), Chappell. COVER: Red and black letters.

728 Career (Paramount, 1959, Dean Martin, Shirley MacLaine).

Love Is a Career—Sammy Cahn (w), James Van Heusen (m), Famous. COVER: Dean Martin, Shirley MacLaine and Others.

729 Careers (First National, 1929, Billie Dove, Thelma Todd).

I Love You, I Hate You/My Sweet Helene—Al Bryan (w), George Meyer (m), Witmark. COVER: Billie Dove.

730 Carefree (RKO, 1938, Fred Astaire, Ginger Rogers).

Change Partners/I Used to Be Color Blind/Night Is Filled with Music, The/Yam, The—Irving Berlin (w, m), Berlin. COVER: Fred Astaire, Ginger Rogers.

731 Careless Age, The (First National, 1929, Douglas Fairbanks, Loretta Young).

Melody Divine—Herman Ruby (w), Norman Spencer (m), Witmark; Say It with a Solitaire—Herman Ruby (w), Ray Perkins (m), Witmark. COVER: Douglas Fairbanks, Carmel Meyers.

732 Careless Lady (Fox, 1932, John Boles, Joan Bennett).

Souvenir of Love—James Hanley

(w,m), Sam Fox; When You Hear This Song, Remember Me—Ralph Freed (w), James Hanley (m), Sam Fox. COVER: John Boles, Joan Bennett.

733 Careless Years, The (United Artists, 1957, Dean Stockwell, Natalie Trundy).

Careless Years, The—Joe Lubin (w,m), Daywin. COVER: Dean Stockwell, Natalie Trundy.

734 Caretakers, The (United Artists, 1963, Robert Stack, Polly Bergen).

Blues for a Four String Guitar— Elmer Bernstein (m), Unart. COVER: Black and white cover with title only.

735 Caribbean Holiday (One Night in the Tropics) (Universal, 1940, Allan Jones, Nancy Kelly).

Back in My Shell/Remind Me/ You and Your Kiss—Dorothy Fields (w), Jerome Kern (m), Harms; Your Dream—Oscar Hammerstein, Otto Harbach (w), Jerome Kern (m), Harms. COVER: Black and white cover with title only.

736 Carmen (Essanay, 1916, Charlie Chaplin, Lawrence Bowes).

Carmen—William McKenna (w,m), Morris. COVER: Charlie Chaplin.

737 Carmen Jones (20th Century-Fox, 1954, Dorothy Dandridge, Henry Belafonte).

Beat Out That Rhythm on a Drum/Dat's Love/My Joe/Stan' Up an' Fight—Oscar Hammerstein (w), Georges Bizet (m), Williamson. COVER: Dorothy Dandridge.

738 Carnation Kid, The (Paramount, 1929, Douglas MacLean, Frances Lee).

Carnations Remind Me of You— Sterling Sherwin (w,m), Sherman Clay. COVER: Douglas MacLean, Frances Lee.

739 Carnegie Hall (United Artists, 1947, William Prince, Marsha Hunt).

All the World Is Mine—Dorothy Dick (w), Mischa Portnoff, Wesley Portnoff (m), Feist; Beware My Heart—Sam Coslow (w,m), Feist; Brown Danube—Hal Borne (m), Crystal; Pleasure's All Mine—Frank Ryerson, Wilton Moore (w,m), Leeds; Romance in Carnegie Hall—Buddy Kaye, D. Artega (w,m), Shapiro Bernstein; Sometime We will Meet Again—William LeBaron, Boris Morros, Gregory Stone (w,m), Feist; Carnegie Hall Piano Selections—Boris Morros, William LeBaron (m), Chappell. COVER: Lily Pons, Harry James, Vaughn Monroe, and Others.

740 Carnival Girl (Young Desire) (Universal, 1930, Mary Nolan, William Janney).

Why Did It Have to Be You?— Bernie Grossman (w), Lou Handman (m), Handman. COVER: Black and white cover with title only.

741 Carnival in Costa Rica (20th Century-Fox, 1947, Dick Haymes, Vera-Ellen).

Another Night Like This/Costa Rica/Gui Pi Pia/I'll Know It's Love/ Maracas/Mi Vida/Rumba Bomba— Harry Ruby (w), Ernesto Lecuona (m), Marks. COVER: Dick Haymes, Vera-Ellen, Cesar Romero, Celeste Holm.

742 Carnival Story (Texas Carnival) (MGM, 1951, Red Skelton, Esther Williams).

It's Dynamite (PC)—Dorothy Fields (w), Harry Warren (m), Miller. COVER: None.

743 Carnival Story (RKO, 1954, Steve Cochran, Anne Baxter).

Ring Down the Curtain—Pony Sherrell, Philip Moody (w), Willy Schmidt Gentner (m), Mills. COVER: Steve Cochran, Anne Baxter.

744 Car of Dreams (Gaumont, 1935, Greta Mosheim, John Mills).

Goodbye Trouble—Frank Eyton (w), Mischa Spoliansky (m), Mills. COVER: Greta Mosheim, John Mills.

745 Carolina (Fox, 1934, Janet Gaynor, Lionel Barrymore).

Carolina—Lew Brown, Jay Gorney (w,m), Movietone; Sun Shines

Brighter, The—William Kernell (w), Louis DeFrancesco (m), Movietone. COVER: Janet Gaynor.

746 Carolina Blues (Columbia, 1944, Kay Kyser, Ann Miller).

Mister Beebe—Jule Styne, Sammy Cahn, Dudley Brooks (w,m), Shapiro Bernstein; Poor Little Rhode Island/ There Goes That Song Again/You Make Me Dream Too Much—Sammy Cahn (w), Jule Styne (m), Shapiro Bernstein. COVER: Kay Kyser, Ann Miller, Victor Moore.

747 Carolina Cannonball (Republic, 1955, Judy Canova, Andy Clyde).

Busy as a Beaver/Carolina Cannonball/Wishin' and Waitin'—Jack Elliott, Donald Kahn (w,m), Kahn. COVER: Judy Canova.

748 Carousel (20th Century-Fox, 1956, Shirley Jones, Gordon MacRae).

Carousel Waltz/If I Loved You/ June Is Bustin' Out All Over/Mister Snow/Real Nice Clambake, A/Soliloquy/What's the Use of Wond'rin'/ When the Children Are Asleep/You'll Never Walk Alone—Oscar Hammerstein (w), Richard Rodgers (m), Williamson. COVER: Shirley Jones, Gordon MacRae.

749 Carpetbaggers, The (Paramount, 1964, George Peppard, Alan Ladd).

Carpetbaggers Love Theme—Elmer Bernstein (m), Famous; Monica —Earl Shuman (w), Elmer Bernstein (m), Famous. COVER: George Peppard, Carroll Baker.

750 Carry on Sergeant (Bairnsfather, 1928, Bruce Bairnsfather).

Far Away Eyes—Bruce Bairnsfather (w), Ernest Dainty (m), Feist. COVER: Man and Woman.

751 Car Wash (Universal, 1976, Franklin Ajaye, Richard Pryor).

Car Wash/I'm Goin' Down/I Wanna Get Next to You/You Gotta Believe—Norman Whitfield (w,m), Duchess. COVER: Cartoon.

752 Casablanca (Warner Bros., 1942, Humphrey Bogart, Ingrid Bergman).

As Time Goes By—Herman Hupfield (w,m), Harms; Song of the Rose (B)—Schreier Bottero (w,m), Ricordi; Casablanca Piano Suite— Max Steiner (m), Warner. COVER: Humphrey Bogart, Ingrid Bergman, Paul Henreid.

753 Casanova Brown (RKO, 1944, Gary Cooper, Teresa Wright).

Casanova Brown—Nick Kenny, Charles Kenny, Abner Silver (w,m), Lincoln. COVER: Gary Cooper, Teresa Wright.

754 Casanova's Big Night (Paramount, 1954, Bob Hope, Joan Fontaine).

Gondolier's Serenade/Pretty Mandolin—Jay Livingston, Ray Evans (w,m), Famous. COVER: Bob Hope, Joan Fontaine.

755 Casbah (Universal, 1948, Tony Martin, Yvonne DeCarlo).

For Every Man There's a Woman/ Hooray for Love/It Was Written in the Stars/What's Good About Goodbye—Leo Robin (w), Harold Arlen (m), Melrose. COVER: Tony Martin, Yvonne DeCarlo.

756 Case Against Brooklyn, The (Columbia, 1957, Maggie Hayes, Darren McGavin).

Jacqueline—Bob Hilliard (w), Mort Garson (m), Columbia. COVER: Darren McGavin, Maggie Hayes.

757 Casey Jones (Ray-Art, 1927, Al St. John, Ralph Lewis).

Casey Jones—Lawrence Seibert (w), Eddie Newton (m), Southern Cal. COVER: Casey Jones and Train.

758 Casino Royale (Columbia, 1967, Peter Sellers, Ursula Andress).

Bond Street—Burt Bacharach (m), Colgems; Look of Love, The—Hal David (w), Burt Bacharach (m), Col-Gems. COVER: Tattooed Lady.

759 Casper (Paramount, 1950, Cartoon).

Casper Casper—Sid Jacobson (w), Jimmy Krondes (m), Harvey; Casper the Friendly Ghost—Mack David

(w), Jerry Livingston (m), Famous.
COVER: Cartoon.

760 Cast a Giant Shadow (United Artists, 1966, Kirk Douglas, Senta Berger).

Cast a Giant Shadow/Love Me True—Ernie Sheldon (w), Elmer Bernstein (m), Unart. COVER: Kirk Douglas, Senta Berger, Frank Sinatra, John Wayne.

761 Castles in the Air (LeBaron, 1938, Cristina Tellez, Eddie Le-Baron).

One Kiss of Love—Harold Raymond (w), Lee Zahler (m), Superior. COVER: Cristina Tellez, Eddie Le-Baron.

762 Casual Sex (Universal, 1988, Lea Thompson, Victoria Jackson).

Hot Hot Hot—Alphonsus Cassell (w,m), Chrysalis. COVER: Buster Poindexter.

763 Cat and the Fiddle, The (MGM, 1934, Jeanette MacDonald, Ramon Novarro).

I Watch the Love Parade/New Love Is Old, A/Night Was Made for Love, The/One Moment Alone/She Didn't Say Yes/Try to Forget—Otto Harbach (w), Jerome Kern (m), Harms. COVER: Jeanette MacDonald, Ramon Novarro.

764 Cat Ballou (Columbia, 1965, Jane Fonda, Lee Marvin).

Ballad of Cat Ballou/They Can't Make Her Cry—Mack David (w), Jerry Livingston (m), Colgems. COVER: King Cole.

765 Cat on a Hot Tin Roof (MGM, 1958, Paul Newman, Elizabeth Taylor).

Cat on a Hot Tin Roof Love Theme—Charles Wolcott (m), Feist. COVER: Black and white cover with title only.

766 Cat People (Universal, 1982, Malcolm MacDowell, Nastassia Kinski).

Cat People-Putting Out Fire—David Bowie (m), Giorgio Moroder (m), MCA. COVER: Blue cover with title only.

767 Cat's Paw, The (Fox, 1934, Harold Lloyd, Una Merkel).

I'm Just That Way—Roy Turk (w), Harry Akst (m), Movietone. COVER: Harold Lloyd.

768 Cattle Queen of Montana (RKO, 1954, Barbara Stanwyck, Ronald Reagan).

Montana—Bob Nolan (w), Louis Forbes (m), Jungnickel. COVER: Barbara Stanwyck, Ronald Reagan.

769 Cattle Raiders (Columbia, 1938, Charles Starrett, Donald Grayson).

Devil's Great Grand Son, The (VS)/This Ain't the Same Old Range (VS)/Welcome to the Spring (VS)—Bob Nolan (w,m), American. COVER: Bob Nolan.

770 Caught in the Draft (Paramount, 1941, Bob Hope, Dorothy Lamour).

Love Me As I Am—Frank Loesser (w), Louis Alter (m), Paramount. COVER: Bob Hope, Dorothy Lamour.

771 Caught Plastered (RKO, 1931, Bert Wheeler, Bob Woolsey).

I'm That Way About You—Victor Schertzinger (w,m), Harms. COVER: Bert Wheeler, Dorothy Lee.

772 Cavalcade (Fox, 1933, Clive Brook, Diana Wynyard).

Cavalcade March Song—Reginald Berkeley (w), Louis DeFrancesco (m), Movietone; Twentieth Century Blues—Noel Coward (w,m), Chappell; You Are My Day Dream—Reginald Berkeley (w), Louis DeFrancesco (m), Movietone. COVER: Horseback Riders.

773 Cavalier (Tiffany Stahl, 1928, Barbara Bedford, Richard Talmadge).

My Cavalier—Meredith Willson (w), Hugo Riesenfeld (m), Bibo. COVER: Masked Man and Woman.

774 Cease Fire (Paramount, 1953, Korean War Documentary).

We Are Brothers in Arms—Ned Washington (w), Dimitri Tiomkin (m), Famous. COVER: Soldiers.

775 Centennial Summer (20th Century-Fox, 1946, Jeanne Crain, Cornel Wilde).

All Thru the Day—Oscar Hammerstein (w), Jerome Kern (m), Williamson; Cinderella Sue—E. Y. Harburg (w), Jerome Kern (m), Harms; In Love in Vain—Leo Robin (w), Jerome Kern (m), Harms; Two Hearts Are Better Than One—Johnny Mercer (w), Jerome Kern (m), Harms; Up with the Lark—Leo Robin (w), Jerome Kern (m), Harms. COVER: Jeanne Crain, Cornel Wilde, Linda Darnell, William Eythe.

776 Certain Smile, A (20th Century-Fox, 1958, Rossano Brazzi, Joan Fontaine).

Certain Smile, A—Paul F. Webster (w), Sammy Fain (m), Miller. COVER: Joan Fontaine, Rossano Brazzi, and Others.

777 Cha-Cha-Cha Boom (Columbia, 1956, Perez Prado, Helen Grayco).

El Marinero—H. Ricardo Rico (w, m), Southern; Lonesome Road, The —Gene Austin (w), Nathaniel Shilkret (m), Paramount; Mambo No. 8 —Perez Prado (m), Peer; Save Your Sorrow—B. G. DeSylva (w), Al Sherman (m), Shapiro Bernstein; Year Round Love—Charles Singleton, Rose McCoy (w,m), Roosevelt. COVER: Perez Prado, Helen Grayco, and Others.

778 Chairman, The (20th Century-Fox, 1969, Gregory Peck, Anne Heywood).

World That Only Lovers See—Hal Shaper (w), Jerry Goldsmith (m), Fox. COVER: Gregory Peck.

779 Chalk Garden, The (Universal, 1964, Deborah Kerr, Hayley Mills).

Madrigal—Mack David (w), Malcolm Arnold (m), Northern. COVER: Black and white cover with title only.

780 Champ, The (MGM, 1978, Jon Voight, Faye Dunaway).

If You Remember Me—Carole B.

Sager, Marvin Hamlisch (w,m), Chappell; T. J.'s Theme—Dave Grusin (m), Columbia; What Matters Most —Alan Bergman, Marilyn Bergman (w), Dave Grusin (m), Columbia. COVER: Jon Voight, Faye Dunaway.

781 Champagne Waltz (Paramount, 1937, Gladys Swarthout, Fred MacMurray).

Blue Danube Waltz—Leo Robin (w), Johann Strauss (m), Popular; Champagne Waltz—Con Conrad, Ben Oakland, Milton Drake (w,m), Famous; Could I Be in Love?—Leo Robin, William Daly (w,m), Popular; Merry-Go-Round, The—Ann Ronell (w,m), Popular; Paradise in Waltz Time—Sam Coslow, Frederick Hollander (w,m), Popular; When Is a Kiss Not a Kiss—Ralph Freed (w), Burton Lane (m), Popular. COVER: Gladys Swarthout, Fred MacMurray.

782 Chance Meeting (Paramount, 1960, Hardy Kruger, Stanley Baker).

Chance Meeting—Ruth Roberts, William Katz (w,m), Famous. COVER: Micheline Presle, Hardy Kruger.

783 Chances Are (Tri-Star, 1989, Cybill Shepherd, Robert Downey).

After All—Dean Pitchford, Tom Snow (w,m), Triple. COVER: Cybill Shepherd, Robert Downey.

784 Chandler (MGM, 1971, Warren Oates, Leslie Caron).

Chandler Theme-Katherine—Geo. Romanis (m), Feist. COVER: Warren Oates.

785 Change of Habit (Universal, 1969, Elvis Presley, Mary Tyler Moore).

Let Us Pray—Buddy Kaye (w), Ben Weisman (m), Aberbach; Rubberneckin'—Dory Jones (w), Bunny Warren (m), Presley. COVER: Elvis Presley.

786 Change of Heart (Fox, 1934, Janet Gaynor, Charles Farrell).

So What?—Harry Akst (w,m), Movietone. COVER: Black and white cover with title only.

787 Change of Seasons (20th Century-Fox, 1980, Shirley Mac-Laine, Bo Derek).

Where Do You Catch the Bus for Tomorrow?—Alan Bergman, Marilyn Bergman (w), Henry Mancini (m), Fox. COVER: Anthony Hopkins, Bo Derek.

788 Chaplin Revue, The (United Artists, 1960, Charlie Chaplin, Sidney Chaplin).

Texas (B)—Charlie Chaplin (w,m), Bourne. COVER: Charlie Chaplin.

789 Chapman Report, The (Warner Bros., 1962, Shelley Winters, Efrem Zimbalist).

Chapman Report Theme—Leonard Rosenman (m), Witmark. COVER: Shelley Winters, Claire Bloom, Jane Fonda.

790 Chapter Two (Columbia, 1979, James Caan, Marsha Mason).

I'm on Your Side—Carole B. Sager, Marvin Hamlisch (w,m), Gold Horizon. COVER: James Caan, Marsha Mason.

791 Charade (Universal, 1963, Cary Grant, Audrey Hepburn).

Charade—Johnny Mercer (w), Henry Mancini (m), Southdale; Charade Music Score-11 Themes—Henry Mancini (m), Southdale. COVER: Cary Grant, Audrey Hepburn.

792 Chariots of Fire (Warner Bros., 1981, Ben Cross, Ian Charleson).

Chariots of Fire Theme—Vangelis (m), Warner; Jerusalem—William Blake (w), Hubert Parry (m), Roberton; Race to the End—Jon Anderson (w), Vangelis (m), Warner; Chariots of Fire Selections/Chariots of Fire Piano Suite—Vangelis (m), Warner. COVER: Runners.

793 Chariots of the Gods (Independent, 1974, Documentary of Outer Space Visitors).

Chariots of the Gods Theme—Peter Thomas (m), Jewel. COVER: Stone Gods.

794 Charlie Bubbles (Universal, 1968, Albert Finney, Liza Minnelli).

Charlie Bubbles Theme—Misha Donat (m), Leeds. COVER: Black and white cover with title only.

795 Charlie Chan in Shanghai (Fox, 1935, Warner Oland, Irene Hervey).

Prince and Ming Lo Fu, The—Troy Sanders (w,m), Movietone. COVER: Black and white cover with title only.

796 Charlie McCarthy, Detective (Universal, 1939, Edgar Bergen, Charlie McCarthy).

Almost—Sam Lerner (w), Ben Oakland (m), Robbins; How Was I to Know—Eddie Cherkose (w), Jacques Press (m), Robbins. COVER: Edgar Bergen, Charlie McCarthy, Constance Moore.

797 Charlotte's Web (Paramount, 1973, Cartoon).

Charlotte's Web/Chin Up/Mother Earth and Father Time (B)/There Must Be Something More (B)/We've Got Lots in Common (B)—Richard Sherman, Robert Sherman (w,m), Ensign. COVER: Cartoon.

798 Charming Deceiver, The (Majestic, 1933, Constance Cummings, Billie Barnes).

Whistling Under the Moon—Robert Hargreaves, Stanley Damerell (w), Montague Ewing (m), Mills. COVER: Constance Cummings.

799 Charm School (Paramount, 1932, Meg Lemonnier, Henry Garat).

It's the Beguine (B)—Jain Laidlow (w), Raoul Moretti (m), Chappell. COVER: Meg Lemonnier, Henry Garat.

800 Charro (National General, 1969, Elvis Presley, Ina Balin).

Charro—Billy Strange, Scott Davis (w,m), Presley. COVER: Elvis Presley.

801 Chase, The (Columbia, 1966, Jane Fonda, Marlon Brando).

Chase, The—Don Black (w), John Barry (m), Colgems. COVER: Marlon Brando, Jane Fonda, Robert Redford.

802 Chase a Crooked Shadow (Warner Bros., 1958, Richard Todd, Anne Baxter).

In Search of a Dream—Robert Mellin (w), Matyas Seiber (m), Blaze. COVER: Anne Baxter.

803 Chasing Rainbows (MGM, 1930, Bessie Love, Charles King).

Everybody Tap/Happy Days Are Here Again—Jack Yellen (w), Milton Ager (m), Ager; Love Ain't Nothin' But the Blues—Joe Goodwin (w), Louis Alter (m), Robbins; Lucky Me-Lovable You—Jack Yellen (w), Milton Ager (m), Ager. COVER: Sketches.

804 Chatterbox (Republic, 1943, Joe D. Brown, Judy Canova).

Guy from Albuquerque/Why Can't I Sing a Love Song—Sol Meyer (w), Harry Akst (m), Mills. COVER: Joe E. Brown, Judy Canova.

805 Che (20th Century-Fox, 1969, Omar Sharif, Jack Palance).

Che—Lalo Schifrin (m), Fox. COVER: Omar Sharif.

806 Cheaper by the Dozen (20th Century-Fox, 1950, Clifton Webb, Jeanne Crain).

When You Wore a Tulip—Jack Mahoney (w), Percy Wenrich (m), Feist. COVER: Clifton Webb, Jeanne Crain.

807 Cheat, The (Paramount, 1923, Pola Negri, Jack Holt).

Carmelita Song (B)—Joan Hastings (w), Nellie Simpson (m), Ricordi. COVER: Pola Negri.

808 Cheaters (Liberty, 1934, Dorothy Mackail, William Boyd).

Without a Man to Love—Marcy Klauber (w), Harry Stoddard (m), Berlin. COVER: Dorothy Mackail, William Boyd, June Collier.

809 Cheating Cheaters (Universal, 1934, Cesar Romero, Fay Wray).

I've Burned My Bridges—Barry Trivers (w), Arthur Morton (m), Harms. COVER: Fay Wray.

810 Check and Double Check (Amos 'n' Andy) (RKO, 1930, Freeman Gosden, Charles Correll).

Nobody Knows But the Lord—Bert Kalmar (w), Harry Ruby (m), Harms; Old Man Blues/Ring Dem Bells—Duke Ellington, Irving Mills (w,m), Harms; Three Little Words—Bert Kalmar (w), Harry Ruby (m), Harms. COVER: Freeman Gosden, Charles Correll.

811 Checkers (Fox, 1919, Thomas Corrigan, Jean Acker).

Checkers—Leo Edwards, Edgar Allen (w,m), McCarthy Fisher. COVER: Thomas Corrigan, Jean Acker.

812 Cheech and Chong's Nice Dreams (Columbia, 1982, Cheech Marin, Thomas Chong).

Nice Dreams—Ruben Guevara (w, m), Golden Torch. COVER: Cheech Marin, Thomas Chong, and Girls.

813 Cheer Up and Smile (Fox, 1930, Arthur Lake, Dixie Lee).

Scamp of the Campus/Shindig/ When You Look in My Eyes/Where Can You Be/You May Not Like It—Ray Klages (w), Jesse Greer (m), Red Star. COVER: Arthur Lake, Dixie Lee.

814 Cherokee Strip (Warner Bros., 1937, Dick Foran, Jane Bryan).

My Little Buckaroo—Jack Scholl (w), M. K. Jerome (m), Witmark. COVER: Dick Foran.

815 Cheyenne Autumn (Warner Bros., 1964, Richard Widmark, Carroll Baker).

Autumn's Ballad—Alex North (m), Witmark. COVER: Richard Widmark, Carroll Baker, Edward G. Robinson.

816 Child Is Waiting, A (United Artists, 1963, Judy Garland, Burt Lancaster).

Snowflakes—Marjorie Kurtz (w, m), Lombardo. COVER: Judy Garland, Burt Lancaster.

817 Children of a Lesser God (Paramount, 1986, Marlee Matlin, William Hurt).

Boomerang—Michael Convertino (w,m), Ensign. COVER: William Hurt, Marlee Matlin.

818 Children of Chance (First National, 1930, Elissa Landi, John Stuart).

He's My Secret Passion (B)—Val Valentine (w), Arthur Young (m), Hawkes. COVER: Elissa Landi, John Stuart.

818a Children of Dreams (Warner, 1931, Paul Gregory, Margaret Schilling).

Children of Dreams Music Score— Oscar Hammerstein (w), Sigmund Romberg (m), Harms. COVER: Black and white cover with title only.

819 Children of Pleasure (MGM, 1930, Lawrence Gray, Wynne Gibson).

Couple of Birds, A—Howard Johnson, George Ward (w), Reggie Montgomery (m), Robbins; Dust—Andy Rice (w), Fred Fisher (m), Robbins; Girl Trouble—Fred Fisher (w,m), Robbins; Leave It That Way—Andy Rice (w), Fred Fisher (m), Robbins; Whole Darned Thing's for You, The —Roy Turk (w), Fred Ahlert (m), Robbins. COVER: Pianist and Girls.

820 Children of the Ritz (First National, 1929, Dorothy Mackaill, Jack Mulhall).

Some Sweet Day—Nat Shilkret, Lew Pollack (w,m), Remick. COVER: Dorothy Mackaill.

821 China Gate (20th Century-Fox, 1957, Gene Barry, King Cole).

China Gate—Harold Adamson (w), Victor Young (m), Young. COVER: King Cole.

822 China Seas (MGM, 1935, Clark Gable, Jean Harlow).

China Seas—Arthur Freed (w), Nacio Herb Brown (m), Robbins. COVER: Clark Gable, Jean Harlow.

823 China Syndrome (Columbia, 1979, Jane Fonda, Jack Lemmon).

Somewhere in Between—Stephen Bishop (w,m), Gold Horizon. COVER: Black and yellow cover with title only.

824 Chinatown   (Paramount, 1974, Jack Nicholson, Faye Dunaway).

Chinatown Theme—Jerry Goldsmith (m), Ensign. COVER: Jack Nicholson, Faye Dunaway.

825 Chip Off the Old Block (Universal, 1944, Donald O'Connor, Peggy Ryan).

It's Mighty Nice to Have Met You —Bill Crago (w), Grace Shannon (m), Lincoln. COVER: Donald O'Connor,

Peggy Ryan, Ann Blyth.

826 Chip of the Flying "U" (Universal, 1940, Bob Baker, Johnny Mack Brown).

Git-a-long/Mister Moon/Ride On— Everett Carter (w), Milton Rosen (m), Robbins. COVER: Bob Baker.

827 Chitty Chitty Bang Bang (United Artists, 1968, Dick Van Dyke, Sally Ann Howes).

Chitty Chitty Bang Bang/Chuchi Face/Hushabye   Mountain/Lovely Lonely Man/Me Ol' Bamboo/Roses of Success, The/Toot Sweets/Truly Scrumptious/You Two/Doll on a Music Box (VS)/Fun Fair (VS)/ Posh (VS)/Vulgarian March (VS)— Richard Sherman, Robert Sherman (w,m), Unart. COVER: Dick Van Dyke, Sally Ann Howes.

828 Chocolate Soldier, The (MGM, 1941, Nelson Eddy, Rise Stevens).

Evening Star—Richard Wagner (w, m), Witmark; My Hero/Sympathy/ Tiralala—Stanislaus Stange (w), Oscar Straus (m), Witmark; While My Lady Sleeps—Gus Kahn (w), Bronislau Kaper (m), Feist. COVER: Nelson Eddy, Rise Stevens.

829 Chorus Line, A (Columbia, 1985, Michael Douglas, Terrance Mann).

Surprise Surprise/What I Did for Love/At the Ballet (VS)/Dance Ten, Looks   Three   (VS)/Hello   Twelve Hello Thirteen (VS)/I Can Do That (VS)/I Hope I Get It (VS)/Let Me Dance for You (VS)/Nothing (VS)/ One (VS)/Who Am I Anyway? (VS) —Edward Kleban (w), Marvin Hamlisch (m), MPL. COVER: Dancers.

830 Christina (Fox, 1929, Janet Gaynor, Charles Morton).

Christina—Archie   Gottler,   Con Conrad,   Sidney   Mitchell   (w,m), DBH. COVER: Janet Gaynor.

831 Christmas Holiday (Universal, 1944, Deanna Durbin, Gene Kelly).

Always—Irving Berlin (w,m), Berlin; Spring Will Be a Little Late This Year—Frank Loesser (w,m), Saunders. COVER: Deanna Durbin.

832 Christmas in Connecticut (Warner Bros., 1945, Barbara Stanwyck, Dennis Morgan).

Wish That I Wish Tonight, The—Jack Scholl (w), M. K. Jerome (m), Witmark. COVER: Barbara Stanwyck, Dennis Morgan.

833 Christmas That Almost Wasn't, The (Childhood, 1966, Rosanno Brazzi, Paul Tripp).

I've Got a Date with Santa/Why Can't Every Day Be Christmas—Paul Tripp (w), Ray Carter (m), Fantasy. COVER: Sketches.

834 Christopher Strong (RKO, 1933, Katharine Hepburn, Colin Clive).

Blue Lagoon/Morena—Max Steiner (m), Sam Fox. COVER: RKO Tower.

835 Chu Chin Chow (GB, 1934, Anna May Wong, George Robey).

Anytime's Kissing Time/Cleopatra's Nile/Cobbler's Song/Corraline/ Here Be Oysters Stewed in Honey/ My Desert Flower/Robbers' March— Oscar Asche (w), Frederick Norton (m), Marks. COVER: Anna May Wong.

836 Cigarette Girl (Columbia, 1947, Leslie Brooks, Jimmy Lloyd).

It's All in the Mind—Allan Roberts, Doris Fisher (w,m), Mood. COVER: Leslie Brooks, Russ Morgan.

837 Cimarron (MGM, 1960, Glenn Ford, Anne Baxter).

Cimarron—Paul F. Webster (w), Franz Waxman (m), Robbins. COVER: Glenn Ford, Maria Schell.

838 Cincinnati Kid, The (MGM, 1965, Steve McQueen, Ann Margret).

Cincinnati Kid, The—Dorcas Cochran (w), Lalo Schifrin (m), Hastings. COVER: Steve McQueen, Ann Margret.

839 Cinderella (RKO Disney, 1949, Cartoon).

Bibbidi-Bobbidi-Boo/Cinderella/ Dream Is a Wish Your Heart Makes, A/Oh Sing Sweet Nightingale/So This Is Love/Work Song, The—Mack David, Al Hoffman, Jerry Livingston (w,m), Disney. COVER: Cartoon.

840 Cinderella Jones (Warner Bros., 1946, Joan Leslie, Robert Alda).

Cinderella Jones/When the One You Love/You Never Know Where You're Goin'—Sammy Cahn (w), Jule Styne (m), Remick. COVER: Joan Leslie, Robert Alda.

841 Cinderella Liberty (20th Century-Fox, 1973, James Caan, Marsha Mason).

Nice to Be Around/Wednesday Special—Paul Williams (w), John Williams (m), 20th Century. COVER: James Caan, Marsha Mason.

842 Cinderfella (Paramount, 1960, Jerry Lewis, Ed Wynn).

Let Me Be a People/Other Fella, The—Jack Brooks (w), Harry Warren (m), Famous; Princess Waltz— Jack Brooks (w), Harry Warren, Walter Scharf (m), Famous; Somebody— Jack Brooks (w), Harry Warren (m), Famous. COVER: Jerry Lewis, Anna Maria Alberghetti, Ed Wynn.

843 Cinerama Holiday (Cinerama, 1955, Fred Troller, Beatrice Troller).

Along a Lonesome Trail/Cinerama Holiday—Jack Lawrence (w), Morton Gould (m), Chappell; Hail to Our Land—James Peterson, Jack Shaindln (w,m), Chappell; Holiday in Rio— Terig Tucci (m), Alpha; Cinerama Themes—Morton Gould (m), Chappell. COVER: Couple on a Carousel.

844 Circle of Danger (RKO, 1951, Ray Milland, Patricia Roc).

White Heather (B)—Michael Carr (w), Robert Farnon (m), Chappell. COVER: Ray Milland, Patricia Roc.

845 Circus, The (United Artists, 1928, Charlie Chaplin, Merna Kennedy).

Thinking of You (Promotion Song)—Joseph Grey (w), Allie Moore (m), Eden. COVER: Charlie Chaplin.

846 Circus, The (Independent, 1979, Stars Unknown).

Computer Game—Haruomi Ho-sono, Ryuichi Sakamoto, Yukihiro Takahashi (w,m), Almo. COVER: Three Young Men.

847 Circus Days (First National, 1923, Jackie Coogan, Peaches Jackson).

Circus Days in Our One Horse Town—Leon DeCosta (w,m), Remick; Circus Days, Oh You Circus Days—Edith Lessing, Jimmie Monaco (w,m), Rossiter. COVER: Jackie Coogan.

848 Circus of Horrors (AIP, 1960, Erika Remberg, Anton Diffring).

Look for a Star—Mark Anthony (w,m), Filmusic. COVER: Anton Diffring, Erika Remberg, Yvonne Monlaur.

849 Circus World (Paramount, 1964, John Wayne, Rita Hayworth).

Circus World—Ned Washington (w), Dimitri Tiomkin (m), Feist; First Dance/Circus World-Ten Themes—Dimitri Tiomkin (m), Feist. COVER: Circus Stars.

850 Cisco Kid, The (Fox, 1932, Warner Baxter, Edmond Lowe).

Song of the Cisco Kid—Warner Baxter (w,m), Movietone; Song of the Fisher Maidens—William Kernell (w,m), Movietone. COVER: Black and white cover with title only.

851 Citizen Saint (Saint Xavier Cabrini) (Elliott, 1947, Carla Dare, Julie Hayden).

Saint Francis Cabrini—Harold Orlob (w,m), Milton; Star That Lights the Midnight Sea—Arthur Norris (w, m), Milton. COVER: Mother Cabrini.

852 City Beneath the Sea (Universal, 1953, Robert Ryan, Mala Powers).

Handle with Care/Time for Love—Fred Herbert (w), Arnold Hughes (m), Mills. COVER: Robert Ryan, and Movie Scenes.

853 City for Conquest (Warner Bros., 1940, Ann Sheridan, James Cagney).

Where Were You When the Moon Came Out? (Q)—Max Steiner (m), Witmark. COVER: Black and white cover with title only.

854 City Girl (Fox, 1930, Charles Farrell, Mary Duncan).

In the Valley of My Dreams—Pierre Norman, James Hanley (w,m), DBH. COVER: Black and white cover with title only.

855 City Lights (United Artists, 1931, Charlie Chaplin, Virginia Cherrill).

City Lights (B)—Reginald Arkell (w), H. M. Tennent (m), Tennett. COVER: Skyscrapers.

856 City That Stopped Hitler, The (Paramount, 1942, War Documentary).

Song of Stalingrad—Harold Rome (w), V. Mokrousov (m), Amrus. COVER: Soldiers.

857 Civilization (Ince, 1916, Howard Hickman, Enid Markey).

Our Own Beloved Land—Thomas Ince (w), Victor Schertzinger (m), Feist; Peace Song—Victor Schertzinger (m), Feist. COVER: Movie Scenes.

858 Clambake (United Artists, Elvis Presley, Shelley Fabares).

Clambake—Sid Wayne (w), Ben Weisman (m), Gladys; Confidence—Sid Tepper, Roy Bennett (w,m), Gladys; Girl I Never Loved, The—Randy Starr (w,m), Gladys; Hey Hey Hey—Joy Byers (w,m), Gladys; House That Has Everything, A—Sid Tepper, Roy Bennett (w,m), Gladys; Who Needs Money?—Randy Starr (w,m), Gladys. COVER: Elvis Presley.

859 Clarence, The Cross-Eyed Lion (MGM, 1965, Marshall Thompson, Betsy Drake).

Clarence the Cross-Eyed Lion—Ray Stevens, Bob Tubert (w,m), Hastings. COVER: Marshall Thompson, Betsy Drake, and Lion.

860 Clash by Night (RKO, 1952, Barbara Stanwyck, Paul Douglas).

Don't Cry—Sunny Skylar (w,m), BMI: Don't Get Married Til You Fall in Love—Billie Webber (w), Imogene Carpenter (m), BMI; I Hear a

Rhapsody—George Fragos, Jack Baker, Dick Gasparre (w,m), BMI. COVER: Barbara Stanwyck, Paul Douglas.

861   Clash of the Titans (United Artists, 1981, Laurence Olivier, Claire Bloom).

Lovers, The—Laurence Rosenthal (m), Warner. COVER: Flying Horse.

862   Class of 1984 (UFD, 1982, Perry King, Merne Lynn).

I Am the Future—Gary Osborne (w), Lalo Schifrin (m), Scherzo. COVER: Punk Rock Hoods.

863   Claudine (20th Century-Fox, 1974, Diahann Carroll, James Earl Jones).

On and On/Claudine-Selections—Curtis Mayfield (w,m), Curtom. COVER: Gladys Knight and Pips.

864   Claws of the Hun (Paramount, 1918, Charles Ray, Jane Novak).

I'm Giving You to Uncle Sam—Thomas Ince (w), Victor Schertzinger (m), Hart. COVER: Soldier and Flag.

865   Clean Shaven Man, A (Paramount, 1936, Cartoon).

I Want a Clean Shaven Man (VS)—Dave Fleischer (w), Sammy Timberg (m), Famous. COVER: Popeye.

866   Cleo from Five to Seven (Zenith, 1962, Corinne Marchand, Antoine Bourseiller).

You're Gone (VS)—Mort Goode (w), Michel Legrand (m), Beaujolais. COVER: Michel Legrand.

867   Cleopatra (Fox, 1918, Theda Bara, Fritz Leiber).

In Egypt—Tom Hill (w,m), Songshop. COVER: Movie Scene.

868   Cleopatra (20th Century-Fox, 1963, Richard Burton, Elizabeth Taylor).

Anthony and Cleopatra Theme/Caesar and Cleopatra Theme—Alex North (m), Robbins; Nile, The—Johnny Mercer (w), Alex North (m), Robbins; World of Love, A—Sid Wayne (w), Alex North (m), Robbins; Cleopatra-Nine Themes—Alex North (m), Robbins. COVER: Elizabeth Taylor, Richard Burton, Rex Harrison.

869   Cleopatra Jones (Warner Bros., 1973, Shelley Winters, Tamara Dobson).

Cleopatra Jones Theme—Joe Simon (m), Warner. COVER: Tamara Dobson.

870   Climax, The (Universal, 1927, Jean Hersholt, Kathryn Crawford).

Chalita/Song of the Soul—Edward Locke (w), Joseph Breil (m), Chappell; You, My Melody of Love—Victor Schertzinger (w,m), Harms. COVER: Jean Hersholt, Kathryn Crawford.

871   Climax, The (Universal, 1944, Susanna Foster, Turhan Bey).

Now at Last/Some Day I Know—George Waggner (w), Edward Ward (m), Robbins. COVER: Susanna Foster, Turhan Bey.

872   Clockwork Orange, A (Warner Bros., 1971, Malcolm MacDowell, Patrick Magee).

Clock-work Orange March—Walter Carlos (m); Clock-work Orange Theme—Rachel Elkind (w), Walter Carlos (m); Pomp and Circumstance #1, #4 (VS)—Edward Elgar (m); Singin' in the Rain (VS)—Arthur Freed (w), Nacio Herb Brown (m); Suicide Scherzo (VS)—Ludwig Von Beethoven (m); Thieving Magpie (VS)—G. Rossini (m); Timesteps (VS)—Walter Carlos (m); Clockwork Orange Title Music (VS)—Walter Carlos (m); William Tell Overture (VS)—G. Rossini (m). PUB. Hansen. COVER: Orange, Clock, and Time Bomb.

873   Close Encounters of the Third Kind (Columbia, 1977, Richard Dreyfuss, Teri Garr).

Close Encounters Theme/Mother Ship and the Mountain (VS)/Mountain (VS)/Close Encounters Complete Theme (VS)—John Williams (m), Gold Horizon; When You Wish Upon a Star (VS)—Ned Washington (w), Leigh Harline (m), Gold Horizon. COVER: Movie Scenes.

874 **Close Harmony** (Paramount, 1929, Nancy Carroll, Charles Rogers).

I'm All A-Twitter/I Wanna Go Places—Leo Robin (w), Richard Whiting (m), Famous; Twelfth Street Rag —Euday Bowman (m), Jenkins. COVER: Charles Rogers, Nancy Carroll.

875 **Clowns, The** (Pickman, 1971, Billi and Scotti).

Clowns, The—Ray Fox (w), Nino Rota (m), Marks; Clowns March, The —Nino Rota (m), Marks; Ebb Tide (VS)—Carl Sigman (w), Robert Maxwell (m), Robbins. COVER: Clowns.

876 **Clue** (Paramount, 1985, Eileen Brennan, Tim Curry).

Clue Theme—John Morris (m), Famous. COVER: Eileen Brennan, Tim Curry, and Other Stars.

877 **"C" Man** (Film Classics, 1949, Dean Jagger, Lottie Elwen).

Do It Now—Larry Neill (w), Gail Kubik (m), Jefferson. COVER: Dean Jagger, Lottie Elwen.

878 **C'Mon Let's Live a Little** (Paramount, 1967, Bobby Vee, Jackie DeShannon).

Back Talk/C'Mon Let's Live a Little/For Granted/Instant Girl/Let's Go Go/Over and Over/Tonight's the Night—Don Crawford (w,m), Tongass. COVER: Movie Scenes.

879 **Coal Miner's Daughter** (Universal, 1980, Sissy Spacek, Tommy Lee Jones).

Coal Miner's Daughter—Loretta Lynn (w,m), Sure Fire. COVER: Sissy Spacek.

880 **Cobra** (Paramount, 1925, Rudolph Valentino, Nita Naldi).

Playing at Love (B)—William Helmore (w,m), Day. COVER: Rudolph Valentino.

881 **Cockeyed Cavaliers** (RKO, 1934, Bert Wheeler, Bob Woolsey).

And the Big Bad Wolf Was Dead/Dilly Dally—Will Jason, Val Burton (w,m), Berlin. COVER: Bert Wheeler, Bob Wollsey.

882 **Cockeyed World** (Fox, 1929, Victor McLaglen, Lili Damita).

So Dear to Me—Con Conrad, Sidney Mitchell, Archie Gottler, DBH. COVER: Victor McLaglen, Lili Damita, Edmond Lowe.

883 **Cockleshell Heroes** (Columbia, 1955, Jose Ferrer, Trevor Howard).

Cockleshell Heroes—Vivian Dunn (m), Chappell; London I Love, The/Something Happened to My Heart—Harold Purcell (w), George Posford (m), Chappell. COVER: Jose Ferrer, Trevor Howard, Yana.

884 **Cock of the Air** (United Artists, 1932, Billie Dove, Chester Morris).

Love Me/Puppets on Parade—Dave Silverstein, Bernie Grossman (w), Alfred Newman (m), Shapiro Bernstein. COVER: Billie Dove, Chester Morris.

885 **Cock o' the Walk** (Sono Art, 1930, Myrna Loy, Joseph Schildkraut).

Play Me a Tango Tune—Lynn Cowan, Paul Titsworth (w,m), Shapiro Bernstein. COVER: Myrna Loy, Joseph Schildkraut.

886 **Cocktail** (Touchstone, 1988, Tom Cruise, Bryan Brown).

Kokomo—Mike Love, Terry Melcher, John Phillips, Scott MacKenzie (w,m), Disney; All Shook Up (VS)—Otis Blackwell, Elvis Presley (w,m), Leonard; Don't Worry Be Happy (VS)—Bobby McFerrin (w,m), Leonard; Hippy Happy Shake (VS)—C. Romero (w,m), Leonard; Oh I Love You So (VS)—Preston Smith (w,m), Leonard; Powerful Stuff (VS)—Wally Wilson, Michael Henderson, Robert Field (w,m), Leonard; Rave On (VS)—Sonny West, Norman Petty, Bill Tilghman (w,m), Leonard; Since When (VS)—Robert Nevil, Brock Walsh (w,m), Leonard; Tutti Frutti (VS)—R. Penniman, D. LaBostrie (w,m), Leonard; Wild Again (VS)—John Bettis, Michael Clark (w, m), Leonard. COVER: Tom Cruise.

887 **Cocktail Hour** (Columbia, 1933, Bebe Daniels, Sidney Blackmer).

Listen Heart of Mine—Victor

Schertzinger (w,m), Harms. COVER: Bebe Daniels, Sidney Blackmer.

888 Cocoanut Grove (Paramount, 1938, Fred MacMurray, Harriet Hilliard).

Cocoanut Grove/Dreamy Hawaiian Moon—Harry Owens (w,m), Famous; Says My Heart—Frank Loesser (w), Burton Lane (m), Famous; You Leave Me Breathless—Ralph Freed (w), Frederick Hollander (m), Famous. COVER: Fred MacMurray, Harriet Hilliard.

889 Cocoanuts (Paramount, 1929, Mary Eaton, Oscar Shaw).

When My Dreams Come True—Irving Berlin (w,m), Berlin. COVER: Mary Eaton, Oscar Shaw.

890 Cohens and Kellys in Hollywood (Universal, 1932, George Sidney, Charlie Murray).

Where Are You, Girl of My Dreams—Bing Crosby, Irving Bibo, Paul McVey (w,m), Bibo. COVER: George Sidney, Charlie Murray.

891 Cold Turkey (United Artists, 1971, Dick Van Dyke, Pippa Scott).

He Gives Us All His Love—Randy Newman (w,m), Unart. COVER: Cartoon.

892 Collector, The (Columbia, 1965, Terence Stamp, Samantha Eggar).

Collector, The—Maurice Jarre (m), Screen Gems. COVER: Terence Stamp, Samantha Eggar.

893 Colleen (Warner Bros., 1936, Dick Powell, Ruby Keeler).

Boulevardier from the Bronx/Evening with You, An/I Don't Have to Dream Again/You Gotta Know How to Dance—Al Dubin (w), Harry Warren (m), Witmark. COVER: Dick Powell, Ruby Keeler.

894 College Coach (Warner Bros., 1933, Dick Powell, Ann Dvorak).

Lonely Lane—Irving Kahal (w), Sammy Fain (m), Remick. COVER: Dick Powell.

895 College Confidential (Universal, 1960, Steve Allen, Jayne Meadows).

College Confidential/Playmates—Randy Sparks (w,m), Northern; So Be It!—Steve Allen (w,m), Rosemeadow. COVER: Randy Sparks, Steve Allen.

896 College Days (So This Is College) (MGM, 1928, Elliott Nugent, Robert Montgomery).

Campus Capers—Charlotte Greenwood (w), Martin Broones (m), MGM; College Days—Al Boasberg (w), Martin Broones (m), MGM; I Don't Want Your Kisses—Fred Fisher, Martin Broones (w,m), MGM; Sophomore Prom—Ray Klages (w), Jesse Greer (m), MGM; Until the End—Fred Fisher, Martin Broones, Al Boasberg (w,m), MGM. COVER: Black and white cover with title only.

897 College Holiday (Paramount, 1936, Jack Benny, George Burns).

I Adore You/Rhyme for Love/So What?—Leo Robin, Ralph Rainger (w,m), Famous; Sweetheart Waltz, The/Who's That Knockin' at My Heart?—Ralph Freed (w), Burton Lane (m), Famous. COVER: Jack Benny, Martha Raye, George Burns, Gracie Allen.

898 College Humor (Paramount, 1933, Bing Crosby, Jack Oakie).

Down the Old Ox Road/Learn to Croon/Moonstruck—Sam Coslow (w), Arthur Johnston (m), Famous. COVER: Bing Crosby, Mary Carlisle, Jack Oakie.

899 College Love (Universal, 1929, George Lewis, Dorothy Gulliver).

It's You/Oh! How We Love Our College—Dave Silverstein, Lee Zahler (w,m), Shapiro Bernstein. COVER: George Lewis, Dorothy Gulliver.

900 College Rhythm (Paramount, 1934, Joe Penner, Lanny Ross).

College Rhythm/Let's Give Three Cheers for Love/Stay as Sweet as You Are/Take a Number from One to Ten—Mack Gordon, Harry Revel (w,m), DBH. COVER: Joe Penner, Jack Oakie, Lanny Ross.

901 College Scandal (Paramount,

1935, Kent Taylor, Arline Judge).

In the Middle of a Kiss—Sam Coslow (w,m), Famous. COVER: Arline Judge.

902 College Swing (Paramount, 1938, George Burns, Gracie Allen).

College Swing—Frank Loesser (w), Hoagy Carmichael (m), Famous; How'dja Like to Love Me—Frank Loesser (w), Burton Lane (m), Famous; I Fall in Love with You Every Day—Frank Loesser (w), Manning Sherwin (m), Famous; Moments Like This—Frank Loesser (w), Burton Lane (m), Famous; What a Rumba Does to Romance—Frank Loesser (w), Manning Sherwin (m), Famous; What Did Romeo Say to Juliet—Frank Loesser (w), Burton Lane (m), Famous; You're a Natural—Frank Loesser (w), Manning Sherwin (m), Famous. COVER: George Burns, Gracie Allen, Martha Raye, Bob Hope, Betty Grable.

903 Collegiate   (Paramount, 1936, Joe Penner, Jack Oakie).

Guess Again/I Feel Like a Feather in the Breeze/Learn to Be Lovely/My Grandfather's Clock in the Hallway/Rhythmatic/Who Am I?/Will I Ever Know/You Hit the Spot—Mack Gordon, Harry Revel (w,m), Famous. COVER: Jack Oakie, Betty Grable, Frances Langford.

904 Colorado Sunset (Republic, 1939, Gene Autry, Smiley Burnette).

Colorado Sunset—L. Wolfe Gilbert (w), Con Conrad (m), Gilbert. COVER: A Sunset.

905 Colorado Trails (Columbia, 1938, Charles Starrett, Iris Meredith).

Bound for the Rio Grande (VS)—Bob Nolan (w,m), American; Cottage in the Clouds (VS)—Bob Nolan, Lloyd Perryman (w,m), American; Lone Buckaroo, A (VS)—Bob Nolan (w,m), American. COVER: Bob Nolan.

906 Color Purple, The (Warner Bros., 1985, Danny Glover, Whoopi Goldberg).

Maybe God Is Tryin' to Tell Me Somethin'—Andrae Crouch, Quincy Jones, William Maxwell, David Del Sesto (w,m), Warner; Miss Celie's Blues, Sister—Quincy Jones, Rod Temperton, Lionel Richie (w,m), Warner; Don't Make Me No Never Mind (VS)—Quincy Jones, James Ingram, Roy Gaines (w,m), Warner; Heaven Belongs to You (VS)—Andrae Crouch, Sandra Crouch (w,m), Warner; J. B. King Road Gang Chant (VS)—Traditional, Warner; Katutoka Corrine (VS)—Caiphus Semenya (w,m), Warner; Mailbox, Proud Theme (VS)—Quincy Jones, Rod Temperton, Jeremy Lubbock (w,m), Warner; Scarification Ceremony (VS)—Caiphus Semenya (w,m), Warner; Sisters Theme (VS)—Quincy Jones, Jeremy Lubbock, Jack Hayes, Rod Temperton (w,m), Warner; Sophia's Walk (VS)—Quincy Jones, Randy Kerber, Jerry Hey (w,m), Warner. COVER: Whoopi Goldberg.

907 Coma (MGM, 1977, Michael Douglas, Genevieve Bujold).

Coma Love Theme—Jerry Goldsmith (m), MGM; Sunday's Moon—Carol Heather (w), Jerry Goldsmith (m), MGM. COVER: A Body.

908 Comancheros, The (20th Century-Fox, 1961, John Wayne, Ina Balin).

Comancheros, The—Tillman Franks (w,m), Robbins. COVER: John Wayne, Ina Balin.

909 Come and Get It (United Artists, 1936, Edward Arnold, Frances Farmer).

Aura Lee—Hugo Frey (w,m), Robbins; Bird on Nellie's Hat, The—Arthur Lamb (w), Alfred Solman (m), Marks. COVER: Frances Farmer.

910 Come Back Charleston Blue (Warner Bros., 1972, Godfrey Cambridge, Raymond St. Jacques).

Come Back Charleston Blue—Quincy Jones, Al Cleveland (w), Don Hathaway (m), Warner. COVER: Godfrey Cambridge, Raymond St. Jacques.

911 Come Blow Your Horn (Paramount, 1963, Frank Sinatra Lee J. Cobb).

Come Blow Your Horn—Sammy Cahn (w), James Van Heusen (m), Maraville. COVER: Frank Sinatra.

912 Comedians, The (MGM, 1967, Richard Burton, Elizabeth Taylor).

Comedians Theme—Laurence Rosenthal (m), Feist. COVER: Richard Burton, Elizabeth Taylor.

913 Come Fly with Me (MGM, 1963, Dolores Hart, Hugh O'Brian).

Come Fly with Me—Sammy Cahn (w), James Van Heusen (m), Maraville. COVER: Hugh O'Brian, Dolores Hart, Pamela Tiffin.

914 Come Next Spring (Republic, 1955, Ann Sheridan, Steve Cochran).

Come Next Spring—Lenny Adelson (w), Max Steiner (m), Frank. COVER: Ann Sheridan, Steve Cochran.

915 Come September (Universal, 1961, Rock Hudson, Gina Lollobrigida).

Come September Theme—Bobby Darin(m), Adaris; Multiplication—Bobby Darin (w,m), Adaris. COVER: Rock Hudson, Gina Lollobrigida, Sandra Dee, Bobby Darin.

916 Come to the Stable (20th Century-Fox, 1949, Celeste Holm, Loretta Young).

Through a Long and Sleepless Night—Mack Gordon (w), Alfred Newman (m), Miller. COVER: Loretta Young, Celeste Holm.

917 Comic, The (Columbia, 1969, Dick Van Dyke, Michele Lee).

Comic, The—Larry Kusik, Eddie Snyder (w), Jack Elliott (m), Valencia. COVER: Dennis Yost and Classics.

918 Coming Out Party (Fox, 1934, Frances Dee, Gene Raymond).

I Think You're Wonderful—Harold Adamson (w), Burton Lane (m), Movietone. COVER: Frances Dee.

919 Coming to America (Paramount, 1988, Eddie Murphy, Arsenio Hall).

Come Into My Life—Paul Chiten, Pamela Phillips Oland (w,m), Ensign; Coming to America—Nile Rodgers, Nancy Huang (w,m), Ensign; Addicted to You (VS)—Gerald Levert, Marc Gordon, Ed Levert (w, m), Ensign; All Dressed Up (VS)—Jonathan Moffett (w,m), Ensign; Better Late Than Never (VS)—Freddie Washington, Alan Scott (w, m), Ensign; Comin' Correct (VS)—Dr. Dre (w,m), Ensign; I Like It That Way (VS)—Michael Rodgers, Lloyd Tolbert (w,m), Ensign; Livin' the Good Life (VS)—Nile Rodgers, Gardner Cole (w,m), Ensign; That's the Way It Is (VS)—Stock Waterman (w,m), Ensign; Transparent (VS)—Danny Sembello, Allee Willis (w,m), Ensign. COVER: Eddie Murphy.

920 Comin' Round the Mountain (Republic, 1936, Gene Autry, Ann Rutherford).

Chiquita (VS)/Don Juan of Sevillio (VS)—Oliver Drake (w), Sam Stept (m), Cole; When the Campfire Is Low on the Prairie (VS)—Sam Stept (w,m), Cole. COVER: Gene Autry.

921 Comin' Round the Mountain (Universal, 1951, Bud Abbott, Lou Costello).

Sagebrush Sadie/Why Don't Someone Marry Mary Anne—George Beatty (w), Britt Wood (m), American. COVER: Dorothy Shay.

922 Commandos Strike at Dawn (Columbia, 1942, Paul Muni, Anna Lee).

Commando's March—Ann Ronell (w), Louis Gruenberg, Ann Ronell (m), Mills; Out to Pick Berries—Ann Ronell (w,m). COVER: Commandos.

923 Command Performance (GFD, 1937, Arthur Tracy, Lili Palmer).

Dance! Gypsy Dance!—Stanley Damerell (w), Tolchard Evans (m), Mills; Whistling Gypsy (B)—Stanley Damerell (w), Tolchard Evans (m), Lennox. COVER: Arthur Tracy.

924 Competition (Columbia, 1980, Amy Irving, Richard Dreyfuss).

Competition Love Theme–Wilbur Jennings (w), Lalo Schifrin (m), Gold Horizon; People Alone–Lalo Schifrin (m), Gold Horizon. COVER: Amy Irving, Richard Dreyfuss.

925 Compulsion (20th Century-Fox, 1959, Orson Welles, Diane Varsi).

Compulsion Theme–Lionel Newman (m), Weiss Barry. COVER: Dean Stockwell, Bradford Dillman, Orson Welles.

926 Condemned (United Artists, 1929, Ronald Colman, Ann Harding).

Song of the Condemned–Jack Meskill (w), Pete Wendling (m), Berlin. COVER: Ronald Colman.

927 Coney Island (20th Century-Fox, 1943, Betty Grable, George Montgomery).

Beautiful Coney Island–Leo Robin (w), Ralph Rainger (m), Miller; Cuddle Up a Little Closer–Otto Harbach (w), Karl Hoschna (m), Witmark; Miss Lulu from Louisville–Leo Robin (w), Ralph Rainger (m), Miller; Put Your Arms Around Me Honey–Junie McCree (w), Albert Von Tilzer (m), Broadway; Take It from There/There's Danger in a Dance–Leo Robin (w), Ralph Rainger (m), Miller; Who Threw the Overalls in Mistress Murphy's Chowder?–George Giefer (w,m), Marks. COVER: Betty Grable, George Montgomery.

928 Congorilla (Fox, 1932, African Documentary).

Congorilla–Al Bryan (w), Louis DeFrancesco (m), Movietone. COVER: Chester Towne, Helen Knott, and Natives.

929 Congress Dances (Der Kongress Tanst) (United Artists, 1932, Lilian Harvey, Conrad Veidt).

Live, Laugh and Love/Just Once for All Time/When the Music Plays –Rowland Leigh (w), Werner Heymann (m), Harms. COVER: Lilian Harvey.

930 Connecticut Yankee in King Arthur's Court, A (Fox, 1921, Harry Myers, Pauline Starke).

Connecticut Yankee, A–Walter Hirsch (w), Robert King (m), Shapiro Bernstein. COVER: Harry Myers.

931 Connecticut Yankee in King Arthur's Court, A (Paramount, 1949, Bing Crosby, Rhonda Fleming).

Busy Doing Nothing/If You Stub Your Toe on the Moon/Once and for Always/Twixt Myself and Me/When Is Sometime?–Johnny Burke (w), James Van Heusen (m), BVH. COVER: Bing Crosby, Rhonda Fleming.

932 Conqueror, The (RKO, 1956, John Wayne, Susan Hayward).

Conqueror, The–Edward Heyman (w), Victor Young (m), Young. COVER: John Wayne, Susan Hayward.

933 Conquerors, The (RKO, 1931, Richard Dix, Ann Harding).

Conquerors Theme–Max Steiner (m), Sam Fox. COVER: RKO Tower.

934 Consolation Marriage (RKO, 1931, Irene Dunne, Pat O'Brien).

Devotion–Myles Connolly (w), Max Steiner (m), Sam Fox. COVER: Irene Dunne.

935 Conspirators, The (Warner Bros., 1944, Hedy Lamarr, Paul Henreid).

Orchid Moon–Al Stillman (w), Max Steiner (m), Sam Fox. COVER: Hedy Lamarr, Paul Henreid.

936 Constant Nymph (Warner Bros., 1943, Charles Boyer, Joan Fontaine).

Tomorrow–Margaret Kennedy (w), Erich W. Korngold (m), Witmark. COVER: A Pianist.

937 Continental Rose (Universal, 1946, Musical Short).

Beautiful Carnation (PC)–Danny Kuana (w), Bernei Kaai (m), Peer. COVER: None.

938 Convention Girl (Universal, 1935, Rose Hobart, Sally O'Neill).

Sand in My Shoes/You Ought to

Be Arrested—Arthur Swanstrom (w), Louis Alter (m), Remick. COVER: Rose Hobart, Herbert Rawlinson.

939 Conversation, The (Paramount, 1974, Gene Hackman, John Cazale).

Conversation Theme—David Shire (m), Ensign. COVER: Gene Hackman.

940 Cool Breeze (MGM, 1972, Thalmus Rasulala, Judy Pace).

We're Almost Home—Solomon Burke, Jr., Solomon Burke, Sr. (w, m), Hastings. COVER: Judy Pace, Jim Watkins.

941 Cool Hand Luke (Warner Bros., 1968, Paul Newman, George Kennedy).

Down Here on the Ground—Gale Garnett (w), Lalo Schifrin (m), Warner. COVER: Paul Newman.

942 Cool Ones, The. (Warner Bros., 1967, Roddy McDowall, Debbie Watson).

High—Billy Strange, Lee Hazlewood (w,m), Remick; It's Your World/This Town—Lee Hazlewood (w,m), Remick. COVER: Roddy McDowall, Phil Harris, Debbie Watson, Gil Peterson.

943 Cop, The (Pathe, 1928, William Boyd, Jacqueline Logan).

Always the Same Sweet Pal—Charles Weinberg, Billy Stone (w,m), Shapiro Bernstein. COVER: William Boyd, Jacqueline Logan.

944 Copacabana (United Artists, 1947, Groucho Marx, Carmen Miranda).

Go West Young Man—Bert Kalmar (w), Harry Ruby (m), Blossom; Je Vous Aime/My Heart Was Doing a Bolero/Stranger Things Have Happened—Sam Coslow (w,m), Crawford. COVER: Groucho Marx, Carmen Miranda, and Other Stars.

945 Copenhagen (MGM, 1937, Travelogue).

Copenhagen Love Song—Sam Ward (w), Jack Shilkret (m), Southern. COVER: Danish Couple.

946 Copper Canyon (Paramount, 1950, Hedy Lamarr, Ray Milland).

Copper Canyon—Jay Livingston, Ray Evans (w,m), Famous. COVER: Hedy Lamarr, Ray Milland.

947 Coquette (United Artists, 1929, Mary Pickford, Johnny Mack Brown).

Coquette—Irving Berlin (w,m), Berlin. COVER: Mary Pickford.

948 Coronado (Paramount, 1935, Johnny Downs, Betty Burgess).

All's Well/Down on the Isle of Oomph/How Do I Rate with You—Sam Coslow, Richard Whiting (w,m), Famous; I've Got Some New Shoes—Sam Coslow, Richard Whiting, Walter Bullock (w,m), Famous; Keep Your Fingers Crossed/You Took My Breath Away—Sam Coslow, Richard Whiting (w,m), Famous. COVER: Johnny Downs, Betty Burgess, Eddy Duchin.

949 Corpse Came C.O.D., The (Columbia, 1947, George Brent, Joan Blondell).

Warm Kiss—Allan Roberts, Doris Fisher (w,m), Mood. COVER: George Brent, Joan Blondell, Adele Jergens.

950 Corruption (Columbia, 1968, Peter Cushing, Sue Lloyd).

Corruption (B)—Bill McGuffie (m), Titan. COVER: Peter Cushing, Sue Lloyd.

951 Corrupt Ones, The (Warner Bros., 1966, Robert Stack, Elke Sommer).

Corrupt Ones, The—Buddy Kaye (w), Georges Carvarentz (m), Raintree. COVER: Elke Sommer.

952 Corvette Summer (United Artists, 1978, Mark Hamill, Annie Potts).

Give Me the Night—Craig Safan (w,m), MGM. COVER: Mark Hamill, Annie Potts.

953 Cossacks, The (MGM, 1928, John Gilbert, Renee Adoree).

Maryana (B)—Ted Pola, Eddie Brandt (w,m), Thornburn. COVER: John Gilbert, Renee Adoree.

954 Costumes of the World (Vitaphone, 1933, Musical Short).

Costumes of the World—David Mendoza (w,m), Witmark. COVER: Black and white cover with title only.

955 Cotton Club, The (Orion, 1985, Richard Gere, Diane Lane).

Best Beats Sandman (VS)—John Barry (m), Belwin Mills; Copper Colored Gal (VS)—Benny Davis, Fred Coots (w,m), Belwin Mills; Cotton Club Stomp #1 & #2 (VS)/Creole Love Call (VS)/Daybreak Express (VS)—Duke Ellington (m), Belwin Mills; Depression Hits (VS)/Dixie Kidnaps Verna (VS)—John Barry (m), Belwin Mills; Drop Me Off in Harlem (VS)—Nick Kenny (w), Duke Ellington (m), Belwin Mills; East St. Louis Toodle-O (VS)—Bob Miley (w), Duke Ellington (m), Belwin Mills; Ill Wind (VS)—Ted Koehler (w), Harold Arlen (m), Belwin Mills; Minnie the Moocher (VS)—Cab Calloway, Irving Mills, Clarence Gaskill (w,m), Belwin Mills; Mooche (VS)—Irving Mills (w), Duke Ellington (m), Belwin Mills; Mood Indigo (VS)—Duke Ellington, Irving Mills, Albany Bigard (w,m), Belwin Mills; Ring Dem Bells (VS)—Duke Ellington, Irving Mills (w,m), Belwin Mills; Truckin' (VS)—Ted Koehler (w), Rube Bloom (m), Belwin Mills. COVER: Machine Gun.

956 Cotton Comes to Harlem (United Artists, 1970, Godfrey Cambridge, Raymond St. Jacques).

Cotton Comes to Harlem—Joe Lewis (w), Galt McDermott (m), Unart. COVER: Godfrey Cambridge, Raymond St. Jacques.

957 Counterfeit Traitor, The (Paramount, 1962, William Holden, Lili Palmer).

Marianna—Paul F. Webster (w), Alfred Newman (m), Paramount. COVER: William Holden, Lili Palmer.

958 Countess from Hong Kong, A (Universal, 1966, Marlon Brando, Sophia Loren).

Ambassador Retires (B)—Charlie Chaplin (m); Bon Jour Madame, (w, m); Chamber Music (B)/Change Partners (B), (m); Countess from Hong Kong, A, (w,m); Countess Sleeps, The (B)/Crossing the Dance Floor (B)/Gipsy Violin Caprice (B)/Hudson Goes to Bed (B)/Ill Fitting Dress (B), (m); My Star, (w,m); Occidental and Oriental (B)/Perdu (B)/Tango Natascha (B)/Taxi Waltz (B)/This Is My Song/Three Ladies (B), (m), Leeds. COVER: Charlie Chaplin.

959 Countess of Monte Cristo, The (Universal, 1948, Sonja Henie, Olga San Juan).

Count Your Blessings/Friendly Polka/Who Believes in Santa Claus—Jack Brooks (w), Saul Chaplin (m), Robert. COVER: Sonja Henie.

960 Count of Monte Cristo, The (United Artists, 1934, Robert Donat, Elissa Landi).

Love Is in Command—Joe Young (w), Lew Pollack (m), DBH; World Is Mine, The—E. Y. Harburg (w), Johnny Green (m), Harms. COVER: Robert Donat, Elissa Landi.

961 Country Cousin, The (Selznick, 1920, Marguerite Sidden, Elaine Hammerstein).

Country Cousin—Alfred Bryan (w), Vincent Youmans (m), Remick. COVER: Elaine Hammerstein.

962 Country Girl, The (Paramount, 1954, Bing Crosby, Grace Kelly).

Dissertation on a State of Bliss/Search Is Through, The—Ira Gershwin (w), Harold Arlen (m), Harwin. COVER: Bing Crosby, Grace Kelly, William Holden.

963 Country Kid, The (Warner Bros., 1923, Wesley Barry, Spec O'Donnell).

That Old Gang of Mine—Billy Rose, Mort Dixon (w), Ray Henderson (m), Berlin. COVER: Wesley Barry.

964 Country Music Holiday (Paramount, 1958, Ferlin Husky, Rocky Graziano).

Country Music Holiday—Hal

David (w), Burt Bacharach (m), Famous; When It Rains It Pours—Slick Slavin (w,m), Central. COVER: Zsa Zsa Gabor, Ferlin Husky.

965   Count Your Blessings (MGM, 1959, Deborah Kerr, Rosanno Brazzi).

Count Your Blessings Theme—Franz Waxman (m), Robbins. COVER: Purple cover with title only.

966   Court Jester, The (Paramount, 1956, Danny Kaye, Glynis Johns).

Baby Let Me Take You Dreaming/Life Could Not Better Be/My Heart Knows a Lovely Song—Sammy Cahn, Sylvia Fine (w,m), Dena. COVER: Danny Kaye, Glynis Johns, Angela Lansbury.

967   Courtship of Eddie's Father, The (MGM, 1963, Glenn Ford, Shirley Jones).

Rose and the Butterfly, The—Stella Unger (w), Victor Young (m), Young; Whistle Bait—Joe Pasternak, Jerry Winn (w), George Stoll, Bob Van Eps (m), Miller. COVER: Glenn Ford, Shirley Jones, Stella Stevens.

968   Courtship of Miles Standish, The (Pathe, 1923, Enid Bennett, Charles Ray).

Why Don't You Speak for Yourself John?—Corinne Ross (w), Gertrude Ross (m), Fischer. COVER: Enid Bennett, Charles Ray.

969   Cousins (Paramount, 1989, Ted Danson, Isabella Rossellini).

Cousins Love Theme—Angelo Badalamenti (m), Famous. COVER: Ted Danson, and Picnic Scene.

970   Covered Wagon, The (Paramount, 1923, J. Warren Kerrigan, Lois Wilson).

Covered Wagon Days—Will Morrissey, Joe Burrowes (w,m), Berlin; In a Covered Wagon with You—Ned Norworth, Harry Stover (w,m), Norworth; Oh Susanna—Stephen Foster (w,m), Haviland; Westward Ho—R. A. Barnet (w), Hugo Riesenfeld (m), Remick. COVER: A Covered Wagon and Pioneers.

971   Cover Girl (Columbia, 1944, Rita Hayworth, Gene Kelly).

Cover Girl/Long Ago—Ira Gershwin (w), Jerome Kern (m), Crawford; Make Way for Tomorrow—Ira Gershwin, E. Y. Harburg (w), Jerome Kern (m), Crawford; Poor John—Fred Leigh (w), Henry Pether (m), Harms; Put Me to the Test/Sure Thing—Ira Gershwin (w), Jerome Kern (m), Crawford. COVER: Rita Hayworth.

972   Cover Me Babe (Run Shadow Run) (20th Century-Fox, 1970, Robert Forster, Sondra Locke).

So You Say—Robb Royer, James Griffin (w), Fred Karlin (m), Fox. COVER: Girl on Beach.

973   Cow and I, The (Cow and the Prisoner) (Zenith, 1961, Fernandel, Marguerite).

Song of the Rain—Mitchell Parish (w), Paul Durand (m), Mills. COVER: Fernandel and Cow.

974   Cow and the Prisoner, The (Cow and I) (Zenith, 1961, Fernandel, Marguerite).

Love Me Some More—Mitchell Parish (w), Paul Durand (m), Mills. COVER: Fernandel and Cow.

975   Cowboy (Columbia, 1958, Glenn Ford, Jack Lemmon).

Cowboy—Dickson Hall (w), George Duning (m), Columbia; Cowboy-Eight Themes—George Duning (m), Columbia. COVER: Glenn Ford, Jack Lemmon.

976   Cowboy and the Lady, The (United Artists, 1938, Gary Cooper, Merle Oberon).

Cowboy and the Lady, The—Arthur Quenzer (w), Lionel Newman (m), Remick; Er-ru-ti-tu-ti—Arthur Quenzer (w), Lionel Newman (m), Stept Mitchell. COVER: Gary Cooper, Merle Oberon.

977   Cowboy Canteen (Columbia, 1944, Charles Starrett, Jane Frazee).

Goin to Lasso a Rainbow for You—Alma Scarberry (w), Connie Glore (m), Southern; Walkin' Down the Lane with You—Jimmy Wakely (w,m), Peer. COVER: Charles Starrett, Jane Frazee, Tex Ritter.

978 Cowboy from Brooklyn (Warner Bros., 1938, Dick Powell, Pat O'Brien).

Cowboy from Brooklyn—Johnny Mercer (w), Harry Warren (m), Witmark; I'll Dream Tonight/I've Got a Heartful of Music/Ride, Tenderfoot, Ride—Johnny Mercer (w), Richard Whiting (m), Witmark. COVER: Dick Powell, Priscilla Lane.

979 Cowboy from Sundown (Monogram, 1940, Tex Ritter, Roscoe Ates).

I've Done the Best I Could (VS)—Tex Ritter, Frank Harford (w,m), Cole. COVER: Tex Ritter.

980 Cowboy in Manhattan (Universal, 1943, Robert Paige, Frances Langford).

Need I Say More/Private Cowboy Jones—Milton Rosen, Everett Carter (w,m), Mills. COVER: Robert Paige, Frances Langford.

981 Cowboy in the Clouds (Columbia, 1943, Charles Starrett, Dub Taylor).

Cowboy in the Clouds—James Cavanaugh, John Redmond, Frank Weldon (w,m), Leeds. COVER: Charles Starrett, Julie Duncan.

982 Cowboy Ridin' High, A (Republic, 1942, Stars Unknown).

Cowboy Ridin' High Over There, A (PC)—Buck Ram (w,m), Noble. COVER: None.

983 Cowboys (Warner Bros., 1972, John Wayne, Bruce Dern).

Cowboys-Piano Overture—John Williams (m), Warner. COVER: Yellow cover with title only.

984 Cowboy Serenade (Republic, 1942, Gene Autry, Smiley Burnette).

Tahiti Honey (PC)—George Brown, Sol Meyer, Jule Styne (w,m), Mills. COVER: None.

985 Cow Cow Boogie (Universal, 1943, Cartoon).

Cow Cow Boogie—Don Raye, Gene DePaul, Benny Carter (w,m), Leeds. COVER: Cartoon.

Leeds. COVER: Cartoon.

986 Crack in the World (Paramount, 1965, Dana Andrews, Janette Scott).

Admiration/Crack in the World—Johnny Douglas (m), Famous; Time—John Davies (w), Johnny Douglas (m), Famous; Crack in the World Music Score—Johnny Douglas (m), Famous. COVER: Movie Scenes.

987 Cradle Song (Paramount, 1933, Dorothea Wieck, Evelyn Venable).

Cradle Song—Leo Robin (w), Ralph Rainger (m), Famous; Lovely Little Senorita—Karl Hajos, Leo Robin, Ralph Rainger (w,m), Famous. COVER: Dorothea Wieck.

988 Crash Donovan (Universal, 1936, Jack Holt, Nan Grey).

California State Highway Patrol—Clarence Marks, William Reardon, Dave Klatzkin (w,m), Sherman-Clay; Devoted to You—Ned Washington (w), Allie Wrubel (m), Robbins. COVER: John King, Jack Holt, Nan Grey.

989 Crazy House (Universal, 1943, Ole Olsen, Chic Johnson).

Get on Board Little Children—Don Raye, Gene DePaul (w,m), Leeds; Pocket Full of Pennies—Eddie Cherkose (w), Franz Steininger (m), Harms; Someday I'll Dream Again—Irving Bibo, Al Piantadosi, Stanley Joseloff (w,m), BMI. COVER: Olsen and Johnson, Martha O'Driscoll.

990 Criminal Lawyer (RKO, 1936, Lee Tracy, Erik Rhodes).

Tonight, Lover, Tonight—Harry Tobias (w), Jack Stern (m), Berlin. COVER: Couple in Window.

991 Cristoforo Colombo (Independent, 1985, Virna Lisi, Gabriel Byrne).

Great Dreamer, The (PC)/Lesson in Love, A (PC)—George D. Weiss (w), Riz Ortolani (m), Sugar. COVER: None.

992 Crook, The (United Artists, 1971, Jean Louis Trintignant, Daniele Deforme).

Crook Theme—Francis Lai (m), Unart. COVER: Jean Louis Trintignant.

993 Crooner (Warner Bros., 1932, Ann Dvorak, David Manners).

Sweethearts Forever—Cliff Friend, Irving Caesar (w,m), Witmark; Three's a Crowd—Al Dubin, Irving Kahal (w), Harry Warren (m), Witmark. COVER: Ann Dvorak.

994 Cross and the Switchblade, The (Ross, 1969, Pat Boone, Eric Estrada).

Bright New World—Flo Price (w, m), Lexicon; God Loves You—Ralph Carmichael (w,m), Lexicon; I've Got Confidence—Andrae Crouch (w,m), Lexicon; Love/Addicts Psalm (VS)/I Just Lost (VS)/When I Think of the Cross (VS)/Where Is It? (VS)/You Gotta Try (VS)—Ralph Carmichael (w,m), Lexicon. COVER: Pat Boone.

995 Crossing, The (China Bound) (MGM, 1930, George Arthur, Karl Dane).

My Universe Is You—Elsie Janis (w), Sam Messenheimer (m), Harms. COVER: George Arthur.

996 Cross My Heart (Paramount, 1946, Betty Hutton, Sonny Tufts).

Cross My Heart—Larry Neill (w), Robert E. Dolan (m), Paramount; Does Baby Feel All Right?/How Do You Do It?/It Hasn't Been Chilly in Chile/Love Is the Darndest Thing/That Little Dream Got Nowhere—Johnny Burke (w), Jimmy Van Heusen (m), Paramount. COVER: Betty Hutton, Sonny Tufts.

997 Crossroads (MGM, 1942, William Powell, Hedy Lamarr).

Till You Return—Howard Dietz (w), Arthur Schwartz (m), Feist. COVER: William Powell, Hedy Lamarr, Claire Trevor.

998 Crosswinds (Paramount, 1951, John Payne, Rhonda Fleming).

Crosswinds—Jay Livingston, Ray Evans (w,m), Paramount. COVER: John Payne, Rhonda Fleming.

999 Cruel Tower, The (Allied Artists, 1956, John Ericson, Mari Blanchard).

Cruel Tower, The—Dick Sherman (w,m), Warman. COVER: Rosalinda.

1000 Crusades, The (Paramount, 1935, Loretta Young, Henry Wilcoxon).

Song of the Crusades—Leo Robin, Richard Whiting, Rudolph Kopp (w, m), Famous. COVER: Loretta Young, Henry Wilcoxon.

1001 Cry for Happy (Columbia, 1950, Glenn Ford, Donald O'Connor).

Cry for Happy—Stanley Styne (w), George Duning (m), Columbia. COVER: Glenn Ford, Donald O'-Connor.

1002 Cry in the Night, A (Warner Bros., 1956, Natalie Wood, Edmund O'Brien).

Cry in the Night, A—Ned Washington (w), David Buttolph (m), Witmark. COVER: Natalie Wood, Richard Anderson.

1003 Cuban Love Song (MGM, 1931, Lawrence Tibbett, Lupe Velez).

Cuban Love Song/Tramps at Sea—Herbert Stothart, Jimmy McHugh, Dorothy Fields (w,m), Robbins. COVER: Lawrence Tibbett, Lupe Velez.

1004 Cuban Pete (Universal, 1946, Desi Arnaz, Ethel Smith).

Cuban Pete—Jose Norman (w,m), Hollywood; El Cumbanchero—Rafael Hernandez (w,m), Peer. COVER: Desi Arnaz.

1005 Cuckoos (RKO, 1930, Bert Wheeler, Bob Woolsey).

All Alone Monday/Dancing the Devil Away—Bert Kalmar (w), Harry Ruby (m), Harms; If I Were a Travelling Salesman (PC)—Al Dubin (w), Joe Burke (m), Witmark; I Love You So Much/Oh! How We Love Our Alma Mater/Wherever You Are—Bert Kalmar (w), Harry Ruby (m), Harms. COVER: Dorothy Lee.

1006 Cuesta Abajo (Paramount, 1934, Carlos Gardel).

Student Loves—Harold Muller

(w), Alfredo Lepera (m), Southern. COVER: Carlos Gardel.

1007 Cup of Fury (Goldwyn, 1919, Helene Chadwick, Rockcliffe Fellowes).

Cup of Fury, The—Annelu Burns (w), Madelyn Sheppard (m), McCarthy Fisher. COVER: Rupert Hughes.

1008 Curly Top (Fox, 1935, Shirley Temple, John Boles).

Animal Crackers in My Soup— Ted Koehler, Irving Caesar (w), Ray Henderson (m), Movietone; Curly Top—Ted Koehler (w), Ray Henderson (m), Movietone; It's All So New to Me—Edward Heyman (w), Ray Henderson (m), Movietone; Simple Things in Life, The—Ted Koehler (w), Ray Henderson (m), Movietone; When I Grow Up—Edward Heyman (w), Ray Henderson (m), Movietone. COVER: Shirley Temple, John Boles, Rochelle Hudson.

1009 Custard Cup, The (Fox, 1923, Mary Carr, Myrta Bonillas).

Mother Darling of Mine—Howard Strow (w), Harold Dryer (m), Henry. COVER: Mary Carr.

1010 Cyclone (Fox, 1920, Tom Mix, Colleen Moore).

High Voltage—Tom Mix (w,m), Shapiro Bernstein. COVER: Tom Mix.

1011 Cyclone Prairie Rangers (Cyclone Prairie Rustlers) (Columbia, 1943, Charles Starrett, Dub Taylor).

When the Prairie Moon Is Shinin' (PC)—Ekko Whelan, Jimmie Davis (w,m), Peer. COVER: None.

1012 Cynthia (MGM, 1947, George Murphy, Elizabeth Taylor).

Melody of Spring—Ralph Freed (w), Josef Strauss, Johnny Green (m), Robbins. COVER: Elizabeth Taylor, George Murphy, Mary Astor.

1013 Czar of Broadway (Universal, 1930, John Wray, Betty Compson).

That Homestead Steady of Mine— Ben Ryan (w), Lou Handman (m), Handman. COVER: Betty Compson.

1014 Daddy Long Legs (First National, 1919, Mary Pickford, Milla Davenport).

Daddy Long Legs—Sam Lewis, Joe Young (w), Harry Ruby (m), Berlin; Dear Old Daddy Long Legs— Neville Fleeson (w), Albert Von Tilzer (m), Broadway. COVER: Mary Pickford.

1015 Daddy Long Legs (20th Century-Fox, 1955, Fred Astaire, Leslie Caron).

C-A-T Spells Cat/Daddy Long Legs/Dancing Through Life—Johnny Mercer (w,m), Robbins; Dream— Johnny Mercer (w,m), Goldsen; Sluefoot/Something's Gotta Give/Welcome Egg-head—Johnny Mercer (w, m), Robbins. COVER: Fred Astaire, Leslie Caron.

1016 Daffy Duck (Warner Bros., 1955, Cartoon).

Daffy Duck/Daffy Duck's Race— Tedd Pierce, Warren Foster (w,m), Witmark. COVER: Cartoon.

1017 Daily Bread (Fox, 1929, Stars Unknown).

Daily Bread—James Hanley, Al Dubin (w), Pierre Norman (m), DBH. COVER: Black and white cover with title only.

1018 Daisy Kenyon (20th Century-Fox, 1947, Joan Crawford, Dana Andrews).

You Can't Run Away from Love— Mack Gordon (w), David Raksin (m), Warren. COVER: Joan Crawford, Dana Andrews, Henry Fonda.

1019 Dakota Lil (20th Century-Fox, 1949, George Montgomery, Marie Windsor).

Rose of Cimarron—Maurice Geraghty (w,m), Alson. COVER: George Montgomery, Marie Windsor, Rod Cameron.

1020 Damaged Love (Sono Art, 1931, June Collyer, Charles Starrett).

In Each Other's Arms—Milton Pascal (w), Homer Pearson (m), Marks. COVER: June Collyer, Charles Starrett.

1021 Dam Busters (Warner Bros.,

1955, Richard Todd, Michael Redgrave).

Dam Busters March—Eric Coates (m), Chappell. COVER: Richard Todd.

1022 Dames (Warner Bros., 1934, Dick Powell, Ruby Keeler).

Dames/Girl at the Ironing Board, The—Al Dubin (w), Harry Warren (m), Remick (Regular Cover and a Special Joan Blondell Cover); I Only Have Eyes for You—Al Dubin (w), Harry Warren (m), Remick; Try to See It My Way—Mort Dixon (w), Allie Wrubel (m), Remick; When You Were a Smile on Your Mother's Lips —Irving Kahal (w), Sammy Fain (m), Remick. COVER: Girls.

1023 Dames Ahoy (Universal, 1929, Glenn Tryon, Otis Harlan).

Barnacle Bill the Sailor—Carson Robison, Frank Luther (w,m), Southern. COVER: Glenn Tryon, and Girls.

1024 Damn the Defiant (H.M.S. Defiant) (Columbia, 1962, Alec Guinness, Dirk Bogarde).

Damn the Defiant—Dorsey Burnette, Johnny Burnette (w,m), Columbia; Damn the Defiant Themes— Clifton Parker (m), Columbia. COVER: Alec Guinness, Dirk Bogarde.

1025 Damn Yankees (Warner Bros., 1958, Tab Hunter, Gwen Verdon).

Goodbye Old Girl/Heart/Shoeless Joe from Hannibal Mo—Richard Adler, Jerry Ross (w,m), Frank; There's Something About an Empty Chair—Richard Adler (w,m), Frank; Two Lost Souls/Whatever Lola Wants/ Who's Got the Pain/Those Were the Good Old Days (VS)—Richard Adler, Jerry Ross (w,m), Frank. COVER: Gwen Verdon.

1026 Damsel in Distress (RKO, 1937, Fred Astaire, Joan Fontaine).

Foggy Day, A/I Can't Be Bothered Now/Jolly Tar and the Milk Maid, The/Nice Work If You Can Get It/Stiff Upper Lip/Things Are Looking Up—Ira Gershwin (w), George Gershwin (m), Chappell.

COVER: Fred Astaire, Joan Fontaine, George Burns, Gracie Allen.

1027 Dance Band (First Division, 1935, Charles Rogers, June Clyde).

Lovey Dovey—Arthur Young (w, m), Chappell; Valparaiso—Desmond Carter (w), Mabel Wayne (m), Chappell. COVER: Charles Rogers, June Clyde.

1028 Dance, Girl, Dance (RKO, 1940, Maureen O'Hara, Lucille Ball).

Morning Star—Chester Forrest, Robert Wright (w), Edward Ward (m), Mills; Oh! Mother—Robert Wright, Chester Forrest (w,m), Mills; Jitterbug Bite—Chester Forrest, Robert Wright (w), Edward Ward (m), Mills. COVER: Lucille Ball, Maureen O'Hara, Louis Hayward.

1029 Dance of Life, The (Paramount, 1929, Hal Skelly, Nancy Carroll).

Cuddlesome Baby/Flippity Flop, The/King of Jazzmania/Ladies of the Dance/Mightiest Matador, The/ True Blue Lou—Sam Coslow, Leo Robin, Richard Whiting (w,m), Spier Coslow. COVER: Hal Skelly, Nancy Carroll.

1030 Dancers, The (Fox, 1930, George O'Brien, Lois Moran).

Love Has Passed Me By—Cliff Friend, Jimmie Monaco (w,m), Red Star. COVER: Lois Moran.

1031 Dancers in the Dark (Paramount, 1932, Jack Oakie, Miriam Hopkins).

I'm in Love with a Tune—Ralph Rainger (w,m), Famous. COVER: Lyda Roberti.

1032 Dance Team (Fox, 1932, James Dunn, Sally Eilers).

I Saw My Future in Your Eyes— James Hanley (w,m), Movietone. COVER: Black and white cover with title only.

1033 Dance Time (Rainbow, 1952, Carol Kieth, Thomas Scott).

Dining and Dancing—Sherman Walker (w,m), Rainbow. COVER: Carol Kieth, Thomas Scott.

1034 Dance with the Devil (Johnny Apollo) (20th Century-Fox, 1940, Dorothy Lamour, Tyrone Power).

This Is the Beginning of the End—Mack Gordon (w,m), Robbins; Your Kiss—Frank Loesser (w), Alfred Newman (m), Robbins. COVER: Black and white cover with title only.

1035 Dancin' Fool (Paramount, 1920, Bebe Daniels, Wallace Reid).

Dancing Fool—Harry B. Smith, Francis Wheeler (w), Ted Snyder (m), Berlin. COVER: Dancing Girl.

1036 Dancing Co-ed (MGM, 1939, Lana Turner, Artie Shaw).

Everything Is Jumpin'—Artie Shaw (w,m), Lincoln; Jungle Drums —Carmen Lombardo, Charles O'-Flynn (w), Ernesto Lecuona (m), Marks; Non Stop Flight—Artie Shaw (w,m), Lincoln; One Foot in the Groove—Artie Shaw, Wen Daury (w, m), Lincoln; Traffic Jam—Artie Shaw, Teddy McRae (m), Lincoln. COVER: Lana Turner, Artie Shaw, Ann Rutherford.

1037 Dancing Daughters (Our Dancing Daughters) (MGM, 1928, Joan Crawford, Johnny Mack Brown).

I Loved You Then as I Love You Now—Ballard MacDonald (w), William Axt, David Mendoza (m), Berlin. COVER: Joan Crawford.

1038 Dancing Feet (Republic 1936, Joan Marsh, Eddie Nugent).

Dancing Feet/Everytime I Look at You—Sidney Mitchell (w), Sam Stept (m), Santly Joy. COVER: Joan Marsh, Eddie Nugent.

1039 Dancing Lady (MGM, 1933, Clark Gable, Joan Crawford).

Everything I Have Is Yours/ Heigh Ho, The Gang's All Here/ Let's Go Bavarian—Harold Adamson (w), Burton Lane (m), Robbins; My Dancing Lady—Dorothy Fields (w), Jimmy McHugh (m), Robbins; Rhythm of the Day—Lorenz Hart (w), Richard Rodgers (m), Robbins. COVER: Clark Gable, Joan Crawford.

1040 Dancing on a Dime (Paramount, 1941, Grace McDonald, Robert Paige).

Dancing on a Dime/I Hear Music—Frank Loesser (w), Burton Lane (m), Famous; Lovable Sort of Person—Frank Loesser (w), Victor Young (m), Famous; Manana—Frank Loesser (w), Burton Lane (m), Famous. COVER: Grace McDonald, Robert Paige.

1041 Dancing on the Moon (Paramount, 1935, Cartoon).

Dancing on the Moon—Charles Tobias (w), Murray Mencher (m), Famous. COVER: Dancing Couple.

1042 Dancing Pirate, The (RKO, 1936, Charles Collins, Steffi Duna).

Are You My Love/When You Are Dancing the Waltz—Lorenz Hart (w), Richard Rodgers (m), Chappell. COVER: Dancing Couple.

1043 Dancing Sweeties (Warner Bros., 1930, Grant Withers, Sue Carol).

Hullabaloo—Walter O'Keefe (w), Bobby Dolan (m), Witmark; Kiss Waltz, The—Al Dubin (w), Joe Burke (m), Witmark. COVER: Grant Withers, Sue Carol.

1044 Dancing with Crime (Paramount, 1947, Richard Attenborough, Sheila Sim).

Bow Bells (B)—Harold Purcell (w), Ben Bernard (m), Kassner. COVER: Richard Attenborough, Sheila Sim.

1045 Dandy in Aspic, A (Columbia, 1968, Mia Farrow, Laurence Harvey).

Spell You Spin, the Web You Weave, The—Bob Russell (w), Quincy Jones, Dave Grusin (m), Colgems. COVER: Mia Farrow, Laurence Harvey.

1046 Danger Love at Work (20th Century-Fox, 1937, Ann Sothern, Jack Haley).

Danger Love at Work—Mack Gordon, Harry Revel (w,m), Miller. COVER: Jack Haley, Ann Sothern, Mary Boland, Edward Everett Horton.

1047 Dangerously Yours (Fox,

1932, Warner Baxter, Miriam Jordan).

Dangerously Yours—Louis De-Francesco (m), Movietone. COVER: Black and white cover with title only.

1048 Dangerous Nan McGrew (Paramount, 1930, Helen Kane, Victor Moore).

Aw!C'mon—Leo Robin (w), Richard Whiting (m), Famous; Dangerous Nan McGrew/I Owe You—Don Hartman (w), Al Goodhart (m), Famous; Once a Gypsy Told Me—Sammy Fain, Irving Kahal, Pierre Norman (w,m), Famous. COVER: Helen Kane.

1049 Dangerous Paradise (Paramount, 1930, Nancy Carroll, Richard Arlen).

Smiling Skies—Leo Robin (w), Richard Whiting (m), Famous. COVER: Nancy Carroll.

1050 Dangerous Partners (MGM, 1945, James Craig, Signe Hasso).

His—Earl Brent (w,m), Feist. COVER: James Craig, Signe Hasso.

1051 Dangerous When Wet (MGM, 1953, Esther Williams, Fernando Lamas).

Ain't Nature Grand/I Got Out of Bed on the Right Side/In My Wildest Dreams—Johnny Mercer (w), Arthur Schwartz (m), Robbins. COVER: Esther Williams, Fernando Lamas.

1052 Danger Valley (Monogram, 1937, Jack Randall, Lois Wilde).

Little Tenderfoot—Johnny Lange (w), Fred Stryker (m), Sam Fox. COVER: Jack Randall.

1053 Danger Within (Break-Out) (Continental, 1959, Richard Todd, Richard Attenborough).

Danger Within (PC)—Garry Blake (w), Henry Himmel (m), Southern. COVER: None.

1054 Daniel Boone (RKO, 1936, George O'Brien, Heather Angel).

In My Garden—Grace Hamilton (w), Jack Stern (m), Sam Fox; Make Way—Jack Stern, Harry Tobias, Grace Hamilton (w,m), Sam Fox. COVER: Green cover with title only.

1055 Dante's Inferno (Fox,

1935, Spencer Tracy, Claire Trevor).

Betty—Sidney Clare (w), Samuel Kaylin (m), Movietone. COVER: Spencer Tracy, Claire Trevor.

1056 Darby O'Gill and the Little People (Buena Vista, 1959, Janet Munro, Albert Sharpe).

Pretty Irish Girl/Wishing Song, The—Lawrence Watkin (w), Oliver Wallace (m), Disney. COVER: Janet Munro, Sean Connery.

1057 Dark at the Top of the Stairs, The (Warner Bros., 1960, Robert Preston, Dorothy McGuire).

Dark at the Top of the Stairs Theme—Max Steiner (m), Witmark. COVER: Robert Preston, Dorothy McGuire.

1058 Dark City (Paramount, 1950, Charlton Heston, Lizabeth Scott).

If I Didn't Have You—Jack Elliott, Harold Spina (w,m), Paramount. COVER: Charlton Heston, Lizabeth Scott.

1059 Darker Than Amber (National General, 1970, Rod Taylor, Suzy Kendall).

Vangie's Theme (PC)—Chip Taylor (w), John Parker (m), Beechwood. COVER:None.

1060 Dark Passage (Warner Bros., 1947, Humphrey Bogart, Lauren Bacall).

Too Marvelous for Words—Johnny Mercer (w), Richard Whiting (m), Harms. COVER: Humphrey Bogart, Lauren Bacall.

1061 Dark Rapture (Universal, 1938, African Documentary).

Dark Rapture—Benny Goodman, Edgar Sampson, Manny Kurz (w,m), BVC. COVER: Benny Goodman.

1062 Dark Skies (Biltmore, 1929, Shirley Mason, Wallace MacDonald).

Juanita—Walter Sheridan (w), Lee Zahler, Walter Sheridan (m), Shapiro Bernstein. COVER: Shirley Mason, Wallace MacDonald.

1063 Dark Star, The (Paramount, 1919, Marion Davies, Norman Kerry).

Dark Star, The—Annelu Burns (w), Madelyn Sheppard (m), Remick. COVER: Marion Davies.

1064 Dark Victory (Warner Bros., 1939, Bette Davis, George Brent).

Oh, Give Me Time for Tenderness —Elsie Janis (w), Edmund Goulding (m), Remick. COVER: Bette Davis, George Brent.

1065 Darling (Embassy, 1964, Laurence Harvey, Dirk Bogarde).

Darling—Gene Lees (w), John Dankworth (m), Legation. COVER: Julie Christie, Laurence Harvey.

1066 Darling How Could You (Paramount, 1951, Joan Fontaine, John Lund).

Darling How Could You—Mack David (w), Jerry Livingston (m), Famous. COVER: Joan Fontaine, John Lund.

1067 Darling Lili (Paramount, 1969, Julie Andrews, Rock Hudson).

Darling Lili/Smile Away Each Rainy Day/Whistling Away the Dark —Johnny Mercer (w), Henry Mancini (m), Holmby; Can Can Cafe, The (VS)—Henry Mancini (m), Holmby; Girl in No Man's Land, The (VS)—Johnny Mercer (w), Henry Mancini (m), Holmby; Gypsy Violins (VS)—Henry Mancini (m), Holmby; I'll Give You Three Guesses (VS)/Little Birds (VS)/Skal (VS)/Your Good-will Ambassador (VS)—Johnny Mercer (w), Henry Mancini (m), Holmby. COVER: Julie Andrews.

1068 Darling of New York, The (Universal, 1923, Baby Peggy, Frank Currier).

Baby Peggy Waltz—M. Winkler (w), J. Titlebaum (m), Belwin. COVER: Baby Peggy.

1069 D.A.R.Y.L. (Paramount, 1985, Mary Beth Hurt, Michael McKean).

Somewhere I Belong—Dean Pitchford (w), Marvin Hamlisch (m), Famous. COVER: Boy and Computers.

1070 Das Lied Ist Aus (The Song Is Over) (ACA, 1932, German Oper-

etta).

Don't Ask Me Why/Goodbye Little Captain of My Heart/If Little IF Were Not a Word—Joe Young (w), Robert Stolz (m), Harms. COVER: Silhouette of Couple.

1071 Date with Judy, A (MGM, 1948, Wallace Beery, Jane Powell).

Cooking with Glass—Ray Gilbert, Luis Oliveira (w,m), Southern; Cuanto Le Gusta—Ray Gilbert (w), Gabriel Ruiz (m), Peer; I'm Strictly on the Corny Side—Stella Unger (w), Alec Templeton (m), Robbins; It's a Most Unusual Day—Harold Adamson (w), Jimmy McHugh (m), Robbins; Judaline—Don Raye, Gene DePaul (w,m), Robbins. COVER: Wallace Beery, Jane Powell, Elizabeth Taylor, Robert Stack.

1072 Daughter of Darkness (Paramount, 1948, Anne Crawford, Maxwell Reed).

Daughter of Darkness—Richard Addinsell (m), Famous. COVER: Black and white cover with title only.

1073 Daughter of Mine (Goldwyn, 1919, Madge Kennedy, John Bowers).

Daughter of Mine—Sidney Mitchell (w), Archie Gottler (m). Feist. COVER: Madge Kennedy.

1074 Daughter of Rosie O'Grady, The (Warner Bros., 1950, June Haver, Gordon MacRae).

As We Are Today—Charles Tobias (w), Ernesto Lecuona (m), Remick; Daughter of Rosie O'Grady, The—Monty Brice (w), Walter Donaldson (m), Witmark; Rose of Tralee—Mordaunt Spencer (w), Charles Glover (m), Remick. COVER: June Haver, Gordon MacRae.

1075 Daughter of the Gods (Fox, 1916, Mark Price, Annette Kellerman).

Daughter of the Gods Piano Score —Robert Hood Bowers (m), Schirmers. COVER: Girl on Beach.

1076 Daughter of Two Worlds (First National, 1920, Norma Talmadge, Jack Crosby).

Daughter of Two Worlds—Paul Sarazan (w), M. K. Jerome (m), Berlin. COVER: Norma Talmadge.

1077 David and Bathsheba (20th Century-Fox, 1951, Gregory Peck, Susan Hayward).

David and Bathsheba—Gordon Jenkins, Robert Allen, Allan Roberts (w,m), Lion; Rapture of Love (VS)/ Twenty Third Psalm, The—Alfred Newman (m), Robbins. COVER: Dancing Girls and Slaves.

1078 David and Lisa (Continental, 1962, Keir Dullea, Janet Margolin).

David and Lisa Love Song—Edward Heyman (w), Mark Lawrence (m), Blackwood; David and Lisa Theme—Mark Lawrence (m). COVER: Keir Dullea, Janet Margolin.

1079 Davy Crockett (Buena Vista, 1955, Fess Parker, Buddy Ebsen).

Ballad of Davy Crockett, The— Tom Blackburn (w), George Bruns (m), Wonderland; Be Sure You're Right—Fess Parker, Buddy Ebsen (w,m), Disney; Old Betsy—George Bruns (w), Gil George (m), Wonderland; Farewell (VS)—Davy Crockett (w), George Bruns (m), Disney; I Gave My Love (VS)/I'm Lonely My Darlin' (VS)—George Bruns, Fess Parker (w,m), Disney. COVER: Fess Parker, Buddy Ebsen.

1080 Day at the Races, A (MGM, 1937, Marx Brothers, Allan Jones).

All God's Chillun Got Rhythm/ Blue Venetian Waters—Gus Kahn (w), Bronislaw Kaper, Walter Jurmann (m), Robbins; Doctor Quackenbush (PC)—Bert Kalmar, Harry Ruby (w,m), Robbins; Message from the Man in the Moon/To-Morrow Is Another Day—Gus Kahn (w), Bronislaw Kaper, Walter Jurmann (m), Robbins. COVER: Marx Brothers, Allan Jones, Maureen O'Sullivan.

1081 Daydreamer, The (Embassy, 1966, Cyril Ritchard, Victor Moore).

Daydreamer/Happy Guy/Isn't It Cozy Here/Luck to Sell/Simply Wonderful/Tivoli Bells/Voyage of the Walnut Shell/Waltz for a Mermaid/ Who Can Tell/Wishes and Teardrops —Jules Bass (w), Maury Laws (m), Morris. COVER: A Boy Dreaming.

1082 Day of Anger (United Artists, 1969, Lee Van Cleef, Giuliana Gemma).

Day of Anger Theme—Riz Ortolani (m), Unart. COVER: Black and white cover with title only.

1083 Day of the Locust, The (Paramount, 1974, Donald Sutherland, Karen Black).

Miss Lonely Hearts—Paul Williams (w), John Barry (m), Famous. COVER: Karen Black.

1084 Day of the Triffids (Allied Artists, 1963, Howard Keel, Nicole Maurey).

Day of the Triffids, Theme (B)— Ron Goodwin (m), Filmusic. COVER: Green cover with title only.

1085 Day of Triumph (Century, 1954, Lee J. Cobb, Robert Wilson).

Day of Triumph—Roger Wagner (w), Daniele Amfitheatrof (m), Hill Range. COVER: Robert Wilson.

1086 Days of Jesse James (Republic, 1939, Roy Rogers, George Hayes).

Echo Mountain/I'm a Son of a Cowboy/Saddle Your Dreams— Peter Tinturin (w,m), Exclusive. COVER: Roy Rogers.

1087 Days of Wine and Roses, The (Warner Bros., 1962, Jack Lemmon, Lee Remick).

Days of Wine and Roses—Johnny Mercer (w), Henry Mancini (m), Witmark. COVER: Jack Lemmon, Lee Remick.

1088 Days of Yesterday (Apex, 1923, Stars Unknown).

Days of Yesterday—Lou Zoeller, Sidney Holden, Art Gillham (w,m), Zipf. COVER: Cowboy Scenes.

1089 Day the Fish Came Out, The (20th Century-Fox, 1967, Tom Courtenay, Sam Wanamaker).

Day the Fish Came Out Theme—Mikis Theodorakis (m), Feist. COVER: Movie Scenes.

1090 Day the World Ended, The (AIP, 1956, Richard Denning, Lori Nelson).

S. F. Blues, The—Ronald Stein (m), BVC. COVER: A Creature Chasing a Woman.

1091 Day They Gave Babies Away, The (All Mine to Give) (RKO, 1957, Cameron Mitchell, Glynis Johns).

My Very, Very Own (PC)—Norman Bennett (w), Max Steiner (m), Lamas. COVER: None.

1092 Deadfall (20th Century-Fox, 1968, Michael Caine, Eric Portman).

My Love Has Two Faces—Jack Lawrence (w), John Barry (m), 20th Century. COVER: Michael Caine, and Movie Scenes.

1093 Dead Heat on a Merry Go Round (Columbia, 1967, James Coburn, Aldo Ray).

Dead Heat on a Merry Go Round—Stu Phillips (m), Colgems. COVER: James Coburn, and Girls.

1094 Deadlier Than the Male (Universal, 1966, Richard Johnson, Elke Sommer).

Deadlier Than the Male—Scott Engel, John Franz (w,m), Shamley; Chess Game, The (B)—Malcolm Lockyer (m), Leeds. COVER: Elke Sommer, Sylvia Koschina, Suzanna Leigh.

1095 Deadly Affair (Columbia, 1966, James Mason, Maximillian Schell).

Who Needs Forever—Howard Greenfield, Quincy Jones (w,m), Colgems. COVER: James Mason, Maximillian Schell, Simone Signoret.

1096 Deadly Bees, The (Paramount, 1968, Guy Doleman, Suzanna Leigh).

Deadly Bees Music Score—Wilfred Josephs (m), Famous. COVER: Green cover with title only.

1097 Deadly Is the Female (Gun Crazy) (United Artists, 1949, Peggy Cummings, John Dall).

Mad About You—Ned Washington (w), Victor Young (m), Weiss. COVER: Frank Sinatra, Kitty Kallen.

1098 Deadly Trap, The (National General, 1971, Faye Dunaway, Frank Langella).

Deadly Trap Theme—Gilbert Becaud (m), Harms; If I Had Never Loved You—Larry Kusik (w), Gilbert Becaud (m), Harms. COVER: Faye Dunaway.

1099 Dead Reckoning (Columbia, 1947, Humphrey Bogart, Lizabeth Scott).

Either It's Love or It Isn't—Allan Roberts, Doris Fisher (w,m), Mood. COVER: Humphrey Bogart, Lizabeth Scott.

1100 Deaf Smith and Johnny Ears (MGM, 1973, Anthony Quinn, Franco Nero).

Ballad of Deaf and Ears, Freedom—Ann Collin (w), Danielle Patucchi (m), Chappell. COVER: Anthony Quinn, Franco Nero.

1101 Dear Heart (The Out of Towners) (Warner Bros., 1964, Glenn Ford, Geraldine Page).

Dear Heart—Jay Livingston, Ray Evans (w), Henry Mancini (m), Northridge; Dear Heart Theme—Henry Mancini (m), Northridge. COVER: Glenn Ford, Geraldine Page.

1102 Dear John (Sigma, 1964, Jari Kulle, Christina Schollin).

Dear John—Dorothy Wayne, Richard Loring (w), Bergt Wallin (m), Overseas. COVER: Black and white cover with title only.

1103 Dear Old Girl (Essanay, 1915, Francis X. Bushman).

My Ship O'Dreams—Francis X. Bushman (w), Frank Suttle (m), Rossiter. COVER: Francis X. Bushman.

1104 Dear Ruth (Paramount, 1947, William Holden, Joan Caulfield).

Fine Thing—Johnny Mercer (w), Robert E. Dolan (m), Paramount.

COVER: William Holden, Joan Caulfield.

1105 Dear Wife (Paramount, 1950, William Holden, Joan Caulfield).

Dear Wife—Jay Livingston, Ray Evans (w,m), Paramount. COVER: William Holden, Joan Caulfield.

1106 Death Driver (Clay, 1977, Earl Owensby, Mike Allen).

Drinking Warm Champagne (PC)/ Every Now and Then (PC)/Honky Tonk Queen (PC)/On the Prowl (PC) —Arthur Smith, Clay Smith (w,m), Clay. COVER: None.

1107 Death in Venice (Warner Bros., 1971, Dirk Bogarde, Marisa Berenson).

Timeless Moment, The (B)— Norman Newell (w), Roger Webb (m), Chappell. COVER: Canal in Venice.

1108 Death of a Scoundrel (RKO, 1956, George Sanders, Yvonne DeCarlo).

Stephanie—Carl Sigman (w), Max Steiner (m), Lamas. COVER: Dead Man and Girls.

1109 Death on the Nile (Paramount, 1978, Peter Ustinov, Bette Davis).

Death on the Nile Love Theme (B)—Nino Rota, EMI. COVER: Peter Ustinov, Bette Davis, Angela Lansbury, and Others.

1110 Deep, The (Columbia, 1977, Robert Shaw, Jacqueline Bisset).

Deep Deep Inside—Donna Summer (w), John Barry (m), Gold Horizon; Deep Theme—John Barry (m), Gold Horizon. COVER: Girl in Water.

1111 Deep Blue Sea, The (20th Century-Fox, 1955, Vivien Leigh, Kenneth Mars).

Deep Blue Sea, The—Roy Hamilton (w), Francis Chagrin (m), Robbins. COVER: Vivien Leigh.

1112 Deep in My Heart (MGM, 1954, Jose Ferrer, Merle Oberon).

Auf Wiedersehn—Herbert Reynolds (w), Sigmund Rombert (m), Schirmer; Deep in My Heart Dear— Dorothy Donnelly (w), Sigmund Romberg (m), Harms; Desert Song— Otto Harbach, Oscar Hammerstein (w), Sigmund Romberg (m), Harms; Faithfully Yours—Sigmund Romberg (m), Harms; Leg of Mutton—Roger Edens (w), Sigmund Romberg (m), Marks; Lover Come Back to Me/ One Kiss—Oscar Hammerstein (w), Sigmund Romberg (m), Harms; Road to Paradise, The—Rida Johnson Young (w), Sigmund Romberg (m), Harms; Serenade—Dorothy Donnelly (w), Sigmund Romberg (m), Harms; Softly as in a Morning Sunrise/Stouthearted Men—Oscar Hammerstein (w), Sigmund Romberg (m), Harms; When I Grow Too Old to Dream— Oscar Hammerstein (w), Sigmund Romberg (m), Robbins; Will You Remember, Sweetheart—Rida Johnson Young (w), Sigmund Romberg (m), Schirmer; You Will Remember Vienna—Oscar Hammerstein (w), Sigmund Romberg (m), Harms; Your Land and My Land—Dorothy Donnelly (w), Sigmund Romberg (m), Harms. COVER: Jose Ferrer, Helen Traubel, and Dancers.

1113 Deep Valley (Warner Bros., 1947, Ida Lupino, Dane Clark).

Deep Valley—Charles Tobias (w), Max Steiner (m), Remick. COVER: Ida Lupino, Dane Clark, Wayne Morris.

1114 Deer Hunter (Universal, 1971, Robert DeNiro, John Savage).

Cavatina—Stanley Myers (m), Glenwood. COVER: Robert De-Niro, and Movie Scenes.

1115 Delicious (Fox, 1931, Janet Gaynor, Charles Farrell).

Blah Blah Blah/Delishious/Katinkitschka/Somebody from Somewhere—Ira Gershwin (w), George Gershwin (m), Harms. COVER: Janet Gaynor.

1116 Delicious Little Devil, The (Universal, 1919, Mae Murray, Rudolpho De Valentino).

Oh, You Delicious Little Devil—Alfred Bryan (w), Buddy DeSylva (m), Remick. COVER: Mae Murray.

1117 Delightfully Dangerous (United Artists, 1945, Jane Powell, Ralph Bellamy).

I'm Only Teasin'/In a Shower of Stars/Once Upon a Song/Thru Your Eyes to Your Heart—Edward Heyman (w), Morton Gould (m), Mills. COVER: Jane Powell, Constance Moore, Ralph Bellamy.

1118 Delightful Rogue, The (RKO, 1929, Rod LaRoque, Rita LaRoy).

Gay Love—Sidney Clare (w), Oscar Levant (m), Harms. COVER: Rod LaRoque, Rita LaRoy.

1119 Delinquents, The (United Artists, 1957, Tom Laughlin, Peter Miller).

Dirty Boogie, The—William Nolan, Ronald Norman (w,m), Bishop. COVER: Movie Scene.

1120 Deliverance (Warner Bros., 1972, Jon Voight, Burt Reynolds).

Duelling Banjos—Eric Weissburg (m), Warner. COVER: Gun and Canoe.

1121 Deputy Marshall (Lippert, 1949, Jon Hall, Frances Langford).

Levis, Plaid Shirt, and Spurs/There's a Hideout in Hidden Valley—John Stephens (w), Irving Bibo (m), Bibo. COVER: Frances Langford.

1122 Derelict (Paramount, 1930, William Boyd, George Bancroft).

Over the Sea of Dreams—Leo Robin (w), Jack King (m), Famous. COVER: George Bancroft.

1123 Der Führer's Face (Donald Duck in Nutzi Land) (Disney, 1942, Cartoon).

Der Führer's Face—Oliver Wallace (w,m), Southern. COVER: Cartoon.

1124 Der Kongress Tanzt (Congress Dances) (United Artists, 1931, Lillian Harvey, Henry Gavat).

Just Once for All Time/Live Love and Laugh/Something from Heaven—Robert Gilbert (w), Werner Heyman (m), Harms. COVER: Dancers.

1125 Der und Seine Schwester (He and His Sister) (Independent, 1931, German Operetta).

Send Me Your Love—Charles Amberg, Leo Robin (w), Jara Benes (m), Harms. COVER: Pen and Ink.

1126 Desert Gold (Hodkinson, 1919, E. K. Lincoln, Margery Wilson).

Desert Gold—Sam Lewis, Joe Young (w), Bert Grant (m), Berlin. COVER: Margery Wilson.

1127 Desert Song, The (Warner Bros., 1929, John Boles, Carlotta King).

Desert Song, The/It/Let's Have a Love Affair/Love's Dear Yearning/One Alone/One Flower Grows Alone in Your Garden/Riff Song, The/Romance—Otto Harbach, Oscar Hammerstein (w), Sigmund Romberg (m), Harms. COVER: Couple on a Camel.

1128 Desert Song, The (Warner Bros., 1943, Dennis Morgan, Irene Manning).

Desert Song, The/One Alone/Riff Song, The/Romance—Otto Harbach, Oscar Hammerstein (w), Sigmund Romberg (m), Harms. COVER: Dennis Morgan, Irene Manning.

1129 Desert Song, The (Warner Bros., 1953, Gordon MacRae, Kathryn Grayson).

Desert Song, The—Otto Harbach, Oscar Hammerstein (w), Sigmund Romberg (m), Harms; Gay Parisienne—Jack Scholl (w), Serge Walter (m), Harms; One Alone/ Riff Song, The/Romance—Otto Harbach, Oscar Hammerstein (w), Sigmund Romberg (m), Harms. COVER: Gordon MacRae, Kathryn Grayson.

1130 Design for Living (Paramount, 1933, Frederic March, Gary Cooper).

My Design for Living—Mack Gordon (w), Harry Revel (m), DBH. COVER: Frederic March, Gary Cooper, Miriam Hopkins.

1131 Designing Woman (Paramount, 1950, Gregory Peck, Lauren Bacall).

Designing Woman—Jack Brooks (w), André Previn (m), Robbins; There'll Be Some Changes Made— Billy Higgins (w), Benton Overstreet (m), Marks. COVER: Gregory Peck, Lauren Bacall, Dolores Gray.

1132 Desire (Paramount, 1936, Gary Cooper, Marlene Dietrich).

Awake in a Dream/Desire—Leo Robin, Frederick Hollander (w,m), Famous. COVER: Gary Cooper, Marlene Dietrich.

1133 Désirée (20th Century-Fox, 1954, Marlon Brando, Jean Simmons).

Song from Désirée-We Meet Again —Ken Darby (w), Alfred Newman (m), Miller. COVER: Marlon Brando, Jean Simmons.

1134 Desire Me (MGM, 1947, Greer Garson, Robert Mitchum).

Why Do You Pass Me By? (B)— Desmond Carter (w), John Hess, Paul Misraki (m), Continental. COVER: Greer Garson.

1135 Desire Under the Elms (Paramount, 1958, Sophia Loren, Tony Perkins).

Desire Under the Elms—Elmer Bernstein (m), Famous. COVER: Sophia Loren, Tony Perkins, Burl Ives.

1136 Desperate Hours, The (Paramount, 1955, Humphrey Bogart, Frederic March).

Desperate Hours, The—Wilson Stone (w), Burt Bacharach (m), Paramount. COVER: A Clock.

1137 Desperately Seeking Susan (Orion, 1985, Madonna, Rosanna Arquette).

Into the Groove—Madonna Ciccone, Steve Bray (w,m), Warner. COVER: Madonna.

1138 Destination Moon (Eagle Lion, 1950, John Archer, Warner Anderson).

Destination Moon—Roy Alfred (w), Marvin Fisher (m), Fisher. COVER: Blue cover with title only.

1139 Destiny (Universal, 1919, Dorothy Phillips, William Stowell).

Destiny—Alfred Bryan (w), Herbert Spencer (m), Remick. COVER: Dorothy Phillips.

1140 Destroyers (Independent, 1942, War Film).

Beloved City—E. Dolmatovsky, N. Bogoslavsky (w,m), Amrus. COVER: Bombers.

1141 Destry Rides Again (Universal, 1939, Marlene Dietrich, James Stewart).

Boys in the Backroom, The/ Little Joe the Wrangler/You've Got That Look—Frank Loesser (w), Frederick Hollander (m), Robbins. COVER: Marlene Dietrich, James Stewart.

1142 Detective, The (20th Century-Fox, 1968, Frank Sinatra, Lee Remick).

Dark Song, The—Estelle Leavitt (w), Jerry Goldsmith (m), Fox. COVER: Frank Sinatra.

1143 Devil and Ten Commandments, The (Union, 1962, Michel Simon, Lucien Baroux).

Warm—Steve Allen (w), Guy Magenia (m), Hansen. COVER: Black and white cover with title only.

1144 Devil in Miss Jones, The (Marvis, 1973, Georgina Spelvin, John Clemens).

I'm Comin' Home—Earl Shuman (w), Alden Shuman (m), Chappell. COVER: Nude Woman.

1145 Devil Is a Woman, The (Paramount, 1935, Marlene Dietrich, Caesar Romero).

Then It Isn't Love—Leo Robin, Ralph Rainger (w,m), Famous. COVER: Marlene Dietrich.

1146 Devil May Care (MGM, 1929, Ramon Novarro, Marion Harris).

Charming/If He Cared/March of the Old Guard/Shepherd's Serenade —Clifford Grey (m), Herbert Stothart (m), Robbins. COVER: Ramon Novarro.

1147 Devil on Horseback (Grand National, 1936, Lili Damita, Fred Keating).

Love Fiesta/Oh Bella Mia/So Divine—Jack Stern, Harry Tobias (w, m), Sam Fox. COVER: Lili Damita.

1148 Devil Riders (PRC, 1943, Buster Crabbe, Al St. John).

It Don't Mean Anything Now/She's Mine—Lew Porter (w), F. J. Tableporter (m), Urban. COVER: Buster Crabbe.

1149 Devil's Brigade, The (United Artists, 1968, William Holden, Cliff Robertson).

Devil's Brigade March/Devil's Brigade Theme—Al Stillman (w), Alex North (m), Unart. COVER: William Holden, and Soldiers.

1150 Devil's Hairpin, The (Paramount, 1957, Cornel Wilde, Jean Wallace).

Swing It Just a Little More—Cornel Wilde (w), Ross Bagdasarian (m), Paramount; Touch of Love, The—Ross Bagdasarian (w,m), Paramount. COVER: Cornel Wilde, Jean Wallace.

1151 Devil's Holiday, The (Paramount, 1930, Nancy Carroll, Phillip Holmes).

You Are a Song—Leo Robin (w), Edmund Goulding (m), Famous. COVER: Nancy Carroll.

1152 Devotion (Associated, 1921, Hazel Dawn, E. K. Lincoln).

Devotion—Jack Stern, Clarence Marks, Norah Haymond (w,m), Remick. COVER: Hazel Dawn.

1153 D. I., The (Warner Bros., 1957, Jack Webb, Don Dubbins).

Somebody Else Will—Fred Weismantel (w), Ray Conniff (m), Pete Kelly. COVER: Jack Webb, Don Dubbins, Monica Lewis.

1154 Dial "M" for Murder (Warner Bros., 1954, Grace Kelly, Ray Milland).

My Favorite Memory—Jack Lawrence (w), Dimitri Tiomkin (m), Witmark. COVER: Grace Kelly.

1155 Diamond from the Sky, A (American, 1915, Lottie Pickford, William Russell).

Like a Diamond from the Sky—

Leo Wood (w), Leo Bennett (m), Cadillac. COVER: Lottie Pickford.

1156 Diamond Head (Columbia, 1961, Charlton Heston, George Chakiris).

Diamond Head—Mack David (w), Hugo Winterhalter (m), Columbia. COVER: Charlton Heston, George Chakiris, James Darren.

1157 Diamond Horseshoe (20th Century-Fox, 1945, Betty Grable, Dick Haymes).

In Acapulco/I Wish I Knew/Mink Lament, The/More I See You, The/Nickel's Worth of Jive/Play Me an Old Fashioned Melody—Mack Gordon (w), Harry Warren (m), BVC. COVER: Betty Grable, Dick Haymes.

1158 Diamonds Are Forever (United Artists, 1971, Sean Connery, Jill St. John).

Diamonds Are Forever—Don Black (w), John Barry (m), Unart. COVER: Sean Connery, and Girls.

1159 Diamonds for Breakfast (Paramount, 1968, Marcello Mastroianni, Rita Tushingham).

Diamonds for Breakfast (B)—Norman Kay, Hal Shaper (w,m), Famous. COVER: Marcello Mastroianni, Rita Tushingham.

1160 Diane (MGM, 1957, Lana Turner, Roger Moore).

Beauty and Grace—Miklos Rozsa (m), Robbins. COVER: Purple cover with title only.

1161 Diary of a Bachelor (American International, 1964, William Traylor, Diane Crane).

Barbara's Theme—Jack Gold (w), Jack Pleis (m), Mansion; Blues for Angie/Girls/I Don't Have to Tell You—Jack Pleis (m), Mansion; Joanna's Theme—Earl Shuman (w), Jack Pleis (m), Mansion; Village Beat—Jack Pleis (m), Mansion; Wise Men—George D. Weiss (w), Jack Pleis (m), Mansion. COVER: Girls on Calendar.

1162 Dich Harich Geliebt (Because I Loved You) (AAFAT, 1930, Walter Dankurn, Mady Christians).

I've Always Loved You—Don Hartman (w), Ed May (m), Harms. COVER: Silhouette of Couple.

1163 Die Lindenwirtin (The Innkeeper of Linden) (ACA, 1931, German Operetta).

Blonde Innkeeper from the Rhine, The—Bruno Hardtwarde (w), Michael Krauz (m), Harms. COVER: Girl on Hill.

1164 Die Lustigen Weiber von Wien (The Merry Wives of Vienna) (CAP, 1931, German Operetta).

I Only Love One—Samuel Lerner (w), Robert Stolz (m), Harma. COVER: Girls.

1165 Digby, The Biggest Dog in the World (Cinerama, 1974, Jim Dale, Angela Douglas).

Digby—Lily Sanderson, Lesley Sanderson (w), Edwin Astley (m), Sherwin. COVER: A Large Dog.

1166 Dime with a Halo (MGM, 1963, Barbara Luna, Roger Mobley).

Dime with a Halo Theme—Ronald Stein (m), Miller. COVER: Barbara Luna, Roger Mobley, Rafael Lopez.

1167 Dimples (The Bowery Princess) (20th Century-Fox, 1936, Shirley Temple, Frank Morgan).

Hey, What Did the Blue Jay Say/ Oh Mister Man Up in the Moon/Picture Me Without You—Ted Koehler (w), Jimmy McHugh (m), Feist. COVER: Shirley Temple.

1168 Dinner at Eight (MGM, 1933, Marie Dressler, Jean Harlow).

Dinner at Eight—Dorothy Fields (w), Jimmy McHugh (m), Robbins. COVER: Marie Dressler, Jean Harlow, Wallace Beery and Others.

1169 Dinty (First National, 1920, Wesley Barry, Colleen Moore).

Dinty—Richard Coburn (w), Vincent Rose (m), Remick. COVER: Wesley Barry.

1170 Diplomaniacs (RKO, 1937, Bert Wheeler, Bob Wollsey).

Sing to Me—Edward Eliscu (w), Harry Akst (m), Witmark. COVER: Bert Wheeler, Bob Woolsey).

1171 Di Que Me Quieres (Tell Me That You Love Me) (RKO, 1936, Eva Ortega, Jorge Lewis).

Slumber Song—Gabriel Luna (w), Miguel Prado (m), Southern. COVER: Eva Ortega, Jorge Lewis.

1172 Dirty Dancing (Vestron, 1987, Patrick Swayze, Jennifer Grey).

Do You Love Me—Berry Gordy (w,m), Jobete; Hey Baby! (PC)—Margaret Cobb, Bruce Channel (w,m), Le Bill; Hungry Eyes—Franke Previte, John DeNicola (w,m), Knockout; I've Had the Time of My Life—Franke Previte, Don Markowitz, John DeNicola (w,m), Knockout; Love Man—Otis Redding (w,m), Irving; He's Like the Wind—Patrick Swayze (w,m), Very Tony. COVER: Patrick Swayze.

1173 Dirty Dingus Magee (MGM, 1970, Frank Sinatra, George Kennedy).

Dirty Dingus Magee—Mack David, Mike Curb (w,m), Feist. COVER: Frank Sinatra, George Kennedy.

1174 Dirty Dozen, The (MGM, 1967, Lee Marvin, Ernest Borgnine).

Bramble Bush, The—Mack David (w), Frank DeVol (m), Feist. COVER: Lee Marvin, Ernest Borgnine.

1175 Dirty Mary Crazy Larry (20th Century-Fox, 1974, Peter Fonda, Susan George).

Dirty Mary Crazy Larry—Jefferey Kanew (w,m), Fox; Time Is Such a Funny Thing—Danny Janssen, Bobby Hart (w,m), Fox. COVER: Peter Fonda, Susan George.

1176 Disc Jockey (Allied Artists, 1951, Ginny Simms, Tom Drake).

After Hours—Roz Gordon (w,m), Kirk; Show Me You Love Me—S. Steuben, Roz Gordon (w,m), Kirk. COVER: Ginny Simms, Tom Drake, and Other Stars.

1177 Discord (Paramount, 1933, Owen Nares, Benita Hume).

When the Shadows Begin (B)—Anona Winn (w), Billy Coomber (m), Day. COVER: Owen Nares, Benita Hume.

1178 Disgraced (Paramount, 1933, Helen Twelvetrees, Bruce Cabot).
Any Place Is Paradise—Sam Coslow (w), Stephan Pasternaki (m), Famous. COVER: Helen Twelvetrees, Bruce Cabot.

1179 Disorderlies (Warner Bros., 1987, Damon Wimbley, Darren Robinson).
I Heard a Rumour—Sarah Dallin, Karen Woodward, Siobban Fahey, Matt Aitken (w,m), Warner. COVER: Bananarama.

1180 Disorderly Orderly, The (Paramount, 1964, Jerry Lewis, Susan Oliver).
Disorderly Orderly, The—Earl Shuman (w), Leon Carr (m), Paramount. COVER: Jerry Lewis.

1181 Dive Bomber (Warner Bros., 1941, Errol Flynn, Fred Mac-Murray).
We Watch the Sky-ways—Gus Kahn (w), Max Steiner (m), Remick. COVER: Black and white cover with title only.

1182 Divine Lady, The (First National, 1927, Corrine Griffith, Victor Varconi).
Lady Divine—Richard Kountz (w), Nathaniel Shilkret (m), Witmark; Pearl o' Mine (B)—Percy Fletcher (m), Hawkes. COVER: Corrine Griffith, Victor Varconi.

1183 Divorce American Style (Columbia, 1967, Debbie Reynolds, Dick Van Dyke).
You Tell Yourself—Arthur Hamilton (w), Dave Grusin (m), Colgems. COVER: Cartoon Sketch.

1184 Divorce Evidence (Evidence) (Warner Bros., 1929, Pauline Frederick, Lowell Sherman).
Little Cavalier—Al Dubin (w), M. K. Jerome (m), Witmark. COVER: Black and white cover with title only.

1185 Divorce Italian Style (Embassy, 1962, Marcello Mastroianni, Stefania Sandrelli).
Canto D'amore—Demi Rustichelli, Carlo Rustichelli (w,m), Embassy. COVER: Cartoon Sketch.

1186 Divorce Made Easy (Paramount, 1929, Douglas MacLean, Marie Prevost).
So Sweet—Sterling Sherwin (w, m), Famous. COVER: Douglas MacLean, Marie Prevost.

1187 Dixianna (RKO, 1930, Bebe Daniels, Everett Marshall).
Dixianna—Bennie Davis (w), Harry Tierney (m), Harms; Guiding Star/Here's to the Old Days/Love Is Like a Song/Mr. and Mrs. Sippi/My One Ambition Is You/Tear, a Kiss, a Smile, A—Anne Caldwell (w), Harry Tierney (m), Harms. COVER: Bebe Daniels, Everett Marshall.

1188 Dixie (Paramount, 1943, Bing Crosby, Dorothy Lamour).
Horse That Knows the Way Back Home/If You Please/Kinda Peculiar Brown/Laughing Tony/Miss Jemima Walks By/She's from Missouri/Sunday, Monday or Always—Johnny Burke (w), Jimmy Van Heusen (m), Mayfair; Dixie-Ana Minstrel Songs/Dixie Minstrel Folio—Traditional. COVER: Bing Crosby, Dorothy Lamour.

1189 Dixie Jamboree (PRC, 1944, Frances Langford, Guy Kibbee).
If It's a Dream—Sam Neuman, Michael Breen (w,m), Mills. COVER: Frances Langford.

1190 Dizzy Dames (Liberty, 1936, Marjorie Rambeau, Florine McKinney).
I Was Taken by Storm—Edward Heyman (w), Louis Alter (m), Harms; Let's Be Frivolous—George Waggner, Howard Jackson (w,m), Harms; Love Is the Thing—Harry Tobias (w), Neil Moret (m), Harms; Martinique, The—Arthur Swanstrom, George Waggner (w), Louis Alter (m), Harms. COVER: Marjorie Rambeau, Lawrence Gray.

1191 Dock Brief, The (Trial and Error) (MGM, 1962, Peter Sellers, Richard Attenborough).

Legal March (B)—Ron Grainer (m), Robbins. COVER: Peter Sellers.

1192 Doctor Doolittle (20th Century-Fox, 1967, Rex Harrison, Samantha Eggar).

After Today/At the Crossroads/ Beautiful Things/Doctor Doolittle/ Fabulous Places/I Think I Like You/ My Friend the Doctor/Something in Your Smile/Talk to the Animals/ When I Look in Your Eyes/Where Are the Words/Like Animals (VS)/ I've Never Seen Anything Like It (VS)/Vegetarian, The (VS)—Leslie Bricusse (w,m), Hastings. COVER: Rex Harrison and Animals.

1193 Doctor Rhythm (Paramount, 1938, Bing Crosby, Mary Carlisle).

Doctor Rhythm/My Heart Is Taking Lessons/On the Sentimental Side/This Is My Night to Dream— John Burke (w), James Monaco (m), Select. COVER: Bing Crosby, Mary Carlisle.

1194 Doctors Wives (Columbia, 1971, Dyan Cannon, Richard Crenna).

Costume Ball, The—Alan Bergman, Marilyn Bergman (w), Elmer Bernstein (m), Colgems. COVER: Dyan Cannon, Richard Crenna, Gene Hackman, and Others.

1195 Doctor You've Got to Be Kidding (MGM, 1966, Sandra Dee, George Hamilton).

I Haven't Got Anything Better to Do/Walk Tall Like a Man—Paul Vance, Lee Pockriss (w,m), Miller. COVER: Sandra Dee, George Hamilton.

1196 Doctor Zhivago (MGM, 1965, Geraldine Chaplin, Julie Christie).

Lara's Theme—Maurice Jarre (m), Robbins; Somewhere My Love—Paul F. Webster (w), Maurice Jarre (m), Robbins; Doctor Zhivago-Ten Themes —Maurice Jarre (m), Robbins. COVER: Omar Sharif, Geraldine Chaplin, Julie Christie.

1197 Dog of Flanders, A (20th Century-Fox, 1960, David Ladd, Donald Crisp).

Dog of Flanders, The—Al Stillman (w), Milton DeLugg (m), Robbins. COVER: David Ladd, Patrasche.

1198 Dollars (Columbia, 1971, Warren Beatty, Goldie Hawn).

Money Runner—Quincy Jones (m), Colgems. COVER: Warren Beatty, Goldie Hawn.

1199 Doll Face (20th Century-Fox, 1946, Vivian Blaine, Dennis O'Keefe).

Chico, Chico/Dig You Later/Here Comes Heaven Again/Red Hot and Beautiful/Somebody's Walking in My Dreams/Wouldn't It Be Nice—Harold Adamson (w), Jimmy McHugh (m), Robbins. COVER: Vivian Blaine, Dennis O'Keefe, Perry Como, Carmen Miranda.

1200 Dolly Sisters (20th Century-Fox, 1945, Betty Grable, June Haver).

Darktown Strutters Ball, The— Shelton Brooks (w,m), Feist; I Can't Begin to Tell You—Mack Gordon (w), James Monaco (m), BVC; I'm Always Chasing Rainbows—Joseph McCarthy (w), Harry Carroll (m), Miller; Vamp, The—Byron Gay (w, m), Feist. COVER: Betty Grable, June Haver, John Payne.

1200a Donald Duck (Disney, 1983, Cartoon).

Happy Happy Birthday to You— Michael Silversher, Patty Silversher (w,m), Wonderland. COVER: Cartoon.

1201 Donald Duck in Nutzi Land (Der Führer's Face) (Disney, 1942, Cartoon).

Der Führer's Face—Oliver Wallace (w,m), Southern. COVER: Cartoon.

1202 Don Juan (Warner Bros., 1927, John Barrymore, Mary Astor).

Don Juan—Harry Lee (w), William Axt (m), Warner; Don Juan Minuet— Wolfgang A. Mozart (m), Century; Don Juan Music Score—Edward Bowes, David Mendoza, William Axt (m), Warner. COVER: John Barrymore, Mary Astor.

1203 Donne Proibite (Angels of Darkness) (Excelsior, 1952, Linda Darnell, Anthony Quinn).

Sciummo-Fiume (B)—E. Bonagura, C. Concina (w,m), Leonardi. COVER: A River.

1204 Do Not Disturb (20th Century-Fox, 1965, Doris Day, Rod Taylor).

Au Revoir Is Goodbye with a Smile—Bob Hilliard (w), Mort Garson (m), Artists; Do Not Disturb—Mark Barkan, Ben Raleigh (w,m), Daywin. COVER: Doris Day, Rod Taylor.

1205 Don't Drink the Water (Embassy, 1969, Jackie Gleason, Estelle Parsons).

Don't Drink the Water—Kelly Gordon (w), Pat Williams (m), Shayne. COVER: Cartoon Sketch.

1206 Don't Fence Me In (Republic, 1945, Roy Rogers, Dale Evans).

Along the Navajo Trail—Larry Markes, Dick Charles, Eddie DeLange (w,m), Leeds. COVER: Roy Rogers, and Trigger.

1207 Don't Get Personal (Universal, 1942, Hugh Herbert, Jane Frazee).

Every Time a Moment Goes By/It Doesn't Make Sense/Now What Do We Do—Jack Brooks (w), Norman Berens (m), Robbins. COVER: Jane Frazee, Robert Paige.

1208 Don't Go Near the Water (MGM, 1957, Glenn Ford, Gia Scala).

Don't Go Near the Water—Sammy Cahn (w), Bronislau Kaper (m), Miller; Melora—Paul F. Webster (w), Bronislaw Kaper (m), Miller. COVER: Glenn Ford, and Girls.

1209 Don't Knock the Rock (Columbia, 1957, Bill Haley, Alan Dale).

Apple Jack—Dave Appell, Ed Appell, Norman Joyce (w,m), Kassner; Country Dance—Ollie Jones (w,m), Wemar; Don't Knock the

Rock—Robert Kent (w), Fred Karger (m), Valley Brook; Hook Line and Sinker/Out of the Bushes—Bill Haley, Ed Khoury, Ronnie Bonner (w,m), Valley Brook; Your Love Is My Love—Francis Edwards (w,m), Peer. COVER: Bill Haley, and Other Stars.

1210 Don't Make Waves (MGM, 1967, Tony Curtis, Claudia Cardinale).

Don't Make Waves—Jim McGunn, Chris Hillman (w,m), Hastings. COVER: Tony Curtis, Claudia Cardinale, Sharon Tate.

1211 Dorothy Vernon of Haddon Hall (United Artists, 1924, Mary Pickford, Allan Forest).

Love Has a Way—Victor Schertzinger (w,m), Flammer. COVER: Mary Pickford.

1212 Do the Right Thing (Universal, 1989, Danny Aiello, Ossie Davis).

My Fantasy—Gene Griffin, William Aquart (w,m), Belwyn. COVER: Danny Aiello.

1213 Double Crossing of Columbus (Vitaphone, 1933, Musical Short).

Rumba Rumble, The—Cliff Hess (w,m), Witmark. COVER: Black and white cover with title only.

1214 Double Crossroads (Fox, 1931, Lila Lee, Robert Ames).

Do You Believe in Love at Sight?—Gus Kahn (w), Ted Fiorito (m), Red Star; My Lonely Heart—William Kernell (w), Charles Cadman (m), Red Star; Show Me the Way—William Kernell (w,m). COVER: Lila Lee, Robert Ames.

1215 Double or Nothing (Vitaphone, 1936, Phil Harris, Leah Ray).

Don't Look Now—Irving Kahal (w), Sanford Green (m), Witmark. COVER: Phil Harris, Leah Ray.

1216 Double or Nothing (Paramount, 1937, Bing Crosby, Martha Raye).

After You—Sam Coslow, Al Siegel (w,m), Popular; All You Want to Do

Is Dance—John Burke (w), Arthur Johnston (m), Select; Double or Nothing—John Burke (w), Victor Young (m), Select; It's on It's Off—Sam Coslow, Al Siegel (w,m), Popular; It's the Natural Thing to Do—John Burke (w), Arthur Johnston (m), Select; Listen My Children and You Shall Hear—Ralph Freed (w), Burton Lane (m), Popular; Moon Got in My Eyes, The—John Burke (w), Arthur Johnston (m), Select; Smarty, You Know It All—Ralph Freed (w), Burton Lane (m), Popular. COVER: Bing Crosby, Martha Raye, Mary Carlisle.

1217 Double Trouble (MGM, 1967, Elvis Presley, Annette Day).

Baby If You'll Give Me All Your Love—Joy Byers (w,m), Presley; City By Night—Bill Giant, Florence Kaye, Bernie Baum (w,m), Presley; Could I Fall in Love—Randy Starr (w,m), Gladys; Double Trouble—Doc Pomus, Mort Shuman (w,m), Presley; I Love Only One Girl—Sid Tepper, Roy Bennett (w,m), Gladys; There's So Much World to See—Sid Wayne (w), Ben Weisman (m), Gladys. COVER: Elvis Presley.

1218 Dough Boys (Forward March) (MGM, 1930, Buster Keaton, Sally Eilers).

Sing—Howard Johnson (w), Joseph Meyer (m), Robbins. COVER: Buster Keaton, Sally Eilers.

1219 Doughboys in Ireland (Columbia, 1943, Kenny Baker, Jeff Donnell).

Little American Boy—Yetta Cohen (w,m), Robbins. COVER: Kenny Baker.

1220 Dove, The (Paramount, 1974, Joseph Bottoms, Deborah Raffin).

Sail the Summer Winds—Don Black (w), John Barry (m), Ensign. COVER: Joseph Bottoms, Deborah Raffin.

1221 Down Among the Sheltering Palms (20th Century-Fox, 1950, William Lundigan, Jane Greer).

Down Among the Sheltering Palms—James Brockman (w), Abe Olman (m), Miller; What Make De Difference?/Who Will It Be When the Time Comes?—Ralph Blane (w), Harold Arlen (m), Harwin. COVER: William Lundigan, Jane Greer, Mitzi Gaynor, Gloria DeHaven.

1222 Down Argentine Way (20th Century-Fox, Don Ameche, Betty Grable).

Down Argentine Way—Mack Gordon (w), Harry Warren (m), Miller; I Want My Mama/Mama Yo Quiero—Al Stillman (w), Jararaca, Vicente Paiva (m), Robbins; Nenita/Sing to Your Senorita/Two Dreams Met—Mack Gordon (w), Harry Warren (m), Miller. COVER: Don Ameche, Betty Grable, Carmen Miranda.

1223 Down Mexico Way (Republic, 1941, Gene Autry, Smiley Burnette).

Down Mexico Way—Jule Styne, Sol Meyer, Eddie Cherkose (w,m), Mills; Maria Elena—S. K. Russell (w), Lorenzo Barcelata (m), Peer. COVER: Gene Autry, Fay McKenzie.

1224 Down Missouri Way (PRC, 1946, Martha O'Driscoll, John Carradine).

Big Town Gal/If Something Doesn't Happen Soon/I'm So in Love with You/Just Can't Get That Guy/Monkey Business/Never Knew That I Could Sing/Old Missouri Hayride/There's a Rose That Grows in the Ozarks—Kim Gannon (w), Walter Kent (m), Southern. COVER: Martha O'Driscoll, John Carradine, and Others.

1225 Down to Earth (Columbia, 1947, Rita Hayworth, Larry Parks).

Let's Stay Young Forever/They Can't Convince Me—Allan Roberts, Doris Fisher (w,m), Mood. COVER: Rita Hayworth, Larry Parks.

1226 Down to Their Last Yacht (RKO, 1934, Mary Boland, Polly Moran).

Beach Boy—Ann Ronell (w,m), Berlin; Funny Little World—Ann Ronell, Max Steiner (w,m), Berlin; There's Nothing to Do in Ma-la-ka-mo-ka-lu—Cliff Friend, Sidney Mitchell (w,m), Berlin. COVER: Yacht Party.

1227 Do You Love Me (Kitten on the Keys) (20th Century-Fox, 1946, Maureen O'Hara, Dick Haymes).

Do You Love Me—Harry Ruby (w,m), BVC; I Didn't Mean a Word I Said—Harold Adamson (w), Jimmy McHugh (m), Robbins; Moonlight Propaganda—Herb Magidson (w), Matty Malneck (m), BVC; St. Louis Blues—W. C. Handy (w,m), Handy; As If I Didn't Have Enough on My Mind—Charles Henderson (w), Harry James, Lionel Newman (m), Melrose. COVER: Dick Haymes, Harry James, Maureen O'Hara.

1228 Dracula (Universal, 1979, Frank Langella, Laurence Olivier).

Dracula Theme—John Williams (m), Duchess. COVER: Frank Langella.

1229 Drag (First National, 1929, Richard Barthelmess, Katherine Parker).

I'm Too Young to Be Careful/My Song of the Nile—Al Bryan (w), George Meyer (m), Witmark. COVER: Richard Barthelmess.

1230 Dragnet (Warner Bros., 1954, Jack Webb, Ben Alexander).

Foggy Night in San Francisco—Sidney Miller (w), Herman Saunders (m), Miller. COVER: Jack Webb.

1231 Dragnet (Universal, 1987, Dan Aykroyd, Tom Hanks).

Just the Facts—James Harris, Terry Lewis (w,m), MCA. COVER: Dan Aykroyd, Tom Hanks.

1232 Dragonslayer (Paramount, 1981, Peter McNicol, Caitlin Clarke).

Dragonslayer Romantic Theme—Alex North (m), Famous. COVER: A Dragon.

1233 Drango (United Artists, 1957, Jeff Chandler, Joanne Dru).

Somehow—Alan Alch (w), Elmer Bernstein (m), Chandler. COVER: Linda Lawson.

1234 Dream a Little Dream (Vestron, 1989, Jason Robards, Piper Laurie).

Rock On—David Essex (w,m), Rock On Music; Dream a Little Dream of Me (VS)—Gus Kahn (w), W. Schwandt, F. Andree (m), Belwyn; Dreams Come True (VS)—Gregg Sutton, Maria McKee (w,m), Belwyn; Into the Mystic (VS)—Van Morrison (w,m), Belwyn; I've Got Dreams to Remember (VS)—Otis Redding, Zelma Redding, Joe Rock (w,m), Belwyn; Never Turn Away (VS)—Tom Whitlock, John Dexter (w,m), Belwyn; Time Runs Wild (VS)—Danny Wilde (w,m), Belwyn; Whenever There's a Night (VS)—Tom Whitlock (w), John Dexter (m), Belwyn; You'd Better Wait (VS)—Rick Neigher, James House (w,m), Belwyn. COVER: Teenagers.

1235 Dream Boat (20th Century-Fox, 1952, Ginger Rogers, Clifton Webb).

You'll Never Know (B)—Mack Gordon (w), Harry Warren (m), Victoria. COVER: Ginger Rogers.

1236 Dreamer (20th Century-Fox, 1979, Tim Matheson, Susan Blakely).

Reach for the Top—Bill Conti, Corey Lerios, David Jenkins (w,m), Fox. COVER: Tim Matheson, Susan Blakely, Jack Warden.

1237 Dream Girl (Paramount, 1948, Betty Hutton, MacDonald Carey).

Dream Girl/Drunk with Love—Jay Livingston, Ray Evans (w,m), Famous. COVER: Betty Hutton, MacDonald Carey.

1238 Dreaming Out Loud (RKO, 1940, Frances Langford, Phil Harris).

Dreaming Out Loud—Sam Coslow (w,m), Coslow. COVER: Frances Langford, Phil Harris, and Others.

1239 Dream of Love (MGM, 1929, Joan Crawford, Warner Oland).

Love o' Mine—Ernst Luz (m), Robbins. COVER: Black and white cover with title only.

1240 Dream Street (United Artists, 1921, Carol Dempster, Ralph Graves).

Someday, You'll Find Your Dream Street—B. G. DeSylva (w), Louis Silvers (m), Harms. COVER: Brown cover with title only.

1241 Dream Wife (MGM, 1952, Cary Grant, Deborah Kerr).

Ghi-li, Ghi-li, Ghi-li—Jamshid Sheibani, Charles Wolcott (w,m), Robbins. COVER: Cary Grant, Deborah Kerr.

1242 Dressed to Thrill (Fox, 1935, Tutta Roff, Clive Brook).

My Heart Is a Violin/My One Big Moment—Paul F. Webster (w), Lew Pollack (m), Movietone. COVER: Black and white cover with title only.

1243 Dress Parade (Pathe, 1926, William Boyd, Bessie Love).

Consolation—Maurice Gunsky (w), Merton Bories (m), Villa Moret. COVER: William Boyd, Bessie Love.

1244 Dr. No (United Artists, 1963, Sean Connery, Ursula Andress).

James Bond Theme/Jamaica Jump Up (VS)/Mango Tree (VS)—Monty Norman (m), Unart. COVER: Sean Connery.

1245 Dr. Strangelove or How I Learned to Stop Worrying and Love the Bomb (Columbia, 1964, Peter Sellers, George C. Scott).

We'll Meet Again—Ross Parker, Hughie Charles (w,m), World. COVER: Cartoon Sketch.

1246 Drum Beat (Warner Bros., 1954, Alan Ladd, Audrey Dalton).

Drum Beat—Ned Washington (w), Victor Young (m), Witmark. COVER: Alan Ladd, Audrey Dalton.

1247 Drums of Africa (MGM, 1962, Frankie Avalon, Mariette Hartley).

River Love—Russell Faith, Robert Marcucci (w,m), Debmar. COVER: Frankie Avalon, and Movie Scenes.

1248 Drums of the Congo (Universal, 1942, Ona Munson, Stuart Erwin).

Hear the Drums Beat Out/River Man/Round the Bend—Everett Carter (w), Milton Rosen (m), Robbins. COVER: Stuart Erwin, Don Terry, Ona Munson.

1249 DuBarry Was a Lady (MGM, 1943, Gene Kelly, Lucille Ball).

There'll Be a Hot Time in the Old Town Tonight (VS)—Joe Hayden, Theo Metz (w,m), Marks. COVER: Blue cover with title only.

1250 Duchess and Dirtwater Fox, The (20th Century-Fox, 1976, George Segal, Goldie Hawn).

Lemon Drops, Lollipops, and Sunbeams/Touch of Love—Sammy Cahn, Melvin Frank, Charles Fox (w, m), Fox. COVER: Cartoon Sketch.

1251 Duchess of Idaho (MGM, 1950, Esther Williams, Van Johnson).

Baby Come Out of the Clouds—Henry Nemo, Lee Pearl (w,m), Robbins; Let's Choo Choo to Idaho/Of All Things/You Can't Do Wrong Doin' Right—Al Rinker, Floyd Huddleston (w,m), Robbins. COVER: Esther Williams, Van Johnson, John Lund, Lena Horne, Eleanor Powell.

1252 Duck and Cover (CD, 1953, War Propaganda Film).

Bert the Turtle-Duck and Cover Song—Leon Carr, Leo Corday, Leo Langlos (w,m), Sheldon. COVER: A Turtle.

1253 Dudes Are Pretty People (United Artists, 1942, Jimmy Rogers, Noah Beery, Jr.).

West Wind Whistlin'—Chet Forrest, Bob Wright (w), Edward Ward (m), Robbins. COVER: Jimmy Rogers, Marjorie Woodworth, Noah Beery Jr.

1254 Duel at Diablo (United Artists, 1966, James Garner, Sidney Poitier).

Duel at Diablo Main Theme—Ernie Sheldon (w), Neal Hefti (m), Unart. COVER: James Garner, Sidney Poitier, and Battle Scene.

1255 Duel in the Jungle (Warner Bros., 1954, Jeanne Crain, Dana Andrews).

Night Belongs to Me, The—Norman Newell (w), Mischa Spoliansky (m), Chappell. COVER: Jeanne Crain, Dana Andrews.

1256 Duel in the Sun (RKO, 1947, Jennifer Jones, Gregory Peck).

Beautiful Dreamer (B)—Stephen Foster (w,m), Chappell; Duel in the Sun—Stanley Adams, Maxson Judell (w), Dimitri Tiomkin (m), Bourne; Gotta Get Me Somebody to Love—Allie Wrubel (w,m), Morris; Headin' Home—Fred Herbert (w), Dimitri Tiomkin (m), Morris; Orizaba Dance, The—Dimitri Tiomkin (m), Morris. COVER: Jennifer Jones, Gregory Peck.

1257 Duffy (Columbia, 1968, James Coburn, James Mason).

I'm Satisfied—Cynthia Weil (w), Barry Mann, Ernie Freeman (m), Colgems. COVER: Lou Rawls.

1258 Duffy's Tavern (Paramount, 1945, Ed Gardner, Bing Crosby).

Hard Way, The—Johnny Burke (w), James Van Heusen (m), Paramount. COVER: Bing Crosby, and Paramount Stars.

1259 Duke of West Point, The (United Artists, 1938, Tom Brown, Louis Hayward).

West Point Hop, The—Arthur Jones (w), Josef Myrow (m), Mills. COVER: Louis Hayward, Joan Fontaine.

1260 Duke Steps Out, The (MGM, 1929, Joan Crawford, William Haines).

Just You—Raymond Klages (w), William Axt, David Mendoza (m), Robbins. COVER: Joan Crawford, William Haines.

1261 Dumbo (RKO, Disney, 1941, Cartoon).

Baby Mine/Casey Junior/Look Out for Mister Stork—Ned Washington (w), Frank Churchill (m), Berlin; Pink Elephants on Parade—Ned Washington (w), Oliver Wallace (m), Berlin; Song of the Roustabouts—Ned Washington (w), Frank Churchill (m), Berlin. When I See an Elephant Fly—Ned Washington (w), Oliver Wallace (m), Berlin. COVER: Cartoon.

1262 Dune (Universal, 1984, Kyle MacLachlan, Francesca Annis).

Dune-Desert Theme—David Paich, Jeff Porcaro, Steve Porcaro, Mike Porcaro (w,m), Columbia; Dune Music Score-17 Themes—David Paich, Jeff Porcaro, Steve Porcaro (m), Columbia. COVER: Kyle MacLachlan, and Movie Scenes.

1263 Dust Be My Destiny (Warner Bros., 1939, John Garfield, Priscilla Lane).

Dust Be My Destiny—M. K. Jerome, Jack Scholl (w), Max Steiner (m), Harms. COVER: John Garfield, Priscilla Lane.

1264 Dynamite (MGM, 1929, Charles Bickford, Kay Johnson).

How Am I to Know—Dorothy Parker (w), Jack King (m), Robbins. COVER: Conrad Nagel, Charles Bickford.

1265 Eadie Was a Lady (Columbia, 1945, Ann Miller, Joe Besser).

Tabby the Cat—Harold Dickinson, Howard Gibeling (w,m), Leeds. COVER: Couple Dancing.

1266 Eagle, The (United Artists, 1925, Rudolph Valentino, Vilma Banky).

Eagle Overture—Lee Erwin (m), General; You My Love—Dailev Paskman (w), Bert Reisfeld (m), Marks. COVER: Rudolph Valentino.

1267 Eagles Brood, The (Paramount, 1935, William Boyd, James Ellison).

Free with Love—Sidney Mitchell (w), Sam Stept (m), Sam Fox. COVER: Nana Martinez.

1268 Earl Carroll Sketchbook (Republic, 1946, Constance Moore, William Marshall).

I've Never Forgotten/Lady with a Mop/Oh Henry/What Makes You

Beautiful, Beautiful?—Sammy Cahn (w), Jule Styne (m), Morros. COVER: Constance Moore, William Marshall.

1269 Earl Carroll Vanities (Republic, 1945, Constance Moore, Dennis O'Keefe).

Endlessly/Rockabye Boogie—Kim Gannon, Walter Kent (w,m), Bourne; Who Dat Up Dere—Bob Russell (w), Walter Kent (m), Morris. COVER: Constance Moore, Dennis O'Keefe, Woody Herman.

1270 Early to Wed (Easy to Wed) (MGM, 1946, Van Johnson, Esther Williams).

Come Closer to Me (PC)—Al Stewart (w), Osualdo Farres (m), Peer. COVER: None.

1271 Earthling, The (Filmways, 1980, William Holden, Ricky Schroeder).

Halfway Home—David Shire, Carol Connors (w,m), Dijon. COVER: Maureen McGovern.

1272 Earthquake (Universal, 1974, Charlton Heston, Ava Gardner).

Earthquake Love Theme/Earthquake Main Title—John Williams (m), Duchess. COVER: Charlton Heston, Ava Gardner, George Kennedy, and Other Stars.

1273 Easter Parade (MGM, 1948, Judy Garland, Fred Astaire).

Beautiful Faces/Better Luck Next Time/Couple of Swells, A/Drum Crazy/Easter Parade (BW)/Everybody's Doin' It/Fella with an Umbrella, A/Girl on the Magazine Cover, The/Happy Easter (BW)/I Love a Piano/I Want to Go Back to Michigan/It Only Happens When I Dance with You/Let's Take an Old Fashioned Walk (BW)/Mrs. Monotony/Ragtime Violin/Shakin' the Blues Away/Snooky Ookums/Steppin' Out with My Baby/When the Midnight Choo Choo Leaves for Alabam'—Irving Berlin (w,m), Berlin. COVER: Judy Garland, Fred Astaire, Peter Lawford, Ann Miller.

1274 East Is East (Independent, 1965, Casey Paxton).

East Is East—David L'Hereux (w, m), Claridge. COVER: Casey Paxton.

1275 East Is West (Universal, 1930, Lupe Velez, Edward G. Robinson).

Chinese Lullaby—Robin Hood Bowers (w,m), Schirmer. COVER: Lupe Velez.

1276 East of Eden (Warner Bros., 1956, Julie Harris, James Dean).

East of Eden Theme—Leonard Rosenman (m), Witmark. COVER: Pink cover with title only.

1277 East River (Under Pressure) (Fox, 1934, Edmund Lowe, Victor McLaglen).

I'll Go to Flannigan—Jack Yellen (w), Dan Dougherty (m), Movietone. COVER: Black and white cover with title only.

1278 Eastside of Heaven (Universal, 1939, Bing Crosby, Joan Blondell).

Eastside of Heaven/Hang Your Heart on a Hickory Limb/Sing a Song of Sunbeams/That Sly Old Gentleman—Johnny Burke (w), James Monaco (m), Santly Joy. COVER: Bing Crosby, Joan Blondell.

1279 Easy Come Easy Go (Paramount, 1947, Barry Fitzgerald, Diana Lynn).

Easy Come Easy Go—Jay Livingston, Ray Evans (w,m), Famous. COVER: Barry Fitzgerald, Diana Lynn, Sonny Tufts.

1280 Easy Come Easy Go (Paramount, 1967, Elvis Presley, Dodie Marshall).

Easy Come Easy Go—Sid Wayne (w), Ben Weisman (m), Gladys; Love Machine—Gerald Nelson, Chuck Taylor, Fred Burch (w,m), Presley. COVER: Elvis Presley.

1281 Easy Going (Way Out West (MGM, 1930, William Haines, Cliff Edwards).

Singing a Song to the Stars—Howard Johnson (w), Joseph Meyer (m), Robbins. COVER: Black and white cover with title only.

1282 Easy Living (Paramount,

1937, Jean Arthur, Edward Arnold).
Easy Living—Leo Robin, Ralph Rainger (w,m), Famous. COVER: Ray Milland, Jean Arthur.
1283 Easy Living (RKO, 1949, Victor Mature, Lucille Ball).
Easy Living—Leo Robin, Ralph Rainger (w,m), Famous. COVER: Victor Mature, Lucille Ball, Lizabeth Scott, Sonny Tufts.
1284 Easy Rider (Columbia, 1969, Peter Fonda, Dennis Hopper).
Ballad of the Easy Rider—Roger McGuinn (w,m), Blackwood; Wasn't Born to Follow—Gerry Goffin, Carole King (w,m), Columbia. COVER: Peter Fonda.
1285 Easy to Love (MGM, 1953, Van Johnson, Esther Williams).
Didja Ever—Mann Curtis (w), Vic Mizzy (m), Miller; Easy to Love—Cole Porter (w,m), Chappell; Look Out I'm Romantic/That's What a Rainy Day Is For—Mann Curtis (w), Vic Mizzy (m), Miller. COVER: Van Johnson, Esther Williams, Tony Martin.
1286 Easy to Wed (Early to Wed) (MGM, 1946, Van Johnson, Esther Williams).
Come Closer to Me—Al Stewart (w), Osvaldo Farres (m), Melody Lane; Continental Polka/Gonna Fall in Love with You—Johnny Green, Ralph Blane (w,m), Feist; Someone Shoulda Told Me—L. L. Kipp (w), Ary Barroso (m), Peer; Viva Mexico—Al Stewart (w), Pedro Galindo (m), Peer. COVER: Van Johnson, Esther Williams, Lucille Ball, and Others.
1287 Ebb Tide (Paramount, 1937, Frances Farmer, Oscar Homolka).
Ebb Tide—Leo Robin, Ralph Rainger (w,m), Paramount. COVER: The Ocean.
1288 Ecco (Olympic, 1965, Documentary on Strange Behaviours).
Ecco Waltz—Riz Ortolani (m), Marks; When Was the Moment?—Alan Bernstein (w), Riz Ortolani (m), Marks; You Know—Alan Brandt (w), Riz Ortolani (m), Marks. COVER

Movie Scenes.
1289 Ecstasy (Elekta, 1937, Hedy Lamarr, Jardmir Rogoz).
Down the Gypsy Trail—Walter Hirsch (w), Emery Heim, Denes Agay (m), Foreign; Lost in Ecstasy—William Colligan, Henry Gershwin (w, m), Foreign; Love Awakens in the Spring—William Colligan (w,m), Foreign; Oh Play Tzigani—William Colligan (w), Kola Jozsef (m), Foreign; What Do Gypsies Dream—William Colligan (w,m), Foreign. COVER: Hedy Lamarr.
1290 Eddie and the Cruisers (Embassy, 1983, Tom Berenger, Michael Pare).
On the Dark Side/Tender Years/Down on My Knees (VS)/Season in Hell, Fire Suite (VS)/Wild Summer Nights (VS)/Boardwalk Angel (VS)—John Cafferty (w,m), Warner. COVER: Michael Pare.
1291 Eddie Cantor Story, The (Warner Bros., 1953, Keefe Brasselle, Marilyn Erskine).
Ida, Sweet as Apple Cider—Eddie Leonard (w), Eddie Munron (m), Marks; If You Knew Susie—B. G. DeSylva, Joseph Meyer (w,m), Shapiro Bernstein; Josephine Please No Lean on the Bell—Ed Nelson, Harry Pease, Duke Leonard (w,m), Mutual; Ma, He's Making Eyes at Me—Sidney Clare (w), Con Conrad (m), Mills; Makin' Whoopee!—Gus Kahn (w), Walter Donaldson (m), BVC; Margie—Benny Davis (w), Con Conrad, J. Russel Robinson (m), Mills; Now's the Time to Fall in Love—Al Sherman, Al Lewis (w,m), DBH; Row Row Row—William Jerome (w), Jimmie Monaco (m), Von Tilzer. COVER: Keefe Brasselle, and Girls.
1292 Eddy Duchin Story, The (Columbia, 1956, Tyrone Power, Kim Novak).
Brazil—Bob Russell (w), Ary Barroso (m), Southern; Chopsticks—Delulli-Liszt (m), Columbia; Dizzy Fingers—Zez Confrey (m), Mills; Exactly Like You—Dorothy Fields

(w), Jimmy McHugh (m), Shapiro Bernstein; I Can't Give You Anything But Love—Dorothy Fields (w), Jimmy McHugh (m), Mills; It Must Be True—Gus Arnheim, Gordon Clifford (w), Harry Barris (m), Mills; Manhattan—Lorenz Hart (w), Richard Rodgers (m), Marks; On the Sunny Side of the Street—Dorothy Fields (w), Jimmy McHugh (m), Shapiro Bernstein; Shine—Cecil Mack, Lew Brown (w), Ford Dabney (m), Shapiro Bernstein; To Love Again—Ned Washington (w), Morris Stoloff, George Sidney (m), Columbia; To Love Again Theme—Morris Stoloff, George Sidney (m), Columbia. COVER: Tyrone Power, Kim Novak.

1293 Education of Sonny Carson, The (Paramount, 1974, Don Gordon, Rony Clanton).

Girl, Girl, Girl/Where Do I Go from Here—Bob Kessler (w), Coleridge Perkinson (m), Famous. COVER: Rony Clanton.

1294 Egg and I, The (Universal, 1947, Claudette Colbert, Fred MacMurray).

Egg and I, The—Harry Akst, Herman Ruby, Bert Kalmar, Al Jolson (w,m), Miller. COVER: Claudette Colbert, Fred MacMurray.

1295 Eggs Don't Bounce (Paramount, 1943, Cartoon).

Now Ya Done It—Buddy Kaye, Fred Wise (w), Sammy Timberg (m), Famous. COVER: Little Lulu.

1296 Eiger Sanction, The (Universal, 1975, Clint Eastwood, George Kennedy).

Eiger Sanction Theme—John Williams (m), Duchess. COVER: Clint Eastwood.

1297 Eight and One-Half (Embassy, 1963, Marcello Mastroianni, Claudia Cardinale).

Eight and One-Half Theme/Eight and One-Half—Six Themes—Nino Rota (m), Marks. COVER: Man, Woman, and Letters.

1298 Eight Girls in a Boat (Para-mount, 1934, Douglass Montgomery, Dorothy Wilson).

Day without You, A—Sam Coslow (w), Arthur Rebner (m), Famous; This Little Piggie Went to Market—Sam Coslow (w), Harold Lewis (m), DBH. Cover: Ethal Shutta and Girls.

1299 El Cid (Allied Artists, 1961, Charlton Heston, Sophia Loren).

El Cid Love Theme-Falcon and the Dove—Paul F. Webster (w), Miklos Rozsa (m), Robbins; El Cid-Ten Themes—Miklos Rozsa (m), Robbins. COVER: Castle and Warriors.

1300 El Dia Que Me Quieras (Day That You Cared) (Paramount, 1935, Carlos Gardel).

Blue Dawn—Jean Herbert (w), Carlos Gardel, Al LePera (m), Southern. COVER: Carlos Gardel.

1301 El Dorado (Paramount, 1966, John Wayne, Robert Mitchum).

El Dorado—John Gabriel (w), Nelson Riddle (m), Ensign. COVER: John Wayne, Robert Mitchum.

1302 Electra Glide in Blue (United Artists, 1973, Robert Blake, Billy Green Bush).

Tell Me—James V. Guercio (w,m), Unart. COVER: Highway Cops.

1303 Electric Dreams (MGM, 1984, Lenny Von Dohlen, Virginia Madsen).

Video—Jeff Lyons (w,m), April. COVER: A Computer.

1304 Electric Horseman, The (Columbia, 1979, Robert Redford, Jane Fonda).

Mammas Don't Let Your Babies Grow Up to Be Cowboys—Ed Bruce, Patsy Bruce (w,m), Tree; My Heroes Have Always Been Cowboys—Sharon Vaughn (w,m), Welk. COVER: Robert Redford, Jane Fonda.

1305 Elephant Walk (Paramount, 1954, Elizabeth Taylor, Dana Andrews).

Many Dreams Ago—Mack David (w), Franz Waxman (m), Paramount. COVER: Elizabeth Taylor, Dana Andrews, Peter Finch.

1306 Eleven Harrow House (20th

Century-Fox, 1974, Charles Grodin, Candice Bergen).

Day After Day/Long Live Love—Hal Shaper, Michael Lewis (w,m), Fox. COVER: Burglar on Roof.

1307 Elmer Fudd (Warner Bros., 1955, Cartoon).

Elmer Fudd/Elmer Fudd Goes Hunting—Jack Segal (w), Maddy Russell (m), Witmark. COVER: Cartoon.

1308 El Super (New Yorker, 1979, Orlando Jiminez Leal, Raymundo Hidalgo Gato).

New York Rush—Enrique Ubieta (m), Schirmer. COVER: Brown cover with title only.

1309 El Trovador de la Radio (Radio Troubadour) (Paramount, 1939, Tito Guizar).

Canto del Pueblo/Mujeres Latinas/Presumida—Nenette Noriega (w), Tito Guizar (m), Famous; Sueno de Amor/Trovador—Nenette Noriega (w), Tito Guizar, Rafael Gama (m), Famous. COVER: Tito Guizar.

1310 Elvira Madigan (Cinema Five, 1969, Pia Degermark, Thommy Berggren).

Elvira—Dorcas Cochran (w), Wolfgang A. Mozart (m), Beechwood; Elvira My Love—Bernard Gasso (w), Wolfgang A. Mozart (m), Lewis; Elvira Theme—Wolfgang A. Mozart (m), Lewis. COVER: A Couple.

1311 Embarrassing Moments (Universal, 1934, Chester Morris, Marion Nixon).

Dreaming a Threadbare Dream—Edward Ward, George Waggner (w, m), Mills; I Won't Think About Tomorrow—Sammy Lerner (w), Jay Gorney (m), Mills. COVER: Chester Morris, Marion Nixon.

1312 Emblems of Love (Progress, 1923, Jane Jennings, Jack Drumier).

Emblems of Love—Sidney Mitchell, Lew Pollack (w), Witmark. COVER: Jane Jennings, Jack Drumier.

1313 Embraceable You (Warner Bros., 1948, Geraldine Brooks, Dane Clark).

Embraceable You (B)—Ira Gershwin (w), George Gershwin (m), Chappell. COVER: Dane Clark, Geraldine Brooks.

1314 Emmanuelle (Columbia, 1975, Sylvia Kristel, Alan Curry).

Emmanuelle—Ken Howard, Alan Blaikley (w), Pierre Bachelet, Herve Roy (m), DeWolfe. COVER: Sylvia Kristel.

1315 Emmanuelle-Joys of a Woman (Paramount, 1976, Sylvia Kristel, Caroline Lawrence).

Emmanuelle, Joys of a Woman—Larry Kusik (w), Francis Lai (m), Famous. COVER: Sylvia Kristel.

1316 Emperor Jones (United Artists, 1933, Paul Robeson, Dudley Diggs).

Emperor Jones—Allie Wrubel (w, m), Harms. COVER: Native Dancer.

1317 Emperor of the North (Emperor of the North Pole) (20th Century-Fox, 1974, Ernest Borgnine, Lee Marvin).

Man and a Train, A—Hal David (w), Frank DeVol (m), Fox. COVER: Lee Marvin, Ernest Borgnine, and Train.

1318 Emperor Waltz, The (Paramount, 1946, Bing Crosby, Joan Fontaine).

Emperor Waltz, The—Johnny Burke (w), Johann Strauss (m), BVH; Friendly Mountains—Johnny Burke (w), Joseph Lilley (m), BVH; I Kiss Your Hand Madame—Sam Lewis, Joe Young (w), Ralph Erwin (m), Harms; Kiss in Your Eyes, The—Johnny Burke (w), R. Heuberger (m), BVH; Whistler and His Dog, The—Arthur Pryor (m), Fischer. COVER: Bing Crosby, Joan Fontaine.

1319 Empire of the Sun (Warner Bros., 1987, Christian Hale, John Malkovitch).

Ex Sultate Justi—John Williams (m), Warner. COVER: A Boy, a Bright Sun, and Plane.

1320 Empire Strikes Back, The (20th Century-Fox, 1980, Mark Hamill, Harrison Ford).

Empire Strikes Back Medley/Han Solo and the Princess/Imperial March and Darth Vader Theme/May the Force Be with You/Yoda's Theme/Empire Strikes Back-Six Themes—John Williams (m), Fox. COVER: Space Man.

1321 Empty Arms (Park Whiteside, 1920, Gail Kane, Thurston Hall).

Empty Arms—Anton Nelson, Thurston Hall (w), George Graff (m), World. COVER: Gail Kane.

1322 Enchanted Cottage, The (RKO, 1945, Robert Young, Dorothy McGuire).

Enchanted Cottage—Jon Gart, Norman Fredbee, Carley Mills (w, m), Southern. COVER: Robert Young, Dorothy McGuire.

1323 Enchanted Island (RKO, 1958, Dana Andrews, Jane Powell).

Enchanted Island—Al Stillman (w), Robert Allen (m), Korwin. COVER: Dana Andrews, Jane Powell.

1324 Enchantment (RKO, 1948, Teresa Wright, David Niven).

Enchantment—Don Raye, Gene DePaul (w,m), Simon. COVER: Teresa Wright, David Niven, Evelyn Keyes, Farley Granger.

1325 End, The (United Artists, 1978, Burt Reynolds, Dom DeLuise).

Here's Another Mess—Paul Williams (w,m), Unart. COVER: Burt Reynolds, Dom DeLuise.

1326 Endless Love (Universal, 1981, Brooke Shields, Martin Hewitt).

Endless Love—Lionel Richie (w, m), Chappell; Dreamin' (VS)—Alan Tarney, Leo Sayer (w,m), Leonard; Dreaming of You (VS)—Lionel Richie, Thomas McClary (w,m), Leonard; I Was Made for Lovin' You (VS)—Paul Stanley, Vini Poncia, Desmond Child (w,m), Leonard. COVER: Brooke Shields, Martin Hewitt.

1327 End of the Affair, The (Columbia, 1955, Van Johnson, Deborah Kerr).

End of the Affair, The (B)—Ken Taylor (w), Red Perksey (m), Southern. COVER: Van Johnson, Deborah Kerr.

1328 Enemies of Women (Paramount, 1923, Lionel Barrymore, Alma Rubens).

Enemies of Women Themes—William Peters (m), Richmond. COVER: Cartoon sketches.

1329 England Made Me (Cineglobe, 1972, Peter Finch, Michael York).

Remembering—Arthur Hamilton (w), John Scott (m), James. COVER: Silhouette of Girl.

1330 Enlighten Thy Daughter (Exploitation, 1933, Herbert Rawlinson, Miriam Battista).

Don't Keep Me in the Dark/Just to Be Alone with You/Romancing with You—Allen Taub (w), Lou Herscher (m), Mills. COVER: Herbert Rawlinson, Miriam Battista.

1331 Ensign Pulver (Warner Bros., 1964, Robert Walker, Burl Ives).

Sentimental Journey—Bud Green, Les Brown, Ben Homer (w,m), Morely. COVER: Robert Walker.

1332 Enter Laughing (Columbia, 1967, Jose Ferrer, Shelley Winters).

Enter Laughing—Mack David (w), Quincy Jones (m), Colgems. COVER: Mel Carter.

1333 Eric Soya's Seventeen (Peppercorn, 1967, Ole Soltoft, Ghita Norby).

Seventeen—Alan Brandt (w), Ole Hoyer (m), Marks. COVER: Boy and Girls.

1334 Errand Boy, The (Paramount, 1961, Jerry Lewis, Brian Donlevy).

That's My Way—Jerry Lewis, Bill Richmond (w), Louis Brown (m), Famous. COVER: Jerry Lewis.

1335 Escapade (MGM, 1935, William Powell, Luise Rainer).

You're All I Need—Gus Kahn (w), Bronislau Kaper, Walter Jurmann (m), Robbins. COVER: William Powell, Luise Rainer.

1336 Escape from Fort Bravo (MGM, 1953, William Holden, Eleanor Parker).
Soothe My Lonely Heart—Jeff Alexander (w,m), Feist. COVER: William Holden, Eleanor Parker.
1337 Escape from the Planet of the Apes (20th Century-Fox, 1971, Roddy McDowell, Kim Hunter).
Escape from the Planet of the Apes Theme—Jerry Goldsmith (m), Fox. COVER: Roddy McDowell, Kim Hunter.
1338 Escape Me Never (Warner Bros., 1947, Errol Flynn, Ida Lupino).
Escape Me Never Ballet Theme (B)—William Walton (m), Day; Love for Love—Ted Koehler (w), Erich W. Korngold (m), Witmark; O'Nene—Erich W. Korngold (m), Witmark. COVER: Errol Flynn, Ida Lupino, Eleanor Parker, Gig Young.
1339 Eternal City, The (First National, 1923, Lionel Barrymore, Barbara Lamarr).
Eternal City of Dreams—Gus Kahn (w), Ted Fiorito (m), Remick. COVER: Lionel Barrymore, Barbara Lamarr.
1340 Eternal Feminine, The (Paramount, 1931, Doria March, Guy Newall).
Bon Soir (B)/Everybody Knows (B)/Rhythmic Melody (B)—Max Gartman, Rock Williams (w), Doria March (m), Ricordi. COVER: Doria March.
1341 Eternal Flame, The (First National, 1922, Norma Talmadge, Conway Tearle).
Eternal Flame, The—J. Keirn Brennan (w), Ernest Ball (m), Witmark. COVER: Norma Talmadge.
1342 Eternal Love (United Artists, 1929, John Barrymore, Camilla Horn).
Eternal Love—Ballard MacDonald, Dave Dreyer, Peter Derose (w,m), Berlin. COVER: John Barrymore, Camilla Horn.
1343 Eternally Yours (United Artists, 1939, Loretta Young, David Niven).
Eternally Yours—L. Wolfe Gilbert (w), Werner Janssen (m), Wolf Gilbert. COVER: Loretta Young, David Niven.
1344 E.T. The Extra Terrestrial (Universal, 1982, Dee Wallace, Henry Thomas).
E.T. Theme/E.T.-Six Themes/Over the Moon—John Williams (m), MCA; Someone in the Dark—Alan Bergman, Marilyn Bergman (w), Rod Temperton (m), MCA. Two Hands.
1345 Evangeline (Fox, 1919, Miriam Cooper, Albert Roscoe).
Evangeline—Joseph McCarthy (w), Fred Fisher (m), McCarthy Fisher. COVER: Miriam Cooper.
1346 Evangeline (United Artists, 1929, Dolores Del Rio, Roland Drew).
Evangeline—Billy Rose (w), Al Jolson (m), Berlin. COVER: Dolores Del Rio.
1347 Eve Knew Her Apples (Columbia, 1945, Ann Miller, William Wright).
I'll Remember April—Don Raye, Gene DePaul, Pat Johnston (w,m), Leeds. COVER: Ann Miller.
1348 Evensong (GP, 1934, Evelyn Laye, Fritz Kortner).
I Wait for You—Edward Knoblock (w), Mischa Spoliansky (m), Harms. COVER: Evelyn Laye.
1349 Evergreen (GB, 1935, Jessie Matthews, Sonnie Hale).
Over My Shoulder/Tinkle Tinkle Tinkle—Harry Woods (w,m), Harms; When You've Got a Little Sunshine in Your Heart—Harry Woods (w,m), Harms. COVER: Jessie Matthews.
1350 Ever Since Eve (Fox, 1934, George O'Brien, Mary Brian).
Horsey—George Marshall (w), Cally Holden (m), Movietone. COVER: Black and white cover with title only.
1351 Ever Since Eve (Warner Bros., 1937, Marion Davies, Robert Montgomery).
Ever Since Eve (PC)—Jack Scholl (w), M. K. Jerome (m), Harms. COVER: None.

1352 Everybody Sing (MGM, 1938, Allan Jones, Judy Garland).

Melody Farm/One I Love, The— Gus Kahn (w), Bronislau Kaper, Walter Jurmann (m), Feist; Quainty, Dainty Me (PC)—Bert Kalmar, Harry Ruby (w,m), Feist; Swing Mister Mendolssohn—Gus Kahn (w), Bronislaw Kaper, Walter Jurman (m), Feist. COVER: Judy Garland, Allan Jones.

1353 Everybody's Old Man (Fox, 1936, Rochelle Hudson, Johnny Downs).

Franklin's Foods—Jack Yellen (w), Lew Pollack (m), Movietone. COVER: Black and white cover with title only.

1354 Every Day's a Holiday (Paramount, 1937, Mae West, Edmund Lowe).

Every Day's a Holiday—Sam Coslow, Barry Trivers (w,m), Famous; Fifi—Sam Coslow (w,m), Famous; Jubilee—Stanley Adams (w), Hoagy Carmichael (m), Famous. COVER: Mae West.

1355 Every Night at Eight (Paramount, 1935, George Raft, Alice Faye).

Every Night at Eight—Dorothy Fields, Jimmy McHugh (w,m), Robbins; I Feel a Song Comin' On—Dorothy Fields, Jimmy McHugh, George Oppenheim (w,m), Robbins; I'm in the Mood for Love/Speaking Confidentially/Take It Easy—Dorothy Fields, Jimmy McHugh (w,m), Robbins; Then You've Never Been Blue —Sam Lewis, Joe Young (w), Ted Fiorito (m), Remick. COVER: George Raft, Alice Faye, Frances Langford, Patsy Kelly.

1356 Every Saturday Night (20th Century-Fox, 1936, June Lang, Thomas Beck).

Breathes There a Man—Herb Magidson (w), Burton Lane (m), Movietone. COVER: Black and white cover with title only.

1357 Everything Happens to Me (Warner Bros., 1938, Max Miller, Chilli Bouchier).

At the Bathing Parade (B)—Fred Godfrey, Max Miller (w,m), Wright. COVER: Max Miller, and Chorus.

1358 Everything in Life (Columbia, 1936, Gitta Alpar, Neil Hamilton).

To Everything in Life (B)—Ruth Feiner (w), Hans May (m), Wright. COVER: Gitta Alpar.

1359 Everything I Have Is Yours (MGM, 1952, Marge Champion, Gower Champion).

Derry Down Dilly—Johnny Mercer (w), Johnny Green (m), Miller; Everything I Have Is Yours—Harold Adamson (w), Burton Lane (m), Robbins; Seventeen Thousand Telephone Poles—Saul Chaplin (w,m), Miller. COVER: Marge and Gower Champion, Dennis O'Keefe, Monica Lewis.

1360 Everything You Always Wanted to Know About Sex But Were Afraid to Ask (United Artists, 1972, Woody Allen, Burt Reynolds).

Everything You Always Wanted to Know-Theme—Mundell Lowe (m), Unart. COVER: Woody Allen, Burt Reynolds, and Others.

1361 Every Which Way but Loose (Warner Bros., 1978, Clint Eastwood, Sondra Locke).

Coca Cola Cowboy—S. Pinkard, I. Dain, S. Dorff, S. Atchley (w,m), Peso; Every Which Way but Loose— Stephen Dorff, Milton Brown, T. Garrett (w,m), Peso; I'll Wake You Up When I Get Home—Stephen Dorff, Milton Brown (w,m), Peso; Send Me Down to Tucson—C. Crofford, T. Garrett (w,m), Peso. COVER: Clint Eastwood, and Monkey.

1362 Evidence (Divorce Evidence) (Warner Bros., 1929, Pauline Frederick, Lowell Sherman).

Little Cavalier—Al Dubin (w), M. K. Jerome (m), Witmark. COVER: Pauline Frederick, Freddie Frederick.

1363 Evil Eye, The (Hallmark, 1920, Benny Leonard, Stuart Holmes).

Evil Eye, The—Benny Leonard, Alex Sullivan, Jack Mills (w,m), Mills. COVER: Benny Leonard.

1364 Evil Under the Sun (Universal, 1982, Peter Ustinov, Colin Blakely).

Anything Goes (VS)/Begin the Beguine (VS)/Get Out of Town (VS)/ I Concentrate on You (VS)/I Get a Kick Out of You (VS)/I'm Going in for Love (VS)/Information Please (VS)/In the Still of the Night (VS)/ It's Delovely (VS)/I've Got my Eyes on You (VS)/I've Got You Under My Skin (VS)/Just One of Those Things (VS)/Longing for Dear Old Broadway (VS)/My Heart Belongs to Daddy (VS)/Night and Day (VS)/ Vite Vite Vite (VS)/You Do Something to Me (VS)/You're the Top (VS)—Cole Porter (w,m), Leonard. COVER: Peter Ustinov, Maggie Smith, and Other Stars.

1365 Excess Baggage (MGM, 1928, William Haines, Josephine Dunn).

In a Little Hideaway—Howard Dietz (w), William Axt, David Mendoza (m), Berlin. COVER: William Haines, Josephine Dunn.

1366 Excuse My Dust (MGM, 1951, Red Skelton, Sally Forrest).

Goin' Steady/I'd Like to Take You Dreaming/Lorelei Brown/Spring Has Sprung/That's for Children— Dorothy Fields (w), Arthur Schwartz (m), Putnam. COVER: Red Skelton, Sally Forrest, and Others.

1367 Exodus (United Artists, 1960, Paul Newman, Eva Marie Saint).

Exodus Song—Pat Boone (w), Ernest Gold (m), Chappell; Exodus Theme/Exodus-Eight Themes—Ernest Gold (m). COVER: A Ship and a Gun.

1368 Exorcist, The (Warner Bros., 1973, Ellen Burstyn, Max Von Sydow).

Tubular Bells—Mike Oldfield (m), Virgin. COVER: Bells.

1369 Experiment in Terror (Columbia, 1962, Glenn Ford, Lee Remick).

Experiment in Terror/Fluters Ball (VS)/White on White (VS)—Henry Mancini (m), Southdale. COVER: Glenn Ford, Lee Remick.

1370 Exploits of Elaine, The (Pathe, 1915, Pearl White, Arnold Daly).

Elaine My Moving Picture Queen —Howard Wesley (w), Charles Elbert (m), Feist; That Clutching Hand —Coleman Goetz (w), Jean Schwartz (m), Berlin. COVER: Pearl White.

1371 Explorers (Paramount, 1985, Ethan Hawke, River Phoenix).

Explorers Theme, Class Reunion— Jerry Goldsmith (m), Ensign. COVER: A Fence and Bicycle.

1372 Expresso Bongo (Continental, 1961, Laurence Harvey, Sylvia Sims).

Voice in the Wilderness—Bunny Lewis (w), Norrie Paramor (m), Chappell. COVER: Cliff Richard.

1373 Eye for Eye (Metro, 1918, Nazimova, Charles Bryant).

Nazimova Valse—Raffaele Paone (m), Ashers. COVER: Nazimova.

1374 Eyes of Laura Mars, The (Columbia, 1978, Faye Dunaway, Tommy Lee Jones).

Eyes of Laura Mars Love Theme-Prisoner—Karen Lawrence, John Desautels (w,m), Diana; Burn (VS)— George Michalski, Niki Odsterveen (w,m), Unichappell; Eyes of Laura Mars Solo (VS)—Karen Lawrence, John Desautels (m), Unichappell; Laura and Neville (VS)—Artie Kane (m), Unichappell; Let's All Chant (VS)—Alvin Fields, Michael Zager (w,m), Unichappell; Native New Yorker (VS)—Denny Randell, Sandy Linzer (w,m), Unichappell; Shake Your Booty (VS)—Harry Casey, Richard Finch (w,m), Unichappell. COVER: Faye Dunaway.

1375 Eyes of the Soul (Paramount, 1919, Elsie Ferguson, Wyndham Standing).

Eyes of the Soul—Ralph Williams (w), Fred Fisher (m), McCarthy Fisher. COVER: Elsie Ferguson.

1376 Eyes of the World (United Artists, 1930, Una Merkel, John Holland).
Love Alone—James Dietrich (w, m), Feist. COVER: Black and white cover with title only.
1377 Eyes of Youth (Paramount, 1919, Clara Kimball Young, Rudolph Valentino).
Eyes of Youth—Irving Berlin (w, m), Berlin. COVER: Clara Kimball Young.
1378 Fabiola (Marinelli, 1920, Elaine DiSangro, Amelaide Poletti).
Fabiola—Alexander Henneman (m), Matre. COVER: Elaine Di-Sangro, Amelaide Poletti.
1378a Fabulous Baker Boys, The (20th Century-Fox, 1989, Jeff Bridges, Beau Bridges).
Makin' Whoopee—Gus Kahn (w), Walter Donaldson (m), Warner. COVER: Jeff Bridges, Beau Bridges, Michelle Pfeiffer.
1379 Fabulous Dorseys, The (United Artists, 1947, Jimmy Dorsey, Tommy Dorsey).
At Sundown—Walter Donaldson (w,m), Feist; Green Eyes—Adolfo Utrera (w), Nilo Menendez (m), Southern; I'm Getting Sentimental Over You—Ned Washington (w), George Bassman (m), Mills; Marie—Irving Berlin (w,m), Berlin; To Me—Don George (w), Allie Wrubel (m), Dorsey. COVER: Tommy Dorsey, Jimmy Dorsey, Janet Blair, Paul Whiteman.
1380 Fabulous Senorita, The (Republic, 1952, Estrelita, Robert Clarke).
You've Changed—Edward Heyman, Tony Martin, Victor Young (w,m), Young. COVER: Estrelita.
1381 Face in the Crowd, A (Warner Bros., 1957, Andy Griffith, Patricia Neal).
Face in the Crowd, A/Free Man in the Morning/Just Plain Folks/Mama Guitar/Old Fashioned Marriage—Tom Glazer, Budd Schulberg (w,m), Remick. COVER: Andy Griffith, Patricia Neal.
1382 Face in the Sky (Fox, 1933, Marion Nixon, Spencer Tracy).
Just Another Dream—Val Burton, Will Jason (w,m), Movietone. COVER: Black and white cover with title only.
1383 Face the Music (The Black Glove) (Lippert, 1954, Alex Nicol, Eleanor Summerfield).
Trumpet Fantasy (B)—Kenny Baker (m), Campbell. COVER: Alex Nicol.
1384 Face to the Wind (Naked Revenge) (Warner Bros., 1974, Cliff Potts, Xochitl).
Ballad of Billy, The—Gerry Browne (w), George Barrie (m), Brut. COVER: Couple on Horse.
1385 Facts of Life, The (United Artists, 1960, Bob Hope, Lucille Ball).
Facts of Life, The—Johnny Mercer (w,m), Commander. COVER: Bob Hope, Lucille Ball.
1386 Fair Co-ed (MGM, 1927, Marion Davies, Johnny Mack Brown).
Fair Co-ed—Alfred Bryan (w), William Axt, David Mendoza (m), Berlin. COVER: College Students.
1387 Faithful in My Fashion (MGM, 1946, Donna Reed, Tom Drake).
I Don't Know Why—Toy Turk (w), Fred Ahlert (m), Feist. COVER: Donna Reed, Tom Drake.
1388 Falcon and the Snow Man, The (Orion, 1985, Sean Penn, Timothy Hutton).
This Is Not America—Pat Metheny, Lyle Mays, David Bowie (w,m), Donna. COVER: Sean Penn, Timothy Hutton.
1389 Fallen Angel (20th Century-Fox, 1945, Alice Faye, Dana Andrews).
Slowly—Kermit Goell (w), David Raksin (m), Vallee. COVER: Alice Faye, Dana Andrews, Linda Darnell.
1390 Fallen Idol, A (Fox, 1919, Evelyn Nesbit, Lillian Lawrence).

Fallen Idols—Alfred Bryan, John Kellette (w), Richard Whiting (m), Remick. COVER: Evelyn Nesbit.

1391 Falling for You (Gainsborough, 1933, Cicely Courtneidge, Jack Hulbert).

Sweep/You Don't Understand—Douglas Furber (w), Vivian Ellis (m), Chappell. COVER: Cicely Courtneidge, Jack Hulbert.

1392 Falling in Love (Paramount, 1984, Robert DeNiro, Meryl Streep).

Falling in Love-Love Theme—Dave Grusin (m), Ensign. COVER: Robert DeNiro, Meryl Streep.

1393 Fall of a Nation (National, 1916, Lorraine Huling, Percy Standing).

Fall of a Nation Love Theme—Victor Herbert (m), Witmark. COVER: Black and white cover with title only.

1394 Fall of Babylon, The (Intolerance) (Griffith, 1916, Constance Talmadge, Alfred Paget).

At the Fall of Babylon—Fred Fisher (w,m), McCarthy Fisher. COVER: Constance Talmadge, and Movie Scene.

1395 Fall of the Roman Empire, The (Paramount, 1964, Sophia Loren, Stephen Boyd).

Fall of Love—Ned Washington (w), Dimitri Tiomkin (m), Feist; Fall of Love Theme/Fall of the Roman Empire-Nine Themes—Dimitri Tiomkin (m), Feist. COVER: Sophia Loren, Stephen Boyd, and Other Stars.

1396 False Faces (Paramount, 1919, Henry Walthall, Lon Chaney).

False Faces—Edgar Leslie (w), Pete Wendling (m), Berlin. COVER: Henry Walthall, Mary Anderson.

1397 False Faces (Republic, 1943, Bill Henry, Veda Ann Borg).

Trifle on the Triflin' Side, A—Ken Darby (w), Walter Scharf (m), Southern. COVER: Bill Henry, Veda Ann Borg.

1398 Fame (Cinema International, 1980, Eddie Barth, Irene Cara).

Fame/I Sing the Body Electric—Dean Pitchford (w), Michael Gore (m), Warner; Out Here on My Own—Lesly Gore (w), Michael Gore (m), Warner; Red Light—Dean Pitchford (w), Michael Gore (m), Warner; Dogs in the Yard (VS)—Dominic Bugatti, Frank Musker (w,m), Warner; Hot Lunch Jam (VS)—Lesly Gore, Michael Gore, Bob Colesberry (w,m), Warner; Is It Okay If I Call You Mine?—Paul McCrane (w,m), Warner; Never Alone (VS)—Anthony Evans (w,m), Warner; Ralph and Monty (VS)—Michael Gore (m), Warner. COVER: Irene Cara, and Students.

1399 Family Jewels, The (Paramount, 1965, Jerry Lewis, Sebastian Cabot).

So Warm My Love—Paul F. Webster (w), Pete King (m), Famous. COVER: Jerry Lewis.

1400 Family Secret, The (Universal, 1924, Baby Peggy, Gladys Hulette).

Baby Peggy Theme (PC)—A. Winkler (w), J. Titlebaum (m), Belwyn. COVER: None.

1401 Family Way, The (Warner Bros., 1966, Hayley Mills, Hywel Bennett).

Family Way, The/Love in the Open Air—Paul McCartney (m), Comet. COVER: George Martin.

1402 Famous Ferguson Case, The (First National, 1932, Tom Brown, Joan Blondell).

Famous Ferguson Case Themes (PC)—Leo Forbstein (m), MPHC. COVER: None.

1403 Fancy Pants (Paramount, 1952, Bob Hope, Lucille Ball).

Fancy Pants/Home Cookin'—Jay Livingston, Ray Evans (w,m), Paramount. COVER: Bob Hope. Lucille Ball.

1404 Fancy That (Pathe, 1929, William Frawley).

Dearest One—Billy Curtis (w), Larry Conley (m), Shapiro Bernstein.

COVER: William Frawley, and Chorus Girls.

1405 Fanny (Warner Bros., 1961, Leslie Caron, Maurice Chevalier).

Fanny—Harold Rome (w,m), Florence. COVER: Leslie Caron, Charles Boyer, Maurice Chevalier, Horst Buchholtz.

1406 Fanny Hill (Favorite, 1964, Miriam Hopkins, Walter Giller).

I Remember Her So Well—Shelly Coburn, Scott English (w), Erwin Halletz (m), Helios. COVER: Sketch of Girl.

1407 Fantasia (RKO, Disney, 1940, Cartoon).

Ave Maria—Rachel Field (w), Franz Schubert (m), Disney; Nutcracker Suite—P. Tchaikovsky (m), Disney; Fantasia-Six Classical Themes —P. Tchaikovsky, L. Beethoven, G. Ponchielli (m), Chappell. COVER: Cartoons.

1408 Farewell to Arms, A (Paramount, 1933, Helen Hayes, Gary Cooper).

Farewell to Arms, A—Allie Wrubel, Abner Silver (w,m), Keit Engel. COVER: Helen Hayes, Gary Cooper.

1409 Farewell to Arms, A (20th Century-Fox, 1957, Rock Hudson, Jennifer Jones).

Farewell to Arms Love Theme—Paul F. Webster (w), Mario Nascimbene (m), Feist. COVER: Rock Hudson, Jennifer Jones.

1410 Far from the Madding Crowd (MGM, 1967, Julie Christie, Terence Stamp).

Far from the Madding Crowd #1—Paul F. Webster (w), Richard R. Bennett (m), Miller; Far from the Madding Crowd #2—Hal Shaper (w), Cyril Ornadel (m), Famous. COVER: Julie Christie, Terence Stamp, Alan Bates, Peter Finch.

1411 Far Horizons, The (Paramount, 1955, Fred MacMurray, Charlton Heston).

Janey—Wilson Stone (w), Hans Salter (m), Paramount. COVER: Charlton Heston, Donna Reed.

1412 Farmer Takes a Wife, The (20th Century-Fox, 1953, Betty Grable, Dale Robertson).

Can You Spell Schenectady/On the Erie Canal/Somethin' Real Special/Today I Love Everybody/We're Doing It for the Natives of Jamaica/We're in Business/When I Close the Door/With the Sun Warm Upon My Face—Dorothy Fields (w), Harold Arlen (m), Harwin. COVER: Betty Grable, Dale Robertson.

1413 Fascination (Metro, 1922, Mae Murray, Creighton Hale).

Fascination—A. Francis, S. Green (w), Louis Silvers (m), Richmond Robbins. COVER: Mae Murray.

1414 Fashion Row (Metro, 1923, Mae Murray, Earle Fox).

Fashion Row—Ormsby Watson (w), Norman Spencer (m), Sunset. COVER: Mae Murray.

1415 Fashions in Love (Paramount, 1929, Fay Compton, Adolphe Menjoy).

Delphine/I Still Believe in You—Leo Robin (w), Victor Schertzinger (m), Famous. COVER: Fay Compton, Adolphe Menjou.

1416 Fashions of 1934 (First National, 1934, Bette Davis, William Powell).

Spin a Little Web of Dreams—Irving Kahal (w), Sammy Fain (m), Harms. COVER: Bette Davis.

1417 Fast Break (Columbia, 1979, Gabriel Kaplan, Harold Sylvester).

Go for It/With You I'm Born Again (PC)—Carol Connors (w), David Shire (m), Check Out. COVER: Gabriel Kaplan.

1418 Fast Forward (Columbia, 1985, John Clough, Don Franklin).

Do You Want It Right Now—China Burton, Nick Straker (w,m), Virgin. COVER: Boys and Girls.

1419 Fast Life (First National, 1929, Douglas Fairbanks, Loretta Young).

Fast Life and a Hot One, A (PC)—Herman Ruby (w), Ray Perkins (m), Witmark; Since I Found You—Herman Ruby (w), Ray Perkins (m), Piantadosi. COVER: Douglas Fairbanks, Loretta Young.

1420 Fast Times at Ridgemont High (Universal, 1982, Sean Penn, Jennifer Leigh).

Somebody's Baby—Jackson Browne, Danny Kortchmar (w,m), Warner; So Much in Love—W. Jackson, G. Williams, R. Straigis (w,m), Abkco. COVER: Jackson Browne.

1421 Fatal Attraction (Paramount, 1987, Glenn Close, Michael Douglas).

Fatal Attraction Theme—Maurice Jarre (m), Famous. COVER: Glenn Close, Michael Douglas.

1422 Fatal Lady (Paramount, 1936, Mary Ellis, Walter Pidgeon).

Je Vous Adore—Sam Coslow, Victor Young (w,m), Famous. COVER: Mary Ellis.

1423 Fatal Ring, The (Pathe, 1915, Pearl White, Warner Oland).

Fatal Ring, The—Charles McCarron, Arthur Jackson (w), James Hanley (m), Shapiro Bernstein. COVER: Pearl White.

1424 Fate Is the Hunter (20th Century-Fox, 1964, Glenn Ford, Nancy Kwan).

Fate Is the Hunter—Don Wolf (w), Jerry Goldsmith (m), Hastings; No Love No Nothin'—Leo Robin (w), Harry Warren (m), Triangle. COVER: Glenn Ford, Nancy Kwan, Jane Russell.

1425 Father Goose (Universal, 1964, Cary Grant, Leslie Caron).

Pass Me By—Carolyn Leigh (w), Cy Coleman (m), Morris. COVER: Leslie Caron, Cary Grant.

1426 Fathom (20th Century-Fox, 1967, Raquel Welch, Tony Franciosa).

Fathom Theme, Sky Girl—John Dankworth (m), Miller. COVER: Raquel Welch.

1427 Fazil (Fox, 1925, Charles Farrell, Greta Nissen).

Neapolitan Nights—Harry Kerr (w), J. S. Zamecnik (m), Sam Fox. COVER: Charles Farrel, Greta Nissen.

1428 F.B.I. Story, The (Warner Bros., 1959, James Stewart, Vera Miles).

What Do I Care—Al Stillman (w), Max Steiner (m), Witmark. COVER: James Stewart, Vera Miles.

1429 Fearless Fagan (MGM, 1952, Janet Leigh, Carlton Carpenter).

What Do You Think I Am (B)—Hugh Martin, Ralph Blane (w,m), Chappell. COVER: Janet Leigh, Carlton Carpenter.

1430 Felix the Cat (Pathe, 1928, Cartoon).

Felix the Cat—Alfred Bryan (w), Pete Wendling, Max Kortlander (m), Sam Fox; Felix the Wonderful Cat—Winston Sharples (w,m), Famous; Felix Kept on Walking (B)—Ed Bryant (w), Hubert David (m), Wright. COVER: Cartoon.

1431 Female on the Beach (Universal, 1955, Joan Crawford, Jeff Chandler).

Female on the Beach Theme—Sonny Burke (m), Northern. COVER: Joan Crawford, Jeff Chandler.

1432 Feminine Touch, The (MGM, 1941, Rosalind Russell, Don Ameche).

Jealous—Tommy Malie, Dick Finch (w), Jack Little (m), Mills. COVER: Rosalind Russell, Don Ameche, Kay Francis.

1433 Ferdinand the Bull (RKO, 1936, Cartoon).

Ferdinand the Bull—Larry Morey (w), Albert Malotte (m), ABC. COVER: Cartoon.

1434 Ferry Cross the Mersey (United Artists, 1964, Gerry Marsden, Cilla Black).

Ferry Cross the Mersey—Gerrard Marsden (w,m), Pacermusic. COVER: Gerrard Marsden.

1435 Feudin' Rhythm (Columbia, 1949, Eddy Arnold, Gloria Henry).

That Ain't in Any Catalog—Kay Evans, Fred Stryker (w,m), Fairway; There's No Wings on My Angel—Cy Coben, Irving Melsher, Eddy Arnold (w,m), Alamo. COVER: Eddy Arnold, Betsy Gay.

1436   Fiddler on the Roof (United Artists, 1971, Topol, Leonard Frey).

Anatevka/Do You Love Me/Far from the Home I Love/Fiddler on the Roof/If I Were a Rich Man/ Matchmaker/Miracle of Miracles/ Now I Have Everything/Sabbath Prayer/Sunrise Sunset/ To Life/ Tradition—Sheldon Harnick (w), Jerry Bock (m), Times. COVER: Topol, and Daughters.

1437   Fiesta (United Artists, 1941, Anne Ayars, George Negrete).

El Relajo—Lamberto Leyva, Jesus Castillion, Oscar Felix (w,m), Robbins; I'll Never Forget Fiesta—Bob Wright, Chet Forrest (w), Nilo Menendez (m), Robbins; Never Trust a Jumping Bean/Quien Sabe, Who Knows?—Bob Wright, Chet Forrest (w), Edward Ward (m), Robbins. COVER: George Negrete, Anne Ayars, Armida.

1438   Fiesta (MGM, 1947, Esther Williams, Ricardo Montalban).

Fantasia Mexicana—Aaron Copland, Johnny Green (m), Boosey Hawkes. COVER: Esther Williams, Ricardo Montalban.

1439   Fifty Five Days at Peking (Allied Artists, 1963, Charlton Heston, Ava Gardner).

Peking Theme, So Little Time—Paul F. Webster (w), Dimitri Tiomkin (m), Bronston. COVER: David Niven, Ava Gardner, Charlton Heston.

1440   Fifty Million Nickels (Juke Box Jenny) (Universal, 1942, Ken Murray, Harriet Hilliard).

Give Out/Macumba/Swing It Mother Goose—Everett Carter (w), Milton Rosen (m), Robbins. COVER: Iris Adrian, Don Douglas, Ken Murray.

1441   Fifty Second Street (United Artists, 1937, Ian Hunter, Leo Carillo).

Don't Save Your Love/Fifty Second Street/I Still Love to Kiss You Goodnight/I'd Like to See Samoa of Samoa/Let Your Hair Down and Sing (BW)/Nothing Can Stop Me Now—Walter Bullock (w), Harold Spina (m), Feist. COVER: Kenny Baker, Pat Paterson, and Movie Scenes.

1442   Fighter, The (United Artists, 1952, Richard Conte, Vanessa Brown).

Vanessa—Bernie Wayne (w,m), Meridian. COVER: Vanessa Brown.

1443   Fighter Attack (Allied Artists, 1953, Sterling Hayden, J. Carroll Naish).

Nina—Sol Meyer (w), Marlin Skiles (m), Tonecraft. COVER: Black and white cover with title only.

1444   Fight for Your Lady (RKO, 1937, John Boles, Jack Oakie).

Blame It on the Danube—Harry Akst (w), Frank Loesser (m), Marlo. COVER: John Boles, Ida Lupino.

1445   Fighting Bill Fargo (Universal, 1942, Johnny Mack Brown, Fuzzy Knight).

Geraldine/Happiness Corral—Everett Carter (w), Milton Rosen (m), Robbins. COVER: Johnny Mack Brown, Fuzzy Knight, Nell O'Day.

1446   Fighting Deputy, The (Spectrum, 1937, Fred Scott, Al St. John).

Old Home Ranch, The (VS)/ Yellow Mellow Moon (VS)—June Hershey (w), Don Swander (m), American. COVER: Fred Scott.

1447   Fighting Engineers, The (Warner Bros., 1943, War Film).

Fighting Engineers, The—Robert Kearney (w), Bob Carlton, Cliff Dixon (m), Vogel. COVER: Soldiers.

1448 Fighting Seabees, The (Republic, 1944, John Wayne, Susan Hayward).
Song of the Seabees, The—Sam Lewis (w), Peter DeRose (m), Robbins. COVER: John Wayne, Susan Hayward, Dennis O'Keefe.

1449 Fincho (Guild, 1957, Stars Unknown).
Fincho (PC)—Sid Robin (w), Alex Lazlo (m), Guild. COVER: None.

1450 Finders Keepers (Universal, 1928, Laura LaPlante, John Barrow).
Finders Keepers Losers Weepers—Paul Corbell, Merton Bories (w,m), Villa. COVER: Laura LaPlante.

1451 Fine Mess, A (Columbia, 1986, Ted Danson, Howie Mandel).
Fine Mess, A—Dennis Lambert, Henry Mancini (w,m), Golden Torch; Walk Like a Man—Bob Crewe, Bob Gaudio (w,m), MPL. COVER: Ted Danson, Howie Mandel.

1452 Finest Hours, The (Columbia, 1964, Documentary on Churchill).
Blenheim Waltz/Churchill March—Ron Grainer (m), Chappell. COVER: Silhouette of Churchill.

1453 Fingers (Brut, 1977, Harvey Keitel, Tisa Farrow).
Now Is Forever—Sammy Cahn (w), George Barrie (m), Brut. COVER: Harvey Keitel.

1454 Finian's Rainbow (Warner Bros., 1968, Fred Astaire, Petula Clark).
Begat, The/How Are Things in Glocca Morra?/If This Isn't Love/Look to the Rainbow/Old Devil Moon/Something Sort of Grandish/That Great Come and Get It Day/When I'm Not Near the Girl I Love/When the Idle Poor Become the Idle Rich—E. Y. Harburg (w), Burton Lane (m), DBH. COVER: Fred Astaire, Petula Clark.

1455 Fire Brigade, The (MGM, 1926, Charles Ray, May McAvoy).
Fire Brigade, The—Alfred Bryan, Ted Snyder (w,m), Berlin. COVER: Charles Ray, May McAvoy.

1456 Fire Down Below (Columbia, 1957, Rita Hayworth, Robert Mitchum).
Fire Down Below—Ned Washington (w), Lester Lee (m), Columbia; Harmonica Theme—Jack Lemmon (m), Columbia; Limbo—Ned Washington (w), Lester Lee (m), Columbia. COVER: Rita Hayworth.

1457 Firefly, The (MGM, 1937, Jeanette MacDonald, Allan Jones).
Donkey Serenade, The—Bob Wright, Chet Forrest (w), Rudolf Friml, Herbert Stothart (m); Schirmer; Giannina Mia—Otto Harbach (w), Rudolf Friml (m), Schirmer; He Who Loves and Runs Away—Gus Kahn (w), Rudolf Friml (m), Schirmer; Love Is Like a Firefly—Bob Wright, Chet Forrest (w), Rudolf Friml (m), Schirmer; Sympathy—Otto Harbach, Gus Kahn (w), Rudolf Friml (m), Schirmer; When a Maid Comes Knocking at Your Heart—Otto Harbach, Bob Wright, Chet Forrest (w), Rudolf Friml (m), Schirmer; Woman's Kiss, A—Bob Wright, Chet Forrest (w), Rudolf Friml (m), Schirmer. COVER: Jeannette MacDonald, Allan Jones.

1458 Fire Power with the Victory Wallop (Westinghouse, 1942, War Film on Tanks).
Men of Iron—W. Mason (w), Larry Sherwood (m), Mason. COVER: Tanks.

1459 Fire Sale (20th Century-Fox, 1977, Alan Arkin, Rob Reiner).
Slam Dunk—Tom Bahler (w), Dave Grusin (m), Fox. COVER: Cartoon Sketch.

1460 Fires of Faith (Paramount, 1919, Eugene O'Brien, Catherine Calvert).
Fires of Faith—Joe Young, Sam Lewis (w), M. K. Jerome (m), Berlin. COVER: Eugene O'Brien.

1461 Fire with Fire (Paramount, 1986, Craig Sheffer, Virginia Madsen).
Fire with Fire Theme—Howard Shore (m), Famous. COVER: Craig Sheffer, Virginia Madsen.

1462 First a Girl (GB, 1935, Jessie Matthews, Sonnie Hale).

Everything's in Rhythm with My Heart/I Can Wiggle My Ears/Little Silkworm/Say the Word and It's Yours—Maurice Sigler, Al Goodhart, Al Hoffman (w,m), Popular. COVER: Jessie Matthews.

1463 First Born (Paramount, 1984, Peter Weller, Teri Garr).

Jake's Theme—Michael Small (m), Ensign. COVER: Chris Collett.

1464 First Kiss (Paramount, 1928, Gary Cooper, Fay Wray).

First Kiss, The—Al Dubin (w), J. Russell Robinson (m), Berlin. COVER: Gary Cooper, Fay Wray.

1465 First Love (Universal, 1939, Deanna Durbin, Robert Stack).

Amapola—Albert Gamse (w), Joseph Lacalle (m), Marks; Home Sweet Home—John Payne (w), Henry Bishop (m), Schirmer; Spring in My Heart—Ralph Freed (w), Johann Strauss (m), Feist. COVER: Deanna Durbin.

1466 First Love (UMC, 1970, Maximillian Schell, Dominique Sanda).

First Love—Don Black (w), Mark London (m), Burlington. COVER: John Brown, Dominique Sanda.

1467 First Traveling Saleslady, The (RKO, 1956, Ginger Rogers, Carol Channing).

Corset Can Do a Lot for a Lady, A/First Traveling Saleslady—Hal Levy (w), Irving Gertz (m), Mills. COVER: Ginger Rogers, Barry Nelson.

1468 First Year, The (Fox, 1926, Matt Moore, Kathryn Perry).

Thinking of You (Promotion Song)—Joseph Grey (w), Allie Moore (m), American. COVER: Matt Moore, Kathryn Perry.

1469 Fisherman's Wharf (RKO, 1938, Bobby Breen, Leo Carrillo).

Blue Italian Waters—Paul F. Webster (w), Frank Churchill (m), Lincoln. COVER: Bobby Breen.

1470 F.I.S.T. (United Artists, 1978, Sylvester Stallone, Rod Steiger).

F.I.S.T. Theme—Bill Conti (m), Unart. COVER: Sylvester Stallone, and Mob.

1471 Fitzwilly (United Artists, 1967, Dick Van Dyke, Barbara Feldon).

Make Me Rainbows—Alan Bergman, Marilyn Bergman (w), Johnny Williams (m), Unart. COVER: Black and white cover with title only.

1472 Five Against the House (Columbia, 1954, Guy Madison, Kim Novak).

Life of the Party—Hal Hackady (w), Billy Mure (m), BMI. COVER: Guy Madison, Kim Novak.

1473 Five Card Stud (Paramount, 1968, Dean Martin, Robert Mitchum).

Five Card Stud—Ned Washington (w), Maurice Jarre (m), Famous. COVER: Dean Martin, Robert Mitchum.

1474 Five Easy Pieces (Columbia, 1968, Jack Nicholson, Karen Black).

Stand By Your Man—Tammy Wynette, Billy Sherrill (w,m), Gallico. COVER: Jack Nicholson.

1475 Five of a Kind (20th Century-Fox, 1938, The Dionne Quintuplets, Jean Hersholt).

All Mixed Up—Sidney Clare (w), Sam Pokrass (m), Robbins. COVER: Dionne Quintuplets.

1476 Five Pennies, The (Paramount, 1959, Danny Kaye, Barbara Bel Geddes).

Five Pennies/Five Pennies Saints/Follow the Leader/Goodnight Sleep Tight/Lullabye in Ragtime—Sylvia Fine (w,m), Dena. COVER: Danny Kaye, Louis Armstrong.

1477 Five Puplets (Fox, 1935, Cartoon).

Five Little Reasons for Happiness—Dave Oppenheim (w), Philip Scheib (m), Sam Fox. COVER: Cartoon.

1478 Five Summer Stories (Fox, 1972, Honk Rock Group).

Pipeline Sequence—S. Wood, R. Stekol, C. Buhler, T. Imboden, D. Whaley (w,m), Granite. COVER: Rock Group.

1479 Five Thousand Fingers of Dr. T., The (Columbia, 1953, Mary Healy, Peter Lind Hayes).

Because We're Kids/Dream Stuff (VS)/Dr. T's Dressing Song (V)/Get Together Weather (VS)/Hypnotic Duel (VS)/Ten Happy Fingers Song (VS)/Ten Happy Fingers Theme (VS)/Victory Procession (VS)—Dr. Seuss (w), Frederick Hollander (m), Mood. COVER: Mary Healy, Peter Lind Hayes.

1480 Five Weeks in a Balloon (20th Century-Fox, 1962, Red Buttons, Fabian).

Give Weeks in a Balloon—Jodi Desmond (w), Urban Thielman (m), Miller. COVER: Red Buttons, Fabian, and Movie Scenes.

1481 Flame and the Flesh, The (MGM, 1953, Lana Turner, Carlos Thompson).

By Candlelight/No One But You/ Peddlar Man—Jack Lawrence (w), Nicholas Brodszky (m), Feist. COVER: Lana Turner, Carlos Thompson, Pier Angeli.

1482 Flame of the Barbary Coast (Republic, 1945, John Wayne, Ann Dvorak).

Lover, Here Is My Heart—Adrian Ross (w), Lao Silesu (m), Feist. COVER: Ann Dvorak.

1483 Flame of the Islands (Republic, 1956, Howard Duff, Yvonne DeCarlo).

Take It or Leave It—Jack Elliott, Sonny Burke (w,m), Morris. COVER: Yvonne DeCarlo.

1484 Flame Within, The (MGM, 1935, Ann Harding, Herbert Marshall).

Dream of a Ladies Cloak Room Attendant (PC)—Jerome Kern (m), MGM. COVER: None.

1485 Flamingo Road (Warner Bros., 1948, Joan Crawford, Zachary Scott).

If I Could Be with You—Henry Creamer, Jimmy Johnson (w,m), Remick. COVER: Joan Crawford, Zachary Scott.

1486 Flaming Star (20th Century-Fox, 1960, Elvis Presley, Steve Forrest).

Flaming Star—Sid Wayne (w), Sherman Edwards (m), Gladys. COVER: Elvis Presley.

1487 Flanagan Boy, The (Bad Blonde) (Lippert, 1953, Barbara Peyton, John Slater).

Let Forever Begin Tonight (B)— Ivor Slaney (w,m), Bradbury. COVER: Barbara Peyton, Tony Wright.

1488 Flash Dance (Paramount, 1983, Jennifer Beals, Michael Nouri).

Flash Dance Love Theme—Giorgio Moroder (m), Famous; Flash Dance What a Feeling—Keith Forsey, Irene Cara (w), Giorgio Moroder (m), Famous; Lady Lady Lady— Keith Forsey (w), Giorgio Moroder (m), Famous; Maniac—Michael Sembello, Dennis Matkosky (w,m), Famous; He's a Dream (VS)—Shandi Sinnamon, Ronald Magness (w,m), Ensign; I'll Be Here Where the Heart Is (VS)—Kim Carnes, Duane Hitchings, Craig Kramf (w,m), Ensign; Imagination (VS)—Mike Boddicker, Jerry Hey, Phil Ramone, Mike Sembello (w,m), Ensign; Manhunt (VS)— Doug Cotler, Richard Gilbert (w,m), Ensign; Romeo (VS)—Pete Bellotte, Sylvester Levay (w,m), Ensign; Seduce Me Tonight (VS)—Keith Forsey (w), Giorgio Moroder (m), Ensign. COVER: Jennifer Beals.

1489 Flash Gordon (Universal, 1980, Sam Jones, Melody Anderson).

Flash/Flash's Theme-aka Flash/ Flash Gordon Themes—Brian May (m), Beechwood. COVER: Shield and Spear.

1490 Flea in Her Ear, A (20th Century-Fox, 1968, Rex Harrison, Rosemary Harris).

Flea in Her Ear, A—Sammy Cahn (w), Bronislau Kaper (m), Fox. COVER: Rex Harrison, Rosemary Harris.

1491 Fleet's In, The (Paramount, 1942, Dorothy Lamour, William Holden).

Arthur Murray Taught Me Dancing in a Hurry/Fleet's In, The/I Remember You/If You Build a Better Mousetrap/Not Mine/Tangerine/When You Hear the Time Signal—Johnny Mercer (w), Victor Schertzinger (m), Paramount. COVER: Dorothy Lamour, William Holden, Jimmy Dorsey, and Others.

1492 Flesh and Blood (CUM, 1922, Lon Chaney, Edith Roberts).

Love's Old Sweet Song—L. Clifton Bingham (w), J. A. Molloy (m), Richmond Robbins. COVER: Lon Chaney.

1493 Flesh and the Devil (MGM, 1927, John Gilbert, Greta Garbo).

Flesh and the Devil Theme—Frank Owens (m), Robbins. COVER: Red cover with title only.

1494 Flight of the Doves (Columbia, 1971, Ron Moody, Jack Wild).

Flight of the Doves Theme—Roy Budd (m), Colgems. COVER: Dorothy McGuire, and Children.

1495 Flight of the Phoenix (20th Century-Fox, 1966, James Stewart, Peter Finch).

Phoenix Love Theme—Alec Wilder (m), TRO. COVER: James Stewart, Peter Finch.

1496 Flight to Hong Kong (United Artists, 1956, Rory Calhoun, Barbara Rush).

Angel's Kiss, An—Bob Hopkins (w), Albert Glasser (m), Coronet; Flight to Hong Kong—Bob Hopkins (w), Monty Kelly (m), Coronet. COVER: Rory Calhoun, Barbara Rush.

1497 Flim Flam Man, The (20th Century-Fox, 1967, George C. Scott, Sue Lyon).

Flim Flam Man Theme—Randy Newman (w), Jerry Goldsmith (m), Hastings. COVER: Cartoon Sketch.

1498 Flipper (MGM, 1963, Chuck Connors, Luke Halpin).

Flipper—By Dunham (w), Henry Vars (m), Feist. COVER: Boy and Dolphin.

1499 Flipper's New Adventure (MGM, 1964, Luke Halpin, Pamela Franklin).

Flipper/Imagine/It's a Cotton Candy World—By Dunham (w), Henry Vars (m), Feist. COVER: Boy and Dolphin.

1500 Flirt, The (Universal, 1923, George Nichols, Lydia Knott).

Flirt, The—Milt Hagen, Victor Nurnberg (w,m), Mittenthal. COVER: Lydia Knott.

1501 Flirtation Walk (First National, 1934, Dick Powell, Ruby Keeler).

Flirtation Walk/Mr. and Mrs. Is the Name/No Horse, No Wife, No Mustache—Mort Dixon (w), Allie Wrubel (m), Remick; Smoking in the Dark (BW)/When Do We Eat? (BW)—Mort Dixon (w), Allie Wrubel (m), Witmark. COVER: Dick Powell, Ruby Keeler.

1502 Florida Special (Paramount, 1936, Jack Oakie, Sally Eilers).

It's You I'm Talkin' About—Mack Gordon, Harry Revel (w,m), Popular. COVER: Jack Oakie, Sally Eilers.

1503 Florodora Girl, The (MGM, 1930, Marion Davies, Lawrence Gray).

My Kind of Man—Clifford Grey, Andy Rice (w), Herbert Stothart (m), Robbins. COVER: Marion Davies.

1504 Flower Drum Song (Universal, 1961, Nancy Kwan, James Shigeta).

Don't Marry Me/Grant Avenue/Hundred Million Miracles, A/I Enjoy Being a Girl/Love Look Away/Sunday/You Are Beautiful—Oscar Hammerstein (w), Richard Rodgers (m), Williamson. COVER: Nancy Kwan, Miyoshi Umeki.

1505 Flower of Night (Paramount, 1925, Pola Negri, Warner Oland).
Magic Love—Carol Raven (w), James Bradford (m), Sam Fox. COVER: Pola Negri.
1506 Flying Down to Rio (RKO, 1933, Dolores Del Rio, Fred Astaire).
Carioca/Flying Down to Rio/ Music Makes Me/Orchids in the Moonlight—Gus Kahn, Edward Eliscu (w), Vincent Youmans (m), Harms. COVER: Dolores Del Rio, Fred Astaire.
1507 Flying Fleet, The (MGM, 1929, Ramon Novarro, Anita Page).
You're the Only One for Me—Ray Klages (w), William Axt, David Mendoza (m), Robbins. COVER: Ramon Novarro, Anita Page.
1508 Flying Fool, The (Pathe, 1929, William Boyd, Marie Prevost).
If I Had My Way/I'm That Way About Baby—George Waggner (w), George Green (m), Ager Yellen. COVER: William Boyd, Marie Prevost.
1509 Flying High (MGM, 1931, Bert Lahr, Charlotte Greenwood).
I'll Make a Happy Landing/ We'll Dance Until Dawn—Dorothy Fields (w), Jimmy McHugh (m), DBH. COVER: Cartoon Sketch.
1510 Flying Hostess, The (Universal, 1936, Judith Barrett, Ella Logan).
Bang the Bell Rang (PC)—Frank Loesser (w), Irving Actman (m), Chappell. COVER: None.
1511 Flying Mouse, The (Disney, 1934, Cartoon).
You're Nothin' but a Nothin'— Larry Morey (w), Frank Churchill (m), Berlin. COVER: Cartoon.
1512 F.M. (Universal, 1978, Michael Brandon, Martin Mull).
F.M.—Donald Fagen, Walter Becker (w,m), Feckless; Bad Man (VS)—J. D. Souther, Glenn Frey (w,m), Warner; Cold as Ice (VS)— Nick Jones, Lou Gramm (w,m), Warner; Do It Again (VS)—Walter

Becker, Donald Fagen (w,m), Warner; Fly Like an Eagle (VS)—Steve Miller (w,m), Warner; It Keeps You Runnin. (VS)—Michael MacDonald (w,m), Warner; Just the Way You Are (VS)—Billy Joel (w,m), Warner; Lido Shuffle (VS)—Boz Scaggs, David Paich (w,m), Warner; Life in the Fast Lane (VS)—Joe Walsh, Don Henley, Glenn Frey (w,m), Warner; Life's Been Good (VS)—Joe Walsh (w,m), Warner; Livingston Saturday Night (VS)—Jimmy Buffett (w,m), Warner; Night Moves (VS)—Bob Seger (w,m), Warner; Poor Poor Pitiful Me (VS)—Warren Zevon (w, m), Warner;There's a Place in the World for a Gambler (VS)—Dan Fogelberg (w,m), Warner; Tumbling Dice (VS)—Mick Jagger, Keith Richards (w,m), Warner; Your Smiling Face (VS)—James Taylor (w,m), Warner. COVER: Silver Letters.
1512a Foghorn Leghorn (Warner Bros., 1960, Cartoon).
Foghorn Leghorn—Tedd Pierce, Warren Foster (w,m), Witmark. COVER: Cartoon.
1513 Folies Bergere de Paris (20th Century-Fox, 1935, Maurice Chevalier, Ann Sothern).
Au Revoir, L'Amour/I Was Lucky/Rhythm of the Rain/Singing a Happy Song—Jack Meskill (w), Jack Stern (m), Robbins; You Took the Words Right Out of My Mouth— Harold Adamson (w), Burton Lane (m), Robbins. COVER: Maurice Chevalier.
1514 Follies (Stand Up and Cheer) (Fox, 1934, Shirley Temple, Warner Baxter).
Broadway's Gone Hill Billy (PC)/ We're Out of the Red (PC)—Lew Brown (w), Jay Gorney (m), Movietone. COVER: None.
1515 Follies Girl (PRC, 1943, Wendy Barrie, Johnny Lone).
Fascination/I Knew Your Father Son—Buddy Kaye, Fred Wise, Sidney Lippman (w,m), Mills; Keep the Flag A'Flying America—Mary Schaeffer

(w,m), Ambassador; Thoity Poiple Boids—Buddy Kaye, Fred Wise, Sidney Lippman (w,m), Mills. COVER: A Follies Girl.

1516 Follow Me Boys (Buena Vista, 1966, Fred MacMurray, Vera Miles).

Follow Me Boys—Richard Sherman, Robert Sherman (w,m), Wonderland. COVER: Fred MacMurray.

1517 Follow That Dream (United Artists, 1962, Elvis Presley, Arthur O'Connell).

Follow That Dream—Fred Wise (w), Ben Weisman (m), Gladys; I'm Not the Marrying Kind—Mack David (w), Sherman Edwards (m), Gladys; What a Wonderful Life—Sid Wayne (w), Jerry Livingston (m), Gladys. COVER: Elvis Presley.

1518 Follow the Band (Universal, 1943, Leo Carrillo, Leon Errol).

Swingin' the Blues—Everett Carter (w), Milton Rosen (m), Robbins. COVER: Mary Beth Hughes, Eddie Quillan.

1519 Follow the Boys (Three Cheers for the Boys) (Universal, 1944, George Raft, Zorina).

I'll Walk Alone—Sammy Cahn (w), Jule Styne (m), Mayfair; Is You Is, or Is You Ain't—Billy Austin, Louis Jordan (w,m), Leeds; Mad About Him, Sad Without Him, How Can I Be Glad Without Him Blues—Larry Markes, Dick Charles (w,m), Leeds; Tonight—Kermit Goell (w), Walter Donaldson (m), Southern; Where Did You Learn to Love?—Jule Styne, Sammy Cahn, Harry Harris (w,m), Morris. COVER: George Raft, Zorina, Andrews Sisters, W. C. Fields, and Others.

1520 Follow the Boys (MGM, 1963, Connie Francis, Paula Prentiss).

Follow the Boys/Waiting for Billy —Benny Davis, Ted Murry (w,m), Francon. COVER: Connie Francis, and Sailors.

1521 Follow the Fleet (RKO, 1936, Fred Astaire, Ginger Rogers).

But Where Are You/Get Thee Behind Me Satan/I'd Rather Lead a Band/I'm Putting All My Eggs in One Basket/Let Yourself Go/Let's Face the Music and Dance/We Saw the Sea —Irving Berlin (w,m), Berlin. COVER: Fred Astaire, Ginger Rogers.

1522 Follow the Leader (Manhattan Mary) (Paramount, 1930, Ed Wynn, Ginger Rogers).

Satan's Holiday—Sammy Fain, Irving Kahal, Pierre Norman, Al Segal (w,m), Famous. COVER: Ed Wynn.

1523 Follow Thru (Paramount, 1930, Charles Rogers, Nancy Carroll).

It Must Be You—Edward Eliscu, Manning Sherwin (w,m), Famous; Peach of a Pair—George Marion (w), Richard Whiting (m), Famous. COVER: Charles Rogers, Nancy Carroll, Jack Haley.

1524 Follow Your Heart (Republic, 1936, Marion Talley, Michael Bartlett).

Follow Your Heart—Sidney Mitchell (w), Victor Schertzinger (m), Sam Fox; Magnolias in the Moonlight/Who Minds 'Bout Me—Walt Bullock (w), Victor Schertzinger (m), Sam Fox. COVER: Marion Talley, Michael Bartlett.

1525 Follow Your Star (Belgrave, 1938, Arthur Tracy, Belle Chrystal).

My Waltz for Those in Love—Jimmy Kennedy, Michael Carr (w, m), Shapiro Bernstein. COVER: Brown cover with title only.

1526 Foolish Wives (Universal, 1923, Eric Von Stroheim, Dale Fuller).

Foolish Wives—Jack Stern, Clarence Marks, Norah Haymond (w, m), Mittenthal. COVER: Eric Von Stroheim, Miss DuPont.

1527 Fools (Cinerama, 1970, Jason Robards, Katherine Ross).

Someone Who Cares—Alex Harvey (w,m), Beechwood. COVER: Jason Robards, Katherine Ross.

1528 Fools for Scandal (Warner Bros., 1938, Carole Lombard, Fernand Gravet).

How Can You Forget/There's a Boy in Harlem—Lorenz Hart (w), Richard Rodgers (m), Harms. COVER: Carole Lombard, Fernand Gravet.

1529 Footlight Parade (Warner Bros., 1933, James Cagney, Joan Blondell).

Ah! The Moon Is Here/By A Waterfall—Irving Kahal (w), Sammy Fain (m), Witmark; Honeymoon Hotel/Shanghai Lil—Al Dubin (w), Harry Warren (m), Witmark; Sittin' on a Backyard Fence—Irving Kahal (w), Sammy Fain (m), Witmark. COVER: James Cagney, Joan Blondell, Ruby Keeler, Dick Powell.

1530 Footlights and Fools (First National, 1929, Colleen Moore, Raymond Hackett).

If I Can't Have You/Ophelia Will Fool You/Pilly Pom Pom Plee/You Can't Believe My Eyes—Al Bryan (w), George Meyer (m), Remick. COVER: Colleen Moore, and Girls.

1531 Footlight Serenade (20th Century-Fox, 1942, John Payne, Betty Grable).

I'll Be Marching to a Love Song/I'm Still Crazy for You—Leo Robin (w), Ralph Rainger (m), Robbins. COVER: John Payne, Betty Grable, Victor Mature.

1532 Footloose (Paramount, 1984, Kevin Bacon, Lori Singer).

Almost Paradise—Dean Pitchford (w), Eric Carmen (m), Ensign; Dancing in the Streets—Dean Pitchford (w), Bill Wolfer (m), Famous; Footloose—Dean Pitchford, Kenny Loggins (w,m), Famous; Holding Out for a Hero—Dean Pitchford (w), Jim Steinman (m), Famous; I'm Free —Dean Pitchford (w), Kenny Loggins (m), Famous; Let's Hear It for the Boy—Dean Pitchford (w), Tom Snow (m), Ensign; Girl Gets Around, The (VS)—Dean Pitchford (w), Sammy Hagar (m), Ensign; Never (VS)—Dean Pitchford (w), Michael Gore (m), Ensign; Somebody's Eyes (VS) —Dean Pitchford (w), Tom Snow (m), Ensign. COVER: Kevin Bacon.

1533 Footsteps in the Fog (Columbia, 1955, Jean Simmons, Stewart Granger).

Lily Watkins Tune, The—Benjamin Frankel (w,m), Chappell. COVER: Jean Simmons, Stewart Granger.

1534 For Art's Sake (Vitaphone, 1929, Musical Short).

Look at Him, My Hero/Look in Any Mirror/Master and Slave/'S Impossible—Jack Murray (w), Bernard Maltin (m), Witmark. COVER: Black and white cover with title only.

1535 For Auld Lang Syne (Warner Bros., 1937, James Cagney, Dick Powell).

Ride Tenderfoot Ride—Johnny Mercer (w), Richard Whiting (m), Witmark. COVER: Black and white cover with title only.

1536 Forbidden (Universal, 1953, Tony Curtis, Joanne Dru).

You Belong to Me—Pee Wee King, Redd Stewart, Chilton Price (w,m), Ridgeway. COVER: Tony Curtis, Joanne Dru.

1537 Forbidden Planet (MGM, 1956, Walter Pidgeon, Anne Francis).

Forbidden Planet—David Rose (m), Robbins. COVER: Purple cover with title only.

1538 Force of Impulse (Sutton, 1960, Robert Alda, Carroll Naish).

Strange Feeling—Mort Goode (w), Joseph Liebman (m), Chappell. COVER: Tony Anthony, Teri Hope.

1539 For Country Life (20th Century-Fox, 1940, Musical Short).

Quaker Hill Polka—Jacques Dallin (m), Sam Fox. COVER: Dancers.

1540 Foreign Affair, A (Paramount, Marlene Dietrich, Jean Arthur).

Black Market/Illusions/Ruins of Berlin—Frederick Hollander (w,m), Famous. COVER: Marlene Dietrich, Jean Arthur, John Lund.

1541 Foreign Intrigue (United Artists, 1956, Robert Mitchum, Genevieve Page).

After You/At the Beaux Art Ball —Paul Durand (w,m), Leeds; Foreign Intrigue Concerto—Charles Norman (m), Leeds; Intrigue—Ervin Drake (w), Paul Durand (m), Leeds. COVER: Robert Mitchum.

1542   Forest Rangers (Paramount, 1942, Fred MacMurray, Paulette Goddard).

Jingle Jangle Jingle—Frank Loesser (w), Joseph Lilley (m), Paramount; Tall Grows the Timber—Frank Loesser (w), Frederick Hollander (m), Paramount. COVER: Fred MacMurray, Paulette Goddard.

1543   Forever Amber (20th Century-Fox, 1947, Linda Darnell, Cornel Wilde).

Forever Amber—Johnny Mercer (w), David Raksin (m), Robbins. COVER: Linda Darnell, Cornel Wilde.

1544   Forever Darling (MGM, 1955, Lucille Ball, Desi Arnaz).

Forever Darling—Sammy Cahn (w), Bronislau Kaper (m), Feist. COVER: Lucille Ball, Desi Arnaz, James Mason.

1545   Forever Female (Paramount, 1954, Ginger Rogers, William Holden).

Change of Heart/Say That You Will—Edward Heyman (w), Victor Young (m), Famous. COVER: Ginger Rogers, William Holden, Paul Douglas.

1546   Forever My Love (Paramount, 1962, Romy Schneider, Karl Boehm).

Forever My Love—Hal David (w), Burt Bacharach (m), Famous. COVER: Romy Schneider, Karl Boehm.

1547   Forget Me Not (Metro, 1922, Irene Hunt, William Machin).

A Million Hearts Are Calling Forget Me Not—Billy Baskette, Ernest Luz (w,m), Marks. COVER: Irene Hunt, William Machin.

1548   Forget Me Not (Forever Yours) (Grand National, 1936, Benjamin Gigli, Joan Gardner).

Say You Will Not Forget—Arthur Wimperis (w), Ernesto DeCurtis (m), Chappell. COVER: Black and white cover with title only.

1549   For Heaven's Sake (Paramount, 1926, Harold Lloyd, Jobyna Ralston).

For Heaven's Sake—Al Bryan (w), Hugo Frey (m), Robbins. COVER: Harold Lloyd.

1550   For Love of Ivy (Cinerama, 1968, Sidney Poitier, Abbey Lincoln).

For Love of Ivy—Bob Russell (w), Quincy Jones (m), Ampco. COVER: Sidney Poitier.

1551   For Me and My Gal (MGM, 1942, Judy Garland, Gene Kelly).

After You've Gone (VS)—Henry Creamer, Turner Layton (w,m), Morley; For Me and My Gal—Edgar Leslie, Ray Goetz (w), George Meyer (m), Mills, (regular cover and a special purple cover with the three stars); How Ya Gonna Keep Em Down on the Farm—Joe Young, Sam Lewis (w), Walter Donaldson (m), Mills; They Go Wild Simply Wild Over Me—Joe McCarthy (w), Fred Fisher (m), Mills; When You Wore a Tulip (B)—Jack Mahoney (w), Percy Wenrich (m), Ascherberg. COVER: Judy Garland.

1552   Formula for Love (Christensen, 1959, Louis Armstrong, Nina and Frederik).

Formula for Love/Hello Pretty One/So Long Lemile/Wondrous Love —Nina Frederik, Arvid Muller (w), Kjeld Bonfils (m), Consolidated. COVER: Louis Armstrong, Nina and Frederik.

1553   For Pete's Sake (World Wide, 1966, Billy Graham, Robert Sampson).

All My Life/Man, The/For Pete's Sake Selections—Ralph Carmichael (w,m), Sacred. COVER: Movie Scenes.

1554   Forsaking All Others (MGM, 1934, Joan Crawford, Clark Gable).

Forsaking All Others—Gus Kahn (w), Walter Donaldson (m), Feist. COVER: Black and white cover with title only.

1555 Fort Apache (RKO, 1950, Henry Fonda, Shirley Temple).

Sweet Genevieve—Harold Potter, Rodd Eddy (w,m), Stasny. COVER: John Wayne, Battle Scene.

1556 Fortune   Cookie,   The (United Artists, 1966, Jack Lemmon, Walter Matthau).

Bad Guys, The—André Previn (m), Unart; Fortune Cookie, The—Dory Previn (w), André Previn (m), Unart; Waltz of the Fortune Cookies, The—André Previn (m), Unart. COVER: Jack Lemmon, Walter Matthau.

1557 Fortune's   Fool (Lubin, 1928, Emil Jannings).

Fortune's Fool—Frank Padwe, Irving Mills (w,m), Mills. COVER: Emil Jannings.

1558 Forty Carats (Columbia, 1973, Liv Ullman, Edward Albert).

In Every Corner of the World—Alan Bergman, Marilyn Bergman (w), Michel Legrand (m), Colgems. COVER: Liv Ullman, Edward Albert.

1559 Forty Eight Hours (Paramount, 1983, Nick Nolte, Eddie Murphy).

Back in Town—Brial O'Neal (w, m), Famous. COVER: Eddie Murphy, Nick Nolte.

1560 Forty Five Minutes from Broadway (First National, 1920, Dorothy Devore, Charles Ray).

Mary's a Grand Old Name/So Long Mary—George M. Cohan (w, m), Richmond. COVER: Charles Ray, Dorothy Devore.

1561 Forty Guns (20th Century-Fox, Barbara Stanwyck, Barry Sullivan).

High Ridin' Woman—Harold Adamson (w), Harry Sukman (m), Globe. COVER: Barbara Stanwyck, Barry Sullivan.

1562 Forty   Little   Mothers (MGM, 1940, Eddie Cantor, Judith Anderson).

Little Curly Hair in a High Chair—Charles Tobias (w), Nat Simon (m), Feist. COVER: Eddie Cantor, and Baby.

1563 Forty Pounds of Trouble (Universal, 1963, Suzanne Pleshette, Tony Curtis).

If You—Sydney Shaw (w), Mort Lindsay (m), Northern. COVER: Suzanne Pleshette, Tony Curtis.

1564 Forty Second Street (Warner Bros., 1933, Dick Powell, Ruby Keeler).

Forty Second Street/Getting Out of Town (PC)/It Must Be June/Shuffle Off to Buffalo/Young and Healthy/You're Getting to Be a Habit with Me—Al Dubin (w), Harry Warren (m), Witmark. COVER: Warner Baxter, Ginger Rogers, Ruby Keeler, Dick Powell, and Others.

1565 Forward   March   (The Doughboys (MGM, 1930, Buster Keaton, Sally Eilers).

Sing—Howard Johnson (w), Joseph Meyer (m), Robbins; You Never Did That Before—Fred Ahlert, Roy Turk (w,m), Robbins. COVER: Black and white cover with title only.

1566 Forward Pass (First National, 1929, Loretta Young, Douglas Fairbanks).

Give It! (PC)/Hello Baby/Huddlin'/ I Gotta Have You/I Love to Hit Myself on the Head with a Hammer (PC)/Nobody But You/One Minute of Heaven—Herb Magidson, Ned Washington, Michael Cleary (w,m), Witmark. COVER: Douglas Fairbanks, Loretta Young.

1567 For Whom the Bell Tolls (Paramount, 1943, Gary Cooper, Ingrid Bergman).

For Whom the Bell Tolls—Milton Drake (w), Walter Kent (m), Famous; Love Like This, A—Ned Washington (w), Victor Young (m), Famous; Love Like This Theme (VS)—Victor Young (m). COVER: Gary Cooper, Ingrid Bergman.

1568 For Your Eyes Only (United Artists, 1981, Roger Moore, Carol Bouquet).

For Your Eyes Only—Michael Lesson (w), Bill Conti (m), Unart. COVER: Roger Moore, and Girl.

1569 Foul Play (Paramount, 1977, Goldie Hawn, Chevy Chase).

Ready to Take a Chance Again—Norman Gimbel (w), Charles Fox (m), Ensign. COVER: Goldie Hawn, Chevy Chase.

1570 Fountain, The (RKO, 1935, Ann Harding, Paul Lukas).

Fountain Waltz—Max Steiner (m), Berlin. COVER: Ann Harding.

1571 Four Devils (Fox, 1928, Janet Gaynor, Mary Duncan).

Destiny/Marion—Lew Pollack (w), Erno Rapee (m), DBH. COVER: Janet Gaynor, Charles Morton.

1572 Four for Texas (Warner Bros., 1963, Frank Sinatra, Dean Martin).

Four for Texas—Sammy Cahn (w), James Van Heusen (m), Sergeant. COVER: Frank Sinatra, Dean Martin, Anita Ekberg, Ursula Andress.

1573 Four Horsemen of the Apocalypse, The (Metro, 1921, Rudolph Valentino, Alice Terry).

Chi Chi—Walter Havenschild (w, m), Photoplay; I Have a Rendezvous with You—Tillie Jay, Nancy Jay (w), Ernst Luz (m), Photoplay; In the Ruins—Leo Kempinski (m), Photoplay; Julio—Ernst Luz (w), Harry Olsen (m), Photoplay; La Serenata De La Argentina—Harry Olsen (m), Photoplay. COVER: Movie Scenes.

1574 Four Horsemen of the Apocalypse, The (MGM, 1961, Glenn Ford, Charles Boyer).

Four Horsemen Theme—André Previn (m), Robbins; Mine for the Moment—Dory Langdon (w), Andre Previn (m), Robbins. COVER: Movie Scenes.

1575 Four Hours to Kill (Paramount, 1935, Richard Barthelmess, Helen Mack).

Hate to Talk About Myself—Leo Robin, Ralph Rainger, Richard Whiting (w,m), Famous; Walking the Floor—Leo Robin, Ralph Rainger (w, m). COVER: Curtains and Spotlight.

1576 Four Jacks and a Jill (RKO, 1941, Ray Bolger, Anne Shirley).

I Haven't a Thing to Wear/I'm in Good Shape/Karanina/Wherever You Are/You Go Your Way—Mort Greene (w), Harry Revel (m), Melody Lane. COVER: Ray Bolger, Anne Shirley.

1577 Four Jills and a Jeep (20th Century-Fox, 1944, Dick Haymes, Jimmy Dorsey).

Crazy Me/How Blue the Night/How Many Times Do I Have to Tell You/You Send Me—Harold Adamson (w), Jimmy McHugh (m), Robbins. COVER: Dick Haymes, Jimmy Dorsey, Kay Francis, Carole Landis, and Others.

1578 Four Mothers (Warner Bros., 1940, Priscilla Lane, Rosemary Lane).

Moonlight and Tears—Jack Scholl (w), Heinz Roemheld (m), Witmark. COVER: Priscilla Lane Rosemary Lane, Lola Lane, Gale Page.

1579 Fourposter, The (Columbia, 1953, Rex Harrison, Lilli Palmer).

If You're in Love—Ned Washington (w), Dimitri Tiomkin (m), Lilli Palmer.

1580 Four Sons (Fox, 1928, Margaret Mann, James Hall).

Little Mother—Erno Rapee, Lew Pollack (w,m), Sherman Clay. COVER: Mother and Sons.

1581 Four Wives (Warner Bros., 1940, Claude Rains, Eddie Albert).

Symphonie Moderne—Max Steiner (m), Remick. COVER: Piano Keys and Notes.

1582 Fox, The (Warner Bros., 1968, Sandy Dennis, Keir Dullea).

Fox Theme—Lalo Schifrin (m), Warner; That Night—Norman Gimbel (w), Lalo Schifrin (m), Warner. COVER: Sketch of Two Girls.

1583 Fox and the Hounds, The (Buena Vista, 1981, Cartoon).

Best of Friends (VS)–Stan Fidel (w), Richard Johnston (m), Wonderland. COVER: A Cartoon.

1584 Foxfire (Universal, 1955, Jane Russell, Jeff Chandler).

Foxfire–Jeff Chandler (w), Henry Mancini (m), Northern. COVER: Jane Russell, Jeff Chandler.

1585 Fox Movietone Follies (Fox, 1929, Sue Carol, Lola Lane).

Big City Blues/Breakaway/Pearl of Old Japan/That's You Baby/Walking with Suzie/Why Can't I Be Like You–Con Conrad, Sidney Mitchell, Archie Gottler (w,m), DBH. COVER: Girls.

1586 Foxy Brown (AIP, 1974, Pam Grier, Antonio Fargas).

Foxy Brown Theme–Willie Hutch (m), Jobete. COVER: Willie Hutch.

1587 Framed (Paramount, 1974, Joe Don Baker, Gabriel Dell).

Nearer My Love to You–Arthur Kent, Frank Stanton (w,m), Famous. COVER: Black and white cover with title only.

1588 Framing of the Shrew (Paramount, 1929, Evelyn Preer).

No Fool Man–Carlton Kelsey, Val Burton, Jack Stern (w,m), Berlin. COVER: A Picture Frame.

1589 Francis (Universal, 1950, Donald O'Connor, Patricia Medina).

Francis the Talking Mule–Sid Tepper, Roy Brodsky, Irving Mills (w,m), Mills. COVER: Donald O'Connor, and Mule.

1590 Francis of Assisi (20th Century-Fox, 1961, Bradford Dillman, Dolores Hart).

Francis of Assisi Theme–Mario Nascimbene (m), Robbins; Hills of Assisti, The–Paul Vance, Lee Pockriss (w,m), Robbins. COVER: Bradford Dillman, Dolores Hart.

1591 Frankie (Frankie and Johnny (Select, 1936, Helen Morgan, Chester Morris).

Get Rhythm in Your Feet/If You Want My Heart–J. Russell Robinson, Bill Livingston (w,m), Engel. COVER: Helen Morgan, Chester Morris.

1592 Frankie and Johnny (Frankie) (Select, 1936, Helen Morgan, Chester Morris).

Give Me a Heart to Sing To–Ned Washington (w), Victor Young (m), Engel; If You Want My Heart–J. Russell Robinson, Bill Livingston (w, m), Engel. COVER: Helen Morgan.

1593 Frankie and Johnny (United Artists, 1966, Elvis Presley, Dora Douglas).

Come Along–David Hess (w,m), Gladys; Down by the Riverside/Everybody Come Aboard–Bill Giant, Bernie Baum, Florence Kaye (w,m), Presley; Frankie and Johnny–Fred Karger, Alex Gottlieb, Ben Weisman (w,m), Gladys; Hard Luck–Ben Weisman, Sid Wayne (w,m), Gladys; Look Out Broadway–Fred Wise, Randy Starr (w,m), Gladys; Petunia the Gardener's Daughter–Sid Tepper, Roy Bennett (w,m), Gladys; Please Don't Stop Loving Me–Joy Byers (w,m), Presley; Shout It Out–Bill Giant, Bernie Baum, Florence Kaye (w,m), Presley; What Every Woman Lives For–Doc Pomus, Mort Shuman (w, m), Presley; When the Saints Come Marching In–Bill Giant, Bernie Baum, Florence Kaye (w,m), Presley. COVER: Elvis Presley.

1594 Fraulein (20th Century-Fox, 1958, Mel Ferrer, Dana Wynter).

My Fraulein–Jay Livingston, Ray Evans (w), Daniele Amfitheatrof (m), Robbins. COVER: Red cover with title only.

1595 Fraulein Doktor (The Betrayal) (Paramount, 1969, Suzy Kendall, Kenneth More).

Fraulein Doktor Theme–Ennio Morricone (m), Famous. COVER: Suzy Kendall, Capucine.

1596 Freaky Friday (Buena Vista, 1976, Barbara Foster, Jodie Foster).

I'd Like to Be You for a Day–Al Kasha, Joel Hirschhorn (w,m), Disney. COVER: Cartoon sketch.

1597 Free and Easy (MGM, 1930, Buster Keaton, Anita Page).

Cubanita (BW)—William Kernell (m), Movietone; Free and Easy, The/ It Must Be You—Roy Turk (w), Fred Ahlert (m), Robbins; Penitentiary Blues (BW)/You've Got Me That Way (BW)—William Kernell (w,m), Movietone. COVER: Buster Keaton.

1598 Freighters of Destiny (RKO, 1931, Tom Keene, Barbara Kent).

At the End of the Trail—Bernie Grossman (w), Arthur Lange (m), Feist. COVER: Tom Keene, Barbara Kent.

1599 French Connection, The (20th Century-Fox, Gene Hackman, Fernando Ray).

French Connection Theme—Don Ellis (m), Fox. COVER: Gene Hackman, Movie Scene.

1600 French Line, The (RKO, 1954, Jane Russell, Gilbert Roland).

Any Gal from Texas/By Madame Firelle/Comment Allez-vous?/French Line, The/Lookin' for Trouble/Wait 'til You See Paris/Well, I'll Be Switched/What Is This That I Feel/ With a Kiss—Ralph Blane, Robert Wells (w), Josef Myrow (m), Mills. COVER: Jane Russell, and Movie Scenes.

1601 French Postcards (Paramount, 1979, Miles Chapin, Blanche Baker).

Thing of It Is, The—Fred Ebb (w), John Kander (m), Ensign. COVER: Movie Scene.

1602 French Without Tears (Paramount, 1940, Ray Milland, Ellen Drew).

French Without Tears (B)—Sonny Miller (w), Nikolas Brodszky (m), Day. COVER: Ray Milland, Ellen Drew.

1603 Fresh from Paris (Paris Follies 1956) (Allied Artists, 1956, Margaret Whiting, Forrest Tucker).

Can This Be Love?—Pony Sherrell, Phil Moody (w,m), American. COVER: Margaret Whiting.

1604 Freshman, The (Pathe, 1925, Harold Lloyd, Jobyna Ral-

ston).

Freshie—Jesse Greer, Harold Berg (w,m), Robbins Engel; College Days (B)—Roland Burnard (m), Wright. COVER: Harold Lloyd.

1605 Freshman Love (Warner Bros., 1936, Frank McHugh, Patricia Ellis).

Collegianna—Jack Scholl (w), M. K. Jerome (m), Witmark. COVER: Frank McHugh, Patricia Ellis.

1606 Friendly Persuasion (Allied Artists, 1956, Gary Cooper, Dorothy McGuire).

Coax Me a Little/Friendly Persuasion/Indiana Holiday/Marry Me Marry Me/Mockingbird in the Willow Tree—Paul F. Webster (w), Dimitri Tiomkin (m), Feist. COVER: Gary Cooper, Dorothy McGuire, Anthony Perkins.

1607 Friends (Paramount, 1970, Sean Bury, Anicee Alvina).

Friends—Elton John, Bernie Taupin (w,m), James. COVER: Elton John.

1608 Fright Night (Columbia, 1985, Chris Sarandon, William Ragsdale).

Fright Night—J. Lamont (w,m), Golden Torch. COVER: A Ghost.

1609 Frisco Sal (Universal, 1945, Susanna Foster, Turhan Bey).

Beloved—George Waggner (w), Edward Ward (m), Southern. COVER: Susanna Foster.

1610 Frisky (Titanus, 1954, Gina Lollobrigida, Vittorio DeSica).

Frisky/Gina—George Thorn (w), Icini (m), Southern. COVER: Gina Lollobrigida.

1611 From Here to Eternity (Columbia, 1955, Burt Lancaster, Deborah Kerr).

From Here to Eternity/I'll See You in Hawaii—Bob Wells (w), Fred Karger (m), Barton; Re-Enlistment Blues—James Jones, Robert Wells, Fred Karger (w,m), Barton. COVER: Burt Lancaster, Deborah Kerr, Frank Sinatra, Montgomery Clift.

1612 From Noon Till Three

(United Artists, 1976, Charles Bronson, Jill Ireland).

Hello and Goodbye—Alan Bergman, Marilyn Bergman (w), Elmer Bernstein (m), Unart. COVER: Charles Bronson, Jill Ireland.

1613 From Russia with Love (United Artists, 1963, Sean Connery, Daniela Bianchi).

From Russia with Love—Lionel Bart (w,m), Unart; "007" (VS)— John Barry (m), Unart. COVER: Sean Connery, and Girls.

1614 From the Earth to the Moon (Warner Bros., 1958, Joseph Cotten, George Sanders).

From the Earth to the Moon— Tom Walton (w), Lou Forbes (m), Robbins. COVER: Space Ship.

1615 From the Mixed-Up Files of Mrs. Basil E. Frankweiler (Cinema Five, 1973, Ingrid Bergman, Sally Prager).

Claudia Theme—Don Devor (m), Morris. COVER: Ingrid Bergman, and Children.

1616 From the Terrace (20th Century-Fox, 1960, Paul Newman, Joanne Woodward).

From the Terrace Love Theme— Elmer Bernstein (m), Miller. COVER: Paul Newman, Joanne Woodward.

1617 From This Day Forward (RKO, 1946, Joan Fontaine, Mark Stevens).

From This Day Forward—Mort Greene (w), Leigh Harline (m), Barton. COVER: Joan Fontaine.

1618 Frontier Woman (Top, 1956, Cindy Carson, Lance Fuller).

Polly Crockett—Theda McCormick, A.L. Royal (w,m), Hill Range. COVER: Cindy Carson.

1619 Front Page (Universal, 1974, Jack Lemmon, Walter Matthau).

Front Page Rag—Billy May (m), Duchess. COVER: Jack Lemmon, Walter Matthau.

1620 Frozen Justice (Fox, 1929, Lenore Ulric, Robert Frazer).

Right Kind of Man, The—L. Wolfe Gilbert (w), Abel Baer (m), DBH. COVER: Lenore Ulric.

1621 Fugitive Kind, The (United Artists, 1960, Marlon Brando, Anna Magnani).

Not a Soul, Blanket Roll Blues— Tennessee Williams (w), Kenyon Hopkins (m), Unart. COVER: Black and white cover with title only.

1622 Full of Life (Columbia, 1956, Judy Holliday, Richard Conte).

Full of Life Theme—Richard Quine (w), George Duning (m), Colgems. COVER: Judy Holliday, Richard Conte.

1623 Fun and Fancy Free (RKO Disney, 1947, Cartoon).

Beanero—Oliver Wallace (w,m); Fee Fi Fo Fum—Arthur Quenzer (w), Paul Smith (m); Fun and Fancy Free —Bennie Benjamin, George Weiss (w, m); Lazy Countryside—Bobby Worth (w,m); My Favorite Dream—William Walsh (w), Ray Noble (m); Say It with a Slap—Eliot Daniel (w,m); Too Good to Be True—Buddy Kaye (w), Eliot Daniel (m). PUB. Santly Joy. COVER: Cartoon.

1624 Funeral in Berlin (Paramount, 1966, Michael Caine, Oscar Homolka).

Funeral in Berlin Theme—Ronald Elfers (m), Famous. COVER: Michael Caine.

1625 Fun in Acapulco (Paramount, 1964, Elvis Presley, Ursula Andress).

Bossa Nova Baby—Jerry Leiber, Mike Stoller (w,m), Presley; Bullfighter Was a Lady, The—Sid Tepper, Roy Bennett (w,m), Gladys; Fun in Acapulco—Sid Wayne (w), Ben Weisman (m), Gladys; I Think I'm Gonna Like It Here—Don Robertson, Hal Blair (w,m), Gladys; Marguerita—Don Robertson (w,m), Gladys; Mexico— Sid Tepper, Roy Bennett (w,m), Gladys; There's No Room to Rumba in a Sports Car—Fred Wise, Dick Manning (w,m), Gladys; Vino Dinero y Amor—Sid Tepper, Roy Bennett (w,m), Gladys; You Can't Say No in Acapulco—Sid Feller, Dee Fuller, Lee Morris (w,m), Presley. COVER: Elvis Presley.

1626 Funny Face (Paramount, 1957, Fred Astaire, Audrey Hepburn).

Funny Face/He Loves and She Loves/How Long Has This Been Going On/Let's Kiss and Make Up/'Swonderful—Ira Gershwin (w), George Gershwin (m), New World. COVER: Fred Astaire, Audrey Hepburn.

1627 Funny Girl (Columbia, 1968, Barbra Streisand, Omar Sharriff).

Don't Rain on My Parade/Funny Girl—Bob Merrill (w), Jule Styne (m), Chappell; I'd Rather Be Blue Over You—Billy Rose (w), Fred Fisher (m), Bourne; I'm the Greatest Star —Bob Merrill (w), Jule Styne (m), Chappell; My Man—Channing Pollack, Maurice Yvain (w,m), Feist; People/ Sadie Sadie—Bob Merrill (w), Jule Styne (m), Chappell; Second Hand Rose—Grant Clarke (w), James Hanley (m), Fisher; You Are Woman, I Am Man/His Love Makes Me Beautiful (VS)/I Am Woman, You Are Man (VS)—Bob Merrill (w), Jule Styne (m), Chappell. COVER: Barbra Streisand.

1628 Funny Lady (Columbia, 1975, Barbra Streisand, James Caan).

Great Day—William Rose, Edward Eliscu (w), Vincent Youmans (m), Miller; How Lucky Can You Get— John Kander, Fred Ebb (w,m), Colgems; More Than You Know—William Rose, Edward Eliscu (w), Vincent Youmans (m), Miller; Beautiful Face Have a Heart (VS)—Billy Rose, James Monaco, Fred Fisher (w,m), Colgems; Fifty Million Frenchmen (VS)—Billy Rose, Willie Raskin (w), Fred Fisher (m), Colgems; Isn't This Better (VS)/Let's Hear It for Me (VS)—John Kander, Fred Ebb (w,m), Colgems; Me and My Shadow (VS)— Billy Rose (w), Al Jolson, Dave Drey-

er (m), Bourne. COVER: Barbra Streisand, James Caan.

1629 Funny Little Bunnies (Disney, 1934, Cartoon).

Funny Little Bunnies (VS)—Larry Morey (w), Frank Churchill (m), Berlin. COVER: Cartoon.

1630 Funny Thing Happened on the Way to the Forum, A (United Artists, 1966, Zero Mostel, Phil Silvers).

Comedy Tonight/Lovely/Everybody Ought to Have a Maid—Stephen Sondheim (w,m), Burthern. COVER: Zero Mostel, Phil Silvers, and Others.

1631 Fun with Dick and Jane (Columbia, 1977, Jane Fonda, George Segal).

Ahead of the Game—Peter Barnes, Michael Morgan (w,m), Colgems. COVER: Jane Fonda, George Segal.

1632 Fury, The (20th Century-Fox, 1978, Kirk Douglas, John Cassavetes).

Hold You/I'm Tired—Joe Williams (w), John Williams (m), Fox. COVER: Movie Scene.

1633 Gable and Lombard (Universal, 1976, James Brolin, Jill Clayburgh).

Gable and Lombard Love Theme —Michel Legrand (m), Leeds. COVER: James Brolin, Jill Clayburgh.

1634 Gaby (MGM, 1956, John Kerr, Leslie Caron).

Gaby—Mitchell Parish (w), Bronislau Kaper (m), Feist; Where or When —Lorenz Hart (w), Richard Rodgers (m), Chappell. COVER: John Kerr, Leslie Caron.

1635 Gaiety George (Show Time) (Warner Bros., 1946, Richard Greene, Ann Todd).

Awake My Heart (B)/Maytime Waltz (B)/One Love (B)—Eric Maschwitz (w), George Posford (m), Prowse. COVER: Richard Greene, Ann Todd.

1636 Gaiety Girls (United Artists, 1938, Jack Hulbert, Patricia Ellis).

Kiss Me Goodnight—William Kernell (w), Mischa Spoliansky (m), Marlo. COVER: Jack Hulbert, Patricia Ellis.

1637 Gaily Gaily (United Artists, 1969, Beau Bridges, Brian Keith).

There's Enough to Go Around/ Tomorrow Is My Friend—Alan Bergman, Marilyn Bergman (w), Henry Mancini (m), Northridge. COVER: Beau Bridges.

1638 Gallant Hours, The (United Artists, 1960, James Cagney, Dennis Weaver).

Gallant Hours Theme—Ward Costello (w,m), United Artists. COVER: Black and white cover with title only.

1639 Gallant Lady (United Artists, 1934, Ann Harding, Clive Brook).

Gallant Lady—Edgar Leslie (w), Fred Ahlert (m), Berlin. COVER: Ann Harding.

1640 Gallegher (Disney, 1965, Roger Mobley, Edmond O'Brien).

Gallegher—Richard Sherman, Robert Sherman (w,m), Wonderland. COVER: Red cover with title only.

1641 Gals, Incorporated (Universal, 1943, Leon Errol, Harriet Hilliard).

All the Time It's You/Hep Hep Hooray/Here's Your Kiss—Everett Carter (w), Milton Rosen (m), Robbins. COVER: Leon Errol, Girls, and Glen Gray Orchestra.

1642 Gambler, The (Lowry, 1980, Kenny Rogers, Bruce Boxleitner).

Gambler (PC)—Don Schlitz (w, m), Wrighters. COVER: None.

1643 Gamblers (Warner Bros., 1929, H. B. Warner, Lois Wilson).

If I Came Back to You and Said I'm Sorry—Will Cobb, Gus Edwards (w,m), Witmark. COVER: H. B. Warner, Lois Wilson.

1644 Gambling (Fox, 1934, George M. Cohan, Dorothy Burgess).

My Little Girl—George M. Cohan (w,m), Witmark. COVER: George M. Cohan.

1645 Gammera-The Invincible (World, 1967, Brian Donlevy, Albert Dekker).

Gammera Theme (PC)—Wes Farrell (m), Picture Tone. COVER: None.

1646 Gandhi (Columbia, 1982, Ben Kingsley, Candice Bergen).

Gandhi Theme-For All Mankind—Ravi Shankar, George Fenton (m), Eaton. COVER: Ben Kingsley, and Crowd.

1647 Gang's All Here, The (20th Century-Fox, 1943, Alice Faye, Carmen Miranda).

Carnival (PC)—Harry Warren (m), Harrison; Journey to a Star/Lady in the Tutti Frutti Hat/Minnie's in the Money/No Love No Nuthin'/Paducah/ Polka Dot Polka, The/You Discover You're in New York—Leo Robin (w), Harry Warren (m), Triangle. COVER: Alice Faye, Carmen Miranda, Benny Goodman, and Movie Scenes.

1648 Gang Show (The Gang) (Wilcox, 1937, Ralph Reader, Gina Malo).

With a Twinkle in Your Eye—Mischa Spoliansky (m), Mills. COVER: Ralph Reader, Gina Malo.

1649 Gang War (FBO, 1928, Olive Borden, Jack Pickford).

My Suppressed Desire—Ned Miller (w), Chester Cohn (m), Feist; Ya Comin' Up Tonight Huh?—Al Sherman, Al Lewis, Abe Lyman (w,m), Feist. COVER: Cartoon sketch.

1650 Gangway (GB, 1937, Jessie Matthews, Barry McKay).

Gangway/Lord and Lady Whoosis/ Moon or No Moon/When You Gotta Sing You Gotta Sing—Sam Lerner, Al Goodhart, Al Hoffman (w,m), Mills. COVER: Jessie Matthews.

1651 Garbo Talks (United Artists, 1984, Anne Bancroft, Ron Silver).

Garbo Talks-Three Themes—Cy Coleman (m), April. COVER: Cartoon Sketch.

1652 Garden of Allah, The (Selig, 1917, Thomas Santschi, Helen Mare).

Garden of Allah, The—George Little, Billy Baskette, Leon Flatow (w, m), Feist. COVER: Movie Scenes.

1653 Garden of Eatin', The (Pathe, 1929, Musical Short).

Pouring Down Rain—Roy Fox (w, m), Spier Coslow. COVER: A Man in a Window.

1654 Garden of the Finzi-Continis, The (Cinema Five, 1971, Dominique Sanda, Lino Catollicchio).

Garden of the Finzi-Continis Theme—Manuel DeSica (m), Sunbury. COVER: Cy Coleman.

1655 Garden of the Moon (Warner Bros., 1938, Pat O'Brien, Margaret Lindsay).

Confidentially/Garden of the Moon/Girl Friend of the Whirling Dervish/Lady on the Two Cent Stamp/Love Is Where You Find It—Al Dubin, Johnny Mercer (w), Harry Warren (m), Harms. COVER: Pat O'Brien, John Payne, Margaret Lindsay.

1656 Gator (United Artists, 1976, Burt Reynolds, Lauren Hutton).

Ballad of Gator McKlusky—Jerry Hubbard (w,m), Unart. COVER: Burt Reynolds, Lauren Hutton.

1657 Gay Bride, The (MGM, 1934, Carole Lombard, Chester Morris).

Mississippi Honeymoon—Gus Kahn (w), Walter Donaldson (m), Robbins. COVER: Carole Lombard, and Movie Scene.

1658 Gay Desperado, The (United Artists, 1936, Nino Martini, Ida Lupino).

Farewell My Country—Sidney Mitchell (w), Miguel Sandoval (m), Sam Fox; Gay Ranchero, A—Abe Tuvim, Francia Luban (w), J. Espinosa (m), Marks; Gypsy Lament—Teddy Powell, Walter Samuels, Leonard Whitcup, Maria Grever (w,m), Southern; World Is Mine—Holt Marvell (w), George Posford (m), Sam Fox. COVER: Nino Martini, Ida Lupino.

1659 Gay Divorcee, The (RKO, 1934, Fred Astaire, Ginger Rogers).

Continental, The—Herb Magidson (w), Con Conrad (m), Harms; Don't Let It Bother You/Let's Knock Knees—Mack Gordon, Harry Revel (w,m), DBH; Needle in a Haystack, A—Herb Magidson (w), Con Conrad (m), Harms; Night and Day—Cole Porter, Harms. COVER: Fred Astaire, Ginger Rogers.

1660 Gay Purr-ee (Warner Bros., 1962, Cartoon—Voices of Judy Garland, Robert Goulet).

Little Drops of Rain/Mewsette/Money Cat, The (PC)/Paris Is a Lonely Town/Roses Red, Violets Blue—E. Y. Harburg (w), Harold Arlen (m), Harwin. COVER: Judy Garland.

1661 Gay Ranchero, A (Republic, 1942, Gene Autry).

Gay Ranchero, A—Abe Tuvim, Francis Luban (w), J. Espinosa (m), Marks. COVER: Gene Autry.

1662 Gay Ranchero, A (Republic, 1948, Roy Rogers, Tito Guizar).

Gay Ranchero, A—Abe Tuvim, Francis Luban (w), J. Espinosa (m), Marks. COVER: Roy Rogers.

1663 Gay Senorita, The (Columbia, 1945, Jinx Falkenburg, Steve Cochran).

Llanero Es/Te Quiero Besar—Manuel Matos (w,m), Peer. COVER: Tito Guizar.

1664 Gazebo, The (MGM, 1959, Glenn Ford, Debbie Reynolds).

Something Called Love—Walton Farrar (w), Walter Kent (m), Miller. COVER: Glenn Ford, Debbie Reynolds.

1665 Geisha Boy, The (Paramount, 1958, Jerry Lewis, Marie MacDonald).

Geisha Boy Song—Jack Brooks (w), Walter Scharf (m), Paramount. COVER: Jerry Lewis.

1666 Gene Krupa Story, The (Columbia, 1959, Sal Mineo, Susan Kohner).

Cherokee (VS)—Ray Noble (w,m),

Shapiro Bernstein; Exactly Like You (VS)—Dorothy Fields (w), Jimmy McHugh (m), Shapiro Bernstein; I Love My Baby (VS)—Bud Green (w), Harry Warren (m), Shapiro Bernstein; Indiana (VS)—Ballard MacDonald (w), James Hanley (m), Shapiro Bernstein; In the Mood (VS)—Joe Garland (m), Shapiro Bernstein; Let There Be Love (VS)—Ian Grant (w), Lionel Rand (m), Shapiro Bernstein; Memories of You (VS)—Andy Razaf (w), Eubie Blake (m), Shapiro Bernstein; On the Sunny Side of the Street (VS)—Dorothy Fields (w), Jimmy McHugh (m), Shapiro Bernstein; Royal Garden Blues (VS)—Clarence Williams, Spencer Williams (w,m), Shapiro Bernstein. COVER: Sal Mineo, Susan Kohner, James Darren.

1667 General Crack (Warner Bros., 1929, John Barrymore, Marion Nixon).

General Crack's Marching Song—Ray Perkins (w,m), Witmark. COVER: Black and white cover with title only.

1668 Generation (Embassy, 1969, David Janssen, Kim Darby).

Generation—Beatrice Verdi, Dino Fekaris, Nick Zesses (w,m), Shayne. COVER: Kim Darby, Pete Duel.

1669 Genevieve (Universal, 1953, Dinah Sheridan, John Gregson).

Genevieve—William Engvick (w), Larry Adler (m), Meridan. COVER: Dinah Sheridan.

1670 Gentleman from Arizona (Call of the Range) (Monogram, 1939, John King, Joan Barclay).

Call of the Range—Ted Cisco (w,m), Golden West. COVER: Desert Scene.

1671 Gentleman from Texas, The (Monogram, 1946, Johnny Mack Brown, Claudia Drake).

With Someone Like You to Love —Meyer Grace (w), Harvey Brooke (m), ChiChi. COVER: Johnny Mack Brown, Claudia Drake.

1672 Gentlemen Marry Brunettes (United Artists, 1955, Jane Russell, Jeanne Crain).

Ain't Misbehavin'—Andy Razaf (w), Thomas Waller, Harry Brooks (m), Mills; Daddy—Bobby Troup (w, m), Republic; Gentlemen Marry Brunettes—Richard Sale (w), Herbert Spencer, Earle Hagen (m), BMI; Have You Met Miss Jones?—Lorenz Hart (w), Richard Rodgers (m), Chappell; I Wanna Be Loved By You—Bert Kalmar (w), Herb Stothart, Harry Ruby (m), Harms; I've Got Five Dollars—Lorenz Hart (w), Richard Rodgers (m), Chappell; Miss Annabelle Lee—Sidney Clare (w), Lew Pollack (m), Bourne; My Funny Valentine—Lorenz Hart (w), Richard Rodgers (m), Chappell; You're Driving Me Crazy—Walter Donaldson (w,m), BVC. COVER: Jane Russell, Jeanne Crain.

1673 Gentlemen Prefer Blondes (20th Century-Fox, 1953, Marilyn Monroe, Jane Russell).

Ain't There Anyone Here for Love—Harold Adamson (w), Hoagy Carmichael (m), Feist; Bye Bye Baby/ Diamonds Are a Girl's Best Friend/ Little Girl from Little Rock, A—Leo Robin (w), Jule Styne (m), Robbins; When Love Goes Wrong—Harold Adamson (w), Hoagy Carmichael (m), Feist. COVER: Jane Russell, Marilyn Monroe.

1674 Gentlemen with Guns (PRC, 1946, Buster Crabbe, Al St. John).

Careless Darlin'—Ernest Tubb, Lou Wayne, Bob Shelton (w,m), Cross. COVER: Eddie Dean.

1675 Gentle Rain, The (Comet, 1966, Christopher George, Lynda Day).

Gentle Rain, The—Luiz Bonita (w,m), Unart. COVER: Black and white cover with title only.

1676 George Raft Story, The (Allied Artists, 1961, Ray Danton, Jayne Mansfield).

Lonely Gal Lonely Guy—Jeff

Alexander (w,m), Miller. COVER: Ray Danton, Jayne Mansfield.

1677 George White's Scandals (Fox, 1934, Alice Faye, Rudy Vallee).

Every Day Is Father's Day with Baby (BW)/Following in Mother's Footsteps (BW)/Hold My Hand—Jack Yellen, Irving Caesar (w), Ray Henderson (m), Movietone; Man on the Flying Trapeze, The—Walter O'Keefe (w,m), Harms; My Dog Loves Your Dog/Nasty Man/Six Women/So Nice/Sweet and Simple—Jack Yellen, Irving Caesar (w), Ray Henderson (m), Movietone. COVER: Alice Faye, Rudy Vallee, Jimmy Durante.

1678 George White Scandals of 1935 (Fox, 1935, Alice Faye, James Dunn).

According to the Moonlight— Jack Yellen, Herb Magidson (w), Joseph Meyer (m), Movietone; Hunkadola/I Got Shoes You Got Shoesies —Jack Yellen, Cliff Friend (w), Joseph Meyer (m), Movietone; It's an Old Southern Custom/I Was Born Too Late—Jack Yellen (w), Joseph Meyer (m), Movietone; Oh, I Didn't Know—Jack Yellen, Cliff Friend (w), Joseph Meyer (m), Movietone; You Belong to Me (BW)—Jack Yellen (w), Cliff Friend (m), Movietone; COVER: Alice Faye, James Dunn.

1679 George White's Scandals (RKO, 1945, Joan Davis, Jack Haley).

How'd You Get Out of My Dreams/ I Want to Be a Drummer—Jack Yellen (w), Sammy Fain (m), Barton; Parrot, The—Ervin Drake (w), Zequinha Abreu (m), Peer. COVER: Joan Davis, Jack Haley, Gene Krupa, Ethel Smith.

1680 Georgy Girl (Columbia, 1966, James Mason, Allan Bates).

Georgy Girl—Jim Dale (w), Tom Springfield (m), Chappell. COVER: James Mason, Allan Bates, Lynn Redgrave.

1681 Geraldine (Pathe, 1929, Marion Nixon, Eddie Quillan).

Geraldine—Charles Tobias (w), El Kay (m), Berlin. COVER: Marion Nixon, Eddie Quillan.

1682 Gertie from Bizerte (Columbia, 1945, War Films).

Fuzzy Wuzzy Wasn't Fuzzy Wuzzy?—Ray Stillwell (w,m), Harmony. COVER: Teddy Bear.

1683 Get Going (Universal, 1943, Robert Paige, Grace McDonald).

Hold That Line—Everett Carter (w), Milton Rosen (m), Robbins. COVER: Robert Paige, Grace McDonald.

1684 Get Hep to Love (Universal, 1942, Gloria Jean, Jane Frazee).

Let's Hitch a Horse to the Automobile—Al Hoffman, Mann Curtis, Jerry Livingston (w,m), Leeds. COVER: Gloria Jean, Jane Frazee, Donald O'Connor, Peggy Ryan.

1685 Get Your Man (Paramount, 1927, Clara Bow, Buddy Rogers).

Thinking of You (Promotion Song)—Joseph Grey (w), Allie Moore (m), Calderone. COVER: Clara Bow.

1686 Get Yourself a College Girl (MGM, 1964, Mary Ann Mobley, Chad Everett).

Get Yourself a College Girl—Sidney Miller, Fred Karger (w,m), Miller. COVER: Dancers and Musical Groups.

1687 Ghostbusters (Columbia, 1984, Bill Murray, Dan Aykroyd).

Cleanin' Up the Town—Kevin O'Neal, Brian O'Neal (w,m), Columbia; Ghostbusters—Ray Parker (w,m, Columbia; Dana's Theme (VS)—Elmer Bernstein (m), Columbia; Hot Night (VS)—Diane Warren, Doctor (w,m), Columbia; I Can Wait Forever (VS)—Graham Russell, David Foster, Jay Graydon (w,m), Columbia; In the Name of Love (VS)—T. Bailey, J. Roog, C. Bell, A. Currie, P. Dodd (w,m), Columbia; Magic (VS)—Mike Smiley (w,m), Columbia; Ghostbusters Title Theme (VS)—Elmer Bernstein (m), Columbia; Savin' the Day (VS)—Bobby Alessi, Dave Immer (w,m), Columbia. COVER: Bill Murray, Dan Aykroyd, Harold Ramis.

1688 Ghostbusters II (Columbia, 1989, Bill Murray, Dan Aykroyd).

On Our Own—L. A. Reid, Baby Face, D. Simmons (w,m), Columbia. COVER: Bill Murray, Dan Aykroyd, Harold Ramis, Ernie Hudson.

1689 Ghost Catchers (Universal, 1944, Ole Olson, Chic Johnson).

Blue Candlelight/Quoth the Raven/ Three Cheers for the Customer— Paul F. Webster (w), Harry Revel (m), Leeds. COVER: Olson and Johnson.

1690 Ghost Goes West, The (United Artists, 1936, Robert Donat, Patricia Hilliard).

Stars Over the Hill (B)—Michael Hodges (w), Michael Spoliansky (m), Chappell. COVER: Robert Donat, Patricia Hilliard.

1691 Giant (Warner Bros., 1956, James Dean, Elizabeth Taylor).

Giant/Jett Rink Ballad/There's Never Been Anyone Else But You— Paul F. Webster (w), Dimitri Tiomkin (m); Yellow Rose of Texas, The—Don George (w,m), Planetary; Giant-Suite for Piano—Dmitri Tiomkin (m), Warner. COVER: Rock Hudson, James Dean, Elizabeth Taylor.

1692 G.I. Blues (Paramount, 1960, Elvis Presley, Juliet Prowse).

Big Boots—Sid Wayne (w), Sherman Edwards (m), Gladys; Blue Suede Shoes—Carl Perkins (w,m), Gladys; Didja Ever—Sid Wayne (w), Sherman Edwards (m), Gladys; Doin' the Best I Can—J. Thomas, W. Schumann (w,m), Gladys; Frankfort Special—Sid Wayne (w), Sherman Edwards (m), Gladys; G.I. Blues—Sid Tepper, Roy Bennett (w,m), Gladys; Pocketful of Rainbows, A—Fred Wise, Ben Weisman (w,m), Gladys; Shoppin' Around—Aaron Schroeder, Sid Tepper, Roy Bennett (w,m), Gladys; Tonight Is So Right for Love—Sid Wayne, Abner Silver (w,m), Gladys; What's She Really Like—Sid Wayne (w), Abner Silver (m), Gladys;

Wooden Heart—Fred Wise, Ben Weisman, Kay Twomey, Bert Kaempfert (w,m), Gladys. COVER: Elvis Presley.

1693 Gidget (Columbia, 1958, Sandra Dee, Cliff Robertson).

Gidget—Patti Washington (w), Fred Karger (m), Colgems; There's No Such Thing—Stanley Styne (w), Fred Karger (m), Colgems. COVER: Sandra Dee, Cliff Robertson, James Darren.

1694 Gidget Goes Hawaiian (Columbia, 1961, James Darren, Michael Callan).

Gidget Goes Hawaiian/Wild About That Girl—Stanley Styne (w), Fred Karger (m), Colgems. COVER: James Darren, Michael Callan, Deborah Walley.

1695 Gidget Goes to Rome (Columbia, 1963, James Darren, Cindy Carol).

Gegetta/Grande Luna Italiana— George Weiss, Al Kasha (w,m), Colgems. COVER: James Darren, Cindy Carol.

1696 Gift of Gab (Universal, 1934, Edmund Lowe, Ruth Etting).

Blue Sky Avenue—Herb Magidson (w), Con Conrad (m), Harms; Don't Let This Waltz Mean Goodbye—Jack Meskill (w), Albert Von Tilzer (m), Harms; I Ain't Gonna Sin No More— Herb Magidson (w), Con Conrad (m), Harms; Somebody Looks Good— George Whiting (w), Albert Von Tilzer (m), Harms; Talkin' to Myself— Herb Magidson (w), Con Conrad (m), Harms. COVER: Ruth Etting, Phil Baker, Ethel Waters, Edmund Lowe, and Others.

1697 Gift of Love, The (20th Century-Fox, 1957, Lauren Bacall, Robert Stack).

Gift of Love—Paul F. Webster (w), Sammy Fain (m), Robbins. COVER: Lauren Bacall, Robert Stack.

1698 Gigi (MGM, 1958, Maurice Chevalier, Leslie Caron).

A Toujours Till Always/Gigi/ I'm Glad I'm Not Young Anymore/

I Remember It Well/It's a Bore (PC)/ Night They Invented Champagne, The/Parisians, The/Say a Prayer for Me Tonight/Thank Heaven for Little Girls/Waltz at Maxim's—Alan Jay Lerner (w), Frederick Loewe (m), Chappell. COVER: Leslie Caron.

1699 Gigolette (RKO, 1935, Adrienne Ames, Ralph Bellamy).

Gigolette—Marcy Klauber (w), Charlie Williams (m), Engel. COVER: Adrienne Ames, and Man.

1700 Gigolo (DeMille, 1926, Rod LaRoque, Jobyna Ralston).

Gigolo—Marian Gillespie (w), John Hagen (m), Witmark. COVER: Rod LaRoque, and Dancer.

1701 Gigot (20th Century-Fox, 1962, Jackie Gleason, Katherine Kath).

Allo Allo Allo—Sammy Cahn, Jackie Gleason (w,m), Songsmith. COVER: Jackie Gleason.

1702 Gilda (Columbia, 1946, Glenn Ford, Rita Hayworth).

Amado Mio/Put the Blame on Mame—Allan Roberts, Doris Fisher (w,m), Sun. COVER: Rita Hayworth.

1703 Gilded Lily, The (Paramount, 1921, Mae Murray, Lowell Sherman).

Without You Sweetheart Mine—Frank Shubert (w,m), Empire. COVER: John Maloy.

1704 Gilded Lily, The (Paramount, 1935, Ray Milland, Claudette Colbert).

Something About Romance—Sam Coslow, Arthur Johnston (w,m), Famous. COVER: Ray Milland, Claudette Colbert, Fred MacMurray.

1705 Ginger (Brenner, 1971, Cheri Caffaro, William Grannell).

Ginger—Kent Evans, Bob Orpin (w,m), Happiness. COVER: Black and white cover with title only.

1706 Girl and the Gambler, The (RKO, 1939, Leo Carrillo, Tim Holt).

Palomita Mia/Timbalero—Aaron Gonzales (w,m), Southern. COVER: Leo Carrillo, Tim Holt, Steffi Duna.

1707 Girl and the Game, The (Signal, 1915, Helen Holmes, J. P. McGowan).

Girl and the Game, The—D. Radford, G. Whiting (w,m), Cadillac. COVER: Car and Train Chase.

1708 Girl Can't Help It, The (20th Century-Fox, 1957, Jayne Mansfield, Edmund O'Brien).

Blue Monday—Dave Bartholomew, Antoine Domino (w,m), Commodore; Girl Can't Help It, The/ Rock Around the Rock Pile—Bobby Troup (w,m), Robbins. COVER: Jayne Mansfield, Edmund O'Brien, Tom Ewell.

1709 Girl Crazy (RKO, 1932, Bert Wheeler, Bob Woolsey).

You've Got What Gets Me—Ira Gershwin (w), George Gershwin (m), New World. COVER: Bert Wheeler, Bob Woolsey, and Girls.

1710 Girl Crazy (MGM, 1943, Mickey Rooney, Judy Garland).

Bidin' My Time/But Not for Me/ Could You Use Me/Embraceable You/I Got Rhythm/Treat Me Rough —Ira Gershwin (w), George Gershwin (m), New World. COVER: Mickey Rooney, Judy Garland, Tommy Dorsey.

1711 Girl Downstairs, The (MGM, 1938, Franciska Gaal, Franchot Tone).

When You're in Love—Bob Wright, Chet Forrest (w,m), Feist. COVER: Franchot Tone, Franciska Gaal.

1712 Girl Friend, The (Columbia, 1935, Ann Sothern, Jack Haley).

Two Together/What Is This Power?—Gus Kahn (w), Arthur Johnston (m), Robbins. COVER: Ann Sothern, Jack Haley, Roger Pryor.

1713 Girl from Brooklyn, The (Barricade) (20th Century-Fox, 1938, Alice Faye, Warner Baxter).

There'll Be Other Nights—Lew Brown (w), Lew Pollack (m), Robbins. COVER: Black and white cover with title only.

1714 Girl from Calgary, The

(Monogram, 1932, Fifi Dorsay, Paul Kelly).

Maybe Perhaps—Albert M. Malotte (w,m), Sherman Clay. COVER: Fifi Dorsay.

1715 Girl from Chicago, The (Warner Bros., 1927, Myrna Loy, Conrad Nagel).

Molly—Harry Lee, Pat Carroll, Ken Macomber (w,m), Witmark. COVER: Black and white cover with title only.

1716 Girl from Frisco, The (Kalem, 1916, Marin Sals).

Girl from Frisco Song—James Brockman (w,m), Cadillac. COVER: Marin Sals.

1717 Girl from Havana, The (Fox, 1929, Lola Lane, Paul Page).

Time Will Tell—L. Wolfe Gilbert (w), Abel Baer (m), DBH. COVER: Lola Lane, Paul Page.

1718 Girl from Jones Beach, The (Warner Bros., 1949, Ronald Reagan, Virginia Mayo).

Girl from Jones Beach, The—Eddie Seiler, Sol Marcus (w,m), Harms. COVER: Ronald Reagan, Virginia Mayo, Eddie Bracken.

1719 Girl from Petrovka, The (Universal, 1974, Goldie Hawn, Hal Holbrook).

Girl from Petrovka Theme—Henry Mancini (m), Leeds. COVER: Goldie Hawn, Hal Holbrook.

1720 Girl from Rio, The (Monogram, 1939, Movita, Warren Hull).

Romance in Rio—Lew Porter, Johnny Lange (w,m), Southern. COVER: Movita.

1721 Girl from Scotland Yard (Paramount, 1937, Karen Morley, Robert Baldwin).

We Haven't a Moment to Lose—John Burke (w), Arthur Johnston (m), Santly Joy. COVER: Milli Monti.

1722 Girl from Woolworth's, The (First National, 1929, Alice White, Charles Delancy).

Someone—Al Bryan (w), George Meyer (m), Witmark; What I Know About Love—Herman Ruby (w), M. K. Jerome (m), Witmark; You Baby Me I'll Baby You—Al Bryan (w), George Meyer (m), Witmark. COVER: Alice White.

1723 Girl Happy (MGM, 1965, Elvis Presley, Shelley Fabares).

Do the Clam—Ben Weisman, Sid Wayne, Dolores Fuller (w,m), Gladys; Fort Lauderdale Chamber of Commerce/Puppet on a String—Sid Tepper, Roy Bennett (w,m), Gladys; Spring Fever/Wolf Call—Bill Giant, Bernie Baum, Florence Kaye (w,m), Presley. COVER: Elvis Presley.

1724 Girl I Loved, The (United Artists, 1923, Charles Ray, Patsy Ruth Miller).

Girl I Loved, The—Harvey Thew (w), Louis Gottschalk (m), Schirmer. COVER: Charles Ray, Patsy Ruth Miller.

1725 Girl Most Likely, The (RKO, 1958, Jane Powell, Cliff Robertson).

All the Colors of the Rainbow/Balboa/Crazy Horse/Girl Most Likely, The/Travelogue/We Gotta Keep Up with the Jones—Hugh Martin, Ralph Blane (w,m), Lamas. COVER: Jane Powell, Cliff Robertson, Keith Andes, Tommy Noonan.

1726 Girl Must Live, A (Universal, 1939, Margaret Lockwood, Renee Houston).

I'm a Savage/Who's Your Love—George Scott, A Robinson (w,m), Mills. COVER: Margaret Lockwood, Renee Houston, and Others.

1727 Girl Named Tamiko, A (Paramount, 1962, Laurence Harvey, Martha Hyer).

Girl Named Tamiko, A—Mack David (w), Elmer Bernstein (m), Famous. COVER: Laurence Harvey, Martha Hyer, France Nuyen.

1728 Girl Next Door, The (20th Century-Fox, 1953, June Haver, Dan Dailey).

I'd Rather Have a Pal Than a Gal Anytime/If I Love You a Mountain/I'm Mad About the Girl Next Door/

Nowhere Guy/Quiet Little Place in the Country, A/You/You're Doin' All Right (BW)—Mack Gordon (w), Josef Myrow (m), Feist. COVER: Dan Dailey, June Haver, Dennis Day.

1729 Girl of the Golden West (First National, 1923, Russel Simpson, Sylvia Breamer).

Girl of the Golden West—Haven Gillespie (w), Charles Cooke, Egbert Van Alstyne (m), Remick. COVER: Sylvia Breamer.

1730 Girl of the Golden West, The (MGM, 1938, Jeanette MacDonald, Nelson Eddy).

Girl of the Golden West/Mariachi/Senorita/Shadows on the Moon/Soldiers of Fortune/Sun-up to Sundown/West Ain't Wild Anymore, The/Who Are We to Say/Wind in the Trees, The—Gus Kahn (w), Sigmund Romberg (m), Feist. COVER: Jeanette MacDonald, Nelson Eddy.

1731 Girl of the Rio (RKO, 1932, Dolores Del Rio, Leo Carrillo).

Querida—Victor Schertzinger (w, m), Harms. COVER: Dolores Del Rio.

1732 Girl on the Barge (Universal, 1929, Jean Hersholt, Sally O'Neill).

When You Were in Love with No One but Me—Roy Turk, Joe Charniousky, Fred Ahlert (w,m), Shapiro Bernstein. COVER: Sally O'Neill, Jean Hersholt.

1733 Girl Rush (RKO, 1944, Frances Langford, Wally Brown).

Annabella's Bustle/If Mother Could Only See Us Now/Rainbow Valley/When I'm Walkin' Arm in Arm with Jim—Harry Harris (w), Lew Pollack (m), Southern. COVER: Frances Langford, Wally Brown.

1734 Girl Rush (Paramount, 1955, Rosalind Russell, Fernando Lamas).

At Last We're Alone/Birmin'ham/Champagne/Girl Rush/Homesick Hillbilly/If You Only Take a Chance/Occasional Man, An/Out of Doors—Hugh Martin, Ralph Blane (w,m), Saunders. COVER: Rosalind Russell,

and Girls.

1735 Girls (Paramount, 1919, Marguerite Clark, Harrison Ford).

Girls—Alfred Bryan (w), Harry Carroll (m), Remick. COVER: Marguerite Clark.

1736 Girls At Sea (Warner Bros., 1958, Guy Rolfe, Alan White).

Merci Beaucoup (B)—John Turner, Geoffrey Parsons (w), Gorni Kramer (m), Mad Mel. COVER: Guy Rolfe, and Girls.

1737 Girls Girls Girls (Paramount, 1962, Elvis Presley, Stella Stevens).

Because of Love—Ruth Batchelor, Bob Roberts (w,m), Presley; Boy Like Me, Girl Like You/Earth Boy—Sid Tepper, Roy Bennett (w,m), Gladys; Girls Girls Girls—Jerry Leiber, Mike Stoller (w,m), Presley; I Don't Wanna Be Tied—Bill Giant, Bernie Baum, Florence Kaye (w,m), Presley; Mama—Charles O'Curran (w), Dudley Brooks (m), Gladys; Return to Sender—Otis Blackwell, Winfield Scott (w,m), Presley; Song of the Shrimp—Sid Tepper, Roy Bennett (w,m), Gladys; Thanks to the Rolling Sea—Ruth Batchelor, Bob Roberts (w,m), Presley; Walls Have Ears—Sid Tepper, Roy Bennett (w, m), Gladys; We'll Be Together—Charles O'Curran (w), Dudley Brooks (m), Gladys; We're Coming in Loaded—Otis Blackwell, Winfield Scott (w,m), Presley; Where Do You Come From—Ruth Batchelor, Bob Roberts, Presley. COVER: Elvis Presley.

1738 Girl Shy (Pathe, 1924, Harold Lloyd, Jobyna Ralston).

Girl Shy—Charles Harris (w), Elizabeth Merrill (m), Harris; Gir-Gir-Girl Shy (B)—Herbert Rule (m), Wright. COVER: Harold Lloyd.

1739 Girls Just Want to Have Fun (New World, 1985, Sara Parker, Leo Montgomery).

Dancing in the Street (PC)—William Stevenson, Marvin Gay, Ivy Hunter (w,m), Jobete; Girls Just

Want to Have Fun—Robert Hazard (w,m), Warner. COVER: Four Girls.

1740 Girls on the Beach (Paramount, 1965, Martin West, Peter Brooks).

Little Honda—Brian Wilson (w, m), Sea Tunes. COVER: The Beach Boys.

1741 Girls on the Loose (Universal, 1958, Mara Corday, Lita Milan).

How Do You Learn to Love—Dixie Phillpott, Ray Whitaker, Dolores Hampton (w,m), Northern; I Was a Little Too Lonely—Jay Livingston, Ray Evans (w,m), Northern. COVER: Movie Scene.

1742 Girls Town (MGM, 1958, Mamie Van Doren, Mel Torme).

Lonely Boy—Paul Anka (w,m), Spanka; Wish It Were Me—Buck Ram (w,m), Robbins. COVER: Paul Anka.

1743 Girl Was Young, The (Young and Innocent) (GB, 1937, Nova Pilbeam, Derrick Demarney).

No One Can Like the Drummer Man—Sam Lerner, Al Goodhart, Al Hoffman (w,m), Mills. COVER: Nova Pilbeam.

1744 Girl with Green Eyes, The (United Artists, 1964, Peter Finch, Rita Tushingham).

Girl with Green Eyes Theme—John Addison (m), Unart. COVER: Black and white cover with title only.

1745 Girl Without a Room (Paramount, 1933, Charles Farrell, Charlie Ruggles).

Rooftop Serenade/You Alone—Val Burton (w), Will Jason (m), Paramount. COVER: Charles Farrell, Marguerite Churchill.

1746 Git Along Little Dogies (Republic, 1937, Gene Autry, Smiley Burnette).

If You Want to Be a Cowboy (VS)—Fleming Allan (w,m), Cole. COVER: Gene Autry.

1747 Give a Girl a Break (MGM, 1953, Gower Champion, Debbie Reynolds).

In Our United State/It Happens

Every Time—Ira Gershwin (w), Burton Lane (m), Feist. COVER:

1748 Give and Take (Universal, 1928, Jean Hersholt, George Sidney).

Give and Take—Dave Dreyer (w), Naceo Pinkard, Joe Charniousky (m), Berlin. COVER: Checkerboard.

1749 Give Me a Sailor (Paramount, 1938, Bob Hope, Martha Raye).

It Don't Make Sense/Little Kiss at Twilight, A/U.S.A. and You, The/What Goes on Here in My Heart—Leo Robin, Ralph Rainger (w,m), Paramount. COVER: Bob Hope, Betty Grable, Martha Raye, Jack Whiting.

1750 Give Me the Simple Life (Wake Up and Dream) (20th Century-Fox, 1945, June Haver, John Payne).

Give Me the Simple Life/I Wish I Could Tell You/Into the Sun—Harry Ruby (w), Rube Bloom (m), Triangle. COVER: June Haver, John Payne, Charlotte Greenwood.

1751 Give My Regards to Broad Street (20th Century-Fox, 1984, Paul McCartney, Bryan Brown).

No More Lonely Nights—Paul McCartney (w,m), MPL; Give My Regards to Broad Street-15 Songs—John Lennon, Paul McCartney (w, m), MPL. COVER: Paul McCartney.

1752 Give My Regards to Broadway (20th Century-Fox, 1948, Dan Dailey, Charles Winninger).

Give My Regards to Broadway—George M. Cohan (w,m), Vogel; Let a Smile Be Your Umbrella—Irving Kahal, Francis Wheeler (w), Sammy Fain (m), Mills. COVER: Dan Dailey, and Girls.

1753 Give Out Sisters (Universal, 1942, Andrews Sisters, Dan Dailey).

Jiggers the Beat—Sid Robins, Al Lerner (w,m), Leeds; New Generation, A—Walter Donaldson (w,m), Leeds; Pennsylvania Polka—Lester Lee, Zeke Manners (w,m), Shapiro Bernstein; Who Do You Think You're Foolin?—Ray Stillwell, Ray Gold (w,m), Leeds; You're Just a Flower from an Old Bouquet—Gwynne Denni, Lucien Denni (w,m), Leeds. COVER: The Andrews Sisters.

1754 Give Us This Night (Paramount, 1936, Jan Kiepura, Gladys Swarthout).

Give Us This Night—Tot Seymour (w), Vee Lawnhurst (m), Famous; I Mean to Say I Love You/Music in the Night/My Love and I/Sweet Melody of Night—Oscar Hammerstein (w), Erich W. Korngold (m), Famous. COVER: Gladys Swarthout, Jan Kiepura.

1755 Glad Rag Doll (Warner Bros., 1929, Dolores Costello, Ralph Graves).

Glad Rag Doll—Jack Yellen (w), Milton Ager, Dan Dougherty (m), Ager Yellen. COVER: Dolores Costello.

1756 Glamour (Universal, 1934, Constance Cummings, Paul Lukas).

Heaven on Earth—Roy Turk, Harry Akst (w,m), Feist. COVER: Constance Cummings, Paul Lukas.

1757 Glamour Boy (Paramount, 1941, Jackie Cooper, Susanna Foster).

Love Is Such an Old Fashioned Thing/Magic of Magnolias, The—Frank Loesser, Victor Schertzinger (w,m), Paramount. COVER: Jackie Cooper, and Girls.

1758 Glamourous Nights (Republic, 1935, Mary Ellis, Otto Kruger).

When the Gipsy Played (B)—Chris Hassall (w), Ivor Novello (m), Chappell. COVER: Mary Ellis.

1759 Glass Menagerie, The (Cineflex, 1987, Joanne Woodward, John Malkovich).

Blue Roses/Tom's Theme—Henry Mancini (m), Hollyweed. COVER: Joanne Woodward, Karen Allen.

1760 Glass Mountain, The (Eagle Lion, 1949, Tito Gobbi, Dulcie Gray).

Legend of the Glass Mountain—Nino Rota (m), Sam Fox; Song of the Mountains—Sonny Miller, Toni Ortelli, Luigi Pigarelli (w,m), Sam Fox; Take the Sun—Emery Bonett (w), Nino Rota (m), Sam Fox; Wayfarer's Song (B)—Emery Bonett (w), Vivien Lambelet, E. Anthony (m), Chappell. COVER: Tito Gobbi, Valentina Cortesa, Michael Denison.

1761 Glass Slipper, The (MGM, 1955, Leslie Caron, Michael Wilding).

Cinderella's Wedding Cake (BW) —Bronislau Kaper (m), Robbins; Take My Love—Helen Deutsch (w), Bronislau Kaper (m), Feist. COVER: Leslie Caron, Michael Wilding.

1762 Glenn Miller Story, The (Universal, 1954, James Stewart, June Allyson).

Adios (PC)—Eddie Woods (w), Enric Madriguera (m), Peer; Basin Street Blues—Spencer Williams (w, m), Mayfair; Chattanooga Choo Choo—Mack Gordon (w), Harry Warren (m), Feist; Glenn Miller Story Love Theme—Henry Mancini (m), Pickwick; In the Mood—Andy Razaf (w), Joe Garland (m), Shapiro Bernstein; Little Brown Jug—J. E. Winner (w,m), Lewis; Moonlight Serenade—Mitchell Parish (w), Glenn Miller (m), Robbins; Pennsylvania 6-5000—Carl Sigman (w), Jerry Gray (m), Robbins; Saint Louis Blues—W. C. Handy (w,m), Handy; String of Pearls, A—Eddie Delange (w), Jerry Gray (m), Mutual; Too Little Time—Don Raye (w), Henry Mancini (m), Pickwick; Tuxedo Junction—Bud Feyne (w), Erskine Hawkins, Bill Johnson, Julian Dash (m), Lewis; At Last (VS) —Mack Gordon (w), Harry Warren (m), United Artists; Elmer's Tune (VS)—E. Albrecht, S. Gallop, Dick Jurgens (w,m), United Artists; Over the Rainbow (VS)—E. Y. Harburg (w), Harold Arlen (m), United Artists; Stairway to the Stars (VS)—Mitchell Parish (w), M. Malneck, F. Signorelli (m), United Artists; I Knew Why (VS)—Mack Gordon (w), Harry Warren (m), United Artists. COVER: June Allyson, James Stewart.

1763   Glimpses of Austria (MGM, 1938, Travel Talk).

Sailing the Blue Danube—James Fitzpatrick (w), Jack Shilkret (m), Southern, COVER: Gabe Drake.

1764   Glimpses of the Moon (Paramount, 1923, Bebe Daniels, Nita Naldi).

Glimpses of the Moon—Phil Cook (w), Tom Johnstone (m), G and J. COVER: Bebe Daniels.

1765   Global Affair, A (MGM, 1963, Bob Hope, Lilo Pulver).

Fais Do Do, Go to Sleep/Global Affair, A/So Wide the World—Dorcas Cochran (w), Dominic Frontiere (m), Hastings. COVER: Bob Hope and Girls.

1766   Gloria's Romance (Kleine, 1916, Billie Burke, David Powell).

Gloria's Romance—Maud Murray (m), Cadillac; Little Billie—Jerome Kern (m), Harms. COVER: Billie Burke.

1767   Glorifying the American Girl (Paramount, 1930, Eddie Cantor, Rudy Vallee).

There Must Be Somebody Waiting for Me—Walter Donaldson (w,m), Donaldson; What Wouldn't I Do for That Man—E. Y. Harburg (w), Jay Gorney (m), Remick. COVER: Helen Morgan, Mary Eaton.

1768   Glorious Lady, The (Selznick, 1919, Matt Moore, Olive Thomas).

Glorious Lady, The—Al Wilson, Lou Klein (w), Irving Bibo (m), Berlin. COVER: Olive Thomas.

1769   Glory (RKO, 1955, Margaret O'Brien, Walter Brennan).

Getting Nowhere Road/Glory/Kentucky Means Paradise—Ted Koehler (w), M. K. Jerome (m), Mills. COVER: Margaret O'Brien.

1770   Glory Alley (MGM, 1952, Leslie Caron, Ralph Meeker).

Glory Alley—Mack David (w), Jerry Livingston (m), Feist. COVER: Leslie Caron, Ralph Meeker, Louis Armstrong.

1771   Glory Guys, The (United Artists, 1965, Tom Tryon, Harve Presnell).

Glory Guys, The—Noel Sherman (w), Riz Ortolani (m), Unart. COVER: Tom Tryon, Harve Presnell, and Battle Scene.

1772   Gnome Mobile (Buena Vista, 1967, Walter Brennan, Matthew Garber).

Gnome Mobile Song—Richard Sherman, Robert Sherman (w,m), Wonderland. COVER: Blue cover with title only.

1773   Go Between, The (Columbia, 1971, Julie Christie, Alan Bates).

Bo Between Theme—Michel Legrand (m), Chappell; I Still See You—Hal Shaper (w), Michel Legrand (m), Chappell. COVER: Julie Christie, Alan Bates.

1774   Goddess, The (Vitagraph, 1915, Anita Stewart, Early Williams).

Celestia Beautiful Goddess of Love—Bart Grant, Joe Young (w,m), Berlin; Goddess, Beautiful Song—Monroe Rosenfield (w), Maud Murray (m), Cadillac; Goddess Valse Hesitation—Maud Murray (m), Cadillac; Goddess Valse Celestia—Lee Orean Smith (m), Feist. COVER: Anita Stewart.

1775   Godfather (Paramount, 1972, Al Pacino, Marlon Brando).

Antico Canto Siciliano—Carmen Coppola (w,m), Famous; Bells of St. Mary's, The—Douglas Furber (w), Emmett Adams (m), Chappell; Come Live Your Life with Me—Larry Kusik, Billy Meshel (w), Nino Rota (m), Famous; Godfather Love Theme —Nino Rota (m), Famous; Godfather Mazurka/Godfather Tarantella—Carmen Coppola (m), Famous; Godfather Waltz—Nino Rota (m), Famous; I Have But One Heart—Marty Symes (w), Johnny Farrow (m), Barton; Many Different People—Norman Simon, Billy Meshel (w), Nino Rota (m), Famous; Michael's Theme —Nino Rota (m), Famous; Non Ci Lasceremo Mai—Italia Pennino (w),

Carmen Coppola (m), Famous; Pick Up—Nino Rota (m), Famous; Speak Softly Love—Larry Kusik (w), Nino Rota (m), Famous; Manhattan Serenade (VS)—Harold Adamson (w), Louis Alter (m), Robbins; Mona Lisa (VS)—Jay Livingston, Ray Evans (w, m), Famous. COVER: Puppet and Strings.

1776 Godfather II (Paramount, 1974, Al Pacino, Robert DeNiro).

Godfather II Theme—Nino Rota (m), Famous; Ho Bisogno Di Te-When I'm with You—Italia Pennino (w), Carmine Coppola (m), Carmit; In a Paris Cafe—Carmine Coppola (m), Carmit; Italian Eyes—Italia Pennino (w), Carmine Coppola (m), Carmit; Kay's Theme—Nino Rota (m), Famous; Love Said Goodbye—Larry Kusik (w), Nino Rota (m), Famous; Napule Ve Salute/ Senza Mamma/Sophia—Italia Pennino (w), Carmine Coppola (m), Carmit. COVER: A Gangster.

1777 God Is My Partner (20th Century-Fox, 1959, Walter Brennan, Marion Ross).

God Is My Partner—Gene Forrell, Max Stein, Jac Thall (w,m), Alamo. COVER: Walter Brennan.

1778 Godless Girl, The (Pathe, 1929, George Duryea, Lina Basquette).

Love, All I Want Is Love—Charles Weinberg, Josiah Zuro (w,m), Berlin. COVER: George Duryea, Lina Basquette.

1779 Godspell (Columbia, 1973, Victor Garber, David Haskell).

Beautiful City—Stephen Schwartz (w,m), Colgems. COVER: Victor Garber, and Movie Scene.

1780 Gog (United Artists, 1954, Richard Egan, Constance Dowling).

Nightfall—Harry Sukman (m), Young. COVER: Two Planets.

1781 Go Go Go World (ABC, 1964, Documentary of Bizarre Behaviour).

I Believe You—Billy Towne (w), Nino Oliviero, Bruno Nicolai (m),

Marks; Only Fools/Sting of the Bee—Alan Brandt (w), Nino Oliviero, Bruno Nicolai (m), Marks. COVER: A Girl and a Native.

1782 Going Highbrow (Warner Bros., 1935, Guy Kibbee, Zasu Pitts).

Moon Crazy/One in a Million—John Scholl (w), Lou Alter (m), Remick. COVER: Guy Kibbee, Zasu Pitts, Edward Everett Horton.

1783 Going Hollywood (MGM, 1933, Marion Davies, Bing Crosby).

After Sundown/Cinderella's Fella/ Going Hollywood/Our Big Love Scene/Temptation/We'll Make Hay While the Sun Shines—Arthur Freed (w), Nacio Herb Brown (m), Robbins. COVER: Marion Davies, Bing Crosby.

1784 Going My Way (Paramount, 1944, Bing Crosby, Rise Stevens).

Day After Forever, The/Going My Way/Swinging on a Star—Johnny Burke (w), Jimmy Van Heusen (m), BVH; Too Ra Loo Ra Loo Ral, That's an Irish Lullaby—J. R. Shannon (w,m), Witmark. COVER: Bing Crosby, Rise Stevens.

1785 Going Places (Warner Bros., 1938, Dick Powell, Anita Page).

Jeepers Creepers—Johnny Mercer (w), Harry Warren (m), Witmark; Mutiny in the Nursery—Johnny Mercer (w,m), Witmark; Say It with a Kiss—Johnny Mercer (w), Harry Warren (m), Witmark. COVER: Dick Powell, Anita Page.

1786 Going Steady (Columbia, 1957, Molly Bee, Alan Reed).

Going Steady-With a Dream—Richard Quine (w), Fred Karger (m), Columbia. COVER: Molly Bee.

1787 Goin' to Town (Paramount, 1935, Mae West, Paul Cavanaugh).

He's a Bad Man—Irving Kahal, Sammy Fain (w,m), Famous; Now I'm a Lady—Irving Kahal, Sam Coslow, Sammy Fain (w,m), Famous. COVER: Mae West.

1788 Go Into Your Dance (Warner Bros., 1935, Al Jolson, Ruby Keeler).

About a Quarter to Nine/Casino De Paree/Go Into Your Dance/Good Old Fashioned Cocktail/Little Things You Used to Do/Mammy I'll Sing About You/She's a Latin from Manhattan—Al Dubin (w), Harry Warren (m), Witmark. COVER: Al Jolson, Ruby Keeler.

1789 Gold (Allied Artists, 1974, Roger Moore, Susannah York).

Wherever Love Takes Me (PC)— Don Black (w), Elmer Bernstein (m), Duchess. COVER: None.

1790 Gold-Diggers, The (Warner Bros., 1925, Louise Fazenda, Hope Hampton).

Gold-digger, The—James Hanley (w,m), Shapiro Bernstein. COVER: Louise Fazenda, Hope Hampton, Wyndham Standing.

1791 Gold-Diggers in Paris (Warner Bros., 1938, Rudy Vallee, Rosemary Lane).

Daydreaming—Johnny Mercer (w), Harry Warren (m), Witmark; I Wanna Go Back to Bali/Latin Quarter—Al Dubin (w), Harry Warren (m), Witmark; My Adventure (BW)—Johnny Mercer (w), Harry Warren (m), Witmark; Put That Down in Writing (BW)/Stranger in Paree, A—Al Dubin, Harry Warren (m), Witmark. COVER: The Eiffel Tower.

1792 Gold-Diggers of Broadway (Warner Bros., 1929, Winnie Lightner, Ann Pennington).

And Still They Fall in Love/Go to Bed/In a Kitchenette/Keeping the Wolf from the Door/Mechanical Man/ Painting the Clouds with Sunshine/ Poison Kiss of That Spaniard (BW)/ Song of the Gold-diggers/Tip Toe Through the Tulips with Me/What Will I Do without You—Al Dubin (w), Joe Burke (m), Witmark. COVER: Winnie Lightner, Ann Pennington, and Others.

1793 Gold-Diggers of 1933 (Warner, 1933, Warren Williams, Joan Blondell).

Gold-diggers' Song, The/I've Got to Sing a Torch Song/Pettin' in the Park/Remember My Forgotten Man/ Shadow Waltz—Al Dubin (w), Harry Warren (m), Remick. COVER: Dick Powell, Ruby Keeler, Joan Blondell.

1794 Gold-Diggers of 1935 (Warner Bros., 1935, Dick Powell, Gloria Stewart).

I'm Goin' Shoppin' with You/Lullaby of Broadway/Words Are in My Heart, The—Al Dubin (w), Harry Warren (m), Witmark. COVER: Girls.

1795 Gold-Diggers of 1937 (Warner Bros., 1936, Dick Powell, Joan Blondell).

All's Fair in Love and War—Al Dubin (w), Harry Warren (m), Harms; Let's Put Our Heads Together/Speaking of the Weather—E. Y. Harburg (w), Harold Arlen (m), Harms; With Plenty of Money and You—Al Dubin (w), Harry Warren (m), Harms. COVER: Dick Powell, Joan Blondell.

1796 Golden Calf, The (Fox, 1930, Sue Carol, Jack Mulhall).

Can I Help It?/I'm Tellin' the World About You/Maybe Someday/ You Gotta Be Modernistic—Cliff Friend (w), Jimmie Monaco (m), Red Star. COVER: Sue Carol, Jack Mulhall.

1797 Golden Child, The (Paramount, 1987, Eddie Murphy, Charles Dance).

Best Man in the World—Ann Wilson, Nancy Wilson, Sue Ennis (w), John Barry (m), Famous. COVER: Eddie Murphy.

1798 Golden Dawn (Warner Bros., 1930, Walter Woolf, Vivienne Segal).

Dawn—Otto Harbach, Oscar Hammerstein (w), Robert Stolz, Herbert Stothart (m), Harms; We Two/Whip, The—Otto Harbach, Oscar Hammerstein (w), Emmerich Kalman, Herbert Stothart (m), Harms. COVER: Sunrise.

1799 Golden Earrings (Paramount, 1947, Marlene Dietrich, Ray Milland).

Golden Earrings—Jay Livingston,

Ray Evans (w), Victor Young (m), Paramount; Golden Earrings Theme (VS)—Victor Young (m). COVER: Marlene Dietrich, Ray Milland.

1800 Golden Girl (20th Century-Fox, 1951, Mitzi Gaynor, Dale Robertson).

California Moon—George Jessel, Sam Lerner (w), Joe Cooper (m), Robbins; Never—Eliot Daniel (w), Lionel Newman (m). COVER: Mitzi Gaynor, Dale Robertson, Dennis Day.

1801 Golden Head, The (Cinerama, 1964, George Sanders, Buddy Hackett).

Things I'd Like to Say—Mitch Murray (w,m), Famous. COVER: George Sanders, Buddy Hackett, and Movie Scenes.

1802 Golden Hoofs (20th Century-Fox, 1941, Jane Withers, Buddy Rogers).

Consider Yourself in Love—Walter Bullock (w), Harold Spina (m), Robbins. COVER: Jane Withers, Buddy Rogers.

1803 Golden Ivory (White Huntress) (AIP, 1954, Robert Urquhart, John Bentley).

Wagon Trail (B)—Philip Green (m), Mills. COVER: Movie Scene.

1804 Golden Stallion, The (Republic, 1949, Roy Rogers, Dale Evans).

Golden Stallion, The—Sid Robin, Foy Willing (w,m), Leeds. COVER: Roy Rogers, Dale Evans.

1805 Golden Touch, The (Disney, 1935, Cartoon).

Golden Touch, The (VS)—Larry Morey (w), Frank Churchill (w), Berlin. COVER: Cartoon.

1806 Golden Trail, The (Monogram, 1940, Tex Ritter, Ina Guest).

Gold Is Where You Find It (VS)—Tex Ritter, Frank Harford (w,m), Cole. COVER: Tex Ritter.

1807 Golden West, The (Fox, 1932, George O'Brien, Janet Chandler).

Home Folks—James Hanley (w, m), Sam Fox. COVER: Covered Wagon Camp.

1808 Goldfinger (United Art-1964, Sean Connery, Gert Frobe).

Goldfinger—Leslie Bricusse, Anthony Newley (w), John Barry (m), Unart. COVER: Sean Connery, Girl, and Statue.

1809 Gold Mine in the Sky (Republic, 1938, Gene Autry, Smiley Burnette).

As Long as I Have My Horse (VS)/ Dude Ranch Cow Hands (VS)—Gene Autry, Fred Rose, Johnny Marvin (w,m), Western; That's How Donkeys Were Born (VS)/Tumbleweed Tenor (VS)—Eddie Cherkose, Smiley Burnette (w,m), Cole. COVER: Gene Autry.

1810 Gold Rush, The (United Artists, 1925, Charlie Chaplin, Mack Swain).

Sing a Song—Charlie Chaplin, Abe Lyman, Gus Arnheim (w,m), Berlin; With You Dear in Bombay—Charlie Chaplin (w,m), Witmark. COVER: Charlie Chaplin.

1811 Goldwyn Follies, The (United Artists, 1938, Adolphe Menjou, Zorina).

Here Pussy Pussy—Ray Golden, Sid Kuller (w,m), Chappell; I Love to Rhyme/I Was Doing All Right/Just Another Rhumba (BW)/Love Is Here to Stay/Love Walked In—Ira Gershwin (w), George Gershwin (m), Chappell; Spring Again—Ira Gershwin (w), Vernon Duke (m), Chappell. COVER: Kenny Baker, Andrea Leeds, Adolphe Menjou, Zorina, Charlie McCarthy, etc.

1812 Go, Man, Go! (United Artists, 1954, Dane Clark, Harlem Globetrotters).

Go, Man, Go!—Sy Oliver, Mike Sher (w,m), Unart. COVER: Dane Clark, Harlem Globetrotters.

1813 Gone Are the Days (Hammer, 1963, Ruby Dee, Ossie Davis).

Good Things—Ruby Dee, Ossie Davis (w), Henry Cowen (m), Lilli. COVER: Ruby Dee, Ossie Davis.

1814 **Gone to Earth (The Wild Heart)** (RKO, 1950, Jennifer Jones, David Farrar).
Gone to Earth-Three Songs (B)—Brian Easdale, W. Shakespeare, Mary Webb (w,m), Chappell. COVER: Jennifer Jones.

1815 **Gone with the Wind** (MGM, 1938, Clark Gable, Vivien leigh).
My Own True Love—Mack David (w), Max Steiner (m), Warner; Tara Theme/Gone with the Wind-Piano Miniatures—Max Steiner (m), Remick. COVER: Clark Gable, Vivien Leigh, and Tara.

1816 **Good Bad Boy, The** (Principal, 1924, Joe Butterworth, Mary Jane Irving).
Who Wants a Bad Little Boy—Joe Burke, Mark Fisher (w,m), Independent. COVER: Joe Butterworth.

1817 **Goodbye Again** (United Artists, 1961, Ingrid Bergman, Yves Montand).
Goodbye Again Theme—George Auric (m), Unart. COVER: Ingrid Bergman, Yves Montand, Tony Perkins.

1818 **Goodbye Charlie** (20th Century-Fox, 1964, Tony Curtis, Debbie Reynolds).
Goodbye Charlie—Dory Langdon (w), André Previn (m), Miller. COVER: Tony Curtis, Debbie Reynolds.

1819 **Goodbye Columbus** (Paramount, 1969, Richard Benjamin, Jack Klugman).
It's Gotta Be Real—Larry Ramos (w,m), Ensign; Love Has a Way—Jay Darrow (w), Charles Fox (m), Ensign; So Kind to Me—Terry Kirkman (w, m), Ensign; Goodbye Columbus-Six Themes—Charles Fox, James Yester (m), Ensign; Goodbye Columbus—James Yester (w,m), Ensign. COVER: Richard Benjamin, Ali Macgraw.

1820 **Goodbye Girl, The** (Warner Bros., 1977, Richard Dreyfuss, Marsha Mason).
Goodbye Girl, The—David Gates (w,m), Warner. COVER: Richard Dreyfuss, Marsha Mason.

1821 **Goodbye Kiss, The** (Warner Bros., 1928, Johnny Burke, Sally Eilers).
Your Goodbye Kiss—Byron Gay, Neil Moret (w,m), Villa Moret. COVER: Johnny Burke, Sally Eilers.

1822 **Goodbye Love** (RKO, 1934, Charlie Ruggles, Verree Teasdale).
Goodbye Love—Con Conrad, Archie Gottler, Sidney Mitchell (w, m), DBH. COVER: Charlie Ruggles, Verree Teesdale.

1823 **Goodbye Mr. Chips** (MGM, 1969, Peter O'Toole, Petula Clark).
Fill the World with Love/What a Lot of Flowers/You and I/And the Sky Smiled (VS)/Apollo (VS)/London Is London (VS)/School Days (VS)/Walk Through the World (VS)/What Shall I Do Today (VS)/When I Am Older (VS)/When I Was Younger (VS)/Where Did My Childhood Go (VS)—Leslie Bricusse (w,m), Hastings. COVER: Peter O'Toole, Petula Clark.

1824 **Goodbye Norma Jean** (Stirling, 1974, Misty Rowe, Terrence Locke).
Norma Jean Wants to Be a Movie Star—Johnny Cunningham (w,m), Chappell. COVER: Misty Rowe.

1825 **Good Companions** (Fox, 1933, Jessie Matthews, Edmund Gwenn).
Let Me Give My Happiness to You/Lucky for Me/Three Wishes—Douglas Furber (w), George Posford (m), Movietone. COVER: Jessie Matthews.

1826 **Good Dame** (Paramount, 1934, Sylvia Sydney, Fredric March).
She's a Good Dame—Leo Robin, Ralph Rainger (w,m), Famous. COVER: Sylvia Sydney, Fredric March.

1827 **Good Gracious Annabelle** (Paramount, 1919, Billie Burke, Herbert Rawlinson).
Good Gracious Annabelle—Ed Rose, George Whiting, Lew Pollack (w,m), McCarthy. COVER: Billie Burke.

1828 **Good Intentions** (Fox, 1930, Edmund Lowe, Marguerite Churchill).

Slave to Love, A—Cliff Friend, James Monaco (w,m), Red Star. COVER: Edmund Lowe, Marguerite Churchill.

1829 **Good Love (Seven Men from Now)** (Warner Bros., 1956, Randolph Scott, Gail Russell).

Good Love—By Dunham (w), Henry Vars (m), Artists. COVER: Randolph Scott, Gail Russell.

1830 **Good Morning Vietnam** (Touchstone, 1988, Robin Williams, Forrest Whittaker).

What a Wonderful World—George D. Weiss, Bob Thiele (w,m), Range. COVER: Louis Armstrong.

1831 **Good News** (MGM, 1930, Bessie Love, Cliff Edwards).

Gee, But I'd Like to Make You Happy—Larry Shay, George Ward, Reggie Montgomery (w,m), DBH; If You're Not Kissing Me/Football—Arthur Freed (w), Nacio Herb Brown (m), DBH; I Feel Pessimistic—George Waggner (w), J. Russel Robinson (m), DBH. COVER: Cartoon Sketch.

1832 **Good News** (MGM, 1947, Peter Lawford, June Allyson).

Best Things in Life Are Free, The/ Good News/Just Imagine/Lucky in Love—B. G. DeSylva, Lew Brown, Ray Henderson (w,m), Crawford; Pass That Peace Pipe—Roger Edens, Hugh Martin, Ralph Blane (w,m), Crawford; Varsity Drag, The—B. G. DeSylva, Lew Brown, Ray Henderson (w,m), Crawford. COVER: Peter Lawford, June Allyson.

1833 **Good Old Soak (The Old Soak)** (MGM, 1937, Wallace Beery, Una Merkel).

You've Got a Certain Something (VS)—Bob Wright, Chet Forrest (w), Walter Donaldson (m), Donaldson. COVER: Walter Donaldson.

1834 **Good, the Bad, and the Ugly, The** (United Artists, 1966, Clint Eastwood, Eli Wallach).

Good, the Bad, and the Ugly, The —Ennio Morricone (m), Unart. COVER: Clint Eastwood, and Movie Scene.

1835 **Goona Goona** (First Division, 1933, Dasnee).

Goona Goona—Mitchell Parish (w), Serge Walter (m), Mills. COVER: Dasnee.

1836 **Goonies, The** (Warner Bros., 1985, Sean Astin, Josh Brolin).

Fourteen K—Teena Marie (w,m), CBS; Goonies Are Good Enough—Cyndi Lauper, Stephen Lunt, Art Stead (w,m), Warner; Eight Arms to Hold You (VS)—Art Baker, Rob Kilgore, Jim Bralower (w,m), Warner; I Got Nothing (VS)—Susannah Hoffs, Vicki Peterson, Jules Shear (w,m), Warner; Love Is Alive (VS)—Philip Bailey, Richard Marx (w,m), Warner; Save the Night (VS)—Joe Williams, Amy La Television (w,m), Warner; She's So Good to Me (VS)—Luther Vandross (w,m), Warner; Goonie's Theme (VS)—Dave Grusin (m), Warner; What a Thrill (VS)—Cyndi Lauper, John Turi (w,m), Warner; Wherever You're Goin' (VS)—Kevin Cronin (w,m), Warner. COVER: Kids.

1837 **Go West** (MGM, 1925, Buster Keaton, Brown Eyes).

She Doesn't—Walter Winchell (w), Jimmie Durante, Chick Endor (m), Waterson. COVER: Buster Keaton, and Cow.

1838 **Go West** (MGM, 1940, Marx Brothers, John Carroll).

As If I Didn't Know—Gus Kahn (w), Bronislau Kaper (m), Feist. COVER: Marx Brothers.

1839 **Go West Young Lady** (Columbia, 1941, Ann Miller, Glenn Ford).

Doggie Take Your Time/Go West Young Lady/I Wish That I Could Be a Singing Cowboy/Most Gentlemen Don't Prefer a Lady/Rise to Arms, Pots and Pans on Parade/Somewhere Along the Trail—Sammy Cahn, Saul

Chaplin (w,m), Mills. COVER: Ann Miller.

1840 Go West Young Man (Paramount, 1936, Mae West, Warren Williams).

Go West Young Man/I Was Saying to the Moon/On a Typical Tropical Night—Johnny Burke (w), Arthur Johnston (m), Santly Joy. COVER: Mae West.

1841 Gracie Allen Murder Case, The (Paramount, 1939, Warren Williams, Gracie Allen).

Snug as a Bug in a Rug—Frank Loesser (w), Matt Malneck (m), Paramount. COVER: Gracie Allen, Warren Williams.

1842 Graduate, The (Embassy, 1967, Anne Bancroft, Dustin Hoffman).

Mrs. Robinson—Paul Simon (w, m), Charing Cross; Scarborough Fair-Canticle—Paul Simon, Art Garfunkel (w,m), Charing Cross; Graduate-Six Themes—Dave Grusin (m), Levine. COVER: Anne Bancroft, Dustin Hoffman.

1843 Grandma's Boy (Associated, 1922, Harold Lloyd, Anna Townsend).

Grandma's Boy—Herb Crooker, Jean Haver, Pete Wendline (w,m), Stark. COVER: Harold Lloyd, Anna Townsend.

1844 Grand Parade, The (Pathe, 1929, Helen Twelvetrees, Fred Scott).

Alone in the Rain/Moanin' for You/Molly—Edmund Goulding, Dan Dougherty (w,m), Agar Yellen. COVER: Helen Twelvetrees.

1845 Grand Prix (MGM, 1966, James Garner, Brian Bedford).

Grand Prix Theme—Maurice Jarre (m), Feist. COVER: James Garner, and Movie Scenes.

1846 Grass-Hopper and the Ants, The (Disney, 1934, Cartoon).

World Owes Me a Living, The—Larry Morey (w), Leigh Harline (m), Berlin. COVER: Cartoon.

1847 Grass Is Greener, The (Universal, 1961, Cary Grant, Deborah Kerr).

Grass Is Greener Theme—Noel Coward (m), Chappell. COVER: Cary Grant, Deborah Kerr, Robert Mitchum, Jean Simmons.

1848 Graustark (First National, 1925, Norma Talmadge, Eugene O'Brien).

Maybe You'll Come Back Someday—Ray Baxter (w), Fred Carbonneau (m), Popular. COVER: Norma Talmadge.

1849 Grease (Paramount, 1978, John Travolta, Olivia Newton-John).

Grease—Barry Gibb (w,m), Warner; Greased Lightnin'—Warren Casey, Jim Jacobs (w,m), Warner; Hopelessly Devoted to You—John Farrar (w, m), Warner; Sandy—Scott Simon (w), Louis St. Louis (m), Warner; Summer Nights—Warren Casey, Jim Jacobs (w,m), Warner; You're the One That I Want—John Farrar (w,m), Warner; Alone at the Drive In Movie (VS)/Beauty School Drop Out (VS)—Warren Casey, Jim Jacobs (w,m), Warner; Blue Moon (VS)—Lorenz Hart (w), Richard Rodgers (m), Warner; Born to Hand Jive (VS)/Freddy My Love (VS)—Warren Casey, Jim Jacobs (w, m), Warner; Hound Dog (VS)—Jerry Leiber, Mike Stoller (w,m), Warner; It's Raining on Prom Night (VS)/Look at Me I'm Sandra Dee (VS)—Warren Casey, Jim Jacobs (w,m), Warner; Love Is a Many Splendored Thing (VS)—Paul F. Webster (w), Sammy Fain (m), Warner; Mooning—Warren Casey, Jim Jacobs (w,m), Warner; Rock and Roll Is Here to Stay (VS)—Dave White (w,m), Warner; Rock 'N' Roll Party Queen (VS)—Warren Casey, Jim Jacobs (w,m), Warner; Tears on My Pillow (VS)—Sylvester Bradford, Al Lewis (w,m), Warner; There Are Worse Things I Could Do (VS)/Those Magic Changes (VS)/We Go Together (VS)—Warren Casey, Jim Jacobs (w,m), Warner. COVER: John Travolta, Olivia Newton-John.

1850 Great Adventure, The (Rochemont, 1955, Anders Norberg, Jack Suckdorff).

Otty the Otter—James Pattarini (w), Jack Shaindlin (m), Triumph. COVER: Anders Norberg, Kjell Sucksdorff, and Otter.

1851 Great Alone, The (West Coast, 1922, Maria Draga, Monroe Salisbury).

Great Alone, The—C. J. Mac-Meekin, J A. MacMeekin (w,m), MacMeekin. COVER: Maria Draga, Monroe Salisbury.

1852 Great American Broadcast, The (20th Century-Fox, 1941, Alice Faye, John Payne).

Great American Broadcast, The/I Take to You/It's All in a Lifetime/I've Got a Bone to Pick with You/Long Ago Last Night/Run Little Raindrop Run (BW)/Where You Are—Mack Gordon (w), Harry Warren (m), Feist. COVER: Alice Faye, John Payne, Jack Oakie.

1853 Great Balls of Fire (Orion, 1989, Dennis Quaid, Winona Ryder).

Great Balls of Fire—Otis Blackwell, Jack Hammer (w,m), Chappell. COVER: Piano Keys and Flames.

1854 Great Caruso, The (MGM, 1951, Mario Lanza, Ann Blyth).

Because—Ed Teschemacher (w), Guy D'Hardelot (m), Chappell; Loveliest Night of the Year—Paul F. Webster (w), Irving Aaronson (m), Robbins; Great Caruso Opera Arias—Various Composers, Robbins. COVER: Mario Lanza, Ann Blyth.

1855 Great Chase, The (Continental, 1960, Buster Keaton, Pearl White).

Way Down East—Larry Adler (m), Saunders. COVER: Sketch.

1856 Great Day (MGM, 1930, Joan Crawford, Johnny Mack Brown).

Great Day (B)—William Rose, Edward Eliscu (w), Vincent Youmans (m), Campbell. COVER: Sunshine Over a River. (NOTE: Movie was cancelled but music was published.)

1857 Great Divide, The (MGM, 1924, Alice Terry, Conway Tearle).

West of the Great Divide—George Whiting (m), Ernest Ball (m), Witmark. COVER: Alice Terry, Conway Tearle.

1858 Great Divide, The (First National, 1930, Dorothy Mackaill, Lucien Littlefield).

End of the Lonesome Trail/Si Si Senor—Herman Ruby (w), Ray Perkins (m), Witmark. COVER: Dorothy Mackaill.

1859 Great Escape, The (United Artists, 1963, Steve McQueen, James Garner).

Great Escape March—Al Stillman (w), Elmer Bernstein (m), Unart. COVER: Steve McQueen, James Garner.

1860 Greatest, The (Columbia, 1977, Muhammad Ali, Ernest Borgnine).

Ali Bombaye 1 and 2 Zaire Chant —Michael Masser (m), Columbia; Greatest Love of All—Linda Creed (w), Michael Masser (m), Columbia; I Always Knew I Had it in Me—Gerry Goffin (w), Michael Masser (m), Columbia. COVER: Mohammad Ali, Ernest Borgnine.

1861 Greatest Question, The (First National, 1919, Lillian Gish, George Fawcett).

Greatest Question, The—Paul Sarazan (w), H. K. Jerome (m), Berlin. COVER: Lillian Gish, George Fawcett.

1862 Greatest Show on Earth, The (Paramount, 1952, Betty Hutton, Cornel Wilde).

Be a Jumping Jack/Greatest Show on Earth—Ned Washington (w), Victor Young (m), Famous; Greatest Show on Earth Theme (PC)—Victor Young (m), Famous; Lovely Luawana Lady—Ray Goetz (w), John R. North (m), Famous; Picnic in the Park/Popcorn and Lemonade/Sing a Happy Song—John M. Anderson (w), Henry Sullivan (m), Famous. COVER: Betty Hutton, Dorothy Lamour, and Circus Acts.

1863 **Greatest Story Ever Told, The** (United Artists, 1965, Charlton Heston, Carroll Baker).
Greatest Story Ever Told Theme—Alfred Newman (m), Unart. COVER: Max Von Sydow.

1864 **Great Expectations** (Universal, 1946, John Mills, Valerie Hobson).
Estella (B)—Walter Goehr (m), Southern. COVER: John Mills, Valerie Hobson.

1865 **Great Gabbo, The** (Sono Art, 1929, Betty Compson, Erich Von Stronheim).
Every Now and Then—Don McNamee, King Zany (w,m), Sherman Clay; Ga Ga Bird—Lynn Cowan, Paul Titsworth (w,m), Sherman Clay; Icky —Don McNamee, King Zany (w,m), Sherman Clay; I'm in Love with You —Lynn Cowan, Paul Titsworth (w, m), Sherman Clay; I'm Laughing—Don McNamee, King Zany (w,m), Sherman Clay; New Step/Web of Love—Lynn Cowan, Paul Titsworth (w,m), Sherman Clay. COVER: Betty Compson, Erich Von Stronheim.

1866 **Great Gatsby, The** (Paramount, 1974, Robert Redford, Mia Farrow).
Five Foot Two, Eyes of Blue—Sam Lewis, Joe Young (w), Ray Henderson (m), Warock; What'll I Do (B)—Irving Berlin, EMI. COVER: Robert Redford, Mia Farrow.

1867 **Great Imposter, The** (Universal, 1960, Tony Curtis, Edmund O'Brien).
Great Imposter, The—Henry Mancini (m), Southdale. COVER: Tony Curtis, and Girls.

1868 **Great Jesse James Raid, The** (Lippert, 1953, Willard Parker, Barbara Payton).
That's the Man for Me (PC)—Bert Shefter, Lou Herschner (w,m), Belt. COVER: None.

1869 **Great John L, The** (United Artists, 1945, Linda Darnell, Greg McClure).

Friend of Yours, A/He Was a Perfect Gentleman—Johnny Burke (w), James Van Heusen (m), BVH; When You Were Sweet Sixteen—James Thornton (w,m), Shapiro Bernstein. COVER: Linda Darnell, Greg McClure.

1870 **Great Lie, The** (Warner Bros., 1941, Bette Davis, Mary Astor).
I Have So Much More—Stanley Adams (w), Max Steiner (m), Witmark; Lilacs and Love—Con Carr, Ted Larrson (w,m), Harmony; Tchaikovsky Concerto Theme—P. Tchaikovsky (m), Robbins. COVER: Bette Davis, George Brent.

1871 **Great Locomotive Chase, The** (Buena Vista, 1955, Fess Parker, Jeffrey Hunter).
Railroadin' Man—Stan Jones (w, m), Disney; Sons of Old Dinah—Larry Watkin (w), Stan Jones, Paul Smith (m), Disney. COVER: Locomotive.

1872 **Great Lover, The** (Paramount, 1949, Bob Hope, Rhonda Fleming).
Lucky Us/Thousand Violins, A—Jay Livingston, Ray Evans (w,m), Paramount. COVER: Bob Hope, Rhonda Fleming.

1873 **Great Man, The** (Universal, 1956, Jose Ferrer, Dean Jagger).
Meaning of the Blues—Bobby Troup, Leah Worth (w,m), Northern. COVER: Julie London.

1874 **Great Mouse Detective, The** (Buena Vista, 1986, Cartoon).
Great Mouse Detective Theme (VS)—Henry Mancini (m), Disney. COVER: Henry Mancini.

1875 **Great Muppet Caper, The** (Universal, 1981, Muppets, Charles Grodin).
First Time It Happens, The/Great Muppet Caper-Twelve Songs—Joe Raposo (w,m), Cherry Lane. COVER: The Muppets.

1876 **Great Race, The** (Warner Bros., 1965, Jack Lemmon, Tony Curtis).

Sweetheart Tree, The—Johnny Mercer (w), Henry Mancini (m), East Hill; Great Race-Ten Themes—Henry Mancini (m), COVER: Cartoon Sketches.

1877 Great Victor Herbert, The (Paramount, 1939, Allan Jones, Mary Martin).

Absinthe Frippe—Glen MacDonough (w), Victor Herbert (m), Witmark; Ah Sweet Mystery of Life—Rida J. Young (w), Victor Herbert (m), Witmark; Al Fresco/All for You —Henry Blossom (w), Victor Herbert (m), Witmark; I Might Be Your Once in a While—Robert Smith (w), Victor Herbert (m), Witmark; I'm Falling in Love with Someone—Rida J. Young (w), Victor Herbert (m), Witmark; Kiss in the Dark, A—B. G. DeSylva (w), Victor Herbert (m), Witmark; Kiss Me Again—Henry Blossom (w), Victor Herbert (m), Witmark; March of the Toys—Glen MacDonough (w), Victor Herbert (m), Witmark; Neapolitan Love Song/Punchinello—Henry Blossom (w), Victor Herbert (m), Witmark; Rose of the World—Glen MacDonough (w), Victor Herbert (m), Witmark; Someday—William LeBaron (w), Victor Herbert (m), Witmark; There Once Was an Owl—Harry B. Smith (w), Victor Herbert (m), Witmark; Thine Alone—Henry Blossom (w), Victor Herbert (m), Witmark;To the Land of My Own Romance—Harry B. Smith (w), Victor Herbert (m), Witmark. COVER: Allan Jones, Mary Martin, and Movie Scenes.

1878 Great Waldo Pepper, The (Universal, 1975, Robert Redford, Bo Swenson).

Great Waldo Pepper March/Waldo's Rag/Waltz for Scooter—Henry Mancini (m), Leeds. COVER: Robert Redford.

1879 Great Waltz, The (MGM, 1938, Luise Rainer, Fernand Gravet).

I'm in Love with Vienna/One Day When We Were Young/Tales from the Vienna Woods/There'll Come a Time/You and You—Oscar Hammerstein (w), Johann Strauss (m), Feist. COVER: Luise Rainer, Fernand Gravet, Miliza Korjus.

1880 Great Waltz, The (MGM, 1972, Horst Bucholz, Nigel Patrick).

Great Waltz-Nine Songs—Robert Wright, George Forrest, Johann Strauss (w,m), Frank. COVER: Movie Scenes.

1881 Great White Way, The (Cosmopolitan, 1924, Anita Stewart, Oscar Shaw).

Great White Way, The—Henry Marshall (w,m), Remick. COVER: Chorus Girls.

1882 Great Ziegfeld, The (MGM, 1936, William Powell, Myrna Loy).

It's Been So Long—Harold Adamson (w), Walter Donaldson (m), Feist; It's Delightful to Be Married—Anna Held (w), V. Scotto (m), Marks; Pretty Girl Is Like a Melody, A—Irving Berlin (w,m), Berlin; Queen of the Jungle (BW)—Harold Adamson (w), Walter Donaldson (m), Feist; Rhapsody in Blue Excerpt (BW)—George Gershwin (m), New World; She's a Follies Girl (BW)/You/You Gotta Pull Strings (BW)/You Never Looked So Beautiful—Harold Adamson (w), Walter Donaldson (m), Feist. COVER: William Powell, Myrna Loy, Luise Rainer.

1883 Greek Street (Latin Love) (GB, 1930, Sari Maritza, William Freshman).

Luna Mia (B)—C. DeCrescenzo (w,m), Rocordi. COVER: Sari Maritza, William Freshman.

1884 Green Dolphin Street (MGM, 1947, Lana Turner, Van Heflin).

On Green Dolphin Street—Ned Washington (w), Bronislau Kaper (m), Feist; COVER: Lana Turner, Van Heflin, Donna Reed, Richard Hart.

1885 Green Fields (New Star, 1937, Michael Goldstein, Helen Beverly).

Green Fields Theme—Vladimer Heifetz (m), Alfred. COVER: Vladimer Heifetz.

1886 Green Fire (MGM, 1954, Grace Kelly, Paul Douglas).

Green Fire—Jack Brooks (w), Miklos Rozsa (m), Robbins. COVER: Grace Kelly, Paul Douglas, Stewart Granger.

1887 Greengage Summer, The (A Loss of Innocence) (Columbia, 1961, Kenneth More, Danielle Darrieux).

Greengage Summer Theme (B)—Richard Addinsell (m), Chappell. COVER: Kenneth More, Danielle Darrieux, Susannah York.

1888 Green Glove, The (United Artists, 1951, Glenn Ford, Geraldine Brooks).

No Regrets—Jerry Morse (w), Joseph Kosma (m), Mills. COVER: Glenn Ford, Geraldine Brooks.

1889 Green Goddess (Warner Bros., 1929, Alice Joyce, George Arliss).

Hindu Chant of Sacrifice—Ray Perkins (m), Witmark. COVER: Black and white cover with title only.

1890 Green Mansions (MGM, 1958, Audrey Hepburn, Anthony Perkins).

Song of Green Mansions—Paul F. Webster (w), Bronislau Kaper (m), Robbins. COVER: Audrey Hepburn, Anthony Perkins.

1891 Green Slime (MGM, 1969, Robert Horton, Richard Jaekel).

Green Slime—Sherry Gaden (w, m), Feist. COVER: Movie Scene.

1892 Greenwich Village (20th Century-Fox, 1944, Carmen Miranda, Vivian Blaine).

Give Me a Band and a Bandana (B)—Leo Robin (w), Nacio Herb Brown (m), Day; I Like to Be Loved by You—Mack Gordon (w), Harry Warren (m), Triangle; I'm Just Wild About Harry (B)—Noble Sissle (w), Eubie Blake (m), Day; Whispering—John Schonberger, Richard Coburn, Vincent Rose (w,m), Miller. COVER: Carmen Miranda, Don Ameche, William Bendix, Vivian Blaine.

1893 Gremlins (Warner Bros., 1984, Zach Galligan, Phoebe Cates).

Gizmo (Gremlin's Theme)—Jerry Goldsmith (m), Warner; Gremlins-Mega Madness—Michael Sembello, Mark Hudson, Don Freeman (w,m), Warner. COVER: Creatures.

1894 Greystoke—The Legend of Tarzan (Warner Bros., 1984, Ralph Richardson, Christopher Lambert).

Tarzan's Theme—John Scott (m), Warner. COVER: Christopher Lambert, and Movie Scenes.

1895 Group, The (United Artists, 1966, Joanna Pettet, Candice Bergen).

We'll Build a Bungalow—Betty Mayhams, Norris Troubadour (w,m), Mellin. COVER: Eight Girls.

1896 Guess Who's Coming to Dinner (Columbia, 1968, Spencer Tracy, Katharine Hepburn).

Glory of Love, The—Billy Hill (w,m), Shapiro Bernstein; Guess Who's Coming to Dinner—Mack David (m), Frank DeVol (m), Colgems. COVER: Spencer Tracy, Katharine Hepburn.

1897 Guide for the Married Man, A (20th Century-Fox, 1967, Walter Matthau, Robert Morse).

Guide for the Married Man—Leslie Bricusse (w), Johnny Williams (m), Hastings. COVER: Walter Matthau, and Movie Scenes.

1898 Gulliver's Travels (Paramount, 1939, Cartoon).

All's Well/Bluebirds in the Moonlight/Faithful/Faithful Forever/Forever/I Hear a Dream—Leo Robin, Ralph Rainger (w,m), Famous; It's a Hap-Hap-Happy Day—Al Neiburg (w), Sammy Timberg, Winston Sharples (m), Famous; We're All Together Now—Leo Robin, Ralph Rainger (w,m), Famous. COVER: Cartoon.

1899 Gunfight at the OK Corral (Paramount, 1957, Burt Lancaster, Kirk Douglas).

Gunfight at the OK Corral—Ned Washington (w), Dimitri Tiomkin (m), Paramount; Gunfight at the OK Corral Theme (VS)—Dimitri Tiomkin (m), Paramount. COVER: Burt Lancaster, Kirk Douglas.

1900 Gunfight in Abilene (Universal, 1967, Bobby Darin, Emily Banks).

Amy—Bobby Darin (w,m), Champion. COVER: Bobby Darin.

1901 Gung Ho (Universal, 1943, Randolph Scott, Alan Curtis).

Gung Ho—Irving Bibo (w), Frank Skinner (m), Words Music. COVER: Randolph Scott, and Marines.

1902 Gunman's Walk (Columbia, 1958, Tab Hunter, Van Heflin).

I'm a Runaway—Richard Quine (w), Fred Karger (m), Colgems. COVER: Tab Hunter.

1903 Gunn (Paramount, 1967, Craig Stevens, Laura Devon).

I Like the Look—Leslie Bricusse (w), Henry Mancini (m), Northridge; Theme for Sam (VS)—Henry Mancini (m). COVER: Craig Stevens, and Movie Scenes.

1904 Guns and Guitars (Republic, 1936, Gene Autry, Smiley Burnette).

Guns and Guitars—Gene Autry, Oliver Drake (w,m), Cole; Ridin' All Day (VS)—Gene Autry, Smiley Burnette (w,m), Cole. COVER: Gene Autry.

1905 Guns at Batasi (20th Century-Fox, 1964, Richard Attenborough, Flora Robson).

Guns at Batasi Love Theme/Guns at Batasi March—John Addison (m), Miller. COVER: Soldiers.

1906 Guns for San Sebastian (MGM, 1968, Anthony Quinn, Anjanette Comer).

Guns for San Sebastian Love Theme—Ennio Morricone (m), Feist. COVER: Anthony Quinn, and Battle Scene.

1907 Gunsmoke   (Universal, 1953, Audie Murphy, Susan Cabot).

True Love—Fred Herbert (w),

Arnold Hughes (m), Mills. COVER: Audie Murphy, Susan Cabot.

1908 Guns of Navarone, The (Columbia, 1961, Gregory Peck, David Niven).

Guns of Navarone—Dimitri Tiomkin (m), Columbia; Yassu-The Wedding Song—Ned Washington (w), Dimitri Tiomkin (m), Columbia. COVER: Gregory Peck, David Niven, Anthony Quinn.

1909 Guns of the Pecos (Warner Bros., 1937, Dick Foran, Anne Nagel).

Prairie Is My Home, The—Jack Scholl (w), M. K. Jerome (m), Harms. COVER: Sketch.

1910 Guns of the Timberland (Warner Bros., 1960, Alan Ladd, Jeanne Crain).

Faithful Kind, The/Gee Whizz Whilikens Golly Gee—Mack David (w), Jerry Livingston (m), Witmark. COVER: Frankie Avalon.

1911 Guy Named Joe, A (MGM, 1943, Irene Dunne, Spencer Tracy).

I'll Get By—Roy Turke (w), Fred Ahlert (m), Berlin. COVER: Irene Dunne, Spencer Tracy.

1912 Guys and Dolls (MGM, 1955, Marlon Brando, Frank Sinatra).

Adelaide/Adelaide's Lament/Follow the Fold/Fugue for Tin Horns/ Guys and Dolls/If I Were a Bell/I'll Know/Luck Be a Lady/My Time of Day/Oldest Established, The/Pet Me Poppa/Sit Down You're Rockin' th the Boat/Sue Me/Take Back Your Mink/Woman in Love, A—Frank Loesser (w,m), Frank. COVER: Marlon Brando, Frank Sinatra, Jean Simmons, Vivian Blaine.

1913 Gypsy (Warner Bros.,1962, Rosalind Russell, Natalie Wood).

All I Need Is the Girl/Everything's Comin' Up Roses/Let Me Entertain You/Little Lamb/Small World/Together Wherever We Go/You'll Never Get Away from Me—Stephen Sondheim (w), Jule Styne (m), Williamson. COVER: Rosalind Russell, Natalie Wood, Karl Malden.

1914 Hail the Conquering Hero (Paramount, 1944, Eddie Bracken, Ella Raines).

Home to the Arms of Mother—Preston Sturges (w,m), Famous. COVER: Eddie Bracken, Ella Raines.

1915 Hair (United Artists, 1979, John Savage, Treat Williams).

Acquarius/Easy to Be Hard/Good Morning Starshine/Hair/Let the Sunshine In/Abie Baby Fourscore (VS)/Air (VS)/Black Boys (VS)/Donna (VS)/Electric Blues (VS)/Frank Mills (VS)/Hashish (VS)/I Got Life (VS)/I'm Black, Ain't Got No (VS)/Manchester England (VS)/Old Fashioned Melody (VS)/Party Music (VS)/Somebody to Love (VS)/3-5-0-0 (VS)/Walking in Space (VS)/What a Piece of Work Is Man (VS)/Where Do I Go (VS)/White Boys (VS)—James Rado, Galt McDermott, Gerome Ragni (w, m), Unart. COVER: Sketches.

1916 Half a House (First American, 1975, Anthony Eisley, Pat Delancy).

World That Never Was, A—Paul F. Webster (w), Sammy Fain (m), Fain. COVER: An Ink Blot.

1917 Half a Sixpence (Paramount, 1967, Tommy Steele, Julia Foster).

Flash, Bang, Wallop/Half a Sixpence/If the Rain's Got to Fall/Long Ago/Money to Burn/Party's on the House, The/She's Too Far Above Me/This Is My World—David Heneker (w,m), Britannia. COVER: Tommy Steele.

1918 Half Breed, The (RKO, 1952, Robert Young, Janis Carter).

Remember the Girl—Mort Greene, Harry Revel (w,m), Chappell. COVER: Robert Young, Janis Carter, Jack Beutel.

1919 Half Marriage (RKO, 1929, Olive Borden, Morgan Farley).

After the Clouds Roll By—Sidney Clare (w), Oscar Levant (m), Harms; To Me, She's Marvelous—Oscar Levant (w,m), Harms. COVER: Olive Borden, Morgan Farley.

1920 Half Naked Truth, The (RKO, 1932, Lupe Velez, Lee Tracy).

O! Mister Carpenter—Edward Eliscu, Harry Akst (w,m), Southern. COVER: Lupe Velez.

1921 Half Shot at Sunrise (RKO, 1930, Bert Wheeler, Bob Woolsey).

Whistling the Blues Away—Anne Caldwell (w), Harry Tierney (m), Feist. COVER: Bert Wheeler, Bob Woolsey.

1922 Half Way Decent (Little Miss Marker) (Paramount, 1934, Shirley Temple, Adolphe Menjou).

Laugh You Son of a Gun (PC)—Leo Robin, Ralph Rainger (w,m), Famous. COVER: None.

1923 Halfway to Heaven (Paramount, 1944, Betty Rhodes, Johnnie Johnston).

Halfway to Heaven—Jerry Seelen (w), Joseph Lilley (m), Paramount. COVER: Betty Rhodes, Johnnie Johnston.

1924 Hallelujah (MGM, 1929, Dan Haymes, Mae McKinney).

Swanee Shuffle/Waiting at the End of the Road—Irving Berlin (w,m), Berlin. COVER: Cartoon sketches.

1925 Hallelujah I'm a Bum (United Artists, 1933, Al Jolson, Madge Evans).

Hallelujah, I'm a Bum/I Gotta Get Back to New York (VS)/I'll Do It Again/What Do You Want with Money/You Are too Beautiful—Lorenz Hart (w), Richard Rodgers (m), Rodart. COVER: Al Jolson, Madge Evans.

1926 Hallelujah Trail, The (United Artists, 1965, Burt Lancaster, Lee Remick).

Hallelujah Trail—Ernie Sheldon (w), Elmer Bernstein (m), Unart. COVER: Covered Wagons and Indians.

1927 Halls of Montezuma (20th Century-Fox, 1950, Richard Widmark, Jack Palance).

Marines Hymn, The—D. Savino (w,m), Robbins. COVER: Marines.

1928 Hand in Hand (Columbia, 1960, Loretta Parry, John Gregson).
Hand in Hand Theme—Stanley Black (m), Witmark. COVER: Loretta Parry, Philip Needs.
1929 Handle with Care (Fox, 1932, James Dunn, Boots Mallory).
Around You/Throw a Little Salt on the Bluebird's Tail—Leo Robin (w), Richard Whiting (m), Movietone. COVER: James Dunn, Boots Mallory.
1930 Hands Across the Border (Republic, 1944, Roy Rogers, Ruth Terry).
Dreaming to Music/Girl with the High Button Shoes—Ned Washington (w), Phil Ohman (m), Southern; Hands Across the Border—Ned Washington (w), Hoagy Carmichael (m), Southern; When Your Heart's on Easy Street—Ned Washington (w), Phil Ohman (m), Southern. COVER: Roy Rogers, Ruth Terry.
1931 Hands Across the Table (Paramount, 1935, Carole Lombard, Fred MacMurray).
Morning After, The—Sam Coslow (w,m), Famous. COVER: Sketch.
1932 Handy Andy (Fox, 1934, Will Rogers, Peggy Wood).
Roses in the Rain—William Conselman (w), Richard Whiting (m), Movietone. COVER: Roses.
1933 Hang 'em High (United Artists, 1968, Clint Eastwood, Inger Stevens).
Hang 'em High—Dominic Frontiere (m), Unart. COVER: Clint Eastwood.
1934 Hanging Tree, The (Warner Bros., 1959, Gary Cooper, Maria Schell).
Hanging Tree, The—Mack David (w), Jerry Livingston (m), Witmark. COVER: Gary Cooper, Maria Schell.
1935 Hangman, The (Angelus, 1944, Stars Unknown).
Where Is My Home?—Leo Erdody (w,m), Mills. COVER: Clouds.
1936 Hangman, The (Paramount, 1959, Robert Taylor, Tina Louise).

Hangman, The—Hal David (w), Burt Bacharach (m), Famous. COVER: Robert Taylor, Tina Louise, Fess Parker.
1937 Hangmen Also Die (United Artists, 1943, Brian Donlevy, Walter Brennan).
No Surrender, Song of the Hostages—Sam Coslow (w), Hanns Eisler (m), BVC. COVER: Brian Donlevy, Anna Lee.
1938 Hangover Square (20th Century-Fox, 1945, Linda Darnell, George Sanders).
All for You/So Close to Paradise—Charles Henderson (w), Lionel Newman (m), Robbins. COVER: Linda Darnell, Laird Cregar, George Sanders.
1939 Hannibal Brooks (United Artists, 1969, Oliver Reed, Michael Pollard).
Looking for Love—Francis Lai (m), Unart. COVER: Black and white cover with title only.
1940 Hans Brinker or the Silver Skates (Independent, 1968, Eleanor Parker, Richard Basehart).
His Love Is Born Anew—Moose Charlap (w,m), Charlice; Hans Brinker-Eight Songs—Moose Charlap (w, m), Leonard. COVER: Robin Askwith, Sheila Whitmill.
1941 Hans Christian Andersen (RKO, 1952, Danny Kaye, Farley Granger).
Anywhere I Wander/I'm Hans Christian Andersen/Inch Worm/King's New Clothes, The/No Two People/Thumbalina/Ugly Duckling/Wonderful Copenhagen—Frank Loesser (w,m), Frank. COVER: Danny Kaye, Farley Granger, Jeanmaire.
1942 Happening, The (Columbia, 1967, Anthony Quinn, Michael Parks).
Happening, The—Eddie Holland, Lamont Dozier, Brian Holland (w), Frank DeVol (m), Jobete. COVER: Movie Scenes.
1943 Happiest Millionaire, The (Buena Vista, 1967, Fred MacMurray, Tommy Steele).

Are We Dancing/Bye Yum Yum Yum/Detroit/Fortuosity/I'll Always Be Irish/Let's Have a Drink/Strengthen the Dwelling/There Are Those/ Valentine Candy/Watch Your Footwork/What's Wrong with That/ When a Man Has a Daughter—Richard Sherman, Robert Sherman (w, m), Wonderland. COVER: Tommy Steele, John Davidson, Leslie Ann Warren.

1944 Happiness (MGM, 1924, Laurette Taylor, Hedda Hopper).

Happiness—William Jerome (w), Ted Barron (m), Barron. COVER: Laurette Taylor.

1945 Happiness Ahead (First National, 1934, Dick Powell, Josephine Hutchinson).

Beauty Must Be Loved—Irving Kahal (w), Sammy Fain (m), Witmark; Happiness Ahead/Pop Goes Your Heart/Strawberry Sundae— Mort Dixon (w), Allie Wrubel (m), Witmark; Window Cleaners, The— Bert Kalmar, Harry Ruby (w,m), Harms. COVER: Dick Powell, Josephine Hutchinson.

1946 Happy Anniversary (United Artists, 1959, David Niven, Mitzi Gaynor).

Happy Anniversary/I Don't Regret a Thing—Al Stillman (w), Robert Allen (m), Korwin. COVER: David Niven, Mitzi Gaynor.

1947 Happy Birthday to Me (Columbia, 1981, Melissa Sue Anderson, Glenn Ford).

Happy Birthday to Me—Molly Ann Leiken (w), Lance Rubin (m), Colgems. COVER: Movie Scene.

1948 Happy Days (Fox, 1930, Will Rogers, Janet Gaynor).

Happy Days—Joseph McCarthy (w), James Hanley (m), Red Star; I'm on a Diet of Love—L. Wolfe Gilbert (w), Abel Baer (m), DBH; Mona—Con Conrad, Sidney Mitchell, Archie Gottler (w,m), DBH; Toast to the Girl I Love, A/We'll Build a Little World of Our Own—James Brockman (w), James Hanley (m),

Red Star. COVER: Will Rogers, Janet Gaynor, Charles Farrell, and others.

1949 Happy Days (Universal, 1943, Musical Short).

Sentimental Women—Johnny Lange (w), Phil Moore (m), Leeds. COVER: Dinah Shore.

1950 Happy Ending, The (United Artists, 1969, Jean Simmons, John Forsythe).

What Are You Doing for the Rest of Your Life?—Alan Bergman, Marilyn Bergman (w), Michel Legrand (m), Unart. COVER: A Trash Can.

1951 Happy Go Lovely (RKO, 1951, David Niven, Vera-Ellen).

Would You (B)—Jack Fishman (w), Mischa Spoliansky (m), Chappell. COVER: David Niven, Vera-Ellen, Cesar Romero.

1952 Happy Go Lucky (Republic, 1936, Phil Regan, Evelyn Venable).

Right or Wrong—Ted Koehler (w), Sam Stept (m), Berlin; Treat for the Eyes, A—Cliff Friend (w), Sam Stept (m), Shapiro Bernstein. COVER: Phil Regan.

1953 Happy Go Lucky (Paramount, 1943, Mary Martin, Dick Powell).

Fuddy Duddy Watchmaker, The/ Happy Go Lucky/Let's Get Lost/ Murder He Says/Sing a Tropical Song (BW)—Frank Loesser (w), Jimmy McHugh (m), Paramount. COVER: Dick Powell, Betty Hutton, Mary Martin, Eddie Bracken.

1954 Happy Landing (20th Century-Fox, 1938, Don Ameche, Sonja Henie).

Gypsy Told Me, A/Hot and Happy/Yonny and His Oompah—Jack Yellen (w), Sam Pokrass (m), Crawford; You Appeal to Me—Walter Bullock (w), Harold Spina (m), Crawford; You Are the Music to the Words in My Heart—Jack Yellen (w), Sam Pokrass (m), Crawford. COVER: Don Ameche, Sonja Henie, Ethel Merman.

1955 Happy Road, The (MGM, 1957, Gene Kelly, Barbara Lange).

Happy Road, The—Gene Kelly (w), Georges Van Parys (m), Robbins. COVER: Gene Kelly, Barbara Lange.

1956 Happy Thieves, The (United Artists, 1962, Rex Harrison, Rita Hayworth).

Eve's Theme/Happy Thieves Theme—Mario Nascimbene (m), Unart. COVER: Rex Harrison, Rita Hayworth.

1957 Happy Time, The (Columbia, 1952, Charles Boyer, Louis Jourdan).

Happy Time, The—Ned Washington (w), Dimitri Tiomkin (m), Laurel. COVER: Charles Boyer, Louis Jourdan, Kurt Kasznar.

1958 Hard Contact (20th Century-Fox, 1969, James Coburn, Lee Remick).

Was It Really Love?—Paul F. Webster (w), Alex North (m), Fox. COVER: James Coburn, Lee Remick.

1959 Hard Day's Night, A (United Artists, 1964, The Beatles).

And I Love Her/Hard Day's Night, A/Ringo's Theme-This Boy/Can't Buy Me Love (VS)/If I Fell (VS)/I'll Cry Instead (VS)/I'm Happy Just to Dance with You (VS)/I Should Have Known Better (VS)/Tell Me Why (VS)—John Lennon, Paul McCartney (w,m), Northern. COVER: The Beatles.

1960 Harder They Fall, The (Columbia, 1956, Humphrey Bogart, Rod Steiger).

Cocktail Lounge—Hugo Friedhofer (m), Colgems. COVER: Blue cover with title only.

1961 Hard Fast and Beautiful (RKO, 1951, Claire Trevor, Sally Forrest).

Hard Fast and Beautiful—Bobby Worth (w,m), Ainsley. COVER: Sally Forrest.

1962 Hard to Get (First National, 1929, Dorothy Mackaill, Louise Fazenda).

Hard to Get—George Meyer, Al Bryan, John McLaughlin (w,m), Witmark. COVER: Dorothy Mackaill.

1963 Hard to Get (Warner Bros., 1938, Dick Powell, Olivia de Havilland).

There's a Sunny Side to Every Situation/You Must Have Been a Beautiful Baby—Johnny Mercer (w), Harry Warren (m), Remick. COVER: Dick Powell, Olivia de Havilland.

1964 Hard to Hold (Universal, 1984, Rick Springfield, Janet Eilber).

Bop Til You Drop/Don't Walk Away/Love Somebody—Rick Springfield (w,m), Welk. COVER: Rick Springfield.

1965 Harlem Nights (Paramount, 1989, Richard Pryor, Eddie Murphy).

It Don't Mean a Thing—Irving Mills (w), Duke Ellington (m), Mills. COVER: Richard Pryor, Eddie Murphy.

1966 Harlem on the Prairie (Associated, 1938, Herb Jeffries, Flourney Miller).

Harlem on the Prairie—Mary Schaeffer, Lew Porter (w,m), Red Star; New Range in Heaven—Jules Loman, Johnny Lang, Fred Stryker (w,m), Mills; Palkadoo—Ira Hardin, Lew Porter (w,m), Mills; Ridin' Down the Trail to Albuquerque—June Hershey (w), Don Swander (m), Cross Winge; Romance in the Rain—Lyle Womack, Mary Schaeffer, Lew Porter (w,m), Red Star. COVER: Herb Jeffries, and other stars.

1967 Harlow (Magna, 1965, Carol Lynley, Ginger Rogers).

I Believed It All/With Open Arms—Alan Bergman, Marilyn Bergman (w), Al Ham (m), Electronic. COVER: Carol Lynley.

1968 Harlow (Paramount, 1965, Carroll Baker, Angela Lansbury).

Girl Talk—Bobby Troup (w), Neal Hefti (m), Consul; Lonely Girl—Jay Livingston, Ray Evans (w), Neal Hefti (m), Consul; Harlow-Piano Suite—Neal Hefti (m), Consul. COVER: Carroll Baker, Angela Lansbury, Red Buttons.

1969 Harmony at Home (Fox, 1930, William Collier, Marguerite Churchill).

Little House to Dream, A—James Brockman (w), James Hanley (m), Red Star. COVER: Man and Woman.

1970 Harold Teen (Warner Bros., 1934, Hal Le Roy, Rochelle Hudson).

Collegiate Wedding/How Do I Know It's Sunday/Simple and Sweet/Two Little Flies on a Lump of Sugar—Irving Kahal (w), Sammy Fain (m), Remick. COVER: Hal LeRoy.

1971 Harper (Warner Bros., 1966, Paul Newman, Lauren Bacall).

Livin' Alone/Quietly There—Dory Previn (w), André Previn (m), Remick; Sure as You're Born—Alan Bergman, Marilyn Bergman (w), Johnny Mandell (m), Remick. COVER: Paul Newman, Lauren Bacall, Shelley Winters.

1972 Harper Valley P.T.A. (April Fool, 1978, Barbara Eden, Ronny Cox).

Harper Valley P.T.A.—Tom Hall (w,m), Chappell. COVER: Cartoon Sketch.

1973 Harrad Experiment, The (Cinerama, 1973, Don Johnson, James Whitmore).

Go Gently/I Hope I'll Have Your Love—Norman Gimbel (w), Charles Fox (m), Beechwood. COVER: Don Johnson, Laurie Walters.

1974 Harris in the Spring (RKO, 1937, Phil Harris).

Sweet Like You, I Want It—Jo Trent (w), Newell Chase (m), Words Music. COVER: Phil Harris.

1975 Harry and Son (Orion, 1984, Paul Newman, Robby Benson).

Harry's Theme (VS)—Henry Mancini (m), OPC. COVER: Henry Mancini.

1976 Harry and the Hendersons (Universal, 1987, John Lithgow, Melinda Dillon).

Love Lives On—Barry Mann, Cynthia Weil, Will Jennings, Bruce Broughton (w,m), MCA. COVER: Eyes and a Rose.

1977 Harry and Tonto (20th Century-Fox, 1974, Art Carney, Ellen Burstyn).

Harry and Tonto—Bill Conti (m), Fox. COVER: Sketch.

1978 Harum Scarum (MGM, 1965, Elvis Presley, Richard Boone).

Animal Instinct/Go East Young Man/Golden Coins—Bill Giant, Bernie Baum, Florence Kaye (w,m), Presley; Harem Holiday—Pete Andreoli, Vince Poncia, Jimmie Crane (w,m), Presley; Hey Little Girl—Joy Byers (w,m), Presley; Kismet—Sid Tepper, Roy Bennett (w,m), Presley; Mirage—Bill Giant, Bernie Baum, Florence Kaye (w,m), Presley; My Desert Serenade—Stanley Gelber (w,m), Presley; Shake That Tambourine—Bill Giant, Bernie Baum, Florence Kaye (w,m), Presley; So Close Yet So Far—Joy Byers (w,m), Presley; Wisdom of the Ages—Bill Giant, Bernie Baum, Florence Kaye (w,m), Presley. COVER: Elvis Presley.

1979 Harvey Girls, The (MGM, 1946, Judy Garland, Angela Lansbury).

In the Valley/It's a Great Big World/My Intuition (BW)/Oh You Kid/March of the Doagies/On the Atchison, Topeka and the Santa Fe/Swing Your Partner Round and Round/Train Must Be Fed, The (BW)/Wait and See/Wild Wild West, The—Johnny Mercer (w), Harry Warren (m), Feist. COVER: Judy Garland.

1980 Has Anybody Seen My Gal (Universal, 1952, Rock Hudson, Piper Laurie).

Five Foot Two Eyes of Blue—Sam Lewis, Joe Young (w), Ray Henderson (m), Feist. COVER: Rock Hudson, Piper Laurie.

1981 Hatari (Paramount, 1961, John Wayne, Hardy Kruger).

Baby Elephant Walk—Hal David (w), Henry Mancini (m), Famous; Baby Elephant Walk Theme—Henry Mancini (m), Famous; Just for Tonight—Johnny Mercer, Hoagy Car-

michael (w,m), Famous; Paraphrase—
Hoagy Carmichael (m), Famous; Soft
Touch, The (VS)/Your Father's
Feathers—Henry Mancini (m), Fa-
mous. COVER: John Wayne, and
Movie Scenes.

1982   Hat Check Girl (Fox, 1932,
Ben Lyons, Ginger Rogers).

You're Worth While Waiting For—
L. Wolfe Gilbert (w), James Hanley
(m), Movietone. COVER: Black and
white cover with title only.

1983   Hat Check Honey (Universal, 1944, Leon Errol, Grace Mac-
Donald).

Nice to Know You/Rockin' with
You/Slightly   Sentimental—Everett
Carter (w), Milton Rosen (m), Urban.
COVER: Grace MacDonald.

1984   Hats Off (Grand National,
1936, Mae Clarke, John Payne).

Hats Off/Let's Have Another/
Little Odd Rhythm/Twinkle Twinkle
Little Star/Where Have You Been All
My Life—Herb Magidson (w), Ben
Oakland (m), Popular. COVER: John
Payne, Mae Clarke.

**1985   Haunting,   The   (MGM,
1963, Julie Harris, Claire Bloom).

Haunting, The—Lalo Schifrin (m),
Hastings. COVER: Julie Harris.

1986   Having a Wild Weekend
(Warner Bros., 1965, Dave Clark,
Barbara Ferris).

Catch Us If You Can—Dave Clark,
Lenny Davidson (w,m), Branston.
COVER: Beach Scene.

1987   Having   Wonderful   Time
(RKO, 1938, Ginger Rogers, Douglas
Fairbanks).

Band Played Out of Tune, The/
My First Impression of You/Nighty
Night—Charles Tobias (w), Sam Stept
(m), Chappell. COVER: Ginger Rogers, Douglas Fairbanks.

1988   Hawaii (United   Artists,
1966, Julie   Andrews, Max   Von
Sydow).

Hawaii/Wishing Doll, The—Mack
David (w), Elmer Bernstein (m),
Unart. COVER: Julie Andrews, Max
Von Sydow, Richard Harris.

1989   Hawaiian   Buckaroo (20th
Century-Fox, 1937, Smith Ballew,
Evelyn Knapp).

Hawaiian Memories—Eddie Grant,
Albert Von Tilzer (w,m), Hollywood;
Ridin' to the Rhythm of the Round-
up—Harry MacPherson, Albert Von
Tilzer (w,m), Hollywood. COVER:
Smith Ballew, Evelyn Knapp.

1990   Hawaiian   Nights (Universal, 1939, Johnny Downs, Mary Carlisle).

Hawaii Sang Me to Sleep/Hey
Good Looking/Then I Wrote the
Minuet in "G"—Frank Loesser (w),
Matty Malneck (m), Miller. COVER:
Johnny Downs, Mary Carlisle, Con-
stance Moore.

1991   Hawaii Calls (RKO, 1938,
Bobby Breen, Ned Sparks).

Down Where the Trade Winds
Blow/Hawaii   Calls—Harry   Owens
m), Select; Macushla—Josephine
Rowe (w), Dermot MacMurrough
(m), Boosey; Song of the Islands—
Charles King (w,m), Marks. COV-
ER: Bobby Breen.

1992   Head (Columbia,   1968,
Victor Mature, The Monkees).

As We Go Along—Carole King,
Toni Stern (w,m), Colgems; Por-
poise Song—Gerry Goffin, Carole
King (w,m), Colgems. COVER:
Black and white cover with title
only.

1993   Headin'   East (Columbia,
1937, Buck Jones, Ruth Coleman).

Irresistable You—Harry Tobias,
Roy Ingraham (w,m), Mills. COV-
ER: Brown cover with title only.

1994   Headin' for the Rio Grande
(Grand National, 1936, Tex Ritter,
Eleanor Stewart).

Headin' for the Rio Grande—Tex
Ritter, Stanley Davis (w,m), Sam
Fox; Jail House Lament—Tex Ritter,
Jack Smith (w,m), Sam Fox. COV-
ER: Tex Ritter.

1995   Head Over Heels in Love
(GB, 1936, Jessie Matthews, Louis
Borrell).

Don't Give a Good Gosh Darn/

Head Over Heels in Love/Lookin' Around Corners for You/May I Have the Next Romance with You?/There's That Look in Your Eyes Again/ Through the Courtesy of Love—Mack Gordon, Harry Revel (w,m), Feist. COVER: Jessie Matthews.

1996 Heads Up (Paramount, 1930, Charles Rogers, Helen Kane).

If I Knew You Better—Don Hartman (w), Victor Schertzinger (m), Harms; My Man Is on the Make—Lorenz Hart (w), Richard Rodgers (m), Harms; Readin' Ritin' Rhythm—Don Hartman (w), Victor Schertzinger (m), Harms; Ship Without a Sail, A— Lorenz Hart (w), Richard Rodgers (m), Harms. COVER: Helen Kane, Charles Rogers.

1997 Hear Me Good (Paramount, 1957, Joe Ross, Hal March).

Hear Me Good—Don McGuire (w, m), Paramount. COVER: Hal March.

1998 Heartbeat (RKO, 1943, Ginger Rogers, Adolphe Menjou).

Can You Guess?—Ervin Drake (w), Paul Misraki (m), Marks. COVER: Ginger Rogers.

1999 Heartbreak Kid, The (20th Century-Fox, 1972, Charles Grodin, Cybill Shepherd).

Heartbreak Kid Theme—Sheldon Harnick (w), Cy Coleman (m), Colgems. COVER: A Heart.

2000 Heartburn (Paramount, 1985, Meryl Streep, Jack Nicholson).

Coming Around Again—Carly Simon (w,m), Famous. COVER: Meryl Streep, Jack Nicholson.

2001 Heart Is a Lonely Hunter, The (Warner Bros., 1968, Alan Arkin, Sondra Locke).

Heart Is a Lonely Hunter, The— Peggy Lee (w), Dave Grusin (m), Warner. COVER: Alan Arkin, Sondra Locke.

2002 Heart Is a Rebel, The (Graham, 1965, Ethel Waters, Georgia Lee).

Heart Is a Rebel—Ralph Carmichael (w,m), Lexicon. COVER: Billy Graham.

2003 Heart of a Child, The (Metro, 1920, Charles Bryant, Nazimova).

As Long as I Have You—John W. Kellette (w,m), Temple of Melody. COVER: Nazimova.

2004 Heart of Humanity (Universal, 1919, Dorothy Phillips, Eric Von Stroheim).

Heart of Humanity—Roy Turk (w), Ray Perkins (m), Berlin. COVER: Dorothy Phillips.

2005 Heart of Ireland (Moore, 1933, Emmett Moore, Mae Fitzgerald).

In My Irish Home Sweet Home/ My Heart Is in Ireland—Mae Fitzgerald (w,m), Moore. COVER: Emmett Moore, Mae Fitzgerald.

2006 Heart of Paula (Paramount, 1916, Lenore Ulrich, Howard Davies).

Paula—Palmelia Woodruff (w), William Charles (m), Schirmer. COVER: Lenore Ulrich.

2007 Heart of the Rio Grande (Republic, 1942, Gene Autry, Smiley Burnette).

Deep in the Heart of Texas (B)— June Hershey (w), Don Swander (m), Southern. COVER: Gene Autry.

2008 Heart of the West (Paramount, 1936, Bill Boyd, Jimmy Ellison).

My Heart's in the Heart of the West—Sam Coslow, Victor Young (w,m), Popular. COVER: Jimmy Ellison, Lynn Gabriel.

2009 Heart of Wetona (Select, 1920, Norma Talmadge, Fred Huntley).

Heart of Wetona—Sidney Mitchell (w), Archie Gottler (m), Feist. COVER: Norma Talmadge.

2010 Heart of Youth Paramount, 1920, Lila Lee, Tom Forman).

Heart of Youth—Jeff Branen, Ed O'Keefe (w,m), Morris. COVER: Lila Lee.

2011 Heart o'the Hills (First National, 1920, Mary Pickford, Allan Sears).

Heart o' the Hills—Sam Lewis, Joe Young (w), Harry Ruby (m), Berlin. COVER: Mary Pickford.

2012 Hearts and Cauliflowers (Universal, 1943, Musical Short).

Just Another Blues—Dick Charles, Larry Markes, Jimmy Paul (w,m), Leeds. COVER: Black and white cover with title only.

2013 Hearts Divided (Warner Bros., 1936, Marion Davies, Dick Powell).

My Kingdom for a Kiss/Two Hearts Divided (BW)—Al Dubin (w), Harry Warren (m), Witmark. COVER: Marion Davies.

2014 Heartsease (Goldwyn, 1919, Tom Moore, Helene Chadwick).

Heartsease—Alfred Bryan (w), Neil Moret (m), Remick; Heartsease Love Theme—Neil Moret (m), Remick. COVER: Tom Moore, Helen Chadwick.

2015 Hearts in Dixie (Fox, 1929, Stepin Fechit, Clarence Muse).

Hearts in Dixie—Walter Weems (w), Howard Jackson (m), DBH. COVER: Sketches.

2016 Hearts in Exile (Warner Bros., 1929, Dolores Costello, Grant Withers).

Like a Breath of Springtime—Al Dubin (w), Joe Burke (m), Piantadosi. COVER: Dolores Costello, and Others.

2017 Hearts of the World (Griffith, 1918, Lillian Gish, Dorothy Gish).

Hearts of the World (#1)—Leo Johnson (w,m), Johnson; Hearts of the World (#2)—Bartley Costello (w), James Casey (m), Forster; Hearts of the World (#3)—George Graff (w), Bert Grant (m), Berlin; Hearts of the World Waltz—James Casey (m), E.C.M.O. COVER: Lillian Gish, Robert Harron.

2018 Heartstrings (Fox, 1920, William Farnum, Gladys Coburn).

Heartstrings—Herman Holland (w, m), Berlin. COVER: William Farnum, Gladys Coburn.

2019 Heat's On, The (Tropicana) (Columbia, 1943, Mae West, Victor Moore).

Hello Mi Amigo/I'm Just a Stranger in Town/There Goes That Guitar/They Looked So Pretty on the Envelope—Henry Myers, Edward Eliscu (w), Jay Gorney (m), Mills; Thinkin' About the Wabash—Sammy Cahn (w), Jule Styne (m), Melrose; White Keys and the Black Keys—Henry Myers, Edward Eliscu (w), Jay Gorney (m), Mills. COVER: Mae West, Victor Moore, William Gaxton.

2020 Heat Wave (Gainsborough, 1935, Les Allen, Anna Lee).

If Your Father Only Knew—Maurice Sigler, Al Goodhart, Al Hoffman (w,m), Mills. COVER: Les Allen, Anna Lee.

2021 Heaven Can Wait (Paramount, 1978, Warren Beatty, Julie Christie).

Heaven Can Wait Love Theme—Dave Grusin (m), Ensign. COVER: Warren Beatty.

2022 Heavenly Bodies (MGM, 1984, Cynthia Dale, Richard Ribiere).

At Last You're Mine—Michael Bolton, Doug James (w,m), April. COVER: Cynthia Dale.

2023 Heavenly Music (MGM, 1943, Fred Brady, Mary Elliott).

Heavenly Music—Sam Coslow (w, m), Feist. COVER: Fred Brady, Mary Elliott.

2024 Heaven Only Knows (United Artists, 1947, Robert Cummings, Brian Donlevy).

Heaven Only Knows—Bill Carey (w), Heinz Roemheld (m), Martin. COVER: Robert Cummings, Brian Donlevy, and Others.

2025 Heaven with a Gun (MGM, 1984, Glenn Ford, Carolyn Jones).

A Lonely Place—Paul F. Webster (w), Johnny Mandel (m), Feist. COVER: Glenn Ford, and Movie Scenes.

2026 Heavy Metal (Columbia, 1981, Animated Feature).

Heavy Metal—Don Felder (w, m), Fingers; Heavy Metal-Sixteen Songs—Don Felder, Donald Fagen, Jerry Riggs (w,m), Columbia. COVER: Cartoon Sketch.

2027 Heidi (20th Century-Fox, 1937, Shirley Temple, Jean Hersholt).

In Our Little Wooden Shoes—Sidney Mitchell (w), Lew Pollack (m), Movietone. COVER: Shirley Temple.

2028 Heidi (Warner Bros., 1968, Gertraud Mittermayr, Eva M. Singhamer).

Heidi—Stanley Styne (w), Franz Grothe (m), Warner. COVER: Eva M. Singhamer, Gustav Knuth.

2029 Heidi's Song (Paramount, 1982, Cartoon)

Christmas-y Day, A/Armful of Sunshine (VS)/Can You Imagine (VS)/Good at Making Friends (VS)/Heidi/Ode to a Rat/She's a Nothing/That's What Friends Are For/Unkind Word—Sammy Cahn (w), Burton Lane (m), Warner. COVER: Cartoon.

2030 Heiress, The (Paramount, 1949, Olivia DeHavilland, Montgomery Clift).

My Love Loves Me—Jay Livingston, Ray Evans (w,m), Paramount. COVER: Montgomery Clift, Olivia DeHavilland.

2031 Hei-Tiki (First Division, 1934, Documentary of South Sea Islands).

Can This Be Heaven?/Hey Ha/Sweethearts in Paradise—Billy Hill (w), Alexander Markey (m), Shapiro Bernstein. COVER: Native Girl.

2032 Helen Morgan Story, The (Both Ends of the Candle) (Warner Bros., 1957, Ann Blyth, Paul Newman).

One I Love Belongs to Somebody Else, The—Gus Kahn (w), Isham Jones (m), Kahn. COVER: Ann Blyth.

2033 Helen of Troy (Warner Bros., 1956, Rossana Podesta, Jack Sernas).

Helen of Troy Theme—Max Steiner (m), Harms. COVER: Rosanna Podesta, Jack Sernas.

2034 Hell-Bound (Tiffany, 1931, Leo Carrillo, Lola Lane).

Is it Love?—Russell Colombo (w, m), Mills. COVER: Lola Lane. and Others.

2035 Hell Harbor (United Artists, 1930, Lupe Velez, Gibson Gowland).

Caribbean Love Song—Eugene Berton (w,m), Feist. COVER: Lupe Velez.

2036 Hellions, The (Columbia, 1962, Richard Todd, Anne Audrey).

Ballad of the Hellions (B)—Larry Adler, Herbert Kretzner (w,m), Adler. COVER: Cowboys.

2037 Hello Dolly (20th Century-Fox, 1969, Barbra Streisand, Walter Matthau).

Before the Parade Passes By/Dancing/Elegance/Hello Dolly/I Put My Hand In/It Only Takes a Moment/It Takes a Woman/Just Leave Everything to Me/Love Is Only Love/Motherhood March/Put on Your Sunday Clothes/Ribbons Down My Back/So Long Dearie—Jerry Herman (w,m), Morris. COVER: Barbra Streisand, Walter Matthau.

2038 Hello Down There (Paramount, 1969, Tony Randall, Janet Leigh).

Hello Down There/I Can Love You—Jeff Barry (w,m), Ensign. COVER: Tony Randall, Janet Leigh.

2039 Hello Everybody (Paramount, 1933, Kate Smith, Randolph Scott).

Moon Song/My Queen of Lullaby Land/Out in the Great Open Spaces/Pickaninnies' Heaven/Twenty Million People—Sam Coslow (w), Arthur Johnston (m), Famous. COVER: Kate Smith.

2040 Hello Frisco Hello (20th Century-Fox, 1943, Alice Faye, John Payne).

Hello Frisco—Gene Buck (w), Louis Hirsch (m), Witmark; I've Gotta Have You (BW)—Mack Gordon (w), Harry Warren (m), BVC; Ragtime Cowboy Joe—Grant Clarke (w), Lewis Muir, Maurice Abrahams (m), Alfred; They Always Pick on Me—Stanley Murphy (w), Harry Von Tilzer (m), Von Tilzer; You'll Never Know—Mack Gordon (w), Harry Warren (m), BVC. COVER: Alice Faye, John Payne, Jack Oakie.

2041 Hello Goodbye (20th Century-Fox, 1970, Michael Crawford, Curt Jurgens).

Hello-Goodbye—Giovanni Dugati (w), Francis Lai (m), Fox. COVER: Genevieve Gilles.

2042 Hello London (London Calling) (20th Century-Fox, 1958, Sonja Henie, Michael Wilding).

Four British Tailors (B)/Girl of My Dreams (B)/Hello London (B)/Magic of You (B)/On Top of a Bus (B)/Petticoat Lane (B)/Truth of the Matter (B)/When You Know Someone Loves You (B)—Phil Green, Michael Carr, Ken Jones (w, m), Bradbury. COVER: Sonja Henie, Stanley Holloway.

2043 Hello Sister (SonoArt, 1930, Olive Borden, Lloyd Hughes).

What Good Am I Without You—Russell Colombo, Jack Gordean (w, m), Shapiro Bernstein. COVER: Olive Borden, Lloyd Hughes.

2044 Hell's Half Acre (Republic, 1953, Wendell Corey, Evelyn Keyes)

Lani—Jack Pitman (w,m), Miller; Polynesian Rhapsody—Jack Pitman (w,m), Criterion. COVER: Wendell Corey, Evelyn Keyes.

2045 Hell Up in Harlem (AIP, 1974, Fred Williamson, Julius Harris).

Escape from Hospital (PC)/Kufus Preaching (PC)/Mafia Boss Stabbed (PC)—Freddie Perren (m), Jobete. COVER: None.

2046 Hellzapoppin (Universal, 1941, Ole Olsen, Chic Johnson).

Watch the Birdie—Don Raye, Gene DePaul (w,m), Leeds; You Were There—Don Raye (w), Vic Schoen, Gene DePaul (m), Leeds. COVER: Olsen and Johnson, Martha Raye.

2047 He Loved the Ladies (Christie, 1929, Helene Millard, Taylor Holmes).

Pretty Words—Harry Cohen, Harry Kerr (w,m), Shapiro Bernstein. COVER: Helene Millard.

2048 Help (United Artists, 1965, The Beatles, Leo McKern).

Another Girl/Help/I Need You/Night Before/Tell Me What You See/Ticket to Ride/You're Going to Lose That Girl/You've Got to Hide Your Love Away—John Lennon, Paul McCartner (w,m), MacLen. COVER: The Beatles.

2049 Help Wanted (GM, 1937, Frankie Mack).

Undying Song, The—Wavavie Lleni (w,m), Lleni. COVER: Sketches.

2050 Hemingway's Adventures of a Young Man (20th Century-Fox, 1962, Richard Beymer, Arthur Kennedy).

Rosanna—Franz Waxman (m), Miller. COVER: Richard Beymer, Susan Strasberg.

2050a Henery Hawk (Warner Bros., 1960, Cartoon).

Henery Hawk—Tedd Pierce, Warren Foster (w,m), Witmark. COVER: Cartoon.

2051 Henriette (Holiday for Henriette) (Regina, 1955, Dany Robin, Hildegard Neff).

Pavements of Paris, The—Sydney Arthur, Sonny Miller (w), Georges Auric (m), Sam Fox. COVER: George Melachrino.

2052 Her Bodyguard (Paramount, 1935, Wynne Gibson, Edmund Lowe).

Where Have I Heard That Melody—Sam Coslow (w), Arthur Johnston (w), Famous. COVER: Wynne Gibson.

2053 Her Cardboard Lover

(MGM, 1942, Norma Shearer, Robert Taylor).

I Dare You—Ralph Freed (w), Burton Lane (m), Feist. COVER: Black and white cover with title only.

2054 Here Comes Carter (The Tattler) (Loud Speaker Lowdown) (First National, 1936, Ross Alexander, Glenda Farrell).

Thru the Courtesy of Love/You on My Mind—Jack Scholl (w), M. K. Jerome (m), Witmark. COVER: Ross Alexander, Glenda Farrell, Ann Nagel.

2055 Here Comes Cookie (Paramount, 1935, Gracie Allen, George Burns).

Vamp of the Pampas—Leo Robin, Richard Whiting (w,m), Famous. COVER: George Burns, Gracie Allen.

2056 Here Comes the Band (MGM, 1935, Virginia Bruce, Ted Lewis).

Headin. Home—Ned Washington (w), Herbert Stothart (m), Robbins; Roll Along Prairie Moon—Ted Fiorito, Harry MacPherson, Albert Von Tilzer (w,m), Robbins; Tender Is the Night—Harold Adamson (w), Walter Donaldson (m), Robbins; You're My Thrill—Ned Washington (w), Burton Lane (m), Robbins. COVER: Virginia Bruce, Harry Stockwell, Ted Lewis.

2057 Here Comes the Groom (Paramount, 1934, Jack Haley, Mary Boland).

I'll Blame the Waltz, Not You— Mack Gordon, Harry Revel (w,m), Paramount. COVER: Jack Haley, Patricia Ellis.

2058 Here Comes the Groom (Paramount, 1951, Bing Crosby, Jane Wyman).

Bonne Nuit—Jay Livingston, Ray Evans (w,m), BVH; In the Cool, Cool, Cool of the Evening—Johnny Mercer (w), Hoagy Carmichael (m), BVH: Misto Christofo Columbo/ Your Own Little House—Jay Livingston, Ray Evans (w,m), BVH. COVER: Bing Crosby, Jane Wyman.

2059 Here Come the Co-eds (Universal, 1945, Bud Abbott, Lou Costello).

I Don't Care If I Never Dream Again/Some Day We will Remember —Jack Brooks (w), Edgar Fairchild (m), Shapiro Bernstein. COVER: Bud Abbott, Lou Costello, Peggy Ryan.

2060 Here Come the Girls (Paramount, 1953, Bob Hope, Rosemary Clooney).

Ali Baba/Girls/Heavenly Days/ It's Torment/Never So Beautiful/ See the Circus/When You Love Someone/Ya Got Class—Jay Livingston, Ray Evans (w,m), Paramount. COVER: Bob Hope, Rosemary Clooney, Arlene Dahl, Tony Martin.

2061 Here Come the Waves (Paramount, 1944, Bing Crosby, Betty Hutton).

Ac-cent-tchu-ate the Positive/Here Come the Waves/I Promise You/Let's Take the Long Way Home/My Mamma Thinks I'm a Star/Navy Song/ There's a Fella Waitin' in Poughkeepsie—Johnny Mercer (w), Harold Arlen (m), Morris. COVER: Bing Crosby, Betty Hutton, Sonny Tufts.

2062 Here Is My Heart (Paramount, 1934, Bing Crosby, Kitty Carlisle).

June in January/Love Is Just Around the Corner/With Every Breath I Take—Leo Robin, Ralph Rainger (w,m), Famous. COVER: Bing Crosby, Kitty Carlisle.

2063 He Restoreth My Soul (Gospel, 1975, Religious Film).

Happy Again—Hal Hackady (w), Lee Pockriss (m), Northern. COVER: Blue Cover with title only.

2064 Here's to Romance (Fox, 1935, Nino Martini, Anita Louise).

Here's to Romance—Con Conrad, Herb Magidson (w,m), Movietone; I Carry You in My Pocket—Ralph Grosvenor (w,m), Ricordi; Midnight in Paris—Con Conrad, Herb Magidson (w,m), Movietone. COVER: Nino Martini.

2065 Here We Go Again (RKO, 1942, Edgar Bergen, Charlie McCarthy).

Delicious Delirium/Until I Live Again—Mort Greene (w), Harry Revel (m), Greene Revel. COVER: Edgar Bergen, Charlie McCarthy, Fibber McGee, Molly, Ginny Simms.

2066 Her First Romance (The Right Man) (Monogram, 1940, Edith Fellows, Wilbur Evans).

Star of Love—Charles Caine (w), Gregory Stone (m), BMI. COVER: Black and white cover with title only.

2067 Her Highness and the Bell Boy (MGM, 1945, Hedy Lamarr, Robert Walker).

Honey—Seymour Simons, Haven Gillespie, Richard Whiting (w,m), Feist. COVER: Hedy Lamarr, Robert Walker, June Allyson.

2068 Her Husband Lies (Paramount, 1937, Gail Patrick, Ricardo Cortez).

No More Tears/You Gambled with Love—Ralph Freed (w), Burton Lane (m), Popular. COVER: Gail Patrick, Ricardo Cortez.

2069 Heritage (French, 1940, Juanita Montenegro, Hubert Preller).

My Heritage—R. Fagin (w), Allan Small, Jean Poueigh (m), BMI. COVER: Juanita Montenegro.

2070 Her Jungle Love (Paramount, 1938, Dorothy Lamour, Ray Milland).

Coffee and Kisses—Ralph Freed (w), Frederick Hollander (m), Paramount; Jungle Love—Leo Robin, Ralph Rainger (w,m), Paramount; Lovelight in the Starlight—Ralph Freed (w), Frederick Hollander (m), Paramount. COVER: Dorothy Lamour, Ray Milland.

2071 Her Kingdom of Dreams (First National, 1919, Anita Stewart, Mahlon Hamilton).

Her Kingdom of Dreams—Anita Stewart (w,m), Berlin. COVER: Anita Stewart.

2072 Her Little Bag of Trix (Independent, 1923, Trixie Friganza).

I'm Gonna Make Los Angeles My Home—Raymond Goldman (w, m), Goldman. COVER: Trixie Friganza.

2073 Her Majesty Love (First National, 1931, Marilyn Miller, W. C. Fields).

Because of You/Though You're Not the First One—Al Dubin (w), Walter Jurmann (m), Harms. COVER: Marilyn Miller.

2074 Her Man (Pathe, 1930, Helen Twelvetrees, Ricardo Cortez).

Far Far Away—Tay Garnett, Joe Seitman (w), George Green (m), Youmans; Somehow I Know—Tay Garnett, Monty Collins (w), George Green (m), Youmans. COVER: Helen Twelvetrees, Ricardo Cortez.

2075 Herman and Katnip (Paramount, 1952, Cartoon).

Skiddle Diddle—Hal David, Leon Carr (w,m), Paramount. COVER: Cartoon.

2076 Her Master's Voice (Paramount, 1936, Peggy Conklin, Edward Everett Horton).

Down by the Old Mill Stream—Traditional, Feist; With All My Heart—Gus Kahn (w), Jimmy McHugh (m), Feist. COVER: Peggy Conklin, Edward Everett Horton.

2077 Hero at Large (MGM, 1979, John Ritter, Anne Archer).

Hero, The—Patrick Williams (m), Warner. COVER: John Ritter, Anne Archer.

2078 Heroes (Universal, 1977, Henry Winkler, Sally Field).

You Are My Tomorrows, Today—Carol Connors (w), Jack Nitzsche (m), Leeds. COVER: Henry Winkler, Sally Field.

2079 Heroes of Liberty (White Seal, 1919, War Film)

Heroes of Liberty—Norrie Bernard (w), Edward Pfeiffer (m), White Seal. COVER: Victory Parade.

2080 Heroes of Telemark, The (Columbia, 1965, Kirk Douglas, Richard Harris).

Heroes of Telemark Love Theme, Main Title—Malcolm Arnold (m), Colgems. COVER: Kirk Douglas, Richard Harris.

2081 Her Private Life (First National, 1929, Billie Dove, Walter Pidgeon).

Love Is Like a Dove—Al Bryan (w), George Meyer (m), Piantadosi. COVER: Billie Dove, Walter Pidgeon.

2082 Hers to Hold (Universal, 1943, Deanna Durbin, Joseph Cotten).

Pale Hands-Kashmiri Song—Lawrence Hope (w), Amy W. Finden (m), Boosey Hawkes; Say a Pray'r for the Boys Over There—Herb Magidson (w), Jimmy McHugh (m), Southern. COVER: Deanna Durbin, Joseph Cotten.

2083 He Was Her Man (We're Going to Be Rich) (20th Century-Fox, 1938, Gracie Fields, Victor McLaglen).

If I Only Hadn't Done What I Did/I'm Glad You Asked Me/Live and Learn/My Only Romance—Sidney Mitchell (w), Lew Pollack (m), Hollywood. COVER: Black and white cover with title only.

2084 Hey Boy Hey Girl (Columbia, 1959, Louis Prima, Keely Smith).

Lazy River—Hoagy Carmichael, Sidney Arodin (w,m), Southern; You Are My Love—Joe Sauter (w, m), Weiss Barry. COVER: Louis Prima, Keely Smith.

2085 Hey Let's Twist (Paramount, 1961, Joey Dee, Kay Armen).

Hey, Let's Twist!—Henry Glover, Joey Dee, Morris Levy (w,m), Jon Ware. COVER: Joey Dee.

2086 Hey Rookie (Columbia, 1943, Ann Miller, Larry Parks).

American Boy—Al Dubin (w), James Monaco (m), Morris; So What Serenade—James Cavanaugh, John Redmond, Nat Simon (w,m), Leeds; Streamlined Sheik/You're Good for My Morale—Henry Myers, Edward Eliscu (w), Jay Gorney (m), Mills.

COVER: Ann Miller, Joe Besser.

2087 Hey Sailor (Here Comes the Navy) (Warner Bros., 1934, James Cagney, Pat O'Brien).

Hey Sailor—Irving Kahal (w), Sammy Fain (m), Remick. COVER: James Cagney.

2088 Hi Beautiful (Universal, 1944, Martha O'Driscoll, Noah Beery).

Hi Beautiful—Roy Newell, Louis Herscher, Dorothy Jan (w,m), Superior. COVER: Martha O'Driscoll.

2089 Hi Buddy (Universal, 1943, Robert Paige, Harriet Hilliard).

Here's to Tomorrow—Charles Newman (w), Lew Pollack (m), Robbins; Hi Buddy Hi/We're the Marines—Everett Carter (w), Milton Rosen (m), Robbins. COVER: Robert Paige, and Girl Orchestra.

2090 Hidden Guns (Republic, 1956, Richard Arlen, Bruce Bennett).

Song of the Sheriff (B)—Hal Levy (w), Al Gannaway (m), Campbell. COVER: Black and white cover with title only.

2091 Hidden Island, The (Panther, 1964, Stars Unknown).

Hello My Love (PC)/Hidden Island (PC)/I Like You All De Time (PC)—Sunny Skylar (w,m), Panther. COVER: None.

2092 Hideaway Girl (Paramount, 1937, Shirley Ross, Robert Cummings).

Beethoven, Mendelssohn, and Liszt—Sam Coslow (w,m), Popular; Dancing Into My Heart/Two Birdies Up a Tree—Ralph Freed (w), Burton Lane (m), Popular; What Is Love?—Leo Robin, Ralph Rainger, Victor Young (w,m), Popular. COVER: Shirley Ross, Robert Cummings.

2093 Hide-out (Universal, 1930, James Murray, Kathryn Crawford).

Just You and I—Clarence Marks (w), Sam Perry (m), Handman. COVER: Kathryn Crawford.

2094 Hiding Out (DeLaurentiis, 1987, Jon Cryer, Keith Coogan).

Live My Life—Allee Willis, Danny Sembello (w,m), MCA. COVER: Green cover with title only.

2095　Hiding Place, The (World Wide, 1975, Julie Harris, Eileen Heckart).

Hiding Place-Five Themes—Tedd Smith (m), Hope. COVER: Movie Scene.

2096　Hi Gaucho (RKO, 1936, John Carroll, Steffi Duna).

Bandit Song/Little White Rose/ Panchita/Song of the Open Road— Albert Malotte (w,m), Berlin. COVER: Sketches.

2097　High and the Mighty, The (Warner Bros., 1954, John Wayne, Laraine Day).

High and the Mighty, The—Ned Washington (w), Dimitri Tiomkin (m), Witmark. COVER: John Wayne, Claire Trevor, Robert Stack, and Others.

2098　High Anxiety (20th Century-Fox, Mel Brooks, Madeline Kahn).

High Anxiety—Mel Brooks (w, m), Fox. COVER: Mel Brooks.

2099　Higher and Higher (RKO, 1943, Frank Sinatra, Michelle Morgan).

I Couldn't Sleep a Wink Last Night/I Saw You First/Lovely Way to Spend an Evening, A/Minuet in Boogie (BW)/Music Stopped, The/ You're on Your Own—Harold Adamson (w), Jimmy McHugh (m), Robbins. COVER: Frank Sinatra, Jack Haley, Michelle Morgan.

2100　High Flight (Columbia, 1957, Ray Milland, Anthony Newley).

High Flight March (B)—Eric Coates (m), Chappell. COVER: Ray Milland.

2101　High Flyers (RKO, 1937, Bert Wheeler, Bob Woolsey).

Keep Your Head Above Water— Herman Ruby (w), Dave Dreyer (m), Berlin. COVER: Black and white cover with title only.

2102　Highly Dangerous (Lippert, 1950, Margaret Lockwood, Dane Clark).

Highly Dangerous (B)—Richard Addinsell (m), Chappell. COVER: Margaret Lockwood.

2103　High Noon (United Artists, 1952, Gary Cooper, Grace Kelly).

High Noon—Ned Washington (w), Dimitri Tiomkin (m), Feist. COVER: Gary Cooper, Grace Kelly, Katy Jurado.

2104　High School Confidential (MGM, 1958, Russ Tamblyn, Jan Sterling).

High School Confidential—Jerry Lee Lewis, Ron Hargrove (w,m), Penron. COVER: Jerry Lee Lewis.

2105　High Society (MGM, 1956, Frank Sinatra, Bing Crosby).

Calypso/I Love You Samantha/ Little One/Mind If I Make Love to You/Now You Has Jazz/True Love/ Well Did You Evah?/Who Wants to Be a Millionaire/You're Sensational/ Let's Vocalize (PC)—Cole Porter (w, m), Buxton. COVER: Bing Crosby, Grace Kelly, Frank Sinatra.

2106　High Society Blues (Fox, 1930, Janet Gaynor, Charles Farrell).

Eleanor/High Society Blues/I'm in the Market for You/Just Like in a Story Book—Joseph McCarthy (w), James Hanley (m), Red Star. COVER: Janet Gaynor, Charles Farrell.

2107　High Tension (20th Century-Fox, 1936, Brian Donlevy, Glenda Farrell).

And That Woman Made a Monkey Out of Me—Sidney Clare (w,m), Movietone. COVER: Black and white cover with title only.

2108　High Time (20th Century-Fox, 1960, Bing Crosby, Fabian).

High Time Theme—Henry Mancini (m), Miller; Second Time Around— Sammy Cahn (w), James Van Heusen (m), Miller. COVER: Bing Crosby, Fabian, Tuesday Weld.

2109　High Coltage (Pathe, 1929, William Boyd, Carole Lombard).

Colleen O'Dare—George Waggner (w), George Green (m), Ager Yellen. COVER: Carole Lombard.

2110 High Wide and Handsome (Paramount, 1937, Randolph Scott, Irene Dunne).

Allegheny Al/Can I Forget You/ Folks Who Live on the Hill, The/ High Wide and Handsome/Things I Want, The/Will You Marry Me Tomorrow Maria—Oscar Hammerstein (w), Jerome Kern (m), Chappell. COVER: Irene Dunne, Randolph Scott.

2111 High Wind in Jamaica (20th Century-Fox, 1965, Anthony Quinn, James Coburn).

High Wind in Jamaica—Christopher Logue (w), Larry Adler (m), Miller. COVER: Anthony Quinn, James Coburn, and Others.

2112 Hi Good Lookin' (Universal, 1944, Harriet Hilliard, Ozzie Nelson).

Deacon Jones—Johnny Lange, Hy Heath, Richard Loring (w,m), Pyramid; You're Just the Sweetest Thing —Basil Adlam, Walter Bishop (w,m), Bishop. COVER: Harriet Hilliard, Ozzie Nelson, Kirby Grant.

2113 Hi Neighbor (Republic, 1942, Jean Parker, John Archer).

Pass the Biscuits Mirandy—Del Porter, Carl Hoefle (w,m), Tune Towne. COVER: Spike Jones.

2114 Hindenburg, The (Universal, 1975, George Scott, Anne Bancroft).

Hindenburg Theme—David Shire (m), Duchess. COVER: The Hindenburg.

2115 Hi Nellie (Warner Bros., 1934, Paul Muni, Glenda Farrell).

Hi Nellie—Mort Dixon (w), Allie Wrubel (m), Remick. COVER: Paul Muni, Glenda Farrell.

2116 Hippodrome (Sascha-Lux, 1961, Gerhard Reidman, Margot Nunke).

Hippodrome Theme—Bert Grund (m), Gil. COVER: Red cover with title only.

2117 Hips Hips Hooray (RKO, 1934, Bert Wheeler, Bob Woolsey).

Keep on Doin' What You're Doin'/ Keep Romance Alive/Tired of It All —Bert Kalmar, Harry Ruby (w,m), Berlin. COVER: Bert Wheeler, Bob Woolsey, Ruth Etting.

2118 His Brother's Wife (MGM, 1936, Barbara Stanwyck, Robert Taylor).

Can't We Fall in Love—Harold Adamson (w), Walter Donaldson (m), Feist. COVER: Black and white cover with title only.

2119 His Butler's Sister (Universal, 1943, Deanna Durbin, Pat O'-Brien).

In the Spirit of the Moment—Bernie Grossman, Walter Jurman (w, m), Southern; When You're Away—Henry Blossom (w), Victor Herbert (m), Witmark. COVER: Deanna Durbin, Pat O'Brien, Franchot Tone.

2120 His Double Life (Paramount, 1933, Lillian Gish, Roland Young).

Someday, Sometime, Somewhere/ Springtime in Old Granada—James Hanley (w), Karl Stark (m), Sam Fox. COVER: Lillian Gish, Roland Young.

2121 His Kind of Woman (RKO, 1951, Robert Mitchum, Jane Russell).

Five Little Miles from San Berdoo —Sam Coslow (w,m), Harman; You'll Know—Harold Adamson (w), Jimmy McHugh (m), Chappell. COVER: Robert Mitchum, Jane Russell.

2122 His Land (Graham, 1969, Cliff Richard, Cliff Barrows).

His Land/New 23rd, The/Over in Bethlehem/His Land-Eight Songs—Ralph Carmichael (w,m), Lexicon. COVER: Cliff Richard, and Movie Scenes.

2123 His Majesty and Company (Fox, 1935, John Garrick, Barbara Waring).

Lover o' Mine (B)—Ord Hamilton (w,m), Ascherberg. COVER: Alfred Campoli.

2124 His Majesty O'Keefe (Warner Bros., 1954, Burt Lancaster, Joan Rice).

Emerald Isle—Paul F. Webster (w), Dimitri Tiomkin (m), Witmark. COVER: Burt Lancaster, Joan Rice.

2125   His Majesty the American (Artcraft, 1919, Douglas Fairbanks, Marjorie Daw).

His Majesty the American—Lew Brown (w), Albert Von Tilzer (m), Broadway. COVER: Douglas Fairbanks.

2126   His Master's Voice (Gotham, 1925, George Hackathorne, Thunder).

His Master's Voice—Howard Johnson, Irving Bibo (w), Gus Edwards (m), Mills. COVER: Thunder, the Dog.

2127   Hit (Paramount, 1973, Billy Dee Williams, Richard Pryor).

Pages of Life—Larry Kusik (w), Lalo Schifrin (m), Ensign. COVER: Billy Dee Williams, Richard Pryor.

2128   Hit Parade, The (Republic, 1937, Frances Langford, Phil Regan).

I'll Reach for a Star (PC)/Last Night I Dreamed of You (PC)—Walter Hirsch (w), Lou Handman (m), Santly Joy; Love Is Good for Anything That Ails You—Cliff Friend, Matt Malneck (w,m), Santly Joy; Sweet Heartache—Ned Washington (w), Sam Stept (m), Santly Joy; Was It Rain—Walter Hirsch (w), Lou Handman (m), Santly Joy. COVER: Frances Langford, Phil Regan.

2129   Hit Parade of 1941 (Republic, 1940, Kenny Baker, Frances Langford).

In the Cool of the Evening/Make Yourself at Home/Swing Low Sweet Rhythm/Who Am I?—Walter Bullock (w), Jule Styne (m), Mills. COVER: Kenny Baker, Frances Langford, Ann Miller.

2130   Hit Parade of 1943 (Republic, 1943, John Carroll, Susan Hayward).

Change of Heart/Do These Old Eyes Deceive Me/Harlem Sandman/ Tahm Boom Bah/That's How to Write a Song/Who Took Me Home Last Night—Harold Adamson (w), Jule Styne (m), Southern. COVER: John Carroll, Susan Hayward, and Others.

2131   Hit Parade of 1947 (Republic, 1947, Eddie Albert, Constance Moore).

I Guess I'll Have That Dream Right Now/Is There Anyone Here from Texas?—Harold Adamson (w), Jimmy McHugh (m), Melrose. COVER: Eddie Albert, Constance Moore, Woody Herman.

2132   Hit the Deck (RKO, 1930, Jack Oakie, Polly Walker).

Hallelujah/Harbor of My Heart—Leo Robin, Clifford Grey (w), Vincent Youmans (m), Harms; Keepin' Myself for You—Sidney Clare (w), Vincent Youmans (m), Youmans; Nothing Could Be Sweeter—Leo Robin, Clifford Grey (w), Vincent Youmans (m), Harms; Sometimes I'm Happy—Irving Caesar (w), Vincent Youmans (m), Harms. COVER: Jack Oakie, Polly Walker.

2133   Hit the Deck (MGM, 1955, Jane Powell, Tony Martin).

Ciribiribin—Howard Johnson (w), A. Pestalozza (m), Robbins; Hallelujah—Leo Robin, Clifford Grey (w), Vincent Youmans (m), Harms; I Know That You Know—Anne Caldwell (w), Vincent Youmans (m), Harms; More Than You Know—William Rose, Edward Eliscu (w), Vincent Youmans (m), Miller; Sometime's I'm Happy—Irving Caesar (w), Vincent Youmans (m), Harms. COVER: Jane Powell, Tony Martin, Debbie Reynolds, Ann Miller.

2134   Hit the Ice (Pardon My Ski) (Universal, 1943, Bud Abbott, Lou Costello).

Happiness Ahead/I'd Like to Set You to Music/I'm Like a Fish Out of Water/Slap Polka, The—Paul F. Webster (w), Harry Revel (m), Miller. COVER: Bud Abbott, Lou Costello, Ginny Simms, Johnny Long.

2135 Hitting a New High (RKO, 1937, Lily Pons, Jack Oakie).

I Hit a New High/Let's Give Love Another Chance/ This Never Happened Before—Harold Adamson (w), Jimmy McHugh (m), Robbins. COVER: Lily Pons, Jack Oakie, Edward Everett Horton.

2136 Hittin' the Trail (Grand National, 1937, Tex Ritter, Jerry Bergh).

Blood on the Saddle (PC)—Everett Cheetham (w,m), Cole; I'm Hittin' the Trail for Home—Harry Miller (w, m), Sam Fox. COVER: Tex Ritter.

2137 Hi Ya Sailor (Universal, 1943, Donald Woods, Elyse Knox).

Dream Ago (PC)/Just a Step Away from Heaven (PC)—Everett Carter (w), Milton Rosen (m), BMI; Oh Brother—Maxine Manners, Jean Miller (w,m), BMI; So Goodnight/ Spell of the Moon (PC)—Everett Carter (w), Milton Rosen (m), BMI. COVER: Donald Woods, Elyse Knox, and Others.

2138 H.M.S. Defiant (Damn the Defiant) (Columbia, 1962, Alec Guinness, Dirk Bogarde).

H.M.S. Defiant—Dorsey Burnette, Johnny Burnette (w,m), Seven Eleven. COVER: Alec Guinness, Dirk Bogarde, Anthony Quayle.

2139 Hoagy Carmichael (Paramount, 1939, Jack Teagarden, Hoagy Carmichael).

That's Right-I'm Wrong—Stanley Adams (w), Hoagy Carmichael (m), Famous. COVER: Hoagy Carmichael, Jack Teagarden.

2140 Hobbit, The (Rankin Bass, 1977, Cartoon).

Hobbit-Thirteen Songs (VS)— Jules Bass (w), Maury Laws (m), Belwin Mills. COVER: Cartoon.

2141 Hobson's Choice (United Artists, 1954, Charles Laughton, John Mills).

Hobson's Choice (B)/Hobson's Choice-Themes (B)/Willie Mossop Theme (B)—Malcolm Arnold (m), Paterson. COVER: Charles Laugh-

ton, John Mills.

2142 Hoedown (Columbia, 1950, Eddy Arnold, Carolina Cotton).

I Betcha I Getcha—Frances Clark, Fred Stryker (w,m), Fairway. COVER: Carolina Cotton.

2143 Hoffman (Levitt Pickman, 1970, Peter Sellers, Sinead Cusack).

If There Ever Is a Next Time (B)— Don Black (w), Ron Grainer (m), Assoc Brit. COVER: Peter Sellers, Sinead Cusack.

2144 Hold Back the Dawn (Paramount, 1941, Charles Boyer, Olivia de Havilland).

Hold Back the Dawn—Richard Loring, Steven Cross (w,m), A I Music; My Boy My Boy—Jim Berg, Fre Fred Jacobson, Frank Loesser (w), Fred Spielman (m), Paramount; Sinner Kissed an Angel, A—Mack David (w), Ray Joseph (m), Famous. COVER: Charles Boyer, Olivia de Havilland, Paulette Goddard.

2145 Hold Back Tomorrow (Universal, 1955, Cleo Moore, John Agar).

Hold Back Tomorrow—Franz Steininger (w), Johnny Rotella (m), Northern. COVER: Cleo Moore, John Agar.

2146 Hold Everything (Warner Bros., 1930, Joe E. Brown, Winnie Lightner).

Girls We Remember, The (BW)/ I'm All Burned Up (BW)/I'm Screwy Over Looey (BW)/Isn't This a Cock-Eyed World/Physically Fit (BW)/ Sing a Little Theme Song/Take It on the Chin (BW)/To Know You Is to Love You/When the Little Red Roses—Al Dubin (w), Joe Burke (m), DBH. COVER: Joe E. Brown, Winnie Lightner.

2147 Hold On (MGM, 1966, Mickey Deems, Herman's Hermits).

Leaning on the Lamp-post—Noel Gay (w,m), Mills. COVER: Herman's Hermits.

2148 Hold That Co-ed (20th Century-Fox, 1938, John Barrymore, Joan Davis).

Heads High (PC)—Lew Brown (w), Lew Pollack (m), Feist; Here Am I Doing It/Hold That Co-ed—Mack Gordon, Harry Revel (w,m), Feist; Limpy Dimp—Jule Styne, Nick Castle, Sidney Clare (w,m), Feist. COVER: Joan Davis, John Barrymore, George Murphy.

2149 Hold That Ghost (Universal, 1941, Ted Lewis, Abbott and Costello).

Aurora—Harold Adamson (w), Mario Lago, Roberto Roberti (m), Robbins; Sleepy Serenade—Mort Greene (w), Lou Singer (m), Leeds; When My Baby Smiles at Me—Andrew Sterling, Ted Lewis (w), Bill Monroe (m), Von Tilzer. COVER: The Andrews Sisters, Ted Lewis.

2150 Hold That Girl (Fox, 1934, James Dunn, Claire Trevor).

Fan Dance—Forman Brown (w), Frederick Hollander (m), Movietone. COVER: Black and white cover with title only.

2151 Hold Your Man (MGM, 1933, Jean Harlow, Clark Gable).

Hold Your Man—Arthur Freed (w), Nacio Herb Brown (m), Robbins. COVER: Jean Harlow, Clark Gable.

2152 Hole in the Head, A (United Artists, 1959, Frank Sinatra, Eleanor Parker).

All My Tomorrows/High Hopes—Sammy Cahn (w), James Van Heusen (m), Barton. COVER: Frank Sinatra, Eleanor Parker, Edward G. Robinson.

2153 Holiday Camp (Universal, 1946, Flora Robson, Dennis Price).

Another Day Is Over (B)—Carlene Muir (w), Al Stone (m), Chappell. COVER: Dennis Price, Hazel Court.

2154 Holiday for Lovers (20th Century-Fox, 1959, Clifton Webb, Jane Wyman).

Holiday for Lovers—Sammy Cahn (w), Jimmy Van Heusen (m), Miller. COVER: Clifton Webb, Jane Wyman, Carol Lynley.

2155 Holiday in Brussels (Randall, 1958, George Jessel, Keefe Brasselle).

Holiday in Brussels—Don George (w), Steve Allen (m), Rosemeadow. COVER: Brussels World Fair.

2156 Holiday in Havana (Columbia, 1949, Desi Arnaz, Mary Hatcher).

Straw Hat Song, The—Allan Roberts, Fred Karger (w,m), Mood. COVER: Desi Arnaz, Mary Hatcher.

2157 Holiday in Mexico (MGM, 1946, Walter Pidgeon, Jane Powell).

I Think of You—Jack Elliott, Don Marcotte (w,m), Embassy; Three Blind Mice—André Previn (m), Robbins; Walter Winchell Rumba—Carl Sigman (w), Noro Morales, Robbins; You Te Amo Mucho—Sam Stept, Xavier Cugat, Ervin Drake (w,m), Bogat; You, So It's You—Nacio Herb Brown, Earl Brent (w,m), Miller. COVER: Jane Powell, Walter Pidgeon, Ilona Massey.

2158 Holiday Inn (Paramount, 1942, Bing Crosby, Fred Astaire).

Abraham/Be Careful It's My Heart/Happy Holiday/I Can't Tell a Lie (BW)/I'll Capture Your Heart Singing/Let's Say It with Firecrackers (BW)/Let's Start the New Year Right/Plenty to Be Thankful For/Song of Freedom/White Christmas/You're Easy to Dance With—Irving Berlin (w,m), Berlin. COVER: Bing Crosby, Fred Astaire, Marjorie Reynolds, Virginia Dale.

2159 Hollywood (Paramount, 1923, Mary Astor, Agnes Ayres).

Hollywood—Aubrey Stauffer (w, m), Sherman Clay. COVER: Paramount Studio and Stars.

2160 Hollywood Canteen (Warner Bros., 1944, Jack Benny, Eddie Cantor).

Corns for My Country—Leah Worth, Jean Barry, Dick Charles (w, m), Remick; Don't Fence Me In—Cole Porter (w,m), Harms; Enlloro—Harold Rome (w), Obdulio Morales, Julio Blanco (m), Leeds; General Jumped at Dawn, The—Larry Neill (w), Jimmy Mundy (m), BVC; Hol-

lywood Canteen—Ted Koehler (w),
M. K. Jerome, Ray Heindorf (m),
Remick; Sweet Dreams Sweetheart—
Ted Koehler (w), M. K. Jermoe (m),
Remick; Tumbling Tumbleweeds—
Bob Nolan (w,m), Sam Fox; What
Are You Doin' the Rest of Your
Life—Ted Koehler (w), Burton Lane
(m), Harms; You Can Always Tell
a Yank—E. Y. Harburg (w), Burton
Lane (m), Remick. COVER: Jack
Benny, Bette Davis, Joan Crawford,
Barbara Stanwyck, and Others.

2161 Hollywood Hotel (Warner
Bros., 1937, Dick Powell, Rosemary
Lane).

Blue Moon (PC)—Lorenz Hart
(w), Richard Rodgers (m), Robbins;
Can't Teach My Old Heart New
Tricks/Hooray for Hollywood/I'm
Like a Fish Out of Water/I've
Hitched My Wagon to a Star/Let
That Be a Lesson to You/Silhouetted
in the Moonlight—Johnny Mercer
(w), Richard Whiting (m), Harms.
COVER: Dick Powell, Benny Good-
man, Rosemary Lane, Lola Lane.

**2162 Hollywood Nights (Let's
Go Places)** (Fox, 1929, Lola Lane,
Walter Catlett).

Hollywood Nights/Out in the
Cold/Parade of the Blues/Reach for
a Rainbow/Um-um-in the Moonlight—Con Conrad, Sidney Mitchell,
Archie Gottler (w,m), DBH. COV-
ER: Black and white cover with title
only.

2163 Hollywood or Bust (Paramount, 1956, Dean Martin, Jerry
Lewis).

Day in the Country, A/Holly-
wood or Bust/It Looks Like Love/
Let's Be Friendly/Wild and Woolly
West—Paul F. Webster (w), Sammy
Fain (m), Paramount. COVER:
Dean Martin, Jerry Lewis, Anita
Ekberg.

2164 Hollywood Party (MGM,
1934, Jimmy Durante, Lupe Velez).

Feelin' High—Walter Donaldson,
Howard Dietz (w,m), Robbins; Hollywood Party—Lorenz Hart (w),

Richard Rodgers (m), Robbins; Hot
Choc'late Soldiers—Arthur Freed
(w), Nacio Herb Brown (m), Robbins; Inka Dinka Doo (VS)—Jimmy
Durante, Ben Ryan, Harry Donnelly
(w,m), Bourne; I've Had My Moments—Gus Kahn (w), Walter Donaldson (m), Robbins. COVER:
Sketch of Three People.

2165 Hollywood Revue (MGM,
1929, Marion Davies, Joan Crawford).

Gotta Feelin' for You—Jo Trent
(w), Louis Alter (m), Robbins; Lon
Chaney's Going to Get You—John
Murray (w), Gus Edwards (m), Rob-
bins; Low Down Rhythm—Raymond
Klages (w), Jesse Greer (m), Robbins;
Nobody But You/Orange Blossom
Time—Joe Goodwin (w), Gus Ed-
wards (m), Robbins; Singin' in the
Rain—Arthur Freed (w), Nacio Herb
Brown (m), Robbins; Your Mother
and Mine—Joe Goodwin (w), Gus Ed-
wards (m), Robbins. COVER: Mar-
ion Davies, Joan Crawford, Jack
Benny, Norma Shearer.

**2166 Hollywood Star Spangled
Revue** (Warner Bros., 1966, Bob
Hope).

Hollywood—William Hendricks
(w), Basil Adlam (m), Warner. COV-
ER: Spotlights at Premiere.

2167 Hollywood Varieties (Lippert, 1950, Robert Alda, Peggy Stewart).

Hollywood Varieties—Dian Man-
ners, Johnny Clark (w,m), Producers.
COVER: Robert Alda, and Movie
Scenes.

2168 Holyland (Vitaphone,
1933, Musical Short).

Holyland—David Mendoza (w,m),
Witmark. COVER: Black and white
cover with title only.

2169 Holy Terror, The (20th
Century-Fox, 1937, Jane Withers,
Leah Ray).

I Don't Know Myself Since I
Know You/There I Go Again—Sid-
ney Clare (w), Harry Akst (m),
Movietone. COVER: Jane Withers.

2170 Hombre (20th Century-

Fox, 1966, Paul Newman, Diane Cilento).

Days of Love—Paul F. Webster (w), David Rose (m), Feist; Hombre —David Rose (m), Feist. COVER: Paul Newman, Diane Cilento.

2171 Home Before Dark (Warner Bros., 1958, Jean Simmons, Rhonda Fleming).

Home Before Dark—Sammy Cahn (w), Jimmy McHugh (m), Witmark. COVER: Jean Simmons.

2172 Homecoming (Paramount, 1928, Dita Parlo, Lars Hanson).

Homecoming (B)—Harry Graham (w), Fraser Simson (m), Ascherberg. COVER: Dita Parlo.

2173 Home from the Hill (MGM, 1959, Robert Mitchum, Eleanor Parker).

Home from the Hill/Young Is Your Lover—Mack David (w), Bronislau Kaper (m), Miller. COVER: Robert Mitchum, Eleanor Parker, George Peppard.

2174 Home in Wyomin' (Republic, 1942, Gene Autry, Smiley Burnette).

Tweedle-O-Twill (VS)—Gene Autry, Fred Rose (w,m), Western. COVER: Gene Autry.

2175 Home on the Prairie (Republic, 1939, Gene Autry, Smiley Burnette).

I'm Gonna Round Up My Blues (VS)—Gene Autry, Johnny Marvin (w,m), Western. COVER: Gene Autry.

2176 Hondo (Warner Bros., 1953, John Wayne, Geraldine Page).

Hondo, Hondo—Emil Newman, Hugo Friedhoffer (w,m), Ronell. COVER: Black and white cover with title only.

2177 Honey (Arthur, 1928, Arlene Jackson).

Honey—Seymour Simons, Haven Gillespie, Richard Whiting (w,m), Feist. COVER: Arlene Jackson.

2178 Honey (Paramount, 1930, Nancy Carroll, Stanley Smith).

I Don't Need Atmosphere/In My Little Hope Chest/Let's Be Domestic/Sing You Sinners/What Is This Power I Have—Sam Coslow, Frank Carling (w,m), Famous. COVER: Nancy Carroll, Stanley Smith.

2179 Honeychile (Republic, 1951, Judy Canova, Eddie Foy).

Honeychile—Jack Elliott (w), Harold Spina (m), Spitzer; More Than I Care To—Ted Johnson, Matt Terry (w,m), Spitzer; Tutti Frutti—Jack Elliott (w), Ann Canova (m), Spitzer. COVER: Judy Canova.

2180 Honeymoon (RKO, 1947, Shirley Temple, Guy Madison).

I Love Geraniums/Ven Aqui—Mort Greene (w), Leigh Harline (m), Morris. COVER: Shirley Temple, Guy Madison.

2181 Honeymoon Hotel (MGM, 1969, Robert Goulet, Robert Morse).

Honeymoon Hotel—Sammy Cahn (w), James Van Heusen (m), Miller. COVER: Robert Goulet, Robert Morse.

2182 Honeymoon Lane (Sono Art, 1931, Eddie Dowling, June Collyer).

Honeymoon Lane—Billy Moll, Eddie Dowling, James Hanley (w,m), Shapiro Bernstein. COVER: Eddie Dowling, June Collyer.

2183 Honeymoon Machine, The (MGM, 1961, Steve McQueen, Jim Hutton).

Honeymoon Machine, The—Jack Brooks (w), Leigh Harline (m), Miller. COVER: Steve McQueen, Brigid Bazlen.

2184 Honey Pot, The (United Artists, 1967, Rex Harrison, Susan Hayward).

Honey Pot Theme—John Addison (m), Unart. COVER: Black and white cover with title only.

2185 Honeysuckle Rose (Warner Bros., 1979, Willie Nelson, Dyan Cannon).

Angel Flying Too Close to the Ground/On the Road Again—Willie Nelson (w,m), Nelson; Honeysuckle

Twenty-Three Songs—Willie Nelson, Kris Kristofferson (w,m), Columbia. COVER: Willie Nelson, Any Irving, Dyan Cannon.

2186 Hong Kong Affair (Allied Artists, 1958, Jack Kelly, May Wynn).

Hong Kong Affair—Paul Herrick (w), Lou Forbes (m), Robbins. COVER: Jack Kelly, May Wynn.

2187 Honkers, The (United Artists, 1972, James Coburn, Slim Pickens).

Easy Made for Lovin'—Bobby Russell (w,m), Unart. COVER: James Coburn, and Girls.

2188 Honky (Harris, 1971, Brenda Sykes, John Nielson).

Something More—Bradford Craig (w), Quincy Jones (m), Getty. COVER: Sketch of Couple.

2189 Honky Tonk (Warner Bros., 1929, Sophie Tucker, Lila Lee).

He's a Good Man to Have Around/ I Don't Want to Get Thin/I'm Doing What I'm Doing for Love/I'm Feathering a Nest/I'm the Last of the Red Hot Mammas—Jack Yellen (w), Milton Ager (m), Ager Yellen; Some of These Days—Shelton Brooks (w,m), Rossiter. COVER: Sophie Tucker.

2190 Honkytonk Man (Warner Bros., 1982, Clint Eastwood, John McIntire).

Honkytonk Man—DeWayne Blackwell (w,m), Peso. COVER: Marty Robbins.

2191 Honolulu (MGM, 1939, Eleanor Powell, Gracie Allen).

Honolulu/Leader Doesn't Like Music, The/This Night—Gus Kahn (w), Harry Warren (m), BVC; Marianina (BW)—Walter Donaldson, Guy Lombardo (w,m), BVC. COVER: Eleanor Powell, Gracie Allen, George Burns, Robert Young.

2192 Honor Caddy (Paramount, 1949, Bing Crosby, Bob Hope).

Tomorrow Is My Lucky Day— Johnny Burke (w), James Van Heusen (m), BVH. COVER: Bing Crosby, Bob Hope, and Golfers.

2193 Hoodlum, The (First Na-

tional, 1919, Mary Pickford, Kenneth Harlan).

Hoodlum, The—Sam Lewis, Joe Young (w), Harry Ruby (m), Berlin. COVER: Mary Pickford.

2194 Hoodlum Saint, The (MGM, 1945, William Powell, Esther Williams).

Sweetheart—Benny Davis (w), Arnold Johnson (m), Miller. COVER: Esther Williams, William Powell, Angela Lansbury.

2195 Hook, The (MGM, 1963, Kirk Douglas, Robert Walker).

Hook Blues Theme/Hook Main Theme—Larry Adler (m), Miller. COVER: Kirk Douglas, Robert Walker, Nick Adams.

2196 Hooray for Love (RKO, 1935, Ann Sothern, Gene Raymond).

Hooray for Love/I'm in Love All Over Again/I'm Livin' in a Great Big Way/You're My Angel—Dorothy Fields, Jimmy McHugh (w,m), Berlin. COVER: Ann Sothern, Gene Raymond.

2197 Hoosier Holiday (Republic, 1943, Dale Evans, George Byron).

Who's Your Little Hoosier (PC)— Johnny Marvin (w,m), Harris. COVER: None.

2198 Hopalong Cassidy (Paramount, 1935, William Boyd, Jimmy Ellison).

Following the Stars—Sam Stept, Dave Franklin (w,m), Shapiro Bernstein. COVER: Jimmy Ellison, Paula Stone.

2199 Horizontal Lieutenant (MGM, 1961, Jim Hutton, Paula Prentiss).

Horizontal Lieutenant—Stella Unger, George Stoll, Jos Pasternak (w, m), Robbins. COVER: Jim Hutton, Paula Prentiss.

2200 Horse Feathers (Paramount, 1932, Thelma Todd, Marx Brothers).

Everybody Says I Love You—Bert Kalmar (w), Harry Ruby (m), Famous. COVER: Marx Brothers.

2201 Horsemasters (Buena Vista,

1960, Annette Funicello, Janet Munro).

Strummin' Song—Richard Sherman, Robert Sherman (w,m), Wonderland. COVER: Annette Funicello.

2202 Horse Shoes (Pathe, 1927, Monty Banks, Ernie Wood).

Horse Shoes—Victor Prospero (w), Menlo Mayfield (m), Alfred. COVER: Monty Banks.

2203 Horse Without a Head, The (Buena Vista, 1962, Jean Pierre Aumont, Herbert Lom).

Horse Without a Head, The—Richard Sherman, Robert Sherman (w, m), Wonderland. COVER: Black and white cover with title only.

2204 Hot Blood (The Wild One) (Columbia, 1954, Marlon Brando, Mary Murphy).

Chino—Leith Stevens (m), Mills; I Could Learn to Love You—R. Bagdasarian (w), Les Baxter (m), Colgems. COVER: Marlon Brando.

2205 Hot Curves (Tiffany, 1930, Benny Rubin, Rex Lease).

If I Only Knew That You Could Care for Me/My Son-ny/Tum Tum Tumble Into Love—Ben Ryan (w), Violinsky (m), Mills. COVER: Benny Lubin, and Girl.

2206 Hotel (Warner Bros., 1967, Rod Taylor, Karl Malden).

This Hotel—Richard Quine (w), Johnny Keating (m), Witmark. COVER: Rod Taylor, Karl Malden, Melvyn Douglas, and Others.

2207 Hotel Variety (Screencraft, 1932, Olive Borden, Hal Skelly).

I Gave the Right Kind of Love—Al Koppell (w), Lou Herscher, Paul Vincent (m), Okay; Rhythm of New York—Lou Herscher, Allen Taub, Paul Vincent (w,m), Okay; Wrapped Up in Nothing at All—Allen Taub, Ben Gordon (w), Lou Herscher (m), Okay. COVER: Olive Borden.

2208 Hot for Paris (Fox, 1929, Victor McLaglen, Fifi Dorsay).

Duke of Ka Ki Ak/If You Want to See Paree/Sweet Nothings of Love—Edgar Leslie, Walter Donaldson (w, m), Donaldson. COVER: Victor McLaglen, Fifi Dorsay, El Brendel.

2209 Hot Heiress (First National, 1931, Ona Munson, Ben Lyons).

Like Ordinary People Do/You're the Cats—Lorenz Hart (w), Richard Rodgers (m), Harms. COVER: Ona Munson, Ben Lyons.

2210 Hot Lead and Cold Feet (Buena Vista, 1977, Jim Dale, Don Knotts).

May the Best Man Win—Al Kasha, Joel Hirshhorn (w,m), Disney; Something Good Is Bound to Happen—Arthur Alsberg, Don Nelson (w), Bud Baker (m), Disney. COVER: Don Knotts.

2211 Hot Millions (MGM, 1968, Maggie Smith, Peter Ustinov).

Hot Millions Theme—Laurie Johnson (m), Feist; There Is Another Song—Herbert Kretzmer (w), Laurie Johnson (m), Feist; This Time—Don Black (w), Laurie Johnson (m), Feist. COVER: Maggie Smith, Peter Ustinov.

2212 Hot Pepper (Fox, 1933, Lupe Velez, Edmund Lowe).

Ain't It Gonna Ring No More/Mon Papa-A French Can Can—Val Burton, Will Jason (w,m), Movietone. COVER: Black and white cover with title only.

2213 Hot Rhythm (Monogram, 1944, Dona Drake, Robert Lowery).

Where Were You—Ruth Herscher (w), Louis Herscher (m), Grand. COVER: Dona Drake, Robert Lowery.

2214 Hot Rock (20th Century-Fox, 1972, Robert Redford, George Segal).

Hot Rock Theme—Quincy Jones (m), Fox; Listen to the Melody—Tay Lihler, Bill Rinehart (w), Quincy Jones (m), Fox. COVER: Robert Redford, George Segal, Ron Liebman, Paul Sands.

2215 Hot Spell (Paramount, 1958, Shirley Booth, Anthony Quinn).

Hot Spell—Mack David (w), Burt

Bacharach (m), Famous. COVER: Shirley Booth, Anthony Quinn.

2216 Hot Stuff (Columbia, 1978, Dom Deluise, Suzanne Pleshette).

Hot Stuff—Jerry Hubbard (w, m), Vector. COVER: Dom Deluise, Suzanne Pleshette.

2217 Hot Summer Night (MGM, 1957, Leslie Nielsen, Colleen Miller).

Hot Summer Night—Bob Russell (w), André Previn (m), Feist. COVER: Leslie Nielsen, Colleen Miller.

2218 Hot Water (Pathe, 1924, Harold Lloyd, Jobyna Ralston).

Hot Water (B)—Saxe Ewart, Herman Darewski (w,m), Strand; Hot Water Fox Trot (B)—Herbert Rule (m), Wright. COVER: Harold Lloyd.

2219 Houdini (Paramount, 1953, Janet Leigh, Tony Curtis).

Golden Years—Jay Livingston, Ray Evans (w,m), Paramount. COVER: Janet Leigh, Tony Curtis.

2220 Hound Dog Man (20th Century-Fox, 1959, Fabian, Carol Lynley).

Got the Feelin'—Richard Sherman, Robert Sherman (w,m), Merge; Hound Dog Man—Doc Pomus, Mort Shuman (w,m), Fabulous; I'm Growin' Up—Robert Marcucci (w), Peter DeAngelis (m), Miller; Single/This Friendly World—Ken Darby (w,m), Miller. COVER: Fabian.

2221 House Across the Bay, The (United Artists, 1940, George Raft, Joan Bennett).

Chula Chihuahua—Jule Styne, Nick Castle, Sidney Clare (w,m), Mills; Hundred Kisses from Now, A— George Brown, Irving Actman (w, m), Mills; I'll Be a Fool Again—Al Seigel (w,m). COVER: George Raft, Joan Bennett.

2222 Houseboat (Paramount, 1958, Cary Grant, Sophia Loren).

Almost in Your Arms/Bing Bang Bong—Jay Livingston, Ray Evans (w, m), Paramount; Houseboat—Steve Allen (w), George Duning (m), Paramount; Houseboat Love Theme—Jay Livingston, Ray Evans (m), Para-

mount. COVER: Cary Grant, Sophia Loren.

2223 House Calls (Universal, 1978, Walter Matthau, Glenda Jackson).

It's All in the Mind (VS)—Leslie Bricusse (w), Henry Mancini (m), Leeds. COVER: Henry Mancini.

2224 House I Live In, The (RKO, 1942, Frank Sinatra).

House I Live In, The— Lewis Allan (w), Earl Robinson (m), Chappell. COVER: Frank Sinatra.

2225 House Is Not a Home, A (Embassy, 1964, Shelley Winters, Robert Taylor).

House Is Not a Home, A—Hal David (w), Burt Bacharach (m), Diplomat. COVER: Shelley Winters, Robert Taylor.

2226 House of Sand, A (Darwin, 1962, Mary Staton, Philippe Forquet).

House of Sand, A—Jerry Winn (w), Les Baxter (m), Miller. COVER: Mary Staton, Philippe Forquet.

2227 House of Seven Gables, The (Universal, 1940, George Sanders, Vincent Price).

Color of Your Eyes—Ralph Freed (w), Frank Skinner (m), Robbins. COVER: Vincent Price, Margaret Lindsay.

2228 Howdy Broadway (Raytone, 1929, Tommy Christian, Jack Clark).

Atta Boy—Billy Moll, Tommy Christian (w,m), Shapiro Bernstein; I Want You to Know I Love You— Art Terker, Tommy Christian (w,m), Shapiro Bernstein. COVER: Tommy Christian, and Band.

2229 How Green Was My Valley (20th Century-Fox, 1941, Walter Pidgeon, Maureen O'Hara).

How Green Was My Valley—Paul F. Webster (w), Alfred Newman (m), Robbins. COVER: Green cover with title only.

2230 How Sweet It Is (National General, 1968, Debbie Reynolds, James Garner).

How Sweet It is/How Sweet It Is-Montage—Jim Webb (w,m), National General. COVER: Debbie Reynolds, James Garner.

2231 How's About It (Universal, 1943, Andrews Sisters, Robert Paige).

Don't Mind the Rain—Ned Miller, Chester Conn (w,m), Feist; East of the Rockies—Sid Robin (w,m), Leeds; Going Up—Irving Gordon, Allen Roth (w,m), Leeds. COVER: Andrews Sisters, Buddy Rich.

2232 How the West Was Won (MGM, 1962, James Stewart, Henry Fonda).

Home in the Meadow—Sammy Cahn (w), Robert Dolan (m), Robbins; How the West Was Won—Ken Darby (w)—Alfred Newman (m), Robbins; Battle Hymn of the Republic (VS)—Alfred Newman, Ken Darby (w,m), Robbins; Come Share My Life (VS)—Ken Darby (w,m), Robbins; I'm Bound for the Promised Land (VS)/Nine Hundred Miles from Home (VS)/No Goodbye (VS)/On the Banks of the Sacramento (VS)—Alfred Newman, Ken Darby (w,m), Robbins; Raise a Ruckus Tonight (VS)—Johnny Mercer (w), Robert Dolan (m), Robbins; Thousand Miles, A (VS)—Ken Darby (w,m), Robbins; What Was Your Name in the States (VS)—Johnny Mercer (w), Robert Dolan (m), Robbins; When Johnny Comes Marching Home (VS)—Alfred Newman, Ken Darby (w,m), Robbins. COVER: Movie Scenes.

2233 How to Be Very Very Popular (20th Century-Fox, 1955, Betty Grable, Robert Cummings).

How to Be Very Very Popular—Sammy Cahn (w), Jule Styne (m), Miller. COVER: Betty Grable, Sheree North.

2234 How to Break Ninety (Vitaphone, 1933, Musical Short).

Down the Fairway—Harry Warren (m), Witmark. COVER: Black and white cover with title only.

2235 How to Marry a Million-aire (20th Century-Fox, 1953, Marilyn Monroe, Betty Grable).

New York—Ken Darby (w,m), Simon. COVER: Marilyn Monroe, Betty Grable, Lauren Bacall.

2236 How to Murder Your Wife (United Artists, 1964, Jack Lemmon, Virna Lisi).

How to Murder Your Wife—Neal Hefti, Lil Mattis (w,m), Unart. COVER: Red and black cover with title only.

2237 How to Save a Marriage and Ruin Your Life (Columbia, 1968, Dean Martin, Stella Stevens).

Winds of Change—Mack David (w), Michel Legrand (m), Colgems. COVER: Stella Stevens.

2238 How to Steal a Million (20th Century-Fox, Audrey Hepburn, Peter O'Toole).

Two Lovers—Leslie Bricusse (w), Johnny Williams (m), Hastings. COVER: Audrey Hepburn, Peter O'Toole.

2239 Huckleberry Finn (United Artists, 1974, Jeff East, Paul Winfield).

Cairo Illinois/Freedom/Huckleberry/Finn/Into His Hands/Rose in a Bible/Rotten Luck/Royal Nonesuch/Royalty/Someday Honey Darlin'/What's Right What's Wrong—Richard Sherman, Robert Sherman (w,m), Unart. COVER: Jeff East, Paul Winfield.

2240 Hucksters, The (MGM, 1947, Ava Gardner, Clark Gable).

Don't Tell Me—Buddy Pepper (w, m), Robbins. COVER: Clark Gable, Deborah Kerr, Ava Gardner.

2241 Hud (Paramount, 1963, Paul Newman, Patricia Neal).

Hud—Mack David (w), Elmer Bernstein (m), Famous. COVER: Paul Newman, Patricia Neal.

2242 Hugo the Hippo (20th Century-Fox, 1972, Cartoon).

Hugo the Hippo-Eleven Songs—Bob Larimer (w,m), Brut. COVER: Cartoon.

2243 Hulda from Holland (Paramount, 1916, Mary Pickford, John Bowers).

Hulda from Holland—George Mack (w), Bob Allan (m), Vandersloot. COVER: Dutch Girl.

2244 Hullabaloo (MGM, 1940, Frank Morgan, Virginia Grey).

Handful of Stars, A—Jack Lawrence, Ted Shapiro (w,m), Feist; We've Come a Long Way Together— Ted Koehler, Sam Stept (w,m), Feist. COVER: Frank Morgan, Virginia Grey, and Girls.

2245 Human Comedy, The (MGM, 1943, Mickey Rooney, Frank Morgan).

Leaning on the Everlasting Arms— E. Hoffman (w), A. Showalter (m), Robbins. COVER: Purple cover with title only.

2246 Human Desire (Columbia, 1954, Glenn Ford, Gloria Grahame).

Human Desire—Bob Wells (w), Daniele Amphitheatrof (m), Mills. COVER: Glenn Ford, Gloria Grahame.

2247 Human Hearts (Universal, 1922, House Peters, Russell Simpson).

Human Hearts—Milt Hagen, Victor Nurnberg (w,m), Feist. COVER: House Peters, Gertrude Claire.

2248 Humanity (Macauley, 1917, Billy Anderson).

Humanity—Grace Bradley (w,m), Berlin. COVER: A Nurse.

2249 Human Jungle (Allied Artists, 1954, Gary Merrill, Jan Sterling).

Tain't Gonna Be You—Max Rich (w,m), Chappell. COVER: Jan Sterling, Gary Merrill.

2250 Humming Bird, The (Paramount, 1924, Gloria Swanson, Edward Burns).

Humming Bird, The—Frank Egan (w), H. Knight Clark (m), Marks. COVER: Gloria Swanson.

2251 Humoresque (Paramount, 1920, Gaston Glass, Alma Rubens).

Humoresque—Alfred Bryan, Coleman Goetz (w), Joe Rosey (m), Remick. COVER: Bobby Connelly, Vera Gordon.

2252 Humoresque (Warner Bros., 1946, John Garfield, Joan Crawford).

Humoresque—William Nameiw (w), Anton Dvorak (m), Remick; Malaguena Theme (B)—Ernesto Lecuona (m), Campbell. COVER: John Garfield, Joan Crawford.

2253 Hunchback of Notre Dame, The (Universal, 1923, Lon Chaney, Patsy Ruth Miller).

Chimes of Notre Dame—Maurice Baron (m), Belwin; Hunchback of Notre Dame Love Theme—Domenico Savino (m), Schirmer; Song of the Bell (B)—Cameron Forrester (w), Montague Clayton (m), Betwyn. COVER: Patsy Ruth Miller, and Notre Dame.

2254 Hungarian Rhapsody (Paramount, 1929, Dita Parlo, Fritz Greiner).

Marika—Allan Stuart (w), William Peters (m), Sam Fox. COVER: Dita Parlo.

2255 Hunter, The (Paramount, 1980, Steve McQueen, Eli Wallach).

Hunter, The—Michel Legrand (m), Famous. COVER: Steve McQueen.

2256 Hunza (National Geographic, 1957, Travelogue).

Hunza-The Himalayan Shangri La—Lyrio Panicali (m), Duchess. COVER: Mountains.

2257 Hurdy Gurdy (Love Live and Laugh) (Fox, 1929, George Jessel, Lila Lee).

Margharita—L. Wolfe Gilbert, Abel Baer (w,m), DBH. COVER: Black and white cover with title only.

2258 Hurricane, The (United Artists, 1937, Dorothy Lamour, Jon Hall).

Moon of Manakoora, The—Frank Loesser (w), Alfred Newman (m), Kalmar. COVER: Dorothy Lamour, Jon Hall.

2259 Hurricane Horseman (Death Rides the Range) (Colony, 1940, Ken Maynard, Kenneth Rhodes).

I'll Roam on Distant Range— Colin MacDonald, Bob McGowan

(m), 20th Century. COVER: Ken Maynard.

2260 Hurry Sundown (Paramount, 1967, Jane Fonda, Michael Caine).

Hurry Sundown—Buddy Kaye (w), Hugo Montenegro (m), Chappell. COVER: Two Hands and Sun.

2261 Hurry Up or I'll Be Thirty (Embassy, 1973, John Lefkowitz, Danny DeVito).

Who Are You Now—Bruce Hart (w), Stephen Lawrence (m), Times. COVER: Black and white cover with title only.

2262 Hushed Hour, The (Garson, 1919, Blanche Sweet, Milton Sills).

Hushed Hour, The—Will Heelan (w), Will Haskins (m), Broadway. COVER: Blanche Sweet.

2263 Hush Hush Sweet Charlotte (20th Century-Fox, 1964, Bette Davis, Olivia de Havilland).

Hush Hush Sweet Charlotte—Mack David (w), Frank DeVol (m), Miller. COVER: Bette Davis, Olivia de Havilland.

2264 Hustle (Paramount, 1976, Burt Reynolds, Catherine Deneuve).

Hustle Theme—Frank DeVol (m), Famous; I Never Loved—Hermine Hilton (w), Frank DeVol (m), Famous. COVER: Burt Reynolds, Catherine Deneuve.

2265 Hustler, The (20th Century-Fox, 1961, Jackie Gleason, Paul Newman).

Hustler Theme—Kenyon Hopkins (m), Miller. COVER: Jackie Gleason, Paul Newman.

2266 Hypnotized (Sono Art, 1932, George Moran, Charlie Mack).

Anywhere with You/In a Gypsy's Heart/Love Bring Back My Love to Me—Bernie Grossman (w), Desider Vecsei (m), Famous. COVER: George Moran, Charlie Mack.

2267 I Accuse My Parents (PRC, 1944, Robert Lowell, Mary Beth Hughes).

Are You Happy in Your Work/ Love Came Between Us/Where Can You Be—Jay Livingston, Ray Evans (w,m), BMI. COVER: Pink cover with title only.

2268 I Aim at the Stars (Columbia, 1960, Curt Jurgens, Victoria Shaw).

I Aim at the Stars—Lionel Bart (w), Laurie Johnson (m), Columbia. COVER: Curt Jurgens, Victoria Shaw.

2269 I Am a Camera (Remus, 1951, Julie Harris, Laurence Harvey).

Why Do I—Carl Sigman (w), Ralph M. Siegel (m), Dartmouth. COVER: Sketches.

2270 I Am Suzanne (Fox, 1934, Lilian Harvey, Gene Raymond).

Eski-o-lay-li-o-mo/Just a Little Garret/St. Moritz Waltz—Forman Brown (w), Frederick Hollander (m), Movietone. COVER: Lilian Harvey.

2271 I Believed in You (Fox, 1934, John Boles, Rosemary Ames).

Out of a Blue Sky—William Kernell (w,m), Movietone. COVER: John Boles, Rosemary Ames.

2272 I Can't Give You Anything But Love (Universal, 1940, Peggy Moran, Johnny Downs).

Day by Day—Paul Smith (w), Frank Skinner (m), Robbins; I Can't Give You Anything But Love—Dorothy Fields (w), Jimmy McHugh (m), Mills; Sweetheart of School Fifty Nine—Paul Smith (w), Frank Skinner (m), Robbins. COVER: Peggy Moran, Johnny Downs.

2273 Ice Capades of 1942 (Republic, 1941, James Ellison, Dorothy Lewis).

Forever and Ever—Sol Meyer, George Brown (w), Jule Styne (m), Mills. COVER: James Ellison, Dorothy Lewis.

2274 Ice Castles (Columbia, 1978, Robby Benson, Colleen Dewhurst).

Through the Eyes of Love—Carole B. Sager (w), Marvin Hamlisch (m), Gold Horizon. COVER: Robby Benson, Lynn Holly Johnson.

2275 Ice Follies of 1939 (MGM, 1939, Joan Crawford, James Stewart).

It's All So New to Me—Marty Symes (w), Bernice Petkere (m), Feist; Something's Gotta Happen Soon—Arthur Freed (w), Nacio Herb Brown (m), Feist. COVER: Joan Crawford.

2276 Iceland (20th Century-Fox, 1942, Sonja Henie, John Payne).

I Like a Military Tune/It's the Lovers' Knot/Let's Bring New Glory to Old Glory/There Will Never Be Another You/You Can't Say No to a Soldier—Mack Gordon (w), Harry Warren (m), Mayfair. COVER: Sonja Henie, John Payne, Jack Oakie, Sammy Kaye.

2277 Ice Pirates (MGM, 1983, Robert Urich, Mary Crosby).

Ice Pirates Love Theme—Bruce Broughton (m), April. COVER: Robert Urich, Mary Crosby.

2278 Ice Station Zebra (MGM, 1968, Rock Hudson, Ernest Borgnine).

Ice Station Zebra Theme—Michel LeGrand (m), Feist; Listen to the Sea—Alan Bergman, Marilyn Bergman (w), Michel Legrand (m), Feist. COVER: Rock Hudson, Ernest Borgnine, and Others.

2279 Ich Will Nicht Wissen Wer Du Bist (Don't Tell Me Who You Are) (Tone, 1933, Liane Haid, Gustav Frolich).

To Think That You Should Care for Me—Mitchell Parish (w), Robert Stolz (m), Mills. COVER: Liane Haid, Gustav Froelich.

2280 I Confess (Warner Bros., 1953, Anne Baxter, Montgomery Clift).

Love Look What You've Done to Me—Ned Washington (w), Dimitri Tiomkin (m), Witmark. COVER: Anne Baxter, Montgomery Clift.

2281 I Could Go on Singing (United Artists, 1963, Judy Garland, Dirk Bogarde).

By Myself (VS)—Howard Dietz (w), Arthur Schwartz (m), DBH; Hello Bluebird (VS)—Cliff Friend (w,m), Remick; I Could Go on Singing—E. Y. Harburg (w), Harold Arlen (m), Harwin. COVER: Judy Garland.

2282 I Cover the Waterfront (United Artists, 1933, Claudette Colbert, Ben Lyons).

I Cover the Waterfront—Edward Heyman (w), John Green (m), Harms; Isn't It Heavenly—E. Y. Harburg (w), Joseph Meyer (m), Harms. COVER: Claudette Colbert, Ben Lyon.

2283 I'd Give My Life (Paramount, 1936, Frances Drake, Tom Brown).

Someday We'll Meet Again—Con Conrad, Herb Magidson (w,m), Famous. COVER: Frances Drake, Tom Brown.

2284 Idiot's Delight (MGM, 1939, Norma Shearer, Clark Gable).

How Strange—Gus Kahn (w), Earl Brent, Herbert Stothart (m), Feist. COVER: Norma Shearer, Clark Gable.

2285 Idle on Parade (Columbia, 1959, Anthony Newley, William Bendix).

Idle on Parade (B)—Len Praverman (w,m), Pan; Sat'day Night Rock-a-boogie (B)—Joe Henderson, Anthony Newley (w,m), Henderson. COVER: Anthony Newley.

2286 Idol Dancer, The (First National, 1920, Clarine Seymour, Richard Barthelmess).

Rainbow Isle—Betty Bentley (w), James Casey (m), Echo. COVER: Dancing Girl.

2287 Idolmaker (United Artists, 1980, Ray Sharkey, Tovah Feldshuh).

Here Is My Love/Idolmaker-Ten Songs—Jeff Barry (w,m), Unart. COVER: Paul Land.

2288 I Don't Care Girl, The (20th Century-Fox, 1953, Mitzi Gaynor, David Wayne).

As Long as You Care—George Jessel (w), Joe Cooper (m), Miller; Here Comes Love Again—George Jessel,

Eliot Daniel (w,m), Miller. COVER: Mitzi Gaynor, David Wayne.

2289 I Dood It (MGM, 1943, Eleanor Powell, Red Skelton).

Shorter Than Me (BW)—Don Raye (w), Gene DePaul (m), Feist; So Long Sarah Jane—Lew Brown, Ralph Freed (w), Sammy Fain (m), Feist; Star Eyes—Don Raye, Gene DePaul (w,m), Feist. COVER: Eleanor Powell, Red Skelton, Jimmy Dorsey.

2290 I'd Rather Be Rich (Universal, 1964, Sandra Dee, Robert Goulet).

Almost There—Jerry Keller, Gloria Shayne (w,m), Northern; I'd Rather Be Rich—Richard Maltby, David Shire (w,m), Northern; Where Are You—Harold Adamson (w), Jimmy McHugh (m), Feist. COVER: Sandra Dee, Robert Goulet, Andy Williams.

2291 I Dream Too Much (RKO, 1935, Lily Pons, Henry Fonda).

I Dream Too Much/I Got Love/I'm the Echo/Jockey on the Carousel, The—Dorothy Fields (w), Jerome Kern (m), Harms. COVER: Lily Pons.

2292 If a Man Answers (Universal, 1962, Sandra Dee, Bobby Darin).

If a Man Answers/True True Love—Bobby Darin (w,m), Adaris. COVER: Sandra Dee, Bobby Darin.

2293 If Ever I See You Again (Columbia, 1977, Shelly Hack, Joe Brooks).

California/Come Share My Love/If Ever I See You Again/When It's Over—Joe Brooks (w,m), Columbia. COVER: Shelly Hack, Joe Brooks.

2294 If I Had My Way (Universal, 1940, Bing Crosby, Gloria Jean).

April Played the Fiddle—Johnny Burke (w), James Monaco (m), Santly Joy; If I Had My Way—Lou Klein (w), James Kendis (m), Paull Pioneer; I Haven't Time to Be a Millionaire/Meet the Sun Half Way/Pessimistic Character, The—Johnny Burke (w), James Monaco (m), Santly Joy. COVER: Bing Crosby, Gloria Jean.

2295 If I'm Lucky (20th Century-Fox, 1946, Vivian Blaine, Perry Como).

Bet Your Bottom Dollar/Follow the Band/If I'm Lucky/Jam Session in Brazil/One More Kiss—Edgar DeLange (w), Josef Myrow (m), Triangle. COVER: Perry Como, Vivian Blaine, Harry James, Carmen Miranda.

2296 If It's Tuesday This Must Be Belgium (United Artists, 1969, Ian McShane, Suzanne Pleshette).

If It's Tuesday This Must Be Belgium—Donovan Leitch (w,m), Donovan. COVER: Donovan.

2297 If This Isn't Love (RKO, 1934, Dorothy Lee, Walter Woolf).

If It Isn't Love—Val Burton, Will Jason (w,m), Engel. COVER: Dorothy Lee, Walter Woolf.

2298 If Winter Comes (Fox, 1922, Percy Marmont, Ann Forrest).

If Winter Comes #1—William Dickson (w), Fred Vanderpool (m), Witmark; If Winter Comes #2 (B)—Reginald Arkell (w), H. M. Tennent (m), Ascherberg. COVER: Percy Marmont, and Others.

2299 If Winter Comes (MGM, 1947, Walter Pidgeon, Deborah Kerr).

If Winter Comes—Kim Gannon (w), Imogen Carpenter (m), Robbins. COVER: Walter Pidgeon, Deborah Kerr, Angela Lansbury.

2300 If You Knew Susie (RKO, Eddie Cantor, Joan Davis).

If You Knew Susie—B. G. DeSylva, Joseph Meyer (w,m), Shapiro Bernstein; My Brooklyn Love Song—George Tibbles, Ramey Driss (w,m), Triangle; My How the Time Goes By—Harold Adamson (w), Jimmy McHugh (m), Chappell. COVER: Eddie Cantor, Joan Davis.

2301 Igloo (Universal, 1932, Chee Ak, Kya Tuk).

Eskimo Melodies (PC)—Val Burton, Corynn Kiehl, Ed Kilenyi, P. Brunell (m), Sam Fox. COVER: None.

2302 I Hear a New Song (Anderson, 1966, Barbara Loren, Greg Loren).

I Hear a New Song—Ken Anderson, Gloria Roe (w,m), Rodeheaver. COVER: Barbara and Greg Loren.

2303 I Kiss Your Hand Madame (Super, 1929, Marlene Dietrich, Harry Leidtke).

I Kiss Your Hand Madame (B)— Andre Mauprey, Ralp Erwin (w,m), Brull. COVER: Marlene Dietrich.

2304 I Know Where I'm Going (Universal, 1947, Wendy Hiller, Roger Livesey).

I Know Where I'm Going—County Antrim (w,m), Boston. COVER: Plaids.

2305 I Like It That Way (Universal, 1934, Gloria Stuart, Roger Pryor).

I Like It That Way/Let's Put Two and Two Together/Miss 1934— Con Conrad, Sidney Mitchell, Archie Gottler (w,m), Sam Fox. COVER: Gloria Stuart, Roger Pryor.

2306 I Live for Love (Warner Bros., 1935, Dolores Del Rio, Everett Marshall).

I Live for Love/I Wanna Play House with You (PC)/Mine Alone/ Silver Wings—Mort Dixon (w), Allie Wrubel (m), Witmark. COVER: Dolores Del Rio, Everett Marshall.

2307 I'll Be Seeing You (United Artists, 1944, Ginger Rogers, Joseph Cotten).

I'll Be Seeing You—Irving Kahal (w), Sammy Fain (m), Williamson. COVER: Ginger Rogers, Joseph Cotten, Shirley Temple.

2308 I'll Be Yours (Universal, 1947, Deanna Durbin, Tom Drake).

It's Dreamtime—Jack Brooks (w), Walter Schuman (m), Santly Joy; Sari Waltz—C. Cushing, E. Heath (w), Emmerich Kalman (m), Marks. COVER: Deanna Durbin.

2309 I'll Cry Tomorrow (MGM, 1956, Susan Hayward, Eddie Albert).

Happiness Is a Thing Called Joe— E. Y. Harburg (w), Harold Arlen (m), Feist; I'll Cry Tomorrow—Johnny Mercer (w), Alex North (m), Rob-

bins; Sing You Sinners—Sam Coslow, Franke Harling (w,m), Famous; When the Red Red Robin Comes Bob Bob Bobbin' Along—Harry Woods (w,m), Feist. COVER: Susan Hayward.

2310 Illegal (Warner Bros., 1931, Margot Grahame, Isobel Elsom).

Can't We Talk It Over (B)—Ned Washington (w), Victor Young (m), Feldman; Now That You're Gone (B)—Gus Kahn (w), Ted Fiorito (m), Feldman; Too Late (B)—Sam Lewis (w), Victor Young (m), Feldman; Was That the Human Thing to Do (B)—Joe Young (w), Sammy Fain (m), Feldman. COVER: Margot Grahame.

2311 I'll Get By (20th Century-Fox, 1950, June Haver, William Lundigan).

Fifth Avenue—Mack Gordon (w), Harry Warren (m), Robbins; I'll Get By—Roy Turk (w), Fred Ahlert (m), Bourne; It's Been a Long Long Time —Sammy Cahn (w), Jule Styne (m), Morris; I've Got the World on a String—Ted Koehler (w), Harold Arlen (m), Mills; Once in a While—Bud Green (w), Michael Edwards (m), Miller; Taking a Chance on Love— John Latouche, Ted Fetter (w), Vernon Duke (m), Miller; There Will Never Be Another You—Mack Gordon (w), Harry Warren (m), Mayfair. COVER: June Haver, William Lundigan, Harry James, Gloria DeHaven.

2312 I'll Remember April (Universal, 1945, Gloria Jean, Kirby Grant).

Cha-da-boom/Dawn—Harry Tobias (w), Al Sherman (m), Hollywood; I'll Remember April—Don Raye, Gene DePaul, Pat Johnston (w,m), Leeds. COVER: Gloria Jean, Kirby Grant.

2313 I'll See You in My Dreams (Warner Bros., 1951, Doris Day, Danny Thomas).

Carolina in the Morning—Gus Kahn (w), Walter Donaldson (m), Remick; I Wish I Had a Girl—Gus

Kahn (w), Grace LeRoy (m), Miller; I'll See You in My Dreams—Gus Kahn (w), Isham Jones (m), Feist; I'm Thru with Love—Gus Kahn (w), Matt Malneck, Fud Livingston (m), Robbins; Love Me or Leave Me/ Makin' Whoopee—Gus Kahn (w), Walter Donaldson (m), BVC; Memories—Gus Kahn (w), Egbert Van Alstyne (m), Remick; My Buddy—Gus Kahn (w), Walter Donaldson (m), Remick; One I Love, The/ Swingin' Down the Lane—Gus Kahn (w), Isham Jones (m), Feist; Toot Toot Tootsie—Gus Kahn, Ernie Erdman, Dan Russo (w,m), Feist. COVER: Doris Day, Danny Thomas.

2314 I'll Take Romance (Columbia, 1937, Grace Moore, Melvyn Douglas).

I'll Take Romance—Oscar Hammerstein (w), Ben Oakland (m), Berlin. COVER: Grace Moore.

2315 I'll Take Sweden (United Artists, 1965, Bob Hope, Tuesday Weld).

I'll Take Sweden—Diane Lampert (w), Kenneth Lauber (m), Unart. COVER: Bob Hope, Tuesday Weld.

2316 I'll Tell the World (Universal, 1934, Lee Tracy, Gloria Stuart).

I'll Tell the World—Louise Townsend (w,m), Browne; I'm Glad That I Found You—Inez Shelley (w), Rosalie Stall (m), Browne; Life Is But a Dream Without You—Otto Riley, Wayne Johnson (w,m), Browne; When Will Our Dreams Come True—B. L. Michel, Clinton Keithley (w,m), Browne. COVER: Lee Tracy, Gloria Stuart.

2317 Illusion (Paramount, 1929, Buddy Rogers, Nancy Carroll).

Levee Love/Revolutionary Rhythm —Lou Davis, Fred Coots, Larry Spier (w,m), Remick; When the Real Thing Comes Your Way—Larry Spier (w,m, Remick. COVER: Buddy Rogers, Nancy Carroll.

2318 I Loved You Wednesday (Fox, 1933, Warner Baxter, Elissa Landi).

Hills of Old New Hampshire—Will Vodery (w,m), Movietone; I Found You, I Lost You, I Found You Again —L. Wolfe Gilbert (w), I. Kornblum (m), Movietone; It's All for the Best —Richard Whiting (w,m), Movietone; Roll Your Bones—Sidney Mitchell, Harry Akst (w,m), Movietone. COVER: Black and white cover with title only.

2319 I Love Melvin (MGM, 1953, Debbie Reynolds, Donald O'Connor).

And There You Are/I Wanna Wander/A Lady Loves/Life Has Its Funny Little Ups and Downs/Saturday Afternoon Before the Game/We Have Never Met as Yet/Where Did You Learn to Dance—Mack Gordon (w), Josef Myrow (m), Feist. COVER: Debbie Reynolds, Donald O'Connor.

2320 I Love You Alice B. Toklas (Warner Bros., 1968, Peter Sellers, Jo Van Fleet).

I Love You Alice B. Toklas—Paul Mazursky, Larry Tucker (w), Elmer Bernstein (m), Warner. COVER: Peter Sellers.

2321 I Married an Angel (MGM, 1942, Nelson Eddy, Jeanette MacDonald).

I Married an Angel (B), Lorenz Hart (w), Richard Rodgers (m), Day. COVER: Nelson Eddy, Jeanette MacDonald.

2322 I'm Cold (Universal, 1954, Cartoon).

Chilly Willy—Mary Jo Rush (w, m), Bibo. COVER: Cartoon.

2323 I Met Him in Paris (Paramount, 1937, Robert Young, Claudette Colbert).

I Met Him in Paris—Helen Mainardi (w), Hoagy Carmichael (m), Famous. COVER: Robert Young, Claudette Colbert, Melvyn Douglas.

2324 I'm from Arkansas (PRC, 1944, El Brendel, Slim Summerville).

Don't Turn Me Down, Little Darlin'—Harry Tobias, Judy Canova, Ed Dean, Zeke Canova (w,m), Leeds. COVER: Judy Canova.

2325 Imitation of Life (Universal, 1959, John Gavin, Lana Turner).
Imitation of Life—Paul F. Webster (w), Sammy Fain (m), Northern. COVER: Lana Turner, John Gavin.

2326 I'm No Angel (Paramount, 1933, Mae West, Cary Grant).
I Found a New Way to Go to Town/I'm No Angel—Gladys DuBois, Ben Ellison (w), Harvey Brooks (m), Shapiro Bernstein; I Want You I Need You—Ben Ellison (w), Harvey Brooks (m), Shapiro Bernstein; That Dallas Man/They Call Me Sister Honky Tonk—Gladys DuBois, Ben Ellison (w), Harvey Brooks (m), Shapiro Bernstein. COVER: Mae West.

2327 I'm Nobody's Sweetheart (Universal, 1940, Dennis O'Keefe, Constance Moore).
Got Love—Everett Carter (w), Milton Rosen (m), Robbins; Nobody's Sweetheart—Gus Kahn, Ernie Erdman, Bill Meyers, Elmer Schoebel (w,m), Mills; There Goes My Romance—Everett Carter (w), Milton Rosen (m), Robbins. COVER: Dennis O'Keefe, Constance Moore.

2328 I, Mobster (20th Century-Fox, 1958, Steve Cochran, Lita Milan).
Give Me Love/Lost Lonely and Looking for Love—Jerry Winn (w), Edward Alpherson (m), Miller. COVER: Steve Cochran, Lita Milan.

2329 Impatient Years, The (Columbia, 1944, Jean Arthur, Lee Bowman).
Who Said Dreams Don't Come True—Harry Akst, Benny Davis, Al Jolson (w,m), Williamson. COVER: Jean Arthur, Lee Bowman.

2330 Impossible Years, The (MGM, 1967, David Niven, Lola Albright).
Impossible Years, The—Mitch Margo, Phil Margo, Hank Nedress, Jay Siegel (w,m), Hastings. COVER: David Niven, Lola Albright.

2331 In a Chinese Temple Garden (Tiffany, 1929, Stars Unknown).
Persianna—Jamie Erickson (m), Quincke. COVER: Pink Flowers.

2332 Inadmissible Evidence (Paramount, 1968, Nicol Williamson, Eleanor Fazan).
Inadmissible Evidence Music Score—Dudley Moore (m), Famous. COVER: Green cover with title only.

2333 In a Lonely Place (Columbia, 1950, Humphrey Bogart, Gloria Grahame).
I Hadn't Anyone Till You—Ray Noble (w,m), ABC. COVER: Humphrey Bogart, Gloria Grahame.

2334 In Caliente (Warner Bros., 1935, Dolores Del Rio, Pat O'Brien).
In Caliente/Lady in Red, The—Mort Dixon (w), Allie Wrubel (m), Remick; Muchacha—Al Dubin (w), Harry Warren (m), Remick; To Call You My Own—Mort Dixon (w), Allie Wrubel (m), Remick. COVER: Dolores Del Rio.

2335 Incendiary Blonde (Paramount, 1945, Betty Hutton, Arturo de Cordova).
Ragtime Cowboy Joe—Grant Clarke (w), Lewis Muir, Maurice Abrahams (m), Alfred; What Do You Want to Make Those Eyes at Me For—Joe McCarthy, Howard Johnson, James Monaco (w,m), Feist. COVER: Betty Hutton.

2336 In Cold Blood (Columbia, 1967, Robert Blake, Scott Wilson).
Lonely Bottles—Quincy Jones (m), Colgems. COVER: Four Eyes.

2337 Incredible Mr. Limpet, The (Warner Bros., 1964, Don Knotts, Carole Cook).
Be Careful How You Wish/Deep Rapture/I Wish I Were a Fish—Harold Adamson (w), Sammy Fain (m), Witmark. COVER: Don Knotts.

2338 Indiana Jones and the Temple of Doom (Paramount, 1984, Harrison Ford, Kate Capshaw).
Anything Goes—Cole Porter (w, m), Warner; Raiders March/Indiana Jones-Three Themes—John Williams (m), Bantha. COVER: Harrison Ford.

2339 Indian Fighter (United Artists, 1956, Kirk Douglas, Elsa Martinelli).

Indian Fighter Theme—Irving Gordon (w), Franz Waxman (m), Cromwell. COVER: Indian Signs.

2340 Indiscreet (United Artists, 1931, Gloria Swanson, Ben Lyon).

Come to Me/If You Haven't Got Love—B. G. DeSylva, Lew Brown, Ray Henderson (w,m), DBH. COVER: Gloria Swanson.

2341 Indiscreet (Warner Bros., 1958, Ingrid Bergman, Cary Grant).

Indiscreet—Sammy Cahn (w), Jimmy Van Heusen (m), Morris. COVER: Ingrid Bergman, Cary Grant.

2342 Indiscretion of an American Wife (Columbia, 1954, Jennifer Jones, Montgomery Clift).

Autumn in Rome/Indiscretion—Sammy Cahn (w), Paul Weston (m), Cromwell. COVER: Jennifer Jones, Montgomery Clift.

2343 I Never Promised You a Rose Garden (New World, 1977, Bibi Anderson, Ben Piazza).

Deborah's Theme—Paul Chihara (m), Shawnee. COVER: A Rose.

2344 I Never Sang for My Father (Columbia, 1971, Melvyn Douglas, Gene Hackman).

Strangers—Cynthia Weil (w), Barry Mann (m), Colgems. COVER: A Cloudy Sky.

2345 In Gay Madrid (MGM, 1930, Ramon Novarro, Dorothy Jordan).

Dark Night—Clifford Grey (w), Herbert Stothart (m), Xavier Cugat (m), Robbins; Into My Heart—Roy Turk (w), Fred Ahlert (m), Robbins; Santiago—Clifford Grey (w), Herbert Stothart, Xavier Cugat (m), Robbins. COVER: Ramon Novarro.

2346 In Harm's Way (Paramount, 1965, John Wayne, Kirk Douglas).

In Harm's Way Love Theme—Jerry Goldsmith (m), Chappell. COVER: A Hand.

2347 Inherit the Wind (United Artists, 1960, Spencer Tracy, Gene Kelly).

Inherit the Wind Theme—Ernest Gold (m), Unart. COVER: Black and white cover with title only.

2348 In Like Flint (20th Century-Fox, 1967, James Coburn, Lee J. Cobb).

Your Zowie Face—Leslie Bricusse (w), Jerry Goldsmith (m), Hastings. COVER: James Coburn, and Girls.

2349 In Mizzoura (Paramount, 1919, Robert Warwick, Monte Blue).

In Mizzoura—Carey Morgan, Abel Green, Lew Porter (w,m), Harris. COVER: Robert Warwick.

2350 Innocent Affair, An (Don't Trust Your Husband) (United Artists, 1948, Fred MacMurray, Madeleine Carroll).

Innocent Affair, An—Walter Kent (w,m), Morris; These Things Are You—Kim Gannon (w), Walter Kent (m), Morris. COVER: Madeleine Carroll, Fred MacMurray.

2351 Innocent Bystanders (Paramount, 1973, Stanley Baker, Geraldine Chaplin).

What Makes the Man—Norman Smith (w), John Keating (m), Famous. COVER: Stanley Baker, Geraldine Chaplin.

2352 Innocents, The (20th Century-Fox, 1961, Deborah Kerr, Peter Wyngarde).

O Willow Waly—Paul Dehn (w), George Auric (m), Robbins. COVER: Deborah Kerr, and Boy.

2353 Innocents of Paris (Paramount, 1929, Maurice Chevalier, Sylvia Beecher).

It's a Habit of Mine/Louise/On Top of the World Alone/Wait Till You See Ma Cherie—Leo Robin (w), Richard Whiting (m), Famous. COVER: Maurice Chevalier, Sylvia Beecher.

2354 Inn of the Sixth Happiness (20th Century-Fox, 1958, Ingrid Bergman, Curt Jurgens).

Children's Marching Song—Malcolm Arnold (m), Miller. COVER: Ingrid Bergman, Curt Jurgens, Robert Donat.

2355 In Old Arizona (Fox, 1929, Warner Baxter, Edmund Lowe).

My Tonia—B. G. DeSylva, Lew Brown, Ray Henderson (w,m), DBH. COVER: Warner Baxter, Dorothy Burgess.

2356 In Old Cheyenne (Republic, 1941, Roy Rogers, George Hayes).

Bonita—Jule Styne, Sol Meyer (w, m), Mills. COVER: Roy Rogers.

2357 In Old Chicago (20th Century-Fox, 1938, Alice Faye, Tyrone Power).

I'll Never Let You Cry—Sydney Mitchell (w), Lew Pollack (m), Hollywood; In Old Chicago—Mack Gordon, Harry Revel (w,m), Feist; I've Taken a Fancy to You/Take a Dip in the Sea—Sydney Mitchell (w), Lew Pollack (m), Hollywood. COVER: Alice Faye, Tyrone Power, Don Ameche.

2358 In Old Kentucky (First National, 1920, Anita Stewart, Edwin Coxen).

In Old Kentucky—Anita Stewart (w,m), Berlin. COVER: Anita Stewart.

2359 In Old Monterey (Republic, 1939, Gene Autry, Smiley Burnette).

Little Pardner—Gene Autry, Fred Rose, Johnny Marvin (w,m), Western. COVER: Gene Autry.

2360 In Old Oklahoma (War of the Wildcats) (Republic, 1943, John Wayne, Martha Scott).

Put Your Arms Around Me Honey—Junie McCree (w), Albert Von Tilzer (m), Vol Tilzer; Red Wing—Thurland Chattaway (w), Kerry Mills (m), Paull Pioneer. COVER: John Wayne, Martha Scott.

2361 In Old Santa Fe (Mascot, 1934, Ken Maynard, Gene Autry).

As Long as I've Got My Dog—Wallace MacDonald (w), Harold Lewis, Bernie Grossman (m), Mills; Down in Old Santa Fe—Bernie Grossman (w), Harold Lewis (m), Mills. COVER: Gene Autry.

2362 In Person (RKO, 1935, Ginger Rogers, George Brent).

Don't Mention Love/Got a New Lease on Life/Out of Sight Out of Mind—Dorothy Fields (w), Oscar Levant (m), Berlin. COVER: Ginger Rogers.

2363 In Search of Castaways (Buena Vista, 1961, Maurice Chevalier, Hayley Mills).

Castaway/Enjoy It/Let's Climb-Grimpons/Merci Beaucoup—Richard Sherman, Robert Sherman (w,m), Wonderland. COVER: Maurice Chevalier, Hayley Mills.

2364 Inside Daisy Clover (Warner Bros., 1965, Natalie Wood, Robert Redford).

Daisy—André Previn (m), Remick; You're Gonna Hear from Me—Dory Previn (w), André Previn (m), Remick. COVER: Natalie Wood, Robert Redford, Christopher Plummer.

2365 Inside Straight (MGM, 1951, David Brian, Arlene Dahl).

Up in a Balloon—H. B. Farnie (w,m), Robbins; What Can a Poor Maiden Do—Earl Brent (w), Charles Horn (m), Robbins. COVER: David Brian, Arlene Dahl.

2366 In Society (Universal, 1944, Bud Abbott, Lou Costello).

My Dreams Are Getting Better All the Time/No Bout Adout It—Mann Curtis (w), Vic Mizzy (m), Santly Joy; Rehearsin'—Bobby Worth, Stanley Cowan (w,m), Morros. COVER: Abbott and Costello, Marion Hutton.

2367 Inspector Clouseau (United Artists, 1968, Alan Arkin, Frank Finlay).

Inspector Clouseau Theme—Ken Thorne (m), Unart. COVER: Black and white cover with title only.

2368 Inspector General, The (Warner Bros., 1949, Danny Kaye, Barbara Bates).

Happy Times—Sylvia Fine (w,m), Harms. COVER: Danny Kaye, Barbara Bates.

2369 Insure Your Wife (Fox, 1935, Conchita Montenegro, Raul Roulien).

Radiante—Enrique Poncela (w), Ernesto Piedra (m), Movietone; Sneezing Love—Enrique Poncela (w), Raul Roulien, Troy Sanders (m), Movietone. COVER: Black and white cover with title only.

2370 Interlude (Universal, 1957, June Allyson, Rossano Brazzi).

Interlude—Paul F. Webster (w), Frank Skinner (m), Northern. COVER: June Allyson, Rossano Brazzi.

2371 Interlude (Columbia, 1967, Oskar Werner, Barbara Ferris).

Interlude—George Delerue (m), Colgems. COVER: Blue cover with title only.

2372 Intermezzo (United Artists, 1939, Ingrid Bergman, Leslie Howard).

Intermezzo—Robert Henning (w), Heinz Provost (m), Schuberth. COVER: Ingrid Bergman, Leslie Howard.

2373 International House (Paramount, 1933, W. C. Fields, Rudy Vallee).

My Blue Bird's Singing the Blues/Thank Heaven for You—Leo Robin (w), Ralph Rainger (m), Famous. COVER: Rudy Vallee, Rose Marie.

2374 International Velvet (MGM, 1978, Tatum O'Neal, Christopher Plummer).

Birth of a Foal/Cross Country/First Love/International Velvet Theme—Francis Lai (m), Variety; Ride (Sarah's Theme)—Leslie Bricusse (w), Francis Lai (m), MGM. COVER: Tatum O'Neal, Nanette Newman, and Others.

2375 Interrupted Melody (MGM, 1955, Glenn Ford, Eleanor Parker).

Over the Rainbow—E. Y. Harburg (w), Harold Arlen (m), Feist. COVER: Glenn Ford, Eleanor Parker.

2376 In the Cool of the Day (MGM, 1962, Peter Finch, Jane Fonda).

In the Cool of the Day—Liam Sullivan (w), Manos Hadjidakis (m), Hastings; In the Cool of the Day Theme—Manos Hadjidakis (m). COVER: Jane Fonda, Angela Lansbury, Peter Finch.

2377 In the Days of St. Patrick (General, 1921, Ira Allen, Vernon Whitten).

In the Days of St. Patrick—William Hart (w), Ed Nelson (m), Sunrise. COVER: A Saint.

2378 In the Good Old Summertime (MGM, 1949, Judy Garland, Van Johnson).

I Don't Care—Jean Lennox (w), Harry Sutton (m), Marks; In the Good Old Summertime—Ren Shields (w), George Evans (m), Marks; Last Night When We Were Young (PC)—E. Y. Harburg (w), Harold Arlen (m), Bourne; Meet Me Tonight in Dreamland—Beth Whitson (w), Leo Friedman (m), Shapiro Bernstein; Merry Christmas—Janice Torre (w), Fred Spielman (m), Robbins; Play That Barber Shop Chord—Bill Tracey, Ballard MacDonald (w), Lewis Muir (m), Shapiro Bernstein; Put Your Arms Around Me Honey—Junie McCree (w), Albert Von Tilzer (m), Broadway. COVER: Van Johnson, Judy Garland.

2379 In the Headlines (Warner Bros., 1929, Marion Nixon, Grant Withers).

Love Will Find a Way—Al Dubin (w), Joe Burke (m), Witmark. COVER: Marion Nixon, Grant Withers.

2380 In the Heat of the Night (United Artists, 1967, Sidney Poitier, Rod Steiger).

In the Heat of the Night—Alan Bergman, Marilyn Bergman (w), Quincy Jones (m), Unart. COVER: Movie Scene.

2381 In the Name of the Law (FBO, 1922, Ralph Lewis, Claire McDowell).

Just Keep on Smiling—Neville Fleeson (w), Albert Von Tilzer (m), Von Tilzer. COVER: A Policeman.

2382 In the Navy (Universal, 1941, Bud Abbott, Lou Costello).

Flotsam and Jetsam—Don Raye, Gene DePaul (w,m), Leeds; Gimmie Some Skin My Friend—Don Raye,

Gene DePaul, Red Mack (w,m), Leeds; Hula Ba Luau/Off to See the World/Sailor's Life for Me, A/Starlight Starbright/We're in the Navy—Don Raye, Gene DePaul (w,m), Leeds. COVER: Andrews Sisters, Abbott and Costello.

2383 In the Nick (Columbia, 1960, Anthony Newley, Anne Aubrey).

In the Nick (B)—Lionel Bart (w, m), Robbins. COVER: Anthony Newley.

2384 Intimate Stranger, The (Finger of Guilt) (RKO, 1956, Richard Basehart, Mary Murphy).

Intimate Stranger Theme (B)—Trevor Duncan (m), Robbins. COVER: Mary Murphy.

2385 Intolerance (Griffith, 1924, [1956 Revival], Mae Marsh, Robert Harron).

Intolerance-Nine Themes—Lee Irwin (m), Marks. COVER: D. W. Griffith.

2386 Intrigue (United Artists, 1947, George Raft, June Havoc).

Intrigue—Sam Lerner, Harry Akst (w,m), Triangle. COVER: George Raft, June Havoc, Helen Carter.

2387 Invitation (MGM, 1952, Van Johnson, Dorothy McGuire).

Invitation—Paul F. Webster (w), Bronislau Kaper (m), Robbins; Invitation-Theme—Bronislau Kaper (m). COVER: An Invitation.

2388 Invitation to a Gun Fighter (United Artists, 1964, Yul Brynner, Janice Rule).

Invitation to a Gun Fighter-Lullabye—David Raksin (m), Unart. COVER: Black and white cover with title only.

2389 In Which We Serve (United Artists, 1942, Noel Coward, John Mills).

In Which We Serve-Seven Themes (B)—Noel Coward (m), Chappell. COVER: A Battleship.

2390 I Only Asked (Columbia, 1958, Bernard Bresslaw, Michael Medwin).

Whistling Sergeant Major, The (B)—Ben Bernard (m), Avenue. COVER: A Soldier.

2391 I Ought to Be in Pictures (20th Century-Fox, 1982, Walter Matthau, Ann Margaret).

One Hello—Carol B. Sager (w), Marvin Hamlisch (m), Warner. COVER: Randy Crawford.

2392 Ipcress File, The (Universal, 1965, Michael Caine, Nigel Green).

A Man Alone—John Barry (m), Northern. COVER: Michael Caine.

2393 Ireland Today (Irish American, 1947, Michael Shannon, Julie Conway).

Ireland Today-Seven Songs—Monte Carlo, Alma Sanders (w,m), Miller. COVER: Michael Shannon, Julie Conway.

2394 Irene (RKO, 1940, Ray Milland, Anna Neagle).

Alice Blue Gown/Alicia/Castle of Dreams/Irene/You've Got Me Out on a Limb—Joseph McCarthy (w), Harry Tierney (m), Feist. COVER: Anna Neagle, Ray Milland, Billie Burke, and Others.

2395 Irish Eyes Are Smiling 20th Century-Fox, 1944, Dick Haymes, June Haver).

Bessie in a Bustle—Mack Gordon (w), James Monaco (m), BVC; Dear Little Boy of Mine—J. Keirn Brennan (w), Ernest Ball (m), Witmark; I'll Forget You—Annella Burns (w), Ernest Ball (m), Witmark; Little Bit of Heaven, A/Let the Rest of the World Go By—J. Keirn Brennan (w), Ernest Ball (m), Witmark; Love Me and the World Is Mine—Dave Reed (w), Ernest Ball (m), Witmark; Mother Machree—Chauncey Olcott (w), Ernest Ball (m), Witmark; When Irish Eyes Are Smiling—Chauncey Olcott, George Graff (w), Ernest Ball (m), Witmark. COVER: Monty Woolley, Dick Haymes, June Haver.

2396 Irma La Douce (United Artists, 1963, Jack Lemmon, Shirley MacLaine).

Irma La Douce Theme—Dory Previn (w), André Previn (m), Unart. COVER: Cartoon Sketches.

2397 Iron Claw, The (Pathe, 1916, Pearl White, Creighton Hale).

Iron Claw Dance—Benjamin Richmond (m), Howley. COVER: Pearl White.

2398 Iron Eagle (Tri-Star, 1985, Louis Gossett, Jason Gedrick).

One Vision—Fred Mercury, Joan Deacon, Brian May, Roger Taylor (w, m), Warner; Hide in the Rainbow (VS)—Ronnie J. Dio (w,m), Columbia; Intense (VS)—George Clinton (w,m), Columbia; It's Too Late (VS) —John Dexter, Paul Hackman (w, m), Columbia; Love Can Make You Cry (VS)—Steve Kehr, Ian Hunter, Michael Kehr (w,m), Columbia; Maniac House (VS)—Kimberley Rew (w,m), Columbia; Never Say Die Iron Eagle (VS)—Jake Hooker, Duane Hitchings (w,m), Columbia; Road of the Gypsy (VS)—Mark Pastoria, Brian Pastoria (w,m), Columbia; These Are the Good Times (VS)— Miles Hunter (w,m), Columbia; This Raging Fire (VS)—Bob Halligan (w, m), Columbia. COVER: Louis Gossett, Jason Gedrick.

2399 Iron Eagle II (Tri-Star, 1988, Louis Gossett, Mark Humphrey).

Enemies Like You and Me—Paul Janz, Elizabeth Janz (w,m), Irving. COVER: Louis Gossett, Pilots, and Planes.

2400 Iron Horse, The (Fox, 1924, George O'Brien, Madge Bellamy).

March of the Iron Horse—Erno Rapee (m), Belwin. COVER: Railroad Workers and Train.

2401 Iron Mask, The (United Artists, 1929, Douglas Fairbanks, Leon Barry).

One for All, All for One—Jo Trent (w), Hugo Riesenfeld, Louis Alter (m), Robbins. COVER: Douglas Fairbanks.

2402 Irreconcilable Differences (Warner Bros., 1985, Ryan O'Neal, Shelley Long).

Harmony—Paul DeSennerville (w,

m), Laadeline; Way I Loved You, The—Oliver Toussaint (w,m), Laadeline. COVER: Richard Clayderman.

2403 Is Everybody Happy (Warner Bros., 1929, Ted Lewis, Alice Day).

I'm Blue for You, New Orleans/ I'm the Medicine Man for the Blues— Grant Clarke (w), Harry Akst (m), Witmark; In the Land of Jazz—J. Keirn Brennan (w), Ray Perkins (m), Witmark; Samoa/Wouldn't It Be Wonderful—Grant Clarke (w), Harry Akst (m), Witmark. COVER: Ted Lewis.

2404 Is Everybody Happy (Columbia, 1943, Ted Lewis, Nan Wynn).

On the Sunny Side of the Street— Dorothy Fields (w), Jimmy McHugh (m), Shapiro Bernstein. COVER: Ted Lewis.

2405 Ishtar (Columbia, 1987, Warren Beatty, Dustin Hoffman).

Little Darlin' (VS)—Maurice Williams (w,m), Columbia. COVER: Black and white cover with title only.

2406 I-Ski Love-Ski You-Ski (Paramount, 1936, Cartoon).

Won't You Come and Climb the Mountain with Me (VS)—Bob Rothberg (w), Sam Timberg (m), Famous. COVER: Popeye.

2407 Island, The (Universal, 1981, Michael Caine, David Warner).

Island, The—Alan Bergman, Marilyn Bergman (w), Victor Martins, Ivin Lins (m), Kidada. COVER: An Island.

2408 Island in the Sky (Warner Bros., 1953, John Wayne, Lloyd Nolan).

Island in the Sky—Emil Newman, John Lehman, Hugo Friedhofer (w, m), Simon. COVER: John Wayne.

2409 Island in the Sun (20th Century-Fox, 1957, James Mason, Joan Fontaine).

Cocoanut Woman/Don't Ever Love Me/Island in the Sun—Harry Belafonte, Lord Burgess (w,m), Clara. COVER: Harry Belafonte.

2410 Island of Lost Men (Paramount, 1939, Anna May Wong, J. Carrol Naish).

Music on the Shore—Frank Loesser (w), Frederick Hollander (m), Paramount. COVER: Anna May Wong.

2411 Island of Love (Warner Bros., 1963, Robert Preston, Tony Randall).

Speak Not a Word—Harold Adamson (w), Sammy Fain (m), Witmark. COVER: Robert Preston, Tony Randall, and Girl.

2412 Islands in Paradise (Independent, 1964, Travelogue).

Red Beard/Tropic Isle—Monte LaFleche (w,m), LaFleche. COVER: Purple cover with title only.

2413 Islands in the Stream (Paramount, 1976, George Scott, David Hemmings).

Islands in the Stream—Jerry Goldsmith (m), Ensign. COVER: George Scott.

2414 Isle of Escape (Warner Bros., 1930, Betty Compson, Myrna Loy).

My Kalua Rose—Al Bryan (w), Eddie Ward (m), Chappell. COVER: Monte Blue, Betty Compson.

2415 Isle of Forgotten Sins (PRC, 1943, John Carradine, Gale Sondergaard).

Sleepy Island Moon—June Stillman, Leo Erdody (w,m), Mills. COVER: Clouds.

2416 Isle of Lost Ships (First National, 1929, Jason Robards, Virginia Valli).

Ship of My Dreams—Al Bryan (w), George Meyers (m), Piantadosi. COVER: Jason Robards, Virginia Valli.

2417 Isle of Zorda (Pathe, 1922, Romuald Joube, Yvette Andreyor).

Isle of Zorda—Milt Hagen, Herb Crooker (w), Victor Nurnberg (m), Caine. COVER: Dancing Girl.

2418 Isn't It Romantic (Paramount, 1948, Mona Freeman, Veronica Lake).

At the Nickelodeon/Indiana Dinner/I Shoulda Quit When I Was Ahead—Jay Livingston, Ray Evans (w,m), Famous; Isn't It Romantic—Lorenz Hart (w), Richard Rodgers (m), Famous; Miss Julie July/Wond'rin' When—Jay Livingston, Ray Evans (w,m), Famous. COVER: Veronica Lake, Mona Freeman, Mary Hatcher, Billy DeWolfe, and Others.

2419 Is Paris Burning (Paramount, 1966, Charles Boyer, Leslie Caron).

Is Paris Burning-Love Theme/ Paris Smiles—Jay Livingston, Ray Evans (w), Maurice Jarre (m), Famous. COVER: Charles Boyer, Leslie Caron, Kirk Douglas, Glenn Ford, and Others.

2420 I Surrender Dear (Columbia, 1948, Gloria Jean, David Street).

There's Nobody Else But Elsie— Allie Wrubel (w,m), Warnow. COVER: David Street.

2421 It (Paramount, 1927, Clara Bow, William Auston).

It—Will Wright, Al Purrington (w, m), Famous. COVER: Clara Bow.

2422 It Ain't Hay (Universal, 1943, Bud Abbott, Lou Costello).

Glory Be/Hang Your Troubles on a Rainbow/Old Timer/Sunbeam Serenade—Paul F. Webster (w), Harry Revel (m), Variety. COVER: Abbott and Costello, Grace McDonald.

2423 It Ain't No Sin (Belle of the Nineties) (Paramount, 1934, Mae West, Roger Pryor).

My American Beauty/My Old Flame/Troubled Waters/When a St. Louis Woman Comes Down to New Orleans—Sam Coslow, Arthur Johnston (w,m), Famous. COVER: Mae West.

2424 Italian Job, The (Paramount, 1969, Michael Caine, Noel Coward).

Getta Bloomin' Move On/On Days Like These—Don Black (w), Quincy Jones (m), Famous. COVER: Michael Caine, and Girl.

2425 It All Came True (Warner Bros., 1940, Ann Sheridan, Jeffrey Lynn).

Angel in Disguise—Kim Gannon (w), Paul Mann, Stephan Weiss (m), Witmark; Gaucho Serenade—James Cavanaugh, John Redmond, Nat Simon (w,m), Remick. COVER: Ann Sheridan, Jeffrey Lynn.

2426 It Can't Last Forever (Columbia, 1937, Ralph Bellamy, Betty Furness).

Crazy Dreams/Lazy Rhythm—Herb Magidson (w), Ben Oakland (m), Berlin. COVER: Black and white cover with title only.

2427 It Had to Be You (Columbia, 1950, Ginger Rogers, Cornel Wilde).

It Had to Be You—Gus Kahn (w), Isham Jones (m), Remick. COVER: Ginger Rogers, Cornel Wilde.

2428 It Happened at the World's Fair (MGM, 1963, Elvis Presley, Joan O'Brien).

Beyond the Bend—Ben Weisman, Fred Wise, Dee Fuller (w,m), Gladys; Cotton Candy Land—Ruth Batchelor, Bob Roberts (w,m), Gladys; Happy Ending—Sid Wayne, Ben Weisman (w,m), Gladys; How Would You Like to Be—Ben Raleigh, Mark Barkran (w,m), Gladys; I'm Falling in Love Tonight—Don Robertson (w,m), Gladys; One Broken Heart for Sale—Otis Blackwell, Winfield Scott (w,m), Gladys; Take Me to the Fair—Sid Tepper, Roy Bennett (w,m), Gladys; They Remind Me Too Much of You—Don Robertson (w,m), Gladys; World of Our Own—Bill Giant, Bernie Baum, Florence Kaye (w,m), Gladys. COVER: Elvis Presley.

2429 It Happened in Athens (20th Century-Fox, 1962, Jayne Mansfield, Trax Colton).

It Happened in Athens—Charles Haldeman (w), Manos Hadjidakis (m), Miller. COVER: Jayne Mansfield, Trax Colton.

2430 It Happened in Brooklyn (MGM, 1947, Frank Sinatra, Jimmy Durante).

Brooklyn Bridge, The/I Believe/It's the Same Old Dream/Songs Gotta Come from the Heart/Time After Time/Whose Baby Are You—Sammy Cahn (w), Jule Styne (m), Sinatra. COVER: Frank Sinatra, Jimmy Durante, Kathryn Grayson, Peter Lawford.

2431 It Happened on Fifth Avenue (Allied Artists, 1947, Don Defore, Ann Harding).

It's a Wonderful Wonderful Feeling/Speak My Heart/That's What Christmas Means to Me/You're Everywhere—Harry Revel (w,m), Chappell. COVER: Don Defore, Gale Storm.

2432 It Happened to Jane (Twinkle and Shine) (Columbia, 1959, Doris Day, Jack Lemmon).

Be Prepared—Richard Quine (w), Fred Karger (m), Artists; It Happened to Jane—Joe Lubin, I. Roth (w,m), Daywin. COVER: Doris Day, Jack Lemmon, Ernie Kovacs.

2433 It Happened Tomorrow (United Artists, 1944, Dick Powell, Linda Darnell).

Cracker Barrel Polka/Girl with the China Blue Eyes/Love Song of the Turkey/Someday, When Tomorrow Comes Along—Edmund Anderson (w), Robert Stolz (m), BMI. COVER: Dick Powell, Linda Darnell.

2434 It Happens Every Spring (20th Century-Fox, 1949, Ray Milland, Jean Peters).

It Happens Every Spring—Mack Gordon (w), Josef Myrow (m), BVC. COVER: Ray Milland, Jean Peters, Paul Douglas.

2435 It's a Date (Universal, 1940, Deanna Durbin, Kay Francis).

Ave Maria—Franz Schubert, Charles Previn (w,m), Robbins; It Happened in Kaloha—Ralph Freed (w), Frank Skinner (m), Robbins; La Boheme, Musetta's Waltz—G. Puccini, Charles Previn (w,m), Robbins; Loch Lomond—Frank Skinner (w, m), Robbins; Love Is All—Harry Tobias (w), Pinky Tomlin (m), Robbins; Rhythm of the Islands—Leon Belasco, Jacques Press, Eddie

Cherkose (w,m), Robbins. COVER: Deanna Durbin, Harry Owens.

2436 It's a Great Feeling (Warner Bros., 1949, Doris Day, Jack Carson).

At the Cafe Rendezvous/Blame It on My Absent Minded Heart/ Fiddle Dee Dee/Give Me a Song with a Beautiful Melody/It's a Great Feeling/That Was a Big Fat Lie/ There's Nothing Rougher Than Love—Sammy Cahn (w), Jule Styne (m), Harms. COVER: Doris Day, Jack Carson, Dennis Morgan.

2437 It's a Great Life (MGM, 1929, Duncan Sisters, Benny Rubin).

Hoosier Hop/I'm Following You/ I'm Sailin' on a Sunbeam—Dave Dreyer, Ballard MacDonald (w,m), Berlin. COVER: The Duncan Sisters.

2438 It's a Great Life (Paramount, 1935, Paul Kelly, Joe Morrison).

I Lost My Heart/Lazy Bone's Gotta Job Now—Leo Rubin, Lewis Gensler (w,m), Famous. COVER: Joe Morrison.

2439 It's a Joke Son (Eagle Lion, 1947, Kenny Delmar, Una Merkle).

Dixie—Dan Emmett (w,m), Mills. COVER: Kenny Delmar.

2440 It's All Happening (The Dream Maker) (Universal, 1965, Tommy Steele, Angela Douglas).

Dream Maker (B)—Norman Newell (w), Philip Green (m), Mutual. COVER: Tommy Steele.

2441 It's All Over Now (Vitaphone, 1936, Travel Short).

Bermuda Buggyride—Mack David (w), Sanford Green (m), Witmark. COVER: Buggy-riders.

2442 It's All Yours (Columbia, 1937, Madeleine Carroll, Francis Lederer).

If They Gave Me a Million—Milton Drake (w), Ben Oakland (m), Berlin. COVER: Black and white cover with title only.

2443 It's Always Fair Weather (MGM, 1955, Gene Kelly, Dan Dailey).

I Like Myself/Thanks a Lot But No Thanks/Time for Parting—Betty Comden, Adolf Green (w), André Previn (m), Feist. COVER: Gene Kelly, Dan Dailey, Cyd Charisse, Dolores Gray.

2444 It's a Mad, Mad, Mad, Mad World (United Artists, 1963, Spencer Tracy, Milton Berle).

It's a Mad, Mad, Mad, Mad World/ Thirty One Flavors—Mack David (w), Ernest Gold (m), Unart. COVER: Cartoon Sketch.

2445 It's a Pleasure (RKO, 1945, Sonja Henie, Michael O'Shea).

Romance—Edgar Leslie (w), Walter Donaldson (m), BVC. COVER: Sonja Henie, Michael O'Shea.

2446 It's Great to Be Alive (Fox, 1933, Gloria Stuart, Raul Roulien).

I'll Build a Nest/Goodbye Ladies/ It's Great to Be the Only Man Alive/ Women—William Kernell (w,m), Movietone. COVER: Gloria Stuart, Raul Roulien (American Version); COVER: Rosita Moreno, Raul Roulien (Spanish Version).

2447 It's Love Again (GB, 1936, Jessie Matthews, Robert Young).

Got to Dance My Way to Heaven —Sam Coslow (w,m), Chappell; I Nearly Let Love Go Slipping Through My Fingers—Harry Woods (w,m), Chappell; It's Love Again—Sam Coslow (w,m), Chappell. COVER: Jessie Matthews.

2448 It's My Turn (Columbia, 1980, Jill Clayburgh, Michael Douglas).

It's My Turn—Carole B. Sager (w), Michael Massner (m), Colgems. COVER: Jill Clayburgh, Michael Douglas.

2449 It's Only Money (Double Dynamite) (RKO, 1951, Frank Sinatra, Jane Russell).

Kisses and Tears—Sammy Cahn (w), Jule Styne (m), Sinatra. COVER: Frank Sinatra, Jane Russell, Groucho Marx.

2450 It Started in Naples (Paramount, 1960, Clark Gable, Sophia Loren).

It Started in Naples—Milt Gabler (w), Alessandro Cicognini, Carlo Savina (m), Famous. COVER: Clark Gable, Sophia Loren.

2451 It Started with a Kiss (MGM, Glenn Ford, Debbie Reynolds).

It Started with a Kiss—Charles Lederer (w), Rudy Render (m), Robbins. COVER: Glenn Ford, Debbie Reynolds.

2452 It Started with Eve (Universal, 1941, Deanna Durbin, Robert Cummings).

Clavelitos—M. Sandwith, J. Valverde (w,m), Schirmer; When I Sing (B)—Sam Lerner (w), P. Tchaikovsky (m), Day. COVER: Deanna Durbin.

2453 I've Always Loved You (Republic, 1946, Philip Dorn, Catherine McLeod).

Beethoven Appassionata Sonata Theme (B)—L. Beethoven (m), Paxton; Full Moon and Empty Arms—Buddy Kaye, Ted Mossman (w), S. Rachmaninoff (m), Barton; I've Always Loved You—Harold Rome (w), S. Rachmaninoff (m), Leeds; I've Always Loved You-Five Themes—S. Rachmaninoff, L. Beethoven (m), Leeds. COVER: Philip Dorn, Catherine McLeod.

2454 I've Been Around (Universal, 1934, Chester Morris, Rochelle Hudson).

I've Been Around—Jack Stern, Jack Meskill (w,m), Harms. COVER: Chester Morris, Rochelle Hudson.

2455 Ivy (Universal, 1947, Joan Fontaine, Patrick Knowles).

Ivy—Hoagy Carmichael (w,m), BVH. COVER: Joan Fontaine.

2456 I Wake Up Screaming (Hot Spot) (20th Century-Fox, 1941, Betty Grable, Victor Mature).

Things I Love, The—Harold Barlow, Lewis Harris (w,m), Campbell. COVER: Carole Landis, Betty Grable, Victor Mature.

2457 I Walk Alone (Paramount, 1947, Lizabeth Scott, Burt Lancaster).

Don't Call It Love—Ned Washington (w), Allie Wrubel (m), Famous. COVER: Lizabeth Scott, Burt Lancaster, Kirk Douglas.

2458 I Walk the Line (Columbia, 1970, Gregory Peck, Tuesday Weld).

Flesh and Blood—Johnny Cash (w,m), Cash. COVER: Gregory Peck, Tuesday Weld.

2459 I Wanna Be a Life Guard (Paramount, 1936, Cartoon).

I Wanna Be a Life Guard (VS)—Bob Rothberg (w), Sammy Timberg (m), Famous. COVER: Popeye.

2460 I Wanted Wings (Paramount, 1941, Veronica Lake, Ray Milland).

Born to Love—Ned Washington (w), Victor Young (m), Famous; Spirit of the Air Corps—William Clinch (w,m), BMI. COVER: Ray Milland, William Holden, Veronica Lake.

2461 I Want to Live (United Artists, 1958, Susan Hayward, Simon Oakland).

I Want to Live-Theme—Johnny Mandel (m), Unart. COVER: Black and white cover with title only.

2462 I Want You (RKO, 1951, Dana Andrews, Dorothy Maguire).

I Want You—Mort Greene (w), Leigh Harline (m), Morris. COVER: Dana Andrews, Dorothy Maguire, Peggy Dow, Farley Granger.

2463 I Was an American Spy (Allied Artists, 1951, Ann Dvorak, Gene Evans).

Because of You—Arthur Hammerstein, Dudley Wilkinson (w,m), BMI. COVER: Tony Bennett.

2464 I Wonder Who's Kissing Her Now (20th Century-Fox, 1947, June Haver, Mark Stevens).

Be Sweet to Me Kid—Will Hough, Frank Adams (w), Joseph Howard (m), Marks; Goodbye My Lady Love —Joseph Howard (w,m), Mills; Hello Ma Baby—Ida Emerson, Joseph Howard (w,m), Robbins; Honeymoon/

I Wonder Who's Kissing Her Now/ Umpire Is a Most Unhappy Man— Will Hough, Frank Adams (w), Joseph Howard (m), Marks; What's the Use of Dreaming—Joseph Howard (w,m), Mills. COVER: June Haver, Mark Stevens.

2465 Jack Ahoy (GB, 1935, Jack Hulbert, Nancy O'Neill).

My Hat's on the Side of My Head —Harry Woods, Claude Hulbert (w, m), Shapiro Bernstein. COVER: Little Jack Little.

2466 Jack and the Beanstalk (Warner Bros., 1952, Bud Abbott, Lou Costello).

Darlene/Dreamer's Cloth/I Fear Nothing/Jack and the Beanstalk/ He Never Looked Better—Lester Lee, Bob Russell (w,m), Remick. COVER: Bud Abbott, Lou Costello.

2467 Jack's the Boy (Gainsborough, 1932, Jack Hulbert, Cicely Courtneidge).

Flies Crawled up the Window, The/I Want to Cling to Ivy—Douglas Furber (w), Vivian Ellis (m), Chappell. COVER: Jack Hulbert, Cicely Courtneidge.

2468 Jailhouse Rock (MGM, 1957, Elvis Presley, Judy Tyler).

Baby I Don't Care—Jerry Leiber, Mike Stoller (w,m), Presley; Don't Leave Me Now—Aaron Schroeder, Ben Weisman (w,m), Gladys; I Want to Be Free/Jailhouse Rock/Treat Me Nice—Jerry Leiber, Mike Stoller (w, m), Presley; Young and Beautiful— Aaron Schroeder, Abner Silver (w, m), Gladys. COVER: Elvis Presley.

2469 Jamboree (Republic, 1944, Ruth Terry, George Byron).

Whittle Out a Whistle—Del Porter, Carl Hoefle (w,m), Cole. COVER: Ernest Tubb.

2470 Jamboree (Warner Bros., 1957, Kay Medford, Robert Pastine).

Broken Promise—Sol Winkler, James Goldsborough (w,m), Jungnickel; Great Balls of Fire—Jack Hammer, Otis Blackwell (w,m), Hill

Range. COVER: Jerry Lee Lewis, Four Coins.

2471 James Dean Story, The (Warner Bros., 1957, Marcus Winslow, Marke Winslow).

Let Me Be Loved—Jay Livingston, Ray Evans (w,m), Livingston Evans. COVER: James Dean.

2472 Jam Session (Columbia, 1944, Ann Miller, Jess Barker).

Victory Polka (B)—Sammy Cahn (w), Jule Styne (m), Chappell. COVER: Ann Miller.

2473 Jango (DQE, 1929, African Documentary).

Dark Moon/Jango—Pat Ballard (w), Kendall Burgess, Paul Van Loan (m), Remick. COVER: Jungle Scene.

2474 Janie (Warner Bros., 1944, Joyce Reynolds, Robert Hutton).

Janie—Lee David (w,m), Remick; Keep Your Powder Dry—Sammy Cahn (w), Jule Styne (m), Remick. COVER: Joyce Reynolds, Robert Hutton.

2475 Jaws (Universal, 1975, Robert Shaw, Roy Scheider).

Jaws Theme—John Williams (m), Duchess. COVER: A Shark and a Swimmer.

2476 Jaws II (Universal, 1978, Roy Scheider, Murray Hamilton).

Jaws Two-Theme—John Williams (m), Duchess. COVER: Shark and Surfer.

2477 Jayhawkers, The (Paramount, 1959, Jeff Chandler, Fess Parker).

Hippy Happy Henny—Phil Boutelje (w,m), Famous; Jayhawkers— Eddie White, Mack Wolfson (w,m), Famous. COVER: Movie Scenes.

2478 Jazz Cinderella (Chesterfield, 1930, Myrna Loy, Jason Robards).

True Love/You're Too Good to Be True—Ray Klages (w), Jesse Greer (m), Bibo Lang. COVER: Jason Robards, Myrna.

2479 Jazz Heaven (RKO, 1929, Johnny Mack Brown, Sally O'neill).

Someone—Sidney Clare (w), Oscar

Levant (m), Harms. COVER: Sketch of Girl.

2480 Jazzmania (Metro, 1923, Mae Murray, Rod LaRoque).

Jazzmania—Lew Brown, N. Granlund, James Hanley (w,m), Shapiro Bernstein. COVER: Mae Murray.

2481 Jazz Singer, The (Warner Bros., 1927, Al Jolson, Warner Oland).

Dirty Hands, Dirty Face—Al Jolson, Grant Clarke, Edgar Leslie, Jim Monaco (w,m), Clarke; Mother of Mine I Still Have You—Al Jolson, Louis Silver, Grant Clarke (w,m), Berlin; Toot Toot Tootsie (PC)—Gus Kahn, Ernie Erdman, Ted Fiorito (w,m), Feist. COVER: Al Jolson.

2482 Jazz Singer, The (Warner Bros., 1953, Danny Thomas, Peggy Lee).

Hushabye/I Hear the Music Now/ Living the Life I Love—Jerry Seelen, Sammy Fain (w,m), Remick; Oh, Moon—Ray Jacobs (w,m), Remick; This Is a Very Special Day—Peggy Lee (w,m), Remick. COVER: Danny Thomas, Peggy Lee.

2483 Jazz Singer, The (Associated, 1980, Neil Diamond, Lucie Arnaz).

America—Neil Diamond (w,m), Stonebridge; Hello Again—Neil Diamond, Alan Lindgren (w,m), Stonebridge; Love on the Rocks/Songs of Life—Neil Diamond, Gilbert Becaud (w,m), Stonebridge; Acapulco (VS)— Neil Diamond, Doug Rhone (w,m), Stonebridge; A Don Olom (VS)—Neil Diamond, Uri Frenkel (w,m), Stonebridge; Amazed and Confused (VS)— Neil Diamond, Richard Bennett (w, m), Stonebridge; Havah Nagilah (VS) —Neil Diamond (w,m), Stonebridge; Hey Louise (VS)—Neil Diamond, Gilbert Becaud (w,m), Stonebridge; Hine Mah Tov (VS)/Jerusalem (VS)— Neil Diamond (w,m), Stonebridge; Koi Nidre (VS)—Neil Diamond, Uri Frenkel (w,m), Stonebridge; On the Robert E Lee (VS)—Neil Diamond, Gilbert Becaud (w,m), Stonebridge;

Shabbat Shalom (VS)—Uri Frankel (w,m), Stonebridge; Summer Love (VS)—Neil Diamond, Gilbert Becaud (w,m), Stonebridge; You Baby (VS) Neil Diamond (w,m), Stonebridge. COVER: Neil Diamond.

2484 Jealousy (UFA, 1928, Lya Deputti).

Jealousy—Charles Weinberg, Al Koppell, Billy Stone (w,m), DeHavilland. COVER: Lya Deputti, and Man.

2485 Jeanne Eagels (Columbia, 1957, Kim Novak, Jeff Chandler).

Half of My Heart—Ned Washington (w), George Duning (m), Colgems. COVER: Kim Novak, Jeff Chandler.

2486 Jennie Gerhardt (Paramount, 1935, Sylvia Sidney, Donald Cook).

Dreaming—L. Heiser (w), J. Anton Dailey (m), Remick. COVER: Sylvia Sidney.

2487 Jennie Was a Lady (MGM, 1946, Stars Unknown).

Bicycle Song, The—Ralph Blane, George Bassman (w,m), Robbins. COVER: Black and white cover with title only.

2488 Jennifer (Allied Artists, 1953, Ida Lupino, Howard Duff).

Angel Eyes—Earl Brent (w), Matt Dennis (m), Simon. COVER: King Cole.

2489 Jenny (Cinerama, 1970, Marlo Thomas, Alan Alda).

Goodbye Young Dreams—Richard Ahlert (w), Bobby Scott (m), Songfest; Jenny—Don Christopher (w), Michael Small (m), Pamco. COVER: Alan Alda, Marlo Thomas.

2490 Jenny Lamour (Vog, 1948, Suzy Delair, Simone Renant).

Whisper to Me—Malcolm Johnson (w), Francis Lopez (m), Aliare. COVER: Suzy Delair.

2491 Jessica (United Artists, 1962, Maurice Chevalier, Angie Dickinson).

It Is Better to Love/Jessica/ Vespa Song/Will You Remember— Dusty Negulesco (w), Marguerite

Monnot (m), Unart. COVER: Angie Dickinson.

2492 Jesus Christ Superstar (Universal, 1973, Ted Neeley, Carl Anderson).

Could We Start Again Please (VS)/Everything's Alright (VS)/Heaven on Their Minds (VS)/Hosanna (VS)/I Don't Know How to Love Him (VS)/I Only Want to Say (VS)/King Herod's Song (VS)/Last Supper, The (VS)/Pilate's Dream (VS)/Superstar (VS)—Tim Rice (w), Andrew Lloyd Webber (m), Leeds. COVER: Movie Scene.

2493 Jet Over the Atlantic (Intercontinent, 1960, Guy Madison, Virginia Mayo).

What Would I Do Without You—Jack Hoffman (w), Lou Forbes (m), Robbins. COVER: Guy Madison, Virginia Mayo, George Raft.

2494 Jewel of the Nile (20th Century-Fox, 1985, Michael Douglas, Kathleen Turner).

When the Going Gets Tough, the Tough Get Going—W. Brathwaite, B. Eastmond, R. Lange, B. Ocean (w, m), Leonard. COVER: Billy Ocean.

2495 Jezebel (Warner Bros., 1938, Bette Davis, Henry Fonda).

Jezebel—Johnny Mercer (w), Harry Warren (m), Remick; Pretty Quadroon (BW)—Nat Vincent, Fred Howard (w,m), Cole. COVER: Bette Davis.

2496 Jiggs and Maggie in Court (Monogram, 1948, Joe Yule, Renie Riano).

All I Have to Have Is You—Ted Mossman, Philip Grace (w,m), Music Art. COVER: Joe Yule, Renie Riano.

2497 Jimmie Lunceford and His Orchestra (Warner Bros., 1937, Jimmie Lunceford and Band).

You Are Just That Kind—A. Sanders, C. Vegge (w,m), Guadagno-Davis. COVER: Jimmie Lunceford and His Orchestra.

2498 Jimmy and Sally (Fox, 1933, James Dunn, Claire Trevor).

Eat Marlowe's Meat (PC)/It's the Irish in Me/You're My Thrill—Sidney Clare (w), Jay Gorney (m), Movietone. COVER: James Dunn, Claire Trevor.

2499 Jim-The World's Greatest (Universal, 1975, Gregory Harrison, Robbie Wolcott).

Story of a Teen-ager, The—Dan Peek, Gerry Beckley (w,m), Warner. COVER: America-Rock Group.

2500 Jinx (Goldwyn, 1920, Mabel Norman, Florence Carpenter).

Jinx—Carrier Worrell (w,m), Remick. COVER: Mabel Norman.

2501 Jitney Bus Elopement, The (Essanay, 1915, Charlie Chaplin, Lloyd Bacon).

Jitney Bus—Edith Lessing (w), Roy Ingraham (m), Rossiter. COVER: Charlie Chaplin, and Bus.

2502 Jitterbugs (20th Century-Fox, 1943, Stan Laurel, Oliver Hardy).

If the Shoe Fits You, Wear It/I've Gotta See for Myself/Moon Kissed the Mississippi, The—Charles Newman (w), Lew Pollack (m), Miller. COVER: Laurel and Hardy, Vivian Blaine.

2503 Jive Junction (PRC, 1943, Dickie Moore, Tina Thayer).

A Doo Dee Doo Doo/Cock a Doodle Doo/In a Little Music Shop/Jive Junction/Mother Earth/We're Just in Between/Where Is Love—Leo Erdody, Lew Porter, June Stillman, F. Tableporter (w,m), Urban. COVER: Dickie Moore, Tina Thayer, and Movie Scenes.

2504 Joanna (20th Century-Fox, 1968, Genevieve Waite, Christian Doermer).

I'll Catch the Sun/Joanna—Rod McKuen (w,m), 20th Century; When Joanna Loved Me—Robert Wells, Jack Segal (w,m), Morris; Joanna-Ten Songs—Rod McKuen (w,m), 20th Century. COVER: Genevieve Waite.

2505 Joan the Woman (Paramount, 1917, Geraldine Farrar, Wallace Reid).

Joan of Arc Song—Robert Roden

(w), James Kendis (m), Cadillac. COVER: Geraldine Farrar.

2506 Joe (Cannon, 1970, Peter Boyle, Dennis Patrick).

Where Are You Going/Hey Joe (VS)/You Can Fly (VS)—Danny Meehan (w), Bobby Scott (m), Cannon Ball. COVER: Peter Boyle.

2507 Joe College (The Sophomore) (Pathe, 1929, Eddie Quillan, Sally O'Neil).

Little by Little—Walter O'Keefe, Bobby Dolan (w,m), DBH. COVER: Black and white cover with title only.

2508 Joe Dakota (Universal, 1957, Jock Mahoney, Luana Patten).

Flower of San Antoine—Mack David (w), Ray Joseph (m), Riverside. COVER: Jock Mahoney, Luana Patten.

2509 Joe Louis Story, The (United Artists, 1954, Paul Stewart, Coley Wallace).

Close to Me—Nat Hiken (w), George Bassman (m), Harman; Theme for Joe—George Bassman (m). COVER: Coley Wallace, Hilda Simms.

2510 Joe MacBeth (Columbia, 1956, Ruth Roman, Paul Douglas).

Joe MacBeth Theme—Trevor Duncan (m), Colgems. COVER: Ruth Roman, Paul Douglas.

2511 Joe Palooka (Palooka) (United Artists, 1934, Jimmy Durante, Lupe Velez).

Count Your Blessings—Irving Caesar (w), Ferde Grofe (m), Harms; Inka Dinka Doo—Ben Ryan (w), Jimmie Durante (m), Berlin; Like Me a Little Bit Less—Harold Adamson (w), Burton Lane (m), Berlin. COVER: Jimmy Durante, Lupe Velez.

2512 Joe Panther (Artists, 1967, Ray Tracey, Brian Keith).

Time Has Come, The—Norman Gimbel (w), Fred Karlin (m), Butterfield. COVER: Ray Tracey, and Movie Scene.

2513 John and Mary (20th Century-Fox, 1969, Dustin Hoffman, Mia Farrow).

Maybe Tomorrow—Alan Bergman, Marilyn Bergman (w), Quincy Jones (m), Fox. COVER: Mia Farrow, Dustin Hoffman.

2514 John Goldfarb Please Come Home (20th Century-Fox, 1965, Shirley MacLaine, Peter Ustinov).

John Goldfarb Please Come Home—Don Wolf (w), Johnny Williams (m), Hastings. COVER: Shirley MacLaine, Peter Ustinov.

2515 Johnny Angel (RKO, George Raft, Claire Trevor).

Memphis in June—Paul F. Webster (w), Hoagy Carmichael (m), BVH. COVER: George Raft, Claire Trevor, Hoagy Carmichael.

2516 Johnny Apollo (Dance with the Devil) (20th Century-Fox, Dorothy Lamour, Tyrone Power).

Dancing for Nickels and Dimes—Frank Loesser (w), Lionel Newman (m), Robbins; This Is the Beginning of the End—Mack Gordon (w,m), Robbins; Your Kiss—Frank Loesser (w), Alfred Newman (m), Robbins. COVER: Dorothy Lamour, Tyrone Power.

2517 Johnny Come Lately (Cagney, 1943, James Cagney, Grace George).

Johnny Come Lately—Jack Scholl (w), Leigh Harline (m), Saunders. COVER: James Cagney.

2518 Johnny Concho (United Artists, 1956, Frank Sinatra, Keenan Wynn).

Johnny Concho Theme, Wait for Me—Dok Stanford (w), Nelson Riddle (m), Barton. COVER: Frank Sinatra, Keenan Wynn, William Conrad.

2519 Johnny Cool (United Artists, 1963, Henry Silva, Elizabeth Montgomery).

Ballad of Johnny Cool—Sammy Cahn (w), James Van Heusen (m), Unart. COVER: Black and white cover with title only.

2520 Johnny Guitar (Republic, 1954, Joan Crawford, Sterling Hayden).

Johnny Guitar—Peggy Lee (w), Victor Young (m), Young. COVER: Joan Crawford, Sterling Hayden.

2521 Johnny Holiday (United Artists, 1950, William Bendix, Allen Martin).

My Christmas Song for You—Furniss Peterson, Paul F. Webster (w), Hoagy Carmichael (m), Sidney. COVER: Hoagy Carmichael.

2522 Johnny Rocco (Allied Artists, 1958, Stephen McNally, Coleen Gray).

Heartstrings—Edward Kay (m), Kay. COVER: Black and white cover with title only.

2523 Johnny Shiloh (Buena Vista, 1963, Kevin Corcoran, Brian Keith).

Johnny Shiloh—Richard Sherman, Robert Sherman (w,m), Wonderland. COVER: Kevin Corcoran.

2524 Johnny Tiger (Universal, 1965, Robert Taylor, Geraldine Brooks).

World of the Heart (Q)—Johnny Mercer (w), Johnny Green (m), Frank. COVER: Black and white cover with title only.

2525 Johnny Tremain (Buena Vista, 1956, Luana Patten, Hal Stalmaster).

Johnny Tremain/Liberty Tree—George Bruns, Tom Blackburn (w,m), Wonderland. COVER: Hal Stalmaster.

2526 Joker Is Wild, The (Paramount, 1957, Frank Sinatra, Mitzi Gaynor).

All the Way—Sammy Cahn (w), James Van Heusen (m), Barton; Chicago—Fred Fisher (w,m), Fisher. COVER: Frank Sinatra, Mitzi Gaynor, Jeanne Crain.

2527 Jokers, The (Universal, 1967, Michael Crawford, Oliver Reed).

Jokers, The—Mike Leander, Charles Mills (w,m), Shamley. COVER: Man with British Flag.

2528 Jolly Little Elves (Universal, 1934, Cartoon).

Dunk Dunk Dunk—Walter Lantz, Victor McLeod (w), James Dietrich (m), Harms. COVER: Cartoon of Elves.

2529 Jolson Sings Again (Columbia, 1949, Larry Parks, Barbara Hale).

April Showers—B. G. DeSylva (w), Louis Silvers (m), Harms; After You've Gone—Henry Creamer, Turner Layton (w,m), Mayfair; Baby Face—Benny Davis, Harry Akst (w,m), Remick; Back in Your Own Backyard (B)—Al Jolson, Billy Rose, Dave Dreyer (w,m), Day; California Here I Come—Al Jolson, Bud DeSylva, Joe Meyer (w,m), Witmark; Carolina in the Morning—Gus Kahn (w), Walter Donaldson (m), Remick; Chinatown, My Chinatown—William Jerome (w), Jean Schwartz (m), Remick; For Me and My Gal—Edgar Leslie, Ray Goetz (w), George Meyer (m), Mills; I Only Have Eyes for You—Al Dubin (w), Harry Warren (m), Remick; I'm Just Wild About Harry—Noble Sissle, Eubie Blake (w,m), Witmark; I'm Looking Over a Four Leaf Clover—Mort Dixon, Harry Woods (w,m), Witmark; Is It True What They Say About Dixie—Irving Caesar, Sam Lerner, Gerald Marks (w,m), Caesar; Learn to Croon—Sam Coslow (w), Arthur Johnston (m), Famous; Let Me Sing and I'm Happy (B)—Irving Berlin (w,m), Day; Ma Blushin' Rose—Edgar Smith (w), John Stromberg (m), Witmark; My Mammy—Sam Lewis, Joe Young (w), Walter Donaldson (m), Bourne; Pretty Baby—Gus Kahn, Tony Jackson, Egbert Van Alstyne (w,m), Witmark; Rock-a-bye Your Baby—Sam Lewis, Joe Young (w), Jean Schwartz (m), Mills; Swanee—Irving Caesar (w), George Gershwin (m), Harms; Toot Toot Tootsie—Gus Kahn, Ernie Erdman, Dan Russo (w,m), Feist; You Made Me Love You—Joe McCarthy (w), James Monaco (m), Broadway. COVER: Silhouette of Al Jolson.

2530 Jolson Story, The (Columbia, 1946, Larry Parks, Evelyn Keyes).

About a Quarter to Nine—Al Dubin (w), Harry Warren (m), Witmark; After the Ball—Charles Harris (w,m), Harris; Anniversary Song—Al Jolson, Saul Chaplin (w,m), Mood; April Showers—B. G. DeSylva (w), Louis

Silvers (m), Harms; Blue Bell—Ed Madden, Dolly Morse (w), Theodore Morse (m), Feist; By the Light of the Silvery Moon—Ed Madden (w), Gus Edwards (m), Remick; California Here I Come—Al Jolson, Bud De-Sylva, Joseph Meyer (w,m), Witmark; Forty Second Street—Al Dubin (w), Harry Warren (m), Witmark; I Want a Girl—William Dillon (w), Harry Von Tilzer (m), Von Tilzer; I'm Sitting on Top of the World—Sam Lewis, Joe Young (w), Ray Henderson (m), Feist; Lullaby of Broadway—Al Dubin (w), Harry Warren (m), Witmark; Ma Blushin' Rose—Edgar Smith (w), John Stromberg (m), Witmark; My Mammy—Sam Lewis, Joe Young (w), Walter Donaldson (m), Bourne; On the Banks of the Wabash —Paul Dresser (w,m), Paull Pioneer; Rock-a-bye Your Baby with a Dixie Melody—Sam Lewis, Joe Young (w), Jean Schwartz (m), Mills; Spaniard That Blighted My Life—Billy Menson (w,m), Harms; Swanee—Irving Caesar (w), George Gershwin (m), Harms; There's a Rainbow Round My Shoulder—Al Jolson, Billy Rose, Dave Dreyer (w,m), Bourne; Toot Toot Tootsie—Gus Kahn, Ernie Erdman, Dan Russo (w,m), Feist; Waiting for the Robert E. Lee—L. Wolfe Gilbert (w), Lewis Muir (m), Alfred; When You Were Sweet Sixteen—James Thornton (w,m), Shapiro Bernstein; You Made Me Love You—Joe McCarthy (w), James Monaco (m), Broadway. COVER: Cartoon Sketches.

2531 Jonathan Livingston Seagull (Paramount, 1973, James Franciscus, Juliet Mills).

Be/Dear Father/Lonely Looking Sky/Skybird/Jonathan Livingston Seagull-12 Songs—Neil Diamond (w,m), Stonebridge. COVER: Neil Diamond.

2532 Josette (20th Century-Fox, 1938, Don Ameche, Simone Simon).

In Any Language/May I Drop a Petal/Where in the World—Mack Gordon, Harry Revel (w,m), Feist. COVER: Don Ameche, Simone Simon,

Robert Young.

2533 Journey Around South America, A (Panagra, 1952, Travelogue).

Peruvian Waltz (PC)—Melle Weersma (m), Morris. COVER: None.

2534 Journey to the Center of the Earth (20th Century-Fox, 1959, Pat Boone, James Mason).

Faithful Heart—Sammy Cahn (w), James Van Heusen (m), Robbins; My Love Is Like a Red Red Rose—Robert Burns (w), James Van Heusen (m), Robbins; To the Center of the Earth—Pat Boone (w,m), Spoone; Twice as Tall—Sammy Cahn (w), James Van Heusen (m), Robbins. COVER: Pat Boone, James Mason, Arlene Dahl.

2535 Joy House (MGM, 1964, Jane Fonda, Alain Delon).

Cat, The—Lalo Schifrin (m), Hastings; Joy House Theme-Just Call Me Love Bird—Peggy Lee (w), Lalo Schifrin (m), Hastings. COVER: Jane Fonda, Alain Delon, Lola Albright.

2536 Joy in the Morning (MGM, 1964, Richard Chamberlain, Yvette Mimieux).

Joy in the Morning—Paul F. Webster (w), Sammy Fain (m), Miller. COVER: Richard Chamberlain, Yvette Mimieux.

2537 Joy of Living (RKO, 1938, Irene Dunne, Douglas Fairbanks).

Heavenly Party/Just Let Me Look at You/What's Good About Goodnight/You Couldn't Be Cuter—Dorothy Fields (w), Jerome Kern (m), Chappell. COVER: Irene Dunne.

2538 Joy of Sex (Paramount, 1984, Ernie Hudson, Colleen Camp).

Dreams—Clydene Jackson, Harold Payne (w,m), Famous. COVER: Ernie Hudson, Colleen Camp, Christopher Lloyd.

2539 Jubilee Trail (Republic, 1953, Vera Ralston, Joan Leslie).

Jubilee Trail—Sidney Clare (w), Victor Young (m), Young. COVER: Vera Ralston, Joan Leslie, Forrest Tucker, and Others.

2540 Jubilo (Goldwyn, 1919, Will Rogers, Josie Sedgwick).

I'm Just a Tramp—Clifford Cake (w), Ed Bergstrom (m), Loveland; Jubilo—Anne Caldwell (w), Jerome Kern (m), Harms. COVER: Will Rogers.

2541 Judgment at Nuremberg (United Artists, 1961, Spencer Tracy, Burt Lancaster).

Care for Me—Al Stillman (w), Ernest Gold (m), Unart; Judgment at Nuremberg Theme/Schwalbenwinkel Theme—Ernest Gold (m), Unart. COVER: S. Tracy, B. Lancaster, R. Widmark, M. Dietrich, J. Garland, and Others.

2542 Judge Priest (Fox, 1934, Will Rogers, Tom Brown).

Massa Jesus Wrote Me a Song—Lamar Trotti, Dudley Nichols (w), Cyril Mockridge (m), Movietone. COVER: Black and white cover with title only.

2543 Judith (Paramount, 1966, Sophia Loren, Peter Finch).

Judith Theme—Sol Kaplan (w,m), Famous. COVER: Sophia Loren, Peter Finch.

2544 Juggler, The (Columbia, 1953, Kirk Douglas, Joey Walsh).

Juggler Dance, The—Rivka Gwily (m), Ludlow. COVER: Black and white cover with title only.

2545 Juke Box Jenny (Fifty Million Nickels) (Universal, 1942, Ken Murray, Harriet Hilliard).

Give Out/Macumba/Swing It Mother Goose—Everett Carter (w), Milton Rosen (m), Robbins. COVER: Iris Adrian, Don Douglas, Ken Murray.

2546 Juke Box Rhythm (Columbia, 1959, Jo Morrow, Jack Jones).

I Feel It Right Here—Steve Graham, Leon Pober (w,m), Criterion; Last Night—Diane Lampert, Leon Pober (w,m), Criterion; Make Room for the Joy—Hal David (w), Burt Bacharach (m), Famous. COVER: Jack Jones, Jo Morrow, and Others.

2547 Jules and Jim (Janus, 1962, Jeanne Moreau, Oscar Werner).

Jules and Jim Theme—Georges Delerue, A. Bassiak (m), Wood. COVER: Jeanne Moreau.

2548 Jules Verne's Rocket to the Moon (Those Fantastic Flying Fools) (Allied Artists, 1967, Burl Ives, Troy Donahue).

Rocket to the Moon (B)—Patrick J. Scott (m), Southern. COVER: Burl Ives, Troy Donahue, and Others.

2549 Julia Misbehaves (MGM, 1948, Greer Garson, Walter Pidgeon).

When You're Playing with Fire—Jerry Seelen (w), Hal Bourne (m), Robbins. COVER: Greer Garson, Walter Pidgeon.

2550 Julie (MGM, 1956, Doris Day, Louis Jourdan).

Julie—Tom Adair (w), Leith Stevens (m), Artists. COVER: Doris Day, Louis Jourdan.

2551 Juliet of the Spirits (Rizzoli, 1965, Giulietta Masina, Sandra Milo).

Amore Per Tutti—Nino Rota (m), Noma; Juliet's Theme—Nino Rota, Marks; Juliet's Dream—Alan Brandt (w), Nino Rota (m), Marks. COVER: Cartoon Sketches.

2552 Jumbo (MGM, 1962, Doris Day, Stephen Boyd).

Circus on Parade/Diavolo/Little Girl Blue/Most Beautiful Girl in the World/My Romance/Over and Over Again/This Can't Be Love—Lorenz Hart (w), Richard Rodgers (m), Harms. COVER: Doris Day, Stephen Boyd, Jimmy Durante, Martha Raye.

2553 Jumping Jacks (Paramount, 1952, Dean Martin, Jerry Lewis).

Big Blue Sky/I Can't Resist a Boy in Uniform/I Know a Dream When I See One/Keep a Little Dream Handy/Parachute Jump/What Have You Done for Me Lately—Mack David (w), Jerry Livingston (m), Paramount. COVER: Dean Martin, Jerry Lewis, Mona Freeman.

2554 Jumpin' Jack Flash (20th Century-Fox, 1986, Whoopi Goldberg, Stephen Collins).

Jumpin' Jack Flash—Mick Jagger, Keith Richards (w,m), ABKCO. COVER: Aretha Franklin, Keith Richards.

2555 Jungle Book, The (Buena Vista, 1966, Cartoon).

Bare Necessities—Terry Gilkyson (w,m), Wonderland; Colonel Hath's March (Elephent Song)/I Wanna Be Like You (Monkey Song)/My Own Home/Trust in Me (Python Song)/That's What Friends Are For (Vulture Song)—Richard Sherman, Robert Sherman (w,m), Wonderland. COVER: Cartoons.

2556 Jungle Jim (Universal, 1937, Grant Withers, Betty Jane Rhodes).

I'm Takin' the Jungle Trail—Kay Kellogg (w,m), Sam Fox. COVER: A Jungle.

2557 Jungle Menace (Columbia, 1938, Frank Buck, John St. Polis).

No More Sleepy Time—Clarence Muse, Elliot Carpenter (w,m), Mills; Rita—Christi Kruger, Lee Zahler (w, m), Southern; Weary Feet—Lee Zahler, Clarence Muse, Elliot Carpenter (w,m), Mills. COVER: Frank Buck.

2558 Jungle Patrol (20th Century-Fox, 1948, Kristine Miller, Arthur Franz).

Forever and Always—Al Rinker, Floyd Huddleston (w,m), BMI. COVER: Kristine Miller.

2559 Jungle Princess (Paramount, 1936, Dorothy Lamour, Ray Milland).

Moonlight and Shadows—Leo Robin, Frederick Hollander (w,m), Popular. COVER: Dorothy Lamour, Ray Milland.

2560 Jupiter's Darling (MGM, 1955, Esther Williams, Howard Keel).

Don't Let This Night Get Away/I Have a Dream—Harold Adamson (w), Burton Lane (m), Chappell. COVER: Esther Williams, Howard Keel.

2561 Just Around the Corner (20th Century-Fox, 1938, Shirley Temple, Joan Davis).

I Love to Walk in the Rain (PC)/This Is a Happy Little Ditty—Walter Bullock (w), Harold Spina (m), Robbins. COVER: Shirley Temple.

2562 Just for You (Paramount, 1952, Bing Crosby, Jane Wyman).

Call Me Tonight/Checkin' My Heart/Flight of Fancy/He's Just Crazy for Me/I'll Si-Si-Ya in Bahia/Just for You/Live Oak Tree/Maiden of Guadalupe/Ol' Spring Fever/On the Ten Ten/Zing a Little Song—Leo Robin (w), Harry Warren (m), Burvan. COVER: Bing Crosby, Jane Wyman.

2563 Just Imagine (Fox, 1930, El Brendel, Maureen O'Sullivan).

Never Swat a Fly/Old Fashioned Girl/You Are the Melody—B. G. DeSylva, Lew Brown, Ray Henderson (w,m), DBH. COVER: Maureen O'Sullivan, and Plane.

2564 Justine (20th Century-Fox, 1969, Anouk Aimee, Dirk Bogarde).

Justine—Hal Shaper (w), Jerry Goldsmith (m), Fox. COVER: Anouk Aimee.

2565 Just Like a Woman (Hodkinson, 1923, Marguerite De La Motte, George Fawcett).

Just Like a Woman—Grace Haskins, Milt Hagen (w,m), Veritas. COVER: Marguerite De La Motte.

2566 Just the Way You Are (MGM, 1984, Kristy McNichol, Michael Ontkean).

Just the Way You Are—Vladimir Cosma (w,m), April. COVER: Kristy McNichol.

2567 Just You and Me Kid (Columbia, 1978, George Burns, Brooke Shields).

Katie—Sammy Fain (w,m), Fain. COVER: George Burns, Brooke Shields.

2568 Kansas City Bomber (MGM, 1972, Raquel Welch, Kevin McCarthy).

Rounds and Spheres—Maria Eckstein (w), Don Ellis (m), Hastings. COVER: Raquel Welch.

2569 Karate Kid, The (I) (Columbia, 1984, Ralph Macchio, Nori-yuki Morita).

Moment of Truth—Dennis Lambert, Peter Beckett (w), Bill Conti (m), Golden Torch; Bop Bop on the Beach (VS)—Mike Love, Adrian Baker (w,m), Columbia; Desire (VS) —Andy Gill, Jon King (w,m), Columbia; Feel the Night (VS)—Baxter Robinson, Bill Conti (w,m), Columbia; It Takes Two to Tango (VS)—Dennis Lambert, Peter Beckett (w, m), Columbia; No Shelter (VS)—John Mark, Richard Fenton (w,m), Columbia; Rhythm Man (VS)—Mark St. Regis, Gregory St. Regis (w,m), Columbia; Rock Around the Clock (VS)—Max Freedman, Jim DeKnight (w,m), Columbia; Tough Love (VS)—A. Shandri, T. Stern (w,m), Columbia; You're the Best (VS)—Bill Conti, Allen Willis (w,m), Columbia; Young Hearts (VS)—David Merenda (w,m), Columbia. COVER: Ralph Macchio, Noriyuki Morita.

2570 Karate Kid, The (II) (Columbia, 1986, Ralph Macchio, Pat Morita).

Earth Angel—Tootsie Williams (w, m), Columbia; Glory of Love—Peter Cetera, David Foster, Diane Nini (w, m), Columbia; This Is the Time—Dennis DeYoung (w,m), Columbia; Fish for Life (VS)—Ian Stanley, Roland Orzabel (w,m), Columbia; Let Me at 'Em (VS)—Richard Wolf, Wayne Perkins (w,m), Columbia; Karate Kid II Love Theme (VS)—Bill Conti (m), Columbia; Rock N Roll Over You (VS)—John Lodge (w,m), Columbia; Storm (VS)—Bill Conti (m), Columbia; Two Looking at One (VS)—Carly Simon, Jacob Brackman, Bill Conti (w,m), Columbia. COVER: Ralph Macchio, Pat Morita.

2571 Karate Kid, The (III) Columbia, 1989, Ralph Macchio, Pat Morita).

Listen to Your Heart—Tom Kelly, Billy Steinberg (w,m), Barry. COVER: Ralph Macchio, Pat Morita.

2572 Kathleen (MGM, 1941, Shirley Temple, Herbert Marshall).

Around the Corner—Roger Edens, Earl Brent (w,m), Feist. COVER: Shirley Temple.

2573 Kathleen Mavourneen (Fox, 1919, Theda Bara, Edward O'Connor).

Kathleen Mavourneen—Will Heelan (w), Albert Von Tilzer (m), Broadway. COVER: Theda Bara, and Movie Scenes.

2574 Kathy-O (Universal, 1958, Dan Duryea, Jan Sterling).

Kathy-O—Charles Tobias, Ray Joseph, Jack Sher (w,m), Northern. COVER: Dan Duryea, Jan Sterling, Patty McCormack.

2575 Katia (Mayer Burstyn, 1940, Danielle Darrieux, John Loder).

Where Is Love, Where Is the Song, Katia—Blance Merrill (w), Wal Berg (m), Mills. COVER: Danielle Darrieux.

2576 Katie Did It (Universal, 1951, Ann Blyth, Mark Stevens).

Little Old Cape Cod Cottage—Lester Lee, Dan Shapiro (w,m), Barton. COVER: Ann Blyth, Mark Stevens.

2577 Keep 'em Flying (Universal, 1941, Bud Abbott, Lou Costello).

Boy with the Wistful Eyes, The—Don Raye, Gene DePaul (w,m), Leeds; I'm Getting Sentimental Over You—Ned Washington (w), George Bassman (m), Mills; Let's Keep 'em Flying/Pig Foot Pete/You Don't Know What Love Is—Don Raye, Gene DePaul (w,m), Leeds. COVER: Abbott and Costello, Carol Bruce, Martha Raye, Dick Foran.

2578 Keep Smiling (Smiling Along) (20th Century-Fox, 1938, Gracie Fields, Roger Livesey).

Swing Your Way to Happiness (B)—Harry P. Davies (w,m), Day; You've Got to Be Smart in the Army Nowadays (B)—Leslie Elliott, Bob Rutherford (w,m), Day. COVER: Gracie Fields.

2579 Keep Your Powder Dry

(MGM, 1945, Laraine Day, Lana Turner).

I'll See You in My Dreams—Gus Kahn (w), Isham Jones (m), Feist. COVER: Laraine Day, Lana Turner, Susan Peters.

2580 Kelly's Heroes (MGM, 1970, Clint Eastwood, Telly Savalas).

All for the Love of Sunshine/Burning Bridges—Mike Curb (w), Lalo Schifrin (m), Hastings. COVER: Clint Eastwood, and War Scenes.

2581 Kentuckian, The (United Artists, 1955, Burt Lancaster, Dianne Foster).

Kentuckian Song—Irving Gordon (w,m), Frank. COVER: Burt Lancaster, Dianne Foster.

2582 Kentucky Kernels (RKO, 1934, Bert Wheeler, Bob Woolsey).

One Little Kiss—Bert Kalmar, Harry Ruby (w,m), Berlin. COVER: Wheeler and Woolsey, Mary Carlisle.

2583 Kentucky Moonshine (20th Century-Fox, 1938, Tony Martin, Marjorie Weaver).

Isn't It Wonderful Isn't It Swell/ Moonshine Over Kentucky—Sidney Mitchell (w), Lew Pollack (m), Robbins; Reuben Reuben I've Been Swingin'/Shall We Dance/Sing a Song of Harvest—Sidney Mitchell (w), Lew Pollack (m), Hollywood. COVER: Ritz Brothers, Tony Martin, Marjorie Weaver.

2584 Key, The (Warner Bros., 1934, William Powell, Edna Best).

There's a Cottage in Kilharney— Mort Dixon (w), Allie Wrubel (m), Witmark. COVER: William Powell.

2585 Key, The (Columbia, 1958, William Holden, Sophia Loren).

Key to Your Heart, The—Al Stillman (w), Malcolm Arnold (m), Colgems. COVER: William Holden, Sophia Loren.

2586 Key to My Heart, The (Paramount, 1940, Frankie Masters, Marion Francis).

Key to My Heart—Frankie Masters, Kahn Keene, Fay Boswell (w,m), Famous. COVER: Frankie Masters,

Marion Francis.

2587 Key Witness (MGM, 1960, Jeffrey Hunter, Pat Crowley).

Ruby Duby Du—Charles Wolcott (m), Robbins. COVER: Pat Crowley, and Movie Scenes.

2588 Khartoum (United Artists, 1966, Charlton Heston, Laurence Olivier).

Khartoum Theme—Frank Cordell (m), Unart. COVER: Charlton Heston, Laurence Olivier.

2589 Kibitzer (Paramount, 1929, Harry Green, Mary Brian).

Just Wait and See Sweetheart— Leo Robin (w), Richard Whiting (m), Famous. COVER: Harry Green, Mary Brian, Neil Hamilton.

2590 Kicking the Moon Around (Play Boy) (Vogue, 1938, Ambrose, Evelyn Dall).

Two Bouquets/You're What's the Matter with Me—Jimmy Kennedy, Michael Carr (w,m), Shapiro Bernstein. COVER: Blue Barron.

2591 Kid, The (First National, 1921, Charlie Chaplin, Jackie Coogan).

Jackie—Vaughn DeLeath (w,m), Witmark; Wonderful Kid—Willie Howard, Sidney Clare (w), Lew Pollack (m), Berlin. COVER: Jackie Coogan.

2592 Kid Boots (Paramount, 1926, Eddie Cantor, Clara Bow).

He Knows His Groceries—Lou Breau, Billy Hueston (w,m), Marks. COVER: Eddie Cantor.

2593 Kid Brother (Paramount, 1927, Harold Lloyd, Jobyna Ralston).

Kid Brother (B)—William Helmore, Vivian Ellis (w,m), Day. COVER: Harold Lloyd.

2594 Kid from Brooklyn, The (RKO, 1946, Danny Kaye, Virginia Mayo).

Hey What's Your Name/I Love an Old Fashioned Song/Josie/You're the Cause of It All—Sammy Cahn (w), Jule Styne (m), Goldwyn. COVER: Danny Kaye, Virginia Mayo, Vera-Ellen.

2595 **Kid from Spain, The** (United Artists, 1932, Eddie Cantor, Lyda Roberti).

In the Moonlight/Look What You-You've Done/What a Perfect Combination—Bert Kalmar, Harry Ruby (w, m), Harms. COVER: Eddie Cantor, Lyda Roberti.

2595a **Kid from Texas** (MGM, 1939, Dennis O'Keefe, Florence Rice).

Right in the Middle O' Texas—Al Mannheimer, Milton Merlin (w), O. Ruthven (m), Loews. COVER: Black and white cover with title only.

2596 **Kid Galahad** (Warner Bros., 1937, Edward G. Robinson, Bette Davis).

Moon Is in Tears Tonight, The—Jack Scholl (w), M. K. Jerome (m), Harms. COVER: Bette Davis.

2597 **Kid Galahad** (United Artists, 1962, Elvis Presley, Lola Albright).

Home Is Where the Heart Is (B)—Hal David (w), Sherman Edwards (m), Belinda; This Is Living (B)—Fred Wise (w), Ben Weisman (m), Hill Range; I Got Lucky (B)—Ben Weisman, Fred Wise, Dee Fuller (w,m), Hill Range. COVER: Elvis Presley.

2598 **Kid Millions** (United Artists, 1934, Eddie Cantor, Ethel Merman).

Earful of Music, An—Gus Kahn (w), Walter Donaldson (m), Robbins; I Want to Be a Minstrel Man—Harold Adamson (w), Burton Lane (m), Robbins; Okay Toots—Gus Kahn (w), Walter Donaldson (m), Robbins; Mandy—Irving Berlin (w,m), Berlin; When My Ship Comes In—Gus Kahn (w), Walter Donaldson (m), Robbins; Your Head on My Shoulder—Harold Adamson (w), Burton Lane (m), Robbins. COVER: Eddie Cantor.

2599 **Kid Nightingale** (Warner Bros., 1939, John Payne, Jane Wyman).

Who Told You I Cared—George Whiting, Bert Reisfeld (w,m), Witmark. COVER: John Payne, Jane Wyman.

2600 **Kid Rodelo** (Paramount, 1965, Don Murray, Janet Leigh).

Love Is Trouble—Tom Glaser (w, m), Famous. COVER: Don Murray, Janet Leigh.

2601 **Kill or Cure** (MGM, 1962, Terry-Thomas, Eric Sykes).

Kill or Cure (B)—Ron Goodwin (m), Robbins. COVER: Terry-Thomas, Eric Sykes.

2602 **King and I, The** (20th Century-Fox, 1956, Yul Brynner, Deborah Kerr).

Getting to Know You/Hello Young Lovers/I Have Dreamed/I Whistle a Happy Tune/March of the Siamese Children/My Lord and Master/Shall We Dance/Something Wonderful/We Kiss in a Shadow—Oscar Hammerstein (w), Richard Rodgers (m), Williamson. COVER: Deborah Kerr, Yul Brynner.

2603 **King and the Chorus Girl** (Warner Bros., 1937, Joan Blondell, Fernand Gravet).

For You—Ted Koehler, Werner Heymann (w,m), Harms. COVER: Joan Blondell, Fernand Gravet.

2604 **King Creole** (Paramount, 1958, Elvis Presley, Carolyn Jones).

As Long as I Have You—Fred Wise (w), Ben Weisman (m), Gladys; Banana—Sid Tepper, Roy Bennett (w, m), Gladys; Danny—Fred Wise (w), Ben Weisman (m), Gladys; Dixieland Rock—Aaron Schroeder, Rachel Frank (w,m), Gladys; Don't Ask Me Why—Fred Wise (w), Ben Weisman (m), Gladys; Hard Headed Woman—Claude DeMetruis (w,m), Gladys; King Creole—Jerry Leiber, Mike Stoller (w,m), Presley; Lover Doll—Sid Wayne (w), Abner Silver (m), Gladys; New Orleans—Sid Tepper, Roy Bennett (w,m), Gladys; Trouble—Jerry Leiber, Mike Stoller (w,m), Presley; Turtles, Berries, and Gumbo—Al Wood, Kay Twomey (w,m), Presley; Young Dreams—Aaron Schroeder, Martin Kalmanoff (w,m), Gladys. COVER: Elvis Presley.

2605 King in New York, A (Archway, 1957, Charlie Chaplin, Dawn Adams).

Mandolin Serenade (B)/Spring Song (B)/King in New York Themes (B)—Charlie Chaplin (m), Bourne. COVER: Charlie Chaplin, Dawn Adams.

2606 King Kelly of the U.S.A. (Monogram, 1934, Guy Robertson, Irene Ware).

Believe Me/Right Next Door to Love/There's a Love Song in the Air —Bernie Grossman (w), Joe Sanders (m), Harms. COVER: Guy Robertson, Irene Ware.

2607 King Kong (RKO, 1933, Fay Wray, Bruce Cabot).

King Kong Theme—Max Steiner (m), Sam Fox. COVER: RKO Tower.

2608 King Kong (Paramount, 1976, Jessica Lange, Jeff Bridges).

Are You in There—David Pomeranz (w), John Barry (m), Ensign; King Kong Theme—John Barry (m), Ensign. COVER: King Kong.

2609 King of Burlesque (Fox, 1935, Alice Faye, Warner Baxter).

I Love to Ride the Horses—Jack Yellen (w), Lew Pollack (m), Movietone; I'm Shooting High/I've Got My Fingers Crossed/Lovely Lady/Spreadin' Rhythm Around/Whose Big Baby Are You—Ted Koehler (w), Jimmy McHugh (m), Robbins. COVER: Alice Faye, Warner Baxter, Jack Oakie, Kenny Baker.

2610 King of Gamblers (Paramount, 1937, Claire Trevor, Lloyd Nolan).

I'm Feelin' High—Ralph Freed (w), Burton Lane (m), Popular. COVER: Claire Trevor, Akim Tamiroff.

2611 King of Jazz (Universal, 1930, Paul Whiteman, John Boles).

Bench in the Park, A/Happy Feet/ I Like to Do Things for You—Jack Yellen (w), Milton Ager (m), Ager Yellen; It Happened in Monterey— Billy Rose (w), Mabel Wayne (m), Feist; Music Hath Charms—Jack Yel-

len (w), Milton Ager (m), Ager Yellen; My Bridal Veil—John M. Anderson, Jack Yellen, Milton Ager (w,m), Feist; My Lover—Jack Yellen (w), Milton Ager (m), Ager Yellen; Ragamuffin Romeo—Harry DeCosta (w), Mabel Wayne (m), Feist; Song of the Dawn—Jack Yellen (w), Milton Ager (m), Ager Yellen; So the Bluebirds and the Blackbirds Got Together— Billy Moll (w), Harry Barris (m), Shapiro Bernstein. COVER: Paul Whiteman.

2612 King of Kings (MGM, 1961, Jeffrey Hunter, Hurd Hatfield).

King of Kings Theme/Prayer of Our Lord/King of Kings-Eleven Themes—Miklos Rozsa (m), Robbins. COVER: Sketch of Movie Scenes.

2613 King of the Congo (Mascot, 1929, Jacqueline Logan, Walter Miller).

Love Thoughts of You—Lois Leeson (w), Lee Zahler (m), Shapiro Bernstein. COVER: Jacqueline Logan, Walter Miller.

2614 King of the Mardi Gras (Paramount, 1935, Cartoon).

I'm King of the Mardi Gras (VS)— Bob Rothberg (w), Sammy Timberg (m), Famous. COVER: Popeye.

2615 King Rat (Columbia, 1965, George Segal, James Fox).

King Rat March—John Barry (m), Colgems. COVER: Movie Scenes.

2616 Kings Go Forth (United Artists, 1958, Frank Sinatra, Tony Curtis).

Kings Go Forth Song-Monique— Sammy Cahn (w), Elmer Bernstein (m), Barton. COVER: Frank Sinatra, Tony Curtis, Natalie Wood.

2617 King Solomon of Broadway (Universal, 1935, Dorothy Page, Edmund Lowe).

Flower in My Lapel—Herb Magidson, Con Conrad (w,m), Harms; Moanin' in the Moonlight—Herb Magidson (w), Con Conrad (m), Harms; That's What You Think— Pinky Tomlin, Ray Jasper, Coy Poe (w,m), Berlin. COVER: Dorothy Page, Edmund Lowe.

2618 King Solomon's Mines (GB, 1937, Paul Robeson, Robert Young).

Climbing Up Climbing Up/Ho Ho the Wagon Song—Eric Maschwitz (w), Mischa Spoliansky (m), Mills. COVER: Paul Robeson.

2619 King's Rhapsody (United Artists, 1955, Errol Flynn, Anna Neagle).

Years Together, The—Chris Hassall (w), Ivor Novello (m), Chappell. COVER: Anna Neagle, Error Flynn, Patrice Wymore.

2620 King's Row (Warner Bros., 1941, Ann Sheridan, Robert Cummings).

King's Row Piano Suite—Erich W. Korngold (m), Warner. COVER: Green cover with title only.

2621 King Steps Out, The (Columbia, 1936, Grace Moore, Franchot Tone).

End Begins, The/Learn How to Love—Dorothy Fields (w), Fritz Kreisler (m), Fischer; Madly in Love/Stars in My Eyes—Dorothy Fields (w), Fritz Kreisler (m), Chappell; What Shall Remain—Dorothy Fields (w), Fritz Kreisler (m), Fischer. COVER: Franchot Tone, Grace Moore.

2622 Kismet (Robertson Cole, 1920, Otis Skinner, Leon Barry).

Kismet—Herschel Henlere, Guido Diero (w,m), Rossiter. COVER: Otis Skinner, Leon Barry.

2623 Kismet (MGM, 1934, Ronald Colman, Marlene Dietrich).

Tell Me Tell Me Evening Star/ Willow in the Wind—E. Y. Harburg (w), Harold Arlen (m), Feist. COVER: Marlene Dietrich, Ronald Colman.

2624 Kismet (MGM, 1955, Howard Keel, Dolores Gray).

And This Is My Beloved/Baubles Bangles and Beads/Bored/Night of My Nights/Sands of Time, The/ Stranger in Paradise, A/He's in Love (VS)/Not Since Nineveh (VS)—Robert Wright, George Forrest, A. Borodin (w,m), Frank. COVER: Arabic Designs.

2625 Kiss and Make Up (Paramount, 1934, Cary Grant, Genevieve Tobin).

Love Divided by Two—Leo Robin, Ralph Rainger (w,m), Famous. COVER: Cary Grant, Genevieve Tobin.

2626 Kiss Before Dying, A (United Artists, 1956, Robert Wagner, Jeffrey Hunter).

Kiss Before Dying, A—Carroll Coates (w), Lionel Newman (m), Weiss Barry. COVER: Robert Wagner, Joanne Woodward.

2627 Kiss Before the Mirror, The (Universal, 1933, Nancy Carroll, Frank Morgan).

A Little Bit of Love—J. Keirn Brennan (w), W. Franke Harling (m), Feist. COVER: Nancy Carroll, Frank Morgan.

2628 Kisses for My President (Warner Bros., 1964, Fred MacMurray, Polly Bergen).

Kisses—Ric Harlow (w), Bronislau Kaper (m), Witmark. COVER: Fred MacMurray, Polly Bergen.

2629 Kissin' Cousins (MGM, 1964, Elvis Presley, Arthur O'Connell).

Anyone—Bennie Benjamin, Sol Marcus, Louis DeJesus (w,m), Gladys; Barefoot Ballad—Dee Fuller, Lee Morris (w,m), Gladys; Catchin' on Fast—Bill Giant, Bernie Baum, Florence Kaye (w,m), Presley; Echoes of Love—Bob Roberts, Patty McMains (w,m), Presley; It's a Long Lonely Highway—Doc Pomus, Mort Shuman (w,m), Presley; Kissin' Cousins #1— Fred Wise, Randy Starr (w,m), Gladys; Kissin' Cousins #2—Bill Giant, Bernie Baum, Florence Kaye (w,m), Presley; Once Is Enough—Sid Tepper, Roy Bennett (w,m), Gladys; One Boy Two Little Girls—Bill Giant, Bernie Baum, Florence Kaye (w,m), Presley; Smokey Mountain Boy—Lenore Rosenblatt, Victor Millrose (w, m), Presley; Tender Feeling/There's Gold in the Mountains—Bill Giant, Bernie Baum, Florence Kaye (w,m), Presley. COVER: Elvis Presley.

2630 Kissing Bandit, The (MGM, 1948, Frank Sinatra, Kathryn Grayson).

If I Steal a Kiss—Edward Heyman (w), Nacio Herb Brown (m), Feist; Love Is Where You Find It/Siesta—Earl Brent (w), Nacio Herb Brown (m), Feist; Senorita—Edward Heyman (w), Nacio Herb Brown (m), Feist; Tomorrow Means Romance—William Katz (w), Nacio Herb Brown (m), Feist; What's Wrong with Me—Edward Heyman (w), Nacio Herb Brown (m), Feist; Latigazos De Pasion—Vicente Gomez, Calvin Jackson (m), Mills. COVER: Frank Sinatra, Kathryn Grayson.

2631 Kissing Time (Vitaphone, 1934, Jane Frohman, George Metaxa).

All My Life I've Waited/Love, Look What You've Done to Me—Cliff Hess (w,m), Witmark. COVER: Black and white cover with title only.

2632 Kiss in the Dark (Warner Bros., 1945, David Niven, Jane Wyman).

Kiss in the Dark, A—B. G. DeSylva (w), Victor Herbert (m), Witmark. COVER: David Niven, Jane Wyman.

2633 Kiss Me Again (Warner Bros., 1925, Marie Prevost, Monte Blue).

Kiss Me Again—Henry Blossom (w), Victor Herbert (m), Witmark. COVER: Marie Prevost, Monte Blue.

2634 Kiss Me Deadly (United Artists, 1955, Ralph Meeker, Albert Dekker).

Blues from Kiss Me Deadly—Frank DeVol (w,m), Winneton. COVER: Ralph Meeker, Gaby Rogers, King Cole.

2635 Kiss Me Kate (MGM, 1953, Howard Keel, Kathryn Grayson).

Always True to You in My Fashion/Bianca/From This Moment On/I Hate Men/So in Love/Were Thine That Special Face/Why Can't You Behave/Wunderbar—Cole Porter (w,m), Harms. COVER: Howard Keel, Kathryn Grayson.

2636 Kiss Me Stupid (United Artists, 1964, Dean Martin, Kim Novak).

All the Live Long Day/I'm a Poached Egg/Sophia—Ira Gershwin (w), George Gershwin (m), Gershwin. COVER: Dean Martin, Kim Novak, Ray Walston.

2637 Kiss of Death (20th Century-Fox, 1947, Victor Mature, Coleen Gray).

Sentimental Rhapsody—Harold Adamson (w), Alfred Newman (m), Robbins. COVER: Victor Mature, Coleen Gray.

2638 Kiss the Boys Goodbye (Paramount, 1941, Mary Martin, Don Ameche).

Find Yourself a Melody/I'll Never Let a Day Pass By/Kiss the Boys Goodbye/Sand in My Shoes/That's How I Got My Start—Frank Loesser (w), Victor Schertzinger (m), Santly Joy. COVER: Mary Martin.

2639 Kiss the Girls and Make Them Die (Columbia, 1967, Michael Connors, Dorothy Provine).

Kiss the Girls and Make Them Die—Howard Greenfield (w), Mario Nascimbene (m), Colgems. COVER: Movie Scenes.

2640 Kiss Them for Me (20th Century-Fox, 1957, Cary Grant, Suzy Parker).

Kiss Them for Me—Carroll Coates (w), Lionel Newman (m), Miller. COVER: Cary Grant, Suzy Parker.

2641 Kit Carson (United Artists, 1940, Jon Hall, Lynn Bari).

Prairie Schooner/With My Concertina—Chet Forrest, Bob Wright (w), Edward Ward (m), Mills. COVER: Jon Hall, Lynn Bari.

2642 Kitten on the Keys (Do You Love Me) (20th Century-Fox, 1945, Dick Haymes, Maureen O'Hara).

I Didn't Mean a Word I Said—Harold Adamson (w), Jimmy McHugh (m), Robbins. COVER: Dick Haymes, Maureen O'Hara, Harry James.

2643 Kitty (Paramount, 1946, Ray Milland, Paulette Goddard).

Kitty—Jay Livingston, Ray Evans (w,m), Paramount. COVER: Ray Milland, Paulette Goddard.

2644 Kitty Foyle (RKO, 1940, Ginger Rogers, Dennis Morgan).

I'll See You in My Dreams (PC)—Gus Kahn (w), Isham Jones (m), Feist. COVER: None.

2645 Kliou the Killer (Duworld, 1937, Henry De La Falaise, Charles Carney).

Kliou the Killer-Music Suite—Heinz Roemheld (m), Meyer. COVER: Black and white cover with title only.

2646 Klondike Annie (Paramount, 1936, Mae West, Victor McLaglen).

Cheer Up Little Sister/Little Bar Butterfly—Gene Austin (w,m), Famous; Mister Deep Blue Sea—Gene Austin, Jimmie Johnson (w,m), Famous; Occidental Women—Gene Austin (w,m), Famous. COVER: Mae West.

2647 Knack-And How to Get It (United Artists, 1965, Michael Crawford, Rita Tushingham).

Knack, The—Leslie Bricusse (w), John Barry (m), Unart. COVER: Rita Tushingham.

2648 Knickerbocker Holiday (United Artists, 1944, Nelson Eddy, Charles Coburn).

Love Has Made This Such a Lovely Day/One More Smile—Sammy Cahn (w), Jule Styne (m), Crawford; September Song—Maxwell Anderson (w), Kurt Weill (m), Crawford. COVER: Nelson Eddy, Constance Dowling, Charles Coburn.

2649 Knights of the Range (Paramount, 1940, William Boyd, Victor Jory).

Covered Wagon Rolled Right Along, The—Britt Wood (w), Hy Heath (m), American; Where the Cimarron Flows—Foster Carling (w), Phil Ohman (m), Famous. COVER: William Boyd, Chill Wills.

2650 Knock Na Gow (Irish, 1919, Fred O'Donovan, Kathleen

Murphy).

In the Valley Near Sleivenamon—Daniel Sullivan (w,m), Witmark. COVER: Black and white cover with title only.

2651 Knock on Wood (Paramount, 1954, Danny Kaye, Mai Zetterling).

All About You—Sylvia Fine (w, m), Famous; End of Spring-Ballet—Sylvia Fine (m), Famous; Knock on Wood—Sylvia Fine (w,m), Famous. COVER: Danny Kaye, Mai Zetterling.

2652 Knowmore College (Paramount, 1931, Rudy Vallee).

Rhyming Song—Sammy Lerner (w), Sammy Timberg (m), Famous. COVER: Rudy Vallee.

2653 Koko the Clown (Red Seal, 1925, Cartoon).

Dixie—Dan Emmett (w,m), Red Seal; Sweet Adeline—Richard Girard, Harry Armstrong (w,m), Red Seal. COVER: Koko.

2654 Kon Tiki (RKO, 1951, Thor Heyerdahl, Knut Haugland).

Kon Tiki—Jose Mendez, Al Jacobs (w,m), Fred Bee. COVER: Native Girl and Boat.

2655 Kotch (Cinerama, 1971, Walter Matthau, Deborah Winters).

Life Is What You Make It—Johnny Mercer (w), Marvin Hamlisch (m), Ampco. COVER: Walter Matthau, and Movie Scenes.

2656 Krakatoa East of Java (Volcano) (Cinerama, 1967, Maximillian Schell, Diane Baker).

East of Java/Just Before Sunrise/ Kee Kana Lu/Nice Old Fashioned Girl—Mack David, Alta. COVER: Movie Scenes.

2657 Kramer vs. Kramer (Columbia, 1979, Dustin Hoffman, Meryl Streep).

Vivaldi Concerto in C—Herb Harris (m), Gold Horizon. COVER: Dustin Hoffman, Meryl Streep, and Boy.

2658 Krazy Kat (Columbia, 1930, Cartoon).

Kat's Meow, The—Joe DeNat, Jimmy Bronis (w,m), Columbia. COVER: Cartoon.

2659 Krull (Columbia, 1983, Ken Marshall, Lysette Anthony).

In Each Other's Arms—Bruce Roberts (w), James Horner (m), Golden Torch; Lyssa's Love Theme—James Horner (m), Golden Torch. COVER: Ken Marshall, Lysette Anthony.

2660 Krush Groove (Warner, 1985, Blair Underwood, Joseph Simmons).

Can't Stop the Street—Dan Hartman, Charlie Midnight (w,m), April; Tender Love—James Harris, Terry Lewis (w,m), Warner. COVER: Chaka Khan.

2661 La Boheme (MGM, 1925, Lillian Gish, John Gilbert).

Appassionato #4/Dramatic Andante #3—William Axt (m), Robbins; Thinking of You (Promotion Song)—Joseph Grey (w), Allie Moore (m), Stern. COVER: Lillian Gish, John Gilbert.

2662 La Bamba (Columbia, 1987, Lou Diamond Phillips, Esai Morales).

Come on Let's Go/Donna—Richie Valens (w,m), Warner; Framed—Jerry Leiber, Mike Stoller (w,m), Warner; La Bamba—Ritchie Valens (w,m), Warner; Summertime Blues—Eddie Cochran, Jerry Capehart (w,m), Warner; Charlena (VS)—Manuel Chavaz, Herman Chaney (w,m), Warner; Crying Waiting Hoping (VS)—Buddy Holly (w,m), Warner; Goodnight My Love, Pleasant Dreams (VS)—George Motola, John Marascalco (w,m), Warner; Lonely Teardrops (VS)—Berry Gordy, Gwen Gordy, Tryan Carlo (w,m), Warner; Ooh, My Head (VS)—Ritchie Valens (w,m), Warner; We Belong Together (VS)—Bob Carr, John Mitchell, Sam Weiss (w,m), Warner; Who Do You Love (VS)—Ellas McDaniel (w,m), Warner. COVER: Lou Diamond Phillips.

2663 Labyrinth (Tri-Star, 1986, David Bowie, Jennifer Connelly).

Labyrinth-Nine Songs—David Bowie, Trevor Jones (w,m), Leonard. COVER: David Bowie, Jennifer Connelly.

2664 La Chamade (United Artists, 1969, Catherine Deneuve, Michel Piccoli).

La Chamade—Dominic Frontiere (m), Unart. COVER: Catherine Deneuve, Michel Piccoli.

2665 La Conga Nights (Universal, 1940, Constance Moore, Dennis O'Keefe).

Carmelita McCoy/Chance of a Lifetime/Havana—Sam Lerner (w), Frank Skinner (m), Robbins. COVER: Constance Moore, Dennis O'—Keefe.

2666 La Cucaracha (RKO, 1934, Steffi Duna, Don Alvarado).

La Cucaracha—Juan Dilorah (w, m), Berlin. COVER: Steffi Duna, Don Alvarado.

2667 Ladies in Love (Chesterfield, 1930, Alice Day, Johnnie Walker).

My Big Boy/Oh How I Love You—Lester Lee, Charles Levison (w,m), Bibo Lang. COVER: Alice Day, Johnnie Walker.

2668 Ladies Man (Paramount, 1947, Eddie Bracken, Cass Daley).

Away Out West/I Gotta Gal I Love/I'm as Ready as I'll Ever Be/What Am I Gonna Do About You—Sammy Cahn (w), Jule Styne (m), Famous. COVER: Eddie Bracken, Spike Jones.

2669 Ladies Man (Paramount, 1961, Jerry Lewis, Helen Traubel).

Don't Go to Paris (BW)/He Doesn't Know—Jack Brooks (w), Harry Warren (m), Paramount. COVER: Jerry Lewis, and Girls.

2670 Ladies Must Live (Warner Bros., 1940, Wayne Morris, Rosemary Lane).

I Could Make You Care—Sammy Cahn (w), Saul Chaplin (m), Witmark. COVER: Wayne Morris, Rosemary Lane.

2671 Ladies Must Love (Universal, 1933, June Knight, Neil Hamilton).

I'd Worship Him Just the Same—Lynn Cowan, Paul Worth (w,m), Sherman Clay; I'm Living with the Bluebirds—Lynn Cowan, Harry Sauber (w,m), Sherman Clay; Someone to Love/Tonight May Never Come Again—Lynn Cowan, Dave Klatzkin (w,m), Sherman Clay. COVER: June Knight.

2672 Ladies of the Big House (Paramount, 1931, Gene Raymond, Sylvia Sidney).

Nearer and Dearer—Haven Gillespie (w), Egbert Van Alstyne (m), Remick. COVER: Sylvia Sidney, Gene Raymond.

2673 Ladies of the Chorus (Columbia, 1949, Marilyn Monroe, Adele Jergens).

Ev'ry Baby Needs a Da-Da-Daddy—Allan Roberts, Lester Lee (w,m), Mood. COVER: Marilyn Monroe, and Chorus.

2674 La Dolce Vita (Astor, 1960, Marcello Mastroianni, Anita Ekberg).

La Dolce Vita—Les Vandyke (w), Nino Rota (m), Robbins. COVER: Anita Ekberg.

2675 Lady and Gent (Paramount, 1932, Wynne Gibson, George Bancroft).

Everyone Knows It But You—Sam Coslow (w), Arthur Johnston (m), Famous. COVER: Wynne Gibson.

2676 Lady and the Tramp (Disney, 1955, Cartoon).

Bella Notte/He's a Tramp—Peggy Lee, Sonny Burke (w,m), Disney; Lady—Sidney Fine, Ed Penner (w), Oliver Wallace (m), Disney; La La Lu/Peace on Earth/Siamese Cat Song—Peggy Lee, Sonny Burke (w,m), Disney. COVER: Cartoons.

2677 Lady Be Good (MGM, 1941, Eleanor Powell, Robert Young).

Fascinating Rhythm—Ira Gershwin (w), George Gershwin (m), Harms; Last Time I Saw Paris, The—Oscar Hammerstein (w), Jerome Kern (m), Chappell; Oh Lady Be Good—Ira Gershwin (w), George Gershwin (m), Harms; You'll Never Know—Roger Edens (w,m), Feist; Your Words and My Music—Roger Edens, Arthur Freed (w,m), Feist. COVER: Eleanor Powell, Robert Young, Ann Sothern.

2678 Lady Fare (Christie, 1929, Leon Herefold).

Hot and Bothered/She's the Hottest Gal in Tennessee—Henry Creamer (w), Jimmy Johnson (m), Shapiro Bernstein. COVER: Black Chorus Girls.

2679 Lady for a Day (Columbia, 1933, Warren Williams, May Robson).

Lady for a Day—Con Conrad, Sidney Mitchell, Archie Gottler (w,m), Berlin. COVER: Black and White cover with title only.

2680 Lady from Shanghai, The (Columbia, 1948, Rita Hayworth, Orson Welles).

Please Don't Kiss Me—Allan Roberts, Doris Fisher (w,m), Mood. COVER: Rita Hayworth.

2681 Lady in Cement (20th Century-Fox, 1968, Frank Sinatra, Raquel Welch).

Lady in Cement/Tony's Theme—Hugo Montenegro (m), Fox. COVER: Sketches.

2682 Lady in Ermine, The (First National, 1927, Francis Bushman, Corinne Griffith).

Just Like a Pure White Rose (B)—Reed Stampa (w,m), David. COVER: Corinne Griffith.

2683 Lady in the Dark (Paramount, 1944, Ginger Rogers, Ray Milland).

Jenny/My Ship—Ira Gershwin (w), Kurt Weill (m), Chappell; Suddenly It's Spring—Johnny Burke (w), Jame James Van Heusen (m), Famous. COVER: Ginger Rogers.

2684 Lady Is Willing, The (Columbia, 1942, Marlene Dietrich, Fred MacMurray).

Strange Thing—Gordon Clifford

(w), Jack King (m), Saunders. COVER: Marlene Dietrich.

2685 Lady "L" (MGM, 1966, Paul Newman, Sophia Loren).

Lady "L" Theme—Jean Francaix, Allesandro Mentrasti (m), Miller. COVER: Sophia Loren, Paul Newman.

2686 Lady Let's Dance (Monogram, 1944, Belita, James Ellison).

Dream of Dreams—Dave Oppenheim, Ted Grouya (w,m), Southern; Silver Shadows and Golden Dreams—Charles Newman (w), Lew Pollack (m), Hollywood; Ten Million Men and a Girl—Dave Oppenheim, Ted Grouya (w,m), Southern. COVER: Belita, and Movie Scenes.

2687 Lady Objects, The (Columbia, 1938, Lanny Ross, Gloria Stuart).

Home in Your Arms/Mist Is Over the Moon, A/Sky High (Q)—Oscar Hammerstein (w), Ben Oakland (m), ABC; That Week in Paris/When You're in the Room—Oscar Hammerstein (w), Ben Oakland (m), Chappell. COVER: Gloria Stuart, Lanny Ross.

2688 Lady of Burlesque (United Artists, 1939, Barbara Stanwyck, Michael O'Shea).

So This Is You/Take It Off the "E" String—Sammy Cahn (w), Harry Akst (m), Fisher. COVER: Barbara Stanwyck, and Girls.

2689 Lady of Chance (MGM, 1928, Norma Shearer, Lowell Sherman).

Just a Little Bit of Driftwood—Benny Davis, Dohl Davis, Abe Lyman (w,m), Robbins. COVER: Norma Shearer.

2690 Lady of the Lake (Fitzpatrick, 1930, Benita Hume, Percy Marmont).

Ellen Sweet Ellen—Morris Ryskind (w), Nat Shilkret (m), Atlas. COVER: Benita Hume.

2691 Lady of the Pavements (Masquerade) (United Artists, 1929, Lupe Velez, William Boyd).

Where Is the Song of Songs for Me —Irving Berlin (w,m), Berlin. COVER: Lupe Velez.

2692 Lady of the Tropics (MGM, 1939, Hedy Lamarr, Robert Taylor).

Each Time You Say Goodbye—Foster Carling (w), Phil Ohman (m), Feist. COVER: Hedy Lamarr, Robert Taylor.

2693 Lady on a Train (Universal, 1945, Deanna Durbin, Ralph Bellamy).

Give Me a Little Kiss—Roy Turk, Jack Smith, Maceo Pinkard (w,m), Bourne; Silent Night Holy Night (B) —King Palmer (w,m), Paxton. COVER: Deanna Durbin.

2694 Lady Sings the Blues (Paramount, 1972, Diana Ross, Billy Dee Williams).

Classy Miss (PC)—Gil Askey (m), Famous; Don't Explain—Arthur Herzog (w), Billie Holiday (m), Northern; Gimme a Pigfoot—Wesley Wilson (w,m), Northern; God Bless the Child —Arthur Herzog, Billie Holiday (w, m), Belwin; Good Morning Heartache —Irene Higginbotham, Ervin Drake, Dan Fisher (w,m), Fisher; Happy—Smokey Robinson (w), Michel Legrand (m), Jobete; Happy Theme—Michel Legrand (m), Jobete; Lady Sings the Blues—Billie Holiday (w), Herbie Nichols (m), Northern; Lady Sings the Blues Love Theme—Michel Legrand (m), Jobete; Lover Man—Jim Davis, Ram Ramirez, Jimmy Sherman (w,m), MCA; Tain't Nobody's Bizness If I Do—Porter Grainger, Everett Robbins (w,m), MCA; Those Shuffle Blues (PC)—Gil Askey (m), Famous; Fine and Mellow (VS)—Billie Holiday (w,m), Marks; Strange Fruit (VS)—Lewis Allan (w,m), Marks. COVER: Diana Ross.

2695 Lady's Morals, A (MGM, 1930, Grace Moore, Wallace Beery).

I Hear Your Voice—Arthur Freed, Clifford Grey (w), Oscar Straus (m), Harms; It Is Destiny—Clifford Grey (w), Oscar Straus (m), Harms; Lovely Hour—Carrie Jacobs Bond (w,m),

Bond; Oh Why—Arthur Freed (w), Herbert Stothart, Harry Woods (m), Robbins. COVER: Grace Moore.

2696 Lady Surrenders, A (Universal, 1944, Margaret Lockwood, Stewart Granger).

Cornish Rhapsody—Hubert Bath (m), Mills. COVER: Margaret Lockwood.

2697 Lady with Red Hair, The (Warner Bros., 1940, Miriam Hopkins, Claude Rains).

Lady with Red Hair, The—Bickley Reichner (w), Guy Wood (m), Remick. COVER: Mirian Hopkins.

2698 La Fayette (Maco, 1963, Orson Welles, Jack Hawkins).

La Fayette Theme-Slowly Slowly —Norbert Terry (w), Steve Laurent, Pierre Duclos (m), Cromwell. COVER: The Brothers Four.

2699 Lafayette Escadrille (Warner Bros., 1957, Tab Hunter, Etchika Choureau).

Learning to Love—Paul F. Webster (w), Leonard Rosenman (m), Witmark. COVER: Tab Hunter, Etchika Choureau.

2700 La Guerre Est Finie (The War Is Over) (Brandon, 1966, Yves Montand, Ingrid Thulin).

Seeing You Like This—Ray Fox (w), G. Fusco (m), Marks. COVER: Yves Montand, and Movie Scenes.

2701 La Inmaculada (United Artists, 1939, Fortunio Bonanova, Andrea Palma).

Divine Temptation—Fortunio Bonanova (w,m), Southern. COVER: Movie Scenes.

2702 Land Before Time, The (Universal, 1988, Cartoon).

If We Hold on Together—James Horner, Will Jennings (w,m), MCA. COVER: Cartoon.

2703 Landlord, The (United Artists, 1970, Lee Grant, Beau Bridges).

Brand New Day/Landlord Love Theme—Al Kooper (w,m), Unart. COVER: Doorbells.

2704 Land of Missing Men, The (Tiffany, 1930, Bob Steele, Caryl Lincoln).

Out at Prairie's End—Jack Scholl (w), Jean Schwartz (m), Feist. COVER: Mountains.

2705 Land of the Giants (Warner Bros., 1970, Stars Unknown).

Land of the Giants (VS)—John Williams (m), Warner. COVER: John Williams.

2706 Land of the Pharaohs (Warner Bros., 1955, Jack Hawkins, Joan Collins).

Land of the Pharaohs—Ned Washington (w), Dimitri Tiomkin (m), Remick; Land of the Pharaohs Theme—Dimitri Tiomkin. COVER: Joan Collins, Dewey Martin.

2707 La Piscine (The Swimming Pool) (Embassy, 1971, Alain Delon, Romy Schneider).

Ask Yourself Why/One at a Time —Alan Bergman, Marilyn Bergman (w), Michel Legrand (m), Unart. COVER: Black and white cover with title only.

2708 Larceny with Music (Universal, 1943, Allan Jones, Kitty Carlisle).

Do You Hear Music—Don Raye, Gene DePaul (w,m), Robbins; For the Want of You—Eddie Cherkose (w), Jule Styne (m), Melrose; Please Louise—Don Raye, Gene DePaul (w, m), Robbins. COVER: Allan Jones, Kitty Carlisle, Alvino Rey, King Sisters.

2709 La Ronde (Commercial, 1950, Anton Walbrook, Simone Signoret).

La Ronde-Merry Go Round—Dorcas Cochran (w), Oscar Straus (m), Hill Range; La Ronde-de l'Amour— Louis Ducreux (w), Oscar Straus (m), Choudens. COVER: Merry Go Round.

2710 La Ronde des Heures (Haik, 1932, Stars Unknown).

I Wouldn't Care-Valse Berceuse— Leo Robin (w), P. Read (m), Harms. COVER: A Clock.

2711 Last American Hero, The

(20th Century-Fox, 1973, Jeff Bridges, Valerie Perrine).

I Got a Name—Norman Gimbel (w), Charles Fox (m), Fox. COVER: Jim Croce.

2712 Last Command, The (Republic, 1955, Sterling Hayden, Anna Maria Alberghetti).

Jim Bowie—Sidney Clare, Sheila MacRae (w), Max Steiner (m), Young. COVER: Sterling Hayden.

2713 Last Dance, The (Audible, 1930, Jason Robards, Vera Reynolds).

Sally, I'm Lovin' You Sally—Haven Gillespie, Neil Moret (w,m), Villa Moret. COVER: Jason Robards, Vera Reynolds.

2714 Last Detail, The (Columbia, 1973, Jack Nicholson, Randy Quaid).

American Patrol—F. Meacham (m), Colgems. COVER: Jack Nicholson.

2715 Last Dragon, The (Tri-Star, 1985, Taimak, Julius Carry).

Peeping Tom—Rockwell, Janet Cole, Antoine Greene (w,m), Jobete; Rhythm of the Night—Diane Warren (w,m), Sunset; Star—Gwen Fuqua, Gregg Crockett, Sharon Barnes (w,m), Jobete; Fire (VS)—Charlene Oliver, Brian Wild, Nigel Wright (w, m), Columbia; First Time on a Ferris Wheel (VS)—Harriet Schock, Misha Segal (w,m), Columbia; Glow (VS)/ Inside You (VS)—Willie Hutch, (w, m), Columbia; Last Dragon, The (VS)—Norman Whitfield, Bruce Miller (w,m), Columbia; Seventh Heaven (VS)—Vanity Wolfer, Bill Wolfer, Columbia; Upset Stomach (VS)—Stevie Wonder (w,m), Columbia. COVER: Taimak, Julius Carry.

2716 Last Frontier, The (Columbia, 1955, Victor Mature, Robert Preston).

Last Frontier, The—Ned Washington (m), Lester Lee (m), Colgems. COVER: Anne Bancroft, Victor Mature.

2717 Last Man on Earth, The (Fox, 1932, Earle Fose, Grace Cunard).

I'll Build a Nest—William Kernell (w,m), Movietone. COVER: Black and white cover with title only.

2718 Last Married Couple in America, The (Universal, 1979, George Segal, Natalie Wood).

We Could Have It all—Norman Gimbel (w), Charles Fox (m), Duchess. COVER: George Segal, Natalie Wood, Richard Benjamin, Valerie Harper.

2719 Last of the Red Hot Lovers, The (Paramount, 1972, Alan Arkin, Sally Kellerman).

I'm There—Alan Bergman, Marilyn Bergman (w), Neal Hefti (m), Famous; Last of the Red Hot Lovers—Mack David, Mike Curb, Alan Osmond (w,m), Famous. COVER: Cartoon Sketch.

2720 Last of the Secret Agents, The (Paramount, 1966, Marty Allen, Steve Rossi).

Don Jose Olé!—Mel Tolkin, Norman Abbott (w), Pete King (m), Famous; Last of the Secret Agents, The —Lee Hazelwood (w,m), Famous; You Are—Neal Hefti (w,m), Paramount. COVER: Marty Allen, Steve Rossi.

2721 Last Outlaw, The (RKO, 1936, Hoot Gibson, Margaret Callahan).

My Heart's on the Trail—Frank Luther (w), Nat Shilkret (m), Southern. COVER: Hoot Gibson, Margaret Callahan.

2722 La Strada (Ponti De Laurentiis, 1954, Anthony Quinn, Giulietta Masina).

La Strada Love Theme—M. Galdiere, Nino Rota (w,m), Leeds; Traveling Down a Lonely Road—Don Raye (w), M. Galdiere, Nino Rota (m), Leeds; You and You Alone/ Zampano—M. Galdiere, Nino Rota (m), Leeds. COVER: Anthony Quinn, Giulietta Masina.

2723 Last Round-Up, The (Columbia, 1947, Gene Autry, Jean Heather).

Hundred and Sixty Acres, A—
David Kapp (w,m), Leeds; Last
Round-Up, The—Billy Hill (w,m),
Shapiro Bernstein. COVER: Gene
Autry.
2724 Last Run, The (MGM,
1971, George Scott, Tony Musante).
Last Run Theme—Jerry Gold-
smith (m), Hastings. COVER: George
Scott.
2725 Last Safari, The (Para-
mount, 1967, Stewart Granger, Kaz
Garas).
Last Safari Theme/Last Safari
Music Score—John Dankworth (m),
Famous. COVER: Stewart Granger,
and Movie Scenes.
2726 Last Stand, The (Univer-
sal, 1938, Bob Baker, Constance
Moore).
Adios My Rose of Laredo—Ho-
mer Gayne (w), Atze Taconis (m),
Davis Schwegler. COVER: Bob
Baker.
2727 Last Summer, The (Allied
Artists, 1969, Richard Thomas, Bar-
bara Hershey).
Last Summer, The—Robert Colby
(w), John Simon (m), Allied Artists.
COVER: Girl on Beach.
2728 Last Sunset, The (Univer-
sal, 1961, Rock Hudson, Kirk Doug-
las).
Pretty Little Girl in the Yellow
Dress—Ned Washington (w), Dimitri
Tiomkin (m), Leeds. COVER: Rock
Hudson, Kirk Douglas, Carol Lynley,
Dorothy Malone.
2729 Last Tango in Paris (United
Artists, 1973, Marlon Brando, Maria
Schneider).
Last Tango in Paris—Dory Previn
(w), Gato Barbieri (m), Unart; Last
Tango in Paris-Theme/Last Tango in
Paris-Twelve Themes—Gato Bar-
bieri (m), Unart. COVER: Marlon
Brando.
2730 Last Time I Saw Archie
(United Artists, 1960, Robert
Mitchum, Jack Webb).
Angel Face—William Bowers (w),
Herm Saunders (m), Feist; At Last—

Mack Gordon (w), Harry Warren (m),
Feist. COVER: Robert Mitchum,
Jack Webb, Martha Hyer, France
Nuyen.
2731 Last Time I Saw Paris, The
(MGM, 1954, Van Johnson, Eliza-
beth Taylor).
Dance Avec Moi—Harold Rome
(w), Andre Hornez, Francis Lopez
(m), Leeds; Last Time I Saw Paris,
The—Oscar Hammerstein (w), Jer-
ome Kern (m), Harms. COVER:
Van Johnson, Elizabeth Taylor.
2732 Last Tycoon, The (Para-
mount, 1976, Tony Curtis, Robert
DeNiro).
Last   Tycoon-Theme—Maurice
Jarre (m), Famous. COVER: Robert
DeNiro.
2733 Last Wagon, The (20th
Century-Fox, 1956, Richard Wid-
mark, Felicia Farr).
Last Wagon Theme—Carroll
Coates (w), Lionel Newman (m),
Weiss Barry. COVER: Richard Wid-
mark, Felicia Farr, and Movie Scene.
2734 Las Vegas Nights (Para-
mount, 1941, Phil Regan, Bert
Wheeler).
Dolores—Frank Loesser (w), Louis
Alter (m), Paramount; I Gotta Ride/
Mary Mary Quite Contrary—Frank
Loesser (w), Burton Lane (m), Para-
mount; On Miami Shore—William Le-
Baron (w), Victor Jacobi (m), Chap-
pell. COVER: Phil Regan, Constance
Moore, Tommy Dorsey, Frank Sina-
tra.
2735 Las Vegas Story, The
(RKO, 1952, Jane Russell, Victor
Mature).
I Get Along without You Very
Well (B)—Hoagy Carmichael (w,m),
Victoria; My Resistance Is Low (B)—
Harold Adamson (w), Hoagy Car-
michael (m), Frank. COVER: Jane
Russell, Hoagy Carmichael.
2736 Latin Lovers (MGM, 1953,
Lana Turner, John Lund).
Carlotta, Ya Gotta Be Mine/I Had
to Kiss You—Leo Robin (w), Nich-
olas Brodszky (m), Morris; Papa

Loves Mambo (B)—Al Hoffman, Dick Manning, Bix Reichner (w,m), Shapiro Bernstein. COVER: Lana Turner, John Lund, Ricardo Montalban.

2737　Laugh Clown Laugh (MGM, 1928, Loretta Young, Lon Chaney).

Laugh Clown Laugh—Sam Lewis, Joe Young (w), Ted Fiorito (m), Remick. COVER: Lon Chaney.

2738　Laughing Boy (MGM, 1934, Lupe Velez, Ramon Novarro).

Call of Love—Gus Kahn (w), Herbert Stothart (m), Robbins. COVER: Ramon Novarro, Lupe Velez.

2739　Laughing Irish Eyes (Republic, 1936, Phil Regan, Evelyn Knapp).

All My Life—Sidney Mitchell (w), Sam Stept (m), Sam Fox; Bless You Darlin' Mother—Sam Stept (w,m), Sam Fox; Laughing Irish Eyes—Sidney Mitchell (w), Sam Stept (m), Sam Fox. COVER: Phil Regan, Evelyn Knapp.

2740　Laughing Lady (Paramount, 1927, Ruth Chatterton, Clive Brook).

Another Kiss—Victor Schertzinger (w,m), Famous. COVER: Ruth Chatterton, Clive Brook.

2741　Laugh It Off (Universal, 1938, Constance Moore, Johnny Downs).

Doin' the 1940/Laugh It Off/My Dreams and I/Who's Gonna Keep Your Wigwam Warm—Sam Lerner (w), Ben Oakland (m), Robbins. COVER: Constance Moore, Johnny Downs.

2742　Lauthter in the Air (Myrt and Marge) (Universal, 1934, Ted Healy, Eddie Foy).

Draggin' My Heels Around/Isle of Blues/What Is Sweeter—Joan Jasmyn (w), M. K. Jerome (m), Witmark. COVER: Eddie Foy, and Girl.

2743　Laugh Your Blues Away (Columbia, 1942, Jinx Falkenberg, Bert Gordon).

Prairie Parade—Larry Marks, Dick Charles (w,m), Leeds. COVER: A Log Cabin.

2744　Laura (20th Century-Fox,

1944, Gene Tierney, Dana Andrews).

Laura—Johnny Mercer (w), David Raksin (m), Robbins; Laura-Theme—David Raksin (m), Robbins. COVER: Gene Tierney, and 20 Different Singers, and Bandleaders.

2745　Laurel and Hardy (MGM, 1931, Stan Laurel, Oliver Hardy).

Dance of the Cuckoos-Laurel and Hardy Film Theme (B)—Marvin Hatley (m), Southern. COVER: Laurel and Hardy.

2746　Law and Disorder (Columbia, 1974, Carroll O'Connor, Ernest Borgnine).

Street of Life—Al Elias (w), Andy Badale (m), Maximas. COVER: Carroll O'Connor, Ernest Borgnine.

2747　Law and Order (Universal, 1940, Johnny Mack Brown, Fuzzy Knight).

Ride 'im Cowboy/Those Happy Old Days—Everett Carter (w), Milton Rosen (m), Robbins. COVER: Johnny Mack Brown, Fuzzy Knight, Nell O'Day.

2748　Lawless Riders (Columbia, 1935, Ken Maynard, Geneva Mitchell).

Rosita Mia My Rose—Louis Herscher, Frank Yaconelli, Leon Leon, Lee Zahler (w,m), Miller. COVER: Ken Maynard.

2749　Law of the Plains (Columbia, 1938, Charles Starrett, Iris Meredity).

No Good Son of a Gun, A (VS)—Bob Nolan (w,m), American. COVER: Bob Nolan.

2750　Law of the Range (Universal, 1941, Johnny Mack Brown, Fuzzy Knight).

Forget Your Boots and Saddle/I Plumb Forget—Everett Carter (w), Milton Rosen (m), Robbins. COVER: Johnny Mack Brown, Fuzzy Knight, Nell O'Day.

2751　Lawrence of Arabia (Columbia, 1962, Peter O'Toole, Alec Guinness).

Lawrence of Arabia Theme—Maurice Jarre (m), Gower; Voice of the

Guns March—Kenneth Alford (m), Boosey Hawkes. COVER: Peter O'Toole.

2752 Lawton Story, The (The Prince of Peace) (Hallmark, 1949, Ginger Prince, Lasses White).

Down in Oklahoma—Lee White (w,m), Kaybee; Right Under My Nose—Steven Edwards, Andy Page (w,m), Kaybee. GOVER: Ginger Prince, Lee White.

2753 Lawyer, The (Paramount, 1970, Barry Newman, Harold Gould).

Winds of Chance—Gloria Nissenson (w), Malcolm Dodds (m), Ensign. COVER: Barry Newman, Diana Muldaur.

2754 Lay That Rifle Down (Republic, 1956, Judy Canova, Robert Lowery).

I'm Glad I Was Born on My Birthday—Jack Elliott, Donald Kahn (w, m), Kahn. COVER: Pinky Lee.

2755 Leadbelly (Paramount, 1976, Roger Mosley, Paul Benjamin).

Cotton Fields—Huddie Ledbetter (w,m), TRO; Goodnight Irene—Huddie Ledbetter, John Lomax (w,m), TRO; Leadbelly-17 Folk Songs—Huddie Ledbetter (w,m), TRO. COVER: Roger Mosley.

2756 League of Gentlemen (Kingsley, 1961, Jack Hawkins, Nigel Patrick).

League of Gentlemen March (B)—Philip Green (m), Filmusic. COVER: Jack Hawkins, Nigel Patrick.

2757 Lean on Me (Warner Bros., 1989, Morgan Freeman, Robert Guillaume).

Lean on Me—Bill Withers (w,m), Warner. COVER: Teacher and Students.

2758 Leatherneck, The (Pathe, 1929, William Boyd, Alan Hale).

Only for You—Josiah Zuro, Francis Cromon, Charles Weinberg (w,m), Berlin. COVER: William Boyd, Diane Ellis.

2759 Leathernecking (RKO, 1930, Irene Dunne, Ken Murray).

All My Life/Careless Kisses/Evening Star/Mighty Nice and So Particular—Benny Davis (w), Harry Akst (m), Harms; Shake It Off and Smile—Sidney Clare (w), Oscar Levant (m), Harms. COVER: Movie Scene.

2760 Leather Saint, The (Paramount, 1956, Paul Douglas, John Derek).

Beyond You—Walter Ruick (w), Richard Whiting (m), Famous. COVER: John Derek, Jody Lawrence.

2761 Leave It to Lester (Paramount, 1930, Lester Allen, Evelyn Hoey).

I'm Yours—E. Y. Harburg (w), John Green (m), Famous. COVER: Lester Allen, and Girls.

2762 Leave It to Susan (Goldwyn, 1920, Wallace MacDonald, Madge Kennedy).

Leave It to Susan Love Theme—G. Borch (m), Belwin. COVER: Madge Kennedy, and Cowboys.

2763 Left Hand of God (20th Century-Fox, 1955, Humphrey Bogart, Gene Tierney).

Loaf of Bread, A—Ken Darby (w, m), Miller. COVER: Black and white cover with title only.

2764 Legal Eagles (Universal, 1986, Robert Redford, Debra Winger).

Love Touch—Holly Knight, Mike Chapman, Gene Black (w,m), Makiki. COVER: Rod Stewart.

2765 Legend of Billie Jean, The (Tri-Star, 1985, Helen Slater, Keith Gordon).

Invincible—Holly Knight, Simon Clime (w,m), Makiki. COVER: Pat Benatar.

2766 Legend of Lobo, The (Disney, 1961, Wild Life Film).

Legend of Lobo, The—Richard Sherman, Robert Sherman (w,m), Wonderland. COVER: A Wolf.

2767 Legend of Lylah Clare, The (MGM, 1968, Kim Novak, Peter Finch).

Lylah—Mack David (w), Frank DeVol (m), Feist. COVER: Kim Novak.

2768 Legend of Nigger Charley, The (Paramount, 1972, Fred Williamson, Durville Martin).

In the Eyes of God/Legend of Nigger Charley—Elnora Bennings (w, m), Famous. COVER: Fred Williamson, Durville Martin.

2769 Legend of the Lost (United Artists, 1957, John Wayne, Sophia Loren).

Legend of the Lost—Don Wolf (w), A. Lavagnino (m), Unart. COVER: John Wayne, Sophia Loren, Movie Scenes.

2770 Legend of Young Dick Turpin, The (Disney, 1966, David Weston, Bernard Lee).

Ballad of Dick Turpin—Norman Newell (w), Ron Grainer (m), Disney. COVER: David Weston.

2771 Legion's Last Patrol (Commando) (AIP, 1962, Stewart Granger, Doran Gray).

Legion's Last Patrol (B)-Concerto—Angelo Lavagnino, Nino Rosso, S. Simoni (m), Filmusic. COVER: Stewart Granger.

2772 Le Million (Clair, 1931, Annabella, Paul Oliver).

If You Were Mine—Sam Lerner (w), A. Bernard, P. Pares, G. Parys (m), Harms. COVER: Girl's Face.

2773 Lemon Drop Kid, The (Paramount, 1951, Bob Hope, Marilyn Maxwell).

It Doesn't Cost a Dime to Dream/Silver Bells/They Obviously Want Me to Sing—Jay Livingston, Ray Evans (w,m), Paramount. COVER: Bob Hope, Marilyn Maxwell.

2774 Lena Rivers (Tiffany, 1932, Charlotte Henry, James Kirkwood).

Creole Moon—Val Burton, Corynn Kiehl (w,m), Sam Fox. COVER: Black and white cover with title only.

2775 Leonard Part Six (Columbia, 1987, Bill Cosby, Tom Courtenay).

Without You—Lamont Dozier (w, m), Gold Horizon. COVER: Bill Cosby.

2776 Leopard, The (20th Century-Fox, 1963, Burt Lancaster, Alain Delon).

Leopard-Themes—Nino Rota (m), Miller. COVER: Burt Lancaster.

2777 Les Girls (MGM, 1957, Gene Kelly, Mitzi Gaynor).

Ca C'est l'Amour/High Flyin' Wings on My Shoes (PC)/I Could Kick Myself (PC)/Les Girls/Why Am I So Gone/You're Just Too Too/You're the Prize Guy of Guys (PC)—Cole Porter (w,m), Buxton. COVER: Gene Kelly, Mitzi Gaynor, Kay Kendall, Taina Elg.

2778 Less Than Zero (20th Century-Fox, 1987, Andrew McCarthy, Jami Gertz).

Hazy Shade of Winter—Paul Simon (w,m), Simon. COVER: The Bangles.

2779 Let Freedom Ring (MGM, 1939, Nelson Eddy, Virginia Bruce).

Dusty Road—Leon Rene, Otis Rene (w,m), Robbins; Love Serenade—Bob Wright, Chet Forrest (w), R. Drigo (m), Fischer; When Irish Eyes Are Smiling—Chauncey Olcott, G. Graff (w), Ernest Ball (m), Witmark; Where Else But Here—Edward Heyman (w), Sigmund Romberg (m), Feist. COVER: Nelson Eddy, Virginia Bruce.

2780 Lethal Weapon (Warner Bros., 1987, Mel Gibson, Danny Glover).

Lethal Weapon—Michael Kamen (w,m), Warner. COVER: Mel Gibson, Danny Glover.

2781 Let It Be (United Artists, 1970, The Beatles).

For You Blue/I, Me, Mine—George Harrison, Harrison; Get Back (VS)/Let It Be (VS)/Long and Winding Road (VS)—John Lennon, Paul McCartney (w,m), Northern. COVER: The Beatles.

2782 Let No Man Write My Epitaph (Columbia, 1960, Burl Ives, Shelley Winters).

Reach for Tomorrow—Ned Washington (w), Jimmy McHugh (m), Colgems. COVER: James Darren, Jean Seberg, Shelley Winters.

2783 Let's Be Happy (Allied Artists, 1957, Tony Martin, Vera-Ellen).

Hold on to Love (B)—Paul F. Webster (w), Nicholas Brodszky (m), Day; One Is a Lonely Number—Paul F. Webster (w), Nicholas Brodszky (m), Miller. COVER: Tony Martin, Vera-Ellen.

2784 Let's Dance (Paramount, 1950, Betty Hutton, Fred Astaire).

Can't Stop Talking/Hyacinth, The/ Jack and the Beanstalk/Oh Them Dudes/Tunnel of Love, The/Why Fight the Feeling—Frank Loesser (w, m), Paramount. COVER: Betty Hutton, Fred Astaire.

2785 Let's Do It Again (Columbia, 1953, Jane Wyman, Ray Milland).

Anyone But You/Call of the Wild/ Gimme a Man Who Makes Music/It Was Great While It Lasted/Let's Do It Again/Takin' a Slow Burn/These Are the Things I Remember—Ned Washington (w), Lester Lee (m), Mills. COVER: Ray Milland, Jane Wyman.

2786 Let's Do It Again (Warner Bros., 1975, Sidney Poitier, Bill Cosby).

Let's Do It Again/New Orleans/ Let's Do It Again-Eight Songs— Curtis Mayfield (w,m), Warner. COVER: Sidney Poitier, Bill Cosby, Jimmie Walker.

2787 Let's Face It (Paramount, 1943, Bob Hope, Betty Hutton).

Who Did? I Did, Yes I Did!—Sammy Cahn (w), Jule Styne (m), Paramount. COVER: Bob Hope, Betty Hutton.

2788 Let's Fall in Love (Columbia, 1934, Edmund Lowe, Ann Sothern).

Let's Fall in Love/Love Is Love Anywhere/This Is Only the Beginning—Ted Koehler (w), Harold Arlen (m), Berlin. COVER: Ann Sothern.

2789 Let's Get Married (Paramount, 1926, Richard Dix, Lois Wilson).

Thinking of You (Promotion Song)—Joseph Grey (w), Allie More (m), Strand. COVER: Cartoon Sketch.

2790 Let's Get Movin' (Paramount, 1936, Cartoon).

Moving Man (VS)—Bob Rothberg (w), Sammy Timberg (m), Famous. COVER: Popeye.

2791 Let's Go Native (Paramount, 1930, Jack Oakie, Jeanette MacDonald).

It Seems to Be Spring/I've Gotta Yen for You/Joe Jazz/Let's Go Native/My Mad Moment—George Marion (w), Richard Whiting (m), Famous. COVER: Jack Oakie, Jeanette MacDonald.

2792 Let's Go Places (Hollywood Nights) (Fox, 1930, Lola Lane, Walter Catlett).

Boop Boop a Doopa Doo Fox Trot—G. Little (w), Johnny Burke (m), Red Star; Fascinating Devil—Joe McCarthy (w), Jimmie Monaco (m), Red Star; Snowball Man, The—James Brockman (w), Jimmie Monaco (m), Red Star. COVER: Lola Lane, Walter Catlett, and Chorus Girls.

2793 Let's Go Steady (Columbia, 1945, Mel Torme, June Preisser).

I Don't Want to Love You—Henry Prichard (w,m), Chelsea. COVER: Phil Brito.

2794 Let's Live Tonight (Columbia, 1935, Tullio Carminati, Lilian Harvey).

Love Passes By—Jack Scholl (w), Victor Schertzinger (m), Santly Joy. COVER: Tullio Carminati, Lilian Harvey.

2795 Let's Make a Night of It (Universal, 1938, June Clyde, Buddy Rogers).

Angel Why Don't You Come Down to Earth—Michael Carr, Ord Hamilton (w,m), Chappell; Let It Rain Let It Pour/My Irish Song/ Something in My Eye/When My Heart Says Sing/You've Got to Take

Your Pick and Swing—Michael Carr, Jimmy Kennedy (w,m), Chappell. COVER: An Artist.

2796 Let's Make Love (20th Century-Fox, 1960, Marilyn Monroe, Yves Montand).

Hey You With the Crazy Eyes/ Incurably Romantic/Let's Make Love —Sammy Cahn (w), James Van Heusen (m), Miller; My Heart Belongs to Daddy—Cole Porter (w,m), Chappell; Specialization—Sammy Cahn (w), James Van Heusen (m), Miller. COVER: Marilyn Monroe, Yves Montand.

2797 Let's Make Music (RKO, 1940, Bob Crosby, Jean Rogers).

Big Noise from Winnetka—Gil Rodin, Bob Crosby, Bob Haggart, Ray Bauduc (w,m), BVC; Central Park—Johnny Mercer (w), Matty Malneck (m), Robbins; You Forgot About Me—Dick Robertson, James Hanley, Sammy Mysels (w,m), Mercer Morris. COVER: Bob Crosby, Jean Rogers.

2798 Let's Rock (Columbia, 1958, Julius LaRosa, Phyliss Newman).

All Love Broke Loose—Hal Hackady (w,m), Roosevelt. COVER: Julius LaRosa, and Movie Scenes.

2799 Let's Sing Again (RKO, 1936, Bobby Breen, Henry Armetta).

Let's Sing Again—Gus Kahn (w), Jimmy McHugh (m), Feist; Lullaby— Selma Hautzik (w), Hugo Riesenfeld (m), Feist. COVER: Bobby Breen.

2800 Let's Talk It Over (Universal, 1934, Chester Morris, Mae Clark).

Long Live Love—Walter Donaldson (w,m), Feist. COVER: Black and white cover with title only.

2801 Letter from an Unknown Woman (Universal, 1948, Joan Fontaine, Louis Jourdan).

A Love Unknown—Sidney Miller, Inez James (w,m), BVC. COVER: Joan Fontaine, Louis Jourdan.

2801a License to Kill (United Artists, 1989, Timothy Dalton, Roberto Davi).

If You Asked Me To—Diane Warren (w,m), Warner. COVER: Patti LaBelle.

2802 Lieutenant Wore Skirts, The (20th Century-Fox, 1955, Tom Ewell, Sheree North).

Rock Around the Island—Ken Darby (w,m), Robbins. COVER: Sheree North.

2803 Life and Times of Grizzly Adams, The (Schicksunn, 1976, Dan Haggerty, Lisa Jones).

Maybe—Thom Pace (w,m), Chippen. COVER: Dan Haggerty, and Bear.

2804 Life and Times of Judge Roy Bean, The (National General, 1972, Paul Newman, Tab Hunter).

Lily's Theme/Maria's Theme— Maurice Jarre (m), Famous; Marmalade, Molasses, and Honey—Alan Bergman, Marilyn Bergman (w), Maurice Jarre (m), Famous. COVER: Paul Newman.

2805 Life at Stake, A (The Key Man) (Gibraltar, 1955, Keith Andes, Angela Lansbury).

Summer Interlude—Ted Koehler (w), Les Baxter, Hank McCune (m), Mills. COVER: Keith Andes, Angela Lansbury.

2806 Life Begins at 8:30 (20th Century-Fox, 1940, Ida Lupino, Monty Woolley).

Your Kiss—Frank Loesser (w), Alfred Newman (m), Robbins. COVER: Black and white cover with title only.

2807 Life Begins in College (20th Century-Fox, 1937, Joan Davis, Tony Martin).

Big Chief Swing It—Sidney Mitchell (w), Lew Pollack (m), Hollywood; Fair Lombardy (BW)/Our Team Is on the Warpath (BW)—Sidney Mitchell (w), Lew Pollack (m), Movietone; Rhumba Goes Collegiate—Sidney Mitchell (w), Lew Pollack (m), Hollywood; Sweet Varsity Sue—Charles Tobias, Al Lewis, Murray Mencher (w,m), Remick; Why Talk About Love?—Sidney Mitchell (w), Lew Pollack (m), Hollywood. COVER:

Ritz Brothers, Joan Davis, Tony Martin, Gloria Stuart.

2808 Life Begins with Love (Columbia, 1937, Edith Fellows, Jean Parker).

What Makes You So Sweet—Bennee Russel (w), Ben Oakland (m), Santly Joy. COVER: Edith Fellows.

2809 Life Guard (Paramount, 1976, Sam Elliott, Anne Archer).

Time and Tide—Paul Williams (w,m), Hobbitron. COVER: Sam Elliott, and Girls.

2810 Life, Love, and Death (United Artists, 1969, Caroline Callier, Janine Magnan).

Life, Love, and Death—Francis Lai (m), Unart. COVER: Black and white cover with title only.

2811 Life of Her Own, A (MGM, 1950, Lana Turner, Ray Milland).

Life of Her Own, A—Paul F. Webster (w), Bronislau Kaper (m), Robbins. COVER: Lana Turner.

2812 Life of the Party (RKO, 1937, Harriet Hilliard, Gene Raymond).

Chirp a Little Ditty/Let's Have Another Cigarette/Life of the Party—Herb Magidson (w), Allie Wrubel (m), Berlin; Roses in December—Herb Magidson, Ben Oakland, George Jessel (w,m), Berlin; So You Won't Sing/Yankee Doodle Band—Herb Magidson (w), Ben Oakland (m), Berlin. COVER: Gene Raymond, Harriet Hilliard, Victor Moore, Joe Penner.

2813 Life With Father (Warner Bros., 1946, William Powell, Irene Dunne).

Sweet Marie—Cy Warman (w), Raymond Moore (m), Remick. COVER: William Powell, Irene Dunne, and Kids.

2814 Light in the Forest, The (Buena Vista, 1958, James MacArthur, Carol Lynley).

I Asked My Love a Favor—Paul Smith, Lawrence Watkin (w,m), Wonderland; Light in the Forest—Paul Smith, Gil George (w,m), Won-

derland. COVER: Black and white cover with title only.

2815 Light in the Piazza, The (MGM, 1962, Olivia de Havilland, Rossano Brazzi).

Light in the Piazza—Arthur Freed (w), Mario Nascimbene (m), Robbins. COVER: Olivia de Havilland, Rossano Brazzi, George Hamilton.

2816 Lights of Old Broadway (MGM, 1925, Marion Davies, Conrad Nagel).

Lights of Old Broadway—Ted Barron (w,m), Barron; Thinking of You (Promotion Song)—Joseph Grey (w), Allie Moore (m), Strand. COVER: Marion Davies.

2817 Lights of the Desert (Fox, 1922, Shirley Mason, Allan Forrest).

For the Sake of Auld Lang Syne —George Graff, Annelu Burns (w), Ernest Ball (m), Witmark. COVER: Shirley Mason, Allan Forrest.

2818 Like Kelly Can (Love in the Rough) (MGM, 1930, Robert Montgomery, Dorothy Jordan).

Dance Fool Dance—Dorothy Fields (w), Jimmy McHugh (m), Robbins. COVER: Black and white cover with title only.

2819 Li'l Abner (RKO, 1940, Granville Owen, Martha O'Driscoll).

Li'l Abner—Ben Oakland, Milton Berle, Milton Drake (w,m), Feist. COVER: Granville Owen, Martha O'Driscoll, and Cartoons.

2820 Li'l Abner (Paramount, 1959, Peter Palmer, Leslie Parrish).

If I Had My Druthers/Jubilation T. Cornpone/Namely You/Otherwise —Johnny Mercer (w), Gene DePaul (m), Commander. COVER: Peter Palmer, Leslie Parrish, and Others.

2821 Lilacs in the Spring (Let's Make Up) (United Artists, 1954, Anna Neagle, Errol Flynn).

We'll Gather Lilacs (B)—Ivor Novello (w,m), Chappell. COVER: Anna Neagle, Errol Flynn.

2822 Lilac Time (First National, 1928, Colleen Moore, Gary Cooper).

Jeanine, I Dream of Lilac Time—

L. Wolfe Gilbert (w), Nat Shilkret (m), Feist. COVER: Colleen Moore.

2823 Lili (MGM, 1953, Leslie Caron, Mel Ferrer).

Hi Lili-Hi-Lo—Helen Deutsch (w), Bronislau Kaper (m), Robbins. COVER: Leslie Caron, Mel Ferrer, Jean Pierre Aumont.

2824 Lilies of the Field (First National, 1930, Corinne Griffith, John Loder).

I'd Like to Be a Gypsy—Ned Washington (w), Michael Cleary (m), Witmark. COVER: Corinne Griffith.

2825 Lilies of the Field (United Artists, 1963, Sidney Poitier, Lilia Skala).

Amen, Theme—Jerry Goldsmith (m), Unart. COVER: Sidney Poitier.

2826 Lilith (Columbia, 1964, Warren Beatty, Jean Seberg).

Lilith-Love Theme—Kenyon Hopkins (m), Colgems. COVER: Jean Seberg.

2827 Lillian Russell (20th Century-Fox, 1940, Don Ameche, Alice Faye).

Adored One—Mack Gordon (w), Alfred Newman (m), Robbins; After the Ball—Charles K. Harris (w,m), Harris; Blue Lovebird—Gus Kahn (w), Bronislaw Kaper (m), Feist; Come Down Ma Evenin' Star—Robert Smith (w), John Stromberg (m), Witmark; Ma Blushin' Rosie—Edgar Smith (w), John Stromberg (m), Witmark. COVER: Alice Faye, Don Ameche.

2828 Lilli Marlene (RKO, 1951, Lisa Daniely, Hugh McDermott).

Lilli Marlene—Hans Leip, Norbert Schultze, Tom Connor (w,m), Marks. COVER: Lisa Daniely, and Soldiers.

2829 Li'l Pedro (Stereotoon, 1958, Cartoon).

Li'l Pedro (PC)—Muzzy Marcellino (w,m), Carmar. COVER: None.

2830 Limbo (Universal, 1972, Kate Jackson, Katherine Justice).

Where Do I Go from Here?—Jay Livingston, Ray Evans (w), Anita Kerr (m), Leeds. COVER: Movie Scene.

2831 Limehouse Blues (Limehouse Nights) (Paramount, 1934, George Raft, Anna May Wong).

Limehouse Nights (PC)—Sam Coslow (w,m), Famous. COVER: None.

2832 Limelight   (Backstage) (Wilcox, 1935, Arthur Tracy, Anna Neagle).

Celebratin'—Harry Woods (w,m), Berlin; Farewell Sweet Senorita/Nirewana/Stay Awhile/ Stranded/We Were Meant to Meet Again/Whistling Waltz—Harry Woods (w,m), Mills. COVER: Anna Neagle, Arthur Tracy.

2833 Limelight (United Artists, 1952, Charlie Chaplin, Claire Bloom).

Eternally—Charlie Chaplin, Geoffrey Parsons (w,m), Bourne; Limelight Theme (B)—Charlie Chaplin (m), Bourne. COVER: Charlie Chaplin.

2834 Linda (First Division, 1929, Warner Baxter, Helen Foster).

Linda—Charles Tobias, Harry Tobias (w), Al Sherman (m), Berlin. COVER: Helen Foster.

2835 Linda Be Good (Eagle Lion, 1947, Elyse Knox, Marie Wilson).

Linda Be Good—Charles Herbert, Jack Mason (w,m), Royal; My Mother Says I Mustn't—Sy Miller, Jack Mason (w,m), Royal; Old Woman with a Rolling Pin/Young Girls of Today—Sir Lancelot (w,m), Royal. COVER: Marie Wilson, Elyse Knox, John Hubbard.

2836 Lion, The (20th Century-Fox, 1961, William Holden, Capucine).

Lion Theme—Malcolm Arnold (m), Miller. COVER: William Holden, Capucine.

2837 Lion Has Wings, The (United Artists, 1939, Merle Oberon, Ralph Richardson).

Cavalry of the Clouds-March (B)—Richard Addinsell (m), Chappell. COVER: Airplanes.

2838 Lion in Winter, The (Embassy, 1968, Katharine Hepburn, Peter O'Toole).

Lion in Winter Theme—John Barry (m), Levine. COVER: Katharine Hepburn, Peter O'Toole.

2839 Lion of the Desert (United, 1981, Anthony Quinn, Oliver Reed).

Lion of the Desert Theme (PC)— Maurice Jarre (m), September. COVER: None.

2840 Lipstick (Paramount, 1976, Margaux Hemingway, Chris Sarandon).

Lipstick—Michel Polnareff (m), Famous. COVER: Margaux Hemingway.

2841 Liquidator, The (MGM, 1966, Rod Taylor, Trevor Howard).

Liquidator, The—Peter Callander (w), Lalo Schifrin (m), Hastings. COVER: Rod Taylor, Jill St. John.

2842 Lisa (The Inspector) (20th Century-Fox, 1962, Stephen Boyd, Dolores Hart).

Lisa—Malcolm Arnold (m), Miller. COVER: Stephen Boyd, Dolores Hart.

2943 Lisbon (Republic, 1954, Ray Milland, Maureen O'Hara).

Lisbon Antiqua—Harry Dupree (w), R. Portela, J. Galhardo, A. Dovale (m), Southern. COVER: Ray Milland, Maureen O'Hara.

2844 Listen Baby! (Pathe, 1929, Eddie Quillan, Dorothy Appleby).

Listen, Baby!—J. R. Robinson, George Green, George Waggner, W. S. Darling (w,m), Berlin. COVER: Eddie Quillan, Dorothy Appleby.

2845 Listen Darling (MGM, 1938, Judy Garland, Freddie Bartholomew).

On the Bumpy Road to Love—Al Hoffman, Al Lewis, Murray Mencher (w,m), Feist; Ten Pins in the Sky—Joseph McCarthy, Milton Ager (w,m), Ager Yellen; Zing! Went the Strings of My Heart—James Hanley (w,m), Harms. COVER: Judy Garland, Freddie Bartholomew.

2846 Little Annie Rooney (United Artists, 1925, Mary Pickford, William Haines).

Little Annie Rooney—Michael Nolan (w,m), Witmark. COVER: Mary Pickford.

2847 Little Ark, The (National General, 1972, Theodore Bikel, Philip Frame).

Come Follow, Follow Me—Marsha Karlin (w), Fred Karlin (m), Blackwood. COVER: Theodore Bikel, and Movie Scene.

2848 Little Audrey (Paramount, 1948, Cartoon).

Little Audrey Says—Buddy Kaye (w), Winston Sharples (m), Famous. COVER: Cartoon.

2849 Little Big Horn (Lippert, 1951, Lloyd Bridges, John Ireland).

On the Little Big Horn—Stanley Adams, Larry Stock, Maurice Sigler (w,m), Flanagan. COVER: Lloyd Bridges, John Ireland, Marie Windsor.

2850 Little Big Shot (Warner Bros., 1935, Sybil Jason, Robert Armstrong).

I'm a Little Big Shot Now—Mort Dixon (w), Allie Wrubel (m), Remick. COVER: Sybil Jason.

2851 Little Bit of Heaven, A (Universal, 1940, Gloria Jean, Robert Stack).

After Ev'ry Rainstorm—Sam Lerner (w), Frank Skinner (m), Robbins; Dawn of Love—Ralph Freed (w), Charles Previn (m), Robbins; Little Bit of Heaven, A—J. Keirn Brennan (w), Ernest Ball (m), Witmark; Nightingale and the Rose— Deems Taylor (w), N. Rimsky Korsakoff (m), Presser; What Did We Learn at School—Vivian Ellis (w, m), Chappell. COVER: Gloria Jean.

2852 Little Boy Lost (Paramount, 1953, Bing Crosby, Claude Dauphin).

Apropos De Rien/If It's All the Same to You/Magic Window, The— Johnny Burke (w), James Van Heusen (m), BVH. COVER: Bing Crosby, and Boy.

2853 Little Church Around the Corner, The (Warner Bros., 1923, Kenneth Harlan, Claire Windsor).

Little Church Around the Corner, The—Gus Arnheim, Ralph Freed, Abe Lyman (w,m), Harris. COVER: A Church and People.

2854 Little Colonel, The (Fox, 1935, Shirley Temple, Bill Robinson).

Little Colonel—Paul F. Webster (w), Lew Pollack (m), Movietone; Love's Young Dream—Thomas Moore (w), Cyril Mockridge (m), Movietone. COVER: Shirley Temple.

2855 Little Fauss and Big Halsy (Paramount, 1970, Robert Redford, Michael Pollard).

Ballad of Little Fauss and Big Halsy—Carl Perkins (w,m), Famous; Little Man/Rollin' Free—Johnny Cash (w,m), Famous; 706 Union Avenue—Carl Perkins (m), Famous; True Love Is Greater Than Friendship—Carl Perkins (w,m), Famous. COVER: Robert Redford, Michael Pollard.

2856 Little Foxes, The (RKO, 1941, Bette Davis, Herbert Marshall).

Never Too Weary to Pray—Meredith Willson (w,m), Willson. COVER: Black and white cover with title only.

2857 Little Fugitive, The (Burstyn, 1953, Richie Andrusco, Richie Brewster).

Joey's Theme—Eddy Manson (m), Trinity. COVER: Richie Andrusco.

2858 Little Giants, The (Olmec, 1959, Angel Macias, Cesar Faz).

Little Boat—Jean Rouverol, George Werker (w), Fred Steiner (m), Bibo. COVER: Young Baseball Team.

2859 Little Gypsy (Rascals) (20th Century-Fox, 1938, Jane Withers, Rochelle Hudson).

Song of the Gypsy Band/Take a Tip from a Gypsy—Sidney Clare (w), Harry Akst (m), Mills. COVER: Black and white cover with title only.

2860 Little Hut, The (MGM, 1957, Ava Gardner, Stewart Granger).

Little Hut, The—Eric Maschwitz, Marcel Stellman (w), Peggy Cochrane (m), Feist. COVER: Ava Gardner, David Niven, Stewart Granger.

2861 Little Johnny Jones (First National, 1929, Eddie Buzzell, Alice Day).

Go Find Somebody to Love/I'd Better Not Try It (BW)—Ned Washington, Herb Magidson, Michael Cleary (w,m), Remick; My Paradise—James Cavanaugh, N. Washington, H. Magidson, M. Cleary (w,m), Remick; She Was Kicked on the Head by a Butterfly—Ned Washington, Herb Magidson, Michael Cleary (w,m), Remick; Straight Place and Show—Herman Ruby (w), M. K. Jerome (m), Remick. COVER: Eddie Buzzell, Alice Day.

2862 Little Lulu (Paramount, 1943, Cartoon).

Little Lulu (Theme Song)—Buddy Kaye, Fred Wise, Sid Lippman (w, m), Famous. COVER: Cartoon.

2863 Little Mermaid, The (Buena Vista, 1989, Cartoon).

Daughter of Triton (VS)/Fathoms Below (VS)/Kiss the Girl (VS)/Les Poissons (VS)/Part of Your World & Reprise (VS)/Poor Unfortunate Souls (VS)/Under the Sea (pub. as single sheet)—Howard Ashman (w), Alan Menken (m), Leonard. COVER: Cartoon.

2864 Little Miss Broadway (20th Century-Fox, 1938, Shirley Temple, George Murphy).

Be Optimistic/How Can I Thank You/If All the World Were Paper/I'll Build a Broadway for You/We Should Be Together—Walter Bullock (w), Harold Spina (m), Robbins. COVER: Shirley Temple.

2865 Little Miss Marker (Half Way Decent) (Paramount, 1934, Shirley Temple, Adolphe Menjou).

I'm a Black Sheep Who's Blue/ Laugh You Son of a Gun/Low Down Lullaby—Leo Robin, Ralph Rainger (w,m), Famous. COVER: Shirley Temple, Adolphe Menjou.

2866 Little Miss Marker (Universal, 1979, Julie Andrews, Walter Matthau).

Little Miss Marker Theme (PC)—Henry Mancini (m), Leeds. COVER: None.

2867 Little Miss Mischief (Vitaphone, 1933, Musical Short).

Little Miss Mischief—David Mendoza (w,m), Witmark. COVER: Black and white cover with title only.

2868 Little Miss Nobody (Fox, 1936, Jane Withers, Jane Darwell).

Then Came the Indians—Harry Tobias, Jack Stern, Henry Tobias (w,m), Movietone. COVER: Jane Withers.

2869 Little Miss Roughneck (Columbia, 1938, Edith Fellows, Leo Carrillo).

As Long as I Love—Milton Drake, George Jessel (w), Ben Oakland (m), Berlin. COVER: Sketch of Couple.

2870 Little Mister Jim (MGM, 1946, Butch Jenkins, James Craig).

Little Jim—Ralph Freed (w), Sammy Fain (m), Robbins. COVER: Butch Jenkins, James Craig, Frances Gifford.

2871 Little Nellie Kelly (MGM, 1940, Judy Garland, George Murphy).

It's a Great Day for the Irish—Roger Edens (w,m), Feist; Nellie Kelly I Love You—George M. Cohan (w,m), Witmark; Pretty Girl Milking Her Cow, A—Roger Edens (w,m), Feist; Singin' in the Rain—Arthur Freed (w), Nacio Herb Brown (m), Robbins. COVER: Judy Garland, George Murphy.

2872 Little Old New York (Cosmopolitan, 1923, Marion Davies, Harrison Ford).

Little Old New York—William LeBaron (w), Victor Herbert (m), Harms. COVER: Marion Davies.

2873 Little Old New York (20th Century-Fox, 1940, Alice Faye, Fred MacMurray).

Who Is the Beau of the Belle of New York—Mack Gordon (w,m),

Robbins. COVER: Alice Faye, Fred MacMurray, Richard Greene.

2874 Little Pal (Say It with Songs) (Warner, 1929, Al Jolson, Davey Lee).

Little Pal—Al Jolson, B. G. DeSylva, Lew Brown, Ray Henderson (w,m), DBH. COVER: Al Jolson.

2875 Little Prince, The (Paramount, 1974, Richard Kiley, Bob Fosse).

Be Happy/Closer and Closer and Closer/I'm on Your Side/I Need Air/I Never Met a Rose/Little Prince/Matters of Consequence/Snake in the Grass/Why Is the Desert/You're a Child—Alan Jay Lerner (w), Frederick Loewe (m), Famous. COVER: Steven Warner.

2876 Little Red Hen, The (Iwerks, 1934, Cartoon).

Little Red Hen, The—Carl Stallings, Otto Englander (w,m), Marks. COVER: Cartoon.

2877 Little Shepherd of Kingdom Come (20th Century-Fox, 1960, Jimmy Rodgers, Luana Patton).

When Love Is Young—By Dunham, Henry Vars (w,m), Planetary. COVER: Black and white cover with title only.

2878 Little Shop of Horrors (Warner Bros., 1987, Steve Martin, Ellen Greene).

Somewhere That's Green/Suddenly Seymour/Da Doo (VS)/Dentist (VS)/Feed Me-Git It (VS)/Finale, Don't Feed the Plants (VS)/Grow for Me (VS)/Mean Green Mother from Outer Space (VS)/Meek Shall Inherit (VS)/Prologue-Little Shop of Horrors (VS)/Skidrow-Downtown (VS)/Some Fun Now (VS)/Suppertime (VS)—Howard Ashman (w), Alan Menken (m), Warner. COVER: Rick Moranis, Ellen Greene.

2879 Littlest Outlaw, The (Buena Vista, 1955, Pedro Armendariz, Joseph Calleia).

Doroteo, The Automobile Song—Edmundo Santos (w,m), Disney; Littlest Outlaw Theme—William Lava (m), Disney. COVER: Andres Velasquez.

2880 Littlest Rebel, The (Fox, 1935, Shirley Temple, John Boles).

Believe Me If All Those Endearing Young Charms (VS)—Thomas Moore (w,m), Movietone; Polly Wolly Doodle—Sidney Clare, B. G. DeSylva (w,m), Movietone. COVER: Shirley Temple, Bill Robinson, John Boles.

2881 Little Teacher, The (The Little School Ma'am) (Triangle, 1916, Dorothy Gish, Elmer Clifton).

Days When We Went to School—John Nilan, Charles Dixon, Roger Halle (w,m), Halle. COVER: Red and black cover with title only.

2882 Little Women (RKO, Katharine Hepburn, Frances Dee).

Josephine—Val Burton, Will Jason (w), Max Steiner (m), Berlin; Little Women—Edgar Leslie (w), Fred Ahlert (m), Berlin; None But the Lonely Heart—Arthur Westbrook (w), P. Tchaikovsky (m), Schirmer. COVER: Katharine Hepburn, Frances Dee, Joan Bennett, Jean Parker.

2883 Live a Little, Love a Little (MGM, 1968, Elvis Presley, Michele Carey).

Almost in Love—Randy Starr (w), Luiz Bonfa (m), Presley; Edge of Reality—Bill Giant, Bernie Baum, Florence Kaye (w,m), Presley; Little Less Conversation, A—Billy Strange, Scott Davis (w,m), Gladys. COVER: Elvis Presley.

2884 Live and Let Die (United Artists, 1973, Roger Moore, Jane Seymour).

Baron Samedi's Dance of Death (VS)—George Martin (m), Unart; Live and Let Die—Paul McCartney, Linda McCartney (w,m), Unart. COVER: Roger Moore, and Girls.

2885 Live for Life (United Artists, 1967, Yves Montand, Candice Bergen).

Live for Life—Norman Gimbel (w), Francis Lai (m), Unart; Live for Life Entracte/Live for Life Theme/Live for Life-Eight Themes—Francis Lai (m), Unart. COVER: Yves Montand, Candice Bergen, Annie Girardot.

2886 Lively Set, The (Universal, 1964, James Darren, Pamela Tiffin).

Boss Barracuda—Terry Melcher (w), Bobby Darin (m), T.M.; If You Love Him/Lively Set, The—Bobby Darin (w,m), T.M. COVER: James Darren, Pamela Tiffin, Doug McClure.

2887 Living Desert, The (Buena Vista, 1953, Wild Life Film).

Living Desert-Three Themes—Paul Smith (m), Disney. COVER: Desert Scene.

2888 Living Free (Columbia, 1972, Susan Hampshire, Nigel Davenport).

Living Free—Fred Douglass (w), Sol Kaplan (m), Colgems. COVER: Lions.

2889 Living Idol, The (MGM, 1956, Steve Forrest, Liliane Montevecchi).

Living Idol, The—Edward Heyman (w), David Campbell (m), Feist. COVER: Steve Forrest, Liliane Montevecchi.

2890 Living in a Big Way (MGM, 1947, Gene Kelly, Marie McDonald).

Fido and Me—Edward Heyman (w), Louis Alter (m), Feist. COVER: Gene Kelly, Marie McDonald.

2891 Living It Up (Paramount, 1954, Dean Martin, Jerry Lewis).

Champagne and Wedding Cake/Every Street's a Boulevard/Money Burns a Hole in the Pocket/That's What I Like/You're Gonna Dance with Me Baby—Bob Hilliard (w), Jule Styne (m), Chappell. COVER: Dean Martin, Jerry Lewis.

2892 Living on Velvet (First National, 1935, Kay Francis, Warren William).

Living on Velvet—Al Dubin (w), Harry Warren (m), Remick. COVER: Kay Francis, Warren William, George Brent.

2893 **Lizzie** (MGM, 1957, Eleanor Parker, Richard Boone).

It's Not for Me to Say—Al Stillman, Robert Allen (w,m), Famous; Warm and Tender—Hal David (w), Burt Bacharach (m), Famous; Lizzie-Four Themes—Leith Stevens, Tom Adair (m), Robbins. COVER: Eleanor Parker.

2894 **Lock Up Your Daughters** (Columbia, 1969, Christopher Plummer, Susannah York).

Hold on to Your Women—Jim Dale (w), Ron Grainer (m), Colgems. COVER: Sketches of Scenes.

2895 **Logan's Run** (MGM, 1976, Michael York, Jenny Agutter).

As We Follow the Sun—Carol Heather (w), Jerry Goldsmith (m), MGM. COVER: Movie Scenes.

2896 **Lola Montes** (Brandon, 1956, Martine Carole, Peter Ustinov).

Surrender to Me—Carl Sigman (w), George Auric (m), Witmark; This Is Real—John Murray (w), George Auric (m), Remick. COVER: Green cover with title only.

2897 **Lolita** (MGM, 1962, James Mason, Shelley Winters).

Lolita Love Theme—Bob Harris (m), Chappell; Lolita Ya Ya—Nelson Riddle, Bob Harris (m), Chappell. COVER: Sue Lyon.

2898 **London Town (My Heart Goes Crazy)** (United Artists, 1946, Greta Gynt, Kay Kendall).

Ampstead Way/Any Way the Wind Blows/Hyde Park on a Sunday/ If Spring Were Only Here to Stay/ My Heart Goes Crazy/So Would I/ You Can't Keep a Good Dreamer Down—Johnny Burke (w), James Van Heusen (m), BVH. COVER: Kay Kendall, Beryl Davis, Pamela Carroll.

2899 **Loneliness of the Long Distance Runner, The** (Continental, 1962, Michael Redgrave, Tom Courtney).

Loneliness of the Long Distance Runner Theme (B)—John Addison (m), Feldman. COVER: Tom Courtney.

2900 **Lonely Man** (Paramount, 1957, Jack Palance, Tony Perkins).

Lonely Man, The—Jack Brooks (w), Nathan Van Cleaves (m), Paramount. COVER: Jack Palance, Tony Perkins.

2901 **Lone Ranger, The** (Republic, 1938, Lee Powell).

Hi Yo Silver—Vaughn DeLeath, Jack Erickson (w,m), Chappell. COVER: Lone Ranger, Silver, Tonto.

2902 **Lonesome** (Universal, 1927, Glenn Tryon, Barbara Kent).

Lonesome—Dave Dreyer, Herman Ruby (w), Joe Cherniovsky (m), Berlin. COVER: Glenn Tryon, Barbara Kent.

2903 **Lonesome Trail, The** (Monogram, 1945, Jimmy Wakely, Lee White).

Lonesome Trail, The (VS)—Jimmy Wakely, Jack Baxley (w,m), Fairway. COVER: Jimmy Wakely.

2904 **Lone Wolf's Daughter, The** (Columbia, 1928, Bert Lytell, Gertrude Olmstead).

You Stole My Heart Away—Ballard MacDonald (w), Peter DeRose (m), Berlin. COVER: Bert Lytell, Gertrude Olmstead.

2905 **Long Ago Tomorrow** (Cinema Five, 1971, Malcolm McDowell, Nanette Newman).

Long Ago Tomorrow—Hal David (w), Burt Bacharach (m), Cinema Five. COVER: Malcolm McDowell, Nanette Newman.

2906 **Long and the Short and the Tall, The (Jungle Fighters)** (Allied Artists, 1961, Laurence Harvey, Richard Todd).

Hi Jig a Jig-Cook a Little Pig— Dory Langdon (w), Sim Simmons (m), Leeds. COVER: Laurence Harvey.

2907 **Long Day's Journey into Night** (Embassy, 1962, Katharine Hepburn, Ralph Richardson).

Long Day's Journey into Night Theme—André Previn (m), Leeds. COVER: Katharine Hepburn, Ralph Richardson, Jason Robards.

2908 Long Duel, The (Paramount, 1967, Yul Brynner, Trevor Howard).

When the World Is Ready—Don Black, Patrick Scott (w,m), Famous. COVER: Yul Brynner, and Movie Scenes.

2909 Longest Day, The (20th Century-Fox, 1962, John Wayne, Robert Mitchum).

Longest Day, The—Paul Anka (w, m), Spanka. COVER: Paul Anka.

2910 Longest Night, The (MGM, 1936, Robert Young, Florence Rice).

Longest Night, The—Bob Wright, Chet Forrest (w,m), Feist. COVER: Robert Young, Florence Rice.

2911 Longest Yard, The (Paramount, 1974, Burt Reynolds, Eddie Albert).

Love Knows the Way—Larry Kusik (w), Frank DeVol (m), Famous. COVER: Burt Reynolds.

2912 Long Goodbye, The (United Artists, 1973, Elliott Gould, Nina Van Pallandt).

Long Goodbye, The—Johnny Mercer (w), John Williams (m), Unart. COVER: Elliott Gould.

2913 Long Haul, The (Columbia, 1957, Victor Mature, Diana Dors).

Long Haul Theme (B)—Trevor Duncan (m), Chappell. COVER: Victor Mature, Diana Dors.

2914 Long Hot Summer, The (20th Century-Fox, 1958, Paul Newman, Joanne Woodward).

Hey, Eula/Long Hot Summer, The —Sammy Cahn (w), Alex North (m), Feist. COVER: Paul Newman, Joanne Woodward, Lee Remick, Anthony Franciosa.

2915 Long John Silver (Kaufman, 1955, Robert Newton, Kit Taylor).

Long John Silver—Irving Gordon, David Buttolph (w,m), Shapiro Bernstein/You're My Treasure—Jeanne Gravelle, David Buttolph (w,m), Shapiro Bernstein. COVER: Robert Newton, and Ship.

2916 Long Night, The (RKO, 1947, Henry Fonda, Barbara Bel Geddes).

Long Night, The—Ned Washington (w), Dimitri Tiomkin (m), Dreyer. COVER: Henry Fonda, Barbara Bel Geddes.

2917, Long Ships, The (Columbia, 1964, Sidney Poitier, Richard Widmark).

Long Ships, The—Charles Albertine, Dusan Radic (w,m), Colgems; Long Ships Themes (B)—Dusan Radic (m), Aldon. COVER: Movie Scenes.

2918 Long Wait, The (United Artists, 1954, Anthony Quinn, Peggie Castle).

Once—Bob Russell (w), Harold Spina (m), Disney. COVER: Anthony Quinn, Peggie Castle.

2919 Look for the Silver Lining (Warner Bros., 1949, June Haver, Ray Bolger).

Look for the Silver Lining—B. G. DeSylva (w), Jerome Kern (m), Harms; Time on My Hands—Harold Adamson, Mack Gordon (w), Vincent Youmans (m), Miller. COVER: Ray Bolger, June Haver, Gordon MacRae.

2920 Look in Any Window (Allied Artists, 1960, Paul Anka, Ruth Roman).

Look in Any Window Theme (PC) —Paul Anka (w,m), Spanka. COVER: None.

2921 Looking for Love (MGM, 1964, Connie Francis, Jim Hutton).

Looking for Love—Hank Hunter, Stan Vincent (w,m), Merna; Whoever You Are, I Love You—Gary Geld, Peter Udell (w,m), Francon. COVER: Connie Francis, Jim Hutton, Danny Thomas.

2922 Looking for Mr. Goodbar (Paramount, 1977, Diane Keaton, Tuesday Weld).

Don't Ask Me to Stay Until Tomorrow/Looking for Mr. Goodbar— Carol Conners, Artie Kane (w,m), Ensign. COVER: Diane Keaton.

2923 Looking Forward (MGM, 1932, Lionel Barrymore, Lewis Stone).
Looking Forward—Benny Davis, Ben Oakland (w,m), American. COVER: Lionel Barrymore, Lewis Stone, Elizabeth Allen.
2924 Looking Glass War, The (Columbia, 1970, Chris Jones, Ralph Richardson).
Fly Away Love—Wally Stott (w, m), Colgems; So Little Time for Lovin'—Wally Stott, Jimmy Walker (w,m), Colgems. COVER: Beach Scene.
2925 Looking on the Bright Side (RKO, 1932, Richard Dolman, Gracie Fields).
You're More Than All the World to Me (B)—Will Haines, M. Beresford, F. Sumner (w,m), Cameo; Looking on the Bright Side (B)—Howard Flynn (w,m), Cameo. COVER: Gracie Fields.
2926 Look Look (Warner Bros., 1948, Rita Rio and Orchestra).
Look! Look! (PC)—Rita Rio, Bill Bird, Tedd Lawrence (w,m), Top. COVER: None.
2927 Look Out for Love (London Melody) (Girls in the Street) (GB, 1937, Anna Neagle, Tullio Carminati).
Eyes of the World Are on You/ Jingle of the Jungle—Maurice Sigler, Al Goodhardt, Al Hoffman (w,m), Mills. COVER: Anna Neagle.
2928 Looping the Loop (Paramount, 1929, Werner Kraus, Jenny Jugo).
Poor Punchinello—Sam Lewis, Joe Young (w), Lew Pollack (m), Remick. COVER: Werner Kraus.
2929 Loose Ankles (First National, 1930, Loretta Young, Douglas Fairbanks).
Loose Ankles/Whoopin' It Up! (BW)—Jack Meskill (w), Pete Wendling (m), Remick. COVER: Loretta Young, Douglas Fairbanks.
2930 Lord Byron of Broadway (MGM, 1930, Cliff Edwards, Benny

Rubin).
Bundle of Old Love Letters, A/ Only Love Is Real/Should I/Woman in the Shoe—Arthur Freed (w), Nacio Herb Brown (m), Robbins. COVER: Sketch of Characters.
2931 Lord Jim (Columbia, 1965, Peter O'Toole, James Mason).
Lord Jim Theme (PC)—Bronislau Kaper (m), Colgems. COVER:None.
2932 Lord Love a Duck (United Artists, 1966, Roddy McDowell, Tuesday Weld).
Lord Love a Duck—Ernie Sheldon (w), Neal Hefti (m), Unart. COVER: A Duck.
2933 Lord of the Flies (Continental, 1963, Tom Chapin, James Aubrey).
Lord of the Flies Theme—Raymond Leppard (m), Saunders. COVER: Eyes.
2934 Lord of the Rings (United Artists, 1978, Cartoon).
Lord of the Rings Theme—Leonard Rosenman (m), Columbia; Mithrandir—Mark Fleischer (w), Leonard Rosenman (m), Columbia; Lord of the Rings-Music Score—Leonard Rosenman (m), Columbia. COVER: Lettering on Concrete.
2935 Lords of Discipline (Paramount, 1983, David Keith, Robert Prosky).
Lords of Discipline Theme—Howard Blake (m), Famous. COVER: David Keith, and Cadets.
2936 Lords of Flatbush (Columbia, 1974, Henry Winkler, Sylvester Stallone).
Lords of Flatbush-Eleven Songs—Joe Brooks (w,m), Big Hill. COVER: Henry Winkler, Sylvester Stallone, Perry King.
2937 Lorna Doone (First National, 1922, Madge Bellamy, John Bowers).
Lorna Doone—Arthur Penn (w), Fred Vanderpool (m), Witmark. COVER: Madge Bellamy.
2938 Loss of Innocence, A (The Greengage Summer) (Columbia,

1961, Kenneth More, Danielle Darrieux).

Loss of Innocence Theme—Richard Addinsell (m), Colgems. COVER: Susannah York.

2939 Lost Boundaries (Film Classics, 1949, Mel Ferrer, Beatrice Pearson).

Guess I'm Thru with Love—Albert Johnston (w,m), BMI; I Wouldn't Mind—Carleton Carpenter (w,m), Chappell; Tanganyika—Louis Applebaum (m), Mills. COVER: Mel Ferrer, Beatrice Pearson.

2940 Lost Boys (Warner Bros., 1987, Jason Patric, Corey Haim).

Good Times—George Young, Harry Vanda (w,m), Columbia. COVER: Red cover with title only.

2941 Lost Command, The (Columbia, 1966, Anthony Quinn, Alain Delon).

Home Again—Franz Waxman (m), Colgems. COVER: Anthony Quinn, Alain Delon, George Segal.

2942 Lost Horizon (Columbia, 1937, Ronald Colman, Jane Wyatt).

Lost Horizon-Love Theme—Gus Kahn (w), Dimitri Tiomkin (m), Berlin; Lost Horizon-Title Song—Clay Boland, Brooks Bowman (w, m), Berlin. COVER: Ronald Colman, and Other Stars.

2943 Lost Horizon (Columbia, 1973, Peter Finch, Liv Ullmann).

Living Together Growing Together/Lost Horizon/Question Me an Answer/Reflections/World Is a Circle, The/Lost Horizon-Eleven Songs—Hal David (w), Burt Bacharach (m), Colgems. COVER: A Buddhist Temple.

2944 Lost in a Harem (MGM, 1944, Bud Abbott, Lou Costello).

John Silver—Ray Krise, Jimmy Dorsey (m), BVC. COVER: Abbott and Costello, Jimmy Dorsey, Marilyn Maxwell.

2945 Lost Moment, The (Universal, 1947, Robert Cummings, Susan Hayward).

Lost Moment, The—Jack Brooks (w), Daniele Amfitheatrof (m), Rob-

ert. COVER: Susan Hayward.

2946 Lost World, The (First National, 1925, Wallace Beery, Bessie Love).

Lost World, The—Harry B. Smith (w), Rudolph Friml (m), Berlin. COVER: Bessie Love, Lloyd Hughes.

2947 Lottery Bride, The (United Artists, 1930, Jeanette MacDonald, John Garrick).

I'll Follow the Trail/My Northern Light/You're an Angel/Yubla—J. Keirn Brennan (w), Rudolph Friml (m), Friml. COVER: #1 Green cover with Jeanette MacDonald, John Garrick. COVER: #2 Yellow cover with Jeanette MacDonald only.

2948 Lottery Lover (Fox, 1935, Lew Ayres, Pat Paterson).

Close Your Eyes and See—Don Hartman (w), Jay Gormey (m), Movietone; Gaby Can Can (PC)—Jay Gormey (m), Movietone; There's a Bit of Paree in You/Ting a Ling a Ling—Don Hartman (w), Jay Gormey (m), Movietone. COVER: Lew Ayres, Pat Paterson, Peggy Fears.

2949 Loud Speaker, The (Monogram, 1934, Ray Walker, Jacqueline Wells).

Doo Ah Doo Ah Doo Ah Know What I'm Doing/Who But You—Roy Turk, Harry Akst (w,m), Harms. COVER: Ray Walker, Jacqueline Wells.

2950 Loud Speaker Lowdown (The Tattler) (Here Comes Carter) (Warner Bros., 1936, Ross Alexander, Ann Nagel).

You on My Mind/Thru the Courtesy of Love—Jack Scholl (w), M. K. Jerome (m), Witmark. COVER: Black and white cover with title only.

2951 Louisiane (Bolling, 1984, Margot Kidder, Len Cariou).

Louisiana Waltz—Felix Landau (w), Claude Bolling (m), Leonard; Louisiana Themes—Claude Bolling (m), Leonard. COVER: Len Cariou, Margot Kidder.

2952 Love (MGM, 1927, Greta Garbo, John Gilbert).

That Melody of Love—Howard Dietz (w), Walter Donaldson (m), Feist. COVER: Greta Garbo, John Gilbert.

2953 Love Affair (RKO, 1939, Irene Dunne, Charles Boyer).

Plaisir d'Amour—Giovanni Martini (w,m), Schirmer; Sing My Heart—Ted Koehler (w), Harold Arlen (m), Crawford; Wishing—B. G. DeSylva (w,m), Crawford. COVER: Irene Dunne, Charles Boyer.

2954 Love Among the Millionaires (Paramount, 1930, Clara Bow, Stanley Smith).

Believe It or Not/Don't Be a Meanie/Love Among the Millionaires—L. Wolfe Gilbert, Abel Baer (w,m), Famous; Rarin' to Go/That's Worth While Waiting For—L. Wolfe Gilbert (w), Abel Baer (m), Famous. COVER: Clara Bow.

2955 Love and Kisses (20th Century-Fox, 1937, Walter Winchell, Ben Bernie).

Be a Good Sport/Broadway's Gone Hawaii—Mack Gordon, Harry Revel (w,m), Feist; Little Love, a Little Kiss, A (B)—Lao Silesu (w,m), Day; I Wanna Be in Winchell's Column/Sweet Someone—Mack Gordon, Harry Revel (w,m), Feist. COVER: Walter Winchell, Ben Bernie, Simone Simon, Bert Lahr, Joan Davis.

2956 Love and Learn (Warner Bros., 1947, Jack Carson, Robert Hutton).

Would You Believe Me—Charles Tobias (w), Ray Heindorf, M. K. Jerome (m), Remick. COVER: Jack Carson, Robert Hutton, Janis Paige, Martha Vickers.

2957 Love and the Devil (First National, 1929, Milton Sills, Maria Korda).

Giovanna, to Thee I Am Calling—Richard Kountz (w), Joe Pasternack (m), Witmark. COVER: Milton Sills, Maria Korda.

2958 Love at First Sight (Chesterfield, 1930, Norman Foster, Paul Specht).

Love at First Sight—Lester Lee, Charles Levison (w,m), Triangle. COVER: Paul Specht, and Orchestra.

2959 Love at Last (Nice Girl) (Universal, 1941, Deanna Durbin, Franchot Tone).

Love at Last—Eddie Cherkose (w), Jacques Press (m), Robbins; Perhaps —Andres DeSegurola (w), Aldo Franchetti (m), Robbins. COVER: Black and white cover with title only.

2960 Love Comes Along (RKO, 1930, Bebe Daniels, Lloyd Hughes).

Night Winds/Until Love Comes Along—Sidney Clare (w), Oscar Levant (m), Harms. COVER: Bebe Daniels.

2961 Love Finds Andy Hardy (MGM, 1938, Mickey Rooney, Judy Garland).

In Between—Roger Edens (w,m), Feist; It Never Rains But When It Pours/Meet the Beat of My Heart/What Do You Know About Love—Mack Gordon, Harry Revel (w,m), Feist. COVER: Mickey Rooney, Judy Garland.

2962 Love Flower (United Artists, 1920, Carol Dempster, Richard Barthelmess).

Love Flower—B. G. DeSylva, Irving Caesar (w), Louis Silvers (m), Harms. COVER: Native Village.

2963 Love Gambler (Fox, 1932, Stars Unknown).

Tree Song—Jose Mojika, Troy Sanders, William Kernell (w,m), Red Star. COVER: Sketch of Woman.

2964 Love Goddesses (Reade, 1965, Mae West, Jean Harlow).

Love Goddess—Mack David (w), Percy Faith (m), Famous. COVER: Sketch of Love Goddess.

2965 Love Happy (United Artists, 1950, Groucho Marx, Harpo Marx).

Love Happy—Ann Ronell (w,m), Jewel. COVER: Marx Brothers, and Girls.

2966 Love Honor and Behave (Warner Bros., 1938, Priscilla Lane, Wayne Morris).

Bei Mir Bist Du Schon—Sammy Cahn (w), Saul Chaplin (m), Harms. COVER: Priscilla Lane, Wayne Morris.

2967 Love in a Goldfish Bowl (Paramount, 1961, Tommy Sands, Fabian).

Love in a Goldfish Bowl—Hal David (w), Burt Bacharach (m), Famous; You're Only Young Once—Russell Faith, Bob Marcucci (w,m), Famous. COVER: Tommy Sands, Fabian, Toby Michaels.

2968 Love in Bloom (Paramount, 1935, George Burns, Gracie Allen).

Got Me Doin' Things/Here Comes Cookie—Mack Gordon (w,m), Crawford; Let Me Sing You to Sleep with a Love Song—Mack Gordon, Harry Revel (w,m), Crawford; My Heart Is an Open Book—Mack Gordon (w,m), Crawford; None but the Lonely Heart—Arthur Westbrook (w), P. Tchaikovsky (m), Famous. COVER: Joe Morrison, Dixie Lee.

2969 Love in Gloom (Columbia, 1941, Musical Short).

How Do I Know It's Real? (PC)—Dan Schapiro, Jerry Seelen, Lester Lee (w,m), Cinema. COVER: None.

2970 Love in the Afternoon (Allied Artists, 1956, Gary Cooper, Audrey Hepburn).

Ariane—Johnny Mercer (w), Matty Malneck (m), Commander; Fascination—Dick Manning (w), F. D. Marchetti (m), Southern; Love in the Afternoon—Johnny Mercer (w), Matty Malneck (m), Commander. COVER: Gary Cooper, Audrey Hepburn, Maurice Chevalier.

2971 Love in the Rough (Like Kelly Can) (MGM, 1930, Robert Montgomery, Dorothy Jordan).

Go Home and Tell Your Mother/ I'm Doing That Thing/I'm Learning a Lot from You/One More Waltz—Dorothy Fields (w), Jimmy McHugh (m), Robbins. COVER: Robert Montgomery, Dorothy Jordan.

2972 Love Is a Ball (United Artists, 1963, Glenn Ford, Hope Lange).

Gather Your Dreams—Bart Howard (w), Michel Legrand (m), Unart; Love Is a Ball—Richard Adler (w), Michel Legrand (m), Unart; Love Is a Ball Theme—Michel Legrand (m), Unart. COVER: Glenn Ford, Hope Lange.

2973 Love Is a Many Splendored Thing (20th Century-Fox, 1955, William Holden, Jennifer Jones).

Love Is a Many Splendored Thing —Paul F. Webster (w), Sammy Fain (m), Miller. COVER: William Holden, Jennifer Jones.

2974 Love Is News (20th Century-Fox, 1937, Loretta Young, Tyrone Power).

Love Is News—Sidney Mitchell (w), Lew Pollack (m), Movietone. COVER: Loretta Young, Tyrone Power.

2975 Love Letters (Paramount, 1917, William Conklin, Dorothy Dalton).

There's No End to My Love for You—Al Dubin (w), James Monaco (m), Witmark. COVER: William Conklin, Dorothy Dalton.

2976 Love Letters (Paramount, 1945, Jennifer Jones, Joseph Cotten).

Love Letters—Edward Heyman (w), Victor Young (m), Famous; Love Letters-Theme/Love Letters-Music Score—Victor Young (m), Famous. COVER: Jennifer Jones, Joseph Cotten.

2977 Love Lines (Tri-Star, 1984, Greg Bradford, Mary Beth Evans).

Love Lines—Al Kasha, Joel Hirschhorn, Michael Lloyd (w,m), Tri-Star. COVER: Boys and Girls with Guitars.

2978 Love Live and Laugh (Hurdy Gurdy) (Fox, 1929, George Jessel, Lila Lee).

Margarita/Two Little Baby Arms —L. Wolfe Gilbert (w), Abel Baer (m), DBH. COVER: George Jessel, Lila Lee.

2979 Lovely to Look At (MGM, 1952, Kathryn Grayson, Howard Keel).

I Won't Dance—Oscar Hammerstein, Otto Harbach, Jerome Kern, Jimmy McHugh, Dorothy Fields (w, m), Harms; I'll Be Hard to Handle—

Bernard Dougall (w), Jerome Kern (m), Harms; Lovely to Look At— Dorothy Fields, Jimmy McHugh (w), Jerome Kern (m), Harms; Smoke Gets in Your Eyes/Touch of Your Hand, The/Yesterdays/You're Devastating—Otto Harbach (w), Jerome Kern (m), Harms. COVER: Kathryn Grayson, Red Skelton, Howard Keel, Ann Miller.

2980 Love Machine, The (Columbia, 1971, John Philip Law, Dyan Cannon).

Amanda—Mark Lindsay (w), Artie Butler (m), Colgems; He's Movin' On —Ruth Batchelor (w), Bryan Wells (m), Colgems. COVER: John Philip Law, Dyan Cannon.

2981 Love Me Forever (Columbia, 1935, Grace Moore, Robert Allen).

Love Me Forever—Gus Kahn (w), Victor Schertzinger (m), Berlin. COVER: Grace Moore.

2982 Love Me or Leave Me (MGM, 1955, Doris Day, James Cagney).

At Sundown—Walter Donaldson (w,m), Feist; Everybody Loves My Baby—Jack Palmer, Spencer Williams (w,m), Pickwick; I'll Never Stop Loving You—Sammy Cahn (w), Nicholas Brodszky (m), Feist; It All Depends on You—B. G. DeSylva, Lew Brown, Ray Henderson (w,m), DBH; Love Me or Leave Me—Gus Kahn (w), Walter Donaldson (m), BVC; Mean to Me—Roy Turk, Fred Ahlert (w,m), DBH; Never Look Back—Chilton Price (w,m), Daywin; Sam the Old Accordion Man—Walter Donaldson (w,m), Feist; Stay on the Right Side Sister—Ted Koehler (w), Rube Bloom (m), Robbins. COVER: Doris Day, James Cagney.

2983 Love Me Tender (20th Century-Fox, 1956, Elvis Presley, Debra Paget).

Let Me/Love Me Tender/Poor Boy/ We're Gonna Move—Elvis Presley, Vera Matson (w,m), Presley. COVER: Elvis Presley.

2984 Love Me Tonight (Paramount, 1932, Maurice Chevalier, Jeanette MacDonald).

Isn't It Romantic/Love Me Tonight/Lover/Mimi/Poor Apache— Lorenz Hart (w), Richard Rodgers (m), Famous. COVER: Maurice Chevalier.

2985 Love of Sunya (United Artists, 1927, Gloria Swanson, John Boles).

Love Waltz—J. Keirn Brennan (w), H. Maurice Jacquet (m), Flammer. COVER: Gloria Swanson.

2986 Love on the Run (MGM, 1936, Joan Crawford, Franchot Tone).

Gone—Gus Kahn (w), Franz Waxman (m), Feist. COVER: Joan Crawford, Franchot Tone.

2987 Love on Toast (Paramount, 1938, John Payne, Grant Richards).

I'd Love to Play a Love Scene— Sam Coslow (w,m), Famous; I Want a New Romance—Sam Coslow (w), Burton Lane (m), Famous. COVER: John Payne, and Girls.

2988 Love Parade, The (Paramount, 1929, Maurice Chevalier, Jeanette MacDonald).

Anything to Please the Queen/ Dream Lover—Clifford Grey (w), Victor Schertzinger (m), Famous; Let's Be Common—Clifford Grey (w), Victor Schertzinger (m), Spier Coslow; March of the Grenadiers/ My Love Parade—Clifford Grey (w), Victor Schertzinger (m), Famous; Nobody's Using It Now—Clifford Grey (w), Victor Schertzinger (m), Remick; Paris Stay the Same—Clifford Grey (w), Victor Schertzinger (m), Famous. COVER: Maurice Chevalier, Jeanette MacDonald.

2989 Lover Come Back (Universal, 1961, Rock Hudson, Doris Day).

Lover Come Back—Alan Spilton, Frank DeVol (w,m), Daywin; Should I Surrender—William Landau (w), Adan Ross (m), Daywin. COVER: Rock Hudson, Doris Day.

2990 Lovers and Lollipops (Trans Lux, 1956, Lori March, Cathy Dunn).

Lovers and Lollipops/Peggy's Theme—Eddy Manson (w,m), Trinity. COVER: Sketch of Movie Scene.

2991 Lovers and Other Strangers (Cinerama, 1970, Bea Arthur, Bonnie Bedelia).

Comin' Thru to Me/For All We Know/Keepin' Free—Robb Wilson, Art James (w), Fred Karlin (m), ABC. COVER: Sketch of Couple.

2992 Loves of an Actress (Paramount, 1927, Pola Negri, Nils Asther).

Sunbeams—J. Keirn Brennan (w), Karl Hajos (m), Shapiro Bernstein. COVER: Pola Negri, Nils Asther.

2993 Loves of Carmen, The (Fox, 1927, Dolores Del Rio, Don Alvarado).

Estrelita—George Davis (w), Manuel Ponce (m), Sherman Clay. COVER: Dolores Del Rio, Don Alvarado.

2994 Loves of Carmen, The (Columbia, 1948, Glenn Ford, Rita Hayworth).

Love of a Gypsy—Moross Stoloff, Fred Karger (w,m), Mood. COVER: Rita Hayworth, Glenn Ford.

2995 Loves of Isadora, The (Universal, 1968, James Fox, Vanessa Redgrave).

Isadora—Don Black (w), Maurice Jarre (m), Shamley. COVER: Vanessa Redgrave.

2996 Love Story (Paramount, 1970, Ali MacGraw, Ryan O'Neal).

Love Story Theme/Snow Frolic—Francis Lai (m), Famous; Where Do I Begin—Carl Sigman (w), Francis Lai (m), Famous; Love Story-Seven Themes—Francis Lai (m), Famous. COVER: Ali MacGraw, Ryan O'Neal.

2997 Love Thy Neighbor (Paramount, 1940, Jack Benny, Mary Martin).

Dearest Dearest I/Do You Know Why/Isn't That Just Like Love—Johnny Burke (w), James Van Heusen (m), Famous. COVER: Jack Benny, Mary Martin, Fred Allen, Rochester.

2998 Love Trader (Tiffany, 1930, Leatrice Joy, Roland Drew).

Love Flower, The—Dick Coburn (w), James Kroe (m), Sherman Clay. COVER: Leatrice Joy, Roland Drew.

2999 Love Under Fire (20th Century-Fox, 1937, Loretta Young, Don Ameche).

Language of Love—Jack Lawrence (w), Sam Pokrass (m), Movietone. COVER: Loretta Young, Don Ameche, Borah Minnevitch.

3000 Love with the Proper Stranger (Paramount, 1964, Natalie Wood, Steve McQueen).

Love with the Proper Stranger—Johnny Mercer (w), Elmer Bernstein (m), Paramount. COVER: Natalie Wood, Steve McQueen.

3001 Loving You (Paramount, 1957, Elvis Presley, Lizabeth Scott).

Got a Lot o' Livin' to Do—Aaron Schroeder, Ben Weisman (w,m), Gladys; Hot Dog—Jerry Leiber, Mike Stoller (w,m), Presley; Lonesome Cowboy—Sid Tepper, Roy Bennett (w,m), Gladys; Loving You—Jerry Leiber, Mike Stoller (w,m), Presley; Mean Woman Blues—Claude DeMetruis (w,m), Gladys; Party—Jessie Mae Robinson (w,m), Gladys; Teddy Bear—Bernie Lowe, Kal Mann (w,m), Gladys. COVER: Elvis Presley.

3002 Lovin' Molly (Columbia, 1873, Anthony Perkins, Beau Bridges).

Lovin' Molly—Fred Hellerman (m), Coral. COVER: Blythe Danner.

3003 L-Shaped Room, The (Columbia, 1962, Leslie Caron, Tom Bell).

T-Shaped Twist, The (B)—John Barry (m), Feldman. COVER: Black and white cover with title only.

3004 Lucia (Graham, 1965, Religious Film).

Life Worth Living (PC)—Ralph Carmichael (w,m), Lexicon. COVER: None.

3005 Lucille Love-Girl of Mystery (Universal, 1914, Francis Ford, Grace Cunard).

Lucille Love, Valse Boston Hesitation—Abe Olman (m), LaSalle. COVER: Grace Cunard.

3006 Luck of Ginger Coffey, The (Continental, 1964, Robert Shaw, Mary Ure).

Luck of Ginger Coffey, The—Will Holt (w), Bernardo Segall (m), Frank. COVER: Man and Woman.

3007 Lucky Boy (Tiffany, 1929, George Jessel, Margaret Quimby).

My Mother's Eyes—L. Wolfe Gilbert (w), Abel Baer (m), Feist. COVER: George Jessel.

3008 Lucky Cowboy (Paramount, 1944, Julie Gibson, Dick Foran).

Headin' Home—Lester Lee, Jerry Seelen (w,m), Famous; Lucky Cowboy—Leo Robin, Ralph Rainger (w, m), Famous; My Old Flame—Sam Coslow, Arthur Johnston (w,m), Famous. COVER: Julie Gibson, Dick Foran.

3009 Lucky in Love (Pathe, 1929, Morton Downey, Betty Lawford).

For the Likes of You and Me/ Love Is a Dreamer/When They Sing the Wearin' of the Green—Bud Green, Sam Stept (w,m), Green Stept. COVER: Morton Downey.

3010 Lucky Lady (20th Century-Fox, 1975, Liza Minelli, Burt Reynolds).

Lucky Lady—Fred Ebb (w), John Kander (m), Chappell. COVER: Gene Hackman, Liza Minnelli, Burt Reynolds.

3011 Lucky Me (Warner Bros., 1954, Doris Day, Robert Cummings).

Blue Bells of Broadway, The/I Speak to the Stars/I Wanna Sing Like an Angel/Love You Dearly/ Lucky Me/Superstition Song/Take a Memo to the Moon—Paul F. Webster (w), Sammy Fain (m), Witmark. COVER: Doris Day, Phil Silvers, Nancy Walker.

3012 Lucky Melodies (Independent, 1950, Ernie George).

That's How I Feel About You— Ernie George (w), Art Behning (m), Clef. COVER: Ernie George.

3013 Lucky Stiff, The (United Artists, 1949, Dorothy Lamour, Brian Donlevy).

Loneliness—Ned Washington (w), Victor Young (m), Famous. COVER: Dorothy Lamour, Brian Donlevy.

3014 Lucretia Lombard (Warner Bros., 1923, Irene Rich, Monte Blue).

Love, My Heart Is Calling You— Sam Lewis, Joe Young (w), Joe Cooper (m), Berlin. COVER: Irene Rich, Monte Blue.

3015 Lucy Gallant (Paramount, 1955, Jane Wyman, Charlton Heston).

How Can I Tell Her—Jay Livingston, Ray Evans (w,m), Famous. COVER: Jane Wyman, Charlton Heston.

3016 Lullaby Land (Disney, 1933, Cartoon).

Dance of the Bogey Man (VS)/ Lullaby Land—Leigh Harline (w,m), Berlin. COVER: Cartoon.

3017 Lullaby of Broadway (Warner Bros., 1951, Doris Day, Gene Nelson).

I Love the Way You Say Goodnight—Eddie Pola, George Wyle (w, m), Remick; In a Shanty in Old Shantytown (B)—Joe Young (w), John Sira, Jack Little (m), Feldman; Lullaby of Broadway—Al Dubin (w), Harry Warren (m), Witmark; Please Don't Talk About Me When I'm Gone—Sidney Clare, Sam Stept, B. Palmer (w,m), Remick. COVER: Doris Day, Gene Nelson.

3018 Lulu Belle (Columbia, 1948, Dorothy Lamour, George Montgomery).

Lulu Belle—Henry Russell, Eddie Delange (w,m), Simon; Sweetie Pie— Henry Russell, Johnny Lehman (w, m), Simon. COVER: Dorothy Lamour.

3019 Lumberjack (United Artists, 1954, William Boyd, Andy Clyde).

That Place Your Heart Calls Home—Forest Johnson, Ozie Waters (w,m), McDaniel. COVER: Ozie Waters.

3020 Lure of the Islands (Monogram, 1942, Robert Lowery, Margie Hart).

Lure of the Islands/Tahiti Sweetie —Edward Kay, Eddie Cherkose (w, m), Chart. COVER: Margie Hart, and Movie Scene.

3021 Luxury Liner (MGM, 1948, George Brent, Jane Powell).

Spring Came Back to Vienna— Fritz Rotter, Janice Torre, Fred Spielman (w,m), Robbins. COVER: Jane Powell, George Brent, Lauritz Melchior.

3022 Lydia (United Artists, 1941, Merle Oberon, Joseph Cotton).

Lydia—Miklos Rozsa (m), Sam Fox. COVER: Sketch of Lady.

3023 Lying Lips (Ince, 1921, House Peters, Florence Vidor).

Lying Lips—King Vidor, Vern Elliott (w,m), Berlin. COVER: Florence Vidor.

3024 Macao (RKO, 1950, Jane Russell, Robert Mitchum).

Ocean Breeze (PC)/You Kill Me (PC)—Leo Robin (w), Jule Styne (m), Morris. COVER: None.

3025 MacArthur (Universal, 1977, Gregory Peck, Ed Flanders).

MacArthur March—Jerry Goldsmith (m), Duchess. COVER: Gregory Peck, and Soldiers.

3026 McConnell Story (Warner Bros., 1945, Alan Ladd, June Allyson).

While You're Away—Stanley Adams (w), Max Steiner (m), Remick. COVER: Alan Ladd, June Allyson.

3027 McFadden's Flats (First National, 1927, Charlie Murray, Chester Conklin).

Down in the Old Neighborhood— William McKenna (w,m), Chilton.

COVER: Sketch of Characters.

3028 MacKenna's Gold (Columbia, 1969, Gregory Peck, Omar Sharif).

Ole Turkey Buzzard—Freddie Douglas (w), Quincy Jones (m), Colgems. COVER: Gregory Peck, Omar Sharif, and Others.

3029 McLintock (United Artists, 1963, John Wayne, Maureen O'Hara).

McLintock's Theme—By Dunham (w), Frank DeVol (m), Unart. COVER: John Wayne, Maureen O'Hara.

3030 McVicar (Crown, 1977, Adam Faith, Roger Daltrey).

Without Your Love—Billy Nichols (w,m), H.G. COVER: Roger Daltrey.

3031 Mad About Music (Universal, 1938, Deanna Durbin, Herbert Marshall).

Chapel Bells/I Love to Whistle/ Serenade to the Stars—Harold Adamson (w), Jimmy McHugh (m), Robbins. COVER: Deanna Durbin.

3032 Madame Bovary (MGM, 1949, Jennifer Jones, Louis Jourdan).

Madame Bovary Waltz—Miklos Rozsa (m), Robbins. COVER: Jennifer Jones, Louis Jourdan.

3033 Madame Satan (MGM, 1930, Roland Young, Reginald Denny).

Live and Love Today—Elsie Janis (w), Jack King (m), Robbins; This Is Love—Clifford Grey (w), Herbert Stothart (m), Robbins. COVER: Kay Johnson, Reginald Denny.

3034 Madame X (MGM, 1937, Gladys George, John Beal).

You're Setting Me on Fire—Bob Wright, Chet Forrest (w), Walter Donaldson (m), Robbins. COVER: Black and white cover with title only.

3035 Madame X (Universal, 1966, Lana Turner, John Forsythe).

Madame X Love Theme—Charles Wildman (m), MCA. COVER: Lana Turner, Keir Dullea.

3036 Mad Dog Coll (Columbia, 1961, John Chandler, Neil Nephew).
Mad Dog Coll—Ed Schreiber (w), Stu Phillips (m), Gower; Tease, The/ Twenty Dollar Gold Piece—Stu Phillips (m), Gower. COVER: Black and white cover with title only.

3037 Made for Each Other (United Artists, 1939, James Stewart, Carole Lombard).
Made for Each Other—Harry Tobias (w), Oscar Levant (m), Crawford. COVER: James Stewart, Carole Lombard.

3038 Made for Each Other (20th Century-Fox, 1971, Renee Taylor, Joseph Bologna).
Panda's Theme—Trade Martin (m), Fox. COVER: Renee Taylor, Joseph Bologna.

3039 Made in Paris (MGM, 1966, Ann Margret, Louis Jourdan).
Made in Paris—Hal David (w), Burt Bacharach (m), Feist; Paris Lullaby—Paul F. Webster (w), Sammy Fain (m), Feist. COVER: Ann Margret, Louis Jourdan.

3040 Madeira, Isle of Romance (MGM, 1938, Travelogue).
On the Island of Madeira—James Fitzpatrick, Nelson Cogan (w), Jack Shilkret (m), Southern. COVER: Jack Arthur.

3041 Mademoiselle from Armentieres (Gaumont, 1926, Estelle Brodie, John Stuart).
Rose of Armentieres—Jack Arthur, Horace Lapp (w,m), Spier Coslow. COVER: Sketch of Girl.

3042 Mad Max-Beyond Thunderdome (Warner Bros., 1985, Mel Gibson, Tina Turner).
One of the Living—Holly Knight (w,m), Makiki; We Don't Need Another Hero—Graham Lyle, Terry Britten (w,m), Almo. COVER: Tina Turner.

3043 Madonna of Avenue "A" (Warner Bros., 1929, Dolores Costello, Grant Withers).
My Madonna—Billy Rose (w), Fred Fisher, Louis Silvers (m), Berlin. COVER: Dolores Costello.

3044 Madonna of the Seven Moons (Universal, 1944, Phyllis Calvert, Stewart Granger).
Rosanna (B)—Sonny Miller (w), Hans May (m), Cinephonic. COVER: Phyllis Calvert.

3045 Madron (Four Stars, 1970, Richard Boone, Leslie Caron).
Till Love Touches Your Life— Arthur Hamilton (w), Riz Ortolani (m), BNP. COVER: Richard Boone, Leslie Caron.

3046 Madwoman of Chaillot (Warner Bros., 1969, Katharine Hepburn, Charles Boyer).
Before We Say Goodbye—Al Stillman (w), Michael Lewis (m), Warner; Lonely Ones—Gil King (w), Michael Lewis (m), Warner; Madwoman of Chaillot/Madwoman of Chaillot-Seven Themes—Michael Lewis (m), Warner. COVER: Katharine Hepburn, Charles Boyer, John Gavin, Yul Brynner.

3047 Maggie, The (High and Dry) (Universal, 1953, Paul Douglas, Alex MacKenzie).
Song of the Maggie (B)—John Addison, Jack Fishman (m), Pickwick. COVER: Paul Douglas, and Boat.

3048 Magic Bow, The (Universal, 1946, Stewart Granger, Phyllis Calvert).
Romance (B)—Phil Green (m), Chappell. COVER: Stewart Granger.

3049 Magic Boy, The (MGM, 1961, Cartoon).
Magic Boy, The—Janice Torre (w), Fred Spielman (m), Robbins. COVER: Cartoon.

3050 Magic Christian (Commonwealth, 1970, Peter Sellers, Ringo Starr).
Come and Get It—Paul McCartney (w,m), Maclen. COVER: Badfinger Rock Group.

3051 Magic Flame, The (Goldwyn, 1927, Ronald Colman, Vilma Banky).
Magic Flame, The—Sigmund Spaeth (w), I. Toselli (m), Boston.

COVER: Ronald Colman, Vilma Banky.

3052 Magic Fountain, The (David, 1962, Hans Conreid, Buddy Baer).

Magic Fountain, The—Steve Allen, Don George (w,m), Rosemeadow. COVER: Movie Scenes.

3053 Magic Garden, The (Pennywhistle Blues) (Swan, 1952, Tommy Ramokgopa, Dolly Rathebe).

Pennywhistle Blues—Willard Cele (m), Leeds. COVER: Buddy De-Franco.

3054 Magic Garden of Stanley Sweetheart, The (MGM, 1970, Don Johnson, Michael Greer).

Nobody Knows/Sweet Gingerbread Man—Alan Bergman, Marilyn Bergman (w), Michel Legrand (m), Feist. COVER: Naked Girl.

3055 Magic Night (United Artists, 1932, Jack Buchanan, Anna Neagle).

Goodnight Vienna/Just Heaven/ Living in Clover/Marching Song/Dear Little Waltz (VS)/My Pretty Flowers (VS)—Holt Marvell (w), George Posford (m), Sam Fox. COVER: Jack Buchanan.

3056 Magic of Lassie, The (International, 1978, Mickey Rooney, Alice Faye).

When You're Loved/Magic of Lassie-Ten Songs—Richard Sherman, Robert Sherman (w,m), Wrather. COVER: Mickey Rooney, Alice Faye, James Stewart, and Lassie.

3057 Magic Town (RKO, 1947, James Stewart, Jane Wyman).

Magic Town—Mel Torme, Robert Wells (w,m), BVH; My Book of Memory—Edward Heyman (w), A. Westendorf (m), BVH. COVER: James Stewart, Jane Wyman.

3058 Magnificent Matador, The (20th Century-Fox, 1955, Maureen O'Hara, Anthony Quinn).

Magnificent Matador, The—Paul Herrick (w), Ed Alpherson (m), Miller. COVER: Anthony Quinn, Maureen O'Hara.

3059 Magnificent Obsession (Universal, 1954, Jane Wyman, Rock Hudson).

Magnificent Obsession—Fred Herbert (w), Frank Skinner (m), Morris. COVER: Sketch of Couple.

3060 Magnificent Seven, The (United Artists, 1960, Yul Brynner, Eli Wallach).

Magnificent Seven Theme—Elmer Bernstein (m), Unart. COVER: Cowboys.

3061 Magus, The (20th Century-Fox, 1968, Michael Caine, Anthony Quinn).

Where Did You Come From—Don Black (w), Mark London (m), Fox. COVER: Red cover with title only.

3062 Ma, He's Making Eyes at Me (Universal, 1940, Constance Moore, Tom Brown).

Ma, He's Making Eyes at Me—Sidney Clare (w), Con Conrad (m), Mills; Unfair to Love—Sam Lerner (w), Frank Skinner (m), Robbins. COVER: Constance Moore, Tom Brown.

3063 Mahogany (Paramount, 1973, Diana Ross, Billy Dee Williams.

Do You Know Where You're Going To—Gerry Goffin (w), Michael Masser (m), Jobete; Mahogany-Twelve Songs—Michael Masser, Gil Askey (w, m), Jobete. COVER: Diana Ross.

3064 Mail Order Bride (MGM, 1963, Buddy Ebsen, Keir Dullea).

Mail Order Bride—Buddy Ebsen (w), George Bassman (m), Miller. COVER: Buddy Ebsen, Keir Dullea, and Girls.

3065 Main Attraction, The (MGM, 1962, Pat Boone, Nancy Kwan).

Amore Baciami (B)—G. Parsons, John Turner, Pat Boone (w), C. Rossi (m), World Wide; Gondoli Gondola—Pat Boone (w), R. Sarosone (m), Spoone; Main Attraction—Pat Boone, Jeff Corey (w,m), Spoone. COVER: Pat Boone, Nancy Kwan.

3066 Main Event, The (Warner Bros., 1979, Barbra Streisand, Ryan O'Neal).

Main Event and Fight—Paul Jabara, Bruce Roberts, Bob Esty (w, m), Warner. COVER: Barbra Streisand, Ryan O'Neal.

3067 Main Street to Broadway (MGM, 1953, Tallulah Bankhead, Ethel Barrymore).

Blue New York/Just a Girl—Ann Ronell (w,m), Ronell; There's Music in You—Oscar Hammerstein (w), Richard Rodgers (m), Williamson. COVER: Mary Martin, Tom Morton, Mary Murphy, and Hirschfeld Sketches.

3068 Maisie Goes to Reno (MGM, 1944, Ann Sothern, John Hodiak).

Panhandle Pete—Ralph Freed (w), Sammy Fain (m), Feist. COVER: Ann Sothern.

3069 Major and the Minor, The (Paramount, 1942, Ginger Rogers, Ray Milland).

Major and the Minor, The—Redd Evans, Earl Bostic (w,m), Famous. COVER: Ginger Rogers, Ray Milland.

3070 Major Dundee (Columbia, 1965, Charlton Heston, Richard Harris).

Laura Lee—Liam Sullivan (w), Forrest Wood (m), Colgems; Major Dundee March—Ned Washington (w), Daniele Amfitheatrof (m), Colgems; To Be with You—Al Stillman (w), Daniele Amfitheatrof (m), Colgems. COVER: Charlton Heston, Richard Harris, and Others.

3071 Majority of One, A (Warner Bros., 1962, Rosalind Russell, Alec Guinness).

Majority of One Theme—Max Steiner (m), Witmark. COVER: Rosalind Russell, Alec Guinness.

3072 Make a Wish (RKO, 1937, Bobby Breen, Basil Rathbone).

Make a Wish/Music in My Heart—Louis Alter, Paul F. Webster (w), Oscar Straus (m), Feist; My Campfire Dreams—Paul F. Webster (w), Louis Alter (m), Feist. COVER: Bobby Breen, Basil Rathbone, Marion Claire.

3073 Make Believe Ballroom (Columbia, 1949, Jerome Courtland, Ruth Warrick).

I'm the Lonesomest Gal in Town—Lew Brown (w), Albert Von Tilzer (m), Broadway; Miss In-Between Blues—Allan Roberts, Lester Lee (w, m), Mood; Way the Twig Is Bent, The—Allan Roberts, Doris Fisher (w,m), Mood. COVER: Jerome Courtland, Virginia Welles.

3074 Make Mine Mink (Continental, 1960, Terry Thomas, Athene Seyler).

Make Mine Mink (B)—Philip Green (w,m), Filmusic. COVER: Terry Thomas, and Others.

3075 Make Mine Music (RKO Disney, 1946, Cartoon).

All the Cats Join In—Alec Wilder, Ray Gilbert (w), Eddie Sauter (m), Regent; Blue Bayou—Ray Gilbert, Bobby Worth (w,m), Southern; Casey the Pride of Them All—Ray Gilbert, Ken Darby, Eliot Daniel (w, m), Southern; Johnny Fedora and Alice Blue Bonnett—Allie Wrubel, Ray Gilbert (w,m), Leeds; Make Mine Music—Ken Darby, Eliot Daniel (w,m), Southern; Peter and the Wolf Themes (B)—S. Prokofiev (m), Campbell; Two Silhouettes—Ray Gilbert (w), Charles Wolcott (m), Southern; Without You—Osvaldo Farres, Ray Gilbert (w,m), Southern. COVER: Andy Russell, Dinah Shore, Jerry Colonna, Benny Goodman, and Cartoons.

3076 Make Way for Tomorrow (Paramount, 1937, Victor Moore, Beulah Bondi).

Make Way for Tomorrow—Leo Robin, Sam Coslow, Jean Schwartz (w,m), Famous. COVER: Victor Moore, Beulah Bondi.

3077 Making It (20th Century-Fox, 1971, Kris Tabori, Marlyn Mason).

Morning Song—Norman Gimbel (w), Charles Fox (m), Fox. COVER: Kris Tabori.

3078 Making Love (20th Century-Fox, 1982, Harry Hamlin, Kate Jackson).

Making Love—Carole B. Sager, Burt Bacharach, Bruce Roberts (w,m), Fox. COVER: Harry Hamlin, Kate Jackson, Michael Ontkean.

3079 Malamondo (Magna, 1964, Documentary of Behaviours).

Funny World—Alan Brandt (w), Ennio Morricone (m), Marks. COVER: Women's Faces.

3080 Male and Female (Paramount, 1919, Gloria Swanson, Bebe Daniels).

Gloria—Tot Seymour (w), M. K. Jerome (m), Berlin. COVER: Gloria Swanson.

3081 Maltese Bippy, The (MGM, 1969, Carol Lynley, Rowan and Martin).

Maltese Bippy Theme—Nelson Riddle (m), Hastings. COVER: Rowan and Martin.

3082 Mambo (Paramount, 1954, Silvana Mangano, Michael Rennie).

Back to Bahia—Katherine Dunham, Wilson Stone (w), Bernard Noriega (m), Paramount; Boogie in Brazil—Wilson Stone (w), Bernard Noriega (m), Paramount; It Wasn't the Wine—Katherine Dunham, Wilson Stone (w), Bernard Noriega (m), Paramount; Silvana Mangano Mambo —Mack David, Wilson Stone (w,m), Paramount; New Love New Wine—Katherine Dunham, Bernard Noriega (w,m), Paramount; Washerwoman—Marion Sunshine, Obdulio Morales (w,m), Paramount. COVER: Silvana Mangano, Michael Rennie.

3083 Mame (Warner Bros., 1974, Lucille Ball, Robert Preston).

Bosom Buddies/Gooch's Song/ If He Walked into My Life/It's Today/Loving You/Mame/Man in the Moon/My Best Girl/Open a New Window/St. Bridget/We Need a Little Christmas—Jerry Herman (w,m), Morris. COVER: Lucille Ball.

3084 Mamele (Sphinx, 1939, Molly Picon, Edmund Zayenda).

Abi Gezunt/Ich Sing/Mazl—Molly Picon, Abraham Ellstein (w,m), Metro. COVER: Molly Picon, Abraham Ellstein.

3085 Mammy (Warner Bros., 1930, Al Jolson, Louise Dresser).

Knights of the Road (BW)/Let Me Sing and I'm Happy/Looking at You/ To My Mammy—Irving Berlin (w,m), Berlin. COVER: Al Jolson.

3086 Man About Town (Paramount, 1939, Jack Benny, Betty Grable).

Fidgety Joe—Frank Loesser (w), Matt Malneck (m), Famous; Man About Town/Strange Enchantment/ That Sentimental Sandwich—Frank Loesser (w), Frederick Hollander (m), Famous. COVER: Jack Benny, Dorothy Lamour, Phil Harris.

3087 Man and a Woman, A (Allied Artists, 1967, Anouk Aimee, Jean Louis Trintignant).

All at Once It's Love/Love Is Stronger Far Then We/Man and a Woman, A—Jerry Keller (w), Francis Lai (m), Northern; My Heart Loves the Samba—Jerry Keller (w), V. DeMoraes, Baden Powell (m), Northern; Shadows of Our Love—Jerry Keller (w), Francis Lai (m), Northern. COVER: Anouk Aimee, Jean Louis Trintignant.

3088 Man and the Moment (First National, 1929, Billie Dove, Rod La-Rocque).

Just a Lucky Moment—Herman Ruby (w), Ray Perkins (m), Witmark. COVER: Billie Dove, Rod La-Rocque.

3089 Man Between, The (United Artists, 1953, James Mason, Claire Bloom).

Man Between Theme (B)—John Addison (m), Dash. COVER: James Mason, Claire Bloom, Hildegarde Neff.

3090 Man Called Back, The (Tiffany, 1932, Conrad Nagel, Doris Kenyon).

Kiss Me Tonight—Val Burton, Corynn Kiehl (w,m), Sam Fox. COV-

ER: Black and white cover with title only.

3091 Man Called Gannon, A (Universal, 1968, Tony Franciosa, Michael Sarrazin).

A Smile, a Memory, and an Extra Shirt—Alan Bergman, Marilyn Bergman (w), Dave Grusin (m), Shamley. COVER: Anthony Franciosa, Susan Oliver.

3092 Man Called Noon, A (National General, 1973, Richard Crenna, Stephen Boyd).

Man Called Noon, A—Sammy Cahn (w), Luis Bacalov (m), Famous. COVER: Richard Crenna.

3093 Man Called Peter, A (20th Century-Fox, 1955, Richard Todd, Jean Peters).

Forever Yours (VS)—Alfred Newman (m), Fox; Give Me That Old Time Religion—Hugo Frey (w,m), Robbins; Man Called Peter, A—Charles Tobias, Max Stein, Ken Sloan (w,m), Jungnickel. COVER: Richard Todd, Jean Peters.

3094 Man Could Get Killed, A (Universal, 1966, James Garner, Melina Mercouri).

But Not Today—Buddy Scott, Jim Radcliff (w), Bert Kaempfert (m), Champion; Strangers in the Night—Charles Singleton, Ed Snyder (w), Bert Kaempfert (m), Champion. COVER: Frank Sinatra.

3095 Mandalay (First National, 1934, Kay Francis, Ricardo Cortez).

When Tomorrow Comes—Irving Kahal (w), Sammy Fain (m), Witmark. COVER: Kay Francis, Ricardo Cortez.

3096 Mandragola (Europix, 1965, Rosanna Schiaffino, Philippe Leroy).

It Seems a Long Long Time—Robert Mellin (w), Gino Marinuzzi (m), Elmwin. COVER: Rosanna Schiaffino.

3097 Man from Glengarry, The (Hodkinson, 1927, Andreas Randolph, Warner Richmond).

Man from Glengarry, The—Menlo Mayfield (m), Veritas. COVER: Al Epps, and Sketch.

3098 Man from Laramie, The (Columbia, 1955, James Stewart, Arthur Kennedy).

Man from Laramie, The—Ned Washington (w), Lester Lee (m), Colgems. COVER: James Stewart, Cathy O'Donnell.

3099 Man from Montana, The (Universal, 1941, Johnny Mack Brown, Fuzzy Knight).

Bananas Make Me Tough/Call of the Range/Western Trail—Everett Carter (w), Milton Rosen (m), Robbins. COVER: Johnny Mack Brown, Fuzzy Knight, Nell O'Day.

3100 Man from Music Mountain, The (Republic, 1938, Gene Autry, Smiley Burnette).

I'm Beginning to Care (VS)—Gene Autry, Fred Rose, Johnny Marvin (w,m), Western. COVER: Gene Autry.

3101 Man from Music Mountain, The (Republic, 1943, Roy Rogers, Ruth Terry).

I'm Thinking Tonight of My Blue Eyes—A. Carter, Don Marcotte (w, m), Southern; Smiles Are Made Out of Sunshine—Ray Gilbert (w,m). COVER: Roy Rogers, Ruth Terry.

3102 Man from Oklahoma, The (Republic, 1945, Roy Rogers, Dale Evans).

I'm Gonna Have a Cowboy Weddin'—Nat Vincent, Milo Sweet (w, m), Chart. COVER: Roy Rogers, Dale Evans.

3103 Man from Snowy River, The (20th Century-Fox, 1982, Kirk Douglas, Jack Thompson).

Jessica's Theme, and Main Title—Bruce Rowland (m), Colgems. COVER: Man, Woman and Horse.

3104 Man from Sundown, The (Columbia, 1939, Charles Starrett, Iris Meridith).

On the Rhythm Range (VS)/Round-up Time Is Over (VS)—Bob Nolan (w,m), American. COVER: Bob Nolan.

3105 Man from Texas, The (Monogram, 1939, Tex Ritter, Ruth Rogers).

Prairie Nights (VS)—Frank Harford (w,m), Cole. COVER: Tex Ritter.

3106 Man from the Alamo, The (Universal, 1953, Glenn Ford, Julie Adams).

Man from the Alamo, Victor Kirk (w), Frank Skinner (m), Skinner. COVER: Glenn Ford, Julie Adams.

3107 Man from the Diners Club, The (Columbia, 1963, Danny Kaye, Cara Williams).

Man from the Diners Club—John Lehmann (w), Steve Lawrence (m), Gower. COVER: Danny Kaye, Cara Williams.

3108 Manhandled (Paramount, 1924, Gloria Swanson, Tom Moore).

In a Little Rendezvous (B)—Sam Lewis, Joe Young (w), Ted Snyder (m), Feldman. COVER: Gloria Swanson.

3109 Manhattan (United Artists, 1978, Woody Allen, Diane Keaton).

But Not for Me (VS)/Do Do Do (VS)/Embraceable You (VS)/He Loves and She Loves (VS)/I've Got a Crush on You (VS)/Love Is Sweeping the Country (VS)/Mine (VS)/Oh Lady Be Good (VS)—Ira Gershwin (w), George Gershwin (m), Warner; Rhapsody in Blue Excerpt (VS)—George Gershwin (m), Warner; 'S Wonderful (VS)/Someone to Watch over Me (VS)/Strike Up the Band (VS)/Sweet and Lowdown (VS)—Ira Gershwin (w), George Gershwin (m), Warner. COVER: Manhattan Skyline and Lettering.

3110 Manhattan Angel (Columbia, 1948, Gloria Jean, Ross Ford).

Candy Store Blues—Herb Jeffries, Nick Castle, Eddie Neal (w,m), Columbia. COVER: Black and white cover with title only.

3111 Manhattan Clock Tale (Vitaphone, 1934, Norma Terris).

Love and Learn—Cliff Hess (w,m), Witmark. COVER: Black and white cover with title only.

3112 Manhattan Cocktail (Paramount, 1927, Nancy Carroll, Richard Arlen).

Another Kiss/Gotta Be Good—Victor Schertzinger (w,m), Famous. COVER: Nancy Carroll, Richard Arlen.

3113 Manhattan Lullaby (Educational, 1934, Helen Morgan).

Stork Song—James Hanley (w, m), Movietone. COVER: Helen Morgan.

3114 Manhattan Mary (Follow the Leader) (Paramount, 1930, Ed Wynn, Ginger Rogers).

Satan's Holiday—Sammy Fain, Irving Kahal, Pierre Norman, Al Segal (w,m), Famous. COVER: Ed Wynn.

3115 Manhattan Melody (Step Lively) (RKO, 1944, Frank Sinatra, Gloria De Haven).

Some Other Time/And Then You Kissed Me—Sammy Cahn (w), Jule Styne (m), Miller. COVER: Black and white cover with title only.

3116 Manhattan Merry Go Round (Republic, 1937, Phil Regan, Ann Dvorak).

All Over Nothing at All/Have You Ever Been to Heaven/I Owe You—Jack Lawrence, Peter Tinturin (w,m), Santly Joy; Mama I Wanna Make Rhythm—Jerome Jerome, Richard Byron, Walter Kent (w,m), Santly Joy; Round Up Time in Texas—Gene Autry, Jack Owens (w,m), Santly Joy. COVER: Phil Regan, Ann Dvorak.

3117 Manhattan Moon (Universal, 1935, Ricardo Cortez, Dorothy Page).

First Kiss—Barry Trivers (w), Arthur Morton (m), Chappell; Manhattan Moon—Barry Trivers (w), Karl Hajos (m), Chappell; My Other Me—E. Y. Harburg (w), Karl Hajos (m), Chappell. COVER: Dorothy Page.

3118 Manhole (Mole, 1973, Stars Unknown).

Manhole Theme (PC)—Grace Slick (w,m), Mole. COVER: None.

3119 **Man I Love, The** (Paramount, 1929, Mary Brian, Richard Arlen).

Celia—Leo Robin, Richard Whiting (w,m), Famous. COVER: Mary Brian, Richard Arlen.

3120 **Man I Love, The** (Warner Bros., 1946, Ida Lupino, Robert Alda).

Man I Love, The—Ira Gershwin (w), George Gershwin (m), Harms. COVER: Ida Lupino, Robert Alda, Bruce Bennett, Andrea King.

3121 **Man Inside, The** (Columbia, 1958, Jack Palance, Anita Ekberg).

Trudie—Joe Henderson (m), Piccadilly. COVER: Anita Ekberg.

3122 **Man in the Fifth Dimension, The** (Graham, 1965, Religious Film).

Beyond All Time (PC)—Ralph Carmichael (w,m), Lexicon. COVER: None.

3123 **Man in the Middle** (20th Century-Fox, 1964, France Nuyen, Robert Mitchum).

No More—Lionel Bart (w,m), Miller. COVER: Robert Mitchum, and Movie Scenes.

3124 **Man in the Saddle** (Columbia, 1951, Randolph Scott, Joan Leslie).

Man in the Saddle—Ralph Murphy (w), Harold Lewis (m), Mills. COVER: Randolph Scott, Joan Leslie, Tennessee Ernie.

3125 **Man in the Vault** (RKO, William Campbell, Karen Sharpe).

Let the Chips Fall—By Dunham (w), Henry Vars (m), BVC. COVER: William Campbell, Karen Sharpe, Anita Ekberg.

3126 **Man in the White Suit, The** (Universal, 1952, Alex Guinness, Cecil Parker).

White Suit Samba (B)—Jack Parnell, T. Clarke (w,m), Chappell. COVER: Alec Guinness.

3127 **Mannequin** (MGM, 1937, Joan Crawford, Spencer Tracy).

Always and Always—Chet Forrest, Bob Wright (w), Edward Ward (m), Feist. COVER: Joan Crawford.

3128 **Mannequin** (20th Century-Fox, 1987, Andrew McCarthy, Kim Cattrall).

Nothing's Gonna Stop Us Now—Albert Hammond, Dianne Warren (w,m), Warner. COVER: Red and white cover with title only.

3129 **Man of Courage** (PRC, 1942, Barton MacLane, Lyle Talbot).

Now and Then—Lew Pollack (w, m), Dorsey. COVER: Barton MacLane, Lyle Talbot, and Others.

3130 **Man of La Mancha** (United Artists, 1972, Peter O'Toole, Sophia Loren).

Aldonza/Dulcinea/Impossible Dream, The/I Really Like Him/ Knight of the Woeful Countenance/ Little Bird Little Bird/Little Gossip, A/Man of La Mancha/To Each His Dulcinea—Joe Darion (w), Mitch Leigh (m), Sam Fox. COVER: Peter O'Toole, Sophia Loren.

3131 **Man of Mayfair** (Paramount, 1931, Jack Buchanan, Joan Barry).

Alone with My Dreams (B)— Frank Leyton, Jack Buchanan (w, m), Victoria. COVER: Jack Buchanan.

3132 **Man of Steel** (Anderson, 1967, Religious Film).

Man of Steel—Ed Lyman (w,m), Rodheaver. COVER: Four People.

3133 **Man of the People** (MGM, 1937, Thomas Mitchell, Joseph Calleia).

Let Me Day Dream—Bob Wright, Chet Forrest (w), Walter Donaldson (m), Feist. COVER: Black and white cover with title only.

3134 **Man on Fire** (MGM, 1957, Bing Crosby, Inger Stevens).

Man on Fire—Paul F. Webster (w), Sammy Fain (m), Robbins. COVER: Bing Crosby, Inger Stevens.

3135 **Man on the Eiffel Tower, The** (RKO, 1950, Charles Laughton, Franchot Tone).

High on the Eiffel Tower—Jay Lynn (w), Michel Michelet (m), Regent. COVER: Franchot Tone, Charles Laughton, Burgess Meredith.

3136   Man on the Flying Trapeze (Paramount, 1935, W. C. Fields, Mary Brian).

Man on the Flying Trapeze, The— Tot Seymour, Vee Lawnhurst (w,m), Famous. COVER: W. C. Fields.

3137   Man's Favorite Sport (Universal, 1964, Rock Hudson, Paula Prentiss).

Man's Favorite Sport—Johnny Mercer (w), Henry Mancini (m), Southdale. COVER: Rock Hudson, Paula Prentiss.

3138   Mansion of Aching Hearts (Schulberg, 1925, Ethel Clayton, Barbara Bedford).

Mansion of Aching Hearts—Arthur Lamb (w), Harry Von Tilzer (m), Von Tilzer. COVER: Movie Scenes.

3139   Man's Man, A (MGM, 1929, William Haines, Josephine Dunn).

My Heart Is Bluer Than Your Eyes—Alfred Bryan (w), Monte Wilhite (m), Hiller. COVER: William Haines, Josephine Dunn.

3140   Man Trouble (Fox, 1930, Dorothy Mackaill, Milton Sills).

Pick Yourself Up/What's the Use of Living Without Love—Joe McCarthy (w), James Hanley (m), Red Star. COVER: Dorothy Mackaill, Milton Sills.

3141   Man Who Came Back (Fox, 1931, Janet Gaynor, Charles Farrell).

My Dream of Love—Albert Malotte (w,m), Movietone; Sweet Hawaiian Mem'ries—William Kernell (w, m), Movietone. COVER: Black and white cover with title only.

3142   Man Who Fell to Earth (B-Lion, 1976, David Bowie, Rip Torn).

Sound and Vision—David Bowie (w,m), Bewlay. COVER: David Bowie.

3143   Man Who Had Power over Woman, The (Embassy, 1971, Carol White, Rod Taylor).

Bend Over Backwards—Hal David (w), Johnny Mandel (m), Shayne. COVER: Little Girl.

3144   Man Who Knew Too Much, The (Paramount, 1955, Doris Day, James Stewart).

We'll Love Again/Whatever Will Be, Will Be—Jay Livingston, Ray Evans (w,m), Artists. COVER: Doris Day, James Stewart.

3145   Man Who Laughs, The (Universal, 1928, Mary Philbin, Conrad Veidt).

When Love Comes Stealing—Erno Rapee, Lew Pollack, Walter Hirsch (w,m), Robbins. COVER: Mary Philbin.

3146   Man Who Loved Redheads, The (United Artists, 1955, Moira Shearer, John Justin).

Man Who Loved Redheads Theme —Benjamin Frankel (m), Day. COVER: Moira Shearer.

3147   Man Who Loved Women, The (Columbia, 1983, Burt Reynolds, Julie Andrews).

Blackie's Tune—Henry Mancini (m), Colgems; Little Boys—Alan Bergman, Marilyn Bergman (w), Henry Mancini (m), Colgems. COVER: Burt Reynolds.

3148   Man Who Shot Liberty Valance, The (Paramount, 1962, James Stewart, John Wayne).

Ann Rutledge Theme—Alfred Newman (m), Robbins; Man Who Shot Liberty Valance, The—Hal David (w), Burt Bacharach (m), Famous. COVER: James Stewart, John Wayne.

3149   Man Who Understood Women, The (20th Century-Fox, 1959, Leslie Caron, Henry Fonda).

Man Who Understood Women Theme—Robert Dolan (m), Robbins; Paris Valentine, A—Paul F. Webster (w), Robert Dolan (m), Robbins. COVER: Leslie Caron, Henry Fonda.

3150   Man Who Would Be King, The (Allied Artists, 1975, Sean Connery, Michael Caine).

Man Who Would Be King, The—Maurice Jarre (m), Colgems. COVER: Sean Connery, Michael Caine.

3151 Man Without a Star (Universal, 1955, Kirk Douglas, Jeanne Crain).

And the Moon Grew Brighter and Brighter—Jimmy Kennedy, Lou Singer (w,m), Disney; Man Without a Star—Fred Herbert (w), Arnold Hughes (m), Leeds. COVER: Kirk Douglas, Jeanne Crain.

3152 Man with the Golden Arm, The (United Artists, 1956, Frank Sinatra, Eleanor Parker).

Delilah Jones—Sylvia Fine, Elmer Bernstein (w,m), Dena; Man with the Golden Arm—Sammy Cahn (w), James Van Heusen (m), Barton; Man with the Golden Arm Title Theme—Sylvia Fine, Elmer Bernstein (m), Dena; Molly-O—Sylvia Fine, Elmer Bernstein (w,m), Dena. COVER: Frank Sinatra, Eleanor Parker, Kim Novak.

3153 Man with the Golden Gun, The (United Artists, 1974, Roger Moore, Britt Ekland).

Man with the Golden Gun—Don Black (w), John Barry (m), Unart. COVER: Roger Moore, and Girls.

3154 Man with the Gun (United Artists, 1955, Robert Mitchum, Jan Sterling).

Handful of Dreams—Paul F. Webster (w), Alex North (m), Marks. COVER: Robert Mitchum, Jan Sterling.

3155 Man Woman and Child (Paramount, 1983, Martin Sheen, Blythe Danner).

Never Gone—David Pomeranz, Buddy Kaye (w), Georges Delerue (m), Famous. COVER: Martin Sheen, Blythe Danner.

3156 Man Woman and Wife (Universal, 1927, Norman Kerry, Marian Nixon).

Love Can Never Die—Herman Ruby (w), Joe Cherniovsky (m), Berlin. COVER: Norman Kerry, Marian Nixon.

3157 Many Happy Returns (Paramount, 1934, George Burns, Gracie Allen).

Boogie Man/Fare Thee Well—Sam Coslow (w,m), Famous; Sweetest Music This Side of Heaven—Cliff Friend (w), Carmen Lombardo (m), Famous. COVER: George Burns, Gracie Allen, Guy Lombardo.

3158 Many Rivers to Cross (MGM, 1954, Robert Taylor, Eleanor Parker).

Berry Tree, The—Saul Chaplin (w, m), Miller. COVER: Robert Taylor, Eleanor Parker.

3159 Maracaibo (Paramount, 1958, Cornel Wilde, Jean Wallace).

Maracaibo—Jefferson Pascal (w), Laurindo Almeida (m), Famous. COVER: Cornel Wilde, Jean Wallace.

3160 Marathon Man (Paramount, 1976, Dustin Hoffman, Laurence Olivier).

Marathon Man Theme—Michael Small (m), Ensign. COVER: Dustin Hoffman.

3161 March of Time (Hollywood Revue of 1930 or Broadway to Hollywood) (MGM, 1930, Frank Morgan, Alice Brady).

Lock Step/Poor Little "G" String —Roy Turk (w), Fred Ahlert (m), Robbins. COVER: Black and white cover with title only.

3162 Marco Polo (AIP, 1962, Rory Calhoun, Yoko Tani).

Amarai (PC)/Marco Polo (PC)/Marco Polo Love Theme (PC)—Les Baxter (m), Harlene. COVER: None.

3163 Marco the Magnificent (MGM, 1965, Anthony Quinn, Horst Buchholz).

Somewhere—Sydney Lee (w), Georges Garvarentz (m), Gil. COVER: Jerry Vale.

3164 Mardi Gras (Vitaphone, 1934, Musical Short).

Alone/Rhythm of the Paddle Wheel—Cliff Hess (w,m), Witmark. COVER: Black and white cover with title only.

3165 Mardi Gras (Paramount,

1943, Betty Rhodes, Johnnie Johnston).

All the Way—Kim Gannon (w), Jule Styne (m), Paramount; At the Mardi Gras—Jerry Seelen (w), Lester Lee (m), Paramount. COVER: Betty Rhodes, Johnnie Johnston.

3166 Mardi Gras (20th Century-Fox, 1958, Pat Boone, Tommy Sands).

Bigger Than Texas/Bourbon Street Blues/A Fiddle, a Rifle, an Axe, and a Bible/I'll Remember Tonight/Loyalty/Mardi Gras March/Stonewall Jackson/That Man Could Sell Me the Brooklyn Bridge—Paul F. Webster (w), Sammy Fain (m), Feist. COVER: Pat Boone, Christine Carere, Tommy Sands, Gary Crosby.

3167 Margie (Universal, 1940, Tom Brown, Nan Grey).

Margie—Benny Davis (w), Con Conrad, Russell Robinson (m), Berlin; When Banana Blossoms Bloom—Sam Lerner (w), Charles Previn (m), Robbins. COVER: Tom Brown, Nan Grey.

3168 Margie (20th Century-Fox, 1946, Jeanne Crain, Lynn Bari).

Margie—Benny Davis (w), Con Conrad, Russell Robinson (m), Mills; Three O'Clock in the Morning—Dorothy Terriss (w), Julian Robeldo (m), Feist; Wonderful One—Dorothy Terriss (w), Ferde Grofe, Paul Whiteman (m), Feist. COVER: Jeanne Crain, Lynn Bari.

3169 Maria Elena (She Devil Island) (Columbia, 1936, Carmen Guerrero, Martiner Casado).

Bamba—Lorenzo Barcelata, Ernesto Cortazar (w,m), Southern; Maria Elena/Flor de Fuego—Lorenzo Barcelata (w,m), Southern. COVER: Movie Scenes.

3170 Marianne (MGM, 1929, Marion Davies, Cliff Edwards).

Blondy—Arthur Freed (w), Nacio Herb Brown (m), Robbins; Hang on to Me/Just You Just Me—Raymond Klages (w), Jesse Greer (m), Robbins; Marianne/Oo-la-la-la-la/That Girl from Noochateau/When I See My Sugar—

Roy Turk (w), Fred Ahlert (m), DBH. COVER: Marion Davies, Cliff Edwards.

3171 Marie Antoinette (MGM, 1938, Tyrone Power, Norma Shearer).

Amour Eternal Amour—Bob Wright, Chet Forrest (w), Herbert Stothart (m), Feist. COVER: Tyrone Power, Norma Shearer.

3172 Marie Galante (Fox, 1934, Spencer Tracy, Ketti Gallian).

It's Home—Jack Yellen (w), Jay Gorney (m), Movietone; Serves Me Right for Treating Him Wrong—Maurice Sigler, Al Goodhart, Al Hoffman (w,m), Movietone; Song of a Dreamer—Don Hartman (w), Jay Gorney (m), Movietone; Un Peu-Beaucoup (BW)—Marcel Silver (w), Arthur Lange (m), Movietone. COVER: Ketti Gallian, Helen Morgan.

3173 Marilyn the Untold Story (Schiller, 1980, Catherine Hicks, Frank Converse).

Candle in the Wind—Elton John, Bernie Taupin (w,m), James. COVER: Catherine Hicks.

3174 Marinella (Caron, 1936, Stars Unknown).

Marinella—Mitchell Parish (w), Vincent Scotto (m), Mills. COVER: Sketch of Man and Woman.

3175 Marine Raiders (RKO, 1940, Pat O'Brien, Robert Ryan).

Bless 'em All—Jim Hughes, Frank Lake, Al Stillman (w,m), Sam Fox. COVER: Robert Ryan, Ruth Hussey, Pat O'Brien.

3176 Marines Let's Go (20th Century-Fox, 1961, Tom Tryon, David Hedison).

Marines Let's Go—Mike Phillips, George Watson (w,m), Miller. COVER: Marines.

3177 Marius (Paramount, 1933, Jules Raimu, Crane Demazis).

Pastorale (PC)—Francis Gromon (m), Famous. COVER: None.

3178 Marjorie Morningstar (Warner Bros., 1958, Gene Kelly, Natalie Wood).

Very Precious Love, A—Paul F.

Webster (w), Sammy Fain (m), Witmark. COVER: Gene Kelly, Natalie Wood.

3179 Marked Woman (Warner Bros., 1937, Bette Davis, Humphrey Bogart).

Silver Dollar (PC)—Al Dubin (w), Harry Warren (m), MPH. COVER: None.

3180 Market of Souls (Paramount, 1919, Dorothy Dalton, Holmes Herbert).

Out of the Market of Souls—Edward Grossman (w,m), Remick. COVER: Dorothy Dalton.

3181 Mark of the Hawk (Universal, 1957, Eartha Kitt, Sidney Poitier).

This Man Is Mine—Don Quinn (w), Ken Darby (m), Longridge. COVER: Eartha Kitt.

3182 Marlowe (MGM, 1968, James Garner, Gayle Hunnicutt).

Little Sister—Norman Gimbel (w), Peter Matz (m), Hastings. COVER: James Garner, Gayle Hunnicutt.

3183 Marnie (Universal, 1964, Tippi Hedren, Sean Connery).

Marnie Theme—Bernard Herrmann, Peter Jason, Gloria Shayne (w,m), Hawaii. COVER: Sean Connery, Tippi Hedren.

3184 Marriage by Contract (Tiffany, 1927, Patsy Ruth Miller, Lawrence Gray).

Come Back to Me—David Goldberg (w), A. Joffe (m), Shapiro Bernstein; When the Right One Comes Along—L. Wolfe Gilbert (w), Mabel Wayne (m), Feist. COVER: Patsy Ruth Miller, Lawrence Gray.

3185 Marriage Go Round (20th Century-Fox, 1960, James Mason, Susan Hayward).

Marriage Go Round—Alan Bergman, Marilyn Bergman (w), Lew Spence (m), Robbins. COVER: James Mason, Susan Hayward, Julie Newmar.

3186 Marriage of a Young Stockbroker (20th Century-Fox, 1971, Richard Benjamin, Joanna Shimkus).

Can It Be True—Tylwyth Kymby (w), Fred Karlin (m), Fox. COVER: Richard Benjamin, Joanna Shimkus.

3187 Married in Hollywood (Fox, 1929, Norma Terris, Harold Murray).

Dance Away the Night—Harlan Thompson (w), Dave Stamper (m), DBH; A Man, a Maid—Harlan Thompson (w), Oscar Straus (m), DBH; Peasant Love Song—Harlan Thompson (w), Dave Stamper (m), DBH. COVER: Movie Scene.

3188 Marry Me! Marry Me! (Allied Artists, 1969, Elizabeth Wiener, Regine).

Marry Me! Marry Me!—Robert Colby (w), Emil Stern (m), Croma. COVER: Cartoon Sketch.

3189 Marshal's Daughter, The (United Artists, 1953, Laurie Anders, Hoot Gibson).

Marshal's Daughter, The—Stan Jones, Ken Murray (w,m), Ranger. COVER: Laurie Anders.

3190 Martin Block's Musical Merry Go Round (MGM, 1947, Musical Short).

Makin' Love Mountain Style—Jack Scholl, Herb Moulton (w,m), Warren. COVER: Dinning Sisters.

3191 Marty (United Artists, 1955, Ernest Borgnine, Betsy Blair).

Marty—Paddy Chayefsky (w), Harry Warren (m), Cromwell; Saturday Night Mambo (PC)—Roy Webb (m). COVER: Ernest Borgnine, Betsy Blair.

3192 Mary Lou (Columbia, 1948, Robert Lowery, Joan Barton).

Mary Lou—Abe Lyman, George Waggner, Russell Robinson (w,m), Mills. COVER: Joan Barton, Frankie Carle, and Others.

3193 Mary Poppins (Buena Vista, 1964, Julie Andrews, Dick Van Dyke).

Chim Chim Cher-ee/Feed the Birds/Let's Go Fly a Kite/Spoonful of Sugar, A/Stay Awake/Supercalifragilisticexpialidocious/Fidelity Fiduciary Bank (VS)/I Love to

Laugh (VS)/Jolly Holiday (VS)/ Life I Lead (VS)/Man Has Dreams, A (VS)/Perfect Nanny (VS)/Sister Suffragette (VS)/Step in Time (VS)/ Synopsis (VS)—Richard Sherman, Robert Sherman (w,m), Disney. COVER: Julie Andrews, Dick Van Dyke.

3194 Mary Queen of Scots (Universal, 1971, Glenda Jackson, Vanessa Redgrave).

Mary Queen of Scots Love Theme —John Barry (m), Leeds; This Way Mary/Wish Now Was Then—Don Black (w), John Barry (m), Leeds. COVER: Glenda Jackson, Vanessa Redgrave.

3195 Mary Regan (First National, 1919, Anita Stewart, Frank Mayo).

Mary Regan—Anita Stewart (w, m), Berlin. COVER: Anita Stewart.

3196 MASH (20th Century-Fox, 1970, Donald Sutherland, Elliott Gould).

Suicide Is Painless-Song from Mash—Mike Altman, Johnny Mandel (w,m), Fox. COVER: A Hand, and Legs.

3197 Masked Phantom (The Adventures of the Masked Phantom) (Browne, 1938, Monte Rawlins, Larry Mason).

Masked Phantom/Prairie Rose/Rip Rip Snortin' Two Gun Gal—Johnny Lange, Lew Porter (w,m), Mills. COVER: Monte Rawlins, Larry Mason, Sonny Lamont.

3198 Masked Rider, The (Universal, 1941, Johnny Mack Brown, Fuzzy Knight).

Carmencita—Everett Carter (w), Milton Rosen (m), Robbins. COVER: Johnny Mack Brown, Fuzzy Knight, Nell O'Day.

3199 Mask of Dijon (PRC, 1946, Eric Von Stroheim, Jeanne Bates).

Disillusion—Billy Austin, Lou Zoeller (w,m), Zoeller. COVER: Eric Von Stroheim, Jeanne Bates.

3200 Masks of the Devil (MGM, 1927, John Gilbert, Alma Rubens).

Live and Love—Raymond Klages (w), William Axt, David Mendoza (m), Robbins. COVER: John Gilbert, Alma Rubens.

3201 Masquerade (Lady of the Pavements) (United Artists, 1929, Lupe Velez, William Boyd).

Where Is the Song of Songs for Me —Irving Berlin (w,m), Berlin. COVER: Lupe Velez.

3202 Masquerade (United Artists, 1965, Cliff Robertson, Jack Hawkins).

Masquerade—Norman Newell (w), Phil Green (m), Unart. COVER: Black and white cover with title only.

3203 Masquerade in Mexico (Paramount, 1945, Dorothy Lamour, Arturo de Cordova).

Adios and Farewell My Lover— Ben Raleigh (w), Marcos Jimenez (m), Peer; Forever Mine—Eddie Lisbona, Bob Musel (w), Maria Lara (m), Southern; Masquerade in Mexico—Ben Raleigh (w), Bernie Wayne (m), Famous; That's Love—Ben Raleigh, Bernie Wayne (w), Agustin Lara (m), Peer. COVER: Dorothy Lamour, Arturo de Cordova, Patric Knowles, Ann Dvorak.

3204 Master of the World (AIP, 1961, Vincent Price, Charles Bronson).

Come Dance My Love—Les Baxter (w,m), Harlene; Master of the World—Lenny Adelson (w), Les Baxter (m), Harlene; Mediterranean/ Over the Rocks—Les Baxter (m), Harlene. COVER: Vincent Price, Henry Hull, Mary Webster, and Dirigible.

3205 Mating Call, The (Paramount, 1928, Thomas Meighan, Renee Adoree).

Mating Call, The—Frances Ring, Martin Broones (w,m), Shapiro Bernstein. COVER: Thomas Meighan, Renee Adoree.

3206 Mating Game, The (MGM, 1959, Debbie Reynolds, Tony Randall).

Mating Game, The—Lee Adams (w), Charles Stouse (m), Robbins. COVER: Tony Randall, Debbie Reynolds.

3207 Mating Season, The (Paramount, 1951, Gene Tierney, John Lund).

Mating Season, The—Jay Livingston, Ray Evans (w,m), Famous; My Lost Melody—Harold Rome (w), Ray Asso, Marguerite Monnot (m), Leeds. COVER: Gene Tierney, John Lund, Thelma Ritter.

3208 Matrimonial Bed, The (Warner Bros., 1930, Lilyan Tashman, Marion Byron).

Fleur D'Amour—Sidney Mitchell, Archie Gottler, George Meyer (w,m), Witmark. COVER: Lilyan Tashman.

3209 Matter of Innocence, A (Universal, 1967, Hayley Mills, Trevor Howard).

Pretty Polly—Don Black (w), Michel Legrand (m), Shamley. COVER: Hayley Mills, Shashi Kapoor.

3210 Matter of Life and Death, A (Stairway to Heaven) (Universal, 1946, David Niven, Raymond Massey).

A Matter of Life and Death-Prelude (B)—Allan Gray (m), Maurice. COVER: Stairway and Clouds.

3211 Matter of Time, A (AIP, 1976, Liza Minnelli, Ingrid Bergman).

Matter of Time, A/Me I Haven't Met Yet, The—Fred Ebb (w), John Kander (m), Chappell. COVER: Liza Minnelli, Ingrid Bergman.

3212 Matter of Who, A (MGM, 1961, Alex Nichol, Sonja Ziemann).

Matter of Who, A (B)—Bob Russell (w,m), Southern. COVER: Terry-Thomas, John Barry, Roy Castle.

3213 Maurie (National General, 1973, Bernie Casey, Bo Swenson).

Winners—Joe Raposo (w,m), Sergeant. COVER: Frank Sinatra.

3214 Maverick Queen, The (Republic, 1956, Barbara Stanwyck, Barry Sullivan).

Maverick Queen, The—Ned Washington (w), Victor Young (m), Young. COVER: Barbara Stanwyck, Barry Sullivan.

3215 Maya (MGM, 1966, Clint Walker, Jay North).

Maya Theme—Riz Ortolani (m), Feist; Stay Close to Me—Paul F. Webster (w), Riz Ortolani (m), Feist. COVER: Sketch of Movie Scene.

3216 Maybe It's Love (Warner Bros., 1930, Joan Bennett, Joe E. Brown).

All American/Maybe It's Love—Sidney Mitchell, Archie Gottler, George Meyer (w,m), Harms. COVER: Joan Bennett, Joe E. Brown.

3217 Mayerling (MGM, 1969, Omar Sharif, Catherine Deneuve).

At Mayerling—Don Black (w), Francis Lai (m), Robbins. COVER: Omar Sharif, Catherine Deneuve.

3218 Mayor of 44th Street, The (RKO, 1942, George Murphy, Anne Shirley).

Heavenly Isn't It?/Million Miles from Manhattan/When There's a Breeze on Lake Louise/You're Bad for Me—Mort Greene (w), Harry Revel (m), Greene Revel. COVER: George Murphy, Anne Shirley, Freddy Martin.

3219 Maytime (Preferred, 1923, Harrison Ford, Ethel Shannon).

Will You Remember-Sweetheart—Rida J. Young (w), Sigmund Romberg (m), Schirmer. COVER: Harrison Ford, Ethel Shannon.

3220 Maytime (MGM, 1937, Jeanette MacDonald, Nelson Eddy).

Carry Me Back to Old Virginny—James Bland (w,m), Feist; Will You Remember-Sweetheart—Rida J. Young (w), Sigmund Romberg (m), Schirmer. COVER: Jeanette MacDonald, Nelson Eddy.

3221 Maytime in Mayfair (Wilcox, 1952, Michael Wilding, Anna Neagle).

Amor, Amor/Do I Love You/I'm Not Going Home/Maytime in Mayfair—Harry Davies, Harold Purcell (w,m), Chappell. COVER: Anna Neagle, Michael Wilding.

3222 Me and Captain Kidd (World, 1919, Evelyn Greeley, Raymond McKee).

Me and Captain Kidd—Will Heelan (w), Will Haskins (m), Haskins. COVER: Evelyn Greeley.

3223 Me and My Gal (Fox, 1933, Spencer Tracy, Joan Bennett).

Oleo the Gigolo—James Hanley (w,m), Movietone. COVER: Black and white cover with title only.

3224 Me and the Colonel (Columbia, 1958, Danny Kaye, Curt Jurgens).

Suzanne—Sylvia Fine (w), George Duning (m), Dena. COVER: Danny Kaye, Curt Jurgens.

3225 Meatballs (Paramount, 1979, Bill Murray, Larry Solway).

Are You Ready for the Summer/ Good Friend/Meatballs/Moondust— Norman Gimbel (w), Elmer Bernstein (m), Bernal. COVER: Bill Murray and Girls.

3226 Meet Danny Wilson (Universal, 1952, Frank Sinatra, Shelley Winters).

Good Man Is Hard to Find, A— Eddie Green (w,m), Mayfair; Lonesome Man Blues—Sy Oliver (w,m), Barton; That Old Black Magic— Johnny Mercer (w), Harold Arlen (m), Famous; When You're Smiling— Mark Fisher, Joe Goodwin, Larry Shay (w,m), Mills. COVER: Frank Sinatra, Shelley Winters.

3227 Meet Me After the Show (20th Century-Fox, 1951, Betty Grable, MacDonald Carey).

I Feel Like Dancing/It's a Hot Night in Alaska—Leo Robin (w), Jule Styne (m), Morris. COVER: Betty Grable, MacDonald Carey.

3228 Meet Me at the Fair (Universal, 1953, Dan Dailey, Diana Lynn).

Meet Me at the Fair—Fred Herbert, Milton Rosen (w,m), Mills; Remember the Time—Kenney Williams, Marvin Wright (w,m), Mills. COVER: Dan Dailey, Diana Lynn, Hugh O'Brien.

3229 Meet Me in Las Vegas (MGM, 1956, Dan Dailey, Cyd Charisse).

Gal with the Yaller Shoes/Hell Hath No Fury/If You Can Dream/My Lucky Charm—Sammy Cahn (w), Nicholas Brodszky (m), Miller; New Frankie and Johnny—Sammy Cahn (w), Johnny Green (m), Feist. COVER: Cyd Charisse.

3230 Meet Me in Moscow (Mosfilm, 1966, Nikita Mikhalkov, Aleksey Loktev).

Romance Romance—Sidney Lee (w), Andrei Petrov (m), Gil. COVER: Boy and Girl in Rain.

3231 Meet Me in St. Louis (MGM, 1944, Judy Garland, Margaret O'Brien).

Boy Next Door, The/Have Yourself a Merry Little Christmas—Hugh Martin, Ralph Blane (w,m), Feist; Meet Me in St. Louis, Louis—Andrew Sterling (w), Kerry Wills (m), Vogel; Skip to My Lou/Trolley Song, The— Hugh Martin, Ralph Blane (w,m), Feist; Under the Bamboo Tree—Bob Cole (w,m), Marks; You and I—Arthur Freed (w), Nacio Herb Brown (m), Feist. COVER: Judy Garland, Margaret O'Brien.

3232 Meet Miss Bobby Socks (Columbia, 1944, Bob Crosby, Lynn Merrick).

Come with Me My Honey—Mack David, Joan Whitney, Alex Kramer (w,m), Santly Joy; Fellow on a Furlough—Bobby Worth (w,m), Block; I'm Not Afraid (PC)—Kim Gannon (w), Walter Kent (m), Mills. COVER: Bob Crosby.

3233 Meet the Baron (MGM, 1932, Jack Pearl, Jimmy Durante).

Clean As a Whistle (PC)—Dorothy Fields (w), Jimmy McHugh (m), Robbins. COVER: None.

3234 Meet the Boy Friend (Republic, 1937, David Carlyle, Carol Hughes).

To Know You Care—Harry Tobias, Roy Ingraham (w,m), Santly Joy.

COVER: David Carlyle, Carol Hughes.

3235 Meet the People (MGM, 1944, Lucille Ball, Dick Powell).

In Times Like These—E. Y. Harburg (w), Sammy Fain (m), Feist; It's Smart to Be People—E. Y. Harburg (w), Burton Lane (m), Feist; Say That We're Sweethearts Again—Earl Brent (w,m), Feist. COVER: Lucille Ball, Virginia O'Brien, Vaughn Monroe.

3236 Melancholy Dame (Paramount, 1929, Stars Unknown).

Melancholy Mama—Sterling Sherwin (w,m), Sherman Clay. COVER: Girl in Evening Gown.

3237 Melba (United Artists, 1952, Patrice Munsel, Robert Morley).

Is This the Beginning of Love/ Melba Waltz—Norman Newell (w), Mischa Spoliansky (m), BVC. COVER: Patrice Munsel, and Movie Scenes.

3238 Melodrama (SAPF, 1936, Elsie Merlini).

Serenade in the Night—C. Bixio, B. Cherubini, Jimmy Kennedy (w, m), Mills. COVER: Man and Guitar.

3239 Melody (Disney, 1953, Cartoon).

The Bird and the Cricket and the Willow Tree—Paul F. Webster (w), Sonny Burke (m), Disney. COVER: Cartoon.

3240 Melody and Moonlight (Republic, 1940, Johnny Downs, Barbara Allen).

Melody and Moonlight/Tahiti Honey/Top of the Norming—George Brown, Sol Meyer, Jule Styne (w,m), Mills. COVER: Johnny Downs, Barbara Allen, Jerry Colonna.

3241 Melody Comes to Town (Wilding, 1941, Stars Unknown).

Beloved America—Louis Herscher, Marvin Hatley (w,m), Mills. COVER: Black and white cover with title only.

3242 Melody Cruise (RKO, 1933, Charles Ruggles, Phil Harris).

Isn't This a Night for Love—Val Burton, Will Jason (w,m), Sam Fox. COVER: Cartoon Sketch.

3243 Melody for Two (Warner Bros., 1937, James Melton, Patricia Ellis).

Excuse for Dancing/Flat in Manhattan, A/Jose O'Neill, the Cuban Heel—Jack Scholl (w), M. K. Jerome (m), Remick; Melody for Two/September in the Rain—Al Dubin (w), Harry Warren (m), Remick. COVER: James Melton, Patricia Ellis, Winifred Shaw.

3244 Melody in Spring (Paramoung, 1934, Lanny Ross, Charles Ruggles).

Ending with a Kiss/It's Psychological/Melody in Spring/Open Road—Harlan Thompson (w), Lewis Gensler (m), Famous. COVER: Lanny Ross, Ann Sothern.

3245 Melody Lane (Universal, 1929, Eddie Leonard, Josephine Dunn).

Beautiful—Eddie Leonard, Grace Stern, Jack Stern (w,m), Berlin; Bogey Man Is Here—Eddie Leonard, Jack Stern (w,m), Berlin; There's Sugar Cane Around My Door—Eddie Leonard, Grace Stern, Jack Stern (w, m), Berlin. COVER: Eddie Leonard.

3246 Melody Lane (Universal, 1941, Leon Errol, Robert Paige).

Changeable Heart/Cherokee Charlie/If It's a Dream/Let's Go to Calia Cabu/Since the Farmer in the Dell Learned to Swing/Swing-a-bye My Baby—Jack Brooks (w), Norman Berens (m), Robbins. COVER: The Merry Macs.

3247 Melody Man (Columbia, 1930, John Sainpolis, William Collier).

Broken Dreams—Dave Dreyer, Ballard MacDonald (w), Arthur Johnston (m), Berlin. COVER: John Sainpolis, William Collier, Alice Day.

3248 Melody of Love (Universal, 1934, Mildred Harris, Walter Pidgeon).

My Sweetheart—Gus Kahn, Larry

Conley, Gene Rodemich (w,m), Weil. COVER: Mildred Harris, Walter Pidgeon, Jane Winton.

3249 Melody of the Plains (Callaghan, 1937, Fred Scott, Louise Small).

Hide Away in Happy Valley/Ridin' Down the Trail to Albuquerque— June Hershey (w), Don Swander (m), Cross Winge. COVER: Fred Scott.

3250 Melody Ranch (Republic, 1940, Gene Autry, Ann Miller).

Rodeo Rose—Jule Styne, Eddie Cherkose (w,m), Mills; Stake Your Claim on Melody Ranch—Eddie Cherkose (w), Jule Styne (m), Mills; Torpedo Joe—Jule Styne, Eddie Cherkose (w,m), Mills; We Never Dream the Same Dream Twice—Gene Autry, Fred Rose (w,m), Mills; What Are Cowboys Made Of—Jule Styne, Eddie Cherkose (w,m), Mills. COVER: Gene Autry, Ann Miller, Jimmy Durate.

3251 Melody Round-up (PRC, 1946, Eddie Dean, Roscoe Ates).

I Can Tell by the Stars (PC)/ Journey's End (PC)/Ride on the Tide of a Song (PC)—Dorcas Cochran, Charles Rosoff (w,m), Rosoff. COVER: None.

3252 Melody Time (Disney, 1948, Cartoon).

Apple Song—Kim Gannon, Walter Kent (w,m), Santly Joy; Blame It on the Samba—Ray Gilbert (w), Ernesto Nazareth (m), Robbins; Blue Shadows on the Trail—Johnny Lange (w), Eliot Daniel (m), Santly Joy; Little Toot—Allie Wrubel (w,m), Santly Joy; Lord Is Good to Me— Kim Gannon, Walter Kent (w,m), Santly Joy; Melody Time—Bennie Benjamin, George Weiss (w,m), Santly Joy; Once Upon a Wintertime— Bobby Worth, Ray Gilbert (w,m) Southern; Pecos Bill—Johnny Lange (w), Eliot Daniel (m), Santly Joy; Pioneer Song—Kim Gannon, Walter Kent (w,m), Santly Joy. COVER: Cartoon Characters.

3253 Melody Trail (Republic,

1935, Gene Autry, Smiley Burnette).

Hold on Little Doggie Hold On (VS)—Gene Autry (w,m), Cole. COVER: Gene Autry.

3254 Men, The (United Artists, 1950, Marlon Brando, Teresa Wright).

Love Like Ours—John Lehman (w), Dimitri Tiomkin (m), Laurel. COVER: Marlon Brando, Teresa Wright.

3255 Me Natalie (National General, 1969, Patty Duke, James Farentino).

Natalie/We—Rod McKuen (w), Henry Mancini (m), Northridge. COVER: Couple on Bridge.

3256 Men of Steel (First National, 1926, Milton Sills, Doris Kenyon).

Thinking of You (Promotion Song) —Joseph Grey (w), Allie Moore (m), Liberty. COVER: Milton Sills, Doris Kenyon.

3257 Men on Her Mind (PRC, 1944, Mary Beth Hughes, Edward Norris).

Heaven on Earth—Pat O'Dea, Lee Zahler (w,m), Morros. COVER: Mary Beth Hughes.

3258 Men with Wings (Paramount, 1938, Ray Milland, Fred MacMurray).

Men with Wings—Frank Loesser (w), Hoagy Carmichael (m), Famous. COVER: Ray Milland, Fred MacMurray, Louise Campbell.

3259 Mephisto Waltz, The (20th Century-Fox, 1971, Alan Alda, Curt Jurgens).

Mephisto Waltz Love Theme— Jerry Goldsmith (m), Fox. COVER: Occult Sign.

3260 Mercenary, The (United Artists, 1970, Franco Nero, Tony Musante).

Mercenaries, The—Ennio Morricone (m), Unart. COVER: Black and white cover with title only.

3261 Merely Mary Ann (Fox, 1931, Janet Gaynor, Charles Farrell).

Kiss Me Goodnight, Not Goodbye —Jules Furthman (w), James Hanley (m), Sam Fox; Mary Ann (PC)—William Kernell (w), Richard Fall (m), Movietone. COVER: Janet Gaynor, Charles Farrell.

3262 Merrily We Live (MGM, 1938, Constance Bennett, Brian Aherne).

Merrily We Live—Arthur Quenzer (w), Phil Charig (m), Feist. COVER: Constance Bennett, Brian Aherne.

3263 Merry Andrew (MGM, 1958, Danny Kaye, Pier Angeli)

Bunnona Fortuna (Q)/Chin Up Stout Fella (Q)/Everything Is Tickety-Boo/Pipes of Pan (Q)/Square of the Hypotenuse/You Can't Always Have What You Want—Johnny Mercer (w), Saul Chaplin (m), Commander. COVER: Danny Kaye, Pier Angeli, and Monkey.

3264 Merry Go Round (Universal, 1923, Erich Von Stroheim, Mary Philbin).

Merry Go Round Waltz—Paul Van Dyke (w,m), Belwin. COVER: Sketch of Characters.

3265 Merry Go Round (Universal, 1937, Bert Lahr, Jimmy Savo).

I'm in My Glory/More Power to You/You're My Dish—Harold Adamson (w), Jimmy McHugh (m), Miller. COVER: Bert Lahr, Jimmy Savo, Mischa Auer, and Others.

3266 Merry Monahans, The (Universal, 1944, Donald O'Connor, Peggy Ryan).

Beautiful to Look At—Irving Bibo (w), Don George (m), Mills; I Hate to Love You—Grant Clarke (w), Archie Gottler (m), Mills; Lovely/Stop Foolin'/We're Having a Wonderful Time—Irving Bibo (w), Don George (m), Mills. COVER: Donald O'Connor, Peggy Ryan, Jack Oakie, Ann Blyth.

3267 Merry Widow, The (MGM, 1925, John Gilbert, Mae Murray).

Merry Widow Waltz—Franz Lehar (m), Century. COVER: John Gilbert, Mae Murray.

3268 Merry Widow, The (MGM, 1934, Jeanette MacDonald, Maurice Chevalier).

Girls Girls Girls/Maxim's/Merry Widow Waltz/Vilia/If Widows Are Rich (VS)/Melody of Laughter (VS)—Lorenz Hart (w), Franz Lehar (m), Robbins. COVER: Jeanette MacDonald, Maurice Chevalier.

3269 Merry Widow, The (MGM, 1952, Lana Turner, Fernando Lamas).

Girls Girls Girls/Merry Widow Waltz/Night/Maxims (VS)/Vilia (VS)—Paul F. Webster (w), Franz Lehar (m), Robbins. COVER: Lana Turner, Fernando Lamas.

3270 Message to Garcia, A (20th Century-Fox, 1936, Barbara Stanwyck, Wallace Beery).

Lita—Sidney Mitchell (w), Lew Pollack (m), Movietone. COVER: Sketch of Barbara Stanwyck.

3271 Metropolis (Paramount, 1926, Gustav Froelich, Brigette Helm).

Metropolis Music Score—Ferde Grofe (m), Robbins. COVER: Futuristic Buildings.

3272 Metropolis (Paramount, 1926 [1984 Revival], Gustav Froelich, Brigette Helm).

Metropolis-Ten Songs—Giorgio Moroder, Pete Bellotte, Billy Squire (w,m), Moroder. COVER: A Robot.

3273 Mexicali Rose (Columbia, 1929, Barbara Stanwyck, Sam Hardy).

Mexicali Rose—Helen Stone (w), Jack Tenney (m), Quincke. COVER: Barbara Stanwyck.

3274 Mexicali Rose (Republic, 1939, Gene Autry, Smiley Burnette).

El Rancho Grande (PC)—Bartley Costello (w), Silvano Ramos (m), Marks. COVER: None.

3275 Mexicana (Republic, 1945, Tito Guizar, Constance Moore).

De Corazon a Corazon/Mexicana—Ned Washington (w), Gabriel Ruiz (m), Southern; Somewhere There's a Rainbow—Ned Washington, Walter Scharf (w,m), Southern. COVER: Tito Guizar, Constance Moore.

3276 **Miami** (Hodkinson, 1924, Betty Compson, Lawford Davidson).

Miami Waltz—William LeBaron (w), Victor Jacobi (m), Chappell. COVER: Betty Compson.

3277 **Miami (Moon Over Miami)** (20th Century-Fox, 1941, Betty Grable, Robert Cummings).

Is That Good/I've Got You All to Myself/Kindergarten Conga, The/ Loveliness and Love/Miami/Solitary Seminole/You Started Something— Leo Robin (w), Ralph Rainger (m), Robbins. COVER: Black and white cover with title only.

3278 **Mickey** (Sennett, 1918, Mabel Normand, Albert Hackett).

Mickey—Harry Williams (w), Neil Moret (m), Berlin. COVER: Mabel Normand.

3279 **Mickey** (Eagle Lion, 1948, Lois Butler, Bill Goodwin).

Dreams in My Heart/Father Goose —Mario Silva, Randolph Van Scoyk (w,m), Johnstone. COVER: Lois Butler.

3280 **Mickey Mouse** (Disney, 1930 to 1988, Cartoons).

Minnie's Yoo Hoo (1930)—Carl Stalling (w,m), Villa Moret; Wedding Party of Mickey Mouse (1931)—Milt Coleman, James Cavanaugh, Robert Bagar—Bibo-Lang; What No Mickey Mouse (1932)—Irving Caesar (w,m), Caesar; Mickey Mouse & Minnie's in Town (1933)—Ann Ronell (w,m), Berlin; March for Mickey Mouse (1934)—Franz Koehler (m), Boston; Mickey Mouse's Birthday Party (1936)—Charles Tobias, Bob Rothberg, Joseph Meyer (w,m), Berlin; Mickey Mouse March (1955)—Jimmie Dodd (m), Disney; It Won't Be Long Till Christmas (1966)—Richard Sherman, Robert Sherman (w, m), Wonderland; Happy Anniversary Mickey Mouse (1988)—Mike Silversher, Pat Silversher (w,m), Leonard; Victory March (1942)—Oliver Wallace (w,m), Disney. COVER: Cartoons.

3281 **Mickey One** (Columbia, 1961, Warren Beatty, Alexandra Stewart).

Once Upon a Time, the Fat Lie/ Taste of Living, A—Eddie Sauter (m), Colgems. COVER: Warren Beatty.

3282 **Micki and Maude** (Columbia, 1984, Dudley Moore, Amy Irving).

Something New in My Life—Alan Bergman, Marilyn Bergman (w), Michel Legrand (m), Golden Torch. COVER: Dudley Moore, Amy Irving, Ann Reinking.

3283 **Middle of the Night** (Columbia, 1959, Kim Novak, Fredric March).

Middle of the Night Theme—Paddy Chayefsky (w), George Bassman (m), Dorsey. COVER: Kim Novak, Fredric March.

3284 **Midnight** (Paramount, 1939, Don Ameche, Claudette Colbert).

Midnight—Ralph Freed (w), Frederick Hollander (m), Famous. COVER: Don Ameche, Claudette Colbert.

3285 **Midnight Cowboy** (United Artists, 1969, Jon Voight, Dustin Hoffman).

Everybody's Talkin'—Fred Neil (w,m), Coconut; Famous Myth, A— Jeffrey Comanor (w,m), Mr. Bones; Midnight Cowboy Theme—John Barry (m), United Artists; Cowboy Song (VS)—Toxey French (m), Big Three; Florida Fantasy (VS)/Fun City (VS)—John Barry (m), Big Three; He Quit Me (VS)—W. W. Zevon (w,m), Big Three; Joe Buck Rides Again (VS)—John Barry (m), Big Three; Jungle Jim at the Zoo (VS)—Stanley Bronstein, Richard Frank (w,m), Big Three; Old Man Willow (VS)—R. Sussman, S. Bronstein, M. Yules, M. Shapiro (w,m), Big Three; Science Fiction (VS)— John Barry (m), Big Three; Tears and Joy (VS)—Jeffrey Comanor (w,m), Big Three. COVER: Dustin Hoffman, Jon Voight.

3286 **Midnight Express** (Columbia, 1978, Brad Davis, Randy Quaid).

Chase, The—Giorgio Moroder (m),

Gold Horizon; Midnight Express Theme—Chris Bennett (w), Giorgio Moroder (m), Gold Horizon. COVER: Brad Davis.

3287 Midnight Girl, The (Philipp, 1919, Adolf Philipp, Marie Pagano).

Midnight Girl, The—Edward Paulton (w), Adolf Philipp (m), Remick. COVER: Adolf Philipp, Marie Pagano.

3288 Midnight in Paris (Distinguished, 1947, Aime Clarand, Charles Granval).

Midnight in Paris—Con Conrad, Herb Magidson (w,m), Movietone. COVER: The Eiffel Tower.

3289 Midnight Lace (Universal, 1960, Doris Day, Rex Harrison).

Midnight Lace—Joe Lubin, Jerome Howard (w,m), Daywin. COVER: Doris Day, Rex Harrison.

3290 Midnight Romance, A First National, 1919, Anita Stewart, Jack Holt).

Midnight Romance, A—Anita Stewart (w,m), Berlin. COVER: Anita Stewart.

3291 Midnight Waltz (DFD, 1948, Ilona Massey, Jean Sablon).

Every Time (PC)—Walton Farrar, Walter Kent (w,m), Southern; Two Things to Worry About—Walton Farrar, Walter Kent (w,m), Block. COVER: Jean Sablon.

3292 Midshipmaid (GB, 1932, Jessie Matthews, Basil Sydney).

One Little Kiss from You—Clifford Grey (w), Noel Gay (m), Chappell. COVER: Jessie Matthews.

3293 Midshipman (MGM, 1925, Ramon Novarro, Harriet Hammond).

Midshipman—Ted Barron (w,m), Barron. COVER: Ramon Novarro, and Movie Scenes.

3294 Midstream (Tiffany, 1929, Claire Windsor, Ricardo Cortez).

Midstream—L. Wolfe Gilbert (w), Abel Baer (m), Feist. COVER: Claire Windsor, Ricardo Cortez.

3295 Midsummer Night's Dream, A (Warner Bros., 1935, James Cag-

ney, Dick Powell).

Midsummer Night's Dream-Themes —F. Mendelssohn, Erich W. Korngold (m), Witmark. COVER: Flowers and Curtains.

3296 Midway (Universal, 1976, Charlton Heston, Henry Fonda).

Men of the Yorktown March/Midway March—John Williams (m), Duchess. COVER: Battle Scene.

3297 Mighty Barnum (United Artists, 1934, Wallace Beery, Virginia Bruce).

Barnum and Beery and Me (PC)— Howard Johnson (w,m), Shapiro Bernstein. COVER: None.

3298 Mikado, The (Universal, 1939, Kenny Baker, Jean Colin).

Flowers That Bloom in the Spring/ Moon and I, The/Three Little Maids/ Tit Willow—W. S. Gilbert, Arthur Sullivan (w,m), Chappell. COVER: Kenny Baker, Jean Colin.

3299 Mike (MGM, 1926, Sally O'Neill, Charles Murray).

Mike—Benny Davis, Jesse Greer (w,m), Shapiro Bernstein. COVER: Sally O'Neill.

3300 Milkman, The (Universal, 1950, Donald O'Connor, Jimmy Durante).

Early Morning Song/It's Bigger Than Both of Us—Jackie Barnett (w), Sammy Fain (m), Chappell; That's My Boy—Jackie Barnett (w), Sammy Fain (m), Durante. COVER: Donald O'Connor, Jimmy Durante.

3301 Milky Way, The (Paramount, 1935, Harold Lloyd, Adolph Menjou).

Milky Way, The—Tot Seymour (w), Vee Lawnhurst (m), Popular. COVER: Harold Lloyd.

3302 Millie (RKO, 1931, Helen Twelvetrees, Joan Blondell).

Millie—Nacio Herb Brown (w, m), Brown. COVER: Helen Twelvetrees.

3303 Millionaire for Christy, A (20th Century-Fox, 1951, Fred MacMurray, Eleanor Parker).

Ghost of a Chance, A—Bing Crosby, Ned Washington (w), Victor Young (m), American. COVER: Fred MacMurray, Eleanor Parker.

3304 Millionairess, The (20th Century-Fox, 1960, Peter Sellers, Sophia Loren).

Goodness Gracious Me (B)—David Lee, Herbert Kretzmer (w,m), Essex. COVER: Peter Sellers, Sophia Loren.

3305 Million Dollar Baby (Warner Bros., 1948, Priscilla Lane, Ronald Reagan).

I Found a Million Dollar Baby—Billy Rose, Mort Dixon (w), Harry Warren (m), Remick. COVER: Priscilla Lane, Jeffrey Lynn, Ronald Reagan.

3306 Million Dollar Melody (Educational, 1933, Lillian Roth, Eddie Craven)

I Feel Like a Million Dollars/Who Is It?—Benny Davis (w), James Hanley (m), Movietone. COVER: Chorus Girls.

3307 Million Dollar Mermaid (MGM, 1952, Esther Williams, Victor Mature).

When You Wore a Tulip (B)—Jack Mahoney (w), Percy Wenrich (m), Feist. COVER: Esther Williams.

3308 Million Dollar Mystery (Randolph, 1914, Florence Labadie, Marguerite Shaw).

You're My Million Dollar Mystery—Wilson Campbell (w), Walter Stone (m), Cullen. COVER: Wilson Campbell.

3309 Million Dollar Ransom (Universal, 1934, Phillips Holmes, Edward Arnold).

You'll Never Know—Walter Donaldson (w,m), Robbins. COVER: Wini Shaw, Edward Arnold, Mary Carlisle.

3310 Millions in the Air (Paramount, 1935, John Howard, Wendy Barrie).

Crooner's Lullaby—Arthur Johnston, Sam Coslow (w,m), Famous; Laughin' at the Weather Man/Penny in My Pocket—Leo Robin, Ralph Rainger (w,m), Famous. COVER:

John Howard, Wendy Barrie.

3311 Mimi (Alliance, 1935, Gertrude Lawrence, Douglas Fairbanks).

Love Over All (B)—G. H. Clutsam (w,m), Prowse. COVER: Gertrude Lawrence, Douglas Fairbanks.

3312 Minstrel Man (PRC, 1944, Alan Dinehart, Benny Fields).

Cindy/I Don't Care If the World Knows It/My Bamboo Cane/Shakin' Hands with the Sun/Remember Me to Carolina—Paul F. Webster (w), Harry Revel (m), Harris. COVER: Benny Fields, Gladys George, and Others.

3313 Minx, The (Cambist, 1969, Jan Sterling, Robert Rodan).

It's a Lovely Game Louise/Squeeze Play—Tom Dawes (w,m), Marks. COVER: Movie Scenes.

3314 Miracle Can Happen, A (On Our Merry Way) (United Artists, 1947, James Stewart, Paulette Goddard).

Mister Miracle Man—Ervin Drake, Jimmy Shirl (w,m), Commercial. COVER: James Stewart, Paulette Goddard, Fred MacMurray.

3315 Miracle in Milan (DeSica, 1951, Francesco Golisano, Brunella Bovo).

Cozy Little Cottage, A—Bert Resifield (w), Inci (m), Southern. COVER: Ray Bloch.

3316 Miracle in the Rain (Warner Bros., 1956, Jane Wyman, Van Johnson).

Miracle in the Rain—Ned Washington (w), Ray Heindorf, M. K. Jerome (m), Remick. COVER: Jane Wyman, Van Johnson.

3317 Miracle Man, The (Paramount, 1919, Thomas Meighan, Betty Compson).

Miracle Man, The—Harry B. Smith (w), Jacques Grandet (m), Berlin. COVER: Thomas Meighan, Betty Compson.

3318 Miracle of Love, The (Times, 1969, Biggi Freyer, Katarina Hartel).

Miracle of Love Theme—Curtis

Lewis (m), Marks. COVER: Biggi Freyer, Katarina Hartel.

3319 Miracle of the Bells (RKO, 1948, Frank Sinatra, Fred MacMurray).

Ever Homeward—Jule Styne, Sammy Cahn (w,m), Sinatra; Miracle of the Bells—Russell Janney (w), Pierre Norman (m), Feist. COVER: Frank Sinatra, Fred MacMurray, Valli.

3320 Miracle of the White Stallions, The (Buena Vista, 1963, Robert Taylor, Lili Palmer).

Just Say Auf Wiedersehen—Richard Sherman, Robert Sherman (w, m), Wonderland. COVER: Horses.

3321 Miracle Worker, The (United Artists, 1960, Anne Bancroft, Patty Duke).

Hush Little Baby-Theme—Arthur Siegel, Don Costa (w,m), Unart. COVER: Anne Bancroft, Patty Duke.

3322 Mirage, The (Possessed) (MGM, 1931, Joan Crawford, Clark Gable).

How Long Will It Last?—Max Lief (w), Joseph Meyer (m), MGM. COVER: Black and white cover with title only.

3323 Misadventures of Merlin Jones, The (Buena Vista, 1964, Annette Funicello, Tommy Kirk).

Merlin Jones—Richard Sherman, Robert Sherman (w,m), Wonderland. COVER: Tommy Kirk, Annette Funicello, and Monkey.

3324 Mis Dos Amores (My Two Loves) (Paramount, 1938, Tito Guizar, Blanca DeCastejon).

Quiubo Quiubo—Nanette Noriega, Tito Guizar (w,m), Southern. COVER: Tito Guizar, Blanca DeCastejon.

3325 Misfits, The (United Artists, 1961, Clark Gable, Marilyn Monroe).

Misfits Theme—Alex North (m), Unart. COVER: Clark Gable, Marilyn Monroe, Montgomery Clift.

3326 Missing (Universal, 1982, Jack Lemmon, Sissy Spacek).

Missing Theme—Vangelis. COVER: Purple cover with title only.

3327 Missions Next Door, The (Crescendo, 1973, Religious Film).

You Don't Have to Go Far to Tell the Story—Ron Owens (w,m), Crescendo. COVER: Yellow cover with title only.

3328 Mission to Moscow (Warner Bros., 1943, Walter Huston, Ann Harding).

From Border Unto Border/Oh It Is Joy—Olga Paul (w), Don Pokrass (m), Marks; Meadowlands—Olga Paul (w), L. Knipper (m), Marks; Moscow/Should Our Land Be Attacked/Song of Our Country/Tachanka/Through the Hills and Vales—Olga Paul (w), Don Pokrass (m), Marks. COVER: Soldiers.

3329 Mississippi (Paramount, 1935, Bing Crosby, Joan Bennett).

Down by the River/It's Easy to Remember—Lorenz Hart (w), Richard Rodgers (m), Famous; Pablo You Are My Heart (B)—Lorenz Hart (w), Richard Rodgers (m), Victoria; Soon—Lorenz Hart (w), Richard Rodgers (m), Famous; Swanee River—Stephen Foster (w,m), Famous. COVER: Bing Crosby, Joan Bennett.

3330 Mississippi Belle (Warner Bros., 1944 [partially filmed movie was canceled]).

I Like Pretty Things (VS)/Mississippi Belle (VS)/When a Woman's in Love (VS)—Cole Porter (w,m), Warner. COVER: Cole Porter.

3331 Mississippi Gambler (Universal, 1929, Joan Bennett, Joseph Shildkraut).

Father Mississippi—L. Wolfe Gilbert (w), Harry Akst (m), Feist. COVER: Joseph Shildkraut.

3332 Missouri Breaks, The (United Artists, 1976, Marlon Brando, Jack Nicholson).

Missouri Breaks Love Theme—John Williams (m), Unart. COVER: Marlon Brando, Jack Nicholson.

3333 Missouri Story, The (Romance of Rosy Ridge) (MGM, 1947, Van Johnson, Janet Leigh).

Far from My Darling—Lewis Allan

(w), Earl Robinson (m), Robbins. COVER: Black and white cover with title only.

3334 Missouri Traveler, The (Buena Vista, 1958, Lee Marvin, Brandon DeWilde).

Missouri Traveler-Biarn's Song and Piney Woods—Johnny Mercer (w), Jack Marshall (m), Disney. COVER: Movie Scenes.

3335 Miss Sadie Thompson (Columbia, 1953, Rita Hayworth, Aldo Ray).

Hear No Evil See No Evil/Heat Is On, The—Ned Washington (w), Lester Lee (m), Mills; A Marine, a Marine, a Marine—Alan Roberts (w), Lester Lee (m), Mills; Sadie Thompson's Song—Ned Washington (w), Lester Lee (m), Mills. COVER: Rita Hayworth, Aldo Ray, and Movie Scenes.

3336 Mister Big (Mr. Big) (Universal, 1943, Peggy Ryan, Donald O'Connor).

Boogie Woogie Sandman/Kitten with My Mittens Laced/Spirit Is in Me, The/Thee and Me/This Must Be a Dream/We're Not Obvious—Buddy Pepper, Inez James (w,m), Robbins. COVER: Peggy Ryan, Donald O'Connor, Gloria Jean.

3337 Mister Roberts (Warner Bros., 1950, Henry Fonda, James Cagney).

Farewell, For Just Awhile—Jack Brooks (w), Eddie Lund (m), Criterion; Let Me Hear You Whisper—Nap Tuiteleleapaga, Ray Evans, Jay Livingston (w,m), Criterion. COVER: Henry Fonda.

3338 Mister Rock and Roll (Paramount, 1957, Alan Freed, Rocky Graziano).

I Was the Last One to Know—Ted Randazzo, Cirino Colacrai, Clyde Otis (w,m), Raleigh; Kiddio—Brook Benton, Clyde Otis (w,m), Raleigh; This Moment of Love—Gene Fiocca (w,m), Raleigh. COVER: Alan Freed, and Rock Stars.

3339 Mlle Modiste (First Nation-al, 1930, Norman Kerry, Corrine Griffith).

Kiss Me Again—Henry Blossom (w), Victor Herbert (m), Witmark. COVER: Corrine Griffith.

3340 Moby Dick (Warner Bros., 1956, Gregory Peck, Richard Basehart).

Departure of the Pequod—Philip Sainton (m), Leeds. COVER: Whaling Ship, and Whale.

3341 Modern Problems (20th Century-Fox, 1981. Chevy Chase, Nell Carter).

Gonna Get It Next Time—Adrienne Anderson (W), Dominic Frontiere (m), Fox. COVER: Chevy Chase, Patti D'Arbanville, Dabney Coleman.

3342 Modern Times (United Artists, 1954, Charlie Chaplin, Paulette Goddard).

Smile—John Turner, Geoffrey Parsons (w), Charlie Chaplin (m), Bourne. COVER: Charlie Chaplin.

3343 Modesty Blaise (20th Century-Fox, 1966, Monica Vitti, Terence Stamp).

Modesty—Benny Green (w), John Dankworth (m), Feist. COVER: Monica Vitti, Terence Stamp.

3344 Mohawk (20th Century-Fox, 1955, Scott Brady, Rita Gam).

Love Plays the Strings of My Banjo—Paul Herrick (w), Edward Alpherson (m), Feist. COVER: Scott Brady, Rita Gam.

3345 Molly and Lawless John (PDC, 1973, Vera Miles, Sam Elliott).

Take Me Home—Alan Bergman, Marilyn Bergman (w), Johnny Mandel (m), Shayne. COVER: Vera Miles.

3346 Molly and Me (Tiffany, 1929, Joe E. Brown, Belle Bennett).

In the Land of Make Believe—L. Wolfe Gilbert (w), Abel Baer (m), Feist. COVER: Joe E. Brown, Belle Bennett.

3347 Molly Maguires, The (Paramount, 1970, Sean Connery, Richard Harris).

Hills of Yesterday—Paul F. Webster (w), Henry Mancini (m), Famous; Molly Maguires Theme—Henry Mancini (m). COVER: Mob Scene.

3348 Molly O (First National, 1921, Mabel Normand, George Nichols).

Molly-O, I Love You—James Emery (w), Norman McNeil (m), Berlin. COVER: Mabel Normand.

3349 Mom and Dad (Hallmark, 1948, June Carlson, Hardie Albright).

Where Shall We Dream Tonight— Eddie Cherkose, Eddie Kay (w,m), Maxwell Key. COVER: June Carlson, Hardie Albright.

3350 Moment by Moment (Universal, 1978, John Travolta, Lily Tomlin).

Momemt by Moment—Molly Ann Leiken (w), Lee Holdridge (m), RSO. COVER: John Travolta, Lily Tomlin.

3351 Moment to Moment (Universal, 1965, Jean Seaberg, Sean Garrison).

Moment to Moment—Johnny Mercer (w), Henry Mancini (m), Southdale. COVER: Jean Seberg, Sean Garrison.

3352 Mommie Dearest (Paramount, Faye Dunaway, Steve Forrest).

Bittersweet—Larry Kusik (w), Henry Mancini (m), Famous; Mommie Dearest Theme—Henry Mancini (m), Famous. COVER: Faye Dunaway.

3353 Mon Amour Mon Amour (Independent, 1967, Jean Louis Trintignant, Valerie LaGrange).

Mon Amour . . . Mon Amour— Carl Sigman (w), Francis Lai (m), TRO. COVER: Robert Goulet.

3354 Mondo Cane (Times, 1962, Documentary of World Behaviours).

More—Norman Newell (w), N. Oliviero, Riz Ortolani, Marks; Mondo Cane-Seven Themes—Riz Ortolani, N. Oliviero (m), Marks. COVER: Seagulls on Beach.

3355 Mondo Cane #2 (Mondo Pazzo) (Rizzoli, 1964, Documentary

of World Behaviours).

I'll Set My Love to Music—Marian Grudeff, Ray Jessell (w), Nino Oliviero (m), Marks. COVER: Pink with title only.

3356 Mondo Pazzo (Mondo Cane #2) (Rizzoli, 1964, Documentary of World Behaviours).

I'll Set My Love to Music—Marian Grudeff, Ray Jessell (w), Nino Oliviero (m), Marks. COVER: Blue with title only.

3357 Money from Home (Paramount, 1954, Dean Martin, Jerry Lewis).

Moments Like This—Frank Loesser (w), Burton Lane (m), Famous. COVER: Dean Martin, Jerry Lewis.

3358 Money in My Pocket (Anson, 1962, Jan Brinker, Graham Archer).

Money in My Pocket (PC)— George Hormel (w,m), Bax. COVER: None.

3359 Monkey Business (20th Century-Fox, 1952, Cary Grant, Ginger Rogers).

Whiffenpoof Song, The (B)—M. Minnigerod, G. Pomeroy, T. Galloway, Rudy Vallee (w,m), Magna. COVER: Cary Grant, Ginger Rogers.

3360 Monkeys Go Home (Disney, 1967, Maurice Chevalier, Dean Jones).

Joie de Vivre—Richard Sherman, Robert Sherman (w,m), Wonderland. COVER: Blue Cover with title only.

3361 Monkey's Uncle, The (Buena Vista, 1964, Tommy Kirk, Annette Funicello).

Monkey's Uncle, The—Richard Sherman, Robert Sherman (w,m), Wonderland. COVER: Annette Funicello, and Monkey.

3362 Monsieur Beaucaire (Paramount, 1924, Rudolph Valentino, Doris Kenyon).

Red Red Rose—Fred Rath (w), Mel Shauer (m), Robbins Engel; Rudolph Valentino's Love Song— Beth Young (w), Ignaz Waghalter (m), Marks. COVER: Rudolph Valentino, Doris Kenyon.

3363 Monsieur Beaucaire (Paramount, 1946, Bob Hope, Joan Caulfield).

Coach and Four/Warm as Wine—Jay Livingston, Ray Evans (w,m), Famous. COVER: Bob Hope, Joan Caulfield.

3364 Monsieur Verdoux (United Artists, 1947, Charlie Chaplin, Martha Raye).

Monsieur Verdoux-Three Themes—Charlie Chaplin (m), Chappell. COVER: Purple and white cover with title only.

3365 Monster That Challenged the World, The (United Artists, 1957, Tim Holt, Hans Conreid).

Full of Love—Alan Bergman, Marilyn Keith (w), Heinz Roemheld (m), Paul. COVER: Green cover with title only.

3366 Montana (Warner Bros., 1950, Errol Flynn, Alexis Smith).

Reckon I'm in Love—Mack David, Al Hoffman, Jerry Livingston (w,m), Harms. COVER: Errol Flynn, Alexis Smith.

3367 Montana Belle (RKO, 1952, Jane Russell, George Brent).

Gilded Lily—Portia Nelson, Margaret Martinez (w,m), Mills. COVER: Jane Russell.

3368 Montana Moon (MGM, 1930, Joan Crawford, Johnny Mack Brown).

Montana Call—Clifford Grey (w), Herbert Stothart (m), Robbins; Moon Is Low, The—Arthur Freed (w), Nacio Herb Brown (m), Robbins. COVER: Joan Crawford.

3369 Monte Carlo (Paramount, 1930, Jack Buchanan, Jeanette MacDonald).

Always in All Ways/Beyond the Blue Horizon/Give Me a Moment Please/Job with a Future, A/She'll Love Me and Like It/Trimmin' the Women/Whatever It Is, It's Grand—Leo Robin (w), Richard Whiting, Franke Harling (m), Famous. COVER: Jack Buchanan, Jeanette MacDonald.

3370 Monte Carlo Madness (The Bombardment of Monte Carlo) (UFA, 1932, Sari Maritz, Hans Albers).

Over the Blue—Jimmy Campbell, Reg Connelly (w), Werner Heymann (m), Harms. COVER: Blue cover with title only.

3371 Monte Carlo Story, The (United Artists, 1957, Marlene Dietrich, Vittorio de Sica).

Monte Carlo Story Theme—Robert Mellin (w), Michael Emer (m), Bishop. COVER: Marlene Dietrich, Vittorio de Sica.

3372 Monte Walsh (National General, 1970, Lee Marvin, Jeanne Moreau).

Good Times Are Comin'—Hal David (w), John Barry (m), April. COVER: Lee Marvin, Jeanne Moreau.

3373 Montmartre (Paramount, 1924, Pola Negri).

Montmartre—Tom Johnstone (w, m), Hinds. COVER: Pola Negri.

3374 Moon and Sixpence, The (United Artists, 1942, George Sanders, Herbert Marshall).

Moon and Sixpence—Bob Reed (w), Harry Miller (m), MPI. COVER: Native Girl.

3375 Moon Is Blue, The (United Artists, 1953, William Holden, David Niven).

Moon Is Blue, The—Sylvia Fine (w), Herschel Gilbert (m), Santly Joy. COVER: William Holden, Maggie McNamara.

3376 Moonlight and Cactus (Universal, 1944, Andrews Sisters, Leo Carrillo).

C'Mere Baby—Roy Jordan, Lanney Grey (w,m), Leeds; Down in the Valley—Frank Luther (w,m), Leeds; Home—Peter Van Steeden, Harry Clarkson, Jeff Clarkson (w,m), Mills; Send Me a Man Amen—Ray Gilbert, Sidney Miller (w,m), Leeds; Sing, It's Good for Ya—Hughie Prince (w), Harold Mooney (m), Luz. COVER: The Andrews Sisters.

3377 Moonlight and Pretzels (Universal, 1933, Leo Carrillo, Mary Brian).

Ah But Is It Love—E. Y. Harburg (w), Jay Gorney (m), Harms; Are You Makin' Any Money—Herman Hupfield (w,m), Harms; Dusty Shoes —E. Y. Harburg (w), Jay Gorney (m), Harms; I've Gotta Get Up and Go to Work—Herman Hupfield (w,m), Harms; Let's Make Love Like the Crocodiles/Moonlight and Pretzels/ There's a Little Bit of You—E. Y. Harburg (w), Jay Gorney (m), Harms. COVER: Girls.

3378 Moonlighter, The (Warner, 1953, Barbara Stanwyck, Fred Mac-Murray).

Moonlighter Song—Carl Sigman (w), Heinz Roemheld (m), Harms. COVER: Barbara Stanwyck, Fred MacMurray.

3379 Moonlight in Vermont (Universal, 1944, Gloria Jean, Ray Malone).

Dobbin and a Wagon of Hay (PC)/ Something Tells Me (PC)—Inez James, Sidney Miller (w,m), Melody Lane. COVER: None.

3380 Moonlight Masquerade (Republic, 1942, Dennis O'Keefe, Jane Frazee).

What Am I Doing Here in Your Arms—Mort Green (w), Harry Revel (m), Mills. COVER: Dennis O'Keefe, Jane Frazee.

3381 Moonlight Melody (Educational, 1935, Musical Short).

Fickle Flo—Jack Yellen (w), Dan Dougherty (m), Movietone; I Like Myself for Liking You—Don Hartman (w), Jay Gorney (m), Movietone. COVER: Black and white cover with title only.

3382 Moonlight on the Prairie (Warner Bros., 1935, Dick Foran, Sheila Manners).

Covered Wagon Days—Joan Jasmyn (w), M. K. Jerome (m), Witmark; Moonlight on the Prairie—Bob Nolan, Vernon Spencer (w,m), Witmark. COVER: Dick Foran.

3383 Moonlight on the Range (Spectrum, 1937, Fred Scott, Lois January).

As Time Goes On (VS)/Ridin' Down the Sundown Trail (VS)/ There's Gonna Be a Shindig (VS)— June Hershey (w), Don Swander (m), American. COVER: Fred Scott.

3384 Moon Over Burma (Paramount, 1940, Dorothy Lamour, Robert Preston).

Mexican Magic—Frank Loesser (w), Harry Revel (m), Paramount; Moon Over Burma—Frank Loesser (w), Frederick Hollander (m), Paramount. COVER: Dorothy Lamour.

3385 Moon Over Harlem (Meteor, 1939, Sidney Bechet, Bud Harris).

Lullaby/Moon Over Harlem/My Hope Chest of Dreams/One More River to Cross/Save Some of Those Roses for Me/Stand Together Children/Teach Me How to Sing Again— Donald Heywood (w,m), Exclusive. COVER: Sketch of Couple and Moon.

3386 Moon Over Her Shoulder (20th Century-Fox, 1941, Lynn Bari, John Sutton).

Girl with the Sugar Brown Hair— Walter Bullock (w), Alfred Newman (m), Robbins. COVER: Lynn Bari, John Sutton.

3387 Moon Over Miami (Miami) (20th Century-Fox, 1941, Betty Grable, Robert Cummings).

Is That Good?/I've Got You All to Myself/Kindergarten Conga/Loveliness and Love/Miami/Solitary Seminole/You Started Something—Leo Robin (w), Ralph Rainger (m), Robbins. COVER: Betty Grable, Don Ameche, Robert Cummings, and Others.

3388 Moon Over Montana (Monogram, 1946, Jimmy Wakely, Lee White).

If You Knew What It Meant to Be Lonesome (VS)—Jimmy Wakely, Lee White (w,m), Mono; Moon Over Montana (VS)—Jimmy Wakely, Oliver Drake (w,m), Mono. COVER: Jimmy Wakely.

3389 Moon Pilot (Buena Vista, 1962, Tom Tryon, Brian Keith).

Moon Pilot Melody, Seven Moons of Beta Lyrae—Richard Sherman, Robert Sherman (w,m), Wonderland. COVER: Tom Tryon, Dany Saval.

3390 Moonraker (United Artists, 1979, Roger Moore, Lois Chiles).

Moonraker—Hal David (w), John Barry (m), Unart. COVER: Roger Moore, and Girls.

3391 Moonrise (Republic, 1948, Dane Clark, Gail Russell).

Moonrise Song—Harry Tobias (w), William Lava (m), Robert. COVER: Dane Clark, Gail Russell.

3392 Moon's Our Home, The (Paramount, 1948, Margaret Sullavan, Henry Fonda).

Moon's Our Home, The—Sam Coslow, Frederick Hollander (w,m), Famous. COVER: Henry Fonda, Margaret Sullavan.

3393 Moonstruck (MGM, 1987, Cher, Nicholas Cage).

That's Amore—Jack Brooks (w), Harry Warren (m), Paramount; Addio Mulberry Street (VS)/Beautiful Signorina (VS)/Canzone Per Loretta (VS)—Dick Hyman (m), Leonard; Donde Lieta Usci (VS)—G. Puccini, Dick Hyman (m), Leonard; It Must Be Him (VS)—M. Vidalin, G. Becaud, Mack David (w,m), Leonard; Moonglow (VS)—Eddie Delange, Will Hudson, Irving Mills (w,m), Leonard; Mr. Moon (VS)—Dick Hyman (m), Leonard; Musetta's Waltz (VS)— G. Puccini, Dick Hyman (m), Leonard; Old Man Mazurka (VS)—Dick Hyman (m), Leonard; O'Soave Fanciulla (VS)—G. Puccini, Dick Hyman (m), Leonard. COVER: Cher.

3394 Moontide (20th Century-Fox, 1942, Ida Lupino, Jean Gabin).

Moontide—Charles Henderson (w), Alfred Newman (m), Robbins. COVER: Ida Lupino, Jean Gabin.

3395 More Than a Miracle (MGM, 1967, Sophia Loren, Omar Sharif).

More Than a Miracle—Larry Kusik, Eddie Snyder (w), Piero Piccioni (m), Feist. COVER: Sophia Loren, Omar Sharif.

3396 More the Merrier, The (Columbia, 1943, Jean Arthur, Joel McCrea).

Damn the Torpedos-Full Speed Ahead—Henry Myers, Edward Eliscu (w), Jay Gorney (m), Robbins. COVER: Eddie Cantor.

3397 Morgan (Cinema Five, 1966, Vanessa Redgrave, David Warner).

Morgan, a Suitable Case for Treatment (B)—Benny Green (w), John Dankworth (m), Feldman. COVER: David Warner, and Movie Scene.

3398 Morituri (20th Century-Fox, 1965, Marlon Brando, Yul Brynner).

Morituri Theme—Jerry Goldsmith (m), Hastings. COVER: Marlon Brando, Yul Brynner.

3399 Morning Glory (RKO, 1933, Katharine Hepburn, Douglas Fairbanks).

Morning Glory—Joe Young (w), Max Steiner (m), Berlin. COVER: Katharine Hepburn.

3400 Morocco (Paramount, 1930, Gary Cooper, Marlene Dietrich).

Give Me the Man—Leo Robin (w), Karl Hajos (m), Famous. COVER: Marlene Dietrich, Adolphe Menjou, Gary Cooper.

3401 Moscow on the Hudson (Columbia, 1984, Robin Williams, Alejandro Rey).

Freedom—David McHugh (w,m), Golden Torch; People Up in Texas— Waylon Jennings (w,m), Jennings. COVER: Robin Williams, and Others.

3402 Most Immoral Lady, A (First National, 1929, Leatrice Joy, Walter Pidgeon).

That's How Much I Need You/ Toujours—Herman Ruby (w), M. K. Jerome (m), Piantadosi. COVER: Leatrice Joy, Walter Pidgeon.

3403 Mother Eternal (Abramson, 1921, Vivian Martin, Thurston Hall).
Mother Eternal—William Duncan (w), Anselm Goetzl (m), Witmark. COVER: Vivian Martin, and Children.

3404 Motherhood (STB, 1928, George Patton, Adelaide Chase).
Motherhood—Edward Grossman, Ted Ward (w,m), Ager Yellen. COVER: Mother and Child.

3405 Mother Knows Best (Fox, 1928, Madge Bellamy, Louise Dresser).
Sally of Our Dreams—William Kernell (w,m), DBH. COVER: Madge Bellamy.

3406 Mother Machree (Fox, 1928, Belle Bennett, Philippe De-Lacy).
Mother Machree—Rida J. Young (w), Chauncey Olcott, Ernest Ball (m), Witmark. COVER: Belle Bennett, Philippe DeLacy.

3407 Mother O' Mine (Ince, 1921, Lloyd Hughes, Betty Blythe).
Mother of Mine—Bob Murphy (w), Elmore White (m), Remick. COVER: Sketch of Mother.

3408 Mother's Boy (RKO, 1929, Morton Downey, Helen Chandler).
I'll Always Be Mother's Boy/ There'll Be You and I—Bud Green, Sam Stept (w,m), Green Stept; There's a Place in the Sun for You—Bud Green, Sammy Fain (w,m), Green Stept; When Nobody Wants You & Nobody Cares, Come to Me—Bud Green, W. Collins, Sam Stept (w, m), Berlin; World Is Yours and Mine—Bud Green, Sam Stept, James Hanley (w,m), Shapiro Bernstein. COVER: Morton Downey, Helen Chandler.

3409 Mother Wore Tights (20th Century-Fox, 1947, Betty Grable, Dan Dailey).
Fare Thee Well, Dear Alma Mater/ Kokomo Indiana/On a Little Two Seat Tandem/There's Nothing Like a Song/This Is my Favorite City—Mack Gordon (w), Josef Myrow (m), BVC; Tra La La La—Mack Gordon (w), Harry Warren (m), Robbins; You Do —Mack Gordon (w), Josef Myrow (m), B V C. COVER: Betty Grable, Dan Dailey.

3410 Moulin Rouge (World Wide, 1929, Olga Chekova, Eve Gray).
My Wonderful Love—William Stone (w), Charles Wynn (m), Harms. COVER: Olga Chekova.

3411 Moulin Rouge (United Artists, 1934, Constance Bennett, Tullio Carminati).
Boulevard of Broken Dreams/ Coffee in the Morning—Al Dubin (w), Harry Warren (m), Remick; Putting It On—Boswell Sisters (w,m), Keit Engel; Song of Surrender—Al Dubin (w), Harry Warren (m), Remick. COVER: Constance Bennett, and Girls.

3412 Moulin Rouge (United Artists, 1952, Jose Ferrer, Zsa Zsa Gabor).
Song from Moulin Rouge—William Engvick (w), George Auric (m), BMI. COVER: Can Can Dancer.

3413 Mountain, The (Paramount, 1956, Spencer Tracy, Robert Wagner).
Mountain—Mack David (w), Daniele Amfitheatrof (m), Famous; Mountain Theme—Daniele Amfitheatrof (m), Famous. COVER: Spencer Tracy, Robert Wagner.

3414 Mountain Men, The (Columbia, 1979, Charlton Heston, Brian Keith).
Last of the Mountain Men—Michel Legrand (m), Golden Torch. COVER: Red Cover with title only.

3415 Mountain Music (Paramount, 1937, Martha Raye, Bob Burns).
Can't You Hear That Mountain Music/Good Mornin'—Sam Coslow (w,m), Famous; If I Put a Heart in My Song—Sam Coslow, Al Siegel (w, m), Famous; Mama Don't Allow It—Charles Davenport (w,m), Select;

Thar She Comes—Sam Coslow (w, m), Famous. COVER: Bob Burns, Martha Raye, Rufe Davis.

3416 Mountain Rhythm (Republic, 1939, Gene Autry, Smiley Burnette).

Highways Are Happy Ways—Larry Shay, Tom Malie, Harry Harris (w, m), Foster. COVER: Gene Autry.

3417 Move (20th Century-Fox, 1970, Elliott Gould, Paula Prentiss).

Move—Alan Bergman, Marilyn Bergman (w), Marvin Hamlisch (m), Fox. COVER: Elliott Gould.

3418 Move Over Darling (20th Century-Fox, 1963, Doris Day, James Garner).

Move Over Darling—Joe Lubin, Hal Kanter, Terry Melcher (w,m), Daywin; Twinkle Lullaby—Joe Lubin (w,m), Daywin. COVER: Doris Day, James Garner.

3419 Movers and Shakers (MGM, 1985, Walter Matthau, Charles Grodin).

Can't We Go Home Again—Mitzie Welch, Ken Welch (w,m), April. COVER: Cartoons.

3420 Mr. Ace (United Artists, 1946, George Raft, Sylvia Sidney).

Now and Then—Sid Silvers, Fred Finklehoff (w,m), Shapiro Bernstein. COVER: George Raft, Sylvia Sidney.

3421 Mr. Big (Mister Big) (Universal, 1943, Donald O'Connor, Peggy Ryan).

We'll Meet Again—Ross Parker, Hughie Charles (w,m), World. COVER: Donald O'Connor.

3422 Mr. Blandings Builds His Dream House (RKO, 1948, Cary Grant, Myrna Loy).

My Dream House—Atra Baer, Martin Kalmanoff (w,m), Shapiro Bernstein. COVER: Cary Grant, Myrna Loy.

3423 Mr. Bug Goes to Town (Hoppity Goes to Town) (Paramount, 1941, Cartoon).

Be My Little Baby Bumble Bee—Stanley Murphy (w), Henry Marshall (m), Remick; Boy Oh Boy—Frank

Loesser (w), Sammy Timberg (m), Famous; I'll Dance At Your Wedding/Katy Did-Katy Didn't/We're the Couple in the Castle—Frank Loesser (w), Hoagy Carmichael (m), Famous. COVER: Cartoon:

3424 Mr. Chump (Warner Bros., 1938, Johnny Davis, Lola Lane).

As Long as You Live (PC)—Johnny Mercer (w), Bernie Hanighen (m), Remick. COVER: None.

3425 Mr. Deeds Goes to Town (Columbia, 1936, Gary Cooper, Jean Arthur).

I'm Pixilated over You—Edward Heyman (w), Harold Spina (m), Santly Joy. COVER: Gary Cooper, Jean Arthur.

3426 Mr. Dodd Takes the Air (Warner Bros., 1937, Kenny Baker, Alice Brady).

Am I in Love/Girl You Used to Be/Here Comes the Sandman/Remember Me—Al Dubin (w), Harry Warren (m), Witmark. COVER: Kenny Baker, Jane Wyman, and Others.

3427 Mr. Emanuel (United Artists, 1945, Greta Gynt, Felix Aylmer).

I Don't Know You—Mischa Spoliansky (w,m), Morris. COVER: Greta Gynt.

3428 Mr. Hobbs Takes a Vacation (20th Century-Fox, 1962, James Stewart, Maureen O'Hara).

Cream Puff—Johnny Mercer (w), Henry Mancini (m), Miller; Mr. Hobbs Theme—Henry Mancini (m), Miller. COVER: James Stewart, Maureen O'Hara.

3429 Mr. Hulot's Holiday (GBD Films, 1953, Jacques Tati, Nathalie Pascaud).

What's the Weather Like in Paris—Mitchell Parish (w), Alain Romans (m), Miller. COVER: Sketches.

3430 Mr. Imperium (MGM, 1951, Lana Turner, Ezio Pinza).

Andiamo/Let Me Look at You/My Love and My Mule—Dorothy Fields (w), Harold Arlen (m), Morris; You Belong to My Heart—Ray Gilbert (w), Agustin Lara (m), La-Salle. COVER: Lana Turner, Ezio Pinza.

3431 Mr. Lemon of Orange (Fox, 1931, Fifi Dorsay, El Brendel).

My Racket Is You—James Hanley (w,m), Red Star. COVER: Fifi Dorsay, El Brendel.

3432 Mr. Music (Paramount, 1950, Bing Crosby, Nancy Olson).

Accidents Will Happen/And You'll Be Home/High on the List/Life Is So Peculiar/Milady/Mister Music/Once More the Blue and White/Wasn't I There/Wouldn't It Be Funny —Johnny Burke (w), James Van Heusen (m), BVH. COVER: Bing Crosby, Nancy Olson, Peggy Lee, Groucho Marx.

3433 Mr. Peabody and the Mermaid (Universal, 1948, William Powell, Ann Blyth).

Caribees—Johnny Mercer (w), Robert Dolan (m), Morris. COVER: William Powell, Ann Blyth.

3434 Mrs. Mike (United Artists, 1949, Dick Powell, Evelyn Keyes).

Kathy—Ned Washington (w), Max Steiner (m), Remick. COVER: Dick Powell, Evelyn Keyes.

3435 Mrs. Miniver (MGM, 1942, Greer Garson, Walter Pidgeon).

Midsummer's Day—Gene Lockhart (w,m), Feist. COVER: Greer Garson, Walter Pidgeon.

3436 Mrs. O'Malley and Mr. Malone (MGM, 1950, Marjorie Main, James Whitmore).

Missus O'Malley and Mister Malone—Paul F. Webster (w), Adolph Deutsch (m), Feist. COVER: Marjorie Main, James Whitmore.

3437 Mr. Sycamore (Capricorn, 1974, Jason Robards, Sandy Dennis).

Time Goes By—Paul F. Webster (m), Maurice Jarre (m), Tower. COVER: Jean Simmons, Jason Robards.

3438 Mr. Texas (Graham, 1951, Redd Harper)

Each Step of the Way/Rally Round the Cross—Redd Harper (w, m), Fiesta. COVER: Redd Harper.

3439 Mr. Topaze (I Like Money) (20th Century-Fox, 1961, Peter Sellers, Herbert Lom).

I Like Money (B)—Herbert Kretzmer (w), Graham Fisher (m), Robbins; Mr. Topaze Theme (B)—Herbert Kretzmer (w), George Van Parys (m), Robbins. COVER: Peter Sellers.

3440 Muppet Movie, The (Associated, 1979, Muppets).

Rainbow Connection, The/Movin' Right Along/Muppet Movie-Nine Songs—Paul Williams, Kenny Ascher (w,m), ATV. COVER: Kermit and Miss Piggy.

3441 Muppets Take Manhattan, The (Universal, 1984, Art Carney, Joan Rivers).

Muppets Take Manhattan-Twelve Songs—Jeff Moss (w,m), Cherry Lane. COVER: Kermit and Miss Piggy.

3442 Murder at the Vanities (Paramount, 1934, Jack Oakie, Kitty Carlisle).

Cocktails for Two/Ebony Rhapsody/Live and Love Tonight/Lovely One/Marahuana/Where Do They Come From—Sam Coslow, Arthur Johnston (w,m), Famous. COVER: Chorus Girls.

3443 Murderers' Row (Columbia, 1967, Dean Martin, Ann Margret).

If You're Thinkin' What I'm Thinkin'—Tommy Boyce, Bobby Hart (w,m), Colgems; I'm Not the Marrying Kind—Howard Greenfield (w), Lalo Schifrin (m), Colgems. COVER: Dean Martin, Ann Margret.

3444 Murder, Inc. (20th Century-Fox, 1961, Stuart Whitman, May Britt).

Awakening/Hey Mister/Fan My Brow—George Weiss (w,m), Aries. COVER: Sara Vaughn, and Movie Scenes.

3445 Murder in the Blue Room (Universal, 1944, Anne Gwynn, Donald Cook).

One Starry Night—Dave Franklin, Don George (w,m), Urban. COVER: Grace McDonald, Anne Gwynne, June Preisser.

3446 Murder in Villa Capri (Burton, 1955, Stars Unknown).

Down in Villa Capri—Florence Mecur (w,m), Citation. COVER: Man and Woman Embracing.

3447 Murder on the Orient Express (Paramount, 1974, Albert Finney, Ingrid Bergman).

Murder on the Orient Express Theme/Orient Express—Richard R. Bennett (m), EMI; Silky—Larry Kusik (w), Richard R. Bennett (m), EMI. COVER: Lauren Bacall, Ingrid Bergman, Sean Connery, Wendy Hiller, and Others.

3448 Musical Doctor (Paramount, 1932, Rudy Vallee).

Keep a Little Song Handy—Sammy Lerner (w), Sammy Timberg (m), Famous. COVER: Rudy Vallee.

3449 Musical Justice (Paramount, 1934, Musical Short).

Don't Take My Boop-oop-a-doop Away—Sammy Lerner (w), Sammy Timberg (m), Famous. COVER: Man at Piano.

3450 Music for Madame (RKO, 1937, Joan Fontaine, Nino Martini).

I Want the World to Know—Gus Kahn (w), Rudolf Friml (m), Schirmer; Music for Madame—Herb Magidson (w), Allie Wrubel (m), Berlin; My Sweet Bambina—Gus Kahn (w), Rudolf Friml (m), Schirmer. COVER: Joan Fontaine, Nino Martini.

3451 Music for Millions (MGM, 1944, Margaret O'Brien, June Allyson).

Umbriago—Irving Caesar, Jimmy Durante (w,m), Robbins. COVER: Jimmy Durante, Margaret O'Brien, June Allyson.

3452 Music Goes Round (Rolling Along) (Columbia, 1936, Harry Richman, Rochelle Hudson).

Let's Go—Harry Richman (w), Victor Schertzinger (m), Berlin; Life Begins When You're in Love—Lew Brown (w), Victor Schertzinger (m), Berlin; Rolling Along—Lew Brown (w), Harry Akst (m), Berlin; Suzannah/There'll Be No South—Lew Brown (w), Harry Akst, Harry Richman (m), Berlin. COVER: Harry Richman, Rochelle Hudson.

3453 Music in Manhattan (RKO, 1944, Anne Shirley, Dennis Day).

Did You Happen to Find a Heart/I Can See You Now/I Like a Man Who Makes Music/One Night in Acapulco Mexico/When Romance Comes Along—Herb Magidson (w), Lew Pollack (m), Southern. COVER: Anne Shirley, Dennis Day, Charlie Barnet.

3454 Music in My Heart (Columbia, 1940, Tony Martin, Rita Hayworth).

It's a Blue World/I've Got Music in My Heart/No Other Love/Oh What a Lovely Dream/Prelude to Love/Punchinello—Bob Wright, Chet Forrest (w,m), ABC. COVER: Tony Martin, Rita Hayworth.

3455 Music in the Air (Fox, 1934, Gloria Swanson, John Boles).

I Am So Eager/I've Told Every Little Star/One More Dance/Song Is You, The/We Belong Together—Oscar Hammerstein (w), Jerome Kern (m), Harms. COVER: Gloria Swanson, John Boles.

3456 Music Is Magic (Fox, 1935, Alice Faye, Ray Walker).

Honey Child—Sidney Clare (w), Oscar Levant (m), Movietone; La Locumba—Sidney Clare (w), Raul Roulien (m), Movietone; Love Is Smiling at Me (BW)—Sidney Clare (w), Oscar Levant (m), Movietone; Music Is Magic—Sidney Clare (w), Arthur Johnston (m), Movietone. COVER: Alice Faye, and Dancers.

3457 Music Lovers, The (United Artists, 1971, Glenda Jackson, Richard Chamberlain).

Music Lovers, The—P. Tchaikovsky, Ferrante-Teicher (m), Unart. COVER: Glenda Jackson, Richard Chamberlain.

3458 Music Man (Monogram,

1948, Freddie Stewart, Jimmy Dorsey).

I Could Swear It Was You—Phil Brito, Larry Stock, Allan Flynn (w, m), Laurel. COVER: Phil Brito.

3459 Music Man, The (Warner Bros., 1962, Robert Preston, Shirley Jones).

Being in Love/Goodnight My Someone/It's You/Lida Rose/Seventy Six Trombones/Till There Was You—Meredith Willson (w,m), Frank. COVER: A Parade.

3460 Mutiny on the Bounty (MGM, 1935, Clark Gable, Franchot Tone).

Love Song of Tahiti—Gus Kahn (w), Bronislau Kaper, Walter Jurmann (m), Robbins. COVER: Clark Gable, and Girl.

3461 Mutiny on the Bounty (MGM, 1962, Marlon Brando, Trevor Howard).

Mutiny on the Bounty Love Song —Paul F. Webster (w), Bronislau Kaper (m), Miller; Mutiny on the Bounty Theme/Mutiny on the Bounty-Ten Themes—Bronislau Kaper (m), Miller. COVER: The Bounty.

2462 My Blue Heaven (20th Century-Fox, Betty Grable, Dan Dailey).

Don't Rock the Boat Dear/Friendly Islands/Halloween/I Love a New Yorker/It's Deductible/Live Hard, Work Hard Love Hard—Ralph Blane (w), Harold Arlen (m), Morris; My Blue Heaven—George Whiting (w), Walter Donaldson (m), Feist. COVER: Betty Grable, Dan Dailey.

3463 My Boy (First National, 1922, Jackie Coogan, Claude Gillingwater).

I'm Just a Lonely Little Kid—Jack Norworth, Al Piantadosi (w,m), Shapiro Bernstein. COVER: Jackie Coogan.

3464 My Dream Is Yours (Warner Bros., 1949, Doris Day, Jack Carson).

I'll String Along with You—Al Dubin (w), Harry Warren (m), Witmark; My Dream Is Yours—Ralph Blane (w), Harry Warren (m), Witmark; Someone Like You/Freddie Get Ready (BW)/ Love Finds a Way (BW)/Tick Tick Tick (BW)—Ralph Blane (w), Harry Warren (m), Harms. COVER: Doris Day, Jack Carson, Lee Bowman.

3465 My Fair Lady (Warner Bros., 1964, Audrey Hepburn, Rex Harrison).

Get Me to the Church on Time/I Could Have Danced All Night/I've Grown Accustomed to Her Face/On the Street Where You Live/Rain in Spain, The/Show Me/With a Little Bit of Luck/Wouldn't It Be Loverly—Alan Jay Lerner (w), Frederick Loewe (m), Chappell. COVER: Rex Harrison, Audrey Hepburn.

3466 My Favorite Brunette (Paramount, 1947, Bob Hope, Dorothy Lamour).

Beside You/My Favorite Brunette —Jay Livingston, Ray Evans (w,m), Famous. COVER: Bob Hope, Dorothy Lamour.

3467 My Favorite Spy (RKO, 1942, Kay Kyser, Robert Armstrong).

Got the Moon in My Pocket/Just Plain Lonesome—Johnny Burke (w), James Van Heusen (m), Mayfair. COVER: Kay Kyser, and Girls.

3468 My Favorite Spy (Paramount, 1951, Bob Hope, Hedy Lamarr).

I Wind Up Taking a Fall—Johnny Mercer (w), Robert Dolan (m), Paramount; Just a Moment More—Jay Livingston, Ray Evans (w,m), Paramount. COVER: Bob Hope, Hedy Lamarr.

3469 My Foolish Heart (RKO, 1949, Susan Hayward, Dana Andrews).

My Foolish Heart—Ned Washington (w), Victor Young (m), Santly Joy. COVER: Dana Andrews, Susan Hayward.

3470 My Friend Irma (Paramount, 1949, Dean Martin, Jerry Lewis).

Here's to Love/Just for Love/My Friend Irma/My Own, My Only, My Pal—Jay Livingston, Ray Evans (w, m), Paramount. COVER: Dean Martin, Jerry Lewis, Marie Wilson, John Lund.

3471 My Friend Irma Goes West (Paramount, 1950, Dean Martin, Jerry Lewis).

Baby Obey Me/Fiddle and Guitar Band/I'll Always Love You—Jay Livingston, Ray Evans (w,m), Famous. COVER: Dean Martin, Jerry Lewis, John Lund, Marie Wilson.

3472 My Gal Loves Music (Universal, 1944, Bob Crosby, Grace McDonald).

Bogo Jo—George Calendar (w,m), Regent; I Need Vitamin "U"—Clarence Gaskill (w,m), Paull Pioneer. COVER: Bob Crosby, Grace McDonald.

3473 My Gal Sal (20th Century-Fox, 1942, Rita Hayworth, Victor Mature).

Come Tell Me What's Your Answer—Paul Dresser (w,m), Paull Pioneer; Here You Are/Me and My Fella—Leo Robin (w), Ralph Rainger (m), Robbins; Mr. Volunteer/My Gal Sal—Paul Dresser (w,m), Paull Pioneer; Oh the Pity of It all—Leo Robin (w), Ralph Rainger (m), Robbins; On the Banks of the Wabash—Paul Dresser (w,m), Paull Pioneer; On the Gay White Way—Leo Robin (w), Ralph Rainger (m), Robbins. COVER: Rita Hayworth, Victor Mature.

3474 My Geisha (Paramount, 1961, Shirley MacLaine, Yves Montand).

My Geisha—Hal David (w), Franz Waxman (m), Famous; My Geisha Theme—Franz Waxman (m), Famous. COVER: Shirley MacLaine, Yves Montand.

3475 My Girl Suzanne (Philipp, 1919, Adolf Philipp, Patsy DeForrest).

My Girl Suzanne—Edward Paulton (w), Adolp Philipp (m), Remick. COVER: Adolf Philipp, Patsy De-

Forrest.

3476 My Gun Is Quick (United Artists, 1957, Robert Bray, Whitney Blake).

Blue Bells—Stanley Styne (w), Marlin Skiles (m), Coronet. COVER: Robert Bray, Whitney Blake.

3477 My Heart Goes Crazy (London Town) (United Artists, 1946, Sid Field, Greta Gynt).

Ampstead Way/Anyway the Wind Blows/Hyde Park on a Sunday/If Spring Were Only Here to Stay/My Heart Goes Crazy/So Would I/You Can't Keep a Good Dreamer Down—Johnny Burke (w), James Van Heusen (m), BVH. COVER: Greta Gynt, Kay Kendall, and Others.

3478 My Heart Is Calling (GB, 1934, Jan Kiepura, Marta Eggerth).

My Heart Is Always Calling You—Harry Pepper (w), Robert Stolz (m), Harms; You Me and Love—Tommie Connor (w), Robert Stolz (m), Harms. COVER: Jan Kiepura, Marta Eggerth.

3479 My Lady's Past (Tiffany, 1928, Joe E. Brown, Belle Bennett).

Kiss to Remember, A—Alfred Bryan (w), Jack Pettis, Al Goering (m), Spier Coslow. COVER: Joe E. Brown, Belle Bennett.

3480 My Lady's Perfumes (Paramount, 1927, Mary Bothwell).

Forgotten Perfumes—Gwynne Denni (w), Lucien Denni (m), Jenkins. COVER: Mary Bothwell.

3481 My Lips Betray (Fox, 1933, John Boles, Lilian Harvey).

His Majesty's Car (BW)/To Romance (BW)/Why Am I Happy?—William Kernell (w,m), Movietone. COVER: John Boles, Lilian Harvey.

3482 My Little Chickadee (Universal, 1940, W. C. Fields, Mae West).

Willie of the Valley—Milton Drake (w), Ben Oakland (m), Robbins. COVER: W. C. Fields, Mae West.

3483 My Lover My Son (MGM, 1970, Romy Schneider, Donald Huston).

Summer's Here—Sue Vickers,

Mike Vickers, Morrie Paramoor (w, m), Feist. COVER: Romy Schneider, Dennis Waterman.

3484 My Lucky Star (20th Century-Fox, 1938, Sonja Henie, Richard Greene).

All American Swing/By a Wishing Well/Could You Pass in Love/I've Got a Date with a Dream/This May Be the Night—Mack Gordon, Harry Revel (w,m), Feist. COVER: Sonja Henie, Richard Greene.

3485 My Man (Warner Bros., 1929, Fannie Brice, Guinn Williams).

I'd Rather Be Blue Over You— Billy Rose (w), Fred Fisher (m), Ber-Lin; If You Want the Rainbow—Billy Rose, Mort Dixon (w), Oscar Levant (m), Remick; I'm an Indian—Blanche Merrill (w), Leo Edwards (m), Mills; I Was a Florodora Baby—Ballard Mac-Donald (w), Harry Carroll (m), Shapiro Bernstein; My Man—Channing Pollock (m), Maurice Yvain (m), Feist; Second Hand Rose—Grant Clarke (w), James Hanley (m), Shapiro Bernstein. COVER: Fannie Brice.

3486 My Old Dutch (Universal, 1926, May McAvoy, Pat O'Malley).

My Old Dutch—Albert Chevalier, Charles Ingle (w,m), Pioneer. COVER: May McAvoy, Pat O'Malley.

3487 My Own True Love (Paramount, 1948, Melvyn Douglas, Phyllis Calvert).

My Own True Love—Jay Livingston, Ray Evans (w,m), Famous. COVER: Melvyn Douglas, Phyllis Calvert.

3488 Myra Breckinridge (20th Century-Fox, 1964, Mae West, John Huston).

Secret Place—John Phillips (w,m), Fox; You Gotta Taste All the Fruit— Alan Bergman, Marilyn Bergman (w), Sammy Fain (m), Chappell. COVER: Mae West.

3489 My Reputation (Warner Bros., 1946, Barbara Stanwyck, George Brent).

While You're Away—Stanley

Adams (w), Max Steiner (m), Remick. COVER: Barbara Stanwyck, George Brent.

3490 Myrt and Marge (Laughter in the Air) (Universal, 1933, Grace Hayes, Trixie Friganza).

Draggin' My Heels Around/Isle of Pines/What Is Sweeter—Joan Jasmyn (w), M. K. Jerome (m), Remick. COVER: Eddie Foy, and Girl.

3491 My Side of the Mountain (Paramount, 1959, Teddy Eccles, Theodore Bikel).

World Like Mine, A—Larry Kusik, Eddie Snyder (w), Wilfred Joseph (m), Famous. COVER: Teddy Eccles.

3492 My Sister Eileen (Columbia, 1955, Janet Leigh, Jack Lemmon).

Give Me a Band and My Baby/It's Bigger Than You and Me/There's Nothing Like Love—Leo Robin (w), Jule Styne (m), Colgems. COVER: Dancers.

3493 My Six Loves (Paramount, 1962, Debbie Reynolds, Cliff Robertson).

It's a Darn Good Thing/My Six Loves—Sammy Cahn (w), James Van Heusen (m), Famous. COVER: Debbie Reynolds, Cliff Robertson, and Family.

3494 My Song for You (GB, 1934, Jan Kiepura, Sonnie Hale).

My Song for You/With All My Heart—Frank Eyton (w), Mischa Spoliansky (m), Harms. COVER: Jan Kiepura, Aileen Marson.

3495 My Son My Son (United Artists, 1940, Brian Aherne, Madeleine Carroll).

My Son My Son—L. Wolfe Gilbert, Lew Pollack (w,m), Gilbert. COVER: Brian Aherne, Madeleine Carroll.

3496 My Stepmother Is an Alien (Columbia, 1989, Dan Aykroyd, Kim Basinger).

Room to Move—Dennis Morgan, Simon Clime, Rob Fisher (w,m), Little Shop. COVER: Animation Rock Group.

3497 Mystery of the Hooded Horseman, The (Grand National, 1937, Tex Ritter, Iris Meredith).
Ride Ride Ride—Fred Rose, Michael David (w,m), Sam Fox. COVER: Tex Ritter.

3498 My Weakness (Fox, 1933, Lilian Harvey, Lew Ayres).
Be Careful/Gather Lip Rouge While You May/How Do I Look?—B. G. DeSylva, Leo Robin, Richard Whiting (w,m), Movietone. COVER: Lilian Harvey, Lew Ayres.

3499 My Wild Irish Rose (Vitagraph, 1922, Pat O'Malley, Helen Howard).
My Wild Irish Rose—Chauncey Olcott (w,m), Witmark. COVER: Helen Howard.

3500 My Wild Irish Rose (Warner Bros., 1947, Dennis Morgan, Arlene Dahl).
Come Down Ma Evenin' Star—Robert Smith (w), John Stromberg (m), Witmark; Hush-a-bye—Ted Koehler (w), M. K. Jerome (m), Witmark; Mother Machree—Rida J. Young (w), Chauncey Olcott, Ernest Ball (m), Witmark; My Nelly's Blue Eyes—William Scanlan (w,m), Harms; My Wild Irish Rose—Chauncey Olcott (w,m), Witmark; When Irish Eyes Are Smiling—Chauncey Olcott, George Graff (w), Ernest Ball (m), Witmark. COVER: Dennis Morgan, Arlene Dahl, Andrea King.

3501 My Woman (Columbia, 1933, Helen Twelvetrees, Victor Jory).
I Knew I Couldn't Hold You—Victor Schertzinger (w,m), Berlin. COVER: Black and white cover with title only.

3502 Naked Brigade, The (Universal, 1965, Shirley Eaton, Ken Scott).
This Is Our Secret Star—Paul F. Webster (w), Theo Fanidi (m), Solo. COVER: Shirley Eaton, Ken Scott.

3503 Naked Dawn, The (Universal, 1955, Arthur Kennedy, Betta St. John).

I Love a Stranger—Edward Heyman (w), Herschel Gilbert (m), Young. COVER: Arthur Kennedy, Betta St. John.

3504 Naked Earth, The (20th Century-Fox, 1958, Richard Todd, Juliette Greco).
Tomorrow My Love (B)—Carey Starr (w), H. Patterson (m), Robbins. COVER: Juliette Greco.

3505 Naked Flame, The (Corona, 1964, Dennis O'Keefe, Kasey Rogers).
Naked Flame, The (PC)/Our Love Was Meant to Be (PC)—Bernie Lewis, Lawrence Matanjki (w,m), Iryce. COVER: None.

3506 Naked Gun-From the Files of the Police Squad, The (Paramount, 1988, Leslie Nielsen, Priscilla Presley).
Naked Gun Theme, The—Ira Newborn (m), Famous. COVER: Leslie Nielsen.

3507 Naked Runner, The (Warner Bros., 1967, Frank Sinatra, Peter Vaughn).
You Are There—Paul F. Webster (w), Harry Sukman (m), Sergeant. COVER: Frank Sinatra.

3508 Naked Sea, The (RKO, 1954, Documentary of the Ocean).
Naked Sea, The—Laurindo Almeida, George Fields (m), Criterion. COVER: Paul Weston.

3509 Namu-The Killer Whale (United Artists, 1966, Robert Lansing, Lee Meriwether).
Ballad of Namu the Killer Whale—Tom Glazer (w,m), Unart. COVER: A Whale.

3510 Nana (United Artists, 1934, Anna Sten, Lionel Atwill).
That's Love—Lorenz Hart (w), Richard Rodgers (m), Berlin. COVER: Anna Sten.

3511 Nancy Goes to Rio (MGM, 1950, Ann Sothern, Jane Powell).
Cae Cae—John Latouche (w), Robert Martins (m), Robbins; Ca Room Pa Pa—Ray Gilbert (w,m), Robbins; Love Is Like This—Ray

Gilbert (w), A. Vianna, Ray Gilbert (m), Robbins; Magic Is the Moonlight —Charles Pasquale (w), Maria Grever (m), Southern; Time and Time Again —Earl Brent (w), Fred Spielman (m), Robbins; Yipseei-o—Ray Gilbert (w, m), Robbins. COVER: Jane Powell, Ann Sothern, Carmen Miranda, and Others.

3512 Nanook of the North (Flaherty, 1922, Documentary of Eskimos)

Nanook of the North—Milt Hagen, Herb Crooker, Victor Nurnberg (w, m), Cameo. COVER: Sketch of Eskimos.

3513 Napoleon (MGM, 1927 [1981 Revival], Gina Manes, Albert Dieudonne).

Napoleon's March—Carmine Coppola (m), Coppola; Thrill of Being in Love, The—Italia Pennino (w), Carmine Coppola (m), Coppola; Victory Song of Napoleon—Italia Pennino, Roxanne Seeman (w), Carmine Coppola (m), Coppola. COVER: Napoleon.

3514 Nashville (Paramount, 1975, Karen Black, Keith Carradine).

I'm Easy/It Don't Worry Me—Keith Carradine (w,m), ABC; Nashville-Twelve Songs—Ronee Blakely, Karen Black, Henry Gibson (w,m), Columbia. COVER: Karen Black, Keith Carradine, Lily Tomlin, Geraldine Chaplin, Others.

3515 National Barn Dance (Paramount, 1944, Jean Heather, Charles Quigley).

Angels Never Leave Heaven—Don Pelosi, Art Noel, Lewis Ilda (w,m), Leeds; Swing Little Indians Swing—Gracie Worth (w,m), Braun. COVER: Dinning Sisters.

3516 National Lampoon's Animal House (Universal, 1978, Thomas Hale, James Widdoes).

Animal House—Stephen Bishop (w,m), Duchess; Shama Lama Ding Dong—Mark Davis (w,m), Duchess. COVER: Cartoon.

3517 National Lampoon's Vacation (Warner Bros., 1983, Chevy Chase, Beverly D'Angelo).

Holiday Road—Lindsey Buckingham (w,m), Now Sounds. COVER: Chevy Chase.

3518 Natural, The (Tri-Star, 1984, Robert Redford, Robert Duvall).

Natural, The—Randy Newman (m), TSP. COVER: Robert Redford.

3519 Naughty But Nice (Warner Bros., 1939, Dick Powell, Ann Sheridan).

Corn Pickin'/Hooray for Spinach/ I'm Happy About the Whole Thing/ In a Moment of Weakness—Johnny Mercer (w), Harry Warren (m), Remick. COVER: Dick Powell, Ann Sheridan.

3520 Naughty Marietta (MGM, 1935, Jeanette MacDonald, Nelson Eddy).

Ah Sweet Mystery of Life/I'm Falling in Love with Someone/Italian Street Song/Neath the Southern Moon/Tramp Tramp Tramp—Rida J. Young (w), Victor Herbert (m), Witmark. COVER: Jeanette MacDonald, Nelson Eddy (published one set in yellow and one set in pink).

3521 Naughty Nineties (Universal, 1945, Bud Abbott, Lou Costello).

I Can't Get You Out of My Mind —Jack Brooks (w), Edgar Fairchild (m), Saunders. COVER: Bud Abbott, Lou Costello, Rita Johnson.

3522 Navy Blues (MGM, 1929, William Haines, Anita Page).

Navy Blues—Roy Turk (w), Fred Ahlert (m), DBH. COVER: William Haines.

3523 Navy Blues (Warner Bros., 1941, Ann Sheridan, Jack Oakie).

In Waikiki/When Are We Going to Land Abroad/You're a Natural— Johnny Mercer (w), Arthur Schwartz (m), Witmark. COVER: Ann Sheridan, Jack Oakie, Martha Raye, Jack Haley.

3524 Navy Lark, The (20th Century-Fox, 1959, Cecil Parker, Ronald Shiner).

Navy Lark, The (B)—Tommy Reilly, James Moody (w,m), Feldman. COVER: Cecil Parker, Ronald Shiner, Leslie Phillips.

3525 Neal of the Navy (Pathe, 1915, Lillian Lorraine, William Gourtleigh).

Neal of the Navy—Douglas Bronston (w,m), Berlin. COVER: Lillian Lorraine.

3526 Nearly Right Won't Do (Good Housekeeping, 1939, Commercial Film).

Nearly Right Won't Do—Three Jesters (w,m), Vogel. COVER: The Three Jesters.

3527 Near the Rainbow's End (Raytone, 1930, Bob Steele, Al Ferguson).

Ro-ro-rollin' Along—Billy Moll, Harry Richman (w), Murray Mencher (m), Shapiro Bernstein. COVER: Ozzie Nelson.

3528 Neil Young and Crazy Horse (Shakey, 1979, Neil Young).

Hey Hey My My-Into the Black—Neil Young (w,m), Silver Fiddle. COVER: Cartoon.

3529 Neither Time Nor Love (Reade, 1966, Venantino Venantini, Elen Faison).

Lovely Lovely—George Cardini, Jan Schaff (w,m), Annica. COVER: Venantino Venantini, Elen Faison.

3530 Nell Gwynn (Paramount, 1926, Dorothy Gish, Rendle Ayrton).

Nell Gwynn—William Helmore (w,m), Feist. COVER: Dorothy Gish.

3531 Neptune's Daughter (MGM, 1949, Esther Williams, Red Skelton).

Baby It's Cold Outside—Frank Loesser (w,m), Morris; My Heart Beats Faster—Frank Loesser (w,m), Miller. COVER: Esther Williams, Red Skelton, Betty Garrett.

3532 Nevada Smith (Paramount, 1956, Steve McQueen, Karl Malden).

Nevada Smith—Hal David (w), Alfred Newman (m), Famous. COVER: Steve McQueen.

3533 Nevada Trail (Universal, 1949, Tex Williams).

Ham 'n Eggs—Country Washburne, Foster Carling (w,m), Sunland. COVER: Tex Williams.

3534 Never a Dull Moment (Universal, 1943, Ritz Brothers, Frances Langford).

He's My Guy (PC)/Mister Five By Five (PC)—Don Raye, Gene De Paul (w,m), Leeds. COVER: None.

3535 Never a Dull Moment (RKO, 1950, Irene Dunne, Fred MacMurray).

Once You Find Your Guy—Kay Swift (w,m), Harms. COVER: Irene Dunne.

3536 Never Ending Story, The (Warner Bros., 1984, Barrett Oliver, Gerald McRaney).

Never Ending Story, The—Giorgio Moroder, Keith Forsey (w,m), Warner. COVER: Limahl.

3537 Never Fear (Young Lovers) (Eagle Lion, 1950, Sally Forrest, Keefe Brasselle).

Guaymas—Bill Earley, John Franco (w,m), Peer; Why Pretend—John Franco (w,m), Peer. COVER: Sally Forrest, Keefe Brasselle.

3538 Never Let Go (Continental, 1960, Richard Todd, Peter Sellers).

Never Let Go Theme (B)—John Barry (m), Filmusic. COVER: Movie Scenes.

3539 Never Love a Stranger (Allied Artists, 1958, John Drew Barrymore, Lita Milan).

Never Love a Stranger/Oh Baby—Lawrence Elow (w), Raymond Scott (m), Feist. COVER: John Drew Barrymore, Lita Milan.

3540 Never on Sunday (United Artists, 1960, Melina Mercouri, Jules Dassin).

Athens by Night—Mel Mandel, Norman Sachs (w), Manos Hadjidakis (m), Esteem; Never on Sunday—Billy Towne (w), Manos Hadjidakis (m), Esteem; Never on Sunday Theme—Manos Hadjidakis (m), Esteem. COVER: Melina Mercouri.

3541 Never Put It in Writing

(Allied Artists, 1963, Pat Boone, Milo O'Shea).

Never Put It in Writing—Pat Boone (w,m), Spoone. COVER: Pat Boone.

3542 Never Say Die (Paramount, 1939, Martha Raye, Bob Hope).

Tra-la-la and the Oom-pah-pah, The—Leo Robin, Ralph Rainger (w, m), Famous. COVER: Martha Raye.

3543 Never Say Goodbye (Warner Bros., 1946, Errol Flynn, Eleanor Parker).

Remember Me—Al Dubin (w), Harry Warren (m), Witmark. COVER: Errol Flynn, Eleanor Parker.

3544 Never Steal Anything Small (Universal, 1959, James Cagney, Shirley Jones).

Helping Our Friends/I Haven't Got a Thing to Wear/I'm Sorry-I Want a Ferrari/It Takes Love to Make a Home/Never Steal Anything Small—Maxwell Anderson (w), Allie Wrubel (m), Morris. COVER: James Cagney, Shirley Jones.

3545 Never Too Late (Warner Bros., 1965, Paul Ford, Connie Stevens).

Never Too Late—Jay Livingston, Ray Evans (w), David Rose (m), Witmark. COVER: Connie Stevens, Maureen O'Sullivan, Paul Ford.

3546 New Faces of 1937 (RKO, 1937, Joe Penner, Milton Berle).

It Goes to Your Feet/Love Is Never Out of Season—Lew Brown (w), Sammy Fain (m), Feist; New Faces—Charles Henderson (w,m), Feist; Our Penthouse on Third Avenue—Lew Brown (w), Sammy Fain (m), Feist; Peckin'—Ben Pollack, Harry James (w,m), Mills; Widow in Lace—Walter Bullock (w), Harold Spina (m), Feist. COVER: Harriet Hilliard, Joe Penner, Milton Berle.

3547 New Interns, The (Columbia, 1964, Michael Callan, Dean Jones).

Come On, Let Yourself Go—Jan Berry, Art Korn (w,m), Colgems. COVER: Michael Callan, Dean Jones,

and Others.

3548 New Kind of Love, A (Paramount, 1963, Paul Newman, Joanne Woodward).

New Kind of Love—Sammy Fain, Irving Kahal, Pierre Norman (w,m), Famous; New Kind of Love Theme/ Paris Mist—Erroll Garner (m), Famous. COVER: Paul Newman, Joanne Woodward.

3549 Newly-Weds and Their Baby, The (Stern, 1926, Comedy Short).

Snookums—James Kendis, Jimmy McHugh (w,m), Mills. COVER: Lovey, Dovey, and Snookums.

3550 New Life, A (Paramount, 1988, Alan Alda, Ann Margret).

A New Life Theme—Joseph Turrin (m), Famous. COVER: Ann Margret, Alan Alda, Veronica Hamel, John Shea.

3551 New Moon (Select, 1919, Norma Talmadge, Stuart Holmes).

New Moon—Irving Berlin (w,m), Berlin. COVER: Norma Talmadge.

3552 New Moon (MGM, 1930, Grace Moore, Lawrence Tibbett).

Lover Come Back to Me/One Kiss/Wanting You—Oscar Hammerstein (w), Sigmund Romberg (m), Harms. COVER: Grace Moore, Lawrence Tibbett.

3553 New Moon (MGM, 1940, Jeanette MacDonald, Nelson Eddy).

Lover Come Back to Me/One Kiss/Softly as in a Morning Sunrise/ Stouthearted Men/Wanting You— Oscar Hammerstein (w), Sigmund Romberg (m), Harms. COVER: Jeanette MacDonald, Nelson Eddy.

3554 New Movietone Follies of 1930 (Fox, 1930, El Brendel, Miriam Seegar).

Cheer Up and Smile/Doing the Derby/Here Comes Emily Brown— Jack Meskill (w), Con Conrad (m), Red Star; I'd Love to Be a Talking Picture Queen—James Brockman (w), James Hanley (m), Red Star. COVER: Mirian Seegar, El Brendel, William Collier, and Others.

3555 New Orleans (Tiffany, 1929, William Collier, Ricardo Cortez).

Pals Forever—Ben Adam (w), Hugo Risenfield, Ted Shapiro (m), Ager Yellen. COVER: William Collier, Ricardo Cortez, Alma Bennett.

3556 New Orleans (United Artists, 1947, Dorothy Patrick, Arturo de Cordova).

Blues Are Brewin', The/Do You Know What It Means to Miss New Orleans/Endie—Eddie DeLange (w), Louis Alter (m), Morris; Farewell to Storyville—Spencer Williams (w,m), Williams; West End Blues—Clarence Williams (w), Joe Oliver (m), Williams; Where the Blues Are Born in New Orleans—Cliff Dixon, Bob Carleton (w,m), Morris. COVER: Louis Armstrong, Billie Holiday, Arturo de Cordova, Dorothy Patrick.

3557 New Spirit, The (Disney, 1942, Cartoon).

Yankee Doodle Spirit, The—Oliver Wallace, Cliff Edwards (w,m), Southern. COVER: Donald Duck, and Airplanes.

3558 New York New York (United Artists, 1977, Liza Minnelli, Robert De Niro).

But the World Goes Round/Happy Endings/New York New York Theme/There Goes the Ball Game—Fred Ebb (w), John Kander (m), Unart; Blue Moon (VS)—Lorenz Hart (w), Richard Rodgers (m), Big Three; Do Nothing Till You Hear from Me (VS)—Bob Russell (w), Duke Ellington (m), Big Three; Don't Be That Way (VS)—Benny Goodman, E. Sampson, Mitchell Parish (w,m), Big Three; Don't Get Around Much Anymore (VS)—Bob Russell (w), Duke Ellington (m), Big Three; Honeysuckle Rose (VS)—Andy Razaf (w), Thomas Waller (m), Big Three; It's a Wonderful World (VS)—Harold Adamson (w), Jan Savitt, John Watson (w,m), Big Three; Just You Just Me (VS)—Ray Klages (w), Jesse Greer (m), Big Three; Man I Love, The (VS)—Ira Gershwin (w), George Gershwin (m), Big Three; New Kind of Love, A (VS)—Sammy Fain, Irving Kahal, Pierre Norman (w,m), Big Three; Once in a While (VS)—Bud Green (w), Michael Edwards (m), Big Three; Taking a Chance on Love (VS)—John LaTouche, Ted Fetter (w), Vernon Duke (m), Big Three; You Are My Lucky Star (VS) —Arthur Freed (w), Nacio Herb Brown (m), Big Three. COVER: Liza Minnelli, Robert De Niro.

3559 New York Nights (United Artists, 1929, Norma Talmadge, John Wray).

Year from Today, A—Al Jolson, Ballard MacDonald, Dave Dreyer (w, m), Berlin. COVER: Norma Talmadge.

3560 New York Town (Columbia, 1934, Musical Short).

Grandfather's Clock—Abner Silver, Nick Kenny, Mack David (w, m), Harms; You Oughta Be in Pictures—Edward Heyman (w), Dana Suesse (m), Harms. COVER: A clock and title.

3561 Niagara (20th Century-Fox, 1952, Marilyn Monroe, Joseph Cotten).

Kiss—Haven Gillespie (w), Lionel Newman (m), Miller; Marilyn—Ervin Drake, Jimmy Shirl (w,m), Starlight. COVER: Marilyn Monroe, Joseph Cotten.

3562 Nice Girl (Love at Last) (Universal, 1941, Deanna Durbin, Franchot Tone).

Beneath the Lights of Home—Bernie Grossman (w), Walter Jurmann (m), Remick; Love at Last—Eddie Cherkose (w), Jacques Press (m), Robbins; Perhaps—Andres DeSegurola (w), Aldo Franchetti (m), Robbins; Thank You America—Bernie Grossman (w), Walter Jurmann (m), Remick; There'll Always Be an England (B)—Ross Parker, Hughie Charles (w,m), Dash. COVER: Deanna Durbin, Franchot Tone, Robert Stack.

3563 Nice Girl Like Me, A (Embassy, 1969, Barbara Ferris, Harry Andrews).

I Will Wait for Love—Hal Shaper (w), Pat Williams (m), Shayne. COVER: A Little Girl.

3564 Nicholas and Alexandra (Columbia, 1971, Michael Jayston, Janet Suzman).

Nicholas and Alexandra Theme —Richard Rodney Bennett (m), Colgems; Too Beautiful to Last—Paul F. Webster (w), Richard R. Bennett (m), Colgems. COVER: Family Crest.

3565 Night and Day (Warner Bros., 1946, Cary Grant, Alexis Smith).

Anything Goes/Begin the Beguine—Cole Porter (w,m), Harms; Easy to Love—Cole Porter (w,m), Chappell; I Get a Kick Out of You— Cole Porter (w,m), Harms; In the Still of the Night/I've Got You under My Skin—Cole Porter (w,m), Chappell; Just One of Those Things/Let's Do It—Cole Porter (w,m), Harms; My Heart Belongs to Daddy—Cole Porter (w,m), Chappell; Night and Day/Old Fashioned Garden—Cole Porter (w,m), Harms; Rosalie—Cole Porter (w,m), Chappell; What Is This Thing Called Love/You Do Something to Me/You're the Top—Cole Porter (w,m), Harms. COVER: Cary Grant, Alexis Smith.

3566 Night at Earl Carroll's, A (Paramount, 1940, Ken Murray, Lillian Cornell).

Cali-conga—Earl Carroll, Dorcas Cochran (w), Nilo Menendez (m), Paramount; I Wanna Make with the Happy Times—Frank Loesser, Gertrude Niesen (w,m), Paramount; Lil Boy Love—Frank Loesser (w), Frederick (m), Paramount; One Look at You—Ned Washington, Earl Carroll (w), Victor Young (m), Paramount. COVER: Lillian Cornell, and Chorus Girls.

3567 Night at the Opera, A (MGM, 1935, Allan Jones, Kitty Carlisle).

Alone—Arthur Freed (w), Nacio Herb Brown (m), Robbins; Cosi Cosa—Ned Washington (w), Bronislau Kaper, Walter Jurmann (m), Robbins. COVER: Allan Jones, Kitty Carlisle, Marx Brothers.

3568 Night Before Xmas, The (Disney, 1934, Cartoon).

Twas the Night Before Xmas (VS) —Leigh Harline (w,m), Berlin. COVER: Cartoon.

3569 Night Club Girl (Universal, 1944, Vivian Austin, Billy Dunn).

What a Wonderful Day—Harry Tobias (w), Al Sherman (m), Shapiro Bernstein. COVER: Vivian Austin, Billy Dunn.

3570 Night Club Queen (Universal, 1934, Mary Clare, Lewis Casson).

Wish I Wuz a Shoe (B)—Sonny Miller (w), Austen Croom Johnson (m), Chappell. COVER: Mary Clare.

3571 Nightfall (Columbia, 1957, Aldo Ray, Anne Bancroft).

Nightfall—Sam Lewis (w), Peter DeRose, Charles Harold (m), Shapiro Bernstein. COVER: Aldo Ray, Anne Bancroft.

3572 Night Has a Thousand Eyes, The (Paramount, 1948, Gail Russell, John Lund).

Night Has a Thousand Eyes, The— Buddy Bernier (w), Jerry Brainin (m), Paramount. COVER: John Lund, Gail Russell.

3573 Night Has Eyes, The (Terror House) (Folks at the Red Wolf Inn) (Scope Three, 1942, James Mason, Mary Clare).

Night Has Eyes Theme (B)— Charles Williams (m), Chappell. COVER: Theatre Curtain and Orchestra.

3574 Night Hawks (Universal, 1981, Sylvester Stallone, Billy Dee Williams).

Brown Sugar (PC)—Mick Jagger, Keith Richards (w,m), ABKCO; COVER: None.

3575 Night Heaven Fell, The (Columbia, 1958, Brigitte Bardot, Stephen Boyd).

Night Heaven Fell, The—Hal David (w), Burt Bacharach (m), Colgems. COVER: Brigitte Bardot, Stephen Boyd.

3576 Night in Casablanca, A (United Artists, 1946, Marx Brothers, Charles Drake).

Who's Sorry Now—Bert Kalmar, Harry Ruby (w), Ted Snyder (m), Mills. COVER: Marx Brothers.

3577 Night in Paradise (United Artists, 1946, Merle Oberon, Turhan Bey).

Night in Paradise—Jack Brooks (w), Frank Skinner (m), Robbins. COVER: Merle Oberon, Turhan Bey.

3578 Night Is Ending, The (Paris After Dark) (20th Century-Fox, 1943, George Sanders, Brenda Marshall).

Sun Will Shine Again, The (PC)— Margot Fragey (w,m), Melody Lane. COVER: None.

3579 Night Is Young, The (MGM, Ramon Novarro, Evelyn Laye).

Night Is Young, The/When I Grow Too Old to Dream—Oscar Hammerstein (w), Sigmund Romberg (m), Robbins. COVER: Ramon Novarro, Evelyn Laye.

3580 Nightmare on Elm Street #3-The Dream Warriors (New Line, 1987, Patricia Arquette, Larry Fishburne).

Dream Warriors Theme—George Lynch, Jeff Pilson (w,m), Warner. COVER: Freddy and People.

3581 Night of Love, The (United Artists, 1927, Ronald Colman, Vilma Banky).

Night of Love—Vilma Banky (w, m), Remick. COVER: Vilma Banky.

3582 Night of the Generals (Columbia, 1967, Peter O'Toole, Omar Sharif).

World Will Smile Again, The— Howard Greenfield (w), Maurice Jarre (m), Colgems. COVER: Peter O'Toole, and Movie Scenes.

3583 Night of the Grizzly, The (Paramount, 1956, Clint Walker,

Martha Hyer).

Angela—Jay Livingston, Ray Evans (w,m), Paramount. COVER: Clint Walker, and Bear.

3584 Night of the Quarter Moon (MGM, 1958, Julie London, John Drew Barrymore).

Night of the Quarter Moon—Sammy Cahn (w), James Van Heusen (m), Miller; To Whom It May Concern—Charlotte Hawkins (w), Nat Cole (m), Comet. COVER: Julie London, John Drew Barrymore.

3585 Night Passage (Universal, 1957, James Stewart, Audie Murphy).

Follow the River/You Can't Get Far Without a Railroad—Ned Washington (w), Dimitri Tiomkin (m), Northern. COVER: James Stewart, Audie Murphy.

3586 Night People (20th Century-Fox, 1954, Gregory Peck, Broderick Crawford).

Two People in the Night (B)— Tommie Connor (w), Karl Bette (m), Chappell. COVER: Gregory Peck.

3587 Night Shift (U.S. Govt., 1942, Kate Smith, Danny Kaye).

Turn Night Into Day—Marc Blitzstein (w,m), Chappell. COVER: Blue cover with title only.

3588 Night Shift (Warner Bros., 1982, Henry Winkler, Michael Keaton).

Jumpin' Jack Flash (PC)—Mick Jagger, Keith Richards (w,m), ABKCO; Night Shift—Burt Bacharach, Carole B. Sager, Marv Ross (w,m), Warner. COVER: Quarterflash.

3589 Night Song (RKO, 1947, Dana Andrews, Merle Oberon).

Who Killed Her?—Hoagy Carmichael, Janice Torre, Fred Spielman (w,m), BVH. COVER: Dana Andrews, Merle Oberon, Hoagy Carmichael.

3590 Night They Raided Minsky's, The (United Artists, 1968, Jason Robards, Britt Ekland).

Dancing Man (VS)—Sammy Cahn (w), Charles Strouse (m), Columbia; Living Alone (VS)—Charles Strouse (w,m), Columbia; Night They Raided Minsky's/Night They Raided Minsky's Love Theme/Take Ten Terrific Girls —Lee Adams (w), Charles Strouse (m), Unart. COVER: Cartoon Sketches.

3591 Night Time in Nevada (Republic, 1948, Roy Rogers, Andy Devine).

When It's Night Time in Nevada— Richard Pascoe (w), Will Dulmage, H. Clint (m), Leeds. COVER: Roy Rogers.

3592 Night Train to Memphis (Republic, 1946, Roy Acuff, Allan Lane).

Night Train to Memphis—Beasley Smith, Marvin Hughes, Owen Bradley (w,m), Peer. COVER: Roy Acuff.

3593 Night Watch (Embassy, 1973, Elizabeth Taylor, Laurence Harvey).

Night Has a Thousand Eyes—Sammy Cahn (w), George Barrie (m), Brut. COVER: Elizabeth Taylor, Laurence Harvey.

3594 Night Without Stars (Rank, 1947, David Farrar, Nadia Gray).

If You Go—Geoffrey Parsons (w), Michel Emer (m), Pickwick; Lingering Down the Lane (B)—Jack Lawrence (w), C. Borel Clerc, Chappell. COVER: Nadia Gray.

3595 Night Work (Pathe, 1930, Sally Starr, Eddie Quillan).

Deep in Your Heart/I'm Gettin' Tired of My Tired Man—Mort Harris (w), Ted Snyder (m), Shapiro Bernstein. COVER: Sally Starr, Eddie Quillan.

3596 Nine and one Half Weeks (MGM, 1986, Mickey Rourke, Kim Basinger).

I Do What I Do—John Taylor, Jonathan Elias, Des Barres (w,m), Famous; I Do What I Do Theme— John Taylor, Jonathan Elias, Des Barres (m), Famous. COVER: John Taylor.

3597 Nine Hours to Rama (20th Century-Fox, 1963, Horst Buchholz, Jose Ferrer).

Nine Hours to Rama Theme (B)— Malcolm Arnold (m). Henrees. COVER: Horst Buchholz, Diane Baker.

3598 Nine Men (United Artists, 1943, Jack Lambert, Gordon Jackson).

Eighth Army March (B)—Eric Coates (m), Chappell. COVER: Soldiers.

3599 Nineteen Hundred (Paramount, 1977, Dominique Sanda, Robert De Niro).

Nineteen Hundred Theme—Ennio Morricone (m), Famous. COVER: Robert De Niro, Burt Lancaster, Donald Sutherland.

3600 Nine to Five (20th Century-Fox, 1980, Jane Fonda, Lily Tomlin).

House of the Rising Sun—Dolly Parton, Mike Post (w,m), Velvet Apple; Nine to Five—Dolly Parton (w,m), Velvet Apple. COVER: Dolly Parton.

3601 Ninety-Nine and Forty-Four Percent Dead (20th Century-Fox, 1974, Richard Harris, Edmond O'Brien).

Easy Baby—Alan Bergman, Marilyn Bergman (w), Henry Mancini (m), Fox; Hangin' Out—Henry Mancini (m), Fox. COVER: Henry Mancini.

3602 Nineteen Eighty-Four (Atlantic, 1984, John Hurt, Richard Burton).

Sex Crime/Nineteen Eighty-Four-Nine Themes—A. Lennox, D. Stewart (w,m), Warner. COVER: John Hurt.

3603 Nitwits (RKO, 1935, Bert Wheeler, Bob Woolsey).

Music in My Heart—Dorothy Fields (w), Jimmy McHugh (m), Berlin; You Opened My Eyes—L. Wolfe Gilbert, Felix Bernard (w,m), Berlin. COVER: Bert Wheeler, Bob Woolsey, Betty Grable.

3604 Noah's Ark (Warner Bros., 1929, Dolores Costello, George O'Brien.

Heart O' Mine/Old Timer—Billy

Rose (w), Louis Silvers (m), Berlin. COVER: Dolores Costello, George O'Brien.

3605 Nob Hill (20th Century-Fox, 1945, George Raft, Joan Bennett).

I Don't Care Who Knows It—Harold Adamson (w), Jimmy McHugh (m), Robbins; I Walked In—Harold Adamson (w), Jimmy McHugh (m), Miller; What Do You Want to Make Those Eyes at Me For?—Joe McCarthy, J. Monaco, H. Johnson (w,m), Feist. COVER: George Raft, Joan Bennett, Vivian Blaine.

3606 No Blade of Grass (MGM, 1970, Lynne Frederick, Nigel Davenport).

No Blade of Grass—Charles Carroll, Louis Nelius (w,m), Feist. COVER: Teenagers.

3607 Nobody's Baby (MGM, 1937, Patsy Kelly, Lyda Roberti).

I've Dreamed About This/Nobody's Baby—Walter Bullock (m), Marvin Hatley (m), Feist. COVER: Black and white cover with title only.

3608 Nobody's Perfekt (Columbia, 1981, Gabe Kaplan, Alex Karras).

Nobody's Perfekt—David McHugh (w,m), Gold Horizon. COVER: Gabe Kaplan, Alex Karras, Susan Clark.

3609 No Control (Metropolitan, 1927, Harrison Ford, Phyllis Haver).

I've No Control of My Heart—Marian Gillespie (w), John Hagen (m), Flammer. COVER: Sketch of Couple.

3610 Nocturne (RKO, 1946, George Raft, Lynn Bari).

Nocturne—Mort Greene (w), Leigh Harline (m), Morris. COVER: George Raft, Lynn Bari.

3611 No Escape (United Artists, 1953, Lew Ayres, Sonny Tufts).

No Escape—Charles Bennett (w), Bert Shefter (m), American. COVER: Tony Craig.

3612 Noisy Neighbors (Pathe,

1928, Eddie Quillan, Alberta Vaughn).

Waiting Through the Night—M. Smoley, B. Seaman, J. Crozier, J. Ricca (w,m), Mercury. COVER: Eddie Quillan, Alberta Vaughn.

3613 No Man (Vitaphone, 1933, Musical Short).

Love Behind a Fan—Cliff Hess (w, m), Witmark. COVER: Black and white cover with title only.

3614 No More West (RKO, 1934, Bert Lahr).

We Said-Hello Again—Charles O'Flynn, Frank Weldon (w,m), Engel. COVER: Ozzie Nelson.

3615 No Leave No Love (MGM, 1946, Van Johnson, Pat Kirkwood).

All the Time—Ralph Freed (w), Sammy Fain (m), Robbins; Caldonia —Fleecie Moore (w,m), Preview; Isn't It Wonderful—Kay Thompson (w,m), Robbins; Love on a Greyhound Bus— Ralph Blane, Kay Thompson (w), George Stoll (m), Robbins; Walter Winchell Rumba (B)—Noro Morales, Carl Sigman (w,m), Albert; When It's Love—Eddie DeLange (w), Nicholas Kharito (m), Robbins. COVER: Van Johnson, Pat Kirkwood, Xavier Cugat, Guy Lombardo.

3616 No No Nanette (First National, 1930, Alexander Gray, Bernice Clare).

As Long as I'm with You—Grant Clarke (w), Harry Akst (m), Witmark; Dance of the Wooden Shoes/ Dancing on Mars (BW)—Ned Washington, Herb Magidson, Mike Cleary (w,m), Witmark; I Want to Be Happy —Irving Caesar (w), Vincent Youmans (m), Harms; No No Nanette— Otto Harbach (w), Vincent Youmans (m), Harms; Tea for Two— Irving Caesar (w), Vincent Youmans (m), Harms; Were You Just Pretending—Herman Ruby (w), M. K. Jerome (m), Witmark. COVER: Alexander Gray, Bernice Clare.

3617 No No Nanette (RKO, 1940, Anna Neagle, Richard Carlson).

I Want to Be Happy—Irving Caesar (w), Vincent Youmans (m), Harms; No No Nanette—Otto Harbach (w), Vincent Youmans (m), Harms; Tea for Two—Irving Caesar (w), Vincent Youmans (m), Harms. COVER: Anna Neagle.

3618 Noose (The Silk Noose) (Monogram, 1950, Carole Landis, Derek Farr).

When Love Has Passed You By (B)—Barry Gray (w), Edward Dryhurst (m), Wright. COVER: Ruth Nixen.

3619 Nora Prentiss (Warner Bros., 1947, Ann Sheridan, Robert Alda).

Who Cares What People Say—Jack Scholl (w), M. K. Jerome (m), Harms. COVER: Ann Sheridan, Robert Alda, Bruce Bennett, Kent Smith.

3620 Norma (Lima, 1972, Stars Unknown).

Leather in the Breeze (PC)/Love Ride (PC)/Norma Love Theme (PC —John Barber (m), Southern. COVER: None.

3621 Norman Is That You? (MGM, 1976, Redd Foxx, Pearl Bailey).

Old Fashioned Man, An—Ron Miller (w), William Goldstein (m), Stone. COVER: Smokey Robinson.

3622 Norma Rae (20th Century-Fox, 1979, Sally Field, Beau Bridges).

It Goes Like It Goes—Norman Gimbel (w), David Shire (m), Fox. COVER: Sally Field, and Factory.

3623 North Avenue Irregulars (Buena Vista, 1977, Barbara Harris, Edward Herriman).

Pass a Little Love Around—Al Kasha, Joel Hirschhorn (w,m), Wonderland. COVER: Barbara Harris, Susan Clark, Patsy Kelly.

3624 North by Northwest (MGM, 1960, Cary Grant, Eva Marie Saint).

North by Northwest Song—Bernard Herrman (m), Robbins. COVER: Cary Grant, Eva Marie Saint.

3625 North of Nome (Columbia, 1937, Jack Holt, Evelyn Ven-

able).

Neath Alaskan Skies—David Ormont (w), Lee Zahler (m), Mills. COVER: Mountain Trail, and Trees.

3626 North of the Yukon (Columbia, 1939, Charles Starrett, Linda Winters).

Still Water Pool (VS)—Bob Nolan (w,m), American. COVER: Bob Nolan.

3627 North Star, The (RKO, 1943, Anne Baxter, Dana Andrews).

No Village Like Mine/Song of the Guerillas/Younger Generation, The— Ira Gershwin (w), Aaron Copland (m), Chappell. COVER: Farley Granger, Anne Baxter, Dana Andrews.

3628 North to Alaska (20th Century-Fox, 1960, John Wayne, Stewart Granger).

North to Alaska—Mike Phillips (w, m), Robbins. COVER: John Wayne, Capucine.

3629 Northwest Frontier (Flame Over India) (20th Century-Fox, 1959, Kenneth More, Lauren Bacall).

Northwest Frontier March (B)— A. Dew (m), Prowse; Northwest Frontier Theme (B)—Mischa Spoliansky (m), Filmusic. COVER: Lauren Bacall, Kenneth More.

3630 Northwest Outpost (Republic, 1947, Nelson Eddy, Ilona Massey).

Love Is the Time/Nearer and Dearer/Raindrops on a Drum/Tell Me with Your Eyes—Edward Heyman (w), Rudolph Friml (m), Morris. COVER: Nelson Eddy, Ilona Massey.

3631 Norwood (Paramount, 1970, Glen Campbell, Kim Darby).

Chicken Out/Country Girl—Al Delory (m), Ensign; Everything a Man Could Ever Need/I'll Paint You a Song—Mac Davis (w,m), Ensign; Marie—Mitchell Torok, Ramona Redd (w,m), Ensign; Norwood—Mac David (w,m), Ensign; Norwood-Fourteen Songs—Mac Davis, Mitchell Torok, Al Delory (w,m), Ensign.

COVER: Glen Campbell, Kim Darby, Joe Namath.

3632 No Small Affair (Columbia, 1984, Jon Cryer, Demi Moore).

Love Makes You Blind—Peppi Marchello (w,m), Gold Horizon. COVER: Jon Cryer, Demi Moore.

3633 No Sun in Venice (Kingsley, 1957, Francoise Arnoul, Christian Marquand).

Love Me—John Lehman (w), John Lewis (m), Ravven; No Sun in Venice-Six Themes—John Lewis (m), Ravven. COVER: Sarah Vaughn, Modern Jazz Quartet.

3634 Not as a Stranger (United Artists, 1955, Frank Sinatra, Robert Mitchum).

Not as a Stranger—Buddy Kaye (w), James Van Heusen (m), Barton. COVER: Frank Sinatra, Olivia de Havilland, Robert Mitchum.

3635 Not Damaged (Fox, 1930, Lois Moran, Walter Byron).

Nothing's Gonna Hold Us Down/ Whisper You Love Me—Cliff Friend, Jimmy Monaco (w,m), Red Star. COVER: Lois Moran, Walter Byron.

3636 Nothing But the Best (Columbia, 1964, Alan Bates, Denholm Elliott).

Nothing But the Best (B)—Fred Raphael (w), Ron Grainer (m), Erle. COVER: Alan Bates, Millicent Martin.

3637 Nothing But the Truth (Paramount, 1929, Helen Kane, Richard Dix).

Do Something—Bud Green, Sam Stept (w,m), Green Stept. COVER: Helen Kane.

3638 Nothing in Common (Tri-Star, 1986, Jackie Gleason, Tom Hanks).

Nothing in Common—Tom Bailey, Alannah Currie (w,m), TSP. COVER: Jackie Gleason, Tom Hanks.

3639 No Time for Sergeants (Warner Bros., 1958, Andy Griffith, Nick Adams).

No Time for Sergeants Theme—Ray Heindorf (m), Witmark. COV-ER: Blue cover with title only.

3640 Notorious Landlady, The (Columbia, 1957, Kim Novak, Jack Lemmon).

Notorious Landlady, The—Mack David (w), Sammy Fain (m), Colgems. COVER: Kim Novak, Jack Lemmon, Fred Astaire.

3641 Not with My Wife, You Don't! (Warner Bros., 1966, Tony Curtis, Virna Lisi).

Big Beautiful Ball/My Inamorata —Johnny Mercer (w), Johnny Williams (m), Harms. COVER: Tony Curtis, Virna Lisi, George C. Scott.

3642 Now and Forever (Paramount, 1934, Shirley Temple, Gary Cooper).

Now and Forever—Joe Young (w), Lew Pollack (m), Famous. COVER: Shirley Temple.

3643 No Way to Treat a Lady (Paramount, 1968, Rod Steiger, Lee Remick).

A Quiet Place—Andrew Belling (w), Stanley Myers (m), Famous. COVER: Rod Steiger, Lee Remick, George Segal.

3644 Now I'll Tell (Fox, 1934, Alice Faye, Spencer Tracy).

Foolin' with the Other Woman's Man/Harlem vs. the Jungle (BW)— Lew Brown, Harry Akst (w,m), Movietone. COVER: Alice Faye, Spencer Tracy, Helen Twelvetrees.

3645 Now Voyager (Warner Bros., 1942, Bette Davis, Paul Henreid).

It Can't Be Wrong—Kim Gannon Max Steiner (m), Harms; Now Voyager Theme (VS)—Max Steiner (m), Warner. COVER: Bette Davis, Paul Henreid.

3646 Nude Bomb, The (Universal, 1980, Don Adams, Sylvia Kristel).

You're Always There When I Need You (PC)—Don Black (w), Lalo Schifrin (m), Duchess. COVER: None.

3647 Nutty Professor, The (Paramount, 1963, Jerry Lewis, Stella Stevens).

We've Got a World That Swings—
Lil Mattis, Louis Y. Brown (w,m),
Paramount. COVER: Jerry Lewis,
Stella Stevens.

3648 Oceans Eleven (Warner
Bros., 1960, Frank Sinatra, Dean
Martin).

Ain't That a Kick in the Head?/
Eee-O-Eleven—Sammy Cahn (w),
James Van Heusen (m), Barton.
COVER: Frank Sinatra, Dean Mar-
tin, Sammy Davis, Angie Dickinson.

3649 Octopussy (United Artists, 1983, Roger Moore, Maud
Adams).

All Time High—Tim Rice (w),
John Barry (m), Blackwood. COV-
ER: Roger Moore, Maud Adams.

3650 Odd Couple, The (Paramount, 1968, Jack Lemmon, Walter
Matthau).

Odd Couple—Sammy Cahn (w),
Neal Hefti (m), Famous; Tomatoes—
Neal Hefti (m), Famous. COVER:
Jack Lemmon, Walter Matthau.

3651 Odessa File, The (Columbia, 1974, Jon Voight, Maximilian
Schell).

Christmas Dream—Tim Rice (w),
Andrew Lloyd Webber (m), Colgems.
COVER: Perry Como.

3652 Ode to Billy Joe (Warner
Bros., 1976, Robby Benson, Glynnis O'Connor).

Ode to Billy Joe—Bobbie Gentry
(w,m), Shayne. COVER: Robby Benson, Glynnis O'Connor.

3653 Odongo (Columbia, 1956,
Rhonda Fleming, MacDonald Carey).

Odongo—Robert Emms (m), Colgems. COVER: Rhonda Fleming,
MacDonald Carey.

**3654 Office Girl, The (Sunshine
Susie)** (RKO, 1932, Renate Muller,
Jack Hulbert).

I Have an Aunt Eliza/Today I Feel
So Happy—Desmond Carter, Frank
Eyton (w), Paul Abraham (w,m),
Harms. COVER: Renate Muller.

**3655 Officer and a Gentleman,
An** (Paramount, 1982, Richard Gere,
Debra Winger).

Up Where We Belong—Will Jen-
nings (w), Buffy Sainte-Marie, Jack
Nitzsche (m), Famous. COVER:
Richard Gere, Debra Winger.

3656 Off Limits (Paramount,
1953, Bob Hope, Mickey Rooney).

All About Love/Military Police-
man/Right or Wrong—Jay Livingston,
Ray Evans (w,m), Famous. COVER:
Bob Hope, Mickey Rooney, Marilyn
Maxwell.

**3657 Off the Beaten Track (Be-
hind the Eight Ball)** (Universal, 1942,
Carol Bruce, Sonny Dunham).

Mister Five By Five—Don Raye,
Gene DePaul (w,m), Leeds. COVER:
A Fat Man.

3658 Of Human Bondage (MGM,
1964, Kim Novak, Laurence Harvey).

Of Human Bondage Theme—Ron
Goodwin (m), Miller. COVER: Kim
Novak.

3659 Of Love and Desire (20th
Century-Fox, 1963, Merle Oberon,
Steve Cochran).

Katherine's Love Theme/Of Love
and Desire—Ronald Stein (w,m),
Feist. COVER: Merle Oberon, Steve
Cochran.

**3660 Of Love Remembered (A
Time for Loving)** (London S.P.,
1971, Mel Ferrer, Britt Ekland).

Of Love Remembered Theme
(PC)—Michel Legrand (m), Beaujo-
lois. COVER: None.

3661 O'Hara's Wife (Davis Pan-
zar, 1982, Edward Asner, Mariette
Hartley).

I'm Never Gonna Say Goodbye—
Molly Leiken (w), Artie Butler (m),
Trans. COVER: Billy Preston.

**3662 Oh Dad Poor Dad Mama's
Hung You in the Closet and I'm
Feelin' So Sad** (Paramount, 1967,
Rosalind Russell, Robert Morse).

Oh Dad Poor Dad—Neal Hefti (w,
m), Famous; Theme for a Boy and
Girl—Neal Hefti (m), Famous. COV-
ER: Rosalind Russell, Robert Morse.

3663 Oh for a Man (Fox, 1931,
Jeanette MacDonald, Reginald
Denny).

I'm Just Nuts About You—William Kernell (w,m), Red Star. COVER: Black and white cover with title only.

3664 Oh God (Warner Bros., 1977, George Burns, John Denver).

Oh God Theme—Jack Elliott (m), Warner. COVER: George Burns.

3665 Oh Johnny How You Can Love (Universal, 1940, Tom Brown, Peggy Moran).

Maybe I Like What You Like/ Swing Chariot Swing—Paul Smith (w), Frank Skinner (m), Robbins. COVER: Tom Brown, Peggy Moran.

3666 Oh Louise (Philipp, 1919, Adolf Philipp, Marie Pagano).

Oh Louise—Edward Paulton (w), Adolf Philipp (m), Remick. COVER: Adolf Philipp, Marie Pagano.

3667 Oh Mabel Behave (Aywon, 1922, Mabel Normand, Mack Sennett).

Oh Mabel Behave—Cliff Friend, Irvin Hup (w,m), Mills. COVER: Mabel Normand.

3668 Oh Sailor Behave (Warner Bros., 1930, Ole Olsen, Chic Johnson).

Highway to Heaven/Leave a Little Smile/Tell Us Which One Do You Love (BW)/When Love Comes in the Moonlight—Al Dubin (w), Joe Burke (m), DBH. COVER: Lotti Loder, Ole Olsen, Chic Johnson.

3669 Oh Susanna (Republic, 1936, Gene Autry, Smiley Burnette).

Dear Old Western Skies (VS)— Gene Autry (w,m), Calumet; I'll Go Ridin' Down That Old Texas Trail (VS)—Gene Autry, Smiley Burnette (w,m), Cole. COVER: Gene Autry.

3670 Oh What a Lovely War (Paramount, 1969, John Rae, Corin Redgrave).

Oh What a Lovely War-Sixteen War Songs (B)—A. Ralston (w,m), Feldman. COVER: War Scenes.

3671 Oh Yeah (RKO, 1929, Zasu Pitts, James Gleason).

Love Found Me—George Waggner, Tay Garnett, George Green (w,m), Shapiro Bernstein. COVER: Robert Armstrong, James Gleason, Zasu Pitts.

3672 Oh You Beautiful Doll (20th Century-Fox, 1949, June Haver, Mark Stevens).

Chicago—Fred Fisher (w,m), Fisher; Come Josephine in My Flying Machine—Alfred Bryan (w), Fred Fisher (m), Shapiro Bernstein; Daddy You've Been a Mother to Me—Fred Fisher (w,m), Fisher; Dardanella— Fred Fisher, Felix Bernard, John Black (w,m), Fisher; Ireland Must Be Heaven—Joe McCarthy, Howard Johnson, Fred Fisher (w,m), Feist; I Want You to Want Me—Bob Schafer, Al Bryan (w), Fred Fisher (m), Mills; Oh You Beautiful Doll (B)— Seymour Brown (w), Nat Ayer (m), Feldman; Peg o' My Heart—Alfred Bryan (w), Fred Fisher (m), Feist; There's a Broken Heart for Every Light on Broadway—H. Johnson (w), Fred Fisher (m), Fisher; When I Get You Alone Tonight—Joe McCarthy, Joe Goodwin (w), Fred Fisher (m), Feist; Who Paid the Rent for Mrs. Rip Van Winkle—Al Bryan (w), Fred Fisher (m), Fisher. COVER: June Haver, Mark Stevens.

3673 Oh You Women (Paramount, 1919, Ernest Truex, Louise Hoff).

Ooooh, You Women—Bud Green (w), Sam Stept (m), Piantadosi. COVER: Ernest Truex, Louise Hoff.

3674 Oil Islands (Independent, 1928, Stars Unknown).

Song of the Brown Islands (PC)— Leon Feuchtwanger (w), Kurt Weill (m), Hampshire House. COVER: None.

3675 Oil Town U.S.A. (Graham, 1952, Redd Harper).

Lord Keep Your Hand on Me— Redd Harper (w,m), Herman; My Testimony Song—Redd Harper (w, m), Fiesta; Oil Town U.S.A.—Cindy Walker (w,m), Oree; Somebody

Bigger Than You and I—J. Lange, H. Heath, S. Burke (w,m), Bullseye. COVER: Redd Harper.

3676 Oklahoma (RKO, 1955, Shirley Jones, Gordon MacRae).

All Er Nothin'/Farmer and the Cowman/I Cain't Say No/Kansas City/Many a New Day/Oh What a Beautiful Mornin'/Oklahoma/Out of My Dreams/People Will Say We're in Love/Pore Jud/Surrey with the Fringe on Top—Oscar Hammerstein (w), Richard Rodgers (m), Williamson. COVER: Shirley Jones, Gordon MacRae.

3677 Oklahoma Annie (Republic, 1952, Judy Canova, John Russell).

Never Never Never—Jack Elliott (w), Sonny Burke (m), Young. COVER: Judy Canova.

3678 Oklahoma Crude (Columbia, 1972, Faye Dunaway, George Scott).

Oklahoma Crude—Henry Mancini (m), Colgems; Send a Little Love My Way—Hal David (w), Henry Mancini (m), Colgems. COVER: Henry Mancini, Anne Murray.

3679 Oklahoma Cyclone (Tiffany, 1930, Bob Steele, Rita Rey).

Let Me Live Out on the Prairie—Jack Scholl, Ernesto Piedra (w,m), Sherman Clay; Song of the Range—Jack Scholl, Carlos Molina (w,m), Sherman Clay. COVER: Bob Steele, Rita Rey.

3680 Oklahoma Kid, The (Warner Bros., 1939, James Cagney, Humphrey Bogart).

Cheer Oklahoma—Joe Hicks (w, m), Moorhead. COVER: James Cagney.

3681 Oklahoma Raiders (Universal, 1945, Tex Ritter, Fuzzy Knight).

Out on the Open Range (PC)—Johnny Bond (w,m), Peer. COVER: None.

3682 Oklahoma Trail (Outlaws of the Panhandle) (Columbia, 1940, Bob Nolan, Charles Starrett).

Saddle the Sun (VS)—Bob Nolan,

Tim Spencer (w,m), American; Trail Dreamin' (VS)/Trail Herdin' Cowboy (VS)—Bob Nolan (w,m), American. COVER: Bob Nolan.

3683 Old Acquaintance (Warner Bros., 1943, Bette Davis, Miriam Hopkins).

Old Acquaintance—Kim Gannon (w), Franz Waxman (m), Witmark. COVER: Bette Davis, Mirian Hopkins.

3684 Old Barn Dance, The (Republic, 1938, Gene Autry, Smiley Burnette).

Roamin' Around the Range (VS)—Smiley Burnette (w,m), Cole; You're the only Star (VS)—Gene Autry (w,m), Shapiro Bernstein. COVER: Gene Autry.

3685 Old Corral, The (Republic, 1936, Gene Autry, Smiley Burnette).

Down Along the Sleepy Rio Grande—Roy Rogers (w,m), American; In the Heart of the West (VS)—Gene Autry, Fleming Allen (w,m), Cole; He's Gone, He's Gone Up the Trail (PC)—Vern Tim Spencer, Cross & Winge. COVER: Nancy Lee and Hilltoppers.

3686 Old Fashioned Way, The (Paramount, 1934, Joe Morrison, W. C. Fields).

Gathering Shells from the Sea Shore (PC)—Will Thompson (w,m), Shapiro Bernstein; Little Bit of Heaven Known as Mother/Rolling in Love—Mack Gordon, Harry Revel (w,m), DBH. COVER: Joe Morrison, W. C. Fields.

3687 Old Gringo (Columbia, 1989, Gregory Peck, Jane Fonda).

Harriet's Theme—Lee Holdridge (m), Burbank. COVER: Gregory Peck, Jane Fonda, Jimmy Smits.

3688 Old Homestead, The (Paramount, 1922, Theodore Roberts, George Fawcett).

Old Homestead, The—Milt Hagen (w,m), Ponce. COVER: Sketches.

3689 Old Homestead, The (Liberty, 1935, Mary Carlisle, Lawrence Gray).

Moonlight in Heaven—Jack Scholl (w), Louis Alter (m), Harms; Plowboy—J. Keirn Brennan (w), Ted Snyder (m), Harms; Somehow I Knew—Charles Rosoff, Harry Tobias, Neil Moret (w,m), Harms; When Our Old Age Pension Check Comes to Our Door—Manny Stone (w,m), Harms. COVER: Mary Carlisle, Lawrence Gray, Lillian Miles.

3690 Old Ironsides (Paramount, 1927, Charles Farrell, Esther Ralston).

Old Ironsides March—Hugo Riesenfeld (m), Robbins; Old Ironsides Music Score—Hugo Riesenfeld, J. S. Zamecnik (m), Sam Fox; Your Love Is All—Harry Kerr (w), J. S. Zamecnik (m), Sam Fox. COVER: Charles Farrell, Esther Ralston, and Ship.

3691 Old Man and the Sea, The (Warner Bros., 1958, Spencer Tracy, Harry Bellavar).

I Am Your Dream—Paul F. Webster (w), Dimitri Tiomkin (m), Witmark; Old Man and the Sea Theme—Dimitri Tiomkin (m). COVER: Spencer Tracy, and Boat.

3692 Old Man Rhythm (RKO, 1935, Buddy Rogers, Betty Grable).

Boys Will Be Boys, Girls Will Be Girls/Comes the Revolution Baby/I Never Saw a Better Night/Old Man Rhythm/There'e Nothing Like a College Education/When You Are in My Arms—Johnny Mercer (w), Lewis Gensler (m), Berlin. COVER: Buddy Rogers, and Girls.

3693 Old Swimming Hole, The (First National, 1921, Charles Ray, Laura Laplante).

Back to the Old Swimming Hole—Clinton Jones (w), Roy Bergstrom, Richard Hays, Edwin Michael (m), Pan. COVER: Charles Ray.

3694 Old West, The (Columbia, 1952, Gene Autry, Pat Buttram).

Somebody Bigger Than You and I—Johnny Lange, Hy Heath, Sonny Burke (w,m), Bullseye. COVER: Gene Autry.

3695 Old Wyoming Trail, The (Columbia, 1937, Charles Starrett, Donald Grayson).

Love Song of the Waterfall—Bob Nolan, Bernard Barnes, Carl Winge (w,m), CrossWinge; Ridin' Home—Bob Nolan (w,m), CrossWinge. COVER: Donald Grayson.

3696 Old Yeller (Buena Vista, 1957, Dorothy McGuire, Fess Parker).

Old Yeller—Gil George (w), Oliver Wallace (m), Disney. COVER: A Dog.

3697 Oliver (Columbia, 1968, Ron Moody, Oliver Reed).

As Long as He Needs Me/Consider Yourself/I'd Do Anything/It's a Fine Life/Oom pah pha/Oliver/Pick a Pocket or Two/Where Is Love?/Who Will Buy?/Be Back Soon (VS)/Boy for Sale (VS)/Food, Glorious Food (VS)/Reviewing the Situation (VS)—Lionel Bart (w,m), TRO. COVER: Mark Lester, and Movie Scenes.

3698 Oliver and Company (Buena Vista, 1988, Cartoon).

Good Company (VS)—Robert Minkoff, Ron Rocha (w,m), Wonderland; Once Upon a Time in New York City (VS)—Howard Ashman (w), Barry Mann (m), Wonderland; Perfect Isn't Easy (VS)—Jack Feldman, Bruce Sussman (w), Barry Manilow (m), Wonderland; Streets of Gold (VS)—Dean Pitchford (w), Tom Snow (m), Wonderland; Why Should I Worry (VS)—Dan Hartman, Charlie Midnight (w,m), Wonderland. COVER: Cartoon.

3699 Oliver's Story (Paramount, 1978, Ryan O'Neal, Candice Bergen).

Music's Too Sweet Not to Dance To, The—John Korty (w), Francis Lai (m), Famous. COVER: Ryan O'Neal, Candice Bergen.

3700 Oliver Twist (First National, 1922, Jackie Coogan, Lon Chaney).

Oliver Twist—Vaughn DeLeath (w,m), Witmark. COVER: Jackie Coogan.

3701 Oliver Twist (Monogram, 1933, Dickie Moore, Irving Pichel).
Poor Oliver Twist—Joan Jasmyn (w), M. K. Jerome (m), Mills. COVER: Dickie Moore.

3702 Oliver Twist (United Artists, 1948, Alec Guinness, Robert Newton).
Oliver Twist-Two Themes (B)—Arnold Bax (m), Chappell. COVER: Black and white cover with title only.

3703 O Lucky Man (Warner Bros., 1973, Malcolm McDowell, Ralph Richardson).
O Lucky Man-Eight Songs—Alan Price (w,m), Warner. COVER: Malcolm McDowell.

3704 Omar Khayyam (Paramount, 1957, Cornel Wilde, Michael Rennie).
Loves of Omar Khayyam—Victor Young (m), Famous; Take My Heart —Mack David (w), Victor Young (m), Famous; Tell My Love—Jay Livingston, Ray Evans (w), Victor Young (m), Famous. COVER: Cornel Wilde, and Movie Scenes.

3705 Omen, The (20th Century-Fox, 1976, Gregory Peck, Lee Remick).
Ave Satani (PC)—Jerry Goldsmith (m), Fox; Piper Dreams, The—Carol Heather (m), Jerry Goldsmith (m), Fox. COVER: Gregory Peck, Lee Remick.

3706 On a Clear Day You Can See Forever (Paramount, 1970, Barbra Streisand, Yves Montand).
Come Back to Me/Go to Sleep (VS)/Hurry, It's Lovely Up Here/ Love with All the Trimmings (VS)/ Melinda/On a Clear Day You Can See Forever/What Did I Have That I Don't Have—Alan Jay Lerner (w), Burton Lane (m), Chappell. COVER: Barbra Streisand.

3707 On Again Off Again (RKO, 1937, Bert Wheeler, Bob Woolsey).
Thanks to You—Dave Dreyer, Herman Ruby (w,m), Santly Joy. COVER: Bert Wheeler, Bob Woolsey, Marjorie Lord.

3708 On an Island with You (MGM, 1948, Esther Williams, Peter Lawford).
Charrisse—William Katz (w), Nacio Herb Brown (m), Miller; If I Were You/On an Island with You—Edward Heyman (w), Nacio Herb Brown (m), Miller; Rhumba at the Waldorf—Xavier Cugat, Jose Murand (m), Pemora; Takin' Miss Mary to the Ball—Edward Heyman (w), Nacio Herb Brown (m), Miller. COVER: Esther Williams, Peter Lawford, Ricardo Montalban, Jimmy Durante.

3709 On Any Sunday (Cinema Give, 1971, Steve McQueen, Malcolm Smith).
On Any Sunday—Sally Stevens (w), Dominic Frontiere (m), Colgems. COVER: Yellow cover with title only.

3710 Once a Thief (United Artists, 1950, June Havoc, Cesar Romero).
Candlelight/He's Good for Nothin'/Tijuana Tilly—John Stephens (w), Michel Michelet (m), BMI. COVER: Cesar Romero, June Havoc.

3711 Once Before I Die (Seven Arts, 1966, John Derek, Ursula Andress).
Once Before I Die—Norman Gimbel, Ralph London (w,m), Seven Arts. COVER: Ursula Andress, John Derek.

3712 Once in a Blue Moon (Paramount, 1936, Jimmy Savo, Nikita Balieff).
Sugar Cookie Mountain—Billy Rose (w), Mabel Wayne (m), Harms. COVER: Cookies.

3713 Once in a Lifetime (Security Benefit, 1941, Commercial Film).
Once in a Lifetime—Larry Sherwood (w,m), Security Benefit. COVER: Sketch of Couple.

3714 Once Is Not Enough (Paramount, 1974, Kirk Douglas, Alexis Smith).
Once Is Not Enough Theme—

Henry Mancini (m), Famous. COVER: Naked Couple.

3715 Once to Every Woman (Universal, 1919, Dorothy Phillips, Rudolph Valentino).

Ben Bolt—Thomas English (w,m), Temple. COVER: Dorothy Phillips.

3716 Once Upon a Dream (That Night With You) (Universal, 1945, Franchot Tone, Susanna Foster).

Once Upon a Dream—Jack Brooks (w), Hans Salter (m), Robbins. COVER: Black and white cover with title only.

3717 Once Upon a Honeymoon (Fairbanks Bell, 1956, Virginia Gibson, Ward Ellis).

Castle in the Sky/Wishing Song, The—Al Stewart (w), Richard Pribor (m), Sigma. COVER: Virginia Gibson, Ward Ellis.

3718 Once Upon a Horse (Universal, 1958, Dick Martin, Dan Rowan).

Once Upon a Horse—Jay Livingston, Ray Evans (w,m), Northern. COVER: Dick Martin, Dan Rowan, Martha Hyer.

3719 Once Upon a Time (Metropolitan Life, 1945, Cartoon).

Think About Your Safety—Frank Speidell (w), Edwin Long (m), Audio. COVER: Cartoon.

3720 Once Upon a Time in America (Warner Bros., 1984, Robert De Niro, James Woods).

Once Upon a Time in America Theme—Ennio Morricone (m), Warner. COVER: Statue of Liberty, Robert De Niro, James Woods.

3721 Once Upon a Time in the West (Paramount, 1969, Henry Fonda, Jason Robards).

Once Upon a Time in the West Theme—Ennio Morricone (m), Famous. COVER: Henry Fonda, Jason Robards, Claudia Cardinale.

3722 One and Only, The (Paramount, 1977, Henry Winkler, Kim Darby).

One and Only, The—Alan Bergman, Marilyn Bergman (w), Patrick Williams (m), Famous. COVER: Henry Winkler, Kim Darby.

3723 One and Only Genuine Original Family Band, The (Buena Vista, 1968, John Davidson, Leslie Ann Warren).

Bout Time/Dakota/Drummin' Drummin' Drummin'/Oh Benjamin Harrison/One and Only Genuine Original Family Band/Ten Feet Off the Ground/West of the Wide Missouri—Richard Sherman, Robert Sherman (w,m), Wonderland. COVER: John Davidson, Leslie Ann Warren, Movie Scenes.

3724 One Dark Night (Million Dollar, 1939, Manton Moreland, Betty Treadville).

Alone Again/Sharpest Man in Town—Johnny Lange, Lew Porter (w,m), Mills. COVER: Green cover with title only.

3725 One Exciting Night (You Can't Do Without Love) (Columbia, 1944, Donald Stewart, Vera Lynn).

One Love—Jack Popplewell (w, m), Maurice; There's a New World Over the Skyline—J. Turner, W. Ridley, David Heneker (w,m), Maurice. COVER: Vera Lynn.

3726 One Eyed Jacks (Paramount, 1959, Marlon Brando, Karl Malden).

Ballad of One Eyed Jacks—McKayla Morgan (w,m), Famous; One Eyed Jacks Love Theme—Hugo Friedhofer (m), Famous. COVER: Marlon Brando.

3727 One Flew Over the Cuckoo's Nest (United Artists, 1975, Jack Nicholson, Louise Fletcher).

One Flew Over the Cuckoo's Nest—Jack Nitzsche (w,m), Prestige; One Flew Over the Cuckoo's Nest-Eleven Themes—Jack Nitzsche (m), Prestige. COVER: Jack Nicholson.

3728 One Heavenly Night (United Artists, 1930, Evelyn Laye, John Boles).

Along the Road of Dreams—Clifford Grey (w), Bruno Granischstaedten (m), Brown; Heavenly Night—

Edward Eliscu (w), Nacio Herb Brown (m), Brown. COVER: Evelyn Laye.

3729 One Hour Late (Paramount, 1935, Joe Morrison, Helen Twelvetrees).

Little Angel Told Me So—Sam Coslow (w,m), Famous; Me Without You—Leo Robin, Lewis Gensler (w, m), Famous. COVER: Joe Morrison, Helen Twelvetrees.

3730 One Hour With You (Paramount, 1932, Maurice Chevalier, Jeanette MacDonald).

Oh That Mitzi—Leo Robin (w), Oscar Straus (m), Famous; One Hour With You—Leo Robin (w), Richard Whiting (m), Famous; We Will Always Be Sweethearts—Leo Robin (w), Oscar Straus (m), Famous; What Would You Do—Leo Robin (w), Richard Whiting (m), Famous. COVER: Maurice Chevalier, Jeanette MacDonald.

3731 One Hundred and One Dalmatians (Buena Vista, 1961, Cartoon).

Cruella DeVille/Dalmatian Plantation—Mel Leven (w,m), Disney; One Hundred and One Dalmatians—Richard Sherman, Robert Sherman (w, m), Disney; Playful Melody—By Dunham, George Bruns (w,m), Disney. COVER: A Dog.

3732 One Hundred Men and a Girl (Universal, 1937, Deanna Dubbin, Adolphe Menjou).

Heart That's Free, A—Thomas Railey (w), Alfred Robyn (m), Feist; Alleluja (VS)—Carl Deis, W. A. Mozart (w,m), Schirmer; It's Raining Sunbeams/Music in My Dreams—Sam Coslow (w), Frederick Hollander (m), Feist. COVER: Deanna Durbin, Leopold Stokowski, Adolphe Menjou.

3733 One Hundred Rifles (20th Century-Fox, 1969, Jim Brown, Raquel Welch).

One Hundred Rifles Theme— Jerry Goldsmith (m), Fox. COVER: Jim Brown, Raquel Welch.

3734 One in a Million (20th Century-Fox, 1936, Sonja Henie, Don Ameche).

Lovely Lady in White/Moonlit Waltz/One in a Million/We're Back in Circulation—Sidney Mitchell (w), Lew Pollack (m), Hollywood. COVER: Sonja Henie, Don Ameche, and Others.

3735 One Mad Kiss (Fox, 1930, Mona Maris, Jose Majica).

Monkey on a String—Joe McCarthy (m), James Hanley (m), Red Star.

3736 One Minute to Zero (RKO, 1952, Robert Mitchum, Ann Blyth).

Golden Moon, China Night—Norman Bennett (w), Nobuyuki Takeoka (m), Clare; When I Fall in Love—Edward Heyman (w), Victor Young (m), COVER: Robert Mitchum, Ann Blyth.

3737 One More Tomorrow (Warner Bros., 1946, Ann Sheridan, Dennis Morgan).

One More Tomorrow—Ernesto Lecuona, Eddie DeLange, Josef Myrow (w,m), Remick. COVER: Ann Sheridan, Dennis Morgan, Jack Carson, Alexis Smith.

3738 One Night in the Tropics (Caribbean Holiday) (Universal, 1940, Allan Jones, Nancy Kelly).

Back in My Shell/Remind Me/ You and Your Kiss—Dorothy Fields (w), Jerome Kern (m), Harms; Your Dream—Oscar Hammerstein, Otto Harbach (w), Jerome Kern (m), Harms. COVER: Allan Jones, Nancy Kelly, Robert Cummings.

3739 One Night of Love (Columbia, 1934, Grace Moore, Tullio Carminati).

One Night of Love—Gus Kahn (w), Victor Schertzinger (m), Berlin. COVER: Grace Moore.

3740 One on One (Warner Bros., 1977, Robby Benson, Annette O'Toole).

My Fair Share/One on One-Five Songs—Paul Williams (w), Charles Fox (m), Warner. COVER: Robby Benson, Annette O'Toole.

3741 One on the House (Vitaphone, 1938, Diane Denise).

Everything You Said Came True—
Cliff Friend, Dave Franklin (w,
m), Remick, COVER: Diane Denise.

3742 One Potato Two Potato
(British Lion, 1964, Barbara Barrie,
Bernie Hamilton).

One Potato, Two Potato—Gerald
Fried (w,m), Cimino. COVER: Barbara Barrie, Bernie Hamilton.

3743 One Rainy Afternoon
(United Artists, 1935, Ida Lupino,
Hugh Herbert).

One Rainy Afternoon—Jack Stern,
Harry Tobias (w), Ralph Erwin (m),
Sam Fox; Secret Rendezvous—Pres-
ton Sturges (w), Ralph Erwin (m),
Sam Fox. COVER: Ida Lupino,
Francis Lederer.

3744 One Stolen Night (Warner
Bros., 1929, Betty Bronson, William
Collier).

My Cairo Love—Harry Kerr (w),
J. S. Zamecnik (m), Sam Fox. COV-
ER: Betty Bronson.

3745 One Sunday Afternoon
(Warner Bros., 1948, Dennis Morgan,
Janis Paige)

Girls Were Made to Take Care of
Boys/One Sunday Afternoon—Ralph
Blane (w,m), Remick. COVER:
Dennis Morgan, Janis Paige, Don
DeFore, Dorothy Malone.

3746 One Third of a Nation
(Paramount, 1939, Sylvia Sidney,
Leif Erikson).

That's How Dreams Should End—
Harold Orlob (w,m), Schirmer.
COVER: Young Boys.

**3747 One Thousand and One
Arabian Nights** (Columbia, 1959,
Cartoon).

Magoo's Blues/You Are My
Dream—Ned Washington (w), George
Duning (m), Colgems. COVER: A
Cartoon.

**3748 One Thousand Dollars a
Touchdown** (Paramount, 1939, Joe
E. Brown, Martha Raye).

Love with a Capital "You"—Leo
Robin, Ralph Rainger (w,m), Paramount. COVER: Martha Raye.

3749 One Too Many (Hallmark,
1951, Ruth Warrick, Ginger Prince).

Everyone Was Meant for Someone
—Nelly Goletti (w,m), Bibo; How
Long—Bunny Lewis (w), Nelly Go-
letti (m), Bibo; I Don't Know Why I
Love You—Bill Copeland, Harmon-
aires (w,m), Bibo; Peace Is Every-
where—John Stephens (w), Nelly
Goletti (m), Music City; Ridin' the
Roller Coaster—John Stephens, Irv-
ing Bibo (w,m), Bibo. COVER: Ruth
Warrick, Ginger Prince, Harmonaires.

3750 One Touch of Venus (Universal, 1948, Robert Walker, Ava
Gardner).

My Heart Is Showing/My Week—
Ann Ronell (w), Kurt Weill (m),
Chappell; Speak Low—Ogden Nash
(w), Kurt Weill (m), Chappell. COV-
ER: Ava Gardner.

3751 One Trick Pony (Warner
Bros., 1979, Paul Simon, Rip Torn).

Late in the Evening/One Trick
Pony/One Trick Pony-Ten Songs—
Paul Simon (w,m), Warner. COVER:
Paul Simon.

3752 One Two Three (United
Artists, 1962, James Cagney, Horst
Buchholz).

One Two Three Waltz—Dory
Previn (w), André Previn (m), Unart.
COVER: Girl With Balloons.

3753 One Week of Life (Goldwyn, 1919, Pauline Frederick,
Thomas Holding).

Greatest Love of All-Leo Wood
(w,m), Wood. COVER: Pauline Frederick.

3754 One Wonderful Night (Essanay, 1914, Francis X. Bushman,
Lillian Drew).

One Wonderful Night You Told
Me You Loved Me—J. Lyons, E.
Keithley, C. Jones (w,m), Root; One
Wonderful Night Waltz—Uriel Davis
(m), Remick. COVER: Francis X.
Bushman.

3755 On Golden Pond (Universal, 1982, Henry Fonda, Jane Fonda).

On Golden Pond Theme—Dave
Grusin (m), ATV. COVER: Henry

Fonda, Jane Fonda, Katharine Hepburn.

3756 On Her Majesty's Secret Service (United Artists, 1969, George Lazenby, Diana Rigg).

Do You Know How Christmas Trees Are Grown—Hal David (w), John Barry (m), Unart; On Her Majesty's Secret Service Theme—John Barry (m), Unart; We Have All the Time in the World—Hal David (w), John Barry (m), Unart. COVER: George Lazenby, and Girls.

3757 Only Saps Work (Paramount, 1930, Leon Errol, Richard Arlen).

Find the Girl—Ballard MacDonald, Dave Dreyer (w,m), Famous. COVER: Leon Errol.

3758 Only When I Larf (Paramount, 1968, David Hemmings, Richard Attenborough).

Only When I Larf/Only When I Larf Music Score—Ron Grainer (m), Famous. COVER: David Hemmings, Richard Attenborough.

3759 Only When I Laugh (Columbia, 1981, Marsha Mason, Kristy McNichols).

Only When I Laugh—Richard Maltby (w), David Shire (m), Gold Horizon. COVER: Marsha Mason, Kristy McNichols.

3760 Only Woman, The (First National, 1924, Eugene O'Brien, Norma Talmadge).

Was It a Dream?—B. G. DeSylva, Larry Spier (w,m), Harms. COVER: Norma Talmadge.

3761 Only Yesterday (Universal, 1933, John Boles, Margaret Sullavan).

Only Yesterday—Walter Donaldson (w,m), Robbins. COVER: John Boles, Margaret Sullavan.

3762 On Moonlight Bay (Warner Bros., 1951 Doris Day, Gordon MacRae).

Christmas Story—Pauline Walsh (w,m), Remick; I'm Forever Blowing Bubbles—Jaan Kenbrovin, John Kellette (w,m), Remick; Love Ya—Charles Tobias (w), Peter DeRose

(m), Harms; Moonlight Bay—Ed Madden (w), Percy Wenrich (m), Remick; Tell Me—J. Will Callahan (w), Max Kortlander (m), Remick; Till We Meet Again—Ray Egan (w), Richard Whiting (m), Remick. COVER: Doris Day, Gordon Macrae.

3763 On My Way to the Crusades, I Met a Girl Who . . .(The Chastity Belt) (Warner Bros., 1969, Tony Curtis, Monica Vitti).

Blue Lace—Bill Jacob, Patti Jacob (w), Riz Ortolani (m), Warner. COVER: Frank Sinatra.

3764 On Stage Everybody (Universal, 1945, Peggy Ryan, Jack Oakie).

Stuff Like That There—Jay Livingston, Ray Evans (w,m), Capitol. COVER: King Sisters.

3765 On the Air and Off (Universal, 1933, Nick Lucas).

Lonely Moonlight Troubadour—Ballard MacDonald (w), Milton Schwarzwald (m), Miller. COVER: Nick Lucas.

3766 On the Avenue (20th Century-Fox, 1937, Alice Faye, Dick Powell).

Girl on the Police Gazette/He Ain't Got Rhythm/I've Got My Love to Keep Me Warm/Slumming on Park Avenue/This Year's Kisses/You're Laughing at Me—Irving Berlin (w, m), Berlin. COVER: Dick Powell, Madeleine Carroll, Alice Faye, Ritz Brothers.

3767 On the Banks of the Wabash (Vitagraph, 1923, Mary Carr, Madge Evans).

On the Banks of the Wabash—Paul Dresser (w,m), Richmond Robbins. COVER: Mary Carr, Madge Evans.

3768 On the Beach (United Artists, 1959, Fred Astaire, Gregory Peck).

On the Beach—Steve Allen (w), Ernest Gold (m), Planetary; There's Still Time Brother—Paul Vance, Jack Segal (w,m), Planetary; Waltzing Matilda—A. Paterson (w), Marie Cowan (m), Fischer. COVER: Fred Astaire,

Gregory Peck, Ava Gardner, Tony Perkins.

3769 On the Double (Paramount, 1961, Danny Kaye, Dana Wynter).

Darlin' Meggie—Sylvia Fine (w,m), Dena. COVER: Danny Kaye, Dana Wynter, Diana Dors.

3770 On the Fiddle (Operation Snafu) (AIP, 1965, Sean Connery, Alfred Lynch).

On the Fiddle (B)—Malcolm Arnold (m), Henrees. COVER: Sean Connery, Alfred Lynch.

3771 On the Old Spanish Trail (Republic, 1947, Roy Rogers, Tito Guizar).

On the Old Spanish Trail—Kenneth Smith, Jimmy Kennedy (w, m), Maurice. COVER: Roy Rogers.

3772 On the Riviera (20th Century-Fox, 1951, Danny Kaye, Gene Tierney).

Ballin' the Jack—Jim Burris (w), Chris Smith (m), Marks; Happy Ending/On the Riviera—Sylvia Fine (w, m), Robbins; Popo the Puppet—Sylvia Fine (w,m), Pickwick; Rhythm of a New Romance—Sylvia Fine (w,m), Robbins. COVER: Danny Kaye, Gene Tierney, Corinne Calvet.

3773 On the Town (MGM, 1949, Frank Sinatra, Gene Kelly).

Count on Me/Main Street—Betty Comden, Adolf Green (w), Roger Edens (m), Witmark; New York New York—Betty Comden, Adolf Green (w), Leonard Bernstein (m), Witmark; On the Town (PC)/You're Awful—Betty Comden, Adolf Green (w), Roger Edens (m), Witmark. COVER: Frank Sinatra, Gene Kelly, Ann Miller, Betty Garrett.

3774 On the Verge of a Merge (Warner Bros., 1928, Bud Morris, Carlyn Nathan).

Because You Belong to Me—Louie Cuim (w,m), Witmark. COVER: Bud Morris, Carlyn Nathan.

3775 On the Waterfront (Columbia, 1954, Marlon Brando, Karl Malden).

On the Waterfront—John Latouche (w), Leonard Bernstein (m), Robbins. COVER: Marlon Brando, Eva Marie Saint.

3776 On Top of Old Smoky (Columbia, 1953, Gene Autry, Smiley Burnette).

If It Wasn't for the Rain (VS)—Gene Autry, Fred Rose (w,m), Western. COVER: Gene Autry.

3777 On with the Show (Warner Bros., 1929, Joe E. Brown, Betty Compson).

Am I Blue/Birmingham Bertha/Don't It Mean a Thing to You/In the Land of Let's Pretend/Let Me Have My Dreams/Lift the Juleps to Your Two Lips/Welcome Home—Grant Clarke (w), Harry Akst (m), Witmark. COVER: Show Girl.

3778 Open the Door and See All the People (Hill, 1964, Charles Rydell, Ellen Martin).

Open the Door and See All the People-Seven Songs—William Engvick (w), Alec Wilder (m), Hollis. COVER: Alec Wilder.

3778a Operation Bikini (AIP, 1963, Tab Hunter, Frankie Avalon).

Operation Bikini Theme (PC)—Les Baxter (m), Harlene. COVER: None.

3779 Operation Eichmann (Allied Artists, 1961, Werner Klemperer, Ruta Lee).

David's Theme—Alex Alexander, June Starr (m), Robbins. COVER: Donald Buka, Barbara Turner.

3780 Operation Madball (Columbia, 1957, Jack Lemmon, Ernie Kovacs).

Mad Ball—Richard Quine (w), Fred Karger (m), Colgems. COVER: Jack Lemmon, Ernie Kovacs, Mickey Rooney.

3781 Operator's Opera (Vitaphone, 1933, Musical Short).

Walkin' in the Wind With You—Cliff Hess (w,m), Witmark. COVER: Black and white cover with title only.

3782 Operator Thirteen (MGM, 1934, Marion Davies, Gary Cooper).

Jungle Fever—Howard Dietz (w), Walter Donaldson (m), Robbins; Once in a Lifetime/Sleepy Head—Gus Kahn (w), Walter Donaldson (m), Robbins. COVER: Marion Davies, Gary Cooper.

3783 Opposite Sex, The (MGM, 1956, June Allyson, Joan Collins).

Now Baby Now/Opposite Sex, The/Perfect Love/Rock and Roll Tumbleweeds—Sammy Cahn (w), Nicholas Brodszky (m), Robbins; Young Man with a Horn—Ralph Freed (w), George Stoll (m), Feist. COVER: June Allyson, Joan Collins, Dolores Gray, Ann Sheridan, Ann Miller.

3784 Orange Bird, The (Buena Vista, 1970, Cartoon).

Orange Bird-Six Songs—Richard Sherman, Robert Sherman (w,m), Wonderland. COVER: A Bird.

3785 Orchestra Wives (20th Century-Fox, 1942, Glenn Miller, George Montgomery).

At Last—Mack Gordon (w), Harry Warren (m), Feist; Kalamazoo/People Like You and Me/Serenade in Blue/That's Sabotage—Mack Gordon (w), Harry Warren (m), BVC. COVER: Glenn Miller, George Montgomery, Ann Rutherford, and Others.

3786 Ordinary People (Paramount, 1980, Donald Sutherland, Mary Tyler Moore).

Ordinary People Theme—Marvin Hamlisch (m), Chappell. COVER: Gray cover with title only.

3787 Orphan Sally (LBR, 1922, Maud Sylvester, Flora Finch).

Sally—Jay Flanagan (w,m), Lee Bradford. COVER: Maud Sylvester.

3788 Orphans of the Storm (United Artists, 1922, Lillian Gish, Dorothy Gish).

Chevalier March—William F. Peters (m), Harms. COVER: Lillian and Dorothy Gish.

3789 Oscar, The (Embassy, 1966, Stephen Boyd, Elke Sommer).

Glass Mountain/Maybe September —Jay Livingston, Ray Evans (w),

Percy Faith (m), Levine. COVER: Stephen Boyd, Elke Sommer, Milton Berle, and Others.

3790 O'Shaughnessy's Boy (MGM, 1934, Wallace Beery, Jackie Cooper).

Tattooed Lady, The—Walter O'—Keefe (w,m), Robbins. COVER: Wallace Beery.

3790a Oswald the Rabbit (Lantz, 1956, Cartoon).

Oswald the Rabbit Hop—Irving Bibo, Clarence Wheeler (w,m), Bibo. COVER: Cartoon.

3791 Other, The (20th Century-Fox, 1972, Uta Hagen, Diana Muldaur).

The Other Theme—Tom Tryon (w), Jerry Goldsmith (m), Fox. COVER: Young Boy.

3792 Other Side of Midnight, The (20th Century-Fox, 1977, John Beck, Marie F. Pisier).

Faded Roses—Carol Connors (w), Michel Legrand (m), Fox; Noelle's Theme—Michel Legrand (m), Fox. COVER: A Man and Woman and Rose.

3793 Other Side of the Mountain (Universal, 1972, Marilyn Hassett, Beau Bridges).

Richard's Window—Norman Gimbel (w), Charles Fox (m), Duchess. COVER: Marilyn Hassett, Beau Bridges.

3794 Other Side of the Mountain-Part Two (Universal, 1978, Marilyn Hassett, Timothy Bottoms).

It's Time to Say I Love You—Molly Ann Leikin (w), Lee Holdridge (m), Leeds. COVER: Marilyn Hassett, Timothy Bottoms.

3795 Otley (Columbia, 1969, Tom Courtenay, Romy Schneider).

Tell Her You Love Her—Hal Shaper (w), Stanley Myers (m), Colgems. COVER: Tom Courtenay, Romy Schneider.

3796 Our Dancing Daughters (Dancing Daughters) (MGM, 1927, Joan Crawford, Johnny Mack Brown).

I Loved You Then—Ballard Mac-

Donald, William Axt, David Mendoza (w,m), Berlin. COVER: Joan Crawford.

3797 Our Gang (Roach, 1925, Allen Farina, Joe Cobb).

L'il Farina—Harrison Smith (w), Alvano Mier (m), Mier. COVER: Allen Farina.

3798 Our Gang (Roach, 1936, Our Gang).

Our Gang—Dave Franklin (w,m), Robbins. COVER: Our Gang.

3799 Our Hearts Were Young and Gay (Paramount, 1944, Gail Russell, Diana Lynn).

Duna—Marjorie Pickthall (w), Josephine McGill (m), Boosey Hawkes; Je Ris—Willis Wager, Nina Koshetz (w,m), Schirmer; When Our Hearts Were Young and Gay—Kermit Goell (w), Ted Grouya (m), Famous. COVER: Gail Russell, Diana Lynn, and Boy Friends.

3800 Our Little Girl (Fox, 1935, Shirley Temple, Rosemary Ames).

Our Little Girl—Paul F. Webster (w), Lew Pollack (m), Movietone. COVER: Shirley Temple.

3801 Our Man Flint (20th Century-Fox, 1965, James Coburn, Lee J. Cobb).

Our Man Flint Theme—Jerry Goldsmith (m), Hastings. COVER: James Coburn, and Girls.

3802 Our Man in Havana (Columbia, 1960, Alec Guinness, Maureen O'Hara).

Love Me Now—Al Stillman (w), Joseph White (m), Chappell. COVER: Maureen O'Hara, Alec Guinness, Burl Ives, Ernie Kovacs.

3803 Our Modern Maidens (MGM, 1929, Joan Crawford, Douglas Fairbanks).

I've Waited a Lifetime for You—Joe Goodwin (w), Gus Edwards (m), Robbins; Should I—Arthur Freed (w), Nacio Herb Brown (m), Robbins. COVER: Joan Crawford.

3804 Our Mother's House (MGM, 1967, Dirk Bogarde, Margaret Brooks).

Our Mother's House Theme—George Delerue (m), Miller. COVER: Dirk Bogarde, and Girl.

3805 Our Town (United Artists, 1945, William Holden, Frank Craven).

Our Town-Piano Excerpts—Aaron Copland (m), Boosey Hawkes. COVER: A Small Town.

3806 Our Very Own (RKO, 1950, Farley Granger, Ann Blyth).

Our Very Own—Jack Elliott (w), Victor Young (m), Spitzer. COVER: Farley Granger, Ann Blyth.

3807 Outlaw, The (RKO, 1950, Jane Russell, Jack Beutel).

Now and Forever—Al Stillman (w), Jan Savitt (m), Robbins. COVER: Jane Russell.

3808 Outlaws of the Prairie (Columbia, 1937, Charles Starrett, Donald Grayson).

Open Range Ahead (VS)—Bob Nolan (w,m), American; Song of the Bandit (VS)—Bob Nolan (w,m), Cross Winge. COVER: Bob Nolan.

3809 Out of Africa (Universal, 1986, Robert Redford, Meryl Streep).

Let the Rest of the World Go By—J. Keirn Brennan (w), Ernest Ball (m), Warner; Music of Goodbye—Alan Bergman, Marilyn Bergman (w), John Barry (m), MCA; Out of Africa Love Theme/Out of Africa-Five Themes—John Barry (m), MCA. COVER: Robert Redford, Meryl Streep.

3810 Out of the Blue (Eagle Lion, 1947, George Brent, Virginia Mayo).

Out of the Blue—Henry Nemo (w), Will Jason (m), Leeds. COVER: Virginia Mayo, George Brent, Carole Landis.

3811 Out of the Depths (Columbia, 1946, Ken Curtis, Ross Hunter).

Home on the Range (VS)—Paul Earlee (w,m), Preview. COVER: Ken Curtis.

3811a Out of the Inkwell (Fleischer, 1923, Cartoon).

Out of the Inkwell—Jack Blue (w,m), Blue. COVER: Cartoon.

3812 Out of This World (Paramount, 1945, Eddie Bracken, Diana Lynn).

I'd Rather Be Me—Sam Coslow, Eddie Cherkose (w), Felix Bernard (m), Morris; June Comes Around Every Year/Out of This World—Johnny Mercer (w), Harold Arlen (m), Morris. COVER: Eddie Bracken, Diana Lynn, Veronica Lake, Bing Crosby.

3813 Out of Towners (Dear Heart) (Warner Bros., 1964, Glenn Ford, Geraldine Page).

Dear Heart—Jay Livingston, Ray Evans (w), Henry Mancini (m), Northridge. COVER: Black and white cover with title only.

3814 Out of Towners (Paramount, 1970, Jack Lemmon, Sandy Dennis).

Out of Towners Theme—Quincy Jones (m), Famous. COVER: Jack Lemmon, Sandy Dennis.

3815 Outrage, The (MGM, 1964, Paul Newman, Claire Bloom).

Outrage-Theme—Alex North (m), Miller. COVER: Paul Newman, Claire Bloom.

3816 Outside of Paradise (Republic, 1938, Phil Regan, Penny Singleton).

Outside of Paradise/Shenanigans/Sweet Irish Sweetheart of Mine—Peter Tinturin, Jack Lawrence (w, m), Santly Joy. COVER: Sketch of Couple.

3817 Outsider, The (Universal, 1961, Tony Curtis, James Franciscus).

Where Are You—Harold Adamson (w), Jimmy McHugh (m), Feist. COVER: Tony Curtis.

3818 Outsiders, The (Warner Bros., 1984, Matt Dillon, Rob Lowe).

Outside In—Italia Pennino, Roxanne Seeman (w), Carmine Coppola (m), Coppola; Stay Gold—Stevie Wonder (w), Carmine Coppola (m), Jobete. COVER: Matt Dillon, Rob

Lowe, Tom Cruise, Patrick Swayze, Emilio Estevez.

3819 Overlanders, The (Universal, 1946, Chips Rafferty, John Hayward).

Overlanders, The (B)—George Dasey (w,m), Nicholson. COVER: Chips Rafferty, John Hayward, Daphne Campbell.

3820 Over Pine Mountain Trails (Calvin, 1941, Commercial Film).

Over Pine Mountain Trail—Larry Sherwood (w,m), Calvin. COVER: Mountain Scene.

3821 Over the Hill (Fox, 1921, Mary Carr, William Welch).

Over the Hill—Lou Klein (w), Edgar Allen, Maurie Rubens (m), Shapiro Bernstein. COVER: A House on a Hill.

3822 Over the Hill (Fox, 1931, James Dunn, Sally Eilers).

Contented—James Hanley (w,m), Sam Fox. COVER: James Dunn, Sally Eilers, Mae Marsh.

3823 Over the Moon (United Artists, 1940, Merle Oberon, Rex Harrison).

An Old Serenade—Leslie Jones (w), Michael Spoliansky (m), Chappell. COVER: Sketch of Girl.

3824 Over the Top (Vitagraph, 1918, Arthur Empey, Lois Meredith).

Liberty Statue Is Looking Right at You/Our Country's in It Now, We've Got to Win It Now/Your Lips Are No Man's Land But Mine—Arthur Empey (w), Charles McCarren, Carey Morgan (m), Stern. COVER: Arthur Empey.

3825 Over the Top (Warner Bros., 1987, Sylvester Stallone, Robert Loggia).

Meet Me Half Way/Winner Takes It All (PC)—Tom Whitlock (w), Giorgio Moroder (m), Columbia. COVER: Red and yellow cover with title only.

3826 Over the Trail (Over the Santa Fe Trail (Columbia, 1947, Ken Curtis, Hoosier Hot Shots).

Have I Told You Lately That I Love You—Scott Wiseman (w,m), Duchess; Look on the Bright Side— W. Farrell, Howard Johnson, E. Welch (w,m), Duchess. COVER: Hoosier Hot Shots.

3827 Overture to Glory (Jewish Education, 1940, Moishe Oysher, Helen Beverly).

Unter Boimer—Alex Olshanetsky, Moishe Oysher (w,m), Olshanetsky. COVER: Moishe Oysher.

3828 Pack Up Your Troubles (20th Century-Fox, 1939, Jane Withers, Lynn Bari).

Who'll Buy My Flowers?—Sidney Clare (w), Jule Styne (m), Robbins. COVER: Black and white cover with title only.

3829 Pad, and How to Use It, The (Universal, 1966, Brian Bedford, James Farentino).

The Pad and How to Use It— Robert Allen (w,m), Leeds. COVER: Sketches.

3830 Paddy (Allied Artists, 1970, Milo O'Shea, Des Cave).

Paddy—David Colloff (w), John Rubenstein (m), Allied Artists. COVER: Des Cave.

3831 Paddy O'Day (Fox, 1935, Jane Withers, Pinky Tomlin).

I Like a Balalaika (BW)/Keep That Twinkle in Your Eye—Edward Eliscu, Sidney Clare (w), Harry Akst (m), Movietone. COVER: Jane Withers.

3832 Paddy the Next Best Thing (Fox, 1933, Janet Gaynor, Warner Baxter).

Paddy—Lester O'Keefe (w), Louis DeFrancesco (m), Movietone. COVER: Janet Gaynor, Warner Baxter.

3833 Pagan, The (MGM, 1929, Ramon Novarro, Renee Adoree).

Pagan Love Song—Arthur Freed (w), Nacio Herb Brown (m), Robbins. COVER: Ramon Novarro.

3834 Pagan Love Song (MGM, 1950, Howard Keel, Esther Williams).

Etiquette (BW)/Here in Tahiti We Make Love (BW)/House of Singing Bamboo—Arthur Freed (w), Harry Warren (m), Four Jays; Pagan Love Song—Arthur Freed (w), Nacio Herb Brown (m), Robbins; Sea of the Moon/Singing in the Sun—Arthur Freed (w), Harry Warren (m), Robbins; Tahiti—Arthur Freed (w), Harry Warren (m), Four Jays; Why Is Love So Crazy—Arthur Freed (w), Harry Warren (m), Robbins. COVER: Howard Keel, Esther Williams.

3835 Page Miss Glory (Warner Bros., 1935, Marion Davies, Dick Powell).

Page Miss Glory—Al Dubin (w), Harry Warren (m), Harms. COVER: Marion Davies.

3836 Paid in Full (Bitter Victory) (Paramount, 1950, Robert Cummings, Lizabeth Scott).

You're Wonderful—Jay Livingston, Ray Evans (w), Victor Young (m), Famous. COVER: Robert Cummings, Lizabeth Scott.

3837 Painted Angel, The (First National, 1929, Billie Dove, Edmund Lowe).

Bride Without a Groom (BW)— Herman Ruby (w), M. K. Jerome (m), Witmark; Everybody's Darling/ Help Yourself to My Love/Only the Girl—Herman Ruby (w), M. K. Jerome (m), Piantadosi. COVER: Billie Dove.

3838 Painted Faces (Tiffany Stahl, 1929, Joe E. Brown, Helen Foster).

Somebody Just Like You—Abner Silver (w,m), Gem. COVER: Joe E. Brown, Helen Foster.

3839 Painting, The (Jarmel, 1962, Documentary).

While I Paint My Dream—Stanley Adams (w), Paul Taubman (m), Saunders. COVER: Painting of Nude Woman.

3840 Painting the Clouds with Sunshine (Warner Bros., 1951, Dennis Morgan, Virginia Mayo).

Birth of the Blues (B)—B. G. DeSylva, Lew Brown, Ray Henderson (w,m), Chappell; Painting the Clouds with Sunshine—Al Dubin (w), Joe Burke (m), Witmark. COVER: Dennis Morgan, Virginia Mayo, Gene Nelson.

3841 Paint Your Wagon (Paramount, 1969, Lee Marvin, Clint Eastwood).

Another Autumn—Alan Jay Lerner (w), Frederick Loewe (m), Chappell; Best Things/First Thing You Know/Gold Fever/Gospel of No Name City—Alan Jay Lerner (w), André Previn (m), Chappell; I Still See Elisa/I Talk to the Trees/I'm on My Way—Alan Jay Lerner (w), Frederick Loewe (m), Chappell; Million Miles Away Behind the Door, A—Alan Jay Lerner (w), André Previn (m), Chappell; They Call the Wind Maria/Wan'-rin' Star—Alan Jay Lerner (w), Frederick Loewe (m), Chappell. COVER: Lee Marvin, Clint Eastwood, Jean Seberg.

3842 Pajama Game, The (Warner Bros., 1957, John Raitt, Doris Day).

Hernando's Hideaway/Hey There/I'm Not at All in Love/Small Talk/Steam Heat/There Once Was a Man/Once a Year Day Polka (VS)—Richard Adler, Jerry Ross (w,m), Frank. COVER: Doris Day.

3843 Paleface, The (Paramount, 1948, Bob Hope, Jane Russell).

Buttons and Bows/Meetcha Round the Corner—Jay Livingston. Ray Evans (w,m), Famous. COVER: Bob Hope, Jane Russell.

3844 Pal Joey (Columbia, 1957, Frank Sinatra, Rita Hayworth).

Bewitched/Den of Iniquity/Do It the Hard Way/Happy Hunting Horn/I Could Write a Book/I Didn't Know What Time It Was/Lady Is a Tramp/My Funny Valentine/Plant You Now Dig You Later/Take Him/There's a Small Hotel/What Is a Man/You Mustn't Kick It Around/Zip—Lorenz Hart (w), Richard Rodgers (m), Chappell. COVER: Frank Sinatra, Kim Novak, Rita Hayworth.

3845 Palm Springs (Paramount, 1936, Frances Langford, Smith Ballew).

Dreaming Out Loud/Hills of Old Wyomin'/I Don't Want to Make History/Palm Springs—Leo Robin, Ralph Rainger (w,m), Famous; Will I Ever Know—Mack Gordon, Harry Revel (w,m), Famous. COVER: Frances Langford, Smith Ballew.

3846 Palm Springs Weekend (Warner Bros., 1963, Troy Donahue, Connie Stevens).

Live Young—Larry Kusik (w), Paul Evans (m), Witmark. COVER: Troy Donahue, Connie Stevens, Stephanie Powers, Robert Conrad.

3847 Palmy Days (United Artists, 1931, Eddie Cantor, Charlotte Greenwood).

Bend Down Sister—Ballard MacDonald, Dave Silverstein (w), Con Conrad (m), Conrad; Dunk Dunk Dunk—Ballard MacDonald (w), Con Conrad (m), Conrad; There's Nothing Too Good for My Baby—Eddie Cantor, Benny Davis, Harry Akst (w,m), Davis; Yes Yes*—Con Conrad, Cliff Friend (w,m), Conrad. COVER: Eddie Cantor, and Chorus Girls. *(Regular Cover and a Special Eddie Cantor Cover.)

3848 Palooka (Joe Palooka) (United Artists, 1934, Jimmy Durante, Lupe Velez).

Inka Dinka Doo—Jimmy Durante, Ben Ryan, Harry Donnelly (w,m), Berlin; Like Me a Little Bit Less—Harold Adamson (w), Burton Lane (m), Berlin; Palooka—Ann Ronell, Johnny Burke (w,m), Berlin. COVER: Jimmy Durante, Lupe Velez, Stuart Erwin.

3849 Panama Hattie (MGM, 1942, Red Skelton, Ann Sothern).

At the Club Savoy—Walter Donaldson (w,m), Chappell; Fresh as a Daisy/I've Still Got My Health/Let's Be Buddies—Cole Porter (w, m), Chappell; Son of a Gun Who Picks on Uncle Sam—E. Y. Harburg (w), Burton Lane (m), Chappell. COVER: Ann Sothern, Red Skelton, Rags Ragland.

3850 Pan Americana (RKO, 1945, Phillip Terry, Audrey Long).

Stars in Your Eyes—Mort Greene (w), Gabriel Ruiz (m), Southern. COVER: Phillip Terry, Audrey Long, and Dancers.

3851 Panamint's Bad Man (20th Century-Fox, 1938, Smith Ballew, Evelyn Daw).

Got Some Ridin' to Do—Mort Greene (w), Fred Stryker (m), Hollywood. COVER: Smith Ballew.

3852 Pandora and the Flying Dutchman (MGM, 1951, Ava Gardner, James Mason).

How Am I to Know—Dorothy Parker (w), Jack King (m), Robbins; Pandora—Albert Lewin (w), Johnny Green (m), Miller. COVER: Ava Gardner.

3853 Panic in Year Zero (AIP, 1962, Ray Milland, Jean Hagen).

Panic in Year Zero-Three Themes (PC)—Les Baxter (m), Harlene. COVER: None.

3854 Papa's Delicate Condition (Paramount, 1963, Jackie Gleason, Glynis Johns).

Call Me Irresponsible—Sammy Cahn (w), James Van Heusen (m), Paramount. COVER: Jackie Gleason.

3855 Paper Chase, The (20th Century-Fox, 1973, Timothy Bottoms, Lindsay Wagner).

I Want to Spend My Life With You—Larry Weiss (w), John Williams (m), Fox. COVER: Timothy Bottoms, Lindsay Wagner.

3856 Paper Tiger (Levine, 1973, David Niven, Hardy Kruger).

My Little Friend/Who Knows the Answers?—Sammy Cahn (w), Roy Budd (m), Famous. COVER: David Niven, and Movie Scene.

3857 Papillon (Allied Artists, 1973, Steve McQueen, Dustin Hoffman).

Free as the Wind—Jerry Goldsmith (m), Soultown. COVER: Steve McQueen, Dustin Hoffman.

3858 Paradise (Embassy, 1982, Willie Aames, Phoebe Cates).

Paradise—Joel Diamond, Russell Brown (w,m), Silver. COVER: Phoebe Cates.

3859 Paradise Hawaiian Style (Paramount, 1966, Elvis Presley, Suzanna Leigh).

Blue Hawaii—Leo Robin, Ralph Rainger (w,m), Famous; Datin'—Fred Wise, Randy Starr (w,m), Gladys; Dog's Life, A—Sid Wayne, Ben Weisman (w,m), Gladys; Drums of the Islands—Sid Tepper, Roy Bennett (w,m), Gladys; House of Sand/Queenie Wahine's Papaya/Scratch My Back/Stop Where You Are/This Is Heaven—Bill Giant, Bernie Baum, Florence Kaye (w,m), Presley. COVER: Elvis Presley.

3860 Paradise Isle (Monogram, 1937, Movita, Warren Hull).

Paradise Isle—Sam Koki (m), Mills. COVER: Movita, Warren Hull.

3861 Paradise Valley (Laurel, 1938, Fred Scott).

Paradise Valley—Harry Tobias, Lew Porter (w,m), Spier. COVER: Fred Scott.

3862 Parallax View, The (Paramount, 1974, Warren Beatty, Paula Prentiss).

Parallax View Theme—Michael Small (m), Ensign. COVER: Warren Beatty.

3863 Paramount on Parade (Paramount, 1930, Maurice Chevalier, Nancy Carroll).

All I Want Is Just One—Leo Robin (w), Richard Whiting (m), Famous; Anytime's the Time to Fall in Love—Elsie Janis (w), Jack King (m), Famous; Dancing to Save Your Sole/Drink to the Girl of My Dreams—L. Wolfe Gilbert (w), Abel Baer (m), Famous; Helen Kane's Schoolroom—Elsie Janis, Jack King (w,m), Famous; I'm in Training for You—L. Wolfe Gilbert (w), Abel Baer (m), Famous; I'm True to the Navy Now—Elsie Janis, Jack King (w,m), Famous; My Marine—Ray Eagan (w), Richard Whiting (m), Famous; Paramount on Parade—Elsie Janis (w), Jack King (m), Famous; Sweepin' the Clouds

Away—Sam Coslow (w,m), Famous. COVER: Maurice Chevalier, Jack Oakie, Gary Cooper, and Other Stars.
3864 Pardners (Paramount, 1956, Dean Martin, Jerry Lewis).
Buckskin Beauty/Me N You N the Moon/Pardners/Win, the Wind—Sammy Cahn (w), James Van Heusen (m), Paramount. COVER: Dean Martin, Jerry Lewis.
3865 Pardon My Gun (RKO, 1930, Tom Keene, Sally Starr).
Deep Down South—Monty Collins (w), George Green (m), Shapiro Bernstein. COVER: Mona Ray, Abe Lyman, and Orchestra.
3866 Pardon My Rhythm (Universal, 1944, Gloria Jean, Evelyn Ankers).
Do You Believe in Dreams—Irving Bibo, Don George, Al Piantadosi (w,m), Forster. COVER: Gloria Jean, Bob Crosby, Mel Torme, and Others.
3867 Pardon My Ski (Hit the Ice) (Universal, 1943, Bud Abbott, Lou Costello).
I'd Like to Set You to Music—Paul F. Webster (w), Harry Revel (m), Miller. COVER: Black and white cover with title only.
3868 Parenthood (Universal, 1989, Steve Martin, Mary Steenburgen).
I Love to See You Smile—Randy Newman (w,m), Warner. COVER: Steve Martin.
3869 Parent Trap, The (Buena Vista, 1961, Brian Keith, Maureen O'Hara).
Let's Get Together/Maggie's Theme, For Now and Always/Parent Trap, The—Richard Sherman, Robert Sherman (w,m), Wonderland. COVER: Maureen O'Hara, Hayley Mills.
3870 Paris (First National, 1930, Irene Bordoni, Jack Buchanan).
Don't Look at Me That Way—Cole Porter (w,m), Harms; I Wonder What Is Really on His Mind/I'm a Little Negative—Al Bryan (w), Eddie Ward

(m), Harms; Land of Going to Be—Ray Goetz, Walter Kollo (w,m), Harms; Miss Wonderful/My Lover/Paris/Somebody Mighty Like You—Al Bryan (w), Eddie Ward (m), Harms. COVER: Irene Bordoni, Jack Buchanan.
3871 Paris (Vitaphone, 1934, Musical Short).
Paris-Themes—David Mendoza (m), Witmark. COVER: Black and white cover with title only.
3872 Paris After Dark (The Night Is Ending) (20th Century-Fox, 1943, George Sanders, Philip Dorn).
Besame Mucho (VS)—Sunny Skylar, Consuelo Velazquez (w,m), Peer. COVER: None.
3873 Paris Blues (United Artists, 1961, Paul Newman, Joanne Woodward).
Paris Blues—Billy Strayhorn, Harold Flender (w), Duke Ellington (m), Unart. COVER: Paul Newman, and Movie Scenes.
3874 Paris Follies of 1956 (Fresh from Paris) (Allied Artists, 1955, Forrest Tucker, Margaret Whiting).
Can This Be Love/I Love a Circus/Lonely Town—Pony Sherrell, Phil Moody (w,m), American. COVER: Margaret Whiting, and Movie Scenes.
3875 Paris Holiday (United Artists, 1958, Bob Hope, Anita Ekberg).
Nothing in Common/Paris Holiday—Sammy Cahn (w), James Van Heusen (m), Morris. COVER: Bob Hope, Fernandel, Martha Hyer, Anita Ekberg.
3876 Paris Honeymoon (Paramount, 1939, Bing Crosby, Franciska Gaal).
Funny Old Hills—Leo Robin, Ralph Rainger (w,m), Paramount; I Ain't Got Nobody—Spencer Williams, Roger Graham (w,m), Davis; I Have Eyes/Joobalai/You're a Sweet Little Headache—Leo Robin, Ralph Rainger (w,m), Paramount. COVER:

Bing Crosby, Shirley Ross, Franciska Gaal.

3877 Paris in Spring (Paramount, 1935, Mary Ellis, Tullio Carminati).

Bon Jour Mamselle/Paris in the Spring/Why Do They Call It Gay Paree—Mack Gordon, Harry Revel (w,m), Crawford. COVER: Mary Ellis, Tullio Carminati.

3878 Parrish (Warner Bros., 1961, Troy Donahue, Claudette Colbert).

Allison's Theme/Ellen's Theme—Max Steiner (m), Witmark; High Spirits—Mann Curtis (w), Joseph Meyer (m), Witmark; Lucy's Theme/Paige's Theme/Parrish-Piano Suite—Max Steiner (m), Witmark. COVER: Troy Donahue, Connie Stevens, Sharon Hugueny, Diane McBain.

3879 Partners of the Plains (Paramount, 1937, William Boyd, Russell Hayden).

Moonlight on the Sunset Trail—Ralph Freed (w), Burton Lane (m), Famous. COVER: William Boyd.

3880 Party, The (United Artists, 1968, Peter Sellers, Claudine Longet).

Nothing to Lose—Don Black (w), Henry Mancini (m), Twinchris. COVER: Cartoon Sketch.

3881 Party Girl (Tiffany, 1930, Douglas Fairbanks, Jeanette Loff).

Farewell/Oh How I Adore You—Harry Stoddard, Marcy Klauber (w, m), Shapiro Bernstein. COVER: Douglas Fairbanks, Jeanette Loff.

3882 Party Girl (MGM, 1958, Robert Taylor, Cyd Charisse).

Party Girl—Sammy Cahn (w), Nicholas Brodszky (m), Miller. COVER: Cyd Charisse.

3883 Passage to Marseilles (Warner Bros., 1944, Humphrey Bogart, Michele Morgan).

Passage to Marseilles Theme (VS) —Max Steiner (m), Warner; Someday I'll Meet You Again—Ned Washington (w), Max Steiner (m), Witmark. COVER: Humphrey Bogart, Nichele Morgan.

3884 Passion (RKO, 1954, Cor-

nel Wilde, Yvonne De Carlo).

Passion Tango—Lou Forbes (m), Young. COVER: Cornel Wilde, Yvonne De Carlo.

3885 Passionate Friends, The (One Woman's Story) (Universal, 1949, Ann Todd, Claude Rains).

Lovers Moon (B)—Richard Addinsell (m), Chappell. COVER: Ann Todd, Trevor Howard.

3886 Passion Flower (First National, 1921, Norma Talmadge, Harrison Ford).

Passion Flower—Eugene Lester (w,m), Lester. COVER: Norma Talmadge.

3887 Patch of Blue, A (MGM, 1965, Sidney Poitier, Elizabeth Hartman).

Patch of Blue, A—Bernie Wayne (w), Jerry Goldsmith (m), Hastings. COVER: Sidney Poitier, Elizabeth Hartman.

3888 Paternity (Paramount, 1981, Burt Reynolds, Beverly D'Angelo).

Baby Talk—Dave Frishberg (w), David Shire (m), Ensign; Love's Gonna Find You—David Shire (m), Ensign. COVER: Burt Reynolds.

3889 Pat Garrett and Billy the Kid (MGM, 1973, James Coburn, Kris Kristofferson).

Knockin' on Heaven's Door—Bob Dylan (w,m), Ranshorn. COVER: A Cowboy.

3890 Pathe All Talking Comedies (Pathe, 1929, Doris McMahon, Evalyn Knapp).

I'll Say She's Pretty—Charles Weinberg, Jack Stanley, Forrest Woods (w,m), Piantadosi. COVER: Bathing Beauties.

3891 Patria (International, 1917, Irene Castle, Warner Oland).

Patria—George Graff (w), Irene Castle (m), Berlin. COVER: Irene Castle.

3892 Patrick the Great (Universal, 1945, Donald O'Connor, Peggy Ryan).

For the First Time—Charles Tobias (w), David Kapp (m), Shapiro Bernstein. COVER: Donald O'Connor.

3893 Patsy, The (Paramount, 1964, Jerry Lewis, Everett Sloane).
I Lost My Heart in a Drive In Movie—Jack Brooks (w), David Raksin (m), Famous. COVER: Jerry Lewis.

3894 Patton (20th Century-Fox, 1970, George C. Scott, Karl Malden).
Patton Theme—Jerry Goldsmith (m), Fox. COVER: George C. Scott.

3895 Paula (Columbia, 1952, Loretta Young, Kent Smith).
Paula—Irving Gordon (w), George Duning (m), Shapiro Bernstein. COVER: Loretta Young.

3896 Pawnbroker, The (Landau, 1965, Rod Steiger, Geraldine Fitzgerald).
Pawnbroker Theme—Jack Lawrence (w), Quincy Jones (m), Pawnbroker. COVER: Pawnbroker Symbol.

3897 Payment on Demand (RKO, 1951, Bette Davis, Barry Sullivan).
A Woman's Intuition—Ned Washington (w), Victor Young (m), Mills. COVER: Bette Davis, Barry Sullivan.

3898 Payroll (Allied Artists, 1961, Michael Craig, Francoise Prevost).
It Happens Every Day (B)—Norman Newell (w), Tony Osborne (m), Filmusic. COVER: Michael Craig, Francoise Prevost.

3899 Peaceful Rafferty (Celtic, 1915, Joe Sullivan).
Peaceful Rafferty—J. Keirn Brennan, Dave Reed (w), Ernest Ball (m), Witmark. COVER: Joe Sullivan.

3900 Peaceful Valley (First National, 1920, Charles Ray, Ann May).
Peaceful Valley Waltz—Joseph Murphy (w,m), Murphy. COVER: A Valley Scene.

3901 Peacemaker, The (United Artists, 1956, James Mitchell, Rose Marie Bowe).
The Peacemaker—George Gree-

ley (m), Jungnickel. COVER: Black and white cover with title only.

3902 Peace of Roaring River, The (Goldwyn, 1919, Pauline Frederick, Thomas Holding).
May Dreams—Gaston Borch (m), Belwin. COVER: Pauline Frederick.

3903 Peacock Alley (Metro, 1921, Mae Murray, Monte Blue).
Peacock Alley—Louis Silvers (w, m), Richmond. COVER: Mae Murray.

3904 Pearl of the South Pacific (RKO, 1955, Virginia Mayo, Dennis Morgan).
I Can't Get Away—Dave Franklin (w), Lou Forbes (m), Jungnickel. COVER: Virginia Mayo, Dennis Morgan.

3905 Peau D'Ane (Donkey Skin) (Paramount, 1971, Jacques Perrin, Catherine Deneuve).
If They Could Talk—Alan Bergman, Marilyn Bergman (w), Michel Legrand (m), Famous. COVER: Black and white cover with title only.

3906 Peck's Bad Boy (First National, 1921, Jackie Coogan, James Corrigan).
Peck's Bad Boy—Paul Sarazan (w,m), Berlin. COVER: Jackie Coogan.

3907 Peculiar Penguins (Disney, 1934, Cartoon).
Peculiar Penguins (VS)—Larry Morey (w), Leigh Harline (m), Berlin. COVER: Cartoon.

3908 Peggy (Ince, 1915, Billie Burke, William Desmond).
Peggy—Thomas Ince (w), Victor Schertzinger (m), Ince. COVER: Billie Burke.

3909 Peggy Sue Got Married (Tri-Star, 1987, Kathleen Turner, Nicholas Cage).
He Don't Love You Like I Love You (VS)—Jerry Butler, Curtis Mayfield, Cal Carter (w,m), Conrad. COVER: Black and white cover with title only.

3910 Peg o' My Heart (Metro,

1924, Laurette Taylor, Nigel Barrie).

Laurette—Ernst Luz, Louis Breau (w,m), Feist; Peg o' My Heart—Alfred Bryan (w), Fred Fischer (m), Feist; Valse Mauve—A. Laraia (m), Southern Cal. COVER: Laurette Taylor.

3911 Peg o' My Heart (MGM, 1933, Marion Davies, Onslow Stevens).

I'll Remember Only You—Arthur Freed (w), Nacio Herb Brown (m), Robbins; Sweetheart Darlin'—Gus Kahn (w), Herbert Stothart (m), Robbins. COVER: Marion Davies.

3912 Peg of Old Drury (Paramount, 1936, Anna Neagle, Jack Hawkins).

A Little Dash of Dublin (B)—Maurice Sigler, Al Goodhart, Al Hoffman (w,m), Cinephonic. COVER: Anna Neagle.

3913 Peg o' the Ring (Universal, 1916, Ruth Stonehouse, Grace Cunard).

Peg o' the Ring—Leo Bennett (w,m), Cadillac. COVER: Grace Cunard.

3914 Penelope (MGM, 1966, Natalie Wood, Dick Shawn).

Penelope—Leslie Bricusse (w), Johnny Williams (m), Hastings; Sun Is Gray, The—Gale Garnett (w, m), Hastings. COVER: Natalie Wood, Ian Bannen, Dick Shawn, Peter Falk.

3915 Pennies from Heaven (Columbia, 1936, Bing Crosby, Madge Evans).

Let's Call a Heart a Heart/One Two Button Your Shoe/Pennies from Heaven/Skeleton in the Closet/So Do I—John Burke (w), Arthur Johnston (m), Select. COVER: Bing Crosby.

3916 Pennies from Heaven (MGM, 1982, Steve Martin, Bernadette Peters).

Clouds Will Soon Roll By (VS)—Harry Brown, George Brown (w,m), Warner; Did You Ever See a Dream Walking (VS)—Mack Gordon (w), Harry Revel (m), Warner; Fancy Our Meeting (VS)—Douglas Furber (w), Philip Charig, Joe Meyer (m), Warner; Glory of Love (VS)—Billy Hill (w,m), Warner; I Want to Be Bad (VS)—B. G. DeSylva, Lew Brown, Ray Henderson (w,m), Warner; I'll Never Have to Dream Again (VS)—Charles Newman (w), Isham Jones (m), Warner; It's a Sin to Tell a Lie (VS)—Billy Mayhew (w,m), Warner; It's the Girl (VS)—Dave Oppenheim (w), Abel Baer (m), Warner; Let's Misbehave (VS)—Cole Porter (w,m), Warner; Let's Put Out the Lights and Go to Sleep (VS)—Herman Hupfield (w,m), Warner; Life Is Just a Bowl of Cherries (VS)—Lew Brown, Ray Henderson (w,m), Warner; Love Is Good for Anything That Ails You (VS)—Cliff Friend, Matt Malneck (w,m), Warner; Pennies from Heaven (VS)—John Burke (w), Arthur Johnston (m), Warner; Roll Along Prairie Moon (VS)—Ted Fiorito, H. MacPherson, Al Von Tilzer (w,m), Warner; Yes Yes (VS)—Con Conrad, Cliff Friend (w,m), Warner. COVER: Bernadette Peters, Steve Martin.

3917 Penny Serenade (Columbia, 1938, Irene Dunne, Cary Grant).

You Were Meant for Me—Arthur Freed (w), Nacio Herb Brown (m), Robbins. COVER: Cary Grant, Irene Dunne.

3918 Penrod (First National, 1922, Freckles Barry, Florence Morrison).

Penrod Song—Bruce Bundy, Frank Egan (w,m), Marks. COVER: Freckles Barry.

3919 Penthouse (Society Lawyer) (MGM, 1939, Virginia Bruce, Walter Pidgeon).

I'm in Love with the Honorable Mr. So and So—Sam Coslow (w, m), Feist. COVER: Black and white Cover with title only.

3920 Penthouse (Paramount, 1967, Suzy Kendall, Terence Morgan).

Penthouse—Shelly Pinz, Paul Leka (w,m), Ensign. COVER: Terence Morgan, Suzy Kendall.

3921 People Are Funny (Paramount, 1946, Jack Haley, Helen Walker).

Every Hour on the Hour—Don George (w), Duke Ellington (m), Melrose; Hey Jose—Jay Livingston, Ray Evans (w), Pepe Guizar (m), Peer; Old Square Dance Is Back Again—Don Reid, Henry Tobias (w, m), Leeds. COVER: Jack Haley, Frances Langford, Rudy Vallee, Helen Walker.

3922 People Next Door, The (Embassy, 1970, Eli Wallach, Julie Harris).

Mama Don't You Wait Up for Me/ Sweet Medusa—Scott English (w), Larry Weiss (m), Legation. COVER: Sketch of Girl.

3923 Pepe (Columbia, 1960, Maurice Chevalier, Bing Crosby).

Faraway Part of Town—Dory Langdon (w), André Previn (m), Columbia; Mimi—Lorenz Hart (w), Richard Rodgers (m), Famous; Pepe —Dory Langdon (w), Hans Wittstatt (m), Shapiro Bernstein; Suzie—Dory Langdon (w), Johnny Green (m), Columbia; That's How It Went All Right—Dory Langdon (w), André Previn (m), Columbia. COVER: Cantinflas.

3924 Perfect (Columbia, 1985, John Travolta, Jamie Lee Curtis).

Closest Thing to Perfect—Michael Omartian, Bruce Sudano, Jermaine Jackson (w,m), Golden Torch. COVER: John Travolta, Jamie Lee Curtis.

3925 Perfect Furlough, The (Universal, 1958, Tony Curtis, Janet Leigh).

Perfect Furlough Theme—Diane Lampert, Richard Loring (w), Frank Skinner (m), Northern. COVER: Tony Curtis, Janet Leigh.

3926 Perfect Lover (Selznick, 1919, Eugene O'Brien, Lucille Stewart).

A Perfect Lover—Alfred Bryan (w), Albert Gumble (m), Remick; The Perfect Lover—Harry B. Smith (w), M. K. Jerome (m), Berlin. COVER: Eugene O'Brien, Lucille Stewart.

3927 Perfect Understanding (United Artists, 1933, Gloria Swanson, Laurence Olivier).

I Love You So Much That I Hate You—Rowland Leigh (w), Henry Sullivan (m), Chappell. COVER: Gloria Swanson, Laurence Olivier.

3928 Perfidia (RKO, 1939, Maria Montoya, Maring Tamayo).

Arriba La Conga/Tu No Comprendes—Rafael Hernandez (w,m), Southern. COVER: Movie Scenes.

3929 Perilous Holiday (Columbia, 1946, Pat O'Brien, Ruth Warrick).

Irishman's Idea of Love—Allan Roberts, Doris Fisher (w,m), Sun. COVER: Pat O'Brien, Ruth Warrick.

3930 Perils of Pauline, The (Eclectic, 1914, Pearl White, Crane Wilbur).

Pauline Waltz—Clarence Jones (m), Root; Poor Pauline—Charles McCarron (w), Raymond Walker (m), Broadway. COVER: Pearl White.

3931 Perils of Pauline, The (Paramount, 1947, Betty Hutton, John Lund).

I Wish I Didn't Love You So— Frank Loesser (w,m), Susan; Poor Pauline—Charles McCarron (w), Raymond Walker (m), Broadway; Poppa Don't Preach to Me/Rumble Rumble Rumble/Sewing Machine, The— Frank Loesser (w,m), Susan. COVER: Betty Hutton, John Lund.

3932 Period of Adjustment (MGM, 1962, Jane Fonda, Anthony Franciosa).

As Big as Texas/Period of Adjustment Love Theme—Mack David (w), Lyn Murray (m), Miller. COVER: Jane Fonda, Anthony Franciosa, Jim Hutton.

3933 Perri (Buena Vista, 1957, True Life Adventure).

Break of Day/Perri—Winston Hibler (w), George Bruns (m), Disney; Now to Sleep—Winston Hibler, Ralph Wright (w), George Bruns (m), Disney; Together Time—Gil George, Winston Hibler (w), Paul Smith (m), Disney. COVER: A Squirrel.

3934 Persuaders, The (ITC, 1971, Tony Curtis, Roger Moore).

The Persuaders Theme—John Barry (m), Kirshner. COVER: Tony Curtis, Roger Moore.

3935 Pete Kelly's Blues (Warner Bros., 1955, Jack Webb, Janet Leigh).

He Needs Me—Arthur Hamilton (w,m), Mark Seven; Pete Kelly's Blues—Sammy Cahn (w), Ray Heindorf (m), Mark Seven; Sing a Rainbow—Arthur Hamilton (w,m), Mark Seven. COVER: Jack Webb, Janet Leigh, Peggy Lee.

3936 Pete 'n' Tillie (Universal, 1972, Walter Matthau, Carol Burnett).

Love's the Only Game in Town—Alan Bergman, Marilyn Bergman (w), John Williams (m), Duchess. COVER: Walter Matthau, Carol Burnett.

3937 Peter Pan (Paramount, 1924, Betty Bronson, Ernest Torrence).

I'd Like to Be Like Peter Pan—Mel Shauer (w,m), Empire; Peter Pan, I Love You (B)—Robert King, Ray Henderson (w,m), Prowse. COVER: Betty Bronson.

3938 Peter Pan (Buena Vista, 1953, Cartoon).

Elegant Captain Hook, The—Sammy Cahn (w), Sammy Fain (m), Disney; Following the Leader—Winston Hibler, Ted Sears (w),Oliver Wallace (m), Disney; Never Smile at a Crocodile—Jack Lawrence (w), Frank Churchill (m), Disney; Peter Pan—Jack Lawrence, Victor Young (w,m), Disney; Second Star to the Right, The/What Made the Red Man Red?/You Can Fly You Can Fly You Can Fly/Your Mother and Mine—Sammy Cahn (w), Sammy Fain (m), Disney; Pirate's Life, A (VS)—Ed

Penner (w), Oliver Wallace (m), Disney. COVER: Cartoon.

3939 Pete's Dragon (Buena Vista, 1977, Helen Reddy, Jim Dale).

Boo Bop Bop Bop Bop/Brazzle Dazzle Day/Candle on the Water/It's Not Easy/There's Room for Everyone/Bill of Sale (VS)/Every Little Piece (VS)/Happiest Home in the Hills (VS)/I Saw a Dragon (VS)/Passa Mash Loddy (VS)—Al Kasha, Joel Hirschhorn (w,m), Disney. COVER: Mickey Rooney, Helen Reddy, Jim Dale, Red Buttons.

3940 Petty Girl, The (Columbia, 1950, Robert Cummings, Joan Caulfield).

Ah Loves Ya/Calypso Song/Fancy Free—Johnny Mercer (w), Harold Arlen (m), Morris. COVER: Joan Caulfield.

3941 Petulia (Warner Bros., 1968, Julie Christie, George C. Scott).

Petulia—Carolyn Leigh (w), John Barry (m), Morris. COVER: Julie Christie, George C. Scott, Richard Chamberlain.

3942 Peyton Place (20th Century-Fox, 1957, Lana Turner, Hope Lange).

Wonderful Season of Love—Paul F. Webster (w), Franz Waxman (m), Robbins. COVER: Diane Varsi, Russ Tamblyn.

3943 Phaedra (United Artists, 1962, Melina Mercouri, Anthony Perkins).

Phaedra Love Theme—Mikis Theodorakis (m), Unart. COVER: Melina Mercouri, Anthony Perkins.

3944 Phantom Broadcast, The (Monogram, 1933, Ralph Forbes, Vivienne Osborne).

My Goodbye to You/Where the Moonbeams Greet the Morning—George Waggner (w), Bernard Brown, Norman Spencer (m), S. Clay. COVER: Ralph Forbes.

3945 Phantom Empire, The (Radio Ranch) (Mascot, 1935, Gene Autry, Frankie Darro).

I'm Getting a Moon's Eye View of

the World/I'm Oscar I'm Pete/Just Come on Back—Gene Autry, Smiley Burnette (w,m), Cole; My Cross Eyed Gal—Gene Autry, Jimmy Long (w,m), Cole; No Need to Worry— Gene Autry, Smiley Burnette (w,m), Cole; That Silver Haired Daddy of Mine—Gene Autry, Jimmy Long (w, m), Cole; Uncle Henry's Vacation/ Uncle Noah's Ark—Gene Autry, Smiley Burnette (w,m), Cole. COVER: Gene Autry, and Movie Scenes.

3946 Phantom of the House (Continental, 1929, Nancy Welford, Ricardo Cortez).

You'll Never Be Forgotten—Abner Silver, Maceo Pinkard (m), Shapiro Bernstein. COVER: Nancy Welford, Ricardo Cortez.

3947 Phantom of the Opera (Universal, 1925, Lon Chaney, Mary Philbin).

Toccata and Fugue-D Minor (PC) —J. Bach (m), Warner. COVER: None.

3948 Phantom of the Opera (Universal, 1943, Nelson Eddy, Claude Rains).

Lullaby of the Bells—George Waggner (w), Edward Ward (m), Robbins; Lullaby of the Bells Concerto (B)— Edward Ward (m), Day. COVER: Nelson Eddy, Susanna Foster.

3949 Phantom of the Paradise (20th Century-Fox, 1974, Paul Williams, William Finley).

Phantom of the Paradise-Nine Songs—Paul Williams (w,m), Triangle. COVER: Paul Williams.

3950 Phantom President, The (Paramount, 1932, George M. Cohan, Claudette Colbert).

Give Her a Kiss—Lorenz Hart (w), Richard Rodgers (m), Famous; We Need a Man—George M. Cohan (w, m), Famous. COVER: George M. Cohan.

3951 Phantom Rider, The (Universal, 1936, Buck Jones, Marla Shelton).

Hidden Valley—Sidney Mitchell (w), Sam Stept (m), Sam Fox. COV-ER: Buck Jones.

3952 Phenix City Story (Allied Artists, 1955, Richard Kiley, Kathryn Grant).

Your Everlovin' Lovin' Arms— Harold Spina (w,m), Morris. COVER: Blue and white cover with title only.

3953 Physical Evidence (Columbia, 1989, Burt Reynolds, Theresa Russell).

Physical Evidence Theme—Henry Mancini (m), Burbank. COVER: Burt Reynolds, Theresa Russell.

3954 Piccadilly Jim (Selznick, 1919, Owen Moore, Zena Keefe).

Piccadilly Jim—Al Wilson, Lou Klein (w), Irving Bibo (m), Berlin. COVER: Owen Moore, and Man.

3955 Piccadilly Jim (MGM, 1936, Robert Montgomery, Frank Morgan).

In the Shadow of the Old Oak Tree—Bob Wright, Chet Forrest (w, m), Feist; Night of Nights—Walter Donaldson (w,m), Feist. COVER: Black and white cover with title only.

3956 Picasso Summer (Warner Bros., 1969, Albert Finney, Yvette Mimieux).

Picasso Summer-Theme—Michel Legrand (m), Warner; Summer Me Winter Me—Alan Bergman, Marilyn Bergman (w), Michel Legrand (m), Warner. COVER: Picasso Painting.

3957 Pick a Star (MGM, 1937, Patsy Kelly, Jack Haley).

Without Your Love—Johnny Lange (w), Fred Stryker (m), Miller. COVER: Laurel and Hardy, Jack Haley, Patsy Kelly, Mischa Auer.

3958 Pick Up Alley (Interpol) (Columbia, 1957, Victor Mature, Anita Ekberg).

Anyone for Love?—Ned Washington (w), Lester Lee (m), Colgems. COVER: Victor Mature, Anita Ekberg.

3959 Pickin' the Winner (Vitaphone, 1933, Musical Short).

Pickin' the Winners/Sweetest Gal

in Town—Cliff Hess (w,m), Witmark. COVER: Black and white cover with title only.

3960 Picnic (Columbia, 1956, William Holden, Kim Novak).

Moon Glow—Will Hudson, Eddie DeLange, Irving Mills (w,m), Mills; Picnic—Steve Allen (w), George Duning (m), Columbia; Picnic Theme —George Duning (m), Columbia. COVER: William Holden, Kim Novak.

3961 Picnic Panic (Van Beuren, 1935, Cartoon).

I Love It When It Rains—Winston Sharples, Ray Kelley, Burt Gillette (w,m), Southern. COVER: Cartoon.

3962 Picture of Dorian Gray, The (MGM, 1945, George Sanders, Hurd Hatfield).

Goodbye Little Yellow Bird—C. Murphy, William Hargreaves, Dan O'Brien (w,m), Shapiro Bernstein. COVER: Angela Lansbury, Hurd Hatfield, George Sanders, Donna Reed.

3963 Picture Palace (Vitaphone, 1933, Musical Short).

If It's Love—Cliff Hess (w,m), Witmark. COVER: Black and white cover with title only.

3964 Pie a la Mode (Vitaphone, 1934, Musical Short).

Jester's Dance—David Mendoza (w,m), Witmark. COVER: Black and white cover with title only.

3965 Pieces of Dreams (United Artists, 1970), Robert Forster, Lauren Hutton).

Little Boy Lost/Pieces of Dreams —Alan Bergman, Marilyn Bergman (w), Michel Legrand (m), Unart. COVER: Robert Forster, Lauren Hutton.

3966 Pied Piper (Disney, 1933, Cartoon).

Pied Piper of Hamelin (VS)—Leigh Harline (w,m), Berlin. COVER: Cartoon.

3967 Pigeon That Took Rome, The (Paramount, 1962, Charlton Heston, Elsa Martinelli).

Pigeon That Took Rome, The— Alessandro Cicognini (m), Famous. COVER: Charlton Heston, Elsa Martinelli.

3968 Pigskin Parade (20th Century-Fox, 1936, Stuart Ervin, Patsy Kelly).

Balboa/Football Songs/It's Love I'm After/You Do the Darndest Things Baby/You're Slightly Terrific —Sidney Mitchell (w), Lew Pollack (m), Movietone. COVER: Football Game.

3969 Pillow Talk (Universal, 1959, Rock Hudson, Doris Day).

Pillow Talk—Buddy Pepper, Inez James (w,m), Artists; Roly Poly (B)—Elsa Doran, Sol Lake (w,m), California. COVER: Rock Hudson, Doris Day.

3970 Pillow to Post (Warner Bros., 1945, Ida Lupino, Sydney Greenstreet).

Whatcha Say?—Ted Koehler (w), Burton Lane (m), Harms. COVER: Ida Lupino, William Prince.

3971 Pink Floyd-The Wall (MGM, 1982, Bob Geldof, Christine Hargreaves).

Another Brick in the Wall, Part Two/When the Tigers Broke Free— Roger Waters (w,m), Floyd; Pink Floyd, The Wall-26 Songs—Roger Waters, David Gilmour (w,m), Floyd. COVER: A Wall.

3972 Pink Panther, The (United Artists, 1964, David Niven, Peter Sellers).

It Had Better Be Tonight—Johnny Mercer (w), Henry Mancini (m), Northridge; Pink Panther Theme/ Pink Panther-Eleven Themes—Henry Mancini (m), Northridge. COVER: David Niven, Peter Sellers, Robert Wagner, Capucine.

3973 Pink Panther Strikes Again, The (United Artists, 1976, Peter Sellers, Herbert Lom).

Come to Me—Don Black (w), Henry Mancini (m), Northridge; Inspector Clouseau Theme—Henry Mancini (m), Northridge; Until You

Love Me—Don Black (w), Henry Mancini (m), Northridge. COVER: Pink Panther.

3974 Pinocchio (RKO, Disney, 1940, Cartoon).

Give a Little Whistle/Hi Diddle Dee Dee/I've Got No Strings/Little Wooden Head/Three Cheers for Anything/Turn on the Old Music Box/When You Wish Upon a Star—Ned Washington (w), Leigh Harline (m), Berlin. COVER: Pinocchio, Jiminy Cricket.

3975 Pinocchio (Special Edition) (RKO Disney, 1940, Cartoon).

Honest John/Jiminy Cricket/Monstro the Whale—Ned Washington (w), Leigh Harline (m), Berlin. COVER: Individual Cartoons of Special Characters.

3976 Pinto Bandit, The (PRC, 1945, Dave O'Brien, Jim Newill).

It's Too Late to Say You're Sorry Now (PC)/Wanderer Wandering Home, A (PC)—Don Weston (w,m), Peer. COVER: None.

3977 Pin-Up Girl (20th Century-Fox, 1944, Betty Grable, John Harvey).

Don't Carry Tales Out of School/Once Too Often/Red Robins, Bob Whites, and Bluebirds/Story of a Very Merry Widow/This Is It/Time Alone Will Tell/Yankee Doodle Hayride/You're My Little Pin-up Girl—Mack Gordon (w), James Monaco (m), BVC. COVER: Betty Grable, Martha Raye, Joe E. Brown, Charlie Spivak.

3978 Pioneers (Monogram, 1941, Tex Ritter, Wanda McKay).

Wild Galoot from Tuzigoot (VS)—Jack Smith, Tex Ritter (w,m), Cole. COVER: Tex Ritter.

3979 Pirate, The (MGM, 1948, Judy Garland, Gene Kelly).

Be a Clown/Love of My Life/Mack the Black/Manuela (VS)/Nina/You Can Do No Wrong—Cole Porter (w,m), Chappell. COVER: Judy Garland, Gene Kelly.

3980 Pirate Movie, The (20th Century-Fox, 1982, Kristy McNichol, Christopher Atkins).

How Can I Live Without Her—Terry Britten, Sue Shifrin (w,m), Hamilton; Pirate Movie-Thirteen Songs—Terry Britten, Kit Hain, Gilbert & Sullivan (w,m), Hamilton. COVER: Kristy McNichol, Christopher Atkins.

3981 Pirates (Cannon, 1986, Walter Matthau, Damian Thomas).

Dolores Love Theme—Daniele Becker (w), Philippe Sarde (m), Lem America; Pirates Main Theme—Philippe Sarde (m), Lem America. COVER: Walter Matthau, and Movie Scene.

3982 P. J. (Universal, 1968, George Peppard, Gayle Hunnicutt).

When Will It End?—Sammy Cahn (w), Neal Hefti (m), Shamley. COVER: George Peppard, Gayle Hunnicutt, Raymond Burr.

3983 Place for Lovers, A (MGM, 1968, Marcello Mastroianni, Faye Dunaway).

Place for Lovers, A—Norman Gimbel (w), Manuel DeSica (m), Hastings. COVER: Marcello Mastroianni, Faye Dunaway.

3984 Place in the Sun, A (Paramount, 1951, Montgomery Clift, Elizabeth Taylor).

Place in the Sun—Jay Livingston, Ray Evans (w), Franz Waxman (m), Paramount; Place in the Sun Theme—Franz Waxman (m). COVER: Montgomery Clift, Elizabeth Taylor.

3985 Plantation Melodies (Warner Bros., 1946, Craig Stevens).

Plantation Melodies (B)—Stephen Foster (w,m), Campbell. COVER: Craig Stevens, and Movie Scene.

3986 Platoon (Orion, 1987, Tom Berenger, Charlie Sheen).

Adagio for Strings—Samuel Barber (m), Schirmer. COVER: Black and white cover with title only.

3987 Playboy of Paris (Paramount, 1930, Maurice Chevalier, Frances Dee).

It's a Great Life/My Ideal—Leo

Robin (w), Richard Whiting, Newell Chase (m), Famous. COVER: Maurice Chevalier.

3988 Play Dirty (United Artists, 1969, Michael Caine, Nigel Davenport).

Play Dirty Theme—Michel Legrand (m), Unart. COVER: Black and white cover with title only.

3989 Players (Paramount, 1979, Ali MacGraw, Dean Paul Martin).

Meant to Be—Carol Heather (w), Jerry Goldsmith (m), Famous. COVER: Ali MacGraw, Dean Paul Martin.

3990 Playful Pluto (Disney, 1934, Cartoon).

Playful Pluto (VS)—Larry Morey (w), Frank Churchill (m), Berlin. COVER: Cartoon.

3991 Playgirl (Universal, 1954, Shelley Winters, Barry Sullivan).

There'll Be Some Changes Made—Billy Higgins (w), W. Benton Overstreet (m), Marks. COVER: Shelley Winters.

3992 Playing Around (First National, 1929, Alice White, Chester Morris).

That's the Low Down on the Low Down/You Learn About Love Every Day—Bud Green, Sam Stept (w,m), Green Stept. COVER: Alice White.

3993 Play It Again Sam (Paramount, 1972, Woody Allen, Diane Keaton).

Blues for Allan Felix—Oscar Peterson (m), Famous; Easy Lovin'—Graeme Kronberg (w), Billy Goldenberg (m), Famous; It's the Same Sad Story All Over Again—Graeme Kronberg (w), Billy Goldenberg (m), Famous; Play It Again Sam Theme—Billy Goldenberg (m), Famous. COVER: Woody Allen, Diane Keaton.

3994 Play It Cool (Allied Artists, 1962, Helen Shapiro, Bobby Vee).

I Don't Care (B)—Norman Newell (w), Norrie Paramor (m), Filmusic. COVER: Helen Shapiro.

3995 Playmates (RKO, 1941, Kay Kyser, John Barrymore).

How Long Did I Dream/Humpty Dumpty Heart/Que Chica/Romeo Smith and Juliet Jones/Thank Your Lucky Stars—Johnny Burke (w), James Van Heusen (m), Southern. COVER: Kay Kyser, Ginny Simms, Patsy Kelly, Lupe Velez, John Barrymore.

3996 Play Misty for Me (Universal, 1971, Clint Eastwood, Jessica Walter).

Misty—Johnny Burke (w), Errol Garner (m), Vernon. COVER: Clint Eastwood.

3997 Plaza Suite (Paramount, 1971, Walter Matthau, Maureen Stapleton).

Plaza Suite Theme—Maurice Jarre (m), Famous. COVER: Walter Matthau, Maureen Stapleton).

3998 Please Don't Eat the Daisies (MGM, 1957, Doris Day, David Niven).

Anyway the Wind Blows—By Dunham (w), Marilyn Hooven, Joe Hooven (m), Artists; Please Don't Eat the Daisies—Joe Lubin (w,m), Daywin. COVER: Doris Day, Janis Paige, David Niven.

3999 Pleasure Crazed (Fox, 1929, Marguerite Churchill, Kenneth MacKenna).

I Only Knew It Was You—Clare Kummer (w,m), DBH. COVER: Black and white cover with title only.

4000 Pleasure Cruise (Fox, 1933, Genevieve Tobin, Roland Young).

Is This a Souvenir?/World Goes Round, The—Val Burton, Will Jason (w,m), Movietone. COVER: Black and white cover with title only.

4001 Pleasure Island (Vitaphone, 1938, Musical Short)

I'm a Little Co-coa-nut—Cliff Hess (w,m), Witmark. COVER: Black and white cover with title only.

4002 Pleasure Mad (Mayer, 1923, Norma Shearer, Huntley Gordon).

Valley of Content—Blanche Upright (w), Albert Gumble (m), Remick. COVER: Norma Shearer, Huntley Gordon.

4003 Pleasure of His Company, The (Paramount, 1961, Fred Astaire, Debbie Reynolds).

Pleasure of His Company—Sammy Cahn (w), Alfred Newman (m), Famous; Pleasure of His Company Theme—Alfred Newman (m), Famous. COVER: Fred Astaire, Debbie Reynolds, Tab Hunter, Lilli Palmer.

4004 Pleasure Seekers, The (20th Century-Fox, 1965, Ann Margret, Tony Franciosa).

Everything Makes Music When You're in Love/Pleasure Seekers, The —Sammy Cahn (w), James Van Heusen (m), Miller. COVER: Ann Margret, Carol Lynley, Pamela Tiffin.

4005 Plough Song (Paramount, 1940, Short Subject).

Song of the Plough (B)—Stanton Jefferies (m), Ascherberg. COVER: Man, Horse, and Plow.

4006 Pocketful of Miracles (United Artists, 1961, Glenn Ford, Bette Davis).

Pocketful of Miracles—Sammy Cahn (w), James Van Heusen (m), Maraville. COVER: Bette Davis, Glenn Ford, Hope Lange.

4007 Pocket Money (National General, 1972, Paul Newman, Lee Marvin).

Pocket Money—Carole King (w, m), Colgems. COVER: Carole King.

4008 Pocono (Elicker, 1949, Clark Ranger, Jane Gray).

Booneville/Chasing That Same Dream/I'll Bet You Did/Little Muffet's Tuffet/Swingin' on the Strings —Joe Elicker (w,m), Elicker. COVER: Clark Ranger.

4009 Poetic Gems (Braunstein, 1935, Home Life Short Subjects from Edgar Guest Poems).

Poetic Gems-Fifteen Songs— Frank Loesser (w), Louis Herscher (m), Mills. COVER: Edgar Guest.

4010 Pointed Heels (Paramount, 1929, William Powell, Helen Kane).

Aintcha?—Mack Gordon, Max Rich (w,m), Shapiro Bernstein; I Have to Have You—Leo Robin (w), Richard Whiting (m), Spier Coslow;

Pointed Heels Ballet—Dimitri Tiomkin (m), Spier Coslow; COVER: Helen Kane, Skeets Gallagher.

4011 Police Academy (Warner, 1984, Steve Guttenberg, Kim Cattrall).

Police Academy March—Robert Folk (m), Warner. COVER: Police Cadets.

4012 Pollyanna (Buena Vista, 1960, Hayley Mills, Jane Wyman).

Pollyanna's Song—David Swift (w), Paul Smith (m), Disney. COVER: Hayley Mills.

4013 Poltergeist (MGM, 1981, Craig Nelson, JoBeth Williams).

Rag Fantasy—William Bolcom (m), Marks. COVER: Ghostly Lettering.

4014 Pony Post (Universal, 1940, Johnny Mack Brown, Fuzzy Knight).

I Don't Like No Cows—Everett Carter (w), Milton Rosen (m), Robbins. COVER: Johnny Mack Brown, Fuzzy Knight, Nell O'Day.

4015 Poor Cinderella (Paramount, 1934, Cartoon).

Poor Cinderella—Charles Tobias, Murray Mencher, Jack Scholl (w,m), Feist. COVER: Betty Boop.

4016 Poor Cow (National General, 1968, Carol White, Terence Stamp).

Poor Cow—Donovan Leitch (w,m), Peer. COVER: Sketch of Boy and Girl.

4017 Poor Little Rich Girl (20th Century-Fox, 1936, Shirley Temple, Alice Faye).

But Definitely/Military Man/Oh My Goodness—Mack Gordon, Harry Revel (w,m), Robbins; Ride a Cock-Horse to Banbury Cross (VS)—John Rochette (w,m), Movietone; When I'm With You/You Gotta Eat Your Spinach Baby—Mack Gordon, Harry Revel (w,m), Robbins. COVER: Shirley Temple, Alice Faye, Jack Haley.

4018 Pope of Greenwich Village (United Artists, 1984, Eric Roberts, Mickey Rourke).

Summer Wind—Johnny Mercer (w), Henry Mayer (m), Warner.

COVER: Eric Roberts, Mickey Rourke.

4019 Popeye (Paramount, 1934, Cartoon).

I'm Popeye the Sailor Man—Sammy Lerner (w,m), Famous. COVER: Popeye.

4020 Popeye (Paramount, 1981, Robin Williams, Shelley Duvall).

I'm Popeye the Sailor Man—Sammy Lerner (w,m), Famous; Popeye-Fourteen Songs—Harry Nilsson (w, m), Famous. COVER: Robin Williams, Shelley Duvall, and Baby.

4021 Popeye the Sailor Meets Sinbad the Sailor (Paramount, 1936, Cartoon).

I'm Sinbad the Sailor (VS)—Bob Rothberg (w), Sammy Timberg (m), Famous. COVER: Popeye.

4022 Popi (United Artists, 1969, Rita Moreno, Alan Arkin).

Popi—Norman Gimbel (w), Dominic Frontiere (m), Unart. COVER: Alan Arkin, and Kids.

4023 Poppin' the Cork (Educational, 1934, Milton Berle, Norma Taylor).

Here's Looking at You/Poppin' the Cork—Benny Davis (w), James Hanley (m), Movietone. COVER: Girls and Champagne Glasses.

4024 Poppy (Paramount, 1936, W. C. Fields, Rochelle Hudson).

Poppy—Sam Coslow, Frederick Hollander (w,m), Famous; Rendezvous with a Dream—Leo Robin, Ralph Rainger (w,m), Famous. COVER: Rochelle Hudson, Richard Cromwell, W. C. Fields.

4025 Porgy and Bess (Columbia, 1959, Sidney Poitier, Dorothy Dandridge).

Bess You Is My Woman/I Got Plenty o' Nuttin'/I Loves You Porgy—Dubose Heyward, Ira Gershwin (w), George Gershwin (m), Gershwin; It Ain't Necessarily So—Ira Gershwin (w), George Gershwin (m), Gershwin; My Man's Gone Now —Dubose Heyward (w), George Gershwin (m), Gershwin; Oh Bess, Oh Where's My Bess—Ira Gershwin (w), George Gershwin (m), Gershwin; Summertime—Dubose Heyward (w), George Gershwin (m), Gershwin; There's a Boat Dat's Leavin' for New York—Ira Gershwin (w), George Gershwin (m), Gershwin; Woman Is a Sometime Thing, A— Dubose Heyward (w), George Gershwin (m), Gershwin. COVER: Sidney Poitier, Dorothy Dandridge, Sammy Davis.

4026 Porky Pig (Warner Bros., 1955, Cartoon).

Porky Pig and Petunia Pig/Porky "Piggeldy Wiggeldy" Pig—Tedd Pierce, Warren Foster (w,m), Witmark. COVER: Porky Pig.

4027 Port Afrique (Columbia, 1956, Pier Angeli, Phil Carey).

Melody from Heaven, A (B)— Jack Fishman (w), Luis Araque (m), Chappell. COVER: Pier Angeli, Phil Carey.

4028 Port of Dreams (Girl Overboard) (Universal, 1929, Mary Philbin, Fred MacKaye).

Today and Tomorrow—Roy Turk, Joe Cherniansky, Fred Ahlert (w, m), Shapiro Bernstein. COVER: Mary Philbin, Fred MacKaye.

4029 Portrait of Jennie (Selznick, 1948, Jennifer Jones, Joseph Cotten).

Portrait of Jennie—Gordon Burdge (w), J. Russel Robinson (m), Chappell. COVER: Jennifer Jones, Joseph Cotten.

4030 Poseidon Adventure, The (20th Century-Fox, 1972, Gene Hackman, Ernest Borgnine).

Morning After, The—Al Kasha, Joel Hirshhorn (w,m), Fox. COVER: Movie Scene.

4031 Posse (Paramount, 1975, Kirk Douglas, Bruce Dern).

Once to Each Man—Paul F. Webster (w), Maurice Jarre (m), Famous. COVER: Cowboys.

4032 Possessed (Mirage) (MGM, 1931, Clark Gable, Joan Crawford).

How Long Will It Last—Max Lief

(w), Joseph Meyer (m), Robbins.
COVER: Clark Gable, Joan Crawford.

4033 Postman Always Rings Twice, The (MGM, 1946, Lana Turner, John Garfield).
She's Funny That Way—Richard Whiting (w), Neil Moret (m), Robbins. COVER: Lana Turner, John Garfield.

4034 Pot o' Gold (United Artists, 1940, James Stewart, Paulette Goddard).
Broadway Caballero—Henry Russell (w,m), BMI; Do You Believe in Fairy Tales—Mack David (w), Vee Lawnhurst (m), Santly Joy; Hi Cy, What's A-Cookin'?—Henry Russell, Lou Forbes (w,m), BMI; Knife, a Fork and a Spoon, A—Dave Franklin (w,m), Shapiro Bernstein; Pete the Piper—Henry Russell (w,m), BMI; When Johnny Toots His Horn—Hy Heath, Fred Rose (w,m), Berlin. COVER: James Stewart, Paulette Goddard, Horace Heidt.

4035 Powder River (Buckaroo from Powder River) (Columbia, 1946, Smiley Burnette, Charles Starrett).
A New Ten Gallon Hat (VS)—Bob Wills, Smiley Burnette, Lee Penny (w,m), Preview. COVER: Ken Curtis.

4036 Power (MGM, 1967, George Hamilton, Suzanne Pleshette).
Power-Theme—Miklos Rozsa (m), Feist. COVER: George Hamilton, Suzanne Pleshette.

4037 Powers Girl, The (United Artists, 1942, George Murphy, Anne Shirley).
Lady Who Didn't Believe in Love/Out of This World/Partners/Three Dreams—Kim Gannon (w), Jule Styne (m), Remick. COVER: George Murphy, Anne Shirley, Carole Landis, Benny Goodman.

4038 Practically Yours (Paramount, 1944, Claudette Colbert, Fred MacMurray).
I Knew It Would Be This Way—Sam Coslow (w,m), Famous. COVER: Claudette Colbert, Fred MacMurray.

4039 Prairie Moon (Republic, 1940, Gene Autry, Smiley Burnette).
Rhythm of the Hoofbeats (VS)—Gene Autry, Fred Rose, Johnny Marvin (w,m), Western. COVER: Gene Autry.

4040 Presenting Lily Mars (MGM, 1943, Judy Garland, Van Heflin).
Broadway Rhythm (VS)—Arthur Freed (w), Nacio Herb Brown (m), Chappell; Every Little Movement (VS)—Otto Harbach (w), Karl Hoschna (m), Chappell; Is It Really Love/When I Look at You—Paul F. Webster (w), Walter Jurmann (m), Feist. COVER: Judy Garland, Bob Crosby.

4041 President's Lady, The (20th Century-Fox, 1953, Susan Hayward, Charlton Heston).
My Love for You—Mack Gordon (w), Alfred Newman (m), Feist; President's Lady, The—Alfred Newman (m), Feist. COVER: Jackie Gleason, Clark Dennis.

4042 Presidio (Paramount, 1988, Sean Connery, Mark Harmon).
Presidio Theme—Bruce Broughton (m), Famous. COVER: Sean Connery, Mark Harmon.

4043 Pretty in Pink (Paramount, 1986, Molly Ringwald, Harry Dean Stanton).
If You Leave—Paul Humphreys, Andy McCluskey (w,m), Virgin; Pretty in Pink—T. Butler, R. Butler, V. Ely, J. Ashton, D. Kilburn, R. Morris (w,m), CBS. COVER: Molly Ringwald, Jon Cryer, Andrew McCarthy.

4044 Pretty Ladies (MGM, 1925, Zasu Pitts, Ann Pennington).
House Fly Blues/I Want a Man/Pretty Ladies—Ted Barron (w,m), Barron. COVER: Ann Pennington, Zasu Pitts, Norma Shearer, Joan Crawford.

4045 Pretty Maids All in a Row (MGM, 1971, Rock Hudson, Angie Dickinson).

Chilly Winds—M. Charles (w), Lalo Schifrin (m), Hastings. COVER: Rock Hudson, and Girls.

4046 Preview Murder Mystery (Paramount, 1936, Gail Patrick, Reginald Denny).

Promise with a Kiss—Leo Robin, Charles Kisco (w,m), Famous. COVER: Gail Patrick, Reginald Denny.

4047 Pride of the Yankees, The (RKO, 1942, Gary Cooper, Teresa Wright).

Always—Irving Berlin (w,m), Berlin. COVER: Gary Cooper, Teresa Wright.

4048 Prime of Miss Jean Brodie, The (20th Century-Fox, 1971, Maggie Smith, Robert Stephens).

Bend Down and Touch Me/Jean —Rod McKuen (w,m), Fox. COVER: Maggie Smith, and Students.

4049 Prince and the Show Girl, The (20th Century-Fox, 1957, Marilyn Monroe, Laurence Olivier).

I Found a Dream—Christopher Hassall (w), Richard Addinsell (m), Chappell. COVER: Marilyn Monroe, Laurence Olivier.

4050 Prince for Cynthia, A (Independent, 1954, Stars Unknown).

A Waltz for Cynthia—Norbert Glanzberg (m), Dartmouth. COVER: Black and white cover with title only.

4051 Prince of Foxes (20th Century-Fox, 1949, Tyrone Power, Orson Welles).

Prince of Foxes-Themes (PC)— Alfred Newman (m), Fox. COVER: None.

4052 Prince of Peace, The (The Lawton Story) (Hallmark, 1951, Ginger Prince, Forrest Taylor).

Down in Oklahoma—Lee White (w,m), Kaybee; Prince of Peace, The —Irving Bibo (w,m), Bibo; Right Under My Nose—Stephen Edwards (w), Andy Page (m), Kaybee. COVER: Ginger Prince, Lee White.

4053 Princess and the Pirate, The (RKO, 1944, Bob Hope, Virginia Mayo).

How Would You Like to Kiss Me in the Moonlight—Harold Adamson (w), Jimmy McHugh (m), Robbins. COVER: Bob Hope, Virginia Mayo.

4054 Princess Bride, The (20th Century-Fox, 1987, Cary Elwes, Robin Wright).

Storybook Love—Willy DeVille (w,m), Irving. COVER: Father and Son.

4055 Princess Charming (GB, 1935, Henry Wilcoxon, Evelyn Laye).

Love Is a Song/Near and Yet So Far—Max Kester (w), Ray Noble (m), Harms. COVER: Henry Wilcoxon, Evelyn Laye.

4056 Princess Comes Across, The (Paramount, 1936, Carole Lombard, Fred MacMurray).

My Concertina—Jack Scholl, Phil Boutelje (w,m), Popular. COVER: Carole Lombard, Fred MacMurray.

4057 Princess O'Rourke (Warner Bros., 1943, Olivia de Havilland, Robert Cummings).

Honorable Moon—Ira Gershwin, E. Y. Harburg (w), Arthur Schwartz (m), Chappell. COVER: Olivia de Havilland, Robert Cummings.

4058 Prince Valiant (20th Century-Fox, 1954, Robert Wagner, Janet Leigh).

I Do—Ken Darby (w), Franz Waxman (m), Miller. COVER: Robert Wagner, Janet Leigh.

4059 Priorities on Parade (Paramount, 1942, Jerry Colonna, Betty Jane Rhodes).

Conchita Marquita Lolita Pepita Rosita Juanita Lopez/Co-operate with Your Air Raid Warden/I'd Love to Know You Better—Herb Magidson (w), Jule Styne (m), Famous; You're in Love with Someone Else— Frank Loesser (w), Jule Styne (m), Famous. COVER: Betty Jane Rhodes, Johnnie Johnston, Anne Miller.

4060 Prisoner of Zenda, The

(Metro, 1922, Alice Terry, Ramon Novarro).

Zenda—Louis Breau, Ernst Luz (w,m), Belwin. COVER: Alice Terry.

4061 Prisoners (Warner Bros., 1929, Corinne Griffith, Ian Keith).

When My Dream of Love Comes True—Herman Ruby (w), Norman Spencer (m), Witmark. COVER: Corinne Griffith.

4062 Private Affairs of Bel Ami, The (United Artists, 1947, George Sanders, Angela Lansbury).

My Bel Ami—Jack Lawrence, Irving Drutman (w,m), Bourne. COVER: Angela Lansbury.

4063 Private Buckaroo (Universal, 1942, Andrews Sisters, Harry James).

Don't Sit Under the Apple Tree (PC)—Lew Brown, Charles Tobias, Sam Stept (w,m), Robbins;Johnny Get Your Gun Again—Don Raye, Gene DePaul (w,m), Leeds; Private Buckaroo—Charles Newman (w), Allie Wrubel (m), Challenge; Six Jerks in a Jeep—Sid Robin (w,m), Leeds; That's the Moon My Son—Art Kassel, Sammy Gallop, Norman Litman (w,m), Leeds; You Made Me Love You—Joseph McCarthy (w), James Monaco (m), Broadway. COVER: Harry James and the Andrews Sisters.

4064 Private Lessons (Vitaphone, 1934, Musical Short).

Snow Song—Cliff Hess (w,m), Witmark. COVER: Black and white cover with title only.

4065 Private Life of Don Juan, The (United Artists, 1934, Douglas Fairbanks, Merle Oberon).

Don Juan—George F. Rubens, Berlin; Senorita Carmencita (B)—Arthur Wimperis (w), Michael Spolianski (m), Campbell. COVER: Douglas Fairbanks, and Girl.

4066 Private Life of Henry VIII, The (United Artists, 1933, Charles Laughton, Robert Donat).

Oh Henry (B)—Arthur DeClero

(w,m), Day. COVER: Charles Laughton.

4067 Private Lives (MGM, 1931, Norma Shearer, Robert Montgomery).

Someday I'll Find You (B)—Noel Coward (w,m), Chappell. COVER: Norma Shearer, Robert Montgomery.

4068 Private Miss Jones (Thousands Cheer) (MGM, 1943, Kathryn Grayson, Gene Kelly).

Just as Long as I Know Katie's Waitin'—Lew Brown, George Brown (w,m), Feist. COVER: Black and white cover with title only.

4069 Private Right (Onyx, 1967, Dimitris Andreas, George Kafkaris).

Private Right Theme—Nicos Mamangakis (m), Peer. COVER: A Soldier.

4070 Private's Affair, A (20th Century-Fox, 1959, Sal Mineo, Christine Carere).

Same Old Army/Thirty Six, Twenty Four, Thirty Six/Warm and Willing—Jay Livingston, Ray Evans, Jimmy McHugh (w,m), Miller. COVER: Sal Mineo, Gary Crosby, Barry Coe, Barbara Eden, Terry Moore.

4071 Private War of Major Benson, The (Universal, 1955, Charlton Heston, Julie Adams).

Toy Tiger—Herman Stein, Henry Mancini (w,m), Northern. COVER: Tim Hovey, Charlton Heston.

4072 Privilege (Universal, 1967, Paul Jones, Jean Shrimpton).

Free Me/I've Been a Bad, Bad Boy/Privilege—Mike Leander (w,m), Shamley. COVER: Paul Jones, Jean Shrimpton.

4073 Prize, The (MGM, 1963, Paul Newman, Elke Sommer).

Prize—Dorcas Cochran (w), Jerry Goldsmith (m), Hastings; Prize Theme—Jerry Goldsmith (m), Hastings. COVER: Paul Newman, Elke Sommer.

4074 Prizefighter and the Lady, The (MGM, 1933, Myrna Loy, Max Baer).

Downstream Drifter—Gus Kahn,

Ray Egan (w), Dave Snell (m), Robbins; You've Got Everything—Gus Kahn (w), Walter Donaldson (m), Robbins. COVER: Myrna Loy, Max Baer.

4075 Prize of Gold (Columbia, 1955, Richard Widmark, Mai Zetterling).

Prize of Gold—Ned Washington (w), Lester Lee (m), Colgems. COVER: Richard Widmark, Mai Zetterling.

4076 Probation Wife (Select, 1919, Norma Talmadge, Thomas Meighan).

I Knew We'd Meet Again—Rodney Powers (w,m), Bluebird. COVER: Norma Talmadge, Thomas Meighan.

4077 Prodigal, The (The Southerner) (MGM, 1931, Lawrence Tibbett, Esther Ralston).

Chidlins—Howard Johnson (w), Herbert Stothart (m), Robbins; Life Is a Dream—Arthur Freed (w), Oscar Straus (m), Robbins; Without a Song—William Rose, Edward Eliscu (w), Vincent Youmans (m), Youmans. COVER: Lawrence Tibbett, Esther Ralston.

4078 Prodigal, The (MGM, 1955, Lana Turner, Edmund Purdom).

Prodigal Love Theme/Samarra—Bronislau Kaper (m), Miller. COVER: Lana Turner.

4079 Prodigal, The (World Wide, 1983, B. J. Thomas).

I Have Today—Dennis Spiegel (w), Bruce Broughton (m), Mama. COVER: B. J. Thomas.

4080 Prodigal's Mother, The (Someone to Remember) (Republic, 1943, Mabel Paige, John Craven).

Susie—Dorcas Cochran (w), Walter Scharf (m), Southern. COVER: Mabel Paige, John Craven, Dorothy Morris.

4081 Producers, The (Embassy, 1967, Zero Mostel, Gene Wilder).

Springtime for Hitler—Mel Brooks (w,m), Legation. COVER: Girl with Mustache.

4082 Professionals, The (Columbia, 1966, Burt Lancaster, Lee Marvin).

Professionals Theme—Maurice Jarre (m), Colgems. COVER: Burt Lancaster, Lee Marvin.

4083 Professional Soldier (20th Century-Fox, 1936, Dixie Dunbar, Victor McLaglen).

Joan of Arkansaw—Edward Heyman (w), John Green (m), Movietone. COVER: Dixie Dunbar.

4084 Professional Sweetheart (RKO, 1933, Ginger Rogers, Norman Foster).

My Imaginary Sweetheart—Edward Eliscu (w), Harry Akst (m), Witmark. COVER: Ginger Rogers.

4085 Promise, The (Universal, 1979, Kathleen Quinlan, Stephen Collins).

I'll Never Say Goodbye—Alan Bergman, Marilyn Bergman (w), David Shire (m), Leeds. COVER: Kathleen Quinlan, Stephen Collins.

4086 Promise Her Anything (Paramount, 1965, Warren Beatty, Leslie Caron).

Promise Her Anything—Hal David (w), Burt Bacharach (m), Famous; Something's Comin' Off Tonight—Ron Grainer (w,m), Famous. COVER: Warren Beatty, Leslie Caron, and Movie Scenes.

4087 Proud and the Profane, The (Paramount, 1956, William Holden, Deborah Kerr).

Proud and the Profane, The—Ross Bagdasarian (w,m), Paramount; To Love You—Mack Gordon (w), Victor Young (m), Paramount. COVER: William Holden, Deborah Kerr.

4088 Proud Ones, The (20th Century-Fox, 1956, Robert Ryan Virginia Mayo).

Proud Ones Theme—Johnny Desmond, Ruth Keddington (w), Lionel Newman (m), Weiss Barry. COVER: Robert Ryan, Virginia Mayo, Jeffrey Hunter.

4089 Proud Rebel (Buena Vista, 1958, Alan Ladd, Olivia de Havilland).

My Rebel Heart—Ned Washington (w), Jerome Moross (m), Chappell. COVER: Alan Ladd, Olivia de Havilland.

4090 Prudence and the Pill (20th Century-Fox, 1968, Deborah Kerr, David Niven).

Too Soon to Tell You—Norman Newell (w), Bernard Ebbinghouse (m), Fox. COVER: David Niven, Deborah Kerr.

4091 Prudence the Pirate (Thanhouser, 1916, Flora Finch, Gladys Hulette).

Prudence Entracte—Ernest Luz (m), Photoplay. COVER: Gladys Hulette.

4092 Prunella (Paramount, 1919, Marguerite Clark, Jules Raucort).

Starlight Love Waltz—Lucien Denni (m), Witmark. COVER: Marguerite Clark, Jules Raucort.

4093 Psycho (Paramount, 1960, Anthony Perkins, Janet Leigh).

Psycho-Prelude—Bernard Hermann (m), Ensign. COVER: Red and black cover with title only.

4094 Public Cowboy Number One (Republic, 1938, Gene Autry, Smiley Burnette).

I Picked Up the Trail When I Found You (VS)/West Ain't What It Used to Be (VS)—Fleming Allan (w,m), Cole. COVER: Gene Autry.

4095 Public Nuisance Number One (Cecil, 1936, Francis Day, Arthur Riscoe).

Between You and Me and the Carpet (B)/Hotsy Totsy (B)/Me and My Dog (B)—Vivian Ellis (w,m), Victoria; Swing—Vivian Ellis (w,m), Chappell. COVER: Frances Day, Arthur Riscoe.

4096 Public Pidgeon Number One (RKO, 1956, Red Skelton, Vivian Blaine).

Don't Be a Chicken, Chicken/Pardon Me Gotta Go Mambo—Eve Marley (w), Matty Malneck (m), Lamas. COVER: Red Skelton, Vivian Blaine, Janet Blair.

4097 Puddin' Head (Republic, 1941, Judy Canova, Eddie Foy Jr.).

Hey Junior/Manhattan Holiday/Minnie Hotcha/Puddin' Head/Sky's the Limit/You're Tellin' I—Eddie Cherkose, Sol Meyer (w), Jule Styne (m), Mills. COVER: Judy Canova, Francis Lederer, and others.

4098 Puf-n-Stuf (Universal, 1971, Jack Wild, Martha Raye).

Puf-n-Stuf—Six Songs—Norman Gimbel (w), Charles Fox (m), Hawaii. COVER: Martha Raye, Mama Cass, Billie Hayes, and little girl.

4099 Puppy Love (Disney, 1933, Cartoon).

Spring Is in the Air (VS)/That's Called Puppy Love (VS)—Frank Churchill (w,m), Berlin. COVER: Cartoon.

4100 Purchase Price, The (Warner Bros., 1932, Barbara Stanwyck, George Brent).

Take Me Away—Sidney Clare, Charles Tobias (w), Peter Tinturin (m), Harms. COVER: Barbara Stanwyck.

4101 Purple Mask, The (Universal, 1916, Grace Cunard, Francis Ford).

Girl in the Purple Mask, The—Harry Ralph (w), Ted Barron (m), Metropolis. COVER: Grace Cunard, Francis Ford.

4102 Purple Rain (Warner Bros., 1984, Prince, Apollonia Kotero).

I Would Die 4 U/Let's Go Crazy/Take Me with U/When Doves Cry/Purple Rain-Eleven Songs—Prince (w, m), Controversy. COVER: Prince.

4103 Pursuit of Happiness, The (Columbia, 1971, Michael Sarrazin, Barbara Hershey).

Let Me Go—Randy Newman (w, m), Colgems. COVER: Michael Sarrazin, Barbara Hershey.

4104 Pusher, The (United Artists, 1958, Kathy Carlisle, Felice Orlandi).

Where Have You Been, Billie Boy—Lawrence Elow (w), Raymond Scott (m), Feist. COVER: Dorothy Collins.

4105   Puss in Boots (Picture Classics, 1931, Stars Unknown).

All I Have Is Spinach/Puss in Boots—Robert Simon (w), Nat Shilkret (m), Fischer. COVER: Dancing Children.

4106   Puttin' on the Ritz (United Artists, 1930, Harry Richman, Joan Bennett).

Alice in Wonderland/Puttin' on the Ritz—Irving Berlin (w,m), Berlin; Singing a Vagabond Song—Harry Richman, Val Burton (w), S. Messenheimer (m), Santly; There's Danger in Your Eyes Cherie—Harry Richman, Jack Meskill, Pete Wendling (w,m), Berlin; With You—Irving Berlin (w,m), Berlin. COVER: Harry Richman.

4107   Quadrophonia (World National, 1979, Phil Daniels, Mark Wingett).

Love Reign over Me—Pete Townsend (w,m), Track; Postcard—John Entwhistle (w,m), Track. COVER: The Who.

4108   Quarterback, The (Paramount, 1940, Wayne Morris, Virginia Dale).

Out with Your Chest—Frank Loesser (w), Matt Malneck (m), Paramount; Sentimental Me—Jack Lawrence (w), Paull Mann, Stephan Weiss (m), Paramount. COVER: Wayne Morris, Virginia Dale.

4109   Queen High (Paramount, 1930, Stanley Smith, Ginger Rogers).

Brother Just Laugh It Off—Arthur Schwartz, Ralph Rainger, E. Y. Harburg (w,m), Famous; I Love a Girl in My Own Peculiar Way—E. Y. Harburg (w), Henry Souvain (m), Famous; I'm Afraid of You—Edward Eliscu (w), Arthur Schwartz, Ralph Rainger (m), Famous; Seems to Me—Dick Howard (w), Ralph Rainger (m), Famous. COVER: Ginger Rogers, Frank Morgan, and others.

4110   Queen of Burlesque (PRC, 1946, Evelyn Ankers, Carleton Young).

How Can I Thank You/Oh, No Not Much—Al Stewart (w), Gene Lucas (m), Peer. COVER: Evelyn Ankers, and Movie Scenes.

4111   Quick Before It Melts (MGM, 1964, George Maharis, Robert Morse).

Quick Before It Melts-Theme—David Rose (m), Robbins. COVER: Robert Morse, George Maharis, and Girls.

4112   Quick on the Trigger (Columbia, 1948, Charles Starrett, Smiley Burnette).

Midnite Flyer—Fred Rose, Hy Heath (w,m), Comdon. COVER: The Sunshine Boys.

4113   Quicksilver (Columbia, 1986, Kevin Bacon, Jami Gertz).

One Sunny Day, Duelling Bikes—Dean Pitchford, Bill Wolfer (w,m), Pitchford; Quicksilver Lightning—Dean Pitchford (w), Giorgio Moroder (m), Gold Horizon; Quicksilver-Ten Songs—Tony Banks, Peter Frampton, Larry McNally, Tom Newman (w,m), Columbia. COVER: Kevin Bacon.

4114   Quiero Llenarme   de Ti (I Want to Be Filled with Thee) (Independent, 1971, Stars Unknown).

Greatest Performance of My Life —Sandro Anderle, Oscar Anderle, R. Allen (w,m), Spier. COVER: Shirley Bassey.

4115   Quiet   American,   The (United Artists, 1958, Audie Murphy, Michael Redgrave).

Stay with Me (Rah hen gay)—Pham Dinh Chuong, Mario Nascimbene (m), Unart. COVER: Audie Murphy.

4116   Quiet Man, The (Republic, 1952, John Wayne, Maureen O'Hara).

Galway   Bay—Arthur   Colahan (w,m), Leeds; Isle of Innisfree—Richard Farrelly (w,m), Leeds; Mush Mush   Mush   Tural-i-addy—Sean O'Casey, Dennis O'Casey   (w,m), Leeds; Wild Colonial Boy, The—Joseph Crofts (w,m), Cox; Young May Moon, The—Thomas Moore,

Dan Howell (w,m), Leeds. COVER: John Wayne, Maureen O'Hara, Barry Fitzgerald.

4117 Quiller Memorandum (20th Century-Fox, 1966, George Segal, Alec Guinness).

Wednesday's Child-Theme—John Barry, Mack David (w,m), Miller. COVER: George Segal, Alec Guinness.

4118 Quilp (The Old Curiosity Shop) (Readers Digest, 1975, David Warner, Anthony Newley).

Every Dog Has His Day/Happiness Pie/Love Has the Longest Memory/Quilp/Somewhere/Sport of Kings/When a Felon Needs a Friend —Anthony Newley (w,m), Morris. COVER: Top Hat and Lettering

4119 Quincannon Frontier Scout (United Artists, 1956, Tony Martin, Peggie Castle).

Quincannon Frontier Scout— Sammy Cahn (w), Hal Borne (m), Hubert. COVER: Tony Martin, Peggie Castle.

4120 Quo Vadis (MGM, 1951, Robert Taylor, Deborah Kerr).

Lygia—Paul F. Webster (w), Miklos Rozsa (m), Robbins; Quo Vadis Music Score—Miklos Rozsa (m), Robbins. COVER: Deborah Kerr, and Movie Scene.

4121 Race for Your Life Charlie Brown (Paramount, 1977, Cartoon).

Greatest Leader, The—Lee Mendelson (w), Ed Bogas (m), Famous; Race for Your Life—Ed Bogas (w, m), Famous. COVER: Cartoon.

4122 Racers, The (20th Century-Fox, 1955, Kirk Douglas, Bella Darvi).

I Belong to You—Jack Brooks (w), Alex North (m), Robbins. COVER: Kirk Douglas, Bella Darvi.

4123 Race Street (RKO, 1948, George Raft, William Bendix).

Love That Boy—Don Raye, Gene DePaul (w,m), Famous. COVER: George Raft, Marilyn Maxwell, William Bendix.

4124 Rachel and the Stranger (RKO, 1948, Loretta Young, William Holden).

Along Came a Tall Dark Stranger/Foolish Pride/Just Like Me/ O He O Hi O Ho/Rachel/Summer Song—Waldo Salt (w), Roy Webb (m), Leeds. COVER: Robert Mitchum.

4125 Racing Blood (Conn, 1938, Frankie Darro, Kane Richmond).

You're So Appealing—Candy Coco (w), Tom Reilly, Jim Franklin (m), Handy. COVER: Frankie Darro, Jones Boys.

4126 Racing with the Moon (Paramount, 1984, Sean Penn, Elizabeth McGovern).

Racing with the Moon-Theme— Dave Grusin (m), Ensign. COVER: Sean Penn, Elizabeth McGovern.

4127 Racketeers in Exile (Columbia, 1937, George Bancroft, Evelyn Venable).

Something Has Happened—Joe Myrow, Milton Royce (w,m), Mills. COVER: George Bancroft, Evelyn Venable, Wynne Gibson.

4128 Rackety Rax (Fox, 1932, Victor McLaglen, Greta Nissen).

Puce and the Green, The (BW)/ Rackety Rax—L. Wolfe Gilbert (w), James Hanley (m), Movietone. COVER: Victor McLaglen, Greta Nissen.

4129 Radio City Revels (RKO, 1938, Bob Burns, Jack Oakie).

Goodnight Angel/I'm Takin' a Shine to You/Speak Your Heart/ Swingin' in the Corn/Take a Tip from the Tulip/There's a New Moon —Herb Magidson (w), Allie Wrubel (m), Berlin. COVER: Bob Burns, Jack Oakie, Ann Miller, Kenny Baker, Jane Froman.

4130 Radio Revels of 1942 (Swing It Soldier) (Universal, 1941, Ken Murray, Frances Langford).

Keep Your Thumbs Up—Jack Brooks (w), Norman Berens (m),

ABC.   COVER: Black and white cover with title only.

4131 Rage to Live, A (United Artists, 1965, Bradford Dillman, Suzanne Pleshette).

A Rage to Live—Noel Sherman (w), Ferrante & Teicher (m), Unart. COVER: Bradford Dillman, Suzanne Pleshette.

4132 Raggedy Ann and Raggedy Andy (Paramount, 1941, Cartoon).

No Speak 'Merican/Raggedy Ann I Love You/You're a Calico Millionaire/You're a Nobody Without a Name—Al Neiberg, Dave Fleischer, Sammy Timberg (w,m), Famous. COVER: Cartoon.

4133 Raggedy Rose (Pathe, 1926, Mabel Normand).

Raggedy Rose—Marian Gillespie (w), John Hagen (m), Marks. COVER: Mabel Normand.

4134 Raging Bull (United Artists, 1980, Robert DeNiro, Cathy Moriarty).

Raging Bull Theme-Cavalleria Rusticana—Harold Wheeler, Joel Diamond (m), Unart. COVER: Red and black cover with title only.

4135 Ragtime (Paramount, 1982, James Cagney, Donald O'Connor).

Change Your Ways/One More Hour/Ragtime-Themes—Randy Newman (w,m), EMI. COVER: Red and black title.

4136 Ragtime Cowboy Joe (Universal, 1940, Johnny Mack Brown, Fuzzy Knight).

Cross Eyed Kate/Do the Oo La La—Everett Carter (w), Milton Rosen (m), Robbins. COVER: Johnny Mack Brown, Fuzzy Knight, Nell O'Day.

4137 Raiders of the Lost Ark (Paramount, 1981, Harrison Ford, Karen Allen).

Marion's Theme/Raiders March/Raiders of the Lost Ark-Four Themes—John Williams (m), Bantha. COVER: Harrison Ford.

4138 Rails into Laramie (Universal, 1954, John Payne, Mari Blanchard).

Laramie—Fred Herbert, Arnold Hughes, Frankie Lee (w,m), Marks. COVER: John Payne, Mari Blanchard.

4139 Rainbow (Tiffany, 1929, Dorothy Sebastian, Laurence Gray).

Song of Gold—Edgar Leslie, Jimmie Monaco (w,m), Donaldson. COVER: Dorothy Sebastian, Laurence Gray.

4140 Rainbow Island (Paramount, 1944, Dorothy Lamour, Eddie Bracken).

Beloved/Boogie Woogie Boogie Man/What a Day—Ted Koehler (w), Burton Lane (m), Paramount. COVER: Dorothy Lamour, Eddie Bracken, Gil Lamb.

4141 Rainbow Man (Sono Art, 1929, Eddie Dowling, Frankie Darrow).

Little Pal/Rainbow Man—Eddie Dowling, James Hanley (w,m), Harms; Sleepy Valley—Andrew Sterling (w), James Hanley (m), Harms; Tambourine Tune—Eddie Dowling, James Hanley (w,m), Harms. COVER: Eddie Dowling (two covers).

4142 Rainbow on the River (RKO, 1936, Bobby Breen, May Robson).

Flower Song—Selma Hautzik (w), Hugo Riesenfeld (m), Feist; Rainbow on the River—Paul F. Webster (w), Louis Alter (m), Feist. COVER: Bobby Breen.

4143 Rainbow Over Broadway (Chesterfield, 1934, Frank Albertson, Joan Marsh).

Dance My Blues Away—Neville Fleeson (w), Albert Von Tilzer (m), Sam Fox; I Must be in Love (BW)—Elizabeth Morgan (w), Albert Von Tilzer (m), Sam Fox; Let's Go Places and Do Things—Harry MacPherson (w), Albert Von Tilzer (m), Sam Fox; Look Up, Not Down—Elizabeth Morgan (w), Albert Von Tilzer (m), Sam Fox; There Ain't

No Substitute for Love (BW) (w), Albert Von Tilzer (m), Sam Fox; While I'm in the Mood—George Whiting (w), Albert Von Tilzer (m), Sam Fox. COVER: Frank Albertson, Joan Marsh.

4144 Rainbow Round My Shoulder (Columbia, 1952, Frankie Laine, Billy Daniels).

Ain't Misbehavin'—Andy Razaf (w), Thomas Waller, Harry Brooks (m), Mills; Bubble, Bubble, Bubble—Robert Wright, George Forrest (w, m), Mills; She's Funny That Way—Richard Whiting (w), Neil Moret (m), Robbins. COVER: Frankie Laine, Billy Daniels.

4145 Rainbow Trail (Fox, 1932, George O'Brien, Cecilia Parker).

My Wife Does Fancy Work—Barry Conners (w), Frank Tresselt, Hugo Friedhofer (m), Movietone. COVER: Black and white cover with title only.

4146 Rainmaker, The (Paramount, 1956, Burt Lancaster, Katharine Hepburn).

Rainmaker, The—Hal David (w), Alex North (m), Famous. COVER: Burt Lancaster, Katharine Hepburn.

4147 Rainmakers, The (RKO, 1935, Bert Wheeler, Bob Woolsey).

Isn't Love the Greatest Thing?—Jack Scholl (w), Louis Alter (m), Feist. COVER: Wheeler and Woolsey, Dorothy Lee.

4148 Rain Man (United Artists, 1988, Dustin Hoffman, Tom Cruise).

Iko Iko—J. Jones, S. Jones, M. Jones, J. Thomas, J. Johnson, B. Hawkins, R. Hawkins (w,m), Trio; I Saw Her Standing There—John Lennon, Paul McCartney (w,m), Warner. COVER: Dustin Hoffman, Tom Cruise.

4149 Rains Came, The (20th Century-Fox, 1939, Tyrone Power, Myrna Loy).

The Rains Came—Mack Gordon (w,m), Robbins. COVER: Myrna Loy, Tyrone Power, George Brent.

4150 Raintree County (MGM,

1957, Elizabeth Taylor, Montgomery Clift).

Never Till Now/Song of Raintree County—Paul F. Webster (w), Johnny Green (m), Robbins; Raintree County-Thirteen Themes—Johnny Green (m), Robbins. COVER: Elizabeth Taylor, Montgomery Clift, Eva Marie Saint.

4151 Rambo-First Blood, Part Two (Tri-Star, 1985, Sylvester Stallone, Richard Crenna).

Peace in Our Life—Frank Stallone, Peter Schless, Jerry Goldsmith (w, m), Warner. COVER: Sylvester Stallone.

4152 Ramona (Clune, 1916, Monroe Salisbury, Adda Gleason).

Ramona-Eight Themes—Lloyd Brown, Emil Biermann (m), Brown. COVER: Adda Gleason.

4153 Ramona (United Artists, 1928, Dolores Del Rio, Warner Baxter).

Dolores—Edward Grossman, Ted Ward (w,m), Harms; Ramona—L. Wolfe Gilbert (w), Mabel Wayne (m), Feist. COVER: Dolores Del Rio.

4154 Ramona (20th Century-Fox, 1936, Don Ameche, Loretta Young).

How the Rabbit Lost His Tail (BW)/Ramona-Three Songs—William Kernell (w,m), Movietone. COVER: Loretta Young.

4155 Rampage (Warner Bros., 1963, Robert Mitchum, Elsa Martinelli).

Anna (B)/Romantic (B)—Elmer Bernstein (m), Blossom. COVER: Black and white cover with title only.

4156 Ramparts We Watch, The (RKO, 1940, John Adair, John Sammers).

Ramparts We Watch, The—J. S. Tolder (w), Gordon Beecher (m), Sam Fox. COVER: American Flag.

4157 Rancho Grande (Republic, 1940, Gene Autry, Smiley Burnette).

I Don't Belong in Your World (VS)—Gene Autry, Fred Rose (w,m),

Western; There'll Never Be Another Pal Like You—Gene Autry, John Marvin, Harry Tobias (w,m), Mills. COVER: Gene Autry.

4158 Rancho Notorious (RKO, Marlene Dietrich, Arthur Kennedy).

Get Away Young Man/Gypsy Davey/Legend of Chuck-a-luck—Ken Darby (w,m), Grammercy. COVER: Marlene Dietrich, Arthur Kennedy, Mel Ferrer.

4159 Rangers Round-Up, The (Spectrum, 1938, Fred Scott, Al St. John).

Hilltop Rendezvous/Jo-Jo-From Mexico/Just a Spanish Shawl/Sing a Song/Terror of Termite Valley—Lew Porter (w,m), Mills. COVER: Fred Scott.

4160 Rapture (20th Century-Fox, 1968, Patricia Gozzi, Melvyn Douglas).

Rapture (B)—Georges Delerue (m), Robbins. COVER: Black and white cover with title only.

4161 Rascal (Buena Vista, 1969, Steve Forrest, Pamela Toll).

Summer Sweet—Bobby Russell (w,m), Disney. COVER: Billy Mumy.

4162 Rascals (Little Gypsy) (20th Century-Fox, 1938, Jane Withers, Rochelle Hudson).

Blue Is the Evening/Song of the Gypsy Band/Take a Tip from a Gypsy—Sidney Clare (w), Harry Akst (m), Mills. COVER: Jane Withers, Rochelle Hudson, Robert Wilcox.

4163 Rat Race, The (Paramount, 1960, Tony Curtis, Debbie Reynolds).

Rat Race Love Theme/Rat Race Main Title Theme—Elmer Bernstein (m), Famous. COVER: Tony Curtis, Debbie Reynolds.

4164 Raven, The (AIP, 1962, Vincent Price, Peter Lorre).

Raven-Two Themes (PC)—Les Baxter (m), Harlene. COVER: None.

4165 Rawhide (20th Century-Fox, 1938, Smith Ballew, Lou Gehrig).

Cowboy's Life—Eddie Cherkose,

Charles Rosoff (w,m), Hollywood; Drifting/When a Cowboy Goes to Town—Albert Von Tilzer, Harry MacPherson (w,m), Hollywood. COVER: Smith Ballew, Lou Gehrig.

4166 Rawhide Rangers (Universal, 1941, Johnny Mack Brown, Fuzzy Knight).

Cowboy Is Happy, A/Huckleberry Pie—Everett Carter (w), Milton Rosen (m), Robbins. COVER: Johnny Mack Brown, Fuzzy Knight, Nell O'Day.

4167 Rawhide Years, The (Universal, 1956, Tony Curtis, Colleen Miller).

Gypsy with the Fire in His Shoes—Peggy Lee, Laurindo Almeida (w, m), Northern. COVER: Tony Curtis, Colleen Miller.

4168 Raw Wind in Eden (Universal, 1958, Jeff Chandler, Esther Williams).

Magic Touch, The—Jay Livingston, Ray Evans (w,m), Northern. COVER: Jeff Chandler, Esther Williams.

4169 Razor's Edge, The (20th Century-Fox, 1946, Tyrone Power, Gene Tierney).

Mamselle—Mack Gordon (w), Edmund Goulding (m), Feist. COVER: Tyrone Power, Gene Tierney.

4170 Reach for the Sky (Rank, 1950, Kenneth More, Muriel Pavlow).

Reach for the Sky Theme—John Addison (m), Mills. COVER: Kenneth More.

4171 Reaching for the Moon (United Artists, 1931, Douglas Fairbanks, Bebe Daniels).

Reaching for the Moon/When the Folks High-Up Do the Mean Low-Down (PC)—Irving Berlin (w,m), Berlin. COVER: Douglas Fairbanks, Bebe Daniels.

4172 Ready Willing and Able (Warner Bros., 1937, Ruby Keeler, Lee Dixon).

Just a Quiet Evening/Sentimental and Melancholy/Too Marvelous for

Words—Johnny Mercer (w), Richard Whiting (m), Harms. COVER: Ruby Keeler, Allen Jenkins, and girls.

4173 Real Genius (Tri-Star, 1985, Val Kilmer, Gabe Jarret).

Real Genius—Thomas Newman (m), Triple. COVER: Val Kilmer.

4174 Reap the Wild Wind (Paramount, 1942, Ray Milland, Paulette Goddard).

Reap the Wild Wind—Ned Washington (w), Lew Pollack (m), Famous. COVER: Ray Milland, Paulette Goddard, John Wayne.

4175 Rear Window (Paramount, 1954, James Stewart, Grace Kelly).

Lisa—Harold Rome (w), Franz Waxman (m), Paramount. COVER: James Stewart, Grace Kelly.

4176 Rebecca of Sunnybrook Farm (20th Century-Fox, 1938, Shirley Temple, Randolph Scott).

Alone with You—Sidney Mitchell (w), Lew Pollack (m), Hollywood; Come and Get Your Happiness—Jack Yellen (w), Sam Pokrass (m), Crawford; Happy Ending—Sidney Mitchell (w), Lew Pollack (m), Hollywood; Old Straw Hat, An—Mack Gordon, Harry Revel (w,m), Feist; Toy Trumpet—Sidney Mitchell, Lew Pollack (w), Ray Scott (m), Circle. COVER: Shirley Temple, Randolph Scott, Gloria Stuart.

4177 Rebel, The (Call Me Genius) (Continental, 1961, Tony Hancock, George Sanders).

Ou la la (B)/Rebel Theme (B)—Frank Cordell (m), Harms. COVER: Tony Hancock.

4178 Rebel in Town (United Artists, 1956, John Payne, Ruth Roman).

Rebel in Town—Lenny Adelson (w), Les Baxter (m), Saunders. COVER: John Payne, Ruth Roman.

4179 Rebel Without a Cause (Warner Bros., 1955, James Dean, Natalie Wood).

Rebel Without a Cause Theme (BW)—Leonard Rosenman (m), Witmark; Secret Doorway—Mack Discant

Leonard Rosenman (m), Witmark. COVER: James Dean, Natalie Wood.

4180 Rebound (RKO, 1931, Ina Claire, Robert Ames).

Same Thing Over Again—Roy Ringwald, Lindsay Macharrie (w,m), Feist. COVER: Ina Claire.

4181 Reckless (MGM, 1935, Jean Harlow, William Powell).

Everything's Been Done Before—Harold Adamson, Edwin Knopf, Jack King (w,m), Robbins; Hi Diddle Dee Dum—Herb Magidson (w), Con Conrad (m), Robbins; Reckless—Oscar Hammerstein (w), Jerome Kern (m), Harms. COVER: William Powell, Jean Harlow.

4182 Reckless Living (Universal, 1938, Nan Grey, Robert Wilcox).

When the Stars Go to Sleep—Harold Adamson (w), Jimmy McHugh (m), Miller. COVER: Nan Grey.

4183 Record Breaker Series (RKO, 1929, Alberta Vaughn).

Crazy Melody—Lee Zahler, Pat O'Dea (w,m), Shapiro Bernstein. COVER: Alberta Vaughn.

4184 Red Circle, The (Pathe, 1915, Ruth Roland, Frank Mayo).

Red Circle Waltz—Abe Olman (m), Morris. COVER: Ruth Roland.

4185 Red Dance (Fox, 1927, Dolores Del Rio, Charles Farrell).

Someday, Somewhere, We'll Meet Again—Lew Pollack (w), Erne Rapee (m), DBH. COVER: Dolores Del Rio.

4186 Redeeming Sin, The (Warner Bros., 1929, Dolores Costello, Conrad Nagel).

Fleurette—Billy Rose (w), Louis Silvers, Fred Fisher (m), Berlin. COVER: Dolores Costello.

4187 Red Garters (Paramount, 1954, Rosemary Clooney, Jack Carson).

Bad News/Brave Man/Dime and a Dollar, A/Good Intentions/Lady Killer/Man and a Woman, A/Meet a Happy Guy/Red Garters/Robin Randall Song/This Is Greater Than

I Thought/Vaquero—Jay Livingston, Ray Evans (w,m), Famous. COVER: Rosemary Clooney, Guy Mitchell.

4188 Red Hair (Paramount, 1928, Clara Bow, Lane Chandler).

Red Hair—Alfred Bryan, Francis Wheeler, Ted Snyder (w,m), Berlin. COVER: Clara Bow.

4189 Red Heads (Pathe, 1930, Nat Carr, Charles Kaley).

Shake Trouble Away/Since I Met You—Walt DeLeon (w), Henry Sullivan (m), Remick. COVER: Chorus Girls.

4190 Red Heads on Parade (Fox, 1935, John Boles, Dixie Lee).

I Found a Dream/I've Got Your Future/Redheads on Parade—Don Hartman (w), Jay Gorney (m), Movietone. COVER: John Boles, Dixie Lee, and girls.

4191 Red Hot and Blue (Paramount, 1949, Betty Hutton, Victor Mature).

Hamlet (PC)/I Wake Up in the Morning Feeling Fine/Now That I Need You/That's Loyalty—Frank Loesser (w,m), Famous. COVER: Betty Hutton, Victor Mature.

4192 Red Lantern, The (Metro, 1919, Nazimova, Darrell Foss).

Red Lantern—Fred Fisher (w,m), McCarthy Fisher. COVER: Nazimova.

4193 Red Line 1000 (Paramount, 1965, James Caan, Laura Devon).

Let Me Find Someone New—Carol Connors (w), Nelson Riddle (m), Ensign. COVER: James Caan, Laura Devon, and others.

4194 Red Mantle, The (Hagbard and Signe) (Prentoulis, 1972, Gitte Haenning, Oleg Vidov).

Red Mantle Love Theme—Sammy Cahn (w), Marc Fredericks (m), Sunbury; When Will the Killing End?—R. Allen (w), Marc Fredericks (m), Sunbury. COVER: Gitte Haenning, Oleg Vidov.

4195 Red Mill, The (MGM, 1926, Marion Davies, Owen Moore).

By the Old Red Mill (B)—H. Davies (m). COVER: Marion Davies.

4196 Red River Valley (Republic, 1936, Gene Autry, Smiley Burnette).

Red River Valley—Nick Manoloff (w,m), Calumet; Where a Water Wheel Keeps Turning on (VS)—Oliver Drake, Sam Stept (w,m), Cole. COVER: Gene Autry, and Movie Scenes.

4197 Reds (Paramount, 1981, Warren Beatty, Diane Keaton).

Goodbye for Now—Stephen Sondheim (w,m), Famous; Reds—Stephen Sondheim (m), Famous. COVER: Warren Beatty, Diane Keaton.

4198 Red Salute (United Artists, 1935, Barbara Stanwyck, Robert Young).

I Wonder Who's Kissing Her Now —Will Hough, Frank Adams (w), Joe Howard (m), Harris. COVER: Barbara Stanwyck, Robert Young.

4199 Red Shoes, The (Rank, 1950, Anton Walbrook, Moira Shearer).

The Red Shoes Ballet—Brian Easdale (m), Chappell. COVER: Red Curtains.

4200 Red Skin (Paramount, 1929, Richard Dix, Gladys Belmont).

Red Skin—Harry Kerr (w), J. S. Zamecnik (m), Sam Fox. COVER: Richard Dix, and Girl.

4201 Red Tanks (Artkino, 1943, War Film).

Song of the Tank Brigade—Dan Pokrass, Dom Pokrass (m), Russ Amer. COVER: An Army Tank.

4202 Red Tent, The (Paramount, 1971, Sean Connery, Claudia Cardinale).

Do Dreams Go On/In My Thoughts of You—Norman Simon, Lowell Mark (w), Ennio Morricone (m), Ensign. COVER: Sean Connery, Claudia Cardinale.

4203 Red White Blue (Picto, 1942, Ken Bennett, Joaquin Grill).

Gentlemen Waits Without/Here Comes a Soldier/Home in the Chu Chu Bean/Saddle and Ride/Skoal/

There'll Always Be a U.S.A./V-I-C-T-O-R-Y—Ruth Elliston (w), Bert Carlson (m), Picto. COVER: Soldiers and Gun.

4204 Regular Girl, A (Selznick, 1919, Elsie Janis, Robert Lytton).

A Regular Girl—Bert Kalmar, Harry Ruby (w), Elsie Janis (m), Berlin. COVER: Elsie Janis.

4205 Reluctant Dragon, The (RKO Disney, 1941, Cartoon).

Reluctant Dragon, The #1—Ed Penner, T. Hee, Charles Wolcott (w,m), BMI; Reluctant Dragon, The #2—Ed Penner, T. Hee, Charles Wolcott (w,m), Wonderland. COVER: Two Different Covers of a Dragon.

4206 Remains to Be Seen (MGM, 1953, June Allyson, Van Johnson).

Taking a Chance on Love—John Latouche, Ted Fetter (w), Vernon Duke (m), Miller; Toot Toot Tootsie —Gus Kahn, Ernie Erdman, Dan Russo (w,m), Feist. COVER: June Allyson, Van Johnson.

4207 Remember Last Night (Universal, 1935, Robert Young, Edward Arnold).

Remember Last Night—Sam Coslow (w,m), Popular. COVER: Robert Young, Constance Cummings, and others.

4208 Remember Pearl Harbor (Republic, 1942, Fay McKenzie, Don Barry).

Because We Are Americans— Emily Head (w,m), Mills. COVER: Don Barry, Alan Curtis, Fay McKenzie.

4209 Remote Control (MGM, 1930, Just a Little Closer—Howard Johnson (w), Joseph Meyer (m), Robbins. COVER: William Haines.

4210 Remo Williams, The Adventure Begins (Orion, 1985, Fred Ward, Joel Grey).

Remo's Theme-What If—Tommy Shaw, Richie Cannata (w,m), Tranquility. COVER: Tommy Shaw.

4211 Renegade Trail, The (Paramount, 1939, William Boyd, George Hayes).

Lazy Rolls the Rio Grande—Foster Carling (w), Phil Ohman (m), Paramount. COVER: William Boyd.

4212 Renfrew of the Royal Mounted (Grand National, 1937, James Newill, Carol Hughes).

Barbecue Bill/Little Son/Mounted Men/Tale of Love—Betty Laidlaw, Robert Lively (w,m), Mills. COVER: James Newill.

4213 Renfrew Rides the Great White Trail (On the Great White Trail) (Grand National, 1938, James Newill, Terry Walker).

Beautiful—Bob Taylor, Lew Porter (w,m), Mills; Je T'Aime—Lew Porter (w,m), Mills. COVER: James Newill.

4214 Reno (Sono Art, 1930, Ruth Roland, Kenneth Thompson).

As Long as We're Together—Ben Bard, Leslie Barton (w,m), Shapiro Bernstein. COVER: Ruth Roland.

4215 Repeat Performance (Eagle Lion, 1947, Louis Hayward, Joan Leslie).

Repeat Performance—Patrece Snyder, Ann Weingarten (w,m), Beverly. COVER: Louis Hayward, Joan Leslie.

4216 Reprieve (Convicts Four) (Allied Artists, 1962, Ben Gazzara, Stuart Whitman).

Reprieve Blues Theme (Ya Hear Me)—Lenny Adelson (w), Leonard Rosenman (m), Robbins. COVER: Designs and Letters.

4217 Requiem for a Heavyweight (Columbia, 1962, Anthony Quinn, Jackie Gleason).

Blues/Grace's Love Theme—Laurence Rosenthal (m), Chappell. COVER: Anthony Quinn, Jackie Gleason, Julie Harris, Mickey Rooney.

4218 Requins de Gibraltar (The Shark of Gibraltar) (Independent, 1953, Stars Unknown).

Melancolie (PC)—Richard Blake (w), Al Romans (m), Romans. COVER: None.

4219 Rescuers, The (Buena Vista, 1977, Cartoon).

Journey—Carol Connors, Ayn Robbins (w), Sammy Fain (m), Disney; R-E-S-C-U-E (Rescue Aid Society)—Carol Connors, Ayn Robbins (w,m), Disney; Someone's Waiting for You—Carol Connors, Ayn Robbins (w), Sammy Fain (m), Disney; Tomorrow Is Another Day—Carol Connors, Ayn Robbins (w,m), Disney. COVER: Cartoon.

4220 Restless Breed, The (20th Century-Fox, 1957, Scott Brady, Anne Bancroft).

Angelita/Restless Breed, The—Dick Hughes, Richard Stapley (w), Ed Alperson (m), Olman. COVER: Anne Bancroft.

4221 Restless Ones, The (World Wide, 1965, Georgia Lee, Robert Sampson).

He's Everything to Me/Numbers Song/Restless Ones-Theme—Ralph Carmichael (w,m), Lexicon. COVER: Georgia Lee, Robert Sampson.

4222 Resurrection (United Artists, 1927, Rod Laroque, Dolores Del Rio).

Brown Eyes—P. Ouglitzky (w,m), Strand. COVER: Russian Dancers.

4223 Resurrection (Universal, 1931, John Boles, Lupe Velez).

Baby's Lullaby/Song of the Gypsies/To Your Eyes/While the Volga's Flowing—Bernard Grossman (w), Dimitri Tiomkin (m), Universal. COVER: John Boles, Lupe Velez.

4224 Return from the Ashes (United Artists, 1965, Maximilian Schell, Samantha Eggar).

Return from the Ashes—Johnny Dankworth (m), Unart. COVER: Naked Girl.

4225 Return of Jack Slade, The (Allied Artists, 1955, John Ericson, Mari Blanchard).

Yellow Rose of Texas—Max Showalter, Jon Shepodd (w,m), Criterion. COVER: Mari Blanchard.

4226 Return of the Cisco Kid (20th Century-Fox, 1939, Warner Baxter, Lynn Bari).

Song of the Cisco Kid—Warner Baxter (w,m), Movietone. COVER: Warner Baxter, Lynn Bari.

4227 Return of the Durango Kid (Columbia, 1944, Charles Starrett, Tex Harding).

When They Fiddle Out the Polka—Eddie Seiler, Al Neiburg, Sol Marcus (w,m), Mutual. COVER: Sketch of Couple Dancing.

4228 Return of the Frontiersman (Warner Bros., 1950, Gordon MacRae, Jack Holt).

Underneath a Western Sky—Jack Scholl (w), M. K. Jerome, Ted Fiorito (m), Remick. COVER: Gordon MacRae, Julie London.

4229 Return of the Jedi (20th Century-Fox, 1983, Mark Hamlin, Harrison Ford).

Ewok Celebration—Joe Williams (w), John Williams (m), Warner; Lapti Nek—Annie Arbogast (w), John Williams (w), Warner; Luke and Leia/Return of the Jedi-Eight Themes—John Williams (m), Warner. COVER: A Sword.

4230 Return of the Pink Panther (United Artists, 1975, Peter Sellers, Christopher Plummer).

Greatest Gift, The—Hal David (w), Henry Mancini (m), Northridge. COVER: The Pink Panther.

4231 Return of the Rough Riders (Riders of the Northland) (Columbia, 1942, Charles Starrett, Russell Hayden).

Miss Liberty (PC)—Johnny Marvin, Jimmy Wakely, Jack Briggs (w, m), Southern. COVER: None.

4232 Return to Paradise (United Artists, 1953, Gary Cooper, Barry Jones).

Return to Paradise—Ned Washington (w), Dimitri Tiomkin (m), Remick. COVER: Gary Cooper, and Native Girl.

4233 Return to Peyton Place (20th Century-Fox, 1961, Carol Lynley, Jeff Chandler).

Return to Peyton Place Theme—Paul F. Webster (w), Franz Waxman (m), Robbins. COVER: Carol Lynley, Jeff Chandler.

4234   Reveille with Beverly (Columbia, 1943, Ann Miller, William Wright).

Cow Cow Boogie—Don Raye, Gene DePaul, Benny Carter (w,m), Leeds; Take the A Train (PC)—Delta Rhythm Boys (w), Billy Strayhorn (m), Tempo. COVER: Ella Mae Morse, Freddie Slack.

4235   Revelation (Metro, 1924, Viola Dana, Monte Blue).

Revelation Melody—G. DeGrandcourt (w), Rodolfo Guarda (m), Schuberth. COVER: Viola Dana, Monte Blue.

4236   Revenge (United Artists, 1928, Dolores Del Rio, Leroy Mason).

Dolores—Edward Grossman, Ted Ward (w,m), Harms; Revenge—Sam Lewis, Joe Young (w), Harry Akst (m), Remick. COVER: Dolores Del Rio.

4237   Revenge of the Nerds Two (20th Century-Fox, 1987, Robert Carradine, Larry Scott).

Back to Paradise—Bryan Adams, Jim Vallance, Pat Giraldo (w,m), Irving. COVER: The Nerds.

4238   Revolt of Mamie Stover, The (20th Century-Fox, 1956, Jane Russell, Richard Egan).

If You Wanna See Mamie Tonight—Paul F. Webster (w), Sammy Fain (m), Miller; Keep Your Eyes on the Hands—Tony Todaro, Mary Johnston (w,m), South Sea. COVER: Jane Russell.

4239   Rhapsody (MGM, 1954, Elizabeth Taylor, Vittorio Gassman).

Rhapsody Piano Themes (B)—P. Tchaikovsky, F. Chopin, F. Liszt (m), Chappell. COVER: Elizabeth Taylor, Vittorio Gassman.

4240   Rhapsody in Blue (Warner Bros., 1945, Robert Alda, Alexis Smith).

Bidin' My Time—Ira Gershwin (w), George Gershwin (m), New World; Clap Yo Hands—Ira Gershwin (w), George Gershwin (m), Harms; Delishious/Embraceable You—Ira Gershwin (w), George Gershwin (m), New World; I Got Rhythm—Ira Gershwin, George Gershwin (m), New World; Liza—Gus Kahn, Ira Gershwin (w), George Gershwin (m), New World; Love Walked In—Ira Gershwin (w), George Gershwin (m), Chappell; Man I Love, The/Oh Lady Be Good—Ira Gershwin (w), George Gershwin (m), Harms; Somebody Loves Me—B. G. DeSylva, Ballard MacDonald (w), George Gershwin (m), Harms; Someone to Watch over Me—Ira Gershwin (w), George Gershwin (m), Harms; Swanee—Irving Caesar (w), George Gershwin (m), Harms; 'S Wonderful—Ira Gershwin (w), George Gershwin (m), New World; Yankee Doodle Blues, The—B. G. DeSylva, Irving Caesar (w), George Gershwin (m), Bourne. COVER: Robert Alda.

4241   Rhinestone (20th Century-Fox, 1984, Dolly Parton, Sylvester Stallone).

God Won't Get You/Tennessee Homesick Blues/Rhinestone-Fourteen Songs—Dolly Parton (w,m), Columbia. COVER: Dolly Parton, Sylvester Stallone.

4242   Rhino (MGM, 1964, Harry Guardino, Shirley Eaton).

Rhino Theme—Lalo Schifrin (m), Hastings. COVER: Harry Guardino, and Movie Scenes.

4243   Rhythm in the Clouds (Republic, 1937, Patricia Ellis, Warren Hull).

Don't Ever Change—Walter Hirsch (w), Lou Handman (m), Santly; Hawaiian Hospitality—Harry Owens, Ray Kinney (w,m), Select; Two Hearts Are Dancing—Walter Hirsch (w), Lou Handman (m), Santly. COVER: Patricia Ellis, Warren Hull.

4244   Rhythm of Paree (Educational, 1935, Niela Goodelle).

Rhythm of Paree—Marcy Klauber, Charles Williams (w,m), Sam Fox. COVER: Niela Goodelle.

4245 Rhythm of the Islands (Universal, 1943, Jane Frazee, Allan Jones).

Bonga Bonga—Louis Herscher, Andy Iona (w,m), Mills; Polynesian Prayer—Dave Franklin (m), Mills. COVER: Allan Jónes, Jane Frazee.

4246 Rhythm of the Rio Grande (Monogram, 1940, Tex Ritter, Susan Dale)

Mexicali Moon (VS)/Rhythm of the Rio Grande (VS)—Frank Harford (w,m), Cole. COVER: Tex Ritter.

4247 Rhythm of the Saddle (Republic, 1938, Gene Autry, Smiley Burnette).

Merry Go Roundup/Old Trail, The (VS)—Gene Autry, Fred Rose, Johnny Marvin (w,m), Western. COVER: Gene Autry, Hoosier Hot Shots.

4248 Rhythm on the Range (Paramount, 1936, Bing Crosby, Frances Farmer).

Empty Saddles—J. Keirn Brennan (w), Billy Hill (m), Shapiro Bernstein; House Jack Built for Jill—Leo Robin, Frederick Hollander (w,m), Famous; I Can't Escape from You—Leo Robin, Richard Whiting (w,m), Famous; I'm an Old Cow Hand—Johnny Mercer (w,m), Feist; Rhythm on the Range—Walter Bullock, Richard Whiting (w,m), Famous; Round Up Lullaby—Badger Clark (w), Gertrude Ross (m), White Smith; You'll Have to Swing It—Sam Coslow (w,m), Famous. Bing Crosby, Frances Farmer.

4249 Rhythm on the River (Paramount, 1940, Bing Crosby, Mary Martin).

Ain't It a Shame About Mame—Johnny Burke (w), James Monaco (m), Santly Joy; I Don't Want to Cry Anymore—Victor Schertzinger (w, m), Famous; Only Forever—Johnny Burke (w), James Monaco (m), Santly Joy; Rhythm on the River/That's for Me/What Would Shakespeare Have Said—Johnny Burke (w), James Monaco (m), Famous; When the Moon Comes over Madison Square Garden—Johnny Burke (w), James Monaco (m), Santly Joy. COVER: Bing Crosby, Mary Martin.

4250 Rhythm Serenade (Columbia, 1943, Vera Lynn, Peter Hill).

With All My Heart (B)—Jack Popplewell (w), Reginald King (m), Maurice. COVER: Vera Lynn.

4251 Rich and Famous (MGM, 1981, Jacqueline Bisset, Candice Bergen).

Rich and Famous Theme—George Delerue (m), Warner. COVER: Jacqueline Bisset, Candice Bergen.

4252 Richard Pryor Live on the Sunset Strip (Columbia, 1982, Richard Pryor).

Richard Pryor Live on the Sunset Strip—Harry Betts (w,m), Gold Horizon. COVER: Richard Pryor.

4253 Rich People (Pathe, 1929, Constance Bennett, Regis Toomey).

One Never Knows—Walter O'-Keefe (w), Bobby Dolan (m), DBH; COVER: Constance Bennett.

4254 Rich Young and Pretty (MGM, 1951, Jane Powell, Vic Damone).

Dark Is the Night/How Dya Like Your Eggs in the Morning/I Can See You/L'Amour Toujours/Paris/We Never Talk Much/Wonder Why—Sammy Cahn (w), Nicholas Brodszky (m), Feist. COVER: Jane Powell, Vic Damone, Danielle Darrieux.

4255 Ricochet Romance (Universal, 1955, Marjorie Main, Chill Wills).

Ricochet Romance—Larry Coleman, Joe Darion, Norman Gimbel (w,m), Sheldon. COVER: Marjorie Main, Chill Wills.

4256 Ride Back, The (United Artists, 1957, Anthony Quinn, William Conrad).

The Ride Back—Frank DeVol (w, m), Meridian. COVER: Anthony Quinn, Ellen Monroe.

4257 Ride 'em Cowboy (Universal, 1942, Bud Abbott, Lou Costello).

Beside the Rio Tonto/Give Me My Saddle—Don Raye, Gene DePaul (w,m), Leeds; I'll Remember April—Don Raye, Gene DePaul, Pat Johnston (w,m), Leeds; Wake Up Jacob—Don Raye, Gene DePaul (w,m), Leeds. COVER: Abbott and Costello, Dick Foran, Anne Gwynne.

4258 Ride Ranger Ride (Republic, 1938, Gene Autry, Smiley Burnette).

On the Sunset Trail—Sidney Mitchell (w), Sam Stept (m), Sam Fox; Ride Ranger Ride/Song of the Pioneers—Tim Spencer (w,m), Cross Winge. COVER: Gene Autry.

4259 Riders in the Sky (Columbia, 1949, Gene Autry, Gloria Henry).

Riders in the Sky (PC)—Stan Jones (w,m), Mayfair. COVER: None.

4260 Riders of Death Valley (Universal, 1941, Dick Foran, Buck Jones).

Ride Along—Everett Carter (w), Milton Rosen (m), Robbins. COVER: Dick Foran, Buck Jones, Leo Carrillo, Noah Beery.

4261 Riders of Pasco Basin (Universal, 1940, Johnny Mack Brown, Bob Baker).

I'm Tying Up My Bridle/Song of the Prairie—Everett Carter (w), Milton Rosen (m), Robbins. COVER: Bob Baker.

4262 Riders of the Dawn (Monogram, 1937, Jack Randall, Peggy Keys).

White Clouds in the Moonlight—Robert Bradbury (w,m), Cross Winge. COVER: Del Courtney.

4263 Riders of the Frontier (Monogram, 1939, Tex Ritter, Jack Rutherford).

Rose of My Dreams (VS)—Frank Harford (w,m), Cole. COVER: Tex Ritter.

4264 Riders to the Stars (United Artists, 1954, William Lundigan, Herbert Marshall).

Riders to the Stars—Lee Pober (w), Harry Sukman (m), Morris. COVER: William Lundigan, Martha

Hyer, Dawn Addams.

4265 Ride the High Country (MGM, 1962, Randolph Scott, Joel McCrea).

Love Me Over and Over/Ride the High Country—Ken Darby (w), George Bassman (m), Miller. COVER: Randolph Scott, Joel McCrea.

4266 Ride the Wild Surf (Columbia, 1964, Fabian, Tab Hunter).

Ride the Wild Surf—Jan Berry, Rober Christian, Brian Wilson (w,m), Colgems. COVER: Jan and Dean.

4267 Ridin' Down the Canyon (Tumbling Tumbleweeds) Republic, 1935, Gene Autry, Smiley Burnette).

Ridin' Down the Canyon—Nick Manoloff, Gene Autry, Smiley Burnette (w,m), Cole. COVER: Gene Autry.

4268 Ridin' Down the Canyon (Republic, 1942, Roy Rogers, George Hayes).

Ridin' Down the Canyon—Nick Manoloff, Gene Autry, Smiley Burnette (w,m), Cole. COVER: Roy Rogers.

4269 Riding High (Paramount, 1943, Dorothy Lamour, Dick Powell).

Injun Gal Heap Hep—Leo Robin, Joe Lilley (w), Ralph Rainger (m), Paramount; Mister Five by Five (VS)—Don Raye, Gene DePaul (w,m), Leeds; Whistling in the Light/You're the Rainbow—Leo Robin (w), Ralph Rainger (m), Paramount. COVER: Dick Powell, Dorothy Lamour.

4270 Riding High (Paramount, 1950, Bing Crosby, Coleen Gray).

Camptown Races (B)—Stephen Foster (w,m), Chappell; Horse Tole Me, The/Someplace on Anywhere Road/Sunshine Cake/Sure Thing—Johnny Burke (w), James Van Heusen (m), BVH; Whiffenpoof Song—Rudy Vallee, M. Minnigerode, G. Pomeroy, T. Galloway (w,m), Miller. COVER: Bing Crosby, Coleen Gray.

4271 Riding on Air (RKO, 1937, Joe E. Brown, Florence Rice).

I'm Tired of Trying to Make You Care—Edward Sedgewick (w), Henry Cohen (m), Sherman-Clay. COVER: Joe E. Brown, Florence Rice, and others.

4272 Ridin' on a Rainbow (Republic, 1941, Gene Autry, Smiley Burnette).

Be Honest with Me—Gene Autry, Fred Rose (w,m), Western; Hunky Dunky Dory/I'm the Only Lonely One—Jule Styne, Sol Meyer (w,m), Mills; Ridin' on a Rainbow—Don George, Jean Herbert, Ted Hall (w, m), Famous; Sing a Song of Laughter/What's Your Favorite Holiday—Jule Styne, Sol Meyer (w,m), Mills. COVER: Gene Autry, Smiley Burnette, Mary Lee.

4273 Ridin' the Cherokee Trail (Monogram, 1941, Tex Ritter, Lloyd Andrews).

Down in Arkansaw (VS)—Slim Andrews (w,m), Cole; Song of the Coyotes (VS)—Jack Smith (w,m), Cole; Tennessee, Tennessee (VS)—Harry Blair, Jack Gillette (w,m), Cole. COVER: Tex Ritter.

4274 Rififi (UMPO, 1956, Jean Servais, Carl Mohner).

Hello to the Blues/Rififi—Jack Lawrence (w), M. Philippe Gerard (m), Chappell. COVER: Blue and green cover with title only.

4275 Right Approach, The (20th Century-Fox, 1960, Juliet Prowse, Frankie Vaughn).

Right Approach—Alan Bergman, Marilyn Keith (w), Lew Spence (m), Miller. COVER: Juliet Prowse, Frankie Vaughn.

4276 Right Stuff, The (Warner Bros., 1984, Charles Frank, Scott Glenn).

The Right Stuff—Bill Conti (m), Warner. COVER: Astronauts.

4277 Right to Happiness, The (Universal, 1919, Dorothy Phillips, William Stowell).

Right to Happiness, The—Alfred Bryan, Abby Green (w,m), Remick. COVER: Dorothy Phillips.

4278 Right to Love, The (Paramount, 1930, Ruth Chatterton, Paul Lukas).

Your True Love and Mine (PC)—Mickey Maslan (w), Ernest Shonfield (m), Maslanka. COVER: None.

4279 Rim of the Canyon (Columbia, 1949, Gene Autry, Nan Leslie).

Rim of the Canyon—Hy Heath, Johnny Lange (w,m), Bulls Eye. COVER: Gene Autry.

4280 Ring of Bright Water (Cinerama, 1969, Bill Travers, Virginia MacKenna).

Ring of Bright Water—Betty Botley (w), Frank Cordell (m), Ampco. COVER: Man, Woman, and an Otter.

4281 Ring of Fire (MGM, 1961, David Janssen, Joyce Taylor).

Bobbie—Edward Alperson, Jerry Winn (w,m), Robbins. COVER: David Janssen, Joyce Taylor, Frank Gorshin.

4282 Rings Around the World (Columbia, 1966, Don Ameche).

Canvas Sky—Howard Greenfield (w), Jacques Belasco (m), Colgems. COVER: Circus Acts.

4283 Ringside Maisie (MGM, 1941, Ann Sothern, George Murphy).

A Bird in a Gilded Cage—Arthur Lamb (w), Harry Von Tilzer (m), Von Tilzer. COVER: Ann Sothern.

4284 Rio (Universal, 1939, Sigrid Gurie, Basil Rathbone).

After the Rain/Heart of Mine/Love Opened My Eyes—Ralph Freed (w), Frank Skinner (m), Robbins. COVER: Sigrid Gurie.

4285 Rio Bravo (Warner Bros., 1959, John Wayne, Dean Martin).

Deguello (No Quarter)—Dimitri Tiomkin (m), Witmark; My Rifle, My Pony, and Me/Rio Bravo—Paul F. Webster (w), Dimitri Tiomkin (m), Witmark. COVER: John Wayne, Dean Martin, Ricky Nelson.

4286 Rio Conchas (20th Century-Fox, 1964, Stuart Whitman, Richard Boone).

Rio Conchas—Bernie Wayne (w), Jerry Goldsmith (m), Hastings. COVER: Stuart Whitman, Richard Boone, Anthony Franciosa.

4287 Rio Grande (Columbia, 1940, Charles Starrett, Ann Doran).

West Is in My Soul, The (VS)—Bob Nolan (w,m), American. COVER: Bob Nolan.

4288 Rio Grande (Republic, 1950, John Wayne, Maureen O'Hara).

My Gal Is Purple—Stan Jones (w, m), Mills. COVER: John Wayne.

4289 Rio Grande Ranger (Columbia, 1937, Bob Allen, Iris Meredith).

In the Gloamin' in Wyomin'—David Ormont (w), Lee Zahler (m), Mills. COVER: River and Trees.

4290 Rio Rita (RKO, 1929, Bebe Daniels, John Boles).

Following the Sun Around/If You're in Love, You'll Waltz/Kinkajou/Rangers Song/Rio Rita/Sweetheart, We Need Each Other/You're Always in My Arms—Joseph McCarthy (w), Harry Tierney (m), Feist. COVER: Bebe Daniels.

4291 Rio Rita (MGM, 1942, Bud Abbott, Lou Costello).

Long Before You Came Along—E. Y. Harburg (w), Harold Arlen (m), Feist; Rangers Song (BW)/Rio Rita (BW)—Joseph McCarthy (w), Harry Tierney (m), Feist. COVER: Abbott and Costello, Kathryn Grayson, John Carroll.

4292 Riot (Paramount, 1970, Jim Brown, Gene Hackman).

One Hundred Years—Robert Wells (w), Chris Komeda (m), Famous. COVER: Jim Brown, Gene Hackman.

4293 Riot in Cell Block Eleven (Allied Artists, 1954, Neville Brand, Emile Meyer).

Riot in Cell Block Eleven Theme (B)—Herschel Burke Gilbert (m), Campbell. COVER: Neville Brand.

4294 Riptide (MGM, 1934, Norma Shearer, Herbert Marshall).

Riptide—Gus Kahn (w), Walter Donaldson (m), Robbins. COVER: Norma Shearer.

4295 Rise and Shine (20th Century-Fox, 1941, Jack Oakie, George Murphy).

Central Two Two Oh Oh/I'm Making a Play for You—Leo Robin (w), Ralph Rainger (m), Robbins. COVER: Jack Oakie, George Murphy, Linda Darnell, Milton Berle.

4296 Rittratto Di Luisa (Portrait of Louise) (Paramount, 1975, Stars Unknown).

Lover or Fool—Richard Ahlert (w), Pasador Sandon (m), Gil. COVER: Black and white cover with title only.

4297 River, The (Fox, 1929, Charles Farrell, Mary Duncan).

I Found Happiness—Lew Pollack (w), Erno Rapee (m), DBH. COVER: Charles Farrell, Mary Duncan.

4298 River, The (United Artists, 1951, Nora Swinbourne, Esmond Knight).

The River—Ann Ronell (w,m), Schirmer. COVER: Radha.

4299 River of No Return (20th Century-Fox, 1954, Marilyn Monroe, Robert Mitchum).

Down in the Meadow/I'm Gonna File My Claim/One Silver Dollar/River of No Return—Ken Darby (w), Lionel Newman (m), Simon. COVER #1: Marilyn Monroe, with Guitar, and Movie Scenes. COVER #2: Marilyn Monroe-Face Only.

4300 River of Romance (Paramount, 1929, Charles Rogers, Mary Brian).

My Lady Love—Sam Coslow, Leo Robin (w,m), Spier Coslow. COVER: Charles Rogers, Mary Brian.

4301 River Rat, The (Paramount, 1984, Tommy Lee Jones, Brian Dennehy).

The River's Song/The River Rat-Ten Songs—Mike Post, Stephen Geyer (w,m), Famous. COVER: Tommy Lee Jones, Brian Dennehy.

4302 River's Edge, The (20th Century-Fox, 1957, Ray Milland, Anthony Quinn).

The River's Edge—Bobby Troup (w), Lou Forbes (m), Miller. COVER: Anthony Quinn, Debra Paget.

4303 River's End, The (First National, 1920, Lewis Stone, Marjorie Daw).

The River's End—Harry Hoch, Arthur Behim (w,m), Berlin. COVER: Marshall Neilan.

4304 Road House (20th Century-Fox, 1948, Ida Lupino, Cornel Wilde).

Again—Dorcas Cochran (w), Lionel Newman (m), Robbins; Right Kind, The—Don George, Charles Henderson, Lionel Newman (w,m), Robbins. COVER: Ida Lupino, Cornel Wilde, Celeste Holm, Richard Widmark.

4305 Roadhouse Nights (Paramount, 1930, Helen Morgan, Charles Ruggles).

It Can't Go on Like This—E. Y. Harburg (w), Jay Gorney (m), Spier Coslow. COVER: Helen Morgan, Charles Ruggles.

4306 Roadhouse Nights (Road House) (GB, 1934, Violet Loraine, Gordon Harker).

What a Little Moonlight Can Do—Harry Woods (w,m), Harms. COVER: The Moon.

4307 Roadie (United Artists, 1980, Kaki Hunter, Art Carney).

Drivin' My Life Away—Even Stevens, Eddie Rabbitt, David Malloy (w,m), Debdave; You Better Run—Felix Cavaliere, Edward Brigati (w, m), Downtown; Your Precious Love—Valerie Simpson, Nicholas Ashford (w,m), Jobete. COVER: Eddie Rabbitt, Pat Benatar, Stephen Bishop, Yvonne Elliman.

4308 Road Is Open Again, The (Vitaphone, 1933, Dick Powell, Charles Middleton).

Road Is Open Again, The—Irving Kahal (w), Sammy Fain (m), Witmark. COVER: Dick Powell, Franklin D. Roosevelt.

4309 Road Show (United Artists, 1941, Adolphe Menjou, Carole Landis).

Caliope Jane/I Should Have Known You Years Ago—Hoagy Carmichael (w,m), BVC; Slav Annie—Stanley Adams (w), Hoagy Carmichael (m), BVC; Yum Yum—Hoagy Carmichael (w,m), BVC. COVER: Adolphe Menjou, Carole Landis, John Hubbard, Patsy Kelly.

4310 Road to Bali (Paramount, 1953, Bob Hope, Bing Crosby).

Chicago Style/Hoot Moon/Merry Go Runaround/Moonflowers/Road to Bali/To See You—Johnny Burke (w), James Van Heusen (m), Burvan. COVER: Bing Crosby, Bob Hope, Dorothy Lamour.

4311 Road to Fortune, The (Paramount, 1930, Doria March, Giy Newall).

Just a Little Song (B)—Brock Williams (w), Doria March (m), Ricordi. COVER: Doria March.

4312 Road to Hong Kong, The (United Artists, 1962, Bob Hope, Bing Crosby).

Let's Not Be Sensible/Road to Hong Kong/Teamwork/Warmer Than a Whisper—Sammy Cahn (w), James Van Heusen (m), Chappell. COVER: Cartoon Sketches.

4313 Road to Morocco (Paramount, 1942, Bob Hope, Bing Crosby).

Ain't Got a Dime to My Name/ Constantly/Moonlight Becomes You/ Road to Morocco, The—Johnny Burke (w), James Van Heusen (m), Paramount. COVER: Bob Hope, Bing Crosby, Dorothy Lamour.

4314 Road to Reno, The (Universal, 1938, Hope Hampton, Randolph Scott).

I Gave My Heart Away/Riding Home/Tonight Is the Night—Harold Adamson (w), Jimmy McHugh (m), Mills. COVER: Randolph Scott, Hope Hampton, Glenda Farrell.

4315 Road to Rio (That Night in Rio) (20th Century-Fox, 1940, Alice Faye, Don Ameche).

Baron Is in Conference (PC)—

Mack Gordon (w), Harry Warren (m), Fox. COVER: None.

4316 Road to Rio (Paramount, 1948, Bob Hope, Bing Crosby).

Apalachicola, Fla./But Beautiful/ Experience—Johnny Burke (w), James Van Heusen (m), BVH; Olha Ella—Russo Do Pandeiro, Peter Pan (w,m), Peer; You Don't Have to Know the Language—Johnny Burke (w), James Van Heusen (m), BVH. COVER: Bob Hope, Dorothy Lamour, Bing Crosby, Andrews Sisters.

4317 Road to Ruin, The (TRG, 1928, Helen Foster, Grant Withers).

Road to Ruin—Lottie Well, Maurice Well (m,w), Wells Alexander. COVER: Sketch of Two Couples in Car.

4318 Road to Singapore, The (Paramount, 1940, Bob Hope, Bing Crosby).

Captain Custard—Johnny Burke (w), Victor Schertzinger (m), Santly Joy; Kaigoon—Johnny Burke (w), James Monaco (m), Paramount; Moon and the Willow Tree—Johnny Burke (w), Victor Schertzinger (m), Paramount; Sweet Potato Piper— Johnny Burke (w), James Monaco (m), Santly Joy; Too Romantic— Johnny Burke (w), James Monaco (m), Paramount. COVER: Bob Hope, Bing Crosby, Dorothy Lamour.

4319 Road to Utopia, The (Paramount, 1945, Bob Hope, Bing Crosby).

Good Time Charlie/It's Anybody's Spring/Personality/Put It There Pal/Welcome to My Dream/ Would You—Johnny Burke (w), James Van Heusen (m), BVH. COVER: Bob Hope, Bing Crosby, Dorothy Lamour.

4320 Road to Zanzibar (Paramount, 1941, Bing Crosby, Bob Hope).

African Etude/Birds of a Feather/ It's Always You/You Lucky People You/You're Dangerous—Johnny Burke (w), James Van Heusen (m), Santly Joy. COVER: Bob Hope, Bing Crosby, Dorothy Lamour.

4321 Roaring Twenties, The (Warner Bros., 1939, James Cagney, Priscilla Lane).

I'm Just Wild About Harry— Noble Sissle, Eubie Blake (w,m), Witmark; It Had to Be You—Gus Kahn (w), Isham Jones (m), Remick; Shantytown—Joe Young, John Siras, Jack Little (w,m), Witmark. COVER: James Cagney, Priscilla Lane.

4322 Robbers Roost (Fox, 1933, George O'Brien, Maureen O'Sullivan).

Cowboy's Heaven (BW)/Gal from Amarillo, The (BW)/I Adore You— Val Burton, Will Jason (w,m), Movietone. COVER: George O'Brien, Maureen O'Sullivan.

4323 Robbers Roost (United Artists, 1955, George Montgomery, Richard Boone).

I Turned It Down—John Bradford (w), Tony Romano (m), Manchester. COVER: Clouds.

4324 Robe, The (20th Century-Fox, 1954, Richard Burton, Jean Simmons).

The Robe-Love Theme—Alfred Newman (m), Robbins. COVER: Alfred Newman.

4325 Roberta (RKO, 1935, Irene Dunne, Ginger Rogers).

I'll Be Hard to Handle—Bernard Dougall (w), Jerome Kern (m), Harms; I Won't Dance—Dorothy Fields, Jimmy McHugh (w), Jerome Kern (m), Harms; Let's Begin—Otto Harbach (w), Jerome Kern (m), Harms; Lovely to Look At—Dorothy Fields, Jimmy McHugh (w), Jerome Kern (m), Harms; Smoke Gets in Your Eyes/Touch of Your Hand/ Yesterdays/You're Devastating—Otto Harbach (w), Jerome Kern (m), Harms. COVER: Ginger Rogers, Fred Astaire, Irene Dunne.

4326 Robin and the Seven Hoods (Warner Bros., 1964, Frank Sinatra, Dean Martin).

All for One and One for All/Any Man Who Loves His Mother/Bang Bang/Charlotte Couldn't Charleston/ Don't Be a Do-Badder/Give Praise!

Give Praise! Give Praise!/I Like to Lead When I Dance/Mister Booze/ My Kind of Town/Style—Sammy Cahn (w), James Van Heusen (m), Sergeant. COVER: Frank Sinatra, Dean Martin, Bing Crosby, Sammy Davis, Peter Falk.

4327 Robin Hood (United Artists, 1922, Douglas Fairbanks, Enid Bennett).

Just an Old Love Song—Sid Grauman (w), Victor Schertzinger (m), Sherman Clay; Robin Hood March (B)—Victor Schertzinger (m), Chappell; Robin Hood Music Score—Victor Schertzinger (m), United Artists. COVER: Douglas Fairbanks.

4328 Robin Hood (Buena Vista, 1973, Cartoon).

Love—Floyd Huddleston (w), George Bruns (m), Disney; Not in Nottingham (VS)/Oh De Lally (VS)—Roger Miller (w,m), Disney; Phony King of England (VS)—Johnny Mercer (w,m), Disney; Whistle Stop (VS)—Roger Miller (w,m), Disney. COVER: Cartoon.

4329 Robin Hood of the Pecos (Republic, 1941, Roy Rogers, George Hayes).

Certain Place I Know—Eddie Cherkose (w,m), Mills; It's a Sad Sad Story—Peter Tinturin (w,m), Mills. COVER: Roy Rogers.

4330 Robinson Crusoe on Mars (Paramount, 1964, Paul Mantee, Victor Lundin).

Robinson Crusoe on Mars—Earl Shuman (w), Leon Carr (m), Famous. COVER: Outer Space Scene.

4331 Rob Roy, the Highland Rogue (Buena Vista, 1954, Richard Todd, Glynis Johns).

Ballad of Rob Roy, The—Irving Gordon (w,m), Disney. COVER: Richard Todd, Glynis Johns.

4332 Rocco and His Brothers (Astor, 1961, Alain Delon, Renato Salvatori).

Rocco's Theme, Far Away Land— Mel Mandel, Norman Sachs (w), Nino Rota (m), Sidmore. COVER: Alain Delon, and Others.

4333 Rock-A-Bye (RKO, 1932, Constance Bennett, Joel McCrea).

Sleep My Sweet—Jean Borlini (w), Nacio Herb Brown (m), Brown. COVER: Black and white cover with title only.

4334 Rock-a-Bye Baby (Paramount, 1958, Jerry Lewis, Marilyn Maxwell).

Dormi, Dormi, Dormi/Land of La La La/Love Is a Lonely Thing/Rock-a-bye Baby/White Virgin of the Nile/ Why Can't He Care for Me—Sammy Cahn (w), Harry Warren (m), Paramount. COVER: Jerry Lewis, Marilyn Maxwell.

4335 Rock Around the Clock (Columbia, 1956, Bill Haley, The Platters).

ABC Boogie—Max Spickol, Al Russell (w,m), Myers; Bacalao Con Papa—Tony Martinez (w,m), Mills; Giddy Up a Ding Dong—Freddie Bell, Pep Lattanzi (w,m), Myers; R O C K—Bill Haley, A. Keefer, R. Keefer (w,m), Valley Brook; Rock Around the Clock—Max Freedman, Jimmy DeKnight (w,m), Kassner; Rudy's Rock—Bill Haley, Rudy Pompillii (w,m), Valley Brook; See You Later Alligator—Robert Guidry (w, m), ABC; Teach You to Rock— Freddie Bell, Pep Lattanzi (w,m), Myers. COVER: Bill Haley, and Rock Stars.

4336 Rock Pretty Baby (Universal, 1957, Sal Mineo, John Saxon).

Can I Feel a Little Love/Happy Is a Boy Named Me/Rock Pretty Baby/ What's It Gonna Be—Phil Tuminello (w,m), Northern. COVER: John Saxon, Sal Mineo, Luana Patten.

4337 Rock Rock Rock (Vanguard, 1956, Frankie Lymon, Lavern Baker).

Tra-La-La—Johnny Parker (w, m), Snapper. COVER: Rock Stars.

4338 Rocky I (United Artists, 1976, Sylvester Stallone, Talia Shire).

Gonna Fly Now/You Take My Heart Away—Carol Connors, Ann

Robbins (w), Bill Conti (m), Unart;
Rocky I-Thirteen Themes—Bill Conti
(m), Unart. COVER: Sylvester Stallone, Talia Shire.

4339 Rocky II (United Artists,
1979, Sylvester Stallone, Talia Shire).

All of My Life—Shelby Conti (w),
Bill Conti (m), Unart; Redemption/
Rocky II-Four Themes—Bill Conti
(m), Unart. COVER: Black and yellow cover with title only.

4340 Rocky III (United Artists,
1982, Sylvester Stallone, Talia Shire).

Eye of the Tiger—Frankie Sullivan, Jim Peterik (w,m), Warner.
COVER: Sylvester Stallone.

4341 Rocky IV (United Artists,
1985, Sylvester Stallone, Talia Shire).

Burning Heart—Frank Sullivan,
Jim Peterik (w,m), Rude; Double or
Nothing—Steve Dorff, Paul Williams
(w,m), Warner; Living in America—
Dan Hartman, Charlie Midnight (w,
m), Unart; No Easy Way Out—Rob-
ert Tepper (w,m), Flowering Stone;
Rocky IV-Six Themes—Vince Di-
Cola, Frank Sullivan, Jim Peterik,
Peter Cox (w,m), Big Three. COV-
ER: Sylvester Stallone.

4342 Rodeo Rhythm (PRC,
1941, Fred Scott, Pat Dunn).

Hitting the Trail/Rodeo Rhythm
—Morrill Moore, Eugene Moore (w,
m), Delcal. COVER: Fred Scott, Pat
Dunn.

4343 Rogue of the Rio Grande
(Sono Art World Wide, 1931, Jose
Bohr, Myrna Loy).

Argentine Moon/Corazon—Oliver
Drake, Herbert Myers (w,m), Saun-
ders. COVER: Myrna Loy, Jose
Bohr, Raymond Hatton.

4344 Rogues and Romance
(Pathe, 1920, June Caprice, George
Seitz).

Alhambra Moon—George Seitz
(w), William Sullivan (m), Seitz.
COVER: A Girl and the Moon.

4345 Rogues Gallery (Paramount, 1968, Roger Smith, Greta
Baldwin).

Valerie—Hal Blair, Jimmie Haskell

(w,m), Famous. COVER: Red and
white cover with title only.

4346 Rogue Song (MGM, 1930,
Lawrence Tibbett, Catherine Owen).

Narrative/Rogue Song, Beyond
the Dawn/When I'm Looking at You
—Clifford Grey (w), Herbert Stothart (m), Robbins; White Dove—Clifford Grey (w), Franz Lehar (m),
Chappell. COVER: Lawrence Tibbett, Catherine Owen.

4347 Rogue's Regiment (Universal, 1948, Dick Powell, Marta
Toren).

Just for a While/Who Can Tell,
Not I—Jack Brooks (w), Serge Walter
(m), Oxford. COVER: Dick Powell,
Marta Toren.

4348 Roll Along Cowboy (20th
Century-Fox, 1937, Smith Ballew,
Cecelia Parker).

On the Sunny Side of the Rockies
—Roy Ingraham, Harry Tobias (w,
m), Hollywood; Roll Along, Ride
Em Cowboy, Roll Along—Lyle War-
mack (w), Lew Porter (m), Holly-
wood; Stars Over the Desert—Roy
Ingraham, Harry Tobias (w,m),
Hollywood. COVER: Smith Ballew.

4349 Rollerball (United Artists, 1975, James Caan, Maud
Adams).

Rollerball Theme—Leroy Holmes
(m), Unart. COVER: Face and
Spikes.

4350 Rollercoaster (Universal,
1977, George Segal, Richard Widmark).

Magic Carousel, The—Lalo Schif-
rin (m), Duchess. COVER: George
Segal, Richard Widmark, Timothy
Bottoms, and Rollercoaster.

**4351 Rolling Along (The Music
Goes Round)** (Columbia, 1936,
Harry Richman, Rochelle Hudson).

Life Begins When You're in Love
(PC)—Lew Brown, Harry Akst, Vic-
tor Schertzinger (w,m), Berlin;
Susannah (PC)—Lew Brown, Harry
Akst, Harry Richman (w,m), Berlin.
COVER: None.

4352 Rolling Caravans (Columbia, 1938, Jack Luden, Eleanor Stewart).

Neath Western Skies—Leon Leon (w), Lee Zahler (m), Mills; Range Ridin' Dreams—David Ormont (w), Lee Zahler (m), Mills. COVER: Desert Scene.

4353 Rolling in Money (Fox, 1934, Anna Lee, Leslie Sarony).

Rolling in Money (B)—James Dyrenforth (w), Carroll Gibbons (m), Movietone. COVER: Anna Lee, Leslie Sarony.

4354 Rollin' Plains (Grand National, 1938, Tex Ritter, Harriet Bennett).

Me and My Pal, My Pony (VS)—Frank Harford (w,m), Cole; Rollin' Plains—Walter Samuels, Leonard Whitcup, Teddy Powell (w,m), Schuster. COVER: Tex Ritter.

4355 Rollin' Westward (Monogram, 1939, Tex Ritter, Dorothy Fay).

Back in 67 (PC)—Johnny Lange, Lew Porter (w,m), Southern; Bold Vaquero—David Guion (w,m), Schirmer; Rollin' Westward (PC)—Ted Choate (w), Bert Pellish (m), Southern. COVER: Tex Ritter.

4356 Roll Wagons Roll (Monogram, 1940, Tex Ritter, Nelson McDowell).

Roll Wagons Roll! (PC)—Dorcas Cochran (w), Charles Rosoff (m), Southern. COVER: None.

4357 Romance (United Artists, 1920, Doris Keane, Basil Sidney).

Romance—Lee David (w,m), Nice. COVER: Doris Keane, Basil Sidney.

4358 Romance (MGM, 1930, Greta Garbo, Lewis Stone).

Romance—Walter Donaldson (w, m), Donaldson. COVER: Greta Garbo Sketch.

4359 Romance and Crinoline (Independent, 1924, Eileen Van Biene, Richard Ford).

Dreams—James Lamont (w), Egbert Van Alstyne (m), Remick. COVER: Eileen Van Biene, Richard Ford.

4360 Romance in the Dark (Paramount, 1938, John Boles, Gladys Swarthout).

Bewitched by the Night—Jay Gorney (w,m), Famous; Blue Dawn—Ned Washington (w), Phil Boutelje (m), Famous; Romance in the Dark—Sam Coslow, Gertrude Niesen (w,m), Paramount; Tonight We Love—Leo Robin, Ralph Rainger (w,m), Famous. COVER: John Boles, Gladys Swarthout.

4361 Romance in the Rain (Universal, 1934, Roger Pryor, Heather Angel).

F'Rinstance/Love At Last—Don Hartman (w), Jay Gorney (m), DBH. COVER: Heather Angel.

4362 Romance of Happy Valley (Paramount, 1919, Lillian Gish, Robert Barron).

Romance of Happy Valley—Miles Overholt (w), Louis Gottschalk (m), Berlin. COVER: Lillian Gish, Robert Barron.

4363 Romance of Rosy Ridge (The Missouri Story) (MGM, 1947, Van Johnson, Janet Leigh).

Far from My Darling/I Come from Missouri—Lewis Allan (w), Earl Robinson (m), Robbins. COVER: Van Johnson, Janet Leigh.

4364 Romance of the Rio Grande (Fox, 1929, Warner Baxter, Mary Duncan).

Ride on Vaquero/You'll Find Your Answer in My Eyes—L. Wolfe Gilbert (w), Abel Baer (m), DBH. COVER: Warner Baxter, Mary Duncan.

4365 Romance of the Underworld (Fox, 1927, Mary Astor, John Boles).

Judy—Jacques Murray (w), Pierre Norman (m), DBH. COVER: Mary Astor.

4366 Romance of the West (PRC, 1946, Eddie Dean, Joan Barton).

Love Song of the Waterfall—Bob Nolan, Bernard Barnes, Carl Winge (w,m), American. COVER: Eddie Dean.

4367 Romance on the High Seas (Warner Bros., 1948, Doris Day, Jack Carson).

I'm in Love/It's Magic/It's You or No One/Put Em in a Box/Run Run Run/Tourist Trade—Sammy Cahn (w), Jule Styne (m), Remick. COVER: Doris Day, Jack Carson, Janis Paige, Don DeFore.

4368 Romancing the Stone (20th Century-Fox, 1984, Michael Douglas, Kathleen Turner).

Romancing the Stone—Eddy Grant (w,m), Leonard. COVER: Eddy Grant.

4369 Romanoff and Juliet (Universal, 1961, Peter Ustinov, Sandra Dee).

Romanoff and Juliet Theme—Mario Nascimbene (m), Northern. COVER: Peter Ustinov, Sandra Dee, John Gavin.

4370 Roman Scandals (United Artists, 1933, Eddie Cantor, Ruth Etting).

Build a Little Home/Keep Young and Beautiful/No More Love—Al Dubin (w), Harry Warren (m), Witmark; Put a Tax on Love—Al Dubin, L. Wolfe Gilbert, Harry Warren (w, m), Witmark; Rome Wasn't Built in a Day—Al Dubin (w), Harry Warren (m), Witmark; Those Eddie Cantor Eyes—L. Wolfe Gilbert (w), Harry Akst (m), Mills. COVER: Eddie Cantor, and Chorus Girls.

4371 Roman Spring of Mrs. Stone, The (Warner Bros., 1961, Vivien Leigh, Warren Beatty).

Roman Spring of Mrs. Stone Theme (B)/Think About a Stranger (B)—Richard Addinsell (m), Henrees. COVER: Vivien Leigh, Warren Beatty.

4372 Romantic Comedy (MGM, Dudley Moore, Mary Steenburgen).

Maybe—Marvin Hamlisch, Carole B. Sager, Burt Bacharach (w,m), April. COVER: Dudley Moore, Mary Steenburgen.

4373 Romany Where Life Runs Wild (Selznick, 1919, Stars Un-

known).

Romany, Where Life Runs Wild— Louis Weslyn (w), H. S. Krouse (m), Stern. COVER: A Gypsy.

4374 Rome Adventure (Warner Bros., 1962, Troy Donahue, Angie Dickinson).

Al Di La—Ervin Drake (w), C. Donida (m), Witmark; Rome Adventure—George Weiss, Hugo Luigi (w), Max Steiner (m), Witmark. COVER: Troy Donahue, Suzanne Pleshette.

4375 Romeo and Juliet (United Artists, 1955, Laurence Harvey, Susan Shentall).

Romeo and Juliet Suite—Roman Vlad, George Terry (m), Ricordi. COVER: Laurence Harvey, Susan Shentall.

4376 Romeo and Juliet (Paramount, 1969, Leonard Whiting, Olivia Hussey).

Romeo and Juliet Love Theme— Nino Rota (m), Famous; Time for Us, A—Nino Rota, Larry Kusik, Eddie Snyder (w,m), Famous; What Is a Youth/Romeo and Juliet Nine Themes—Eugene Walter (w), Nino Rota (m), Famous. COVER: Leonard Whiting, Olivia Hussey.

4377 Romola (Metro, 1924, Lillian Gish, Dorothy Gish).

Sunshine of Love—Dailey Paskman (w), Louis Gottschalk (m), Robbins Engel. COVER: Lillian Gish.

4378 Ronny (UFA, 1932, German Operetta).

Ronny-Four Songs—E. Y. Harburg (w), Emmerich Kalman (m), Harms. COVER: Man and Woman.

4379 Rookies on Parade (Republic, 1941, Bob Crosby, Ruth Terry).

Chula Chihuahua/I Love You More/Mother Never Told Me Why/ My Kinda Music/Rookies on Parade/ What More Do You Want/You'll Never Get Rich—Sammy Cahn (w), Saul Chaplin (m), Mills. COVER: Bob Crosby, Ruth Terry, Eddie Foy, Gertrude Neisen.

4380 Room at the Top (Continental, 1959, Simone Signoret, Laurence Harvey).

Susan Theme—Mario Nascimbene (m), Robbins. COVER: Simone Signoret, Laurence Harvey.

4381 Roosevelt Story, The (United Artists, 1947, Story of Franklin D. Roosevelt).

Toward the Sun—Lewis Allen (w), Earl Robinson (m), Chappell. COVER: Franklin D. Roosevelt.

4382 Rootin' Tootin' Rhythm (Republic, 1937, Gene Autry, Smiley Burnette).

Little Black Bronc/Trail of the Mountain Rose—Al Clauser, Tex Hoepner (w,m), Cross Winge. COVER: The Oklahoma Outlaws.

4383 Roots of Heaven, The (20th Century-Fox, 1958, Errol Flynn, Juliette Greco).

Roots of Heaven, The—Ned Washington (w), Henri Patterson (m), Robbins. COVER: Errol Flynn, Juliette Greco, and Elephants.

4384 Rosalie (MGM, 1937, Nelson Eddy, Eleanor Powell).

Close/I've a Strange New Rhythm/In the Still of the Night/Rosalie/Who Knows/Why Should I Care/I Know It's Not Meant for Me (VS)—Cole Porter (w,m), Chappell. COVER #1: Nelson Eddy, Eleanor Powell. COVER #2: Sketch of Soldiers and Girl.

4385 Rosary, The (First National, 1922, Jane Novak, Robert Gordon).

The Rosary—Ethelbert Nevin (w, m), Boston. COVER: Jane Novak, Robert Gordon.

4386 Rose, The (20th Century-Fox, 1979, Bette Midler, Alan Bates).

Rose, The—Amanda McBroom (w, m), Fox; Stay with Me—Jerry Ragavoy, George Weiss (w,m), Chappell; When a Man Loves a Woman—Calvin Lewis, Andrew Wright (w,m), Pronto; Camellia (VS)—Stephen Hunter (m), Columbia; Keep on Rockin' (VS) —Sam Hagar, John Carter (w,m), Co-

lumbia; Let Me Call You Sweetheart (VS)—Beth Whitson (w), Leo Friedman (m), Columbia; Love with a Feeling (VS)—Hudson Whitaker (w,m), Columbia; Midnight in Memphis (VS) —Tony Johnson (w,m), Columbia; Sold My Soul to Rock and Roll (VS)— Gene Pistilli (w,m), Columbia; Who's Side Are You On (VS)—Ken Hopkins, Charlie Williams (w,m), Columbia. COVER: Bette Midler.

4387 Roseanna McCoy (RKO, 1949, Farley Granger, Charles Bickford).

Roseanna—Frank Loesser (w,m), Sidney. COVER: Farley Granger, Joan Evans.

4388 Rose Bowl, The (Paramount, 1936, Tom Brown, Eleanor Whitney).

At the Rose Bowl/Son of Sierra —Irving Taylor (w), Vic Mizzy (m), Popular. COVER: Black and white cover with title only.

4389 Rose Marie (MGM, 1936, Nelson Eddy, Jeanette MacDonald).

Indian Love Call—Otto Harbach, Oscar Hammerstein (w), Rudolf Friml (m), Harms; Just for You—Gus Kahn (w), Rudolf Friml, Herbert Stothart (m), Harms; Mounties—Otto Harbach, Oscar Hammerstein (w), Rudolf Friml, H. Stothart (m), Harms; Pardon Me Madame—Gus Kahn (w), Herbert Stothart (m), Robbins; Rose Marie—Otto Harbach, Oscar Hammerstein (w), Rudolf Friml (m), Harms. COVER: Nelson Eddy, Jeanette MacDonald.

4390 Rose Marie (MGM, 1954, Howard Keel, Ann Blyth).

I Have the Love—Paul F. Webster (w), Rudolf Friml (m), Robbins; Indian Love Call—Otto Harbach, Oscar Hammerstein (w), Rudolf Friml (m), Harms; Mounties—Otto Harbach, O. Hammerstein (w), H. Stothart, Rudolf Friml (m), Harms; Rose Marie— Otto Harbach, Oscar Hammerstein (w), Rudolf Friml (m), Harms; Totem Tom Tom—Otto Harbach, O. Hammerstein (w), H. Stothart, Rudolf Friml (m), Harms. COVER:

Ann Blyth, Howard Keel, Fernando Lamas.

4391 Rosemary (Roxy, 1958, Nadja Tiller, Peter Van Eyck).

Rosemary/Rosemary Mambo—Leon Pober (w), Norbert Schultze (m), Criterion. COVER: Nadja Tiller.

4392 Rosemary's Baby (Paramount, 1968, Mia Farrow, John Cassavetes).

Rosemary's Baby Lullaby—Christopher Komeda (m), Famous; Sleep Safe and Warm—Larry Kusik, Eddie Snyder (w), Christopher Komeda (m), Famous. COVER: Mia Farrow, and Baby Coach.

4393 Rose of the Golden West (First National, 1927, Mary Astor, Gilbert Roland).

Rose of Monterey—Byron Gay (w), Neil Moret (m), Villa Moret. COVER: Mary Astor, Gilbert Roland.

4394 Rose of the Rancho (Paramount, 1936, John Boles, Gladys Swarthout).

Got a Gal in California/If I Should Lose You/Little Rose of the Rancho/Thunder Over Paradise/Where Is My Love—Leo Robin, Ralph Rainger (w, m), Famous. COVER: Gladys Swarthout.

4395 Rose of the Rio Grande (Monogram, 1938, Movita, John Carroll).

Ride Amigos Ride/Song of the Rose/What Care I?—Eddie Cherkose (w), Charles Rosoff (m), Mills. COVER: Movita, John Carroll.

4396 Rose of Washington Square (20th Century-Fox, 1939, Alice Faye, Tyrone Power).

Curse of An Aching Heart—Henry Fink (w), Al Piantadosi (m), Feist; I'm Always Chasing Rainbows—Joseph McCarthy (w), Harroll Carroll (m), Robbins; I'm Sorry I Made You Cry—N. J. Cesi (w,m), Feist; I Never Knew Heaven Could Speak—Mack Gordon, Harry Revel (w,m), Robbins; My Mammy—Sam Lewis, Joe Young (w), Walter Donaldson (m), Berlin; My Man—Channing Pollock

(w), Maurice Yvain (m), Feist; Rose of Washington Square—Ballard Mac-Donald (w), James Hanley (m), Shapiro Bernstein; Toot Toot Tootsie—Gus Kahn, Ernie Erdman, Dan Russo (w,m), Feist; Vamp, The—Byron Gay (w,m), Feist. COVER: Alice Faye, Al Jolson, Tyrone Power, Louis Prima.

4397 Rose Tattoo, The (Paramount, 1955, Burt Lancaster, Anna Magnani).

Rose Tattoo, The—Jack Brooks (w), Harry Warren (m), Paramount; Vino Vino—Hal David (w), Alex North (m), Paramount. COVER: Burt Lancaster, Anna Magnani.

4398 Rosie (Universal, 1957, Rosalind Russell, Sandra Dee).

Rosie—Johnny Mercer (w), Harry Warren (m), Shamley. COVER: Rosalind Russell.

4399 Rosita (United Artists, 1923, George Walsh, Mary Pickford).

La Rosita Song—Allan Stuart (w), Paul DuPont (m), Sam Fox. COVER: Senorita and Rose.

4400 Rough Night in Jericho (Universal, 1967, Dean Martin, George Peppard).

Devil Rides in Jericho—Phil Zeller, Martin Rackin (w), Don Costa (m), Hawaii; Hold Me Now and Forever—Phil Zeller (w), Don Costa (m), Hawaii. COVER: Dean Martin, George Peppard, Jean Simmons.

4401 Rough Riders (Paramount, 1927, Mary Astor, Charles Farrell).

Goodbye Dolly Gray—Will Cobb, Paul Barnes (w,m), Pioneer; Rough Riders March—Hugo Riesenfeld (m), Sam Fox. COVER: Mary Astor, Charles Farrell, and Rough Rider.

4402 Rough Romance (Fox, 1931, George O'Brien, Helen Chandler).

Nobody Knows/She's Somebody's Baby—George Little (w), Johnny Burke (m), Red Star. COVER: Colored Designs.

4403 Rough Sketch (Columbia, 1949, Desi Arnaz).

Balada Romantica—Marco Rizo (w,m), Peer. COVER: Desi Arnaz.

4404 Round Midnight (Warner Bros., 1986, Dexter Gordon, Gabrielle Baker).

Round Midnight Jazz Themes (41)—Various Composers, Warner. COVER: Dexter Gordon.

4405 Round the Clock with Music (Baldwin, 1921, Commercial Film).

Round the Clock with Music-Themes—Various Composers, Presser. COVER: Family at Piano.

4406 Round Up Time in Texas (Republic, 1938, Gene Autry, Smiley Burnette).

Indian Song (VS)—Fleming Allan (w,m), Cole; Prairie Rose—Sidney Mitchell (w), Sam Stept (m), Sam Fox. COVER: Gene Autry.

4407 Roustabout (Paramount, 1964, Elvis Presley, Barbara Stanwyck).

Big Love Big Heartache—Dolores Fuller, Lee Morris, Sonny Hendrix (w,m), Gladys; Carny Town—Fred Wise, Randy Starr (w,m), Gladys; Hard Knocks—Joy Byers (w,m), Presley; It's a Wonderful World—Sid Tepper, Roy Bennett (w,m), Gladys; Little Egypt—Jerry Leiber, Mike Stoller (w,m), Progressive; One Track Heart/Poison Ivy League/Roustabout—Bill Giant, Bernie Baum, Florence Kaye (w,m), Presley, There's a Brand New Day on the Horizon—Joy Byers (w,m), Presley; Wheels on My Heels—Sid Tepper, Roy Bennett (w,m), Gladys. COVER: Elvis Presley.

4408 Roving Tumbleweeds (Washington Cowboy) (Republic, 1939, Gene Autry, Smiley Burnette).

Back in the Saddle Again—Ray Whitley, Gene Autry (w,m), Chappell. COVER: Gene Autry.

4409 Royal Bed, The (Abdullah the Great) (Fox, 1955, Kay Kendall).

If Hearts Could Talk—Kay Twomey, Fred Wise (w), Georges Auric (m), Hill Range. COVER: Percy Faith.

4410 Royal Wedding (MGM, 1951, Fred Astaire, Jane Powell).

Ev'ry Night at Seven/Happiest Day of My Life/How Could You Believe Me When I Said I Love You When You Know I've Been a Liar All My Life/I Left My Hat in Haiti/Open Your Eyes/Too Late Now/You're All the World to Me—Alan Jay Lerner (w), Burton Lane (m), Feist. COVER: Fred Astaire, Jane Powell, Peter Lawford.

4411 R.P.M. (Revolutions Per Minute) (Columbia, 1970, Anthony Quinn, Ann Margret).

Stop, I Don't Wanna Hear It Anymore—Perry Botkin, B. DeVorzon, M. Safka (w,m), Colgems. COVER: Black Letters.

4412 Rubaiyat of Omar Khayyam, The (Earle, 1921, Stars Unknown).

Rubaiyat of Omar Khayyam-Piano Suite—Charles W. Cadman (m), White Smith. COVER: A Temple.

4413 Rubeville (Pathe, 1929, Josephine Fontaine).

When You're Seeing Sweetie Home—Sam Lewis, Joe Young (w), Harry Warren (m), Remick. COVER: Josephine Fontaine.

4414 Ruby Gentry (20th Century-Fox, 1951, Jennifer Jones, Charlton Heston).

Ruby—Mitchell Parish (w), Heinz Roemheld (m), Miller; Ruby-Theme —Heinz Roemheld (m), Miller. COVER: Jennifer Jones.

4415 Rudolph and Frosty (Rankin Bass, 1979, Cartoon).

Everything I've Always Wanted/No Bed of Roses—Johnny Marks (w, m), St. Nicholas; Rudolph and Frosty-Thirteen Songs—Johnny Marks (w, m), Columbia. COVER: Porter Wagoner, and Cartoons.

4416 Ruling Class, The (Embassy, 1972, Peter O'Toole, Alastair Sim).

My Jack/Ruling Class Theme—

John Cameron (m), Embassy. COVER: Peter O'Toole.

4417 Rumba (Paramount, 1935, Carole Lombard, George Raft).

I'm Yours for Tonight/Magic of You, The/Rhythm of the Rumba—Ralph Rainger (w,m), Famous. COVER: Carole Lombard, George Raft.

4418 Runaway (Tri-Star, 1984, Tom Selleck, Cynthia Rhodes).

Runaway Theme—Jerry Goldsmith (m), Triple. COVER: Tom Selleck, Cynthia Rhodes.

4419 Runaway June (Reliance, 1915, Norma Phillips, J. Johnston).

Runaway June—Harold Freeman (w,m), Witmark. COVER: Norma Phillips.

4420 Run for Cover (Paramount, 1955, James Cagney, John Derek).

Run for Cover—Jack Brooks (w), Howard Jackson (m), Famous. COVER: James Cagney, John Derek, Viveca Lindfors.

4421 Run for the Sun (United Artists, 1956, Trevor Howard, Richard Widmark).

Bueno Taco/My Hacienda—Buddy Kaye (w), Fred Steiner (m), Coronet. COVER: Richard Widmark, and Jungle Scene.

4422 Run for Your Money (Universal, 1950, Alec Guinness, Moira Lister).

Thro' the Night (B)—Ray Oliven (m), Campbell. COVER: Moira Lister, Donald Houston.

4423 Run for Your Wife (Allied Artists, 1965, Marina Vlady, Ugo Tognazzi).

All—Ray Jessel, Marian Grudeff (w), Nino Oliviero (m), Marks. COVER: Ugo Tognazzi, and Girls.

4424 Running Scared (MGM, 1986, Gregory Hines, Billy Crystal).

Man Size Love/Sweet Freedom—Rod Temperton (w,m), Rodsongs. COVER: Gregory Hines, Billy Crystal.

4425 Running Target (United Artists, 1956, Doris Dowling, Arthur Franz).

Summer Game—Fred Jordan (w), Ernest Gold (m), Criterion. COVER: Arthur Franz, Doris Dowling.

4426 Running Wild (Universal, 1955, William Campbell, Mamie Van Doren).

Razzle Dazzle—Charles Calhoun (w,m), Roosevelt. COVER: Mamie Van Doren.

4427 Run of the Arrow (RKO, 1957, Rod Steiger, Sarita Montiel).

Purple Hills—Milton Berle, Buddy Arnold (w), Victor Young (m), Young. COVER: Soldiers and an Indian.

4428 Run Shadow Run (Cover Me Babe) (20th Century-Fox, 1970, Robert Forster, Sandra Locke).

Cover Me Babe—Randy Newman (w), Fred Karlin (m), Fox; So You Say—Robb Royer, James Griffin (w), Fred Karlin (m), Fox. COVER: Beach Scene.

4429 Run Wild Run Free (Columbia, 1969, John Mills, Sylvia Syms).

Run Wild Run Free—Don Black (w), David Whitaker (m), Colgems. COVER: Mark Lester, and Others.

4430 Russians Are Coming, The Russians Are Coming, The (United Artists, 1966, Carl Reiner, Eva Marie Saint).

The Russians Are Coming, The Russians Are Coming—Johnny Mandell (m), Unart. COVER: Cartoon Sketches.

4431 Rustlers of the Badlands (Columbia, 1945, Charles Starrett, Sally Bliss).

Dusty Saddle on the Ole Barn Wall—Mickey Stoner (w), Burt Rice (m), BVC. COVER: Black and white cover with title only.

4432 Rustlers Rhapsody (Paramount, 1985, Tom Berenger, Marilu Henner).

I Break Horses, Not Hearts—Steve Dorff, Milt Brown, Nancy Masters (w,m), Ensign; I Ride Alone/Lasso the Moon—Steve Dorff, Milt

Brown (w,m), Ensign. COVER: Tom Berenger.

4433 Ruthless People (Buena Vista, 1986, Danny DeVito, Bette Midler).

Give Me the Reason (PC)—Luther Vandross, Nat Adderly (w,m), Columbia; Modern Woman—Billy Joel (w,m), Joel. COVER: Billy Joel.

4434 Ryan's Daughter (MGM, 1970, Robert Mitchum, Trevor Howard).

It Was a Good Time—Mack David, Mike Curb (w), Maurice Jarre (m), Feist; Major—Maurice Jarre (m), Hastings; Rosy's Theme—Maurice Jarre (m), Feist; Where Was I When the Parade Went By—Mack David, Mike Curbe (w), Maurice Jarre (m), Hastings. COVER: A Girl Facing the Sea.

4435 Saadia (MGM, 1953, Cornel Wilde, Mel Ferrer).

Saadia Theme—Bronislau Kaper (m), Miller. COVER: Purple and white cover with title only.

4436 Sabrina (Paramount, 1954, Audrey Hepburn, William Holden).

Sabrina—Wilson Stone (w,m), Famous. COVER: Humphrey Bogart, Audrey Hepburn, William Holden.

4437 Sacco and Vanzetti (UMC, 1971, Gian Maria Volonte, Riccardo Cucciolla).

Here's to You—Joan Baez, Ennio Morricone (w,m), Sunbury. COVER: Gian Maria Volonte, Riccardo Cucciolla.

4338 Sacred Flame, The (SCI, 1920, Emily Stevens, Maud Hill).

Sacred Flame, The—Will Heelan (w), Will Haskins (m), Cohen. COVER: Emily Stevens.

4439 Sacred Flame, The (Warner Bros., 1929, Pauline Frederick, Lila Lee).

Sacred Flame, The—Grant Clarke (w), Harry Akst (m), Remick. COVER: Conrad Nagel.

4440 Saddle Pals (Republic, 1947, Gene Autry, Lynn Roberts).

I Wish I'd Never Met Sunshine

(PC)—Gene Autry, Dale Evans, L. Halderman (w,m), Cole. COVER: None.

4441 Saddle the Wind (MGM, 1958, Robert Taylor, Julie London).

Saddle the Wind—Jay Livingston, Ray Evans (w,m), Robbins. COVER: Robert Taylor, Julie London.

4442 Sad Horse, The (20th Century-Fox, 1959, David Ladd, Chill Wills).

Sad Horse, The—Walter Kent, Tom Walton (w,m), Feist. COVER: A Boy, a Horse, and a Dog.

4443 Sadie Love (Paramount, 1919, Billie Burke, James Crane).

Sadie Love—L. Wolfe Gilbert, Leon Flatow (w,m), Gilbert. COVER: Billie Burke.

4444 Sadie McKee (MGM, 1934, Joan Crawford, Gene Raymond).

All I Do Is Dream of You—Arthur Freed (w), Nacio Herb Brown (m), Robbins. COVER: Joan Crawford.

4445 Sadie Thompson (United Artists, 1928, Gloria Swanson, Lionel Barrymore).

Good Time Sadie—Seymour Simons (w,m), Berlin. COVER: Gloria Swanson.

4446 Sad Sack, The (Paramount, 1957, Jerry Lewis, David Wayne).

Sad Sack, The—Hal David (w), Burt Bacharach (m), Famous; Why You Pay (BW)—F. Miller, Ch. O'Curran, Dudley Brooks (w,m), Famous. COVER: Jerry Lewis.

4447 Safari (Columbia, 1956, Victor Mature, Janet Leigh).

Safari (B)—Paddy Roberts (w), Muir Mathieson (m), Maurice. COVER: Victor Mature, Janet Leigh.

4448 Safe Place, A (Columbia, 1971, Tuesday Weld, Jack Nicholson).

Beyond the Sea—Jack Lawrence (w), Charles Trenet (m), Belwin Mills. COVER: Black and blue cover with title only.

4449 Safety in Numbers (Paramount, 1930, Charles Rogers, Josephine Dunn).

Bee in Your Boudoir/Business Girl/Do You Play Madame/Pick Up/ My Future Just Passed/You Appeal to Me—George Marion (w), Richard Whiting (m), Famous. COVER: Charles Rogers, and Girls.

4450 Safety Last (Pathe, 1923, Harold Lloyd, Mildred Davis).

Harold and Maude (B)—Herman Finck (w,m), Hawkes. COVER: Harold Lloyd.

4451 Saga of Death Valley (Republic, 1939, Roy Rogers, Gabby Hayes).

I've Sold My Saddle for an Old Guitar—Roy Rogers, Fleming Allan (w,m), Cole. COVER: Roy Rogers.

4452 Sagebrush Troubadour (Republic, 1935, Gene Autry, Smiley Burnette).

End of the Trail (VS)—Gene Autry (w,m), Cole; Hurdy Gurdy Man (VS)—Smiley Burnette (w,m), Cole; I'd Love a Home in the Mountains (VS)—Gene Autry, Smiley Burnette (w,m), Cole; Lookin' for the Lost Chord (VS)/My Prayer for Tonight (VS)/On the Prairie (VS)—Smiley Burnette (w,m), Cole; Way Out West in Texas (VS)—Gene Autry (w,m), Cole; When the Moon Shines (VS)—Gene Autry, Smiley Burnette (w,m), Cole. COVER: Gene Autry.

4453 Sahara (Hodkinson, 1919, Louise Glaum, Matt Moore).

Sahara—William Wells (w), Harold Kay, Fred Bowers (m), Bowers. COVER: Louise Glaum.

4454 Sail a Crooked Ship (Columbia, 1961, Robert Wagner, Dolores Hart).

Opposites Attract—Bob Marcucci, Russ Faith (w,m), Colgems. COVER: Cartoon sketches.

4455 Sailing Along (GB, 1936, Jessie Matthews, Roland Young).

My River/Souvenir of Love/ Trusting My Luck/Your Heart Skips a Beat—Maurice Sigler (w), Arthur Johnston (m), Santly Joy. COVER: Jessie Matthews.

4456 Sailing the South Seas (Ingris, 1969, Sailing Documentary).

Blue Sea (PC)—Ed Ingris, Henry Taft (w,m), Ingris. COVER: None.

4457 Sailor Beware (Paramount, 1951, Dean Martin, Jerry Lewis).

Merci Beaucoup/Never Before/Old Calliope/Sailor's Polka/Today Tomorrow Forever—Mack David (w), Jerry Livingston (m), Paramount. COVER: Dean Martin, Jerry Lewis, Corinne Calvet.

4458 Sailor's Luck (Fox, 1933, James Dunn, Sally Eilers).

A Sailor's Luck—A. Ryan (w), Val Burton, Will Jason (m), Movietone. COVER: Black and white cover with title only.

4459 Sailors on Leave (Republic, 1941, William Lundigan, Shirley Ross).

Since You—Frank Loesser (w), Jule Styne (m), Mercer Morris. COVER: Shirley Ross.

4460 Saint Joan (United Artists, 1957, Jean Seberg, Richard Widmark).

Saint Joan Theme—Mischa Spoliansky (m), Carlot; The Dream Minuet (B)—Mischa Spoliansky (m), Chappell. COVER: Jean Seberg.

4461 Saint Xavier Cabrini (Citizen Saint) (Elliott, 1947, Carla Dare, Julie Hayden).

Saint Xavier Cabrini Theme (PC) —Harold Orlob (w,m), Milton. COVER: None.

4462 Sally (First National, 1925, Colleen Moore, Leon Errol).

Sally's in the Movies Now—Harry Seymour, Irving Abrahamson (w,m), Seymour. COVER: Colleen Moore.

4463 Sally (First National, 1929, Marilyn Miller, Joe E. Brown).

After Business Hours/All I Want to Do Do Do Is Dance/If I'm Dreaming—Al Dubin (w), Joe Burke (m), Harms; Look for the Silver Lining— P. G. Wodehouse (w), Jerome Kern (m), Harms; Sally—Al Dubin (w), Joe Burke (m), Harms; Wild Rose—Clifford Grey (w), Jerome Kern (m), Harms. COVER: Marilyn Miller.

4464 Sally Irene and Mary (20th Century-Fox, 1938, Alice Faye, Fred Allen).

Got My Mind on Music—Mack Gordon, Harry Revel (w,m), Robbins; Half Moon on the Hudson/I Could Use a Dream—Walter Bullock (w), Harold Spina (m), Robbins; Sweet as a Song—Mack Gordon, Harry Revel (w,m), Robbins; This Is Where I Came In (BW)—Walter Bullock (w), Harold Spina (m), Robbins. COVER: Alice Faye, Fred Allen, Tony Martin, Joan Davis.

4465 Sal of Singapore (RKO Pathe, 1929, Phyllis Haver, Alan Hale).

Singapore Sal—Billy Stone, Al Koppell, C. Weinberg (w,m), Witmark; Singapore Sal's Lullaby—Charley Wynn (w), Jack Grun (m), Mills. COVER: Phyllis Haver.

4466 Salome (Columbia, 1953, Rita Hayworth, Stewart Granger).

Salome (B)—Philip Green (m), Chappell. COVER: Rita Hayworth, Stewart Granger, and Movie Scenes.

4467 Salome vs. Shenandoah (Sennett, 1919, Ben Turpin, Louise Fazenda).

Salome vs. Shenandoah—Ray Perkins (w,m), Berlin. COVER: Ben Turpin, Phyllis Haver, Mack Sennett.

4468 Salt and Pepper (United Artists, 1968, Sammy Davis, Peter Lawford).

Salt and Pepper—Leslie Bricusse (w,m), Unart. COVER: Peter Lawford, Sammy Davis.

4469 Saludos (Saludos Amigos) (Disney, 1942, Cartoon).

Brazil—S. K. Russell (w), Ary Barroso (m), Southern; Saludos Amigos —Ned Washington (w), Charles Wolcott (m), Southern. COVER: Cartoon.

4470 Saludos Amigos (Saludos) (Disney, 1942, Cartoon).

Brazil—S. K. Russell (w), Ary Barroso (m), Southern; Saludos Amigos —Ned Washington (w), Charles Wolcott (m), Southern. COVER: Cartoon.

4471 Salute for Three (Paramount, 1943, MacDonald Carey, Betty Rhodes).

Don't Worry/I'll Do It for You— Kim Gannon (w), Jule Styne (m), Paramount; Left, Right—Kim Gannon, Sol Meyer (w), Jule Styne (m), Paramount; My Wife's a WAAC/ Whadya Do When It Rains—Kim Gannon (w), Jule Styne (m), Paramount. COVER: Betty Rhodes, MacDonald Carey, Dona Drake.

4472 Salute to Courage (Goodwill, 1952, Peggy Dew, Marvin Press).

The Goodwill Song—Don Dixon (w,m), Goodwill. COVER: Joe E. Brown, Peggy Dew, and Cartoon.

4473 Samarang (United Artists, 1933, Sai Yu, Ah Mang).

Out of the Deep, Samarang Love Song—Gus Kahn (w), D. Snell, C. Schonberg (m), Robbins. COVER: Sai Yu, Ah Mang.

4474 Same Old Town (Paramount, 1915, Stars Unknown).

Same Old Town—L. Wolfe Gilbert (w), Dave Levy (m), Stern. COVER: A Man and a Woman.

4475 Same Time Next Year (Universal, 1978, Ellen Burstyn, Alan Alda).

Last Time I Felt Like This—Alan Bergman, Marilyn Bergman (w), Marvin Hamlisch (m), Leeds. COVER: Johnny Mathis.

4476 Samson and Delilah (Paramount, 1949, Victor Mature, Hedy Lamarr).

Song of Delilah—Jay Livingston, Ray Evans (w), Victor Young (m), Famous. COVER: Hedy Lamarr, Victor Mature.

4477 Sam Whiskey (United Artists, 1969, Burt Reynolds, Clint Walker).

Sam Whiskey Theme—Herschel Burke Gilbert (m), Unart. COVER: Black and white cover with title only.

4478 San Antonio (Warner Bros., 1945, Errol Flynn, Alexis Smith).

Put Your Little Foot Right Out—
Larry Spier (w,m), Spier; Some Sunday Morning—Ted Koehler (w), M. K. Jerome, Ray Heindorf (m), Harms; Somewhere in Monterey—Jack Scholl (w), Charlie Kisco (m), Harms. COVER: Errol Flynn, Alexis Smith.

4479 San Antonio Rose (Universal, 1941, Jane Frazee, Robert Paige).
Hi Neighbor—Jack Owens (w,m), BMI; Mexican Jumping Beat—Don Raye, Gene DePaul (w,m), Leeds. COVER: Jane Frazee, The Merry Macs.

4480 Sanctuary (20th Century-Fox, 1961, Lee Remick, Yves Montand).
Sanctuary—Alan Bergman, Marilyn Keith (w), Alex North (m), Feist. COVER: Lee Remick, Yves Montand, Bradford Dillman.

4481 Sanders of the River (United Artists, 1935, Paul Robeson, Leslie Banks).
Canoe Song/Congo Lullaby/Killing Song—Arthur Wimperis (w), Mischa Spoliansky (m), Mills. COVER: African Dancers.

4482 Sand Pebbles (20th Century-Fox, 1966, Steve McQueen, Candice Bergen).
And We Were Lovers—Leslie Bricusse (w), Jerry Goldsmith (m), Hastings; Sand Pebbles Theme—Jerry Goldsmith (m), Hastings. COVER: Movie Scenes.

4483 Sandpiper, The (MGM, 1965, Elizabeth Taylor, Richard Burton).
Sandpiper Love Theme—Johnny Mandel (m), Miller; Shadow of Your Smile, The—Paul F. Webster (w), Johnny Mandel (m), Miller. COVER: Elizabeth Taylor, Richard Burton.

4484 Sands of the Kalahari (Paramount, 1965, Stuart Whitman, Stanley Baker).
Sands of the Kalahari Theme/ Sands of the Kalahari-Music Score— John Dankworth (m), Famous. COVER: Stuart Whitman, and Movie Scenes.

4485 San Fernando Valley (Republic, 1944, Roy Rogers, Dale Evans).
San Fernando Valley (B)—Gordon Jenkins (w,m), Chappell. COVER: Roy Rogers.

4486 San Francisco (MGM, 1936, Clark Gable, Jeanette MacDonald).
San Francisco (#1) (PC-CUT)— Harold Adamson (w), Walter Donaldson (m), Robbins; San Francisco (#2)—Gus Kahn (w), Bronislau Kaper, Walter Jurmann (m), Robbins; Would You—Arthur Freed (w), Nacio Herb Brown (m), Robbins. COVER: Clark Gable, Jeanette MacDonald.

4487 Sangaree (Paramount, 1953, Fernando Lamas, Arlene Dahl).
Sangaree—Jay Livingston, Ray Evans (w,m), Paramount. COVER: Fernando Lamas, Arlene Dahl.

4488 San Quentin (Warner Bros., 1937, Humphrey Bogart, Pat O'Brien).
How Could You?—Al Dubin (w), Harry Warren (m), Remick. COVER: Ann Sheridan, Pat O'Brien, Humphrey Bogart.

4489 Santa Claus-The Movie (Tri-Star, 1985, Dudley Moore, John Lithgow).
Santa Claus, The Movie—Twelve Songs and Themes—Henry Mancini, Leslie Bricusse (w,m), Leonard. COVER: Santa Claus.

4490 Santa Fe Trail, The (Arrow, 1923, Neva Gerber, Jack Perrin).
Santa Fe Trail, The—Ed Chenette (w,m), Brown. COVER: Neva Gerber, and Covered Wagon.

4491 Sap from Syracuse, The (Paramount, 1930, Ginger Rogers, Jack Oakie).
How I Wish I Could Sing a Love Song—E. Y. Harburg (w), John Green (m), Famous. COVER: Ginger Rogers, Jack Oakie.

4492 Saratoga (MGM, 1937, Clark Gable, Jean Harlow).

Horse with the Dreamy Eyes, The/Saratoga—Bob Wright, Chet Forrest (w), W. Donaldson (m), Robbins. COVER: Jean Harlow, Clark Gable.

4493 Saratoga Trunk (Warner Bros., 1945, Gary Cooper, Ingrid Bergman).

As Long as I Live/Goin' Home—Charles Tobias (w), Max Steiner (m), Witmark; Saratoga Trunk Theme (VS)—Max Steiner (m), Warner. COVER: Gary Cooper, Ingrid Bergman.

4494 Sarong Girl (Monogram, 1943, Ann Corio, Tim Ryan).

Saronga/Woogie Hula—Louis Herscher, Marvin Hatley (w,m), Southern. COVER: Ann Corio.

4495 Sarumba (Eagle Lion, 1954, Doris Dowling, Tommy Wonder).

Low Tide—Marla Forbes, Hugo Rubens (w,m), Peer. COVER: A Guitar, a Hat, a Serape.

4496 Satan Never Sleeps (20th Century-Fox, 1961, William Holden, Clifton Webb).

Satan Never Sleeps—Harold Adamson, Leo McCarey (w), Harry Warren (m), Feist. COVER: William Holden, Clifton Webb, France Nuyen.

4497 Satan's Holiday (Paramount, 1930, Stars Unknown).

That's When I Felt Blue—Larry Rich, Charles Roddick (w,m), Shapiro Bernstein. COVER: Black and white cover with title only.

4498 Saturday Night and Sunday Morning (Continental, 1960, Rachel Roberts, Albert Finney).

Let's Slip Away (B)—David Dearlove (w), John Dankworth (m), Feldman. COVER: Albert Finney, Rachel Roberts, Shirley Ann Field.

4499 Saturday Night Fever (Paramount, 1977, John Travolta, Barry Miller).

Barracuda Hangout—David Shire (m), Ensign; How Deep Is Your Love/ If I Can't Have You—Barry Gibb, Robin Gibb, Maurice Gibb (w,m), RSO; Manhattan Skyline—David Shire (m), Ensign; More Than a Woman/Night Fever—Barry Gibb, Robin Gibb, Maurice Gibb (w,m), RSO; Night on Disco Mountain/ Salsation—David Shire (m), Ensign; Saturday Night Fever Medley/Stayin' Alive/Saturday Night Fever-16 Songs —Barry Gibb, Robin Gibb, Maurice Gibb (m), RSO. COVER: John Travolta.

4500 Saturday's Children (First National, 1929, Corinne Griffith, Grant Withers).

I Still Believe in You—Grant Clark, Benny Davis (w), Harry Akst (m), Witmark. COVER: Corinne Griffith.

4501 Saturday's Children (Warner Bros., 1940, John Garfield, Anne Shirley).

Saturday's Children—Jack Scholl (w), M. K. Jerome (m), Remick. COVER: John Garfield, Anne Shirley.

4502 Saturday's Millions (Universal, 1933, Robert Young, Leila Hyams).

Darling of the Campus—Al Jacobs, Jerry Herst (w,m), Sherman Clay; This Time It's Love—Sam Lewis (w), Fred Coots (m), Feist. COVER: Robert Young, Leila Hyams.

4503 Savage Sam (Disney, 1964, Tommy Kirk, Brian Keith).

Savage Sam and Me—Terry Gilkyson (w,m), Wonderland. COVER: A Dog.

4504 Save the Tiger (Paramount, 1972, Jack Lemmon, Jack Gilford).

Save the Tiger Theme/Where Are All My Dreams Now?—Marvin Hamlisch (m), Famous. COVER: Jack Lemmon.

4505 Saxon Charm, The (Universal, 1945, Robert Montgomery, Susan Hayward).

I'm in the Mood for Love—Dorothy Fields (w), Jimmy McHugh (m), Robbins. COVER: Susan Hayward, Robert Montgomery, John Payne, Audrey Totter.

4506 Say It in French (Paramount, 1938, Ray Milland, Olympe Bradna).

April in My Heart—Helen Meinardi, Hoagy Carmichael (w,m), Paramount. COVER: Ray Milland, Olympe Bradna.

4507 Say It with Music (BD, 1932, Jack Payne, Percy Marmont).

I'll Do My Best to Make You Happy/Love Is the Sweetest Thing—Ray Noble (w,m), Harms. COVER: Sketch of Couple.

4508 Say It with Songs (Little Pal) (Warner Bros., 1929, Al Jolson, Marion Nixon).

Little Pal—Al Jolson, B. G. De-Sylva, Lew Brown, Ray Henderson (w,m), DBH; Mem'ries of One Sweet Kiss—Al Jolson, Dave Dreyer (w,m), Berlin; Seventh Heaven/Used to You/Why Can't You—Al Jolson, B. G. DeSylva, Lew Brown, Ray Henderson (w,m), DBH. COVER: Al Jolson.

4509 Sayonara (Warner Bros., 1957, Marlon Brando, Red Buttons).

Katzumi Love Theme—Franz Waxman (m), Witmark; Mountains Beyond the Moon—Carl Sigman (w), Franz Waxman (m), Witmark; Sayonara—Irving Berlin (w,m), Berlin. COVER: Marlon Brando, Miko Taka.

4510 Say One for Me (20th Century-Fox, 1959, Bing Crosby, Robert Wagner).

Chico's Choo Choo/Girl Most Likely to Succeed/Night That Rock and Roll Died/Say One for Me/Secret of Christmas, The/You Can't Love 'Em All—Sammy Cahn (w), James Van Heusen (m), Feist. COVER: Bing Crosby, Robert Wagner, Debbie Reynolds.

4511 Scalphunters, The (United Artists, 1968, Burt Lancaster, Shelley Winters).

Scalphunters' Theme—Elmer Bernstein (m), Unart. COVER: Burt Lancaster, Ossie Davis.

4512 Scandal in Sorrento (Titanus, 1957, Sophia Loren, Vittorio DeSica).

Bread, Love, and Tears—Robert Mellin (w), Ic Ini (m), Mellin. COV-

ER: Sophia Loren, Vittorio De-Sica.

4513 Scandalous John (Disney, 1971, Brian Keith, Alfonso Arau).

Pastures Green/Scandalous John-Fourteen Songs—Rod McKuen (w, m), Ed-Chan. COVER: Brian Keith.

4514 Scapegoat, The (MGM, 1959, Alec Guinness, Bette Davis).

Scapegoat Theme (B)—Bronislau Kaper (m), Robbins. COVER: Alec Guinness, Irene Worth.

4515 Scaramouche (MGM, 1923, Ramon Novarro, Alice Terry).

Scaramouche-Fox Trot March—Joseph Jordan (m), Photoplay; Scaramouche-Minuet (B)—P. S. Robinson (w), L. Beethoven (m), Boosey Hawkes. COVER: Ramon Novarro, Alice Terry.

4516 Scaramouche (MGM, 1952, Eleanor Parker, Stewart Granger).

My Heart's Desire—Edward Heyman (w), Victor Young (m), Lion. COVER: Eleanor Parker, Stewart Granger, Janet Leigh.

4517 Scared Stiff (Paramount, 1953, Dean Martin, Jerry Lewis).

Enchilada Man/San Domingo/What Have You Done for Me Lately?/When Someone Wonderful Thinks You're Wonderful—Mack David (w), Jerry Livingston (m), Paramount. COVER: Dean Martin, Jerry Lewis, Carmen Miranda.

4518 Scarlet Hour, The (Paramount, 1956, Tom Tryon, Carol Ohmart).

Never Let Me Go—Jay Livingston, Ray Evans (w,m), Famous; Scarlet Hour Mambo—Bebe Blake (w), Leith Stevens (m), Famous. COVER: Tom Tryon, Carol Ohmart.

4519 Scarlet Lady, The (Columbia, 1928, Lya De Putti, Don Alvarado).

My Heart Belongs to You—Lou Herschner (w,m), Lewis. COVER: Lya De Putti, and Men.

4520 Scatterbrain (Republic, 1940, Judy Canova, Alan Mowbray).

Benny the Beaver—Hy Heath,

Johnny Lange, Lew Porter (w,m), Mills. COVER: Judy Canova.

4521 Scent of Mystery (Todd, 1959, Peter Lorre, Denholm Elliott).

Chase—Harold Adamson (w), Mario Nascimbene (m), Liza; Scent of Mystery—Harold Adamson, J. Ramin (w), Mario Nascimbene, J. Ramin (m), Liza. COVER: A Gun and a Rose.

4522 School Days (Warner Bros., 1922, Wesley Barry, George Lessey).

School Days—Will Cobb, Gus Edwards (w,m), Edwards. COVER: Wesley Barry.

4523 School Daze (Columbia, 1988, Larry Fishbourne, Giancarlo Esposito).

Da Butt—Marcus Miller, Mark Stevens (w,m), MCA. COVER: Red cover with title only.

4524 School for Wives (Vitagraph, 1925, Conway Tearle, Peggy Kelly).

School for Wives—Jimmy Clark (w,m), Whiteway. COVER: Conway Tearle, Peggy Kelly.

4525 Scotland Yard Commands (Grant National, 1936, Clive Brook, Victoria Hooper).

If You're Going My Way—Jimmy Kennedy, Wally Ridley (w,m), Crawford. COVER: Clive Brook.

4526 Script Girl (Vitaphone, 1937, Musical Short).

Just a Simple Melody—Sammy Cahn (w), Saul Chaplin (m), Witmark. COVER: Tommy Dorsey.

4527 Scrooge (United Artists, 1951, Alastair Sim, Kathleen Harrison).

Tiny Tim's Tune (B)—Richard Addinsell (m), Chappell. COVER: Alastair Sim.

4528 Scrooge (National General, 1970, Albert Finney, Alec Guinness).

Beautiful Day/Christmas Carol/ Christmas Children/Father Christmas/ Good Times/Happiness/I Like Life/ I'll Begin Again/Thank You Very Much/You, You—Leslie Bricusse (w, m), Stage-Screen. COVER: Albert Finney, and Movie Scene.

4529 Scrooged (Paramount, 1988, Bill Murray, Karen Allen).

Put a Little Love in Your Heart— Jim Holiday, Randy Myers, Jackie DeShannon (w,m), Unart; Scrooged Theme (VS)—Danny Elfman (m), Unart. COVER: Bill Murray.

4530 Sea, The (Warner Bros., 1967, Documentary on Oceans).

The Ever Constant Sea/The Sea— Fourteen Songs—Rod McKuen (w), Anita Kerr (m), Warm. COVER: The Ocean and Rocks.

4531 Sea Bat, The (MGM, 1930, Charles Bickford, John Miljan).

Lo Lo—F. Feist, Howard Johnson (w), R. Montgomery, George Ward (m), Robbins. COVER: Native Girl.

4532 Sea Beneath, The (Fox, 1932, George O'Brien, Marion Lessing).

Sailor Lad—Maria Grever (w,m), Red Star. COVER: A Lighthouse and a Girl.

4533 Sea Devils (RKO, 1953, Rock Hudson, Yvonne De Carlo).

Sea Devils Prologue (B)—Richard Addinsell (m), Prowse. COVER: Black and white cover with title only.

4534 Sea Hawk, The (First National, 1924, Enid Bennett, Milton Sills).

The Sea Hawk (#1)—J. Johnston (w), M. Altschuler (m), Mills; The Sea Hawk (#2) (B)—P. Rogers, E. Valentine, J. Tunbridge (w,m), Feldman. COVER: Milton Sills, and Ship.

4535 Sea Hawk, The (Warner Bros., 1940, Erroll Flynn, Brenda Marshall).

The Sea Hawk-Piano Suite—Erich W. Korngold (m), Warner. COVER: Brown cover with title only.

4536 Sea Hornet, The (Republic, 1951, Rod Cameron, Adele Mara).

A Dream or Two Ago—Jack Elliott (w,m), Young. COVER: Rod Cameron, Adele Mara.

4537 Sealed Hearts (Selznick, 1919, Eugene O'Brien, Robert Edeson).

Sealed Hearts—Alex Sullivan (w), Irving Bibo (m), Berlin. COVER: Eugene O'Brien, Lucille Stewart.

4538 Sea Legs (Paramount, 1930, Jack Oakie, Harry Green).

This Must Be Illegal—George Marion (w), Ralph Rainger, Franke Harling (m), Famous. COVER: Jack Oakie, Lillian Roth.

4539 Sea of Sand (Desert Patrol) (Universal, 1940, Richard Attenborough, John Gregson).

Sea of Sand March (B)—Clifton Parker (m), Filmusic. COVER: Soldiers.

4540 Searchers, The (Warner Bros., 1956, John Wayne, Natalie Wood).

The Searchers-Ride Away—Stan Jones (w,m), Witmark. COVER: John Wayne, Jeffrey Hunter, Vera Miles.

4541 Search for Beauty (Paramount, 1934, Ida Lupino, Buster Crabbe).

I'm a Seeker of Beauty—Sam Coslow (w), Arthur Johnston (m), Famous. COVER: Cartoon Sketch.

4542 Search for Paradise (Cinerama, 1957, Travel Documentary).

Happy Land of Hunza/Kashmir/ Search for Paradise/Shalimar—Ned Washington, Lowell Thomas (w), Dimitri Tiomkin (m), Witmark. COVER: Movie Scenes.

4543 Searching Generation, The (Carmichael, 1968, Religious Film).

I Looked for Love—Ralph Carmichael (w,m), Lexicon. COVER: A Guitar.

4544 Searching Wind, The (Paramount, 1946, Robert Young, Sylvia Sidney).

Searching Wind—Edward Heyman (w), Victor Young (m), Famous; Searching Wind Theme—Victor Young (m), Famous. COVER: Robert Young, Sylvia Sidney, Ann Richards.

4545 Seasoned Greetings (Vitaphone, 1933, Lita Grey Chaplin).

Sunny Weather—Cliff Hess (w,m), Witmark. COVER: Black and white cover with title only.

4546 Sea Wife, The (20th Century-Fox, 1957, Joan Collins, Richard Burton).

I'll Find You—Richard Mullan (w), Tolchard Evans (m), Robbins. COVER: Joan Collins, and Ship.

4547 Sebastian (Paramount, 1967, Dirk Bogarde, Susannah York).

Comes the Night/Hey There, Who Are You—Hal Shaper (w), Jerry Goldsmith (m), Ensign. COVER: Dirk Bogarde, and Girls.

4548 Second Best Secret Agent in the Whole Wide World, The (Embassy, 1966, Tom Adams, Karel Stepanek).

Second Best Secret Agent, The— Sammy Cahn (w), James Van Heusen (m), Levine. COVER: Tom Adams, Karel Stepanek.

4549 Second Chance (RKO, 1953, Robert Mitchum, Linda Darnell).

Second Chance—Roy Webb (m), Mills. COVER: Robert Mitchum, Linda Darnell.

4550 Second Choice (Warner Bros., 1930, Dolores Costello, Chester Morris).

Life Can Be Lonesome—Al Dubin, Joe Burke (w), M. K. Jerome (m), Witmark. COVER: Black and white cover with title only.

4551 Second Chorus (Paramount, Fred Astaire, Paulette Goddard).

Dig It—Johnny Mercer (w), Hal Borne (m), Mercer Morris; Love of My Life—Johnny Mercer (w), Artie Shaw (m), Mercer Morris; Poor Mr. Chisolm (B)—Johnny Mercer (w), Bernie Hanighen (m), Victoria. COVER: Fred Astaire, Paulette Goddard.

4552 Second Fiddle (20th Century-Fox, 1939, Sonja Henie, Tyrone Power).

Back to Back/I Poured My Heart into a Song/I'm Sorry for Myself/Old Fashioned Tune Always Is New, An/ Song of the Metronome/When Winter Comes—Irving Berlin (w,m), Berlin.

COVER: Sonja Henie, Tyrone Power, Rudy Vallee.

4553 Second Greatest Sex, The (Universal, 1955, George Nader, Jeanne Crain).

How Lonely Can I Get—Joan Whitney, Alex Kramer (w,m), Northern; I'm a Travelin' Man/Lysistrata/ My Love Is Yours—Pony Sherrell, Phil Moody (w,m), American; Second Greatest Sex, The—Jay Livingston, Ray Evans (w,m), Northern; Send Us a Miracle/There's Gonna Be a Wedding/What Good Is a Woman Without a Man—Pony Sherrell, Phil Moody (w,m), American. COVER: George Nader, Jeanne Crain, and others.

4554 Second Hand Rose (Universal, 1922, Gladys Walton, George Williams).

Second Hand Rose—Grant Clarke (w), James Hanley (m), Shapiro Bernstein. COVER: Gladys Walton.

4555 Second Time Around, The (20th Century-Fox, 1961, Debbie Reynolds, Steve Forrest).

Second Time Around, The—Sammy Cahn (w), James Van Heusen (m), Miller. COVER: Debbie Reynolds.

4556 Secret Ceremony (Universal, 1968, Elizabeth Taylor, Mia Farrow).

Secret Ceremony Themes (B)— Richard Rodney Bennett (m), Leeds. COVER: Black and white cover with title only.

4557 Secret Door, The (Allied Artists, 1964, Robert Hutton, Sandra Dorne).

Lisboa (B)—Charles Baldour (w, m), BMI. COVER: Tony Osbourne.

4558 Secret Heart, The (MGM, 1950, Claudette Colbert, Walter Pidgeon).

I Can't Give You Anything but Love—Dorothy Fields (w), Jimmy McHugh (m), Mills. COVER: Claudette Colbert, Walter Pidgeon, June Allyson.

4559 Secret Hour, The (Para-

mount, 1927, Pola Negri, Jean Hersholt).

Beggar—Francis Wheeler, Irving Kahal (w), Ted Snyder (m), Berlin. COVER: Pola Negri.

4560 Secret Life of Walter Mitty, The (RKO, 1947, Danny Kaye, Virginia Mayo).

Beautiful Dreamer—Stephen Foster (w,m), Mills. COVER: Danny Kaye, Virginia Mayo.

4561 Secret of My Success (MGM, 1965, Shirley Jones, Stella Stevens).

I've Got a Little Secret—Joao Baptista Laurenco (m), Robbins. COVER: Cartoon Sketches.

4562 Secret of My Success, The (Universal, 1987), Michael Fox, Helen Slater).

Secret of My Success—Tom Keane, David Foster, J. Blades, M. Landau (w,m), MCA. COVER: Michael Fox.

4563 Secret of NIMH, The (MGM, 1982, Cartoon).

Flying Dreams—Paul Williams (w), Jerry Goldsmith (m), Unart. COVER: Cartoons.

4564 Secret of Santa Vittoria, The (United Artists, 1969, Anthony Quinn, Virna Lisi).

Song of Santa Vittoria—Norman Gimbel (w), Ernest Gold (m), Unart. COVER: Anthony Quinn, Anna Magnani.

4565 Secrets (First National, 1924, Norma Talmadge, Eugene O'Brien).

Secrets—Egbert Van Alstyne, Haven Gillespie, Al Sobler (w,m), Remick. COVER: Norma Talmadge.

4566 Secret Service (Paramount, 1919, Robert Warwick, Wanda Hawley).

In Secret Service, I Won Her Heart —Alfred Bryan (w), Herbert Spencer (m), Remick. COVER: Robert Warwick.

4567 Secrets of a Co-ed (PRC, 1942, Otto Kruger, Tina Thayer).

Brazilly Willy—Jay Livingston,

Ray Evans (w), H. Lobo, M. DuOliveira (m), Southern. COVER: Otto Kruger, Tina Thayer, Diana Del Rio.

4568 Secrets of the Wasteland (Paramount, 1941, William Boyd, Andy Clyde).

Blue Moon on the Silver Sage—Ralph Freed (w), Sam Stept (m), Famous. COVER: William Boyd.

4569 Secret Ways (Universal, 1961, Richard Widmark, Sonja Ziemann).

Secret Ways—Johnny Williams (m), Champion. COVER: Richard Widmark, Sonja Ziemann.

4570 See America Thirst (Universal, 1930, Harry Langdon, Slim Summerville).

Doya, Doncha, Wontcha?—Bernie Grossman (w), Lou Handman (m), Universal. COVER: Harry Langdon, Slim Summerville.

4571 See Here Private Hargrove (MGM, 1944, Robert Walker, Donna Reed).

In My Arms—Frank Loesser, Ted Grouya (w,m), Saunders. COVER: Donna Reed, Robert Walker.

4572 Seems Like Old Times (Columbia, 1980, Chevy Chase, Goldie Hawn).

Seems Like Old Times—Marvin Hamlisch (m), Golden Torch. COVER: Red and yellow cover with title only.

4573 Sein Liebeslied (His Love Song) (Associated, 1931, German Operetta).

Little Mascot—Joe Young (w), Robert Stolz (m), Harms; My Sunshine Is Yours—John Greenhaigh (w), Robert Stolz (m), Harms. COVER: Sketch of Dancers.

4574 Send Me No Flowers (Universal, 1964, Rock Hudson, Doris Day).

Send Me No Flowers—Hal David (w), Burt Bacharach (m), Artists. COVER: Rock Hudson, Doris Day.

4575 Senior Prom (Columbia, 1958, Jill Corey, Paul Hampton).

Longer I Love You—Hal Hackady (w), Don Gohman (m), Columbia; That Old Black Magic—Johnny Mercer (w), Harold Arlen (m), Famous. COVER: Jill Corey, Paul Hampton, and Singers.

4576 Senor Americano (Universal, 1929, Ken Maynard, Kathryn Crawford).

Estrellita—Manuel Ponce, George Davis, George Hulten (w,m), Sherman Clay. COVER: Ken Maynard, Kathryn Crawford.

4577 Sensation Hunters (Monogram, 1933, Arline Judge, Preston Foster).

Something in the Air—Bernie Grossman, Harold Lewis (w,m), Harms. COVER: Arline Judge.

4578 Sensations of 1945 (United Artists, 1944, Eleanor Powell, Dennis O'Keefe).

Kiss Serenade—Harry Tobias (w), Al Sherman (m), Mills; Mr. Hepster's Dictionary—Harry Tobias (w), Al Sherman (m), Leeds; No Never/One Love/Spin Little Pin Ball—Harry Tobias (w), Al Sherman (m), Mills; Wake Up Man, You're Slippin'—Harry Tobias (w), Al Sherman (m), Leeds. COVER: Eleanor Powell, Dennis O'Keefe, Woody Herman, W. C. Fields.

4579 Separate Tables (United Artists, 1958, Rita Hayworth, Deborah Kerr).

Separate Tables—Harold Adamson (w), Harry Warren (m), Hecht-Lancaster. COVER: Rita Hayworth, Deborah Kerr, David Niven, Burt Lancaster.

4580 September Affair (Paramount, 1951, Joan Fontaine, Joseph Cotten).

September Song—Maxwell Anderson (w), Kurt Weill (m), Crawford. COVER: Joan Fontaine, Joseph Cotten.

4581 Serenade (Warner Bros., 1956, Mario Lanza, Joan Fontaine).

Come Back to Sorrento—Claire Stafford (w), Ernest DeCurtis (m), Remick; My Destiny/Serenade—

Sammy Cahn (w), Nicholas Brodszky (m), Harms. COVER: Mario Lanza, Sarita Montiel.

4582 Sergeant Rutledge (Warner Bros., 1960, Constance Towers, Jeffrey Hunter).

Captain Buffalo—Mack David (w), Jerry Livingston (m), Witmark. COVER: Constance Towers, Jeffrey Hunter.

4583 Serial (Paramount, 1980, Tuesday Weld, Martin Mull).

Changing World—Norman Gimbel (w), Lalo Schifrin (m), Famous. COVER: Movie Scene.

4584 Serpico (Paramount, 1973, Al Pacino, John Randolph).

Beyond Tomorrow—Larry Kusik (w), Mikis Theodorakis (m), Famous; Serpico Theme—Mikis Theodorakis (m), Famous. COVER: Al Pacino.

4585 Sesame Street Presents Follow That Bird (Warner Bros., 1985, Jim Henson, Frank Oz).

Ain't No Road Too Long—Steve Pippin, Jeff Harrington, Jeff Pennig (w,m), Warner; Sesame Street-Follow That Bird-Ten Songs—V. D. Parks, L. Niehaus, Jeff Moss (w,m), Warner. COVER: Big Bird.

4586 Seven Beauties (Cinema Five, 1976, Giancarlo Giannini, Fernando Ray).

Seven Beauties Theme—E. Jannacci, L. Wertmuller, G. Viola (m), Famous. COVER: Giancarlo Giannini.

4587 Seven Brides for Seven Brothers (MGM, 1954, Howard Keel, Jane Powell).

Bless Yore Beautiful Hide/Goin' Co'tin/June Bride/Lonesome Polecat/Sobbin' Women/Spring Spring Spring/When You're in Love/Wonderful Wonderful Day—Johnny Mercer (w), Gene DePaul (m), Robbins. COVER: Howard Keel, Jane Powell, Six Boys, Six Girls.

4588 Seven Capital Sins (Embassy, 1962, Nicole Mirel, Eddie Constantine).

Good Life, The—Jack Reardon (w), Sacha Distel (m), Paris; Seven Capital Sins Theme—Michel Legrand (m), Wood. COVER: Movie Scenes.

4589 Seven Days Ashore (RKO, 1944, Wally Brown, Alan Carney).

Apple Blossoms in the Rain/Hail and Farewell/Ready, Aim, Kiss/Sioux City Sue—Mort Greene (w), Lew Pollack (m), Southern. COVER: Marcy McGuire, Wally Brown, Alan Carny, Freddie Slack.

4590 Seven Days in May (Paramount, 1964, Burt Lancaster, Kirk Douglas).

Seven Days in May—Richard Stratford (m), Famous. COVER: Burt Lancaster, Ava Gardner, Kirk Douglas, Fredric March.

4591 Seven Days Leave (RKO, 1942, Victor Mature, Lucille Ball).

Baby/Can't Get out of This Mood/I Get the Neck of the Chicken/Please Won't You Leave My Girl Alone/Puerto Rico/Soft Hearted/Touch of Texas/You Speak My Language—Frank Loesser (w), Jimmy McHugh (m), Southern. COVER: Victor Mature, Lucille Ball, Ginny Simms.

4592 Seven Faces of Dr. Lao, The (United Artists, 1963, Tony Randall, Barbara Eden).

Seven Faces of Dr. Lao Theme—Leigh Harline (m), Miller. COVER: Tony Randall.

4593 Seven Golden Men (United Artists, 1966, Phillipe Leroy, Rosanna Podesta).

It Happens All the Time—Al Stillman (w), Armando Trovajoli (m), Marks; Rossana's Theme—Armando Trovajoli (m), Marks. COVER: Rosanna Podesta.

4594 Seven Hills of Rome (MGM, 1958, Mario Lanza, Renato Rascel).

Come Dance With Me—George Blake (w), Dick Leibert (m), Bloom; Goodbye to Rome—Carl Sigman (w), R. Rascel (m), Connelly; Seven Hills of Rome—Harold Adamson (w), Victor Young (m), Young; There's Gonna Be a Party Tonight—George Stoll (w,m), Robbins; When the Saints Go Marching On—David Nelson, George Stoll (w,m), Robbins. COVER: Mario Lanza, Renato Rascel.

4595 Seven Little Foys, The (Paramount, 1955, Bob Hope, Eddie Foy).

I'm the Greatest Father of Them All—W. Jerome, J. Lilley, B. Foy (w, m), Famous; Mary's a Grand Old Name—George M. Cohan (w,m), Cohan; Nobody—Alex Rogers (w), Bert Williams (m), Marks; Yankee Doodle Boy—George M. Cohan (w,m), Cohan; You're Here, My Love—Johnny Burke (w), Joseph Lilley (m), Famous. COVER: Bob Hope, James Cagney, and Seven Foys.

4596 Seven Minutes, The (20th Century-Fox, 1971, Wayne Maunder, Marianne McAndrew).

Seven Minutes—Stu Phillips, Bob Stone (w,m), Fox. COVER: A Book and a Girl.

4597 Seven Per Cent Solution (Universal, 1977, Alan Arkin, Vanessa Redgrave).

I Never Do Anything Twice, The Madam's Song—Stephen Sondheim (w,m), Leeds. COVER: Blue cover with title only.

4598 Seven Sinners (Universal, 1940, Marlene Dietrich, John Wayne).

I Fall Overboard/I've Been in Love Before/Man's in the Navy, The/ Frank Loesser (w), Frederick Hollander (m), Robbins. COVER: Marlene Dietrich.

4599 Seven Sweethearts (MGM, 1942, Kathryn Grayson, Van Heflin).

You and the Waltz and I—Paul F. Webster (w), Walter Jurmann (m), Feist. COVER: Kathryn Grayson, Van Heflin.

4600 Seventeen (Paramount, 1940, Jackie Cooper, Betty Field).

Seventeen—Frank Loesser (w,m), Paramount. COVER: Jackie Cooper, Betty Field.

4601 Seventh Dawn, The (United Artists, 1964, William Holden, Capu-

cine).

Seventh Dawn, The—Paul F. Webster (w), Riz Ortolani (m), Unart. COVER: William Holden, Capucine, Susannah York.

4602 Seventh Heaven (Fox, 1927, Janet Gaynor, Charles Farrell).

Diane—Erno Rapee, Lew Pollack (w,m), Sherman Clay. COVER: Janet Gaynor, Charles Farrell.

4603 Seventh Heaven (20th Century-Fox, 1937, James Stewart, Simone Simon).

Diane—Erno Rapee, Lew Pollack (w,m), Sherman Clay; Seventh Heaven—Sidney Mitchell (w), Lew Pollack (m), Hollywood. COVER: James Stewart, Simone Simon.

4604 Seventh Veil, The (Universal, 1945, Ann Todd, James Mason).

Seventh Veil Waltz (B)—Ben Bernard (m), Southern. COVER: Ann Todd.

4605 Seven Wonders of the World (Cinerama, 1957, Travel Documentary).

Japanese Parasols—Kazuo Totoki (m), Hill Range; Seven Wonders of the World Theme—Emil Newman, Lionel Newman (m), Hill Range; Taj Mahal—Emil Newman (m), Hill Range. COVER: Movie Scenes.

4606 Seven Year Itch, The (20th Century-Fox, 1955, Tom Ewell, Marilyn Monroe).

Girl Upstairs—Sammy Cahn (w), Alfred Newman (m), Robbins; Girl Upstairs Theme—Alfred Newman (m), Robbins. COVER: Marilyn Monroe, Tom Ewell.

4607 Sex and the Single Girl (Warner Bros., 1964, Tony Curtis, Natalie Wood).

Sex and the Single Girl—Richard Quine (w,m), Witmark. COVER: Tony Curtis, Natalie Wood.

4608 Sgt. Pepper's Lonely Heart's Club Band (Universal, 1978, Peter Frampton, George Burns).

Come Together/Get Back/Got to Get You Into My Life/Oh Darling/ Sgt. Pepper's Lonely Heart's Club

Band/With a Little Help from My Friends/Day in the Life, A (PC)/ Lucy in the Sky with Diamonds (PC) —John Lennon, Paul McCartney (w, m), ATV. COVER: Musical Instruments.

4609 Shadow of a Doubt (MGM, 1935, Ricardo Cortez, Virginia Bruce).

Beyond the Shadow of a Doubt— Harold Adamson (w), Burton Lane (m), Robbins. COVER: Isabel Jewell.

4610 Shadow of a Doubt (Universal, 1943, Joseph Cotten, Teresa Wright).

Shadow of a Doubt—Bob Reed (w), Harry Miller (m), MPI. COVER: Teresa Wright.

4611 Shadow of the Boomerang (Graham, 1960, Religious Film).

Return to the One Who Loves You—Ralph Carmichael, Dick Ross (w,m), Herman. COVER: Man, Woman, and Dog.

4612 Shadows (Goldwyn, 1918, Geraldine Farrar, Thomas Santschi).

Shadows—Ray Sherwood (w), Howard Lutter (m), Vandersloot; Shadows Love Theme—L. Beethoven (m), Belwin. COVER: Geraldine Farrar.

4613 Shadows (Preferred, 1923, Lon Cheney, Marguerite De La Motte).

Ching Ching Chinaman—Eve Unsell (w), Louis Gottschalk (m), Remick. COVER: Lon Chaney.

4614 Shady Lady (RKO, 1929, Phyllis Haver, Robert Armstrong).

Shady Lady—Howard Johnson (w), Z. Zuro, Francis Gromon, Jack Grun (m), Shapiro Bernstein. COVER: Phyllis Haver, Robert Armstrong.

4615 Shady Lady (Universal, 1945, Charles Coburn, Robert Paige).

In Love with Love—George Waggner (w), Milt Rosen (m), Viking; Xango, Chongo—George Waggner (w), Edgar Fairchild (m), Viking. COVER: Charles Coburn, Robert Paige, Ginny Simms.

4616 Shaft (MGM, 1971, Richard Roundtree, Moses Gunn).

Do Your Thing/Shaft Theme— Isaac Hayes (w,m), East Memphis. COVER: Richard Roundtree.

4617 Shaft in Africa (MGM, 1971, Richard Roundtree, Vonetta McGee).

Are You Man Enough?—Dennis Lambert, Brian Potter (w,m), Hastings. COVER: Richard Roundtree.

4618 Shaft's Big Score (MGM, 1972, Richard Roundtree, Moses Gunn).

Blowin' Your Mind/Don't Understand/Move on In—Gordon Parks (w,m), Feist. COVER: Richard Roundtree.

4619 Shaggy Dog, The (Buena Vista, 1959, Fred MacMurray, Jean Hagen).

Shaggy Dog, The—Gil George (w), Paul Smith (m), Disney. COVER: A Dog.

4620 Shakiest Gun in the West (Universal, 1968, Don Knotts, Barbara Rhoades).

Shakiest Gun in the West, The— Jerry Keller, Dave Blume (w,m), Northern. COVER: Don Knotts.

4621 Shalako (Cinerama, 1968, Sean Connery, Brigitte Bardot).

Irena/Shalako—Jim Dale (w), Robert Farnon (m), AMPCO. COVER: Sean Connery, Brigitte Bardot.

4622 Shall We Dance (RKO, 1937, Fred Astaire, Ginger Rogers).

Beginner's Luck/Let's Call the Whole Thing Off/Shall We Dance/ Slap That Bass/They All Laughed/ They Can't Take That Away from Me/Wake Up Brother and Dance (PC)/ Walking the Dog-Promenade (PC)— Ira Gershwin (w), George Gershwin (m), Chappell. COVER: Fred Astaire, Ginger Rogers.

4623 Shane (Paramount, 1953, Alan Ladd, Jean Arthur).

Call of the Faraway Hills—Mack David (w), Victor Young (m), Paramount; Call of the Faraway Hills Theme—Victor Young (m), Paramount; Eyes of Blue—Wilson Stone (w), Victor Young (m), Paramount. COVER: Alan Ladd, Jean Arthur, Van Heflin.

4624 Shanghai Lady (Universal, 1929, Mary Nolan, James Murray).

I Wonder If It's Really Love—Bernie Grossman, Arthur Sizemore (w,m), Shapiro Bernstein. COVER: Mary Nolan.

4625 Shannons of Broadway, The (Universal, 1929, James Gleason, Lucille Gleason).

Get Happy/Somebody to Love Me—Ray Klages (w), Jesse Greer (m), Robbins. COVER: James Gleason, Lucille Gleason.

4626 Shanty Town (Republic, 1943, Mary Lee, John Archer).

On the Corner of Sunshine and Main—Kim Gannon (w), Jule Styne (m), Witmark. COVER: Mary Lee.

4627 Shark Fighters (United Artists, 1956, Victor Mature, Karen Steele).

Shark Fighters Theme—Jerome Moross (m), Chappell. COVER: A Shark.

4628 She Couldn't Say No (Warner Bros., 1930, Winnie Lightner, Chester Morris).

Bouncing the Baby Around (BW)/Darn Fool Woman Like Me/Watching My Dreams Go By—Al Dubin (w), Joe Burke (m), Witmark. COVER: Winnie Lightner.

4629 She Done Him Wrong (Paramount, 1933, Mae West, Cary Grant).

Frankie and Johnny—Leighton Bros, Ren Shields (w,m), Shapiro Bernstein; A Guy What Takes His Time—Ralph Rainger (w,m), Famous. COVER: Mae West.

4630 Sheer Luck (Big Four, 1931, Jobyna Ralston, Nick Stuart).

Imagine!—Earl Burtnett, Jim Base, Jess Kirkpatrick, Ray Canfield (w, m), Hollywood. COVER: Jobyna Ralston, Nick Stuart.

4631 She Goes to War (United Artists, 1929, Al St. John, Glen Walters).

Joan/There Is a Happy Land—Sam Lewis, Joe Young (w), Harry Akst (m), Remick. COVER: Eleanor Boardman.

4632 She Had to Eat (20th Century-Fox, 1937, Jack Haley, Rochelle Hudson).

Living on the Town/When a Gal from Alabama Meets a Boy from Tennessee—Sidney Clare (w), Harry Akst (m), Movietone. COVER: Black and white cover with title only.

4633 She Has What It Takes (Columbia, 1943, Jinx Falkenberg, The Vagabonds).

Honk, Honk, The Rumble Seat Song—Roy Jordan, Gene DePaul (w, m), Leeds; Timber Timber Timber, The Woodchoppers Song—Don Reid, Henry Tobias (w,m), Shapiro Bernstein. COVER: The Vagabonds.

4634 Sheila Levine Is Dead and Living in New York (Paramount, 1975, Jeannie Berlin, Roy Scheider).

Sheila Levine Theme—Michel Legrand (m), Famous. COVER: Jeannie Berlin.

4635 She Learned About Sailors (Fox, 1934, Alice Faye, Lew Ayres).

Here's the Key to My Heart/She Learned About Sailors (BW)—Sidney Clare (w), Richard Whiting (m), Movietone. COVER: Alice Faye, Lew Ayres.

4636 She Loves Me Not (Paramount, 1934, Bing Crosby, Miriam Hopkins).

I'm Hummin', I'm Whistlin', I'm Singin'—Mack Gordon, Harry Revel (w,m), DBH; Love in Bloom—Leo Robin, Ralph Rainger (w,m), Famous; Straight from the Shoulder—Mack Gordon, Harry Revel (w,m), DBH. COVER: Bing Crosby.

4637 She Married a Cop (Republic, 1939, Phil Regan, Jean Parker).

I Can't Imagine/I'll Remember—Ralph Freed (w), Burton Lane (m), Miller. COVER: Phil Regan, Jean Parker.

4638 Shenandoah (Universal, 1965, James Stewart, Doug McClure).

Legend of Shenandoah—Gloria Shayne, Jerry Keller (w,m), Northern. COVER: James Stewart, Doug McClure, and Movie Scenes.

4639 Shepherd of the Hills (First National, 1927, John Boles, Molly O'Day).

The Shepherd of the Hills—Edgar Leslie (w), Horatio Nicholls (m), Berlin. COVER: Molly O'Day.

4640 Shepherd of the Hills (Paramount, 1941, Betty Field, John Wayne).

There's a Happy Hunting Ground —Sam Coslow (w,m), Paramount. COVER: John Wayne, Betty Field.

4641 Sheriff of Fractured Jaw (20th Century-Fox, 1958, Kenneth More, Jayne Mansfield).

If the San Francisco Hills Could Only Talk/In the Valley of Love/ Strolling Down the Lane with Bill— Harry Harris (w,m), Robbins. COVER: Jayne Mansfield, Kenneth More.

4642 She's a Sweetheart (Columbia, 1944, Jane Frazee, Larry Parks).

Peggy the Pin Up Girl—Redd Evans, John Loeb (w,m), Mutual. COVER: Jane Frazee.

4643 She's Back on Broadway (Warner, 1952, Virginia Mayo, Gene Nelson).

Ties That Bind—Bob Hilliard (w), Carl Sigman (m), Witmark. COVER: Virginia Mayo.

4644 She's for Me (Universal, 1943, Grace McDonald, David Bruce).

Ain't You Got No Time for Love? —Lottie Wells, Maurice Wells (w,m), Wells. COVER: Grace McDonald.

4645 She's Got Everything (RKO, 1938, Ann Sothern, Gene Raymond).

It's Sleepy Time in Hawaii—Leon Rene, Otis Rene (w,m), Berlin. COVER: Ann Sothern, Gene Raymond.

4646 She Shall Have Music (Twickenham, 1935, Jack Hylton, June Clyde).

Band That Jack Built—Maurice Sigler, Al Goodhart, Al Hoffman (w, m), Mills; Leader of the Band—Jimmy Kennedy, Michael Carr (w,m), Mills; My First Thrill—Maurice Sigler, Al Goodhart, Al Hoffman (w,m), Berlin; She Shall Have Music—Maurice Sigler, Al Goodhart, Al Hoffman (w,m), Chappell. COVER: Jack Hylton, Kate Smith.

4647 She's Working Her Way Through College (Warner Bros., 1952, Virginia Mayo, Gene Nelson).

I'll Be Loving You/Stuff That Dreams Are Made Of—Sammy Cahn (w), Vernon Duke (m), Witmark. COVER: Virginia Mayo, Gene Nelson.

4648 She Wolf, The (La Lupa) (Ponti De Laurentis, 1954, Kerima, Ettore Manni).

La Lupa—Barry Fremont, Fred Wise, Ben Weisman (w,m), Alamo. COVER: Kerima, Ettore Manni.

4649 She Wore a Yellow Ribbon (RKO, 1949, John Wayne, Joanne Dru).

She Wore a Yellow Ribbon—M. Ottner, Leroy Parker (w,m), Regent. COVER: John Wayne, Joanne Dru.

4650 Shifting Sands (Hodkinson, 1923, Peggy Hyland, Lewis Willoughby).

Shifting Sands—Victor Dale, Wyn Ewart (w,m), Song Success. COVER: Peggy Hyland, Lewis Willoughby.

4651 Shine on Harvest Moon (Republic, 1938, Roy Rogers, Mary Hart).

Man in the Moon Is a Cowhand, The (VS)—Roy Rogers (w,m), Marks. COVER: Roy Rogers.

4652 Shine on Harvest Moon (Warner Bros., 1944, Ann Sheridan, Dennis Morgan).

I Go for You—Kim Gannon (w), M. K. Jerome (m), Remick; Shine on Harvest Moon—Nora Bayes, Jack Norworth (w,m), Remick; So Dumb But So Beautiful—Kim Gannon (w), M. K. Jerome (m), Remick; Time Waits for No One—Cliff Friend, Charles Tobias (w,m), Remick. When It's Apple Blossom Time in Normandy—T. Mellor, H. Gifford, H.

Trevor (w,m), Remick. COVER: Ann Sheridan, Dennis Morgan.

4653 Ship Ahoy (MGM, 1942, Eleanor Powell, Red Skelton).

Hawaiian War Chant—Ralph Freed (w), John Noble, Leleiahaku (m), Miller; I'll Take Tallulah—E. Y. Harburg (w), Burton Lane (m), Feist; I'm Getting Sentimental Over You—Ned Washington (w), George Bassman (m), Mills; Last Call for Love, The—E. Y. Harburg, M. Cummings, Burton Lane (w,m), Feist; Poor You —E. Y. Harburg (w), Burton Lane (m), Feist. COVER: Eleanor Powell, Red Skelton, Tommy Dorsey, Bert Lahr.

4654 Ship Cafe (Paramount, 1935, Carl Brisson, Arline Judge).

Change Your Mind—Ray Noble (w,m), Popular; Fatal Fascination—Harlan Thompson, Lewis Gensler (w, m), Popular. COVER: Carl Brisson, Arline Judge.

4655 Shipmates Forever (First National, 1935, Dick Powell, Ruby Keeler).

Don't Give Up the Ship/I'd Love to Take Orders from You/I'd Rather Listen to Your Eyes—Al Dubin (w), Harry Warren (m), Remick; COVER: Dick Powell, Ruby Keeler.

4656 Ship of Fools (Columbia, 1965, Vivien Leigh, Jose Ferrer).

Ship of Fools—Ned Washington (w), Ernest Gold (m), Colgems. COVER: Ship.

4657 Ships With Wings (United Artists, 1941, John Clements, Leslie Banks).

When Did It Begin? (B)—Diana Morgan, Robert MacDermot (w), Geoffrey Wright (m), Chappell. COVER: Jane Baxter, Ann Todd, and Warship.

4658 Shipyard Sally (20th Century-Fox, 1939, Gracie Fields, Sydney Howard).

Wish Me Luck—Phil Park (w), Harry Davis (m), Chappell. COVER: Gracie Fields.

4659 Shiralee (MGM, 1957,

Peter Finch, Dana Wilson).

Shiralee (B)—Tommy Steele (w, m), Robbins. COVER: Peter Finch, Dana Wilson.

4660 Shirley Valentine (Paramount, 1989, Pauline Collins, Tom Conti).

Girl Who Used to Be Me, The—Alan Bergman, Marilyn Bergman (w), Marvin Hamlisch (m), Famous. COVER: Pauline Collins.

4661 Shocking Miss Pilgrim, The (20th Century-Fox, 1947, Betty Grable, Dick Haymes).

Aren't You Kind of Glad We Did?/ Back Bay Polka, The/Changing My Tune/For You, For Me, Forevermore/One, Two, Three—Ira Gershwin (w), George Gershwin (m), Gershwin. COVER: Betty Grable, Dick Haymes.

4662 Shoes of the Fisherman (MGM, 1968, Anthony Quinn, Oskar Werner).

Reconciliation/Shoes of the Fisherman—Alex North (m), Feist; Singing Wind, The—Paul F. Webster (w), Alex North (m), Feist. COVER: Anthony Quinn, Oskar Werner, and Others.

4663 Shooting High (20th Century-Fox, 1940, Jane Withers, Gene Autry).

In Our Little Shanty of Dreams—Gene Autry, Johnny Marvin (w,m), Robbins; On the Rancho with My Pancho—Sidney Clare (w), Harry Akst (m), Robbins; There's Only One Love in a Lifetime—Gene Autry, Harry Tobias, Johnny Marvin (w,m), Robbins. COVER: Jane Withers, Gene Autry.

4664 Shootist, The (Paramount, 1976, John Wayne, Lauren Bacall).

The Shootist Theme—Elmer Bernstein (m), Ensign. COVER: John Wayne, Lauren Bacall.

4665 Shoot Out at Medicine Bend (Warner Bros., 1957, Randolph Scott, James Craig).

Kiss Me Quick—Wayne Shanklin (w), Ray Heindorf (m), Witmark.

COVER: Randolph Scott, Angie Dickinson, Dani Crayne.

4666 Shoot the Man (Universal, 1974, Stars Unknown).

Play with Fire (PC)—Nanker Phelge (w,m), ABKCO. COVER: None.

4667 Shoot the Moon (MGM, 1981, Albert Finney, Diane Keaton).

Don't Blame Me—Dorothy Fields (w), Jimmy McHugh (m), Unart. COVER: Albert Finney, Diane Keaton.

4668 Shoot the Works (Paramount, 1934, Jack Oakie, Dorothy Dell).

Bowl of Chop Suey and You-ey—Ben Bernie, Al Goering, Walt Bullock (w,m), Famous; Do I Love You?—Leo Robin, Ralph Rainger (w,m), Famous; In the Good Old Wintertime—Mack Gordon, Harold Adamson, Harry Revel (w,m), DBH; Take a Lesson from the Lark—Leo Robin, Ralph Rainger (w,m), Famous; Were Your Ears Burning Baby?—Mack Gordon, Harry Revel (w,m), DBH; With My Eyes Wide Open I'm Dreaming—Mack Gordon, Harry Revel (w, m), DBH. COVER: Ben Bernie, Jack Oakie, Dorothy Dell.

4669 Shop on Main Street, The (Prominent, 1955, Josef Kroner, Ida Kaminska).

Shop on Main Street Theme—Zoener Liska (w,m), Marks. COVER: Man and Woman.

4670 Shopworn Angel (Paramount, 1929, Nancy Carroll, Gary Cooper).

A Precious Little Thing Called Love—Lou Davis, Fred Coots (w,m), Remick. COVER: Nancy Carroll, Gary Cooper.

4671 Shopworn Angel (MGM, 1938, Margaret Sullavan, James Stewart).

Let's Pretend It's True—Bob Wright, Chet Forrest (w), Edward Ward (m), Feist. COVER: Black and white cover with title only.

4672 Shore Acres (Metro, 1920, Alice Lake, Frank Brownlee).

Love's Ship—Nellie Morrison (w), Alice Morrison (m), Morrison. COVER: A Ship.

4673 Short Circuit (Tri-Star, 1986, Ally Sheedy, Steve Guttenberg).

Who's Johnny—Peter Wolf, Ina Wolf (w,m), Chappell. COVER: El DeBarge.

4674 Shot in the Dark, A (United Artists, 1964, Peter Sellers, Elke Sommer).

Shadows of Paris—Robert Wells (w), Henry Mancini (m), Twin Chris; Shot in the Dark, A—Henry Mancini (m), Twin Chris. COVER: Sketches.

4675 Should a Girl Marry? (Rayart, 1929, Helen Foster, Donald Keith).

Haunting Memories—Irving Bibo (w,m), Bibo Lang. COVER: Helen Foster.

4676 Should a Husband Forgive? (Fox, 1919, Miriam Cooper, Eric Mayne).

Should a Husband Forgive?—Herman Holland, George Rupert (w,m), Remick. COVER: Sketch of Girl.

4677 Show Boat (Universal, 1929, Laura La Plante, Joseph Schildkraut).

Bill—P. G. Wodehouse, Oscar Hammerstein (w), Jerome Kern (m), Harms; Can't Help Lovin' Dat Man—Oscar Hammerstein (w), Jerome Kern (m), Harms; Down South—Sigmund Spaeth (w), William Middleton (m), Marks; Here Comes the Show Boat—Billy Rose (w), Maceo Pinkard (m), Shapiro Bernstein; Lonesome Road, The—Gene Austin (w), Nathaniel Shilkret (m), Spier Coslow; Love Sings a Song in My Heart—Clarence Marks (w), Joe Cherniavsky (m), Sherman Clay; Make Believe/ Ol' Man River/Why Do I Love You/ You Are Love—Oscar Hammerstein (w), Jerome Kern (m), Harms. COVER: Laura La Plante, Joseph Schildkraut.

4678 Show Boat (Universal, 1936, Irene Dunne, Allan Jones).

Bill—P. G, Wodehouse, Oscar

Hammerstein (w), Jerome Kern (m), Harms; Can't Help Lovin' Dat Man/ I Have the Room Above/I Still Suits Me/Make Believe/Ol' Man River/Why Do I Love You/You Are Love/Show Boat-Piano Selections—Oscar Hammerstein (w), Jerome Kern (m), Harms. COVER: Irene Dunne, Helen Morgan, Allan Jones, Paul Robeson.

4679 Show Boat (MGM, 1951, Kathryn Grayson, Howard Keel).

After the Ball—Charles Harris (w, m), Lewis; Bill—P. G. Wodehouse, Oscar Hammerstein (w), Jerome Kern (m), Harms; Can't Help Lovin' Dat Man/Cotton Blossom (VS)/I Might Fall Back on You/I Still Suits Me/Life Upon the Wicked Stage/ Make Believe/Ol' Man River/Why Do I Love You/You Are Love— Oscar Hammerstein (w), Jerome Kern (m), Harms. COVER: Kathryn Grayson, Howard Keel, Joe E. Brown, Ava Gardner, and others.

4680 Show Business (RKO, 1944, Eddie Cantor, George Murphy).

Dinah—Sam Lewis, Joe Young (w), Harry Akst (m), Mills; I Want a Girl—William Dillon (w), Harry Von Tilzer (m), Von Tilzer; It Had to Be You—Gus Kahn (w), Isham Jones (m), Remick; Makin' Whoopee—Gus Kahn (w), Walter Donaldson (m), BVC; You May Not Remember— George Jessel (w), Ben Oakland (m), Southern. COVER: Eddie Cantor, George Murphy, Joan Davis, Constance Moore.

4681 Show Folks (Pathe, 1928, Eddie Quillan, Lina Basquette).

Love's First Kiss—Sam Perry, Lew Porter (w,m), Lewis; No One But Me Only Me—Billy Stone, Al Koppell, Charles Weinberg (w,m), Denton. COVER: Eddie Quillan, Lina Basquette.

4682 Show Girl (First National, 1927, Alice White, Lee Moran).

Buy Buy for Baby—Irving Caesar (w), Joseph Meyer (m), Famous; Show Girl—Ted Ward, Edward Gross-man (w,m), Famous. COVER: Alice White.

4683 Show Girl in Hollywood (First National, 1930, Alice White, Jack Mulhall).

Hang Onto a Rainbow/I've Got My Eye on You/There's a Tear for Every Smile on Broadway—Bud Green (w), Sam Stept (m), DBH. COVER: Alice White.

4684 Show Goes On, The (ATP, 1937, Gracie Fields, Owen Nares).

My Love for You—Harry P. Davies, Eddie Pola (w,m), Chappell; Smile When You Say Goodbye (B)/ Song in Your Heart (B)—Harry P. Davies (w,m), Wright. COVER: Gracie Fields.

4685 Show of Shows (Warner Bros., 1929, Hobart Bosworth, Johnny Arthur).

If I Could Learn to Love (BW)— Herman Ruby (w), M. K. Jerome (m), Witmark; If Your Best Friend Won't Tell You (BW)—Al Dubin (w), Joe Burke (m), Witmark; Just an Hour of Love—Al Bryan (w), Eddie Ward (m), Witmark; Lady Luck—Ray Perkins (w,m), Witmark; Only Song I Know—J. Keirn Brennan (w), Ray Perkins (m), Witmark; Singin' in the Bathtub—Herb Magidson, Ned Washington, Mike Cleary (w,m), Witmark; Your Love Is All That I Crave—Al Dubin, Perry Bradford (w), Jimmy Johnson (m), Witmark. COVER: Red, White and Blue, with Stars.

4686 Show People (MGM, 1927, Marion Davies, William Haines).

Cross Roads—Ray Klages (w), William Axt, David Mendoza (m), Robbins. COVER: Marion Davies, William Haines.

4687 Shrike, The (Universal, 1955, Jose Ferrer, June Allyson).

The Shrike (B)—Jose Ferrer (m), Morris. COVER: Jose Ferrer, June Allyson.

4688 Sicilian Clan, The (20th Century-Fox, 1969, Alain Delon, Jean Gabin).

I Have Felt the Fire—Carl Sigman

(w), Ennio Morricone (m), Fox; Sicilian Clan-Song—Ennio Morricone (m), Fox. COVER: Alain Delon, and Others.

4689 Sidewalks of London (St. Martin's Lane) (Paramount, 1940, Vivien Leigh, Charles Laughton).

Liza/London Love Song/Wear a Straw Hat in the Rain—Eddie Pola (w), Arthur Johnston (m), Mills. COVER: Vivien Leigh, Charles Laughton.

4690 Sign of the Ram, The (Columbia, 1948, Susan Peters, Alexander Knox).

I'll Never Say I Love You—Allan Roberts, Lester Lee (w,m), Shapiro Bernstein. COVER: Susan Peters.

4691 Sign of the Rose, The (Independent, 1923, George Beban).

Sign of the Rose, The—Lew Brown (w), Leo Edwards (m), Shapiro Bernstein. COVER: George Beban.

4692 Sign o' the Times (Cineplex, 1987, Prince, Sheena Easton).

U Got the Look/Sign o' the Times/ Sign o' the Times-16 Songs—Prince (w,m), Controversy. COVER: Prince.

4693 Silencers (Columbia, 1966, Dean Martin, Stella Stevens).

Lovey Kravesit—Howard Greenfield, Jack Keller, Colgems; Santiago/ Silencers Theme—Mack David (w), Elmer Bernstein (m), Colgems; Anniversary Song (VS)— Al Jolson, Saul Chaplin (w,m), Shapiro Bernstein; Empty Saddles (VS)/Glory of Love (VS)— Billy Hill (w,m), Shapiro Bernstein; If You Knew Susie (VS)—B. G. DeSylva, Joe Meyer (w,m), Shapiro Bernstein; Last Round Up (VS)— Billy Hill (w,m), Shapiro Bernstein; Lord You Made the Night Too Long (VS)—Sam Lewis (w), Victor Young (m), Shapiro Bernstein; On the Sunny Side of the Street (VS)—Dorothy Fields (w), Jimmy McHugh (m), Shapiro Bernstein; Red Sails in the Sunset (VS)— Jimmy Kennedy (w), Hugh Williams (m), Shapiro Bernstein; Side By Side (VS)—Harry Woods (w,m), Shapiro Bernstein; South of the Border (VS) —Jimmy Kennedy, Michael Carr (w, m), Shapiro Bernstein. COVER: Dean Martin, and Girls.

4694 Silent Enemy, The (Paramount, 1930, Chief Yellow Robe, Chief Long Lance).

Rain Flower—Leo Robin (w), Massard Kurzhene (m), Famous; Song of the Waters—Sam Coslow, Newell Chase (w,m), Famous. COVER: Chief Yellow Robe.

4695 Silent Movie (20th Century-Fox, 1976, Mel Brooks, Marty Feldman).

Silent Movie March—John Morris (m), Fox. COVER: Mel Brooks.

4696 Silent Rage (Columbia, 1981, Chuck Norris, Ron Silver).

Time for Love—Morgan Stoddard (w,m), Golden Torch. COVER: Chuck Norris.

4697 Silent Running (Universal, 1971, Bruce Dern, Cliff Potts).

Silent Running—Diane Lampert (w), Peter Schickele (m), Leeds. COVER: Bruce Dern, and Movie Scenes.

4698 Silhouettes (La Strad, 1982, George Weiss, Susan Monts).

Silhouettes—George David Weiss, Guseppe Murolo, Nino Tassone (w, m), Abilene. COVER: Silhouettes.

4699 Silken Affair (RKO, 1957, David Niven, Genevieve Page).

Romance Is a Silken Affair—Carl Sigman (w), Peggy Stuart (m), Torch. COVER: David Niven, Genevieve Page.

4700 Silk Stockings (MGM, 1957, Fred Astaire, Cyd Charisse).

All of You/Fated to Be Mated/ Paris Loves Lovers/Ritz Rock and Roll, The/Siberia/Silk Stockings/ Without Love—Cole Porter (w,m), Buxton Hill. COVER: Fred Astaire, Cyd Charisse.

4701 Silly Billies (RKO, 1936, Bert Wheeler, Bob Woolsey).

Tumble on Tumbleweed—Dave Dreyer, Jack Scholl (w,m), Berlin. COVER: Bert Wheeler, Bob Woolsey, Dorothy Lee.

4702 Silverado (Columbia, 1986, Kevin Kline, Scott Glenn).

Silverado Theme—Bruce Broughton (m), Golden Torch. COVER: Cowboys.

4703 Silver Fleet, The (PRC, 1943, Ralph Richardson, Googie Withers).

Helene (B)—Allan Gray (m), Maurice. COVER: Black and white cover with title only.

4704 Silver Skates (Monogram, 1943, Kenny Baker, Belita).

Calling from the Mountain/Dancing on Top of the World/Girl Like You, Boy Like Me/Love Is a Beautiful Thing/Lovely Lady/Victory Party —Dave Oppenheim, Roy Ingraham (w,m), Mills. COVER: Kenny Baker, Patricia Morison, Belita.

4705 Silver Streak (20th Century-Fox, 1976, Gene Wilder, Jill Clayburgh).

Hilly's Theme—Henry Mancini (m), Fox. COVER: Gene Wilder, Richard Pryor, Jill Clayburgh.

4706 Simba (Wilson, 1928, African Safari).

Song of Safari—Sam Stept (w,m), Green Stept. COVER: Mr. and Mrs. Martin Johnson.

4707 Sincerely Yours (Warner Bros., 1955, Joanne Dru, Liberace).

Sincerely Yours—Paul F. Webster (w), Liberace (m), Witmark. COVER: Liberace.

4708 Since You Went Away (United Artists, 1944, Claudette Colbert, Jennifer Jones).

Since You Went Away—Kermit Goell (w), Ted Grouya, Lou Forbes (m), Chappell; Together—B. G. De-Sylva, Lew Brown, Ray Henderson (w,m), Crawford. COVER: Claudette Colbert, Jennifer Jones, Shirley Temple, Robert Walker.

4709 Sing (Tri-Star, 1989, Lorraine Bracco, Peter Dobson).

Birthday Suit—Dean Pitchford, Rhett Lawrence (w,m), Triple Star; Romance—Dean Pitchford, Patrick Leonard (w,m), Triple Star; Sing—Dean Pitchford, Jonathan Cain, Martin Page (w,m), Triple Star; Sing-Eleven Songs—Dean Pitchford, Tom Snow, Richard Marx, Tom Kelly (w, m), Belwin. COVER: A Boy Dancing.

4710 Sing a Jingle (Universal, 1944, Allan Jones, Jerome Cowan).

Beautiful Love—Haven Gillespie (w), Victor Young, Wayne King, E. Van Alstyne (m), Movietone. COVER: Allan Jones.

4711 Sing and Be Happy (20th Century-Fox, 1937, Tony Martin, Leah Ray).

Pickles (BW)/Sing and Be Happy/Travellin' Light/What a Beautiful Beginning—Sidney Clare (w), Harry Akst (m), Movietone. COVER: Tony Martin, Leah Ray.

4712 Sing Another Chorus (Universal, 1941, Johnny Downs, Jane Frazee).

Boogie Woogie Man/Dancin' on Air/Mister Yankee Doodle/Two Weeks Vacation with Pay/Walk with Me—Everett Carter (w), Milton Rosen (m), Robbins; We Too Can Sing—Paul Smith, Everett Carter (w), Milton Rosen (m), Robbins. COVER: Iris Adrian, Johnny Downs, Jane Frazee.

4713 Sing as You Swing (Rock, 1937, Evelyn Dall, Claude Dampier).

Sing as You Swing—Cyril Ray, Clifford Grey (w,m), Mills. COVER: Evelyn Dall, and Movie Scene.

4714 Sing, Baby, Sing (20th Century-Fox, 1936, Alice Faye, Adolphe Menjou).

Continental Parody (BW)—Joe Glover (m), Movietone; Love Will Tell/Sing, Baby, Sing—Jack Yellen (w), Lew Pollack (m), Movietone; When Did You Leave Heaven?—Walter Bullock (w), Richard Whiting (m), Robbins; You Turned the Tables on Me—Sidney Mitchell (w), Louis Alter (m), Movietone. COVER: Alice Faye, Adolphe Menjou, Ritz Brothers.

4715 Sing, Boy, Sing (20th Century-Fox, 1958, Tommy Sands, Edmund O'Brien).

Bundle of Dreams—Billy Strange, Homer Escamilla (w,m), Opal; Crazy Cause I Love You—Spade Cooley (w, m), Hill Range; Sing Boy Sing—Tommy Sands, Rod McKuen (w,m), Snyder; Soda Pop Pop—Betty Daret, Darla Daret (w,m), Central; Your Daddy Wants to Be Right—Tommy Sands (w,m), Snyder. COVER: Tommy Sands, Lili Gentle, and Movie Scenes.

4716 Sing, Cowboy, Sing (Grand National, 1937, Tex Ritter, Louise Stanley).

Goodbye Old Paint/Sing Cowboy Sing—Tex Ritter, Ted Choate (w,m), Sam Fox. COVER: Tex Ritter.

4717 Singed Wings (Paramount, 1922, Bebe Daniels, Conrad Nagel).

Singed Wings—Kathrine Hazzard (w), Salvatore Tomaso (m), Clifford. COVER: Girl in Butterfly Costume.

4718 Singer of Seville (Call of the Flesh) (MGM, 1930, Ramon Novarro, Dorothy Jordan).

Lonely—Clifford Grey (w), Ramon Novarro, Herbert Stothart (m), Robbins. COVER: Black and white cover with title only.

4719 Singing Blacksmith, The (New Star, 1938, Moishe Oysher, Miriam Riselle).

The Singing Blacksmith—Olga Paul (w), Jacob Weinberg (m), Marks. COVER: Moishe Oysher.

4720 Singing Cowboy, The (Republic, 1936, Gene Autry, Smiley Burnette).

My Old Saddle Pal (VS)—Gene Autry, Oddie Thompson (w,m), Cole; Rainbow Trail (VS)—Oliver Drake, Smiley Burnette (w,m), Cole. COVER: Gene Autry.

4721 Singing Cowgirl, The (Grand National, 1938, Dorothy Page, David O'Brien).

Prairie Boy—Milton Drake (w), Al Sherman (m), Morris. COVER: Dorothy Page.

4722 Singing Fool, The (Warner Bros., 1929, Al Jolson, Betty Bronson).

It All Depends on You (B)—B. G. DeSylva, Lew Brown, Ray Henderson (w,m), Chappell; Sonny Boy—Al Jolson, B. G. DeSylva, Lew Brown, Ray Henderson (w,m), DBH; There's a Rainbow Round My Shoulder—Al Jolson, Billy Rose, Dave Dreyer (w,m), Berlin. COVER: Al Jolson.

4723 Singing Guns (Republic, 1950, Vaughn Monroe, Ella Raines).

Mule Train—Johnny Lange, Hy Heath, Fred Glickman (w,m), Disney; Singin' My Way Back Home—Wilton Moore, Al Vann (w,m), Mutual. COVER: Vaughn Monroe.

4724 Singing Kid, The (First National, 1936, Al Jolson, Sybil Jason).

I Love to Sing A/Save Me Sister/You're the Cure for What Ails Me—E. Y. Harburg (w), Harold Arlen (m), Remick. COVER: Al Jolson, Sybil Jason.

4725 Singing Marine, The (Warner Bros., 1937, Dick Powell, Doris Weston).

Cause My Baby Says It's So/I Know Now/Lady Who Couldn't Be Kissed, The—Al Dubin (w), Harry Warren (m), Remick; Night Over Shanghai—Johnny Mercer (w), Harry Warren (m), Remick; Song of the Marines/You Can't Run Away from Love—Al Dubin (w), Harry Warren (m), Remick. COVER: Dick Powell, Doris Weston.

4726 Singing Nun, The (MGM, 1966, Debbie Reynolds, Ricardo Montalban).

Reyond the Stars—Randy Sparks (w), Soeur Sourire (m), General; Brother John—Randy Sparks (w,m), Miller; Dominique/It's a Miracle—Randy Sparks (w), Soeur Sourire (m), General; Lovely—Randy Sparks (w,m), Miller; Pied Piper/Raindrops—Randy Sparks (w), Soeur Sourire (m), MRC; Sister Adele—Randy Sparks (w), Soeur Sourire (m), General; Singing Nun-Eleven Songs— John Dee, Soeur Sourire (w,m), General. COVER: Debbie Reynolds, and other stars.

4727 Singing Outlaw, The (Universal, 1938, Bob Baker, Joan Barclay).

Jail Song (VS)/There's a Ring Around the Moon (VS)—Fleming Allan (w,m), Cole. COVER: Gene Autry.

4728 Singing Vagabond, The (Republic, 1935, Gene Autry, Smiley Burnette).

Friends of the Prairie Farewell (VS)—Smiley Burnette (w,m), Cole; Wagon Trail (VS)—Gene Autry, Smiley Burnette (w,m), Cole. COVER: Gene Autry.

4729 Singing Wheels (AMA, 1941, Commercial Film).

Song of the Trucker—Maurice Stoller (w), Edwin Ludig (m), AMA; COVER: Sketch of Trucker.

4730 Singin' in the Corn (Columbia, 1946, Judy Canova, Allen Jenkins).

I'm a Gal of Property/An Old Love Is a True Love—Allan Roberts, Doris Fisher (w,m), Mood. COVER: Judy Canova.

4731 Singin' in the Rain (MGM, 1952, Gene Kelly, Donald O'Connor).

All I Do Is Dream of You/Beautiful Girl/Broadway Rhythm/Good Morning/Make Em Laugh (B)/Should I/Singin' in the Rain/Wedding of the Painted Doll/Would You/You Are My Lucky Star/You Were Meant for Me—Arthur Freed (w), Nacio Herb Brown (m), Robbins. COVER: Gene Kelly, Debbie Reynolds, Donald O'Connor.

4732 Singin' Kid from Pine Ridge (Yodelin' Kid from Pine Ridge) (Republic, 1938, Gene Autry, Smiley Burnette).

At the Millhouse Wild West Show (VS)—Fleming Allan (w,m), Cole. COVER: Gene Autry.

4733 Sing Me a Love Song (First

National, 1936, James Melton, Patricia Ellis).

Little House That Love Built, The/ Summer Night/That's the Least You Can Do for the Lady—Al Dubin (w), Harry Warren (m), Remick; Your Eyes Have Told Me So—Gus Kahn, Egbert Van Alstyne (w), Walter Blaufuss (m), Remick. COVER: James Melton, Patricia Ellis, Hugh Herbert, Zasu Pitts.

4734 Sing Me a Song of Texas (Columbia, 1945, Tom Tyler, Rosemary Lane).

She Never Said a Word—Allan Roberts, Doris Fisher (w,m), Northern. COVER: Hoosier Hot Shots.

4735 Sing, Neighbor, Sing (Republic, 1944, Ruth Terry, Brad Taylor).

Have I Told You Lately—Scott Wiseman (w,m), Duchess; Sing Neighbor Sing—Fred Rose (w,m), Forster. COVER: Jack Owens.

4736 Sing, Sinner, Sing (Majestic, 1933, Paul Lucas, Leila Hyams).

He's Mine—George Waggner (w), Howard Jackson (m), Mills. COVER: Leila Hyams.

4737 Sing While You're Able (Melody, 1937, Pinky Tomlin, Toby Wing).

I'm Gonna Sing While I'm Able— Connie Lee (w), Paul Parks (m), Mills; I'M Just a Country Boy at Heart—Connie Lee, Paul Parks, Pinky Tomlin (w,m), Mills; Leave It Up to Uncle Jake—Paul Parks, Connie Lee, Al Heath, Bud LeRoux (w, m), Mills; One Girl in My Arms— Harry Tobias (w), Roy Ingraham (m), Mills; Swing Brother Swing— Bud LeRoux (w), Al Heath (m), Mills; You're My Strongest Weakness—Coy Poe, Bud LeRoux, Al Heath (w,m), Mills. COVER: Pinky Tomlin.

4738 Sing Your Way Home (RKO, 1945, Jack Haley, Marcy McGuire).

I'll Buy That Dream—Herb Magidson (w), Allie Wrubel (m), BVH.

COVER: Jack Haley, Marcy Mc-Guire, Anne Jeffreys.

4739 Sing You Sinners (Paramount, 1938, Bing Crosby, Fred MacMurray).

Don't Let That Moon Get Away/ I've Got a Pocketful of Dreams/ Laugh and Call It Love—John Burke (w), James Monaco (m), Santly Joy; Sing You Sinners—Sam Coslow, Franke Harling (w,m), Famous; Small Fry—Frank Loesser (w), Hoagy Carmichael (m), Famous. COVER: Bing Crosby, Fred MacMurray, Donald O'Connor.

4740 Sing Your Worries Away (RKO, 1942, Bert Lahr, June Havoc).

Cindy Lou McWilliams/How Do You Fall in Love?/Sing Your Worries Away—Mort Greene (w), Harry Revel (m), Greene Revel. COVER: Bert Lahr, June Havoc, and The King Sisters.

4741 Sink the Bismarck! (20th Century-Fox, 1960, Kenneth More, Dana Wynter).

Sink the Bismarck!—Johnny Horton, Tillman Franks (w,m), Cajun. COVER: Kenneth More, Dana Wynter, and Ship.

4742 Sinner Take All (MGM, 1936, Bruce Cabot, Margaret Lindsay).

I'd Be Lost Without You—Bob Wright, Chet Forrest (w), Walter Donaldson (m), Feist. COVER: Bruce Cabot, Margaret Lindsay.

4743 Sioux City Sue (Republic, 1946, Gene Autry, Lynne Roberts).

Ridin' Double—John Rox (w,m), BMI; Sioux City Sue—Ray Freedman (w), Dick Thomas (m), Morris. COVER: Gene Autry, Lynne Roberts, and Champion.

4744 Siren of the Tropics (Gold, 1928, Josephine Baker).

Love for a Day—Joe Jordan, Porter Grainger (w,m), Mills. COVER: Checkerboard Design.

4745 Siren's Song, The (Fox, 1919, Alfred Freemont, Theda Bara).

The Siren's Song—Roy Turk (w), Ray Perkins (m), Berlin. COVER: Theda Bara.

4746 Sis Hopkins (Goldwyn, 1919, Mabel Normand, John Bowers).

Sunshine Sis—Raymond Egan (w), Richard Whiting (m), Remick. COVER: Mabel Normand.

4747 Sis Hopkins (Republic, 1941, Judy Canova, Bob Crosby).

Cracker Barrel County/If You're in Love/Look at You, Look at Me/ That Ain't Hay/Well! Well!—Frank Loesser (w), Jule Styne (m), Mills. COVER: Judy Canova, Bob Crosby.

4748 Sitting Bull (United Artists, 1954, Dale Robertson, Mary Murphy).

The Great Spirit—Max Rich (w, m), Chappell. COVER: Movie Scenes.

4749 Sitting on the Moon (Republic, 1936, Roger Pryor, Grace Bradley).

How'm I Doin' with You/Lost in My Dreams/Sitting on the Moon/ Who Am I—Sidney Mitchell (w), Sam Stept (m), Sam Fox. COVER: Roger Pryor, Grace Bradley.

4750 Sitting Pretty (Paramount, 1933, Jack Oakie, Jack Haley).

Ballad of the South-Lazy Lazy Lisa/Did You Ever See a Dream Walking/Good Morning Glory/I Wanna Meander with Miranda/Many Moons Ago/You're Such a Comfort to Me—Mack Gordon (w), Harry Revel (m), DBH. COVER: Jack Oakie, Ginger Rogers, Jack Haley.

4751 Sitting Pretty (20th Century-Fox, 1948, Clifton Webb, Maureen O'Hara).

Pretty Baby (B)—Gus Kahn (w), Tony Jackson, Egbert Van Alstyne (m), Day. COVER: Robert Young, Clifton Webb, Maureen O'Hara.

4752 Situation Hopeless But Not Serious (Paramount, 1965, Alec Guinness, Robert Redford).

Situation Hopeless But Not Serious—Earl Schuman (w), Leon Carr (m), Famous. COVER: Alec Guinness, Michael Connors, Robert Redford.

4753 **Six Bridges to Cross** (Universal, 1955, Tony Curtis, Julie Adams).
Six Bridges to Cross—Jeff Chandler (w), Henry Mancini (m), Leeds. COVER: Tony Curtis, Julie Adams, George Nader.

4754 **Six Gun Rhythm** (Grand National, 1939, Tex Fletcher, Joan Barclay).
Rock Me in the Cradle of the Rockies—Al Jacobs, Dave Oppenheim (w,m), Stasny. COVER: Tex Fletcher.

4755 **Six Lessons from Madame La Zonga** (Universal, 1941, Lupe Velez, Leon Errol).
Jitterumba/Matador's Wife—Everett Carter (w), Milton Rosen (m), Robbins; Six Lessons from Madame La Zonga (B)—Charles Newman, James Monaco (w,m), Albert. COVER: Lupe Velez, Leon Errol, Helen Parrish.

4756 **Six Pack** (20th Century-Fox, 1982, Kenny Rogers, Diane Lane).
Love Will Turn You Around—Kenny Rogers, E. Stevens, T. Schuyler, D. Malloy (w,m), Debdave. COVER: Kenny Rogers.

4757 **Six Thirty Three Squadron** (United Artists, 1964, Cliff Robertson, George Maharis).
Six Thirty Three Squadron Theme (B)—Ron Goodwin (m), Unart. COVER: Air Battle.

4758 **Skidoo** (Paramount, 1968, Jackie Gleason, Carol Channing).
I Will Take You There—Harry Nilsson (w,m), Dunbar. COVER: Sketch of a Convict.

4759 **Skin Deep** (First National, 1922, Milton Sills, Florence Vidor).
My Buddy—Gus Kahn (w), Walter Donaldson (m), Remick. COVER: Milton Sills, Florence Vidor.

4760 **Skin Deep** (Warner Bros., 1929, Monte Blue, Betty Compson).
I Came to You—Con Conrad, Sidney Mitchell, Archie Gottler (w,m), Remick. COVER: Betty Compson.

4761 **Skinner's Big Idea** (FBO, 1928, Martha Sleeper, Hugh Trevor).
One Moment of Madness—Eugene West (w), Charles Harris (m), Harris. COVER: Martha Sleeper, Hugh Trevor.

4762 **Skippy** (Paramount, 1931, Jackie Cooper, Mitzi Green).
Skippy—Benny Davis (w), Con Conrad (m), Feist. COVER: Jackie Cooper.

4763 **Skirts Ahoy** (MGM, 1952, Esther Williams, Vivian Blaine).
Glad to Have You Aboard (BW)/Hold Me Close to You/I Get a Funny Feeling/Navy Waltz—Ralph Blane (w), Harry Warren (m), Four Jays; Oh By Jingo—Lew Brown (w), Albert Von Tilzer (m), Broadway; Skirts Ahoy (BW)/What Good Is a Gal?/What Makes a Wave? (BW)—Ralph Blane (w), Harry Warren (m), Four Jays. COVER: Esther Williams, Joan Evans, Vivian Blaine.

4764 **Sky Hawk** (Fox, 1929, Helen Chandler, John Garrick).
The Song of Courage—Edward Lynn (w), Charles Cadman (m), DBH. COVER: Black and white cover with title only.

4765 **Skyjacked** (MGM, 1972, Charlton Heston, James Brolin).
Love Is the Answer—Paul F. Webster (w), Perry Botkin (m), Hastings; Skyjacked Love Theme—Perry Botkin (m), Hastings. COVER: An Airplane.

4766 **Sky Rocket** (Associated, 1926, Peggy Hopkins Joyce, Owen Moore).
Wonderful One—Dorothy Terriss (w), Paul Whiteman, Ferdie Grofe (m), Feist. COVER: Peggy Hopkins Joyce.

4767 **Sky's the Limit, The** (RKO, 1943, Fred Astaire, Joan Leslie).
Cuban Sugar Mill—Freddie Slack (m), Robbins; Harvey the Victory Garden Man/I've Got a Lot in Common with You/My Shining Hour/One for My Baby—Johnny Mercer (w), Harold Arlen (m), Morris. COVER: Fred Astaire, Joan Leslie.

4768 Sky Symphony (Vitaphone, 1933, Musical Short).

I'm Happy When It Rains/Men of Steel/Spell of the Moon, The—Cliff Hess (w,m) Witmark. COVER: Black and white cover with title only.

4769 Sky West and Crooked (Gypsy Girl) (Continental, 1965, Hayley Mills, Ian McShane).

Sky West and Crooked Theme (B)—Malcolm Arnold (m), Henrees. COVER: Hayley Mills.

4770 Slaughter (American International, 1972, Jim Brown, Stella Stevens).

Slaughter—Billy Preston (w,m), Irving. COVER: Jim Brown, Stella Stevens.

4771 Slaughter on Tenth Avenue (Universal, 1957, Richard Egan, Jan Sterling).

Slaughter on Tenth Avenue Theme/Slaughter on Tenth Avenue-Complete—Richard Rodgers (m), Chappell. COVER: Richard Egan, Jan Sterling, Julie Adams.

4772 Slaughter Trail (RKO, 1951, Brian Donlevy, Gig Young).

I Wish I Wuz—Sid Kuller, Lyn Murray (w,m), United. COVER: Brian Donlevy, Gig Young, Virginia Grey.

4773 Slaves (Continental, 1969, Ossie Davis, Nancy Coleman).

Slaves—Bob Kessler (w), Bobby Scott (m), Reade. COVER: Dionne Warwick.

4774 Sleeping Beauty (Buena Vista, 1959, Cartoon).

I Wonder—Winston Hibler, Ted Sears (w), George Bruns (m), Disney; Once Upon a Dream—Sammy Fain, Jack Lawrence (w,m), Disney; Sing a Smiling Song/Sleeping Beauty—Tom Adair (w), George Bruns (m), Disney; Sleeping Beauty Love Theme—George Bruns (m), Disney; Sleeping Beauty Song—Tom Adair (w), George Bruns (m), Disney. COVER: Cartoon.

4775 Sleeping Partners (Paramount, 1930, Seymour Hicks, Edna Best).

Playing with Fire (B)—Harry Graham (w), Noel Gay (m), Wright. COVER: Saymour Hicks, Edna Best.

4776 Sleep My Love (United Artists, 1947, Claudette Colbert, Robert Cummings).

Sleep My Love—Sam Coslow (w, m), Chappell. COVER: Claudette Colbert, Robert Cummings, Don Ameche.

4777 Sleepy Time Gal (Republic, 1942, Judy Canova, Tom Brown).

Barrelhouse Bessie from Basin Street/When the Cat's Away—Herb Magidson (w), Jule Styne (m), ABC. COVER: Judy Canova.

4778 Slender Thread, The (Paramount, 1965, Sidney Poitier, Anne Bancroft).

The Slender Thread—Mack David (w), Quincy Jones (m), Famous. COVER: Sidney Poitier, Anne Bancroft.

4779 Sleuth (20th Century-Fox, 1972, Laurence Olivier, Michael Caine).

Deception—Sammy Cahn (w), John Addison (m), Godspell. COVER: Magnifying Glass.

4780 Slightly French (Columbia, 1949, Dorothy Lamour, Don Ameche).

I Want to Learn About Love—Allan Roberts, Lester Lee (w,m), Mood. COVER: Dorothy Lamour, Don Ameche, Janis Carter.

4781 Slightly Honorable (United Artists, 1940, Pat O'Brien, Edward Arnold).

Cupid's After Me—Jule Styne, George Brown, Irving Actman (w, m), Mills. COVER: Pat O'Brien, Ruth Terry.

4782 Slightly Scarlet (Paramount, 1930, Evelyn Brent, Clive Brook).

You Still Belong to Me—Elsie Janis (w), Jack King (m), Famous. COVER: Evelyn Brent, Clive Brook.

4783 Slim Carter (Universal, 1957, Jock Mahoney, Julie Adams).

Gold—Ralph Freed, Beasley Smith

(w,m), Northern. COVER: Jock Mahoney, Julie Adams, Tim Hovey.

4784 Slim Shoulders (Hodkinson, 1922, Irene Castle, Rod LaRoque).

Slim Shoulders—Charles Harris (w, m), Harris. COVER: Irene Castle.

4785 Slipper and the Rose, The (Universal, 1976, Richard Chamberlain, Gemma Craven).

Once I Was Loved (B)/Slipper and the Rose Waltz/Tell Him Anything (B)—Richard Sherman, Robert Sherman (w,m), Duchess. COVER: Richard Chamberlain, Gemma Craven.

4786 Slow Dancing in the Big City (United Artists, 1978, Paul Sorvino, Anne Ditchburn).

Dancin' Slow—Randy Edelman (w), Bill Conti (m), Unart. COVER: Paul Sorvino, Anne Ditchburn.

4787 Small One, The (Disney, 1978, Cartoon).

Small One-Three Songs—Don Bluth, Richard Rich (w,m), Disney. COVER: Boy and Donkey.

4788 Small Town Girl (MGM, 1936, Robert Taylor, Janet Gaynor).

Small Town Girl—Gus Kahn (w), Herbert Stothart, Edward Ward (m), Robbins. COVER: Robert Taylor, Janet Gaynor.

4789 Small Town Girl (MGM, 1953, Jane Powell, Farley Granger).

Fine, Fine, Fine/I've Gotta Hear the Beat (VS)/Lullaby of the Lord/My Flaming Heart/Small Towns Are Smile Towns—Leo Robin (w), Nicholas Brodszky (m), Robbins. COVER: Jane Powell, Farley Granger, Ann Miller.

4790 Smartest Girl in Town, The (RKO, 1936, Gene Raymond, Ann Sothern).

Will You?—Gene Raymond (w, m), Berlin. COVER: Gene Raymond.

4791 Smash-up (Universal, 1947, Susan Hayward, Lee Bowman).

Hush-a-bye Island/I Miss That Feeling/Life Can Be Beautiful—Harold Adamson (w), Jimmy McHugh

(m), Melrose. COVER: Susan Hayward, Lee Bowman.

4792 Smiles of a Summer Night (Svensk, 1958, Ulla Jacobson, Harriet Anderson).

Smiles of a Summer Night Theme—Erik Nordgren (m), Robbins. COVER: Blue and white cover with title only.

4793 Smiley Gets a Gun (20th Century-Fox, 1956, Chips Rafferty, Sybil Thorndike).

Little Boy Called Smiley, A—Clyde Collins (w,m), Robbins. COVER: Keith Calvert.

4794 Smilin' Through (First National, 1922, Norma Talmadge, Harrison Ford).

Smilin' Through—Arthur Penn (w,m), Witmark. COVER: Norma Talmadge.

4795 Smilin' Through (MGM, 1932, Norma Shearer, Leslie Howard).

Smilin' Through—Arthur Penn (w, m), Witmark. COVER: Norma Shearer.

4796 Smilin' Through (MGM, 1941, Jeanette MacDonald, Gene Raymond).

I'm Forever Blowin' Bubbles—Jaan Kenbrovin, John Kellette (w, m), Chappell; A Little Love, a Little Kiss—Adrian Ross (w), Lao Silesu (m), Chappell; Smiles—Will Callaghan, Lee Roberts (w,m), Chappell; Smilin' Through—Arthur Penn (w, m), Witmark. COVER: Jeanette MacDonald, Gene Raymond.

4797 Smiling Irish Eyes (First National, 1929, Colleen Moore, James Hall).

Smiling Irish Eyes/Wee Bit o' Love—Herman Ruby (w), Ray Perkins (m), Witmark. COVER: Colleen Moore.

4798 Smiling Lieutenant, The (Paramount, 1931, Maurice Chevalier, Claudette Colbert).

Breakfast Table Love/One More Hour of Love/Toujours l'Amour in the Army/While Hearts Are Singing—

Clifford Grey (w), Oscar Straus (m), Famous. COVER: Maurice Chevalier, and Soldiers.

4799 Smoke Bellew (Big Four, 1929, Conway Tearle, Barbara Bedford).

At the End of the Trail I Found You—Mitchell Parish (w), David Broekman (m), Mills. COVER: Conway Tearle, Barbara Bedford.

4800 Smokey and the Bandit I (Universal, 1977, Sally Field, Burt Reynolds).

Bandit—Dick Feller (w,m), Cuchess; West (East) Bound and Down—Jerry Hubbard, Dick Feller (w,m), Duchess. COVER: Jackie Gleason, Sally Field, Burt Reynolds.

4801 Smokey and the Bandit II (Universal, 1980, Burt Reynolds, Sally Field).

Charlotte's Web—John Durrill, Cliff Croford, Snuff Garrett (w,m), Peso; Pecos Promenade—Larry Collins, Sandy Pinkard, Snuff Garrett (w,m), Peso; Texas Bound and Flyin' —Jerry Hubbard (w,m), Duchess; Smokey and the Bandit Two-Twelve Songs—Danny Flowers, Snuff Garrett (w,m), Big 3. COVER: Jackie Gleason, Burt Reynolds, Sally Field.

4802 Smoky (20th Century-Fox, 1946, Fred MacMurray, Anne Baxter).

Smoky-Twenty One Folk Songs—Traditional, Leeds. COVER: Burl Ives.

4803 Smoky (20th Century-Fox, 1966, Fess Parker, Diana Hyland).

Five Dollar Bill—Hoyt Axton (w, m), Hastings; Smoky—Ernie Sheldon (w), Leith Stevens (m), Hastings. COVER: Fess Parker, and Horse.

4804 Snoopy Come Home (National General, 1972, Cartoon).

Snoopy Come Home-Ten Songs—Richard Sherman, Robert Sherman (w,m), CBS. COVER: Snoopy.

4805 Snow Queen, The (Universal, 1959, Cartoon).

Do It While You're Young/Jolly Robbers/Snow Queen, The—Diane

Lampert, Richard Loring (w,m), Northern. COVER: Cartoon.

4806 Snows of Kilimanjaro, The (20th Century-Fox, 1956, Gregory Peck, Susan Hayward).

To Ava (VS)—Alfred Newman (m), Fox. COVER: None.

4807 Snow Train (Macone, 1949, Cartoon).

The Snow Train—Jesse Richardson, Bernice Richardson (w,m), Macone. COVER: Cartoon of Train.

4808 Snow White and the Seven Dwarfs (RKO, Disney, 1937, Cartoon).

Bluddle-uddle-um-dum/Dwarf's Yodel Song/Heigh-Ho/I'm Wishing/ One Song/Snow White/Some Day My Prince Will Come/Whistle While You Work/With a Smile and a Song—Larry Morey (w), Frank Churchill (m), Berlin. COVER: Cartoon.

4809 Snow White and the Three Stooges (20th Century-Fox, 1961, Carol Heiss, The Three Stooges).

A Place Called Happiness—Harry Harris (w,m), Miller. COVER: Carol Heiss and The Three Stooges.

4810 So Big (First National, 1925, Wallace Beery, Colleen Moore).

How Big Is Baby? So Big!—Leo Wood, Fred Phillips (w,m), Feist. COVER: Colleen Moore.

4811 So Big (Warner Bros., 1953, Jane Wyman, Sterling Hayden).

Selena's Waltz—Max Steiner (m), Witmark; So Big—Ned Washington (w), Max Steiner (m), Witmark; So Big Theme (VS)—Max Steiner (m), Warner. COVER: Jane Wyman, Sterling Hayden.

4812 Social Register (Columbia, 1934, Colleen Moore, Alexander Kirkland).

Honey Dear—Edward Heyman (w), Ford Dabney, Con Conrad (m), Harms; I Didn't Want to Love You—Ned Washington (w), Con Conrad (m), Harms; Why Not?—Edward Heyman (w), Con Conrad (m), Harms. COVER: Sketch of Girl.

4813 Society Lawyer (Penthouse) (MGM, 1939, Walter Pidgeon, Virginia Bruce).

I'm in Love with the Honorable Mr. So and So—Sam Coslow (w,m), Feist. COVER: Walter Pidgeon, Virginia Bruce.

4814 So Dear to My Heart (RKO, Disney, 1948, Bobby Driscoll, Beulah Bondi).

County Fair—Mel Torme, Robert Wells (w,m), BVH; It's Whatcha Do with Whatcha Got—Don Raye, Gene DePaul (w,m), Santly Joy; Lavender Blue Dilly Dilly—Larry Morey (w), Eliot Daniel (m), Santly Joy; So Dear to My Heart—Irving Taylor (w), Ticker Freeman (m), Santly Joy; Stick-to-it-ivity—Larry Morey (w), Eliot Daniel (m), Santly Joy. COVER: Cartoon.

4815 Sodom and Gomorrah (20th Century-Fox, 1962, Stewart Granger, Pier Angeli).

Answer to a Dream/Sodom and Gomorrah—Miklos Rozsa (m), Robbins. COVER: Movie Scenes.

4816 So Ends Our Night (United Artists, 1941, Frederic March, Margaret Sullavan).

So Ends Our Night—Sylvia Dee (w), Joseph Shalit (m), BMI. COVER: Frederic March, Margaret Sullavan, Glenn Ford, Frances Dee.

4817 Sofia—City of Intrigue (ARPI, 1948, Gene Raymond, Sigrid Gurie).

Lucky Star/My Beloved/Wake Up, It's Love—Karen Walter (w), Serge Walter (m), Harris. COVER: Patricia Morison, Gene Raymond.

4818 Soft Drinks—Sweet Music (Vitaphone, 1935, Georgie Price, Sylvia Froos).

I'd Like to Dance the Whole Night Through—Mack David (w), Sanford Green (m), Remick. COVER: Georgie Price, Sylvia Froos.

4819 So Goes My Love (Universal, 1946, Myrna Loy, Don Ameche).

So Goes My Love—Jack Brooks (w), H. J. Salter (m), Robbins. COVER: Myrna Loy, Don Ameche.

4820 Soldier Blue (Embassy, 1970, Candice Bergen, Peter Strauss).

Soldier Blue, This Is My Country—Buffy Sainte-Marie (w,m), Levine. COVER: Candice Bergen, and Battle Scene.

4821 Soldier in the Rain (Allied Artists, 1963, Jackie Gleason, Steve McQueen).

Soldier in the Rain—Alan Bergman, Marilyn Bergman (w), Henry Mancini (m), East Hill; Soldier in the Rain Theme—Henry Mancini (m), East Hill. COVER: Green and white cover with title only.

4822 Soldier of Fortune (20th Century-Fox, 1955, Susan Hayward, Clark Gable).

Soldier of Fortune—Ken Darby (w), Hugo Friedhofer (m), Miller. COVER: Clark Gable, Susan Hayward.

4823 Soldiers of Fortune (Pathe, 1920, Norman Kerry, Pauline Starke).

Soldiers of Fortune March—Arthur Pryor (m), Fischer. COVER: A Parade.

4824 Soldiers of the King (The Woman in Command) (Gainsborough, 1933, Cicely Courtneidge, Edward Everett Horton).

There's Something About a Soldier—Noel Gay (w,m), Mills. COVER: Cicely Courtneidge.

4825 Soldier's Story, A (Columbia, 1984, Howard Rollins, Adolph Caesar).

Pourin' Whiskey Blues—Patti LaBelle, James Ellison, Armstead Edwards (w,m), Gold Horizon. COVER: Howard Rollins.

4826 Solid Gold Cadillac, The (Columbia, 1956, Judy Holliday, Paul Douglas).

The Solid Gold Cadillac—William Bowers, Russ Black (w,m), Colgems. COVER: Judy Holliday, Paul Douglas.

4827 Sol Madrid (MGM, 1968, David McCallum, Stella Stevens).

Nice to Know—Norman Gimbel

(w), Lalo Schifrin (m), Hastings; Sol Madrid Theme—Lalo Schifrin (m), Hastings. COVER: David McCallum, Stella Stevens, Telly Savalas.

4828 Solomon and Sheba (United Artists, 1959, Yul Brynner, Gina Lollobrigida).

Solomon and Sheba Theme—Johnny Lehmann (w), Mario Nascimbene (m), Unart. COVER: Black and white cover with title only.

4829 So Long Letty (Warner Bros., 1929, Charlotte Greenwood, Grant Withers).

My Strongest Weakness Is You/One Sweet Little Yes—Grant Clarke (w), Harry Akst (m), Piantadosi; Clowning (BW)—Grant Clarke (w), Harry Akst (m), Witmark. COVER: Cartoon Sketch.

4830 Somebody Loves Me (Paramount, 1952, Betty Hutton, Ralph Meeker).

Honey Oh My Honey—Jay Livingston, Ray Evans (w,m), Paramount; I Cried for You—Arthur Freed, Gus Arnheim, Abe Lyman (w, m), Miller; Love Him—Jay Livingston, Ray Evans (w,m), Paramount; Rose Room—Harry Williams (w), Art Hickman (m), Miller; Somebody Loves Me—B. G. DeSylva, Ballard MacDonald (w), George Gershwin (m), New World; Thanks to You—Jay Livingston, Ray Evans (w,m), Paramount. COVER: Betty Hutton, Ralph Meeker.

4831 Somebody Up There Likes Me (MGM, 1956, Paul Newman, Pier Angeli).

Somebody Up There Likes Me—Sammy Cahn (w), Bronislau Kaper (m), Feist. COVER: Perry Como.

4832 Sombrero (MGM, 1953, Vittorio Gassman, Yvonne De Carlo).

Ufemia-Cartas a Ufemia—Saul Chaplin (w), Ruben Fuentes, Ruben Mendez (m), Southern. COVER: Pier Angeli, Ricardo Montalban.

4833 Some Came Running (MGM, 1959, Frank Sinatra, Dean Martin).

To Love and Be Loved—Sammy Cahn (w), James Van Heusen (m), Barton. COVER: Shirley MacLaine, Frank Sinatra, Dean Martin.

4834 Some Kind of Hero (Paramount, 1982, Richard Pryor, Margot Kidder).

Some Kind of Hero—Will Jennings (w), Patrick Williams (m), Ensign. COVER: Richard Pryor.

4835 Some Like It Hot (Paramount, 1939, Bob Hope, Shirley Ross).

Lady's in Love with You, The—Frank Loesser (w), Burton Lane (m), Paramount; Some Like It Hot—Frank Loesser (w), Gene Krupa, Remmo Biondi (m), Paramount. COVER: Bob Hope, Shirley Ross, Gene Krupa.

4836 Some Like It Hot (United Artists, 1959, Marilyn Monroe, Jack Lemmon).

I'm Thru with Love—Gus Kahn (w), Matt Malneck, Fud Livingston (m), Robbins; Stairway to the Stars (PC)—Mitchell Parish (w), Matt Malneck, Frank Signorelli (m), Robbins. COVER: Marilyn Monroe.

4837 Something Big (National General, 1971, Dean Martin, Brian Keith).

Something Big—Hal David (w), Burt Bacharach (m), Hidden Valley. COVER: Dean Martin, Brian Keith.

4838 Something for the Boys (20th Century-Fox, 1944, Carmen Miranda, Michael O'Shea).

Eighty Miles Outside of Atlanta/I Wish We Didn't Have to Say Goodnight/In the Middle of Nowhere/Wouldn't It Be Nice—Harold Adamson (w), Jimmy McHugh (m), Chappell. COVER: Carmen Miranda, Michael O'Shea, Phil Silvers, Perry Como, Vivian Blaine.

4839 Something in the Wind (Universal, 1947, Deanna Durbin, Donald O'Connor).

I Love a Mystery/I'm Happy Go Lucky and Free/It's Only Love/Something in the Wind/Turntable Song/You Wanna Keep Your Baby

Lookin' Right—Leo Robin (w), Johnny Green (m), Robbins. COVER: Deanna Durbin.

4840 Something Money Can't Buy (Universal, 1953, Patricia Roc, Anthony Steel).

Something Money Can't Buy—Nino Rota (m), Sam Fox. COVER: Richard Hayman.

4841 Something to Live For (Paramount, 1952, Joan Fontaine, Ray Milland).

Alone at Last—Bob Hilliard (w), Victor Young (m), Paramount. COVER: Joan Fontaine, Ray Milland.

4842 Something to Shout About (Columbia, 1943, Don Ameche, Janet Blair).

Hasta Luego/I Always Knew/It Might Have Been/Lotus Bloom/Something to Shout About/You'd Be So Nice to Come Home To—Cole Porter (w,m), Chappell. COVER: Don Ameche, Janet Blair, Jack Oakie.

4843 Something to Sing About (Grand National, 1937, James Cagney, Evelyn Daw).

Any Old Love—Victor Schertzinger (w,m), Schirmer; Loving You—Victor Schertzinger, Myrl Alderman (w,m), Schirmer; Out of the Blue/Right or Wrong/Something to Sing About—Victor Schertzinger (w,m), Schirmer. COVER: James Cagney, Evelyn Daw.

4844 Sometimes a Great Notion (Universal, 1971, Paul Newman, Henry Fonda).

All His Children—Alan Bergman, Marilyn Bergman (w), Henry Mancini (m), Leeds. COVER: Paul Newman, Henry Fonda, Lee Remick.

4845 Somewhere in Time (Universal, 1980, Jane Seymour, Christopher Reeves).

Somewhere in Time—John Barry (m), Duchess. COVER: Christopher Reeves, Jane Seymour.

4846 Song and Dance Man (20th Century-Fox, 1936, Claire Trevor, Paul Kelly).

In My Playroom (BW)/Join the Party/Let's Get Goin' Baby (BW)—Sidney Clare (w,m), Movietone; You're My Favorite One—Sidney Clare (w), Lew Pollack (m), Movietone. COVER: Claire Trevor, Paul Kelly.

4847 Song for Miss Julie, A (Republic, 1945, Shirley Ross, Barton Hepburn).

That's What I Like About You—Maria Shelton, Louis Herschner (w, m), Mills. COVER: Shirley Ross.

4848 Song Is Born, A (Paramount, 1938, Larry Clinton, Bea Wain).

Devil with the Devil, The—Larry Clinton (w,m), Famous; Heart and Soul—Frank Loesser, Hoagy Carmichael (w,m), Famous; I Fell Up to Heaven—Leo Robin, Ralph Rainger (w,m), Famous; Love Doesn't Grow on Trees—Ralph Freed, Burton Lane (w,m), Famous. COVER: Larry Clinton.

4849 Song Is Born, A (RKO, 1948, Danny Kaye, Virginia Mayo).

Anitra's Boogie—Marvin Wright, Jimmy Grier (w,m), Crystal; Blind Barnabus—Willie Johnson (w,m), Leeds; Daddy-o—Don Raye, Gene DePaul (w,m), Simon; Flying Home—Sid Robin (w), Benny Goodman, Lionel Hampton (m), Regent; I'm Getting Sentimental Over You—Ned Washington (w), George Bassman (m), Mills. COVER: Danny Kaye, Virginia Mayo, Benny Goodman, Tommy Dorsey.

4850 Song of Bernadette, The (20th Century-Fox, 1956, Jennifer Jones, William Eythe).

Song of Bernadette (VS)—Alfred Newman (m), Fox. COVER: None.

4851 Song of Freedom (BL, 1936, Paul Robeson, Elizabeth Welch).

Lonely Road (B)—Henrik Ege (w), Eric Ansell (m), Dix; Sleepy River (B)/Song of Freedom Themes (B)—Eric Ansell (m), Dix. COVER: Paul Robeson.

4852 Song of Kentucky, A (Fox, 1929, Lois Moran, Joseph Wagstaff).

Night of Happiness/Sitting by the Window—Con Conrad, Sidney Mitchell, Archie Gottler (w,m), DBH. COVER: Lois Moran, Joseph Wagstaff.

4853 Song of Love, The (First National, 1924, Norma Talmadge, Joseph Schildkraut).

Life Sings a Song—Mabel Livingstone (w), Muriel Pollock (m), Remick. COVER: Norma Talmadge.

4854 Song of Love (Columbia, 1929, Belle Baker, Ralph Graves).

I'll Still Go on Wanting You—Bernie Grossman, M. Kippell, Art Sizemore (w,m), SB; I'm Somebody's Baby Now—Mack Gordon, Max Rich (w,m), Gordon; I'm Walking with the Moonbeams—Mack Gordon, Max Rich, M. Abrahams (w,m), Gordon; Take Everything But You—Maurice Abrahams, Elmer Colby (w,m), DBH; White Way Blues—Mack Gordon, Max Rich, George Weist (w,m), Gordon. COVER: Belle Baker.

4855 Song of Love (MGM, 1947, Katharine Hepburn, Paul Henreid).

As Years Go By—Charles Tobias, Peter DeRose (w,m), Miller; Dedication—Ted Mossman (w,m), Robbins; Fantasy—Ted Mossman, Jack Segal (w,m), Robbins; Love Story—Ted Mossman, Jack Fina (w,m), Robbins; Love Will Keep Us Young—Edgar Leslie, J. Brahms (w,m), Lombardo; Song of Love-Seventeen Themes—Robert Schuman, Johannes Brahms (m), Robbins. COVER: Katharine Hepburn, Paul Henreid, Robert Walker.

4856 Song of My Heart (Allied Artists, 1947, Frank Sundstrum, Audrey Long).

Story of a Starry Night, The—Al Hoffman, Mann Curtis, Jerry Livingston (w,m), Mutual; Song of My Heart-Sixteen Themes—P. Tchaikovsky (m), Hansen. COVER: Frank Sundstrum, Audrey Long.

4857 Song of Norway (Cinerama, Florence Henderson, Toralv Maurstad).

Strange Music/Song of Norway-Twenty One Songs—Bob Wright, Chest Forrest, E. Grieg (w,m), Chappell. COVER: Florence Henderson, Toralv Maurstad, Frank Porreta.

4858 Song of Russia (MGM, 1943, Robert Taylor, Susan Peters).

And Russia Is Her Name—E. Y. Harburg (w), Jerome Kern (m), Chappell. COVER: Robert Taylor, Susan Peters.

4859 Song of Scheherazade (Universal, 1947, Yvonne De Carlo, Jean Pierre Aumont).

Bazaar Song—S. Rachmaninoff, Jack Edwards (w,m), Edwards; Hymn to the Sun—N. Rimsky-Korsakoff, Harold Potter (m), Edwards; Piano Concerto Themes—S. Rachmaninoff (m), Edwards; Scheherazade Song—N. Rimsky-Korsakoff, Jack Edwards (w,m), Edwards; Scheherazade Themes—N. Rimsky-Korsakoff (m), Edwards; Song of India—N. Rimsky-Korsakoff, Jack Edwards (w, m), Edwards; Thousand and One Nights, A—Ted Mossman, Jack Segal (w,m), Barton; Song of Scheherazade-Four Themes—N. Rimsky-Korsakoff (m), Leeds; Song of Scheherazade-Eight Themes—N. Rimsky-Korsakoff, Miklos Rozsa (m), Robbins. COVER: Yvonne De Carlo, Jean Pierre Aumont, and Movie Scenes.

4860 Song of Songs (Paramount, 1933, Marlene Dietrich, Brian Aherne).

Johnny—Edward Heyman (w), Frederick Hollander (m), Famous; Marlene, You Are My Song of Songs—Edward Heyman (w), Richard Myers (m), Famous. COVER: Marlene Dietrich.

4861 Song of Surrender (Paramount, 1949, Wanda Hendrix, Claude Rains).

Song of Surrender—Jay Livingston, Ray Evans (w,m), Victor Young (m), Paramount. COVER: Wanda Hendrix, MacDonald Carey.

4862 Song of the Buckaroo (Monogram, 1939, Tex Ritter, Jinx Falkenberg).

I Promise You (VS)—Tex Ritter, Frank Harford (w,m), Cole. COVER: Tex Ritter.

4863 Song of the Caballero (Universal, 1930, Ken Maynard, Doris Hill).

Mi Caballero—Joe Seitman (w), Sam Perry (m), Handman Kent. COVER: Ken Maynard.

4864 Song of the Eagle (Paramount, 1933, Charles Bickford, Richard Arlen).

Hey Hey! We're Gonna Be Free—Bernie Grossman (w), Harold Lewis (m), Famous. COVER: Richard Arlen, Mary Brian.

4865 Song of the Flame (First National, 1930, Alexander Gray, Bernice Claire).

Cossack Love Song—Otto Harbach, Oscar Hammerstein (w), Herbert Stothart, George Gershwin (m), Harms; One Little Drink—Grant Clarke (w), Harry Akst (m), Harms; Song of the Flame—Otto Harbach, Oscar Hammerstein (w), Herbert Stothart, George Gershwin (m), Harms; When Love Calls—Grant Clarke (w), Eddie Ward (m), Harms. COVER: Alexander Gray, Bernice Claire.

4866 Song of the Gringo (Grand National, 1936, Tex Ritter, Joan Woodbury).

My Sweet Chiquita—Tex Ritter (w,m), Sam Fox; Out on the Lone Prairie—Harry Miller (w,m), Sam Fox. COVER: Tex Ritter.

4867 Song of the Islands (20th Century-Fox, 1942, Betty Grable, Victor Mature).

Blue Shadows and White Gardenias/Down on Ami Ami Oni Oni Isle/Maluna Malalo Mawaena/O'Brien Has Gone Hawaiian/Sing Me a Song of the Islands—Mack Gordon, Harry Owens (w,m), BVC; Song of the Islands—Charles King (w,m), Marks; What's Buzzin' Cousin?—Mack Gor-

don, Harry Owens (w,m), BVC. COVER: Betty Grable, Victor Mature.

4868 Song of the Open Road (United Artists, 1944, Edgar Bergen, Charlie McCarthy).

Delightfully Dangerous/Fun in the Sun/Here It Is Monday/Rollin' Down the Road/Too Much in Love—Kim Gannon (w), Walter Kent (m), Barton. COVER: Edgar Bergen, W. C. Fields, Sammy Kaye, Jane Powell, Charlie McCarthy.

4869 Song of the Saddle (Warner Bros., 1936, Dick Foran, Alma Lloyd).

Underneath a Western Sky—Jack Scholl (w), M. K. Jerome, Ted Fiorito (m), Remick. COVER: Dick Foran.

4870 Song of the South (RKO Disney, 1946, Ruth Warwick, Lucille Watson).

Ev'ry Body Has a Laughing Place —Ray Gilbert (w), Allie Wrubel (m), Santly Joy; How Do You Do—Robert MacGimsey (w,m), Santly Joy; Song of the South—Sam Coslow (w), Arthur Johnston (m), Santly Joy; Sooner or Later—Charles Wolcott, Ray Gilbert (w,m), Santly Joy; Uncle Remus Said—Johnny Lange, Hy Heath, Eliot Daniel (w,m), Santly Joy; Zip-a-dee-doo-dah—Ray Gilbert (w), Allie Wrubel (m), Santly Joy. COVER: Cartoon.

4871 Song of the Thin Man (MGM, 1947, William Powell, Myrna Loy).

You're Not So Easy to Forget—Herb Magidson (w), Ben Oakland (m), Feist. COVER: William Powell, Myrna Loy, Gloria Grahame.

4872 Song of the West (Warner Bros., 1930, John Boles, Vivienne Segal).

Bride Was Dressed in White—Oscar Hammerstein (w), Vincent Youmans (m), Youmans; Come Back to Me—Grant Clarke (w), Harry Akst (m), Witmark; Hay Straw/I Like You as You Are/Let Me Give All My Love to Thee/My Mother Told Me Not to Trust a Sailor/One Girl—Oscar Hammerstein (w), Vincent Youmans (m), Youmans; West Wind—Russell Robinson (w), Vincent Youmans (m), Youmans. COVER: John Boles, Vivienne Segal.

4873 Song o' My Heart (Fox, 1930, John McCormack, Alice Joyce).

I Feel You Near Me—Joseph McCarthy (w), James Hanley (m), Red Star; I Hear You Calling Me—Harold Harford (w), Charles Marshall (m), Boosey; Ireland, Mother Ireland— P. J. O'Reilly (w), Ray Loughborough (m), Boosey; Just for a Day— Charles Glover, Mordaunt Spencer (w,m), Red Star; Little Boy Blue— Eugene Field (w), Ethelbert Nevin (m), Boston; Pair of Blue Eyes, A— William Kernell (w,m), Red Star; Rose of Tralee, The—Mordaunt Spencer (w), Charles Glover (m), Red Star; Song o' My Heart—Joseph McCarthy (w), James Hanley (m), Red Star. COVER: John McCormack, Maureen O'Sullivan.

4874 Song Plugger (Educational, 1935, Sylvia Froos).

Tell Me an Old Fashioned Story— Cliff Friend, Irving Caesar (w,m), Sam Fox. COVER: Silhouettes of Man and Woman.

4875 Song Service (Paramount, 1930, Lee Morse).

Just Another Dream Gone Wrong —E. Y. Harburg (w), Peter DeRose (m), Famous. COVER: Lee Morse.

4876 Song to Remember, A (Columbia, 1945, Cornel Wilde, Merle Oberon).

Chopin Polonaise—Harold Potter, Eddie Dorr (w,m), Edwards; Chopin Polonaise Theme—F. Chopin, Harold Potter (m), Edwards; So Deep Is the Night—Sonny Miller (w), F. Chopin (m), Sam Fox; Song to Remember, A—Sammy Cahn, Saul Chaplin, Morris Stoloff (w,m), Pacific; Song to Remember-Six Themes—F. Chopin (m), Leeds. COVER: Merle Oberon,

Cornel Wilde.

4877 Song Without End (Columbia, 1960, Capucine, Dirk Bogarde).

My Consolation—Ned Washington (w), Morris Stoloff, Harry Sukman (m), Columbia; Song Without End— Ned Washington (w), Morris Stoloff, George Duning (m), Columbia; Song Without End-Eight Themes—L. Beethoven, F. Liszt (m), Columbia. COVER: Capucine, Dirk Bogarde.

4878 Songwriter (Tri-Star, 1984, Willie Nelson, Kris Kristofferson).

How Do You Feel About Foolin' Around?—Kris Kristofferson, M. Utley, S. Bruton (w,m), Resaca; Songwriter-Eleven Songs—Kris Kristofferson, Willie Nelson (w,m), Resaca. COVER: Willie Nelson, Kris Kristofferson.

4879 Son of Dracula (Cinemation, 1974, Ringo Starr, Harry Nilsson)

Daybreak/Remember—Harry Nilsson (w,m), Blackwood; Son of Dracula-Seven Songs—Harry Nilsson, Peter Ham, Tom Evans (w,m), Blackwood. COVER: Harry Nilsson.

4880 Son of Fury (20th Century-Fox, 1942, Tyrone Power, Gene Tierney).

Blue Tahitian Moon—Mack Gordon (w), Alfred Newman (m), Triangle. COVER: Tyrone Power, Gene Tierney.

4881 Son of Paleface (Paramount, 1952, Bob Hope, Jane Russell).

Am I in Love—Jack Brooks (w, m), Famous; California Rose—Jay Livingston, Ray Evans (w,m), Famous; Four Legged Friend—Jack Brooks (w,m), Famous; There's a Cloud in My Valley of Sunshine— Jack Hope, Lyle Moraine (w,m), Famous; What a Dirty Shame/Wing Ding Tonight—Jay Livingston, Ray Evans (w,m), Famous. COVER: Bob Hope, Jane Russell, Roy Rogers, Trigger.

4882 Son of Roaring Dan (Universal, 1940, Johnny Mack Brown, Fuzzy Knight).

And Then I Got Married/Sing Yippi-ki-yi—Everett Carter (w), Milton Rosen (m), Robbins. COVER: Johnny Mack Brown, Fuzzy Knight, Nell O'Day.

4883 Son of Robin Hood (20th Century-Fox, 1959, Al Hedison, June Laverick).

Son of Robin Hood—Sid Tepper, Roy Bennett (w,m), Miller. COVER: Al Hedison.

4884 Son of Tarzan (National, 1920, Dempsey Tabler, Karia Schram).

Tarzan-My Jungle King—Osborne Tedman (w), N. Stuckey (m), Howells. COVER: Tarzan and Jane.

4885 Son of the Gods (First National, 1930, Richard Barthelmess, Constance Bennett).

Pretty Little You—Ben Ryan (w), Violinsky (m), Witmark; Allana (BW) —Leo Forbstein, Tom Satterfield, John Murry (w,m), Witmark. COVER: Sketch of Man and Woman.

4886 Son of the Sheik (United Artists, 1926, Rudolph Valentino, Vilma Banky).

My One Arabian Night—James Bradford, Art Gutman, Art Jones (w,m), Mills; Son of the Sheik—Edwin Powell (w), Miro Mosay (m), Chilton; That Night in Araby—Billy Rose (w), Ted Snyder (m), Waterson. COVER: Rudolph Valentino, Vilma Banky.

4887 Sons and Lovers (20th Century-Fox, 1960, Trevor Howard, Dean Stockwell).

Sons and Lovers Theme—Mario Nascimbene (m), Feist. COVER: Dean Stockwell, Mary Ure.

4888 Sons of Katie Elder (Paramount, 1965, John Wayne, Dean Martin).

Sons of Katie Elder—Ernie Sheldon (w), Elmer Bernstein (m), Famous. COVER: John Wayne, Dean Martin, Earl Holliman.

4889 Sons of Matthew (The Rugged O'Riordans) (Universal, 1938, Michael Pate, Wendy Gibb).

Goanna Song, The (B)—Rod Mansfield (w,m), Chappell. COVER: Five Men.

4890 Sons of New Mexico (Columbia, 1950, Gene Autry, Gail Davis).

There's a Rainbow on the Rio Colorado (VS)—Gene Autry, Fred Rose (w,m), Western. COVER: Gene Autry.

4891 Sons of the Desert (MGM, 1934, Oliver Hardy, Stan Laurel).

Honolulu Baby (PC)—Marvin Hatley (w,m), Belwin. COVER: None.

4892 Sons of the Legion (Paramount, 1938, Lynne Overman, Evelyn Keyes).

Sons of the Legion—Ralph Freed (w), Frederick Hollander (m), Famous. COVER: Young Legionnaires.

4893 Sons o' Guns (Warner Bros., 1936, Joe E. Brown, Joan Blondell).

For a Buck and a Quarter (BW)/ In the Arms of an Army Man (BW) —Al Dubin (w), Harry Warren (m), Witmark. COVER: None.

4894 Sooner or Later (Hart, 1978, Rex Smith, Denise Miller).

Sooner or Later/You Take My Breath Away—Bruce Hart (w), Stephen Lawrence (m), L. Willow. COVER: Rex Smith.

4895 Sophie's Choice (Universal, 1982, Meryl Streep, Kevin Kline).

Sophie's Choice Theme—Marvin Hamlisch (m), ATV. COVER: Meryl Street, Kevin Kline.

4896 Sophomore, The (Joe College) (Pathe, 1929, Eddie Quillan, Sally O'Neill).

Little By Little—Walter O'Keefe, Bobby Dolan (w,m), DBH. COVER: Eddie Quillan, Sally O'Neill.

4897 So Proudly We Hail (Paramount, 1943, Claudette Colbert, Paulette Goddard).

Loved One—Eddie Heyman (w), Miklos Rozsa (m), Paramount. COVER: Black and white cover with only.

4898 So Red the Rose (Paramount, 1935, Margaret Sullavan, Randolph Scott).

So Red the Rose—Jack Lawrence, Arthur Altman (w,m), Popular. COVER: Margaret Sullavan.

4899 Sorrowful Jones (Paramount, 1949, Bob Hope, Lucille Ball).

Havin' a Wonderful Wish—Jay Livingston, Ray Evans (w,m), Paramount. COVER: Bob Hope, Lucille Ball.

4900 So This Is College (College Days) (MGM, 1929, Elliot Nugent, Robert Montgomery).

Campus Capers—Charlotte Greenwood (w), Martin Broones (m), Robbins; College Days—Al Boasberg (w), Martin Broones (m), Robbins; I Don't Want Your Kisses—Fred Fisher, Martin Broones (m), Robbins; Sophomore Prom—Raymond Klages (w), Jesse Greer (m), Robbins; Until the End—Fred Fisher, Martin Broones, Al Boasberg (w,m), Robbins. COVER: Cartoon Sketch.

4901 So This Is Harris (RKO, 1933, Phil Harris).

It Can Happen to You—Val Burton, Will Jason (w,m), Sam Fox. COVER: Phil Harris.

4902 So This Is Love (Warner Bros., 1953, Kathryn Grayson, Merv Griffin).

So This Is Love—E. Ray Goetz (w, m), Harms. COVER: Kathryn Grayson.

4903 So This Is Marriage (Pathe, 1930, Maurice Holland, Katherine Skidmore).

After You Say I Love You—Billy Curtis (w), Larry Conley (m), Shapiro Bernstein. COVER: Dancing Couples.

4904 So This Is Paris (Universal, 1955, Tony Curtis, Gene Nelson).

Dame's a Dame, A/I Can't Do a Single—Pony Sherrell, Phil Moody (w,m), American; I Can't Give You Anything But Love—Dorothy Fields (w), Jimmy McHugh (m), Mills; If You Were There/It's Really Up to You/Looking for Someone to Love/So This Is Paris/Three Bon Vivants/Two of Us/Wait Till Paris Sees Us—Pony Sherrell, Phil Moody (w,m), American. COVER: Tony Curtis, Gene Nelson, Gloria De Haven, Paul Gilbert.

4905 So This Is Paris Green (Paramount, 1930, Louise Fazenda).

La La Mama—Irving Bibo, Henry Cohen (w,m), Bibo Lang. COVER: Louise Fazenda.

4906 Souls at Sea (Paramount, 1937, Gary Cooper, George Raft).

Susie Sapple—Leo Robin, Ralph Rainger (w,m), Popular. COVER: Gary Cooper, George Raft, Frances Dee.

4907 Souls in Conflict (Commission, 1955, Joan Winmill, Eric Micklewood).

I Found What I Wanted—Ralph Carmichael (w,m), Herman. COVER: The Ralph Carmichael Singers.

4908 Sound and the Fury, The (20th Century-Fox, 1959, Yul Brynner, Joanne Woodward).

The Sound and the Fury—Sammy Cahn (w), Alex North (m), Feist. COVER: Yul Brynner, Joanne Woodward, Ethel Waters, Margaret Leighton.

4909 Sound Defects (Vitaphone, 1937, Musical Short).

Fifty Second Street—Sammy Cahn (w), Saul Chaplin (m), Harms. COVER: Sketch of Night Clubs.

4910 Sound Off (Columbia, 1952, Mickey Rooney, Anne James).

Lady Love—Lester Lee, Bob Russell (w,m), Cromwell; Sound Off—Willie Lee Duckworth (w,m), Shapiro Bernstein. COVER: Mickey Rooney.

4911 Sound of Music, The (20th Century-Fox, 1965, Julie Andrews, Christopher Plummer).

Climb Ev'ry Mountain/Do Re Mi/Edelweiss/I Have Confidence/Lonely Goatherd/Maria/My Favorite Things/

Ordinary Couple/Sixteen Going on Seventeen/So Long Farewell/Something Good/Sound of Music, The/ Wedding Processional—Oscar Hammerstein (w), Richard Rodgers (m), Williamson. COVER: Julie Andrews, Christopher Plummer.

4912 Soup to Nuts (Fox, 1930, Ted Healey, Stanley Smith).

One Pair of Pants at a Time—Cliff Friend, Jimmie Monaco (w,m), Red Star. COVER: Ted Healey and Girl.

4913 Sous Les Toits de Paris (Under the Roofs of Paris) (Tobis, 1930, Pola Illery, Albert Prejean).

Under a Roof in Paree—Irving Caesar (w), R. Moretti (m), Harms. COVER: Parisian Buildings.

4914 Southerner, The (The Prodigal) (MGM, 1931, Lawrence Tibbett, Esther Ralston).

Chidlins—Howard Johnson (w), Herbert Stothart (m), Robbins; Life Is a Dream—Arthur Freed (w), Oscar Straus (m), Robbins; Without a Song —William Rose, Edward Eliscu (w), Vincent Youmans (m), Youmans. COVER: Lawrence Tibbett, Esther Ralston.

4915 Southern Star, The (Columbia, 1969, George Segal, Ursula Andress).

Southern Star—Don Black (w), Georges Garvarentz (m), Colgems. COVER: George Segal, Ursula Andress.

4916 South of Arizona (Columbia, 1938, Charles Starrett, Iris Meredith).

Saddle Your Worries to the Wind (VS)/When Pay Day Rolls Around (VS)—Bob Nolan (w,m), American. COVER: Bob Nolan.

4917 South of Pago Pago (United Artists, 1940, Victor McLaglen, Jon Hall).

South of Pago Pago—Bob Wright, Chet Forrest (w), Lew Pollack (m), Mills. COVER: Jon Hall, Frances Farmer.

4918 South of Panama (PRC, 1940, Roger Pryor, Virginia Vale).

Madame Will Drop Her Shawl— Sam Brown (w), Herb Pine (m), BMI. COVER: Roger Pryor, Virginia Vale.

4919 South of St. Louis (Warner Bros., 1948, Joel McCrea, Alexis Smith).

Too Much Love—Ralph Blane (w), Ray Heindorf (m), Harms. COVER: Alexis Smith, Joel McCrea, Zachary Scott.

4920 South of Tahiti (Universal, 1941, Brian Donlevy, Broderick Crawford).

Melahi—George Waggner (w), Frank Skinner (m), Robbins. COVER: Brian Donlevy, Maria Montez.

4921 South of the Border (Republic, 1939, Gene Autry, Smiley Burnette).

Girl of My Dreams—Sunny Clapp (w,m), Mills; Goodbye Little Darlin' Goodbye—Johnny Marvin, Gene Autry (w,m), Western; South of the Border—Jimmy Kennedy, Michael Carr (w,m), Shapiro Bernstein. COVER: Gene Autry.

4922 South Pacific (20th Century-Fox, 1958, Mitzi Gaynor, Rossano Brazzi).

Bali Ha'i/Cock-eyed Optimist, A/ Dites Moi/Happy Talk/Honey Bun/ I'm Gonna Wash That Man Right Outa My Hair/My Girl Back Home/ Some Enchanted Evening/There Is Nothin' Like a Dame/This Nearly Was Mine/Wonderful Guy/Younger Than Springtime/You've Got to Be Carefully Taught—Oscar Hammerstein (w), Richard Rodgers (m), Williamson. COVER: Mitzi Gaynor, Rossano Brazzi.

4923 South Sea Rose (Fox, 1929, Ilka Chase, Lenore Ulrich).

South Sea Rose—L. Wolfe Gilbert (w), Abel Baer (m), DBH. COVER: Lenore Ulrich.

4924 South Seas Adventure (Cinerama, 1958, Kay Johnson, Marlene Hunter).

Click Go the Shears—Alex North, Norman Luboff (w,m), Jungnickel;

Kangaroo Hop—Alex North (m), Jungnickel. COVER: Natives.

4925 South Sea Sinner (Universal, 1950, Shelley Winters, MacDonald Carey).

Blue Lagoon—Fred Herbert (w), Arnold Hughes (m), Spitzer. COVER: Shelley Winters.

4926 Spacehunter Adventures in the Forbidden Zone (Columbia, 1983, Peter Strauss, Molly Ringwald).

Spacehunter-Adventures in the Forbidden Zone—Elmer Bernstein (m), Golden Torch. COVER: Peter Strauss, Molly Ringwald.

4927 Spanish Affair (Paramount, 1958, Richard Kiley, Carmen Sevilla).

Flaming Rose—Mack David (w), Daniele Amfitheatrof (m), Famous. COVER: Richard Kiley, Carmen Sevilla.

4928 Spanish Dancer, The (Paramount, 1923, Pola Negri, Adolphe Menjou).

A Cross, a Heart, a Crown (B)— Jack Gartman, Louis Chapman (w, m), Ricordi; Spanish Dancer, The— Lorenz Hart (w), Mel Shauer (m), Globe. COVER: Pola Negri.

4929 Spanish Fly (Emerson, 1975, Leslie Phillips, Terry Thomas).

Fly Me (B)—Bill Martin, Phil Coulter (w,m), EMI. COVER: Leslie Phillips, Terry Thomas.

4930 Sparkle (Warner Bros., 1976, Irene Cara, Lonette McKee).

Jump/Look Into Your Heart/ Something He Can Feel—Curtis Mayfield (w,m), Warner. COVER: Aretha Franklin.

4931 Sparrows (United Artists, 1926, Mary Pickford, Roy Stewart).

Thinking of You (Promotion Song)—Joseph Grey (w), Allie Moore (m), Weequahic. COVER: Mary Pickford.

4932 Spartacus (Universal, 1960, Kirk Douglas, Laurence Olivier).

Spartacus Love Theme—Alex North (m), Northern. COVER: Black and white cover with title only.

4933 Spartakiada Days (Inde-

pendent, 1962, Russian Film).

Moscow Nights—Mann Curtis (w), Vassili Soloviev-Sedoy (m), Leeds. COVER: Russian Buildings.

4934 Spawn of the North (Paramount, 1938, Henry Fonda, George Raft).

I Wish I Was the Willow—Frank Loesser (w), Burton Lane (m), Famous. COVER: Henry Fonda, George Raft, Dorothy Lamour.

4935 Speak Easily (MGM, 1932, Jimmy Durante, Buster Keaton).

Singin' in the Rain (VS)—Arthur Freed (w), Nacio Herb Brown (m), Robbins. COVER: None.

4936 Speak Easy (Fox, 1929, Stuart Erwin, Lola Lane).

Song of Broadway—Pal Denell, Eddy Eckels (w,m), Denell. COVER: Sketch of Broadway.

4937 Speaking of Operations (Vitaphone, 1933, Musical Short).

Lonesome Levee/Sure Cure for the Blues/Under the Cotton Moon— Cliff Hess (w,m), Witmark. COVER: Black and white cover with title only.

4938 Speedway (MGM, 1968, Elvis Presley, Nancy Sinatra).

He's Your Uncle Not Your Dad— Sid Wayne (w), Ben Weisman (m), Gladys; Let Yourself Go—Joy Byers (w,m), Presley; Speedway—Mel Glazer, Stephen Schlaks (w,m), Gladys; There Ain't Nothing Like a Song—Joy Byers, Bob Johnston (w, m), Presley; Who Are You, Who Am I—Sid Wayne (w), Ben Weisman (m), Gladys; Your Time Hasn't Come Yet—Joel Hirschhorn, Al Kasha (w, m), Presley. COVER: Elvis Presley.

4939 Speedy (Paramount, 1927, Harold Lloyd, Ann Cristy).

Speedy Boy—Raymond Klages (w), Jesse Greer (m), Robbins. COVER: Harold Lloyd.

4940 Spellbound (United Artists, 1945, Ingrid Bergman, Gregory Peck).

Spellbound—Mack David (w), Miklos Rozsa (m), Chappell; Spellbound Concerto Theme/Spellbound Concerto Complete—Miklos Rozsa (m), Chappell. COVER: Ingrid Bergman, Gregory Peck.

4941 Spies Like Us (Warner Bros., 1985, Chevy Chase, Dan Aykroyd).

Spies Like Us—Paul McCartney (w,m), MPL. COVER: Chevy Chase, Dan Aykroyd.

4942 Spinout (MGM, 1966, Elvis Presley, Deborah Walley).

Adam and Evil—Fred Wise, Randy Starr (w,m), Gladys; All That I Am/Am I Ready—Sid Tepper, Roy Bennett (w,m), Gladys; Beach Shack—Bill Giant, Florence Kaye, Bernie Baum (w,m), Presley; I'll Be Back—Sid Wayne (w), Ben Weisman (m), Gladys; Smorgasbord—Sid Tepper, Roy Bennett (w,m), Gladys; Spinout—Sid Wayne, Ben Weisman, Darrell Fuller (w,m), Gladys; Stop Look and Listen—Joy Byers (w,m), Presley. COVER: Elvis Presley.

4943 Spirit of the U.S.A., The (Johnson, 1924, Mary Carr, Johnnie Walker).

That Wonderful Mother of Mine—Clyde Hager (w), Walter Goodwin (m), Witmark. COVER: Mary Carr, Johnnie Walker.

4944 Spirit of Youth (Grand National, 1938, Joe Louis, Clarence Muse).

Blue, What For?/Little Things You Do/Magic Lover/No More Sleepy Time/Spirit of Youth—Clarence Muse, Elliot Carpenter (w,m), Mills. COVER: Clarence Muse, Edna Mae Harris.

4945 Spite Bride, The (Selznick, 1919, Olive Thomas, Robert Ellis).

The Spite Bride—Joe Young, Sam Lewis (w), Harry Ruby (m), Berlin. COVER: Olive Thomas.

4946 Splash (Buena Vista, 1984, Tom Hanks, Daryl Hannah).

Love Came for Me—Will Jennings (w), Lee Holdridge (m), Wonderland. COVER: Daryl Hannah.

4947 Splendor in the Grass (Warner Bros., 1961, Warren Beatty, Natalie Wood).

Splendor in the Grass Theme—David Amram (m), Witmark. COVER: Warren Beatty, Natalie Wood.

4948 Split, The (MGM, 1968, Jim Brown, Diahann Carroll).

Good Woman's Love—Sheb Wooley (w), Quincy Jones (m), Feist; It's Just a Game Love/Split—Ernie Shelby (w), Quincy Jones (m), Hastings. COVER: Jim Brown, Diahann Carroll, Julie Harris, Ernest Borgnine.

4949 Sporting Chance (Paramount, 1920, James Hall, William Colier).

Old Playmate—Gus Kahn (w), Matt Malneck (m), Robbins. COVER: Claudia Dell.

4950 Sport of the Gods (Real, 1921, Elizabeth Boyer, Edward Abrams).

Dear Old Virginia—Harry Diggs (w), Otto Standhart (m), Mills. COVER: Sketch of Mansion.

4951 Spring Break (Columbia, 1983, David Knell, Perry Lang).

Spring Break—Rick Nielsen (w, m), Gold Horizon. COVER: Beach Scene.

4952 Spring Is Here (First National, 1930, Lawrence Gray, Bernice Claire).

Absence Makes the Heart Grow Fonder/Bad Baby/Cryin' for the Carolines/Have a Little Faith in Me/How Shall I Tell/What's the Big Idea—Sam Lewis, Joe Young (w), Harry Warren (m), Remick; With a Song in My Heart/Yours Sincerely—Lorenz Hart (w), Richard Rodgers (m), Harms. COVER: Lawrence Gray, Bernice Claire.

4953 Spring Parade (Universal, 1940, Deanna Durbin, Robert Cummings).

Blue Danube Dream—Gus Kahn (w), Johann Strauss (m), Robbins; In a Spring Parade—Gus Kahn (w), Charles Previn (m), Robbins; It's Foolish But It's Fun/Waltzing in the Clouds/When April Sings—Gus Kahn (w), Robert Stolz (m), Robbins. COVER: Robert Cummings, Deanna Durbin.

4954 Spring Reunion (United Artists, 1957, Betty Hutton, Dana Andrews).

Spring Reunion—Johnny Mercer (w), Harry Warren (m), Four Jays. COVER: Black and white cover with title only.

4955 Springtime for Henry (Fox, 1934, Otto Kruger, Nancy Carroll).

Forbidden Lips—Don Hartman (w), Jay Gorney (m), Movietone. COVER: Otto Kruger, Nancy Carroll.

4956 Springtime in Holland (Vitaphone, 1935, Dorothy Dare, Felix Knight).

Girl on the Little Blue Plate—Jack Scholl (w), Lou Alter (m), Remick. COVER: Dorothy Dare, Felix Knight.

4957 Springtime in Texas (Monogram, 1946, Jimmy Wakely, Dennis Moore).

Springtime in Texas/You're the Sweetest Rose in Texas—Jimmy Wakely (w,m), Peer. COVER: Jimmy Wakely.

4958 Springtime in the Rockies (Republic, 1937, Gene Autry, Smiley Burnette).

Give Me a Pony and an Open Prairie—Gene Autry, Frank Harford (w, m), Southern. COVER: Couple on Horseback.

4959 Springtime in the Rockies (20th Century-Fox, 1942, Betty Grable, John Payne).

I Had the Craziest Dream/I Like to Be Loved by You (BW)—Mack Gordon (w), Harry Warren (m), BVC; O Tic Tac Do Meu Coracao —Vermelbo Silva (w,m), Southern; Pan Americana Jubilee—Mack Gordon (w), Harry Warren (m), BVC; Poem Set to Music, A—Mack Gordon (w), Harry Warren (m), BVC; Run Little Raindrop Run—Mack Gordon (w), Harry Warren (m), Feist; You Made Me Love You—Joe McCarthy

(w), James Monaco (m), BMI. COVER: Betty Grable, John Payne, Harry James, Carmen Miranda.

4960 Spring Tonic (Fox, 1935, Lew Ayres, Claire Trevor).

There's a Spell on the Moon Tonight—Jay Gorney (w,m), Movietone. COVER: Sketch of Man and Woman.

4961 Spy Who Came in from the Cold, The (Paramount, 1965, Richard Burton, Claire Bloom).

Spy Who Came in from the Cold Theme—Sol Kaplan (m), Famous. COVER: Richard Burton, Claire Bloom.

4962 Spy Who Loved Me, The (United Artists, 1977, Roger Moore, Curt Jurgens).

Nobody Does It Better—Carole B. Sager (w), Marvin Hamlisch (m), Unart. COVER: Roger Moore, Barbara Bach.

4963 Spy with the Cold Nose, The (Embassy, 1966, Laurence Harvey, Daliah Lavi).

Spy with the Cold Nose-Theme—Riz Ortolani (m), Levine. COVER: Cartoon Sketch.

4964 Squall, The (First National, 1929, Myrna Loy, Alice Joyce).

Gypsy Charmer—Grant Clarke (w), Harry Akst (m), Witmark. COVER: Myrna Loy.

4965 Square Dance Jubilee (Lippert, 1949, Don Harry, Wally Vernon).

Hangman's Boogie—Larry Cassidy (w,m), Fairway. COVER: Cowboy Copas.

4966 Square Dance Katy (Monogram, 1950, Vera Vague, Phil Brito).

You Hold the Reins, While I Kiss You—Raleigh Keith (w,m), BMI. COVER: Vera Vague, Phil Brito.

4967 Square Root (Independent, 1969, Stars Unknown).

We Gotta All Get Together—Freddy Weller (w,m), Equinox. COVER: Paul Revere and Raiders.

4968 Squaw Man (De Mille, 1914, Dustin Farnum, Red Wing).

Nat-u-ritch, An Indian Idyll—Theodore Bendix (m), Stern. COVER: Red Wing.

4969 Squeaker, The (Murder on Diamond Row) (United Artists, 1937, Edmund Lowe, Sebastian Shaw).

I Can't Get Along Without You (B)—William Kernell (w,m), Chappell. COVER: Tamara Desni.

4970 Stagecoach (United Artists, 1939, John Wayne, Claire Trevor).

Song of the Sage—Joe Inge (w, m), Davis Schweiger. COVER: John Wayne.

4971 Stagecoach (20th Century-Fox, 1966, Bing Crosby, Ann Margret).

I Will Follow-Theme from Stagecoach—Ruth Batchelor (w), Jerry Goldsmith (m), Hastings; Stagecoach to Cheyenne—Lee Pockriss, Paul Vance (w,m), Miller. COVER: Stagecoach and Indians.

4972 Stagecoach Buckaroo (Universal, 1942, Johnny Mack Brown, Fuzzy Knight).

Don't You Ever Be a Cowboy/Put It There—Everett Carter (w), Milton Rosen (m), Robbins. COVER: Johnny Mack Brown, Fuzzy Knight, Nell O'Day.

4973 Stagecoach Days (Columbia, 1938, Jack Luden, Eleanor Stewart).

Prairie Dreams—Lee Zahler, Harold Raymond, Carroll Cooper (w,m), Superior. COVER: Jack Luden.

4974 Stage Door Canteen (United Artists, 1943, Kenny Baker, Tallulah Bankhead).

Alligator and the Crocodile (BW)/American Boy (BW)/Don't Worry Island—Al Dubin (w), James Monaco (m), Morris; Machine Gun Song—A. Hoffman, M. Curtis, Jerry Livingston, C. Corbin (w,m), Morris; Quicksands/Rookie and His Rhythm, A/She's a Bombshell from Brooklyn/Sleep Baby Sleep/We'll Meet in the Funniest Places/We Mustn't Say Goodbye/You're Pretty Terrific Yourself (BW)—Al Dubin (w), James Monaco (m), Morris; Marching Through Berlin—Bob Reed, Harry Miller (w,m), MPI. COVER: Sketch of Couple, and Star.

4975 Stage Fright (Warner Bros., 1950, Marlene Dietrich, Jane Wyman).

Eve's Rhapsody (B)—Leighton Lucas (m), Feldman; Laziest Gal in Town (B)—Cole Porter (w,m), Chappell. COVER: Marlene Dietrich.

4976 Stage Mother (MGM, 1933, Maureen O'Sullivan, Alice Brady).

Beautiful Girl/Dancin' on a Rainbow—Arthur Freed (w), Nacio Herb Brown (m), Robbins. COVER: Maureen O'Sullivan, Alice Brady, and Girls.

4977 Stage Struck (Warner Bros., 1936, Dick Powell, Joan Blondell).

Fancy Meeting You/In Your Own Quiet Way—E. Y. Harburg (w), Harold Arlen (m), Harms. COVER: Dick Powell, Joan Blondell.

4978 Staircase (20th Century-Fox, 1969, Rex Harrison, Richard Burton).

The Staircase—Stanley Donen, Dudley Moore (w,m), Fox. COVER: Richard Burton, Rex Harrison.

4979 Stalag Seventeen (Paramount, 1953, William Holden, Don Taylor).

I Love You—Franz Waxman (m), Famous. COVER: Black and white cover with title only.

4980 Stallion Canyon (Astor Kanab, 1949, Ken Curtis, Carolina Cotton).

Hills of Utah—Hy Heath (w,m), Astor. COVER: Ken Curtis, Carolina Cotton.

4981 Stand and Deliver (Warner Bros., 1988, Edward Olmos, Lou Phillips).

Stand and Deliver—Richard Page, Steve George, John Lang (w,m), Warner. COVER: Edward Olmos, Lou Phillips.

4982 Stand By Me (Columbia, 1986, Wil Wheaton, River Phoenix).

Book of Love (PC)—Warren Davis, George Malone, Charles Patrick (w, m), Columbia; Every Day (PC)—Norman Petty, Charles Hardin (w,m), Columbia; Stand By Me—Ben King, Mike Stoller, Jerry Lieber (w,m), Warner. COVER: Ben King.

4983 Stand Up and Cheer (Follies) (Fox, 1934, Shirley Temple, Warner Baxter).

Baby Take a Bow/Broadway's Gone Hill Billy/I'm Laughin'—Lew Brown, Jay Gorney (w,m), Movietone; She's Way Up Thar—Lew Brown (w,m), Movietone; Stand Up and Cheer—Lew Brown, Harry Akst (w,m), Movietone; This Is Our Last Night Together—Lew Brown, Jay Gorney (w,m), Movietone; We're Out of the Red—Lew Brown (w), Jay Gorney (m), Movietone. COVER: Sketch of Chorus Girls.

4984 Star, The (20th Century-Fox, 1952, Bette Davis, Sterling Hayden).

Moonlight Serenade—Victor Young (m), Young; Summer Love—Milton Berle, Buddy Arnold (w), Victor Young (m), Young. COVER: Red cover with title only.

4985 Star! (20th Century-Fox, 1968, Julie Andrews, Richard Crenna).

Burlington Bertie from Bow (B)— William Hargreaves (w,m), Wright; Clap Yo' Hands/Dear Little Girl/Do Do Do—Ira Gershwin (w), George Gershwin (m), New World; Has Anybody Seen Our Ship—Noel Coward (w,m), Chappell; In My Garden of Joy—Saul Chaplin (w,m), Fox; Jenny —Ira Gershwin (w), Kurt Weill (m), Chappell; Limehouse Blues—Douglas Furber (w), Philip Braham (m), Warner; Maybe—Ira Gershwin (w), George Gershwin (m), New World; My Ship—Ira Gershwin (w), Kurt Weill (m), Chappell; Someday I'll Find You—Noel Coward (w,m), Chappell; Star!—Sammy Cahn (w), James Van Heusen (m), Fox; N Everything (VS)—B. G. DeSylva, Gus Kahn, Al Jolson (w,m), Warner; Parisian Pierrot (VS)—Noel Coward (w,m), Warner; Physician, The (VS)— Cole Porter (w,m), Warner; Someone to Watch Over Me (VS)—Ira Gershwin (w), George Gershwin (m), Warner; You Were Meant for Me (VS)— Noble Sissle (w), Eubie Blake (m), Warner. COVER: Julie Andrews.

4986 Stardust (20th Century-Fox, 1940, John Payne, Linda Darnell).

Don't Let It Get You Down/ Secrets in the Moonlight—Mack Gordon (w,m), Robbins; Stardust—Mitchell Parish (w), Hoagy Carmichael (m), Mills. COVER: John Payne, Linda Darnell.

4987 Stardust on the Sage (Republic, 1942, Gene Autry, Gabby Hayes).

You'll Be Sorry (VS)—Gene Autry, Fred Rose (w,m), Western. COVER: Gene Autry.

4988 Star for a Night (20th Century-Fox, 1936, Claire Trevor, Jane Darwell).

Down Aroun' Malibu Way/Over a Cup of Coffee—Sidney Clare (w), Harry Akst (m), Movietone. COVER: Claire Trevor, and Chorus.

4989 Star Is Born, A (United Artists, 1937, Janet Gaynor, Fredric March).

A Star Is Born—Dorothy Dick (w), Max Steiner (m), Berlin. COVER: Janet Gaynor, Fredric March.

4990 Star Is Born, A (Warner Bros., 1954, Judy Garland, James Mason).

Gotta Have Me Go With You/I'm Off the Downbeat (PC)/It's a New World/Lose That Long Face/Man That Got Away, The—Ira Gershwin (w), Harold Arlen (m), Harwin; Peanut Vendor, The—Marion Sunshine, L. Wolfe Gilbert (w), M. Simons (m), Marks; Swanee (VS)—Irving Caesar (w), George Gershwin (m), New World; Born in a Trunk (VS)—Leonard Gershe (w,m), Warner; Here's What I'm Here For (VS)/Someone at Last (VS)—Ira Gershwin (w), Harold Arlen (m), Harwin. COVER: Judy Garland.

4991 Star Is Born, A (Warner Bros., 1976, Barbra Streisand, Kris Kristofferson).

Evergreen—Paul Williams (w), Barbra Streisand (m), Warner; I Believe in Love—Alan Bergman, Marilyn Bergman (w), Kenny Loggins (m), Warner; Watch Closely Now—Paul Williams, Kenny Ascher (w,m), Warner; A Star Is Born-Ten Songs—Rupert Holmes, Paul Williams, Kenny Ascher (w,m), Warner. COVER: Barbra Streisand, Kris Kristofferson.

4992 Starlight Over Texas (Monogram, 1938, Tex Ritter, Carmen Laroux).

Starlight Over Texas—Harry Tobias, Ray Ingraham (w,m), Schuster. COVER: Tex Ritter.

4993 Starmaker, The (Paramount, 1939, Bing Crosby, Louise Campbell).

Apple for the Teacher—Johnny Burke (w), James Monaco (m), Sanly Joy; Go Fly a Kite—Johnny Burke (w), James Monaco (m), Famous; I Can't Tell Why I Love You But I Do/If I Was a Millionaire—Will Cobb (w), Gus Edwards (m), Paull Pioneer; I Wonder Who's Kissing Her Now—Will Hough, Frank Adams (w), Joe Howard (m), Marks; Man and His Dream, A—Johnny Burke (w), James Monaco (m), Santly Joy; School Days—Will Cobb (w), Gus Edwards (m), Mills; Still the Bluebird Sings—Johnny Burke (w), James Monaco (m), Famous; Sunbonnet Sue—Will Cobb (w), Gus Edwards (m), Shapiro Bernstein; Starmaker-Ten Songs—Will Cobb (w), Gus Edwards (m), Witmark. COVER: Bing Crosby, Louise Campbell.

4994 Star of Midnight (RKO, 1935, William Powell, Ginger Rogers).

Midnight in Manhattan—Jack

Scholl (w), Max Steiner (m), Berlin. COVER: Black and white cover with title only.

4995 Stars and Stripes Forever (20th Century-Fox, 1952, Clifton Webb, Robert Wagner).

Stars and Stripes Forever/Stars and Stripes Forever-Ten Marches—John Philip Sousa (m), Presser. COVER: Clifton Webb.

4996 Stars Are Singing, The (Paramount, 1953, Rosemary Clooney, Anna Maria Alberghetti).

Haven't Got a Worry/I Do! I Do! I Do!/Lovely Weather for Ducks/ My Heart Is Home/My King O'Day —Jay Livingston, Ray Evans (w,m), Famous. COVER: Rosemary Clooney, Anna Maria Alberghetti, Lauritz Melchior.

4997 Stars in the Backyard (Paradise Alley) (20th Century-Fox, 1961, Marie Windsor, Hugo Haas).

Stars in the Backyard—Frans Steininger (w,m), Feist. COVER: Black and white cover with title only.

4998 Stars Over Arizona (Monogram, 1937, Jack Randall, Kathleen Elliot).

Headin' for the Trail—Johnny Lange (w), Fred Stryker (m), Sam Fox. COVER: Jack Randall.

4999 Stars Over Broadway (Warner Bros., 1935, Pat O'Brien, Jane Froman).

At Your Service Madame/Broadway Cinderella/Brownstone Baby (BW)—Al Dubin (w), Harry Warren (m), Harms; Carry Me Back to the Lone Prairie—Caason Robison (w, m), Mills; Where Am I?/You Let Me Down—Al Dubin (w), Harry Warren (m), Harms. COVER: Pat O'Brien, Jane Froman, James Melton, Phil Regan.

5000 Star Spangled Girl (Paramount, 1971, Sandy Duncan, Tony Roberts).

Girl—Norman Gimbel (w), Charles Fox (m), Ensign. COVER: Sandy Duncan.

5001 Star Spangled Rhythm (Paramount, 1942, Bob Hope, Bing Crosby).

Hit the Road to Dreamland/I'm Doing It for Defense/Old Glory/On the Swing Shift/Sharp as a Tack/Sweater, a Sarong, a Peek-aboo Bang/That Old Black Magic—Johnny Mercer (w), Harold Arlen (m), Famous. COVER: Bing Crosby, Dorothy Lamour, Bob Hope, and Paramount Stars.

5002 Start Cheering (Columbia, 1938, Jimmy Durante, Walter Connolly).

Am I in Another World/Love Takes a Holiday—Ted Koehler (w), Johnny Green (m), Witmark; My Heaven on Earth—Charlie Tobias (w), S. Pokrass, Phil Baker (m), Witmark; Naughty Naught (BW)—Milton Drake (w), Ben Oakland (m), Witmark; Paper Says Rain, The (BW)—Max Lief, Nat Lief (w), Samuel Pokrass (m), Witmark; Rockin' the Town—Red Koehler (w), Johnny Green (m), Witmark. COVER: Sketches of People.

5003 Starting Over (Paramount, 1979, Burt Reynolds, Jill Clayburgh).

Better than Ever/Easy for You/Starting Over—Carole B. Sager (w), Marvin Hamlisch (m), Famous; Starting Over Love Theme—Marvin Hamlisch (m), Famous. COVER: Burt Reynolds, Candice Bergen, Jill Clayburgh.

5004 Star Trek I-The Motion Picture (Paramount, 1979, William Shatner, Leonard Nimoy).

A Star Beyond Time—Larry Kusik (w), Jerry Goldsmith (m), Ensign. COVER: William Shatner, Leonard Nimoy.

5005 Star Trek II-The Wrath of Khan (Paramount, 1982, William Shatner, Leonard Nimoy).

The Wrath of Khan-Main Theme—James Horner (m), Famous. COVER: Futuristic Signs.

5006 Star Trek III-Search for Spock (Paramount, 1984, William Shatner, DeForest Kelley).

Search for Spock Theme/Returning to Vulcan-Spock's Theme/Star Trek III-Nine Themes—James Horner (m), Famous. COVER: Spock.

5007 Star Trek IV-The Voyage Home (Paramount, 1987, William Shatner, Leonard Nimoy).

Star Trek IV-The Voyage Home Theme—Leonard Rosenman (m), Famous. COVER: William Shatner, Leonard Nimoy.

5008 Star Trek V-The Final Frontier (Paramount, 1989, William Shatner, Leonard Nimoy).

The Moon's a Window to Heaven—John Bettis (w), Jerry Goldsmith (m), Ensign. COVER: William Shatner, Leonard Nimoy.

5009 Star Wars (20th Century-Fox, 1977, Harrison Ford, Mark Hamill).

Cantina Band/Princess Leia's Theme/Star Wars Main Title/Star Wars Piano Suite—John Williams (m), Fox. COVER: Black cover with title only.

5010 State Fair (Fox, 1933, Janet Gaynor, Will Rogers).

Romantic—Val Burton, Will Jason (w), Louis DeFrancesco (m), Movietone; Shanty or Levee Song (BW)—Fred Rycroft (w,m), Movietone. COVER: Janet Gaynor.

5011 State Fair (20th Century-Fox, 1945, Dick Haymes, Vivian Blaine).

All I Owe Ioway/Isn't It Kinda Fun/It Might as Well Be Spring/It's a Grand Night for Singing/That's for Me/We Will Be Together (PC)—Oscar Hammerstein (w), Richard Rodgers (m), Williamson. COVER: Dick Haymes, Vivian Blaine, Jeanne Crain.

5012 State Fair (20th Century-Fox, 1962, Pat Boone, Ann Margret).

Isn't It Kinda Fun/It Might as Well Be Spring/It's a Grand Night for Singing—Oscar Hammerstein (w), Richard Rodgers (m), William-

son; It's the Little Things in Texas/
More Than Just a Friend/Never
Say No—Richard Rodgers (w,m),
Williamson; Our State Fair/That's
for Me—Oscar Hammerstein (w),
Richard Rodgers (m), Williamson;
This Isn't Heaven/Willing and Eager
—Richard Rodgers (w,m), Williamson. COVER: Pat Boone, Ann Margret, and Movie Scenes.

5013 State Police (Universal,
1938, Constance Moore, William
Lundigan).
You, You Darlin'—Jack Scholl
(w), M. K. Jerome (m), Harms.
COVER: Larry Clinton.

5014 Station Six Sahara (Allied
Artists, 1964, Carroll Baker, Ian
Bannen).
Station Six Sahara Theme (B)—
Ron Grainer (m), Erle. COVER:
Carroll Baker, and Men.

5015 Station West (RKO, 1948,
Dick Powell, Jane Greer).
Man Can't Grow Old/Sometime
Remind Me to Tell You—Mort
Greene (w), Leigh Harline (m), Famous. COVER: Dick Powell, Jane
Greer.

5016 Stay Away Joe (MGM,
1968, Elvis Presley, Burgess Meredith).
Stay Away Joe—Sid Wayne (w),
Ben Weisman (m), Hill Range.
COVER: Elvis Presley.

5017 Staying Alive (Paramount,
1983, John Travolta, Cynthia
Rhodes).
Far from Over—Frank Stallone,
Vince DiCola (w,m), Famous; Look
Out for Number One (PC)—Bruce
Foster, Tom Marolda (w,m), Famous; So Close to the Fire (PC)—
Randy Bishop, Tommy Faragher
(w,m), Ensign; Someone Belonging
to Someone/Stayin' Alive/Woman
in You, The—Barry Gibb, Robin
Gibb, Maurice Gibb (w,m), Gibb;
Staying Alive-Twelve Songs—Barry
Gibb, Robin Gibb, Maurice Gibb
(w,m), Leonard. COVER: John Travolta.

5018 St. Benny the Dip (United
Artists, 1951, Dick Haymes, Nina
Foch).
I Believe—Robert Stringer (w,m),
BVC. COVER: Dick Haymes, Nina
Foch.

**5019 Steamboat Round the
Bend** (Fox, 1935, Will Rogers, Anne
Shirley).
Steamboat Round the Bend—Sidney Clare (w), Oscar Levant (m),
Movietone. COVER: Black and white
cover with title only.

5020 Steel Trap, The (20th Century-Fox, 1952, Joseph Cotten,
Teresa Wright).
You Mean So Much to Me—Stan
Jones (w), Dimitri Tiomkin (m),
Feist. COVER: Joseph Cotten,
Teresa Wright.

5021 Stella (20th Century-Fox,
1950, Victor Mature, Ann Sheridan).
Stella—Allan Roberts (w), Alfred
Newman (m), Miller. COVER: Victor
Mature, Ann Sheridan.

5022 Stella Dallas (United Artists, 1925, Belle Bennett, Ronald
Colman).
Mother Song—S. L. Rothafel, Graham Harris, Anton Dvorak (w,m),
Unart; Songs That My Mother Taught
—Hugo Frey (w), Anton Dvorak (m),
Robbins Engel. COVER: Belle Bennett, Lois Moran.

5023 St. Elmo's Fire (Columbia,
1985, Emilio Estevez, Rob Lowe).
For Just a Moment—Cynthia Weil
(w), David Foster (m), Gold Horizon;
St. Elmo's Fire-Man in Motion—John
Parr (w), David Foster (m), Gold
Horizon; St. Elmo's Fire-Love Theme
—David Foster (m), Gold Horizon;
St. Elmo's Fire-Ten Songs—David
Foster, Steve Lukather (w,m), Gold
Horizon. COVER: Emilio Estevez,
Rob Lowe, Andrew McCarthy, and
others.

**5024 Step Lively (Manhattan
Melody)** (RKO, 1944, Frank Sinatra,
George Murphy).
And Then You Kissed Me/As
Long as There's Music/Come Out,

Come Out, Wherever You Are/Some Other Time/Where Does Love Begin —Sammy Cahn (w), Jule Styne (m), Miller. COVER: Frank Sinatra.

5025 Stepmother, The (Crown, 1973, Alejandro Rey, John Anderson).
Strange Are the Ways of Love— Paul F. Webster (w), Sammy Fain (m), Webster Fain. COVER: Blue Cover with title only.

5026 Stepping Out (Paramount, 1919, Enid Bennett, Niles Welch).
Stepping Out—Edward Grossman (w,m), Remick. COVER: Enid Bennett, Niles Welch.

5027 Stepping Sisters (Fox, 1932, Louise Dresser, Minna Gombell).
Look Here Comes a Rainbow/My World Begins and Ends with You— James Hanley (w,m), Sam Fox. COVER: Louise Dresser, Minna Gombell, Jobyna Howland.

5028 Steptoe and Son (MGM, 1972, Wilfrid Brambell, Harry Corbett).
The Streets of London (B)—Roy Budd, Jack Fishman (w,m)—Coronado. COVER: Wilfrid Brambell, Harry Corbett.

5029 Sterile Cuckoo, The (Paramount, 1969, Liza Minelli, Wendell Burton).
Come Saturday Morning—Dory Previn (w), Fred Karlin (m), Famous. COVER: Liza Minelli.

5030 Stevie (Paramount, 1973, Steven Hawkes, Samson).
Born to Love—William F. Lawson (w,m), Popular. COVER: Steven Hawkes, Samson, Delilah.

5031 Stick to Your Guns (Paramount, 1941, William Boyd, Andy Clyde).
Blue Moon on the Silver Sage— Smiley Burnette (w,m), Famous. COVER: William Boyd.

5032 Stiletto (Embassy, 1969, Alex Cord, Britt Ekland).
Stiletto—Sid Ramin (m), Levine; Sugar in the Rain—Alan Bergman,

Marilyn Bergman (w), Sid Ramin (m), Levine. COVER: Alex Cord.

5033 Sting, The (Universal, 1974, Paul Newman, Robert Redford).
Entertainer—Scott Joplin (m), Hansen; Gladiolus Rag—Scott Joplin (m), Marks; Pineapple Rag—Scott Joplin (m), Belwin Mills; Solace— Scott Joplin (m), Leeds; Sting-Ten Songs—Scott Joplin (m), MCA. COVER: Paul Newman, Robert Redford).

5034 Stingaree (RKO, 1934, Irene Dunne, Richard Dix).
Tonight Is Mine—Gus Kahn (w), Frank Harling (m), Berlin. COVER: Irene Dunne, Richard Dix.

5035 Stir Crazy (Columbia, 1980, Gene Wilder, Richard Pryor).
Crazy/Love/Nothing Can Stop Us Now—Randy Goodrum, Michael Masser (w,m), Golden Torch. COVER: Gene Wilder, Richard Pryor.

5036 St. Louis Blues (Paramount, 1939, Dorothy Lamour, Lloyd Nolan).
Blue Nightfall—Frank Loesser (w), Burton Lane (m), Famous; I Go for That—Frank Loesser (w), Matt Malneck (m), Famous; Junior—Frank Loesser (w), Burton Lane (m), Famous; Kinda Lonesome—Leo Robin, Sam Coslow, Hoagy Carmichael (w, m), Famous; Let's Dream in the Moonlight—Raoul Walsh, Matt Malneck (w,m), Famous; St. Louis Blues —W. C. Handy (w,m), Handy. COVER: Dorothy Lamour.

5037 St. Louis Blues (Paramount, 1958, Nat King Cole, Eartha Kitt).
Aunt Hagar's Children Blues—Tim Brymn (w), W. C. Handy (m), Handy; Beale Street Blues/Careless Love/ Chantez Les Bas/Friendless Blues/ Harlem Blues/Hesitation Blues/Memphis Blues—W. C. Handy (w,m), Handy; Morning Star—Mack David (w), W. C. Handy (m), Comet; St. Louis Blues/Way Down South Where the Blues Began/Yellow Dog Blues— W. C. Handy (w,m), Handy. COVER: Nat King Cole, Eartha Kitt, Pearl Bailey, Ella Fitzgerald.

5038 St. Louis Woman (Showmen, 1935, John Mack Brown, Jeanette Loff).

St. Louis Woman/You're Indispensable to Me—Betty Laidlaw, Bob Lively (w,m), Mills. COVER: Jeanette Loff, and girls.

5039 Stolen Harmony (Paramount, 1935, George Raft, Ben Bernie).

Let's Spill the Beans—Mack Gordon, Harry Revel (w,m), Crawford; Stolen Harmony—Joe Young, Art Altman, Jack Lawrence (w,m), Famous; Would There Be Love—Mack Gordon, Harry Revel (w,m), Crawford. COVER: Ben Bernie.

5040 Stolen Heaven (Paramount, 1938, Gene Raymond, Olympe Bradna).

Stolen Heaven—Ralph Freed (w), Frederick Hollander (m), Famous. COVER: Gene Raymond, Olympe Bradna.

5041 Stolen Holiday (Warner Bros., 1936, Kay Francis, Claude Rains).

Stolen Holiday—Al Dubin (w), Harry Warren (m), Remick. COVER: Green and white cover with title only.

5042 Stolen Hours (United Artists, 1963, Susan Hayward, Michael Craig).

Non Finisce in Una Sera-Theme—Mort Lindsay (m), Unart; Stolen Hours—Alan Bergman, Marilyn Bergman (w), Mort Lindsay (m), Unart. COVER: Black and white cover with title only.

5043 Stooge, The (Paramount, 1952, Dean Martin, Jerry Lewis).

Girl Named Mary and a Boy Named Bill—Mack David (w), Jerry Livingston (m), Paramount; Just One More Chance (B)—Sam Coslow (w), Arthur Johnston (m), Victoria. COVER: Dean Martin, Jerry Lewis.

5044 Stop Flirting (PDC, 1925, John Murray, Wanda Hawley).

Stop Flirting—Henri Sloane (w), Russell Tarbox (m), Brean Tobias. COVER: Wanda Hawley.

5045 Stop Look and Love (20th Century-Fox, 1939, Jean Rogers, William Frawley).

Let's Start Where We Left Off—Sidney Clare (w), Jule Styne (m), Robbins. COVER: Jean Rogers, William Frawley, Robert Kellard.

5046 Stop You're Killing Me (Warner Bros., 1953, Broderick Crawford, Claire Trevor).

My Ever Lovin'—Bob Hilliard (w), Carl Sigman (m), Witmark. COVER: Broderick Crawford, Claire Trevor.

5047 Stork Club, The (Paramount, 1945, Betty Hutton, Barry Fitzgerald).

Doctor Lawyer Indian Chief—Paul F. Webster (w), Hoagy Carmichael (m), Melrose; If I Had a Dozen Hearts—Paul F. Webster (w), Harry Revel (m), Paramount; Love Me—Sammy Cahn (w), Jule Styne (m), Famous; Square in a Social Circle, A—Jay Livingston, Ray Evans (w,m), Famous. COVER: Betty Hutton, Barry Fitzgerald, Don Defore, Andy Russell.

5048 Storm, The (Universal, 1922, Virginia Valli, House Peters).

You Know How Tis—Arthur Penn (w,m), Witmark. COVER: Virginia Valli.

5049 Storm, The (Universal, 1930, Lupe Velez, William Boyd).

Chansonette of Pierrot and Pierrette—Bernie Grossman (w), Heinz Roemheld (m), HKG. COVER: Lupe Velez.

5050 Storm Boy (Aus, 1976, Greg Rowe, Peter Cummins).

Storm Boy (PC)—Leslie Bricusse (w,m), Stage Screen. COVER: None.

5051 Stormy (Universal, 1935, Jean Rogers, Noah Beery, Jr.).

Ridge Runnin' Roan—Curley Fletcher (w,m), Cole. COVER: Noah Beery Jr. and Movie Scenes.

5052 Stormy Weather (20th Century-Fox, 1943, Lena Horne, Bill Robinson).

Ain't Misbehavin'—Andy Razaf

(w), Thomas Waller, Harry Brooks (m), Mills; Diga Diga Doo/I Can't Give You Anything But Love—Dorothy Fields (w), Jimmy McHugh (m), Mills; Geechy Joe—Cab Calloway, Jack Palmer, Andy Gibson (w,m), Mills; I Lost My Sugar in Salt Lake City—Leon Rene, Johnny Lange (w, m), Mills; Moppin' and Boppin'—Fats Waller, Benny Carter, Ed Kirkeby (w,m), Mills; My My Ain't That Somethin'—Harry Tobias, Pinky Tomlin (w,m), Mills; Stormy Weather —Ted Koehler (w), Harold Arlen (m), Mills; That Ain't Right—King Cole, Irving Mills (w,m), American; There's No Two Ways About Love— Ted Koehler (w), James Johnson, Irving Mills (m), Mills. COVER: Lena Horne, Fats Waller, Bill Robinson.

5053 Story of G.I. Joe, The (United Artists, 1945, Burgess Mereeith, Robert Mitchum).

Ernie Pyle Infantry March/I'm Comin' Back/Linda—Ann Ronell (w, m), Picture. COVER: Burgess Meredith, and others.

5054 Story of Gilbert and Sullivan (The Great Gilbert and Sullivan) (United Artists, 1954, Robert Morley, Maurice Evans).

Story of Gilbert and Sullivan— Piano Selections (B)—W. S. Gilbert, A. Sullivan (w,m), Chappell; Story of Gilbert and Sullivan-Seven Songs (B)—W. S. Gilbert, A. Sullivan (w, m), Day. COVER: Movie Scenes.

5055 Story of Robin Hood, The (RKO Disney, 1950, Richard Todd, Joan Rice).

Riddle De Diddle De Day/Whistle My Love—Eddie Pola, George Wyle (w,m), Disney. COVER: Richard Todd, Joan Rice.

5056 Story of Ruth, The (20th Century-Fox, 1961, Stuart Whitman, Tom Tryon).

The Song of Ruth—Paul F. Webster (w), Franz Waxman (m), Robbins. COVER: Elana Eden.

5057 Story of Shirley Yorke,

The (Butscher, 1949, Derek Farr, Dinah Sheridan).

Portrait of a Lady—George Melanchrino (m), Mills. COVER: Black and white cover with title only.

5058 Story of Three Loves, The (MGM, 1953, Pier Angeli, Ethel Barrymore).

Rachmaninoff's Eighteenth Variation—S. Rachmaninoff (m), Foley. COVER: Black and white cover with title only.

5059 Story of Vernon and Irene Castle, The (RKO, 1939, Fred Astaire, Ginger Rogers).

Only When You're in Love—Con Conrad, Bert Kalmar, Herman Ruby (w,m), Crawford; Too Much Mustard—Cecil Macklin (m), Schuberth; Waiting for the Robert E. Lee—L. Wolfe Gilbert (w), Lewis Muir (m), Alfred; Yama Yama Man, The (BW)— Collin Davis (w), Karl Hoschna (m), Witmark. COVER: Fred Astaire, Ginger Rogers.

5060 Stowaway (20th Century-Fox, 1936, Shirley Temple, Alice Faye).

Goodnight My Love/I Wanna Go to the Zoo/One Never Knows, Does One?—Mack Gordon, Harry Revel (w,m), Robbins; That's What I Want for Christmas—Irving Caesar (w), Gerald Marks (m), Caesar; You Gotta S M I L E to Be H A Double P Y—Mack Gordon, Harry Revel (w, m), Robbins. COVER: Shirley Temple, Robert Young, Alice Faye.

5061 Stowaway in the Sky (Voyage of the Balloon) (Lopert, 1962, Jack Lemmon).

Stowaway in the Sky-Theme— Eddy Marnay (w), Jean Prodromides (m), Piedmont. COVER: People in a Balloon.

5062 Straight Place and Show (20th Century-Fox, 1938, Richard Arlen, Ethel Merman).

Why Not String Along With Me/ With You on My Mind—Lew Brown (w), Lew Pollack (m), Robbins. COVER: Ethel Merman, The Ritz Brothers.

5063 Straight to Heaven (Domino, 1939, Jackie Ward, Jack Carter).

Don't Stop/Headin' Straight to Heaven/When the Dawn Became Dark/You Can Count on Me—Robert Maxwell (w), Josef Myrow (m), Exclusive. COVER: Clouds and Music Notes.

5064 Strange Affair, The Paramount, 1968, Michael York, Jeremy Kemp).

The Strange Affair-Music Score—Basil Kirchin, Jack Nathan (w,m), Famous. COVER: Green cover with title only.

5065 Strange Ceremonies of the World (Vitaphone, 1933, Musical Short).

Ceremonies of the World—David Mendoza (w,m), Witmark. COVER: Black and white cover with title only.

5066 Strange Lady in Town (Warner Bros., 1955, Greer Garson, Dana Andrews).

Strange Lady in Town—Ned Washington (w), Dimitri Tiomkin (m), Witmark. COVER: Greer Garson, Dana Andrews.

5067 Strange Love of Martha Ivers, The (Paramount, 1946, Barbara Stanwyck, Kirk Douglas).

Strange Love—Edward Heyman (w), Miklos Rozsa (m), Famous; Strange Love Theme—Miklos Rozsa (m), Famous. COVER: Barbara Stanwyck, Kirk Douglas, Lizabeth Scott, Van Heflin.

5068 Strange One, The (Columbia, 1957, Ben Gazzara, Julie Wilson).

The Strange One—Ralph Douglas (w), Kenyon Hopkins (m), Horizon. COVER: Ben Gazzara.

5069 Stranger Left No Card, The (Arthur, 1953, Alan Badel, Cameron Hall).

Swedish Rhapsody, Midsummer Vigil—Hugo Alfren (m), Cromwell. COVER: Black and white cover with title only.

5070 Stranger on the Run (World Premiere, 1967, Henry Fonda, Anne Baxter).

Stranger on the Run—Kay Scott, Bill Anderson (w,m), Shamley. COVER: Henry Fonda.

5071 Stranger Returns, The (MGM, 1968, Tony Anthony, Dan Vadis).

A Man, a Horse, and a Gun—Stelvio Cipriani (m), Marks. COVER: Henry Mancini.

5072 Strangers When We Meet (Columbia, 1960, Kirk Douglas, Kim Novak).

Strangers When We Meet—Richard Quine (w), George Duning (m), Colgems. COVER: Kirk Douglas, Kim Novak.

5073 Strategic Air Command (Paramount, 1954, James Stewart, June Allyson).

Air Force Takes Command—Ned Washington, Tom Thomson (w), Victor Young (m), Paramount; World Is Mine—Stanley Adams (w), Victor Young (m), Paramount; World Is Mine Theme—Victor Young (m), Paramount. COVER: James Stewart, June Allyson.

5074 Stratton Story, The (MGM, 1949, James Stewart, June Allyson).

You Are My Lucky Star—Arthur Freed (w), Nacio Herb Brown (m), Robbins. COVER: Black and white cover with title only.

5075 Strawberry Blonde, The (Warner Bros., 1945, James Cagney, Olivia de Havilland).

Band Played On, The—John Palmer (w), Charles Ward (m), Harms; Goodbye Little Girl—Will Cobb (w), Gus Edwards (m), Witmark. COVER: James Cagney, Olivia de Havilland.

5076 Strawberry Roan (Universal, 1933, Ken Maynard, Ruth Hall).

Strawberry Roan—Fred Howard, Nat Vincent, Curley Fletcher (w,m), Cole. COVER: Ken Maynard.

5077 Strawberry Roan (Columbia, 1948, Gene Autry, Gloria Henry).

Texas Sandman—Allan Roberts, Doris Fisher (w,m), Mood. COVER: Gene Autry, Gloria Henry.

5078 Street Angel (Fox, 1928, Janet Gaynor, Charles Farrell).

Angela Mia—Lew Pollack (w), Erno Rapee (m), DBH. COVER: Janet Gaynor, Charles Farrell.

5079 Streetcar Named Desire, A (Warner Bros., 1951, Marlon Brando, Vivien Leigh).

Streetcar Named Desire-Nine Themes—Alex North (m), Witmark; Streetcar Named Desire Piano Suite —Alex North (m), Warner. COVER: The French Quarter.

5080 Street Girl (RKO, 1929, Betty Compson, Jack Oakie).

Broken Up Tune/Lovable and Sweet/My Dream Memory—Sidney Clare (w), Oscar Levant (m), Harms. COVER: Betty Compson.

5081 Streets of Fire (Universal, 1984, Michael Pare, Diane Lane).

I Can Dream About You—Dan Hartman (w,m), Multi-level; Streets of Fire-Ten Songs—Jim Steinman, Jerry Leiber, Mike Stoller (w, m), Columbia. COVER: Michael Pare.

5082 Streets of Laredo (Paramount, 1948, William Holden, MacDonald Carey).

Streets of Laredo—Jay Livingston, Ray Evans (w,m), Famous. COVER: William Holden, MacDonald Carey, William Bendix.

5083 Streets of New York (Arrow, 1922, Barbara Castleton, Leslie King).

Dear Old New York—Larry Urbach (w), Victor Nurnberg (m), Cameo. COVER: Barbara Castleton, and Movie Scenes.

5084 Strictly   Dishonorable (MGM, 1951, Ezio Pinza, Janet Leigh).

Everything I Have Is Yours— Harold Adamson (w), Burton Lane (m), Miller; I'll See You in My Dreams—Gus Kahn (w), Isham Jones (m), Feist. COVER: Ezio Pinza, Janet Leigh.

5085 Strictly Dynamite (RKO, 1934, Jimmy Durante, Lupe Velez).

Oh Me! Oh My! Oh You!—Harold Adamson (w), Burton Lane (m), Berlin. COVER: Lupe Velez, Jimmy Durante.

5086 Strictly   Illegal   (Here Comes   a   Policeman) (Universal, 1935, Leslie Fuller, Betty Astell).

I Can't Do Without You—Georgie Harris, Cyril Ray (w,m), Mills. COVER: Black and white cover with title only.

5087 Strike Me Pink (United Artists, 1936, Eddie Cantor, Ethel Merman).

Calabash Pipe/First You Have Me High/Lady Dances/Shake It Off— Lew Brown (w), Harold Arlen (m), Harms. COVER: Eddie Cantor, and Girls.

5088 Strike Up the Band (MGM, 1940, Judy Garland, Mickey Rooney).

Drummer   Boy/Nobody—Roger Edens (w,m), Feist; Our Love Affair —Arthur Freed (w), Roger Edens (m), Feist; Strike Up the Band—Ira Gershwin (w), George Gershwin (m), Harms. COVER: Judy Garland, Mickey Rooney.

5089 Strip, The (MGM, 1951, Mickey Rooney, Sally Forrest).

Don't Blame Me—Dorothy Fields (w), Jimmy McHugh (m), Robbins; Kiss to Build a Dream On—Bert Kalmar, Harry Ruby, Oscar Hammerstein (w,m), Miller; La Bota—Haven Gillespie (w), Charles Wolcott (m), Southern. COVER: Mickey Rooney, Louis Armstrong, Sally Forrest, Vic Damone.

5090 Stripes (Columbia, 1981, Bill Murray, Warren Oates).

Stripes-Theme—Elmer   Bernstein (m), Golden Torch. COVER: Bill Murray.

5091 Stripper, The (20th Century-Fox, 1962, Joanne Woodward, Richard Beymer).

Lila's   Theme—Jerry   Goldsmith

(m), Hastings. COVER: Joanne Woodward, Richard Beymer.

5092 Student Life in Merry Springtime (PRX, 1931, German Operetta).

Just Say That You Love Me—J. Buchhorn, F. Baumann, H. Gilder, E. Buder (w,m), Sesac. COVER: Man and Woman.

5093 Student Prince, The (MGM, 1954, Ann Blyth, Edmund Purdom).

Beloved—Paul F. Webster (w), Nicholas Brodszky (m), Harms; Deep in My Heart Dear/Drinking Song/Golden Days—Dorothy Donnelly (w), Sigmund Romberg (m), Harms; I'll Walk with God—Paul F. Webster (w), Nicholas Brodszky (m), Harms; Serenade—Dorothy Donnelly (w), Sigmund Romberg (m), Harms; Summertime in Heidelberg—Paul F. Webster (w), Nicholas Brodszky (m), Harms. COVER: Ann Blyth, Edmund Purdom, John Ericson.

5094 Student Tour, The (MGM, 1934, Jimmy Durante, Charles Butterworth).

By the Taj Mahal/Carlo/From Now On/New Moon Is Over My Shoulder/Snake Dance—Arthur Freed (w), Nacio Herb Brown (m), Robbins. COVER: Phil Regan, and Girls.

5095 Stunt Man, The (20th Century-Fox, 1980, Peter O'Toole, Barbara Hershey).

Bits and Pieces—Norman Gimbel (w), Dominic Frontiere (m), Fox. COVER: Man and Camera.

5096 St. Valentine's Day Massacre (20th Century-Fox, 1967, Jason Robards, George Segal).

Smarty—Lee Hale (w), Lionel Newman (m), Hastings. COVER: Jason Robards, and movie scenes.

5097 Submarine (Columbia, 1928, Jack Holt, Dorothy Reveir).

Pals, Just Pals—Dave Dreyer, Herman Ruby (w,m), Berlin. COVER: Jack Holt, Ralph Graves.

5098 Submarine Eye, The (Williamson, 1917, Chester Barnett, Lindsay Hall).

Fourteen Fathoms Deep—M. L. Lake (m), Fischer. COVER: Underwater Scene.

5099 Subterraneans, The (MGM, 1960, Leslie Caron, George Peppard).

Why Are We Afraid—Dory Langdon (w), André Previn (m), Robbins. COVER: Leslie Caron, George Peppard.

5100 Such Good Friends (Paramount, 1971, Dyan Cannon, James Coco).

Suddenly, It's All Tomorrow—Robert Brittain (w), Thomas Shepard (m), Ensign. COVER: A Pair of Legs.

5101 Such Men Are Dangerous (Fox, 1931, Warner Baxter, Hedda Hopper).

Bridal Hymn—George Gramlich (w), Albert Malotte (m), Red Star; Cinderella by the Fire—Dave Stamper (w,m), Red Star. COVER: Black and white cover with title only.

5102 Sudden Bill Dorn (Universal, 1937, Buck Jones, Noel Francis).

Don't Jump the Gun (VS)—Fleming Allan (w,m), Cole. COVER: Gene Autry.

5103 Sudden Fear (RKO, 1952, Joan Crawford, Jack Palance).

Afraid—Jack Brooks (w), Elmer Bernstein (m), Mutual; Sudden Fear—Irving Taylor (w), Arthur Altman (m), Fred Bee. COVER: Joan Crawford.

5104 Sudden Impact (Warner Bros., 1980, Clint Eastwood, Sondra Locke).

This Side of Forever—DeWayne Blackwell (w), Lalo Schifrin (m), Peso. COVER: Clint Eastwood.

5105 Suddenly It's Spring (Paramount, 1962, Paulette Goddard, Fred MacMurray).

Suddenly It's Spring—Johnny Burke (w), Jimmy Van Heusen (m), Famous. COVER: Paulette Goddard, Fred MacMurray, MacDonald Carey.

5106 Sugarfoot (Warner Bros., 1951, Randolph Scott, Adele Jergens).

Oh! He Looked Like He Might Buy Wine—Sammy Cahn, Ray Heindorf (w,m), Remick. COVER: Randolph Scott, Adele Jergens.

5107 Suicide Squadron (Dangerous Moonlight) (Republic, 1941, Anton Walbrook, Sally Gray).

Warsaw Concerto—Richard Addinsell (m), Chappell. COVER: Anton Walbrook, Sally Gray.

5108 Sultan's Daughter, The (Monogram, 1943, Ann Corio, Charles Butterworth).

Clickity Clack Jack—Mort Greene (w,m), Southern; I'd Love to Make Love to You/Sultan's Daughter, The —Mort Greene (w), Karl Hajos (m), Southern. COVER: Ann Corio, and movie scenes.

5109 Summer and Smoke (Paramount, 1961, Laurence Harvey, Geraldine Page).

Summer and Smoke Theme—Elmer Bernstein (m), Famous. COVER: Laurence Harvey, Geraldine Page.

5110 Summer Holiday (MGM, 1948, Mickey Rooney, Gloria De Haven).

Afraid to Fall in Love/Brave Heart (BW)/Dan Dan Danville High/Independence Day/Our Home Town (BW)/Spring Isn't Everything (BW)/Stanley Steamer/Sweetest Kid I Ever Saw (BW)/Weary Blues/While the Men Are All Drinking (BW)/You're Next—Ralph Blane (w), Harry Warren (m), Warren. COVER: Mickey Rooney, Gloria De Haven, Marilyn Maxwell.

5111 Summer Holiday (AIP, 1962, Cliff Richards, Ron Moody).

Bachelor Boy (B)—Bruce Welch, Cliff Richard (w,m), Elstree. COVER: Cliff Richard.

5112 Summer Love (Universal, 1958, John Saxon, Fay Wray).

Love Is Something—Malvina Reynolds (w,m), Northern; Summer Love/To Know You Is to Love You—Bill Carey (w), Henry Mancini (m), Northern.COVER: John Saxon, Judy

Meredith.

5113 Summer Lovers (Orion, 1982, Peter Gallagher, Daryl Hannah).

Hard to Say I'm Sorry—Peter Cetera, David Foster (w,m), Double V; Summer Lovers—Michael Sembello, Dennis Matkosby, David Batteau (w, m), Warner. COVER: Black and white cover with title only.

5114 Summer Magic (Buena Vista, 1963, Burl Ives, Hayley Mills).

Beautiful Beulah/Femininity/Flitterin'/On the Front Porch/Pink of Perfection/Summer Magic Song/Ugly Bug Ball—Richard Sherman, Robert Sherman (w,m), Wonderland. COVER: Porch Railing.

5115 Summer of '42 (Warner Bros., 1971, Gary Grimes, Jennifer O'Neill).

Summer Knows, The—Alan Bergman, Marilyn Bergman (w), Michel Legrand (m), Warner; Summer of '42 Themes—Michel Legrand. COVER: Gary Grimes, Jennifer O'Neill.

5116 Summer Place, A (Warner Bros., 1959, Richard Egan, Dorothy McGuire).

Summer Place, A—Mack Discount (w), Max Steiner (m), Witmark; Summer Place '76/Summer Place Theme —Max Steiner (m), Witmark. COVER: Richard Egan, Dorothy McGuire.

5117 Summer Rental (Paramount, 1985, John Candy, Richard Crenna).

Summer Rental Theme—Alan Silvestri (m), Famous. COVER: John Candy.

5118 Summer School (Paramount, 1987, Mark Harmon, Kirstie Alley).

Mind Over Matter—Michael Jay, Rick Palombi (w,m), Famous. COVER: Mark Harmon.

5119 Summer Stock (MGM, 1950, Judy Garland, Gene Kelly).

Dig Dig Dig Dig for Your Dinner—Mack Gordon (w), Harry Warren (m), Miller; Friendly Star—Mack Gordon (w), Harry Warren (m), Feist; Get Happy—Ted Koehler (w), Harold Arlen (m), Remick; Happy Harvest Howdy Neighbor—Mack Gordon (w), Harry Warren (m), Feist; If You Feel Like Singing Sing—Mack Gordon (w), Harry Warren (m), Miller; Mem'ry Island—Mack Gordon (w), Harry Warren (m), Feist; You Wonderful You—Jack Brooks, Saul Chaplin (w), Harry Warren (m), Miller. COVER: Judy Garland, Gene Kelly.

5120 Summer Storm (United Artists, 1944, George Sanders, Linda Darnell).

Summer Storm—Rowland Leigh (w), Karl Hajos (m), Mills. COVER: George Sanders, Linda Darnell.

5121 Summertime (Summer Madness) (United Artists, 1955, Katharine Hepburn, Rossano Brazzi).

Believe in Me/Summertime in Venice—Carl Sigman (w), Icini (m), Pickwick; Summertime in Venice Theme—Icini (m), Pickwick. COVER: Katharine Hepburn, Rossano Brazzi.

5122 Sun Also Rises, The (20th Century-Fox, 1957, Tyrone Power, Ava Gardner).

The Lights of Paris—Charles Henderson (w), Hugo Friedhofer (m), Robbins. COVER: Tyrone Power, Ava Gardner, Mel Ferrer, Errol Flynn.

5123 Sunbonnet Sue (Monogram, 1945, Gale Storm, Phil Regan).

Sunbonnet Sue—Will Cobb (w), Gus Edwards (m), Shapiro Bernstein. COVER: Gale Storm, Phil Regan.

5124 Sun Comes Up, The (MGM, 1949, Jeanette MacDonald, Lloyd Nolan).

Cousin Ebenezer—William Katz (w), André Previn (m), Robbins. COVER: Jeanette MacDonald, Lloyd Nolan.

5125 Sunday in New York (MGM, 1963, Cliff Robertson, Jane Fonda).

Hello—Roland Everett (w), Peter Nero (m), Hastings; More in Love/ Sunday in New York—Carroll Coates (w), Peter Nero (m), Hastings. COVER: Cliff Robertson, Jane Fonda, Rod Taylor.

5126 Sundown (United Artists, 1941, Gene Tierney, Bruce Cabot).

I'll Meet You at Sundown—Jack Betzner, Irving Mills (w,m), Mills. COVER: Bruce Cabot, Gene Tierney.

5127 Sundowners, The (Warner Bros., 1960, Robert Mitchum, Deborah Kerr).

Sundowners Theme—Dimitri Tiomkin (m), Witmark. COVER: Robert Mitchum, Deborah Kerr.

5128 Sundown on the Prairie (Monogram, 1939, Tex Ritter, Dorothy Faye).

Sundown on the Prairie—Albert Von Tilzer, Harry MacPherson (w, m), Southern. COVER: Tex Ritter.

5129 Sunflower (Embassy, 1969, Sophia Loren, Marcello Mastroianni).

Loss of Love—Bob Merrill (w), Henry Mancini (m), Northridge. COVER: Sophia Loren, Marcello Mastroianni.

5130 Sunny (First National, 1930, Marilyn Miller, Laurence Gray).

I Was Alone/Who—Otto Harbach, Oscar Hammerstein (w), Jerome Kern (m), Harms. COVER: Marilyn Miller.

5131 Sunny (RKO, 1941, Anna Neagle, Ray Bolger).

Dye Love Me/Sunny/Sunshine/ Two Little Lovebirds/Who—Otto Harbach, Oscar Hammerstein (w), Jerome Kern (m), Harms. COVER: Anna Neagle, John Carroll.

5132 Sunny Side of the Street (Columbia, 1951, Frankie Laine, Billy Daniels).

I'm Gonna Live Till I Die (B)— Al Hoffman, Walter Kent, Mann Curtis (w,m), Feldman; Love of a

Gypsy—Morris Stoloff, Fred Karger (w,m), Mood; On the Sunny Side of the Street—Dorothy Fields (w), Jimmy McHugh (m), Shapiro Bernstein. COVER: Frankie Laine, Billy Daniels, Terry Moore.

5133 Sunny Side Up (Fox, 1929, Janet Gaynor, Charles Farrell).

Aren't We All/If I Had a Talking Picture of You/Pickin' Petals Off o' Daisies/Sunny Side Up/Turn on the Heat/You Find the Time, I'll Find the Place—B. G. DeSylva, Lew Brown, Ray Henderson (w,m), DBH. COVER: Janet Gaynor.

5134 Sunny Skies (Tiffany, 1930, Benny Rubin, Marceline Day).

Laugh Song—Val Burton, Will Jason, Benny Rubin (w,m), Sunkist; Must Be Love/Sunny Days/Wanna Find a Boy/You for Me—Val Burton, Will Jason (w,m), Bibo Lang. COVER: Benny Rubin, Marceline Day, Rex Lease, Marjorie Kane.

5135 Sunrise (Fox, 1927, Janet Gaynor, George O'Brien).

Sunrise and You—Arthur Penn (w, m), Witmark. COVER: Janet Gaynor, George O'Brien.

5136 Sunset Boulevard (Paramount, 1950, William Holden, Gloria Swanson).

Charmaine/Diane—Erno Rapee, Lew Pollack (w,m), Miller; Paramount-Don't-Want-Me Blues—Jay Livingston, Ray Evans (w,m), Paramount. COVER: William Holden, Nancy Olson, Jay Livingston, Ray Evans, and girls.

5137 Sunset Strip Case, The (Grand National, 1938, Sally Rand, Reed Hadley).

I'd Rather Look at You—Sam Coslow (w,m), Mills. COVER: Sally Rand.

5138 Sunshine Ahead (Universal, 1940, Eddie Pola, Betty Astell).

Sunshine Ahead (B)—Reg Connelly, Jack Rolls (w,m), Campbell. COVER: Jack Payne.

5139 Sunshine of Paradise Alley (Chadwick, 1926, Barbara Bed-

ford, Kenneth McDonald).

Sunshine of Paradise Alley (B)—Walter Ford (w), John Bratton (m), Witmark. COVER: Barbara Bedford.

5140 Sunshine Susie (The Office Girl) (RKO, 1932, Renate Muller, Jack Hulbert).

Today I Feel So Happy—Desmond Carter, Frank Eyton (w), Paul Abraham (m), Harms. COVER: Renata Muller.

5141 Sunshine Trail, The (First National, 1923, Douglas MacLean, Edith Roberts).

The Sunshine Trail—Arthur Francis(w), George Gershwin (m), Harms. COVER: Douglas MacLean.

5142 Sun-Up (MGM, 1925, Lucille LaVerne, Conrad Nagel).

It's Sun-up Now—Eugene Lockhart (w,m), Lockhart. COVER: Lucille LaVerne.

5143 Sun Valley Serenade (20th Century-Fox, 1941, Sonja Henie, John Payne).

Chattanooga Choo Choo/I Know Why/It Happened in Sun Valley/Kiss Polka—Mack Gordon (w), Harry Warren (m), Feist. COVER: Glenn Miller, Sonja Henie, John Payne, Milton Berle, Lynn Bari.

5144 Super Dad (Buena Vista, 1974, Bob Crane, Kurt Russell).

Los Angeles/These Are the Best Times/When I'm Near You—Shane Tatum (w,m), Wonderland. COVER: Kurt Russell, Bob Crane, Kathleen Cody.

5145 Superfly (Warner, 1972, Ron O'Neal, Carl Lee).

Freddie's Dead/Superfly—Curtis Mayfield (w,m), Curtom. COVER: Ron O'Neal.

5146 Superman (Warner, 1978, Gene Hackman, Marlon Brando).

Can You Read My Mind?—Leslie Bricusse (w), John Williams (m), Warner; Superman Theme/Superman Piano Suite/Superman-Seven Themes —John Williams (m), Warner. COVER: Christopher Reeves.

5147 Superman III (Warner,

1983, Christopher Reeves, Richard Pryor).

Superman III-Love Theme—Giorgio Moroder (m), Warner; Superman III-Five Themes—John Williams, Giorgio Moroder, Keith Forsey (w, m), Warner. COVER: Christopher Reeves, Richard Pryor.

5148 Surf Party (20th Century-Fox, 1964, Bobby Vinton, Pat Morrow).

Pearly Shells—Webley Edwards, Leon Pober (w,m), Criterion. COVER: Blue and white cover with title only.

5149 Surrender (Universal, 1927, Mary Philbin, Ivan Mosjukine).

Surrender—Jeff Edwards, Haven Gillespie, Egbert Van Alstyne (w, m), Remick. COVER: Mary Philbin.

5150 Surrender (Fox, 1931, Warner Baxter, Leila Hyams).

Zulu Chant—F. Tresselt (w,m), Movietone. COVER: Black and white cover with title only.

5151 Survive (Paramount, 1976, Hugo Stiglitz, Norma Lazaran).

Survive Theme—Gerald Fried (m), RSO. COVER: Plane Crash and Survivors.

5152 Survivors (Columbia, 1983, Walter Matthau, Robin Williams).

Survivors Theme—Paul Chihara (m), Golden Torch. COVER: Walter Matthau, Robin Williams.

5153 Susan Slept Here (RKO, 1954, Dick Powell, Debbie Reynolds).

Hold My Hand—Jack Lawrence, Richard Myers (w,m), Raphael. COVER: Dick Powell, Debbie Reynolds.

5154 Susie Steps Out (United Artists, 1946, David Bruce, Nita Hunter).

Bop Bop That Did It! (PC)—Eddie Cherkose (w), Hal Borne (m), Crystal; When You're Near (PC)—Hal Borne (w,m), Crystal. COVER: None.

5155 Suspense (Monogram, 1946, Belita, Barry Sullivan).

With You in My Arms—B. A. Dunham (w), Dan Alexander (m), Crystal. COVER: Barry Sullivan, Belita.

5156 Suzanna (United Artists, 1922, Mabel Normand, Leon Barry).

Suzanna—Benny Davis, Archie Gottler (w,m), Witmark. COVER: Mabel Normand.

5157 Suzy (MGM, 1936, Jean Harlow, Franchot Tone).

Did I Remember—Harold Adamson, Walter Donaldson (w,m), Feist. COVER: Jean Harlow, Franchot Tone, Cary Grant.

5158 Swan, The (MGM, 1956, Grace Kelly, Alec Guinness).

The Swan-Theme—Bronislau Kaper (m), Miller. COVER: Grace Kelly.

5159 Swanee River (Sono Art World Wide, 1931, Grant Withers, Thelma Todd).

River Stay 'Way from My Door—Mort Dixon (w), Harry Woods (m), Shapiro Bernstein. COVER: Black and white cover with title only.

5160 Swanee River (20th Century-Fox, 1939, Don Ameche, Andrea Leeds).

Jeannie with the Light Brown Hair (PC)—Stephen Foster (w,m), Acwell; Swanee River-39 Songs—Stephen Foster (w,m), ABC. COVER: Don Ameche, Andrea Leeds—(Al Jolson with movie scenes on back cover).

5161 Swashbuckler, The (Universal, 1976, Robert Shaw, James Earl Jones).

Swashbuckler Love Theme—John Addison (m), Leeds. COVER: Robert Shaw.

5162 Sweater Girl (Paramount, 1942, Eddie Bracken, June Preisser).

I Don't Want to Walk Without You/I Said No/Sweater Girl/What Gives Out Now—Frank Loesser (w), Jule Styne (m), Paramount. COVER: Eddie Bracken, and College Students.

5163 Sweden Heaven or Hell (Embassy, 1969, Documentary on Swedish Behaviors).

Mah-Na Mah-Na—Piero Umiliani

(m), Marks; You Tried to Warn Me—
L. MacDonald (w), Piero Umiliani
(m), Marks. COVER: Movie Scenes.

5164 Sweepings (RKO, 1933,
Lionel Barrymore, Gregory Ratoff).

Sweepings-Theme—Max   Steiner
(m), Sam Fox. COVER: RKO
Tower.

5165 Sweepstakes (RKO, 1931,
Eddie Quinlan, James Gleason).

My Sweetheart—Mort Harris (w),
Ted Snyder (m), Feist. COVER:
Eddie Quinlan, Marion Nixon.

5166 Sweet Adeline (Chadwick,
1926, Charles Ray, Gertrude Olmstead).

Sweet Adeline—Richard Girard
(w), Harry Armstrong (m), Witmark.
COVER: Charles Ray, Gertrude Olmstead.

5167 Sweet Adeline (Warner
Bros., 1935, Irene Dunne, Donald
Woods).

Don't Ever Leave Me/Here Am I/
Lonely Feet/Twas Not So Long Ago/
We Were So Young/Why Was I Born
—Oscar Hammerstein (w), Jerome
Kern (m), Harms. COVER: Irene
Dunne.

5168 Sweet and Lowdown (20th
Century-Fox, 1944, Linda Darnell,
Lynn Bari).

Chug Chug Choo Choo Chug/Hey
Bub! Let's Have a Ball/I'm Making
Believe—Mack Gordon (w), James
Monaco (m), BVC; I've Found a
New Baby—Jack Palmer, Spencer
Williams (w,m), Williams; Ten Days
with Baby—Mack Gordon (w), James
Monaco (m), BVC. COVER: Lynn
Bari, Jack Oakie, Linda Darnell,
Benny Goodman.

5169 Sweet Bird of Youth
(MGM, 1962, Paul Newman, Geraldine Page).

Ebb Tide—Carl Sigman (w), Robert Maxwell (m), Columbia. COV-
ER: Blue and white cover with title
only.

5170 Sweet Charity (Universal,
1969, Shirley MacLaine, John Mc-
Martin).

Big Spender/If My Friends Could
See Me Now/I Love to Cry at Wed-
dings/I'm a Brass Band/It's a Nice
Face/My Personal Property/Rhythm
of Life/Sweet Charity/There's Gotta
Be Something Better Than This/
Where Am I Going?—Dorothy Fields
(w), Cy Coleman (m), Notable.
COVER: Shirley MacLaine, John
McMartin, Chita Rivera, Paula Kelly.

5171 Sweet Dreams (Tri-Star,
1986, Jessica Lange, Ed Harris).

Sweet Dreams-Twelve Songs—
Hank Williams, Willie Nelson, Bob
Wills (w,m), Columbia. COVER:
Jessica Lange, Ed Harris.

5172 Sweetheart of Sigma Chi
(Monogram, 1933, Mary Carlisle,
Buster Crabbe).

Fraternity Walk/It's Spring Again
—Ted FioRito, Edward Ward, George
Waggner (w,m), Remick. COVER:
Mary Carlisle, Buster Crabbe.

5173 Sweetheart of Sigma Chi
(Monogram, 1946, Elyse Knox, Ross
Hunter).

And Then It's Heaven—Eddie Sei-
ler, Sol Marcus, Al Kaufman (w,m),
Remick; Five Minutes More—Sammy
Cahn (w), Jule Styne (m), Melrose;
Penthouse Serenade—Will Jason, Val
Burton (m), Paramount; Sweetheart
of Sigma Chi—Byron Stokes, Dud-
leigh Vernor (w,m), Melrose; Wolf
Song—Merle Maddern, Lanier Dar-
win (w,m), Melrose. COVER: Elyse
Knox.

5174 Sweetheart of the Campus
(Columbia, 1941, Ruby Keeler,
Ozzie Nelson).

Beat It Out/Here We Go Again/
Tap Happy—Eddie Cherkose (w),
Jacques Press (m), Mills; Tom Tom—
Walter Samuels (w,m), Mills; When
the Glee Club Swings the Alma Mater
—Charles Newman, Walter Samuels
(w,m), Mills; Where?—Jacques Kra-
keur (w,m), Mills; Zig Me Baby with
a Gentle Zag—Eddie Cherkose (w),
Jacques Press (m), Mills. COVER:
Ruby Keeler, Ozzie Nelson, Harriet
Hilliard.

5175 Sweetheart of the Fleet (Columbia, 1942, Joan Davis, Jinx Falkenburg).

All Over the Place—Frank Eyton, Noel Gay (w,m), Mills; I Surrender Dear—Gordon Clifford (w), Harry Barris (m), Mills. COVER: Joan Davis, Jinx Falkenburg, and Movie Scene.

5176 Sweetheart of the Navy (Grand National, 1937, Eric Linden, Cecilia Parker).

I Want You to Want Me/Sweetheart of the Navy—Jack Stern, Harry Tobias (w,m), Mills. COVER: Eric Linden, Cecilia Parker.

5177 Sweethearts (MGM, 1938, Jeanette MacDonald, Nelson Eddy).

Cricket on the Hearth—Robert Smith (w), Victor Herbert (m), Schirmer; Every Lover Must Meet His Fate/ Mademoiselle/On Parade/Pretty as a Picture/Summer Serenade/Sweethearts/Wooden Shoes—Bob Wright, Chet Forrest (w), Victor Herbert (m), Schirmer. COVER: Jeanette MacDonald, Nelson Eddy.

5178 Sweethearts of the U.S.A. (Monogram, 1944, Una Merkel, Parkya Karkus).

All the Latin I Know Is "Si Si"/ That Reminds Me—Charles Newman (w), Lew Pollack (m), Southern. COVER: Una Merkel, Parkya Karkus, Donald Novis, Lillian Cornell.

5179 Sweetie (Paramount, 1929, Nancy Carroll, Helen Kane).

Alma Mammy/Bear Down Pelham—George Marion (w), Richard Whiting (m), Famous; He's So Unusual—Abner Silver, Al Sherman, Sam Lewis (w,m), Shapiro Bernstein; I Think You'll Like It/My Sweeter Than Sweet/Prep Step—George Marion (w), Richard Whiting (m), Famous. COVER: Nancy Carroll, Jack Oakie, Helen Kane.

5180 Sweet Kitty Bellairs (Warner Bros., 1930, Claudia Dell, Walter Pidgeon).

Here Is My Heart/Highwayman's Song/My Love, I'll Be Waiting for You/You, I Love But You—Walter O'Keefe, Bobby Dolan (w,m), Harms. COVER: Claudia Dell.

5181 Sweet Love Bitter (Film Two, 1965, Don Murray, Dick Gregory).

Della's Dream—Mal Waldron (m), Piedmont; Loser's Lament—Paul Evans, Paul Parnes (w), Mal Waldron (m), Piedmont. COVER: Don Murray, Dick Gregory.

5182 Sweet Moments (Paramount, 1939, Russ Morgan and Orchestra).

Am I Proud—Teddy Powell, Leonard Whitcup (w,m), Sun; Holiday in Toyland/ Old Heart of Mine—Teddy Powell, Leonard Whitcup (w,m), Famous; Sweet Moments—Dave Franklin, Russ Morgan (w,m), Famous. COVER: Russ Morgan.

5183 Sweet Music (Warner Bros., 1935, Rudy Vallee, Ann Dvorak).

Ev'ry Day—Irving Kahal (w), Sammy Fain (m), Remick; Fare Thee Well Annabelle—Mort Dixon (w), Allie Wrubel (m), Remick; Good Green Acres of Home—Irving Kahal (w), Sammy Fain (m), Remick; I See Two Lovers/Outside—Mort Dixon (w), Allie Wrubel (m), Remick; Sweet Music—Al Dubin (w), Harry Warren (m), Remick; There Is a Tavern in the Town—William Hills (w, m), Shapiro Bernstein; There's a Different You in Your Heart—Irving Kahal (w), Sammy Fain (m), Remick. COVER: Rudy Vallee.

5184 Sweet November (Warner Bros., 1968, Sandy Dennis, Anthony Newley).

Sweet November—Leslie Bricusse, Anthony Newley (w,m), Warner. COVER: Sandy Dennis, Anthony Newley.

5185 Sweet Ride, The (20th Century-Fox, 1968, Tony Franciosa, Michael Sarrazin).

The Sweet Ride—Lee Hazlewood (w,m), Fox. COVER: Movie Scenes.

5186 Sweet Rosie O'Grady (20th Century-Fox, 1943, Betty Grable, Robert Young).

Get Your Police Gazette (BW)/ Goin' to the County Fair/My Heart Tells Me/My Sam—Mack Gordon (w), Harry Warren (m), BVC; Sweet Rosie O'Grady—Maude Nugent (w,m), Mills; Waitin' at the Church—Fred Leigh (w), Henry Pether (m), Harms; Where, Oh Where Is the Groom (BW)/ Wishing Waltz—Mack Gordon (w), Harry Warren (m), BVC. COVER: Betty Grable, Robert Young, Adolphe Menjou.

5187   Sweet Smell of Success (United Artists, 1957, Burt Lancaster, Tony Curtis).

Goodbye Baby—William Engvick (w), Fred Katz, Chico Hamilton (m), Calyork. COVER: Burt Lancaster, Tony Curtis.

5188   Sweet Surrender (Universal, 1935, Frank Parker, Helen Lind).

Day You Were Born (BW)/I'm So Happy I Could Cry—Edward Heyman (w), Dana Suesse (m), Harms; Let Us Have Peace—Neville Fleeson (w), Mabel Wayne (m), Chappell; Love Makes the World Go Round—Edward Heyman (w), Dana Suesse (m), Harms; Please Put on Your Wraps and Toddle Home—Neville Fleeson (w), Mabel Wayne (m), Chappell; Sweet Surrender/Take This Ring— Edward Heyman (w), Dana Suesse (m), Harms; Twenty-Four Hours a Day—Arthur Swanstrom (w), James Hanley (m), Harms. COVER: Frank Parker, Tamara, Helen Lynd, Russ Brown, Abe Lyman.

5189   Swimmer, The (Columbia, 1968, Burt Lancaster, Janice Rule).

Carnival (PC)—Marvin Hamlisch (m), April; Send for Me in Summer (PC)—Charles Burr (w), Marvin Hamlisch (m), April. COVER: None.

5190   Swinger, The (Paramount, 1966, Ann Margret, Tony Franciosa).

The Swinger—Dory Previn (w), André Previn (m), Famous. COVER: Ann Margret, Tony Franciosa.

5191   Swing Fever (MGM, 1943, Kay Kyser, Marilyn Maxwell).

I Planted a Rose—Lew Brown, Nacio Herb Brown, Ralph Freed (w, m), Feist; Mississippi Dream Boat— Lew Brown, Ralph Freed (w), Sammy Fain (m), Feist; You're So Indifferent—Mitchell Parish (w), Sammy Fain (m), Feist. COVER: Kay Kyser, Lena Horne, Marilyn Maxwell.

5192   Swing for Sale (Vitaphone, 1936, Hal Le Roy).

Swing for Sale—Sammy Cahn (w), Saul Chaplin (m), Remick. COVER: Hal Le Roy.

5193   Swing High (RKO, 1930, Helen Twelvetrees, Fred Scott).

Do You Think That I Could Grow on You?—Mack Gordon (w), Abner Silver (m), Shapiro Bernstein; It Must Be Love—Mack Gordon (w), Abner Silver (w), Shapiro Bernstein; Shoo The Hoo-Doo Away—Mort Harris (w), Ted Snyder (m), Sherman Clay; There's Happiness Over the Hill— Ray Egan (w), Henry Sullivan (m), Shapiro Bernstein; With My Guitar and You—Mort Harris, Ed Heyman (w), Ted Snyder (m), Sherman Clay. COVER: Helen Twelvetrees, Fred Scott.

5194   Swing High Swing Low (Paramount, 1937, Carole Lombard, Fred MacMurray).

I Hear a Call to Arms/Panamania —Sam Coslow, Al Siegel (w,m), Famous; Spring Is in the Air—Ralph Freed (w), Charley Kisco (m), Famous; Swing High Swing Low— Ralph Freed (w), Burton Lane (m), Famous; Then It Isn't Love—Leo Robin, Ralph Rainger (w,m), Famous. COVER: Carole Lombard, Fred MacMurray.

5195   Swing Hostess (PRC, 1945, Martha Tilton, Iris Adrian).

Say It with Love—Jay Livingston, Ray Evans, Lewis Bellim (w,m), Global. COVER: Black and white cover with title only.

5196   Swing It Professor (Ambassador, 1937, Pinky Tomlin, Paula Stone).

I'm Richer Than a Millionaire/ I'm Sorta Kinda Glad I Met You/ Old Fashioned Melody—Connie Lee, Al Heath, Buddy LeRoux (w,m), Mills. COVER: Pinky Tomlin.

5197 Swing It Soldier (Radio Revels of 1942) (Universal, 1941, Ken Murray, Don Wilson).

I'm Gonna Swing My Way Up to Heaven—Eddie Cherkose (w), Jacques Press (m), American. COVER: Frances Langford, Don Wilson, Ken Murray.

5198 Swing Parade of 1946 (Monogram, 1946, Gale Storm, Phil Regan).

After All This Time—Ken Thompson, Paul DeFur (w,m), Chelsea; Caldonia—Fleecie Moore (w,m), Morris; Don't Worry Bout That Mule—William Davis, Duke Groner, Charles Stewart (w,m), Preview. COVER: Gale Storm, Phil Regan, Three Stooges, Connee Boswell.

5199 Swing Shift (Warner Bros., 1984, Goldie Hawn, Kurt Russell).

Someone Waits for You—Will Jennings (w), Peter Allen (m), Warner. COVER: Goldie Hawn.

5200 Swing Time (RKO, 1936, Fred Astaire, Ginger Rogers).

Bojangles of Harlem/Fine Romance/Never Gonna Dance/Pick Yourself Up/Waltz in Swingtime/ Way You Look Tonight—Dorothy Fields (w), Jerome Kern (m), Chappell. COVER: Fred Astaire, Ginger Rogers.

5201 Swing Your Lady (Warner Bros., 1938, Humphrey Bogart, Frank McHugh).

Hill Billy from Tenth Avenue/Old Apple Tree, The—Jack Scholl (w), M. K. Jerome (m), Witmark. COVER: Humphrey Bogart, Frank McHugh, Louise Fazenda.

5202 Swiss Family Robinson (Buena Vista, 1960, John Mills, Dorothy McGuire).

My Heart Was an Island-Theme— Terry Gilkyson (w,m), Wonderland. COVER: Sketch of Movie Scenes.

5203 Swiss Miss (MGM, 1938, Stan Laurel, Oliver Hardy).

Cricket Song/I Can't Get Over the Alps/Yo Ho Dee O Lay Hee— Arthur Quenzer (w), Phil Charig (m), Shapiro Bernstein. COVER: Laurel and Hardy, Della Lind, Walter Woolf King.

5204 Sword and the Rose, The (Buena Vista, 1963, Richard Todd, Glynis Johns).

Sword and the Rose, The—Fred Spielman, George Brown (w,m), Wonderland. COVER: Movie Scenes.

5205 Sword in the Stone, The (Buena Vista, 1963, Ricky Sorenson, Sebastian Cabot).

Sword in the Stone-Six Songs— Richard Sherman, Robert Sherman (w,m), Wonderland. COVER: Cartoon.

5206 Sylvester the Cat (Warner Bros., 1950, Cartoon).

Sylvester the Cat/Sylvester the Cat's Nine Lives—Tedd Pierce, Warren Foster (w,m), Witmark. COVER: Cartoon.

5207 Sylvia (Paramount, 1965, George Maharis, Carroll Baker).

Sylvia—Paul F. Webster (w), David Raksin (m), Famous. COVER: George Maharis, Carroll Baker.

5208 Symphony for a Massacre (Seven Arts, 1965, Michel Auclair, Claude Dauphin).

Symphony for a Massacre-Theme (PC)—Michel Magne (m), Warner. COVER: None.

5209 Syncopation (RKO, 1929, Morton Downey, Dorothy Lee).

Do Something—Bud Green, Sam Stept (w,m), Green Stept; I'll Always Be in Love with You—Herman Ruby, Bud Green, Sam Stept (w,m), Green Stept; Jericho—Leo Robin (w), Richard Myers (m), Harms; Mine Alone— Clifford Grey (w), Richard Myers (m), Harms. COVER: Morton Downey, Dorothy Lee.

5210 Syncopation (RKO, 1942, Adolphe Menjou, Jackie Cooper).

Under a Falling Star—Rich Hall

(w), Leith Stevens (m), Peer. COVER: Adolphe Menjou, Jackie Cooper, Bonita Granville.

5211 Synthetic Sin (First National, 1929, Colleen Moore, Antonio Moreno).

Betty—Harold Christy (w), Nat Shilkret (m), Feist. COVER: Colleen Moore.

5212 Tabu (Paramount, 1931, Documentary of South Sea Islands).

Tabu—Sam Coslow (w), Franke Harling (m), Famous. COVER: Natives.

5213 Tahiti Honey (Republic, 1943, Simone Simon, Dennis O'-Keefe).

Any Old Port in a Storm/I'm a Cossack/In a Ten Gallon Hat/Koni Plenty Hu Hu—Charles Newman (w), Lew Pollack (m), Carmichael; Tahiti Honey—Jule Styne, George Brown, Sol Meyer (w,m), Mills; This Gets Better Ev'ry Minute/You Could Hear a Pin Drop—Charles Newman (w), Lew Pollack (m), Carmichael. COVER: Simone Simon, Dennis O'Keefe.

5214 Tahiti My Island (Shoestring, 1951, Paul Moe, Adeline Tetahamani).

Tahiti My Island—Mack David, Lela Rogers (w), Victor Young (m), Paramount. COVER: Natives.

5215 Tahiti Nights (Columbia, 1945, Mary Treen, Jinx Falkenburg).

Cockeyed Mayor of Kaunakakai—A. Anderson, Al Stillman (w), A. Anderson (m), Marks. COVER: Native Girl.

5216 Tail Spin (20th Century-Fox, 1939, Alice Faye, Constance Bennett).

Are You in the Mood for Mischief?—Mack Gordon, Harry Revel (w,m), Robbins; Go In and Out the Window—Lew Pollack, Walter Bullock (w,m), Mills. COVER: Alice Faye.

5217 Take a Chance (Paramount, James Dunn, Cliff Edwards).

Come Up and See Me Sometime—Arthur Swanstrom (w), Louis Alter (m), Harms; Eadie Was a Lady—B. G. DeSylva (w), Richard Whiting, Herb Nacio Brown (m), Harms; It's Only a Paper Moon—Billy Rose, E. Y. Harburg (w), Harold Arlen (m), Harms; New Deal Rhythm—E. Y. Harburg (w), Roger Edens (m), Harms; Night Owl—Herman Hupfield (w,m), Harms; Should I Be Sweet?—B. G. DeSylva (w), Vincent Youmans (m), Harms. COVER: Lillian Roth, June Knight, Buddy Rogers.

5218 Take a Giant Step (United Artists, 1959, Johnny Nash, Estelle Henley).

Take a Giant Step—Jay Livingston, Ray Evans (w,m), Hecht-Lancaster. COVER: Johnny Nash.

5219 Take It Big (Paramount, 1944, Jack Haley, Harriet Hilliard).

Love and Learn/Take It Big—Jerry Seelen, Lester Lee (w,m), Paramount. COVER: Jack Haley, Harriet Hilliard, Ozzie Nelson.

5220 Take Me Out to the Ball Game (MGM, 1949, Frank Sinatra, Gene Kelly).

If It Weren't for the Irish (PC)—Ralph Blane (w), Harry Warren (m), Four Jays; It's Fate Baby It's Fate/O'Brien to Ryan to Goldberg/Right Girl for Me—Betty Comden, Adolph Green (w), Roger Edens (m), Robbins; Strictly U.S.A.—Roger Edens (w,m), Robbins; Take Me Out to the Ball Game—Jack Norworth (w), Albert Von Tilzer (m), Broadway; Yes Indeedy—Betty Comden, Adolph Green (w), Roger Edens (m), Robbins. COVER: Frank Sinatra, Gene Kelly, Esther Williams.

5221 Take My Tip (GB, 1937, Jack Hulbert, Cecily Courtneidge).

Birdie Out of a Cage/I Was Anything But Sentimental—Sam Lerner, Al Goodhart, Al Hoffman (w,m), Mills. COVER: Jack Hulbert, Cicely Courtneidge.

5222 Take the Heir (Big Four, 1929, Edward Everett Horton, Dorothy Devore).

I Always Knew It Would Be You—

Cliff Hess (w), J. M. Coopersmith (m), Remick. COVER: Edward Everett Horton, Dorothy Devore.

5223 Take the High Ground (MGM, 1953, Richard Widmark, Karl Malden).

Julie—Charles Wolcott (w), Dimitri Tiomkin (m), Miller; Take the High Ground—Ned Washington (w), Dimitri Tiomkin (m), Robbins. COVER: Richard Widmark, Karl Malden, Elaine Stewart.

5224 Take the Money and Run (Cinerama, 1969, Woody Allen, Janet Margolin).

Get Yourself a Dream—Walter Marks (w), Marvin Hamlisch (m), Ampco. COVER: Woody Allen.

5225 Talent Scout (Warner Bros., 1937, Donald Woods, Jeanne Madden).

Born to Love—Jack Scholl (w), M. K. Jerome (m), Harms. COVER: Donald Woods, Jeanne Madden.

5226 Tale of Two Cities, A (Rank America, 1958, Dirk Bogarde, Dorothy Tutin).

A Tale of Two Cities (B)—Richard Addinsell (m), Chappell. COVER: Dirk Bogarde.

5227 Tales of Beatrix Potter (Peter Rabbit and the Tales of Beatrix Potter) (MGM, 1971, Erin Geraghty, Joan Benham).

Tales of Beatrix Potter-Eight Songs—John Lanchbery (m), Sam Fox. COVER: Animals.

5228 Tales of Manhattan (20th Century-Fox, 1942, Charles Boyer, Rita Hayworth).

Fare Thee Well to El Dorado—Paul F. Webster (w), Sol Kaplan (m), Mills; Glory Day—Leo Robin (w), Ralph Rainger (m), Robbins; Journey to Your Lips/Tale of Manhattan—Paul F. Webster (w), Sol Kaplan (m), Mills. COVER: Charles Boyer, Ginger Rogers, Rita Hayworth, Henry Fonda, and Others.

5229 Talk About a Lady (Columbia, 1946, Jinx Falkenberg, Forrest Tucker).

Avocado/I Never Had a Dream Come True/You Gotta Do Whatcha Gotta Do—Allan Roberts, Doris Fisher (w,m), Sun. COVER: Jinx Falkenberg, Forrest Tucker, Stan Kenton.

5230 Talk of Hollywood, The (World Wide, 1929, Nat Carr, Fay Marbe).

Daughter of Mine/I Get It from My Daddy/No No Babie/Sarah/They Say Goodnight in the Morning—Al Piantadosi, Nat Carr, Jack Glogan (w,m), Triangle. COVER: Nat Carr, Fay Marbe.

5231 Tall Dark and Handsome (20th Century-Fox, 1941, Cesar Romero, Virginia Gilmore).

Hello Ma! I Done It Again/I'm Alive and Kickin'/Wishful Thinking—Leo Robin (w), Ralph Rainger (m), Robbins. COVER: Cesar Romero, Virginia Gilmore, Milton Berle, Charlotte Greenwood.

5232 Tall Men, The (20th Century-Fox, 1955, Clark Gable, Jane Russell).

Tall Men—Ken Darby (w,m), Robbins. COVER: Clark Gable, Jane Russell, Robert Ryan.

5233 Tall Story (Warner Bros., 1960, Anthony Perkins, Jane Fonda).

Tall Story—Dory Langdon (w), André Previn, Shelly Manne (m), Mansfield. COVER: Anthony Perkins, Jane Fonda.

5234 Tall Tan and Terrific (Astor, 1946, Mantan Moreland, Monte Hawley).

Stop This Tune/Sweetness of You—Eugene Roland, Mickey Castle (w, m), Casey Sisson; Teasing Me—Eugene Roland, Mickey Castle, LeRoy Hodges (w,m), Casey Sisson. COVER: Mantan Moreland, Francine Everett, Monte Hawley, and Others.

5235 Tamahine (MGM, 1963, Nancy Kwan, John Fraser).

Tamahine (B)—Malcolm Arnold (m), Harms. COVER: Black and white cover with title only.

5236 Tammy and the Bachelor

(Universal, 1957, Debbie Reynolds, Leslie Nielsen).

Tammy—Jay Livingston, Ray Evans (w,m), Northern. COVER: Debbie Reynolds.

5237 Tammy Tell Me True (Universal, 1961, Sandra Dee, John Gavin).

Tammy Tell Me True—Dorothy Squires (w,m), Hunter. COVER: Sandra Dee.

5238 Tangier (Universal, 1946, Maria Montez, Robert Paige).

Love Me Tonight—George Waggner (w), Gabriel Ruiz (m), Southern. COVER: Maria Montez, Robert Paige, Sabu.

5239 Tango Bar (Paramount, 1935, Carlos Gardel, Rosite Moreno).

Arrabel Amargo—A. LePera, Carlos Gardel (w,m), Famous. COVER: Carlos Gardel.

5240 Tanned Legs (RKO, 1929, Ann Pennington, June Clyde).

Tanned Legs/With You, With Me/You're Responsible—Sydney Clare (w), Oscar Levant (m), Harms. COVER: Legs.

5241 Tap (Tri-Star, 1989, Gregory Hines, Suzzanne Douglas).

All I Want Is Forever—Diane Warren (w,m), Realsongs. COVER: Gregory Hines.

5242 Tap Roots (Universal, 1948, Van Heflin, Susan Hayward).

Tap Roots-Themes—Frank Skinner (m), Skinner. COVER: Black and white cover with title only.

5243 Taras Bulba (United Artists, 1962, Tony Curtis, Yul Brynner).

Wishing Star-Theme—Mack David (w), Franz Waxman (m), Unart. COVER: Tony Curtis, Yul Brynner.

5244 Tarnished Angel (RKO, 1938, Ann Miller, Sally Eilers).

It's the Doctor's Orders—Lew Brown (w), Sammy Fain (m), Feist. COVER: Ann Miller.

5245 Tars and Spars (Columbia, 1946, Alfred Drake, Janet Blair).

I'm Glad I Waited for You/Kiss Me Hello/Love Is a Merry Go Round —Sammy Cahn (w), Jule Styne (m), Shapiro Bernstein. COVER: Alfred Drake, Janet Blair.

5246 Tarzan the Fearless (Principal, 1933, Buster Crabbe, Jacqueline Wells).

Call of Tarzan—Felton Kaufman, Bernie Grossman (w), Jerry Herst (m), Southern. COVER: Buster Crabbe, Jacqueline Wells.

5247 Task Force (Warner Bros., 1949, Jane Wyatt, Gary Cooper).

If You Could Care—Arthur Wimperis (w), Herman Darewski (m), Remick. COVER: Gary Cooper, Jane Wyatt.

5248 Tattered Dress, The (Universal, 1957, Jeff Chandler, Elaine Stewart).

Remember When? (PC)—Al Skinner (w), Frank Skinner (m), Skinner. COVER: None.

5249 Tattler, The (Here Comes Carter, or Loud Speaker Lowdown) (Warner Bros., 1936, Ross Alexander, Ann Nagel).

Thru the Courtesy of Love/You on My Mind—Jack Scholl (w), M. K. Jerome (m), Witmark. COVER: Ross Alexander, Ann Nagel, Glenda Farrell.

5250 Taxi Driver (Columbia, 1976, Robert DeNiro, Jodie Foster).

Taxi Driver Theme—Bernard Herrmann (m), Colgems. COVER: Robert DeNiro.

5251 Teachers (MGM, 1984, Nick Nolte, JoBeth Williams).

Edge of a Dream—Adams Vallance (w,m), Irving; Interstate Love Affair—Jack Blades (w,m), Kid Bird; Teacher, Teacher—Adams Vallance (w,m), Irving; Understanding—Bob Seger (w,m), Gear. COVER: An Apple with a Fuse.

5252 Teacher's Pet (Paramount, 1956, Clark Gable, Doris Day).

Girl Who Invented Rock and Roll/Teacher's Pet—Joe Lubin (w,m), Daywin; Teacher's Pet Mambo—Joe

Lubin, Luis Alvarez (w,m), Daywin. COVER: Clark Gable, Doris Day.

5253   Tea for Two (Warner Bros., 1950, Doris Day, Gordon MacRae).

Crazy Rhythm—Irving Caesar (w), Joseph Meyer, Roger Kahn (m), Harms; Do Do Do—Ira Gershwin (w), George Gershwin (m), Harms; I Know That You Know—Anne Caldwell (w), Vincent Youmans (m), Harms; I Want to Be Happy/Tea for Two—Irving Caesar (w), Vincent Youmans (m), Harms. COVER: Doris Day, Gordon MacRae.

5254   Teenage Rebel (20th Century-Fox, 1956, Ginger Rogers, Michael Rennie).

Cool It Baby—Carroll Coates (w), Lionel Newman (m), Weiss Barry; Dodie—Edmund Goulding, Ralph Freed (w,m), Miller. COVER: Ginger Rogers, Michael Rennie, Betty Lou Keim.

5255   Tell It to a Star (Republic, 1945, Ruth Terry, Robert Livingston).

Tell It to a Star—Shirley Botwin (w,m), Indigo. COVER: Ruth Terry.

5256   Tell Me That You Love Me Junie Moon (Paramount, 1970, Liza Minelli, Ken Howard).

Tell Me That You Love Me Junie Moon—Philip Springer (w,m), Famous. COVER: Liza Minelli.

5257   Temperamental Wife, A (First National, 1919, Constance Talmadge, Wyndham Standing).

Temp'rament—Ernest Luz, Cheerfull Willoughby (w,m), Berlin. COVER: Constance Talmadge, Wyndham Standing.

5258   Tempest (United Artists, 1928, John Barrymore, Camilla Horn).

Out of the Tempest—Edward Grossman, Ted Ward (w,m), Harms. COVER: John Barrymore, Camilla Horn.

5259   Tempest (Paramount,1959, Sylvana Mangano, Van Heflin).

Tempest—Eddie White, Mack Wolfson (w,m), Famous. COVER: Van

Heflin, and Movie Scenes.

5260   Tempo of Tomorrow (Paramount, 1939, Richard Himber and Orchestra).

Alone in the Station—Richard Himber, Naomi Shaw (w,m), Famous; Gettin' Off—Tot Seymour, Vee Lawnhurst (w,m), Famous; Listen to My Heart—Abner Silver, Lanny Ross, Al Neiburg (w,m), Famous; Prom Waltz—Leo Robin, Ralph Rainger (w,m), Famous. COVER: Richard Himber.

5261   "10" (Ten) (Orion, 1979, Julie Andrews, Dudley Moore).

It's Easy to Say—Robert Wells (w), Henry Mancini (m), Warner; Ravel's Bolero—Maurice Ravel (m), Presser. COVER: Dudley Moore, Bo Derek.

5262   Ten Cents a Dance (Columbia, 1935, Barbara Stanwyck, Ricardo Cortez).

Ten Cents a Dance—Lorenz Hart (w), Richard Rodgers (m), Harms. COVER: Barbara Stanwyck.

5263   Ten Cents a Dance (Columbia, 1944, Jilly Lloyd, Jane Frazee).

Someday Somewhere—Joan Brooks, Jack Segal, Dick Miles (w,m), Chelsea. COVER: Jimmy Lloyd, Jane Frazee.

5264   Ten Commandments, The (Paramount, 1929, Richard Dix, Rod LaRoque).

Love's Old Sweet Song—Clifton Bingham (w), J. A. Molloy (m), Richmond Robbins. COVER: Richard Dix, Edythe Chapman.

5265   Ten Commandments, The (Paramount, 1956, Charlton Heston, Anne Baxter).

Ten Commandments-Love and Ambition/Ten Commandments-Piano Score—Elmer Bernstein (m), Famous. COVER: Charlton Heston, Yul Brynner.

5266   Tender Is the Night (20th Century-Fox, 1961, Jennifer Jones, Jason Robards).

Tender Is the Night—Paul F. Webster (w), Sammy Fain (m), Miller.

COVER: Jennifer Jones, Jason Robards.

5267 Tender Mercies (UAFD, 1983, Robert Duvall, Tess Harper).

Over You—Austin Roberts, Bobby Hart (w,m), Colgems. COVER: Brown and white cover with title only.

5268 Tender Moment, The (Maron, 1971, Natalie Delon, Renaud Verley).

Where Did Our Summers Go?—Don Black (w), Francis Lai (m), Regent. COVER: Natalie Delon, Renaud Verley.

5269 Tender Trap, The (MGM, 1955, Frank Sinatra, Debbie Reynolds).

Tender Trap, The—Sammy Cahn (w), James Van Heusen (m), Barton. COVER: Frank Sinatra, Debbie Reynolds.

5270 Ten Gentlemen from West Point (20th Century-Fox, 1945, Maureen O'Hara, George Montgomery).

Caissons Go Rolling Along, The—Edmund Gruber (w,m), Shapiro Bernstein. COVER: Maureen O'Hara, George Montgomery, John Sutton, and Cadets.

5271 Tennessee's Partner (RKO, 1955, John Payne, Ronald Reagan).

Heart of Gold—Dave Franklin (w), Lou Forbes (m), HR Music. COVER: Rhonda Fleming.

5272 Tension at Table Rock (RKO, 1956, Richard Egan, Dorothy Malone).

Ballad of Wes Tancred/Wait for Love—Robert Wells (w), Josef Myrow (m), Mills. COVER: Richard Egan, Dorothy Malone.

5273 Ten Thousand Bedrooms (MGM, 1957, Dean Martin, Anna Maria Alberghetti).

Man Who Plays the Mandolin—Marilyn Keith, Alan Bergman (w), G. Faniciulli (m), Raphael; Money Is a Problem/Only Trust Your Heart/Ten Thousand Bedrooms/You I Love—Sammy Cahn (w), Nicholas

Brodszky (m), Feist. COVER: Dean Martin, Anna Maria Alberghetti, Eva Bartok.

5274 Ten Who Dared (Buena Vista, 1960, Brian Keith, John Beal).

Jolly Rovers/Roll Along—Lawrence Watkin, Stan Jones (w,m), Wonderland; Ten Who Dared—Stan Jones (w,m), Wonderland. COVER: Black and white cover with title only.

5275 Tequila Sunrise (Warner Bros., 1988, Mel Gibson, Kurt Russell).

Surrender to Me—Richard Marx, Ross Vannelli (w,m), SBX. COVER: Clouds and Sunrise.

5276 Teresa (MGM, 1951, Pier Angeli, John Ericson).

Teresa—Mack David (w), Jerry Livingston (m), Robbins. COVER: Pier Angeli.

5277 Terms of Endearment (Paramount, 1983, Shirley MacLaine, Debra Winger).

Terms of Endearment Theme—Michael Gore (m), Ensign. COVER: Shirley MacLaine, Debra Winger.

5278 Terror of Tiny Town, The (Columbia, 1938, Billy Curtis, Yvone Moray).

Daughter of Sweet Caroline/Down on the Sunset Trail/Hey Look Out I'm Gonna Make Love to You/Laugh Your Troubles Away/Missus Jack and Missus Jill—Lew Porter (w, m), Gilbert. COVER: Billy Curtis, and Movie Scenes.

5279 Tess (Columbia, 1979, Nastassia Kinski, Peter Firth).

Tess-Love Theme—Philippe Sarde (m), Renn. COVER: Nastassia Kinski.

5280 Tess of the Storm Country (Famous, 1915, Mary Pickford, Jean Hersholt).

Tess o' the Storm Country, My Fisher Maid—Charles Patrick (w), Bob Allen (m), Rossiter. COVER: Mary Pickford, Jean Hersholt.

5281 Tess of the Storm Country

(Paramount, 1933, Janet Gaynor, Charles Farrell).

Tess of the Storm Country-Love Theme—Louis DeFrancesco (m), Movietone. COVER: Black and white cover with title only.

5282 Testing Block, The (Paramount, 1920, Eve Novak, William Hart).

Darling Nellie Grey—B. R. Hanby (w,m), Remick. COVER: William Hart, and Movie Scenes.

5283 Texan, The (Paramount, 1930, Gary Cooper, Fay Wray).

To Hold You—L. Wolfe Gilbert, Abel Baer (w,m), Famous. COVER: A Dancing Couple.

5284 Texans, The (Paramount, 1938, Randolph Scott, Joan Bennett).

Silver on the Sage—Leo Robin, Ralph Rainger (w,m), Paramount. COVER: Randolph Scott, Joan Bennett.

5285 Texans Never Cry (Columbia, 1951, Gene Autry, Pat Buttram).

Texans Never Cry—Gene Autry, Oakley Haldeman, Hank Fort (w,m), Western. COVER: Gene Autry.

5286 Texas Across the River (Universal, 1966, Dean Martin, Alain Delon).

Texas Across the River—Sammy Cahn (w), James Van Heusen (m), Northern. COVER: Dean Martin, Alain Delon, Joey Bishop.

5287 Texas Brooklyn and Heaven (United Artists, 1948, Guy Madison, Diana Lynn).

Texas Brooklyn and Heaven—Ervin Drake, Jimmy Shirl (w,m), Unart. COVER: Guy Madison, Diana Lynn.

5288 Texas Carnival (Carnival Story) (MGM, 1951, Esther Williams, Red Skelton).

It's Dynamite (BW)/Whoa Emma!/Young Folks Should Get Married—Dorothy Fields (w), Harry Warren (m), Miller. COVER: Esther Williams, Red Skelton, Howard Keel, Ann Miller.

5288a Texas John Slaughter (Disney, 1958, Tom Tryon, Norma Moore).

Texas John Slaughter—Stan Jones (w,m), Disney. COVER: Black and white cover with title only.

5289 Texas Lady (RKO, 1955, Claudette Colbert, Barry Sullivan).

Texas Lady—Johnnie Mann (w), Paul Sawtell (m), Deerheaven. COVER: Claudette Colbert.

5290 Texas Rangers (Paramount, 1936, Fred MacMurray, Jack Oakie).

I Can't Play My Banjo (PC)—Jack Scholl (w), Phil Boutjalie (m), Paramount; Texas Rangers Song—Sam Coslow, Harry Behn (w,m), Famous. COVER: Fred MacMurray, Jean Parker.

5291 Texas Romance, A (Janua, 1964, Documentary of Texas Town).

A Texas Romance-Ten Themes—Harvey Schmidt (m), Chappell. COVER: Black and white cover with title only.

5292 Texas Stampede (Columbia, 1939, Charles Starrett, Iris Meredith).

Boss Is Hangin' Out a Rainbow, The (VS)/Chant of the Wanderer (VS)/Grab Your Saddle Horn and Blow (VS)/Rise an' Shine (VS)—Bob Nolan (w,m), American. COVER: Bob Nolan.

5293 Tex Rides with the Boy Scouts (Grand National, 1938, Tex Ritter, Marjorie Reynolds).

Girl of the Prairie (VS)—Tex Ritter, Ted Choate (w,m), Cole; Headin' for My Texas Home—Frank Sanucci (w,m), Sam Fox. COVER: Tex Ritter.

5294 Thank God It's Friday (Columbia, 1978, Terri Nunn, Valerie Landsburg).

Je T'aime Moi Non Plus—Serge Gainsbourg (m), Painted Desert; Last Dance, The—Paul Jabara (w,m), Primus; Love Masterpiece—Josef Powell, Art Posey, Hal Davis (w,m), Jobete; Lovin' Livin' and Givin'—Kenneth Stover, Pam Davis (w,m), Jobete; Thank God It's Friday—Alec

Costandinos (w,m), Cafe Americana; Thank God It's Friday-Eighteen Songs—Paul Jabara, Donna Summer, Giorgio Moroder (w,m), Almo. COVER: Cartoon Sketches.

5295 Thanks a Million (20th Century-Fox, 1935, Dick Powell, Ann Dvorak).

I'm Sittin' High on a Hilltop/I've Got a Pocket Full of Sunshine/New Orleans/Sugar Plum/Thanks a Million —Gus Kahn (w), Arthur Johnston (m), Robbins. COVER: Dick Powell, Fred Allen, Paul Whiteman, Ann Dvorak, Patsy Kelly.

5296 Thanks for Everything (20th Century-Fox, 1938, Adolphe Menjou, Jack Oakie).

Thanks for Everything/You're the World's Fairest—Mack Gordon, Harry Revel (w,m), Robbins. COVER: Tony Martin, Jack Oakie, Binnie Barnes, Adolphe Menjou, Jack Haley.

5297 Thanks for Listening (Conn, 1937, Pinky Tomlin, Aileen Pringle).

I Like to Make Music—Connie Lee, Al Heath, Buddy LeRoux (w, m), Gilbert; In the Name of Love— Connie Lee, Pinky Tomlin (w,m), Gilbert. COVER: Pinky Tomlin.

5298 Thanks for the Memory (Paramount, 1938, Bob Hope, Shirley Ross).

Two Sleepy People—Frank Loesser (w), Hoagy Carmichael (m), Famous. COVER: Bob Hope, Shirley Ross.

5299 Thank Your Lucky Stars (Warner Bros., 1943, Bette Davis, Humphrey Bogart).

Dreamer, The/Goodnight Good Neighbor/How Sweet You Are/ I'm Ridin' for a Fall/Ice Cold Katy/ Love Isn't Born/Thank Your Lucky Stars/They're Either Too Young or Too Old—Frank Loesser (w), Arthur Schwartz (m), Harms. COVER: Bette Davis, Humphrey Bogart, Errol Flynn, John Garfield, and others.

5300 That Certain Age (Univer-

sal, 1938, Deanna Durbin, Jackie Cooper).

Be a Good Scout—Harold Adamson (w), Jimmy McHugh (m), Robbins; Daydreams—Ann Ronell (w), Charles Gounod (m), Schirmer; Girls of Cadiz—Ann Ronell (w), Leo Delibes (m), Schirmer; My Own—Harold Adamson (w), Jimmy McHugh (m), Robbins; Romeo and Juliet Waltz—Ann Ronell (w), Charles Gounod (m), Schirmer; That Certain Age/You're Pretty As a Picture—Harold Adamson (w), Jimmy McHugh (m), Robbins. COVER: Deanna Durbin.

5301 That Certain Feeling (Paramount, 1957, Bob Hope, Eva Marie Saint).

Hit the Road to Dreamland— Johnny Mercer (w), Harold Arlen (m), Famous. COVER: Bob Hope, Eva Marie Saint.

5302 That Dangerous Age (If This Be Sin) (United Artists, 1949, Myrna Loy, Roger Livesey).

Song of Capri (B)—Norman Newell (w), Mischa Spoliansky (m), Chappell. COVER: Myrna Loy, Roger Livesey.

5303 That Darn Cat (Buena Vista, 1965, Hayley Mills, Dean Jones).

That Darn Cat—Richard Sherman, Robert Sherman (w,m), Wonderland. COVER: A Cat.

5304 That Funny Feeling (Universal, 1965, Bobby Darin, Sandra Dee).

That Funny Feeling—Bobby Darin (w,m), TM Music. COVER: Bobby Darin, Sandra Dee.

5305 That Girl from Paris (RKO, 1937, Lily Pons, Gene Raymond).

Call to Arms, The/Love and Learn/ Moon Face/My Nephew from Nice/ Seal It with a Kiss—Edward Heyman (w), Arthur Schwartz (m), Chappell. COVER: Sketch of Girl.

5306 That Kind of Woman (Paramount, 1959, Sophia Loren, Tab Hunter).

That Kind of Woman—Hal David (w), Burt Bacharach (m), Paramount. COVER: Sophia Loren, Tab Hunter.

5307 That Lady in Ermine (20th Century-Fox, 1948, Betty Grable, Douglas Fairbanks).

Melody Has to Be Right, The/Ooh! What I'll Do/There's Something About Midnight/This Is the Moment—Leo Robin (w), Frederick Hollander (m), Miller. COVER: Betty Grable.

5308 That Midnight Kiss (MGM, 1949, Mario Lanza, Kathryn Grayson).

I Know, I Know, I Know—Bob Russell (w), Bronislau Kaper (m), Robbins; They Didn't Believe Me—Herbert Reynolds (w), Jerome Kern (m), Harms; Mamma Mia, Che Vo Sape? (VS)—Walter Hirsch (w), E. Nutile (m), Robbins; Una Furtiva Lagrima (VS)—Walter Hirsch (w), G. Donizetti (m), Robbins. COVER: Mario Lanza, Kathryn Grayson, Ethel Barrymore, Keenan Wynn.

5309 That Night in Rio (Road to Rio) (20th Century-Fox, 1941, Alice Faye, Don Ameche).

Baron Is in Conference, The (BW)—Mack Gordon (w), Harry Warren (m), Robbins; Boa Noite—Mack Gordon (w), Harry Warren (m), Miller; Cae Cae—Roberto Martins (w,m), Peer; Chic Chica Bum Chic—Mack Gordon (w), Harry Warren (m), Robbins; I Yi Yi Yi Yi/They Met in Rio—Mack Gordon (w), Harry Warren (m), Miller. COVER: Alice Faye, Don Ameche, Carmen Miranda.

5310 That Night with You (Once Upon a Dream) (Universal, 1945, Franchot Tone, Susanna Foster).

Once Upon a Dream—Jack Brooks (w), Hans Salter (m), Robbins. COVER: Franchot Tone, Susanna Foster, David Bruce, Louise Allbritton.

5311 That's a Good Girl (United Artists, 1934, Jack Buchanan, Elsie Randolph).

Now That I've Found You (B)—Douglas Furber (w), Philip Braham (m), Chappell; Oo! La La! (B)—Douglas Furber (w), Walter Jurmann (m), Chappell. COVER: Jack Buchanan, Elsie Randolph.

5312 That's Dancing (MGM, 1984, Ray Bolger, Mikhail Baryshnikov).

Invitation to Dance—K. Carnes, Dave Ellingson, B. Fairweather, M. Page (w,m), April; That's Dancing—Larry Grossman, Ellen Fitzhugh (w), Henry Mancini (m), April. COVER: Movie Scenes with Dancers.

5313 That's Entertainment I (MGM, 1974, Bing Crosby, Judy Garland).

Boy Next Door, The—Hugh Martin, Ralph Blane (w,m), Feist; If I Only Had a Brain/Over the Rainbow—E. Y. Harburg (w), Harold Arlen (m), Feist; San Francisco—Gus Kahn (w), Bronislau Kaper, Walter Jurmann (m), Robbins; Singin' in the Rain—Arthur Freed (w), Nacio Herb Brown (m), Robbins; Take Me Out to the Ball Game—Jack Norworth (w), Albert Von Tilzer (m), Vogel; That's Entertainment—Howard Dietz (w), Arthur Schwartz (m), Chappell; Trolley Song, The—Hugh Martin, Ralph Blane (w,m), United Artists; We're Off to See the Wizard—E. Y. Harburg (w), Harold Arlen (m), Feist; That's Entertainment I-Sixty Songs—Various Composers, Big Three. COVER: Bing Crosby, Frank Sinatra, Gene Kelly, and others.

5314 That's Entertainment II (MGM, 1976, Fred Astaire, Gene Kelly).

That's Entertainment II-Forty Songs—Various Composers, Big Three. COVER: Fred Astaire, Gene Kelly, Frank Sinatra, and others.

5315 That's Life (Columbia, 1986, Julie Andrews, Jack Lemmon).

Life in a Looking Glass—Leslie Bricusse (w), Henry Mancini (m), Golden Torch. COVER: Jack Lemmon.

5316 That's My Boy (Paramount, 1951, Jerry Lewis, Dean Martin).

Ballin' the Jack—Jim Burris (w), Chris Smith (m), Marks; I'm in the Mood for Love—Dorothy Fields, Jimmy McHugh (w,m), Robbins. COVER: Jerry Lewis, Dean Martin, Polly Bergen.

5317 That's Right, You're Wrong (RKO, 1939, Kay Kyser, Adolphe Menjou).

Answer Is Love, The—Charles Newman (w), Sam Stept (m), BVC; Chatterbox—Allan Roberts (w), Jerome Brainin (m), Chappell; Happy Birthday to Love—Dave Franklin (w, m), BVC; I'm Fit to Be Tied—Walter Donaldson (w,m), Feist; Little Red Fox, The—Jim Kern, Hy Heath, Johnny Lange (w), Lew Porter (m), Feist; Scatterbrain (BW)—Johnny Burke (w), Keene Bean, Frankie Masters (m), BVC; Thinking of You—Walter Donaldson, Paul Ash (w,m), Feist. COVER: Kay Kyser, Ginny Simms, Harry Babbitt.

5318 That's the Spirit (Universal, 1945, Peggy Ryan, Jack Oakie).

Baby Won't You Please Come Home—Clarence Williams, Charles Warfield (w,m), Williams. COVER: Peggy Ryan, Johnny Coy.

5319 That's the Way It Is (MGM, 1970, Elvis Presley Documentary).

How the Web Was Woven—Clive Westlake, David Most (w,m), Aberbach; Stranger in the Crowd—Winfield Scott (w,m), Aberbach. COVER: Elvis Presley.

5320 That Tennessee Beat (20th Century-Fox, 1966, Sharon DeBord, Earl Richards).

I'm Sorry (PC)/That Tennessee Beat (PC)—Merle Travis (w,m), Tree. COVER: None.

5321 That Texas Jamboree (Columbia, 1947, Ken Curtis, Jeff Donnell).

Never Tangle with Old John Law (VS)—Ken Curtis, Lee Penny (w,m), Preview. COVER: Ken Curtis.

5322 That Uncertain Feeling (United Artists, 1941, Merle Oberon, Melvin Douglas).

That Uncertain Feeling—Sylvia Dee (w), Joseph Shalit (m), BMI. COVER: Merle Oberon, Melvyn Douglas, Burgess Meredith.

5323 Theft of the Mona Lisa, The (RKO, 1932, Willy Forst, Trude Von Molo).

Tell Me Why You Smile, Mona Lisa?—Raymond Egan (w), Robert Stolz (m), Feist. COVER: Mona Lisa.

5324 Their Mad Moment (Fox, 1932, Warner Baxter, Dorothy Mackaill).

Fiesta Song—William Kernell (w), Jose Mojica (m), Movietone; Hold My Hand/Little Flower of Love—William Kernell (w,m), Movietone. COVER: Black and white cover with title only.

5325 Their Own Desire (MGM, 1929, Norma Shearer, Belle Bennett).

Blue Is the Night—Fred Fisher (w, m), Robbins. COVER: Norma Shearer.

5326 Them (Warner Bros., 1954, James Whitmore, Edmund Gwenn).

Them—Al Hoffman, Dick Manning (w,m), Spinlan. COVER: Animals.

5327 Then I'll Come Back to You (World, 1916, Alice Brady, Jack Sherrill).

Then I'll Come Back to You—Robert Roden (w), Peter DeRose, Ivan Reid (m), Havilland. COVER: Alice Brady.

5328 Then She'll Be Mine (Capa, 1968, Stars Unknown).

You Came Along (PC)—R. Kipling (w,m), Capa. COVER: None.

5329 Theodora Goes Wild (Columbia, 1934, Irene Dunne, Melvyn Douglas).

Be Still My Heart—Allan Flynn, Jack Egan (w,m), Broadway. COVER: Gray and orange cover with title only.

5330 There's a Girl in My Heart (Allied Artists, 1949, Lee Bowman, Elyse Knox).

Roller Skating Song, The—Robert Bilder (w,m), Mass. COVER: Guy Lombardo.

5331 There's Magic in Music (Paramount, 1941, Allan Jones, Susanna Foster).

Fireflies on Parade—Ann Ronell (w,m), Famous. COVER: Allan Jones, Susanna Foster.

5332 There's No Business Like Show Business (20th Century-Fox, 1954, Ethel Merman, Marilyn Monroe).

After You Get What You Want You Don't Want It/Heat Wave/If You Believe/Lazy/Let's Have Another Cup of Coffee/Man Chases a Girl, A/Marie/Play a Simple Melody/ Pretty Girl Is Like a Melody, A/Remember/Sailor's Not a Sailor, A/ There's No Business Like Show Business/When the Midnight Choo Choo Leaves for Alabam'/You'd Be Surprised—Irving Berlin (w,m), Berlin. COVER: Ethel Merman, Marilyn Monroe, Donald O'Connor, Dan Dailey, Mitzi Gaynor.

5333 There Was a Time (Renhall, 1972, Stars Unknown).

Monty Bloom (PC)—George Bounds (w), June Cool (m), Renhall. COVER: None.

5334 These Dangerous Years (Dangerous Youth) (Warner Bros., 1957, Frankie Vaughan, George Baker).

Isn't This a Lovely Evening (B)— Bert Waller, Peter Moreton (w,m), Robbins. COVER: Frankie Vaughan.

5335 These Glamour Girls (MGM, 1939, Lana Turner, Lew Ayres).

Loveliness—Bob Wright, Chet Forrest (w), Edward Ward (m), Feist. COVER: Lana Turner, Lew Ayres.

5336 These Thousand Hills (20th Century-Fox, Don Murray, Richard Egan).

These Thousand Hills—Ned Washington (w), Harry Warren (m), Robbins. COVER: Don Murray, Richard Egan, Lee Remick.

5337 They All Laughed (20th Century-Fox, 1981, Audrey Hepburn, Ben Gazzara).

Kentucky Nights—Eric Kaz (w,m), Unart; One Day Since Yesterday— Earl Poole, Peter Bogdanovich (w, m), House Cash. COVER: Audrey Hepburn, Ben Gazzara, John Ritter, and others.

5338 They Came to Cordura (Columbia, 1959, Gary Cooper, Rita Hayworth).

They Came to Cordura—Sammy Cahn (w), James Van Heusen (m), Barton. COVER: Gary Cooper, Rita Hayworth, Van Heflin, Tab Hunter.

5339 They Gave Him a Gun (MGM, 1937, Spencer Tracy, Gladys George).

A Love Song of Long Ago—Gus Kahn (w), Sigmund Romberg (m), Feist. COVER: Spencer Tracy, Franchot Tone, Gladys George.

5340 They Got Me Covered (RKO, 1943, Bob Hope, Dorothy Lamour).

Palsy-Walsy—Johnny Mercer (w), Harold Arlen (m), Mills. COVER: Bob Hope, Dorothy Lamour.

5341 They Had to See Paris (Fox, 1929, Will Rogers, Irene Rich).

I Could Do It for You—Con Conrad, Sidney Mitchell, Archie Gottler (w,m), DBH. COVER: Will Rogers.

5342 They Learned About Women (MGM, 1929, Bessie Love, J. C. Nugent).

Ain't You Baby?/Does My Baby Love?/Harlem Madness/He's the Kind of a Pal/Man of My Own, A/ There Will Never Be Another Mary— Jack Yellen (w), Milton Ager (m), AYD. COVER: Van and Schenck.

5343 They Meet Again (RKO, 1940, Jean Hersholt, Dorothy Lovett).

Rhythm Is Red an' White an' Blue, The—David Greggory (w), Al Moss (m), BMI; When Love Is New—Jack Owens (w), Claude Sweeten (m), BMI. COVER: Jean Hersholt, Dorothy Lovett.

5344 They Met in Argentina (RKO, 1941, Maureen O'Hara, James Ellison).

Amarillo/Cutting the Cane/Simpatica/You've Got the Best of Me—Lorenz Hart (w), Richard Rodgers (m), Chappell. COVER: Maureen O'Hara, James Ellison.

5345 They Shoot Horses, Don't They? (ABC, 1969, Jane Fonda, Michael Sarrazin).

Easy Come, Easy Go—Edward Heyman (w), John Green (m), Warner. COVER: Jane Fonda, Gig Young, and Others.

5346 They Were Expendable (MGM, 1945, Robert Montgomery, John Wayne).

Marcheta—Victor Schertzinger (w, m), Cole; To the End of the End of the World—Earl Brent (w), Herbert Stochart (m), Feist. COVER: Robert Montgomery, Donna Reed, John Wayne.

5347 Thief in New York City, A (Dimension Seventy, 1969, Stars Unknown).

Slpendor in the Dark—Tony Villa (w,m), Euclidean. COVER: A Man and a Car.

5348 Thief in Paradise, A (First National, 1925, Ronald Colman, Aileen Pringle).

Thief in Paradise, A—Bartley Costello (w), Alfred Solman (m), Sam Fox. COVER: Ronald Colman, Aileen Pringle.

5349 Thief of Bagdad (United Artists, 1929, Douglas Fairbanks, Julanne Johnston).

The Thief of Bagdad—Dailey Paskman (w,m), Marks. COVER: Douglas Fairbanks.

5350 Thief of Bagdad (United Artists, 1940, Conrad Veidt, Sabu).

I Want to Be a Sailor—Robert Denham (w), Miklos Rozsa (m), Chappell; Since Time Began—William Kernell (w), Nic Roger (m), Chappell. COVER: Sabu.

5351 Thief of Hearts (Paramount, 1984, Steven Bauer, Barbara Williams).

Thief of Hearts-Love Theme—Harold Faltermeyer (m), Famous. COVER: Steven Bauer.

5352 Thief Who Came to Dinner (Warner Bros., 1973, Ryan O'Neal, Jacqueline Bisset).

Thief Who Came to Dinner-Theme—Henry Mancini (m), Warner. COVER: Ryan O'Neal, Jacqueline Bisset.

5353 Thieves (Paramount, 1976, Marlo Thomas, Charles Grodin).

Thieves—Sammy Cahn (w), George Barrie (m), Brut. COVER: Marlo Thomas, Charles Grodin.

5354 Things Are Tough All Over (Columbia, 1982, Cheech Marin, Tommy Chong).

Chilly Winds of Chicago—Richard Marin, Gaye DeLorne (w,m), Colgems. COVER: Cheech and Chong.

5355 Things of Life, The (Columbia, 1970, Romy Schneider, Michel Piccoli).

Things of Life, The—Hal Shaper (w), Philippe Sarde (m), Arcola. COVER: Romy Schneider, Michel Piccoli.

5356 Things to Come (United Artists, 1936, Raymond Massey, Ralph Richardson).

Ballet for Children (B)/Things to Come-March (B)/Things to Come Prologue-Epilogue (B)—Arthur Bliss (m), Chappell. COVER: A Large Telescope.

5357 Thin Ice (20th Century-Fox, 1937, Sonja Henie, Tyrone Power).

My Secret Love Affair/My Swiss Hilly Billy/Overnight—Sidney Mitchell (w), Lew Pollack (m), Movietone. COVER: Sonja Henie.

5358 Think Fast Mr. Moto (20th Century-Fox, 1937, Peter Lorre, Virginia Field).

Shy Violet—Sidney Clare (w), Harry Akst (m), Movietone. COVER: Purple and white cover with title only.

5359 Third Alarm, The (FBO, 1923, Ralph Lewis, John Walker).

A Fire Laddie, Just Like My Daddy—Bartley Costello (w), Johnnie Tucker (m), Mittenthal. COVER: A Fireman.

5360 Third Day, The (Warner Bros., 1965, Elizabeth Ashley, George Peppard).

Love Me Now—Jay Livingston, Ray Evans (w), Percy Faith (m), Witmark. COVER: Elizabeth Ashley, George Peppard.

5361 Third Kiss, The (Paramount, 1919, Vivian Martin, Harrison Ford).

The Third Kiss—Bernie Grossman (w), Billy Frisch (m), Stern. COVER: Vivian Martin, Harrison Ford.

5362 Third Man, The (Selznick, 1950, Joseph Cotten, Orson Welles).

Cafe Mozart Waltz/Harry Lime Theme—Anton Karas (m), Chappell; Third Man Theme—Walter Lord (w), Anton Karas (m), Chappell. COVER: Orson Welles, Joseph Cotten, Valli.

5363 Third Man on the Mountain (Buena Vista, 1959, James MacArthur, Michael Rennie).

Climb the Mountain—By Dunham (w), Franklyn Marks (m), Disney; Good Night Valais—G. Haenni, Tom Adair (w,m), Disney. COVER: James MacArthur, Janet Munro.

5364 Thirteenth Man, The (Monogram, 1937, Weldon Heyburn, Inez Courtney).

My Topic of Conversation—Joseph Myrow, Milton Royce (w,m), Mills. COVER: Eadie Adams, Weldon Heyburn, Inez Courtney.

5365 Thirty (Warner Bros., 1959, Jack Webb, William Conrad).

Boy!—W. Bowers, N. Beckman, B. Rosen, S. Lipkin (w), Don Ralke (m), Mark VII. COVER: Jack Webb.

5366 Thirty Nine Steps, The (United Artists, 1978, David Warner, Robert Powell).

Thirty Nine Steps Main Theme and Hannah's Theme—Ed Welch (m), Unart. COVER: Robert Powell.

5367 Thirty Seconds Over To- kyo (MGM, 1944, Spencer Tracy, Van Johnson).

Sweetheart of All My Dreams—Art Fitch, Kay Fitch, Bert Lowe (w, m), Shapiro Bernstein. COVER: Spencer Tracy, Van Johnson, Phyllis Thaxter.

5368 Thirty-Six Hours (MGM, 1965, James Garner, Eva Marie Saint).

A Heart Must Learn to Cry—Paul F. Webster (w), Dimitri Tiomkin (m), Feist. COVER: James Garner, Eva Marie Saint, Rod Taylor.

5369 This Angry Age (Columbia, 1958, Anthony Perkins, Silvana Mangano).

Uh-Huh! The Crawl!—Nino Rota (m), Raleigh. COVER: Anthony Perkins, Silvana Mangano.

5370 This Could Be the Night (MGM, 1957, Jean Simmons, Paul Douglas).

This Could Be the Night—Sammy Cahn (w), Nicholas Brodszky (m), Robbins. COVER: Jean Simmons, Paul Douglas, Anthony Franciosa.

5371 This Earth Is Mine (Universal, 1959, Rock Hudson, Jean Simmons).

This Earth Is Mine—Sammy Cahn (w), James Van Heusen (m), Northern. COVER: Rock Hudson, Jean Simmons.

5372 This Happy Feeling (Universal, 1958, Debbie Reynolds, Curt Jurgens).

This Happy Feeling—Jay Livingston, Ray Evans (w,m), Carrie. COVER: Debbie Reynolds.

5373 This Is Cinerama Cinerama, 1952, Lowell Thomas).

America the Beautiful—Katharine Lee Bates, Samuel Ward (w,m), Cinerama. COVER: Red and black cover with title only.

5374 This Is Heaven (United Artists, 1929, Vilma Banky, James Hall).

Tell Me Daisy—Harry B. Smith (w), Hugo Riesenfeld (m), Berlin; This Is Heaven—Jack Yellen (w),

Harry Akst (m), AYB. COVER: Vilma Banky.

5375 This Is My Affair (His Affair) (20th Century-Fox, 1937, Robert Taylor, Barbara Stanwyck).

I Hum a Waltz—Mack Gordon, Harry Revel (w,m), Miller. COVER: Robert Taylor, Barbara Stanwyck.

5376 This Is My Love (RKO, 1954, Linda Darnell, Rick Jason).

This Is My Love—Hugh Brooke (w), Franz Waxman (m), Goldshen. COVER: Linda Darnell, Rick Jason.

5377 This Is the Army (Warner Bros., 1943, Irving Berlin, George Murphy).

American Eagles/Army's Made a Man Out of Me, The/How About a Cheer for the Navy/I Left My Heart at the Stage Door Canteen/I'm Getting Tired So I Can Sleep/That's What the Well Dressed Man in Harlem Will Wear/This Is the Army, Mr. Jones/What Does He Look Like That Boy of Mine/With My Head in the Clouds—Irving Berlin (w,m), This Is the Army Music. COVER: Soldiers.

5378 This Is the Life (20th Century-Fox, 1935, Jane Withers, Sally Blane).

Fresh from the Country/Got a New Kind-a Rhythm/Sandy and Me—Sidney Clare (w), Sam Stept (m), Movietone. COVER: Black and white cover with title only.

5379 This Is the Life (Universal, 1944, Donald O'Connor, Peggy Ryan).

You're a La La Palooza—Grace Shannon, Bill Crago (w,m), Southern. COVER: Donald O'Connor, Peggy Ryan.

5380 This Is the Night (Paramount, 1932, Lily Damita, Charles Ruggles).

This Is the Night-Sam Coslow (w), Ralph Rainger (m), Famous. COVER: Lily Damita.

5381 This Property Is Condemned (Paramount, 1966, Natalie Wood, Robert Redford).

Wish Me a Rainbow—Jay Livingston, Ray Evans (w,m), Famous. COVER: Natalie Wood, Robert Redford.

5382 This Time for Keeps (MGM, 1947, Esther Williams, Jimmy Durante).

Easy to Love—Cole Porter (w,m), Chappell; Hokey Joe—Juan Ricardo (w), Don Swan (m), Vanguard; I Love to Dance—Ralph Freed (w), Burton Lane (m), Feist; Un Poquito De Amor—Ralph Freed (w), Raul Soler, Xavier Cugat (m), Robbins; When It's Lilac Time on Mackinac Island—Lesley Kirk (w,m), Robbins. COVER: Esther Williams, Jimmy Durante, Lauritz Melchior, Johnnie Johnston.

5383 This Way Please (Paramount, 1937, Buddy Rogers, Betty Grable).

Delighted to Meet You—Sam Coslow (w,m), Popular; Love or Infatuation—Sam Coslow, Frederick Hollander (w,m), Popular; This Way Please—Sam Coslow, Al Siegel (w,m), Popular; Voom Voom—Sam Coslow (w,m), Popular. COVER: Buddy Rogers, Betty Grable, Mary Livingstone.

5384 This Week of Grace (RKO, 1933, Gracie Fields, Henry Kendall).

Mary Rose (B)—Harry Parr Davies (w,m), Day. COVER: Gracie Fields.

5385 Thomas Crown Affair, The (United Artists, 1968, Steve McQueen, Faye Dunaway).

His Eyes, Her Eyes (PC)/Windmills of Your Mind, The—Alan Bergman, Marilyn Bergman (w), Michel Legrand (m), Unart. COVER: Steve McQueen, Faye Dunaway.

5386 Thoroughbreds Don't Cry (MGM, 1937, Judy Garland, Mickey Rooney).

Got a Pair of New Shoes—Arthur Freed (w), Nacio Herb Brown (m), Robbins. COVER: Judy Garland, Mickey Rooney.

5387 Thoroughly Modern Millie (Universal, 1967, Julie Andrews, Mary Tyler Moore).

Baby Face—Benny Davis, Harry Akst (w,m), Remick; Charmaine—Erno Rapee, Lew Pollack (w,m), Miller; Do It Again—B. G. DeSylva (w), George Gershwin (m), New World; I Can't Believe That You're in Love with Me—Clarence Gaskill, Jimmy McHugh (w,m), Mills; Japanese Sandman—Raymond Egan (w), Richard Whiting (m), Remick; Jazz Baby—Blanche Merrill (w), M. K, Jerome (m), Mills; Jewish Wedding Song—Sylvia Neufeld (w,m), Northern: Jimmy—Jay Thompson (w,m), Northern; Poor Butterfly—John Golden (w), Raymond Hubbell (m), Harms; Rose of Washington Square—Ballard MacDonald, James Hanley (w,m), Shapiro Bernstein; Stumbling—Zez Confrey (w,m), Mills; Tapioca/Thoroughly Modern Millie—Sammy Cahn (w), James Van Heusen (m), Northern; Everybody Loves My Baby (VS)/I Found a New Baby (VS)—Jack Palmer, Spencer Williams (w,m), MCA; Looking at the World (VS)—Tommy Malie, Jimmy Steiger (w,m), MCA. COVER: Julie Andrews.

5388 Those Calloways (Buena Vista, 1964, Brian Keith, Vera Miles).

Angel—Jay Livingston, Ray Evans (w), Max Steiner (m), Disney; Cabin Raising Song—Richard Sherman, Robert Sherman (w,m), Disney. COVER: Johnny Tillotson.

5389 Those Daring Young Men in Their Jaunty Jalopies (Paramount, 1969, Tony Curtis, Susan Hampshire).

They're Playing Chester's Song/ Those Daring Young Men in Their Jaunty Jalopies— Ron Goodwin (w, m), Famous. COVER: Movie Scenes.

5390 Those Magnificent Men in Their Flying Machines (20th Century-Fox, 1966, Stuart Whitman, Sarah Miles).

Those Magnificent Men in Their Flying Machines—Ron Goodwin (w, m), Miller. COVER: Stuart Whitman, Sarah Miles, James Fox, Robert Morley.

5391 Those Redheads from Seattle (Paramount, 1953, Rhonda Fleming, Gene Barry).

Baby, Baby, Baby—Mack David (w), Jerry Livingston (m), Famous; Chica Boom—Bob Merrill (w,m), Santly Joy; I Guess It Was You All the Time—Johnny Mercer (w), Hoagy Carmichael (m), Famous; Mr. Banjo Man—Jay Livingston, Ray Evans (w, m), Famous; Once More—Bebe Blake (w), Leo Shukein (m), Famous. COVER: Rhonda Fleming, Teresa Brewer, Cynthia Bell.

5392 Those Three French Girls (MGM, 1930, Fifi D'Orsay, Cliff Edwards).

You're Simply Delish—Arthur Freed (w), Joseph Meyer (m), Robbins. COVER: Fifi D'Orsay, Yola D'Avril, Sandra Ravel.

5393 Those Who Dance (First National, 1924, Blanche Sweet, Warner Baxter).

I Love to Dance with You—Jack Bauer, Joe Mayer, James Scott (w, m), Bauer. COVER: Blanche Sweet.

5394 Thousand Clowns, A (United Artists, 1964, Jason Robards, Barbara Harris).

A Thousand Clowns—Gerry Mulligan, Judy Holiday (w,m), Unart. COVER: Jason Robards, Barbara Harris, Barry Gordon.

5395 Thousands Cheer (Private Miss Jones) (MGM, 1943, Judy Garland, Kathryn Grayson).

Honeysuckle Rose—Andy Razaf (w), Thomas Waller (m), Santly Joy; I Dug a Ditch—Lew Brown, Ralph Freed (w), Burton Lane (m), Feist; Joint Is Really Jumpin' in Carnegie Hall—Roger Edens, Ralph Blane, Hugh Martin (w,m), Feist; Let There Be Music—E. Y. Harburg (w), Earl Brent (m), Feist; Three Letters in the Mail Box—Paul F. Webster (w), Walter Jurmann (m), Feist; United Nations on the March—Harold Rome (w), D. Shostakovich (m), Feist; Daybreak (B)—Harold Adamson (w), Ferde Grofe (m), Albert. COVER: Lena Horne, Judy Garland, Kathryn Grayson, Jose Iturbi.

5396 Three Bad Men (Wild and Woolly) (20th Century-Fox, 1937, Jane Withers, Walter Brennan).

Whoa Whoopee Whoa Whipee— Sidney Clare (w), Harry Akst (m), Movietone. COVER: Red and white cover with title only.

5397 Three Bites of the Apple (MGM, 1967, David McCallum, Sylvia Koscina).

In the Garden Under the Tree— Paul F. Webster (w), David McCallum (m), Miller. COVER: David McCallum, and Girls.

5398 Three Blind Mice (20th Century-Fox, 1948, Loretta Young, Joel McCrea).

Isn't It Wonderful, Isn't It Swell— Sidney Mitchell (w), Lew Pollack (m), Miller. COVER: Loretta Young, Joel McCrea.

5399 Three Caballeros, The (RKO Disney, 1945, Aurora Miranda, Carmen Molina).

Angel-May-Care—Ervin Drake (w), Ary Barroso (m), Southern; Baia —Ray Gilbert (w), Ary Barroso (m), Southern; Jesusita En Chihuahua-Cactus Polka—Erwin Drake (w), Edward Plumb (m), Southern; Mexico—Ray Gilbert (w), Charles Wolcott (m), Southern; Three Caballeros, The—Ray Gilbert (w), Manuel Esperon (m), Harris; You Belong to My Heart—Ray Gilbert (w), Agustin Lara (m), LaSalle; Arroz Con Leche (VS)—Paul Smith (w,m), Melody Lane; Hey Mister Sunshine (VS)— Ray Gilbert (w), Charles Wolcott (m), Melody Lane; Zandunga-Cancion, Ranchera (VS)—Charles Wolcott (m), Melody Lane. COVER: Aurora Miranda, Carmen Molina, Dora Luz.

5400 Three Cheers for Love (Paramount, 1936, Robert Cummings, Eleanore Whitney).

Long Ago and Far Away/Swing Tap/Where Is My Heart—Leo Robin, Ralph Rainger (w,m), Popular. COVER: Robert Cummings, Eleanore Whitney.

5401 Three Cheers for the Boys (Follow the Boys) (Universal, 1945, George Raft, Vera Zorina).

Shoo Shoo Baby—Phil Moore (w,m), Leeds. COVER: The Andrews Sisters.

5402 Three Coins in the Fountain (20th Century-Fox, 1954, Clifton Webb, Dorothy McGuire).

Three Coins in the Fountain— Sammy Cahn (w), Jule Styne (m), Robbins. COVER: Clifton Webb, Dorothy McGuire, Jean Peters, Louis Jourdan.

5403 Three Daring Daughters (MGM, 1948, Jeanette MacDonald, Jose Iturbi).

Dickey Bird Song—Howard Dietz (w), Sammy Fain (m), Robbins; Where There's Love—Earl Brent (w), R. Strauss (m), Boosey Hawkes. COVER: Jeanette MacDonald, Jane Powell, Jose Iturbi.

5404 Three Days of the Condor (Paramount, 1975, Robert Redford, Faye Dunaway).

Three Days of the Condor Theme —David Grusin (m), Ensign. COVER: Robert Redford, Faye Dunaway.

5405 Three Flights Up (Dancing Sweeties) (Warner Bros., 1930, Grant Withers, Sue Carol).

Hullabaloo—Walter O'Keefe (w), Bobby Dolan (m), Witmark. COVER: Black and white cover with title only.

5406 Three for the Show (Columbia, 1955, Betty Grable, Jack Lemmon).

Down Boy—Harold Adamson (w), Hoagy Carmichael (m), Mills; How Come You Do Me Like You Do— Gene Austin, Roy Bergere (w,m), Mills. COVER: Betty Grable, Jack Lemmon, Marge and Gower Champion.

5407 365 Nights in Hollywood (Fox, 1934, Alice Faye, James Dunn).

My Future Star/Yes to You—
Sidney Clare (w), Richard Whiting
(m), Movietone. COVER: Alice
Faye, James Dunn.

**5408 Three in the Cellar (Up in
the Cellar)** (AIP, 1970, Wes Stern,
Joan Collins).

Didn't I Turn Out Nice?—Dory
Previn (w,m), Harlene. COVER:
Girls.

5409 Three Little Girls in Blue
(20th Century-Fox, 1946, June
Haver, Vivian Blaine).

Always the Lady/Farmer's Life
Is a Very Merry Life, A—Mack Gordon (w), Josef Myrow (m), BVC;
If You Can't Get a Girl in the Summertime—Bert Kalmar (w), Harry
Tierney (m), Mills; I Like Mike/On
the Boardwalk in Atlantic City—
Mack Gordon (w), Josef Myrow (m),
BVC; Somewhere in the Night—
Mack Gordon (w), Josef Myrow (m),
Triangle; This Is Always/Three Little
Girls in Blue/You Make Me Feel So
Young—Mack Gordon (w), Josef
Myrow (m), BVC. COVER: June
Haver, George Montgomery, Vivian
Blaine, Vera-Ellen.

5410 Three Little Pigs (Disney,
1933, Cartoon).

Who's Afraid of the Big Bad
Wolf? #1/Who's Afraid of the Big
Bad Wolf? #2—Frank Churchill, Ann
Ronell (w,m), Berlin. COVER: #1
Outside Scene, #2 Inside Scene.

5411 Three Little Sisters (Republic, 1944, Mary Lee, Cheryl
Walker).

Don't Forget the Girl Back Home
—Kim Gannon (w), Walter Kent
(m), Mills. COVER: Black and white
cover with title only.

5412 Three Little Words (MGM,
1950, Fred Astaire, Red Skelton).

All Alone Monday—Bert Kalmar
(w), Harry Ruby (m), Harms; Come
on Papa—Edgar Leslie, Harry Ruby
(w,m), Mills; I Love You So Much—
Bert Kalmar (w), Harry Ruby (m),
Harms; I Wanna Be Loved by You—
Bert Kalmar (w), Herbert Stothart,

Harry Ruby (m), Harms; My Sunny
Tennessee—Bert Kalmar, Harry
Ruby, Herman Ruby (w,m), Mills;
Nevertheless—Bert Kalmar, Harry
Ruby (w,m), Crawford; She's Mine
All Mine/So Long! Oo-Long—Bert
Kalmar, Harry Ruby (w,m), Mills;
Thinking of You/Three Little Words
—Bert Kalmar (w), Harry Ruby (m),
Harms; Where Did You Get That
Girl?—Bert Kalmar (w), Harry Puck
(m), Fisher; Who's Sorry Now?—Bert
Kalmar, Harry Ruby (w), Ted Snyder
(m), Mills. COVER: Fred Astaire,
Red Skelton, Vera-Ellen, Arlene
Dahl.

**5413 Three Lives of Thomasina,
The** (Buena Vista, 1964, Patrick
McGoohan, Susan Hampshire).

Thomasina—Terry Gilkyson (w,
m), Wonderland. COVER: Black and
orange cover with title only.

5414 Three Loves (Associated
Cinema, 1931, Marlene Dietrich,
Fritz Kortner).

Stasha—Sam Lerner (w), Walter
Bransen (m), Harms. COVER: Marlene Dietrich.

5415 Three Men and a Baby
(Buena Vista, 1987, Tom Selleck,
Steve Guttenberg).

Bad Boy (PC)—Lawrence Dermer,
Joe Galdo, Rafael Vigil (w,m), Columbia. COVER: None.

5416 Three Musketeers, The
(20th Century-Fox, 1939, Don
Ameche, The Ritz Brothers).

My Lady/Song of the Musketeers/Voila—Walter Bullock (w), Sam
Pokrass (m), Robbins. COVER: Don
Ameche, Ritz Brothers.

5417 Three on a Couch (Columbia, 1966, Jerry Lewis, Janet Leigh).

A Now and Later Love—Jerry
Lewis, Lil Mattis (w), Lewis Brown
(m), Consolidated. COVER: Jerry
Lewis, Janet Leigh.

5418 Three on a Honeymoon
(Fox, 1934, Sally Eilers, Zasu Pitts).

Desert Nights—William Kernell
(w,m), Movietone. COVER: Desert
Scene with Camel.

5419 Three Ring Circus (Paramount, 1954, Jerry Lewis, Dean Martin).

Hey Punchinello—Jay Livingston, Ray Evans (w,m), Paramount; Three Ring Circus—Wilson Stone (w), Walter Schaff, Paramount. COVER: Dean Martin, Jerry Lewis.

5420 Three Sailors and a Girl (Warner Bros., 1953, Jane Powell, Gordon MacRae).

Face to Face/Home Is Where the Heart Is/Kiss Me or I'll Scream/Lately Song, The/My Heart Is a Singing Heart/Show Me a Happy Woman/There Must Be a Reason— Sammy Cahn (w), Sammy Fain (m), Witmark; When It's Love—Sammy Cahn, Earl Brent (w,m), Witmark. COVER: Jane Powell, Gordon MacRae, Gene Nelson, Jack E. Leonard.

5421 Three Sisters, The (Fox, 1930, Tom Patricola, Louise Dresser).

Italian Kisses—L. Wolfe Gilbert (w), Abel Baer (m), DBH. COVER: Tom Patricola, Louise Dresser.

5422 Three Smart Girls (Universal, 1937, Deanna Durbin, Ray Milland).

My Heart Is Singing/Someone to Care for Me—Gus Kahn (w), Bronislau Kaper, Walter Jurmann (m), Feist. COVER: Deanna Durbin, Ray Milland, Binnie Barnes, Alice Brady.

5423 Three Smart Girls Grow Up (Universal, 1938, Deanna Durbin, Robert Cummings).

Invitation to the Dance—Charles Henderson (w), Carl Von Weber (m), Feist; Tis the Last Rose of Summer— Thomas Moore (w,m), Feist; The Wren—Howard Johnson (w), J. Benedict (m), Feist; Because (B)—Edward Teschemacher (w), Duy D'Hardelot (m), Chappell. COVER: Deanna Durbin.

5424 3:10 to Yuma (Columbia, 1957, Glenn Ford, Van Heflin).

3:10 to Yuma—Ned Washington (w), George Duning (m), Colgems.

COVER: Glenn Ford, Felicia Farr.

5425 Three Violent People (Paramount, 1956, Anne Baxter, Charlton Heston).

My Wild and Reckless Heart— Bebe Blake (w), Walter Scharf (m), Famous; Una Momento—Mack David (w), Martita (m), Famous. COVER: Anne Baxter, Charlton Heston, Gilbert Roland.

5426 Three Worlds of Gulliver, The (Columbia, 1960, Kerwin Mathews, Jo Morrow).

Gentle Love (B)—Ned Washington (w), George Duning (m), Chappell. COVER: Kerwin Mathews and Movie Scenes.

5427 Thrill of a Lifetime (Paramount, 1937, Betty Grable, Dorothy Lamour).

Paris in Swing—Sam Coslow, Frederick Hollander (w,m), Famous; Sweetheart Time—Sam Coslow (w), Frederick Hollander (w,m), Marlo; Thrill of a Lifetime—Frederick Hollander, Sam Coslow, Carmen Lombardo (w,m), Marlo. COVER: Betty Grable, Dorothy Lamour, Buster Crabbe.

5428 Thrill of a Romance (MGM, 1945, Esther Williams, Van Johnson).

I Should Care—Sammy Cahn, Axel Stordahl, Paul Weston (w, m), Dorsey; Lonely Night—Richard Connell (w), George Stoll (m), Feist; Please Don't Say No-Ralph Freed (w), Sammy Fain (m), Feist; Serenade—M. Meskill, Earl Brent (w), Franz Schubert (m), Feist; Viva d'Amour—George Stoll, Ralph Blane, Kay Thompson (w,m), Feist. COVER: Lauritz Melchior, Esther Williams, Van Johnson, Tommy Dorsey.

5429 Thrill of Brazil, The (Columbia, 1946, Evelyn Keyes, Keenan Wynn).

Copa Cabana/Man Is a Brother to a Mule, A—Allan Roberts, Doris Fisher (w,m), Mood; Minute Samba— Enric Madriguera (m), Riviera; That's

Good Enough for Me/Thrill of Brazil, The—Allan Roberts, Doris Fisher (w, m), Mood. COVER: Evelyn Keyes, Keenan Wynn, Ann Miller, Allyn Joslyn.

5430 Thrill of It All, The (Universal, 1963, Doris Day, James Garner).

Thrill of It All, The—Frederick Herbert (w), Arnold Schwarzwald (m), Northern. COVER: Doris Day, James Garner.

5430a Through the Wrong Door (Goldwyn, 1919, Madge Kennedy, John Bowers).

Visions No.—William Buse (m), Belwyn. COVER: Madge Kennedy, John Bowers.

5431 Throw a Saddle on a Star (Columbia, 1946, Ken Curtis, Adelle Roberts).

Throw a Saddle on a Star—Andy Parker, Hank Caldwell (w,m), Nordyke. COVER: Ken Curtis, Adella Roberts.

5432 Thru Different Eyes (Fox, 1929, Mary Duncan, Warner Baxter).

I'm Saving All My Loving—William Kernell, Dave Stamper (w,m), DBH. COVER: Mary Duncan.

5433 Thumbs Up (Republic, 1943, Brenda Joyce, Richard Fraser).

From Here on In/Love Is a Corny Thing/Who Are the British?—Sammy Cahn (w), Jule Styne (m), Southern. COVER: Brenda Joyce, Richard Fraser, Gertrude Neisen, and Movie Scenes.

5434 Thumb Tipping (Embassy, 1972, Michael Burns, Meg Forster).

Thumb Tipping—S. Black, R. Cork, Harry Elston, Floyd Butler (w, m), Levine. COVER: Two Hitchhikers.

5435 Thunderball (United Artists, 1965, Sean Connery, Claudine Auger).

Mister Kiss Kiss Bang Bang—Leslie Bricusse (w), John Barry (m), Unart; Thunderball—Don Black (w), John Barry (m), Unart. COVER: Sean Connery, and Movie Scene.

5436 Thunder Before Lightning (Independent, 1961, Stars Unknown).

Pony Express-Theme—Robert Robbins (w), Hal Shutz (m), Leeds. COVER: Brown and white cover with title only.

5437 Thunder Birds (Republic, 1953, John Derek, Mona Freeman).

Wintertime of Love—Edward Heyman (w), Victor Young (m), Young. COVER: Purple cover with title only.

5438 Thunderbirds Are Go (United Artists, 1966, Animated Feature).

Lady Penelope (B)—Bruce Welch, Brian Bennett, John Rostill (w,m), Shadows. COVER: Movie Scene.

5439 Thunderbolt (Paramount, 1929, George Bancroft, Richard Arlen).

Daddy Won't You Please Come Home/Thinkin' About My Baby—Sam Coslow (w,m), Spier Coslow. COVER: George Bancroft, Fay Wray, Richard Arlen.

5440 Thundering Jets (20th Century-Fox, 1958, Rex Reason, Dick Foran).

Blast Off!—Walter Kent, Tom Walton (w,m), Robbins. COVER: Rex Reason, and Jets.

5441 Thundering West, The (Columbia, 1940, Charles Starrett, Iris Meredith).

Cody of the Pony Express (VS)—Bob Nolan (w,m), American. COVER: Bob Nolan.

5442 Thunder in the East (Paramount, 1953, Alan Ladd, Deborah Kerr).

Ruby and the Pearl, The—Jay Livingston, Ray Evans (w,m), Famous. COVER: Alan Ladd, Deborah Kerr.

5443 Thunder in the Sun (Paramount, 1959, Susan Hayward, Jeff Chandler).

Mon Petit/Thunder in the Sun—Ned Washington (w), Cyril Mockridge (m), Paramount. COVER: Susan Hayward, Jeff Chandler.

5444 Thunder of Drums, A (MGM, 1961, George Hamilton, Richard Boone).
A Thunder of Drums Theme—Harry Sukman (m), Miller. COVER: George Hamilton, Luana Patten, Richard Boone.

5445 Thunder Road (United Artists, 1958, Robert Mitchum, Gene Barry).
Ballad of Thunder Road, The—Don Raye, Robert Mitchum (w,m), Leeds; Thunder Road Chase—Jack Marshall (m), Leeds; Whippoorwill—Don Raye, Robert Mitchum (w, m), Leeds. COVER: Robert Mitchum, Keely Smith.

5446 Tickle Me (Allied Artists, 1965, Elvis Presley, Julie Adams).
Easy Question—Otis Blackwell, Winfield Scott (w,m), Presley; Night Rider—Doc Pomus, Mort Shuman (w,m), Presley; I Feel That I've Known You Forever—Doc Pomus, Alan Jeffreys (w,m), Presley. COVER: Elvis Presley.

5447 Ticklish Affair, A (MGM, 1963, Shirley Jones, Gig Young).
Love Is a Ticklish Affair/Tandy—Harold Adamson (w), George Stoll, Bob Van Eps (m), Feist. COVER: Shirley Jones, Gig Young, Red Buttons.

5448 Tide of Empire (MGM, 1929, Renee Adoree, George Duryea).
Josephita—Raymond Klages (w), Jesse Greer (m), Robbins. COVER: Renee Adoree.

5449 Tiger Bay (Continental, 1959, John Mills, Horst Buchholz).
Tiger Bay Theme (B)—Laurie Johnson (m), Filmusic. COVER: Hayley Mills, Horst Buchholz.

5450 Tiger Rose (Warner Bros., 1923, Lenore Ulric, Forrest Stanley).
Tiger Rose Waltz and Song—Ivan Reid, Peter DeRose (w,m), Havilland. COVER: Lenore Ulric.

5451 Tiger Rose (Warner Bros., 1929, Lupe Velez, Monte Blue).

Day You Fall in Love, The—Ned Washington, Herb Magidson, Mike Cleary (w,m), Witmark. COVER: Lupe Velez.

5452 Tight Spot (Columbia, 1955, Ginger Rogers, Brian Keith).
Forbidden Love—Tom Glazer (w), George Duning (m), Colgems. COVER: Ginger Rogers, Brian Keith.

5453 Till the Clouds Roll By (MGM, 1946, Robert Walker, Van Heflin).
All the Things You Are/Can't Help Lovin' Dat Man—Oscar Hammerstein (w), Jerome Kern (m), Harms; How'd You Like to Spoon with Me?—Edward Laska (w), Jerome Kern (m), Harms; I Won't Dance—Otto Harbach, Oscar Hammerstein (w), Jerome Kern (m), Harms; Land Where Good Songs Go—P. G. Wodehouse (w), Jerome Kern (m), Harms; Last Time I Saw Paris, The—Oscar Hammerstein (w), Jerome Kern (m), Harms; Look for the Silver Lining—Bud DeSylva (w), Jerome Kern (m), Harms; Ol' Man River—Oscar Hammerstein (w), Jerome Kern (m), Harms; She Didn't Say Yes/Smoke Gets in Your Eyes—Otto Harbach (w), Jerome Kern (m), Harms; They Didn't Believe Me—Herbert Reynolds (w), Jerome Kern (m), Harms; Till the Clouds Roll By—P. G. Wodehouse, Guy Bolton (w), Jerome Kern (m), Harms; Who?—Otto Harbach, Oscar Hammerstein (w), Jerome Kern (m), Harms; Why Was I Born—Oscar Hammerstein (w), Jerome Kern (m), Harms; Yesterdays—Otto Harbach (w), Jerome Kern (m), Harms. COVER: Judy Garland, Frank Sinatra, Robert Walker, Lena Horne, and Others.

5454 Till the End of Time (RKO, 1945, Guy Madison, Dorothy McGuire).
Till the End of Time—Buddy Kaye, Ted Mossman (w,m), Santly Joy. COVER: Guy Madison, Dorothy McGuire.

5455 Til We Meet Again (Warner

Bros., 1940, Merle Oberon, George Brent).

Where Was I?—Al Dubin (w), Franke Harling (m), Remick. COVER: Merle Oberon, George Brent.

5456 Timberjack (Republic, 1954, Sterling Hayden, Vera Ralston).

He's Dead But He Won't Lie Down—Johnny Mercer (w), Hoagy Carmichael (m), Famous; Timberjack—Ned Washington (w), Victor Young (m), Young. COVER: Sterling Hayden, Vera Ralston, and Movie Scenes.

5457 Time Machine, The (MGM, 1960, Rod Taylor, Alan Young).

Time Machine Theme—Russel Garcia (m), Robbins. COVER: Rod Taylor, Yvette Mimieux, and Movie Scene.

5458 Time Out for Rhythm (Columbia, 1941, Rudy Vallee, Rosemary Lane).

As If You Didn't Know/Boogie Woogie Man/Did Anyone Ever Tell You?/Obviously the Gentleman Prefers to Dance/Twiddlin' My Thumbs —Sammy Cahn (w), Saul Chaplin (m), Mills. COVER: Rudy Vallee, Rosemary Lane, Ann Miller, Glen Gray and Orchestra.

5459 Time Out of Mind (Universal, 1947, Phyllis Calvert, Robert Hutton).

Time Out of Mind—Jayne Glyde (w), Miklos Rozsa (m), Sam Fox. COVER: Black and white cover with title only.

5460 Times Square (Vitaphone, 1928, Alice Day, Arthur Lubin).

My Heart's Longing for You Elaine—Johnny Tucker, Joe Schuster (w,m), Witmark. COVER: Alice Day.

5461 Times Square (AFD, 1980, Trini Alvarado, Robin Johnson).

Help Me!—Robin Gibb, Blue Weaver (w,m), Chappell; Times Square-Nineteen Songs—David Byrne, Joe Jackson, Lou Reed (w,m), Chappell. COVER: Trini Alvarado, Robin

Johnson.

5462 Times Square Lady (MGM, 1935, Robert Taylor, Virginia Bruce).

What's the Reason?—Coy Poe, Jim Grier (w), Pinky Tomlin, Earl Hatch (m), Berlin. COVER: Virginia Bruce.

5463 Time, the Place, the Girl, The (Warner Bros., 1929, Betty Compson, Grant Withers).

Honeymoon—Will Hough, Frank Adams (w), Joseph Howard (m), Harris. COVER: Betty Compson.

5464 Time, the Place and the Girl, The (Warner Bros., 1946, Dennis Morgan, Jack Carson).

Gal in Calico, A/Oh But I Do/ Rainy Night in Rio, A/Through a Thousand Dreams—Leo Robin (w), Arthur Schwartz (m), Remick. COVER: Dennis Morgan, Jack Carson, Martha Vickers, Janis Paige.

5465 Time to Love and a Time to Die, A (Universal, 1958, John Gavin, Lilo Pulver).

A Time to Love—Charles Henderson (w), Miklos Rozsa (m), Northern. COVER: John Gavin, Lilo Pulver.

5466 Time to Run (World Wide, 1973, Ed Nelson, Randall Carver).

I Love You—Larry Norman, Randy Stonehill (w,m), Glenwood. COVER: Randy Stonehill.

5467 Time to Sing, A (MGM, 1968, Hank Williams, Jr., Shelley Fabares).

Hummingbird Line, The/It's All Over But the Crying—Hank Williams, Jr., Hastings; Man Is on His Own, A—Hank Williams, Jr., John Scoggins (w, m), Hastings; Money Can't Buy Happiness—Steve Karliski (w,m), Hastings; Next Time I Say Goodbye I'm Leavin'—Larry Kusik, Ed Snyder (w, m), Feist; Old Before My Time—Steve Karliski (w,m), Hastings; Rock in My Shoe—Hank Williams, Jr. (w, m), Hastings; There's Gotta Be Much More to Life Than You—Steve Karliski (w,m), Hastings; Time to Sing, A—John Scoggins (w,m), Hastings.

COVER: Hank Williams, Jr., Shelley Fabares.

5468 Tin Pan Alley (20th Century-Fox, 1940, Betty Grable, Alice Faye).

America I Love You—Edgar Leslie (w), Archie Gottler (m), Mills; K-K-K-Katy—Geoffrey O'Hara (w,m), Feist; Sheik of Araby, The—Harry B. Smith, Francis Wheeler (w), Ted Snyder (m), Mills; You Say the Sweetest Things Baby—Mack Gordon (w), Harry Warren (m), Feist. COVER: Betty Grable, John Payne, Alice Faye, Jack Oakie.

5469 Tin Star, The (Paramount, 1957, Henry Fonda, Anthony Perkins).

Tin Star, The—Jack Brooks (w), Elmer Bernstein (m), Paramount. COVER: Henry Fonda, Anthony Perkins.

5470 Tisa (My Girl Tisa) (Warner Bros., 1948, Lilli Palmer, Sam Wanamaker).

At the Candlelight Cafe—Mack David (w,m), Witmark. COVER: Lilli Palmer, Sam Wanamaker.

5471 Titanic (20th Century-Fox, 1953, Barbara Stanwyck, Clifton Webb).

Here's to the Ladies—Eddie Mc-Mullen, Henry Jerome (w,m), Jerome. COVER: Musical Notes.

5472 Toast of New Orleans, The (MGM, 1950, Kathryn Grayson, Mario Lanza).

Bayou Lullaby, The/Be My Love/ Boom Biddy Boom Boom/I'll Never Love You/Tina Lina, The—Sammy Cahn (w), Nicholas Brodszky (m), Robbins; Brindisi (VS)—Walter Hirsch (w), Giuseppe Verdi (m), Robbins; La Fleur Que Tu M'Avais Jetée (VS)—Carolyn Davies (w), Georges Bizet (m), Miller; O Paradis Sorti de Londe (VS)—Walter Hirsch (w), Giacomo Meyerbeer (m), Robbins. COVER: Kathryn Grayson, Mario Lanza.

5473 Toast of New York, The (RKO, 1937, Edward Arnold, Cary Grant).

First Time I Saw You, The—Allie Wrubel (w), Nathaniel Shilkret (m), Santly Joy. COVER: Edward Arnold, Cary Grant, Jack Oakie, Frances Farmer.

5474 To Beat the Band (RKO, 1935, Hugh Herbert, Helen Broderick).

Eeny Meeny Miney Mo/If You Were Mine/I Saw Her at Eight o'-Clock/Meet Miss America—Johnny Mercer, Matt Malneck (w,m), Berlin; Santa Claus Came in the Spring—Johnny Mercer (w,m), Berlin. COVER: A Girl and a Band.

5475 To Be or Not to Be (United Artists, 1940, Carole Lombard, Jack Benny).

Bless Em All—Jinny Hughes, Frank Lake, Al Stillman (w,m), Sam Fox. COVER: Jack Benny, Carole Lombard.

5476 Toby Tyler (Buena Vista, 1959, Kevin Corcoran, Henry Calvin).

Biddle Dee Dee/Toby Tyler—Diane Lampert, Richard Loring (w, m), Disney. COVER: Black and white cover with title only.

5477 To Catch a Thief (Paramount, 1955, Grace Kelly, Cary Grant).

Francie's Theme—Lyn Murray (m), Famous; Unexpectedly—Edward Heyman (w), Lyn Murray (m), Famous; Your Kiss—Pat Auld, George Auld, George Cates (w,m), Famous. COVER: Grace Kelly, Cary Grant.

5478 To Die of Love (MGM, 1972, Annie Girardot, Bruno Pradal).

To Die of Love—Howard Liebling (w), Charles Aznavour (m), Chappell. COVER: Charles Aznavour.

5479 To Each His Own (Paramount, 1946, John Lund, Olivia de Havilland).

To Each His Own—Jay Livingston, Ray Evans (w,m), Paramount. COVER: John Lund, Olivia de Havilland.

5480 Together Again (Columbia, 1944, Irene Dunne, Charles Boyer).

Pablo the Dreamer (B)—Roberto

Lopez (w), Julio Sanders (m), Southern. COVER: A Camera and Film.

5481 To Have and Have Not (Warner Bros., 1943, Humphrey Bogart, Lauren Bacall).

Baltimore Oriole—Paul F. Webster (w), Hoagy Carmichael (m), Witmark; Hong Kong Blues—Hoagy Carmichael (w,m), Spier; How Little We Know—Johnny Mercer (w), Hoagy Carmichael (m), Witmark. COVER: Humphrey Bogart, Lauren Bacall, Hoagy Carmichael.

5482 To Have and to Hold (Paramount, 1922, Betty Compson, Bert Lytell).

To Have and to Hold—Arthur Glendale (w), Menlo Mayfield (m), Mittenthal. COVER: Betty Compson, Bert Lytell.

5483 To Hell and Back (Universal, 1955, Audie Murphy, Marshall Thompson).

Dogface Soldier—Bert Gold, Ken Hart, Jack Dolph (w,m), Shawnee. COVER: Audie Murphy.

5484 To Kill a Mockingbird (Universal, 1962, Gregory Peck, Mary Badham).

To Kill a Mockingbird—Mack David (w), Elmer Bernstein (m), Northern. COVER: Gregory Peck, and Children.

5485 Told in the Hills (Paramount, 1919, Robert Warwick, Ann Little).

Told in the Hills—Bernie Grossman (w), Billy Frisch (m), Stern. COVER: Robert Warwick, Ann Little.

5486 To Live and Die in L.A. (United Artists, 1985, William Peterson, John Pankow).

To Live and Die in L.A.—Jack Hues, Nick Feldman (w,m), Warner. COVER: Nick Feldman, Jack Hues.

5487 Tom and Jerry (MGM, 1960, Cartoon).

Cat Chasing Mouse—William Scher (w,m), Witmark. COVER: Cartoon.

5488 To Mary with Love (20th

Century-Fox, 1936, Myrna Loy, Warner Baxter).

To Mary with Love—Mack Gordon, Harry Revel (w,m), Feist. COVER: Warner Baxter, Myrna Loy.

5489 Tom Brown of Culver (Universal, 1932, Tom Brown, Slim Summerville).

Culver Military Band, The—Clarence Marks, Harry Brown, Irving Bibo (w,m), Bibo Lang. COVER: Tom Brown, and Cadets.

5490 Tom Jones (United Artists, 1963, Albert Finney, Susannah York).

Love Song of Tom Jones—Mack David (w), John Addison (m), Unart. COVER: A Bed.

5491 Tommy (Columbia, 1975, Ann Margret, Oliver Reed).

Eyesight to the Blind—Willie Williamson (w,m), Mellin; Tommy-31 Songs—Pete Townsend, Keith Moon, John Entwhistle (w,m), Fabulous. COVER: Roger Daltrey.

5492 Tomorrow Is Forever (RKO, 1946, Claudette Colbert, Orson Welles).

Tomorrow Is Forever—Charles Tobias (w), Max Steiner (m), Witmark; Tumblin' Tim—Marilyn Lang (w,m), Irwin. COVER: Claudette Colbert, Natalie Wood.

5493 Tomorrow We Live (PRC, 1942, Jean Parker, Ricardo Cortez).

Senorita Chula (PC)—A. Levitt, Leo Erdody (w,m), Southern. COVER: None.

5494 Tom Sawyer (United Artists, 1973, Celeste Holm, Johnny Whitaker).

Freebootin'/Gratification/How Come/If'n I Was God/A Man's Gotta Be/River Song-Theme/Aunt Polly's Soliloguy (VS)/Hannibal Mo-Zouree (VS)/Tom Sawyer (VS)—Richard Sherman, Robert Sherman (w,m), Unart. COVER: Celeste Holm, Johnny Whitaker, Jess East, Warren Oates.

5495 Tom Thumb (MGM, 1958, Russ Tamblyn, Alan Young).

After All These Years—Janice Torre (w), Fred Spielman (m), Robbins; Are You a Dream—Peggy Lee (w,m), Robbins; Talented Shoes—Janice Toree (w), Fred Spielman (m), Robbins; Tom Thumb's Tune—Peggy Lee (w,m), Robbins; Yawning Song—Kermit Goell (w), Fred Spielman (m), Robbins. COVER: Russ Tamblyn.

5496 Tonight and Every Night (Columbia, 1945, Rita Hayworth, Janet Blair).

Anywhere/Cry and You Cry Alone/ Tonight and Every Night/You Excite Me—Sammy Cahn (w), Jule Styne (m), Bourne. COVER: Rita Hayworth, Janet Blair, Lee Bowman.

5497 Tonight or Never (United Artists, 1931, Gloria Swanson, Melvyn Douglas).

Tell Me Tonight—Bernie Grossman (w), Alfred Newman, C. M. Ziehrer (m), Harms. COVER: Gloria Swanson.

5498 Tonka (Disney, 1958, Sal Mineo, Philip Carey).

Tonka—Gil George, George Bruns (w,m), Wonderland. COVER: Black and white cover with title only.

5499 Tony Fontane Story (Independent, 1962, Religious Film).

Tony Fontane Story-Three Themes—Nat Haag, Tony Fontane, Lyle Murphy (w,m), Grandview. COVER: Black and white cover with title only.

5500 Tony Rome (20th Century-Fox, 1967, Frank Sinatra, Jill St. John).

Tony Rome—Lee Hazlewood (w, m), Sergeant. COVER: Nancy Sinatra.

5501 Too Busy to Work (Fox, 1932, Will Rogers, Dick Powell).

Jubilo-Kingdom Come—Henry C. Work (w,m), Movietone. COVER: Black and white cover with title only.

5502 Too Late Blues (Paramount, 1961, Bobby Darin, Stella

Stevens).

Too Late Blues-Theme—David Raksin (m), Famous. COVER: Stella Stevens, Bobby Darin.

5503 Too Many Blondes (Universal, 1941, Rudy Vallee, Helen Parrish).

Don't Mind If I Do/Let's Love Again—Everett Carter (w), Milton Rosen (m), Robbins; Man on the Flying Trapeze—Walter O'Keefe (w, m), Robbins; Whistle Your Blues to a Bluebird—Everett Carter (w), Milton Rosen (m), Robbins. COVER: Rudy Vallee, Helen Parrish.

5504 Too Many Crooks (United Artists, 1959, Terry Thomas, George Cole).

Too Many Crooks-Theme (B)—Stanley Black (m), Filmusic. COVER: Terry Thomas, George Cole, Brenda DeBanzie.

5505 Too Many Girls (RKO, 1940, Lucille Ball, Ann Miller).

I Didn't Know What Time It Was/ Love Never Went to College/You're Nearer—Lorenz Hart (w), Richard Rodgers (m), Harms. COVER: Lucille Ball, Football Players and Girls.

5506 Toomorrow (Rank, 1970, Olivia Newton-John, Benny Thomas).

You're My Baby Now—Mark Barkan, Ritchie Adams (w,m), Kirshner. COVER: Toomorrow Rock Group.

5507 Too Much Harmony (Paramount, 1933, Bing Crosby, Jack Oakie).

Black Moonlight/Boo Boo Boo/ Buckin' the Wind/Day You Came Along/I Guess It Had to Be That Way/ Thanks—Sam Coslow, Arthur Johnston (w,m), Famous. COVER: Bing Crosby, Judith Allen.

5508 Too Much Too Soon (Warner Bros., 1958, Dorothy Malone, Errol Flynn).

Too Much Too Soon—Al Stillman (w), Ernest Gold (m), Witmark. COVER: Dorothy Malone.

5509 Tootsie (Columbia, 1982, Dustin Hoffman, Jessica Lange).

It Might Be You—Alan Bergman, Marilyn Bergman (w), Dave Grusin (m), Columbia; That's All—Alan Brandt, Bob Haymes (w,m), Mixed Bag; Tootsie—Alan Bergman, Marilyn Bergman (w), Dave Grusin (m), Columbia. COVER: Dustin Hoffman.

5510 Toot Whistle Plunk and Boom (Disney, 1953, Musical Short).

Toot and a Whistle and a Plunk and a Boom—Jack Elliott (w), Sonny Burke (m), Disney. COVER: Cartoons.

5511 Too Young to Know (Warner Bros., 1945, Joan Leslie, Robert Hutton).

It's Only a Paper Moon—Billy Rose, E. Y. Harburg (w), Harold Arlen (m), Harms. COVER: Joan Leslie, Robert Hutton.

5512 To Paris with Love (Rank, 1955, Alex Guinness, Odile Versois).

People Like Us—Bob Musel (w), Franklin King (m), Hollis. COVER: Red and white cover with title only.

5513 Topa Topa (Pennant, 1938, Helen Hughes, James Bush).

Rocky Mountain Trail—Rudy Sooter (w,m), Cross Winge. COVER: Black and white cover with title only.

5514 Top Gun (Paramount, 1986, Tom Cruise, Kelly McGillis).

Danger Zone—Giorgio Moroder, Tom Whitlock (w,m), Famous; Heaven in Your Eyes—Paul Dean, Mike Reno, John Dexter, Mae Moore (w, m), Famous; Lead Me On—Giorgio Moroder, Tom Whitlock (w,m), Famous; Memories—Harold Faltermeyer (m), Famous; Mighty Wings—Harold Faltermeyer, Mark Spiro (w, m), Famous; Playing with the Boys—Kenny Loggins, Peter Wolf, Ina Wolf (w,m), Famous; Take My Breath Away—Giorgio Moroder, Tom Whitlock (w,m), Famous; Top Gun Anthem—Harold Faltermeyer (m), Famous; Top Gun-Eleven Songs—Giorgio Moroder, Tom Whitlock (w,m), Famous. COVER: Tom Cruise, Kelly McGillis.

5515 Top Hat (RKO, 1935, Fred Astaire, Ginger Robers).

Cheek to Cheek/Isn't This a Lovely Day?/No Strings, I'm Fancy Free/Piccolino, The/Top Hat, White Tie, and Tails—Irving Berlin (w,m), Berlin. Cover #1: Gold Cover with Fred Astaire and Ginger Rogers Dancing Together; COVER #2: Pink Cover with Fred Astaire and Ginger Rogers Dancing Separately.

5516 Topkapi (United Artists, 1964, Melina Mercouri, Peter Ustinov).

Topkapi—Noel Sherman (w), Manos Hadjidakis (m), Unart. COVER: Green and black cover with title only.

5517 To Please a Lady (MGM, 1950, Clark Gable, Barbara Stanwyck).

Wonderful One—Dorothy Terriss (w), Paul Whiteman, Ferde Grofe (m), Feist. COVER: Clark Gable, Barbara Stanwyck.

5518 Top of the Town (Universal, 1937, George Murphy, Hugh Herbert).

Blame It on the Rhumba/Jamboree/That Foolish Feeling/There's No Two Ways About It/Top of the Town/Where Are You—Harold Adamson (w), Jimmy McHugh (m), Feist. COVER: Sketch of Roofs and People.

5519 Top of the World (Vitaphone, 1933, Musical Short).

Top of the World—David Mendoza (w,m), Witmark. COVER: Black and white cover with title only.

5520 Top o' the Morning (Paramount, 1949, Bing Crosby, Ann Blyth).

Donovans—Francis Fahy (w), Alicia A. Needham (m), Boosey Hawkes; My Lagan Love—Seosamh MacCathmhaoil (w,m), Boosey Hawkes; Oh Tis Sweet to Think—Thomas Moore (w,m), BVH; Top o' the Morning/You're in Love with McGillis.

Someone—Johnny Burke (w), James Van Heusen (m), BVH. COVER: Bing Crosby, Ann Blyth, Barry Fitzgerald.

5521 Topper (MGM, 1937, Constance Bennett, Cary Grant).

Old Man Moon—Hoagy Carmichael (w,m), Witmark. COVER: Constance Bennett, Cary Grant, Roland Young, Billie Burke.

5522 Top Secret (Paramount, 1984, Omar Sharif, Jeremy Kemp).

How Silly Can You Get—Phil Pickett (w,m), Famous; Spend This Night with Me—D. Zucker, J. Zucker, J. Abrahams, M. Noran (w,m), Famous; Straighten Out the Rug—Paul Hudson (w,m), Famous. COVER: A Cow.

5523 Top Sergeant (Universal, 1942, Leo Carrillo, Andy Devine).

Engineer's Song, The—Don Brown (w,m), Robbins. COVER: Leo Carrillo, Andy Devine, Don Terry, Elyse Knox.

5524 Top Speed (First National, 1930, Joe E. Brown, Bernice Clare).

As Long as I Have You/Knock Knees/Looking for the Lovelight in the Dark—Al Dubin (w), Joe Burke (m), Harms. COVER: Joe E. Brown, Bernice Clare, Jack Whiting.

5525 Tora! Tora! Tora! (20th Century-Fox, 1970, Martin Balsam, Joseph Cotten).

Tora! Tora! Tora!—Jerry Goldsmith (m), Fox. COVER: Battle Scene-Planes and Ships.

5526 Torch Singer (Paramount, 1933, Claudette Colbert, Ricardo Cortez).

Don't Be a Cry Baby/Give Me Liberty or Give Me Love/It's a Long Dark Night/Torch Singer—Leo Robin (w), Ralph Rainger (m), Famous. COVER: Claudette Colbert, Ricardo Cortez, David Manners.

5527 Torch Song (The Laughing Sinners) (MGM, 1931, Joan Crawford, Neil Hamilton).

I Love That Man, What Can I Do—Arthur Freed (w), Martin Broones

(m), Robbins. COVER: Joan Crawford, Neil Hamilton.

5528 Torch Song (MGM, 1953, Joan Crawford, Michael Wilding).

Follow Me—Adolph Deutsch (w, m), Feist; You Won't Forget Me—Kermit Goell (w), Fred Spielman (m), Feist. COVER: Joan Crawford, Michael Wilding.

5529 Tornado (Paramount, 1943, Chester Morris, Nancy Kelly).

I'm Afraid of You—Ralph Freed (w), Frederick Hollander (m), Fisher; There Goes My Dream—Frank Loesser (w), Frederick Hollander (m), Fisher. COVER: Chester Morris, Nancy Kelly, and Movie Scenes.

5530 Torn Curtain (Universal, 1966, Julie Andrews, Paul Newman).

Green Years—Love Theme—Jay Livingston, Ray Evans (w), John Addison (m), Shamley. COVER: Julie Andrews, Paul Newman, Alfred Hitchcock.

5531 Torpedo Boat (Paramount, 1942, Richard Arlen, Jean Parker).

Heaven Is a Moment in Your Arms—Nat Winecoff (w), Marian Boyle (m), Famous. COVER: Richard Arlen, Jean Parker, Philip Terry.

5532 Torrid Zone (Warner Bros., 1940, James Cagney, Ann Sheridan).

Mi Caballero—Jack Scholl (w), M. K. Jerome (m), Harms. COVER: James Cagney, Pat O'Brien, Ann Sheridan.

5533 Tortoise and the Hare, The (Disney, 1935, Cartoon).

Slow But Sure (VS)—Larry Morey (w), Frank Churchill (m), Berlin. COVER: Cartoon.

5534 To Sir with Love (Columbia, 1967, Sidney Poitier, Suzy Kendall).

It's Getting Harder All the Time—Ben Raleigh, Charles Albertine (w, m), Colgems; To Sir with Love—Don Black (w), Marc London (m), Colgems; To Sir with Love-Twelve Songs—Ron Grainer, Marc London, Carole B. Sager (w,m), Colgems. COVER: Sidney Poitier, Judy Geeson, and Others.

5535 To the Shores of Tripoli (20th Century-Fox, 1942, Maureen O'Hara, John Payne).

Marines Hymn, The—L. Z. Phillips (w,m), Marks. COVER: Maureen O'Hara, John Payne, Randolph Scott.

5536 To the Victor (Warner Bros., 1948, Dennis Morgan, Viveca Lindfors).

You're Too Dangerous, Cherie— Mack David (w), Louiguy (m), Harms. COVER: Dennis Morgan, Viveca Lindfors.

5537 Touchables, The (20th Century-Fox, 1968, Judy Huxtable, Esther Anderson).

All of Us—Alex Spyropoulos, Pat Campbell Lyons (w,m), Fox. COVER: A Boy and Four Girls.

5538 Touch and Go (The Light Touch) (Universal, 1955, Jack Hawkins, Margaret Johnston).

Mirror Waltz, The (B)—John Addison (m), Anglo-Continental. COVER: Margaret Johnston.

5539 Touchez Pas au Grisbi (Don't Touch the Loot) (Becker, 1953, Jean Gabin, Jeanne Moreau).

Le Grisbi-The Touch—Norman Gimbel (w), Jean Wiener (m), Duchess. COVER: A Girl's Face.

5540 Touch of Class, A (Embassy, 1973, George Segal, Glenda Jackson).

All That Love Went to Waste/ Amor Mio/Nudge Me Every Morning/ Touch of Class, A—Sammy Cahn (w), George Barrie (m), Brut. COVER: George Segal, Glenda Jackson.

5541 Touch of Evil (Universal, 1958, Charlton Heston, Janet Leigh).

Tana's Theme—Henry Mancini (m), Northern. COVER: Stars and Lines.

5542 Touch of Larceny, A (Paramount, 1959, James Mason, George Sanders).

The Nearness of You—Ned Washington (w), Hoagy Carmichael (m), Famous. COVER: James Mason, Vera Miles, George Sanders.

5543 Toughest Man in Arizona, The (Republic, 1952, Vaughn Monroe, Joan Leslie).

The Man Don't Live Who Can Die Alone—Johnny Schram (w), Bobby Sherwood (m), Morris. COVER: Vaughn Monroe.

5544 Tough Guys (Touchstone, 1986, Burt Lancaster, Kirk Douglas).

They Don't Make Em Like They Used To—Carole B. Sager (w), Burt Bacharach (m), Leonard. COVER: Burt Lancaster, Kirk Douglas.

5545 Tough to Handle (Syndicate, 1937, Frankie Darro, Kane Richmond).

What You've Got Is Love (PC)— Connie Lee (w,m), Schwiter Miller. COVER: None.

5546 Towering Inferno, The (20th Century-Fox, 1974, Steve McQueen, Paul Newman).

We May Never Love Like This Again—Al Kasha, Joel Hirschhorn (w,m), Fox. COVER: A Building in Flames.

5547 Town Tamer (Paramount, 1965, Dana Andrews, Terry Moore).

Town Tamer—By Dunham (w), Jimmie Haskell (m), Ensign. COVER: Dana Andrews, Terry Moore.

5548 Town Without Pity (United Artists, 1961, Kirk Douglas, Robert Blake).

Town Without Pity—Ned Washington (w), Dimitri Tiomkin (m), Unart. COVER: Kirk Douglas.

5549 Toy, The (Columbia, 1982, Richard Pryor, Jackie Gleason).

I Just Want to Be Your Friend— Frank Musker, Trevor Lawrence (w, m), Gold Horizon. COVER: Richard Pryor, Jackie Gleason.

5550 Toys in the Attic (United Artists, 1963, Dean Martin, Geraldine Page).

Toys in the Attic—George Duning, Joe Sherman, George D. Weiss (w,m), Unart. COVER: Dean Martin, Yvette Mimieux.

5551 Toy Tiger (Universal, 1956, Jeff Chandler, Laraine Day).

Toy Tiger—Leah Worth (w), Henry Mancini, Herman Stein (m), Northern. COVER: Jeff Chandler, Laraine Day, Tim Hovey.

5552 Trade Winds (United Artists, 1938, Fredric March, Joan Bennett).

Trade Winds—Arthur Quenzer (w), Alfred Newman (m), BVC. COVER: Black and white cover with title only.

5553   Traffic in Souls (Universal, 1914, Ethel Grandin, Matt Moore).

Traffic in Souls—Al Dubin (w), Horatio Buckley (m), Welch. COVER: Matt Moore, and Newspaper Cover.

5554 Trail Drive (Trail Herd) (Universal, 1933, Ken Maynard, Cecelia Parker).

Trail Herd (VS)—Ken Maynard (w,m), Cole. COVER: Ken Maynard.

5555 Trail Dust (Paramount, 1936, William Boyd, Jimmy Ellison).

Beneath a Western Sky/Take Me Back to Those Wide Open Spaces—Harry Tobias, Jack Stern (w,m), Popular; Trail Dust—Claudia Humphrey (w,m), Popular. COVER: William Boyd.

5556 Trailin' Trouble (Universal, 1930, Hoot Gibson, Margaret Quimby).

Mi Caballero—Joe Seitman (w), Sam Perry (m), Handman Kent Goodman. COVER: Black and white cover with title only.

5557 Trailin' West (First National, 1937, Dick Foran, Paula Stone).

Moonlight Valley—Jack Scholl (w), M. K. Jerome (m), Witmark. COVER: Black and white cover with title only.

5558 Trail of 98 (MGM, 1928, Dolores Del Rio, Ralph Forbes).

I Found Gold When I Found You —Hazel Mooney, Ev E. Lyn (w), William Axt (m), Berlin. COVER: Dolores Del Rio, Ralph Forbes.

5559 Trail of Robin Hood (Re-public, 1950, Roy Rogers, Penny Edwards).

Trail of Robin Hood—Jack Elliott (w,m), Mills. COVER: Roy Rogers.

5560 Trail of the Lonesome Pine, The (Paramount, 1936, Fred MacMurray, Sylvia Sidney).

Melody from the Sky—Sidney Mitchell, Louis Alter (w,m), Famous; Trail of the Lonesome Pine, The-Ballard MacDonald (w), Harry Carroll (m), Shapiro Bernstein; Twilight on the Trail—Sidney Mitchell, Louis Alter (w,m), Famous. COVER: Fred MacMurray, Sylvia Sidney.

5561 Trail of the Tumbleweed (Columbia, 1938, Charles Starrett).

Rocky Roads (VS)—Bob Nolan (w,m), American. COVER: Bob Nolan.

5562 Trail to San Antone (Republic, 1947, Gene Autry, Peggy Stewart).

That's My Home—Sid Rubin (w, m), Leeds. COVER: Cowboy and Horse.

5563 Traitors, The (The Accursed) (Allied Artists, 1957, Donald Wolfit, Robert Bray).

Prelude Without a Name (B)—Jackie Brown (m), Day. COVER: Black and white cover with title only.

5564 Transatlantic Merry Go Round (United Artists, 1934, Jack Benny, Gene Raymond).

If I Had a Million Dollars—Johnny Mercer (w), Matt Malneck (m), Berlin; It Was Sweet of You/Oh, Leo/ Rock and Roll—Sidney Clare (w), Richard Whiting (m), Berlin. COVER: Jack Benny, Gene Raymond, Nancy Carroll, Frank Parker.

5565 Trapeze (United Artists, 1956, Burt Lancaster, Tony Curtis).

Lola—Al Stillman (w), Malcolm Arnold (m), Hecht Lancaster. COVER: Gina Lollobrigida.

5566 Traveling Husbands (RKO, 1931, Evelyn Brent, Frank Albertson).

There's a Sob in My Heart—Humphrey Pearson (w), Max Steiner (m), Fiest. COVER: Evelyn Brent.

5567 Travels with My Aunt (MGM, 1972, Maggie Smith, Alec McCowen).

Serenade of Love—Jackie Trent (w), Tony Hatch (m), Robbins. COVER: Maggie Smith.

5568 Trav'lling the Road (Educational, 1934, Alexander Grey).

Trav'lling the Road—Sammy Lerner (w), Gerald Marks (m), Movietone. COVER: A Railroad Train.

5569 T. R. Baskin (Paramount, 1971, Candice Bergen, Peter Boyle).

I Got a Feeling/It's a Mixed Up World—June Jackson (w), Jack Elliott (m), Ensign; Love Is All—Norman Gimbel, Jack Elliott (w,m), Ensign. COVER: Candice Bergen, Peter Boyle.

5570 Treasure Island (Paramount, 1920, Lon Chaney, Shirley Mason).

Treasure Island—Louis Weslyn (w), Joe Meyer (m), Daniels Wilson. COVER: Pirates and Treasure Chest.

5571 Treasure of San Gennaro (Paramount, 1968, Senta Berger, Nino Manfredi).

Man on My Mind, The—Al Stillman (w), Armando Travajoli (m), Marks. COVER: Senta Berger, Nino Manfredi, and Movie Scenes.

5572 Treasure of Sierra Madre, The (Warner Bros., 1947, Humphrey Bogart, Walter Huston).

The Treasure of Sierra Madre— Buddy Kaye (w), Dick Manning (m), Remick. COVER: Cactus and Mountains.

5573 Trespasser, The (United Artists, 1929, Gloria Swanson, Robert Ames).

Love Your Spell Is Everywhere— Elsie Janis (w), Edmund Goulding (m), Berlin; Serenade (Rimpianto)— Sigmund Spaeth (w), Enrico Toselli (m), Boston. COVER: Gloria Swanson.

5574 Trial Marriage (Columbia, 1928, Sally Eilers, Norman Kerry).

Dear Little Boy of Mine—J. Keirn Brennan (w), Ernest Ball (m), Witmark; I'll Never Forget—Gus Kahn (w), Spike Hamilton (m), Berlin. COVER: Sally Eilers, Norman Kerry.

5575 Trial of Vivienne Ware (Fox, 1932, Joan Bennett, Donald Cook).

If I Were Adam and You Were Eve —James Hanley (w,m), Movietone; Together Again—Ralph Freed (w), James Hanley (m), Movietone. COVER: Black and white cover with title only.

5576 Trick or Treat (Disney, 1952, Cartoon).

Trick or Treat-For Halloween— Mack David, Al Hoffman, Jerry Livingston (w,m), Disney. COVER: Cartoon.

5577 Trifling Women (MGM, 1922, Ramon Novarro, Barbara LaMarr).

Trifling—George Kershaw (w), Ernst Luz, A. Breau (m), Von Tilzer. COVER: Ramon Novarro, Barbara LaMarr.

5578 Trigger, Jr. (Republic, 1950, Roy Rogers, Dale Evans).

May the Good Lord Take a Liking to You—Roy Rogers, Peter Tinturin (w,m), Tindale. COVER: Roy Rogers, Dale Evans.

5579 Trigger Pals (Grand National, 1939, Art Jarrett, Lee Powell).

Lullaby Trail—Johnny Lange (w), Lew Porter (m), Marks. COVER: Art Jarrett.

5580 Trocadero (Republic, 1944, Rosemary Lane, Johnny Downs).

Bullfrog Jump—Lew Porter (w, m), Urban; Can't Take the Place of You—Walter Colmes, Lew Porter (w, m), Urban; How Could You Do That to Me—Lew Porter (w,m), Urban; In a Round-a-bout Way—B. Urban, Evelyn Claire, Lew Porter (w,m), Urban; Louisiana Lulu—Teepee Mitchell, Lew Porter (w,m), Urban; Shoo Shoo Baby—Phil Moore (w,m), Leeds; Trocadero, The—Lew Porter (w,m), Urban. COVER: Bob Chester and His Orchestra.

5581 Trooper Hook (United Artists, 1957, Barbara Stanwyck, Joel McCrea).

Trooper Hook—Mitzi Cummings (w), Gerald Fried (m), Ritter. COVER: Joel McCrea, Barbara Stanwyck.

5582 Troopers Three (Tiffany, 1930, Rex Lease, Dorothy Gulliver).

As Long as You Love Me—George Waggner, Abner Silver (w,m), Shapiro Bernstein. COVER: Rex Lease, Dorothy Gulliver, Roscoe Karns, Slim Summerville.

5583 Troopship (Farewell Again) (United Artists, 1937, Leslie Banks, Flora Robson).

Hold Your Hats On (B)—Sonny Miller (w), Richard Addinsell (m), Keith Prowse. COVER: Soldiers.

5584 Tropicana (The Heat's On) (Columbia, 1943, Mae West, Victor Moore).

Thinkin' About the Wabash—Sammy Cahn, Walter Bullock (w), Jule Styne (m), Morley; Victory Polka—Sammy Cahn (w), Jule Styne (m), Chappell. COVER: Sammy Kaye on American Version; Mae West on British Version.

5585 Tropic Holiday (Paramount, 1938, Dorothy Lamour, Ray Milland).

Havin' Myself a Time—Leo Robin, Ralph Rainger (w,m), Paramount; Lamp on the Corner, The/My First Love/On a Tropic Night/Tonight Will Live—Ned Washington, Agustin Lara (w,m), Paramount. COVER: Dorothy Lamour, Ray Milland, and Movie Scenes.

5586 Tropic of Cancer (Paramount, 1970, Rip Torn, David Bauer).

Tropic of Cancer Love Theme-Germaine—Jay Darrow (w), Stanley Myers (m), Famous. COVER: Black and white cover with title only.

5587 Trouble in Paradise (Paramount, 1932, Miriam Hopkins, Kay Francis).

Trouble in Paradise (PC)—Leo Robin (w), W. Franke Harling (m), Famous. COVER: None.

5588 Trouble in Texas (Grand National, 1937, Tex Ritter, Rita Hayworth).

Down the Colorado Trail—Al Bryan (w), A. Stock (m), Sam Fox; Song of the Rodeo—Tex Ritter, Frank Sanucci (w,m), Sam Fox. COVER: Tex Ritter.

5589 Troublemaker, The (Janus, 1964, Thomas Aldredge, Joan Darling).

Troublemaker Theme—Cy Coleman (m), Morris. COVER: A Bomb and Buildings.

5590 Trouble Man (20th Century-Fox, 1972, Robert Hooks, Paul Winfield).

Trouble Man—Marvin Gaye (w,m), Jobete. COVER: Marvin Gaye.

5591 Trouble with Angels, The (Columbia, 1966, Rosalind Russell, Hayley Mills).

Trouble with Angels, The—Ernie Sheldon (w), Jerry Goldsmith (m), Colgems. COVER: Rosalind Russell, Hayley Mills.

5592 Trouble with Girls, The (MGM, 1969, Elvis Presley, Marlyn Mason).

Almost/Clean Up Your Own Back Yard—Scott Davis, Billy Strange (w, m), Presley. COVER: Elvis Presley.

5593 Trouble with Harry, The (Paramount, 1956, Shirley MacLaine, John Forsythe).

Flaggin' the Train to Tuscaloosa—Mack David (w), Raymond Scott (m), Frank; Trouble with Harry, The—Floyd Huddleston, H. Eiseman (w), Mark McIntyre (m), Frank. COVER: Shirley MacLaine, John Forsythe, Edmund Gwenn.

5594 Truck That Flew, The (Paramount, 1943, Pal Puppetoon).

Moonlight Holiday—Del Porter (w), Maurice DePackh (m), Paramount. COVER: Cartoon.

5595 True Confession (Paramount, 1937, Carole Lombard, Fred MacMurray).

True Confession—Sam Coslow, Frederick Hollander (w,m), Famous. COVER: Carole Lombard, Fred Mac-Murray.

5596 True Grit (Paramount, 1969, John Wayne, Glen Campbell).

True Grit—Don Black (w), Elmer Bernstein (m), Famous; True Grit Medley-Five Themes—Elmer Bernstein (m), Famous. COVER: John Wayne, Glen Campbell, Kim Darby.

5597 True Heaven (Fox, 1929, George O'Brien, Lois Moran).

True Heaven—Dave Stamper, William Kernell (w,m), DBH. COVER: George O'Brien, Lois Moran.

5598 True Story of the Song Lili Marlene, The (Universal, 1943, Stars Unknown).

Lili Marlene—Mack David (w), Phil Park (m), Chappell. COVER: Perry Como.

5599 True to Life (Paramount, 1943, Mary Martin, Dick Powell).

Mister Pollyanna/Old Music Master, The—Johnny Mercer (w), Hoagy Carmichael (m), Famous; There She Was—Hoagy Carmichael (w,m), Famous. COVER: Mary Martin, Dick Powell, Franchot Tone, Victor Moore.

5600 True to the Army (Paramount, 1942, Judy Canova, Ann Miller).

Jitterbug's Lullaby/Need I Speak—Frank Loesser (w), Harold Spina (m), Paramount. COVER: Judy Canova, Ann Miller, and Soldiers.

5601 True to the Navy (Paramount, 1930, Clara Bow, Fredric March).

Believe It or Not, I Lost My Man/There's Only One—L. Wolfe Gilbert, Abel Baer (w,m), Famous. COVER: Clara Bow.

5602 Trumpet Blows, The (Paramount, 1934, George Raft, Adolphe Menjou).

Pancho/This Night—Leo Robin, Ralph Rainger (w,m), Famous. COVER: George Raft, Frances Drake.

5603 Truth About Spring, The (Universal, 1965, Hayley Mills, James MacArthur).

The Truth About Spring (B)—David Heneker (w), Robert Farnon (m), Chappell. COVER: Hayley Mills, James MacArthur, John Mills.

5604 Tubby the Tuba (Paramount, 1947, Pal Puppetoon).

Tubby the Tuba Song—Paul Tripp (w), George Kleinsinger (m), General; Tubby the Tuba-Six Themes—Paul Tripp (w), George Kleinsinger (m), Schirmer. COVER: Cartoon.

5605 Tucker, The Man and His Dream (Paramount, 1988, Jeff Bridges, Joan Allen).

Captain of Industry Overture—Joe Jackson (m), Famous. COVER: Jeff Bridges, and Car.

5606 Tulsa (Eagle Lion, 1949, Robert Preston, Susan Hayward).

Tulsa—Mort Greene (w), Allie Wrubel (m), Advanced. COVER: Susan Hayward, Robert Preston.

5607 Tumbledown Ranch in Arizona (Monogram, 1941, Crash Corrigan, John King).

Tumbledown Range in Arizona/Wake Up with the Dawn—Bill Waters (w), Howard Steiner (m), Broadway. COVER: Crash Corrigan, John King, Max Terhune.

5608 Tumbling Tumbleweeds (Republic, 1935, Gene Autry, Smiley Burnette).

Riding Down the Canyon—Gene Autry, Smiley Burnette (w,m), Cole; That Silver Haired Daddy of Mine—Jimmy Long, Gene Autry (w,m), Cole; Tumbling Tumbleweeds—Bob Nolan (w,m), Sam Fox. COVER: Gene Autry.

5609 Tunes of Glory (United Artists, 1960, Alec Guinness, John Mills).

Black Bear, The—Malcolm Arnold (m), Unart; Tunes of Glory—Mel Mandel, Norman Sachs (w), Malcolm Arnold (m), Unart. COVER: Alec Guinness, John Mills.

5610 Tunnel of Love, The

(MGM, 1958, Doris Day, Richard Widmark).

Have Lips Will Kiss in the Tunnel of Love—Patty Fisher, Bob Roberts (w,m), Daywin; Run Away Skidaddle Skidoo—Ruth Roberts, Bill Katz (w, m), Daywin. COVER: Doris Day, Richard Widmark.

5611 Turn Off the Moon (Paramount, 1937, Johnny Downs, Eleanor Whitney).

Easy on the Eyes/Jammin'/That's Southern Hospitality/Turn Off the Moon—Sam Coslow (w,m), Popular. COVER: Kenny Baker, Phil Baker.

5612 Turn to the Right (MGM, 1927, Alice Terry, Jack Mulhall).

Turn to the Right—William Jerome (w), Milton Ager (m), Berlin. COVER: Alice Terry, Jack Mulhall.

5613 Tweety and Sylvester (Warner Bros., 1950 Cartoon).

I Taut I Taw a Puddy Tat—Alan Livingston, Billy May, Warren Foster (w,m), Remick. COVER: Cartoon.

5614 Twelve Angry Men (United Artists, 1957, Henry Fonda, Lee J. Cobb).

Twelve Angry Men-The Boy's Theme (PC)—Kenyon Hopkins (m), Unart. COVER: None.

5615 Twenty-Fifth Hour, The (MGM, 1967, Anthony Quinn, Virna Lisi).

The Twenty-Fifth Hour Theme—Georges Delerue (m), Miller. COVER: Anthony Quinn, Virna Lisi.

5616 Twenty-Four Hours of a Woman's Life (Affair in Monte Carlo) (Allied Artists, 1953, Merle Oberon, Richard Todd).

The Hour of Meditation (B)—Philip Green (m), Chappell. COVER: Merle Oberon, Richard Todd.

5617 Twenty Million Sweethearts (Warner Bros., 1934, Dick Powell, Ginger Rogers).

Fair and Warmer/I'll String Along with You—Al Dubin (w), Harry Warren (m), Witmark; Man on the Flying Trapeze, The—Ted Eastwood (w,m), Witmark; Out

for no Good/What Are Your Intentions?—Al Dubin (w), Harry Warren (m), Witmark. COVER: Dick Powell, Ginger Rogers, Pat O'Brien.

5618 Twenty-One Dollars a Day, Once a Month (Universal, 1941, Cartoon).

Twenty-One Dollars a Day, Once a Month—Ray Klages (w), Felix Bernard (m), Leeds. COVER: Cartoon.

5619 Twenty Thousand Cheers for a Chain Gang (Vitaphone, 1933, Musical Short).

The Sing Sing Serenade—Cliff Hess (w,m), Witmark. COVER: Black and white cover with title only.

5620 Twenty Thousand Leagues Under the Sea (Buena Vista, 1954, Kirk Douglas, James Mason).

A Whale of a Tale—Al Hoffman, Norman Gimbel (w,m), Wonderland. COVER: Kirk Douglas, and Sailors.

5621 Twenty Three and One Half Hours Leave (Grand National, 1937, James Ellison, Terry Walker).

Army Song, The/Goodnight My Lucky Day/It Must Be Love—Ted Koehler (w), Sam Stept (m), Select; Now You're Talking My Language—Sidney Mitchell, Ted Koehler (w), Sam Stept (m), Select. COVER: James Ellison, Terry Walker.

5622 Twice Blessed (MGM, 1950, Preston Foster, Wilde Twins).

Bem-te-vi Atrevido (Chorinho)—Lina Pesce (w,m), Peer; Lero-lero (Marcha Carnavesca)—B. Lacerda, E. Frazao (w,m), Peer. COVER: Ethel Smith.

5623 Twilight Melodies (Independent, 1929, Stars Unknown).

Twilight Melodies—Don Bernard, Nat Natoli, Vic Young (w,m), Grossman Lewis. COVER: Satyr Playing Flute.

5624 Twilight of Honor (MGM, 1963, Richard Chamberlain, Nick Adams).

I Knew It Then, I Know It Now—John Green (w,m), Miller. COVER:

Richard Chamberlain, Joan Blackman, Joey Heatherton.

5625 Twilight on the Prairie (Universal, 1944, Johnny Downs, Leon Errol).

Texas Polka—Vick Knight, Oakley Haldeman, Lew Porter (w,m), Urban. COVER: Jimmie Dodd, Connie Haines.

5626 Twilight Zone (Warner Bros., 1983, Vic Morrow, Scatman Crothers).

Nights Are Forever—John Bettis (w), Jerry Goldsmith (m), Warner. COVER: Twilight on Mountain.

5627 Twin Beds (First National, 1929, Jack Mulhall, Patsy Miller).

Chicken Walk/If You Were Mine—Al Bryan (w), George Meyer (m), Witmark. COVER: Patsy Miller, Jack Mulhall.

5628 Twinkle and Shine (It Happened to Jane) (Columbia, 1959, Doris Day, Jack Lemmon).

Twinkle and Shine—By Dunham (w,m), Artists. COVER: Doris Day, Jack Lemmon.

5629 Twinkle in God's Eye (Republic, 1955, Mickey Rooney, Coleen Gray).

Twinkle in God's Eye, The—Mickey Rooney (w,m), Rooney. COVER: Mickey Rooney.

5630 Twist Around the Clock (Columbia, 1962, Chubby Checker, Dion).

Twist Around the Clock—Buddy Kaye, Philip Springer, Clay Cole (w,m), Columbia. COVER: Chubby Checker, Dion, and Rock Stars.

5631 Two for the Road (20th Century-Fox, 1967, Audrey Hepburn, Albert Finney).

Happy Barefoot Boy—Henry Mancini (m), Northridge; Two for the Road—Leslie Bricusse (w), Henry Mancini (m), Northridge. COVER: Audrey Hepburn, Albert Finney.

5632 Two for the Seesaw (United Artists, 1962, Robert Mitchum, Shirley MacLaine).

Second Chance, A—Dory Langdon (w), André Previn (m), Unart.

COVER: Robert Mitchum, Shirley MacLaine.

5633 Two for Tonight (Paramount, 1935, Bing Crosby, Joan Bennett).

From the Top of Your Head to the Tip of Your Toes/I Wish I Were Aladdin/Takes Two to Make a Bargain/Two for Tonight/Without a Word of Warning—Mack Gordon, Harry Revel (w,m), Crawford. COVER: Bing Crosby, Joan Bennett.

5634 Two Girls and a Sailor (MGM, 1944, Van Johnson, June Allyson).

Babalu/Cachita—Margarita Lecuona (w,m), Peer; Estrellita—Manuel Ponce (w,m), Assoc. Music; In a Moment of Madness—Ralph Freed (w), Jimmy McHugh (m), Feist; Granada—Dorothy Dodd (w), Agustin Lara (m), Peer; La Mulata Rumbera—Alejandro Rodriguez (w,m), Peer; Love Like Ours, A—Mann Holiner (w), Alberta Nichols (m), Feist; My Mother Told Me—Ralph Freed (w), Jimmy McHugh (m), Feist; Rumba, Rumba—Sammy Gallop (w), Jose Pafumy (m), Peer; Sweet and Lovely—Gus Arnheim, Harry Tobias, Jules Lemare (w,m), Robbins; Take It Easy—Al DeBau, Irving Taylor, Vic Mizzy (w,m), Santly Joy; You Dear—Ralph Freed (w), Sammy Fain (m), Feist; Young Man with a Horn—Ralph Freed (w), George Stoll (m), Feist. COVER: Van Johnson, Gloria De Haven, June Allyson, Harry James, Helen Forrest.

5635 Two Girls on Broadway (MGM, 1940, Lana Turner, Joan Blondell).

Maybe It's the Moon (BW)—Bob Wright, Chet Forrest (w), Walter Donaldson (m), Donaldson; My Wonderful One Let's Dance—Nacio Herb Brown, Arthur Freed, Roger Edens (w,m), Feist; Rancho Santa Fe (BW)/True Love (BW)—Gus Kahn (w), Walter Donaldson (m), Feist. COVER: Lana Turner, George Murphy, Joan Blondell.

5636 Two Gun Rusty (Paramount, 1944, Pal Puppetoon).

Down in Santa Fe—Rudy Sooter (w), Maurice DePackh (m), Famous. COVER: Rudy Sooter.

5637 Two Gun Troubadour (Spectrum, 1939, Fred Scott, Claire Rochelle).

Cowboy and the School Marm, The (VS)—Martha Zimmer, D. Jarrel, Fred Scott (w,m), American; Ride Cowboy Ride (VS)—E. Jennings, C. Junkins, Fred Scott (w, m), American. COVER: Fred Scott.

5638 Two Guys from Texas (Warner Bros., 1948, Dennis Morgan, Jack Carson).

At the Rodeo—Sammy Cahn (w), Jule Styne (m), Remick; Ev'ry Day I Love You—Sammy Cahn (w), Jule Styne (m), Harms; Hankerin'— Sammy Cahn (w), Jule Styne (m), Remick; I Don't Care If It Rains All Night/I Never Met a Texan/I Wanna Be a Cowboy in the Movies—Sammy Cahn (w), Jule Styne (m), Witmark; There's Music in the Land—Sammy Cahn (w), Jule Styne (m), Harms. COVER: Dennis Morgan, Jack Carson, Janis Paige.

5639 Two Heads on a Pillow (Liberty, 1934, Miriam Jordan, Neil Hamilton).

Oh, Why?—Herbert Stahlberg (w), Hugo Riesenfeld (m), Southern. COVER: Neil Hamilton, Miriam Jordan.

5640 Two Hearts in Harmony (Time, 1935, Bernice Clare, George Curzon).

Sleep, My Baby, Sleep—Eddie Pola, Franz Steininger (w,m), Shapiro Bernstein. COVER: Bobby Breen, Judy Garland.

5641 Two Hearts in Waltz Time (Associated Cinema, 1930, Walter Janseen, Oscar Karlweiss).

I See Vienna in Your Eyes of Blue/ Song of Vienna/Two Hearts/You Too—Joe Young (w), Robert Stolz (m), Harms. COVER: Silhouette of Couple Drinking.

5642 Two Latins from Manhattan (Columbia, 1941, Joan Davis, Jinx Falkenburg).

Daddy—Bob Troup (w,m), Republic. COVER: Joan Davis, Jinx Falkenburg.

5643 Two Lovers (United Artists, 1927, Vilma Banky, Ronald Colman).

Grieving—Wayland Axtell (w,m), Forster; Lenora-Waltz Song—L. Wolfe Gilbert (w), Hugo Riesenfeld (m), Feist. COVER: Vilma Banky.

5644 Two Loves (MGM, 1961, Laurence Harvey, Shirley MacLaine).

Children's Picnic Song—Walton Farrar (w), Bronislau Kaper (m), Robbins; Two Loves-Theme—Bronislau Kaper (m), Robbins. COVER: Laurence Harvey, Shirley MacLaine.

5645 Two Men and a Maid (Tiffany, 1929, Eddie Gribbon, Alma Bennett).

Love Will Find You—L. Wolfe Gilbert (w), Abel Baer (m), Feist; Rose of Algiers (PC)—John Rafael (w), Ted Shapiro (m), Ager Yellen. COVER: Eddie Gribbon, Alma Bennett, William Collier.

5646 Two Men of Karamoja (Tomorrow, 1974, Iaian Ross, Paul Ssalii).

Two Men of Karamoja—Charles Grean (m), Galahad. COVER: Iaian Ross, Paul Ssalii, and Animals.

5647 Two of a Kind (20th Century-Fox, 1983, John Travolta, Olivia Newton-John).

Take a Chance—David Foster, Steve Lukather, Olivia Newton-John (w,m), Foster; Two of a Kind-Ten Songs—David Foster, Tom Snow, Steve Kipner (w,m), Columbia. COVER: John Travolta, Olivia Newton-John.

5648 Two of Us, The (Gainsborough, 1935, Jack Hulbert, Gina Malo).

Where There's You There's Me/ You're Sweeter Than I Thought You Were—Maurice Sigler, Al Goodhart,

Al Hoffman (w,m), Feist. COVER: Jack Hulbert.

5649 Two on a Guillotine (Warner Bros., 1965, Connie Stevens, Dean Jones).

Right to Love, The—Ervin Drake (w), Max Steiner (m), Witmark. COVER: Connie Stevens, Dean Jones.

5650 Two People (Universal, 1972, Peter Fonda, Lindsay Wagner).

Time Will Tell—Richard Maltby (w), David Shire (m), Duchess. COVER: Peter Fonda, Lindsay Wagner.

5651 Two Rode Together (Columbia, 1961, James Stewart, Richard Widmark).

Two Rode Together (PC)—Stanley Styne (w), George Duning (m), Columbia. COVER: None.

5652 Two Shadows (Vitaphone, 1938, Sharkey Ronano and His Band).

Two Shadows—Bobby Byrnes (w), Guy Wood (m), Witmark. COVER: George Hall.

5653 Two Sisters from Boston (MGM, 1946, Kathryn Grayson, June Allyson).

When Romance Passes By—Earl Brent (w), Leo Delibes (m), Feist; After the Show (VS)/Down by the Ocean (VS)/Fire Chief's Daughter (VS)/G'wan Home, Your Mudder's Callin' (VS)/Nellie Martin (VS)/ There Are Two Sides to Every Girl (VS)—Ralph Freed (w), Sammy Fain (m), Feist. COVER: Jimmy Durante, June Allyson, Kathryn Grayson, Peter Lawford.

5654 Two Smart People (MGM, 1946, Lucille Ball, John Hodiak).

Dangerous (Peligrosa)—Ralph Blane, George Bassman (w,m), Robbins. COVER: Lucille Ball, John Hodiak.

5655 2001: A Space Odyssey (MGM, 1968, Keir Dullea, Gary Lockwood).

2001 Space Odyssey Theme—

Richard Strauss (m), Lewis. COVER: The Earth from Space.

5656 2010 (MGM, 1984, John Lithgow, Helen Mirren).

New World's Theme—David Shire (m), Blackwood. COVER: A Baby.

5657 Two Tickets to Broadway (RKO, 1951, Tony Martin, Janet Leigh).

Closer You Are, The/Let the Worry Bird Worry for You—Leo Robin (w), Jule Styne (m), Morris; Manhattan—Lorenz Hart (w), Richard Rodgers (m), Marks. COVER: Tony Martin, Janet Leigh, Dinah Shore.

5658 Two Weeks in Another Town (MGM, 1962, Kirk Douglas, Edward G. Robinson).

Two Weeks in Another Town-Theme—David Raksin (m), Miller. COVER: Kirk Douglas, Cyd Charisse.

5659 Two Weeks Off (First National, 1929, Jack Mulhall, Dorothy Mackaill).

Love Thrills—Al Bryan (w), George Meyer (m), Witmark. COVER: Jack Mulhall, Dorothy Mackaill.

5660 Two Weeks with Love (MGM, Jane Powell, Ricardo Montalban).

Aba Daba Honeymoon, The—Arthur Fields, Walter Donovan (w,m), Feist; Heart That's Free, A—Thomas Railey (w), Alfred Robyn (m), Feist; That's How I Need You—Joe McCarthy, Joe Goodwin (w), Al Piantadosi (m), Feist. COVER: Jane Powell, Ricardo Montalban, Debbie Reynolds, Carlton Carpenter.

5661 Typhoon (Paramount, 1940, Dorothy Lamour, Robert Preston).

Palms of Paradise—Frank Loesser (w), Frederick Hollander (m), Famous. COVER: Dorothy Lamour, Robert Preston.

5662 Uei Paesano (Argentina Sono, 1954, Nicola Paone).

Way, Paesano—Tom Glazer (w),

Nicola Paone (m), Shapiro Bernstein. COVER: Al Martino.

5663 Umbrellas of Cherbourg, The (Landau, 1964, Catherine Deneuve, Nino Castelnuovo).

I'm Falling in Love Again—Bill Barberis, Ted Randazzo (w), Michel Legrand (m), Vogue; I Will Wait for You/Watch What Happens—Norman Gimbel (w), Michel Legrand (m), Vogue; Where's the Love—Bobby Weinstein (w), Michel Legrand (m), Vogue; Day They Closed the Carousel (VS)—Ruth Allison (w), Michel Legrand (m), Vogue; Two Voices (VS)—Bill Barberis, Ted Randazzo (w), Michel Legrand (m), Vogue. COVER: Couple with Umbrella.

5664 Uncertain Glory (Warner Bros., 1944, Errol Flynn, Jean Sullivan).

Marianne—Ernesto Lecuona, Josef Myrow, Eddie DeLange (w,m), Remick. COVER: Errol Flynn, Jean Sullivan.

5665 Unchained (Warner Bros., 1955, Elroy Hirsch, Barbara Hale).

Unchained Melody—Hy Zaret (w), Alex North (m), Frank. COVER: Elroy Hirsch, Barbara Hale.

5666 Uncle Tom's Cabin (Universal, 1927, James Lowe, Virginia Grey).

Old Noah's Ark (B)—Noble Sissle (w), Eubie Blake (m), Keith Prowse. COVER: Movie Scene.

5667 Uncommon Valor (Paramount, 1984, Gene Hackman, Robert Stack).

Brothers in the Night—Ray Kennedy, David Ritz, Kevin Dukes (w, m), Famous. COVER: Soldiers.

5668 Undefeated, The (20th Century-Fox, 1969, John Wayne, Rock Hudson).

The Undefeated—Hugo Montenegro (m), Twentieth Century. COVER: John Wayne, Rock Hudson, and Others.

5669 Under a Texas Moon (Warner Bros., 1930, Frank Fay, Myrna Loy).

Under a Texas Moon—Ray Perkins (w,m), Witmark. COVER: Frank Fay, Myrna Loy.

5670 Under Capricorn (Warner Bros., 1948, Ingrid Bergman, Joseph Cotten).

One Magic Wish—Kay Twomey (w), Richard Addinsell (m), Chappell; Under Capricorn Themes (B)—Richard Addinsell (m). COVER: Ingrid Bergman, Joseph Cotten, Michael Wilding.

5671 Undercurrent (MGM, 1947, Katharine Hepburn, Robert Taylor).

Undercurrent—J. Brahms, Herbert Stothart (m), Robbins. COVER: Katharine Hepburn, Robert Taylor.

5672 Under Fiesta Stars (Republic, 1941, Gene Autry, Gabby Hayes).

Under Fiesta Stars—Gene Autry, Fred Rose (w,m), Western. COVER: Gene Autry.

5673 Under My Skin (20th Century-Fox, 1950, John Garfield, Micheline Prelle).

Stranger in the Night—Mack Gordon (w), Alfred Newman (m), Robbins. COVER: John Garfield, Micheline Prelle.

5674 Under Paris Skies (Regina, 1951, Brigette Auber, Jean Brochard).

Under Paris Skies—Kim Gannon (w), Hubert Giraud (m), Leeds; Under Paris Skies-Theme—Hubert Giraud (m), Leeds. COVER: Georgia Gibbs.

5675 Underpup, The (Universal, 1939, Gloria Jean, Robert Cummings).

I'm Like a Bird—Harold Adamson (w), Charles Previn (m), Feist; Shepherd Lullaby—Ralph Freed (w), W. A. Mozart (m), Feist. COVER: Gloria Jean.

5676 Under Suspicion (Fox, 1930, Lois Moran, Harold Murray).

Round My Kingdom's Door/Sas-Katch-A/Whisper to the Whisp'ring Pines—Joe McCarthy (w), James Hanley (m), Red Star. COVER: Black and white cover with title only.

5677 Under Ten Flags (Paramount, 1960, Van Heflin, Charles Laughton).
Under Ten Flags—Ruth Roberts, William Katz (w,m), Famous. COVER: Van Heflin, Charles Laughton.
5678 Under the Cherry Moon (Warner Bros., 1986, Prince, Jerome Benton).
Kiss/Mountains—Prince (w,m), Warner. COVER: Prince.
5679 Under the Pampas Moon (Fox, 1935, Warner Baxter, Ketti Gallian).
The Gaucho—B. G. DeSylva (w), Walter Samuels (m), Harms. COVER: Warner Baxter.
5680 Under the Yum Yum Tree (Columbia, 1963, Jack Lemmon, Carol Lynley).
Under the Yum Yum Tree—Sammy Cahn (w), James Van Heusen (m), Colgems. COVER: Jack Lemmon, Carol Lynley.
5681 Under Two Flags (Universal, 1922, Priscilla Dean, James Kirkwood).
Cigarette—Guy Sampsel (w), Don Mathews (m), Shapiro Bernstein. COVER: Priscilla Dean.
5682 Under Two Flags (20th Century-Fox, 1936, Ronald Colman, Claudette Colbert).
One-Two-Three-Four-Hey!—Sidney Mitchell (w), Lew Pollack (m), Movietone. COVER: Brown and white cover with title only.
5683 Underwater (RKO, 1955, Gilbert Roland, Jane Russell).
Cherry Pink and Apple Blossom White—Mack David (w), Louiguy (m), Chappell. COVER: Jane Russell.
5684 Under Western Stars (Republic, 1938, Roy Rogers, Smiley Burnette).
Dust—Johnny Marvin (w,m), Santly Joy; That Pioneer Mother of Mine—Tim Spencer (w,m), American. COVER: Roy Rogers, Sons of the Pioneers.
5685 Under Your Spell (20th Century-Fox, 1936, Lawrence Tibbett, Wendy Barrie).
Amigo, My Friend/My Little Mule Wagon/Under Your Spell—Howard Dietz (w), Arthur Schwartz (m), Movietone. COVER: Lawrence Tibbett.
5686 Unfaithful (Paramount, 1931, Ruth Chatterton, Paul Lukas).
Mama's in the Doghouse Now—Sam Coslow (w,m), Famous. COVER: Ruth Chatterton.
5687 Unfaithfully Yours (20th Century-Fox, 1984, Dudley Moore, Nastassja Kinski).
Unfaithfully Yours—Stephen Bishop (w,m), Bishop. COVER: Stephen Bishop.
5688 Unfinished Business (Universal, 1939, Irene Dunne, Robert Montgomery).
I Love Thee—Henry Chapman (w), Edvard Grieg (m), Schirmer. COVER: Irene Dunne.
5689 Unfinished Dance, The (MGM, 1947, Margaret O'Brien, Cyd Charisse).
Holiday for Strings (B)—David Rose (m), Chappell; I Went Merrily Merrily on My Way—Irving Kahal (w), Sammy Fain (m), Crawford; Minor Melody—Ray Jacobs, Danny Thomas (w,m), Robbins. COVER: Margaret O'Brien, Danny Thomas, and Girls.
5690 Unforgiven, The (United Artists, 1960, Burt Lancaster, Audrey Hepburn).
The Need for Love-The Unforgiven—Ned Washington (w), Dimitri Tiomkin (m), Hecht. COVER: Burt Lancaster, Audrey Hepburn.
5691 Unholy Beebes, The (Sing You Sinners) (Paramount, 1938, Bing Crosby, Fred MacMurray).
Don't Let That Moon Get Away/I've Got a Pocketful of Dreams/Laugh and Call It Love—John Burke (w), James Monaco (m), Santly Joy. COVER: Bing Crosby, Fred MacMurray, Donald O'Connor.
5692 Uninvited, The (Paramount, 1946, Ray Milland, Ruth Hussey).

Stella by Starlight—Ned Washington (w), Victor Young (m), Famous; Stella by Starlight Solo/Stella by Starlight Theme—Victor Young (m), Famous. COVER: A Girl and a Moon.

5693 United We Stand (20th Century-Fox, 1942, War Film).

United We Stand—Herb Rikles, Howard Dressner (w), Samuel Meade (m), Mills. COVER: Flags of Allies.

5694 Unknown Soldier, The (Hoffman, 1926, Charles Mack, Marguerite De La Motte).

The Unknown Soldier's Grave—Annabelle Lee (w,m), Shapiro Bernstein. COVER: Charles Mack, Marguerite De La Motte.

5695 Unmarried Woman, An (20th Century-Fox, 1978, Alan Bates, Jill Clayburgh).

An Unmarried Woman—Michelle Wiley (w), Bill Conti (m), 20th Century. COVER: Jill Clayburgh.

5696 Unmasked (Weiss, 1929, Robert Warwick, Milton Krims).

I'll Climb the Highway to Your Heart—John Steel Abner Silver (w, m), Remick. COVER: Robert Warwick, Sam Ash, and Girls.

5697 Unpardonable Sin, The (Garson, 1919, Blanche Sweet, Bobby Connelly).

The Unpardonable Sin—Arthur Lamb (w), Frederick Bowers (m), Bowers. COVER: Blanche Sweet.

5698 Unsinkable Molly Brown, The (MGM, 1964, Debbie Reynolds, Harve Presnell).

Belly up to the Bar Boys/Colorado My Home/Dolce Far Niente/He's My Friend/I Ain't Down Yet/I'll Never Say No/Bon Jour (VS)/If I Knew (VS)/Leadville Johnny Brown (VS)—Meredith Willson (w, m), Frank. COVER: Debbie Reynolds.

5699 Untamed (MGM, 1929, Joan Crawford, Robert Montgomery).

Chant of the Jungle—Arthur Freed (w), Nacio Herb Brown (m),

Robbins; That Wonderful Something —Joe Goodwin (w), Louis Alter (m), Robbins. COVER: Joan Crawford.

5700 Untamed Youth (Warner Bros., 1957, Lori Nelson, Mamie Van Doren).

Go Go Calypso—Les Baxter (w, m), Witmark; Oo La La Baby—Les Baxter, L. Adelson, E. Cochran, J. Capehart (w,m), Witmark; Rolling Stone—Lenny Adelson (w), Les Baxter (m), Witmark; Salamander—Les Baxter (w,m), Witmark. COVER: Mamie Van Doren.

5701 Until They Sail (MGM, 1957, Jean Simmons, Joan Fontaine).

Until They Sail—Sammy Cahn (w), David Raksin (m), Miller. COVER: Jean Simmons, Paul Newman.

5702 Untouchables, The (Paramount, 1987, Kevin Costner, Robert De Niro).

Untouchables Theme, The/Untouchables-Three Themes—Ennio Morricone (m), Famous. COVER: Kevin Costner, Robert De Niro, Sean Connery.

5703 Up from the Beach (20th Century-Fox, 1965, Cliff Robertson, Red Buttons).

No Time to Love—Lorraine Williams (w), Edgar Cosma (m), Miller; Up from the Beach-March—Edgar Cosma (m), Miller. COVER: Cliff Robertson, Irina Demick, and Soldiers.

5704 Up in Arms (RKO, 1944, Danny Kaye, Dinah Shore).

All Out for Freedom/Now I Know/Tess's Torch Song, I Had a Man—Ted Koehler (w), Harold Arlen (m), Harms. COVER: Danny Kaye, Dinah Shore.

5705 Up in Central Park (Universal, 1948, Deanna Durbin, Dick Haymes).

Carousel in the Park (B)/Close as Pages in a Book (B)/When You Walk in the Room (B)—Dorothy Fields (w), Sigmund Romberg (m), Williamson. COVER: Deanna Durbin, Dick Haymes.

5706 Up in Mary's Attic (Fine Arts, 1920, Eva Novak, Harry Bribbon).
Up in Mary's Attic—Ethel Broaker, Dwight Conn (w,m), Broaker-Conn. COVER: Eva Novak, and Baby.
5707 Upstairs and Down (Selznick, 1919, Olive Thomas, Robert Ellis).
Upstairs and Down—Sam Lewis, Joe Young (w), Walter Donaldson (m), Berlin. COVER: Olive Thomas.
5708 Up the Junction (Paramount, 1968, Dennis Waterman, Suzy Kendall).
Up the Junction—Mike Hugg (w, m), Famous. COVER: Dennis Waterman, Suzy Kendall.
5709 Up the River (20th Century-Fox, 1938, Tony Martin, Preston Foster).
It's the Strangest Thing—Sidney Clare, Harry Akst (w,m), Mills. COVER: Tony Martin, Phyllis Brooks.
5710 Up Tight (Paramount, 1968, Raymond St. Jacques, Ruby Dee).
Johnny I Love You/Time Is Tight—Booker T. Jones (w,m), East Memphis. COVER: Raymond St. Jacques.
5711 Uptown New York (Tiffany, 1932, Jack Oakie, Shirley Grey).
A Viennese Waltz Song—Hazel Bruster (w,m), Sam Fox. COVER: Black and white cover with title only.
5712 Urban Cowboy (Paramount, 1980, John Travolta, Debra Winger).
Could I Have This Dance—Wayland Holyfield, Bob House (w,m), Maplehill; Hello Texas—Brian Collins, Robby Campbell (w,m), Beef Baron; Lookin' for Love—Wanda Mallette, Patti Ryan, Bob Morrison (w,m), Southern Nights; Love the World Away—Bob Morrison, Johnny Wilson (w,m), Southern Nights; Stand by Me—Ben King, Mike Stoller, Jerry Lieber (w,m), Chappell; Urban Cowboy-17 Songs—Joe Walsh,

Mike Murphy, J. D. Souther, Rusty Wier (w,m), Warner. COVER: John Travolta, Debra Winger, and Movie Scenes.
5713 Used Cars (Columbia, 1980, Jack Warden, Kurt Russell).
Used Cars—Norman Gimbel (w), Patrick Williams (m), Colgems. COVER: Field of Grass and the Sun.
5714 Use Your Imagination (Vitaphone, 1933, Musical Short).
Wouldn't It Be Nice—Cliff Hess (w,m), Witmark. COVER: Black and white cover with title only.
5715 Utah Trail, The (Grand National, 1938, Tex Ritter, Adele Pearce).
The Utah Trail—Bob Palmer (w, m), Southern. COVER: Tex Ritter.
5716 U-2—Rattle and Hum (Paramount, 1988, U-2 Rock Group).
Angel of Harlem/Desire/U-2 Rattle and Hum-17 Songs—Bono (w), U-2 (m), U-2. COVER: U-2 Rock Group.
5717 Vacation from Love (MGM, 1938, Dennis O'Keefe, Florence Rice).
Let's Pretend It's True—Bob Wright, Chet Forrest (w), Edward Ward (m), Feist. COVER: Dennis O'Keefe, Florence Rice.
5718 Vagabond King, The (Paramount, 1930, Jeanette MacDonald, Dennis King).
Love for Sale/Love Me Tonight/Only a Rose/Some Day/Song of the Vagabonds/Vagabond King Waltz—Brian Hooker (w), Rudolph Friml (m), Famous. COVER: Jeanette MacDonald, Dennis King.
5719 Vagabond King, The (Paramount, 1956, Kathryn Grayson, Oreste).
Bon Jour/Comparisons—Johnny Burke (w), Rudolf Friml (m), Famous; Lord I'm Glad That I Know Thee—Johnny Burke (w), Victor Young (m), Famous; Only a Rose/Some Day/Song of the Vagabonds—Brian Hooker (w), Rudolf Friml (m), Famous; This Same Heart—Johnny

Burke (w), Rudolf Friml (m), Famous; Vagabond King Waltz—Brian Hooker (w), Rudolf Friml (m), Famous; Vive La You/Watch Out for the Devil—Johnny Burke (w), Rudolf Friml (m), Famous. COVER: Kathryn Grayson, Oreste, and Movie Scenes.

5720 Vagabond Lover, The (RKO, 1929, Rudy Vallee, Sally Blane).

If You Were the Only Girl—Clifford Grey (w), Nat Ayer (m), Chappell Harms; I Love You Believe Me I Love You—Rubey Cowan (w), Phil Boutelje (m), Harms; Little Kiss Each Morning, A—Harry Woods (w,m), Harms; Nobody's Sweetheart—Gus Kahn, E. Erdman, B. Meyers, E. Schoebel (w,m), Mills; Then I'll Be Reminded of You—Ed Heyman (w), Ken Smith (m), Harms. COVER: Rudy Vallee.

5721 Valachi Papers, The (Columbia, 1972, Charles Bronson, Joseph Wiseman).

Valachi Papers Love Theme—Hal Hackady (w), Riz Ortolani (m), Dramatis. COVER: Charles Bronson, Lino Venturi.

5722 Valentino (Columbia, 1950, Eleanor Parker, Anthony Dexter).

La Comparita—The Masked One—Olga Paul (w), G. Rodriguez (m), Marks; Sheik of Araby, The—Harry B. Smith, Francis Wheeler (w), Ted Snyder (m), Mills; Valentino Tango, The—Jack Lawrence (w), Heinz Roemheld (m), Leeds. COVER: Eleanor Parker, Anthony Dexter, Patricia Medina.

5723 Valley of the Dolls (20th Century-Fox, 1967, Barbara Parkins, Patty Duke).

Give a Little More/I'll Plant My Own Tree/It's Impossible/Valley of the Dolls-Theme—Dory Previn (w), André Previn (m), Feist. COVER: Barbara Parkins, Patty Duke, Sharon Tate.

5724 Valley of the Giants (Paramount, 1919, Wallace Reid, Grace Darmond).

Valley of the Giants—Sam Lewis, Joe Young (w), Bert Grant (m), Berlin. COVER: Wallace Reid, Grace Darmond.

5725 Vampire, The (United Artists, 1957, John Beal, Coleen Gray).

The Vampire!—Alan Bergman, Marilyn Keith (w), Gerald Fried, H. Gilbert (m), Paul. COVER: Green cover with title only.

5726 Vanishing American, The (Paramount, 1925, Richard Dix, Lois Wilson).

Little White Rose—Wells Hively (w), Charles Cadman (m), Sherman Clay. COVER: An Indian Facing a City.

5727 Vanishing Point (20th Century-Fox, 1971, Barry Newman, Cleavon Little).

Vanishing Point-Love Theme—Jimmy Bowen, Pete Carpenter (m), Fox. COVER: Hippies and an Automobile.

5728 Vanishing Prairie, The (Buena Vista, 1954, Wild Life Adventure).

Prairie Home—Gil George (w), Paul Smith (m), Disney. COVER: Prairie and Sky.

5729 Vanishing Virginian, The (MGM, 1941, Frank Morgan, Kathryn Grayson).

The World Was Made for You—Earl Brent (w), Johann Strauss (m), Feist. COVER: Kathryn Grayson.

5730 Variety Girl (Paramount, 1947, Mary Hatcher, Olga San Juan).

Harmony—Johnny Burke (w), James Van Heusen (m), BVH; He Can Waltz/Tallahassee—Frank Loesser (w,m), Famous; Tired—Allan Roberts, Doris Fisher (w,m), Barton; Your Heart Calling Mine—Frank Loesser (w,m), Famous. COVER: Bing Crosby, Bob Hope, and 45 Paramount Stars.

5731 Variety Parade (Butcher, 1936, Mrs. Jack Hylton and Her Boys).

Taking a Stroll Around the Park—

Clive Erard (w,m), Mills. COVER: Mrs. Jack Hylton.

5732 Varsitans, The (First Consolidated, 1929, Anna Ross, Buddy Shaw).

Varsity Rhythm—Haven Gillespie, Ray Canfield, Neil Moret (w,m), Villa Moret. COVER: Anna Ross, Buddy Shaw.

5733 Varsity (Paramount, 1927, Buddy Rogers, Chester Conklin).

My Varsity Girl, I'll Cling to You —Alfred Bryan (w), Frank Harling (m), Famous. COVER: Buddy Rogers, Mary Brian.

5734 Varsity Show (Warner Bros., 1937, Dick Powell, Priscilla Lane).

Give Us a Drink—Pat Ballard, Charles Henderson, Tom Waring (w, m), Words Music; Have You Got Any Castles Baby?—Johnny Mercer (w), Richard Whiting (m), Harms; I'm Dependable—Don Raye (w), Tom Waring (m), Words Music; Let That Be a Lesson to You—Johnny Mercer (w), Richard Whiting (m), Harms; Little Fraternity Pin—Paul Gibbons (w), Roy Ringwald (m), Words Music; Love Is on the Air Tonight/Moonlight on the Campus/Old King Cole/ On with the Dance/We're Working Our Way Through College/You've Got Something There—Johnny Mercer (w), Richard Whiting (m), Harms. COVER: Dick Powell, Priscilla Lane, Rosemary Lane, Fred Waring.

5735 Vega$ (Spelling, 1978, Robert Urich, Tony Curtis).

Vegas-Theme—Dominic Frontiere (m), Columbia. COVER: Robert Urich, and Other Stars.

5736 Velvet Touch, The (RKO, 1948, Rosalind Russell, Leo Genn).

The Velvet Touch—Mort Greene (w), Leigh Harline (m), Sinatra. COVER: Rosalind Russell.

5737 Venere Imperiale (Imperial Love) (Cineriz, 1964, Gina Lollobrigida, Stephen Boyd).

Venere Imperiale Theme (PC)— A. F. Lavagnino (m), Marks. COVER: None.

5738 Venetian Affair, The (MGM, 1967, Robert Vaughn, Elke Sommer).

Our Venetian Affair—Hal Winn (w), Lalo Schifrin (m), Hastings. COVER: Robert Vaughn, Elke Sommer.

5739 Vengeance (Columbia, 1928, Jack Holt, Dorothy Revier).

Vengeance (PC)—Harry Akst (m), Remick. COVER: None.

5740 Vera Cruz (United Artists, 1954, Gary Cooper, Burt Lancaster).

Vera Cruz—Sammy Cahn (w), Hugo Friedhofer (m), Feist. COVER: Gary Cooper, Burt Lancaster.

5741 Verboten (RKO, 1959, James Best, Susan Cummings).

Verboten (Forbidden)—Mack David (w), Harry Sukman (m), Feist. COVER: James Best, Susan Cummings.

5742 Vertigo (Paramount, 1958, James Stewart, Kim Novak).

Vertigo—Jay Livingston, Ray Evans (w,m), Famous. COVER: James Stewart, Kim Novak.

5743 Very Thought of You, The (Warner Bros., 1945, Dennis Morgan, Eleanor Parker).

The Very Thought of You—Ray Noble (w,m), Witmark. COVER: Dennis Morgan, Eleanor Parker.

5744 Vicious Breed, The (Sedish, 1961, Stars Unknown).

The Lonely Whistler—Charles Norman, Les Baxter (m), Robbins. COVER: A Grand Piano.

5745 Vicki (20th Century-Fox, 1953, Jeanne Crain, Jean Peters).

Vicki—Ken Darby (w), Max Showalter (m), Frank. COVER: Jean Peters.

5746 Victoria the Great (RKO, 1937, Anna Neagle, Anton Walbrook).

Victoria the Great-Incidental Music (B)—Anthony Collins (m), Keith Prowse. COVER: A Scroll with Fancy Lettering.

5747 Victors, The (Columbia, 1963, Vincent Edwards, Albert Finney).

Does Goodnight Mean Goodbye—Howard Greenfield, Gerry Goffin, Jack Keller (w,m), Colgems; Magda's Song/March of the Victors—Freddy Douglas (w), Sol Kaplan (m), Colgems; Victors Theme-My Special Dream—Freddy Douglas, Howard Greenfield (w), Sol Kaplan (m), Colgems. COVER: Soldiers.

5748 Victor/Victoria (MGM, 1982, Julie Andrews, Robert Preston).

Crazy World/You and Me—Leslie Bricusse (w), Henry Mancini (m), MGM; Alone in Paris (VS)/Cat and Mouse (VS)—Henry Mancini (m), Big Three; Chicago Illinois (VS)/Gay Paree (VS)/Le Jazz Hot (VS)/Shady Dame from Seville (VS)—Leslie Bricusse (w), Henry Mancini (m), Big Three. COVER: A Pair of Lips and a Mustache.

5749 Victory at Sea (United Artists, 1954, War Documentary).

Guadalcanal March/Song of the High Seas/Victory at Sea Symphonic Scenario—Richard Rodgers (m), Williamson. COVER: Red, white, and blue cover with title only.

5750 Victory of Virtue, The (Exclusive Films, 1915, Gerda Holmes, Bert Howard).

Penelope—Richard Carroll (w), Bert Howard (m), Remick. COVER: Gerda Holmes.

5751 Victory Through Air Power (United Artists, 1943, War Cartoon).

Song of the Eagle-Bombs Away—Oliver Wallace (w,m), Forster. COVER: An Eagle and an Octopus.

5752 Victory Vehicles (Disney, 1943, Cartoon).

Hop on Your Pogo Stick—Ned Washington (w), Oliver Wallace (m), Southern. COVER: Cartoon.

5753 Viennese Nights (Warner Bros., 1930, Vivienne Segal, Alexander Gray).

Here We Are/I Bring a Love Song/I'm Lonely/Ja Ja Ja/Regimental March/You Will Remember Vienna—Oscar Hammerstein (w), Sigmund Romberg (m), Harms. COVER: A Castle on a Mountain.

5754 View to a Kill, A (MGM, 1985, Roger Moore, Christopher Walken).

A View to a Kill—Duran Duran, John Barry (w,m), Blackwood. COVER: Roger Moore, and Grace Jones.

5755 Vikings, The (United Artists, 1958, Kirk Douglas, Tony Curtis).

Vikings Love Theme/Vikings March—Joe Lubin (w), Mario Nascimbene (m), Unart. COVER: Kirk Douglas, Tony Curtis.

5756 Village of Daughters (MGM, 1962, Eric Sykes, Scilla Gabel).

Village of Daughters (B)—Ron Goodwin (m), Robbins. COVER: Eric Sykes, Scilla Gabel.

5757 Villain Still Pursued Her, The (RKO, 1940, Hugh Herbert, Alan Mowbray).

The Villain Still Pursued Her—Charles Tobias, Nat Simon, Harry Tobias (w,m), Shapiro Bernstein. COVER: Alan Mowbray, Anita Louise.

5758 Villa Rides (Paramount, 1968, Yul Brynner, Robert Mitchum).

Villa Rides-Theme—Maurice Jarre (m), Famous. COVER: Yul Brynner, Robert Mitchum.

5759 V.I.P.'s, The (MGM, 1963, Elizabeth Taylor, Richard Burton).

V.I.P.s Theme—Miklos Rozsa (m), Robbins; V.I.P.s Theme-The Willow—Mack David (w), Miklos Rozsa (m), Robbins. COVER: Elizabeth Taylor, Richard Burton.

5760 Virginian, The (Lasky, 1914, Dustin Farnum, Billy Elmer).

My Virginian—Charles Harris (w, m), Harris; Ten Thousand Cattle Straying—Owen Wister (w,m), Harris. COVER: Dustin Farnum.

5761 Virgin Soldiers, The (Columbia, 1970, Lynn Redgrave, Hywel Bennett).

The Ballad of the Virgin Soldiers—Larry Kusik, Eddie Snyder (w),

Ray Davies (m), Colgems. COVER: Hywel Bennett.

5762 Virtuous Vamp, A (First National, 1919, Gilda Gray, Conway Tearle).

Beautiful Gwendolyn—Paul Sarazan (w), Cliff Friend (m), Berlin. COVER: Gilda Gray.

5763 Vision Quest (Warner Bros., 1985, Matthew Modine, Linda Fiorentino).

Change—Holly Knight (w,m), Arista; Crazy for You—Jon Lind, John Bettis (w,m), Warner; Vision Quest-Ten Songs—Madonna Ciccone, Sammy Hagar, Paul Weller (w,m), Warner. COVER: Matthew Modine, Linda Fiorentino.

5764 Visit to a Small Planet (Paramount, 1960, Jerry Lewis, Joan Blackman).

Desdemona's Lament—Doc Pomus, Mort Shuman (w,m), Brenner. COVER: Jerry Lewis.

5765 Vivacious Lady (RKO, 1938, James Stewart, Ginger Rogers).

You'll Be Reminded of Me—George Jessel, Jack Meskill, Ted Shapiro (w,m), Berlin. COVER: James Stewart, Ginger Rogers.

5766 Viva Las Vegas (MGM, 1964, Elvis Presley, Ann Margret).

Come On Everybody—Joy Byers (w,m), Presley; If You Think I Don't Need You—Bob West, Joe Cooper (w,m), Presley; I Need Somebody to Lean On/Viva Las Vegas—Doc Pomus, Mort Shuman (w,m), Presley. COVER: Elvis Presley.

5767 Viva Maria (United Artists, 1965, Brigitte Bardot, Jeanne Moreau).

Viva Maria—Georges Delerue, Leroy Holmes, Noel Sherman (w,m), Unart. COVER: Brigitte Bardot, Jeanne Moreau.

5768 Viva Villa (MGM, 1934, Wallace Beery, Fay Wray).

La Cucaracha—Ned Washington (w), D. Savino (m), Robbins. COVER: Wallace Beery, Fay Wray.

5769 Vogliamoci Bene (IFA,

1954, Patrizia Mangano).

Please Tell Me—Al Alberts, Fred Moritt (w), C. Icini (m), Signet. COVER: Black and white cover with title only.

5770 Vogues of 1938 (United Artists, 1937, Joan Bennett, Warner Baxter).

Lovely One—Frank Loesser (w), Manning Sherwin (m), Feist; That Old Feeling—Lew Brown, Sammy Fain (w,m), Feist; Turn on the Red Hot Heat—Paul F. Webster (w), Louis Alter (m), COVER: Joan Bennett, Warner Baxter, and Movie Scenes.

5771 Voice in the Mirror (Universal, 1958, Julie London, Richard Egan).

Voice in the Mirror—Bobby Troup, Julie London (w,m), Northern. COVER: Julie London.

5772 Voice in the Wind (United Artists, 1944, Francis Lederer, Sigrid Gurie).

I Hear Your Voice in the Wind—Eddie Heyman (w), Michel Michelet (m), Saunders. COVER: The Ocean and Clouds.

5773 Voice Is Born, A (Columbia, 1947, Miklos Gagai).

With All My Heart (PC)—George Blake (w), Peter Lukas (m), Mutual. COVER: None.

5774 Voice on the Wire, The (Universal, 1917, Ben Wilson, Neva Gerber).

The Voice on the Wire Is Calling—Harry Ralph (w), Ted Barron (m), Metropolis. COVER: Ben Wilson, Neva Gerber.

5775 Voices (United Artists, 1978, Amy Irving, Michael Ontkean).

Children's Song/Disco If You Want To/Drunk as a Punk/I Will Always Wait for You/On a Stage—Jimmy Webb (w,m), MGM. COVER: Amy Irving, Michael Ontkean.

5776 Volcano (United Artists, 1950, Anna Magnani, Rossano Brazzi).

Volcano—Buddy Kaye (w), V.

Finni (m), Symphony. COVER: Anna Magnani, Rossano Brazzi.

5777 Volga Boatman, The (De-Mille, 1926, William Boyd, Elinor Fair).

Song of the Volga Boatman—Sigmund Spaath (w), Carl Deis (m), Schirmer. COVER: William Boyd.

5778 Von Ryan's Express (20th Century-Fox, 1965, Frank Sinatra, Trevor Howard).

Von Ryan March—Jerry Goldsmith (m), Hastings. COVER: Frank Sinatra, Trevor Howard, Raffaella Carra.

5779 Voyage of the Rock Aliens (Inter-curb, 1985, Pia Zadora, Tom Nolan).

When the Rain Begins to Fall—Mike Bradley, Peggy March, Steve Wittmark (w,m), Arista. COVER: Jermaine Jackson, Pia Zadora.

5780 Voyage to the Bottom of the Sea (20th Century-Fox, 1961, Walter Pidgeon, Joan Fontaine).

Voyage to the Bottom of the Sea—Russell Faith (w,m), Miller. COVER: Walter Pidgeon, Joan Fontaine, Barbara Eden.

5781 Vulture, The (Paramount, 1968, Robert Hutton, Akim Tamiroff).

The Vulture-Music Score—Eric Spear (m), Famous. COVER: Brown cover with title only.

5782 Wabash Avenue (20th Century-Fox, 1950, Betty Grable, Victor Mature).

Baby Won't You Say You Love Me—Mack Gordon (w), Josef Myrow (m), Feist; Billy—Joe Goodwin (w), James Kendis, Herman Paley (m), Mills; I've Been Floating Down the Old Green River—Bert Kalmar (w), Joe Cooper (m), Mills; I Wish I Could Shimmy Like My Sister Kate—A. J. Piron (w,m), Vogel; Wilhelmina—Mack Gordon (w), Josef Myrow (m), Feist. COVER: Betty Grable, Phil Harris, Victor Mature.

5783 Waco (Paramount, 1966, Howard Keel, Jane Russell).

All But the Remembering/Waco—Hal Blair (w), Jimmie Haskell (m), Ensign. COVER: Howard Keel, Jane Russell.

5784 Wagon Master (RKO, 1950, Ben Johnson, Joanne Dru).

Chuckawalla Swing/Rollin' Dust/Song of the Wagonmaster/Wagons West—Stan Jones (w,m), Alamo. COVER: Ben Johnson, and Covered Wagon.

5785 Waikiki Wedding (Paramount, 1937, Bing Crosby, Shirley Ross).

Blue Hawaii/In a Little Hula Heaven—Leo Robin, Ralph Rainger (w, m), Famous; Okolehao—Leo Robin, Ralph Rainger, Don Hartman (w,m), Famous; Sweet Is the Word for You—Leo Robin, Ralph Rainger (w,m), Famous; Sweet Leilani—Harry Owens (w,m), Select. COVER: Bing Crosby, Shirley Ross, Martha Raye.

5786 Waiting for Love (Movietone, 1931, Musical Short).

Bugle Song—Maria Grever (w,m), Red Star. COVER: Black and white cover with title only.

5787 Wait Till the Sun Shines Nellie (20th Century-Fox, 1952, David Wayne, Jean Peters).

Wait Till the Sun Shines Nellie—A. B. Sterling (w), Harry Von Tilzer (m), Von Tilzer; Wait Till the Sun Shines Nellie-Blues—A. Sterling, George Jessel (w), Harry Von Tilzer (m), Von Tilzer. COVER: David Wayne, Jean Peters.

5788 Wait Until Dark (Warner Bros., 1967, Audrey Hepburn, Efrem Zimbalist).

Wait Until Dark—Jay Livingston, Ray Evans (w), Henry Mancini (m), Witmark. COVER: Audrey Hepburn.

5789 Wake Me When It's Over (20th Century-Fox, 1959, Ernie Kovacs, Margo Moore).

Wake Me When It's Over—Sammy Cahn (w), James Van Heusen (m), Robbins. COVER: Ernie Kovacs, Margo Moore, Dick Shawn, Nobu McCarthy.

5790 Wake Up and Dream (Universal, 1934, Russ Colombo, June Knight).

Let's Pretend There's a Moon—Russ Colombo, G. Hamilton, Jack Stern (w,m), Harms; Too Beautiful for Words/When You're in Love—Russ Columbo, Bernie Grossman, Jack Stern (w,m), Harms. COVER: Russ Colombo, June Knight, Wini Shaw.

5791 Wake Up and Dream (Give Me the Simple Life) (20th Century-Fox, 1946, June Haver, John Payne).

Give Me the Simple Life/I Wish I Could Tell You/Into the Sun—Harry Ruby (w), Rube Bloom (m), Triangle. COVER: John Payne, June Haver, Charlotte Greenwood.

5792 Wake Up and Live (20th Century-Fox, 1937, Alice Faye, Patsy Kelly).

I Love You Much Too Much Muchacha/I'm Bubbling Over/It's Swell of You/Never in a Million Years/Ooh But I'm Happy/There's a Lull in My Life/Wake Up and Live—Mack Gordon, Harry Revel (w,m), Robbins. COVER: Alice Faye, Walter Winchell, Ben Bernie.

5793 Walkabout (20th Century-Fox, 1971, Lucien John, Jenny Agutter).

Walkabout—Don Black (w), John Barry (m), Morris. COVER: A Boy, a Girl and a Native.

5794 Walk Don't Run (Universal, 1971, Cary Grant, Samantha Eggar).

Stay with Me, Just Stay with Me/Happy Feet—Peggy Lee (w), Quincy Jones (m), Colgems. COVER: Cary Grant, Samantha Eggar.

5795 Walking on Air (RKO, 1936, Gene Raymond, Ann Sothern).

Cabin on the Hilltop—Bert Kalmar, Harry Ruby (w,m), Berlin; Let's Make a Wish/My Heart Wants to Dance—Bert Kalmar, Sid Silvers (w), Harry Ruby (m), Berlin. COVER: Gene Raymond, Ann Sothern.

5796 Walking Tall—Part Two (AIP, 1975, Bo Swenson, Luke Askew).

Walking Tall—Don Black (w), Walter Scharf (m), ASCO. COVER: Bo Swenson, and Others.

5797 Walk in the Spring Rain, A (Columbia, 1970, Anthony Quinn, Ingrid Bergman).

A Walk in the Spring Rain—Don Black (w), Elmer Bernstein (m), Colgems. COVER: Ingrid Bergman, Anthony Quinn.

5798 Walk Like a Dragon (Paramount, 1960, Jack Lord, Nobu McCarthy).

Walk Like a Dragon—Mel Torme (w,m), Paramount. COVER: Jack Lord, Nobu McCarthy.

5799 Walk on the Wild Side, A (Columbia, 1961, Jane Fonda, Barbara Stanwyck).

Somewhere in the Used to Be/Walk on the Wild Side, A—Mack David (w), Elmer Bernstein (m), Columbia. COVER: Barbara Stanwyck, Jane Fonda, Capucine, Anne Baxter, Laurence Harvey.

5800 Wallflower (Warner Bros., 1947, Robert Hutton, Joyce Reynolds).

I May Be Wrong—Harry Ruskin (w), Henry Sullivan (m), Advanced. COVER: Robert Hutton, Joyce Reynolds.

5801 Waltz Dream, A (MGM, 1926, Willy Fritsch, Xenia Desni).

A Waltz Dream Waltz—Oscar Strauss (m), Belwin. COVER: Willy Fritsch, Xenia Desni.

5802 Waltz Time (GB, 1933, Evelyn Laye, Fritz Schultze).

Come Out Vienna—A. P. Herbert (w), Johann Strauss (m), Chappell Harms. COVER: Evelyn Laye.

5803 Wanderer, The (Vitaphone, 1930, Douglas Stanbury).

Cottage for Sale, A—Larry Conley (w), Willard Robison (m), DBH. COVER: Douglas Stanbury.

5804 Wanderers, The (Warner Bros., 1979, Ken Wahl, John Friedrich).

The Wanderer (PC)—Ernie Maresca (w,m), Schwartz. COVER: None.

5805 Wanted (Pursued) (Fox, 1935, Rosemary Ames, Victor Jory).

Wanted-Someone—Sidney Clare (w), Harry Akst (m), Movietone. COVER: Black and white cover with title only.

5806 Wanted for Murder (20th Century-Fox, 1946, Eric Portman, Dulcie Gray).

A Voice in the Night (B)—Mischa Spoliansky (w,m), Southern. COVER: Eric Portman.

5807 War and Peace (Paramount, 1956, Audrey Hepburn, Mel Ferrer).

Maid of Novgorod, The—Nino Rota (m), Famous; War and Peace—Wilson Stone (w), Nino Rota (m), Famous; War and Peace Theme—Nino Rota (m), Famous. COVER: Audrey Hepburn, Henry Fonda, Mel Ferrer.

5808 War Between Men and Women, The (National General, 1972, Jack Lemmon, Barbara Harris).

You and Me (PC)—Howard Liebling (w), Marvin Hamlisch (m), April. COVER: None.

5809 War Brides (Selznick, 1916, Nazimova, Robert Whitworth).

War Brides—John Calhoun (w, m), Shapiro Bernstein. COVER: Nazimova.

5810 War Games (MGM, 1983, Matthew Broderick, Dabney Coleman).

Video Fever—Cynthia Morrow (w), Arthur Rubenstein (m), Unart. COVER: Matthew Broderick, and Computer.

5811 War Lord, The (Universal, 1965, Charlton Heston, Richard Boone).

War Lord Theme (B)—Jerome Moross (m), Leeds. COVER: Charlton Heston.

5812 War Lover, The (Columbia, 1962, Steve McQueen, Robert Wagner).

War Lover Theme-They Say—Mack David (w), Richard Addinsell (m), Columbia. COVER: Steve McQueen, Robert Wagner, and Movie Scenes.

5813 Warming Up (Paramount, 1928, Richard Dix, Jean Arthur).

Out of the Dawn—Walter Donaldson (w,m), Donaldson. COVER: Richard Dix.

5814 Warning Shot (Paramount, 1967, David Janssen, Steve Allen).

Warning Shot Theme—Jerry Goldsmith (m), Ensign. COVER: David Janssen, George Grizzard, Eleanor Parker, Stephanie Powers.

5815 Warrior's Husband, The (Fox, 1933, Elissa Landi, Ernest Truex).

Amazon Blues—Arthur Lange, Val Burton, Will Jasson (w,m), Red Star. COVER: Black and white cover with title only.

5816 War Wagon, The (Universal, 1967, John Wayne, Kirk Douglas).

Ballad of the War Wagon—Ned Washington (w), Dimitri Tiomkin (m), Shamley. COVER: John Wayne, Kirk Douglas.

5817 Washington Behind Closed Doors (Paramount, 1977, Cliff Robertson, Jason Robards).

America Nation Song—Norman Gimbel (w), Dominic Frontiere (m), Bruin; March of the Elephants—Dominic Frontiere (m), Bruin. COVER: Capitol Building.

5818 Washington Cowboy (Republic, 1939, Gene Autry).

Ole Peaceful River—Johnny Marvin (w,m), Western. COVER: Gene Autry.

5819 Waterhole #3 (Paramount, 1967, James Coburn, Carroll O'Connor).

Ballad of Waterhole #3/Rainbow Valley/Waterhole #3-Nine Themes—Robert Wells (w), Dave Grusin (m), Famous. COVER: James Coburn, and Others.

5820 Waterloo Bridge (MGM, 1940, Robert Taylor, Vivien Leigh).

Auld Lang Syne (B)—Herbert Stothart (m), Feist; Candlelight Waltz (B)—Arthur Beul (w), E. Flat (m), Melodie. COVER: Robert Taylor, Vivien Leigh.

5821 WAVE, a WAC, a Marine, A (Monogram, 1944, Henny Youngman, Elyse Knox).

We Stopped for a Kiss—Lucien Denni (w,m), Denni; You Have Me So Excited—Gwynne Denni (w), Lucien Denni (m), Denni. COVER: Marjorie Woodworth.

5822 Way Ahead, The (20th Century-Fox, 1945, David Niven, James Donald).

Way Ahead March (B)—William Alwyn (m), Chappell. COVER: David Niven.

5823 Way Back Home (RKO, 1932, Phillips Lord, Effie Palmer).

You Go to Your Church and I'll Go to Mine—Phillips H. Lord (w, m), Fischer. COVER: Phillips Lord.

5824 Way Down East (United Artists, 1919, Lillian Gish, Richard Barthelmess).

Chatterbox—Jean Havez (w), Louis Silvers (m), Harms; If You Knew, Would You Care—Guy Wellington (w), Louis Silvers (m), Forster. COVER: Lillian Gish.

5825 Way Down South (RKO, 1939, Bobby Breen, Alan Mowbray).

Louisiana—Clarence Muse, Langston Hughes (w,m), Chappell. COVER: Bobby Breen.

5826 Way Out (Valley Forge, 1966, Frank Rodriguez, James Dunleavy).

Lament—John Gimenez (w,m), Sam Fox. COVER: Roy Hamilton.

5827 Way Out West (Easy Going) (MGM, 1930, William Haines, Leila Hyams).

Singing a Song to the Stars—Howard Johnson (w), Joseph Meyer (m), Robbins. COVER: William Haines, and Girls.

5828 Way to Love, The (Paramount, 1933, Maurice Chevalier, Ann Dvorak).

In a One Room Flat/It's Oh-It's Ah—Leo Robin (w), Ralph Rainger (m), Famous; Way to Love, The—Sam Coslow, Arthur Johnston (w, m), Famous. COVER: Maurice Chevalier, Ann Dvorak.

5829 Way to the Stars, The (Johnny in the Clouds) (United Artists, 1945, Michael Redgrave, John Mills).

The Way to the Stars (B)—Nicholas Brodszky (m), Chappell. COVER: John Mills, Michael Redgrave.

5830 Wayward (Paramount, 1932, Nancy Carroll, Richard Arlen).

What's the Difference—Edward Heyman (w), John Green (m), Famous. COVER: Nancy Carroll.

5831 Wayward Wife, The (Electra, 1955, Gina Lollobrigida, Gabriele Ferzetti).

Wayward Wife—Joanne Towne (w), Dick Jacobs (m), Tee Kaye. COVER: Gina Lollobrigida, Gabriele Ferzetti.

5832 Way West, The (United Artists, 1967, Kirk Douglas, Robert Mitchum).

The Way West—Mack David (w), Bronislau Kaper (m), Unart. COVER: Kirk Douglas, Robert Mitchum, Richard Widmark.

5833 Way We Were, The (Columbia, 1973, Barbra Streisand, Robert Redford).

The Way We Were—Alan Bergman, Marilyn Bergman (w), Marvin Hamlisch (m), Colgems; Did You Know It Was Me? (VS)—Marvin Hamlisch (m), Colgems; In the Mood (VS)—Joe Garland (m), Colgems; Katie (VS)/Like Pretty (VS)/Look What I've Got (VS) —Marvin Hamlisch (m), Colgems; Red Sails in the Sunset (VS)—Jimmy Kennedy, Hugh Williams (w,m), Colgems; Remembering (VS)—Marvin Hamlisch (m), Colgems; River Stay 'Way from My Door (VS)—Mort Dixon, Harry Woods (w,m), Colgems; Way We Were Theme and Finale (VS) —Marvin Hamlisch (m), Colgems; Wrap Your Troubles in Dreams (VS)

—Ted Koehler, Billy Moll, Harry Barris (w,m), Colgems. COVER: Barbra Streisand, Robert Redford.

5834 W. C. Fields and Me (Universal, 1976, Rod Steiger, Valerie Perrine).

The Joke's on Me—Jay Livingston, Ray Evans (w), Henry Mancini (m), Leeds. COVER: Rod Steiger, Valerie Perrine.

5835 We Are the Marines (20th Century-Fox, 1942, War Film on Marines).

Hail the U.S.A. Marines—Esther Van Seiver (w), Jack Shaindlin (m), Miller. COVER: Marines.

5836 Weary River (First National, 1929, Richard Barthelmess, Betty Compson).

It's Up to You/Weary River—Grant Clarke (w), Louis Silvers (m), Berlin. COVER: Richard Barthelmess.

5837 Wedding March, The (Paramount, 1927, Fay Wray, Eric Von Stroheim).

Paradise—Harry Kerr (w), J. S. Zamecnik (m), Sam Fox. COVER: Fay Wray.

5838 Wedding Rings (First National, 1930, Lois Wilson, H. B. Warner).

Love Will Last Forever/That's My Business (BW)—Al Bryan (w), Eddie Ward (m), Witmark. COVER: Lois Wilson, H. B. Warner.

5839 Weekend at the Waldorf (MGM, 1945, Ginger Rogers, Lana Turner).

And There You Are—Ted Koehler (w), Sammy Fain (m), Feist; Guadalajara—Pepe Guizar (w,m), Peer. COVER: Ginger Rogers, Lana Turner, Walter Pidgeon, Van Johnson.

5840 Weekend in Havana (20th Century-Fox, 1941, Alice Faye, John Payne).

Man with the Lollypop Song, The/Nango-Nyango—Mack Gordon (w), Harry Warren (m), BVC; Romance and Rhumba—Mack Gordon (w), James Monaco (m), BVC; Tropical Magic/Weekend in Havana/When I Love I Love—Mack Gordon (w), Harry Warren (m), BVC. COVER: Alice Faye, John Payne, Carmen Miranda, Cesar Romero.

5841 Week End Italian Style (Telegraff, 1966, Enrico Salerno, Sandra Milo).

Take a Week End Italian Style—Leonard Whitcup, Jon Graff (w,m), Cinimo. COVER: Enrico Salerno, Sandra Milo.

5842 Weekend Pass (Universal, 1944, Martha O'Driscoll, Noah Beery).

I Am, Are You?/I Like to Be Loved—Everett Carter (w), Milton Rosen (m), Variety. COVER: Martha O'Driscoll, Noah Beery.

5843 Week Ends Only (Fox, 1932, Joan Bennett, Ben Lyon).

Am I Too Fresh—James Hanley (w,m), Movietone. COVER: Black and white cover with title only.

5844 Weekend with Lulu, A (Columbia, 1961, Leslie Phillips, Bob Monkhouse).

Lulu (B)—Trevor Stanford (w, m), Clover Conway. COVER: Leslie Phillips, Bob Monkhouse.

5845 Weird Science (Universal, 1985, Anthony Hall, Kelly LeBrock).

Weird Science—D. Elfman (w,m), MCA. COVER: Red and blue cover with title only.

5846 Welcome Danger (Paramount, 1929, Harold Lloyd, Barbara Kent).

Billie/When You Are Mine—Lynn Cowan, Paul Titsworth (w,m), Davis Coots. COVER: Harold Lloyd, Barbara Kent.

5847 Welcome Home (Fox, 1935, James Dunn, Arline Judge).

Hail Hail Hail to Ellum Dale—B. G. DeSylva (w,m), Movietone. COVER: Black and white cover with title only.

5848 Welcome Home (Columbia, 1989, JoBeth Williams, Kris Kristofferson).

Welcome Home—Alan Bergman, Marilyn Bergman (w), Henry Mancini (m), Burbank. COVER: JoBeth Williams, Kris Kristofferson.

5849 Welcome Stranger (Paramount, 1947, Bing Crosby, Joan Caulfield).

As Long as I'm Dreaming/Country Style Square Dance/My Heart Is a Hobo/Smile Right Back at the Sun—Johnny Burke (w), James Van Heusen (m), BVH. COVER: Bing Crosby, Joan Caulfield.

5850 Welcome to Arrow Beach (The Tender Flesh) (Warner, 1974, Laurence Harvey, Joanna Pettet).

Who Can Tell Us Why?—Sammy Cahn (w), George Barrie, Bert Keys (m), Brut. COVER: Lou Rawls.

5851 We'll Meet Again (Columbia, 1942, Vera Lynn, Patricia Roc).

All the World Sings a Lullaby (B) —B. Gordon, B. Thomas (w), Harry Davies (m), Chappell; Be Like the Kettle and Sing (B)—T. Connor, W. Ridley, D. O'Connor (w,m), Maurice. COVER: Vera Lynn.

5852 Wells Fargo (Paramount, 1937, Joel McCrea, Bob Burns).

Where I Ain't Been Yet—Ralph Freed (w), Burton Lane (m), Famous. COVER: Joel McCrea, Frances Dee, Bob Burns.

5853 We're Going to Be Rich (He Was Her Man) (20th Century-Fox, 1940, Gracie Fields, Victor McLaglen).

Sweetest Song in the World, The (B)—Harry P. Davies (w,m), Day; Trek Song, The—Harry P. Davies (w,m), Chappell. COVER: Gracie Fields.

5854 We're in the Money (Warner Bros., 1935, Joan Blondell, Glenda Farrell).

So Nice Seeing You Again—Mort Dixon (w), Allie Wrubel (m), Harms. COVER: Joan Blondell, Ross Alexander.

5855 We're No Angels (Paramount, 1960, Humphrey Bogart, Aldo Ray).

Sentimental Moments—Ralph Freed (w), Frederick Hollander (m), Para-

mount. COVER: Humphrey Bogart, Aldo Ray, Peter Ustinov, Joan Bennett.

5856 We're Not Dressing (Paramount, 1934, Bing Crosby, Carole Lombard).

Goodnight Lovely Little Lady/It's Just a New Spanish Custom/It's the Animal in Me/Love Thy Neighbor/May I/Once in a Blue Moon/She Reminds Me of You—Mack Gordon (w), Harry Revel (m), DBH. COVER: Bing Crosby, Carole Lombard, Ethel Merman.

5857 Werewolf in a Girl's Dormitory (MGM, 1963, Carl Schell, Barbara Lass).

The Ghoul in School—Marilyn Stewart (w), Frank Owens (m), Hastings. COVER: Werewolf and Girl.

5858 Wer Wird Denn Weinen (No Use Crying) (International, 1922, German Operetta).

No Use Crying—Alice Mattullath (w), Hugo Hirsch (m), Marks. COVER: A Sad Woman.

5859 Westbound Stage (Monogram, 1940, Tex Ritter, Muriel Evans).

It's All Over Now (PC)—Johnny Lange, Lew Porter (w,m), Southern. COVER: None.

5860 Westerner, The (United Artists, 1940, Gary Cooper, Walter Brennan).

You're So Lovely—Sara Colton, Max Mann, Maurie Hartmann (w,m), Cherio. COVER: Lilian Bond.

5861 Western Gold (20th Century-Fox, 1938, Smith Ballew, Heather Angel).

Echoes of the Trail—Fleming Allen, Gene Autry (w,m), Sam Fox. COVER: Smith Ballew.

5862 Western Grandeur (20th Century-Fox, 1937, Short Subject on Western Scenery).

Home Road—Lew Lehr (w), James Hanley (m), Movietone. COVER: Western Scenes.

5863 Western Jamboree (Republic, 1938, Gene Autry, Smiley Burnette).

Old November Moon—Johnny Marvin, Gene Autry (w,m), West'rn; Paradise in the Moonlight—Gene Autry, Fred Rose (w,m), West'rn. COVER: Gene Autry.

5864 West of Carson City (Universal, 1940, Johnny Mack Brown, Bob Baker).

Let's Go/On the Trail of Tomorrow—Everett Carter (w), Milton Rosen (m), Robbins. COVER: Bob Baker.

5865 West of Cheyenne (Columbia, 1938, Charles Starrett, Iris Meredith).

Biscuit Blues (VS)—Bob Nolan (w,m), American; Night Falls on the Prairie (VS)—Bob Nolan, Lloyd Perrys (w,m), American. COVER: Bob Nolan.

5866 West of Laramie (Universal, 1949, Tex Williams, Smokey Rogers).

Cowpuncher's Waltz—Foster Carling (m), Sunland. COVER: Tex Williams.

5867 West of Santa Fe (Columbia, 1938, Charles Starrett, Iris Meredith).

Good Mornin' (VS)—Bob Nolan (w,m), American. COVER: Bob Nolan.

5868 West of the Alamo (Monogram, 1946, Jimmy Wakely, Lee White).

I'm Always Blue for You (VS)—Jimmy Wakely, Arthur Smith (w, m), Fairway. COVER: Jimmy Wakely.

5869 West of Zanzibar (Universal, 1954, Anthony Steel, Sheila Sim).

Jambo-West of Zanzibar—Georges Sigara (w,m), Leeds. COVER: Anthony Steel, Sheila Sim.

5870 West Point Story (Warner Bros., 1950, Doris Day, James Cagney).

By the Kissing Rock/It's Raining Sundrops/Long Before I Knew You/ Military Polka/Ten Thousand Four Hundred and Thirty Two Sheep/ You Love Me—Sammy Cahn (w), Jule Styne (m), Witmark. COVER: James Cagney, Doris Day, Gordon MacRae, Gene Nelson.

5871 West Side Story (United Artists, 1961, Natalie Wood, Richard Beymer).

America/Cool/Gee Officer Krupke/I Feel Pretty/Maria/One Hand One Heart/Something's Coming/Somewhere/Tonight/Jet Song, The (VS)/ Boy Like That, A (VS)/I Have a Love (VS)—Stephen Sondheim (w), Leonard Bernstein (m), Schirmer. COVER: A Fire Escape.

5872 Westward Ho (Republic, 1935, John Wayne, Sheila Manners).

Westward Ho—Tim Spencer (w, m), Cross Winge. COVER: The Murray Sisters.

5873 Westward Ho the Wagons (Buena Vista, 1956, Fess Parker, Jeff York).

Green Grow the Lilacs—Tex Ritter (w,m), Ritter; Westward Ho the Wagons—Tom Blackburn (w), George Bruns (m), Wonderland; Wringle Wrangle—Stan Jones (w,m), Disney. COVER: Fess Parker, Tex Ritter.

5874 Wharf Angel (Paramount, 1934, Victor McLaglen, Dorothy Dell).

Down Home—Leo Robin, Ralph Rainger (w,m), Famous. COVER: Dorothy Dell.

5875 What a Way to Go (20th Century-Fox, 1964, Paul Newman, Shirley MacLaine).

I Think That You and I Should Get Acquainted—Betty Comden, Adolph Green (w), Jule Styne (m), Miller; Louisa's Theme—Nelson Riddle (m), Hastings; Our Houseboat on the Hudson—Betty Comden, Adolph Green (w), Jule Styne (m), Miller. COVER: Shirley MacLaine, Paul Newman, Robert Mitchum, Gene Kelly, Dean Martin.

5876 What a Widow (United Artists, 1930, Gloria Swanson, Owen Moore).

Love Is Like a Song/Say "Oui" Cherie/You're the One—Russel Robinson, George Waggner (w), Vincent Youmans (m), Youmans. COVER: Gloria Swanson.

5877 What Did You Do in the War Daddy? (United Artists, 1966, James Coburn, Dick Shawn).

In the Arms of Love—Jay Livingston, Ray Evans (w), Henry Mancini (m), Shayne. COVER: Cartoon Sketch.

5878 What Do You Say to a Naked Lady? (United Artists, 1970, Joie Addison, Laura Huston).

What Do You Say to a Naked Lady?—Steve Karmen (w,m), Unart. COVER: Naked Lady and Students.

5879 Whatever Happened to Baby Jane? (Warner Bros., 1962, Bette Davis, Joan Crawford).

I've Written a Letter to Daddy (B) —Frank DeVol (w,m), Bradbury. COVER: Bette Davis, Joan Crawford.

5880 What Men Want (Universal, 1930, Pauline Starke, Robert Ellis).

My Baby An' Me—Bernie Grossman (w), Lou Handman (m), Handman Kent; What a Perfect Night for Love—C. Lenzen, A. Cameron, P. Dontsema (w,m), Handman Kent. COVER: Pauline Starke, Robert Ellis.

5881 What—No Spinach! (Paramount, 1936, Popeye Cartoon).

Hamburger Mine (VS)—Bob Rothberg (w), Sammy Timberg (m), Famous. COVER: Popeye.

5882 What Price Glory (Fox, 1926, Edmund Lowe, Dolores Del Rio).

Charmaine—Erno Rapee, Lew Pollack (w,m), Sherman Clay; Charmaine-Love Theme—Louis Leazer (w), Erno Rapee (m), Belwin; I'll See You Again (B)—Clark Lewis, Reed Stampa (w,m), Wright. COVER: Sketch of Man and Woman.

5883 What Price Glory (20th Century-Fox, 1952, James Cagney,

Dan Dailey).

My Love My Life—Jay Livingston, Ray Evans (w,m), Paramount. COVER: James Cagney, Corinne Calvet, Dan Dailey.

5884 What's Buzzin' Cousin? (Columbia, 1943, Ann Miller, John Hubbard).

Ain't That Just Like a Man?/ Blue Ridge Mountain Blues (PC)— Don Raye, Gene DePaul (w,m), Leeds; In Grandpaw's Beard—Charles Newman (w), Lew Pollack (m), West'rn; Nevada—Mort Greene, Walter Donaldson (w,m), Dorsey; Short Fat and 4 F/Taffy (PC)—Don Raye, Gene DePaul (w,m), Leeds. COVER: Ann Miller, Rochester, Freddy Martin, John Hubbard.

5885 What's Cookin' (Universal, 1942, Andrews Sisters, Jane Frazee).

Amen (Yea-Man)—Roger Segure, Bill Hardy, Vic Schoen (w,m), Olman; One Kiss, Il Bacio—Sid Robin (w,m), Leeds; What To Do—Sid Robin (w,m), Olman; Woodchoppers Ball—Joe Bishop, Woody Herman (m), Leeds; You Can't Hold a Memory in Your Arms—Hy Zaret (w), Art Altman (m), Olman. COVER: Andrews Sisters, Woody Herman, Gloria Jean, Jane Frazee.

5886 What Shall I Do (Hodkinson, 1924, Dorothy Mackaill, John Harrow).

What'll I Do—Irving Berlin (w,m), Berlin. COVER: Dorothy Mackaill.

5887 What's New Pussycat? (United Artists, 1965, Peter Sellers, Peter O'Toole).

Dance Mamma, Dance Pappa, Dance (PC)/Here I Am/My Little Red Book/What's New Pussycat?— Hal David (w), Burt Bacharach (m), Unart. COVER: Peter Sellers, Capucine, Woody Allen, Romy Schneider.

5888 What's So Bad About Feeling Good? (Universal, 1968, George Peppard, Mary Tyler Moore).

What's So Bad About Feeling Good?—Jerry Keller, Dave Blume

(w,m), Northern. COVER: George Peppard, Mary Tyler Moore.

5889 What Would You Do in a Case Like This? (Modern, 1928, Stars Unknown).

What Would You Do in a Case Like This?—Nat Cordish, Irving Mills (w,m), Mills. COVER: Movie Scene.

5890 Wheeler Dealers, The (MGM, 1963, Lee Remick, James Garner).

The Wheeler Dealers—Randy Sparks (w,m), Miller. COVER: James Garner, Lee Remick.

5891 Wheel of Life, The (Paramount, 1929, Richard Dix, Esther Ralston).

I Wonder Why I Love You—Victor Schertzinger (w,m), Famous. COVER: Richard Dix, Esther Ralston.

5892 Wheels of Destiny (Universal, 1934, Ken Maynard, Dorothy Dix).

Wheels of Destiny (VS)—Ken Maynard (w,m), Cole. COVER: Ken Maynard.

5893 When a Fellow Needs a Friend (Paramount, 1919, Comedy Short).

When a Fellow Needs a Friend—Bernie Grossman (w), Joseph Stern, Billy Frisch (m), Stern. COVER: Cartoons and Movie Scenes.

5894 When a Girl's Beautiful (Columbia, 1947, Adele Jergens, Marc Platt).

I'm Sorry I Didn't Say I'm Sorry—Allan Roberts, Lester Lee (w,m), Mood. COVER: Adele Jergens, Marc Platt.

5895 When Dawn Came (Producers Security, 1920, Colleen Moore, James Barrows).

When Dawn Came—E. Van Pelt (w), Hampton Durand (m), Dierker. COVER: A Sunrise.

5896 When Harry Met Sally (Castle Rock, 1989, Billy Crystal, Meg Ryan).

It Had to Be You—Gus Kahn (w), Isham Jones (m), Warner. COVER: Billy Crystal, Meg Ryan.

5897 When It Strikes Home (Harris World, 1915, Grace Washburn, Edwin August).

When It Strikes Home—Charles Harris (w,m), Harris. COVER: Grace Washburn.

5898 When Johnny Comes Marching Home (Universal, 1942, Allan Jones, Jane Frazee).

Green Eyes (VS)—E. Rivera, E. Woods (w), Nilo Menendez (m), Peer; Romance—Edgar Leslie (w), Walter Donaldson (m), BVC; We Must Be Vigilant—Edgar Leslie (w), Joseph Burke (m), BVC. COVER: Allan Jones, Jane Frazee, Donald O'Connor, Gloria Jean, Phil Spitalny.

5899 When Knighthood Was in Flower (Paramount, 1922, Marion Davies, William Powell).

Marion Davies March, The—Victor Herbert (m), Harms; When Knighthood Was in Flower—William LeBaron (w), Victor Herbert (m), Harms. COVER: Marion Davies, and Movie Scenes.

5900 When Love Grows Cold (FBO, 1926, Natacha Rambove, Clive Brook).

When Love Grows Cold—Jack Ellis (w), J. Fred Coots (m), Harms; When Love Grows Cold Waltz (B)—Billy Sunday, Roy York (w,m), David. COVER: Natacha Rambova.

5901 When Love Is Young (Universal, 1937, Virginia Bruce, Kent Taylor).

Did Anyone Ever Tell You?/When Love Is Young—Harold Adamson (w), Jimmy McHugh (m), Miller. COVER: Virginia Bruce, Kent Taylor.

5902 When My Baby Smiles at Me (20th Century-Fox, 1948, Betty Grable, Dan Dailey).

By the Way—Mack Gordon (w), Josef Myrow (m), BVC; Oui Oui Marie—Al Bryan, Joe McCarthy (w), Fred Fisher (m), Fisher; What Did I Do?—Mack Gordon (w), Josef Myrow (m), Triangle; When My Baby Smiles at Me—Harry Von Tilzer, A. Sterling, B. Munro, Ted Lewis (w, m), Von Tilzer. COVER: Betty Grable, Dan Dailey.

5903 When's Your Birthday (RKO, 1937, Joe E. Brown, Marion Marsh).

I Love You from Coast to Coast—Al Stillman, Alex Hyde, Basil Adlam (w,m), Berlin. COVER: Frank LaMarr, and Map of U.S.A.

5904 When the Boys Meet the Girls (MGM, 1965, Connie Francis, Harve Presnell).

Listen People—Graham Gouldman (w,m), New World; When the Boys Meet the Girls—Howard Greenfield, Jack Keller (w,m), New World. COVER: Connie Francis, Harve Presnell, Louis Armstrong, Liberace.

5905 When Willie Comes Marching Home (20th Century-Fox, 1946, Dan Dailey, Corinne Calvet).

Somebody Stole My Gal—Leo Wood (w,m), Robbins. COVER: Dan Dailey, Corinne Calvet, Colleen Townsend.

5906 When Worlds Collide (Paramount, 1951, Richard Derr, Barbara Rush).

When Worlds Collide—Jay Livingston, Ray Evans (w), Leith Stevens (m), Paramount. COVER: Richard Derr, Barbara Rush.

5907 When You're in Love (Columbia, 1937, Grace Moore, Cary Grant).

Minnie the Moocher—Cab Calloway, Irving Mills, Clarence Gaskill (w,m), Mills; Our Song/Whistling Boy—Dorothy Fields (w), Jerome Kern (m), Chappell. COVER: Grace Moore.

5908 When You're Smiling (Columbia, 1950, Jerome Courtland, Frankie Laine).

When You're Smiling—Mark Fisher, Joe Goodwin, Larry Shay (w, m), Mills. COVER: Frankie Laine, Jerome Courtland, Lola Albright.

5909 Where Angels Go-Trouble

Follows! (Columbia, 1968, Rosalind Russell, Stella Stevens).

Where Angels Go, Trouble Follows—Lalo Schifrin, Tommy Boyce, Bob Hart (w,m), Colgems. COVER: Tommy Boyce, Bob Hart.

5910 Where Danger Lives (RKO, 1950, Robert Mitchum, Faith Domergue).

Margot-Love Theme—Ray Carter (w), Roy Webb (m), Paxton. COVER: Robert Mitchum, Faith Domergue.

5911 Where Did You Get that Girl (Universal, 1941, Leon Errol, Charles Lang).

Rug Cuttin' Romeo/Sergeant Swing—Everett Carter (w), Milton Rosen (m), Robbins; Where Did You Get That Girl—Bert Kalmar (w), Harry Puck (m), Mills. COVER: Leon Errol, Franklin Pangborn, Charles Lang, Eddie Quillan.

5912 Where Do We Go from Here? (20th Century-Fox, 1945, Joan Leslie, Fred MacMurray).

All at Once/If Love Remains/ Nina, the Pinta, the Santa Maria/ Song of the Rhineland—Ira Gershwin (w), Kurt Weill (m), Chappell. COVER: Fred MacMurray, Joan Leslie, June Haver.

5913 Where Eagles Dare (MGM, 1969, Richard Burton, Clint Eastwood).

Where Eagles Dare-Theme—Ron Goodwin (m), Miller. COVER: Richard Burton, Clint Eastwood.

5914 Where Love Has Gone (Paramount, 1964, Bette Davis, Susan Hayward).

Where Love Has Gone—Sammy Cahn (w), James Van Heusen (m), Famous. COVER: Bette Davis, Susan Hayward, Michael Connors, Joey Heatherton.

5915 Where's Jack? (Paramount, 1969, Tommy Steele, Stanley Baker).

Ballad of Jack Shepherd/Where's Jack? (B)—Don Black (w), Elmer Bernstein (m), Famous. COVER: Timmy Steele, Stanley Baker.

5916 Where's Poppa? (United Artists, 1970, George Segal, Ruth Gordon).

Where's Poppa?—Norman Gimbel (w), Jack Elliott (m), Unart. COVER: George Segal, Ruth Gordon.

5917 Where the Boys Are (MGM, 1960, Dolores Hart, George Hamilton).

Have You Met Miss Fandango—Stella Unger (w), Victor Young (m), Young; Turn on the Sunshine/Where the Boys Are—Howard Greenfield (w), Neil Sedaka (m), Aldon. COVER: Connie Francis, and Girls.

5918 Where the Boys Are (Tri-Star, 1984, Lisa Hartman, Lorna Luft).

Where the Boys Are—Howard Greenfield (w), Neil Sedaka (m), Warner. COVER: Lisa Hartman, Lorna Luft.

5919 Where the Buffalo Roam (Monogram, 1938, Tex Ritter, Dorothy Short).

Troubadour of the Prairie—Frank Harford (w,m), Southern; Where the Buffalo Roam (VS)—Frank Sanucci, Frank Harford (w,m), Cole. COVER: Tex Ritter.

5920 Where the Hot Wind Blows (MGM, 1960, Gina Lollobrigida, Yves Montand).

Where the Hot Wind Blows—Buddy Kaye (w), Jimmy McHugh (m), Levine McHugh. COVER: Piano Keys.

5921 Where the Pavement Ends (MGM, 1923, Ramon Novarro, Alice Terry).

Neath the Passion Vine—Bert Herbert (w), Walter Hauenschild (m), Photoplay. COVER: Ramon Novarro, Alice Terry.

5922 Where Were You When the Lights Went Out? (MGM, 1968, Doris Day, Robert Morse).

Where Were You When the Lights Went Out?—Kelly Gordon (w), Dave Grusin (m), Hastings. COVER: Doris Day, Robert Morse, Terry Thomas, Patrick O'Neal.

5923 Which Way Is Up? (Universal, 1977, Richard Pryor, Lonette McKee).

Which Way Is Up?—Norman Whitfield (m), Warner. COVER: Stargard Girls.

5924 Whiffs (20th Century-Fox, 1975, Elliott Gould, Eddie Albert).

Now That We're in Love—Sammy Cahn (w), George Barrie (m), Brut. COVER: Cartoon Sketches.

5925 While Paris Sleeps (Fox, 1932, Victor McLaglen, Helen Mack).

Cherie, Paree Is Mine—James Hanley (w,m), Movietone. COVER: Victor McLaglen, Helen Mack.

5926 While the City Sleeps (RKO, 1956, Dana Andrews, Ida Lupino).

While the City Sleeps—Joe Mullendorf, Herschel B. Gilbert (w,m), Bourne. COVER: Blue and white cover with title only.

5927 Whip, The (Paragon, 1917, Alma Hanlon, June Elvidge).

The Whip-March and Two Step—Abe Holzmann (m), Remick. COVER: Train Wreck.

5928 Whip, The (First National, 1928, Dorothy Mackaill, Ralph Forbes).

Just Because It's You—Lou Klein (w), Franke Harling (m), Robbins. COVER: Dorothy Mackaill, Ralph Forbes.

5929 Whiplash (Warner, 1948, Dane Clark, Alexis Smith).

Just for Now—Dick Redmond (w, m), Advanced. COVER: Dane Clark, Alexis Smith.

5930 Whispering Whoopee (MGM, 1930, Charley Chase, Thelma Todd).

Smile When the Raindrops Fall—Alice Howlett, Will Livernash (w,m), Quincke. COVER: Charley Chase, Oliver Hardy, Stan Laurel, Our Gang, Thelma Todd.

5931 Whispering Winds (Tiffany, 1929, Patsy Ruth Miller, Malcolm McGregor).

Whenever I Think of You—Harry

Kerr (w), H. J. Tandler (m), Feist. COVER: Black and white cover with title only.

5932 Whistle at Eaton Falls (Columbia, 1951, Lloyd Bridges, Dorothy Gish).

Ev'ry Other Day—Carleton Carpenter (w,m), Simon. COVER: Lloyd Bridges, Carleton Carpenter, Anne Francis.

5933 Whistle Down the Wind (Pathe, 1961, Hayley Mills, Alan Bates).

Whistle Down the Wind—Marge Singleton (w), Malcolm Arnold (m), Harvard. COVER: Hayley Mills.

5934 White Cargo (MGM, 1942, Hedy Lamarr, Walter Pidgeon).

Tondelayo—Howard Dietz (w), Vernon Duke (m), Feist. COVER: Hedy Lamarr.

5935 White Christmas (Paramount, 1954, Bing Crosby, Danny Kaye).

Best Things Happen When You're Dancing/Choreography/Count Your Blessings/Gee I Wish I Was Back in the Army/Love You Didn't Do Right By Me/Mandy/Old Man, The/Sisters/Snow/What Can You Do With a General/White Christmas—Irving Berlin (w,m), Berlin. COVER: Bing Crosby, Danny Kaye, Rosemary Clooney, Vera-Ellen.

5936 White Dawn, The (Paramount, Warren Oates, Timothy Bottoms).

Whalehunters Theme/Wooley Booger Hornpipe—Henry Mancini (m), Famous. COVER: Warren Oates, Timothy Bottoms, Lou Gossett, and Bears.

5937 White Heather, The (Paramount, 1919, Mabel Ballin, Ralph Graves).

The White Heather—Alfred Haase (w), J. Fred Coots (m), McKinley. COVER: Mabel Ballin, Ralph Graves.

5938 White Hell of Pitz-Palu (Universal, 1930, Gustav Diesel, Leni Riefensthal).

Loving You—Bernie Grossman (w), Heinz Roemheld (m), Handman Kent. COVER: Mountain Peak and Airplane.

5939 White Hunter, The (20th Century-Fox, 1937, Warner Baxter, June Lang).

Swahili Songs—C. Court Treatt (w,m), Movietone. COVER: Black and white cover with title only.

5940 White Nights (Columbia, 1985, Gregory Hines, Mikhail Baryshnikov).

Other Side of the World, The—B. Robertson, Michael Rutherford (w, m), Warner; Say You Say Me—Lionel Richie (w,m), Brockman; Separate Lives—Stephen Bishop (w,m), Gold Horizon; Snake Charmer—John Hiatt (w,m), Gold Horizon; White Nights-Ten Songs—Nile Rodgers, Walt Aldridge, David Pack (w,m), Columbia. COVER: Gregory Hines, Mikhail Baryshnikov.

5941 White Orchid, The (United Artists, 1954, William Lundigan, Peggie Castle).

The White Orchid—Reginald LeBorg (w), Chuy Hernandez (m), Southern. COVER: William Lundigan, Peggie Castle.

5942 White Parade, The (Fox, 1934, John Boles, Loretta Young).

White Parade March—Louis DeFrancesco (m), Movietone. COVER: Orange and white cover with title only.

5943 White Shadows in the South Seas (MGM, 1928, Monte Blue, Racquel Torres).

Flower of Love—Dave Dreyer, Herman Ruby (w), William Axt, Dave Mendoza (m), Berlin. COVER: Monte Blue, Racquel Torres.

5944 White Sister, The (MGM, 1923, Lillian Gish, Ronald Colman).

Love Will Forgive—Millard Thomas (w), Fred Carbonneau (m), Radio; Tis Springtime Again—Ray Baxter (w), Fred Carbonneau (m), Radio; When the Convent Bell Rings Out (B)—Reed Stampa (w,m), David. COVER: Lillian Gish, Ronald Colman.

5945 White Woman (Paramount, 1933, Carole Lombard, Charles Laughton).
Yes My Dear—Mack Gordon (w), Harry Revel (m), DBH. COVER: Carole Lombard.
5946 Who Is Killing the Great Chefs of Europe? (Warner Bros., 1978, George Segal, Jacqueline Bisset).
Natasha's Theme—Henry Mancini (m), Hollywood; Who Is Killing the Great Chefs of Europe-Theme—Henry Mancini (m), Hollywood. COVER: George Segal, Jacqueline Bisset, Robert Morley.
5947 Who Is That Girl (Vitaphone, 1934, Bernice Claire, J. Harold Murray).
Is This Love/That Melody from Out the Past—Cliff Hess (w,m), Witmark. COVER: Black and white cover with title only.
5948 Who Killed Cock Robin? (Disney, 1935, Cartoon).
Somebody Rubbed Out My Robin (VS)/Who Killed Cock Robin (VS)—Larry Morey (w), Frank Churchill (m), Berlin. COVER: Cartoon.
5949 Wholly Moses (Columbia, 1980, Dudley Moore, Laraine Newman).
Wholly Moses-Theme—Patrick Williams (m), Gold Horizon. COVER: Red and yellow cover with title only.
5950 Whoopee (United Artists, 1930, Eddie Cantor, Eleanor Hunt).
Come West Little Girl Come West/Girl Friend of a Boy Friend of Mine—Gus Kahn (w), Walter Donaldson (m), Donaldson; I'll Still Belong to You—Edward Eliscu (w), Nacio Herb Brown (m), Brown; Makin' Whoopee/My Baby Just Cares for Me—Gus Kahn (w), Walter Donaldson (m), Donaldson. COVER: Eddie Cantor.
5951 Who's Afraid of Virginia Woolf? (Warner Bros., 1966, Elizabeth Taylor, Richard Burton).
Who's Afraid?—Paul F. Webster (w), Alex North (m), Harms. COVER: Elizabeth Taylor, Richard Burton.
5952 Who's Been Sleeping in My Bed? (Paramount, 1964, Dean Martin, Elizabeth Montgomery).
Who's Been Sleeping in My Bed?—Hal David (w), Burt Bacharach (m), Famous. COVER: Dean Martin, Elizabeth Montgomery, Jill St. John.
5953 Who's Got the Action? (Paramount, 1963, Lana Turner, Dean Martin).
Who's Got the Action?—Jack Brooks (w), George Duning (m), Famous. COVER: Lana Turner, Dean Martin.
5954 Who's That Girl (Warner Bros., 1987, Madonna, Griffith Dunne).
Causing a Commotion—Madonna Ciccone, Steve Bray (w,m), Warner; Who's That Girl—Madonna Ciccone, Patrick Leonard (w,m), Warner; Who's That Girl-Nine Songs—Madonna Ciccone, Steve Bray, Pat Leonard (w,m), Warner. COVER: Madonna, Griffith Dunne.
5955 Who Was That Lady? (Columbia, 1960, Tony Curtis, Dean Martin).
Who Was That Lady?—Sammy Cahn (w), James Van Heusen (m), Saunders; Your Smile—Dory Langdon (w), André Previn (m), Columbia. COVER: Dean Martin, Tony Curtis, Janet Leigh.
5956 Why Be Good? (First National, 1929, Colleen Moore, Neil Hamilton).
I'm Thirsty for Kisses, Hungry for Love—Lou Davis, J. Fred Coots (w,m), Witmark. COVER: Colleen Moore.
5957 Why Bring That Up? (Paramount, 1929, George Moran, Charles Mack).
Shoo Shoo Boogie Boo/While I'm in Love—Leo Robin, Sam Coslow, Richard Whiting (w,m), Famous. COVER: George Moran, Charles Mack.
5958 Why Change Your Wife?

(Paramount, 1920, Gloria Swanson, Thomas Meighan).

Why Change Your Wife?—Bert Kalmar, Harry Ruby (w), Hugo Riesenfeld (m), Berlin. COVER: Gloria Swanson.

5959 Why Girls Go Wrong (Road Show, 1929, Nina Vanna).

That's Why Girls Go Wrong—Irving Bibo, Charles Weinberg (w,m), Bibo Lang. COVER: Nina Vanna.

5960 Why Girls Leave Home (PRC, 1946, Pamela Blake, Sheldon Leonard).

Cat and the Canary, The (PC)—Jay Livingston, Ray Evans (w,m), Livingston Evans. COVER: None.

5961 Why Leave Home? (Fox, 1929, Sue Carol, Nick Stuart).

Look What You've Done to Me—Con Conrad, Sidney Mitchell, Archie Gottler (w,m), DBH. COVER: Sue Carol, Nick Stuart, and Others.

5962 Why Men Leave Home (Hallmark, 1951, Ginger Prince).

The Big Parade—John Stephens (w), Bert Shefter (m), Bibo. COVER: Ginger Prince.

5963 Why Worry (Pathe, 1923, Harold Lloyd, Jobyna Ralston).

Why Worry Blues (B)—B. Sheppard, G. Webb, V. Bell, J. Prentice (w, m), Wilford. COVER: Harold Lloyd.

5964 Wichita (Allied Artists, 1955, Joel McCrea, Vera Miles).

The Marshal of Wichita—Ned Washington (w), Hans Salter (m), Feist. COVER: Joel McCrea.

5965 Wicked Lady, The (Universal, 1945, James Mason, Margaret Lockwood).

Love Steals Your Heart—Alan Stranks (w), Hans May (m), Chappell. COVER: James Mason, Margaret Lockwood.

5966 Wicked Woman (United Artists, 1954, Beverly Michaels, Richard Egan).

One Night in Acapulco/Wicked Woman—Buddy Baker, Joe Mullendore (w,m), Teri. COVER: Beverly Michaels.

5967 Wien Du Stadt der Lieder (Vienna Home of Songs) (Brecker, 1931, German Operetta).

Vienna, Home of Songs—Joe Young (w), Hans May (m), Harms. COVER: Man with Violin.

5968 Wife Husband and Friend (20th Century-Fox, 1939, Loretta Young, Warner Baxter).

Drink from the Cup of Tomorrow—Sam Pockrass, Walter Bullock (w,m), Tomorrow. COVER: Loretta Young, Warner Baxter, Binnie Barnes.

5969 Wild and the Innocent, The (Universal, 1959, Audie Murphy, Sandra Dee).

A Touch of Pink—Diane Lampert, Richard Loring (w,m), Northern. COVER: Audie Murphy, Sandra Dee.

5970 Wild and the Willing, The (Young and Willing) (Universal, 1962, Virginia Maskell, Paul Rogers).

Zulu Warriors (B)—Bob Sloman, Laurence Doble (w), Norrie Paramor (m), Filmusic. COVER: Virginia Maskell, Paul Rogers, Ian McShane.

5971 Wild and Woolly (Three Bad Men) (20th Century-Fox, 1937, Jane Withers, Walter Brennan).

Whoa Whoopee Whoa Whipee (PC)—Sidney Clare (w), Harry Akst (m), Movietone. COVER: None.

5972 Wild Blue Yonder, The (Republic, 1951, Vera Ralston, Wendell Corey).

Heavy Bomber Song, The—Ned Washington (w), Victor Young (m), Young; U.S. Air Force—Robert Crawford (w,m), Fischer. COVER: Wendell Corey, Vera Ralston, and Movie Scenes.

5973 Wild Bunch, The (Warner Bros., 1969, William Holden, Ernest Borgnine).

The Mirror of Morning—Bob Russell (w), Jerry Fielding (m), Warner. COVER: Cowboys.

5974 Wild Company (Fox, 1930, Frank Albertson, Sharon Lynn).

Joe!—Jack Meskill (w), Con Conrad (m), Red Star; That's What I Like

About You—Cliff Friend, Jimmy Monaco (w,m), Red Star. COVER: Frank Albertson, Sharon Lynn.

5975 Wild Gold (Fox, 1934, Claire Trevor, John Boles).

I've Got You on the Top of My List—Sidney Clare (w), Jay Gorney (m), Movietone. COVER: Claire Trevor.

5976 Wild Horse Rodeo (Republic, 1938, Bob Livingston, Ray Corrigan).

When the Round Up Days Are Over (VS)—Fleming Allan (w,m), Cole. COVER: Gene Autry.

5977 Wild in the Country (20th Century-Fox, 1961, Elvis Presley, Hope Lange).

In My Way/I Slipped, I Stumbled, I Fell—Fred Wise (w), Ben Weisman (m), Gladys. Wild in the Country—Hugo Peretti, Luigi Creatore, George Weiss (w,m), Gladys. COVER: Elvis Presley.

5978 Wild in the Streets (AIP, 1968, Shelley Winters, Christopher Jones).

Fifty Two Per Cent/Sally Leroy/Shape of Things to Come—Barry Mann, Cynthia Weil (w,m), Colgems. COVER: Tony Butala.

5979 Wild Is the Wind (Paramount, 1957, Anna Magnani, Anthony Quinn).

Wild Is the Wind—Ned Washington (w), Dimitri Tiomkin (m), Hill Range. COVER: Anna Magnani, Anthony Quinn, Tony Franciosa.

5980 Wild Oats (Cummings, 1919, William Jefferson, Emily Marceau).

Wild Oats—Jeff Branen (w), Ed O'Keefe (m), Morris. COVER: William Jefferson, Emily Marceau.

5981 Wild One, The (Hot Blood) (Columbia, 1953, Marlon Brando, Mary Murphy).

Beetle/Black Rebel's Ride/Blues for Brando/Chino/Drag for Beer/Hotshoe/Lonely Way/Scramble/Wild One/Windswept—Leith Stevens (m), Mills. COVER: Marlon Brando, Mary Murphy.

5982 Wild Orchids (MGM, 1929, Greta Garbo, Lewis Stone).

Wild Orchids—Ray Klages (w), William Axt, David Mendoza (m), Robbins. COVER: Greta Garbo.

5983 Wild Party, The (Paramount, 1929, Clara Bow, Fredric March).

My Wild Party Girl—Leo Robin (w), Richard Whiting (m), Famous. COVER: Clara Bow.

5984 Wild Party, The (AIP, 1975, James Coco, Raquel Welch).

Ain't Nothin' Bad About Feeling Good/Sunday Mornin' Blues—Walter Marks (w,m), Promco. COVER: Raquel Welch, James Coco, and Others.

5985 Wild River (20th Century-Fox, 1960, Lee Remick, Montgomery Clift).

Wild River—Kenyon Hopkins (m), Miller. COVER: Montgomery Clift, Lee Remick, Jo Van Fleet.

5986 Wild Rovers (MGM, 1971, William Holden, Ryan O'Neal).

Wild Rovers Theme—Jerry Goldsmith (m), Hastings. COVER: William Holden, Ryan O'Neal.

5987 Wild West Days (Universal, 1937, Johnny Mack Brown, Lynn Gilbert).

Get Along Little Pony Get Along/Song of the Sage—Kay Kellogg (w, m), Sam Fox. COVER: Johnny Mack Brown.

5988 Willow (MGM, 1988, Val Kilmer, Joanne Whalley).

Willow Theme—James Horner (m), Warner. COVER: Val Kilmer, Joanne Whalley, Warwick Davis.

5989 Willow Tree, The (MGM, 1920, Viola Dana, Edward Connelly).

The Willow Tree—Will Heelan (w), Will Haskins (m), Morris. COVER: Viola Dana.

5990 Will Penny (Paramount, 1968, Charlton Heston, Joan Hackett).

Lonely Rider—Robert Wells (w), David Raksin (m), Famous. COVER: Charlton Heston, and Movie Scenes.

5991   Willy Wonka and the Chocolate Factory (Paramount, 1971, Gene Wilder, Jack Albertson).

Candy Man, The/Pure Imagination/Willy Wonka and the Chocolate Factory-Six Songs—Leslie Bricusse, Anthony Newley (w,m), Taradam. COVER: Gene Wilder, and Kids.

5992   Wilson (20th Century-Fox, 1945, Alexander Knox, Charles Coburn).

By the Light of the Silvery Moon —Ed Madden (w), Gus Edwards (m), Remick; Madelon—Al Bryan, Louis Bousquet, Camille Robert (w,m), Remick; Moonlight Bay—Ed Madden (w), Percy Wenrich (m), Remick; Put on Your Old Grey Bonnet—Stan Murphy (w), Percy Wenrich (m), Remick; Smiles—Will Callahan, Lee Roberts (w,m), Remick. COVER: Alexander Knox, Geraldine Fitzgerald, and Movie Scenes.

5993   Wind, The (MGM, 1928, Lillian Gish, Lars Hanson).

Love Brought the Sunshine—Herman Ruby, Dave Dreyer (w), William Axt, Dave Mendoza (m), Berlin. COVER: Lillian Gish.

5994   Windjammer   (National, 1957, Pablo Casals, Arthur Fiedler).

Kari Waits for Me—Terry Gilkyson, Richard Dehr, Frank Miller (w, m), Montclare; Night Watch/Windjammer—Morton Gould (m), G and C. COVER: Sailing Ship.

5995   Window on Moscow (Independent, 1968, Stars Unknown).

Window on Moscow—Richard Ahlert (w), P. Chreniakow (m), Pincus. COVER: Red cover with title only.

5996   Windsplitter, The (POP, 1971, Jim McMullan, Paul Lambert).

The Road Home—Joyce Taylor (w,m), Green Apple. COVER: Sketch of Couple and Motorcycle.

5997   Wine Women and Song (Chadwick, 1934, Lilyan Tashman, Lew Cody).

When You Are Mine/Wine Women and Song—Con Conrad, Sidney Mitchell, Archie Gottler (w,m),

Harms. COVER: Lilyan Tashman, Lew Cody.

5998   Winged Victory (20th Century-Fox, 1944, Lon McCallister, Jeanne Crain).

Spirit of the Air Force—William J. Clinch (w,m), Peer; Whiffenpoof Song, The—M. Minnigerode, G. Pomeroy, T. Galloway, R. Vallee (w,m), Miller; You're So Sweet to Remember—Leo Robin (w), David Rose (m), BVC. COVER: Lon McCallister, Jeanne Crain, Barry Nelson, Movie Scenes.

5999   Wings (Paramount, 1927, Clara Bow, Buddy Rogers).

Wings—Ballard MacDonald (w), J. S. Zamecnik (m), Sam Fox. COVER: Clara Bow, Buddy Rogers.

6000   Wings of Eagles, The (MGM, 1957, John Wayne, Dan Dailey).

The Wings of Eagles—Jack Brooks (w), Jeff Alexander (m), Feist. COVER: John Wayne, Maureen O'Hara.

6001   Wings of the Morning (Fox, 1919, William Farnum, Hershall Mayall).

Wings of the Morning—Jean Lefaure (w), W. C. Pola (m), Church. COVER: A Sailing Ship.

6002   Wings of the Navy (Warner Bros., 1939, George Brent, Olivia de Havilland).

Wings Over the Navy—Johnny Mercer (w), Harry Warren (m), Witmark. COVER: Navy Planes.

6003   Winners of the West (Universal, 1940, Dick Foran, Vyola Vonn).

The Drinks Are on the House— Everett Carter (w), Milton Rosen (m), Robbins. COVER: Dick Foran, Vyola Vonn.

6004   Winnie the Pooh and the Blustery Day (Disney, 1968, Cartoon).

The Wonderful Thing About Tiggers—Richard Sherman, Robert Sherman (w,m), Wonderland. COVER: Cartoon.

6005   Winnie the Pooh and the

Honey Tree (Disney, 1966, Cartoon).

Winnie the Pooh—Richard Sherman (w), Robert Sherman (m), Disney. COVER: Cartoon.

6006 Winning (Universal, 1969, Paul Newman, Joanne Woodward).

California Montage—Dave Grusin (m), Shamley. COVER: Paul Newman, Joanne Woodward, Robert Wagner.

6007 Winter A-Go-Go (Columbia, 1966, James Stacy, Beverly Adams).

King of the Mountain/Ski City/ Winter A-Go-Go—Howard Greenfield, Jack Keller (w,m), Colgems. COVER: James Stacy, Beverly Adams.

6008 Winter Carnival (United Artists, 1939, Ann Sheridan, Richard Carlson).

Winter Blossoms—L. Wolfe Gilbert (w), Werner Janssen (m), Gilbert. COVER: Ann Sheridan.

6009 Wintertime (20th Century-Fox, 1943, Sonja Henie, Jack Oakie).

I Like It Here/Later Tonight/Wintertime—Leo Robin (w), Nacio Herb Brown (m), Robbins. COVER: Sonja Henie, Jack Oakie, Woody Herman, Carole Landis.

6010 Wiretapper (Vaus, 1955, Bill Williams, Georgia Lee).

I Cannot Hide from God—Ralph Carmichael (w,m), Herman. COVER: Evangeline Carmichael.

6011 Wise Little Hen, The (Disney, 1934, Cartoon).

The Wise Little Hen (VS)—Larry Morey (w), Leigh Harline (m), Berlin. COVER: Cartoon.

6012 Witches of Eastwick, The (Warner Bros., 1987, Jack Nicholson, Cher).

The Devil's Dance—John Williams (m), Warner. COVER: Jack Nicholson, Cher, Michelle Pfeiffer, Susan Sarandon.

6013 Witchfinder General (The Conqueror Worm) (AIP, 1968, Vincent Price, Ian Ogilvy)..

Witchfinder General Love Theme (B)—Paul Ferris (m), Shadows. COVER: Vincent Price, Hilary Dwyer.

6014 With a Song in My Heart (20th Century-Fox, 1952, Susan Hayward, Rory Calhoun).

Blue Moon—Lorenz Hart (w), Richard Rodgers (m), Robbins; I'll Walk Alone—Sammy Cahn (w), Jule Styne (m), Mayfair; It's a Good Day —Peggy Lee, Dave Barbour (w,m), Criterion; That Old Feeling—Lew Brown (w), Sammy Fain (m), Feist; With a Song in My Heart—Lorenz Hart (w), Richard Rodgers (m), Harms. COVER: Susan Hayward, Rory Calhoun, and Movie Scenes.

6015 With Byrd at the South Pole (Paramount, 1930, Richard Byrd, Clair Alexander).

Back Home—Irving Kahal, Sammy Fain, Pierre Norman (w,m), Famous. COVER: Richard Byrd.

6016 With Love and Kisses (Melody, 1936, Pinky Tomlin, Toby Wing).

I'm Right Back Where I Started— Pinky Tomlin, Coy Poe (w,m), Mills; Sittin' on the Edge of My Chair—Paul Parks, Pinky Tomlin, Coy Poe (w, m), Mills; Sweet—Pinky Tomlin, Al Heath, Bud LeRoux (w,m), Mills; Trouble with Me Is You—Pinky Tomlin, Harry Tobias (w,m), Mills; With Love and Kisses—Connie Lee (w,m), Mills. COVER: Pinky Tomlin, Toby Wing.

6017 Without You (British Lion, 1938, Henry Kendall, Wendy Barrie).

Without You—Cliff Marsh, Len Harley, Irving King (w,m), Mills. COVER: Margot Grahame.

6018 With Poopdeck Pappy (Paramount, 1940, Popeye Cartoon).

I'm Popeye's Poopdeck Pappy— Al Neiburg (w), Sammy Timberg (m), Famous. COVER: Cartoon.

6019 Witness (Paramount, 1985, Harrison Ford, Kelly McGillis).

Party Down—Scott Shelly, Alan Brackett (w,m), Famous; Witness-

Main Theme—Maurice Jarre (m), Famous. COVER: Harrison Ford, and Boy.

6020 Witness for the Prosecution (United Artists, 1957, Tyrone Power, Marlene Dietrich).

I May Never Go Home Anymore—Jack Brooks (w), Ralph Roberts (m), Unart. COVER: Tyrone Power, Marlene Dietrich.

6021 Wives and Lovers (Paramount, 1963, Janet Leigh, Van Johnson).

Golly Walk—Lyn Murray (m), Famous; Wives and Lovers—Hal David (w), Burt Bacharach (m), Famous. COVER: Janet Leigh, Van Johnson, Shelley Winters, Martha Hyer, Ray Walston.

6022 Wiz, The (Universal, 1978, Diana Ross, Michael Jackson).

Believe in Yourself—Charlie Smalls (w,m), Fox; Brand New Day, A—Luther Vandross (w,m), Fox; Don't Nobody Bring Me No Bad News/ Ease on Down the Road/Home—Charlie Smalls (w,m), Fox; Is This What Feeling Gets?—Quincy Jones, Nick Ashford, Valerie Simpson (w, m), Fox; You Can't Win—Charlie Smalls (w,m), Fox; The Wiz-Sixteen Songs—Charles Smalls, Quincy Jones (w,m), Warner. COVER: Diana Ross, Michael Jackson, Nipsey Russell, Ted Ross.

6023 Wizard of Baghdad, The (20th Century-Fox, 1961, Dick Shawn, Diane Baker).

The Wizard of Baghdad—Diane Lampert, Peter Farrow (w), David Saxon (m), Miller. COVER: Dick Shawn, and Movie Scenes.

6024 Wizard of Oz, The (MGM, 1939, Judy Garland, Ray Bolger).

Ding Dong the Witch Is Dead/If I Only Had a Brain/Jitterbug, The/ Merry Old Land of Oz/Over the Rainbow/We're Off to See the Wizard/If I Were King of the Forest (VS/ Lullaby League and Lollypop Guild (VS)/Munchkinland (VS)/Optimistic Voices (VS)—E. Y. Harburg (w),

Harold Arlen (m), Feist. COVER: Judy Garland, Frank Morgan, Ray Bolger, Jack Haley, Bert Lahr.

6025 Wolf of Wall Street, The (Paramount, 1929, George Bancroft, Nancy Carroll).

Love Take My Heart—Harold Christy (w), Joseph Meyer (m), Famous. COVER: George Bancroft, Olga Baclanova.

6026 Wolf Song, The (Paramount, 1929, Lupe Velez, Gary Cooper).

Dolly Dean—Arthur Lamb, A. Teres (w,m), T and K; Mi Amado—Sam Lewis, Joe Young (w), Harry Warren (m), Famous; Yo Te Amo Means I Love You—Alfred Bryan (w), Richard Whiting (m), Famous. COVER: Lupe Velez, Gary Cooper.

6027 Woman Between, The (RKO, 1931, Lester Vail, Lili Damita).

Close to Me—Victor Schertzinger (w,m), Harms. COVER: Lester Vail, Lili Damita.

6028 Woman Commands, A (RKO, 1931, Roland Young, Pola Negri).

Paradise—Gordon Clifford, Nacio Herb Brown (w,m), Brown; Promise You'll Remember Me—Charles Whittaker, Nacio Herb Brown (w,m), Brown. COVER: Pola Negri.

6029 Woman Disputed, The (United Artists, 1927, Norma Talmadge, Gilbert Roland).

Woman Disputed-I Love You—Ed Grossman, Ted Ward (w,m), Witmark. COVER: Norma Talmadge, Gilbert Roland.

6030 Woman Hater (Universal, 1949, Stewart Granger, Edwige Feuillere).

People in Love (B)—Harold Purcell, Lambert Williamson (w,m), Chappell. COVER: Stewart Granger, Edwige Feuillere.

6031 Woman in a Dressing Gown, **A** (Warner Bros., 1957, Yvonne Mitchell, Anthony Quayle).

Invitation Waltz (B)—Richard Addinsell (m), Chappell. COVER: Yvonne Mitchell, Anthony Quayle, Sylvia Syms.

6032 Woman in Red, The (Orion, 1984, Gene Wilder, Charles Grodin).

I Just Called to Say I Love You/ Love Light in Flight—Stevie Wonder (w,m), Jobete; Woman in Red—Eight Songs—Stevie Wonder (w,m), Columbia. COVER: Stevie Wonder.

6033 Woman in Room 13 (Fox, 1932, Ralph Bellamy, Elissa Landi).

Love at Dusk—Robert Browning (w), James Hanley (m), Movietone. COVER: Black and white cover with title only.

6034 Woman in the Window, The (RKO, 1944, Joan Bennett, Edward G. Robinson).

Modern Galatea—Arthur Lange (w,m), Mills. COVER: Joan Bennett.

6035 Woman of Affairs, A (MGM, 1929, Greta Garbo, John Gilbert).

Love's First Kiss—Ray Klages (w), William Axt, David Mendoza (m), Robbins. COVER: Greta Garbo, John Gilbert.

6036 Woman of Paris, A (United Artists, 1923, Edna Purviance, Adolphe Menjou).

Woman of Paris Music Score—Charlie Chaplin (m), United Artists. COVER: Blue and white cover with title only.

6037 Woman of the River (Columbia, 1955, Sophia Loren, Gerard Oury).

Woman of the River—Franco Giordano (w), Roman Vatro (m), Hollis. COVER: Sophia Loren, Gerard Oury.

6038 Woman on Trial, The (Paramount, 1927, Pola Negri, Andre Sarti).

Thinking of You All the Time (Promotion Song)—Joseph Grey (w), Allie Moore (m), Beacon. COVER: Pola Negri, Andre Sarti.

6039 Woman's Devotion, A (Republic, 1956, Ralph Meeker, Janice Rule).

A Woman's Devotion—Gwen Davis (w), Les Baxter (m), Criterion. COVER: Ralph Meeker, Janice Rule.

6040 Woman's World (20th Century-Fox, 1954, Clifton Webb, June Allyson).

It's a Woman's World—Sammy Cahn (w), Cyril Mockridge (m), Robbins. COVER: Clifton Webb, June Allyson, Van Heflin, Lauren Bacall, Fred MacMurray.

6041 Woman Spy, The (After Tonight) (RKO, 1933, Constance Bennett, Gilbert Roland).

Buy a Kiss—Val Burton, Will Jason (w), Max Steiner (m), Berlin. COVER: Black and white cover with title only.

6042 Woman Thou Gavest Me, The (Paramount, 1919, Jack Holt, Katharine MacDonald).

The Woman Thou Gavest Me—Al Piantadosi (w,m), Piantadosi. COVER: Jack Holt, Katharine MacDonald.

6043 Woman Times Seven (Embassy, 1967, Alan Arkin, Shirley MacLaine).

What to Do—Al Stillman (w), Riz Ortolani (m), Levine. COVER: Shirley MacLaine, Alan Arkin, Rossano Brazzi, Michael Caine, Peter Sellers.

6044 Woman to Woman (Tiffany, 1929, Betty Compson, George Barraud).

Parisian Doll/Sunshine of My Heart/To You—Jay Whidden, Fred May (w,m), Feist. COVER: Betty Compson, George Barraud.

6045 Woman Who Was Forgotten, The (Goetz, 1929, Belle Bennett, Leroy Mason).

Give to the World the Best You Have—Haven Gillespie, R. Canfield, S. Rockman (w,m), Feist. COVER: Belle Bennett, and Young Couple.

6046 Woman Wise (20th Century-Fox, 1937, Rochelle Hudson, Michael Whalen).

You're a Knock-out—Sidney

Clare (w), Harry Akst (m), Movietone. COVER: Rochelle Hudson, Michael Whalen.

6047 Women, The (MGM, 1939, Joan Crawford, Norma Shearer).

Forevermore—Bob Wright, Chet Forrest (w), Edward Ward (m), Feist. COVER: Black and white cover with title only.

6048 Women Everywhere (Fox, 1930, Harold Murray, Fifi Dorsay).

Beware of Love/Bonjour/Good Time Fifi/One Day/Where Is Honky Tonk Town/Women Everywhere—William Kernell (w,m), Red Star. COVER: Fifi Dorsay, Harold Murray.

6049 Women of the World (Embassy, 1963, Documentary on Women).

La Donna nel Mondo/Women of the World Theme—Riz Ortolani (m), Marks. COVER: A Woman with a Globe.

6050 Wonder Bar (First National, 1934, Dick Powell, Kay Francis).

Dark Eyes—Carol Raven (w), A. Fassio (m), Marks; Don't Say Goodnight/Goin' to Heaven on a Mule/ Vive la France/Why Do I Dream Those Dreams/Wonder Bar—Al Dubin (w), Harry Warren (m), Witmark. COVER: Kay Francis, Dick Powell, Dolores Del Rio, Al Jolson.

6051 Wonderful Country (United Artists, 1959, Robert Mitchum, Julie London).

Wonderful Country Theme—Alex North (m), Unart. COVER: Robert Mitchum, Julie London.

6052 Wonderful to Be Young (The Young Ones) (Paramount, 1962, Cliff Richard, Robert Morley).

Wonderful to Be Young—Hal David (w), Burt Bacharach (m), Famous. COVER: Cliff Richard, and Movie Scenes.

6053 Wonderful World of the Brothers Grimm, The (MGM, 1962, Laurence Harvey, Claire Bloom).

Above the Stars/Dancing Princess, The—Bob Merrill (m), Hansen; Singing Bone—Charles Beaumont (w), Bob Merrill (m), Hansen; Wonderful World of the Brothers Grimm Theme —Bob Merrill (m), Hansen; Wine Festival Waltz—Robert Armbruster (m), Robbins; Wonderful World of the Brothers Grimm-Seven Songs—Bob Merrill (w,m), Hansen. COVER: Movie Scenes.

6054 Wonder Man (RKO, 1945, Danny Kaye, Virginia Mayo).

So-o-o-o in Love—Leo Robin (w), David Rose (m), BVC. COVER: Danny Kaye, Virginia Mayo.

6055 Wonder of Women (MGM, 1929, Lewis Stone, Peggy Wood).

At Close of Day—Ray Klages, Jesse Greer, Martin Broones (w,m), Robbins; Ich Liebe Dich, I Love You —Fred Fisher, Martin Broones (w,m), Robbins. COVER: Lewis Stone, Peggy Wood.

6056 Wonder Valley (Independent, 1952, Gloria Jean).

Beautiful Arkansas—Pat Patrick, Marge Patrick (w,m), Patrick. COVER: Gloria Jean.

6057 Won Ton Ton, the Dog Who Saved Hollywood (Paramount, 1976, Art Carney, Madeline Kahn).

Won Ton Ton Rag—Neal Hefti (m), Famous. COVER: Bruce Dern, Madeline Kahn, Art Carney, Won Ton Ton.

6058 Woodstock (Warner Bros., 1970, Documentary of Rock Concert).

Woodstock #1-23 Songs—Sylvester Stewart, Arlo Guthrie, etc. (w, m), Warner; Woodstock #2-15 Songs —Jimi Hendrix, David Crosby, etc. (w,m), Warner. COVER: Concert Scenes.

6059 Woody Woodpecker (Universal, 1948, Cartoon).

Woody Woodpecker-March—Irving Bibo, Eugene Pondazy (w,m), Bibo; Woody Woodpecker-Theme—George Tibbles, Ramey Idriss (w,m), Leeds; Woody Woodpecker-Waltz—Irving Bibo, Clarence Waltz (w,m), Bibo. COVER: Cartoons.

6060 Words and Music (Fox, 1929, Lois Moran, Helen Twelvetrees).

Steppin' Along—William Kernell (w,m), DBH; Too Wonderful for Words—Harlan Thompson (w), Dave Stemper (m), DBH. COVER: Lois Moran, Tom Patricola, Frank Albertson.

6061 Words and Music (MGM, 1948, Mickey Rooney, Judy Garland).

Blue Moon/Blue Room/I Wish I Were in Love Again/Johnny One Note/Lady Is a Tramp, The/Lover (B)/Manhattan/Mountain Greenery/There's a Small Hotel/This Can't Be Love (B)/Thou Swell/Where or When/Where's That Rainbow/With a Song in My Heart—Lorenz Hart (w), Richard Rodgers (m), Robbins. COVER: June Allyson, Judy Garland, Lena Horne, Mickey Rooney, Gene Kelly.

6062 Working Girl (20th Century-Fox, 1988, Harrison Ford, Sigourney Weaver).

Let the River Run—Carly Simon (w,m), Warner. COVER: Harrison Ford, Sigourney Weaver, Melanie Griffith.

6063 Work Is a Four Letter Word (Universal, 1967, David Warner, Cilla Black).

Work Is a Four Letter Word Theme (B)—Guy Woolfenden (m), Leeds. COVER: Black and white cover with title only.

6064 World in His Arms, The (Universal, 1952, Gregory Peck, Ann Blyth).

The World in His Arms—Fred Herbert (w), Frank Skinner (m), Marks. COVER: Gregory Peck, Ann Blyth.

6065 World in My Corner, The (Universal, 1956, Audie Murphy, Barbara Rush).

The World in My Corner (PC)—Roy Carroll (w), Henry Mancini (m), Northern. COVER: None.

6066 World Moves On, The (Fox, 1934, Madeleine Carroll, Franchot Tone).

Should She Desire Me Not—Reginald Berkeley (w), Louis DeFrancesco (m), Movietone. COVER: Red and black cover with title only.

6067 World of Suzie Wong, The (Paramount, 1960, William Holden, Nancy Kwan).

Suzie Wong—Sammy Cahn (w), James Van Heusen (m), Famous; Suzie Wong Love Theme—George Duning (m), Famous. COVER: William Holden, Nancy Kwan.

6068 World's Apart (Singspiration, 1966, Religious Film).

Am I in Love/Here's to a Soldier Here/Higher Hands/Katarina/Kiss of the Street/Of Love I Sing/Shepherd of Love/That's What It's Like in the Army/Together/World's Apart—John Peterson (w,m), Singspiration. COVER: Movie Scenes.

6069 World's Fair Encounter (Graham, 1965, Ralph Carmichael, The Young People).

Miracle of Grace—Ralph Carmichael (w,m), Lexicon. COVER: Ralph Carmichael.

6070 World's Greatest Athlete, The (Disney, 1973, John Amos, Jan Michael Vincent).

World's Greatest Athlete-Love Theme/World's Greatest Athlete-Ragtime Theme—Marvin Hamlisch (m), Disney. COVER: Marvin Hamlisch.

6071 World's Greatest Lover, The (20th Century-Fox, 1977, Gene Wilder, Carol Kane).

Ain't It Kind of Wonderful—Gene Wilder (w,m), Fox. COVER: Gene Wilder.

6072 World, the Flesh, and the Devil, The (MGM, 1959, Harry Belafonte, Mel Ferrer).

Fifteen—Alan Greene, Robert Nemiroff (w,m), Clara. COVER: Harry Belafonte.

6073 Worst Woman in Paris, The (Fox, 1933, Benita Hume, Adolphe Menjou).

Love Passes Me By—Robert Burkhardt, Allan Stuart (w), Arthur

Lange (w), Movietone. COVER: Benita Hume, Adolphe Menjou.

6074 Wranglers Roost (Monogram, 1941, Ray Corrigan, John King).

Joggin' (PC)/Rodeo in Heaven (PC)—Ekko Whelan (w), Roger Lohrman (m), Newmusic. COVER: None.

6075 Wrecker, The (Tiffany, 1929, Carlyle Blackwell, Benita Hume).

Are You Really Mine—Irving Caesar (w), Joseph Santly (m), Santly Bros. COVER: Carlyle Blackwell, Benita Hume.

6076 Written on the Wind (Universal, 1957, Rock Hudson, Lauren Bacall).

Written on the Wind—Sammy Cahn (w), Victor Young (m), Northern. COVER: Rock Hudson, Lauren Bacall.

6077 Wrong Box, The (Columbia, 1966, John Mills, Ralph Richardson).

The Wrong Box—John Barry (m), Colgems. COVER: Michael Caine, Nanette Newman.

6078 Wrong Is Right (Columbia, 1982, Sean Connery, George Grizzard).

He's Our Man—Sally Stephens (w), Artie Kane (m), Gold Horizon. COVER: Sean Connery.

6079 W.U.S.A. (Paramount, 1970, Paul Newman, Joanne Woodward).

Glory Road—Neil Diamond (w, m), Stonebridge. COVER: Paul Newman, Joanne Woodward.

6080 Wuthering Heights (AIP, 1971, Anna Calder-Marshall, Timothy Dalton).

I Was Born in Love with You——Alan Bergman, Marilyn Bergman (w), Michel Legrand (m), Buckminster. COVER: Anna Calder-Marshall, Timothy Dalton.

6081 W. W. and the Dixie Dance Kings (20th Century-Fox, 1975, Burt Reynolds, Jerry Reed).

A Friend—Jerry Hubbard (w,m), Fox. COVER: Burt Reynolds, and Movie Scenes.

6082 Wynken, Blynken, and Nod (Disney, 1938, Cartoon).

Wynken, Blynken, and Nod—Eugene Field (w), Leigh Harline (m), ABC. COVER: Weather Vane, and Stars.

6083 Wyoming Mail (Universal, 1950, Alexis Smith, Stephen McNally).

Endlessly/Take Me to Town—Dan Shapiro, Lester Lee (w,m), Barton. COVER: Alexis Smith, Stephen McNally.

6084 X-15 (United Artists, 1961, Charles Bronson, David McLean).

Concerto for the X-15—Carl Prior, Euro Testi (m), Ding Dong. COVER: Air Force Fighter.

6085 Xanadu (Universal, 1980, Gene Kelly, Olivia Newton-John).

All over the World/I'm Alive—Jeff Lynne (w,m), United Artists; Magic—John Farrar (w,m), Farrar; Xanadu—Jeff Lynne (w,m), United Artists; Xanadu-Ten Songs—Jeff Lynne, John Farrar (w,m), Big Three. COVER: Olivia Newton-John.

6086 X, Y, and Zee (Columbia, 1972, Elizabeth Taylor, Michael Caine).

Going in Circles—Ted Myers, Jai Ananda (w,m), Colgems. COVER: Brown cover with title only.

6087 Yankee Doodle Dandy (Warner Bros., 1942, James Cagney, Joan Leslie).

Forty Five Minutes from Broadway/Give My Regards to Broadway/Harrigan/I Was Born in Virginia/Mary's a Grand Old Name—George M. Cohan (w,m), Vogel; Over There—George M. Cohan (w,m), Feist; So Long Mary/Yankee Doodle Boy/You're a Grand Old Flag—George M. Cohan (w,m), Vogel. COVER: James Cagney, George M. Cohan.

6088 Yankee Doodle in Berlin (Lesser, 1919, Bothwell Browne, Ford Sterling).

Yankee Doodle in Berlin—Harry

Williams (w), Charles Daniels (m), Daniels. COVER: Mack Sennett, and Girls.

6089 Yankee Pasha (Universal, 1954, Jeff Chandler, Rhonda Fleming).

More Than Anyone—Don Raye, Gene DePaul (w,m), Hub. COVER: Jeff Chandler.

6090 Yank in the R.A.F., A (20th Century-Fox, 1941, Betty Grable, Tyrone Power).

Another Little Dream Won't Do Us Any Harm/Hi Ya Love—Leo Robin (w), Ralph Rainger (m), Robbins. COVER: Betty Grable, Tyrone Power.

6091 Yanks (Universal, 1979, Richard Gere, Lisa Eichhorn).

Yanks Love Theme (PC)—Richard Rodney Bennett (m), Leeds. COVER: None.

6092 Yanks Are Coming, The (PRC, 1943, Henry King, Mary Healey).

Don't Fool Around with My Heart/I Must Have Priorities on Your Love/There Will Be No Blackout of Democracy/Yanks Are Coming, The/Zip Your Lip—Herman Ruby, Sidney Clare (w), Lew Pollack (m), Southern. COVER: Henry King.

6093 Yellow Rolls Royce, The (MGM, 1965, Ingrid Bergman, Shirley MacLaine).

Eloise—Riz Ortolani (m), Miller; Forget Domani—Norman Newell (w), Riz Ortolani (m), Miller; Mae—Riz Ortolani (m), Miller; Now and Then —Norman Newell (w), Riz Ortolani (m), Miller; She's Just a Quiet Girl —Paul Vance (w), Riz Ortolani (m), Miller; Yellow Rolls Royce Theme—Riz Ortolani (m), Miller. COVER: Shirley MacLaine, Rex Harrison, Ingrid Bergman, George Scott.

6094 Yellow Rose of Texas, The (Republic, 1944, Roy Rogers, Dale Evans).

Down in the Old Town Hall/ Lucky Me, Unlucky You—Charles

Henderson (w,m), Mills; Two Seated Saddle and a One Gaited Horse—Tim Spencer (w,m), Cross; Western Wonderland—Guy Savage (w), Hugh Carson (m), Peer. COVER: Roy Rogers, Dale Evans, and Movie Scenes.

6095 Yellow Submarine (Apple, 1968, Beatles Cartoon).

All Together Now/Hey Bulldog—John Lennon, Paul McCartney (w,,m), Northern; It's All Too Much/Only a Northern Song—George Harrison (w,m), Northern; Yellow Submarine—John Lennon, Paul McCartney (w,m), Northern. COVER: Sketch of Beatles.

6096 Yentl (United Artists, 1983, Barbra Streisand, Amy Irving).

Papa, Can You Hear Me?/Way He Makes Me Feel, The—Alan Bergman, Marilyn Bergman (w), Michel LeGrand (m), EMM; Yentl-Ten Songs—Alan Bergman, Marilyn Bergman (w), Michel Legrand (m), Columbia. COVER: Barbra Streisand.

6097 Yes Giorgio (MGM, 1982, Kathryn Harrold, Luciano Pavarotti).

If We Were in Love—Alan Bergman, Marilyn Bergman (w), John Williams (m), Warner. COVER: Kathryn Harrold, Luciano Pavarotti.

6098 Yes Mr. Brown (United Artists, 1932, Jack Buchanan, Elsie Randolph).

If You Would Learn to Live (B)/ Leave a Little for Me (B)/Yes Mr. Brown (B)—Douglas Furber (w), Paul Abraham (m), Chappell. COVER: Jack Buchanan.

6099 Yes Sir That's My Baby (Universal, 1949, Donald O'Connor, Gloria DeHaven).

Look at Me/Men Are Little Children/They've Never Figured Out a Woman—Jack Brooks (w), Walter Scarf (m), Jewel. COVER: Donald O'Connor, Gloria De Haven, Charles Coburn.

6100 Yesterday, Today and Tomorrow (Embassy, 1964, Sophia Loren, Marcello Mastroianni).

Descansado (B)—A. J. Trovajoli

(m), Diplomat; Romeo—Jimmy Kennedy (w), Robert Stolz (m), Marks. COVER: Sophia Loren, Marcello Mastroianni.

6101 Yodelin' Kid from Pine Ridge (Singin' Kid from Pine Ridge) (Republic, 1937, Gene Autry, Smiley Burnette).

Sing Me a Song of the Saddle (VS)—Frank Harford, Gene Autry (w,m), Cole. COVER: None.

6102 Yokel Boy (Republic, 1942, Joan Davis, Albert Dekker).

Jim (VS)—Caesar Petrillo, Edward Ross, Nelson Shawn (w,m), Leeds. COVER: None.

6103 Yolanda and the Thief (MGM, 1945, Fred Astaire, Lucille Bremer).

Angel—Arthur Freed (w), Harry Warren (m), Miller; Coffee Time—Arthur Freed (w), Harry Warren (m), Morris. This Is a Day for Love/Will You Marry Me?/Yolanda—Arthur Freed (w), Harry Warren (m), Miller. COVER: Fred Astaire, Lucille Bremer.

6104 Yor the Hunter from the Future (Columbia, 1983, Reb Brown, Corinne Clery).

Yor's World—B. Antonia, P. Hanna, S. D. Smith (w), G. DeAngelis, M. DeAngelis (m), Golden Torch. COVER: Reb Brown, Corinne Clery.

6105 Yosemite Sam (Warner Bros., 1955, Cartoon).

Yosemite Sam/Yosemite Sam and Bugs Bunny/Yosemite Sam and the Hold Up Man—Tedd Pierce, Warren Foster (w,m), Witmark. COVER: Cartoon.

6106 You and Me (Paramount, 1938, Sylvia Sidney, George Raft).

Right Guy for Me, The—Sam Coslow (w), Kurt Weill (m), Famous; You and Me—Ralph Freed (w), Frederick Hollander (m), Famous. COVER: Sylvia Sidney, George Raft.

6107 You Belong to Me (Paramount, 1934, Helen Morgan, Lee Tracy).

When He Comes Home to Me—Leo Robin, Sam Coslow (w,m), Famous. COVER: Helen Morgan.

6108 You Came Along (Paramount, 1945, Lizabeth Scott, Robert Cummings).

You Came Along—Edward Heyman (w), John Green (m), Famous. COVER: Lizabeth Scott, Robert Cummings, Helen Forrest, Don DeFore.

6109 You Can Change the World (Paramount, 1950, Jack Benny, Bing Crosby).

Early American—Johnny Burke (w), James Van Heusen (m), BVH. COVER: Bing Crosby, Jack Benny, Bob Hope, Irene Dunne, Rochester, William Holden.

6110 You Can Do Without Love (One Exciting Night) (Columbia, 1946, Vera Lynn, Donald Stewart).

One Love—Jack Popplewell (w, m), Shapiro Bernstein. COVER: Vera Lynn.

6111 You Can't Have Everything (20th Century-Fox, 1937, Alice Faye, Don Ameche).

Afraid to Dream/Danger Love at Work—Mack Gordon, Harry Revel (w,m), Miller; Long Underwear (BW)—Sam Pokrass, Sid Kuller, Ray Golden (w,m), Movietone; Loveliness of You, The/Please Pardon Us, We're in Love—Mack Gordon, Harry Revel (w,m), Miller; Rhythm of the Radio (BW)—Louis Prima (w,m), Hollywood; You Can't Have Everything—Mack Gordon, Harry Revel (w,m), Miller. COVER: Alice Faye, Don Ameche, Ritz Brothers, Tony Martin.

6112 You Can't Ration Love (Paramount, 1944, Betty Rhodes, Johnnie Johnston).

How Did It Happen/Look What You Did to Me—Jerry Seelen, Lester Lee (w,m), Paramount; Louise—Leo Robin (w), Richard Whiting (m), Famous; Love Is This/Nothing Can Replace a Man/Ooh-Ah-Oh—Jerry Seelen, Lester Lee (w,m), Paramount.

COVER: Betty Rhodes, Johnnie Johnston.

6113 You Can't Run Away from It (Columbia, 1956, Jack Lemmon, June Allyson).

Howdy Friends and Neighbors/ It Happened One Night/Temporarily/ Thumbin' a Ride/What Cha Ma Call It/You Can't Run Away from It— Johnny Mercer (w), Gene DePaul (m), Columbia. COVER: Jack Lemmon, June Allyson.

6114 You Know What Sailors Are (United Artists, 1953, Akim Tamiroff, Donald Sinden).

When You Love (B)—Michael Carr, Leo Towers (w,m), Southern. COVER: Eileen Sands.

6115 You Light Up My Life (Columbia, 1977, Didi Conn, Joe Silver).

You Light Up My Life—Joe Brooks (w,m), Big Hill; You Light Up My Life-Ten Songs—Joe Brooks (w,m), Columbia. COVER: Didi Conn, Joe Silver.

6116 You'll Find Out (RKO, 1940, Kay Kyser, Peter Lorre).

Bad Humor Man, The/Don't Think This Ain't Been Charming/I'd Know You Anywhere/I've Got a One Track Mind/Like the Fella Once Said/You've Got Me This Way— Johnny Mercer (w), Jimmy McHugh (m), BVC. COVER: Kay Kyser, Peter Lorre, Boris Karloff, Bela Lugosi, Ginny Simms.

6117 You'll Never Get Rich (Columbia, 1941, Fred Astaire, Rita Hayworth).

Boogie Barcarolle/Dream Dancing/Shootin' the Works for Uncle Sam/Since I Kissed My Baby Goodbye/So Near and Yet So Far/Wedding Cake-Walk—Cole Porter (w,m), Chappell. COVER: Fred Astaire, Rita Hayworth.

6118 You Made Me Love You (BIP, 1933, Thelma Todd, Stanley Lupino).

Miss What's Her Name—Stanley Lupino (w), Noel Gay (m), Mills.

COVER: Thelma Todd, Stanley Lupino.

6119 You Must Be Joking (Columbia, 1955, Michael Callan, Lionel Jeffries).

I'll Always Be True to You Baby (B)/I'm with You (B)—Hal Shaper, Buddy Bregman (w,m), Essex. COVER: Terry Thomas.

6120 Young and Beautiful (Mascot, 1934, William Haines, Judith Allen).

Hush Your Fuss/Pretty Girl, A Lovely Evening—Ted Fiorito, Harry Tobias, Neil Moret (w,m), Mills. COVER: Ted Fiorito.

6121 Young as You Feel (Fox, 1931, Will Rogers, Fifi D'Orsay).

The Cute Little Things You Do— James Hanley (w,m), Sam Fox. COVER: Will Rogers, Fifi D'Orsay.

6122 Young at Heart (Warner Bros., 1954, Frank Sinatra, Doris Day).

Hold Me in Your Arms—Ray Heindorf, Charles Henderson, Don Pippin (w,m), Artists; Ready Willing and Able—Al Rinker, Floyd Huddleston, Dick Gleason (w,m), Daywin; There's a Rising Moon—Paul F. Webster (w), Sammy Fain (m), Artists; Til My Love Comes to Me—Paul F. Webster (w), Ray Heindorf (m), Artists; You, My Love—Mack Gordon (w), James Van Heusen (m), Barton. COVER: Doris Day, Frank Sinatra.

6123 Young Billy Young (United Artists, 1969, Robert Mitchum, Robert Walker).

Young Billy Young—Shelley Manne, Ernie Sheldon (w,m), Unart. COVER: Black and white cover with title only.

6124 Youngblood Hawke (Warner Bros., 1964, James Franciscus, Suzanne Pleshette).

On My Way—Jay Livingston, Ray Evans (w), Max Steiner (m), Witmark. COVER: James Franciscus, Suzanne Pleshette.

6125 Young Cassidy (MGM, 1965, Rod Taylor, Julie Christie).

Young Cassidy—Tommy Maken (w), Sean O'Riada (m), Hastings. COVER: Rod Taylor, Julie Christie.

6126 Young Desire (Universal, 1930, Mary Nolan, William Janey).

Hello Margot—Milton Pascal (w), Fred David (m), Marks. COVER: Sketch of Man and Woman.

6127 Younger Generation, The (Columbia, 1929, Lina Basquette, Jean Hersholt).

Always in My Heart—Don Drew (w), Sam Perry (m), Lewis; Because You Flew Away—Andrew Sterling (w), David Prince (m), Lewis; Bird Flew into My Heart—Lou Herscher (w,m), Lewis. COVER: Lina Basquette, and Sketches.

6128 Young Frankenstein (20th Century-Fox, 1975, Gene Wilder, Peter Boyle).

Transylvania Lullaby—John Morris (m), 20th Century. COVER: Gene Wilder, Peter Boyle.

6129 Young Girls at Rochefort (Warner Bros., 1968, Catharine Deneuve, Francoise Dorleac).

Love Discover Me (VS)—Earl Shuman (w), Michel Legrand (m), Legrand; To Love (VS)—Julian More, Earl Brown (w), Michel Legrand (m), Legrand; You Must Believe in Spring (VS)—Alan Bergman, Marilyn Bergman (w), Michel Legrand (m), Legrand. COVER: Michel Legrand.

6130 Young in Heart (United Artists, 1938, Janet Gaynor, Douglas Fairbanks).

Young in Heart—Harry Tobias (w), Franz Waxman (m), Feist; COVER: Janet Gaynor, Douglas Fairbanks, Paulette Goddard.

6131 Young Land, The (Columbia, 1959, Pat Wayne, Yvonne Craig).

Strange Are the Ways of Love— Ned Washington (w), Dimitri Tiomkin (m), Feist. COVER: Pat Wayne, Yvonne Craig.

6132 Young Lovers, The (MGM, 1964, Peter Fonda, Sharon Hugueny).

The Young Lovers—Bob Russell (w), Sol Kaplan (m), Sollari. COVER: Peter Fonda, Sharon Hugueny.

6133 Young Man in Manhattan (Paramount, 1930, Claudette Colbert, Norman Foster).

I'd Fall in Love All Over Again— Irving Kahal, Pierre Norman, Sammy Fain (w,m), Famous; I'll Bob Up with the Bob-o-link—Sammy Fain, I. Kahal, W. Raskin, P. Norman (w, m), Famous; I've Got It—Sammy Fain, Irving Kahal, Pierre Norman (w,m), Famous. COVER: Claudette Colbert, Ginger Rogers, Norman Foster, Charles Ruggles.

6134 Young Man with a Horn (Warner Bros., 1950, Kirk Douglas, Lauren Bacall).

Melancholy Rhapsody—Sammy Cahn (w), Ray Heindorf (m), Witmark. COVER: Kirk Douglas.

6135 Young Ones, The (Wonderful to Be Young) (Paramount, 1961, Cliff Richard, Robert Morley).

When the Boy in Your Arms—Sid Tepper, Roy Bennett (w,m), Pickwick; Young Ones, The—Sid Tepper, Roy Bennett (w,m), Witmark. COVER: Connie Francis.

6136 Young People (20th Century-Fox, 1940, Shirley Temple, Jack Oakie).

Fifth Avenue/I Wouldn't Take a Million/Tra La La/Young People— Mack Gordon (w), Harry Warren (m), Robbins. COVER: Shirley Temple, Jack Oakie, Charlotte Greenwood.

6137 Young Racers, The (AIP, 1963, Mark Damon, William Campbell).

Young Racers-Three Themes (PC) —Les Baxter (m), Harlene. COVER: None.

6138 Young Rajah, The (Paramount, 1922, Rudolph Valentino, Wanda Hawley).

The Young Rajah—Aubrey Stauffer (m), M. Schwartz. COVER: Rudolph Valentino.

6139 Young Sherlock Holmes (Paramount, 1986, Nicholas Rowe, Alan Cox).

Young Sherlock Holmes-Love Theme/Young Sherlock Holmes-Main Theme—Bruce Broughton (m), Famous. COVER: Nicholas Rowe.

6140 Young Sinners (Fox, 1931, Dorothy Jordan, Thomas Meighan).

Better Wait Till You're Eighteen—James Hanley (w,m), Red Star; Keep Doing It (BW)—James Hanley (w,m), Movietone; You Called It Love—James Hanley (w,m), Red Star. COVER: Hardie Albright, Dorothy Jordan.

6141 Young Widow (United Artists, 1946, Jane Russell, Marie Wilson).

My Heart Sings—Harold Rome, Jamblan Herpin (w,m), Leeds. COVER: Johnny Clark.

6142 Young Winston (Columbia, 1972, Robert Shaw, Anne Bancroft).

Jennie's Theme—Alfred Ralston (m), Colgems. COVER: Anne Bancroft.

6143 You Only Live Once (United Artists, 1938, Sylvia Sidney, Henry Fonda).

A Thousand Dreams of You—Paul F. Webster (w), Louis Alter (m), Robbins. COVER: Sylvia Sidney, Henry Fonda.

6144 You Only Live Twice (United Artists, 1967, Sean Connery, Charles Gray).

You Only Live Twice—Leslie Bricusse (w), John Barry (m), Unart. COVER: Sean Connery, and Girls.

6145 Your Cheatin' Heart (MGM, 1965, George Hamilton, Susan Oliver).

Your Cheatin' Heart-Ten Songs—Hank Williams (w,m), Rose. COVER: George Hamilton.

6146 You're a Big Boy Now (Warner Bros., 1966, Elizabeth Hartman, Geraldine Page).

Darling, Be Home Soon—John Sebastian (w,m), Faithful Virtue. COVER: Lovin' Spoonful Rock Group.

6147 You're a Sweetheart (Universal, 1937, Alice Faye, George Murphy).

Broadway Jamboree/My Fine Feathered Friend—Harold Adamson (w), Jimmy McHugh (m), Robbins; Scrapin' the Toast—Charles Tobias (w), Murray Mencher (m), Robbins; So It's Love—Mickey Bloom (w), Lou Bring, Art Quenzer (m), Robbins; You're a Sweetheart—Harold Adamson (w), Jimmy McHugh (m), Robbins. COVER: Alice Faye, George Murphy, Ken Murray, Andy Devine.

6148 You're in the Army Now (GB, 1937, Grace Bradley, Wallace Ford).

Turning the Town Upside Down—Maurice Sigler, Al Goodhart, Al Hoffmann (w,m), Crawford. COVER: Grace Bradley, and Girls.

6149 You're My Everything (20th Century-Fox, 1949, Dan Dailey, Anne Baxter).

On the Good Ship Lollipop—Sidney Clare, Richard Whiting (w,m), Movietone; You're My Everything—Mort Dixon, Joe Young (w), Harry Warren (m), Harms. COVER: Anne Baxter, Dan Dailey, Shari Robinson.

6150 You're Never Too Young (Paramount, 1955, Dean Martin, Jerry Lewis).

Face the Music/I Know Your Mother Loves You/I Like to Hike/Love Is All That Matters/Relax-ay-voo/Simpatico—Sammy Cahn (w), Arthur Schwartz (m), Leeds. COVER: Dean Martin, Jerry Lewis.

6151 You're Only Young Once (MGM, 1938, Mickey Rooney, Lewis Stone).

You're Only Young Once—Bob Wright, Chet Forrest (w), Alex Hyde (m), Feist. COVER: Mickey Rooney, Lewis Stone, Fay Holden, Sara Haden.

6152 You're Telling Me (Paramount, 1934, W. C. Fields, Joan Marsh).

Sympathizin' with Me—Arthur Johnston, Sam Coslow (w,m), Famous. COVER: Joan Marsh, Buster Crabbe.

6153 You're the One (Paramount, 1941, Bonnie Baker, Orrin Tucker).

Gee, I Wish I'd Listened to My Mother/I Could Kiss You for That/Strawberry Lane/Yogi-Who Lost His Will Power/You're the One-For Me—Johnny Mercer (w), Jimmy McHugh (m), Paramount. COVER: Bonnie Baker, Orrin Tucker.

6154 Your Own Back Yard (Roach, 1925, Our Gang).

Stay in Your Own Back Yard—Karl Kenneth (w), Lyn Udall (m), Witmark. COVER: Our Gang.

6155 Your Red Wagon (They Live By Night) (RKO, 1940, Cathy O'Donnell, Farley Granger).

Your Red Wagon—Don Raye (w), Gene DePaul, Richard Jones (m), Leeds. COVER: Cathy O'Donnell, Farley Granger.

6156 Yours Mine and Ours (United Artists, 1968, Lucille Ball, Henry Fonda).

Yours Mine and Ours—Ernie Sheldon (w), Fred Karlin (m), Unart. COVER: Lucille Ball, Henry Fonda, and Kids.

6157 Your Uncle Dudley (Fox, 1936, Edward Everett Horton, Lois Wilson).

I Sing of Spring—Sidney Clare (w), Troy Sanders (m), Movietone. COVER: Green and white cover with title only.

6158 Youth Marches On (Oxford, 1937, Cecil Broadhurst).

New Frontiersman—Fred Watt, George Fraser (w,m), Fischer; Wise Old Horsey—George Fraser (w,m), Fischer. COVER: Cecil Broadhurst.

6159 Youth on Parade (Republic, 1942, John Hubbard, Ruth Terry).

I've Heard That Song Before/You're So Good to Me—Sammy Cahn (w), Jule Styne (m), Morris. COVER: John Hubbard, Ruth Terry.

6160 Youth Takes a Fling (Universal, 1938, Andrea Leeds, Joel McCrea).

For the First Time/Heigh-Ho, The Merry-O—Harold Adamson (w), Jimmy McHugh (m), Feist. COVER: Andrea Leeds, Joel McCrea.

6161 Youth Will Be Served (20th Century-Fox, 1941, Jane Withers, Jane Darwell).

Hot Catfish and Corn Dodgers—Frank Loesser (w), Louis Alter (m), Robbins. COVER: Purple cover with title only.

6162 You Were Meant for Me (20th Century-Fox, 1948, Jeanne Crain, Dan Dailey).

Ain't Misbehavin'—Andy Razaf (w), Thomas Waller, Harry Brooks (m), Mills; I'll Get By—Roy Turk (w), Fred Ahlert (m), Bourne; You Were Meant for Me—Arthur Freed (w), Nacio Herb Brown (m), Miller. COVER: Jeanne Crain, Dan Dailey.

6163 You Were Never Lovelier (Columbia, 1942, Fred Astaire, Rita Hayworth).

Chiu Chiu—Alan Surgal (w), Nicanor Molinare (m), Chart; Dearly Beloved/I'm Old Fashioned/On the Beam/Shorty George/Wedding in the Spring/You Were Never Lovelier—Johnny Mercer (w), Jerome Kern (m), Chappell. COVER: Fred Astaire, Rita Hayworth, Xavier Cugat, Adolphe Menjou.

6164 "Z" (Cinema Five, 1969, Yves Montand, Irene Pappas).

"Z" Theme—Mikis Theodorakis (m), Blackwood. COVER: A Large "Z."

6165 Zarak (Columbia, 1957, Victor Mature, Michael Wilding).

Climb Up the Wall—Norman Gimbel (w), Auyar Hossein (m), Sheldon. COVER: Anita Ekberg, Victor Mature.

6166 Zaza (Paramount, 1939, Claudette Colbert, Herbert Marshall).

Hello, My Darling—Frank Loesser (w), Frederick Hollander (m), Paramount. COVER: Claudette Colbert, Herbert Marshall.

6167 Zebra in the Kitchen (MGM, 1965, Jay North, Martin Milner).

Zebra in the Kitchen—Hal Hopper (w,m), Miller. COVER: Jay North and a Lion.

6168 Zero Hour (Paramount, 1957, Dana Andrews, Linda Darnell).

Zero Hour—Arthur Hamilton (w, m), Saunders. COVER: Dana Andrews, Linda Darnell, Sterling Hayden.

6169 Ziegfeld Follies (MGM, 1946, Fred Astaire, Lucille Bremer).

If Swing Goes, I Go Too—Fred Astaire (w,m), Feist; If You Knew Susie—B. G. DeSylva (w,m), Shapiro Bernstein; Limehouse Blues—Douglas Furber (w), Philip Braham (m), Harms; Love—Ralph Blane, Hugh Martin (w,m), Feist; There's Beauty Everywhere/This Heart of Mine—Arthur Freed (w), Harry Warren (m), Triangle. COVER: Fred Astaire, Lucille Bremer, Lena Horne, Lucille Ball.

6170 Ziegfeld Girl (MGM, 1941, James Stewart, Judy Garland).

Caribbean Love Song—Ralph Freed (w), Roger Edens (m), Feist; I'm Always Chasing Rainbows—Joe McCarthy (w), Harry Carroll (m), Robbins; Minnie from Trinidad—Roger Edens (w,m), Feist; Mister Gallagher and Mister Shean—Ed Gallagher, Al Shean (w,m), Mills; Too Beautiful to Last—Marty Symes (w), Ruth Lowe (m), Feist; We Must Have Music (BW)/You Stepped Out of a Dream—Gus Kahn (w), Nacio Herb Brown (m), Feist. COVER: James Stewart, Judy Garland, Hedy Lamarr, Lana Turner, Tony Martin.

6171 Zis Boom Bah (Monogram, 1941, Grace Hayes, Peter Lind Hayes).

Put Your Trust in the Moon—June Baldwin (w), Charles Callender (m), Art. COVER: Peter Lind Hayes, Mary Healy.

6172 Zorba the Greek (20th Century-Fox, 1964, Anthony Quinn, Alan Bates).

Dance My Trouble Away—Al Stillman (w), Mikis Theodorakis (m), Miller; Life Goes On/Piraeus Theme—Mikis Theodorakis (m), Miller. COVER: Anthony Quinn.

6173 Zudora (Thanhouser, 1914, James Cruze, Marguerite Snow).

Zudora—J. R. Shannon (m), Forster. COVER: Marguerite Snow.

6174 Zulu (Paramount, 1964, Stanley Baker, Jack Hawkins).

Monkey Feathers/Zulu Stamp—John Barry (m), Famous. COVER: Stanley Baker, and Movie Scenes.

Bibliography

Adams, Lee and Buck Rainey. *Shoot-Em-Ups: The Complete Reference Guide to Westerns of the Sound Era.* New Rochelle, New York: Arlington House Publishers, 1978.

American Film Institute Catalog of Feature Films, 1911-1920. Berkeley, California: University of California Press, 1988.

American Film Institute Catalog of Feature Films, 1921-1930. Berkeley, California: University of California Press, 1983.

Anderson, Gillian B. *Music for Silent Films, 1894-1929, A Guide.* Washington, D.C.: Library of Congress, 1988.

Autry, Gene and Mickey Herskowitz. *Back in the Saddle Again.* Garden City, New York: Doubleday and Company, 1978.

Baer, D. Richard. *The Film Buff's Checklist of Motion Pictures, 1912-1979.* Hollywood, California: Hollywood Film Archives, 1979.

Bergan, Ronald. *The United Artists Story.* New York: Crown Publishers, 1986.

Blum, Daniel. *A Pictorial History of the Silent Screen.* New York: G. P. Putnam's Sons, 1953.

Bodeen, DeWitt. *From Hollywood, the Careers of 15 Great American Stars.* Cranbury, New Jersey: A. S. Barnes and Company, 1976.

————. *More from Hollywood, the Careers of 15 Great American Stars.* Cranbury, New Jersey: A. S. Barnes and Company, 1977.

Burton, Jack. *The Blue Book of Hollywood Musicals.* Watkins Glen, New York: Century House, 1953.

Connelly, Robert. *The Motion Picture Guide—Silent Films, 1910-1936.* Chicago, Illinois: Cinebooks, Inc., 1986.

Dixon, Wheeler. *Producers Releasing Corporation, A Comprehensive Filmography and History.* Jefferson, North Carolina: McFarland and Company, 1986.

Eames, John Douglas. *The M-G-M Story, The Complete History of 57 Roaring Years.* New York: Crown Publishers, 1983.

Eames, John Douglas. *The Paramount Story.* New York: Crown Publishers, 1985.

Film Daily Year Book of Motion Pictures—1964 Edition. New York: The Film Daily, 1964.

Franklin, Joe. *Classics of the Silent Screen.* New York: Cadillac Publishing Co., 1959.

Gifford, Denis. *The British Film Catalogue, 1895-1985, A Reference Guide.* Oxford, England: Facts on File Publications, 1986.

Gish, Lillian. *Dorothy and Lillian Gish.* New York: Charles Scribner's Sons, 1973.

Hirschhorn, Clive. *The Hollywood Musical.* New York: Crown Publishers, 1981.

————. *The Warner Brothers Story.* New York: Crown Publishers, 1982.

————. *The Universal Story.* New York: Crown Publishers, 1983.

_____. *The Columbia Story*. New York: Crown Publishers, 1989.

Holliss, Richard and Brian Sibley. *The Disney Studio Story*. New York: Crown Publishers, 1988.

Hurst, Richard Maurice. *Republic Studios, Between Poverty Row and the Majors*. Metuchen, New Jersey: Scarecrow Press, 1979.

Jewell, Richard B. and Vernon Harbin. *The R-K-O Story*. New York: Arlington House, 1982.

Lahue, Kalton C. *Continued Next Week, A History of the Moving Picture Serial*. Norman, Oklahoma: University of Oklahoma Publishing Division, 1964.

McCarthy, Todd and Charles Flynn. *King of the B's: Working within the Hollywood System*. New York: E. P. Dutton and Co., 1975.

McGee, Mark Thomas. *Fast and Furious: The Story of American International Pictures*. Jefferson, North Carolina: McFarland and Company, 1984.

Maltin, Leonard. *The Great Movie Shorts*. New York: Bonanza Books, 1972.

_____. *The Disney Films*. New York: Crown Publishers, 1984.

_____. *TV Movies and Video Guide–1989 Edition*. New York: New American Library, 1989.

Marill, Alvin H. *Samuel Goldwyn Presents*. Cranbury, New Jersey: A. S. Barnes and Co., 1976.

Meeker, David. *Jazz in the Movies*. New York: DeCapo Press, 1981.

Nash, Jay Robert and Stanley Ralph Ross. *The Motion Picture Guide–1927-1984* (9 Volumes). Chicago, Illinois: Cinebooks, Inc., 1987.

New York Times Directory of the Film. New York: Arno Press, 1974.

Okuda, Ted. *The Monogram Checklist, The Films of Monogram Pictures Corporation, 1931-1952*. Jefferson, North Carolina: McFarland and Company, 1987.

_____. *Grand National, Producers Releasing Corporation, and Screen Guild/ Lippert*. Jefferson, North Carolina: McFarland and Company, 1989.

Parish, James Robert. *The Paramount Pretties*. New York: Arlington House, 1972.

_____. *The R-K-O Gals*. New York: Arlington House, 1974.

Pitts, Michael R. *Western Movies, A TV and Video Guide to 4200 Genre Films*. Jefferson, North Carolina. McFarland and Company, 1986.

Quinlan, David. *Quinlan's Illustrated Directory of Film Stars*. New York: Hippocrene Books, Inc., 1986.

Shull, Michael S. and David E. Wilt. *Doing Their Bit, Wartime American Animated Short Films, 1939-1945*. Jefferson, North Carolina: McFarland and Company, 1987.

Sigoloff, Marc. *The Films of the Seventies, A Filmography of American, British and Canadian Films 1970-1979*. Jefferson, North Carolina: McFarland and Company, 1984.

Sweeney, Russell, C. *Coming Next Week, A Pictorial History of Film Advertising*. New York: Castle Books, 1973.

Thomas, Tony and Aubrey Solomon. *The Films of 20th Century-Fox*. Secaucus, New Jersey: Citadel Press, 1985.

Tuska, Jon. *The Vanishing Legion, A History of Mascot Pictures, 1927-1935*. Jefferson, North Carolina: McFarland and Company, 1982.

Vallance, Tom. *The American Musical*. New York: Castle Books, 1970.

Variety Film Reviews, 1907-1980 (16 Volumes). Hollywood, California: Hollywood Film Archives, 1983.

Warner, Alan. *Who Sang What on the Screen.* North Ryde, Australia: Angus and Robertson Publishers, 1984.

Weiss, Ken and Ed Goodgold. *To Be Continued.* . . . New York: Bonanza Books, 1972.

Willis, John and Daniel Blum. *Screen World* (40 Volumes). New York: Crown Publishers, 1949-1989.

Appendix A:
Songs from Selections Books

Numbers in bold refer to entry numbers.

Judy Garland Songbook (Chappell, 1975) **234**

Gene Autry Movie Hits (Western, 1945) **252**

Ella Mae Morse Sings (Leeds, 1944) **326**

Movie Songbook of 1988/1989 (Belwin) **393**

Disney Silly Symphony (Berlin, 1936) **394**

Red Foley Cowboy Songs (Cole, 1941) **431**

Gene Autry Republic Picture Songs (Western, 1940) **501**

Gene Autry Movie Hits (Western, 1945) **501**

Popeye Song Folio (Famous, 1936) **573**

Popeye Song Folio (Famous, 1936) **613**

Disney Silly Symphony (Berlin, 1934) **626**

Bob Nolan Cowboy Classics (American, 1939) **686**

Disney Silly Symphony (Berlin, 1934) **696**

Bob Nolan Cowboy Classics (American, 1939) **769**

Popeye Song Folio (Famous, 1936) **865**

Michel Legrand Anthology (Big Three, 1971) **866**

Movie Stoppers (Columbia, 1987) **875**

Bob Nolan Cowboy Classics (American, 1939) **905**

Gene Autry Cowboy Songs (Cole, 1938) **920**

Tex Ritter Cowboy Songs (Cole, 1941) **979**

Alfred Newman Serenade (Robbins, 1956) **1077**

James Bond Songbook (United Artists, 1963) **1244**

Henry Mancini Songbook (Columbia, 1987) **1369**

Fred Scott Songs (American, 1939) **1446**

Judy Garland Songbook (Chappell, 1975) **1551**

Motion Picture Musical Themes (Famous, 1962) **1567**

Disney Songbook (Abrams, 1986) **1583**

James Bond's Greatest Hits (Columbia, 1986) **1613**

Disney Silly Symphony (Berlin, 1936) **1629**

Gene Autry Cowboy Songs (Cole, 1938) **1746**

Motion Picture Musical Themes (Famous, 1962) **1799**

Disney Silly Symphony (Berlin, 1936) **1805**

Tex Ritter Cowboy Songs (Cole, 1941) **1806**

Gene Autry Republic Picture Songs (Western, 1940) **1809**

Gene Autry Cowboy Songs (Cole, 1938) **1809**

Henry Mancini Songbook (Columbia, 1987) **1874**

Motion Picture Musical Themes (Famous, 1962) **1899**

Henry Mancini Piano Solos Hansen, 1969) **1903**

461

Gene Autry Cowboy Songs (Cole, 1938) **1904**

Rodgers and Hart Musical Anthology (Leonard, 1984) **1925**

Henry Mancini Songbook (Columbia, 1987) **1975**

Henry Mancini Piano Solos (Hansen, 1969) **1981**

That's Entertainment #2–1976 (Big Three) **2164**

Gene Autry Movie Hits (Western, 1945) **2174**

Gene Autry Movie Hits (Western, 1945) **2175**

Henry Mancini Songbook (Columbia, 1987) **2223**

Judy Garland Songbook (Chappell, 1975) **2281**

Cinema Sounds of 1987/1988 (Columbia) **2405**

Popeye Song Folio (Famous, 1936) **2459**

Popeye Song Folio (Famous, 1936) **2614**

John Williams Anthology (Warner, 1987) **2705**

Bob Nolan Cowboy Classics American, 1939) **2749**

Popeye Song Folio (Famous, 1936) **2790**

Jimmy Wakely Song Parade (Mono, 1947) **2903**

Disney Silly Symphony (Berlin, 1934) **3016**

Alfred Newman Serenade (Robbins, 1956) **3089**

Gene Autry Republic Picture Songs (Western, 1940) **3096**

Bob Nolan Cowboy Classics (American, 1940) **3100**

Tex Ritter Cowboy Songs (Cole, 1941) **3101**

Gene Autry Cowboy Songs (Cole, 1938) **3253**

Unpublished Cole Porter (Simon and Schuster, 1975) **3330**

Fred Scott Songs (American, 1939) **3383**

Disney Silly Symphony (Berlin, 1936) **3568**

Charles Strouse Songbook (Columbia, 1983) **3590**

Bob Nolan Cowboy Classics (American, 1940) **3626**

Best of Max Steiner (Warner, 1989) **3645**

Gene Autry Cowboy Songs (Cole, 1936), **3669**

Bob Nolan Cowboy Classics (American, 1940) **3682**

Gene Autry Cowboy Songs (Cole, 1938) **3684**

Gene Autry Cowboy Songs (Cole, 1938) **3685**

Gene Autry Movie Hits (Western, 1945) **3776**

Bob Nolan Cowboy Classics (American, 1939) **3808**

Ken Curtis Song Corral (Preview, 1947) **3811**

Golden Movie Themes (Columbia, 1981) **3872**

Disney Silly Symphony (Berlin, 1936) **3907**

Disney Silly Symphony (Berlin, 1936) **3966**

Tex Ritter Cowboy Songs (Cole, 1941) **3978**

Unpublished Cole Porter (Simon and Schuster, 1975) **3979**

Disney Silly Symphony (Berlin, 1936) **3990**

Shirley Temple Song Album (Movietone, 1936) **4017**

Popeye Song Folio (Famous, 1936) **4021**

Ken Curtis Song Corral (Preview, 1947) **4035**

Gene Autry Republic Pictures Songs (Western, 1940) **4039**

Judy Garland Songbook (Chappell, 1975) **4040**

Gene Autry Cowboy Songs (Cole, 1938) **4094**

Disney Silly Symphony (Berlin, 1936) **4099**

Gene Autry Movie Hits (Western, 1945) **4157**

Tex Ritter Cowboy Songs (Cole, 1941) **4246**

Gene Autry Movie Hits (Western, 1945) **4247**

Tex Ritter Cowboy Songs (Cole, 1941) **4263**

Ella Mae Morse Sings (Leeds, 1944) **4269**

Tex Ritter Cowboy Songs (Cole, 1941) **4273**

Bob Nolan Cowboy Classics (American, 1940) **4287**

Tex Ritter Cowboy Songs (Cole, 1941) **4354**

Unpublished Cole Porter (Simon and Schuster, 1975) **4384**

Gene Autry Cowboy Songs (Cole, 1938) **4406**

Gene Autry Cowboy Songs (Cole, 1938) **4452**

Gene Autry Cowboy Songs (Cole, 1934) **4452**

Best of Max Steiner (Warner, 1989) **4493**

Cinema Sounds 1988/1989 (Belwin) **4529**

That's Entertainment #1—1974 (Big Three) **4679**

Gene Autry Cowboy Songs (Cole, 1938) **4720**

Gene Autry Cowboy Songs (Cole, 1938) **4728**

Gene Autry Cowboy Songs (Cole, 1938) **4732**

That's Entertainment #1—1974 (Big Three) **4789**

Alfred Newman Serenade (Robbins, 1956) **4806**

Best of Max Steiner (Warner, 1989) **4811**

Alfred Newman Serenade (Robbins, 1956) **4850**

Tex Ritter Cowboy Songs (Cole, 1941) **4862**

Bob Nolan Cowboy Classics (American, 1939) **4916**

That's Entertainment #1—1974 (Big Three) **4935**

Gene Autry Movie Hits (Western, 1945) **4987**

Gene Autry Cowboy Songs (Cole, 1938) **5102**

Bob Nolan Cowboy Classics (American, 1940) **5292**

Tex Ritter Cowboy Songs (Cole, 1940) **5293**

Mario Lanza Movie Songs (Robbins, 1951) **5308**

Ken Curtis Song Corral (Preview, 1947) **5321**

Bob Nolan Cowboy Classics (American, 1940) **5441**

Mario Lanza Movie Songs (Robbins, 1951) **5472**

Disney Silly Symphony (Berlin, 1936) **5533**

Ken Maynard Songs (Cole, 1935) **5554**

Bob Nolan Cowboy Classics (American, 1939) **5561**

Fred Scott Songs (American, 1939) **5637**

Bob Nolan Cowboy Classics (American, 1939) **5865**

Bob Nolan Cowboy Classics (American, 1939) **5867**

Popeye Song Folio (Famous, 1936) **5881**

Ken Maynard Songs (Cole, 1935) **5892**

Golden Movie Themes (Columbia, 1981) **5898**

Tex Ritter Cowboy Songs (Cole, 1941) **5919**

Disney Silly Symphony (Berlin, 1936) **5948**

Gene Autry Cowboy Songs (Cole, 1938) **5976**

Disney Silly Symphony (Berlin, 1936) **6011**

Gene Autry Cowboy Songs (Cole, 1938) **6101**

Ella Mae Morse Sings (Leeds, 1944) **6102**

Michel Legrand Anthology (Big Three, 1978) **6129**

Appendix B:
Thematic Cue Sheets

These cue sheets are listed for information only, as they were composed of music phrases by many different composers—both popular and classical.

1928 Across to Singapore (MGM)
1928 Actress, The (MGM)
1928 Adoration (Warner Bros.)
1928 Air Circus (Fox)
1928 Air Legion (FBO)
1925 Ancient Highway, The (Paramount)
1927 Annapolis (Pathé)
1928 Anybody Here Seen Kelly (Universal)
1929 Apache (Columbia)
1925 Are Parents People (Paramount)
1928 Arizona Wildcat (Fox)
1928 Avalanche (Paramount)
1928 Bare Knees (Gotham)
1928 Beau Broadway (MGM)
1927 Beau Geste (Paramount)
1926 Behind the Front (Paramount)
1929 Betrayal (Paramount)
1926 Beverly of Graustark (MGM)
1926 Blue Eagle (Fox)
1922 Bond Boy (First National)
1925 Bright Lights (MGM)
1923 Bright Shawl (First National)
1929 Broadway Melody (MGM)
1928 Broken Mask (Anchor)
1926 Brown Derby (First National)
1926 Buckaroo Kids (Universal)
1927 Bugle Call (MGM)
1926 Campus Flirt, The (Paramount)
1928 Captain Lash (Fox)
1929 Case of Lena Smith (Paramount)
1927 Casey Jones (Ray-Art)
1927 Cat and the Canary, The (Universal)
1927 Catch as Catch Can (Gotham)
1929 China Bound (MGM)
1929 Chinatown Nights (Paramount)
1925 Clothes Make the Pirate (First National)
1928 Cohens and Kellys in Paris (Universal)
1926 Cowboy and the Countess, The (Fox)
1928 Crazy to Fly (Paramount)
1928 Crowd, The (MGM)
1925 Crowded Hour, The (Paramount)
1920 Dangerous Age (First National)
1929 Dangerous Curves (Paramount)
1928 Dawn (Columbia)
1929 Desert Nights (MGM)
1925 Desert's Price (Fox)
1927 Desired Woman (Warner Bros.)
1928 Divine Woman (MGM)
1928 Docks of New York (Paramount)
1922 Domestic Relations (First National)
1915 Double Trouble (Triangle)
1928 Dragnet (Paramount)
1929 Dream of Love (MGM)
1928 Dressed to Kill (Fox)
1925 Drusilla with a Million (FBO)
1929 Duke Steps Out, The (MGM)
1926 Eagle of the Sea (Paramount)
1926 Ella Cinders (First National)
1926 Enchanted Hill, The (Paramount)

1927	Enemy, The (MGM)
1926	Everybody's Acting (Paramount)
1925	Exchange of Wives (MGM)
1924	Family Secret (Universal)
1925	Fazil (Fox)
1925	Fighting Heart, The (Fox)
1928	Finders Keepers (Universal)
1929	Find the King (Paramount)
1928	First Kiss (Paramount)
1928	Flirty Four Flushers (Pathé)
1929	Flying Fleet, The (MGM)
1928	Forbidden Hours (MGM)
1928	Forbidden Love (Pathé)
1928	Foreign Legion (Universal)
1928	Four Sons (Fox)
1928	Freckles (FBO)
1928	Free Lips (First Division)
1929	Fugitives (Fox)
1923	Fury, The (First National)
1927	General, The (United Artists)
1930	Girl in the Show (MGM)
1930	Girl Said No, The (MGM)
1929	Girls Who Dare (Trinity)
1928	Glorious Betsy (Warner Bros.)
1928	Goodbye Kiss, The (First National)
1928	Good Morning Judge (Universal)
1925	Goose Hangs High, The (Paramount)
1925	Go West (MGM)
1926	Graustark (First National)
1925	Great Deception, The (First National)
1925	Great Divide, The (MGM)
1923	Grumpy (Paramount)
1929	Hallelujah (MGM)
1928	Harold Teen (First National)
1928	Heart of a Follies Girl (First National)
1919	Heartsease (Goldwyn)
1928	Heart to Heart (First National)
1926	Her Big Night (Universal)
1922	He Who Gets Slapped (MGM)
1928	His Tiger Lady (Paramount)
1926	Hold That Lion (Paramount)
1928	Home James (Universal)
1928	Hot Papa (Paramount)
1920	Hurricane's Gal (First National)
1930	In Gay Madrid (MGM)
1925	In the Name of Love (Paramount)
1926	Into Her Kingdom (First National)
1928	Into No Man's Land (Excellent)
1924	Iron Horse, The (Fox)
1928	Jazz Land (Quality)
1927	Jesse James (Paramount)
1926	Just Suppose (First National)
1926	Kosher Kitty Kelly (FBO)
1928	Ladies Night in a Turkish Bath (First National)
1928	Lady Be Good (First National)
1925	Lady Who Lied (First National)
1924	Last of the Duanes (Fox)
1928	Latest from Paris (MGM)
1928	Laugh, Clown, Laugh (MGM)
1927	Law of the Range (MGM)
1927	Les Misérables (Universal)
1927	Life of Riley (First National)
1927	Lightning Reporter (Elbee)
1925	Lights of Old Broadway (MGM)
1915	Lily and the Rose, The (Triangle)
1928	Lingerie (Tiffany)
1923	Little Johnny Jones (Warner Bros.)
1922	Lorna Doone (First National)
1925	Lost World, The (First National)
1927	Love's Greatest Mistake (Paramount)
1929	Lucky Star (Fox)
1928	Mad Hour (First National)
1928	Magnificent Flirt, The (Paramount)
1928	Making the Varsity (Excellent)
1928	Man Crazy (First National)
1929	Man from Nevada (Syndicate)
1926	Mannequin (Paramount)
1927	Man, Woman and Wife (Universal)
1929	Marquis Preferred (Paramount)
1927	Marriage by Contract (Tiffany)
1928	Masked Angel (Chadwick)

1922	Masquerader, The (First National)
1926	Meet the Prince (PDC)
1928	Me, Gangster (Fox)
1925	Merry Widow, The (MGM)
1926	Michael Strogoff (Ciné France)
1928	Michigan Kid, The (Universal)
1923	Mighty Like a Rose (First National)
1926	Mike (MGM)
1926	Moana (Paramount)
1923	Money, Money, Money (First National)
1926	Money Talks (MGM)
1928	Moran of the Movies (Paramount)
1927	Mr. Wu (MGM)
1926	Mystery Club, The (Universal)
1925	Mystic, The (MGM)
1927	Napoleon (MGM)
1927	Nevada (Paramount)
1925	Never the Twain Shall Meet (MGM)
1927	New York (Paramount)
1928	Night Bird (Universal)
1928	Noose, The (First National)
1925	Not So Long Ago (Paramount)
1923	"NTH" Commandment, The (Paramount)
1928	Oh Kay (First National)
1922	Oliver Twist (First National)
1922	Omar, The Tentmaker (First National)
1925	Only Thing, The (MGM)
1927	On Your Toes (Universal)
1927	Orchids and Ermines (First National)
1929	Our Modern Maidens (MGM)
1926	Padlocked (Paramount)
1928	Painted Post (Fox)
1926	Paradise (First National)
1928	Patsy, The (MGM)
1919	Peace of Roaring River (Goldwyn)
1925	Phantom or the Opera (Universal)
1028	Pioneer Scout (Paramount)
1925	Pony Express (Paramount)
1920	Prodigal's Daughters, The (Paramount)

1926	Quarterback, The (Paramount)
1928	Ramona (United Artists)
1927	Red Dance, The (Fox)
1929	Red Hot Speed (Universal)
1928	Red Lips (Universal)
1929	Red Wine (Fox)
1927	Riding to Fame (Elbee)
1928	Road House (Fox)
1928	Romance of a Rogue (Quality)
1927	Romance of the Underworld (Fox)
1927	Rubber Heels (Paramount)
1925	Rugged Water (Paramount)
1926	Runaway (Paramount)
1925	Sally, Irene and Mary (MGM)
1927	Service for Ladies (Paramount)
1928	Sharpshooters (Fox)
1924	Silent Accuser, The (MGM)
1929	Sin Sister (Fox)
1930	Sins of the Children (MGM)
1929	Sins of the Father (Paramount)
1925	Slave of Fashion (MGM)
1928	Smith's Picnic (Pathé)
1925	Son of His Father (Paramount)
1929	So This Is College (MGM)
1926	Spangles (Universal)
1925	Splendid Crime, A (Paramount)
1923	Spook Ranch (Universal)
1925	Sporting Life (Universal)
1927	Spotlight (Paramount)
1925	Stage Struck (Paramount)
1929	Stairs of Sand (Paramount)
1927	Stolen Bride (First National)
1929	Stolen Love (FBO)
1927	Stop That Man (Universal)
1928	Street Angel (Fox)
1928	Streets of Shanghai (Tiffany)
1929	Strong Boy (Fox)
1927	Student Prince, The (MGM)
1928	Submarine (Columbia)
1929	Sunset Pass (Paramount)
1925	Sun-up (MGM)
1928	Take Me Home (Paramount)
1929	Taking a Chance (Fox)
1928	Tenderloin (Warner Bros.)
1926	Texas Streak, A (Universal)
1928	That Royale Girl (Paramount)
1928	That's My Daddy (Universal)

1922	Thorns and Orange Blossoms (Preferred)	1928	Wagon Show (First National)
1927	Three Miles Up (Universal)	1926	Waltz Dream, A (MGM)
1928	Three Weekends (Paramount)	1928	We Americans (Universal)
1919	Through the Wrong Door (Goldwyn)	1929	Wheel of Life, The (Paramount)
1929	Thunderbolt (Paramount)	1920	When Dawn Came (Producers Security)
1925	Thundering Herd (Paramount)	1925	When the Door Opened (Fox)
1926	Tin Gods (Paramount)	1927	Where East Is East (MGM)
1928	Tired Business Men (Pathé)	1928	White Shadows in the South Seas (MGM)
1928	Toilers, The (Tiffany)		
1925	Tommy Atkins (World Wide)	1926	Whole Town's Talking, The (Universal)
1925	Tower of Lies (MGM)		
1928	Trick of Hearts (Universal)	1929	Wild Party, The (Paramount)
1926	Two Gun Man (FBO)	1915	Winged Idol (Triangle)
1928	Two Time Mama (Pathé)	1927	Wings (Paramount)
1927	Uncle Tom's Cabin (Universal)	1929	Wolf of Wall Street (Paramount)
1928	Under the Tonto Rim (Paramount)	1929	Wolf Song, The (Paramount)
		1918	Woman and Wife (Select)
1925	Unholy Three, The (MGM)	1927	Woman Disputed (United Artists)
1926	Unknown Cavalier, The (First National)	1925	Woman Handled (Paramount)
1926	Unknown Soldier, The (Hoffman)	1923	Woman of Paris (United Artists)
1927	Valley of the Giants (First National)	1928	Woman Wise (Fox)
		1925	Zander the Great (MGM)

Appendix C:
Music Collectors Groups

There are four collecting groups in the United States. Each group issues periodicals and two of them hold monthly meetings. Members of these groups meet and correspond with the intention of buying, selling and trading music in addition to giving and gaining knowledge on the subject. Anyone who is searching for any of the songs listed in this book could contact any of these groups for information as to how to obtain them.

Lois Cordrey
Remember That Song
Suite 103/306
5821 N. 67th Avenue
Glendale, Arizona 85301

Monthly publication

Pat Cleveland
Sheet Music Exchange
P.O. Box 69
Quicksburg, Virginia 22847-0069

Bi-monthly publication

Bob Lippet
New York Sheet Music Society
P.O. Box 1214
Great Neck, New York 11023

Monthly newsletter and monthly meeting in New York City

National Sheet Music Society
1597 Fair Park Avenue
Los Angeles, California 90041

Monthly newsletter and monthly meeting in Los Angeles

Composer Index

Only major composers are listed.

1174, 1305, 1332, 1517, 1727,
1770, 1815, 1896, 1910, 1934,
1988, 2144, 2173, 2215, 2237,
2241, 2263, 2441, 2444, 2508,
2553, 2656, 2719, 2767, 2964,
3078, 3232, 3366, 3393, 3413,
3560, 3640, 3704, 3932, 4034,
4117, 4434, 4457, 4517, 4582,
4623, 4693, 4778, 4818, 4927,
4940, 5037, 5043, 5214, 5243,
5276, 5391, 5425, 5470, 5484,
5490, 5536, 5576, 5593, 5598,
5683, 5741, 5759, 5799, 5812,
5832

DAVIS, BENNY
146, 586, 955, 1187, 1291, 1520,
2194, 2329, 2529, 2689, 2759,
2923, 3163, 3164, 2299, 3306,
3847, 4023, 4500, 4762, 5156,
5387

DEFRANCESCO, LOUIS
92, 745, 772, 928, 1047, 3832,
5010, 5281, 5942, 6066

DELANGE, EDDIE
109, 365, 443, 716, 1206, 1762,
2295, 3018, 3393, 3556, 3615,
3737, 3960, 5664

DELERUE, GEORGES
160, 2371, 2547, 3151, 3804,
4160, 4251, 5615, 5767

DEPAUL, GENE
32, 79, 270, 343, 602, 985, 989,
1071, 1324, 1347, 2046, 2289,
2312, 2382, 2577, 2708, 2820,
3534, 3657, 4063, 4123, 4234,
4257, 4269, 4479, 4587, 4633,
4814, 4849, 5884, 6089, 6113,
6155

DESYLVA, B. G.
131, 184, 185, 374, 425, 442,
520, 777, 1116, 1240, 1291,
1832, 1877, 2146, 2300, 2340,
2355, 2529, 2530, 2563, 2632,
2874, 2880, 2919, 2953, 2962,
2982, 3498, 3760, 3840, 3916,
4240, 4508, 4693, 4708, 4722,
4830, 4985, 5133, 5217, 5387,
5453, 5679, 5847, 6169

DEVOL, FRANK
1174, 1317, 1896, 1942, 2263,
2264, 2634, 2767, 2911, 2989,
3220, 4256, 5879

DIETZ, HOWARD
280, 531, 669, 997, 1365, 2164,
2281, 2952, 3782, 5313, 5403,
5685, 5934

DIXON, MORT
582, 596, 597, 963, 1022, 1501,
1945, 2115, 2306, 2334, 2529,
2584, 2850, 3305, 3485, 5159,
5183, 5833, 5854, 6149

DOLAN, ROBERT
231, 996, 1043, 1104, 2232,
2507, 3145, 3433, 3468, 4253,
4896, 5180, 5405

DONALDSON, WALTER
54, 326, 365, 693, 1074, 1291,
1379, 1519, 1551, 1554, 1657,
1672, 1753, 1767, 1833, 1882,
2056, 2118, 2164, 2208, 2313,
2445, 2529, 2530, 2598, 2800,
2952, 2982, 3030, 3129, 3309,
3462, 3761, 3782, 3849, 3955,
4074, 4294, 4358, 4396, 4486,
4492, 4680, 4742, 4759, 5157,
5317, 5635, 5707, 5813, 5884,
5898, 5950, 6179

DRAKE, ERVIN
18, 189, 302, 310, 1541, 1679,
1998, 2157, 2694, 3314, 3561,
4374, 5287, 5399, 5649

DRAKE, MILTON
421, 781, 1567, 2442, 2819,
2869, 3482, 4721, 5002

DREYER, DAVE
309, 604, 1342, 1748, 1628,
2101, 2437, 2529, 2530, 2902,
3247, 3559, 3707, 3757, 4508,
4701, 4722, 5097, 5943, 5993

DUBIN, AL
110, 469, 520, 594, 667, 893,
993, 1005, 1017, 1022, 1043,
1184, 1362, 1464, 1529, 1564,
1655, 1788, 1791, 1792, 1793,
1794, 1795, 2013, 2016, 2073,
2086, 2146, 2334, 2379, 2529,
2530, 2892, 2975, 3017, 3175,
3243, 3411, 3426, 3464, 3543,
3668, 3835, 3840, 4370, 4463,
4488, 4550, 4628, 4655, 4685,
4725, 4733, 4893, 4974, 4999,
5041, 5183, 5455, 5524, 5553,
5617, 6050

DUKE, VERNON
182, 365, 657, 1811, 2311, 3558, 4206, 4647, 5934
DUNHAM, BY
458, 1498, 1499, 1829, 2877, 3121, 3220, 3731, 3998, 5155, 5363, 5547, 5628
DUNING, GEORGE
100, 172, 347, 975, 1001, 1622, 2222, 2485, 3224, 3747, 3895, 3960, 4877, 5072, 5424, 5426, 5452, 5550, 5651, 5953, 6067
EBB, FRED
655, 1601, 1628, 3010, 3207, 3558
EDENS, ROGER
237, 1112, 1832, 2572, 2677, 2871, 2961, 3773, 5088, 5217, 5220, 5395, 5635, 6170
EDWARDS, GUS
73, 352, 442, 653, 1643, 2126, 2165, 2530, 3803, 4522, 4993, 5075, 5123, 5992
EGAN, RAYMOND
653, 3762, 3863, 4074, 4746, 5193, 5323, 5387
ELISCU, EDWARD
434, 1170, 1506, 1523, 1628, 1856, 1920, 2019, 2086, 2133, 3396, 3728, 3831, 4077, 4084, 4109, 4914, 5950
ELLINGTON, DUKE
139, 365, 810, 955, 1965, 3558, 3873, 3921
ELLIOTT, JACK
272, 747, 917, 1058, 1483, 2157, 2179, 2754, 3664, 3677, 3806, 4536, 5510, 5559, 5569, 5916
ELLIS, VIVIAN
1391, 2467, 2593, 2851, 4095
FAIN, SAMMY
61, 79, 140, 183, 405, 416, 670, 682, 776, 894, 1048, 1416, 1529, 1679, 1697, 1752, 1787, 1849, 1916, 1945, 1970, 2087, 2163, 2289, 2307, 2310, 2325, 2337, 2411, 2482, 2536, 2567, 2870, 2973, 3011, 3035, 3064, 3091, 3110, 3130, 3162, 3174, 3235, 3300, 3377, 3408, 3488, 3546, 3548, 3615, 3640, 3938, 4219, 4238, 4308, 4774, 5025, 5183,

5191, 5244, 5266, 5403, 5420, 5428, 5634, 5653, 5689, 5770, 5839, 6014, 6015, 6122, 6133
FIELDS, DOROTHY
77, 212, 406, 535, 735, 742, 1003, 1039, 1168, 1292, 1355, 1366, 1412, 1509, 1666, 2196, 2272, 2291, 2362, 2404, 2537, 2621, 2818, 2971, 2979, 3233, 3430, 3603, 3738, 4325, 4505, 4558, 4667, 4693, 4904, 5052, 5089, 5132, 5170, 5200, 5288, 5316, 5705, 5907
FINE, SYLVIA
966, 1476, 2368, 2651, 3148, 3224, 3375, 3769, 3772
FIORITO, TED
1214, 1339, 1355, 2056, 2310, 2481, 2737, 4228, 4869, 5172, 6120
FISHER, DORIS
836, 949, 1099, 1225, 1702, 2680, 3069, 3929, 4730, 4734, 5077, 5229, 5429, 5730
FISHER, FRED
152, 495, 819, 896, 1345, 1375, 1394, 1551, 1627, 1628, 2526, 3039, 3485, 3604, 3672, 3910, 4186, 4192, 4900, 5325, 5902, 6055
FORBES, LOU
301, 768, 1614, 2186, 2493, 3884, 3904, 4034, 4302, 4708, 5271
FORREST, CHET AND BOB WRIGHT
54, 269, 479, 551, 605, 1028, 1253, 1437, 1457, 1711, 1833, 1880, 2624, 2641, 2779, 2910, 3030, 3123, 3129, 3167, 3454, 3955, 4144, 4492, 4671, 4742, 4857, 4917, 5177, 5335, 5635, 5717, 6047, 6151
FOSTER, WARREN
624, 1016, 4026, 5206, 5613, 6105, 6176, 6177
FOX, CHARLES
285, 1250, 1569, 1819, 1973, 2711, 2718, 3073, 3740, 3793, 4098, 5000
FRANKLIN, DAVE
78, 300, 542, 595, 604, 2198,

2340, 2355, 2530, 2563, 2874,
2982, 3840, 3916, 3937, 4508,
4708, 4722, 5133
HERBERT, VICTOR
235, 236, 1393, 1877, 2119,
2632, 2633, 2872, 3339, 3520,
5177, 5899
HERMAN, JERRY
2037, 3079
HERRMAN, BERNARD
3624, 4093, 5250
HERSCHNER, LOUIS
38, 1330, 1868, 2088, 2207,
2213, 2748, 3241, 4245, 4494,
4519, 4847, 6127
HESS, CLIFF
21, 1213, 2631, 2867, 3107,
3160, 3613, 3781, 3959, 3963,
4001, 4064, 4545, 4768, 4937,
5222, 5619, 5714, 5947
HEYMAN, EDWARD
143, 170, 379, 447, 510, 932,
1008, 1078, 1117, 1190, 1380,
1545, 2282, 2630, 2779, 2889,
2890, 2976, 3053, 3425, 3503,
3560, 3630, 3708, 3736, 4083,
4516, 4544, 4812, 4860, 4897,
5067, 5188, 5193, 5305, 5345,
5437, 5477, 5720, 5772, 3850,
6108
HILL, BILLY
1896, 2031, 2723, 3916, 4248,
4693
HILLIARD, BOB
79, 756, 1204, 2891, 4643, 4841,
5046
HIRSCHHORN, JOEL
181, 1596, 2210, 2977, 3623,
3939, 4030, 4938, 5546
HOFFMAN, AL
79, 839, 1462, 1650, 1684, 1743,
2020, 2736, 2845, 2927, 3168,
3366, 3912, 4646, 4856, 4974,
5132, 5221, 5326, 5576, 5620,
5648, 6148
HOLLANDER, FREDERICK
106, 149, 170, 193, 206, 490,
523, 781, 888, 1132, 1141, 1479,
1540, 1542, 2070, 2150, 2270,
2410, 2559, 3082, 3284, 3384,
3392, 3566, 3732, 4024, 4248,
4598, 4860, 4892, 5040, 5307,

5383, 5427, 5529, 5595, 5661,
5855, 6106, 6166
HOPKINS, KENYON
238, 2265, 2826, 5068, 5614,
5985
HORNER, JAMES
134, 2659, 2702, 5005, 5006,
5988
INGRAHAM, ROY
419, 1993, 2501, 3234, 4348,
4704, 4737, 4992
JAMES, INEZ
86, 191, 406, 2801, 3336, 3379,
3969
JANIS, ELSIE
995, 1064, 3029, 3863, 4204,
4782, 5573
JANSSEN, WALTER
476, 1343, 6008
JARRE, MAURICE
211, 892, 1196, 1421, 1473,
1845, 2419, 2732, 2751, 2804,
2839, 2995, 3146, 3437, 3582,
3997, 4031, 4082, 4434, 5758,
6019
JASON, WILL
57, 372, 518, 527, 879, 1382,
1745, 2212, 2297, 2882, 3242,
3810, 4000, 4322, 4458, 4901,
5010, 5134, 5173, 5815, 6041
JEROME, M. K.
126, 517, 596, 722, 814, 832,
1076, 1184, 1263, 1291, 1351,
1362, 1460, 1605, 1722, 1769,
1861, 1909, 2054, 2160, 2529,
2596, 2742, 2861, 2950, 2956,
3076, 3243, 3316, 3382, 3402,
3490, 3500, 3616, 3619, 3701,
3837, 3926, 4228, 4478, 4501,
4550, 4595, 4652, 4685, 4869,
5013, 5201, 5225, 5249, 5387,
5532, 5557
JESSEL, GEORGE
159, 1800, 2288, 2812, 2869,
4680, 5787
JOHNSON, HOWARD
819, 1218, 1281, 1565, 2126,
2133, 2335, 3297, 3672, 3826,
4077, 4209, 4531, 4614, 5423,
5827
JOHNSTONE, ARTHUR
351, 898, 1216, 1704, 1712,

3916, 4096, 4108, 4836, 4949,
5036, 5474, 5564
MANCINI, HENRY
188, 0244, 253, 471, 557, 787,
791, 1067, 1087, 1101, 1369,
1451, 1584, 1637, 1719, 1759,
1762, 1867, 1874, 1876, 1878,
1903, 1975, 1981, 2108, 2223,
2866, 3133, 3143, 3255, 3347,
3351, 3352, 3428, 3601, 3678,
3714, 3813, 3880, 3953, 3972,
3973, 4071, 4230, 4489, 4674,
4705, 4753, 4821, 4844, 5112,
5129, 5261, 5312, 5315, 5352,
5541, 5551, 5631, 5748, 5788,
5834, 5877, 5936, 5848, 5946,
6065
MANDEL, JOHNNY
127, 132, 1971, 2025, 2461,
3139, 3192, 3345, 4430, 4483
MANN, BARRY
134, 1257, 1976, 2344, 3698,
5978
MARKS, GERALD
578, 2529, 5060, 5568
MARTIN, HUGH
217, 368, 602, 621, 1429, 1725,
1734, 1832, 3231, 5313, 5395,
6169
MARVIN, JOHNNY
293, 501, 1809, 2175, 2197,
2359, 3096, 4039, 4157, 4231,
4247, 4663, 4921, 5684, 5818,
5863
MENDOZA, DAVE
74, 954, 1202, 1260, 1365, 1386,
1507, 2168, 2867, 3196, 3796,
3871, 3964, 4686, 5065, 5519,
5943, 5982, 5993, 6035
MERCER, JOHNNY
101, 112, 132, 144, 175, 289,
350, 365, 366, 410, 442, 503,
557, 656, 723, 775, 791, 868,
978, 1015, 1051, 1060, 1067,
1087, 1104, 1359, 1385, 1491,
1535, 1543, 1655, 1785, 1791,
1876, 1963, 1979, 1981, 2058,
2061, 2161, 2232, 2309, 2495,
2524, 2655, 2744, 2797, 2820,
2912, 2970, 3000, 3133, 3226,
3263, 3334, 3351, 3424, 3428,
3433, 3468, 3519, 3523, 3641,

3692, 3812, 3940, 3972, 4018,
4172, 4248, 4328, 4398, 4551,
4575, 4587, 4725, 4767, 4954,
5001, 5301, 5340, 5391, 5456,
5474, 5481, 5564, 5599, 5734,
6002, 6113, 6116, 6153, 6163
MERRILL, BOB
1627, 5129, 5391, 6053
MEYER, GEORGE
356, 396, 589, 729, 1229, 1530,
1551, 1722, 1962, 2081, 2416,
2529, 3204, 3212, 5627, 5659
MEYER, JOSEPH
243, 1218, 1565, 1678, 2300,
2529, 2530, 3280, 3322, 3878,
3916, 4032, 4209, 4682, 4693,
5253, 5392, 5570, 5827, 6025
MEYER, SOL
252, 804, 984, 1223, 1443, 2273,
2356, 3240, 4097, 4272, 4471,
5213
MILLS, IRVING
365, 606, 810, 955, 1557, 1589,
1965, 3393, 3960, 5052, 5126,
5889, 5907
MITCHELL, SIDNEY
396, 588, 590, 654, 718, 830,
882, 1038, 1073, 1226, 1267,
1312, 1524, 1585, 1658, 1822,
1948, 2009, 2027, 2083, 2162,
2305, 2318, 2357, 2583, 2679,
2739, 2807, 2974, 3204, 3212,
3270, 3734, 3951, 3968, 4176,
4258, 4406, 4603, 4714, 4749,
4760, 4852, 5341, 5357, 5398,
5560, 5621, 5682, 5961, 5997
MONACO, JAMES
600, 847, 1030, 1193, 1200,
1278, 1291, 1628, 1796, 1828,
2086, 2294, 2335, 2395, 2481,
2529, 2530, 2792, 2975, 3605,
3635, 3977, 4063, 4139, 4318,
4249, 4739, 4755, 4912, 4959,
4974, 4993, 5168, 5691, 5840,
5974
MOORE, ALLIE
845, 1468, 1685, 2661, 2789,
2816, 3256, 4931, 6038
MORET, NEIL
1190, 1821, 2014, 2713, 3278,
3689, 4033, 4144, 4393, 5732,
6120

Song Index

Aba Daba Honeymoon 5660
A Batucada Comecou 556
A B C Boogie 4335
A B C's of Love 130
Abie Baby Fourscore 1915
Abie's Irish Rose 4
Abi Gezunt 3080
Abou Ben Boogie 6
About a Quarter to Nine 1788, 2530
Above the Stars 6053
Abraham 2158
Absence Makes the Heart Grow Fonder 4952
Absence of Malice 10
Absent Minded Professor March 11
Absinthe Frippe 1877
Acapulco 173, 2483
Accent on Youth 12
Ac-cent-tchu-ate the Positive 2061
Accidental Tourist Theme 13
Accidents Will Happen 3432
According to the Moonlight 1678
Accused Theme 14
Acquarius 1915
Across 110th Street 17
Across the Wide Missouri 18
Ada 20
Adagio for Strings 3986
Adam and Evil 4942
Addicted to You 919
Addicts Psalm 994
Addio Mulberry Street 3393
Adelaide 1912
Adelaide's Lament 1912
Adios 1762
Adios Amigo 23
Adios and Farewell My Lover 3203
Adios My Rose of Laredo 2726
Admiration 986
A Don Olom 2483
A Doo Dee Doo Doo 2503
Adorable 25

Adoration 26
Adoration of the Maji 363
Adored One 2827
Adventure 29
Adventures of Robin Hood Piano Suite 35
Advise and Consent-Main Theme 39
Advise and Consent-Song 39
A E I O U-The Caterpillar Song 79
Aesop and His Funny Fables 40
Affair to Remember 44
Affair to Remember Theme 44
Affair with a Stranger 45
Afraid 5103
Afraid to Dream 6111
Afraid to Fall in Love 5110
Africa Addio Theme 46
African Etude 4320
African Serenade 48
After All 783
After All These Years 5495
After All This Time 5198
After a Million Dreams 693
After Business Hours 4463
After Ev'ry Rainstorm 2851
After Hours 1176
After Sundown 1783
After the Ball, 51, 233, 2530, 2827, 4679
After the Clouds Roll By 1919
After the Fox 52
After the Rain 4284
After the Show 5653
After Today 1192
After Tomorrow 56
After You 1216, 1541
After You Get What You Want 5332
After You Say I Love You 4903
After You've Gone 218, 1551, 2529
Again 4304
Against All Odds 58
Age of Not Believing 336

Go Home and Tell Your Mother
2971
Go in and out the Window
5216
Goin' Back to Texas 466
Goin' Co'tin' 4587
Going Hollywood 1783
Going in Circles 6086
Going My Way 1784
Going Steady with a Dream 1786
Going Up 2231
Goin' Home 4493
Goin' Steady 1366
Goin' to Heaven on a Mule 6050
Goin' to Lasso a Rainbow for You
977
Goin' to the County Fair 5186
Go Into Your Dance 1788
Gold 4783
Gold-digger 1790
Golddiggers' Song 520, 1793
Golden Coins 1978
Golden Days 5093
Golden Earrings 1799
Golden Earrings Theme 1799
Golden Moon China Night 3736
Golden Stallion 1804
Golden Touch 1805
Golden Years 2219
Gold Fever 3841
Goldfinger 1808
Gold Is Where You Find It 1806
Golly Walk 6021
Golphers Blues 95
Go Man Go 1812
Gondoliers Serenade 754
Gondoli Gondola 3061
Gone 2986
Gone to Earth-Three Songs 1814
Gone with the Wind-Piano Minia-
tures 1815
Gonna Fall in Love with You
1286
Gonna Fly Now 4338
Gonna Get It Next Time 3341
Gooch's Song 3079
Good at Making Friends 2029
Goodbye 365
Goodbye Again Theme 1817
Goodbye Baby 5187
Goodbye Charlie 1818
Goodbye Columbus, with lyrics

1819
Goodbye Columbus, Six Themes
1819
Goodbye Dolly Gray 4401
Goodbye for Now 4197
Goodbye Girl 1820
Goodbye Ladies 2446
Goodbye Little Captain of My Heart
1070
Goodbye Little Darlin' Goodbye
4921
Goodbye Little Girl 5075
Goodbye Little Yellow Bird 3962
Goodbye Love 1822
Goodbye My Dreams Goodbye
561
Goodbye My Lady Love 2464
Goodbye Old Girl 1025
Goodbye Old Paint 4716
Goodbye to Rome 4594
Goodbye Tristesse 454
Goodbye Trouble 744
Goodbye Young Dreams 2489
Good Company 3698
Good for Nothin' But Love 415
Good Friend 3225
Good Gracious Annabelle 1827
Good Green Acres of Home 5183
Good Intentions 4187
Good Life 4588
Good Love 1829
Good Lovin' 404
Good Man Is Hard to Find 3226
Good Mornin' 3415, 5867
Good Morning 234, 4731
Good Morning Glory 4750
Good Morning Heartache 2694
Good Morning Starshine 1915
Goodness Gracious Me 3304
Good News 1832
Goodnight Angel 4129
Goodnight Good Neighbor 5299
Goodnight Irene 2755
Goodnight It's Time to Go 130
Goodnight Lovely Little Lady
5856
Goodnight My Love 5060
Goodnight My Love Pleasant Dreams
2662
Goodnight My Lucky Day 5621
Goodnight My Someone 3459
Goodnight Sleep Tight 1476

I Always Knew 4842
I Always Knew I Had It in Me 1860
I Always Knew It Would Be You
    5222
I Am, Are You 5842
I Am in Love 699
I Am So Eager 3455
I Am the Future 862
I Am Woman, You Are Man 1627
I Am Your Dream 3691
I Asked My Love a Favor 2814
I Begged Her 140
I Believe 2430, 5018
I Believe in Love 4991
I Believed It All 1967
I Believe You 1781
I Belong to You 4122
I Betcha I Getcha 2142
I Break Horses, Not Hearts 4432
I Bring a Love Song 5753
I Bring You a Song 274
I Cain't Say No 3676
I Came to You 4760
I Can Do That 829
I Can Do Without You 670
I Can Dream About You 5081
I Can Live Without Love 659
I Can Love You 2038
I Cannot Hide from God 6010
I Can See You 4254
I Can See You Now 3453
I Can't Be Bothered Now 1026
I Can't Begin to Tell You 1200
I Can't Believe That You're in Love
    with Me 668, 5387
I Can't Do a Single 4904
I Can't Do the Sum 235, 236
I Can't Do Without You 5086
I Can Tell By the Stars 3251
I Can't Escape from You 4248
I Can't Get Along Without You
    4969
I Can't Get Away 3904
I Can't Get You Out of My Mind
    3521
I Can't Give You Anything But Love
    535, 1292, 2272, 4558, 4904,
    5052
I Can't Play My Banjo 5290
I Can't Get Over the Alps 5203
I Can't Remember 4637
I Can't Resist a Boy in Uniform

2553
I Can't Tell a Lie 2158
I Can't Tell Why I Love You But I
    Do 352, 4993
I Can't Waltz Alone 77
I Can Wait Forever 1687
I Can Wiggle My Ears 1462
I Carry You in My Pocket 2064
Ice Cold Katy 5299
Ice Pirates-Love Theme 2277
Ice Station Zebra-Theme 2278
Ichabod 32
Ich Liebe Dich, I Love You 6055
Icky 1865
Ich Sing 3084
I Come from Missouri 4363
I Concentrate on You 601, 1364
I Could Be Happy with You 544
I Could Do It for You 5341
I Could Go on Singing 2281
I Could Have Danced All Night 3465
I Could Kick Myself 2777
I Could Kiss You for That 6153
I Could Learn to Love You 2204
I Could Make You Care 2670
I Couldn't Be More Annoyed 478
I Couldn't Sleep a Wink Last Night
    2099
I Could Swear It Was You 3458
I Could Use a Dream 4464
I Could Write a Book 3844
I Cover the Waterfront 2282
I Cried for You 234, 4830
I Dare You 2053
Ida, Sweet as Apple Cider 1291
I'd Be Lost Without You 4742
I'd Better Not Try It 2861
I Did It Teacher 38
I Didn't Know What Time It Was
    3844, 5505
I Didn't Know You 3427
I Didn't Mean a Word I Said 1227,
    2642
I Didn't Want to Love You 4812
I'd Do Anything 3697
I'd Fall in Love All Over Again 6133
I'd Know You Anywhere 6116
Idle on Parade 2285
I'd Like to Baby You 1
I'd Like to Be a Gypsy 2824
I'd Like to Be Like Peter Pan 3937
I'd Like to Be You for a Day 1596

La Parisienne 436
Lapti Nek 4229
Laramie 4138
Lara's Theme 1196
La Ronde-de l'Amour 2709
La Ronde-Merry Go Round 2709
La Rosita Song 4399
La Serenata De La Argentina 1573
Lasso the Moon 4432
Last Call for Love 4653
Last Dance 5294
Last Dragon 2715
Last Frontier 2716
Last Night 2546
Last Night I Dreamed 507
Last Night I Dreamed of You 2128
Last Night When We Were Young 2378
Last of the Mountain Men 3414
Last of the Red Hot Lovers 2719
Last of the Secret Agents 2710
La Strada-Love Theme 2722
Last Round Up 2723, 4693
Last Run-Theme 2724
Last Safari-Theme 2725
Last Safari-Music Score 2725
Last Summer 2727
Last Supper 2492
Last Tango in Paris 2729
Last Tango in Paris Theme 2729
Last Tango in Paris-12 Themes 2729
Last Time I Felt Like This 4475
Last Time I Saw Paris 2677, 2731, 5453
Last Tycoon-Theme 2732
Last Wagon-Theme 2733
Late in the Evening 3751
Lately Song 5420
Later Tonight 6009
Latigazos de Pasión 2630
Latin Quarter 1791
Laugh and Call It Love 5691, 4739
Laugh Clown Laugh 2737
Laughin' at the Weather Man 3310
Laughing Irish Eyes 2739
Laughing Tony 1188
Laugh It Off 2741
Laugh Song 5134
Laugh Your Troubles Away 5278
Laugh Your Way Through Life 75
Laugh You Son of a Gun 1922, 2865

Laura 2744
Laure-Theme 2744
Laura and Neville 1374
Laure Lee 3070
Laurette 3910
Lavender Blue, Dilly Dilly 4814
La Venta 716
Lawrence of Arabia-Theme 2751
La Zarabanda 716
Laziest Gal in Town 4975
Lazy 68, 5332
Lazy Bone's Got a Job Now 2438
Lazy Countryside 1623
Lazy Love 395
Lazy Rhythm 2426
Lazy River 375, 2084
Lazy Rolls the Rio Grande 4211
Lazy Summer Night 145
Leadbelly-17 Folk Songs 2755
Leader Doesn't Like the Music 2191
Leader of the Band 4646
Lead Me On 5514
Leadville Johnny Brown 5698
League of Gentlemen-March 2756
Leaning on the Everlasting Arms 2245
Leaning on the Lamp Post 2147
Lean on Me 2757
Learn How to Love 2621
Learning to Love 2699
Learn to Be Lovely 903
Learn to Croon 898, 2529
Leather in the Breeze 3620
Leave a Little for Me 6098
Leave a Little Smile 3668
Leave It That Way 819
Leave It to Susan-Love Theme 2762
Leave It Up to Uncle Jake 4737
Lee Ah Loo 333
Left, Right 4471
Legal March 1191
Legend of Chuck-a-luck 4158
Legend of Lobo 2766
Legend of Nigger Charley 2768
Legend of Shenandoah 4638
Legend of the Glass Mountain 1760
Legend of the Lost 2769
Legion's Last Patrol-Concerto 2771
Leg of Mutton 1112
Le Grisbi, the Touch 5539
Le Jazz Hot 5748
Lemonade 236

Live and Let Die 2884
Live and Let Live 699
Live and Love 3200
Live and Love Today 3033
Live and Love Tonight 3442
Live for Life 2885
Live for Life-Eight Themes 2885
Live for Life-Entracte 2885
Live for Life-Theme 2885
Live Hard, Work Hard, Love Hard
  3462
Live, Laugh, and Love 929
Live, Love, and Laugh 1124
Lively Set 2886
Live My Life 2094
Live Oak Tree 2562
Live to Tell 216
Live Young 3846
Livin' Alone 1971
Living Alone 3590
Living Desert-Three Themes 2887
Living Free 2888
Living Idol 2889
Living in America 4341
Living in Clover 3055
Living Inside My Heart 8
Living on the Town 4632
Living on Velvet 2892
Livingston Saturday Night 1512
Living the Life I Love 2482
Living Together, Growing Together
  2943
Livin' in the Sunlight, Lovin' in the
  Moonlight 416
Livin' the Good Life 919
Liza 131, 4240, 4689
Liza Lee 396
Lizzie-Four Themes 2893
Llanero Es 1663
Loaf of Bread 2763
Lobster Quadrille 78
Loch Lomond 2435
Lock Step 3161
Loco in Acapulco 642
Lola 5565
Lola, Lola 491
Lolita Love Theme 2897
Lolita, Ya, Ya 2897
Lollipop Lane 293
Lo Lo 4531
Lon Chaney's Going to Get You
  2165

London I Love 883
London Is London 1823
London Love Song 4689
Lone Buckaroo 905
Loneliness 3013
Loneliness of the Long Distance
  Runner-Theme 2899
Lonely 683, 4718
Lonely Bottles 2336
Lonely Boy 1742
Lonely Feet 5167
Lonely Gal, Lonely Guy 1676
Lonely Girl 1968
Lonely Goatherd 4911
Lonely Gondolier 594
Lonely Lane 894
Lonely Looking Sky 2531
Lonely Man-Theme 2900
Lonely Moonlight Troubadour 3765
Lonely Night 5428
Lonely Ones 3046
Lonely Place 2025
Lonely Rider 5990
Lonely Road 4851
Lonely Room 177
Lonely Teardrops 2662
Lonely Town 3874
Lonely Way 5981
Lonely Whistler 5744
Lonesome 2902
Lonesome Cowboy 3001
Lonesome Levee 4937
Lonesome Man Blues 3226
Lonesome Polecat 4587
Lonesome Road 777, 4677
Lonesome Trail 2903
Long After Tonight 189
Long Ago 971, 1917
Long Ago and Far Away 5400
Long Ago Last Night 1852
Long Ago Tomorrow 2905
Long and Winding Road 2781
Long Before I Knew You 354, 5870
Long Before You Came Along 4291
Longer I Love You 4575
Long Day's Journey Into Night-
  Theme 2907
Longest Day 2909
Longest Night 2910
Long Goodbye 2912
Long Haul-Theme 2913
Long Hot Summer 2914

My Future Star 5407
My Gal Is Purple 4288
My Gal Sal 3473
My Geisha-Theme 3474
My Girl 404
My Girl Back Home 4922
My Girl Suzanne 3475
My Goodbye to You 3944
My Grandfather's Clock in the Hallway 903
My Hacienda 4421
My Hat's on the Side of My Head 2465
My Heart and I 170
My Heart Beats Faster 3531
My Heart Belongs to Daddy 1364, 2796, 3565
My Heart Belongs to You 4519
My Heart Goes Crazy 2898, 3477
My Heart Is a Hobo 5849
My Heart Is Always Calling You 3478
My Heart Is an Open Book 2968
My Heart Is a Singing Heart 5420
My Heart Is a Violin 1242
My Heart Is Bluer Than Your Eyes 3139
My Heart Is Home 4996
My Heart Is in Ireland 2005
My Heart Isn't in It 678
My Heart Is Showing 3750
My Heart Is Singing 5422
My Heart Is Taking Lessons 1193
My Heart Knows a Lovely Thing 966
My Heart Loves to Samba 3087
My Heart's Desire 25, 4516
My Heart Sings 6141
My Heart's in the Heart of the West 2008
My Heart's Longing for You, Elaine 5460
My Heart's on the Trail 2721
My Heart's Wrapped Up in Gingham 144
My Heart Tells Me 5186
My Heart Wants to Dance 5795
My Heart Was an Island 5202
My Heart Was Doing a Bolero 944
My Heaven on Earth 5002
My Heritage 2069
My Hero 828

My Heroes Have Always Been Cowboys 1304
My Hope Chest of Dreams 3385
My, How the Time Goes By 2300
My Ideal 3987
My Imaginary Sweetheart 4084
My Inamorata 3641
My Intuition 1979
My Irish Song 2795
My Jack 4416
My Joe 737
My Kalua Rose 2414
My Kinda Music 4379
My Kind o' Day 4996
My Kind of Country 618
My Kind of Man 1503
My Kind of Town 4326
My Kingdom for a Kiss 2013
My Lady 5416
My Lady Love 4300
My Lagan Love 5520
My Little Buckaroo 814
My Little Friend 3856
My Little Girl 1644
My Little Mule Wagon 5685
My Little Red Book 5887
My Lonely Heart 1214
My Lord and Master 2602
My Lost Melody 3207
My Love and I 1754
My Love and My Mule 3430
My Love for You 4041, 4684
My Love Has Two Faces 1092
My Love, I'll Be Waiting for You 5180
My Love Is Like a Red Red Rose 136, 2534
My Love Is Yours 4553
My Love Loves Me 2030
My Love, My Life 5883
My Love Parade 2988
My Lover 2611, 3870
My Lucky Charm 3229
My Mad Moment 2791
My Madonna 3043
My Male Curiosity 58
My Mamma Thinks I'm a Star 2061
My Mammy 2529, 2530, 4396
My Man Is on the Make 1996
My Man's Gone Now 4025
My Marine 3863
My Melancholy Baby 442

Poor Little Pitiful Me 1512
Poor Punchinello 2928
Poor Rich Boy 204
Poor Unfortunate Souls 2863
Poor You 4653
Poor Young Millionaire 221
Popcorn and Lemonade 1862
Popeye-Fourteen Songs 4020
Pop Goes the Bubble 206
Pop Goes Your Heart 1945
Popi 4022
Popo the Puppet 3772
Poppa Don't Preach to Me 3931
Poppin' the Cork 4023
Poppin' the Corn 293
Poppy 4024
Pore Jud 3676
Porky Pig and Petunia Pig 4026
Porky Piggeldy Wiggeldy Pig 4026
Porpoise Song 1992
Portobello Road 336
Portobello Road Street Dance 336
Portrait of a Lady 5057
Portrait of Jennie 4029
Posh 827
Postcard 4107
Pourin' Down Rain 1653
Pourin' Whiskey Blues 4825
Powerful Stuff 886
Power of Love 259
Power-Theme 4036
Prairie Boy 4721
Prairie Dreams 4973
Prairie Home 5728
Prairie Is My Home 1909
Prairieland Lullaby 197
Prairie Nights 3101
Prairie Parade 2743
Prairie Rose 3193, 4406
Prairie Schooner 2641
Prayer of Our Lord 2612
Precious Little Thing Called Love 4670
Prelude to Love 3454
Prelude Without a Name 5563
Prep Step 5179
President's Lady 4041
Presidio-Theme 4042
Presumida 1309
Pretty as a Picture 5177
Pretty Baby 602, 2529, 4751
Pretty Girl, a Lonely Evening 6120

Pretty Girl Is Like a Melody 68, 504, 1882, 5332
Pretty Girl Milking Her Cow 2871
Pretty in Pink 4043
Pretty Irish Girl 1056
Pretty Ladies 4044
Pretty Little Girl in the Yellow Dress 2728
Pretty Little You 4885
Pretty Mandolin 754
Pretty Melody 194
Pretty Polly 3209
Pretty Quadroon 2495
Pretty Words 2047
Prince and Ming Lo Pu 795
Prince in Patches 38
Princess Leia's Theme 5009
Princess Waltz 842
Prince of Foxes-Themes 4051
Prince of Peace 4052
Private Buckaroo 4063
Private Cowboy Jones 980
Private Right-Theme 4069
Privilege 4072
Prize of Gold 4075
Prize 4073
Prize-Theme 4073
Prodigal-Love Theme 4078
Professional-Theme 4082
Prologue to Little Shop of Horrors 2878
Promise Her Anything 4086
Promise with a Kiss 4046
Promise You'll Remember Me 6028
Prom Waltz 5260
Proud Ones-Theme 4088
Proud and the Profane 4087
Prudence-Entracte 4091
Psycho-Prelude 4093
Public Melody Number One 206
Puce and the Green 4128
Puddin' Head 4097
Puerto Rico 4591
Puf-n-Stuf–Six Songs 4098
Pull Down the Blind 566
Punchinello 1877, 3454
Puppet on a String 1723
Puppets on Parade 884
Pure Imagination 5991
Purple Hills 4427
Purple Rain-11 Songs 4102
Purt Nigh But Not Plumb 1

Think About Your Safety 3719
Thinkin' About My Baby 5439
Thinkin' About the Wabash 2019, 5584
Thinking of You 845, 1468, 1685, 2661, 2789, 2816, 3256, 4931, 5317, 5412
Thinking of You All the Time 6038
Third Kiss 5361
Third Man Theme 5362
Thirty Nine Steps-Themes 5366
Thirty One Flavors 2444
Thirty Six, Twenty Four, Thirty Six 4070
This Ain't the Same Old Range 769
This Can't Be Love 548, 2552, 6061
This Could Be the Night 5370
This Earth Is Mine 5371
This Friendly World 2220
This Gets Better Ev'ry Minute 5213
This Happy Feeling 5372
This Heart of Mine 6169
This Hotel 2206
This Is a Day for Love 6103
This Is a Happy Little Ditty 2561
This Is Always 5409
This Is a Very Special Day 2482
This Is Canada 698
This Is Greater Than I Thought 4187
This Is Heaven 5374
This Is It 3977
This Is Living 2597
This Is Love 3033
This Is Madness 671
This Is My Favorite City 3409
This Is My Heaven 3859
This Is My Love 5376
This Is My Night to Dream 1193
This Is My Song 958
This Is My World 1917
This Is Not America 1388
This Isn't Heaven 5012
This Is Only the Beginning 2788
This Is Our Last Night Together 4983
This Is Our Secret Star 3502
This Is Real 2896
This Is the Army, Mr. Jones 5377
This Is the Beginning of the End 1034, 2516
This Is the Life 68

This Is the Moment 5307
This Is the Night 5380
This is the Time 2570
This Is Where I Came In 4464
This Little Piggie Went to Market 1298
This Little Ripple Had Rhythm 400
This Man Is Mine 3181
This May Be the Night 3484
This Moment of Love 3338
This Must Be a Dream 3336
This Must Be Illegal 4538
This Nearly Was Mine 4922
This Never Happened Before 2135
This Night 2191, 5602
This Raging Fire 2398
This Same Heart 5719
This Side of Forever 5104
This Time 2211
This Time It's Love 4502
This Time the Dream's on Me 503
This Town 942
This Was Mary 3190
This Way Please 5383
This World Is Yours 174
This Year's Kisses 3766
Thoity Poiple Boids 1515
Thomasina 5413
Thomas O'Malley Cat 194
Thoroughly Modern Millie 5387
Those Daring Young Men in Their Jaunty Jalopies 5389
Those Eddie Cantor Eyes 4370
Those Happy Old Days 2747
Those Magic Changes 1849
Those Magnificent Men in Their Flying Machines 5390
Those Shufflin' Blues 2694
Those Were the Good Old Days 1025
Though You're Not the First One 2073
Thousand and One Nights 4859
Thousand Clowns 5394
Thousand Dreams of You 6143
Thousand Miles 2232
Thousand Miles Away 130
Thousand Violins 1872
Thou Swell 6061
Three Blind Mice 2157
Three Bon Vivants 4904
Three Caballeros 5399
Three Cheers for Anything 3974

T. J.'s Theme 780
Toast to the Girl I Love 1948
To Ava 4806
To Be the One You Love 164
To Be with You 3070
Toby Tyler 5476
To Call You My Own 2334
Toccata and Fugue 3947
Today 27
Today and Tomorrow 4028
Today I Feel So Happy 3654, 5140
Today I Love Everybody 1412
Today, Tomorrow and Forever 4457
Toddlin' Along with You 582, 597
To Die of Love 5478
To Each His Dulcinea 3130
To Each His Own 5479
To Everything in Life 1358
Together 374, 4708, 6068
Together Again 5575
Together Time 3933
Together Wherever We Go 1913
To Have and to Hold 5482
To Hold You 5283
To Kill a Mockingbird 5484
To Know You Care 3238
To Know You Is to Love You 2146, 5112
Told in the Hills 5485
To Life 1436
To Live and Die in L.A. 5486
To Love 6129
To Love Again 1292
To Love Again-Theme 1292
To Love and Be Loved 4833
To Love You 4087
Tom and Mary 236
To Mary with Love 5488
Tomatoes 3650
Tombstone Arizona 196
To Me, She's Marvelous 1919
Tommy-31 Songs 5491
Tomorrow 161, 936
Tomorrow Belongs to Me 655
Tomorrow Is Another Day 396, 1080, 4219
Tomorrow Is Forever 5492
Tomorrow Is My Friend 1637
Tomorrow Is My Lucky Day 2192
Tomorrowland 44
Tomorrow Means Romance 2630
Tomorrow My Love 3504

Tom Sawyer 5494
Tom's Theme 1759
Tom Thumb's Tune 5495
Tom Tom 5174
To My Mammy 3085
Tonda Wanda Hoy 224
Tondelayo 5934
Tonight 1519, 5871
Tonight and Every Night 5496
Tonight Is Mine 5034
Tonight Is So Right for Love 1692
Tonight Is the Night 4314
Tonight Lover Tonight 990
Tonight May Never Come Again 2671
Tonight's the Night 878
Tonight We Love 4360
Tonight Will Live 5585
Tonight You're Mine 556
Tonka 5498
Tony Fontane Story-Themes 5499
Tony Rome 5500
Tony's Theme 2681
Too Beautiful for Words 5790
Too Beautiful to Last 3564, 6170
Too Good to Be True 1623
Too Late 2310
Too Late Blues-Theme 5502
Too Late Now 4410
Too-Lee Roll-um 195
Too Little Time 1762
Too Many Crooks-Theme 5504
Too Many Fish in the Sea 404
Too Marvelous for Words 1060, 4172
Too Much in Love 4868
Too Much Love 4919
Too Much Mustard 5059
Too Much Too Soon 5508
Too Ra Loo Ra Loo Ral 1784
Too Romantic 4318
Too Soon to Tell You 4090
Toot and a Whistle and a Plunk and a Boom 5510
Tootsie 5509
Toot Sweets 827
Toot Toot Tootsie 2313, 2481, 2529, 2530, 4206, 4396
Too Wonderful for Words 6060
Top Gun-Anthem 5514
Top Gun-11 Songs 5514
Top Hat, White Tie and Tails 5515

Wedding Party of Mickey Mouse 3280
Wedding Processional 4911
Wednesday's Child-Theme 4117
Wednesday Special 841
We Don't Need Another Hero 3042
Wee Bit of Love 4797
Weekend in Havana 5840
Weekend in the Country 291
We Got Annie 161
We Gotta All Get Together 4967
We Gotta Keep Up with the Jones' 1725
We Go Together 1849
We Hate to Leave 140
We Have All the Time in the World 3756
We Have Never Met as Yet 2319
We Haven't a Moment to Lose 1721
Weight 404
Weird Science 5845
We Kiss in a Shadow 2602
Welcome Egghead 1015
Welcome Home 465, 3777, 5848
Welcome to My Dream 4319
Welcome to the Spring 769
We'll All Be Riding on a Rainbow 227
We'll All Go Riding 108
Well All Right 622
We'll Be Together 1737, 5011
We'll Build a Bungalow 1895
We'll Build a Little World of Our Own 1948
We'll Dance Until Dawn 1509
Well Did You Evah 221, 2105
We'll Gather Lilacs 2821
Well, I'll Be Switched 1600
We'll Love Again 3144
We'll Make Hay While the Sun Shines 1783
We'll Meet Again 1245, 3421
We'll Meet in the Funniest Places 4974
Well! Well! 4747
We May Never Love Like This Again 5546
We Must Be Vigilant 5898
We Must Have Music 6170
We Mustn't Say Goodbye 4974
We Need a Little Christmas 3083
We Need a Man 3950

We Never Dream the Same Dream Twice 3250
We Never Talk Much 4254
We're All Together Now 1898
We're Almost Home 940
We're Back in Circulation 3734
We're Coming in Loaded 1737
We're Doing It for the Natives of Jamaica 1412
We're Gonna Move 2983
We're Having a Wonderful Time 3266
We're in Business 1412
We're in the Navy 2382
We're Just in Between 2503
We're Not Obvious 3336
We're Off to See the Wizard 5313, 6024
We're on Our Way to France 68
We're Out of the Red 1514, 4983
We're the Couple in the Castle 3423
We're the Marines 2089
Were Thing That Special Face 2635
We're Working Our Way Through College 5734
Were You Just Pretending 3616
Were Your Ears Burning Baby 4668
We Said Hello Again 3614
We Saw the Sea 504, 1521
We Should Be Together 2864
West Ain't What It Used to Be 4094
West Ain't Wild Anymore 1730
West (East) Bound and Down 4800
West End Blues 3556
Western Trail 3095
Western Wonderland 6094
West Is My Soul 4287
West of the Great Divide 1857
West of the Missouri 3723
We Stopped for a Kiss 5821
West Point Hop 1259
Westward Ho 970, 5872
Westward Ho, the Wagons 5873
West Wind 4872
West Wind Whistlin' 1253
We Too Can Sing 4712
We Two 1798
We've Come a Long Way Together 2244
We've Got a World That Swings 3647
We've Got Lots in Common 797